THE BLACKWELL COMPANION TO GLOBALIZATION

The Blackwell Companion to Globalization

Edited by

George Ritzer

© 2007 by Blackwell Publishing Ltd

BLACKWELL PUBLISHING
350 Main Street, Malden, MA 02148-5020, USA
9600 Garsington Road, Oxford OX4 2DQ, UK
550 Swanston Street, Carlton, Victoria 3053, Australia

First published 2007 by Blackwell Publishing Ltd

Library of Congress Cataloging-in-Publication Data

The Blackwell companion to globalization / edited by George Ritzer.
  p. cm.
  Includes bibliographical references and index.
  ISBN 978-1-4051-3274-9 (hardback : alk. paper)
  1. Globalization. I. Ritzer, George.

  JZ1318.B615 2007
  303.48′2–dc22
                                                                2007001203

A catalogue record for this title is available from the British Library.

For further information on
Blackwell Publishing, visit our website:
www.blackwellpublishing.com

Contents

Illustrations

BOXES

Contributors

David L. Andrews is an Associate Professor of Sport Commerce and Culture in the Department of Kinesiology at the University of Maryland at College Park, USA, and an affiliate faculty member of the Departments of American Studies and Sociology. He is assistant editor of the *Journal of Sport and Social Issues*, and an editorial board member of the *Sociology of Sport Journal*, *Leisure Studies*, and *Quest*. He has published on a variety of topics related to the critical analysis of sport as an aspect of contemporary commercial culture. His recent publications include *Sport–Commerce–Culture: Essays on Sport in Late Capitalist America* (2006), *Sport, Culture, and Advertising: Identities, Commodities, and the Politics of Representation* (with S.J. Jackson, 2005), *Sport and Corporate Nationalisms* (with M.L. Silk and C.L. Cole, 2005), and *Manchester United: A Thematic Study* (2004). He has also guest edited special issues of the *Journal of Sport and Social Issues*, the *Sociology of Sport Journal*, *Cultural Studies–Critical Methodologies* and *South Atlantic Quarterly*.

Robert J. Antonio teaches sociology at the University of Kansas, USA. He is the editor of *Marx and Modernity: Key Readings and Commentary* (Blackwell, 2003). He has written widely on classical, contemporary and critical theory. He also has done work on various facets of globalization, frequently collaborating on that topic with Alessandro Bonanno.

Salvatore Babones is Assistant Professor of Sociology at the University of Pittsburgh, USA, with secondary appointments in Pitt's Graduate Schools of Public Health and Public and International Affairs. He is co-editor with Christopher Chase-Dunn of the forthcoming volume *Global Social Change: Historical and Comparative Perspectives*. His research focuses on the causes and consequences of social stratification in broad cross-national perspective. He is currently studying the relationship between economic globalization and domestic income inequality at the country level.

Ulrich Beck is Professor for Sociology at the University of Munich, Germany; British Journal of Sociology Visiting Centennial Professor of the London School of Economics and Political Science, UK; and director of a research centre 'Reflexive Modernization' (Deutsche Forschungsgemeinschaft). His numerous books include *Risk Society* (1992) and *Power in the Global Age* (2005).

Peter Beyer is Professor of Religious Studies in the Department of Classics and Religious Studies at the University of Ottawa, Canada. His publications include *Religion and Globalization* (1994), *Religion in the Process of Globalization* (2001), *Religions in Global Society* (2006) and numerous articles in diverse journals and collected volumes. His current research focuses on religion among second generation Hindu, Muslim and Buddhist youth in Canada.

Tim Blackman is Professor of Sociology and Social Policy at Durham University, UK and Head of the University's School of Applied Social Sciences. He is an adviser to the UK Office of the Deputy Prime Minister on neighbourhood renewal. Among his publications are books on urban planning, urban policy, comparative social policy and health inequalities. He is currently working on a major project looking at the role of performance management in public health across England, Wales and Scotland. His previous posts include Dean of the School of Social Sciences and Law at Teesside University and Director of the Oxford Dementia Centre.

John Boli is Professor of Sociology at Emory University, USA. A native Californian and Stanford graduate, he studies world culture, global organizations, education, citizenship, and state power and authority. Recent books include *World Culture: Origins and Consequences* (with Frank Lechner; Blackwell, 2005) and *Constructing World Culture: International Nongovernmental Organizations since 1875* (with George Thomas; 1999).

Melissa L. Caldwell is Assistant Professor of Anthropology at the University of California, Santa Cruz, USA. She is the author of *Not by Bread Alone: Social Support in the New Russia* (2004), and co-editor with James L. Watson of *The Cultural Politics of Food and Eating* (Blackwell, 2005). Her research on food, globalization and post-socialism in Russia has been published in journals such as *The Journal of Consumer Culture* and *Ethnos*. She is currently writing a book on summer gardens and personal agriculture in Russia.

Chris Carter is Reader in Management at the University of St Andrews, UK. He also holds a Visiting Appointment with the University of Technology, Sydney, Australia. He travels globally quite a lot, especially in the Scottish winter.

Stewart Clegg is Professor of Management at the University of Technology, Sydney, Australia. He also holds appointments at the University of Aston Business School, Maastricht University and the Vrije Universiteit, Amsterdam, the Netherlands. He travels globally a great deal.

Gerard Delanty is Professor of Sociology at the University of Liverpool, UK. His most recent publications include *Community* (2003) and (with Chris Rumford) *Rethinking Europe: Social Theory and the Implications of Europeanization* (2005). He has edited the *Handbook of Contemporary European Social Theory* (2005), and (with Krishan Kumar) *Handbook of Nations and Nationalism* (2006).

Nicholas C. DelSordi is a doctoral candidate in the Department of Sociology at Arizona State University, USA. He is currently working on a dissertation that analyzes the ethnic, cultural and structural integration of Mexican Americans in the United States and migrant groups in Europe from a global comparative/historical perspective. His general research covers issues of immigration, ethnicity and globalization, and how class polarization is implicated with broader global processes. He is also conducting research on the political participation and modes of incorporation among recent immigrants in the south-west.

Peter Dicken is Emeritus Professor of Geography in the School of Environment and Development at the University of Manchester, UK. He has held visiting academic appointments at universities and research institutes in Australia, Canada, China, Hong Kong, Mexico, Singapore, Sweden and the United States and lectured in many other countries throughout Europe and Asia. He is an Academician of the Social Sciences, a recipient of the Victoria Medal of the Royal Geographical Society (with the Institute of British Geographers) and of an Honorary Doctorate of the University of Uppsala, Sweden. He has served as a consultant to UNCTAD and to the Commission on Global Governance as well as to private organizations. He is recognized as a world authority on the geography of economic globalization through his extensive contributions to leading international journals and books and, especially, through his internationally acclaimed book, *Global Shift: Reshaping the Global Economic Map in the 21st Century* (4th edn, 2003).

Kathryn Farr is Professor Emerita in the Department of Sociology at Portland State University, USA and the author of *Sex Trafficking: The Global Market in Women and Children* (2005). Her research interests are in transnational experiences of women with violence and feminist understandings of gender-based violence.

Glenn Firebaugh is Liberal Arts Research Professor of Sociology and Demography at Pennsylvania State University, USA and former editor of the *American Sociological Review* (1997–9). During the 2004–5 academic year he was a Visiting Scholar in the Sociology Department at Harvard University. Recent books include *The New Geography of Global Income Inequality* (2003) and *Seven Rules for More Effective Social Science Research* (forthcoming).

Brian Goesling is a post-doctoral fellow in the Population Research Center at the University of Michigan, USA. He received his PhD from Pennsylvania State University in 2003 and was a Robert Wood Johnson Foundation Fellow at Michigan from 2003 to 2005. In addition to global inequality, his research interests include the study of health disparities in the United States.

Douglas J. Goodman is an Assistant Professor at the University of Puget Sound, USA. He has published on consumer culture including *Consumer Culture: A Handbook* (ABC-CLIO, 2003) and 'Consumption as a Social Problem', in *The International Handbook of Social Problems* (2004); sociological theory including three texts with George Ritzer, *Sociological Theory* (2003), *Classical Sociological Theory* (2004) and *Modern Sociological Theory* (2004); and law and society including 'Defending Liberal Education From the Law', (with Susan Silbey) in *Law in the Liberal Arts* (2004). His current work focuses on the nexus between law and popular culture and he has a forthcoming article, 'Approaches to Popular Culture and Law', in *Law and Social Inquiry*.

Andrew D. Grainger is a doctoral candidate in the Department of Kinesiology, University of Maryland, College Park. His research examines sport's role in the construction and negotiation of identities – both 'local' and 'global' – within, and between, Polynesia and the broader Pacific. Of particular interest is how the notion of diaspora may be employed as a means of understanding the lives, travels and migration of Pacific peoples, and Polynesian athletes in particular, throughout the Pacific and beyond.

Subhrajit Guhathakurta is an Associate Professor with appointments in the School of Planning and the International Institute for Sustainability at Arizona State University, USA. His research interests include land and regional economics, small industries in developing countries, housing policies, land use and environmental planning. His publications appear in journals such as *World Development, Economic Development and Cultural Change, Urban Affairs Review, Berkeley Planning Journal, Mortgage Banking* and the *Journal of Planning Education and Research*. He has held visiting appointments at the Center for Urban Spatial Analysis at University College London, and at the Center for Sustainable Urban and Regional Futures at the University of Queensland in Brisbane.

Farnoosh Hashemian is a Research Associate in the Department of Global Health at the Yale University School of Public Health, USA. Her research focus is on the nexus of global health policy and universal access to quality healthcare. She has worked extensively on health and human rights issues in the Middle East. Farnoosh Hashemian has compiled a two-volume Farsi book entitled *The Trial and Diary of Abbass Amir Entezam*, Iran's deputy Prime Minister in 1979 and the longest-held prisoner of conscience in the Middle East. Published in the spring of 2001, the book has sold over 21,000 copies and stirred much political debate in Iran. Most recently, she was the recipient of a Yale's Deans Award for Outstanding MPH thesis.

David Jacobson is the founding director of the School of Global Studies at Arizona State University, USA. His research and teaching is in politics from a global and legal perspective, with a particular focus on international and regional institutions, international law and human rights issues, and he works extensively in the area of immigration and citizenship. His books include *Rights Across Borders: Immigration and the Decline of Citizenship* (1996), *Place and Belonging in America* (2002) and editor of *The Immigration Reader: America in Multidisciplinary Perspective* (Blackwell, 1998).

Richard Kahn is a doctoral candidate at the UCLA Graduate School of Education, USA and is the co-editor of the recent book *Theory, Facts, and Interpretation in Educational and Social Research* (2004).

Douglas Kellner is George Kneller Chair in the Philosophy of Education at University of California Los Angeles, USA and is author of many books on social theory, politics, history and culture, including *Critical Theory, Marxism, and Modernity* (1989); *Jean Baudrillard: From Marxism to Postmodernism and Beyond* (1990); works in cultural studies such as *Media Culture and Media Spectacle*; a trilogy of books on postmodern theory with Steve Best; a trilogy of books on the Bush administration, including *Grand Theft 2000* (2001); and his latest book *Media Spectacle and the Crisis of Democracy* (2005). His website is at http://www.gseis.ucla.edu/faculty/kellner/kellner.html.

Roberto Patricio Korzeniewicz is Associate Professor of Sociology at the University of Maryland, USA and Professor Titular at the Escuela de Política y Gobierno of the Universidad Nacional de San Martín, Argentina. He co-edited (with William Smith) *Latin America in the World-Economy* (1996), and *Politics, Social Change, and Economic Restructuring in Latin America* (1997). His articles have appeared in the *American Journal of Sociology*, *Comparative Studies in Society and History*, *Desarrollo Económico*, *Economic Development and Cultural Change*, *Hispanic American Historical Review*, *Latin American Research Review* and *Revista Mexicana de Sociología*. His current research focuses on global income inequality and on social movements in Latin America.

Craig Lair is a doctoral candidate at the University of Maryland, USA. Craig attended Arizona State University where he received the John D. Hudson Memorial Award for the Outstanding Graduate in Sociology. Craig's general interests include social theory, the sociology of work and the social processes of individualization. He is currently working on a project with George Ritzer on the sociology of outsourcing. His dissertation will concentrate on the outsourcing of intimate matters. Craig has co-authored a number of pieces for edited volumes dealing with such topics as the labour process of computer programming firms and the relevance of the McDonaldization thesis to service work. He has also published work on the relationship between communication technology and social relationships.

Eriberto P. Lozada Jr is Assistant Professor of Anthropology and Director of Asian Studies at Davidson College in North Carolina, USA and the author of *God Aboveground: Catholic Church, Postsocialist State, and Transnational Processes in a Chinese Village* (2002). He has also published articles on his research on globalization and its impact on food and popular culture, various issues in science and religion, and is currently exploring the relationship between sports and civil society in China and the United States.

Xiulian Ma is a doctoral student in sociology at the University of Utah, USA. She earned a Master's degree in Mass Communications and Journalism at Remin University of China in 2000. She is also a journalist, having worked for China's *The Economic Daily* from 2000 to 2002, winning the China News Award ('Zhongguo Xinwenjiang') in 2002, for her coverage of rural communities' poverty and related policy issues in Yan'an.

Anthony McGrew is Professor of International Relations at the University of Southampton, UK and Head of the School of Social Sciences. He has held Visiting Professorships at Ritsumeikan University, Kyoto; Trinity College, Dublin; the Australian National University, Canberra; and the Centre for Global Governance, London School of Economics. Research interests embrace globalization, global governance (with particular reference to issues of accountability and democracy) and international relations theory. Recent publications include: (ed.) *The Transformation of Democracy? Democracy Beyond Borders* (1997); *Global Transformations* (with D. Held; 1999); *The Global Transformations Reader* (ed. with D. Held; 2003); (ed.) *Empire: The United States in the Twentieth Century* (2000); *Globalization/ Anti-Globalization* (ed. with D. Held; 2002); *Governing the Global Polity: From Government to Global Governance* (2002); *Understanding Globalization* (ed. with D. Held; 2006); and *Globalization, Human Security and Development* (ed. with N. Poku; 2006).

Philip McMichael is an International Professor of Development Sociology at Cornell University, USA. His research focuses on food regime analysis, global development and transnational social movements. Recently he has authored *Development and Social Change: A Global Perspective* (2004), and co-edited *New Directions in the Sociology of Global Development* (2005).

Peter Manicas is currently Director of Interdisciplinary Studies at the University of Hawai'i at Manoa. He has published many books and articles, including *A History and Philosophy of the Social Sciences* (Blackwell, 1987), *War and Democracy* (Blackwell, 1989) and most recently *A Realist Philosophy of the Social Sciences: Explanation and Understanding* (2006).

Gus Martin is Assistant Vice President for Faculty Affairs at California State University, Dominguez Hills, USA. He is former Chair of the Department of Public Administration and Public Policy, where he also coordinated and taught in the Criminal Justice Administration programme. His research and teaching interests are terrorism and extremism, criminal justice administration and juvenile justice process. Dr Martin was educated at the University of Pittsburgh's Graduate School of Public and International Affairs, Duquesne University Law School and Harvard College.

Timothy Patrick Moran is Assistant Professor of Sociology and Faculty Director of the International Studies Undergraduate Program at Stony Brook University, SUNY, USA. His research and writing is currently focused on subjects related to global inequality in its various dimensions and forms. He also writes on issues related to the historical application of quantitative methods in the social sciences, specifically focusing on global measurement and comparative statistical techniques. His research has been supported by the Universidad Nacional de General San Martín, Argentina, and the Luxembourg Income Study Project.

Velina Petrova is a PhD candidate and Woodruff Fellow in the Department of Sociology at Emory University, USA. Her research interests include development, globalization and comparative democratization. She is currently constructing a system-level analysis of foreign aid for development covering all DAC donor countries since the Marshall Plan.

Clayton Pierce is a doctoral student in Education at the University of California Los Angeles, USA, with a specialization in philosophy and history of education. He is co-author of multiple encyclopaedia articles with Douglas Kellner including one for Blackwell's *Encyclopedia of Sociology* on media and consumer culture.

George Ritzer is Distinguished University Professor at the University of Maryland. In addition to globalization, his other main areas of interest are social theory and the sociology of consumption. Among his works on globalization are *The Mcdonaldization of Society* (2004), *The Globalization of Nothing 2* (2007), *The Outsourcing of Everything* (with Craig Lair, forthcoming), as well as a forthcoming textbook on globalization to be published by Blackwell.

Roland Robertson is Professor of Sociology and Global Society at the University of Aberdeen, Scotland and Distinguished Service Professor Emeritus of Sociology, University of Pittsburgh. He is the author, co-author, editor or co-editor of many published items, including *Globalization: Basic Concepts in Sociology* (6 vols, 2003) and *The Encyclopedia of Globalization* (4 vols, 2006). His current interests are primarily in glocalization, cosmopolitanism and global millennialism.

William I. Robinson is Professor of Sociology, Global and International Studies and Latin American and Iberian Studies at the University of California-Santa Barbara, USA. His most recent books are *A Theory of Global Capitalism: Production, Class and State in a Transnational World* (2004) and *Transnational Conflicts: Central America, Social Change, and Globalization* (2003). Pine Forge Press will publish his new manuscript, *Theories of Globalization*, in 2007.

Chris Rumford is Senior Lecturer in Political Sociology at Royal Holloway, University of London, UK. His most recent publications include (with Gerard Delanty) *Rethinking Europe: Social Theory and the Implications of Europeanization* (Routledge, 2005), and *The European Union: A Political Sociology* (Blackwell, 2002). He is currently editing the *Handbook of European Studies*, and completing a new book entitled *Cosmopolitan Spaces: Europe, Globalization, Theory*.

Gerald Schneider is, since 1997, Professor of Political Science at the University of Konstanz, Germany, where he holds the International Relations Chair. He is also

Executive Editor of *European Union Politics* and has authored or co-authored around 100 scholarly articles. His main areas of research are decision-making in the European Union as well as the economic causes and consequences of armed conflict. Recent publications have appeared in *European Journal of International Relations, European Journal of Political Research, Journal of Conflict Resolution, Political Studies* and *Rationality and Society.*

Manfred B. Steger is Professor of Global Studies and Head of School of International and Community Studies at RMIT University, Australia. He is also a Senior Research Fellow at the Globalization Research Center at the University of Hawai'i at Manoa. His academic fields of expertise include global studies, political and social theory, international politics and theories of non-violence. His most recent publications include *Globalism: Market Ideology Meets Terrorism* (2nd edn., 2005); *Judging Nonviolence: The Dispute Between Realists and Idealists* (2003); *Globalization* (2003); *Gandhi's Dilemma: Nonviolent Principles and Nationalist Power* (2000); and *The Quest for Evolutionary Socialism: Eduard Bernstein and Social Democracy* (1996). He is currently working on a book manuscript titled *Ideology in the Global Age: Transforming the National Imaginary.*

George M. Thomas holds a PhD in Sociology from Stanford University and is Professor of Global Studies at Arizona State University, USA. His research and teaching focus on world cultural processes and their constitutive effects on authority and identity. He has a long-term research programme on how religious groups engage global rationalism. He is co-editor with John Boli of *Constructing World Culture: International Nongovernmental Organizations since 1875* (1999).

Michael Timberlake is Professor of Sociology and Department Chair at the University of Utah, USA. His research has contributed to developing scholarship on cities and urbanization that takes into account social, economic, cultural and political processes operating across national borders, at the world level. He is currently involved in studying global networks of cities through research partly supported by the National Science Foundation.

John Tomlinson is Professor of Cultural Sociology and Director of the Institute for Cultural Analysis, Nottingham (ICAn) at Nottingham Trent University, UK. His many publications on the themes of globalization, cosmopolitanism, cultural modernity and mediated cultural experience include *Cultural Imperialism* (Continuum, 1991) and *Globalization and Culture* (Polity Press, 1999). He is currently writing a book on the relationship between speed and cultural modernity.

Howard Tumber is Professor of Sociology at City University London, UK and founder and co-editor of the journal *Journalism.* He is author of several books, including *Reporting Crime: The Media Politics of Criminal Justice* (with Philip Schlesinger; 1994), *News: A Reader* (1999) and *Media at War* (with Jerry Palmer; 2004). Tumber and Webster published *Journalism under Fire: Information War and Journalistic Practices* in 2006.

Bryan S. Turner was Professor of Sociology at the University of Cambridge, UK (1998–2005) and is currently Professor of Sociology in the Asia Research Institute, National University of Singapore. He is the research leader of the cluster on globalization and religion, and is currently writing a three-volume study of the sociology of religion and editing the *Dictionary of Sociology* for Cambridge University Press. A book on human rights and vulnerability is to be published in 2006 by Penn State University Press. Professor Turner is a research associate of GEMAS (Centre National de la Recherche Scientifique, Paris), a professorial Research Associate of SOAS, University of London, and an honorary professor of Deakin University, Australia. Professor Turner's recent publications include *Classical Sociology* (1999) and *The New Medical Sociology* (2004). With Chris Rojek, he published *Society and Culture: Principles of Scarcity and Solidarity* (2001) and with Engin Isin he edited the *Handbook of Citizenship Studies* (2002).

Carolyn Warner is Associate Professor in the School of Global Studies and Affiliated Faculty in the Department of Political Science at Arizona State University, USA, and a research fellow with the Center on Democracy, Development and the Rule of Law at Stanford University. Her book, *Corruption in the European Union*, is forthcoming with Cornell University Press, and her works on patronage and fraud have appeared in *Party Politics*, *The Independent Review* and *Clientelism, Interests, and Democratic Representation* (edited by Simona Piattoni; 2001). Her major work on rent seeking by a religious organization is *Confessions of an Interest Group: The Catholic Church and Political Parties in Post-War Europe* (2000).

Frank Webster is Professor of Sociology at City University London, UK. He has written many books, including *The Virtual University? Knowledge, Markets and Managements* (with Kevin Robins; 2002), *Theories of the Information Society* (Routledge, 2002), *The Intensification of Surveillance* (with Kirstie Ball; 2003) and *The Information Society Reader* (2004).

Kathleen E. White is an educational researcher and consultant in global education. She has been a pioneer in global and international education in the United States and has authored, co-authored and edited numerous items in this and the general field of globalization. She has co-edited *Globalization: Critical Concepts in Sociology* (6 vols., 2003).

Derek Yach is currently a Professor of Public Health and head of the Division of Global Health at the Yale University School of Public Health, USA. He joined Yale after a long career with the World Health Organization where he was responsible for developing a new 'Health for All' Policy, which was adopted by all governments at the May 1998 World Health Assembly. He established the Tobacco Free Initiative and ensured that the Framework Convention for Tobacco Control (WHO's first treaty) was accepted by all governments, and also placed chronic diseases and injuries higher on the global health agenda. Derek Yach has studied and written extensively about the breadth and depth of health issues as well as the challenges of globalization for health and the new era of global health governance.

Steve Yearley is Professor of the Sociology of Scientific Knowledge and Senior Professorial Fellow of the ESRC Genomics Policy and Research Forum at the University of Edinburgh in Scotland. He specializes in environmental sociology and the sociology of science and, in particular, in areas where these fields overlap. His recent books include *Cultures of Environmentalism* (2005), *Making Sense of Science* (2005) and (with Steve Bruce) *The SAGE Dictionary of Sociology* (2006).

Introduction

George Ritzer

While this essay constitutes an introduction to this volume, it is being written after all the chapters have been submitted (and revised, sometimes several times) and the introductions to each of the three parts of the book have been completed. It is actually more of an epilogue than an introduction; a reflection on the chapters in the volume and, more importantly, on what they have to tell us about the state and quality of our knowledge and understanding of one of the most important phenomena of our times – globalization.

One of the points that is almost always made about the study of globalization is how contested almost everything is, including the definition of globalization itself. In terms of the latter, it is interesting how many authors of the chapters to follow found it necessary to define globalization, often in the first paragraph or so of the chapter. That act indicates, I think, that there is no consensus on the definition and each of the authors who offered one wanted to make something clear that they felt was not clear or agreed-upon.

If the need to define globalization indicated a lack of consensus, most of the definitions proffered used similar ideas and demonstrated more consensus than is usually assumed (including by the authors represented here). Among the terms usually included in the definitions offered were, in order of frequency, speed and time (accelerating, rapidly developing etc.), processes and flows, space (encompassing ever greater amounts of it), and increasing integration and interconnectivity. A composite definition, therefore, might be: Globalization is an accelerating set of processes involving flows that encompass ever-greater numbers of the world's spaces and that lead to increasing integration and interconnectivity among those spaces.

A basic distinction among positions taken on globalization, one made several times in this book, is *globophilia* versus *globophobia*. In fact, the chapters in this volume, indeed in much of the social science literature on globalization (contrary to what Turner argues in the concluding chapter), are much more informed by globophobia than globophilia. While most of the authors here lean toward the former, it is almost always from the political left (rather than the right), and involves a wide range of criticisms of globalization in general, as well as the specific aspects of it of concern to them.

Globophilia is generally associated with a view, the mainstream neoliberal, 'Washington Consensus', that tends to be disliked, if not despised, by most of the authors represented here (see, especially, Antonio and his critique of a well-known cheerleader for this position, Thomas Friedman; neoliberalism has pride of place in Steger's delineation of the elements of 'globalism' as the hegemonic ideology in the epoch of globalization). It is generally associated by its critics with economic domination, exploitation and growing global inequality. McMichael focuses, specifically, on neoliberal agricultural policies such as the 'law of comparative advantage' which has had a variety of devastating effects (for example, de-agrarianization and de-peasantization) on the agriculture of the South. And, it has led, among many other things, to the growth of rural industrialization (e.g. *maquiladores*) and to the underpaid jobs associated with it that force workers to supplement their wages in various ways. Yearley suggests that neo-liberal policies have led to many of the devastating environmental problems that have faced, are facing and are increasingly likely to face much, if not all, of the globe.

Relatedly, in an analysis of a key economic aspect of globalization – outsourcing – Ritzer and Lair take on a favourite theoretical perspective of the neoliberals, Schumpeter's (1950) 'creative destruction', and argue (at least in the case of outsourcing), contrary to the theory and its adherents, that destruction is *not* always creative (for a similar use of creative destruction, see Korzeniewicz and Moran). Thus, in terms of issues discussed above, it may well be that the destruction of Southern peasants and agriculture is just destructive, at least for them; there is little or no construction (save the highly exploitative *macquiladores*) taking place at least in the South to compensate for the losses. More clearly, the destruction of the environment is certainly not accompanied by *any* constructive ecological developments. At a more general level, many of the inadequacies of the theory of creative destruction, at least as Schumpeter envisioned it, are traceable to the fact that it was created to deal with an economic world that existed long before the current boom in globalization and it is ill-suited to dealing with new global realities where destruction is at least as prevalent in many domains as creation.

Before we leave globophilia in general and Friedman (2005) in particular, it is worth mentioning, and casting a critical eye on, his recent and highly positive view that globalization is leading to a flat world. Among many other things, this means that barriers to participation are coming down throughout the world and, as a result, involvement is growing more democratic and the world less unequal (see below; Firebaugh and Goesling). While a laudable view, and one with at least some merit, the fact remains that it flies in the face of not only the considerable (although debatable, see below) evidence on increasing inequality, but virtually the entirety of the field of sociology and its study of innumerable structures and institutions that are erected, and often serve as barriers (sometimes insuperable mountains), on the global landscape. From a sociological view, the world is, and is likely to remain, at least hilly, if not downright mountainous, impeding the development of easy participation, greater democracy and less inequality. Among those hills, if not mountains, are cities (Timberlake and Ma), nation-states (Delanty and Rumford), transnational corporations (Dicken), educational (especially higher education) systems (Manicas), systems of healthcare (Hashemian and Yach), organized corruption (Warner) and so on. Were the flat world envisioned by Friedman ever to come about, we would either need to abandon sociology (an act that would be welcomed by many) or so alter it to make it unrecognizable.

This view on the continuation of barriers in the world is supported by Guhathakurta, Jacobson and DelSordi who take on the issue of the idea of the 'end of globalization' in the context of migration. Some argue that globalization has ended because we have achieved free and easy movement of people through and across borders. Guhathakurta et al. contend, however, that creating borders is 'natural' (an essentializing view that is questionable in light of postmodern theory) and the continued creation of such barriers means that we are unlikely ever to see the free movement of people and therefore the end of globalization (at least in the sense they are using that idea here).

In spite of the predominance of globophobia in this volume, none of the authors rejects globalization outright and in its entirety. Rather, their view is that the problem lies *not* in globalization per se, but in the way globalization currently operates. There is a widespread sense that globalization is with us for the foreseeable future, if not forever (it is often portrayed here as 'inevitable or 'inexorable'; see, for example, Steger), so the issue is one of what is needed in order to create a 'better' form of globalization. For example, the problems of globalization are often associated with its economic[1] aspects (usually accorded pride of place in the process) and, more specifically, its domination by capitalism. Capitalism, by its very nature, is seen as leading to various problems such as global inequality and exploitation. Thus, for some, the answer lies in the creation of a different kind of economic globalization that leads to greater equality, and less exploitation, in the world (e.g. Antonio; more below).

This, of course, bears on the normative aspects of globalization and, as with all aspects of this phenomenon, there are great differences and important disputes. For example, there are those more radical than Antonio who would reject a role for all forms of capitalism in globalization, while there are others, more to the right, who would find his ideas on the sources of a reformed type of globalization far too radical.

But much more is in dispute in the study of globalization including fundamental images of the nature of the subject matter in globalization studies (McGrew), as well as basic theories (Robinson) and methods (Babones). One way of looking at this is to say that there is great richness in globalization studies with a wide range of perspectives, normative orientations, theories and methods to choose from. But another is to suggest that these profound differences, this near-total lack of agreement, are representative of a 'crisis' that can only be resolved through a paradigmatic revolution and the creation of a new paradigm not only for the study of globalization, but for the social sciences in general. Such a new paradigm – cosmopolitanism – is suggested in this volume (and in many other works) by Ulrich Beck who argues that the social sciences (e.g. sociology, political science, international relations) are still locked into older paradigms which, among other commonalities, take the nation-state as their basic unit of analysis (this is also criticized by Korzeniewicz and Moran). Suggested in Beck's position is a paradigmatic revolution in which the globe becomes the basic unit of analysis (for Korzeniewicz and

Moran it is the world-system) and new normative orientations, overarching perspectives, theories and methods are created to fit better with such a revolutionary new focus.

While we await such a paradigmatic revolution, which of course may never come, we are left with all sorts of intellectual differences in the study of globalization. However, those differences pale in comparison to those to be found in work on a wide range of substantive issues that relate to globalization. These include whether there is any such thing as globalization and, if there is, when it began and how is it different from prior stages in the history of the globe. Obviously, by its very existence, this volume indicates support for the view that there *is* such a thing as globalization, but that is not terribly helpful because under that heading there exist a bewildering array of players (Thomas) and every conceivable social structure and social institution (Boli and Petrova, as well as at least all of the chapters in Part II of this book). In addition, there are all sorts of new players (learning the names of, and the difference between, international governmental organizations [IGOs] and international non-governmental organizations [INGOs] is a necessity) and more are coming into existence all the time. Furthermore, virtually every aspect of the social world, including all social structures and institutions, is undergoing dramatic changes because, at least in part, of globalization. As a result, the global is a near-impossible world to master both because our intellectual tools are inadequate, in dispute and perhaps out of date and because we are trying to deal with so much and everything we seek to analyze is changing, coming into existence and disappearing. Paraphrasing Marx in his analysis of capitalism, in globalization all that has seemed to be solid is melting into thin air and that which is to be re-formed or newly created seems likely to melt away very soon.

The result of all of this is that everything in globalization studies seems to be up-for-grabs. Much of the field appears to be dominated by debates of all sorts. Let us enumerate at least some of those debates that are dealt with, or touched on, in these pages.

Perhaps the most important substantive debate is whether globalization brings with it more (Korzeniewicz and Moran; relatedly, Blackman wonders whether globalization is causing greater inequality) or less (Firebaugh and Goesling) inequality. (Babones both casts light on this issue and seems to suggest that at least from a methodological ground the former are on the stronger footing.)

At a scholarly level, Beck makes the point that the tendency to take the state as the unit of analysis leads to a focus on, and concern for, the relatively small inequalities within nation-states. More importantly, this leads to a tendency to ignore the glaring and enormous inequalities that exist at a global level. This is a key reason why he argues for a paradigmatic shift involving, among other things, a change in the unit of analysis from the nation-state to the globe.

Beyond these general issues, inequality comes up in many other ways both in the literature on globalization as a whole and in this volume. A range of positions are represented here including the oft-repeated view that the dominant neo-liberal approach inevitably leads to global inequality (Antonio) and that there is relatively little that can be done about it within the confines of that orientation versus what Steger calls 'universalist protectionism', which seeks at least a reduction in global inequality (as do, as Blackman shows, various government policies). Then there is the fact that some IGOs support this unequal system and even serve to increase such inequality. However it is also true that this inequality has spawned various organizations (especially INGOs) seeking to combat this tendency toward increasing inequality.

While there is much debate, there are areas of some agreement on the issue of inequality and globalization. For example, inequality can be seen as a major cause of migration. The poverty in the South and relative affluence in the North can be viewed as push-pull factors in migration from the former to the latter. Of course, inequalities are also caused by migration as, for example, those that result from the fact that highly skilled and educated migrants are more likely to be welcomed in the North (and virtually everywhere else) and to fare better than their less skilled and educated compatriots (with illegal migrants apt to fare worst of all). Remittances home from those who have successfully migrated (to the North) enhance the economic status of some back home (in the South), while others lag behind. The loss by the South of highly trained and skilled workers tends to increase the economic gap between it and the North. Huge agricultural inequalities, especially between North and South, are being exacerbated by such aspects of globalization as the development of international standards for foodstuffs that adversely affect the economically worse off countries that may be unable to afford to do what is necessary to meet these standards. This tends to worsen their situation and to increase the likelihood of poverty and hunger amidst abundance (McMichael). There are also inequalities between global/world cities and the rest, as well as inequalities within all types of cities (Timberlake and Ma). There are certainly gross inequalities in healthcare between the developed and less developed (especially Africa) world (Hashemian and Yach). Finally, there is the narrower issue of the degree to which sex work draws on and increases inequality (Farr).

Closely related to the issue of inequality is power, especially the unequal division of power in the globe; the ability of some to exercise enormous power over others (North over South; United States and/or the West over the rest). This is implicit in many chapters in this volume, and explicit in several others such as Steger's discussion of the asymmetrical power relations in the world and the fact that the ideology of globalism is used to support that system.

Technology (and its relationship to power) also gets a great deal of attention here as, for example, in Kellner and Pierce's discussion of the technologies associated with the global media. (Relatedly, Tumber and Webster detail the increasing role of advanced technologies in 'soft' and especially 'hard' information war. This emphasis on technology also informs, at least in part, their grand narrative of the transition from 'industrial' war to 'information' war.) While, as Marcuse (1964) pointed out long ago, technology itself is neutral (in contrast to McLuhan's [1964] view that the 'medium is the message'), it is clear that it is being used and controlled by those who gain from globalization to further their gains and to better entrench them in their powerful and enriching position. However, the media and their technologies are also employed by forces opposing the elites. This is clearest in Kahn and Kellner's discussion of the technopolitics of the resistors of globalization. Thus, the issue is whether, in the end, technology favours the further entrenchment of those who gain from globalization or those who are seeking an alternative global system.

Another pervasive debate is between those who see globalization producing greater heterogeneity and those who view it as leading to increasing homogeneity. This issue arises over and over in this book with virtually all of those who address it coming down in the end squarely on the side of the idea that globalization leads to increased heterogenization. This great consensus is a bit bothersome, especially to me, since I perceive a tendency to underplay the degree and significance of homogenization in globalization. Further, I think, as suggested by Goodman, that having to choose sides on this issue is probably the wrong thing to do and a waste of effort. It is probably well past time for declaration of a hiatus on the useless debate between homogenization and heterogenization (especially when the former is usually set up as a 'straw man' in the debate). I very much like Goodman's notions that *both* homogenization and heterogenization are *always* involved and that globalization, especially of consumer culture, 'makes people more different, but in a similar way'. Similar viewpoints are expressed by the ideas that 'diversity takes standardized form', and at least global consumer culture is a 'global system of common difference'.

Related to the consensus on heterogenization (even though those who support it almost always tend, self-consciously, to critique any hint of the idea of homogenization) is the widespread acceptance and use of the idea of glocalization (Robertson and White). Indeed that term, and related concepts like hybridization and creolization, derive their popularity from the fact that they all imply heterogeneity *and* the absence of homogenization). The power of this idea is reflected in McGrew's chapter in which he identifies the glocal as one of the four 'modes' of analyzing globalization. Not only does this serve to give exaggerated significance to this idea, but seeing it as a mode of analysis seems inconsistent with the other three modes identified by McGrew – defensive globalization, post-globalizing and critical globalism – because all of them are much broader theoretically than glocalism. That is, glocalism seems of an entirely different order than the other three.

The rush to accept the glocal position is best seen in the chapters by Robertson and White, Andrews and Grainger, and Caldwell and Lozada. While I think they are too accepting of this idea (Robertson and White even imply that glocalization *is* globalization), I do think nonetheless that they produce some useful ideas that can help move work in this area forward. For example, Caldwell and Lozada suggest that it is better to see the (g)local not so much as a thing to be discovered, but rather as a set of processes of social change. The issue, then, becomes how to best represent these processes. The focus should be on the processes through which the (g)local is generated; on 'location-work'. In general, (g)localism is a dynamic, interactive and continually renegotiated process. From my perspective, such a view does not prejudge whether something is glocal (or local), but rather focuses on ongoing processes that may, or may not, involve glocalization. Or, if it is glocalization that is seen as occurring, the issue becomes the relative mix of homogenization and heterogenization involved.

Also useful is Andrews and Grainger's distinction between two types of glocalization – the *organic glocal* involving the incorporation of globalized, internationalized sport (and much else) into the local and the *strategic glocal* which involves transnational corporations (TNCs) exploiting the local, through either 'interiorized glocal strategizing' (global sport coopting and exploiting sport's local dimension) or 'exteriorized glocal strategizing' (importation and mobilization of sporting differences into the local market).

However, my problem with all of this is the continued hegemony of the idea of the glocal (as well as heterogenization), no matter how much more nuanced it becomes as a result of the contributions of Caldwell and Lozada and Andrews and Grainger. As I have argued elsewhere (Ritzer 2004a), the emphasis on glocalization and heterogeneity needs to be complemented (*not* replaced) by a concern with *grobalization* (defined as the growing imperialistic influences of business, states and so on) and homogeneity. In terms of Caldwell and Lozada's location work, in my view that takes place in the context of *both* glocal and grobal influences. And, when we look at the conceptual elaboration of Grainger and Andrews what we see there is not just glocalization, but substantial grobalization (in both types, 'grobal' sport is 'incorporating' itself into, or coopting, local sport). All of this makes the Robertson and White position highly questionable (in spite of their brief and undeveloped recognition of grobalization), especially when they go so far as to say that as 'a homogenizing force, globalization really makes no sense'. To me globalization makes no sense without examining *both* the homogenizing *and* heterogenizing effects of, the grobalization *and* glocalization involved in, globalization.

Related to, but more general than, the various global–local issues is the idea that globalization is a *contingent* phenomenon. In the case of the global/local relationship, the contingency is in effect the local (although it is also possible to see the global in contingent terms). That is, the nature of the impact of the global depends on, is contingent on, the nature of the local (and the agents involved, see below), as well as the ways in which the global and local interact. Since no two local settings are exactly alike, the impact of globalization will vary from one local setting to another. However, this is far from the only contingency of interest and importance in globalization in general and in the global–local relationship in particular.

A second key phenomenon is agency (the local and agency are directly linked by Caldwell and Lozada; Turner integrates agency into his 'neo-Malthusian' approach; but agency is devalued by the dominant ideology of globalism; see Steger) and another important contingency involves the differences among people and therefore the differences in the way they react to, and interact with, globalization. This is consistent with poststructuralist or constructivist approaches to globalization (McGrew) which, in turn, alerts us to the idea that it is not the inherent nature of globalization (if there is such a thing) that is of greatest importance, but rather agents' highly variable social constructions of that process. Ultimately, what matter most from this perspective are those constructions and *not* globalization *per se*. This obviously accords great (too much?) power to agents and their constructions. It also leads to the possibility of constructions that run counter to globalization and ultimately to the possibility of alternative globalizations (see below for more on resistance and revolution).

Much of the preceding discussion can be subsumed under a distinction that appears at several points in this book between *globalization from above* and *globalization from below*. While we need to be wary of *all* such binaries in this post-postmodern era, especially the gross oversimplifications that they involve, it is clear that this distinction is intimately related to important issues such as inequality, power and the global–local relationship. That is, globalization from above clearly

favours wealthy nations, especially the economic elites in those countries, as well
as the well-to-do in less well-off nations. The poor are exploited across the board
and they do not share in the wealth generated by globalization from above. Similarly, power is linked to globalization from above while a relative lack of power is
linked to globalization from below. And, grobalization is associated, and may be
nearly synonymous with, globalization from above, while glocalization is more tied
to globalization from below. The local is even more linked to the latter perspective,
but it can be argued that the 'truly' local is increasingly difficult, if not impossible,
to find in a globalizing world (in fact, I have gone so far as to discuss the 'death of
the local' [Ritzer 2004a]).

As a result of these associations, globalization from below describes not only a
process, but also a rallying cry and a political programme to be followed by the
have-nots in society in order to attempt to create, among other things, an equal, or
at least a less unequal, global system. In fact, Kahn and Kellner suggest that we use
the idea of globalization from below (or others such as *alter globalization*) instead
of the popular idea (and movement) of anti-globalization. The point that is often
made is that people and groups associated with this idea and movement do not
oppose globalization *per se* (hence they are not anti-globalization), but they oppose
more specifically the current form of globalization dominated by neoliberalism that
is exploitative of the poor, the weak and the local of less developed nations.

Another perennial issue and subject of debate is the continuing importance of
the nation-state in general, and the United States in particular, in the era of globalization. Let us begin with the latter, especially in the form of the process of
Americanization, since it is directly related to preceding discussions of the glocal and
of agency. According great importance to the glocal (or local) and/or the agent leads
to a de-emphasis on all grobal forces, especially those emanating from the United
States. However, one of the interesting things about the chapters in this volume is the
fact that a number of them accord great significance to Americanization. For
example, Antonio recognizes (albeit critically) the importance of the neoliberal,
Washington Consensus in the process of globalization. McMichael gives great centrality to the exportation of American consumption patterns, its agro-business, and
the supermarket (to say nothing of the fast food restaurant [Ritzer 2004b]).

Clegg and Carter see much of global business having its roots in the United States,
including the global proliferation of America's MBA programmes and the importance and power it grants to those with MBAs ('neo-colonial domination of an
American educational model on a global scale'), American management gurus (e.g.
Tom Peters) and American business 'fashions'. Clegg and Carter argue, correctly in
my view, that Americanization is *not* primarily about the consumption of American
products (Big Macs, Whoppers), but about the global spread of a given way of
doing business; a particular 'system'. However, Clegg and Carter do not accept a
totalizing conception of Americanization, but argue that there are other models,
and reverse processes of colonization, that lead to hybrid forms of business that
reflect, only in part, Americanization.

Americanization is also important in Kellner and Pierce's discussion of the media
and of even greater importance in Manicas's discussion of the globalization of the
American model of higher education. Warner sees the United States as the global
leader in efforts to reduce corruption (many would question this) and in seeking to

create Americanized anti-corruption norms and laws throughout the world. These essays indicate that in spite of a rejection of the importance of Americanization in much of the general literature on globalization, when it comes to analyses of more concrete and specific institutions and structures, there is far greater recognition of its importance and, in my view, a far more realistic assessment of its true and continuing significance. This suggests, more generally, that highly abstract and general discussions of globalization may be of far less utility than those that have greater concreteness.

One issue that is implicit in many of the chapters mentioned above and in much of the literature on Americanization is the fact that it is often not the best that America has to offer that is being exported throughout globe. Manicas makes this point in terms of the various deleterious aspects of American higher education (over-specialization, for-profit universities) that are being globalized. Much of my work has dealt with a variety of American exports – fast food restaurants, credit cards (Ritzer 1995), shopping malls (Ritzer 2005) and so on – that bring with them that which is, for example, mediocre, dangerous in terms of leading to high levels of debt and hyper-consumption, empty and ultimately 'nothing' (Ritzer 2004a).

Turning to the more general issue of the significance of the nation-state in contemporary globalization, there is as much disagreement among the authors represented here as there is in the globalization literature as a whole. Thomas sees the nation-state as one of the two strong actors in the world today; to Dicken the nation-state has been overwhelmed by TNCs (but is still one of their important adversaries); Beck, and Robertson and White see it as of continuing importance but only as one of many elements of, actors in, the global world (Delanty and Rumford offer a similar view); late modern and postmodern theories tend to see the state as being of declining importance; Kellner and Pierce and Tumber and Webster see the nation-state as increasingly porous; the emergence of 'enemies without states' (e.g. Al-Qaeda) and 'states without enemies' (as a result of increasingly open and porous borders, especially in the EU) both suggest a decline in the significance of the nation-state as does the literature on the increasing importance of global civil society; and finally to those who accept the post-globalizing orientation (McGrew), the nation-state may have declined, but it is now in the process of reasserting itself (through, for example, a reassertion of the importance of borders). Whether the nation-state is of continued importance in the era of globalization is one of the most contentious issues in the field of globalization studies today.

Clearly, this debate, and most others, cannot be settled at a general level. What is needed is more analyses of specific nation-states and the role of each in globalization. Furthermore, the importance of the nation-state should be discussed in the context of specific substantive issues – trade, migration, media, criminal networks and so on – and not in airy general terms. Clearly, at least some nation-states remain important (especially the United States) and on some issues the nation-state is more important than on others. Rather than endlessly and fruitlessly debating the fate of the nation-state in general, we might gain much more through such more limited analyses.

In addition to all of the problematic aspects of globalization dealt with above (e.g. poverty, powerlessness, the loss of the local), there is also the much more obvious and blatant 'dark side' of globalization (Delanty and Rumford). For example, Martin analyzes the 'new' terrorism, Farr deals with sex trafficking and Warner works with corruption, but there are other dark sides of globalization such as the global drug trade and international criminal cartels that are only touched on in various places in this volume. While it is not usually included under this heading, we might also discuss, as another of globalization's dark sides, the increasing danger posed by so-called *borderless diseases* such as AIDS and the threat of avian flu (Hashemian and Yach).

Given all of the problems associated with globalization, reforms of various types are on the minds of many of the authors in this volume, especially reforms that address the centrally important issue of inequality stemming especially from the workings of global capitalism. On a practical level, there are already in existence many groups, most notably a number of well-known INGOs, that seek to combat some of the worst excesses of capitalism. Most abstractly and generally, one of the things that defines the transformationalist perspective identified by McGrew is democratic reform in search of a better combination of economic efficiency and social justice. Following his critique of neo-liberalism (as expressed in Friedman's work), Antonio argues for the need for a more just society and world. Thus, Antonio accepts the idea (inevitability) of capitalism and its advance, but argues that it needs to be a democratic form of capitalism. Such a form of capitalism needs to be both socially regulated and embedded in, and controlled by, a number of institutions, not just the economic institution. Thus, Antonio wants a new form of global capitalism that draws on an array of older democratic and socialist ideas. While laudable, one wonders whether the solution to the problems created by such a new and emergent world as global capitalism can be dealt with by a system that takes as its basis ideas created decades, if not centuries, ago to respond to a very different world and form of capitalism (this is similar to the critique of the theory of creative destruction; see above).

Kahn and Kellner review a wide range of types of resistance to globalization (see also McMichael on rural resistance) from conservative to moderate and even radical forms. While Kahn and Kellner's underlying sympathies seem to lie with a more radical approach, in the end they urge, at least theoretically, for a more moderate orientation that avoids the extremes of globophilia and globophobia. Of course, there are some who do not think reform is enough and are in favour of more revolutionary change. In McGrew's typology, the critical globalists, especially those oriented to Marxian theory, adopt such an orientation. Perhaps the best-known example of this orientation is Hardt and Negri's (2000, 2004) approach (critiqued by Kahn and Kellner) that favours a revolution by the multitude and its triumph over the emerging global hegemony of empire.

While much of the conventional wisdom on globalization (e.g. the [over-] emphasis of glocalization) is affirmed in this collection of essays, there are occasions when it is challenged. For example, Yearley takes on the idea that environmental problems are global problems arguing that not everyone or every part of the world contributes equally to those problems; not everyone and all areas of the world are affected in the same way; there are great differences in the importance accorded, and the dangers associated with, these problems; there are other possibilities as globally important environmental problems; and the causes of environmental problems change, especially in terms of their geographical source(s). Among other things, this implies not only a lack of consensus on global environmental problems, but also then a lack of agreement on what, if anything, can or should be done about them. This, obviously, has grave implications for the future of those problems and the likelihood that anything substantial will be done about them. Indeed, it supports the idea that nothing of any great consequence will be done until, and if, a global ecological catastrophe (the results of global warming seem like the most likely possibility now) occurs.

In another example of this kind of counter-hegemonic thinking, Dicken challenges the idea that TNCs are as powerful as many laypeople and globalization scholars seem to feel. In addition, Dicken takes on the 'placelessness' idea that pervades various perspectives on globalization such as those that emphasize flows (Castells 1996 and Appadurai 1996), networks (Castells 1996), and non-places (Auge 1995; Ritzer 2004a). He argues that the place of origin continues to affect large organizations long after they have become multinationals (and this tends to support the idea of Americanization since so many of these organizations have their roots there).

There is a tendency in the globalization literature to deal with globalization in a totalizing, even reified, way and thereby to overlook the significance of other aspects of the social world. This is clear, for example, in Ritzer and Lair's discussion of outsourcing (and other forms of sourcing), an idea that is closely associated in the public mind, especially in the United States, with globalization. However, outsourcing (as well as related ideas) is far broader and has far wider implications than simply those associated with globalization. Thus, Ritzer and Lair go 'beyond' globalization to discuss outsourcing at the meso- and micro-levels (although, of course, globalization can be implicated at those levels, as well). The irony is that while thinking on globalization seems to offer something approaching an all-inclusive perspective, its very 'globalness' causes it to lose sight of many important social issues and phenomena. It is important to focus on global issues, but in doing so analysts ought not to lose sight of other dimensions involved in what they are studying.

The conceptual elaborations in Ritzer and Lair's discussion of outsourcing remind us, as do other chapters in this volume (e.g. Andrews and Grainger on elaborations of the glocal; see above), of the need to refine our conceptual arsenal in the area of globalization. It is clear that far too many things are discussed under the heading of the concept of outsourcing and that teasing out a range of related concepts greatly refines our ability to think about all this. For example, the distinction between outsourcing and in-sourcing permits us to understand that all forms of outsourcing in the realm of globalization (and elsewhere) from one part of the world involve in-sourcing in other parts of the world. Furthermore, this makes it clear that critics of outsourcing, especially in the United States, such as Lou Dobbs (2004), ignore the fact that the United States is not only outsourcing work, but also in-sourcing it. While there are legitimate criticisms of, and problems with, outsourcing, the fact is that the United States gains by *both* outsourcing (getting lower priced goods and services in return) and in-sourcing (new jobs to replace those that are lost due to outsourcing). This is not to say that the United States overall is a net gainer in global sourcing (although it may be), but it is to suggest that we need to take a deeper and more nuanced look at this than is characteristic of examinations by critics like Dobbs.

Above all, what emerges from these essays is a sense of the complexity of globalization and its widely diverse, even conflicting, effects. For example, Kellner and Pierce discuss the use of the media to exert hegemony, but also its increasing utilization by the forces of globalization from below (e.g. Indymedia) to oppose successfully such efforts and exercise counter-hegemonic power from below. Staying within the media, complexity is increasing as conflicting messages emerge from the mainstream media and from the increasingly important alternative media forms (e.g. the publication of photos of the Abu Ghraib atrocities appearing first on the Internet thereby forcing their publication in mainstream media, many of which would have undoubtedly preferred that they not be published).

In warfare, the media once were employed and controlled by the motherland to supply a uniform message, but now that control has eroded with the result that innumerable complex and ambiguous messages emerge in wartime from highly diverse media outlets. The latter, in turn, makes becoming involved in war, and remaining in it, much more complicated. Warner points out how globalization is simultaneously increasing and reducing the possibilities of corruption. Schneider advances a theory of war that includes the view that globalization can both increase and decrease the possibility of war. Globalization simultaneously creates the new terrorism as well as the means to combat it (Martin). One could go on with this kind of enumeration, but it is clear that globalization is, to put it mildly, a complex process with many diverse and conflicting effects.

While the vast majority of the analyses represented in this volume are largely critical of globalization (especially Turner's concluding chapter), there are positive images and evaluations to be found in these pages. For example, several argue that we are witnessing an increase in democracy and democratization as a result of globalization (Delanty and Rumford; Tumber and Webster; the same view, albeit more critical, is found in Steger's outline of the ideology of globalism).

Another positive aspect of globalization for many (e.g. Tumber and Webster) is the growth of global civil society (such a development is consistent with Beck's cosmopolitanism). Indeed, Tumber and Webster argue that we should be 'grateful' for its development and the common orientation associated with it. Delanty and Rumford are extremely strong on the importance of global civil society arguing that it is of growing importance (Thomas discusses the possibility of the World Social Forum offering the possibility of such a global civil society) on such issues as human rights, the environment, health and security, the development of a global normative culture and the ability of both that culture and global civil society to confront the abuses of globalization, especially in the economic sphere.

Thus, this introduction ends on several positive notes about globalization. However, while globalization certainly has its positive sides, it is important to remember that the thrust of these essays, and of the literature in the social sciences on this topic, is globophobic. It may not be uplifting to read this literature, but it does have the merit of offering a nuanced (contra the gross criticisms of someone like Lou Dobbs) and detailed critique (contra the cheerleading of someone like Thomas Friedman) of globalization. It is only by understanding the problems associated with globalization that we can begin to address what needs to be done to redress them.

Note

1 Many of the authors in this volume (Tomlinson, Steger, Beyer et al.) feel that their focal interest, be it culture, ideology or religion, and its relationship to globalization, have tended to be downplayed or ignored because of the overwhelming focus on the economy.

References

Appadurai, A. 1996. *Modernity at Large: Cultural Dimension of Globalization.* Minneapolis: University of Minnesota Press.

Auge, M. 1995. *Non-Places: An Introduction to an Anthropology of Supermodernity.* London: Verso.

Castells, M. 1996. *The Rise of the Network Society.* Vol. I of *The Information Age: Economy, Society and Culture.* Malden, MA: Blackwell.

Dobbs, L. 2004. *Exporting America: Why Corporate Greed Is Shipping American Jobs Overseas.* New York: Warner Business Books.

Friedman, T. 2005. *The World Is Flat.* New York: Farrar, Strauss and Giroux.

Hardt, M. and Negri, A. 2000. *Empire.* Cambridge, MA: Harvard University Press.

McLuhan, M. 1964. *Understanding Media: The Extensions of Man.* New York: McGraw-Hill.

Marcuse, H. 1964. *One-Dimensional Man: Studies in the Ideology of Advanced Industrial Society.* London: Routledge.

Ritzer, G. 1995. *Expressing America: A Critique of the Global Credit Card Society.* Thousand Oaks, CA: Pine Forge Press.

Ritzer, G. 2004a. *The Globalization of Nothing.* Thousand Oaks, CA: Pine Forge Press.

Ritzer, G. 2004b. *The McDonaldization of Society,* rev. New Century edn. Thousand Oaks, CA: Pine Forge Press.

Ritzer, G. 2005. *Enchanting a Disenchanted World: Revolutionizing the Means of Consumption,* 2nd edn. Thousand Oaks, CA: Pine Forge Press.

Part I
Introduction

Introduction to Part I

GEORGE RITZER

Part I offers a series of essays that, in combination, constitute a general introduction to the study and phenomenon of globalization, especially from the point of view of sociology and the other social sciences.

We begin with Anthony McGrew's wide-ranging and magisterial overview of globalization studies from both an intellectual and political perspective. In fact, the issue of globalization, and the debate over it, has served to invigorate *both* scholarly work and political action. On the one hand, many scholars have been drawn to the study of globalization and, because it is such a highly contested idea, into many scholarly debates, as well. On the other hand, many politicians, lay people and activists (and some scholars) have become enmeshed in the red-hot political debates on problems, and protests over them, associated with many of the real-world effects of contemporary globalization. Since the process of globalization is not going away anytime soon, if ever, public discussion, protests and scholarly work will continue and, if anything, accelerate. At the same time, the political issues that surround globalization (for example, the inequities that seem endemic to the process), like the scholarly ones, show every sign of continuing, and likely increasing in number and intensity.

Broadly speaking, the debate involves, as discussed in the Introduction to this volume, those who have 'globophilia' versus those who suffer from 'globophobia'. The former group includes, among others, those who adopt a neoliberal approach, especially capitalists and politicians who see their firms and countries benefiting from globalization. Those who can be said to suffer from globophobia include those who adopt both far right and far left political positions. Those on the right often see their nation and identity being threatened by global flows, while those on the left are enraged by the injustices associated with globalization. Many activists, both from the right and especially the left, can be seen as having globophilia.

Among scholars, especially sociologists, another source of their interest in, and concern about, globalization is that it threatens some of their most basic and long-lasting ideas. Many of the basic units of analysis in sociology – economy, polity, society and especially the state – are threatened, if not undermined, by globalization. All of these phenomena seem to interpenetrate in a global world and are increasingly difficult to clearly distinguish from one another. Many of them, but especially the state, seem to be undermined by the process of globalization. Most generally, there are those who believe that the basic unit of analysis in today's world should be the globe rather than social science's traditional units of analysis.

At its most extreme, this indicates that the social sciences in general, and sociology in particular, are in need of, if not undergoing, a paradigm shift. In Thomas Kuhn's (1962/1970) now classic work on paradigms and revolutions in scientific fields, basic to any paradigm is its fundamental image of the subject matter of the science in question (Ritzer 1975/1980). It is arguable that in the past sociology, at least at the macro-level, has focused on society in general and the nation-state in particular, but such foci seem weak in the era of globalization since society and the nation-state are being penetrated and eroded by the process of globalization. This is leading to a shift towards the globe as the fundamental unit of analysis, at least in macro-sociology. Such a shift would have profound implications for much of sociology, especially its theories and methods (see Robinson and Babones in this part of the book). It could be argued that sociology, and other social sciences, are undergoing a paradigm shift, a revolution, as a result of the growing power and importance of globalization.

McGrew offers two basic ways of mapping globalization scholarship. The first involves outlining four 'waves' that have framed academic scholarship on the topic. The second is four 'modes' of analyzing globalization.

The first 'wave' is *theoreticist* involving theoretical work that addresses several basic issues, all of which are contested and hotly debated. First, there is the issue of how to conceptualize globalization. This issue, and differences among scholars on it, will reappear throughout this book, especially in the various efforts to define globalization. Indeed, the very fact that there are such differences in definition makes it clear just how contested the entire idea of globalization is and remains. Second, there is the question of what are the basic dynamics involved in the process of globalization. Finally, there is the question of the systemic and structural consequences of globalization as a secular process of social change. That is, what is its impact on, among others, social structures, social institutions and so on.

A second wave of scholarship is *historicist*. Here a key issue, indeed a central issue in globalization scholarship in general, is what, if anything, is new about globalization today in comparison to other periods in history. There are those who see globalization as beginning with the fall of the Soviet Union, others who trace it to the end of World War II, still others who see its beginnings centuries ago, and even those who argue that globalization can be traced back thousands of years. For those who see globalization today as something unique in history, there is the issue of its general implications, and most specifically its implications for progressive values and projects of human emancipation. Most generally, the issue is whether globalization improves or worsens the overall human condition. A key question is whether globalization promises to reduce or exacerbate social inequality within given nations (say, the United States) and the world (say, between the global North and the South).

The third wave identified by McGrew is *institutionalist* (the Thomas and Boli and Petrova chapters in this section are strongly affected by this wave). Here the focus is on social institutions, especially economic, political and cultural institutions. The issue is, most generally, whether – and in what ways – globalization is leading to change in these institutions, especially whether there is continued global divergence, or increasing convergence, throughout the world in these institutions. This bears on a general issue that is central to the globalization literature in general, and this volume in particular, and that is whether globalization brings with it increasing homogenization, supports extant heterogenization or even brings with it further heterogeneity.

The final wave identified by McGrew is the *poststructuralist* (or *constructivist*). This involves several shifts in focus in globalization scholarship. For one thing, concern moves from globalization as an all-encompassing macro-process to one that is contingent and that involves the importance of agents and the ways in which they construct it as a process. Relatedly, this involves a shift in the direction of the importance of ideas about globalization, especially as both hegemonic and counter-hegemonic discourse. This focus leads to several key issues such as whether the definitions of agents and the rise of counter-globalization discourse is leading to the demise of globalization; whether we are in, or moving toward, a post-global age. At the minimum, it leads to the view that there is not one form of globalization, but multiple globalizations. That is, we should think in terms of globalization*s* rather than globalization.

Given these four waves of globalization scholarship, McGrew turns to a second mapping device – four modes for analyzing globalization, the first of which is *defensive globalization*. In this view, globalization is a really existing and enduring condition (although far from inexorable or irresistible) that is changing societies throughout the world. It can be divided into liberal and transformationalist perspectives.

In the liberal view (for an overview and critique, see Antonio, below), globalization is generally seen as a benign process that has continuities with the past and historical changes. It is primarily economic in nature and leads to increasing integration through the market and technology. While liberals see merit in globalization, they can be differentiated from the crude neoliberal, Washington Consensus view that globalization is an unmitigated good producing increased prosperity, democratization, cosmopolitanism and peace throughout the world. The liberals recognize that there are problems associated with globalization, but adopt the view that it can be made to function better.

In contrast, the transformationalist position is that globalization today is unique in history and that it involves much more than simply economic changes. Not only are there political, cultural and social manifestations of globalization above and beyond the economic manifestations, but all of them, including the economic, can be distinguished from one another and are often contradictory. While there are benefits to globalization, especially market-led globalization, there are also problems such as great inequality in and across societies. Democratic reforms are needed to produce a process of globalization that leads to both economic efficiency and social justice.

Post-globalizing is the second mode of analysis. Here the view is that globalization either never occurred, or that it is in decline or disappearing as borders of nation-states are being reasserted (e.g. between the United States and Mexico), nationalism is being revived and so on (all of these changes can be seen as involving 'deglobalization'). In any case, in this view the whole idea of globalization has been 'oversold' as a description of social reality, an explanation of social change and as an ideology of social progress. Rather than a global world, we continue to live in a world dominated by national societies and states. Thus, the issue is the construction of a better world either through the better use of extant state power or by taking control over and transforming the uses to which it is put.

Whatever its status in the real world, globalization remains important as an idea and as discourse (in the speeches of politicians and the rhetoric of protestors). It provides people with social means and with frames with which to think about and act in the social world. Ideas associated with globalization also serve to both legitimate and de-legitimate social and political change.

The third mode is *critical globalism*. As its title suggests, this view is critical of globalization because it is associated with the extension and transnationalization of power. The best-known idea associated with this perspective is Hardt and Negri's (2000) 'empire'. However, this mode goes beyond critique to point to new subjective and transnational forms of resistance to this extension of power (Hardt and Negri's [2004] 'multitude'). Agency, subjectivity and social struggle are central to this resistance. The conflict between, for example, empire and multitude is leading to struggles over the distribution of the world's resources and over recognition and identity (ethnic, gender and so on). Globalization is generally accepted as a social reality, but the issue is how to realize its progressive, even more its revolutionary, potential.

The final mode of analysis is *glocalism*. This involves the widely accepted view among contemporary globalization scholars that the focus of studies on this topic should be on *both* the global and the local in combination with one another, the dialectical relationship between the two. There is a great deal of work in the field that focuses on the issue of glocalization, or on the closely related ideas of hybridization and creolization. In fact, this mode of analysis is so hegemonic that I recently suggested the idea of 'grobalization' as a complement to the concept of glocalization (Ritzer 2004a). That is, it is important not only to focus on the integration of the global and the local, but also on the imposition of the latter on the former. The need for both ideas is clear in a distinction made by McGrew and others in this volume (e.g. Kahn and Kellner) between 'globalization from below' (McGrew associates this with critical globalism) and 'globalization from above'. Glocalization would be more in tune with the former while grobalization well expresses the latter.

McGrew offers one of many possible road maps for understanding the literature on globalization, as well as the remainder of the chapters in this volume. Given the diversity of approaches, McGrew anticipates the continuation of disagreements in the study of globalization and that the concept itself is likely to remain fiercely contested.

Robertson and White outline their thinking on globalization which is informed by the glocalization perspective discussed by McGrew and which is closely associated with the work of the senior author of that chapter. That concept plays a role in this piece, but it is subordinated to a larger set of arguments about globalization. The main point made here about glocalization is that it means that globalization is a self-limiting process, at least as far as homogenization is concerned. That is, because all ideas and practices must adapt to the local, there can be no such thing as globalization; the latter 'makes no sense'. In making this move Robertson and White seem to be reducing globalization to glocalization and thereby are largely ignoring the importance of what has been called above grobalization (although they do touch on its importance briefly, including the fact that it is *not* self-limiting).

The more general argument made by Robertson and White is that globalization follows a pattern composed of four basic elements. First, in contrast to a number of scholars in the field, they argue that the nation-state, while it is changing, must continue to be seen as part of globalization. Second, globalization should not be seen as solely a macroscopic process and 'individual selves' must be included as part of it. Third, globalization involves an international system. Finally, even more broadly it encompasses humanity as a whole including such issues as our relationship to the environment, animals and human rights. These four elements and their interrelationship constitute Robertson and White's broadest answer to the question: What is globalization?

Antonio critically analyses an updated version of the liberal theory discussed by McGrew – neoliberalism, or what is sometimes referred to as the 'Washington Consensus'. He does so in a critique of the popular and influential work of the journalist Thomas Friedman, especially his most recent book, *The World Is Flat* (Friedman 2005). Antonio's critique is based on his argument that neoliberalism in general, and Friedman's position in particular, has much in common with an outdated and discredited theory, *social Darwinism* (as well as Malthusian theory; see Turner, concluding chapter of this volume).

Neoliberalism (and the Washington Consensus) have strong roots in, and overtones of, America and Americanization. Antonio associates the following ideas with neoliberalism – a free market, deregulation, tax cuts, minimization of welfare, limited government, free trade and global capitalism. Support for these policies (for a very different view on government policy, see Blackman, Part II) is seen as the motor force of globalization.

Antonio focuses on Friedman's ideas not only because of his wide readership and influence, but also because the main sources of his thinking are interviews with high-level corporate and political leaders. Thus, his reportage offers much insight into how these leaders view and justify neoliberalism. Friedman's work is *not* highly regarded by scholars; it is often seen as 'trite' and 'lightweight' (although, to be fair, his 2005 book offers, among other things, useful insight into a topic – outsourcing – that scholars have tended to ignore [see Ritzer and Lair, Part II]). Nonetheless, Antonio sees his work as offering 'what may be the most comprehensive, widely read defence of neoliberal globalization'.

Friedman uses a term – 'inexorable' – to describe globalization (other similar ideas in his work are 'irreversible' and globalization as a 'Golden straitjacket') and, as we will see, this idea recurs in several definitions of that process in this volume. Such an idea not only justifies the future expansion of globalization, but in this context it justifies the continued expansion of *one type* – neoliberal – of globalization (as we will see at a number of points [especially, Kahn and Kellner in Part III] in this book, and Antonio will argue, there are, or could be, other varieties of globalization).

Antonio offers the following enumeration of Friedman's basic cultural and institutional ideas: the fall of communism was a key step in the increasing flatness of the world; technology, especially information-communicative, is key but the main driver of globalization is still neoliberal policymaking; globalization is defined by fluid, loosely coupled, flexible networks (rather than traditional bureaucracies) that, among other things, make it easier for individuals anywhere in the globe to compete and collaborate (central to the idea of the flat world); nomadic individuals are on the move not only spatially but also in the creation of new identities; some inequality is inevitable and although Friedman is 'compassionate' and suggests palliatives, no major social programmes are suggested; the democratization of ownership by the 'electronic herd' (no one is in charge) through the democratization of technology, finance, information and decision-making; the reactionary backlash against globalization by a wide range of anti-globalization forces (made increasingly dangerous by the flatness of the world) that slows the process; self-regulation of the global system; and the lead role played by the United States in globalization as its model (and flattest spot) taking the lead in such key neoliberal processes as downsizing, privatizing, streamlining and outsourcing.

Antonio associates Friedman's ideas with the work of a number of social theorists (Herbert Spencer, William Graham Sumner and Talcott Parsons) and theories (modernization, classical liberalism, social Darwinism) that have been discredited and have few supporters today in the social sciences. Such theoretical roots are the source of the neoliberal emphasis on the laissez-faire economy that leads inevitably to great inequality which, in turn, makes it difficult to integrate and legitimate society. Instead of reiterations of old ideas in a neoliberal guise, we need in Antonio's view to decouple the concepts and processes of neoliberalism and globalization. To do so, we need to create a 'more just, institutionally embedded, social regulated democratic capitalism' that draws on an array of perspectives such as 'postwar democratic socialism, social democracy and other liberal democratic models'.

Thomas offers us another kind of road map than the one presented by McGrew, this one of the key players in the process of globalization. He begins with the two strong actors in the process – transnational corporations and states, nation-states. The thrust of much of the literature in globalization is to accord transnational corporations the greatest power over the process (e.g. Sklair 2002). The state is often accorded a secondary role because it is either a pawn in the hands of transnational corporations or unable to contain or control their necessarily transnational operations. However, Thomas argues that the power of the transnational corporations may be overestimated because, for example, of internal differences among them, because of the power of other actors (especially the state), or because they are being modified by globalization itself. While transnational corporations and the state retain pride of place at the top of the hierarchy of global actors, even they need to be viewed within a global institutional context to which they must both react and adapt. This serves to moderate not only their power, but the power of all of the other key actors.

Next Thomas deals with international governmental organizations (IGOs) which, while they are created and used by states, have become significant collective actors themselves. Among the key IGOs are the International Monetary Fund (IMF) and the World Bank (both created by the 1944 Bretton Woods agreements), as well as the 1947 General Agreement on Tariffs and Trade (GATT). Among other things, these IGOs were oriented to reconstructing the post-World War II world economy; providing support for national development; keeping poorer nations viable in the capitalist system and resistant to (communist) revolution; and facilitating the flow of raw materials from peripheral to core nations and the reverse flow of finished products. Later came the Group of 77, formed by developing nations to counter the deleterious effects on them of the global economic system. This was followed by the Group of 7 (later 8) of core nations that were more interested in maintaining the global economic system as it was, or even getting it to operate even more to their benefit.

By the 1980s there was a global shift in focus from national development to economic liberalization and this new orientation was firmly established by 1989. A series of GATT meetings (the Uruguay Round) beginning in 1986 culminated in the formation of the World Trade Organization (WTO) in 1995. This became the organization whose primary task was the development and enforcement of that which liberalized trade or, in other words, supported the much ballyhooed idea of 'free trade'. This was linked to the development of regional free trade IGOs such as the controversial North Atlantic Free Trade Association (NAFTA) and the hotly debated proposal for the creation of a Free Trade Area of the Americas (FTAA).

These IGOs are key players in the global economic system and their influence extends to other areas such as population and women's rights. However, many of their actions are hotly contested because they are seen as not being truly democratic, not being accountable to all interested parties, and as serving to support an unjust system and even to further inequality and injustice. A series of global actors have emerged to combat these IGOs and some see them as forming the basis of a global civil society. In any case, the system of IGOs and the opposition to them have come to form a global field in which a wide array of both supporters and opponents act. While the opposition seeks to undermine these IGOs, Thomas argues that they may inadvertently be furthering them by defining them as the key actors in the global field.

Also of note as an IGO is, of course, the United Nations which while it is strongly influenced by powerful states, is also autonomous of them, at least to some degree. Then there are a variety of increasingly important international courts (e.g. International Court of Justice, World Court, the more recent International Criminal Court) and tribunals (ad hoc courts that have dealt with human rights issues in Rwanda, Yugoslavia and elsewhere).

Then there are the international non-governmental organizations (INGOs). These are distinguished from IGOs by the fact that they are not established and run by states. They are independent, not-for-profit organizations whose major goal is to exert influence (largely moral) over other major players – transnational corporations, states, IGOs and other international organizations. Among the best-known of the INGOs are Amnesty International, Greenpeace, World Wildlife Fund. Of increasing importance are INGOs like the International Organization for Standardization (ISO) which are moving to create a variety of global standards for products, accounting, ethics and a wide array of other technical matters and issues. There is a trend towards at least some INGOs cooperating in the formation of supermovements such as the World Social Forum (established in Porto Alegre in 2001). It claims not to be an actor *per se* and, controversially, it does not take political positions and make political pronouncements. Rather it sees itself as a formal space for a global civil society; a space for various groups to come together. While many IGOs are increasingly successful, others such as those associated with labour have been less so.

Thomas then discusses a wide range of other global actors, perhaps the most notable of which are religious and terrorist (e.g. Al-Qaeda) groups. Finally, he includes individual professionals, scientists, writers and celebrities (e.g. Bono) as important actors on the global stage.

Overall, Thomas envisions a world in which the results of unbridled individual interest have brought into being collectivities that see such action as a problem and are oriented to dealing with it, as well as the many other problems that arise on the global stage.

Yet another kind of mapping is undertaken by Boli and Petrova. What is of primary interest to us is the various social entities that they see being globalized, but they begin with other forms of globalization. First, they argue that everyday experience has been globalized. On a day-to-day basis we increasingly find the process inescapable, but we usually do not object to this (in fact, we desire it) because it has become so much a part of our lives and because we find it legitimate rather than feeling as if it has been imposed on us. Second, globalization has become a taken-for-granted reality; we see it as less and less exotic. Third, globalization encompasses more and more people; it has descended the social ladder and become more democratized. However, Boli and Petrova recognize that there are still poor people who are not enmeshed in the global system. They are likely to be on the receiving end of that system, to be driven by it rather than drivers of it, and they have little or no access to the advantages, let alone the niceties, of globalization.

Their discussion of the various social entities that have been globalized is shaped by a (fluid) distinction between cultural forms and organizations. Cultural forms are abstract, disembodied models of social entities that form part of the constituting edifice of world culture. Organizations are the more or less formalized institutions of world society that are built around, embed and sustain particular types of entities. These cultural models and institutions are primarily cognitive, but also normative, both enable and constrain actors, and have served to accelerate globalization, making it increasingly elaborate, but also more incoherent.

Turning to the social entities, Boli and Petrova begin with the globalization of the individual, of individual personhood. Fundamental to this is the globalization of schooling and of standardized models of how the individual is to be developed in the educational process. The individual is also at the heart of the exchange economy (e.g. is paid, has property rights). An ideology of human rights has become increasingly pervasive around the world. And, the World Values Survey confirms that people increasingly see the self as belonging to the world.

Next as a social entity is the state and the view that there is greater global acceptance of the view that a viable state is central to contemporary world culture, of what constitutes a model state and for the need for performance assessment to ascertain how well a state measures up to the model. In that model, the state has a series of responsibilities to its citizens including schooling, medical care, economic development, gender empowerment and reduction or elimination of state corruption. Further the state has a responsibility to the environment and affluent states have the added responsibility of aiding poorer countries. Just as there is a model state, there is an increasing global model of what constitutes a failed state including one rife with poverty, violence and social disorder traceable to state inadequacies.

Like the state in the political realm, the corporation (or transnational corporation) has become the globally favoured organizational form within the economy. In addition, also like the state, the corporation has become a global model(s) for economic organizations throughout the world. This process has been expedited by the ISO (see Chapter 4), the major global accounting and management consulting firms and a wide range of consultants with their various standards and models for organization structure and quality, employee relations and so forth. These organizational forms are not restricted to corporations, but through 'organizational isomorphism' have become models for universities, sports teams, clubs, professional associations, even hobby groups.

Corporations have also come under increasing moral pressure from global critics. There are, for example, general statements on the moral responsibilities of corporations (Sullivan Principles, UN Global Compact). INGOs like Corpwatch and INFACT focus on the need for corporations to have a triple bottom line focusing not just on financial matters, but also their environmental and social impacts (INFACT has a Hall of Shame for those that fail to measure up on such dimensions). Then there are INGOs like Social Accountability 8000 and AA 1000 that focus on such things as measuring the social responsibility and ecological sustainability achievements of corporations. Also of note here is the growing attractiveness of social choice investments.

Civil society, that evanescent world that exists between the state and markets, has become globalized. Involved here are a wide range of scientific, medical, technical, professional, educational, recreational and sporting INGOs. Many INGOs come together at the World Social Forum which, as we will see (Thomas), has become a critical counterpoint to the World Economic Forum in Davos. Overall, Boli and Petrova see greater standardization of voluntary associations throughout the world, although they also see greater variety through the process of glocalization (see above).

Finally, even the transcendental has been globalized in great concern for the planet as a whole (climate change, global diseases etc.), cosmologies and more specifically in religion in which ecumenicism, fundamentalism and evangelism are all global in their reach.

In conclusion, Boli and Petrova address an issue that is of central concern among scholars of globalization and will reappear throughout this volume (for example, Caldwell and Lozada). That is, once again, the issue of global homogenization versus heterogenization. While they certainly see homogenization through the proliferation of global cultural models and organization forms (isomorphism), they also see local resistance to them. However, in their view a model of homogenization and resistance is too simplistic. They argue that globalization itself produces and legitimates differences and diversity; that there are many conflicts and contradictions in world cultural models, and that globalization produces both homogenization and new forms and levels of competition and conflict.

The next two chapters deal with efforts to map two critical aspects of the study of globalization – theories of globalization and the methods that are used to study it empirically. Clearly, we must venture forth and collect data on this process, but also just as clearly we cannot be content with the simple accumulation of such data; we must reflect theoretically on the meaning and importance of the data and of globalization more generally.

As Robinson makes clear, mapping theories of globalization is no easy matter. However, before we get to that we should make clear that Robinson traces most theory, indeed the entire field of globalization studies, to the 1970s. This bears on the issue, discussed above, of whether or not globalization is something new. While Robinson is not necessarily taking a position on this issue (and in fact sees the debate over the beginnings of globalization as one the key domain questions in the field), he is arguing that the theoretical and other scholarly work on globalization boomed, indeed became an increasingly identifiable field of globalization studies, after 1970. This is traceable to a series of developments that included the emergence of a globalized economy, culture and political processes; the unprecedented multidirectional movement of people around the world with profound effects on identities and communities; as well as new patterns of global inequality and domination. All of these became central topics in globalization studies and to them have been added significant work on global corruption, the media, sexuality and so on. All of these topics, and many more, will be covered in this volume.

There is a large variety of theories of globalization derived from a number of different fields. Furthermore, theories are rapidly changing and new theoretical perspectives are continually emerging. Thus, Robinson eschews trying to come up with a definitive classification system, but rather simply offers an enumeration of the major theories while recognizing that it is far from being comprehensive.

World-system theory, created by and closely associated with Immanuel Wallerstein, is interesting in that it can be seen as a globalization theory even though many of those associated with it (including Wallerstein himself), as well as observers of globalization theory, do not see it in that way. Yet, its primary focus is the capitalist world system that had become a global system by the late nineteenth century.

Theories of global capitalism (Sklair 2002; Robinson 2004; Hardt and Negri 2000) have several things in common with world-system theory including a critique of capitalism, emphasis on long-term, large-scale changes that culminated in globalization, and the central importance of global economic structures. Among the differences with world-system theory are that theories of global capitalism see globalization today as a qualitatively new stage in the history of capitalism ('capitalist globalization'), involving new global and production systems that have supplanted earlier national ones, systems that cannot be put into traditional frameworks that focus on nation-states or the inter-state system (as does world-system theory).

Network society theory is traceable to the work of Manuel Castells (1996). Here the focus shifts from capitalism to technology as the motor force in globalization. Recent technological changes associated with computers and the Internet have led to a new mode of development: informationalism. Capitalists used this new technology to create a 'new economy', 'informational capitalism'. Thus, the new economy is knowledge and information based, is characterized by production on a global scale, and productivity is generated through networks. The latter is a key idea to Castells who associates it with the networked enterprise and ultimately the network society. Indeed, networks and networked enterprises are linked to the new post-Fordist more horizontal and flexible corporate structures. This more flexible and fluid system is tied into Castells' view that we have moved from a world characterized by 'spaces of places' to one of increasingly important 'spaces of flows' (and similarly fluid 'timeless time'). Castells offers a more positive view of globalization than the previous two types of theories, although that may be because he ignores a variety of problems, especially the 'digital divide' (Drori 2005).

Another set of theories deals with the relationship between space, place and globalization. Spaces and places have been restructured in both a general sense (spaces have tended to replace places, or as Auge [1996], Ritzer [2004a] and others put it, 'non-places' have replaced 'places'), as well as in global capitalism. As Harvey (1989) (and Giddens 2000) sees it, time and space have been compressed, so that the constraints of both have been greatly reduced. Business can be conducted in almost any place at any time and this permits not only the increasing globalization of capitalism but a whole new stage in the history of capitalism.

Also under this broad heading is the body of work that sees a new spatial order in the world with the growing importance of global and world cities.

Next is a series of theories of transnationality and transnationalism. Among the concerns here is the issue of increasing migration and its role in globalization. In many cases, these migrants are forming transnational communities made possible by an inexpensive and readily available international telephone service, the Internet and international travel. More generally, transnationality is not restricted to immigrants, an increasing number of people are having transnational experiences.

Then there is a series of theories surrounding the issue of modernity and postmodernity. On the one hand, there are theorists (Giddens 2000; Beck 2005; Bauman 1998) who argue that even with globalization we continue to live in the modern, albeit a late-modern, world. Others, such as Albrow (1997), see a much more profound change from a modern age to a global age in which, among other things, the nation-state has lost its centrality and various institutions relate directly to the globe thereby rendering the nation-state increasingly less important. It is the globe, rather than the nation state, that is the primary source of identity and major arena for action.

A wide range of theories have addressed global culture. Much of it surrounds the issue, once again, of whether, from a cultural point of view, the world is growing increasingly homogeneous or heterogeneous. Tending to emphasize homogeneity are theories that stress such ideas as global culture (see Thomas; Boli and Petrova), coca-colonization, McWorld (Barber 1995) and Ritzer's ideas on McDonaldization (2004b) and the globalization of 'nothing' (2004a). On the heterogeneity side are a set of theories mentioned above that focus on glocalization, hybridity and creolization as well as Appadurai's (1996) work on global landscapes and their disjunctures.

In a parallel essay, Babones seeks to chart methodologies involved in the study of globalization. He differentiates between quantitative and qualitative studies of globalization, but focuses most of his attention on the former. Most of the most sophisticated quantitative work in globalization is in the economic realm and this work tends to rely on published compilations of existing data rather than involving the collection of new data. Three variables have typically been used in cross-national panel studies of economic globalization – foreign trade, foreign direct investment and foreign portfolio investment.

Other studies have focused on national income, most commonly measured by gross domestic product (GDP) and gross national product (GNP). A big issue among those who work with such data is the conversion of the different currencies into a common currency, usually US dollars. The issue of conversion has led to huge debate in the globalization literature between world-system theorists and demographers. In fact, the major protagonists (Firebaugh and Goesling; Korzeniewicz and Moran) in this debate discuss this issue and others in later chapters in this volume.

Turning to non-economic issues, Babones discusses studies of cultural globalization that rely on the World Values Survey. In this survey, researchers in 80 countries have asked parallel questions on values and beliefs in four waves between 1981 and 2001. This is an invaluable source on various cultural issues such as whether there is increasing homogeneity or heterogeneity throughout the globe.

Political globalization can be studied through the use of various published data sources on diplomatic relationships between countries (*Europa World Year Book*), military matters (*The Military Balance* and the Armed Conflict Database) and terrorism (*Patterns of Global Terrorism*).

While all of the other chapters in Part I map a variety of issues that relate to globalization, this part closes with a much more focused essay by one of the world's most important theorists, Ulrich Beck. In this chapter Beck argues for the need to replace a focus on the nation-state with a more cosmopolitan orientation that adopts an inherently critical perspective on globalization and the place of the nation-state in it. While Beck does not see the nation-state as disappearing, he sees it as only one of many actors in a global power game. The focus needs to be on that global power game and not the nation-state.

Such a shift in focus requires the restructuring of the social sciences conceptually, theoretically, methodologically and organizationally. All of their fundamental concepts – especially the nation-state – need to be re-examined. Many are 'zombie concepts' that continue to live on even though the world that they related to at one time no longer exists.

Cosmopolitanism, as pointed out above, not only involves a fundamental reorientation of the social sciences, and a dramatic shift in focus, but it also must be critical in its orientation. The critical focus must be on the increasing inequality in the world. The focus on the nation-state has led to a concern with comparatively 'small' inequalities within nations, but it has also led to a shameful neglect of the 'large' global inequalities. A cosmopolitan orientation overcomes the blinders of a national orientation and attunes us to global issues.

Thus, we have not only surveyed a wide range of realities of, and approaches to, the global world, but also included one view on the need for a total overhaul of, a paradigm revolution in, the social sciences in general and especially in their approach to the issue of globalization.

References

Albrow, M. 1997. *The Global Age*. Stanford, CA: Stanford University Press.

Appadurai, A. 1996. *Modernity at Large: Cultural Dimension of Globalization*. Minneapolis: University of Minnesota Press.

Auge, M. 1996. *Non-Places: An Introduction to an Anthropology of Supermodernity*. London: Verso.

Barber, B. 1995. *Jihad vs. McWorld*. New York: Times Books.

Bauman, Z. 1998. *Globalization: The Human Consequences*. New York: Columbia University Press.

Beck, U. 2005. *Power in the Global Age*. Cambridge: Polity Press.

Castells, M. 1996. *The Rise of the Network Society*. Vol. I of *The Information Age: Economy, Society and Culture*. Malden, MA: Blackwell.

Drori, G. 2005. *Global E-Litism: Digital Technology, Social Inequality, and Transnationality*. New York: Worth.

Friedman, T. 2005. *The World Is Flat*. New York: Farrar, Strauss and Giroux.

Giddens, A. 2000. *Runaway World: How Globalization Is Reshaping Our Lives*. New York: Routledge.

Hardt, M. and Negri, A. 2000. *Empire*. Cambridge, MA: Harvard University Press.

Hardt, M. and Negri, A. 2004. *Multitude*. New York: Penguin.

Harvey, D. 1989. *The Condition of Postmodernity*. Oxford: Blackwell.

Kuhn, T. 1962/1970. *The Structure of Scientific Revolutions*. Chicago: University of Chicago Press.

Ritzer, G. 1975/1980. *Sociology: A Multiple Paradigm Science*. Boston: Allyn and Bacon.

Ritzer, G. 2004a. *The Globalization of Nothing*. Thousand Oaks, CA: Pine Forge Press.

Ritzer, G. 2004b. *The McDonaldization of Society*, rev. New Century edn. Thousand Oaks, CA: Pine Forge Press.

Ritzer, G. 2005. *Enchanting a Disenchanted World: Revolutionizing the Means of Consumption*, 2nd edn. Thousand Oaks, CA: Pine Forge Press.

Robinson, W.I. 2004. *A Global Theory of Capitalism: Production, Class and State in a Transnational World*. Baltimore, MD: The Johns Hopkins University Press.

Sklair, L. 2002. *Globalization: Capitalism and Its Alternatives*. New York: Oxford University Press.

Chapter 1

Globalization in Hard Times: Contention in the Academy and Beyond

Anthony McGrew

Introduction

Globalization incites controversy. Both within and beyond the academy it provokes vociferous debate and contradictory responses. Within the academy opinion divides over the reality and significance of contemporary globalization but more especially with respect to its supposed revolutionary implications for the classical paradigms of the human sciences. In the wider public sphere globalization elicits sharply divergent responses and fuels radically different political projects, from the globaphobia of the extreme right to the globaphilia of neoliberals. On closer inspection, however, this apparent polarization of views dissolves into a far more complex and nuanced set of arguments which cut across orthodox ideological and disciplinary fault lines. Globalization has not imposed a 'golden straitjacket', to use Friedman's phrase, on the academy nor upon social activism either. On the contrary it has provoked a radical resurgence, if not renaissance, of social and political theory not to mention popular mobilization and dissent. This chapter seeks to map the intellectual and political controversy surrounding the idea of globalization, explaining why it has become such a fiercely contested and detested idea amongst academics and activists alike.

In the first part of the chapter the discussion focuses upon what is at stake in the great globalization controversy and, by implication, why it matters so much both academically and politically. This anchors the subsequent elaboration of a heuristic framework for mapping this diversity and the identification of the principal contending schools of thought. The remaining sections discuss and critically evaluate each of these broad schools, relating these to the contentious politics of globalization. In the conclusion the discussion reflects upon the current controversy about globalization and why it is likely to remain of central concern to social scientists and social activists well into the twenty-first century.

BEYOND THE ANTIMONIES OF GLOBALIZATION

There is some validity in the phrase that 'globalization is what we make of it'. How globalization is socially constructed, in the media and academic discourses, frames, if not constrains, its meaning for both academics and activists. Contemporary discourses of globalization tend too readily to construct its meaning in terms of a titanic struggle between its advocates and its opponents, between the forces of globalization and those of anti-globalization, between globalists and sceptics, between cosmopolitans and communitarians, or between the global and the particular. Such antimonies certainly have heuristic value in helping define what is at stake – in the intellectual and social realms – if globalization is to be taken seriously. Too often, however, such antimonies oversimplify the complexity of academic and political contestation about the nature and meaning of globalization. If taken too literally they can readily tend towards the substitution of rhetoric for rigorous analysis. To move beyond such antinomies is the principal task of this chapter. Before confronting this task, however, it will be useful to rehearse some of the reasons why globalization has become such a contested and detested idea within and beyond the academy.

In the inaugural edition of the journal *Globalizations*, V. Spike Petersen argues that, 'We cannot makes sense of globalizations through conventional analytical and disciplinary frameworks' (Petersen 2004: 50). Jim Rosenau, also in the same edition, observes that 'Social scientists, like the people they study, are prone to habitual modes of behaviour, and thus are more likely to cast their inquiries into habitual frameworks that are taken for granted than to treat their organizing principles as problematic' (Rosenau 2004: 12), while Martin Shaw calls for the 'the global transformation of the social sciences' (Shaw 2003: 35). What globalization brings into question are the core organizing principles of modern social science – namely the state, society, political community, the economy – and the classical inheritance of modern social theory which takes them for granted as the units or focus of social explanation – sometimes referred to as methodological nationalism. Recursive patterns of worldwide interconnectedness challenge the very principle of the bounded society and the presumption that its dynamics and development can be comprehended principally by reference to endogenous social forces. By eroding the distinctions between the domestic and the international, endogenous and exogenous, internal and external, the idea of globalization directly challenges the 'methodological nationalism' which finds its most acute expression in modern social theory. It implies, as Scholte and others conclude, the need for 'a paradigm shift in social analysis' in order that the emerging condition of globality in all its complexity can be explained and understood (Scholte 2000: 18).

Such revolutionary claims have not gone uncontested. Many reject such a hasty dismissal of classical social theory and consider the 'globalization turn' as simply the folly of much liberal and radical social science in which advocacy has displaced scepticism or 'balanced social scientific reflection' (Rosenberg 2005: 66). Rather than presenting an insurmountable intellectual challenge to orthodox social science, however, globalization has been largely incorporated into contemporary social analysis through a concern with spatiality, and by implication globality, in the development and functioning of modern societies (Brenner 2004). Aspirations for a globalization theory have given way to a proliferation of theories of globalization as different traditions and disciplines, from anthropology to world history, seek to incorporate its dynamics into their explanatory schemas. Although this 'global turn' has not displaced classical social theory, the idea of globalization has now colonized the human sciences. Amongst those of a sceptical disposition, what is principally at stake in this 'colonization' process is not so much the displacement of social theory as the descriptive and explanatory purchase of the very concept of globalization itself. This strikes at the very *raison d'être* of globalization studies since, as Rosenberg amongst others argues, if the concept provides no convincing 'guide to the interpretation of empirical events' it must in any meaningful sense be analytically redundant (Rosenberg 2005: 1; Hay 2004). For both Rosenau and Rosenberg, as representatives of opposing arguments, what is at stake in these academic disputes is nothing less than the very soul of the social sciences as a reflexive and critical undertaking which seeks to explain and understand the principal forces shaping the contemporary human condition. In short, globalization constitutes either the new 'social imaginary' of the human sciences – as explanans or explanandum – or alternatively a subversive conceptual 'folly' (Taylor 2004; Rosenberg 2000).

If one critical source of academic contention over globalization stems from competing assessments of its descriptive (ontological) and explanatory (epistemological) value a second, but no less important source, issues from differing normative and ethical positions. These are inextricably bound together with matters of empirics and theory in so far as analyses of globalization are necessarily imbued with ethical judgments about its tendencies and consequences. Whether globalization is good for the poor, to take an obvious example, involves not just empirical assessments but judgments about what is good for the poor. Deliberations about globalization, whether in the academy or beyond, are inescapably inflected – whether explicitly or implicitly – with normative reasoning. To paraphrase Sandel, 'Everyday we live out many of the concepts of normative theory' (Sandel 1996). Whether it is considered benign, malign or both is a judgment conditioned by normative reasoning and ethical assessments of its consequences for the human condition. But there is no simple correspondence between particular normative positions – such as left or right – and attitudes towards globalization. Rather, as Tormey has suggested, the more significant distinction is between what might be broadly defined as ideological and post-ideological reasoning, between those who judge globalization in relation to how far it advances or constrains progress towards a particular ideal of the 'good life' and those who judge it in relation to how far it facilitates or hinders different and multiple 'ways of life' or what Haber refers to as 'radical pluralism' (Tormey 2004: 75; Haber in Noonan 2003: 92). In this respect ethical assessments of globalization do not mirror a traditional left–right binary opposition but on the contrary dissolve it. Ethical critiques of globalization, whether on the grounds of justice or community, transcend orthodox left/right thinking as do ethical defences of globalization, whether rooted in cosmopolitanism or conservatism. Tracking these broader intellectual currents within the social sciences the controversy about globalization has become increasingly framed by normative and ethical deliberations concerning whether different or better worlds are either imaginable or possible.

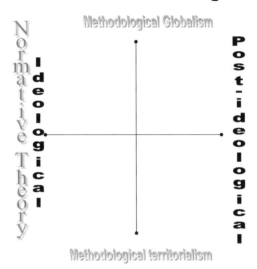

Figure 1.1   Debating globalization

To recap: two key issues are at stake in the academic controversy about globalization. The first concerns the contested intellectual hegemony of the concept of globalization in the social sciences: its descriptive, analytical and explanatory purchase. The second concerns the normative trajectory of globalization: whether on ethical grounds it is to be defended, transformed, resisted or rejected. When combined these two axes provide a conceptual space for thinking about what distinguishes the many different voices and contributions to the controversy about globalization. Figure 1.1 attempts a mapping of this space. The vertical axis represents the contest over the intellectual hegemony of globalization characterized by a privileging of either globalist forms of analysis (methodological globalism) or alternatively statist or societal forms of analysis (methodological territorialism). The horizontal axis represents the normative domain differentiating between ideological and post-ideological forms of reasoning: that is, the privileging of a vision of the 'good community' as opposed to the advocacy of many coexisting 'good communities' (ideological versus post-ideological reasoning). This figure constitutes a heuristic device for identifying, mapping and differentiating between the multiplicity of globalization scholarship. It provides the basis for the construction of a simple typology, one which moves beyond existing binary oppositions – for and against globalization, globalizers versus anti-globalizers, or globalists versus sceptics – to acknowledge the nuanced nature of current controversies.

As Holton and others have suggested, globalization scholarship has come in three overlapping but distinctive waves: the hyper-globalist, the sceptical and the post-sceptical (Holton 2005: 5; Bruff 2005). The wave analogy is useful in so far as it alludes to the successive diffusion and churning of distinct research programmes over time in which core research problematiques come to be reappropriated and redefined by new research agendas. Significantly, too, it does not imply a notion of cumulative knowledge or epistemic progress. Building upon Holton's schema, but inevitably modifying it, four successive waves of globalization scholarship can be identified: the theoreticist, the historicist, the institutionalist and the deconstructivist. As with all such schema it is neither definitive nor exhaustive but rather a partial way of organizing a highly complex field of study.

As manifest in the works of, amongst others, Giddens, Robertson, Rosenau, Albrow, Ohmae, Harvey and Lawrence the initial theoreticist wave was generally concerned with debates about the conceptualization of globalization, its principal dynamics and its systemic and structural consequences as a secular process of world-wide social change (Albrow 1996; Giddens 1990; Robertson 1992; Rosenau 1990; Ohmae 1990; Harvey 1989; Lawrence 1996). By contrast, the historicist wave, drawing upon the historical sociology of global development, was principally concerned with exploring in what ways, if any, contemporary globalization could be considered novel or unique, whether it defined a new epoch, or transformation, in the socio-economic and political organization of human affairs and, if so, its implications for the realization of progressive values and projects of human emancipation (see amongst others, Held et al. 1999; Hirst and Thompson 1999; Frank 1998; Castells 1996; Bordo et al. 2003; Dicken 1998; Baldwin and Martin 1999; Gilpin 2001; Gill 2003; Scholte 2000; Mann 1997; Hopkins 2002; Sassen 1996; Hardt and Negri 2000; Hoogvelt 1997; O'Rourke and Williamson 2000; Boyer and Drache 1996; Appadurai 1998; Amin 1997; Tomlinson 1994; Taylor 1995). Sceptical of these arguments about structural transformation, the third (institutionalist) wave sought to assess claims about global convergence (and divergence) by concentrating upon questions of institutional change and resilience, whether in national models of capitalism, state restructuring or cultural life (see amongst others here Garrett 1998, 2000; Swank 2002; Held 2004; Keohane and Milner 1996; Campbell 2004; Mosley 2003; Cowen 2004; Hay and Watson 2000; Pogge 2001). Finally, the fourth and most recent wave reflects the influence of poststructuralist and constructivist thinking across the social sciences, from Open Marxism to postmodernism. As a consequence there is an emphasis upon the importance of ideas, agency, communication, contingency and normative change to any convincing analysis of the making, unmaking and remaking of globalization understood as both a historical process and a hegemonic discourse. Central to this wave is a debate about whether the current historical conjuncture is best understood as a post-global age, in which globalization (as aspiration, discourse, material process and explanatory category) is (or should be) in retreat, or on the contrary an epoch of sometimes competing and alternative globalizations (in the plural), what Hoffman has referred to as the 'clash of globalizatons' (Hoffman 2002; Rosenberg 2005; Hay 2004; Urry 2003; Bello 2002; Held and McGrew 2002; Callinicos 2003; Keohane and Nye 2000; Rosamond 2003; Wolf 2004; Saul 2005; Eschele 2005; Beck 2004; Harvey 2003).

These four waves of analysis frame contemporary academic deliberations about globalization. As will be discussed subsequently, they also significantly influence how the wider public debate is constructed. Since they draw upon different epistemic traditions in the human sciences the contention over globalization is defined as much by contests over substantive matters as it is by competing, although not necessarily

Figure 1.2   Modes of analysis

incommensurable, modes of social enquiry. That said even within similar modes of enquiry conflicting views of globalization are in evidence. This suggests, as noted earlier, that simple binary oppositions or antinomies do little justice to the complexity of the controversies about globalization.

Returning to the task of mapping, the general field of enquiry involves, in the first instance, drawing together this discussion of the sources or dimensions of contention and the four waves of scholarship. Figure 1.1 identifies at least four different modes of analysis: that which takes globalization to be a really existing condition and considers it either on balance broadly benign or, subject to greater political direction, that it can be harnessed to progressive ideals and the creation of a 'better world'; that again which takes it seriously although as a new form of domination to be resisted along with any grand projects for remaking the world according to abstract universal principles; that which is deeply sceptical of the idea of globalization, or its presumed benign nature, emphasizing instead the continued importance of 'methodological territorialism' to social theory and the centrality of state power to the improvement of the human condition; and that which also rejects the privileging of the global in social theory emphasizing the intermeshing of processes of globalization and localization but with a normative attachment to community, autonomism, sustainability and difference. These four modes of analysis are referred to here as: defensive globalism, critical globalism, post-globalism and glocalism respectively (see Figure 1.2). Clearly these are generic labels which themselves conceal a spectrum of arguments from the more orthodox to the more radical. This does not invalidate the heuristic value of the typology as a tool for more systematic analysis and comparative enquiry into the question of why globalization, as a concept and/or really existing condition, is the source of so much controversy within and beyond the academy.

DECONSTRUCTING THE GLOBALIZATION CONTROVERSY: IDENTIFYING THE SOURCES OF CONTENTION

In identifying these four general modes of analysis within globalization scholarship the principal aim is to understand the substantive sources of their disagreement and agreement. This, in the first instance, requires some explication of their core arguments and assumptions.

Defensive globalism

There are broadly two main strands of literature which can be located under this label: liberal and transformationalist. Both acknowledge that recent decades have witnessed a new historical phase of globalization although they tend to disagree as to whether it is unprecedented. Liberal theory tends to emphasize continuities with the past, especially with the 'first global age' of 1870–1914, whereas transformationalist theory tends to emphasize globalization's unique and radical consequences. Nevertheless, both consider it central to understanding and explaining the current human condition and the possibilities for creating a 'better world'. However, both differ considerably in how globalization is conceived and whether it is to be judged broadly benign or malign. Whereas liberal theory offers a primarily economistic reading of globalization, as the growing integration of the world through market-led and technological forces, the transformationalist literature emphasizes its distinct, and often times contradictory, political, cultural, economic and social manifestations, that is, its multidimensional character. Moreover, whereas liberal theory stresses its generally benign character, the transformationalist literature offers a far more circumspect and critical assessment. This is associated with very different normative prescriptions for improving the global human condition – one rooted in an individualist market philosophy and the other in a collectivist philosophy of global regulation and control. What both share, however, is the belief that contemporary globalization, though far from inevitable or irresistible, is an enduring phenomenon which is changing societies across the world.

Amongst the most thoughtful liberal accounts of globalization are those offered by Martin Wolf (in his *Why Globalization Works*, 2004) and Jagdish Bhagwati (*In Defense of Globalization*, 2004). Both defend a sophisticated liberal position which is, in part, a critique of the rather crude neoliberalism which informs the 'Washington Consensus' and the ideology of corporate globalization. This crude neoliberalism asserts that the globalization of markets, through amongst other things free trade and unrestricted capital movements, is the harbinger of a more prosperous, democratic, cosmopolitan and peaceful world. Rooted in the 'commercial liberalism' of Adam Smith, and nineteenth-century thinkers such as Cobden and Bright, it views the 'creative destruction' of globalizing markets as a source of social progress and prosperity which provide the conditions within which democracy, cosmopolitanism and world peace may flourish.

Whilst both Wolf and Bhagwati argue that contemporary globalization has been principally benign their analysis is nuanced and qualified. Both emphasize how globalization is re-structuring the world economy as freer trade and the transnationalization of production create a new world division of labour, eroding the North–South hierarchy, and facilitate the rise of new economic powers such as China, India, and Brazil. This shift, they argue, has brought worldwide material benefits, in so far as it has reduced world poverty, inequality, and contributed to democratization and social progress in many parts of the world (Bhagwati 2004; Wolf 2004). It has, according to Cowen, also contributed to the renaissance, rather than the destruction, of local cultures (Cowen 2004). However, its benefits have not been uniformly experienced since, for various institutional and structural reasons, its transformative potential is unevenly realized (Wolf 2006; Bhagwati 2004). Moreover, as Wolf observes, globalization has not necessarily created the basis of a more stable or cooperative world nor overcome 'humanity's characteristic tribalism' (Wolf 2004, 2006). To address its distributional consequences they argue, in different ways, for more 'appropriate governance' to ' preserve and celebrate the good effects that globalization generally brings but supplement the good outcomes and address the phenomenon's occasional downsides' (Bhagwati 2004). Although this distinguishes them from the neo-liberal advocates of market globalization it is essentially an argument for making liberal globalization work better rather than for effectively regulating or restraining it.

In contrast transformationalist theory presents a much less benign and economistic reading of globalization. Amongst the principal works which share such a perspective, although rooted within different theoretical and methodological traditions, are those of Castells (1997), Rosenau (1990, 2003), Giddens (1990), Held et al. (1999), Held and McGrew (2002) and Scholte (2000). Rooted in the theoreticist and historicist waves of analysis they present a rich account of the distinctive features of contemporary globalization from within a broadly historical sociology tradition. This maps the scale and complexity of worldwide social relations, across all dimensions from the economic to the cultural, arguing that their historically unprecedented extensity and intensity represents a significant 'global shift' in the social organization of human affairs.

Contrary to an economistic analysis, globalization is conceived as operating across different domains, from the cultural to the political. Nor does it display a simple logic of global integration or convergence. On the contrary it is considered dialectical, integrating and fragmenting, uniting and dividing the world by creating winners and losers, including and excluding locales, as it proceeds. Whilst it generates pressures for socio-economic convergence these are mediated by domestic factors such that significant divergence, whether in levels of national social spending or economic growth, may often be the result. Rather than imposing a 'golden straitjacket' on all states its consequences are significantly differentiated. Yet increasingly states and societies confront similar problems of boundary control as the separation of the global and the domestic becomes less tenable. Political problems, from people trafficking to the management of the national economy, are simultaneously both domestic and global matters. This erosion of the internal and external, domestic and international, articulates the growing compression of time and space in an epoch of instant global communications. A resultant structural consequence is that the relationships between territory, economy, society, identity, sovereignty and the state no longer appear as historically fixed and congruent – even if this was imaginary – but rather as relatively fluid and disjointed. For the transformationalists it is this apparent dislocation or destabilizing of the institutional coordinates of modern social life that is the source of both heightened conflict and insecurity at all levels from the local to the global. This dislocation takes many forms, from the political to the cultural. It finds, for example, particular expression in the political domain in the apparent disjuncture between national sovereignty and the suprastate locus of many aspects of the actual business of contemporary government.

Unlike neoliberal thinking, the transformationalist account does not imbue globalization with any particular telos, neither an inevitably more prosperous nor peaceful world, nor the inevitable emergence of a singular world society or the coming anarchy. However, there is broad agreement that its structural consequences do much to multiply the complexity of modern societies and thereby their governance whilst simultaneously creating a range of new transnational problems, from global warming to global financial stability, which such complexity makes even more difficult to resolve. One consequence is the restructuring of the state evidenced in the shift from government to governance. Furthermore, since decisions in one country can directly impact on the interests of citizens of other societies a whole new range of trans-boundary problems is generated which challenge the efficacy of national democracy. Beyond the political domain, the consequences of globalization present comparable challenges to the organization and functioning of modern societies.

In addition to its structural consequences the transformationalist literature has much to say about the distributional consequences of globalization. In particular Castells, amongst others, argues, contra the Washington Consensus and liberal accounts, that economic globalization is associated with a polarizing and divided world, as the gap between rich and poor widens, whilst much of humanity remains on the margins or is excluded from its benefits (Castells 2000). This structural exclusion and structural inequality, it is argued, is an inevitable consequence of market-led globalization. However, this need not be the case if globalization could be harnessed to the ideals of social justice. The normative thrust of the transformationalist analysis is thus an argument for an ethical or humane globalization that combines economic efficiency with equity or social justice. This is a demand for nothing less than a fundamental transformation of contemporary globalization itself in so far as its 'challenges are likely to be of enduring significance' (Held 2004: 11). For Held, Castells, and others this takes the form of variations on a project for global democracy (Held 2004; Castells 2005; Scholte 2005) – a project that, building upon the reform of existing infrastructures of global governance and civil society, seeks the democratic regulation of globalization in order to address its more socially malignant structural and distributional consequences.

Post-globalism

Post-globalist scholarship echoes Joseph Stiglitz's quip that 'globalization today has been oversold' (Stiglitz 2005: 229). It is oversold in at least three senses: as a description of social reality (a social ontology), as an explanation of social change (an explanans) and as an ideology of social progress (a political project). In all these respects, most particularly in the wake of 9/11, globalist rhetoric increasingly appears rather hollow. Amongst others, the historian Niall Ferguson (2005) writes of 'sinking globalization', Saul (2005) 'the end of globalism' and Rosenberg (2005) 'the age of globalization is unexpectedly over'. These critiques of globalization have inherited from the historicist and deconstructivist waves of analysis a theoretically informed and empirically rich scepticism which points to the demise of globalization (deglobalization) both as description and prescription.

Central to this scepticism is the work of, amongst others, Hirst and Thompson (1999), Hay (2004), Rugman (2000) and Gilpin (2002). Though their analyses differ in significant ways their studies concur that contemporary globalization is not historically unprecedented, that the dominant economic trends are towards internationalization and regionalization, and that the idea of globalization has been much more significant than its descriptive or explanatory utility. In effect, they argue that radical, liberal and transformationalist scholarship significantly exaggerates its empirical and normative significance arguing that the world remains principally one of discrete national societies or states. Accordingly much contemporary theory exaggerates the significance of the global in explanations of the social world often by disregarding the continuing significance of endogenous sources of social change and the powerful insights of classical social theory. In short, globalization is both bad description and bad theory.

Qualifying this scepticism, however, Hay argues that there is one sense in which globalization remains absolutely central to any account of the current epoch: as an idea or discourse which provides social meaning and frames, as well as legitimates, social and political change (Hay 2004). As an idea or discourse, globalization finds expression across the world in the speeches of politicians and the rhetoric of protesters as a rationale for social and political action. Within an interpretative tradition, globalization, as the discursive construction of the social world, remains essential to understanding the contemporary epoch.

These sceptical arguments have acquired particular force in the current context. For today, borders and boundaries, nationalism and protectionism, localism and ethnicity appear to define an epoch of radical deglobalization, the disintegration of the liberal world order and the demise of globalism. Ferguson suggests that the current epoch has many similarities with the 'sinking' of the 'last age of globalization', which ended in the destruction of World War I and the subsequent world depression (Ferguson 2005). J.R. Saul, in similar vein, argues that the ideology or discourse of globalism, upon which globalization as a 'social fact' or social ontology depends, is rapidly receding in the face of the resurgence of nationalism, ethnicity, religious fundamentalism and geo-politics (Saul 2005). As Rosenberg concludes, the current conjuncture demonstrates the follies of globalization theory not to mention just how far its proponents misread and misunderstood the 1990s period in the context of world historical development (Rosenberg 2005). The rapidity of the slide 'backwards' towards an increasingly deglobalized world demonstrates not only the intellectual bankruptcy of globalization as description, explanation and ideology but also paradoxically that '"globalization" did not even exist'(Rosenberg 2005: 65).

Post-globalism, on the whole, does not mourn the passing of globalization. On the contrary, for many, but admittedly not all, of its adherents it constitutes a welcome return to grounded or immanent critique, to understanding both the real possibilities and real obstacles to the construction of a better world. For those of a historical materialist persuasion this requires capturing state power, building a post-capitalist society and developing a progressive internationalism as opposed to the utopia of global democracy; more anti-capitalism perhaps than anti-globalism *per se* (Tormey 2004). Amongst those of liberal persuasion it means using state power to create the conditions of a more just international order – a form of liberal internationalism. What both share is a commitment to the state as the principal, but not the sole, agent of social and political progress, or building a better world from the inside out rather than the outside in.

Critical globalism

Although it spans a diverse set of literatures critical globalism is perhaps best described as encompassing that 'engaged' scholarship which takes globalization seriously because it is constitutive of new global structures and systems of transnational domination (Mittleman 2000; Rupert and Solomon 2005; Gill 2003; Hardt and Negri 2000; Eschele 2005; Petersen 2004). As such, critical globalist scholarship not only acknowledges the ways in which the organization and exercise of social power is being radically extended and transnationalized by the social forces of globalization but also how, in the process, new subjectivities and transnational collectivities of resistance are formed. Variously referred to as the 'global matrix', 'global market civilization' or 'Empire', a new globalized social formation is held to be in the making which, according to critical globalist theory, requires new ways of thinking about and acting in the world (James and Nairn 2005; Gill 2003; Hardt and Negri 2000). Issuing principally from first and fourth wave theorizing it draws upon critical theory, poststructural and post-Marxist scholarship to understand the making and unmaking of these new globalized forms of domination as well as the possibilities for their remaking or progressive transformation.

Amongst the more influential of this scholarship is the work of Hardt and Negri. In *Empire* they theorize and explain the emergence of a historically unique form of global domination with globalization at its core. Though they refer to this as 'Empire' it is distinguished from classic imperialism:

> By 'Empire,' . . . we understand something altogether different from 'imperialism.' . . . Imperialism was really an extension of the sovereignty of the European nation-states beyond their own boundaries. . . . In contrast to imperialism, Empire establishes no territorial center of power and does not rely on fixed boundaries or barriers. It is a decentered and deterritorializing apparatus of rule that progressively incorporates the entire global realm within its open, expanding frontiers . . . (Hardt and Negri 2000: Introduction)

Central to the making of Empire, they argue, are processes of globalization which they consider enduring rather than contingent. These same processes, however, engender projects of transnational resistance which create the social basis for alternative globalizations in opposition to the totalizing logic of Empire:

> The passage to Empire and its processes of globalization offer new possibilities to the forces of liberation. Globalization, of course, is not one thing, and the multiple

processes that we recognize as globalization are not unified or univocal. Our political task, we will argue, is not simply to resist these processes but to reorganize them and redirect them toward new ends. The creative forces of the multitude that sustain Empire are also capable of autonomously constructing a counter-Empire, an alternative politi-cal organization of global flows and exchanges. The struggles to contest and subvert Empire, as well as those to construct a real alternative, will thus take place on the imperial terrain itself – indeed, such new struggles have already begun to emerge . . . (Hardt and Negri 2000: Introduction)

Hardt and Negri's 'Empire' has much in common with Gill's neo-Gramscian account of the hegemony of a globalized capitalist order (Gill 2003). Both consider globalization as a historically distinctive mode of domination which is not only economic but cultural, social, ideological and political. Both also emphasize the highly contested nature of this domination articulated in diverse local and transna-tional struggles of resistance and recognition, from the Zapatistas in Mexico to the World Social Forum, which constitute the solidarist networks of alternative globalizations.

Agency, subjectivity and social struggle are thus vital expository concepts in the critical globalist lexicon. As Evans, amongst many others, observes, globalization has been associated with the emergence of a globalized contentious politics in which local and global struggles are conjoined since 'the defence of difference and quests for local power require global strategies and connections, likewise transnational social movements must have local social roots' (Evans 2005: 7). These alternative globalizations, which are not necessarily progressive, partly reflect both the rise of identity politics and global consciousness constituting new subjectivities, or ways of thinking about and acting in the world. The sources of alternative globalizations are thus to be located not simply in distributional struggles but also in struggles over recognition, whether of indigenous peoples or gender discrimination. This 'globalization from below' perspective focuses attention on the significance of indi-vidual and collective agency, from fair trade consumerism to G8 protests, in the making and remaking of global society.

In certain respects, as with the transformationalists, there is an assumption that, irrespective of its particular form, globalization *per se* is integral to (post)modernity or (post)modern social life. Corporate globalization is neither its sole face nor is it inevitably hegemonic. Nor is globalization *per se* inherently malign but rather harbours, as in the multitude, progressive potential. The principal normative and political question is whether and how that potential is to be realized. In this regard critical globalism resists the valorization of any singular normative vision of ethical globalization or its institutionalization, whether global democracy or a post-capitalist order, in favour of a radical pluralism, that is the positive prospect of a multiplicity of alternative globalizations (Tormey 2004).

Glocalism

Contrary to the claims of Rosenberg, globalization theory has far from colonized the human sciences. Indeed poststructuralism has encouraged a shift away from macro-social analysis to a concern with the particular, the local and the micro-social.

Glocalist scholarship takes this shift seriously. It seeks to problematize the local–global complex rather than *a priori* to assert, or presume, the causal primacy of either or to conceive them in a structurally contradictory relationship. In simple terms glocalist analysis, which inherits much from third and fourth wave thinking, takes both globalization and localization seriously without necessarily privileging either in explanations of the social. Holton refers to this as 'methodological glocalism' because it is an approach whose 'defining characteristic . . . is to observe the interpenetration of the two [local and global]' and to 'recognize the co-existence and inter-relations between these various layers of social life' acknowledging that such inter-relations 'are not necessarily corrosive or incompatible' since 'the global and the national or local may under certain circumstances depend on each other' (Holton 2005: 191). Glocalist scholarship charts via media between the divergent approaches of 'methodological globalism' and 'methodological nationalism' which inform much contemporary social theory.

Some of the more influential work in this genre is located within cultural studies, anthropology, social and urban geography. Brenner, for example, argues that capitalism has always operated at different spatial scales, from the local to the global, but that the restructuring of capitalism in the 1990s brought with it a more complex spatiality (Brenner 2004). Social relations increasingly are articulated and rearticulated simultaneously across a multiplicity of spatial scales, from the sub-local to the local, national, transational, regional and global. Thus much of the work on global cities illuminates how they are simultaneously local, national, transnational, regional and global centres of power (Smith 2001; Taylor 1995). Rather than conceiving this multiplicity of spatial scales as necessarily organized in a hierarchical or contradictory fashion Brenner argues that they are mutually constitutive (Brenner 2004). By this he does not mean that the global and local can simply be dissolved into one another, for they retain their distinctive forms, but rather that explanation of one necessarily requires an account of the other. Brenner's work is a critique of that globalization scholarship which privileges any particular spatial scale: in other words that suggests social relations are becoming increasingly deterritorialized, denationalized or alternatively regionalized or nationalized. On the contrary, he argues, the multiplicity of spatial scales are relational not containers of social relations. Territory still matters but not in the way in which it is conventionally theorized – as deterritorialization or reterritorialization. Within this spatial matrix state power and sovereignty may be far from being eroded by globalization but is being restructured and rearticulated across a multiplicity of spatial scales.

Similar arguments are made in many studies of cultural globalization. Whereas much first wave thinking about globalization associated it with cultural convergence or homogenization – McDonaldization – second wave thinking emphasized its polarizing dynamics in strengthening traditional identities and leading to the resurgence of nationalism and ethnicity (Ritzer 1995; Barber 1996). By contrast, Hannerz and Appadurai, amongst others, have argued that it is associated with cultural hybridization, fusion or creolism (Hannerz 1992; Appadurai 1998). Stressing the social construction, rather than primordial origins, of individual and collective identity, they point to ways in which local and global cultural resources are conjoined in the production of new kinds of identities and cultural imaginings, from the self-identification of Irish-Americans to the indigenization of world religions. To

explain these processes of cultural hybridization requires moving beyond the antinomies of the global and the local to a recognition of their mutual imbrication.

Recognition of the complexity and contingency of this mutual imbrication informs
the normative thinking of much glocalist scholarship. Although it is animated by a
concern to identify the structures and processes of domination which range in,
across and through societies it necessarily rejects the crude binary division of the
global as the principal source of domination and the local as the principal source
of resistance or emancipation. Transnational domination, as with the politics of
resistance, is constituted through complex interrelationships between the local and
global. This produces a scepticism both towards visions of an ethical globalization,
with its emphasis both upon the remaking of global institutions, and towards
unqualified faith in the politics of resistance, namely Hardt and Negri's 'multitude'
(2004). Some emphasize the significance of the new localism through which regimes
of urban governance harness local, national and global social forces to the realization of progressive social purposes (Smith 2001; Brenner 2004). Others the new
(global) regionalism which, Hettne argues, provides a cooperative framework for
states to manage collectively their engagement with the world economy in socially
progressive ways (Hettne 2000). And others still, strategies of autonomous development as articulated by the Zapatista movement which Olesen notes relies upon 'a
growing imbrication of local, national and transnational levels of interaction rather
than their increasing disconnection' (Olesen 2005: 54). As with critical globalism,
there is no singular normative vision of a better world only an aspiration for
'a world in which many worlds fit' (Olesen 2005: 12).

ONE GLOBALIZATION OR MANY?

These distinctive ways of thinking about globalization represent general modes of
analysis in the existing literature, rather than discrete theories. They differ as discussed in respect of their substantive and normative interpretations of globalization.
This does not mean, however, that at some level they are necessarily incommensurable or incompatible. But the disagreements between them are significant for they
arise from disagreements about matters of social ontology, epistemology and theory
(both explanatory and normative).

Much of the controversy about globalization, and its consequences, is a disagreement about whether or not it represents a valid or convincing social ontology: a
description of a really existing condition. Thus for Rosenberg and others such as
Hirst and Thompson, globalization is a highly misleading description of contemporary social reality (Rosenberg 2005; Hirst and Thompson 1999). It distorts and
misinterprets social reality since it posits a world in which social relations transcend
states and societies, whether as Empire or the global market, when the actuality is
that the world remains organized into territorially bounded capitalist societies. If
globalization means anything more than simply interdependence between societies,
it is more prescription rather than accurate description. Only to the extent, as Hay
suggests, that globalization is an important idea or dominant discourse does it
constitute a really existing condition (Hay 2004). By contrast, much contemporary
social theory accepts, implicitly or explicitly, that it is, both materially and

discursively, a principal facet, if not the dominant feature, of the contemporary human condition. Whilst its significance and impact on societies may be debated its existence is both undeniable and enduring. In part this is because, moving beyond the economism which informs the more sceptical position, globalization – and by definition social ontology – tends to be conceived more expansively not just simply in terms of market globalism or the social relations of production. Rather than economic globalization *per se* emphasis is placed upon multiple globalizations, from the cultural to the criminal, the corporate to the religious. This more Weberian approach engenders a focus upon the multiple ways in which globalization pervades social existence, not just in terms of abstract systems binding people's material fate together, whether in finance or trade, but also with respect to the life world. Globality, as the consciousness or awareness of the global, many argue, is an important aspect of the contemporary life world in so far as it constitutes a social imaginary, that is, how people locate themselves and act in the world.

Discussion of social ontology necessarily connects to matters of epistemology, or the meta-theories of knowledge and explanation. Controversies about many substantive questions, from whether globalization is good or bad for the poor, or whether it encourages cultural homogeneity or heterogeneity, are infused with epistemological questions. Different aspects of globalization appear to lend themselves to different forms of social enquiry, from the econometric studies of its causal links with world inequality, to the post-positivist studies of its discursive construction. This divide between the broadly orthodox, fallibalist or historicist social science and post-positivist, hermeneutic epistemologies is highly significant. It is not just that there is simply (ontological) disagreement about whether globalization is a historical or social fact but that there is also (epistemological) disagreement about what constitutes valid knowledge of globalization in the first instance. Since there can be no objective resolution of this problem aspirations for a singular theory of globalization are likely to remain unrealized. It is also why there is effectively no globalization *debate* – since this implies the possibility of shared judgment – but rather enduring deliberation. This is intellectually uncomfortable although it demonstrates the importance of identifying whether disagreement is of a substantive or epistemological kind.

Arguably the most critical sources of disagreement are theoretical. Globalization theory as such does not exist. Rather, for the most part, it has been incorporated into the explanatory frameworks of existing social theory, both as explanans and explanandum, from historical materialism to postmodernism. It is hardly surprising, therefore, that there are competing, if not contradictory, readings of its causal powers, the significance of agency, dialectics and social transformation. Many discussions of globalization confuse cause and effect, that is, whether it is the phenomenon doing the work of explanation (the explanans) or alternatively that which is the object of explanation (the explanandum). Tendencies to elide the two, such that the social phenomenon to which globalization refers become effectively its causes, are clearly problematic. However, the real issue which courts disagreement is not the inversion of explanans and explanandum, on which there is probably general agreement, but rather whether globalization is essentially *epiphenomenal*. If, as historical materialist accounts argue, it is solely the consequence of the expansionary logic of capitalist societies, then it has no independent causal powers, that is, it is clearly epiphenomenal. By contrast much of the work on globalization disagrees fundamentally with this line of reasoning, including most other neo-Marxist and Weberian historical sociological analyses. These argue instead that globalization, whatever its underlying causes, has systemic or emergent properties which make it causally significant, rather than simply epiphenomenal, in effect it structures social action or social change. This interpretation shares much in common with those historical materialist or historical sociology accounts of imperialism which conceive it as a product of capitalist logics but also nevertheless causally significant.

At least some of the tension between different interpretations of globalization is attributable to embedded conceptions of structure and agency. To the extent that, as with world systems theory or neoliberalism, globalization is understood in primarily economistic or technological terms it appears inevitable and irresistible: a structural imperative of capitalist or technological development. Within such accounts agency, institutions or cultural difference tend to be undervalued leading to overly deterministic explanations which have some implicit teleology of global convergence, or a singular modernity. By contrast much second and third wave thinking, as noted, has contributed to a greater focus on agency and the making, or unmaking, of globalization. This is not a return to voluntarism but on the contrary draws upon the idea of *structuration* to explain globalization as both structure and process, as a social phenomenon that is both constructed and reproduced through human agency (Scholte 2000). This leads to a recognition of the contingency of globalization, its potential limits, and the significance of agency, ideas and institutions to mediating and shaping its impact. Rather than global convergence it implies a more dialectical understanding of the world: one which emphasizes simultaneous integration and fragmentation, convergence and divergence, particularism and universalism, and localism and globalism. It also brings to the fore the idea of alternative and multiple globalisms whilst highlighting the multiple scales at which both local and global processes operate. However, for those of a more structuralist persuasion the extent to which difference prevails over the convergent pressures of globalization, whether in respect of different national capitalisms or resurgent cultures, is powerful evidence of its social limits and limited explanatory power. This underdetermination of theories of globalization remains in part rooted in different meta-conceptions of agency and structure.

Some of the fiercest disagreements about contemporary globalization concern the invocation of epochal change: that it represents a profound organizational shift in the spatio-temporal constitution of modern societies and world order. Whether understood as the emergence of a global informational capitalism, the global market civilization, the post-Westphalian world order or the new global complexity, there is, as noted, a powerful tendency in the existing literature to emphasize its epochal nature. This remains deeply contested, as discussed earlier, by a range of work which points to the continuing significance of territory, the state, endogenous forces of change and the general overselling of globalization and its historical novelty. What is at issue in these disagreements are not just substantive matters of empirics and historical interpretation but differing theoretical conceptions of conjunctural and epochal social change. Whereas historical materialists calibrate epochal change principally by reference to transformations in the organization of production those of a neo-Weberian persuasion do so with reference to the multiple domains of social production and reproduction, including the economic, the cultural, the political and so on. Put simply the differences can be construed in terms of restrictive or expansive criteria of epochal change. Of course these are only given meaning in the context of some broader theory of social change. In this respect differences of interpretation are not just matters of empirics but also importantly theorization. Theories of social change influenced by an economism or alternatively post-positivism, tend to produce rather different assessments of the transformative potential and impact of globalization. But even where economism dominates, as in historical materialist and liberal accounts of the global, significant differences arise because of very different theoretical and also normative commitments. Normative assumptions and outlooks, as discussed above, have a central role in shaping academic controversies about globalization.

Amongst the most significant normative debates is that between cosmopolitanism and communitarianism. Although best thought of as a normative continuum, in so far as both are tendencies not absolutes, there remain sufficient principled differences between both to suggest the distinction remains useful. Whilst there are many variants of cosmopolitanism, nevertheless it embodies a general tendency, which though critical of market globalization accepts some notion of its perfectibility or the possibility of constructing alternative globalisms for progressive ends. By contrast much communitarian thinking is sceptical of globalization because of its universalizing tendencies and therefore doubts its assumed perfectibility or its progressive potential emphasizing instead an ethical preference for difference, diversity, the local and self-determination. Of course the same ideological and post-ideological continuum can be grafted onto this binary divide, highlighting the significance of grand visions versus multiple possibilities within both ethical camps. Thus ideas of cosmopolitan democracy – the democratization of globalization – share ethical ground with radical notions of alternative globalizations but both differ radically in their understanding of whether a better world is to be designed or to emerge out of ethical and political struggle. Similarly, despite common ethical outlooks, there are important differences between statism and communitarianism (see Figure 1.3). Since all explanatory theories of globalization are implicitly, if not explicitly, normative, disagreement about its essential nature is, in part at least, often rooted in different ethical outlooks. Indeed the most contentious aspect of the study of contemporary globalization concerns the ethical and the political: whether it hinders or assists the pursuit of a better world and whether that better world should be defined by cosmopolitan or communitarian principles or both?

THE POLITICS OF GLOBALIZATION: REFORM, RESISTANCE OR REVOLUTION?

Beyond the academy, the struggle for globalization's soul finds its most visible expression in the annual summits of the World Social Forum, the critics of corporate globalization, and the World Economic Forum – the elite defenders of cosmopolitan capitalism. Porto Alegre and Davos have become symbols of the 'clash of globalizations', a contest of ideas and projects for forging very different worlds. In the media

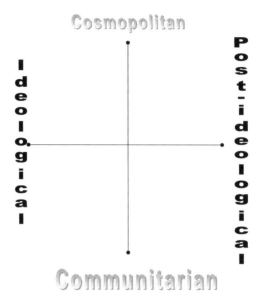

Figure 1.3 Normative spaces

this is largely represented as a clash between elite globalizers and the people's anti-globalizers but, as most studies conclude, this is a significant misrepresentation. At its core the politics of globalization is shaped by the contest between the advocates of capitalism and a liberal world order and those who seek a world order 'within which many worlds are possible'. It is in crude terms principally a clash between the social forces of globalizing capitalism and those of anti-capitalism. It is, too, a historic political development in an age in which 'bowling alone' is the dominant metaphor since it brings collective agency 'back in' and opens up social imaginaries to the possibility that 'other worlds' might indeed be desirable, if not necessary.

To the extent that globalization is the foil for capitalism much of the rhetoric and politics of capitalism/anti-capitalism revolves around globalization. It draws, too, in complex and often inconsistent ways, upon academic controversies about globalization such that in significant ways these have become overlapping discourses. As studies of the anti-capitalist movement conclude, the organizing master frame of ideas which binds these disparate causes together is opposition to the Washington Consensus as the modernizing project of global capital (Ayres 2004). The liberalizing and free market logic of the Washington Consensus is conceived as extending the reach and reproducing the power of a globalizing capitalist order, a system of domination which is responsible for growing global poverty, inequality and the extinction of alternative and sustainable 'ways of life'. This juggernaut of globalizing capitalist modernity, far from benign as the liberals might have it, is structurally malign. By contrast, the advocates of global capitalism consider it the sole route to a more prosperous, stable and democratic world in which different ways of life remain quite possible.

What is at stake in this political contest is of vital importance to humanity, for it is nothing less than a struggle over the trajectory of global development: put simply, over who rules, on whose terms, by what means and for what purposes.

Figure 1.4 Contentious politics: the remaking of globalization

Central to this is the issue of whether globalization can or should be made good or better: whether it can be made to serve human interests and wider social objectives as well as economic efficiency, or whether alternative post-global, post-capitalist futures are both necessary and more desirable. In this respect the political contest cuts across the traditional left–right and red–green divides, bringing together unlikely allies, of reds, greens and blues on both sides of the globalization/post-globalization fracture. Thus in the 1999 Seattle demonstrations, which influenced the collapse of the WTO talks, environmentalists, trade unionists and protectionists protested together against trade liberalization whilst corporate leaders, social democratic politicians and global social justice campaigners sought to defend it. This illustrates the remarkably complex and heterogeneous social composition of the various constituencies in this political contest which is interpreted by some as delineating a new kind of globalized contentious politics transcending the conventional political categories of left, right, green and red/blue. Moreover, whilst there remain avid defenders of a Hayekian free market globalized capitalism or alternatively the radical re-localization of social life, increasingly the locus of contention has come to revolve around the questions of how contemporary globalization can be regulated, transformed or alternative globalizations pursued, as opposed to an *a priori* rejection or unqualified advocacy of its current form. Thus Joseph Stiglitz, one time arch-defender of the Washington Consensus, now advocates its greater regulation, whilst Subcommandante Marcos of the Chiapas Zapatista movement calls for alternative globalizations. Constructing the politics of globalization, as with the academic controversy, in terms of adversarial pro- and anti-globalization factions is no longer convincing.

One way to envisage this contentious politics of globalization is to draw on the earlier distinctions between cosmopolitan and communitarian, and ideological and post-ideological thinking. Figure 1.4 locates some of the more significant political projects or constituencies according to their underlying cosmopolitan or communitarian sensibilities and the extent to which they coalesce around a singular institutionalized vision of a better world (ideological) or seek 'merely to establish that worlds other than the neoliberal variety are possible' (post-ideological) (Tormey 2004: 167). These projects differ not only in substantive terms but also with respect to their radicalism, from reform to rejection, and political strategies, from lobbying to protest. Here the focus is necessarily limited to a brief overview of the broad projects which define the parameters of the current politics of globalization rather than a detailed survey of its myriad constituencies.

Market globalists defend neoliberal globalization but in qualified ways whilst recognizing that it has to be, by necessity, rule-governed (Wolf 2004; Bhagwati 2004). Rather than simply the triumph of markets they advocate essential but limited global and national regulation, the social embedding of markets, as well as differential integration of poorer countries into the global economy. In many respects such thinking informs the emerging post-Washington Consensus. By contrast reformist globalists, as with the transformationalists discussed above, seek in varying degrees to regulate or reconstruct globalization primarily through global institutional change or its transformation. This encompasses both notions of incremental reform, making the global governance complex more transparent and sensitive to the needs of the world's most needy, and the advocacy of global social democracy, the fundamental transformation of global institutions in order to realize a more just and democratic world order (Held 2004). Whilst the motivations of reformists may be admired, those of a more radical persuasion remain sceptical of the possibilities of authentic reform because of the problem of cooptation – of being socialized into the values and logics of the 'system'. This leads to greater emphasis upon projects of resistance, to the activities of both global governance institutions and global corporations, but also to constructing alternative networks of transnational solidarity, of promoting alternative globalisms to the dominant neoliberal variety. Such ideas are effectively rooted in a cosmopolitanism from below rather than, as with the reformers, from above. In its more revolutionary expressions it leads to the advocacy, drawing upon neo-Gramscian Marxism, of a counter-hegemonic global politics which emphasizes the construction of broad coalitions of globalization's discontented confronting and eroding from without the institutional and ideological legitimacy of market globalism. It is a project for the democratization of global and national governance from without, rather than from within, and it seeks not the regulation of global capital but its transformation towards a post-capitalist world order.

Although the notion of a counter-hegemonic politics finds resonance amongst many radical critics of capitalism some remain convinced that its principal focus should remain the national in so far as the levers of global power remain firmly rooted within states, or at least the most powerful states. Thus for many of a radical or reformist persuasion 'capturing' the state, as an instrument for realizing progressive social change, is both the proper and more convincing response to the challenges of globalization. Moreover, it provides the institutional platform for creating more progressive forms of multilateralism and global governance. And for some, since capitalism remains essentially national capitalism, it is the only realistic political strategy for constructing not just a better world but a post-capitalist world.

Interestingly, those constituencies of a more conservative persuasion also advocate a stronger focus on state power but principally to protect the 'nation' from the modernizing and corrosive consequences of globalization from without. This leads to an emphasis upon protectionism, deglobalization and a form of neo-mercantilism which prioritizes national autonomy over other values or obligations.

Finally, there are those constituencies which are somewhat distrustful of both the idea that the state can, or should, be the primary locus of governance in a globalizing world and of vesting power with remote global institutions. Accordingly, many politicians and civil society groups across the globe advocate forms of suprastate regionalism as a political strategy for combining effective collective governance of globalizing forces with the decentralization of power away from global institutions (Schirm 2002). This new regionalism has become increasingly significant especially beyond the Western core of the global order. In large part this is because it is conceived as the basis for a multicentric or pluralistic world order in which different versions of the good life simultaneously can be nurtured whilst coexisting with each other in a globalizing world (Amin 1997). In contrast, others – most especially from within the environmental movement – advocate a much more radical decentralization of power away from the global and national to localities and communities. This resonates with notions of autonomism, of the recovery of local and communal self-determination, whether at the city or neighbourhood level. It reflects an incipient desire for the deglobalization of social life although it is not necessarily incompatible with notions of alternative globalisms.

As this brief discussion has attempted to demonstrate, the politics of globalization is more complex than the simple popularized versions of the antimony of 'pro and anti' factions. It embodies both progressive and reactionary forces. It is this complexity which has in many respects confounded those who argued that, in the wake of 9/11, the 'anti-globalization' movement would wither away. Not only has this not transpired but on the contrary the contentious politics of globalization has been reignited by the prosecution of the 'global war on terror' and the resurgence of global justice as the political terrain on which that contention is mobilized. Whether this contentious politics ultimately proves a progressive or reactionary force remains to be realized. Historical studies of contentious politics suggest that for progressive change to be successful requires, in the first instance, a growing recognition that the world could be otherwise, that the future is more contingent than predictable, that agency, collective or otherwise, does matter (Tilly 2004). If this is the only achievement of progressive forces today that in itself may prove, as with earlier struggles for democracy, a significant but enduring development in the politics of globalization (Tormey 2004).

CONCLUSION: A POST-MORTEM FOR GLOBALIZATION?

This chapter has sought to explain why globalization is the source of so much contention within and beyond the academy. In so doing it has identified and elaborated some of the principal contending modes of analysis and how these are inflected in the current contentious politics of globalization. It has argued throughout that the academic and political disagreements concerning globalization no longer, if they ever did, coalesce around polarized arguments or factions captured by the labels 'pro' and 'anti'. On the contrary the controversies are far more nuanced and complex reflecting, in part, differences of an ontological, epistemelogical, theoretical and normative kind. Not all take globalization seriously either as explanans or explanandum, and even amongst those that do there exist competing interpretations of its sources, consequences and dynamics. Moreover, the contentious politics of globalization transcends not only orthodox political alignments but also the crude 'pro' and 'anti' labelling. Radical critics of corporate globalization often defend alternative forms of globalization whilst national capital often advocates deglobalization.

To understand why globalization is so contested, what is at stake, and the under-lying sources of disagreement requires moving beyond the metaphor of debate to that of the web metaphor of a multi-logue, a conversation between multiple differently situated – spatially and epistemically – participants. To this extent globalization, whether real or imaginary, has been associated, for good or ill, with a powerful renaissance of social and political theorizing as well as social and political activism. For these reasons alone it is likely to remain, for the foreseeable future, a fiercely contested idea within and outside the academy.

References

Albrow, M. 1996. *The Global Age*. Cambridge: Polity Press.

Amin, S. 1997. *Capitalism in the Age of Globalization*. London: Zed Press.

Appadurai, A. 1998. *Modernity at Large*. Minneapolis: Minnesota University Press.

Ayres, J. 2004. 'Framing collective action against neoliberalism', *Journal of World Systems Theory*, 10(1), 11–34.

Baldwin, R.E. and Martin, P. 1999. 'Two waves of globalisation: Superficial similarities, fundamental differences'. NBER Working Paper No. 6904.

Barber, B. 1996. *Jihad versus McWorld*. New York: Ballantine Books.

Beck, U. 2000. *What Is Globalization?* Cambridge: Polity Press.

Beck, U. 2004. 'Cosmopolitical realism: On the distinction between cosmopolitanism in philosophy and the social sciences', *Global Networks*, 4 (2), 131–56.

Bello, W. 2002. *Deglobalization: Ideas for a New Global Economy*. London: Zed Press.

Bhagwati, J. 2004. *In Defense of Globalization*. Oxford: Oxford University Press.

Bordo, M., Taylor, A.M. and Williamson, J.G. (eds) 2003. *Globalization in Historical Perspective*. Chicago: NBER/Chicago University Press.

Boyer, R. and Drache, D. (eds) 1996. *States against Markets*. London: Routledge.

Brenner, N. 2004. *New State Spaces: Urban Governance and the Rescaling of Statehood*. Oxford: Oxford University Press.

Bruff, I. 2005. 'Making sense of the globalization debate when engaging in political economy analysis', *British Journal of Politics and International Relations*, 7 (3), 261–80.

Callinicos, A. 2003. *An Anti-Capitalist Manifesto*. Cambridge: Polity Press.

Campbell, J.L. 2004. *Institutional Change and Globalization*. Ithaca, NY: Cornell University Press.

Castells, M. 1996. *The Rise of the Network Society*. Vol. I of *The Information Age: Economy, Society and Culture*. Oxford: Blackwell.

Castells, M. 1997. *The Power of Identity*. Vol. II of *The Information Age: Economy, Society and Culture*. Oxford: Blackwell.

Castells, M. 2000. *The Rise of the Network Society*. Vol. I of *The Information Age: Economy, Society and Culture*, 2nd edn. Oxford: Blackwell.

Castells, M. 2005. 'Global governance and global politics', *PS Online*, January, 9–16.

Cowen, T. 2004. *Creative Destruction: How Globalization Is Changing the World's Cultures*. Princeton, NJ: Princeton University Press.

Dicken, P. 1998. *Global Shift*. London: Paul Chapman.

Dicken, P. 2000. *Global Shift: Transforming the World Economy*. London: Chapman.

Dollar, D. and Kraay, A. 2000. *Growth Is Good for the Poor*, World Bank Report, Washington DC, www.worldbank.org

Eschele, C. 2005. 'Constructing the antiglobalization movement'. In C. Eshele and B. Maiguashia (eds), *Critical Theories, International Relations and the 'Anti Globalization Movement': The Politics of Resistance*, 17–35. London: Routledge.

Evans, P. 2005. 'Counter hegemonic globalization: Transnational social movements in the contemporary global political economy.' Retrieved 29 September 2005 from http://sociology.berkeley.edu/faculty/evans/evans_pdf/Evans%20Transnational_Movements.pdf.

Falk, R. 2002. *Predatory Globalization*. Cambridge: Polity Press.

Ferguson, N. 2005. 'Sinking globalization', *Foreign Affairs*, 84 (2), 64–77.

Frank, A.G. 1998. *Re-Orient: Global Economy in the Asian Age*. New York: University of California Press.

Garrett, G. 1998. *Partisan Politics in the Global Economy*. Cambridge: Cambridge University Press.

Garrett, G. 2000. 'The causes of globalization', *Comparative Political Studies*, 33 (6), 945–91.

Giddens, A. 1990. *The Consequences of Modernity*. Cambridge: Polity Press.

Gill, S. 2003. *Power and Resistance in the New World Order*. Basingstoke: Palgrave.

Gilpin, R. 2001. *Global Political Economy*. Princeton, NJ: Princeton University Press.

Gilpin, R. 2002. *The Challenge of Global Capitalism*. Princeton, NJ: Princeton University Press.

Hannerz, U. 1992. *Global Complexity*. New York: Columbia University Press.

Hannerz, U. 1996. *Transcultural Connections: Culture, People, Places*. London: Routledge.

Hardt, M. and Negri, A. 2000. *Empire*. Cambridge MA: Harvard University Press.

Hardt, M. and Negri, A. 2004. *Multitude*. New York: The Penguin Press.

Harvey, D. 1989. *The Condition of Postmodernity*. Oxford: Basil Blackwell.

Harvey, D. 2003. *The New Imperialism*. Oxford: Oxford University Press.

Hay, C. 2004. 'Globalization and the state'. In J. Ravenhill (ed.), *Global Political Economy*. Oxford: Oxford University Press.

Hay, C. and Watson, M. 2000. 'Globalization and the British political economy', mimeo.

Held, D. 2004. *Global Covenant*. Cambridge: Polity Press.

Held, D. and McGrew, A. 2002. *Globalization/Antiglobalization*. Cambridge: Polity Press.

Held, D., McGrew, A., Goldblatt, D. and Perraton, J. 1999. *Global Transformations*. Cambridge: Polity Press.

Hettne, B. 2000. 'Global market versus regionalism'. In D. Held and A. McGrew (eds), *The Global Transformations Reader*, 156–66. Cambridge: Polity Press.

Hirst, P. and Thompson, G. 1999. *Globalization in Question*. Cambridge: Polity Press.

Hoffmann, S. 2002. 'The clash of globalizations', *Foreign Affairs*, July.

Holton, R. 2005. *Making Globalization*. Basingstoke: Palgrave.

Hoogvelt, A. 1997. *Globalization and the Post-Colonial World*. Basingstoke: Macmillan.

Hopkins. A. 2002. *Globalization in World History*. London: Pimlico.

James, H. 2001. *The End of Globalization*. Cambridge, MA: Harvard University Press.

James, P. 2005. *Globalism, Nationalism, Tribalism: Bringing Theory Back In*. London: Routledge.

James, P. and Nairn, T. 2005. *Global Matrix: Nationalism, Globalization, and Terrorism*. London: Routledge.

Keane, J. 2003. *Global Civil Society*. Cambridge: Cambridge University Press.

Keohane, R.O. and Milner, H.V. (eds) 1996. *Internationalization and Domestic Politics*. Cambridge: Cambridge University Press.

Keohane, R. and Nye, J. 2000. 'Globalization: What's new and what's not so new?' *Foreign Policy*, 118, 104–19.

Khor, M. 2001. *Rethinking Globalization*. London: Zed Press.

Lawrence, R. 1996. *Single World, Divided Nations? International Trade and OECD Labor Markets*. Washington DC: Brookings Institution.

Mann, M. 1997. 'Has globalization ended the rise and rise of the nation-state?' *Review of International Political Economy*, 4 (3), 472–96.

Mittleman, J. 2000. *The Globalization Syndrome*. Princeton, NJ: Princeton University Press.

Mosley, L. 2003. *Global Capital and National Governments*. Cambridge: Cambridge University Press.

Noonan, J. 2003. *Critical Humanism and the Politics of Difference*. Montreal: McGill-Queens University Press.

Ohmae, K. 1996. *The End of the Nation-State*. London: Harper Collins.

Ohmae, K. 1990. *The Borderless World*. London: Collins.

Olesen, T. 2005. *International Zapatismo: The Construction of Solidarity in the Age of Globalization*. London: Zed Books.

O'Rourke, K.H. and Williamson, J.G. 2000. *Globalization and History*. Boston, MA: MIT Press.

Petersen, V.S. 2004. 'Plural processes, patterned connections', *Globalizations*, 1 (1), 50–68.

Phillips, N. 2005. 'Whither IPE?' in N. Phillips (ed.), *Globalizing International Political Economy*, 246–70. Basingstoke: Palgrave.

Pogge, T.W. 2001. 'Priorities of global justice'. In T.W. Pogge, *Global Justice*, 6–24. Oxford: Blackwell.

Ritzer, G. 1995. *The McDonaldization of Society*. Thousand Oaks, CA: Pine Forge Press.

Robertson, R. 1992. *Globalization: Social Theory and Global Culture*. London: Sage.

Rosamond, B. 2003. 'Babylon and on? Globalization and international political economy', *Review of International Political Economy*, 10(4), 661–71.

Rosamond, B. 2004. *Globalization and the European Union*. Basingstoke: Palgrave.

Rosenau, J. 1990. *Turbulence in World Politics*. Princeton, NJ: Princeton University Press.

Rosenau, J. 1995. *Along the Domestic Foreign Frontier*. Cambridge: Cambridge University Press.

Rosenau, J. 2003. *Distant Proximities*. Princeton, NJ: Princeton University Press.

Rosenau, J. 2004. 'Many globalizations, one international relations', *Globalizations*, 1(1), 7–14.

Rosenberg, J. 2000. *The Follies of Globalisation Theory*. London: Verso Press.

Rosenberg, J. 2005. 'Globalization theory: A post mortem', *International Politics*, 42, 2–74.

Rugman, A. 2000. *The End of Globalization*. New York: Random House.

Rupert, M. and Solomon, S. 2005. *Globalization and International Political Economy*. New York: Rowman and Littlefield.

Sandel, M. 1996. *Democracy's Discontent*. Cambridge, MA: Harvard University Press.

Sassen, S. 1996. *Losing Control? Sovereignty in an Age of Globalization*. New York: Columbia University Press.

Saul, J.R. 2005. *The Collapse of Globalism*. London: Atlantic Books.

Schirm, S.A. 2002. *Globalization and the New Regionalism*. Cambridge: Polity Press.

Scholte, J. 2000. *Globalization: A Critical Introduction*. Basingstoke: Palgrave.

Scholte, J. 2005. *Globalization: A Critical Introduction*, 2nd edn. Basingstoke: Palgrave.

Shaw, M. 2003. 'The global transformation of the social sciences'. In M. Kaldor et al. (eds.), *The Global Civil Society Yearbook*, 35–44. London: Sage.

Smith, M.P. 2001. *Transnational Urbanism: Locating Globalization*. Oxford: Blackwell.

Stiglitz, J. 2002. *Globalization and Its Discontents*. New York: Norton.

Stiglitz, J.P. 2005. 'The overselling of globalization'. In M.M. Weinstein (ed.), *Globalization: What's New?*, 228–62. New York: Columbia University Press.

Swank, D. 2002. *Global Capital, Political Institutions, and Policy Change in Developed Welfare States*. Cambridge: Cambridge University Press.

Taylor, C. 2004. *Modern Social Imaginaries*. Durham, NC: Duke University Press.

Taylor, P.J. 1995. 'Beyond containers: Internationality, interstateness, interterritoriality', *Progress in Human Geography*, 19 (March), 1–15.

Tilly, C. 2004. *Contention and Democracy in Europe, 1650–2000*. Cambridge: Cambridge University Press.

Tomlinson, J. 1994. 'A phenomenology of globalization? Giddens on global modernity', *European Journal of Communication*, 9, 149–72.

Tormey, S. 2004. *Anticapitalism*. Oxford: Oneworld.

Urry, J. 2003. *Global Complexity*. Cambridge: Polity Press.

Wallerstein, I. 1979. *The Capitalist World Economy*. Cambridge: Cambridge University Press.

Weiss, L. 1998. *The Myth of the Powerless State*. Cambridge: Polity Press.

Wolf, M. 2004. *Why Globalization Works*. Oxford: Oxford University Press.

Wolf, M. 2006. 'Will globalization survive?' *World Economics*, 6 (4).

Chapter 2

What Is Globalization?

Roland Robertson and Kathleen E. White

The question we address in this chapter is both very general and very specific. It is general because it almost inevitably covers a number of disciplinary standpoints as well as worldviews to be found in different parts of the world. It is specific because we are concerned with the demarcation of the distinctive features of what has come to be called globalization. The general sense of the question 'What is globalization?' is continuously latent in what follows, whereas specification is much more explicit. Many different topics are included under the rubric of globalization, such as global governance, global citizenship, human rights, migration and the creation of diasporas, transnational connections of various kinds and so on. We are not concerned here with the matter of particular topics within the general frame of what we might loosely call the globalization paradigm.

Notwithstanding our attempt here to produce a definitely systematic way of analysing globalization, it should be strongly emphasized that in a major respect globalization is, in the frequently used phrase, an essentially contested concept. Many books and articles purporting to be talking about globalization indicate at the outset that there is no accepted definition of globalization but that the author or authors are about to provide one. To some degree this phenomenon is a manifestation of the relative newness of this topic on the academic agenda, not to speak of political discourse. (It is also in many cases a somewhat gratuitous effort to claim uniqueness, when such is completely unnecessary in view of the large number of similarities between many definitions of globalization.) Nonetheless, we attempt in what follows to supply as coherent a statement as is possible in full recognition of the disputed nature of the concept. Some of the disputes arise from differences in perspective across the world. Understandably, many people in developing countries are not exactly eager to accept definitions of globalization deriving from more privileged societal contexts. And there is much deviation with respect to ideas about globalization from one civilizational context to another. For these reasons a number of scholars speak of *globalizations* in the plural, as opposed to a single process of globalization.

Velho (1997) has spoken of globalization as an object, a perspective and a horizon. The object approach involves thinking of globalization as a single process, as if 'it' were being addressed from an Archimedean standpoint. This is not entirely possible, but nonetheless with sufficient reflexivity, one may continue to aim for a focus upon a particular object 'in an objective way', meaning that there is a wide degree of inter-subjectivity. As far as the perspectival position is concerned, Velho himself argues that, from within the 'community' of scholars and observers of global processes, the world takes on a different complexion when viewed in global terms. This, indeed, is one of the primary goals of the growing field of global education. Finally, in the Velho paradigm, globalization may be understood as the direction in which the world considered as a whole is moving. This brief synopsis of Velho's discussion indicates the range of presuppositions of which any contributor to the debate should be very conscious. It should be added that there are also different presuppositions resulting from disciplinary standpoints (Robertson and Khondker 1998). Indeed, the study of globalization is marked by the great mingling of disciplinary orientations, and the resultant debate has been and still is being conducted on a site of major disciplinary mutations, such that it may well be called a transdisciplinary development.

Globalization was discussed by that explicit name in sociology and anthropology, as well as in religious studies, as long ago as the late 1970s and early 1980s. However, as has become increasingly apparent in recent years, concern with globalization in effect began many centuries ago. To complicate matters a little, we have to recognize clearly that the idea of globalization did not fully enter academic, not to speak of wider political and intellectual, discourse until the late 1980s or early 1990s. In fact, the widespread use across the world of this term began only after the fall of the Berlin Wall in 1989 and the subsequent, if only partial, collapse of communism. The cleavage – because that is what it is – between those who take a mainly economic position on globalization, in reference to the eventual end of capitalism, and those who have adopted a broader view, is a strong characteristic of the currency of the concept.

The necessity to recognize the two, initially very separate but now converging, uses of the term globalization can be recognized quite simply in the following example. During the late 1990s there arose what was popularly called the anti-globalization movement, situated mainly but certainly not exclusively in Western societies. As this movement grew, through often massive, sometimes violent, demonstrations at meetings of such organizations as the World Trade Organization (WTO), the International Monetary Fund (IMF) and the G7/8 assemblies, largely through the increasingly instrumental use of the Internet in the facilitation of such global movements, so too did the development of a global consciousness about what were perceived to be the great inequalities produced by globalization, in its *mainly economic* sense. As the protest against capitalistic globalization grew rapidly, so too did the sense that the movement itself was a part of the globalization process. Hence, the distinction that emerged in the early 2000s between the notions of globalization from above (the 'enemy') and globalization from below (the 'good guys'). Meanwhile, ever since the early 1990s there has indeed developed a policy, promoted particularly by the more affluent nations, in favour of the desirability of open markets, free trade, deregulation and privatization. Accompanying the advocacy of such a policy – one which has usually been labelled neoliberalism – has been the growing significance in the economic life of the world as a whole of transnational corporations (TNCs). Indeed, it is the latter which have often become the most iconic representatives of what many think of as the 'nasty' side of globalization.

In the concentration upon the capitalistic conception of globalization a number of crucial social scientific factors were greatly neglected. The kind of approach that had developed in the late 1970s and early 1980s to the phenomenon had been and still remains much more multidimensional. From the outset, those adopting a more multidimensional, as opposed to a unidimensional (economic), approach to the discussion and study of globalization drew upon a wider set of intellectual resources and were not, on the face of it, so obviously ideological as were those adopting the economic posture. This more general view of globalization had its roots in a different set of premises. In the background of the rise of globalization theory was the relatively simple observation that the world was increasingly becoming a 'single place'. This emphasis upon the world as becoming singular – as characterized by unicity (Robertson 1992) – was to have important ramifications in the development of various social sciences. In one way or another it has greatly affected the intellectual trajectory of the disciplines of sociology, political science and anthropology. For example, the idea of the world as a single place has brought into great question the sociological tendency to conceive of the basic and largest unit of sociology as being society (Mann 1986, 1993; Urry 2000; cf. Outhwaithe 2006). In political science and international relations, the rapid growth of interest in globalization has led to an increasing questioning of such heretofore central themes as sovereignty and territory. And in anthropology, attention has rather rapidly been turned from the study of societies, particularly of so-called primal societies, as if they were more or less completely isolated, towards a more inclusive view of the variety of different types of society and in particular, of the transcendence of societal boundaries by various globalizing processes, such as migration and hybridization.

THE PARAMETERS OF THE GENERAL PROCESS OF GLOBALIZATION

It is very widely, if somewhat misleadingly, thought that the most important single defining feature of globalization – whether considered as a very long-term process or a rather short one – is that of increasing connectivity (sometimes called interconnectedness). Thus, for those who think of globalization as being pivoted upon this, little attention is given directly to what could, in general terms, be considered as a combination of both subjective and cultural factors. It is here maintained that increasing global consciousness runs in complex ways, hand in hand, so to speak, with increasing connectivity. Both connectivity and consciousness have to be unravelled, but the most essential point to grasp here is the significance of the relative neglect of the latter in favour of the former. Indeed, some disciplines have given much more attention to one or the other; in particular, while connectivity has been considered by political scientists, international relations specialists and economists as the defining feature of globalization, consciousness has been studied more by anthropologists, sociologists and cultural historians.

In his original journal article (1993), Samuel Huntington predicted that, with the assumed end of the Cold War, centred as it was upon the conflict between the United States and (former) USSR, the major world conflicts from there on would not be ideologically based, but rather focused more on civilizational issues. So when President Bush announced within a few hours of the tragedy of 9/11 that there had to be a *crusade* against mainly Muslim 'terrorism', we could say that, within the contexts of a narrow definition of globalization, there had suddenly appeared a recognition that indeed globalization involved much more. Bush's proclamation has to be seen against the background of Huntington's well-known (and controversial) thesis about the clash of civilizations (1993, 1996).

In Huntington's argument, civilizational conflicts would revolve above all upon profound differences in conceptions of the nature and purpose of human life. When all was said and done – and this became particularly evident when Huntington published a book based on the original article – the real and most salient civiliza-tional conflict was between the 'Judeo-Christian' West and the Islamic Middle East plus the larger portion of Muslims in south and south-east Asia. Some have said that Huntington, in effect, wrote the script for the trauma of 9/11. It must, however, be emphasized that the growing perception of an Islamic threat to the West (in particular to the United States) had been evident since the Iranian Revolution of 1979. The drama of the conflict between the West and mainly Middle Eastern Islam lay relatively dormant between the Iranian Revolution, which brought into power an aggressive theocracy in Iran, and the first attack on the World Trade Center in 1993. But it took nearly a decade for the full significance of the so-called clash to become fully evident. From the perspective of globalization theory, this seeming failure to acknowledge fully the cultural aspect of globalization can now clearly be seen as a very costly mistake. For much of the 1990s and indeed up to the present time, there has been considerable talk of the 'real' clash or conflict, having to do more with scarce resources, in particular oil, and more recently, water. It was in this way that it was possible for many to think of increasing connectivity as well as global consciousness as being either economic-materialistic or about policies and ideologies surrounding access to such resources. Few were able to see that the esca-lating conflicts around the world, with the Islamic/Judeo-Christian conflict at the core, were not at all helpfully described in terms of conflicts over material resources. To be sure, it would be extremely foolish to deny the significance of the material resource aspects of recent international conflicts or to neglect the great salience of military and strategic considerations.

THE DIMENSIONS OF GLOBALIZATION

Many books and articles on globalization, not least written by sociologists, stipulate that there are three major dimensions of such: the economic, the political and the cultural. The latter, the cultural, has come increasingly to the fore partly *because of* the concern with economic globalization. There has been much talk of what Ritzer has influentially called McDonaldization (2000). Even though Ritzer has not in an entirely explicit way spoken of McDonaldization as a form of cultural globalization or indeed as cultural imperialism, such ideas are at least latent in his important contributions. Ritzer has been primarily concerned with the spread from America to much of the rest of the world of certain social and economic practices that have been spread not simply by the McDonald's Corporation, but by such others as Nike, Starbucks, the Gap, Kentucky Fried Chicken (KFC) and so on. Nevertheless, it has been found that in spite of attempts to spread the consumption of goods or services around the world in a relatively homogeneous way it is necessary to adapt brands to local circumstances. Moreover, the generalized mode of such adaptation can well constitute a form of homogeneity. In other words, even though adaptation to the local may promote heterogeneity, the way in which such projects of this kind are implemented is frequently very similar across much of the world. This has been evident, to take but one example, in the way in which McDonald's has had to alter the making of their burgers in the Indian context in which the eating of beef is taboo. (This issue is more adequately discussed under the concept of glocalization to which we will turn in due course.) The central thrust of this brief comment on the relationship between economic and cultural factors is that, somewhat paradoxically, the expansion of capitalism around the world has of seeming necessity involved the elevation of the cultural themes. This well illustrates the complexity of thinking in multidimensional terms yet at the same time brings sharply into focus the poverty of thinking in unidimensional terms.

Since much of thinking about globalization has been undertaken by sociologists, the neglect of the social dimension is rather glaring. In other words, many sociologists, speaking as prominent participants in (some would even say, the initiators of) the debate about globalization, have more often than not overlooked the very important social aspects of this general theme. One of the major exceptions to this generalization about the neglect of the social is Ritzer who does deal very directly with the globalization of social practices and relations in his influential work on McDonaldization. Others include scholars who have promoted the network approach to globalization, most distinctively Castells (1996, 1997, 1998) and Knorr Cetina (2001; Knorr Cetina and Bruegger 2001). Notwithstanding the irony of this relative neglect of the social by sociologists in numerous books on globalization, suffice it to say that the spread, the diffusion of, styles of social interaction and communication around the world has surely been pivotal in the process of globalization. When all is said and done, it is impossible to conceive of connectivity without attending to social interaction, particularly but not only long-distance interaction (such as that via the Internet). One of the major sites of this kind of social interaction is to be seen in communications in previous decades – for example, by correspondence between migrants and those they have left behind, the classic case study being that of Thomas and Znaniecki's *The Polish Peasant in Europe and America* (1918–20).

In sum, it can here be stipulated that the major dimensions of globalization are indeed the cultural, the social, the political and the economic. It should be stressed that in referring to the social dimension, we are including the communicative. Furthermore, this listing is not to suggest that any one of these dimensions is more important than the other. Nor is it to maintain that such factors as environmental or ecological change are excluded. After all, it is human perception of the environment which is the crucial element; in other words, the concern with the environment is part of contemporary human culture.

THE FORM OF GLOBALIZATION

The issue of the form (or the pattern) of globalization was raised most sharply by Immanuel Wallerstein (1974, 1980, 1989), even though Wallerstein himself does not approve of the concept of globalization as such. Many scholars, nonetheless, have used aspects of his work in addressing this topic. Thus, Wallerstein raised an extremely important point in the early stages of his crucial work on the making of what he calls the modern world-system – the world capitalist system – when he spoke of the different ways in which the world could have become the singular 'system' that it has now more or less actually become. He cogently argued at that time that there were other ways in which the world could have become what we have here called a single place, a term which is certainly not meant to imply that we live in a world in which every nation or segment is totally integrated. We may say, following Wallerstein, that the world has not become a single place under the aegis, for example, of a particular religious institution, in spite of the attempts of the Vatican periodically having acted along such lines. The world could have become singular through the activities of an ideologically based, vanguard organization, such as the Soviet Communist Party, or through the expansion of German Fascism. It could, to take yet another example, have become a world-system along the lines planned by some Japanese politicians and intellectuals during the Second World War. Numerous other possibilities could be provided. The most important consideration at the present time is that, in the 1970s and subsequently, Wallerstein has ruled out the argument that the modern world could be systematized and coordinated along imperial lines. However, in the present circumstance it has to be said that there has recently been a great discussion of the new imperialism, a discussion which has brought into sharp focus the part played by ancient empires – most notably the Roman Empire. Here we should say in more than an *en passant* manner that this discussion of the role of imperial moves in the making of the modern world has brought into sharp relief the whole question of the ancient origins of the overall globalization process (Robertson and Inglis 2004; Inglis and Robertson 2004). The entire question as to the ancient origins of globalization – or, at least, protoglobalization – is currently being pursued by scholars from a number of disciplines, particularly sociological history.

However, leaving on one side the question of imperialism, the issue of the form of globalization can be addressed directly. From Wallerstein's point of view, the present world-system – or what some other writers have called world society, the global ecumene, global society and so on – has been produced primarily by the expansion of capitalism over the past five or six hundred years. This expansion Wallerstein regards as now being increasingly challenged by what he calls anti-systemic movements. He has not, however, regarded the latter in such an optimistic way as have some anti-globalization movements. In so far as we have rejected the unidimensional, economic approach to globalization (a term which we have already emphasized, but Wallerstein and his numerous followers have largely rejected or considered as only a particular phase of capitalistic expansion), we are constrained to think of the overall process of globalization in a more multifaceted way.

It is necessary to stress that in speaking of multidimensionality in the previous section, we have not exhausted the ways in which this methodological principle may be applied. Thus, in the immediate context of discussion of what we are calling the *form* of globalization we speak of there being different dimensions or facets of this form. In much of the present authors' work on globalization it has been proposed, not uninfluentially, that it is useful to think of the process of globalization as having conformed in a general way to the following pattern. First, and most obviously, there is what can, for simplicity's sake, be called the international-systemic aspect. Second, there is the aspect which covers the most general feature of global-human life, namely the concept of humanity. Third, there is another component which we have called (the totality of) individual selves. Finally, there is the principal 'container' of human beings for many centuries, namely the nation-state.

There are a number of important things to say about this proposal. In the first place, attention should quickly be drawn to the inclusion of the nation-state in the process of globalization. Many contributors to the debate have argued, from a variety of different disciplinary perspectives, that globalization is a process which has been challenged by nation-states. From the reverse angle, it has been argued that the nation-state as we know it, is being rapidly undermined, notably – but not only – by economic forces. Contrary to this perspective, we contend – not without some reservation – that the nation-state should actually be regarded as an *aspect* of globalization. We would almost certainly not be talking about globalization were it not for the existence of nation-states. For example, much of the discussion of increasing connectivity has been centred on the increasing intensity of and the organization of the relationships between nation-states; even though connectivity refers to all kinds of connections that involve bypassing nation-states. In any case, the preference in the work of the present authors has been not to think so much about the alleged decline of the nation-state, but rather about its *changing nature*. Here we think particularly of the rapidly growing concern with the problems of the so-called multicultural society. Widespread and extensive migration has contributed a great deal to these. At this time the debates in a number of societies about their identities is an excellent example of the centrality of the nation-state to any discussion of globalization. One might well say that the idea of national identity has itself been globalized with increasing but intermittent intensity since the early years of the twentieth century. The multiculturality or polyethnicity of most societies has become an issue of great political contention. It would seem that nativistic, right-wing movements notwithstanding, forms of multiculturality are becoming the global norm (McNeill 1986).

Next, the inclusion of selves within the general frame of global change has been motored by the conviction that it is not viable to exclude individuals – or, more generally, local life – from the scope of global change, more specifically globalization. This is why we consider it to be very misleading to think of globalization as being a solely macroscopic process, a process which excludes the individual, or indeed everyday life, from the realm of global change. Currently we may pinpoint considerable change with respect to the self – more especially, processes of individualization (Beck and Beck-Gernsheim 2002). Admittedly these changes tend to apply most clearly to the West, although there are intimations of these occurring well beyond the West. Individualization does, in one sense, isolate the individual and makes her or him more and more responsible for her/his actions. Increasingly, societies, including global society, depend on the inputs of individuals. It should be hastily emphasized that this societal reliance upon the individual is a phenomenon that can all too easily be transformed into a manipulation of the individual and her/his identity. In fact, the growth in the manipulation of individual identities by the state is all too apparent in much of the Western world. One notices this tendency particularly in the United Kingdom and the United States. At the same time, the identity of selves becomes increasingly differentiated in the sense that the self can and does assume a variety of forms and modes of representation, such as the 'racial', the national, the class, the religious, the gender and so on. This ability to manipulate one's own identity is greatly facilitated by the anonymity of Internet communications. Indeed self-identity is a crucial site of the complex relationship between homogeneity and heterogeneity, between sameness and difference. Here we find a paradoxical convergence of similarity and uniqueness. Specifically, individuals exhibit their uniqueness in terms of a common mode of presentation, most clearly manifested in fashion.

We move now to the international system – sometimes called the system of societies (Parsons 1966). Since the so-called end of the Cold War, we have witnessed an end to bipolarity. For much of the period since 1989 we have lived in a unipolar world dominated by the United States. However, in spite of the 'promise' of the European Union and the rise and rise of East Asia, the world now is to a large degree seen in terms of the West versus 'Terror'. Specifically, ever since the disaster of 9/11, in much of the world the major axis has been perceived as radical Islamists – sometimes called Jihadists. On the other hand, in spite of the seeming ability of the United States to act unilaterally, not merely has the Jihadist challenge rendered US domination less and less secure, consideration also has to be given to the rapidly expanding strength of China and, to a lesser degree, of Russia. In other words, the present international system is in a state of great and puzzling flux. Moreover, in this and in other respects, also including the life of individuals, we presently inhabit a world where millennialist views have great consequence. In particular reference to the international system we have a rapidly burgeoning discourse concerning the possible end of the world. Needless to say, environmental issues are much at stake, especially with reference to the international system.

Finally, we attend to the component of humanity. Here we find much increasing thematization and problematization. For example, the relationship between the human species and its natural and physical environment is clearly changing rapidly. Similarly the relationship between human and animal life is being thematized in a number of respects. For example, the globally expanding debate about the claims of creationists' and intelligent designists' conceptions of the origins and making of human life are in great confrontation with the inherited forms of Darwinian evolutionary theory. The very notion of human rights is also in a state of great flux, notably in the many rights which are being inserted into this realm. To the more conventional of human rights are being added a number of others, such as various categories of physical and psychological handicap, additional categories of gender and expanding rights for children and for the aged.

GLOCALIZATION

We turn now to an issue that has been intermittently invoked in the preceding pages. The concept of glocalization is one which has received considerable attention within the confines of business studies. Indeed, some claim that it is within that intellectual territory that the concept was first used. On the other hand, it has become with particular rapidity in recent years a relatively central concept in the discussion of globalization (Robertson 1992, 1995; Robertson and White 2003, 2004, 2005; Syngedouw 1989) in a much broader way. The problem that precipitated the introduction of the concept of glocalization was that concerning the relationship between the global and the local. Indeed, to this day it is not at all unusual to find the local being regarded as the opposite of the global. However, a few scholars began to see about 15 years ago that it was relatively fruitless to continue with this binary or antinomic line of thought. To put it very briefly, the alleged problem of the relationship between the local and the global could be overcome by a deceptively simple conceptual move. Rather than speaking of an inevitable tension between the local and the global it might be possible to think of the two as not being opposites but rather as being different sides of the same coin. We may illustrate this from the realm of business, although the same point could be made with reference to any other sphere of human activity. In order to produce goods for a market of diverse consumers, it is necessary for any producer, large or small, to adapt his/her product in some way to particular features of the envisaged set of consumers. Nevertheless, there is great variation in the degree to which such actions may straightforwardly be a form of adaptation or, on the other hand, more a matter of imposition. The latter important issue is addressed by Ritzer via his concept of grobalization (2004). The significant point here is that, far from seeing the local/global problem as one needing extensive academic discussion, real life producers as well as advertisers have simply *assumed* that coping 'globally' with 'local' circumstances is a necessary and an accomplishable project. Thus, the real sociological or anthropological question becomes that of examining the ways in which the relationship between the global and the local is *actually* undertaken.

Inherent in much of the discussion of globalization is the old sociological and anthropological concept of diffusion. Indeed, it could be argued that much of the literature on globalization involves a recasting of ideas from these two disciplines dating back, particularly in the case of diffusion, many years. In sociology, the concept of diffusion has involved concentration upon the ways in which ideas and practices spread (or do not spread) from one locale to another. (This approach was developed mainly in the field of rural sociology, notably in reference to the spread of agricultural innovations.) Broadly speaking, diffusion theory thus anticipated what we now call glocalization in very important respects. This is one of the reasons why some of the ideas produced in work on globalization are sometimes said to be exaggerated in their claims as to novelty.

There is a particularly significant set of ramifications of the concept of glocalization. This has to do with the ways in which one might sensibly answer the question: What happens after globalization? We have already indicated that globalization involves a strong shift in the direction of unicity, the world as one place.

Yet some people, very misleadingly, speak of 'a globalized world'. It should be clear, however, that there can be no criterion as to what a fully globalized world might look like. In this sense, a globalized world is an impossible world. Approaching this problem via the concept of glocalization, it can be seen that globalization is, in fact, inevitably and increasingly a *self-limiting* process. In other words, in so far as all ideas and practices have to adapt to contexts and niches, then in the sense of it being a homogenizing force, globalization really makes no sense. Globalization, when considered with due respect to the glocalizing aspects of diffusion, inherently limits itself. However, on the other hand, if we think more along the lines of Ritzer's grobalization, then globalization cannot be regarded as self-limiting since, as we see it, grobalization as a homogenizing force would be in theory a perpetually ongoing process until everything in the world has been enveloped by it.

GLOBALIZATION AND GLOBAL HISTORY

It is not surprising, given all that has been said about our now living in a global age (Albrow 1996), that the historical perspectives of our time are being greatly affected by this enhanced sense of globality (Robertson 1983). At any point in historical time, the matters which interest us about the past are very much framed by what are thought to be the main features and problems of the present. It is in this way that rather large number of historians and historically minded social scientists have become greatly concerned with the antecedents of this present globality – more specifically, a time of great connectivity and global consciousness. It is in this way that history as a discipline is being greatly affected by discussions within the framework of globalization analysis (Hopkins 2002). At the same time, there have been a number of developments among analysts of globalization leading to fairly widespread concern with the relationship between globalization and history or globalizations and histories, emphasizing that globalization is a narrower concept than that of 'mere' global change. Indeed, one of the most striking features of the highly compressed world in which we presently live is an often contentious rewriting of histories of ethnic groups, nation-states and regions in order that the members of such entities may have an 'authentic identity'. Clearly, the current almost worldwide concern on the part of not only intellectuals but also politicians and religious leaders with national identities is a very good example of this. Indeed, this interrelationship between globalization and concern with 'local identity' is a very good example of the apparently paradoxical relationship between the nation-state and processes of globalization, as was indicated earlier in this chapter.

There has been rather a lot of interest in mapping the different phases of globalization (e.g. Robertson 1992; Scholte 2005). This is indeed, transparently, a historical problem. Much more work needs to be, and to a considerable extent is being, done on this particular theme. This is ultimately leading, as has been indicated above, to new understandings of globalization, in spatial as well as temporal respects.

CONCLUSION

At the centre of our attempt to characterize globalization are the following. First, globalization consists primarily of two major directional tendencies, increasing global connectivity and increasing global consciousness. Consciousness does not imply consensus, merely a shared sense of the world as a whole. Second, globalization has a particular form, one which has been, to all intents and purposes, consummated by the founding of the United Nations organization. This means that, like the operations of the UN, globalization is focused upon four points of reference: nation-states; world politics; individuals; and humankind. Third, globalization is constituted by four major facets of human life – namely, the cultural, the social, the political and the economic. These dimensions are in reality heavily intertwined, one or two aspects being more prominent at any given time or place. For example, in the modern world the cultural and the economic are closely interpenetrative.

We have also highlighted the importance of not reifying globalization. Globalization is not a thing, not an 'it'. Recognition of its conceptual status, as opposed to its being an ontological matter, is of prime importance. This is vital in view of the global nature of the interest in, the discourse about and the analysis of globalization – a debate which brings ever sharper into focus what we have described as the inevitably contested nature of globalization talk. The very globality of this talk about globalization must surely lead to an appreciation of the impossibility of definitively answering, in an essentialistic way, the question, 'What is globalization?' This should *not*, however, be regarded as an open invitation for a proliferation of narratives of globalization as a matter of course. Rather the aim should be, with due regard for variation, both spatial and temporal, to aspire to the never-totally-attainable goal of locating an Archimedean fulcrum from which to view the world.

A particular concern here has been to push back the views of those who would prefer to swim in the seas of cultural relativism. Having said this, we do not deny in any way whatsoever that what have been called *critical* analyses of globalization are inappropriate. Far from it. The many injustices and forms of exploitation which are rampant in the world demand continuing attention. But we insist that the attainment of ever more sophisticated frameworks for the very discussion of globalization is required in order for effective and plausible critical analysis to take place. One of the dangers of undisciplined critique is that globalization simply becomes a negative buzzword, something to employ as a source of blame for each and every 'problem' on this planet – indeed, in the cosmos. In spite of much rigorous elaboration of globalization theory in recent years, we still unfortunately see a great deal of such indulgence around us.

References

Albrow, M. 1996. *The Global Age: State and Society beyond Modernity.* Stanford, CA: Stanford University Press.
Beck, U. and Beck-Gernsheim, E. 2002. *Individualization.* London: Sage.

Castells, M. 1996. *The Rise of the Network Society*. Vol. I of *The Information Age: Economy, Society and Culture*. Oxford: Blackwell.

Castells, M. 1997. *The Power of Identity*. Vol. II of *The Information Age: Economy, Society and Culture*. Oxford: Blackwell.

Castells, M. 1998. *End of Millennium*. Vol. III of *The Information Age: Economy, Society and Culture*. Oxford: Blackwell.

Holton, R.J. 2005. *Making Globalization*. Basingstoke: Palgrave Macmillan.

Hopkins, A.G. (ed.) 2002. *Globalization in World History*. London: Pimlico.

Huntington, S.P. 1993. 'The clash of civilizations', *Foreign Affairs*, 72 (3), 22–8.

Huntington, S.P. 1996. *The Clash of Civilizations and the Remaking of World Order*. New York: Simon and Schuster.

Inglis, D. and Robertson, R. 2004. 'Beyond the gates of the *polis*: Reconfiguring sociology's ancient inheritance', *Journal of Classical Sociology*, 4 (2), 165–89.

Knorr Cetina, K. 2001. 'Postsocial relations: Theorizing sociality in a postsocial environment'. In G. Ritzer and B. Smart (eds), *Handbook of Social Theory*, 520–34. London: Sage.

Knorr Cetina, K. and Bruegger, U. 2001. 'Global microstructures: The virtual societies of financial markets', *American Journal of Sociology*, 107 (4), 905–50.

Lechner, F.J. and Boli, J. 2005. *World Culture: Origins and Consequences*. Malden, MA: Blackwell.

McNeill, W.H. 1986. *Polyethnicity and National Unity in World History*. Toronto: University of Toronto Press.

Mann, M. 1986. *The Sources of Social Power*, vol. 1. Cambridge: Cambridge University Press.

Mann, M. 1993. *The Sources of Social Power*, vol. 2. Cambridge: Cambridge University Press.

Outhwaithe, W. 2006. *The Future of Society*. Oxford: Blackwell.

Parsons, T. 1966. *The System of Modern Societies*. Englewood Cliffs, NJ: Prentice-Hall.

Ritzer, G. 2000. *The McDonaldization of Society*, rev. New Century edn. London: Sage.

Ritzer, G. 2004. *The Globalization of Nothing*. Thousand Oaks, CA: Pine Forge Press.

Robertson, R. 1983. 'Interpreting globality'. In *World Realities and International Studies Today*, 7–19. Glenside, PA: Pennsylvania Council on International Education.

Robertson, R. 1992. *Globalization: Social Theory and Global Culture*. London: Sage.

Robertson, R. 1995. 'Glocalization: Time-space and homogeneity-homogeneity'. In M. Featherstone, S. Lash and R. Robertson (eds), *Global Modernities*, 25–44. London: Sage.

Robertson, R. and Inglis, D. 2004. 'The global *animus*: In the tracks of world-consciousness', *Globalizations*, 1 (1), 38–49.

Robertson, R. and Khondker, H.H. 1998. 'Discourses of globalization: Preliminary considerations', *International Sociology*, 13 (1), 25–40.

Robertson, R. and White, K.E. 2003. 'Globalization: An overview'. In R. Robertson and K.E. White (eds), *Globalization: Critical Concepts in Sociology*, Vol. 1: *Analytical Perspectives*, 1–44. London: Routledge.

Robertson, R. and White, K.E. 2004. 'La glocalizzazione rivisitata ed elaborate'. In F. Sedda (ed.), *Glocal: Sul presente a venire*, 13–41. Rome: Luca Sossella Editore.

Robertson, R. and White, K.E. 2005. 'Globalization: Sociology and cross-disciplinarity'. In C. Calhoun, C. Rojek and B. Turner (eds), *The Sage Handbook of Sociology*, 345–66. London: Sage.

Scholte, J.A. 2005. *Globalization: A Critical Introduction*. Basingstoke: Palgrave Macmillan.

Syngedouw, E. 1989. 'In the heart of the place: The resurrection of locality in an age of hyperspace', *Geographiska Annaler*, B, 71B, n.1.

Thomas, W.I. and Znaniecki, F. 1918–20. *The Polish Peasant in Europe and America: Monograph of an Immigrant Group*, 5 vols. Boston: Richard G. Badger.

Urry, J. 2000. *Sociology beyond Societies*. London: Routledge.

Velho, O. 1997. 'Globalization: Object, perspective, horizon'. In L.E. Soares (ed.), *Cultural Pluralism, Identity, and Globalization*, 98–125. Rio de Janiero: UNESCO and Candido Mendes University.

Wallerstein, I. 1974, 1980, 1989. *The Modern World System*, 3 vols. New York: Cambridge University Press.

Wittel, A. 2001. 'Toward a network sociality', *Theory Culture and Society*, 18 (6), 51–76.

Chapter 3

The Cultural Construction of Neoliberal Globalization

Robert J. Antonio

Honey, . . . I think the world is flat. (Friedman 2005a: 5)

Globalization is a multi-sided process, but the most intense debates over it have stressed its connections to a new global political economic regime with a distinct 'American template' – *neoliberalism* (e.g. Barber 1996; Gray 1998). Neoliberals champion free-market policy, deregulation and tax cuts. They seek to minimize health, education, welfare and other social spending, and they contend that limited government, free trade and global capitalism offer the only road to reduced poverty and increased prosperity. They hold that neoliberalism is the main engine of globalization *per se* and that the process's progress can be furthered only by fuller global implementation of their programme. Social Darwinism has been an important part of US political culture for more than a century; it has been reconstructed during major technological and financial bubbles. Neoliberals have revived it again (Foner 1998; Phillips 2002). They do not identify as social Darwinists, and their views usually lack the nineteenth-century version's racially tinted Malthusianism. They combine their highly optimistic claims about exceptional wealth creation, global opportunity and hybrid culture with emphases on the free market, unrestricted property rights, and self-reliance and opposition to welfare and redistribution. This chapter will explore the work of the highly influential globalization advocate, Thomas L. Friedman, with the aim of elaborating his tacit social theory, which maps and justifies neoliberal globalization.

New Age Globalization and the US-led New World Order

. . . America was, and for now, still is, the world's greatest dream machine. (Friedman 2005a: 469)

By the late 1980s, the Thatcher–Reagan liberalization, new information-communication technologies, freer movement of goods, capital, images and people across national borders and geopolitical realignment stirred globalization discourse. Reported widely in the US media, Francis Fukuyama's 'end of history' thesis announced triumphantly a hegemonic, made-in-America, global political-economic regime and new unipolar world arising in the wake of the collapsing Soviet bloc. He argued that the US model of liberal democracy, stripped of its post-World War II era social democratic or welfarist facets, was dominant globally. Fukuyama held that modern peoples can no longer imagine a practical alternative that would 'represent a fundamental improvement over our current order' (1992: 51; 1989). Critics from the left and the hard right decried his celebratory view of ascendent neoliberalism, but their broadsides about the 'end of left and right' and 'end of alternatives' and critiques of the new breed of market-oriented, 'third way' politicians (e.g. Clinton, Blair, Schroeder) affirmed his claims about zero options. The first Iraq War, won quickly and decisively by a US-led international coalition, including former Cold War, American arch-enemy, Russia, was scripted by the first President Bush as the opening act of the 'new world order'. Globalization's lead nation also had become the lone superpower in post-Cold War geopolitical dynamics.

President Clinton was an outspoken champion of neoliberal globalization. Former Clinton Administration economic adviser and Nobel Prize winning economist, Joseph E. Stiglitz, states that Clinton was elected on a 'putting the people first' agenda; he aimed to chart a 'third way' between New Deal policy and Reaganomics, but neoliberalism ruled in his Administration. Stiglitz argues that they saw financial markets as a disciplining force that increases efficiency and prosperity. The Clinton Administration's domestic programme of neoliberal deregulation, privatization and securitization, he holds, constituted the core of their globalization policy, put forward in the US-dominated IMF and G8. Stiglitz asserts that their reigning idea was that 'what is good for Goldman Sachs, or Wall Street, is good for America and the world' (2003: xiv–xv, 24–6, 275–6, 281). And their neoliberal strategy seemed to work; the US economy grew rapidly, with low unemployment, low inflation and substantial income growth (especially for the wealthy). Between 1994 and early 2000, the New York Stock Exchange Composite soared over 125 per cent and the NASDAQ rocketed up over 500 per cent, stimulating much wider public discourse about globalization and enthusiasm about its prospects (Phillips 2002: 100; Henwood 2003: 4, 146). The boom in financial markets sparked claims that the Dow was on a 'permanent high plateau' and would climb to 30,000. Globalization advocates held that the 'New Economy' creates wealth so effectively that a post-scarcity culture is in sight. Clintonians considered the 1990s to be the 'fabulous Decade' (Blinder and Yellen 2001). By contrast, *New Left Review* editor Perry Anderson asserted, critically, that the decade's chief event was 'the virtually uncontested consolidation, and universal diffusion of neoliberalism' (2000: 10).

Framed in the roaring nineties boom, Clinton-supporter Thomas L. Friedman's best-selling *The Lexus and the Olive Tree* (2000) has been an extremely influential piece of globalization advocacy. Even after the NASDAQ bubble burst and after 9/11, Friedman has maintained his glowing optimism about the process. His recent best seller *The World Is Flat* (2005a) builds on the earlier book. Other writers have done parallel works on neoliberal globalization (e.g. Micklethwait and Wooldridge 2000) and more scholarly defences of it (e.g. Wolf 2004). However, Friedman is heralded as the top globalization advocate. His regular column for America's paper of record, *The New York Times*, adds force to his views. The back cover of his first globalization book quotes Fukuyama, who declares that the text defines 'the real character of the new world order'. On the recent book's dust-jacket, Stiglitz and other notables praise how lucidly Friedman expresses complex processes and makes them accessible to a mass audience. Even his scathing critics stress his importance, i.e. as top 'publicist of neoliberal ideas', pundit to 'presidents, policymakers, and captains of industry', or as 'the most important columnist in America today' (Gray 2005; Gonzalez 2005; Taibbi 2005). Friedman's copious references to his schmoozing with top corporate and political globalization advocates make it hard to tell who influences whom. For example, he thanks informants, Clinton Administration, Treasury Secretaries Robert Rubin and Larry Summers, Federal Reserve Chair Alan Greenspan, World Bank president James Wolfensohn, Cisco Systems head John Chambers and hedge fund manager Leon Cooperman. He also credits Microsoft's Bill Gates, Rolls-Royce's Sir John Rose, Dell's Michael Dell and Netscape's Mark Andreessen for commenting on draft sections of his latest book. Friedman also thanks intellectuals, such as economist Paul Romer and political theorists Michael Sandel and Robert Kagen (Friedman 2000: 478; 2005a: 472). Many more corporate heads and top globalizers, from diverse regions of the world, appear in his texts as informants. Friedman's reportage offers insight into the way that they construct and justify the neoliberal regime. Some academic analyses of globalizers, working in transnational organizations and US government, converge, at key points, with Friedman's accounts (e.g. Hunter and Yates 2002; Stiglitz 2003: 281–319). His critics lampoon his trite terms and lightweight tone, but he articulates what may be the most comprehensive, widely read, influential defence of neoliberal globalization. Perry Anderson (2000: 11) identified *The Lexus and the Olive Tree* as 'the most ambitious and intransigent theorization of ultra-capitalism as a global order'.

Friedman is a public intellectual aiming to generate support for the neoliberal policy regime. Although his works have been bestsellers, reaching diverse segments of the public, he directs his writing especially at the secure segment of the professional middle class. This highly educated, affluent stratum cuts across political parties and occupations, including corporate managers, entrepreneurs, financiers, advertisers, stock-brokers, technical experts, government officials and many other occupants of influential roles, who belong to the so-called 'investor class'. Even some higher education leaders find Friedman's work attractive because he provides a rationale for supporting education. He arguably seeks to mobilize his readers into a public to rally support for neoliberal globalization in the face of mounting domestic criticism about its negative impacts and increasing resistance to it abroad. I will analyze his tacit social theory of neoliberal globalization, mapping its core features and contradictory facets and addressing critically its ideological thrust. Friedman's theory is not in the foreground of his texts. It must be teased out of his respondents' points as well as his interpretations and summary arguments.

Mr Friedman's Planet: Globalization's Emergent Consumer-Stockholder Republic

We Americans are the apostles of the Fast World, the enemies of tradition, the prophets of the free market and the high priests of high tech. We want 'enlargement' of both our values and our Pizza Huts. We want the world to follow our lead and become democratic, capitalistic, with a Web site in every pot, a Pepsi on every lip, Microsoft Windows on every computer and most of all – most of all – with everyone pumping their own gas. (Friedman 2000: 384)

Friedman defines globalization as the unparalleled 'inexorable, integration of markets, nation-states, and technologies', which enables 'individuals, corporations and nation-states to reach around the world farther, faster, deeper, and cheaper than ever before, and in a way that is enabling the world to reach into individuals, corporations and nation-states farther, faster, deeper, and cheaper than ever before' (2000: 9). Below I explain his view of the overall cultural and institutional regime that drives and structures the process. Friedman poses his mapping of the 'globalization system' with normative intent; he defends global neoliberalism on the basis of claims about its impacts – its putative, beneficial socio-cultural and economic consequences for 'what is' and 'what is coming to be'.

Post-communist globalism

Friedman holds that a shift from the 'Cold War system' to the 'globalization system' occurred by the year 2000. He claims that capitalism's new phase, 'Globalization 3.0', will be, at least, as momentous as the two earlier globalization waves (i.e. 300 years of European mercantalist expansion and 200 years of modern capitalist development). Friedman contends that the November 1989 fall of the Berlin Wall was the first of a series of 'flatteners' that brought the globalization system into being. He treats the event as a fundamental step that opened the way for the others and as an iconic representation of the overall shift. Employing the metaphor 'falling walls' to refer to the chief causes and effects of Globalization 3.0, he argues that the Soviet bloc and East–West split stunted capitalism's global extension and consolidation; the Soviet state's monopoly of power, puppet states, secrecy and massive interference in private life, civic associations and, especially, economics generated paralysing fixity and unfreedom. Besides controlling a major portion of the world, Friedman implies, the USSR helped cultivate anticapitalist sensibilities and movements and a global climate favouring statist alternatives. Although not monopolizing power, he holds, Cold War era liberal democracies still concentrated it too greatly and deployed it too widely. Identifying power almost entirely with states, parties and politically motivated individuals, he sees politics to be *the* main wall or barrier to the flatness that he contends is the globalization system's prime characteristic and virtue. He believes that the tearing down of the Berlin Wall inspired forward-looking people everywhere to shrink political power's grip over social life. In liberal democracies, Friedman argues, this meant cutting state regulation, social programmes and redistribution. Stopping far short of declaring the state's end, he holds that individual states and the nation-state system constitute a necessary infrastructure for capitalism that helps coordinate, provision and defend the globalization system. He and his respondents see state intervention that serves capitalist development, without undue regulatory interference or major business costs, to be virtuous and not politics at all (Friedman 2000: 7–16, 44–6; 2005a: 8–11, 48–55).

Extreme capitalism

Perhaps misleadingly, Friedman claims to be a *'technological determinist'* and *'not a historical determinist'*. After communism, he holds, nine flatteners (i.e. Netscape's IPO, work flow software, open-sourcing, outsourcing, offshoring, supply-chaining, in-sourcing, in-forming and wireless innovations) forged a new 'flat world platform' that greatly accelerates, intensifies and extends global capitalism. Friedman's flatteners combine business and technological innovations. He considers neoliberal policymaking to be the decisive force that gave rise to third-wave globalization, albeit not its singular, sufficient cause. He portrays the new information-communication technology as a core, necessary facet of the process. Friedman sees this electronic connective tissue to be the enabling mechanism for realizing the potential of the unparalleled 'opening, deregulating, and privatizing' of the economy that drove the move to Globalization 3.0 (2000: 9–16; 2005a: 374–5). Other globalization analysts argue that deregulation and new technologies produced world-shrinking, spatial-temporal compression, generating much speedier, much more extensive and much freer global movement of capital, goods, messages, images and people (e.g. Harvey 1989). However, Friedman holds that Globalization 3.0 provides unparalleled democratic access to the means of communication and collaboration; the new 'playing field' allows enterprising individuals from all over the globe to plug in and to employ their creativity, skills and disciplined work habits to engage unregulated capitalism's vast opportunities (2005a: 8–11, 173–200). Friedman quotes Netscape's Marc Andreessen's assertion that 'a 14-year-old in Romania or Bangalore or the Soviet Union [*sic*] or Vietnam has all the information, all the tools, all the software easily available to apply knowledge however they want' (Friedman 2005b). Friedman contends that nations obeying the globalization system's free-market rules and employing its new technologies don a 'golden straitjacket' that makes their economies grow and politics shrink; 'political choices get reduced to Pepsi or Coke' (2000: 101–6). He holds that the flat world accelerates greatly the later twentieth century's already sweeping deregulation; Darwinian-like selection compels serious players to remove more and more sources of 'friction', or regulatory, redistributive and other social blockages that limit capitalist property rights and exchange. Friedman and his respondents imply that the consequent flat playing field is the heart of a knowledge-based economy with nearly frictionless, transnational capitalist intercourse and drastically reduced transaction costs. Tepidly qualifying the argument, however, he defends a minimal social safety-net and modest protections for certain highly valued public goods, which have inherent worth and secure the public trust that sustains markets. Still Friedman sees New Deal programmes and European-style social democracy to be moribund; social policy must rely almost entirely on market-centred strategies and public–private cooperation (policies largely already in operation) (2000: 276–305, 437–40). He considers Globalization 3.0's unparalleled prosperity and consumer freedom to be far too beneficial for informed publics to allow statist backsliding. In his view, neoliberal globalization has so much momentum that its further worldwide expansion and consolidation is inevitable (Friedman 2005a: 204–5, 469).

Fluid networks

Breaking radically from the Cold War system's 'frozen' structures, Friedman argues, today's globalization is 'a dynamic ongoing process' (2000: 8–9). Many other think-ers argue that complex organizations have been restructured to fit the imperatives of globalization's new technological, economic and regulatory environments. They argue that the postwar era's vertically integrated firms have been made more flexible, more dispersed and leaner. However, they stress that slightly modified bureaucracies operate successfully in most major business sectors and that more sweepingly trans-formed organizations often retain key elements of postwar firms and rationalize more rigorously and in new ways *vertical* ownership structures, managerial hierar-chies, work relations and technical controls (e.g. 'neo-Fordism' replaces 'Fordism' – Prechel 2000). By contrast, Friedman portrays a dawning post-bureaucratic era in which new technologies forge *lateral* collaboration rather than hierarchical control. He claims that the new flat world platform supplants rigid, coercive, vertical organizations with flexible, voluntary, horizontal networks; lateral communication and collaboration replace the mechanical obedience demanded by hierarchical line-authority and constrictive roles, jurisdictions and offices; and multitudinous indi-vidual decisions and initiatives establish dynamic 'non-linear' patterns of association. Although Cold War-type organizations remain, Friedman and his informants imply that a flat, seamlessly integrated *Web*, fashioned on the model of Internet, is the globalization system's ascendent organizational logic (2000: 8). This loosely coupled, flexible system is shaped by innumerable rational choices, myriad individual responses to vast complexes of shifting local conditions. In constant aleatory flux, it allows players to gravitate to locations that best fit their abilities and characters, and, thus, generates legitimacy and social integration. The new network offers enormous opportunities to enterprising people and penalizes severely free-riders. Highly talented, motivated individuals find more felicitous locations and work better deals, while unskilled, undisciplined players, who do not adapt readily to constant changes, are left to drift on their own without handouts. Friedman holds that Globalization 3.0's 'unique character' derives from 'the newfound power of *individuals* to collaborate and compete globally' and that globalization is 'increas-ingly driven by the *individual*' (2005a: 10, 183).

Nomadic subjects

A Goldman Sachs vice-chair tells Friedman that it is useful to think about globaliza-tion from the standpoint of an 'intellectual nomad', because the process lacks fixed grounds (2000: 27). However, Friedman implies that nomadic qualities are necessary for everyone navigating Globalization 3.0. Stretching from Nietzsche to postmodernist thinkers, cultural theorists have long predicted the arrival of the postmodern subject; this post-traditional individual usually is described as a many-sided, hybrid nomad, uprooted from fixed space, multi-perspectival in purview, at home with otherness, and, thus, free to create his or her own values, identities and cultural forms. Friedman contends that third-wave globalization has added more than one and a half billion new global players; millions of these exceptionally diverse people already communicate and collaborate instantly, flexibly and regularly via new computer and telecommunication technologies. He argues that players must be ready to move to new positions in an instant; lifetime job security and long-term social contracts between firms and employees ended with Globalization 2.0. Friedman and his respondents see flexible labour laws, allowing untrammelled hiring and firing with maximal speed and minimal cost, to be essential to the flat world's open competition and voluntary integration. Friedman holds that its multi-sided nomads thrive on the consequent challenges and opportunities; they are formed to operate in uncertain, ever changing circumstances and, thus, lack any sense of entitlement. He touts them as human equivalents to 'Swiss Army Knives' (i.e. famous for their multiple blades and other retractable tools fashioned for different tasks). Friedman argues that these brave new workers make themselves ever more multiple as the situation demands and that they constantly upgrade their capacities so that their skills cannot be easily outsourced. Replacing the Cold War era's inflexible specialists, these 'versatilists' welcome the fresh experiences, relationships and activities entailed by new jobs. Friedman implies that being fired and having to move to a new position makes talented people more multifaceted and, thus, ultimately, more successful (2005a: 238–49, 290–3). He quotes an Asian business writer's portrayal of globalization's techno-capitalist, postmodern subjects, or 'Zippies' – 'Belongs to generation Z. Can be male or female, studying or working. Oozes attitude, ambition, and aspiration. Cool, confidant, and creative. Seeks challenges, loves risks and shuns fear.' Friedman adds that they are guilt free about 'making money or spending it' (2005a: 181–4). In his view, Globalization 3.0 not only produces the type of subjects that ensure system reproduction, but it also nurtures multicultural sensibilities, tolerance and even cyberspace spirituality. Stopping just short of the fully deterritorialized subject, Friedman asserts, islands of tradition survive (e.g. religion), constituting another side to the globalization system's multiplicity and providing alternative sources for sustenance of the self (2000: 468–75). He seldom mentions consumption directly and does not even list the term in his indexes, but brand names suffuse his storytelling. For example, he says: 'globalization often wears Mickey Mouse ears, eats Big Macs, drinks Coke or Pepsi, and does its computing on an IBM PC, using Windows 98, with an Intel Pentium II processor and a network link from Cisco Systems' (Friedman 2000: 382). Unlimited consumer freedom and pleasure is the unspoken presupposition and chief virtue of the *golden* straitjacket and its irreversible, post-political globalized world. His postmodern nomads constitute their dynamic, largely deterritorialized, plural subjectivity by consuming global commodities as well as by multitasking and telecommuting. On Friedman's planet, accumulating 'More' and consuming it is the main inspiration for choosing a path that entails so much frenetic competition, intense work and profound uncertainty. Declaring that 'culture matters', Friedman holds, 'outward looking' nations 'glocalize', absorbing the best foreign ideas, practices and commodities into their local cultures (2005: 324–9). His brand-name world is so thick with commercial messages and commodities that the borders between markets and extra-economic institutions are porous or obliterated. Celebrating unabashedly this blurring as another facet of falling walls, Friedman does not hesitate to ponder critically self-formation by participation in niche markets or reflect seriously how traditional institutions can reproduce in such a fluid, materialistic world.

Legitimate inequality

Friedman's flat world has skill and reward hierarchies, based on divergences in character (e.g. work habits, flexibility, ambition), intelligence and, in part, good or bad fortune. However, his idea of flatness implies a nascent just meritocracy based on ample opportunity in a worldwide free market. Friedman holds that the globalization system generates so much wealth that nearly everyone benefits; even if inequalities grow sharper, the ever larger basket of commodities available to consumers means that the process is not a zero-sum game. He implies that wealth gushes towards the globalization system's most talented people and delivers substantial rewards to almost all disciplined, motivated and, at least, moderately skilled people. Friedman points to NBA superstar, basketball player Michael Jordan's $80 million yearly income. However, he argues that marginally skilled, substitute Joe Klein's hefty $270,000 NBA minimum salary was buoyed by Jordan's worldwide popularity and consequent growth of the league's global market. Friedman holds that players, such as Klein, know that they benefit enormously from Jordan's success and, thus, do not begrudge his wealth (2000: 306–24). Friedman implies that this type of mutually beneficial inequality, although usually involving more modest rewards, pervades Globalization 3.0. He acknowledges that extreme inequalities and misery exist outside the flat world (i.e. poor nations and even unskilled, non-wired sectors of wealthy nations), and admits that flat world growth will not soften all inequalities or eliminate all poverty. However, Friedman holds that hope for a better life rides on joining the globalization system and benefiting from its technology transfers, free trade and market-based growth. He says that 'there is no alternative' except 'to go backward' to a Cuban-style command economy that impoverishes and oppresses everyone. Friedman contends that oil-based command states, such as Saudi Arabia and Venezuela, spread wealth a bit more widely than other statist regimes, but at the cost of very substantial waste, unfreedom and backwardness (2000: 318, 355–7; 2005a: 309–36, 460–3). Advocating 'compassionate flatism', Friedman argues that Globalization 3.0 nations should provide some welfare for their poorest, sickest, weakest people. For others, he advises 'portable' pensions and healthcare plans that do not discourage work and that go with workers to new jobs (2005a: 284–93). However, Friedman neither suggests that sharp economic inequality is problematic *per se* nor advocates redistribution or other programmes to reduce it. He implies that empowering individuals results in inevitable inequalities; not everyone can master Globalization 3.0. But Friedman portrays its intense international competition as a 'race to the top' for the vast majority of participants; its successful players' enterprise and productivity have significant spillover benefits for those on its margins (2005a: 233; 2005b).

Ownership society and stockholder direct democracy

Besides the new possibilities for collaborative work and consumption, Friedman and his respondents hold that Globalization 3.0 offers unparalleled opportunities for owning financial assets and participating in an electronic stockholders' democracy. Friedman describes a four-faceted democratization: 'democratization of technology' dispersed the means of communication, information and wealth creation (e.g.

miniaturization, digitalization, telecommunications, computerization and compression technologies) to a much greater number of diverse people over wider spaces than ever before; 'democratization of finance' ended insurance companies', investment banks' and commercial banks' monopoly control over financial instruments and provided inexpensive easy access to credit and means of investment (e.g. cut-rate brokers, online trading, 401K pension plans); 'democratization of information' made the tools for creating, gathering, storing and transmitting information (e.g. cable TV, satellite dishes, DVD players, mobile phones, e-mail and, especially, Internet and its hyperlinks) nearly universally available and much cheaper, faster and more efficient than ever before; 'democratization . . . of decision-making and the deconcentration of power and information' opened the way for the other flatteners and year 2000 flat world platform (2000: 44–72, 86; 2005a: 48–172). These conditions, Friedman contends, allow a highly dispersed, inclusive 'Electronic Herd' of investors to drive financial markets and ultimately direct politics and socio-cultural development. For example, he holds that their purchases and sales in currency markets constitute daily 'votes' on the management of entire nations, which discipline political leaders' actions and sometimes lead to their removal. Stressing Gobalization 3.0 deregulation, financialization, privatization and securitization, he suggests that the Electronic Herd's 'votes' ensure that stockholder interests determine policy trajectories in more institutional domains than ever before. Friedman does not deny electronic democracy's inequalities or 'one dollar, one vote' processes (i.e. the extent of participation and influence depend on ownership share – large investors' access and clout overshadow that of small investors and non-investors have no voice at all). He also acknowledges that financial speculators sometimes start stampedes, causing national or regional crises. However, Friedman holds that, in Globalization 3.0's nearly frictionless, transparent markets, large investors and small investors react to the same signals, share common information and have parallel, if not equal, outcomes. He and his respondents propound the rationality of stockholder democracy – that the Electronic Herd's decision-making power operates, on average, in the best interest of nearly everyone, including vast numbers of people from the unflat world, who do not own stock or 'vote' (2000: 112–42). He contends that stockholding is growing rapidly as more people benefit from the flat world platform and neoliberal reform. Friedman sees electronic traders to be radically dispersing power, turning the 'whole world into a parliamentary system'. Globalization's 'most basic truth', Friedman declares, is that 'No one is in charge' (2000: 112; also pp. 72, 137, 168; 2005a: *passim*).

Self-regulation

Friedman acknowledges that Enron, Tyco and WorldCom used the new information and communications technologies to fleece their stockholders, workers and customers. The leadership of these firms took advantage of a control and regulatory environment that lagged behind the extremely rapid development of new financial instruments, information technologies and means of communication. Prior to the scandals, Friedman mistook Enron as a model fast company. He now portrays it as a prime example of a firm led by enterprising, super-empowered crooks, who exploit the resources of Globalization 3.0. However, he sees predations by occasional corporate violators to pale by the side of statist regimes' top-to-bottom corruption. Moreover, he holds that the self-regulating system adjusted to the new conditions rapidly and worked; US financial markets' exceptional transparency and regulatory mechanisms facilitated identification and punishment of the corporate criminals (Friedman 2000: 387–8; 2005a: 198, 245). Friedman also holds that the globalization system fosters geopolitical self-regulation *within* its borders; countries with McDonald's franchises or branches of Dell supply chains do not want to go to war with each other; linked by trade and foreign direct investment, they avert conflicts that upset global interdependence and economic security. He argues that Globalization 3.0's seamless webs of collaboration and consequent affluence raise the potential costs of war to the highest level ever and act as a deterrent to it. Friedman asserts that people, wearing the golden straitjacket, want to preserve the system that delivers the goods; their engaged work habits and comfortable consumer lifestyles reduce tolerance for disrupted lives and weaken the will to fight bloody battles and suffer casualties (2000: 248–56; 2005a: 422–9).

Backlash

Stressing an inherent tension between capitalism and tradition, Friedman refers to Karl Marx's famous passages, in the Communist Manifesto, about how globalization knocks down 'Chinese walls' and pulverizes the traditional world (i.e. 'All that is solid melts into air, all that is holy is profaned . . . '). Friedman also mentions twentieth-century economist Joseph Schumpeter's argument, inspired, in part, by Marx, that 'creative destruction', or constant economic change, is capitalism's essence (Friedman 2005a: 201–4; 2000: 11, 213). He holds that Marx's and Schumpeter's points about capitalism's exceptionally powerful, restlessly creative, productive forces and ever more extensive markets constantly making obsolescent its own products, creating new ones and transforming the wider culture pertain more to today's third-wave globalization than to Globalization 2.0. Friedman's repeated references to 'falling walls' and 'flatness' imply that barriers to capitalism are being smashed more rapidly and completely than ever before. He suggests that the tension between capitalism and tradition is manageable within the flat world and that it even produces laudable hybridity. However, he contends that sudden inclusion of vast unflat areas of the globe into fast capitalism generates resentment, anger and resistance within traditional cultures. Friedman also holds that the new flatteners extend unparalleled opportunities to, or super-empower, talented individuals who want to cheat, oppose or destroy the globalization system; Globalization 3.0's new technologies are as important to outliers' practices as they are to the system's legitimate, honest players. Thus, he is not surprised that corporate scandals, antiglobalization protests and 9/11 occurred at the moment that the flat world platform came into being. Friedman implies that Globalization 3.0's political and cultural enemies pose much more dangerous threats than violators, motivated by personal economic gain. Holding that the anti-globalization movement exploits capitalism's tensions with tradition, he argues that it is a reactionary backlash by people lacking the discipline, courage, energy, imagination and skill to adjust to post-Cold War realities. He says that anti-globalization critics offer no programmes that can reduce poverty or protect the environment. Contending that their political successes deprive the poorest people of Globalization 3.0's bonanza, Friedman asserts that they need a 'policy lobotomy' or simply to 'grow up' – accept the golden straitjacket as the only path to a prosperous, peaceful world. He contends that Third World opposition to globalization and related anti-Americanism manifest wounded pride, humiliation and unreason. He claims that especially strong backlash comes from middle-class segments of former statist regimes, who, under neoliberal reform, lose the security and benefits of their old bureaucratic positions. Friedman criticizes most emphatically the globalization system's radical, violent, anti-modern opposition. Prior to 9/11, he warned presciently about grave threats posed by Osama bin Laden and other anti-American, 'super-empowered angry men'. He holds that the new flatteners make such individuals all the more dangerous; telecommunications technologies provide them with better means than ever to incite anti-Americanism, acquire vital information about weapons of mass destruction (WMDs), link global terror cells and coordinate terrorist acts. Believing that Globalization 3.0 reduces poverty, fosters openness to difference and leaves spaces for tradition, Friedman argues that its extension and consequent empowerment will defuse humiliation and resentment in now unflat parts of the world and that their peoples will overcome the shock of de-traditionalization and embrace globalization (Friedman 2000: 327–47, 395, 405; 2005a: 197–200, 429–38).

Globalization's lead society and its 'quiet crisis'

Friedman has moderated recently his earlier triumphant declaration that 'Globalization is Americanization', and he no longer refers to 'Americanization-Globalization' (2000: xix, 293–4, 379–84; 2005a: *passim*). The sobering impacts of the NASDAQ crash, 9/11 and, especially, China's and India's ascendence in the global economy have tempered his tone. But he still touts the United States as the globalization system's lead society and Globalization 3.0 as an American invention. He does not retreat from his earlier claims that 'there is no better model . . . on earth today than America' and that even a 'visionary geoarchitect' could not have imagined a better regime to 'compete and win' in global economic competition (Friedman 2000: 368, 475). In his view, the United States is the globe's flattest spot; it has the best regulated, most efficient capital markets, most transparent firms, strongest protections for private property rights, best designed tax and regulatory laws, most creative entrepreneurial culture, most flexible labour laws, largest consumer market, best political system and most open society. He sees neoliberal 'downsizing, privatizing, networking, deregulation, re-engineering, streamlining, and restructuring' to have given the United States a substantial edge over other rich nations, which often have bloated welfare systems, overly powerful labour unions, excessively regulated workplaces and markets, and inflexible labour laws. However, Friedman warns that tough new competitors, especially India and China, may soon challenge US global economic leadership. He argues that individuals from these and other developing nations, now climbing onto the flat world platform, share exceptional intensity, discipline and motivation. Friedman holds that many of them are well educated and skilled, and nearly all are driven by the will to escape poverty. Referring to the pitiful performance by pampered American NBA stars in the 2004 Olympics, Friedman concurs with a sportswriter who attributes the US fall from basketball dominance to its players' insouciant attitude about its competitors' progress and lack of ambition and discipline. He employs this example to illustrate a broader 'quiet crisis' – Americans feeling entitled to their affluence, being complacent and expressing insufficient effort, discipline and preparation. He warns that there may be taints of truth in the crude generalization that younger Americans 'get fat, dumb, and slowly squander it all' (i.e. US wealth) (Friedman 2005a: 250–2). Friedman asserts that: 'I am now telling my own daughters, "girls finish your home work – people in China and India are starving for your jobs"' (2005b). Still he hopes that competitive pressure will push younger Americans to study harder (e.g. stress maths, science, engineering), work more intensely and abandon any sense of entitlement. Friedman implies that they must become the brave new nomadic, worker bees described above (2000: 368–75; 2005a: 243–75, 469).

Unipolar geopolitics

Friedman holds that the United States leads geopolitically as well as economically and that the lone superpower after communism is not an imperialist power. Before 9/11, Friedman declared the United States to be the 'Michael Jordan of geopolitics', identifying it as the globalization system's 'benign hegemon and reluctant enforcer' and legitimate leader to 'most of the world'. He acknowledges that foreign views of the United States have darkened in 9/11's militarized aftermath, but he sees this negativity to derive, in good part, from the Bush Administration's execution of the Iraq War and War on Terror. Friedman supports the Iraq intervention and employment of US power to democratize the region. He also holds that the US defence of the globalization system must not be deterred by allies, such as France, who refuse to contribute to conjoint actions. However, he contends that Clinton-style, American-led multinationalism would be much more effective than Bush's unilateralism. Friedman argues that the long-term solution for global problems is integration of all unflat parts of the world into Globalization 3.0, but even if this ideal condition were to be achieved, he implies, the globalization system would still benefit from US strategic leadership (2000: 389, 464–6; 2003: 4–5, 290–9, *passim*).

MODERNIZATION THEORY REDUX: ELECTRONIC SOCIAL DARWINISM

> Liberalism stands for the freedom of the individual *versus* the control of the state.
> (Spencer 1912: 585)

Quoting Crane Brinton, Talcott Parsons (1968 [1937]: 3) began his *magnum opus* with the parenthetical question: 'Who now reads Spencer?' Parsons held that Herbert Spencer had been cast into history's dustbin. Opening the prologue to the 'creative destruction' argument, Schumpeter (1962 [1942]: 61) asked: 'Can capitalism survive?' He declared: 'No. I do not think it can.' He was no fan of socialism, but he thought that increased public management of economic affairs was becoming the rule in liberal democracies and communist regimes. In the wartime command economy, renascent classical liberalism was hard to imagine. Although conservative opposition grew after the war, liberal-democratic modernization theories, including the dominant Parsonsian model, advocated Keynesian state regulation and redistribution to correct market failures and provision of health, education and welfare. This trend peaked, in the United States, with the mid-1960s wave of social legislation and argument that greater attention be given to 'equality of conditions'. However, splits over race, welfare and the Vietnam War festered, the New Deal coalition crumbled and postwar growth slowed. Libertarians argued that restoring economic growth and vitalizing democracy hinged on the United States recovering its *laissez-faire* roots. In this climate, the Reagan Administration instituted the neoliberal policy regime. When the Soviet bloc was collapsing, Fukuyama vindicated modernization theory and its core claims that history is progressive and that liberal democracy is its endpoint. Reversing New Deal policy, neoliberals held that the state's regulatory, redistributive and welfare arms must be eliminated or reduced. They also argued that all nations, aspiring to be modern, must adopt this US model. The New Democratic Coalition and Clinton Administration offered a moderate sounding version of the market fundamentalism advocated by the Republican right. This bipartisan, stripped-down, neoliberal modernization theory revived Social Darwinism with free-market ideology.

Friedman's flat world is a global, electronic version of the classical liberal equation of the *laissez-faire*, 'regime of contracts' with direct democracy. Arguing that Globalization 3.0 empowers individuals as never before, Friedman updates Spencer's market-based individualism. The quote from Spencer, at the head of this section, illustrates his view of states as the realm of compulsion and power and markets as the sphere of liberty and choice. Classical liberals argued that capitalist firms' vertical facets do not compromise voluntary cooperation, because they are embedded in competitive markets and are based on contractual relations (i.e. employers can hire and fire at will and employees are free to seek other jobs). Classical liberals sometimes spoke sympathetically about the workers' plight, but they opposed redistribution and welfare, holding that such policies impose statist oppression, violate property rights, the foundation of individual liberty, and encourage worker sloth. At least implicitly, classical liberals saw full citizenship to be anchored in property ownership. Friedman's stockholder's republic converges with their view. His individually negotiated, contractual, fluid webs are today's version of Spencerian 'spontaneous' orders. Friedman contends that the flat world's transparency, readily available information, 'weightless' goods, instant exchanges, vast numbers of players and low transaction costs approximate neoclassical economics' ideal of frictionless, perfect markets. He suggests that nearly all disciplined, educated individuals can succeed by plugging into the Internet, forging collaborative ventures, employing their skills online and accumulating resources needed for full citizenship in the ownership society. By contrast to the state's command structure, classical liberals saw markets to be horizontal systems of voluntary association, which suffuse market-like, contractual relations throughout associational life. They believed that these webs of voluntary cooperation forge integrative interdependence across class lines, liberating individuals, eliminating violent conflicts and cultivating people's better angels. Friedman concurs heartily.

Affirming mass consumption, Friedman has a sunnier view than nineteenth-century social Darwinists, who held that 'poverty is the best policy' (i.e. to discipline profligate workers) (Sumner, 1883: 13–27). However, even leading twentieth-century classical liberal, Hayek (1944: 120) advocated 'a given minimum subsistence for all', implying more generous provisioning of the least talented, infirm and aged than the minimal safety-net proposed by Friedman. Portraying Americans' beliefs in capitalism, he stresses that, '*most of all*' [emphasis added], they want 'everyone pumping their own gas', or making it on their own, without dependence on public support (2000: 384). Friedman shares the classical liberal view that capitalism's class hierarchy is the product of a meritocratic struggle that rewards individual achievement and punishes free-riders, and, thus, is a legitimate, even pivotal facet of democracy. Friedman says that being middle class is a 'state of mind' in the United States, shared by low-wage (even '$2 a day') workers, which spurs their drive for success (2005a: 375–6). His assessment of the American class situation and 'quiet crisis' (i.e. with its driven, low-wage, Indian tech workers and slacker, nouveau riche, Afro-American NBA players) manifests taints of classical liberal beliefs in the virtue of poverty and danger of affluence. Like his predecessors, Friedman does not fret about great wealth compromising his fabulously rich corporate respondents' motivation. He sees the astronomical compensation enjoyed by top CEOs and the Electronic Herd's biggest investors to be a fast capitalist version of what William Graham Sumner (1883: 52) called 'wages of superintendence'; copious rewards for directing investment capital to the most important areas. Friedman implies that this hard-earned income seldom corrupts these driven innovators.

Neoliberal promises about tax cuts and growth fuel hopes about getting rich or, at least, improving substantially one's lot. However, while some Americans have flourished, many more have been forced to work more hours for lower wages in top-down, dead-end workplaces and to face much increased costs for healthcare, homes and education. While the stock market soared, incomes, benefits, vacation time and security of less advantaged workers shrank. Productivity gains, from the technological innovations lauded by Friedman, have been captured largely by people in the upper brackets, like himself, who also benefited enormously from huge tax cuts (e.g. Phillips 2002). Friedman insists that neoliberalism's sharply divergent economic outcomes have legitimacy and do not diminish globalization's supposed seamless integration. However, he stresses mostly technical connections, especially telecommunications links, and procedural equality, which have enormously divergent outcomes for different strata and hardly constitute *per se* the voluntary collaboration and substantive freedom that he implies. Émile Durkheim's and John Dewey's classic critiques of 'forced' or 'mechanistic' interdependence remain timely – undemocratically regulated 'free markets' and high levels of intergenerational inequality erode the *socio-cultural* integration needed to cultivate the smooth, uncoerced cooperation that Friedman claims rule. His rhetorical celebration of the flat world does not address the grossly unequal opportunities faced by poor Americans, especially minority children in underclass schools, and others on the margin. Substantive injustice is a chief breeding ground for 'super-empowered angry men [and women]'. However, it also spurs humane criticism, alternative visions of the future, and democratic resistance and reconstruction. Friedman dismisses as mere resentment all but the most tepid, market-friendly opposition to economic injustice. Although expressing keen insight into some facets of neoliberal globalization, his celebration of 'flatness' and 'democracy' transfigure and sanctify the plutocratic tendencies signified in his own portrayal of the United States as a 'winners take all' society (Friedman 2000: 306–24). *The world is unflat!*

Friedman argues that Globalization 3.0 has added 3.5 billion people and 1.5 billion new workers to the global economy since the mid-1980s (150 million skilled workers). He holds that the flat world platform ensures continuing rapid growth of worker numbers and increased exportation of portable skilled tasks to India and other rapidly developing regions with educated workers and lower wages. He also implies that technical rationalization and automation will continue to accelerate with no end in sight. Friedman stresses that American workers have to 'work harder, run faster, and become smarter' to get their share (2005a: 182–3, 469). He quotes a business leader's assertion that grasping the employment problem takes 'a leap of faith based on economics'. As in past capitalist technical transformations, Friedman holds, new jobs will arise to meet the demand (2005a: 232–3). Can we trust his assessment if we accept his own portrayal of Globalization 3.0 as a sea change altering the rules of the game? Hundreds of millions of people, in China alone, remain on peasant plots, in unprofitable state enterprises and in the informal economy, or they lack jobs. Given Friedman's scenario, why will the ever larger pool of global workers *not* far outstrip the demand for them? In neoliberal labour markets, why should wages for less skilled workers *not* drop below subsistence? Arguably, this is the case already for US minimum-wage workers. And how will economic well-being increase without well-organized countervailing power? Friedman dismisses strong unions and reform politics as sources of friction. However, historically, they have been the counterforces that have pushed for higher minimum wages, safer work conditions, shorter hours and better benefits. What happens if the ranks of low-wage, US workers continue to grow and their wages decline further? Can US consumption, which drives global production, be maintained? If China and India greatly expand their domestic consumption to generate demand, how can the pressure on global resources and the environment be mediated? How can Friedman be so sure that the neoliberal policy regime and massively expanded global labour force are *'racing us to the top'*? Friedman mentioned Marx's points about capitalism's awesome productive powers and worldwide markets. However, he also should have addressed Marx's related prediction that advanced capitalist globalization, driven increasingly by sophisticated technology and scientific knowledge, would expand greatly the global proletariat, accelerate automation and create a permanent, massive 'surplus army' of underemployed, unemployed and unemployable workers. If this scenario is emergent, neoliberal policymaking hastens the probability of a fundamental social, political and environmental crisis.

Friedman declares that he is 'a journalist, not a salesman for globalization' and that he is 'keenly aware of globalization's downsides' (2000: xxii). However, he does not engage globalization's non-corporate participants and, essentially, dismisses its critics. He contends that neoliberal restructuring is the greatest source of socio-economic good and that it does little or no harm. Seeing Globalization 3.0's major problems to be exogenous, he holds that universalizing neoliberalism is the only way to mitigate or eliminate them. Friedman's kinder-gentler sounding market fundamentalism ironically plays into the hands of virulently anti-liberal forces that Friedman opposes (i.e. the European New Right, US paleoconservatives, many fundamentalists and some radical leftists); they see his sanguine scenario to be proof of the tendencies that they detest. Equating neoliberalism and globalization, they hold that US-led global capitalism is a runaway locomotive that homogenizes everything in its path; genuine culture, community and politics are flattened by untrammelled, deracinated individualism, economism and consumerism. Arguing that neoliberalism inheres in liberalism *per se*, they aim to scuttle liberal democracy with globalization. Liberal approaches that deny alternatives to neoliberalism, celebrate uncritically shareholder power and conflate democracy with free markets and consumerism should be addressed critically. We need social theories that decouple neoliberalism from globalization *per se* and that formulate paths to socio-economic reconstruction and visions of global capitalism 'with a human face'. The burning theoretical and cultural question for those who value liberal-democratic institutions, substantive freedom and the planet's survival is how to cultivate a more just, democratically embedded, socially regulated, environmentally sustainable capitalism. This means coming to terms with social Darwinism, addressing environmental limits, re-engaging critically postwar versions of democratic socialism, social democracy and other liberal democratic models, and formulating post-neoliberal visions of democracy and modernization. After 9/11 and after the War on Terror, Americans must rethink prudently and more modestly the US role in the world. Reigniting American *political vision and sociological imagination* might begin with critical reconstruction, for a globalist era, of what Dewey called the prophetic side of US democracy, which once called out to the world something much more substantial and inspirational than 'political choices . . . reduced to Pepsi and Coke'!

References

Anderson, P. 2000. 'Renewals', *New Left Review* (Second Series) 1 (January/February), 5–24.

Barber, B.R. 1996. *Jihad vs. McWorld: How Globalism and Tribalism Are Reshaping the World*. New York: Ballantine Books.

Blinder, A. and Yellen, J. 2001. *The Fabulous Decade: Macroeconomic Lessons from the 1990s*. New York: Century Foundation Press.

Foner, E. 1998. *The Story of American Freedom*. New York: W.W. Norton and Company.

Friedman, T.L. 2000. *The Lexus and the Olive Tree*. New York: Anchor Books.

Friedman, T.L. 2003. *Longitudes and Attitudes: The World in the Age of Terrorism*. New York: Anchor Books.

Friedman, T.L. 2005a. *The World Is Flat: A Brief History of the Twenty-first Century*. New York: Farrar, Strauss and Giroux.

Friedman, T.L. 2005b. 'It's a flat world after all', *The New York Times*, 3 April <http://www.nytimes.com>.

Fukuyama, F. 1989. 'The end of history?' *National Interest*, 16 (Summer), 3–18.

Fukuyama, F. 1992. *The End of History and the Last Man*. London: Penguin Books.

Gonzalez, R.J. 2005. 'Falling flat: As the world boundaries are worn smooth, Friedman examines changing horizons', *San Francisco Chronicle*, 15 May <http://www.sfgate.com>.

Gray, J. 1998. *False Dawn: The Delusions of Global Capitalism*. New York: The New Press.

Gray, J. 2005. 'The world is round', *New York Review of Books*, 52 (11 August), 13 <http://www.nybooks>.

Harvey, D. 1989. *The Condition of Postmodernity: An Enquiry into the Origins of Cultural Change*. Oxford: Blackwell.

Hayek, F.A. 1944. *The Road to Serfdom*. Chicago: University of Chicago Press.

Henwood, D. 2003. *After the New Economy*. New York: The New Press.

Hunter, J.D. and Yates, J. 2002. 'In the vanguard of globalization: The world of American globalizers'. In P.L. Berger and S.P. Huntington (eds), *Many Globalizations: Cultural Diversity in the Contemporary World*, 323–57. Oxford: Oxford University Press.

Micklethwait, J. and Wooldridge, A. 2000. *A Future Perfect: The Challenge and Promise of Globalization*. New York: Crown Business.

Parsons, T. 1968 [1937]. *The Structure of Social Action: A Study in Social Theory with Special Reference to a Group of Recent Writers*, vol. 1. New York: Free Press.

Phillips, K. 2002. *Wealth and Democracy: A Political History of the American Rich*. New York: Broadway Books.

Prechel, H. 2000. *Big Business and the State: Historical Transitions and Corporate Transformation, 1880s–1990s*. Albany, NY: State University of New York Press.

Schumpeter, J.A. 1962 [1942]. *Capitalism, Socialism, and Democracy*, 3rd edn. New York: Harper Torchbooks.

Spencer, H. 1912. *The Principles of Sociology*, vol. 1. New York: D. Appleton and Company.

Stiglitz, J.E. 2002. *Globalization and its Discontents*. New York: W.W. Norton & Company.

Stiglitz, J.E. 2003. *The Roaring Nineties: A New History of the World's Most Prosperous Decade*. New York: W.W. Norton.

Sumner, W.G. 1883. *What the Social Classes Owe Each Other*. New York: Harper and Brothers.

Taibbi, M. 2005. 'Flathead', *New York Press*, 27 April <http://www.nypress.com>.

Wolf, M. 2004. *Why Globalization Works*. New Haven: Yale University Press.

Further reading

Dicken, P. 2003. *Global Shift: Reshaping the Economic Map in the 21st Century*, 4th edn. New York: Guilford Press.

Frank, P. 2000. *One Market under God: Extreme Capitalism, Market Populism, and the End of Economic Democracy*. New York: Doubleday.

Friedman, B.M. 2005. *The Moral Consequences of Economic Growth*. New York: Alfred A. Knopf.

Friedman, T.L. 2005. 'The world is flat: A brief history of the 20th century', *Carnegie Council on Ethics and International Affairs*, 6 May <http://www.cceia.org>.

Harvey, D. 2003. *The New Imperialism*. Oxford: Oxford University Press.

Pink, D.H. 2005. 'Why the world is flat' (interview with T.L. Friedman), *Wired Magazine*, 13.5 (May) <http://www.wired.com>.

Ritzer, G. 2004. *The Globalization of Nothing*. Thousand Oaks, CA: Pine Forge Press.

Chapter 4

Globalization: The Major Players

George M. Thomas

An area of study operating under the nominalization as powerful as 'globalization' is bound to be fraught with visions of larger than life forces, structures and processes that toss actors to and fro, from the small boats of individuals to ships of states. It also is understandable that there would be reactions against these visions – waves of attempts to re-centre discussions around the actions and agencies of individual actors as an antidote to the massive scale of globalization.

Whatever your take on these issues might be, it is important to understand the players involved in globalization and to understand that each is both actor and acted upon. It is not difficult to produce immediately a list of the players: nation-states, firms, international governmental organizations (IGOs), international non-governmental organizations (INGOs), a host of other associations and individuals. It is a little more difficult to catalogue their interrelations and to understand who they are, what they are doing and why. That is, it is more difficult to delineate their identities, interests, actions and interrelations, and just how they relate to globalization and its processes.

It is reasonable to begin with one type of actor with clear identities and interests and then map out its relation to globalization – how it reacts and how globalization influences it. Those who study one type of actor, commonly states or firms, tend to depict that actor as the most important and simply as a given. This is very natural. It means that most studies of nation-states and firms as the drivers of globalization tend towards a realist theoretical position – a position that assumes particular actors with presumably clear, coherent interests.

Because of the nature of globalization, we take seriously how the world as a whole is influencing actors and how actors are interacting in a world context that is, or at least recently has become, out of the control of any set of actors. This means that there is a tendency to soften the assumptions about actors as free agents and to give more weight to the impact of global processes. Many still retain realist assumptions: actors with clear organizational interests find themselves reacting to more complex environments. Going a step further, we can point to how globalization has an impact on the very identities and interests of actors. In this view, it is not only the global playing field that is continually shifting, it is also the nature of the state, firm, association and individual that is in flux.

In this chapter, I take up the various actors in turn and for each, begin with a realist view and then, following the scholarly and practical literatures, soften this approach to understand better their interrelations and the dynamics of globalization.

STRONG ACTORS AND REALIST, ACTOR-CENTRED APPROACHES

Transnational corporations

From the very origins of global capitalism in the sixteenth and seventeenth centuries, trading companies and financial houses which worked closely with mercantile states replaced the 'pre-national' guilds and trading leagues. They helped create global capitalism, and their descendants – modern corporations – continue to reproduce capitalism as they pursue their interests worldwide. Capitalist firms – corporate bureaucracies pursuing profit within competitive markets – are the bourgeois revolutionaries that range throughout the world, as so vividly depicted by Karl Marx. Corporations historically have had great influence over their states. In a classic overstatement, Marx depicted the state as the manager of capitalists' interests. In scholarly, policy and activist circles, they are the strong actors pursuing clear economic interests, influencing states and pushing globalization for good or for bad.

Transnational corporations are both competitive and collusive. Corporations that are able to gain competitive advantage, often through the policies and geo-military support of their states, become the most powerful players: they are able to bully and outdo competing corporations and have the greatest influence on states often at the expense of other corporations. At the same time, corporate capitalist interests confront state, society and local cultures as a united force of capitalists or 'big business'. This might at times be due to a unified corporate collusion or it might be more structural despite intense competition among corporations themselves. Their interests are, for example, directly tied to outcomes of globalization. It is wise to not treat corporate capitalists as a class as a singular unified actor but rather as a set of competing actors that have broadly common interests for pursuing profit and power, but it is an empirical issue and it must be documented to what extent they have formed coalitions for concerted action.

From the time of the mercantile state which actively managed markets for national interest through the *laissez-faire* nineteenth century to the middle of the twentieth century, multinational corporations were linked to nation-states, supported by state policies and associated with nationalism and national development. While multinational in nature, corporations were vehicles for concentrating capital in their home state and furthering national development, at the expense of development in other countries. Dependency theorists pointed to this as the key mechanism for underdevelopment and poverty in regions throughout the world.

The influence of the well-known global corporations is difficult to overestimate, but they are only part of the picture. The familiar global firms are the historically influential ones (General Motors and the auto industry), ones that make massive profits (ExxonMobil and the oil industry), those at the cutting edge of technology (Microsoft and computer hardware/software) and ones associated with consumer culture (McDonald's, Coca-Cola). Yet lesser known firms have tremendous power and influence: construction (Halliburton, Vivendi, Cemex); and consulting and accounting (PricewaterhouseCoopers, Deloitte Touche Tohmatsu). Nearly invisible are the trading conglomerates (Mitsui, Mitsubishi), legal firms (Baker & McKenzie, White & Case) and other middleman companies.

Focusing exclusively on capitalist corporations, while natural and insightful, can be misleading because it is incomplete. Powerful corporations do influence state policies and gain advantage over other firms. Societal associations and local communities are no match for the political-economic clout and clear interests of these actors. But it is too easy and obvious an explanation that firms are the drivers of global capitalism and globalization. What this approach gains in its simplicity is offset by its underestimating the role of other powerful players, namely the state. Moreover, it has to be modified extensively to understand the intensity, speed and forms of globalization at the turn of the twenty-first century. Globalization has an impact on the very nature of firms: the striking thing about successful contemporary firms is not simply that they adapt through quick reactions to complex global environments (which they do), but also that they pioneer new organizational forms with flexibility and fuzziness built into their organizations.

States

The nation-state is the other obviously strong actor in the world. The titanic struggles of states and blocs of states are the stuff of history. The modern nation-state has many dimensions to it, and one or another has been used to define it: rational-legal authority, effective administrative control or monopoly of legitimate violence over a territory; the incorporation of a population through citizenship; the pursuit of national interest. The study of the world has been the study of international relations – that is, the relations among nation-states – rooted firmly in the real interests and interactions of nation-states. States act in national interests vis-à-vis other states, firms and domestic actors.

By focusing on the pursuit of national geo-political and economic interests on the global stage, observers tend to presume that states have a coherent set of national interests centred on military security and attained through force and realpolitik methods such as balance of power and coalition formation. States integrate the demands of domestic groups and the realities of geo-politics into coherent national interests. Meeting the demands of domestic groups might shape foreign policy and a state's pursuit of international interests might require national mobilization and centralization.

In state-centred views, nation-states are 'relatively autonomous' from firms and classes. They recognize the complex nature of state–firm relations and do not presume that states always follow the interests of powerful economic actors. On the contrary, state-centred theorists are quick to point to the progressive nature of the state as an agent of change: corporations were and continue to be as reactionary as much as they are revolutionary. While states depend on capitalist corporations for revenues and competitive advantage, the capitalist firm also depends on state support. Since its origins in the centralizing monarchies in Europe, nation-states have established internal sovereignty over populations and territories even as they contend externally with other states. In the process, states were crucial in the rise of the capitalist corporation over the entrenched guilds and leagues, relying heavily on their revenues.

After World War II, and as nations became politically independent nation-states, they pursued interests of security, but an increasingly dominant *raison d'état* was development. States mobilize societies around national goals of economic development. They entice and coerce firms and classes to support national programmes and goals. They pursue development models set by international organizations such as the World Bank, models patterned after core industrial policies and articulated by Western academic economists. The mobilizing, modernizing state is the epitome of our understanding of the contemporary nation-state. In this view, the state is a relatively unitary, powerful apparatus imposing bureaucratic logics and control internally (Scott 1998) and competing externally around military, geo-political interests.

The realist view that the firm and the state are the most powerful global players dominates popular, policy, activist and scholarly discussions of globalization. In this view, states and firms, as they together use and expand new technologies, form the juggernaut known as globalization.

Strong actors and globalization

With increased globalization, the limits of this realist or actor-centred view have become more apparent, and there is a growing recognition that we have to understand how actors are shaped by global institutional environments. Many observers have emphasized that it is the very nature of globalization that requires firms and states to adapt and be flexible to new technologies and trends. The writings of Thomas Friedman (1999, 2005), for example, underscore the need for firms and states to see the technological and market trends and to position themselves to take advantage of them. The image of firms and states that one gets from Friedman's insights is not the rugged, autonomous actors anchored solidly from where they direct globalization but rather of ships of state and commerce that must weather raging storms at sea.

Today we observe firms from across the world looking for cheap labour and lucrative niche markets, not as Marx depicted as revolutionaries, but as adaptive players hoping to turn the short-term profit or meet their quarterly projections. Those who support the liberalization of markets (pro-globalization in the sense of an economic policy and thus better termed pro-globalism), such as the editors of the *Economist*, present this image by arguing that only the adaptive, flexible, innovative and opportunistic firms will survive. They also argue that states will produce wealth within their populations if they too have these adaptive qualities, opening themselves to globalization forces so as to take advantage of them. States, for example, must not protect national labour, but rather must adopt policies that take best advantage of global labour markets. Activists against the liberalization of markets (referred to by the misnomer anti-globalization and better termed anti-globalism) tend to retain a more realist model, depicting a collusion of powerful firms and states that are able to structure global markets to their advantage. Even for these activists, however, the sense is that state and firms require expansive international organizations and institutions.

Globalization at the turn of the twenty-first century thus creates conditions in which the realist, actor-centred views are limited: the intensification of globalization reveals that these strong actors are reactive and adaptive to globalization processes.

WORLD CONTEXTS OF ACTORS

This rethinking of actors and agency is taken further by those who argue that actors and their interests are themselves shaped by their environments. In other words realist, actor-centred views of global processes were always only part of the story, they argue, and this is more fully revealed by recent globalization. One line of argument is that global capitalism and the interstate system are global contexts that shape actors' identities and interests. A complementary line of argument is to see global contexts as world institutional and cultural structures.

According to neo-Marxist critiques of the autonomous actor, such as world-systems theory, firms and capitalists individually and as a class are embedded in processes of capital accumulation. The latter are determining. The interests, strategies and actions of states and firms as well as the ultimate outcomes are interpreted in terms of global exchange relations and flows of capital. Strong capitalists concentrated within a region and who benefit from unequal exchanges with other regions in the global division of labour are the source of strong states. These are the core countries over and against the periphery. Core countries are powerful and can have their way in the world-system, yet world-systems theorists are quick to point to the competition among core countries and the larger capitalist processes that make and break core states and firms.

State-centred theory and world-system theory have shifted their focus from individual states to the system of states (e.g. Chase-Dunn 1989; Wendt 1999). The policies and actions of states can be understood only as part of a system of states. The system rarely acts as an actor itself, although this line of thinking raises the issue of how states might associate, organize and act together, and opens an avenue for conceptualizing international institutions.

International institutions have garnered increasing attention. Scholars have been very cautious, initially extending conventional theories to conceptualize them. The most common interpretation is that as firms and states interact in increasingly complex environments marked by high levels of interdependence, simple interactions or exchanges cannot meet everyone's interests; that is, they cannot attain a social optimum. Thus there is a need to form institutions for coordination and control (Keohane and Nye 2000). In these observations, globalization is comprised of the most obvious forces of technology and economic flows, geo-political shifts and immigration flows: that is, material and social problems that have technical solutions requiring adaptation, coordination and control. Neoliberal theories see this process as actors naturally creating norms and institutions – international organizations – in order to produce a social optimum. That is, under complex conditions in which everyday exchanges do not result in optimal outcomes for the players, they establish institutions that allow them to coordinate and control these complexities (Baldwin 1993). Neo-Marxist versions of this type of explanation have the same functional reasoning: powerful states and firms in the face of increased complexity find it necessary to increase coordination and control through the establishment of institutions. Institutions can take on a life of their own, affecting the incentive structures of states and firms, but in these views they have little agency that is not determined by the states and firms that created them or the powerful ones running them.

Amenable to the analyses of rational actors, institutions provide the incentive structures that shape the strategies and actions of states, firms and other actors. In short, there is great explanatory gain by allowing for complex, non-reductionist relations between the major players and their environments.

This trend towards understanding actors in their environments is furthered by conceptualizing actors' environments as cultural and institutional contexts, as argued by sociological institutionalism and constructivism in international relations theory. In these views, culture is not essentially comprised of values internalized by individuals and organizations. Rather, culture is comprised of institutions: cognitive models of and blueprints for reality in which identities are enacted and interests are pursued. Institutions are not natural reactions to complexity; rather, they are the assumed reality underlying actor identities and interests that define problems and their solutions. They are constitutive in the sense that they define the nature of the firm or state. These cognitive blueprints, moreover, are not only built into legal systems, they tend to have moral weight: pursuing interest, enacting sovereignty, and organizing for collective goals are virtuous and the means of progress. By maximizing our view that actors are embedded in institutional structures, this view shifts our attention to these institutional structures and to the sources of authority and agency that actors wield. It also broadens our view of actors other than states and firms (Meyer et al. 1997).

The concept of institution is somewhat distinct: any category, principle or model that is used to organize reality, identity and action (Berger and Luckmann 1966; Douglas 1966). Markets, following Karl Polanyi's (1944) early insights, are institutions. Contracts are institutions: culturally defined agreements bound by assumptions about reality (rational individuals and commodities) anchored in legal arrangements. Put another way, not only are the World Bank and World Trade Organization institutions, so also are private property, profit, chief executive officers and quarterly reports. Like other formal organizations, the identities, interests and formal structures of firms are shaped by their institutional environments. Lawyers, economists and consultants as well as psychologists, leadership gurus and motivational speakers are global-local actors propping up the firm.

This approach helps us to understand a peculiar aspect of business leaders: they adopt globalization strategies not only to survive, but also as a moral project. While the idea that what is good for business is good for the world certainly is a rhetorical device to legitimate all types of business practices and narrow interests, all evidence suggests that they believe this: Max Weber's 'spirit of capitalism', that business is virtuous, is alive and well in the world (Hunter and Yates 2002).

The nation-state also exhibits these qualities. Historically the modern nation-state was consolidated by the Treaty of Westphalia (1648) through which the boundaries and sovereignty of the different monarchies were recognized and the principle of territorial sovereignty was established. That is, it was the system of states that recognized both the general principles underlying nation-states and the particular monarchies and their boundaries. These arrangements embodied and derived from broader cultural imperatives inherited from Christendom: secular authority and thus every nation-state had the mandate and authority to establish peace and justice (Strayer 1970; Meyer et al. 1987). Their authority thus was anchored in external cultural understandings which eventually were woven into a narrative of progress. Monarchies consequently supported the arts and sciences as ways of displaying the legitimacy of their sovereignty (Wuthnow 1987; Drori et al. 2003). These monies did not begin to have material returns until the nineteenth century when the arts and sciences were linked to industry and research universities.

The mandate for peace and justice remains, although in the twentieth century it has transposed to 'development' and specifically economic development and gross domestic product per capita. The contemporary mandate for development is no less externally derived. State definitions and methods of development are highly stylized global models. For about a quarter century after World War II, the dominant model of national development was to industrialize to produce goods for domestic markets to be less dependent on export agriculture and on importing manufactured goods from developed core countries. In the 1980s there was a shift such that by the end of the Cold War free market liberalization or globalism – what often is referred to as globalization itself – came to dominate development models (McMichael 2004).

In myriad ways the state reacts to external demands requiring that it adopt, at least formally, policies in diverse areas: human rights, population policy, immigration, environment, education and labour. No state is able to deliver on all of these mandates. State agencies (e.g. ministries of the interior, energy, education and consumer rights) must each adapt to differentiated global policy sectors resulting in loosely coupled state agencies that often work at cross-purposes (e.g. economic development, environmental standards, education, rights). The image that emerges is a much more fractured, penetrated state than a highly integrated, coherent bureaucracy (Meyer 1999).

Pressing the constitutive nature and complexity of world contexts draws attention to the nature and sources of authority and actorhood which is important for understanding the nature of actors, the diversity of types of actors and the contentions over globalization. Rational-legal authority is the primary source of actorhood and agency for nation-states and for firms. We see, however, in addition what can be termed rational-moral authority that endows these actors with moral force. Rational-moral authority also encompasses a rational-voluntarism that animates a host of collectivist associations, including IGOs and INGOs. Associations of states, firms and individuals take on the role of a disinterested technical and moral expert that gives actors professional and moral guidance and accountability (Haas 1992; Meyer 1994; Boli and Thomas 1999).

DIVERSE GLOBAL ACTORS AND GLOBAL GOVERNANCE

The contextualization of strong actors opens up our understanding of what is happening 'beyond' the firm and the state. Greater attention is given to institutions not reducible to interests of strong actors and within which states and firms are embedded. This conceptual opening coincided with the collapse of the Soviet Union and the end of the Cold War which cleared space for the workings of more types of actors and also for observers without bipolar lenses seeing more clearly the diverse types of actors. Whatever one's understanding of actors and their environment, an increasing amount of scholarly, policy and practical work examines a full field of global players: IGOs, international courts, INGOs, a panoply of professional and legal actors, and their interrelations.

International governmental organizations

IGOs are created by states and have states as members. They are arenas for coordinating interactions and the organization of collective action. Taking a multi-layered approach that incorporates various theoretical perspectives: IGOs are influenced by powerful member states and internal politics, they take on a life of their own such that they constrain even powerful member states, and they confer collective purpose and legitimacy that shape and constitute even powerful member states. Put another way, IGOs are institutional arrangements created and used by state actors, are collective actors themselves, and they embody cultural assumptions about the world. They set global policies, provide incentive structures for states and other actors, and carry world cultural principles and models.

ECONOMIC INSTITUTIONS

Much attention is given to those IGOs that set global economic policy and thus are viewed as the most immediately responsible for globalization and its effects. Three organizations were established immediately after World War II: the International Monetary Fund (IMF), the World Bank and the General Agreement on Tariffs and Trade (GATT).

The World Bank and IMF were created through the Bretton Woods agreements of 1944 and GATT was established in 1947 with several explicit purposes and practical effects: to reconstruct the world economy, provide support for national development, keep poorer peripheral countries within the capitalist world system and resistant to revolution, facilitate the flow of primary foods and materials from the periphery to the core and manufactured goods from the core to the periphery. Subsequent informal associations were formed. Developing countries in the 1960s formed the influential Group of 77 in an attempt to counter the deleterious effects of the economic system; this was followed shortly by the Group of 7 formed by core industrial countries (now the G8).

Economic liberalization in the 1980s began to replace the older national development models, and it was firmly established as orthodox economic policy after 1989. A series of meetings of GATT (known as the Uruguay Round) beginning in 1986 culminated in the creation in 1995 of the World Trade Organization (WTO) which became the primary organization that develops and enforces rules of free trade or liberalization. Contemporary free markets, as with their historical predecessors (e.g. Polanyi 1944), are created and managed by states and governance bodies. This fact is also seen in the creation of regional free trade agreements such as the North American Free Trade Agreement (NAFTA) and the political processes and controversies surrounding the proposed Free Trade Area of the Americas (FTAA).

Global policies are enforced or conformity is elicited through several mechanisms. Member states of the WTO and of regional free trade agreements are bound by the decisions of governing boards, and states are expected to act as enforcement agents of the decisions. Political manoeuvring to affect or undermine decisions and the influence of powerful states are typical, as in any political process. Loans from the IMF and World Bank are contingent on states adopting elements of the liberalization model, from economic to education policies. The prestige of participating in decision making, being a member in good standing and adopting the most cutting-edge models of development are general incentives for states. The elements imposed on states go beyond narrow economic policies. For example, by adopting world population policy principles, states signal that they are serious about development and receive more aid dollars from the United States (Barrett and Tsui 1999). When women's INGOs helped convince organizations like the World Bank that women's rights were important for development, these organizations made women's rights part of development programmes, thereby expanding women's issues across nation-states (Berkovitch 1999).

Contention over global economic policies generates a field of collective action – a global civil society (Scholte 2003). Activists (and many states) demand greater democratic participation and accountability and they demand a revision of liberalization policy to create more just outcomes. With the embodiment of liberalization policy in the WTO, longstanding activist contentions over global economic policy have come to focus on and target it. One by-product of this symbiotic relationship is that activists have gained greater visibility through their actions surrounding WTO meetings. Activist contentions over liberalization might threaten particular interests of powerful actors, but this contention tends to increase the visibility and significance of the organizations and policies, even as it creates a global public space. Anti-globalization activists, by targeting the WTO, the World Bank and other international organizations, are furthering the status of these organizations as the definitive arenas and actors involved in formulating world policies. Activists are anti-globalization in the narrow sense of being against economic liberalization or globalism, but they further globalization in the broad sense of legitimating the authority of international institutions: limiting authority and making it rationally accountable legitimates it.

UNITED NATIONS

The United Nations is the universal global political arena, comprised of politically independent nation-states. Within it we witness a full range of power politics, the creation of factions, coalition formation, the brokering of deals and betrayal. It is strongly influenced by powerful states but is just as clearly relatively autonomous from them. For example, the United States can get its way in this and other global arenas, but it is just as evident that in many instances it cannot. While its power gives it a greater ability to not conform to any given UN resolution or declaration, there are costs involved and even the most powerful country in the world has to be strategic in its nonconformity.

Through its universalism and ideology of voluntary participation of all nations, the UN provides fundamental legitimacy and identity to states. This is most obvious in the myriad island societies that exist as modern nation-states primarily due to their membership in the UN. Legitimacy and prestige flow even to the most powerful through their participation in the UN and its functioning. Despite the prominent cases of states not conforming to UN resolutions and declarations, the degree of participation and at least formal conformity is striking. It helps too that resources also flow along with legitimacy. The mechanisms through which universalism and volunteerism operate are precisely the legitimacy and prestige of participating in the universal political arena.

The universalism and the ideology of voluntary participation – democracy, albeit very limited and open to a whole range of criticisms – provide the UN with the authority for collective action. As globalization intensifies, more and more global problems are identified and in each case something needs to be done by someone. In the absence of a world state that is authorized to take such action, the UN and, to a degree, regional organizations (from the European Union to the Organization of American States) are able to deputize actors to take action. States of course can take action without the formal sanctioning of the UN, and there are in fact many examples not the least of which is the US invasion of Iraq in 2003. But there are costs of legitimacy, support and resources: without a UN mandate, the actions are interpretable as furthering the particular interests of the actors whereas with such a mandate, the actors can sustain the claim of acting for the global collective good.

After the Cold War and especially with the scandal involving the Oil-for-Food Program with Iraq, the reform of the UN has emerged as a major global problem. Claims that the UN is unduly influenced by powerful Northern states, not representative and soft on corruption undermine the very basis of its authority – universalism, democracy, equality – and thereby question its ability to effectively deliver its goals of justice and development (Rittberger 2001). The UN's structure so reflects the particular immediate post-World War II world it would seem that such reform will have to be foundational. UN leaders, in turn, have argued for the need to strengthen the UN, largely in terms of the legitimacy of its use of force to establish peace and justice. Such reforms will likely be marked by many crises that will continually raise the questions, 'What must be done? Who must do it?'

International courts and tribunals

International law has expanded greatly, governing the interactions of states, firms and individuals. International courts were established after World War II, but case loads were light until the 1970s and 1980s. Courts early on had jurisdiction either between states (the International Court of Justice or World Court) or over individual rights and in which individuals could appeal domestic cases (e.g. European Court of Human Rights). These courts have expanded to include individuals and groups taking foreign states to court. This process has advanced the furthest in Europe in which national courts draw on decisions from international courts and national legislatures craft laws with international law and precedents in mind. More recently, the claims of some national courts to universal jurisdiction and the establishment of the International Criminal Court mark steps beyond a state-centric legal model. Tribunals are *ad hoc* courts instituted to establish justice and give closure to particular incidents such as in the former Yugoslavia and Rwanda. The imperative is that those who committed war crimes must be brought to justice, and these tribunals are the means to accomplish that.

Human rights treaties, like all international treaties, rely on states to implement international law, and international courts and tribunals depend on state cooperation for obtaining evidence, witnesses and even the accused. International courts and UN investigations are forced to rely on information from NGOs (e.g. Gaer 1996). States usually are at least formally and rhetorically committed to these institutions, but they might in fact act on countervailing interests. Furthermore, there is no capacity for the courts and treaty institutions to coerce states to comply with decisions. States not recognizing negative decisions by international courts and the fragility of the reach of tribunals are notorious. The Rwanda Tribunal, for example, is located in Arusha, Tanzania, and witnesses having to fly from Rwanda travelled at the mercy of the government (Peskin 2005). Certainly this speaks to the weakness of these global legal actors. Still, we see historically that the establishment of sovereignty by centralizing monarchies through the expansion of their judicial system was no less tenuous (Strayer 1970). The lesson we see is that if states strategically comply with some decisions but not others, over time there is an accumulation of legitimacy and recognition for the courts.

A lot of the success of the tribunals has to do with their ability to relate world legal procedures and principles to those of the local population experiencing the atrocities. The tribunal in Rwanda, for example, is extremely handicapped by its location in Arusha, Tanzania (Peskin 2005). This opens space for sub-national actors (tribal institutions or nations within nations) with alternative or complementary judicial mechanisms. Effective governance is that which bridges the local–global divide.

IGOs and international courts and tribunals are all creatures of the interstate system. States participate for a variety of reasons even if a narrow calculation of interests might make them hesitant. States, for example, strategize to be where the action is (to be at the table where decisions are made) in the hope of influencing future decisions and general directions of world institutions. Moreover, as states manage their identities in world society, they find it necessary to participate in civilized governance structures. Woven through the institutional incentives are the institutional sources of authority and identity. Rational-legal authority of the nation-state is implicated in the rational-moral authority of voluntary participation: the moral project of the nation-state is at risk if it will not participate in collective action. This interface between nation-states and world institutions is a major focal point of current research and policy analysis.

International non-governmental organizations and global civil society

INGOs are not-for-profit organizations not established or run by states. Those that attract the most scholarly, political and media attention are those such as Amnesty International, Greenpeace and the World Wildlife Fund that mobilize collective action to influence states, international institutions and firms (Charnovitz 1997; Florini 2003; Guidry et al. 2000; Keck and Sikkink 1998). Many others such as the International Organization for Standardization function behind the scenes working out legal, accounting, technical and ethical standards in many sectors (Loya and Boli 1999; Brunsson and Jacobsson 2000; Abbott et al. 2004; Prakash and Potoski 2006).

The growth and operation of INGOs have a close association with world society at large. The first modern INGOs emerged in the late nineteenth century and have experienced remarkable growth. Reflecting their correspondence to the interstate and world-economic systems, this growth was interrupted twice, first with World War I and then during the period marked by the Great Depression and World War II. Subsequently, there has been sustained phenomenal growth in the number of INGOs paralleling the growth in other global indicators such as world trade, energy production, interstate treaties and IGOs. They are everywhere and involved in all sectors of global policy (Boli and Thomas 1999). They elicit diverse responses from other players who view them as harbingers of a democratic global civil society, elitist autocrats imposing inappropriate universal plans on local settings or annoying busybodies.

Whatever their reputation, INGOs wield a substantial amount of influence. They lack, of course, rational-legal authority and for the most part they have little economic power, although large INGOs in the development sector mediate the administration of increasingly high amounts of development monies (e.g. Oxfam, CARE, Action AID, Catholic Relief Services). Their influence has its source in rational-moral authority deriving from their voluntarism. INGOs claim to represent and express universal human interests, are individualistic and democratic in their goals and organization, and are committed to global rationalism or progress. These principles are woven together and embodied in the authorizing of individuals as world citizens to act globally (Boli and Thomas 1999). In practice, they provide expertise, sometimes in the form of abstract scientific knowledge (e.g. about the ozone), sometimes in the form of information (e.g. the disappearance of political dissidents), and thereby have an impact on the decisions of other players (Haas 1992; Gaer 1996). They provide this expertise to the full range of actors, and their relationship with the UN can be formalized in gaining official consultative status. Their neutrality and disinterestedness except for the common good is crucial to their ability to have morally compelling influence (Meyer 1994).

At the most general level, INGOs frame global policy issues within different issue areas. Women's INGOs historically have framed the nature of and arguments for women's rights, ranging from protection early in the century to labour issues to individual rights (e.g. the International Council of Women, International Federation of Working Women, Women's International Democratic Federation, International Women's Rights Watch) (Berkovitch 1999). INGOs shaped population policies at the turn of the twentieth century in terms of neo-Malthusian principles and then eugenics (International Union of Scientific Investigation of Population Problems); after World War II, INGOs such as the International Planned Parenthood Federation framed the anti-natalism of development and individual choice (Barrett and Frank 1999). INGOs (e.g. World Education, Action Aid International) spread the gospel of education reform throughout the world (Spring 2004), and myriad INGOs frame issues and amass scientific evidence concerning environmental issues (Frank et al. 1999; Wapner 1996).

The trend in activist INGOs is to cooperate in supermovements. Cooperatives and associations of INGOs form within and across functional issue areas. This trend has been transformed qualitatively by the World Social Forum (WSF). The WSF was established in Porto Alegre, Brazil, in 2001. It has grown from 5,000 participants at that meeting to tens of thousands of official delegates and participants by 2004 in Mumbai and 2005 in Porto Alegre. The qualitative difference with the WSF is its claim to be not an actor *per se* but a formal civil society space for groups and movements to come together. It has resisted (not without substantial internal controversy) taking political positions or making political pronouncements (Patomäki and Teivainen 2004).

INGOs target nation-states directly in a 'top-down' fashion, but they also become involved with domestic movements. They work from the top down in part by linking state purposes and policies to universal models of progress and moral principles. INGOs often attempt to mobilize directly domestic groups and thereby become involved in national and local power politics. Conversely local and national groups including indigenous peoples attempt to gain leverage over their states by involving INGOs (Keck and Sikkink 1998; Brysk 2000). This is not without tension because some domestic groups might prefer different frames and strategies than those espoused by INGOs and their local partners.

INGOs also target IGOs such as the UN, the World Bank and the WTO, with some acting as consultants working closely with them and others as activists attempting policy reform. Given their influence, affecting their policies has ripple effects throughout the world. When, for example, women's rights and development became intertwined within the UN through the work of many INGOs in the 1970s, women's issues such as education and labour force participation diffused throughout the UN and became global priorities (Berkovitch 1999). The World Bank uses development INGOs as experts to help administer development money locally. At the same time, activist INGOs attempt to influence World Bank 'best practices' that stipulate how development and education reform projects are to be worked out. Not all movements are success stories. Labour as an international player (e.g. International Confederation of Free Trade Unions) is active in lobbying IGOs such as the International Labor Organization and WTO, but it has had limited success in an environment dominated by liberalization policies (O'Brien 2004).

INGOs play an important role in the operation of international courts. Indeed, they were active in the establishment of the International Criminal Court (Potec 2003; Tornquist-Chesnier 2004). For courts in general, but especially in cases in which states are accused of rights violations, INGOs are crucial. In the absence of state cooperation, INGOs are the primary alternative source of information (Peskin 2005). Amnesty International, for example, is able to draw on volunteers to provide evidence and find and deliver witnesses, well beyond the limited resources of the courts or UN agencies and against the obstruction of states (e.g. Gaer 1996).

There is a dense network of states, firms, IGOs and INGOs that work together across global policy issue areas, technical sectors and markets to develop and institute standards ranging from measurements and labels to safety and to ethical accountability. The diverse actors form a variety of governance structures (Brunsson and Jacobsson 2000; Abbott et al. 2004). Two major players in standardization are the International Organization for Standardization (ISO) and the International Electrotechnical Commission (IEC) that have published, respectively, over 9,000 and 3,000 sets of standards. But they are only the major players in a dense network of a myriad of organizations (Loya and Boli 1999).

Firms comply with these standards for a variety of reasons. Technical, ethical and accountability standards are fundamental rules of the game and thus there is overriding pressure for actors to participate. Focused pressure also occurs; for example, in the case of ethical standards, diverse organizations such as the Global Compact function as moral entrepreneurs that put pressure on firms, bringing to bear global public opinion (Colonomos and Santiso 2005). Yet firms have strong interests apart from such pressures. By signing onto technical standards, they are able to function in an interdependent world. By meeting environmental, safety, ethical and accounting standards, they are able to display to other actors, including clients and customers, that they are responsible partners. Because of the nature of commodity chains, the compliance of one firm has ripple effects. A corporation marketing products in the United States, for example, that has been awarded an ISO 14001 certificate for environmental standards, will require all of its suppliers throughout the commodity chain reaching across many countries to be so certified (Prakash and Potoski 2006).

Actors beyond the nation-state, especially IGOs, INGOs and professional associations, in many respects are qualitatively different from other actors. As first described by John Meyer (1994, 1999), they exist and act to tell actors such as states, firms and individuals how to act, how to be proper players. To press the metaphor of player, they themselves are not players; if actors are players in the field or on the court, then these others are more like coaches, referees, groundskeepers, sporting associations and committees, sportswriters, impresarios, physical therapists, agents and advertisers. They are consultants, experts and advisers. IGOs prescribe goals and policies; INGOs advise actors and monitor their performance; professionals and intellectuals (economists, scientists, lawyers and academics) articulate models and give advice on implementing them.

Other players

The interactions of states, firms, IGOs and INGOs are complex enough, but things are even more complex because the distinctions among these different types of actors can become fuzzy. In a study of standardization, Abbott et al. (2004) depict a triangle with the vertices representing states, NGOs and firms. There are unambiguous examples of each of the three types of actors, but this framework reveals hybrid types of actors. For example, the Council for Environmentally Responsible Economies is comprised of investor groups and environmental INGOs. The Global

Compact is a hybrid of state and firm that was created to address issues of globalization and accountability. Its formation was at the initiative of the UN with voluntary participation by firms with a lesser involvement of NGOs. The Kimberly Process, formed to address conflict or 'blood' diamonds, was a multi-stakeholder initiative of states, INGOs and firms. While INGOs go out of their way to remain independent of states and firms to maintain their claim to disinterested universalism, hybrid actors attempt the same thing by bringing the various players together.

A significant trend in governance is toward regionalism, both supra- and sub-national. One aspect of globalization is the direct (i.e. not mediated by the nation-state) links between local actors and the global field. Cities, for example, directly market themselves and their industries throughout the world. There has been a proliferation of national and local NGOs that often cluster around INGOs. Large development INGOs, for example, will bring a large amount of international money into local contexts (e.g. in India) giving rise to the creation of local entrepreneurial NGOs attempting to partner with them. This interface between the large INGO and the local indigenous NGO is a major source of both cooperation and conflict.

Religious organizations, groups and movements are important players. Like INGOs, many influential ones work quietly behind the scenes whereas a few that politically engage nation-states or attempt to appeal to global public opinion attract more attention. Many religions are themselves transnational organizations, from the Roman Catholic Church to the Assemblies of God to smaller international denominations. Other religions such as Sunni Islam or Shi'a Islam, despite not having a singular bureaucratic organization, are transnational in scope and action. Important mainline religious organizations, such as the World Council of Churches, are comprised of different religions and have long histories, but they tend to lack the influence of individual charismatic leaders such as Bishop Tutu or the more revivalistic religions. Religious organizations that press for religious revival tend to be involved in missionary activity throughout the world, and missionary boards within Christianity have been global players for centuries. More recently religious organizations that tend toward religious revival (Evangelical Protestant or schools within Islam) have been able to mobilize and target issues of interest. For example, at population conferences, typically the Roman Catholic Church, associations of Evangelical Protestants and Muslim clerics lobby IGOs and states. Obviously, those organizations that politically mobilize violently attract more attention and arguably are having a profound impact in global civil society. Nevertheless, one of the most important ways in which religious players have an impact on the global field is through their sponsorship of a range of humanitarian, relief and development INGOs such as Catholic Relief Services: they have been in the vanguard of innovations in this area (Mei 2003).

Terrorist groups since the end of the Cold War have become prominent players and some such as Al-Qaeda can be conceptualized as a type of INGO. Terrorist groups have been especially innovative in organizational structure and use of the global media to further global agendas. Al-Qaeda seemingly has developed into a franchised brand name with local, loosely affiliated cells taking on the *modus oper-andi* of the brand name. This is not to be dismissive or flippant, but to acknowledge the fluidity of this and other organizational players.

Individuals

The tendency is to think of individuals at the 'micro' level of interactions that comprise collective actors that are global players. But this is a false distinction. Certainly the meeting of the United Nations Security Council or the board of directors of a transnational firm is just as micro as any face-to-face interaction among a small group of people. The distinction is 'as whose agent is the person acting?' As part of globalization and global rationalism, the individual is viewed as a global citizen with the authority and obligation to act globally. The modern markers that demarcate the individual are still largely national (censuses, public opinion surveys, passports), but individuals are important actors as they organize globally.

Intellectuals of all stripes are especially influential individuals. Professionals, lawyers and scientists are highly organized, and have influence through their INGOs; for example, there has been a substantial increase in the number of science INGOs oriented to social problems (Schofer 1999). It is important, however, to recognize their impact in the form of individual works, writings and lectures through which they articulate world principles and the interests of diverse players. This conjunction of charismatic individual and member of a profession and organization produces powerful players and scripts of world citizenship on the world stage. Religious personages are especially notable, even though they receive little attention in the scholarly literatures. Pope John Paul II worked to present himself as the first among world citizens; the Dali Lama also. Others such as Bishop Tutu and Mother Theresa combine a spirituality with working through situations of suffering, service and reconciliation. Many celebrities, often rock stars such as Bono, have also come to embody world citizenship.

CONCLUSIONS

There are a large number of important global players and a range of types of actors. Ability, authority and obligation are important dimensions of global players: players vary in their degree and extent of power, they exhibit different types of authority, and they to varying degrees all present their actions and purposes as moral projects. Our understanding of states and firms as the strong players in history forming the juggernaut of globalization has been furthered by acknowledging their embeddedness in global contexts and appreciating the complexity of those contexts. This, in turn, has called attention to the many important others: international governmental organizations, international courts and tribunals, international non-governmental organizations, intellectuals and world citizens. Early polemics about whether these other players are in the game only at the whim of powerful states and firms have given way to empirical studies of just how they operate, influence other actors and play a role in globalization processes.

The world is dominated by rational-legal authority and by rational-moral authority. States and firms are firmly anchored in rational-legal authority, technical rationality and science. We now have a better understanding that they also derive rational-moral authority, defining their goals and interests in terms of moral progress.

We also have a clearer picture of the myriad collective actors driven by the rational-moral authority of their universalism and volunteerism.

The sea-wave that is globalization is such an inexorable force in part due to the imperative for collective action. A good part of the dynamism is of course due to the seemingly unbridled agency to pursue individual interest, but it is unlikely that we would be witnessing the intensity and scale of globalization – the consciousness of one world in one time and one place as described by Roland Robertson (1992) – to the degree that we do without this imperative for collective action that views that unbridled quality as a problem. Individual players are authorized to discover problems and to take action to solve them, resulting in a continual uncovering of social problems – gaps between discursive claims and on-the-ground reality. There are the gaps between global ideals of peace, justice, progress, equality and democracy on the one hand and the way things actually work and turn out on the other. And there are the related problems of the players themselves: accountability, corruption, global–local tensions, implementation and compliance. What must be done? Who must do it? We understand a little better that all types of players and others equipped with technical and moral authority have the agency and obligation to ask, and answer, these questions.

References

Abbott, K.W., Sceats, S. and Snidal, D. 2004. 'The governance triangle: States, firms, NGOs and global business standards'. Paper presentation, Roundtable on Interdisciplinary Approaches to International Law, Vanderbilt University Law School, 12–13 November.

Baldwin, D.A. 1993. *Neorealism and Neoliberalism: The Contemporary Debate*. New York: Columbia University Press.

Barrett, D. and Frank, D. 1999. 'Population control for national development: From world discourse to national policies'. In J. Boli and G.M. Thomas (eds), *Constructing World Culture*, 198–221. Stanford, CA: Stanford University Press.

Barrett, D. and Tsui, A.O. 1999. 'Policy as symbolic statement: International response to national population policies', *Social Forces*, 78, 213–34.

Berger, P. and Luckman, T. 1966. *The Social Construction of Reality*. Garden City, NY: Anchor Books.

Berkovitch, N. 1999. *From Motherhood to Citizenship: Women's Rights and International Organizations*. Baltimore, MD: The Johns Hopkins University Press.

Boli, J. and Thomas, G.M. (eds.) 1999. *Constructing World Culture: International Non-governmental Organizations since 1875*. Stanford, CA: Stanford University Press.

Brunsson, N. and Jacobsson, B. 2000. *A World of Standards*. Oxford: Oxford University Press.

Brysk, A. 2000. *From Tribal Village to Global Village: Indian Rights and International Relations in Latin America*. Stanford, CA: Stanford University Press.

Charnovitz, S. 1997. 'Two centuries of participation: NGOs and international governance', *Michigan Journal of International Law*, 18 (2), 183–286.

Chase-Dunn, C. 1989. *Global Formation: Structures of the World Economy*. Oxford: Blackwell.

Colonomos, A. and Santiso, J. 2005. 'Vive la France! French multinationals and human rights', *Human Rights Quarterly*, 27 (4), 1307–45.

Douglas, M. 1966. *Purity and Danger*. London: Routledge & Kegan Paul.

Drori, G.S., Meyer, J.W., Ramirez, F.O. and Schofer, E. 2003. *Science in the Modern World Polity: Institutionalization and Globalization*. Stanford, CA: Stanford University Press.

Florini, A. 2003. *The Coming Democracy: New Rules for Running a New World.* Washington DC: Brookings Institution Press.

Frank, D., Hironaka, A., Meyer, J., Schofer, E. and Tuma, N. 1999. 'The rationalization and organization of nature in world culture'. In J. Boli and G.M. Thomas (eds), *Constructing World Culture*, 81–99. Stanford, CA: Stanford University Press.

Friedman, T. 1999. *The Lexus and the Olive Tree*. New York: Anchor Books.

Friedman, T. 2005. *The World Is Flat: A Brief History of the Twenty-First Century*. New York: Farrar, Straus and Giroux.

Gaer, F.D. 1996. 'Reality check: Human rights NGOs confront governments at the UN'. In T.G. Weiss and L. Gordenker (eds), *NGOs, the UN, and Global Governance*, ch. 2. Boulder, CO: Lynne Rienner.

Guidry, J.A., Kennedy, M.D. and Zald, M.N. (eds.) 2000. *Globalizations and Social Movements: Culture, Power, and the Transnational Public Sphere*. Ann Arbor: University of Michigan Press.

Haas, P.M. 1992. 'Introduction: Epistemic communities and international policy coordination', *International Organization*, 46 (1) Winter, 1–35.

Hunter, J.D. and Yates, J. 2002. 'In the vanguard of globalization: The world of American globalizers'. In P. Berger and S.P. Huntington (eds), *Many Globalizations: Cultural Diversity in the Contemporary World*, 323-57. Oxford: Oxford University Press.

Keck, M. and Sikkink, K. 1998. *Activists beyond Borders: Advocacy Networks in International Politics*. Ithaca, NY: Cornell University Press.

Keohane, R. and Nye, J. 2000. *Power and Interdependence*, 3rd edn. New York: Longman.

Loya, T. and Boli, J. 1999. 'Standardization in the world polity: Technical rationality over power'. In J. Boli and G.M. Thomas (eds), *Constructing World Culture*, 169–97. Stanford, CA: Stanford University Press.

McMichael, P. 2004. *Development and Social Change*, 3rd edn. Thousand Oaks, CA: Pine Forge Press.

Mei, Y. 2003. 'The changing discourse of international humanitarian charitable-relief NGOs'. Doctoral dissertation, Arizona State University.

Meyer, J. 1994. 'Rationalized environments'. In W.R. Scott and J.W. Meyer (eds), *Institutional Environments and Organizations*, 28–54. Thousand Oaks, CA: Sage.

Meyer, J. 1999. 'The changing cultural content of the nation-state: A world society perspective'. In G. Steinmetz (ed.), *State/Culture*, 123–43. Ithaca, NY: Cornell University Press.

Meyer, J.W., Boli, J. and Thomas, G.M. 1987. 'Ontology and rationalization in the Western cultural account'. In G.M. Thomas, J.W. Meyer, F.O. Ramirez and J. Boli (eds), *Institutional Structure: Constituting State, Society and the Individual*, 12–27. Newbury Park, CA: Sage.

Meyer, J., Boli, J., Thomas, G.M. and Ramirez, F.O. 1997. 'World society and the nation-state', *American Journal of Sociology*, 103 (1), 144–81.

O'Brien, R. 2004. 'Continuing incivility: Labor rights in a global economy', *Journal of Human Rights*, 3 (June), 203–14.

Patomäki, H. and Teivainen, T. 2004. 'The World Social Forum: An open space or a movement of movements?' *Theory, Culture & Society*, 21 (6), 145–54.

Peskin, V. 2005. 'Trials and tribulations: International criminal tribunals and the politics of state cooperation'. Doctoral dissertation, University of California, Berkeley.

Polanyi, K. 1944. *The Great Transformation*. Boston: Beacon Press.

Potec, L. 2003. 'Transnational advocacy networks as agents of change in international relations: The case of the coalition for an international criminal court'. Paper presented at the meetings of the Central and East European International Studies Association, Budapest, Hungary, 26–28 June.

Prakash, A. and Potoski, M. 2006. *The Voluntary Environmentalists: Green Clubs, ISO 14001, and Voluntary Environmental Regulations*. Cambridge: Cambridge University Press (forthcoming).

Rittberger, V. 2001. *Global Governance and the United Nations System*. New York: United Nations University Press.

Robertson, R. 1992. *Globalization: Social Theory and Global Culture*. Newbury Park, CA: Sage.

Schofer, E. 1999. 'Science associations in the international sphere, 1875–1990: The rationalization of science and the scientization of society'. In J. Boli and G.M. Thomas (eds), *Constructing World Culture*, 249–66. Stanford, CA: Stanford University Press.

Scholte, J.A. 2003. *Democratizing the Global Economy: The Role of Civil Society*. Coventry: Centre for the Study of Globalisation and Regionalisation.

Scott, J.C. 1998. *Seeing Like a State*. New Haven, CT: Yale University Press.

Spring, J. 2004. *How Educational Ideologies Are Shaping Global Society: Intergovernmental Organizations, NGOs, and the Decline of the Nation-state*. Mahwah, NJ: Lawrence Erlbaum.

Strayer, J.R. 1970. *On the Medieval Origins of the Modern State*. Princeton, NJ: Princeton University Press.

Tornquist-Chesnier, M. 2004. 'NGOs and international law', *Journal of Human Rights*, 3 (2), 253–63.

Wapner, P. 1996. *Environmental Activism and World Civic Politics*. Albany, NY: SUNY Press.

Wendt, A. 1999. *Social Theory of International Politics*. Cambridge: Cambridge University Press.

Wuthnow, R. 1987. *Meaning and Moral Order*. Berkeley: California University Press.

Chapter 5

Globalization Today

JOHN BOLI AND VELINA PETROVA

Globalization signifies becoming global or worldwide. Expanding on Roland Robertson's well-known framework, globalization entails conceiving the world as a single social space – for example, an all-encompassing world society, polity, culture or economy. It is evident in the 'making global', or 'universalization' (Boli and Thomas 1999), of social entities, organizations, authority structures, knowledge and accounting systems, news and entertainment media and so on. Globalization thus entails the making global of such elemental social entities as the individual, the corporation, the state and nature. It entails the construction of globe-spanning authority (global governance) in the form of international governmental organizations (IGOs) and international non-governmental organizations (INGOs). It signifies the development and worldwide propagation of scientific principles, research methods, engineering techniques and management methods that are presumed to be useful everywhere. Globalization also involves universalization in the moral domain – the 'making global' of principles of sacred value, equality and propriety that define an ever-expanding array of rights and obligations of globalizing entities.

The presumptuousness of this chapter's assignment – to review the essentials of globalization today – cannot be overstated. Begging indulgence for our necessary selectivity and the many points of contention that cannot be addressed, we have chosen to highlight the present globalization of social entities and authority structures. Along the way, we bring in conventionally discussed domains of globalization – the world economy, popular culture, environmentalism, human rights and so on[1] – but mainly in terms of processes within these domains that contribute to the globalization of social entities and authority. Thus, our concern is to emphasize the globalizing aspect of globalization, that is, the making global of the social world, rather than the degree to which the world has become interconnected. This emphasis reflects our desire to avoid the ubiquitous but unfortunate practice of discussing globalization as if it were chiefly a matter of international or interregional interaction and exchange.

The chapter begins on an experiential level, offering some general reflections on globalization today as it is evident and experienced in everyday life. We then turn to the globalization of the individual, the state and the corporation, complemented by brief discussions of the globalization of two more diffuse collective social entities, global civil society and the transcendental. The conclusion draws together some thoughts on the dynamics and tensions of globalization today.

THE GLOBALIZATION OF EXPERIENCE

In a nutshell, everyday experience suggests that globalization is inescapable, taken for granted and inclusive (Sernau 2000; Appadurai 1996) – despite a variety of objections to such characterizations, particularly the common lament that globalization excludes the poor and the marginalized (e.g. Mander and Goldsmith 1997; Korten 2001).

Inescapable globalization

The European explorers of the fifteenth and sixteenth centuries, financed by monarchs and merchants, went in search of the globe, establishing new trade routes and founding new colonies to expand competing empires. They experienced globalization by doing it; the peoples they encountered experienced globalization by having it done to them. This sense of imposition by powerful globalizing forces – mercantile capitalism, competing states, evangelistic religions – remains a common experience but its character has changed. On the one hand, large portions of the social milieu, whether national or local, are constituted by globalizing forces. We are, as it were, immersed in globalization to such an extent that we often cannot recognize it. On the other hand, and as a corollary, even those who are often seen as primary drivers of globalization – such as the corporate executives, state officials and high-level technicians that Sklair (2001) calls the 'transnational capitalist class' – are subject to these ubiquitous forces.

Globalization's inescapability is based in large part on a shift in the nature of globalizing forces, which are increasingly based not on power but on forms of authoritative legitimacy – scientific, professional, credentialed, moral (Meyer 1980; Drori et al. 2003; Boli and Thomas 1999). These authority complexes are more welcomed than imposed, representing as they do the purported pathways to economic growth, social progress, environmental sustainability and the like. At the same time, the increasingly integrated global stratification structure leads to common symbols and systems of value and desirability everywhere in the world, be it high fashion, pop music, advanced technogadgets, investment instruments, anime or pseudo-spiritual exercises. Those who are barely plugged in seek to plug in more; those who are immersed strive mightily to reach the leading edge of globalization. Inescapability for many is not a problem so much as it is a desired condition.

At the everyday level, of course, the mass media and their real-time images are important elements in this inescapable immersion of and in the globalized. But the media carry mainly images and talk; of greater import, for many people, are the flows of people, goods, media products and subcultures that swirl around them.

While in earlier eras it took a voyage around the world to come into contact with exotic, mysterious others, today the world has come to the local neighbourhood (Albrow 1997). Among London's schoolchildren, some 300 different languages are spoken (UNDP 2004). American grandparents make birthday calls to their Peace Corps-volunteering grandchildren halfway around the world. A primary export of the Philippines is highly trained nurses, while a primary import of Mexico is remittances from brothers, fathers, sisters and cousins working in the United States (remittances to Latin America from just California, New York, Texas, Florida, Illinois and New Jersey exceed $1 billion a year; IADB 2005). In economic terms, remittances reflect financial globalization, labour globalization and the globalization of, say, Mexican, Nicaraguan and Colombian cultures. In terms of human experience, these examples show how, for more and more families around the world, globalization has become an inescapable aspect of everyday life.

Taken-for-granted globalization

Before the globalization of economic exchange that has been driven largely by expansive capitalism, for most people the clothes they wore and the food they ate were local products, self-produced or traded within a narrowly circumscribed area. For the richest classes, limited long-distance trade brought high-value products much appreciated for their rarity and inaccessibility. Today, we hardly consider it remarkable that our clothes are sewn in China or Romania or Guatemala, that fruits and vegetables are flown in from Chile or Kenya, that coffee from three continents and nine countries is available in neat rows on supermarket shelves. None of this is exotic any longer, especially not for the wealthier segment of the world's population. We take it for granted that global markets stretching to 40 or 60 or 100 countries are fairly well integrated, that goods travel thousands of miles, that information and propaganda and mindless entertainment products reach us instantaneously from around the world. We take it for granted, in short, that the world is globalized, and that we can – if not this summer, then next year, or the year after – go on that Caribbean cruise or Himalayan trek or African safari. The world will be there waiting for us.

Globalization for everyone

Who is this 'we' whom we so blithely invoke in claiming globalization's taken-for-granted character? Who experiences globalization every day as inescapable, as routine contact with the far side of the globe, as routine purchases of the products of global commodity chains? Surely not everyone – but the unevenness and inequalities of globalization are not quite what they seem.

In earlier eras when globalization was primarily an elite prerogative, lumps of sugar from Brazil ended up only in the Indian tea of the wealthy. Silk textiles graced the shoulders of the nobility, not the peasants; higher education in the intellectual centres of Europe was reserved for the well-born. In recent decades, the experience of globalization has plunged down the social pyramid. Travel in foreign lands has become a routine middle-class luxury and a common imperative for the poor illegal immigrant or refugee. The cell phone warms the hands of hundreds of millions of people living well below the level of the middle classes. International students in the universities of affluent countries come from all rungs of the stratification ladder in their home countries. The rivers of clothing flowing from Chinese sweatshops flood not only the discount megastores of the West but also the outdoor markets of African cities and towns. Not to mention the torrents of pop culture – Mexican telenovelas, Asian fusion cuisine, 'world music' from a hundred different production centres in the Third World – that swirl through even remote villages in peripheral lands.

All this is not to say that the poor, the peripheral, the marginalized are equally enmeshed in globalization, far from it. They are on the receiving end, the driven rather than the drivers, with little or no access to many of the bells and whistles of globalized systems. But a strong ethos of inclusion permeates world culture, decrying the 'digital divide' (the Digital Divide Network's [2005] slogan: 'Knowledge to help everyone succeed in the digital age') and all the other pernicious forms of exclusion, inequality and unrepresentativeness of globalized modernity. Efforts to broaden globalization appear at every turn: professional associations offer lower membership fees for members in poor countries, Englishman Trevor Baylis reinvented the hand-crank radio so aid organizations and NGOs could plug in villagers in electricity-less locales (Drake 2001), NGO conferences subsidize the travel expenses of poor delegates, and on and on. Globalization is for everyone, or it should be – this is the ethos, and increasingly the ethos is actualized in the everyday experience of ever more of the world's population.

GLOBALIZATION OF SOCIAL ENTITIES: INDIVIDUAL, STATE, CORPORATION

The globalization of social entities takes two primary forms; for simplicity's sake we denote them as cultural and organizational forms. The former refers to abstract, disembodied models of social entities that form part of the constituting edifice of world culture (Meyer et al. 1997; Boli and Thomas 1999; Lechner and Boli 2005). The latter points to the more or less formalized institutions of world society that are built around, embed and sustain particular types of entities. While the distinction is somewhat artificial in that the organizational is always also cultural, its significance should become clear as we discuss the three main entities undergoing globalization.

The dual nature of these models and institutions must be stressed at the outset. Primarily cognitive in nature – that is, defining and shaping the properties, capacities, identities, limitations and foibles of the entities – the models are also normative in that they specify the rights, duties and expectations associated with the entities. By the same token, the institutions both enable and constrain entities, prompting them to actualize the abstract models. Both models and institutions have globalized rapidly, especially since the latter half of the nineteenth century (cf. Robertson 1992; Lechner and Boli 2005). They have become much more elaborate and incoherent as well.

While discussions of global cultural models often have a rather diffuse and imprecise character, we can give them more substance and specificity by cataloguing the types of measures or scales that are routinely used to assess social entities in world society. Consider these examples: for individuals, one common metric of accomplishment is the highest educational degree obtained; for states, one metric of accomplishment is the proportion of the nation's population that is literate (literacy is also a metric for individuals); for research-intensive corporations, one metric is the proportion of doctoral degree holders among its researchers. The first example tells us that the 'individual' is an entity that is (cognitively) capable of becoming educated and (normatively) expected to do so. As a global abstraction, this element of the model of the individual is presumed to apply to all individuals everywhere and, according to the ideology of education as a human right, all individuals everywhere must have the opportunity to become educated. The globalized institution of relevance to this aspect of the globalized individual is, of course, mass schooling, which is to be organized and funded by each and every state. From this it follows that global models of the state assume that the state is capable of such crucial functions as society-wide taxation, school construction, teacher certification and so on, while the state is also normatively obligated to undertake mass schooling to help its citizens actualize global models of the individual. All of this is also inherent in the second example, the metric of population literacy, which is tied to global models of both the individual and the state.

The third example, the metric of doctoral-degree research intensity, implies that global models of the corporation extend well beyond notions of production and profit-seeking. The corporation is presumed to be (cognitively) capable of organizing the production of scientific knowledge that is universally (globally) applicable. The normative situation regarding this metric is rather complex. On the one hand, the knowledge generated should contribute to the advancement of general human welfare (new medicines, faster chips, safer products); on the other hand, the corporation is authorized to treat this knowledge as proprietary, controlling its release and use. Note that this metric also ups the ante, as it were, for global models of the individual and the state. Individuals are not only capable of being educated; they (or, at least, some individuals) can become sufficiently informed and skilled to operate on the frontiers of knowledge and help make the world a better place, that is, contribute to progress. At the same time, the state is presumed – and expected – to be capable of organizing universities that can operate doctoral programmes that produce leading-edge researchers, a weighty and complex responsibility indeed. We hardly need stress that, on the organizational side, the university is a quintessentially globalized institution (Riddle 1993).

With this background in mind, let us turn to the globalization of the individual.

The individual

Many globalizing forces embed the individual as the fundamental unit of social action and meaning. Most central in this respect is mass schooling, as indicated above. Schooling treats children primarily as individuals whose capacities and character are to be developed in line with standardized global models of the productive, loyal, efficacious and rights-endowed actor (Meyer et al. 1992). The ideology of egalitarian schooling, widely embraced rhetorically and imperfectly implemented practically, shoves aside identities based on primordial or ascribed collectivities (the family, village, ethnicity etc.) in favour of individual development, industry and achievement (cf. Frank and Meyer 2002). Schooling confers individualized credentials that constitute significant status and identity markers (Collins 1979), both general (the secondary school graduate, the university degree holder) and specific (the certified accountant, the agricultural adviser). In counterpoint, school failure also confers a significant individualized status (the high-school dropout). Schooling is crucial to the occupational trajectories of individuals and their life chances across a great many domains (Levin et al. 1971), thanks in no small part to its capacity to convince the schooled that they possess individuality that overrides the stereotyped qualities and capacities associated with collective identities.

The globalization of schooling has been a massive enterprise in the postwar era, both in terms of global organizations (IGOs, especially UNESCO, and many education-related INGOs) that propagate global schooling models and aid in the construction of school systems, and in the state-directed schooling expansion process that has rapidly incorporated most of the world's children in schools (Meyer et al. 1992). The enrolment data are remarkable: in 2001–2, some 84 per cent of the world's children were enrolled in primary schools, 55 per cent of the world's youth population was enrolled in secondary schools and tertiary education enrolments amounted to 23 per cent of the world's young adults (UNESCO 2005). Not entirely coincidentally, literacy has greatly increased as well, rising from about 56 per cent of the world's population in 1970 (UIS 2002) to about 82 per cent at the turn of the century (UNESCO 2005). And, as Ramirez and colleagues have shown in numerous studies (e.g. Ramirez and Wotipka 2001; Bradley and Ramirez 1996), this expansion has become almost gender-blind, at all educational levels. Worldwide, in 2001–2 girls accounted for 48.5 per cent of primary enrolments, 47.1 per cent of secondary enrolments and 50.5 per cent of tertiary enrolments, with more women than men enrolled in higher education in 90 of the 144 countries reporting data, including most of the large-population countries (UNESCO 2005). Global models of the individual carried by schooling are truly universalized to a remarkable degree.

Also of great significance for the globalization of the individual is the complex of institutions that make up the modern exchange economy. Monetarized exchange systems assume individuals as their fundamental units in almost every respect. Individuals – not groups – possess human capital (education, skills, experience) that enables them to produce value. Individuals – not groups – are paid for their production. Individuals purchase goods and services through recurrent interaction rituals of individualized exchange. Individuals have unique value storage facilities (bank or investment accounts) and individual property rights to their possessions. Of course, in many instances the household remains an active collective entity – individuals may contribute their earnings to the household, make purchases on behalf of the household, or own property jointly (especially with spouses). But exchange is, primarily, overwhelmingly individualized and individualizing.

Such globalization of the individual is one of the deeper institutional effects of the world economy. Conventional measures of economic globalization – trade as a proportion of world product or the mean value of trade as a proportion of national product – only indirectly measure this institutional effect, and these measures are rather poor indicators of economic globalization in any case. Not all trade across national boundaries involves global structures or processes; much trade is local or regional, based on simple commodity chains that hardly qualify as global. But, as is often lamented, nation-states so dominate the accounting of economic flows that meaningful measures of exchange that do not reify national units are practically unavailable.

Besides the globalization of the individual as the fundamental social entity, we should also note the globalization of individual personhood. Most striking in this respect is the ideology of human rights, an ever more elaborate set of documents and doctrines (Elliott forthcoming) that specify the fundamental meaning of personhood in terms of rights to various forms of protection, empowerment and well-being. While not uncontested, particularly with respect to women's rights, human rights doctrines are increasingly important as normative frameworks for policy making and judicial decisions at all levels, and as stimuli to global social movements. Another striking development, not yet studied systematically, is the spread of standard models of the interior of the individual, as depicted in the *Diagnostic and Statistical Manual of Mental Disorders* (DSM), a project of the American Psychiatric Association (2000), and its global counterpart, the ICD-10 Classification of Mental and Behavioural Disorders (part of the International Statistical Classification of Diseases, overseen by WHO 1993). The DSM, first published in 1952 and currently in process toward its fifth iteration, is now in use in most countries around the world. It has been translated into 22 languages, including major non-European languages (Chinese, Japanese, Arabic etc.), and its publisher proudly proclaims it 'the most widely used psychiatric reference in the world' (Psychiatry Online 2005).

A final aspect of the globalization of the individual, modest though it may be, emerges in the World Values Survey (WVS) data (see Inglehart et al. 2004; Inglehart and Baker 2000) that explore values and attitudes in 81 countries around the world. One item asks, 'To which of these geographical groups would you say you belong first of all?', presenting the alternatives of 'locality or town where you live', 'state or region of country where you live', '[name of country] as a whole', '[name of continent]' or 'the world as a whole'. The next item asks for respondents to name their second locus of belonging. During the first three waves of this massive survey project (1981–4, 1990–3, 1995–7), the combined figures for respondents choosing 'world as a whole' as the first or second locus of belonging rose from 14.0 per cent to 16.7 per cent to 21.0 per cent; those choosing the world as the first locus rose from 6.5 per cent to 10.1 per cent. In other words, about a fifth of respondents saw themselves, in the third wave, as 'world citizens' first or second. Analyses of the WVS data show that choosing the world as a crucial locus of belonging is more common among younger people, those with more education, those who have a professional, supervisory or managerial occupation (or who live in a household where someone has such an occupation) and those in larger urban areas. Class identity and income matter rather little, remarkably enough. In a world of rising education, expanding professionalism and growing urbanism, these findings suggest a gradual increase in this tendency to see the globe as one's home above all other possibilities.

The state

The globalization of the state in terms of world models, expectations and demands is rather far advanced. Here the number of concrete measures and indicators is legion; states are monitored and ranked on their performance in more ways than we can count. To give but a few examples: states are evaluated in terms of their success in providing education (primary schooling enrolment ratios, secondary school graduation rates), medical care (rates of infectious diseases, physicians per thousand population, immunization rates) and welfare services (pensions, maternity leave, unemployment compensation). Broader measures of 'development' have become common, such as the Human Poverty Index (HPI) that is at the core of the UN Development Programme's annual *Human Development Report* (UNDP 2004). The HPI is a summary indicator based on life expectancy, education and per capita income, and states in countries that fare poorly on the HPI are states that are not meeting their responsibilities.

Besides these conventional development indicators, states must also cope with assessments of their social, political and cultural 'progress'. A whole battery of measures of women's rights and participation have emerged, including the Gender Empowerment Measure and the Gender-Related Development Index (UNDP 2000), which combine more specific measures such as the female share of education enrolments, women's shares of professional occupations, women's share of parliamentarians, women's literacy relative to that of men and so on. Environmental performance is assessed through measures of sulphuric air contamination, mercury parts per million in water and many more. The degree of democratic governance is assessed by the Freedom House's (2005) Political Rights and Civil Liberties index, while the degree of state corruption is measured by Transparency International's (2005) Corruption Perceptions Index. Even the health of national civil societies is formally tracked, for example by USAID's (2005) NGO Sustainability Index, which assesses both the NGO population and state policies that affect the conditions for civil society development in numerous countries.

The globalized measures mentioned so far relate primarily to state responsibilities to their own citizens. Other indices measure state willingness to behave responsibly in relation to the 'international community', or world society. For the environment, for instance, a common measure is a country's share of total world emissions of a noxious substance or greenhouse gas (NO, CO_2). For conformity to the principles of the global moral order (Boli 2006b), various INGOs and research communities monitor state signatures and ratifications of treaties, declarations and protocols on the environment, human rights, non-discrimination and so on. The rankings that emerge identify both global exemplars – states and countries that actualize the ideal global models in particular dimensions – and, more importantly, global laggards and failures. The latter know that they must improve their performance or try to explain away their failure (as a function of too little or too much foreign investment, too much or not enough openness to global markets, too strong or too weak a central state etc.). What they cannot do is challenge the globalized models of the state, except in marginal terms about specific particularistic matters.

For states in richer countries a special set of expectations applies. These states are to aid their poorer cousins around the world through generous foreign aid (the

UN standard, which is met by only a few small welfare-state countries, is 0.7 per cent of GNI). Their aid should be unrestricted in use, consist mainly of grants rather than loans and further the development of local civil society (Petrova 2006). Richer states must also give generously for emergency relief (consider the controversy about slow-in-coming US commitments following the calamitous 2004 Asian tsunami), they are to accept generous quotas of refugee immigrants and they are under growing pressure (to which they are increasingly acceding) to forgive the debts of the poorest countries.

Taken together, these multifarious dimensions of globalized state modelling and performance assessment put heavy constraints on state managers, legislators and adjudicators. Most of their tasks are embedded in the goals encapsulated in the globalized state, and countless globalized actors of other sorts – experts, consultants, advisers, activists and bureaucrats in IGOs, INGOs, domestic NGOs, firms etc. – swarm about states to ensure that they make good-faith efforts to actualize the globalized models, or take them to task for not doing so (cf. Boli and Thomas 1999). The most formalized version of this process is found in IGOs, which often act as supranational bodies with quasi-authoritative jurisdiction over their member states and, as with the WTO, can even impose sanctions on misbehaving states (Ougaard 2004).[2] The most widespread version of the process, however, is the more diffuse mechanism whereby world-cultural authority is exercised by non-governmental actors whose long-term reshaping of state identities and interests leads to sweeping changes in particular social sectors (see the chapters in Boli and Thomas 1999).

Globalized models of state performance are sufficiently influential that the 'failed state' is no longer one whose territorial integrity has been compromised, as in earlier periods of state formation and consolidation (e.g. Tilly 1992), but a state whose population is trapped in poverty, violence and social disorder due to the incapacity, ineptitude, corruption or negligence of the state. Note, however, that the proliferation of globalized models of state behaviour and performance, and the diffusion of authority among many globalized non-state or transnational organizations, have also increased the authority and reach of states (contrary to proclamations of the state's demise by Strange 1996, Sassen 1996, and others). All states, both rich and poor, are not only authorized but expected to take action in many arenas that once were deemed part of the private sphere of life, for example reproductive health and family planning (Barrett and Frank 1999), religious instruction (a standard subject in most school systems), job training and so on. Following the models of state performance pushed by authoritative globalized entities enhances the authority of the state vis-à-vis its citizens.

In terms of their authority, legitimacy and effectiveness, states are best off if they actually make progress on at least some measures of performance. If progress is difficult, however, they still gain if they make a good-faith effort, perhaps by setting up appropriate agencies and developing ambitious five-year plans (see Meyer 1980). At the same time, conveniently enough, the available range of excuses for inadequate state performance is always expanding. When states fail to make progress, they can blame the very same transnational and non-governmental actors whose demands for state conformity to world models are so insistent, either for specific restrictions and conditions imposed on them by IGOs or for the more diffuse 'interference' or 'imperialism' or 'infringement on sovereignty' that outside actors represent.

States are not supposed to fail, and numerous global governance structures are dedicated to ensuring that states do not fail. In the worst instances, when states are unable to maintain even minimal public services, rich states provide 'subsistence foreign aid' that directly constitutes a share of the state budget. Such aid helps prevent the breakdown of order, though it usually fails to increase the state's long-term viability and it suppresses the emergence of political alternatives to a non-viable regime (Morgenthau 1962). Some states have become almost entirely dependent on foreign subsistence aid, for example Mali, for which official development assistance averaged 9 per cent of GDP between 2000 and 2004 (World Bank 2005). With external debt reaching 100 per cent of GDP in 2001, only through debt relief assistance under the IMF/World Bank Highly Indebted Poor Country (HIPC) initiative was Mali able to service its debt, an expenditure greater than total state spending on health and education (see AFRODAD 2005). With subsistence foreign aid, the Malian state has been able to devote some resources to such areas as poverty relief, education and health sector development and HIV/AIDS projects, but the very existence of the state and its capacity to act have been wholly dependent on the international community (Glenzer 2004 reports that up to 80 per cent of the Malian state budget has come from official development assistance in recent years).

Such is the importance of the globalized state, however, that the very thought of abandoning Mali to its fate cannot be entertained by the international community. The IMF and World Bank, CARE and World Vision, the Swedish International Development Agency and the US Agency for International Development (USAID) would be entirely derelict in their duties if they were to allow the Malian state to collapse. In contemporary world culture, the only legitimate form of political organization is the democratic, bureaucratized, progress-oriented, inclusive state, and 'everyone' has the responsibility to help weak or poor or inordinately corrupt states clean up their act and live up to their globally defined obligations. If such help means that the sovereign autonomy of many states is more fiction than fact, so be it – as long as the fiction can be maintained, and as long as some degree of progress is evident in some of the measures of state performance that are crucial to the identity of the state as such.

The corporation

Most obvious and widely discussed with regard to the globalization of the corporation is the emergence of globalized enterprises (multinational or transnational corporations, MNCs/TNCs) over the past two centuries, in the tradition of the early trading companies (e.g. the Dutch East India Company and Hudson's Bay Company) that were key global diffusers of capitalism. While TNCs number in the tens of thousands (Gabel and Bruner 2003), just the largest 500 companies have total revenues equal to a quarter or more of world economic product and account for half or more of total world trade in goods and services. Lists of these behemoths (e.g. *Fortune*'s Global 500) confirm that capital concentration is greatest in the highly developed core countries – the United States, Japan, Germany, the United Kingdom, France, Switzerland etc. – in that most of them are headquartered in these countries. Over time, however, non-core countries such as China, South Korea, Brazil and India, among others, have an increasing presence among the world's economic giants, indicating a decentralization of capital accumulation among rising economic powers.

We concentrate here on less frequently discussed aspects of the globalization of the corporation, one cluster of which relates to instrumental and technical dimensions of corporate globalization while the other cluster relates to moral and normative dimensions.

INSTRUMENTAL DIMENSIONS

Like the state in the political realm, in the economic realm the corporation has become the globally favoured organizational form. Also like the state, the corporation has become a global model, or, rather, a variety of models based on a common core of characteristics – what organizational theorists like Scott (2002) might call the 'technical core', except that many aspects of the core are now more social than technical. The common core includes such basic features as formalized structures, job descriptions, mission statements, cost accounting (double-entry bookkeeping, formal audits), lines of authority, cost-benefit analysis and so on. Equally well, it now includes personnel departments, the use of psychological testing, corporate culture management, environmental impact and pollution control structures, regulatory compliance officers and a host of other relatively recent additions to the globalized models.

A good number of these dimensions are formally globalized through particular INGOs. Most prominent, due to their highly public nature, are efforts in technical standardization and accounting: the ISO 9000 family of standards for organizational quality (Hoyle 2001), the ISO 14000 family of standards for environmental performance (Sayre 1996) and the many accounting standardization rules and principles developed by the International Accounting Standards Board (IASB; see Tamm Hallström 2004a). In all these areas, adoption of the globalized models is formally voluntary, but in practice companies often come to regard adoption as virtually compulsory because their legitimacy as rational, responsible actors depends on it (Loya and Boli 1999).

Instrumentally focused globalized models are most easily identified in these public arenas, but the strongest global forces influencing corporations to seek out, adopt or adapt to global models surely are the great global accounting and management consulting firms (now down to the Big Four: Deloitte Touche Tohmatsu, KPMG, PricewaterhouseCoopers, Ernst & Young). Their business is, in essence, the elaboration and propagation of globally standardized models – of corporate accounting, to be sure, but also of organizational structure, internal processes, employee relations, relationships with the external environment (clients and customers, regulators, IGOs, social movements and so on) and a host of other aspects. They are, or aim to be, in the vanguard of global development, constantly on the hunt for the Next Big Thing in management philosophy, investment strategy, financial instruments or tax-evasion devices. Add to them the bewildering array of other types of consultant firms – for employment practices, benefits packages, information technology, software development, production techniques, marketing strategies and all the rest – and it is clear that, to a large extent, the contemporary TNC is a quintessentially boundary-less organization (Scott and Meyer 1994) that is highly permeated by all kinds of globalized modelling forces. The really remarkable thing about all this, besides the fact that TNCs so eagerly subject themselves to globalized modelling, is how little noticed it is. TNCs are the gigantic, commanding power-houses of the world economy, in most accounts. That they are continually shaped and reshaped by external globalizing forces – including, of course, their fellow TNCs – is not much discussed.

We could easily broaden this discussion of the instrumental dimensions of glo-balized corporation models to include a variety of other organizational types, such as the university, the sports club, the political activist collective, the hobby group and the professional association. These and many more types have been globalized, with fairly standard models available globally for organizations that may operate locally, nationally or transnationally. In many cases, such models are fairly highly formalized in the rules specified by INGOs regarding the nature and characteristics of their members (especially for INGOs that have national associations as members, like ISO or the World Medical Association) and in the guidelines INGOs promulgate to help new local chapters or national sections get off the ground (cf. Boli 2006a). The larger point is that, regardless of locale, to an increasing extent a university is a university, a club is a club, a social movement organization is a social movement organization – recognizably so, in familiar terms, to all kinds of people from all kinds of places. Organizational isomorphism (DiMaggio and Powell 1983) is clearly on the march in today's globalization.

MORAL DIMENSIONS

The moral dimensions of the globalization of the corporation are much more promi-nent in the global public realm than the instrumental dimensions, no doubt because they involve highly visible struggles pitting a ragtag army of slingshot-bearing Davids against the overwhelming concentration of firepower represented by TNC Goliaths. We have in mind here, above all, the so-called anti-globalization move-ments that challenge corporate domination, neoliberal worship of the free market and the infamous 'race to the bottom' that they decry as the inevitable consequence of competitive global capitalism dominated by profit-obsessed TNCs. Much of their vitriol is directed against the IMF, WTO and the World Bank, which are seen as crucial bulwarks of global capitalism and its consequent global stratification, but the list of individual TNCs that corporate-critical organizations have targeted is long and ever growing, from such perennial targets as Nestlé, Nike and Dow Chemical to more obscure companies like Freeport McMoRan and Rio Tinto, Cow & Gate and Cargill, Novartis and Eskom.

The critics of TNCs are moral gadflies and entrepreneurs, drawing on principles embedded in the global moral order to broaden the framework of obligations and concerns that corporations are expected to adopt (Boli et al. 2004). Many of these principles have been formalized in official UN and other IGO human rights docu-ments, ILO conventions regarding labour rights and employer/worker relations, and declarations and treaties derived from global conferences (e.g. the Kyoto protocol on global warming, the declarations emanating from the series of UN conferences for women). Often directed at states, such documents and declarations also impli-cate TNCs, raising expectations for them to help address a range of problems that historically have been seen as not the 'business of business'. More directly, of course, TNCs and domestic companies, particularly subcontractors in the less developed countries producing goods for TNCs, are the prime targets of a growing set of statements of principles, codes of conduct, specifications of corporate social responsibility and monitoring efforts.

The most general declarations regarding the moral (social responsibility) obligations of corporations are the Sullivan Principles (originated in connection with the global movement against South African apartheid; see Sethi and Williams 2001) and the UN Global Compact of nine principles concerning human rights, labour and the environment, pushed by Secretary-General Kofi Annan since the late 1990s. Also well known are several exemplars produced by non-governmental and business organizations, such as the CERES environmental guidelines by the Coalition for Environmentally Responsible Economies (from 1989, prompted by the Exxon Valdez disaster) and the Caux Roundtable principles created by an association of Japanese, German and US businesspeople.[3]

What drives the development and propagation of these 'triple bottom line' (financial, environmental, social) declarations and principles? For the most part, the drivers are the global social movements involving international and domestic non-governmental organizations, often working in loosely coordinated networks, that seek out and publicize corporate violations of the global moral order (Boli 2006b). For example, Amnesty International regularly publishes reports of human rights abuses in the workplace, Corpwatch monitors TNCs for their human rights and environmental transgressions, and INFACT has developed a Hall of Shame campaign to identify and expose the worst corporate offenders each year. Some movements are industry- or company-specific, such as the numerous organizations that have emerged to end child labour and improve working conditions in the global apparel industry (e.g. The Clean Clothes Campaign, which pushes its 'Code of labor practices for the apparel industry') and groups directing their efforts at the global toy industry (e.g. the label Rugmark, or 'De l'éthique sur l'étiquette', whose goal is to induce consumers to buy goods of socially responsible origins only).

Like most organizations, initially TNCs typically reject outside efforts to influence their behaviour, but more and more they are acceding rhetorically to their critics and even backing up their rhetoric with meaningful action. Rhetorical conformity in moral dimensions appears in company or industry codes of conduct, which posit voluntary compliance but normally omit enforcement mechanisms. Thousands of global companies and hundreds of industries now have such codes, in the latter case usually developed by the leading business INGO in the sector. Not infrequently, one or more companies adopt the role of moral trailblazer, making systematic and costly efforts to comply with conduct expectations – e.g. Levi-Strauss in apparel, the Body Shop in cosmetics and skin care, Max Havelaar in fair-trade agricultural products – and may well find it profitable to do so in a certain market niche. Because voluntary compliance normally is not particularly effective, however, social movement (I)NGOs have become vigorous monitors of corporate behaviour, even in formal ways, for example by developing joint monitoring programmes with TNCs – and thereby exposing themselves to the dangers and charges of co-optation by corporate capitalism.

The past decade has witnessed the development of more systematic approaches to the globalization of corporate morality (i.e. the assessment and certification of socially responsible behaviour), building on the logic of the ISO 14000 family of standards but going well beyond their environmental focus. Most notable are the AA1000 system by AccountAbility, a standard for measuring social responsibility and sustainability achievements of companies (initiated in 1999), and the Social Accountability 8000 (SA 8000) certification effort by the Council on Economic Priorities Accreditation Agency (CEPAA), from 1997, on labour rights, workplace standards and trade. CEPAA (2005) reports that 655 facilities in 44 countries, with over 430,000 workers, are currently SA 8000 certified; these numbers have risen quickly in recent years. Of potentially greater consequence are the recent rounds of intensive discussion within ISO regarding standards for corporate social responsibility (Tamm Hallström 2004b). While ISO appears to be a long way from undertaking the huge project that would be required, the fact that ISO would even consider the matter indicates a widespread perception on the part of the world's largest corporations (many of which are heavily involved in ISO work) that social responsibility principles are too well legitimated globally to ignore. Given the rapidity with which ISO's other major standards for corporate behaviour (the ISO 9000 and 14000 standards mentioned above) have become quasi-mandatory for large companies, ISO's discussion may indicate that serious voluntary compliance with these principles is well underway already.

A final force that should be mentioned, that powers the spread of morally globalized corporate models, is the socially responsible investment movement, which emerged in the latter part of the 1960s (e.g. the Interfaith Center on Corporate Responsibility, an international coalition of institutional investors, was founded in 1972) and expanded rapidly with the anti-apartheid movement. It has succeeded well enough that practically all large investment fund families offer one or more 'social choice' investment vehicles and some such funds have become fairly prominent.

How much change has actually occurred worldwide in the implementation of social responsibility principles through these voluntary conduct codes, independent monitoring mechanisms and social responsibility investment funds is impossible to assess. Rhetorical compliance certainly outstrips concrete action – for medium to large companies, flashy social responsibility pages on their websites are practically mandatory irrespective of company behaviour – but the pile of well-documented examples of meaningful change and good-faith adherence is growing rapidly (Hollender and Fenichell 2003). In any case, the moral dimensions of TNC globalization are undergoing considerable institutionalization and are likely to become more effective in coming decades (see Braithwaite and Drahos 2000).

Globalization of civil society

Individuals, states and corporations are seen in world culture as discrete, bounded, integrated actors. They make up, are immersed in and help shape more diffuse entities, known as 'societies', which most commonly are designated as national, tribal or local-communal rather than global. Most important by far in the organization of daily life are national societies, managed by states and serving as the primary form of identity and orientation for most actors. Conventionally, national societies are conceived as consisting of three sectors: the economic, the political and a third sector, civil society, that is 'between states and markets' (Wuthnow 1991). Civil society is made up of individuals and organizations engaged in a great variety of social and cultural sectors on a voluntary, associational, autonomous basis, without the interference of states or business enterprises. The condition of civil society is widely seen as essential to the condition of society in general; a well-functioning, vibrant civil society is essential to democracy, to social cohesion and social justice, to harmonious international relations, to environmental prudence and so on (Keane 2003; Young 2001).

Such assertions about civil society's importance for the 'good society' are fully globalized; they have become conventional wisdom that is taken entirely seriously by many global governance organizations, by the global development sector (cf. Glenzer 2004), by states and IGOs and INGOs. Since at least the late 1980s, encouraging states to promote civil society's expansion and organization, and directly aiding in the construction of civil society structures and programmes where civil society is deemed to be insufficiently developed, have been major goals for many of the relevant organizations, both IGOs and INGOs, as well as official development assistance organizations.

Beyond the national level, global civil society has flourished remarkably in the postwar period. Organized primarily by INGOs, generating ever more and ever more varied global social movements, interconnected by ever more elaborate, often evanescent networks, global civil society has become a major force in the world-cultural processes that shape the interests and identities of global actors (Boli and Thomas 1999; Lechner and Boli 2005). Scholarly alertness about global civil society has increased sharply, epitomized by the annual Global Civil Society yearbooks initiated at the London School of Economics that even include an index for measuring the development of global civil society as a whole (Anheier et al. 2001). Particularly prominent in discussions of global civil society are the vociferous, proliferating movements and organizations attempting to reorient globalization or explore 'alternative' globalizations (Starr 2000; Held and McGrew 2002), many of which come together every year at the World Social Forum as a critical counterpoint to the World Economic Forum in Davos. Far more numerous and influential in the actual shaping of global development, however, are the legions of INGOs and national NGOs that organize the many highly differentiated sectors of global civil society that do not receive public attention – in scientific, medical, technical, professional, educational, recreational, sports and other domains in which globalized organization is routine, even humdrum (Boli 2006a).

The globalization of civil society puts strong pressure on other (tribal, local-communal) societal types to organize and mobilize as civil-society actors rather than as primordial collective entities. These societal types have considerable legitimacy thanks to the world-cultural embrace of cultural authenticity (a kind of reworked noble-savage ideology) but the conditions for their cultural continuity are steadily undermined from without and within by the many external global actors seeking to foster civil-society development – and by savvy chiefs, leaders, students and activists who come to understand the advantages of organized mobilization for obtaining resources that will help ensure societal integrity. The end result is ever greater standardization of societies, voluntary associations and civil society itself, but with ever greater variety as global models are glocalized (Robertson 1994) through adaptation to local circumstances.

Globalization of the transcendental

The final aspect of globalization today that we will discuss is the transcendental dimension – the realm of the cosmos and beyond. We begin with the physical or material world, having in mind the globalization of planet Earth, of nature and of the universe writ large. Like so many others, these three globalizations gained serious world-cultural purchase only after the middle of the nineteenth century, with the Darwinian revolution (Frank 1997), the development of high-powered telescopy across the electromagnetic spectrum, the rise of globe-spanning geological exploration (particularly for oil and gas prospecting), the development of nuclear and, hence, astrophysics, and so on. The planet became a single integrated entity with a single integrated geological history (heavily shaped by extra-terrestrial natural forces) and a single integrated biological history (possibly also shaped by extra-terrestrial forces) that have resulted in an integrated but highly complex ecosystem. This singularizing conceptual shift led to all sorts of globalizations – of climate, of the hydrosphere, of species migration, of disease and so on. It also greatly boosted tendencies to see the entire planet as a single organism, a living being (Lovelock's [1995] Gaia hypothesis).

Beyond the planetary level, the entire cosmos has been subject to a kind of globalization that expands the scope of human hubris almost limitlessly. Naturalistic human knowledge is assumed to apply everywhere in the most literal sense, enabling 'theories of everything' (Big Bang, string, unified field theories) that explain the very origins and development of the universe as a multiple not-so-well-integrated whole. The resulting cosmologies have become strong competitors with traditional religion-based tales (though many of the latter have been adjusted to accommodate the empirical findings of the sciences) and spawned innumerable half-baked lay versions of varying attractiveness and implausibility. All of this is today so routine as to be part of globalization's taken-for-grantedness, despite the suddenness with which it has emerged (e.g. as late as 1900 the sun was generally believed to be less than 100 million years old; the concept of the light-year emerged only after 1870 as the vast size of the galaxy began to become clear).

Outside the material realm, the transcendental in the more conventional sense has been globalized in three main forms. The first is ecumenicism, the ongoing effort of mutual spiritual accommodation among many religions that seeks to globalize the gods around a vision of a unitary deity that has historically been manifested in many different forms. Ecumenicism is fairly well institutionalized through the World Council of Churches, the Council for a Parliament of the World's Religions and other INGOs, as well as by some religious movements like Baha'i whose very doctrine is ecumenical. The second is fundamentalism, experiencing another resurgence in recent decades through highly globalized social movements and organizations, and the third is evangelism, long a globalized practice by some of the world religions but more recently globalized in many new forms by numerous and varied denominations and movements (cf. chapter 8 in Lechner and Boli 2005;

Marty and Appleby 1991). Purely local transcendentalisms and cosmologies are rapidly disappearing; to a large extent, the logic of contemporary spirituality assumes that, if it is not done globally, it is not worth doing at all.

The result of this multifaceted globalization of the transcendental is a peculiarly inchoate and eclectic array of world-cultural elements and complexes. In principle, any given global citizen can now believe in almost anything, from mathematical theories of parallel universes to pseudo-scientific folk tales (e.g. 'intelligent design') purporting to prove the existence of a cosmic bioengineering god. *Requiescat in pace* conventional concerns about the modern world's meaninglessness; in today's globalization the world citizen must learn to cope with too many meanings propagated by too many intense adherents, whose capacities for proselytizing are increasing in tandem with globalization itself.

CONCLUSION: GLOBALIZED TENSIONS IN WORLD SOCIETY

Globalization of the individual, state, corporation and other entities involves a wide variety of dynamic, tension-filled processes. At issue is the reconstruction of the social world, all over the world, in line with globalized models, principles, role expectations and identities. Powerful actors with great resources (TNCs, states, IGOs) and powerless actors imbued with prodigious amounts of rationalized or moral legitimacy and authority (international and local NGOs, social movements, bodies of knowledge, technical systems and so on) carry world-cultural models and principles to the far corners of the earth. Obviously, collisions between global and local models generate high social heat; dislocation is widespread, forced adaptation can be brutal and many of the complaints about cultural or capitalist imperialism are well grounded. The global steamroller that threatens to flatten and homogenize all cultures charges along, engendering all kinds of resistance and counter-movements rooted in local and particularistic models of varying degrees of staying power – but rooted more commonly in universalistic models and principles that are applied to the local context.

Much more is at work than the simplistic idea of globalized homogenization producing local resistance, however. For one thing, globalization forces also produce and legitimate difference and diversity. Global transportation and communication networks facilitate migration and relocation, making all the world's cities increasingly diverse. Many people find that daily life enmeshes them in far more diversity and difference than the lives of their parents or grandparents, even if there is a kind of 'sameness of diversity' that characterizes the world's cities (Lechner and Boli 2005). In addition, world cultural principles and movements champion indigenous peoples, push for equality and inclusion, and raise cultural authenticity to a supreme value. Thus, the value of difference has become a principal organizing force, strengthening efforts to limit and reinterpret the global at the local level.

For another thing, given their inchoate and complex character, world-cultural models and principles contain within them many contradictions and inherent conflicts, for example the clashes between freedom and equality, development and environmentalism, individualism and collective welfare. Movements organized around extreme individualism (e.g. neoliberalism) run headlong into movements prizing collective goods (e.g. social democracy), with much resulting tension-fraught dynamism. Third, to the extent that globalization today does homogenize societies and cultures, it thereby generates new forms and levels of competition and conflict. As cultural models of the individual become more standardized, for example, so too do individuals' ambitions and aspirations – for more material possessions, greater physical comforts, exotic vacations, sympathetic therapists and so on. Demands on the resources that make high-consumption, self-expansive life possible tend to grow exponentially; niche diversification and local subsistence production become less significant sources of livelihood support. From this perspective, sameness produces scarcity, with the attendant tragedies of domestic and international strife that the struggle for scarce resources entails.

Globalization today is thus a set of forces and actors generating both greater homogeneity and increasing diversity, more cooperative relationships and new kinds of conflicts, greater wealth and opportunity along with rising inequalities. Globalization has become, to many minds, a grand source of progress and salvation; to many others, it is a merciless juggernaut that levels all in its path. On both sides of this grand debate, one thing stands out: globalization has become a central axis of social change like never before.

Notes

1 About the world economy, for example, analysts stress its long globalizing history (Wallerstein and followers), the emergence of mammoth transnational corporations controlling large percentages of world trade (de Carlo 2005), the proliferation of global commodity chains (Gereffi and Korzeniewicz 1994), rising economic integration as measured by international trade, capital flows and currency trading, and so on. Big numbers are thrown about: total world merchandise imports and exports grew from $4.1 trillion in 1980 to $15.1 trillion in 2003, trade in services rose over the same period from $824 billion to $3.7 trillion, foreign direct investment stocks grew from $3.74 trillion in 1990 to $16.4 trillion in 2003 (UNCTAD 2005). All this is so widely discussed that we see little utility in reiterating it here.

2 The most controversial exercises of supranational authority along these lines are the International Monetary Fund's imposition of strict conditions on state behaviour as part of its structural adjustment programmes (Vreeland 2003) and World Bank conditionalities that supersede state law for the duration of its projects (Randeria 2003). For example, the IMF demands cuts in social programmes while the Bank dictates how states will compensate indigenous peoples displaced by new dams or highways. That such measures are so controversial, having given rise to numerous social movement organizations opposing them (e.g. 50 Years Is Enough, Jubilee 2000), is especially revealing: the IMF and World Bank are preventing receiving states from meeting their broader (globalized) responsibilities to their populations, such as health and pension support, poverty relief and the like. Note, however, that the World Bank also ensures that states act in accordance with global expectations, e.g. by insisting that they care for displaced populations and indigenous cultures (Randeria 2003). Much of the discord, then, is about who has authority to decide how global models will be implemented, INGOs and social movements or IGOs like the World Bank. That the models must be implemented is often taken for granted.

3 The earliest codes of conduct were established by IGOs in the mid-1970s: the OECD Guidelines for Multinational Enterprises in 1976, the ILO Tripartite Declaration of Principles concerning Multinational Enterprises and Social Policy of 1977 and the UN Centre on Transnational Corporations' Draft Code of Conduct, also 1977. This early wave of concern for the non-financial behaviour and impact of corporations gained little traction, however, in an era of severe economic dislocation (the oil shocks, stagflation, Latin American debt crisis, recessions) and trapping up of the Cold War by the Reagan administration in the early 1980s.

References

AFRODAD. 2005. *Debt Profiles: Mali*. Available at <http://www.afrodad.org/debt/mali.htm>.

Albrow, M. 1997. *The Global Age: State and Society beyond Modernity*. Stanford, CA: Stanford University Press.

American Psychiatric Association. 2000. *Diagnostic and Statistical Manual of Mental Disorders*, 4th edn, text revision. Arlington, VA: American Psychiatric Publishing.

Anheier, H., Glasius, M. and Kaldor, M. (eds) 2001. *Global Civil Society 2001*. Oxford: Oxford University Press.

Appadurai, A. 1996. *Modernity at Large: Cultural Dimensions of Globalization* (Public Worlds, Vol. 1). Minneapolis, MN: University of Minnesota Press.

Barrett, D. and Frank, D.J. 1999. 'Population control for national development: From world discourse to national policies'. In J. Boli and G.M. Thomas (eds), *Constructing World Culture: International Nongovernmental Organizations since 1875*, 198–221. Stanford, CA: Stanford University Press.

Boli, J. 2006a. 'International nongovernmental organizations'. In W.W. Powell and R. Steinberg (eds), *The Nonprofit Sector*, 2nd edn, ch. 24. New Haven, CT: Yale University Press.

Boli, J. 2006b. 'The rationalization of virtue and virtuosity in world society'. In M.-L. Djelic and K. Sahlin-Andersson (eds), *Transnational Regulation in the Making*, 95–118. Cambridge: Cambridge University Press.

Boli, J., Elliott, M.A. and Bieri, F. 2004. 'Globalization'. In G.M. Ritzer (ed.), *Handbook of Social Problems: A Comparative International Perspective*, 389–415. Newbury Park, CA: Sage.

Boli, J. and Thomas, G.M. (eds) 1999. *Constructing World Culture: International Nongovernmental Organizations since 1875*. Stanford, CA: Stanford University Press.

Bradley, K. and Ramirez, F.O. 1996. 'World polity and gender parity: Women's share of higher education, 1965–1985', *Research in Sociology of Education and Socialization*, 11, 63–91.

Braithwaite, J. and Drahos, P. 2000. *Global Business Regulation*. Cambridge: Cambridge University Press.

CEPAA (Council on Economic Priorities Accreditation Agency). 2005. 'SA8000 Certified Facilities – as of March 31, 2005'. Available at <http://www.sa-intl.org/Accreditation/SummaryStatistics.htm>.

Collins, R. 1979. *The Credential Society*. New York: Academic Press.

Digital Divide Network. 2005. 'Welcome to the Digital Divide Network!' Available at <http://www.digitaldivide.net/>.

DiMaggio, P.J. and Powell, W.W. 1983. 'The iron cage revisited: Institutional isomorphism and collective rationality in organizational fields', *American Sociological Review*, 48, 147–60.

Drake, J. 2001. 'The greatest shoe on earth', *Wired Magazine* 9.02, February. Available at <http://www.wired.com/wired/archive/9.02/>.

Drori, G.S., Meyer, J.W., Ramirez, F.O. and Schofer, E. 2003. *Science in the Modern World Polity: Institutionalization and Globalization*. Stanford, CA: Stanford University Press.

De Carlo, S. 2005. 'Special report: The Forbes Global 2000'. Available at <http://www.forbes.com/2005/03/30/05f2000land.html>.

Elliott, M.A. forthcoming. 'Human Rights and the Triumph of the Individual in World Culture'. *Cultural Sociology*.

Frank, D.J. 1997. 'Science, nature, and the globalization of the environment, 1870–1990', *Social Forces*, 76 (December), 409–35.

Frank, D.J. and Meyer, J.W. 2002. 'The profusion of individual roles and identities in the postwar period', *Sociological Theory*, 20 (1), 86–105.

Freedom House. 2005. *Freedom in the World: The Annual Survey of Political Rights and Civil Liberties*. Available at <http://www.freedomhouse.org/research/index.htm>.

Gabel, M. and Bruner, H. 2003. *Global Inc.: An Atlas of the Multinational Corporation*. New York: New Press.

Gereffi, G. and Korzeniewicz, M. (eds.) 1994. *Commodity Chains and Global Capitalism*. Westport, CT: Praeger.

Glenzer, K. 2004. ' "Politics is a thing that passes": A historical ethnography of power, democracy, and development in the Pondori Flood Plain, Mali, c. 1818–2004'. Unpublished doctoral dissertation. Graduate Institute of Liberal Arts, Emory University.

Held, D. and McGrew, A. 2002. *Globalization/Anti-Globalization*. Cambridge: Polity Press.

Hollender, J. and Fenichell, S. 2003. *What Matters Most: How a Small Group of Pioneers Is Teaching Social Responsibility to Big Business, and Why Big Business Is Listening*. New York: Basic Books.

Hoyle, D. 2001. *ISO 9000 Quality Systems Handbook*, 4th edn. Burlington, MA: Butterworth-Heinemann.

IABD (Inter-American Development Bank). 2005. 'Remittances'. Available at <http://www.iadb.org/exr/remittances/index.cfm>.

Inglehart, R., Basanez, M., Diez-Medrano, J., Halman, L. and Luijk, R. (eds) 2004. *Human Beliefs and Values*. Mexico City: Siglo XXI.

Inglehart, R. and Baker, W.E. 2000. 'Modernization, cultural change, and the persistence of traditional values', *American Sociological Review*, 65 (1), 19–51.

Keane, J. 2003. *Global Civil Society?* Cambridge: Cambridge University Press.

Korten, D. 2001. *When Corporations Rule the World*. San Francisco: Berrett-Koehler Publishers.

Lechner, F.J. and Boli, J. 2005. *World Culture: Origins and Consequences*. Malden, MA: Blackwell.

Levin, H.M., Guthrie, J.W., Kleindorfer, G.B. and Stout, R.T. 1971. 'School achievement and post-school success: A review', *Review of Educational Research*, 41 (1), 1–16.

Lovelock, J. E. 1995. *The Ages of Gaia: A Biography of Our Living Earth*, rev. edn. New York: W.W. Norton.

Loya, T.A. and Boli, J. 1999. 'Standardization in the world polity: Technical rationality over power'. In J. Boli and G.M. Thomas (eds), *Constructing World Culture: International Nongovernmental Organizations since 1875*, 169–97. Stanford, CA: Stanford University Press.

Mander, J. and Goldsmith, E. (eds) 1997. *The Case against the Global Economy: And for a Turn Toward the Local*. San Francisco: Sierra Club Books.

Marty, M. and Appleby, R.S. (eds) 1991. *Fundamentalisms Observed*. Chicago: University of Chicago Press.

Meyer, J.W. 1980. 'The world polity and the authority of the nation-state'. In A.J. Bergesen (ed.), *Studies of the Modern World-System*, 109–37. New York: Academic Press.

Meyer, J.W., Boli, J., Thomas, G.M. and Ramirez, F.O. 1997. 'World society and the nation-state', *American Journal of Sociology*, 103 (1), 144–81.

Meyer, J.W., Ramirez, F.O. and Soysal, Y. 1992. 'World expansion of mass education, 1870–1970', *Sociology of Education*, 65 (2), 128–49.

Morgenthau, H. 1962. 'A political theory of foreign aid', *American Political Science Review*, 56 (2), 301–9.

Ougaard, M. 2004. *Political Globalization: State, Power, and Social Forces*. New York: Palgrave Macmillan.

Petrova, V.P. 2006. 'The Marshall Plan is dead, long live foreign aid: The shape of foreign development assistance after WW II'. Unpublished doctoral dissertation. Department of Sociology, Emory University.

Psychiatry Online. 2005. 'Reference works'. Available at <http://www.psychiatryonline.com/referral.aspx>.

Ramirez, F.O. and Wotipka, C.M. 2001. 'Slowly but surely? The global expansion of women's participation in science and engineering fields of study, 1972–92', *Sociology of Education*, 74 (3), 231–51.

Randeria, S. 2003. 'Glocalization of the law: Environmental justice, World Bank, NGOs and the cunning state in India', *Current Sociology*, 51 (3/4), 305–28.

Riddle, P. 1993. 'Political authority and university formation in Europe, 1200–1800', *Sociological Perspectives*, 36, 45–62.

Robertson, R. 1992. *Globalization: Social Theory and Global Culture*. Thousand Oaks, CA: Sage.

Robertson, R. 1994. 'Globalization or glocalization', *Journal of International Communication*, 1 (1), 33–52.

Sassen, S. 1996. *Losing Control? Sovereignty in an Age of Globalization*. New York: Columbia University Press.

Sayre, D. 1996. *Inside ISO 14000: The Competitive Advantage of Environmental Management*. Delray Beach, FL: St Lucie Press.

Scott, W.R. 2002. *Organizations: Rational, Natural and Open Systems*, 5th edn. Englewood Cliffs, NJ: Prentice-Hall.

Scott, W.R. and Meyer, J.W. 1994. *Institutional Environments and Organizations: Structural Complexity and Individualism*. Thousand Oaks, CA: Sage.

Sernau, S. 2000. *Bound: Living in the Globalized World*. Bloomfield, CT: Kumarian Press.

Sethi, S.P. and Williams, O.F. 2001. *Economic Imperatives and Ethical Values in Global Business: The South African Experience and Global Codes Today*. Notre Dame, IN: University of Notre Dame Press.

Sklair, L. 2001. *The Transnational Capitalist Class*. Cambridge, MA: Blackwell.

Starr, A. 2000. *Naming the Enemy: Anti-corporate Movements Confront Globalization*. New York: Zed Books.

Strange, S. 1996. *The Retreat of the State: The Diffusion of Power in the World Economy*. Cambridge: Cambridge University Press.

Tamm Hallström, K. 2004a. *Organizing International Standardization: ISO and IASC in Quest for Authority*. Cheltenham: Edward Elgar.

Tamm Hallström, K. 2004b. 'ISO enters the field of social responsibility'. Presented at the WZB/CARR conference, 'Global Governance and the Role of Non-State Actors,' London, 4–5 November 2004. Stockholm: Stockholm Centre for Organizational Research.

Tilly, C. 1992. *Coercion, Capital and European States, AD 1990–1992.* Cambridge, MA: Blackwell.

Transparency International. 2005. 'Corruption Perceptions Index'. Available at <http://www.transparency.org/surveys/index.html#cpi>.

UNDP (United Nations Development Programme). 2000. *Human Development Report 2000.* New York: UNDP.

UNDP. 2004. *Human Development Report 2004.* New York: UNDP.

UNESCO. 2005. *Education for All Global Monitoring Report 2005 – The Quality Imperative.* Paris: UNESCO.

UIS (UNESCO Institute for Statistics). 2002. 'Estimated illiteracy rate and illiterate population aged 15 years and older, by country, 1970–2015.' Available at <http://www.uis.unesco.org/TEMPLATE/html/Exceltables/education/View_Table_Literacy_Country_Age15+.xls>. Montreal: UIS.

UNCTAD (United Nations Conference on Trade and Development). 2005. 'Handbook of Statistics On-Line'. Available at <http://www.unctad.org/Templates/Page.asp?intItemID=1890&lang=1>.

USAID (United States Agency for International Development). 2005. *The 2004 NGO Sustainability Index for Central and Eastern Europe and Eurasia.* Washington, DC: USAID.

Vreeland, J.R. 2003. *The IMF and Economic Development.* Cambridge: Cambridge University Press.

World Bank. 2005. *Country Brief: Mali.* Available at <http://web.worldbank.org/WBSITE/EXTERNAL/COUNTRIES/AFRICAEXT/MALIEXTN/0,,menuPK:362193~pagePK:141132~piPK:141107~theSitePK:362183,00.html>.

World Health Organization. 1993. *The ICD-10 Classification of Mental and Behavioural Disorders: Diagnostic Criteria for Research.* Geneva: WHO.

Wuthnow, R. 1991. *Between States and Markets: The Voluntary Sector in Comparative Perspective.* Princeton, NJ: Princeton University Press.

Young, O.R. (ed.) 2001. *Global Governance: Drawing Insights from the Environmental Experience.* Cambridge, MA: MIT Press.

Chapter 6

Theories of Globalization

WILLIAM I. ROBINSON

THEORY AND THE RISE OF GLOBALIZATION STUDIES

Globalization is reshaping how we have traditionally gone about studying the social world and human culture and a field of globalization studies is now emerging across the disciplines (Appelbaum and Robinson, 2005). These globalization studies arose around several sets of phenomena that drew researchers' attention from the 1970s onwards. One was the emergence of a globalized economy involving new systems of production, finance and consumption and worldwide economic integration. A second was new transnational or global cultural patterns, practices and flows, and the idea of 'global culture(s)'. A third was global political processes, the rise of new transnational institutions and, concomitantly, the spread of global governance and authority structures of diverse sorts. A fourth was the unprecedented multi-directional movement of peoples around the world involving new patterns of transnational migration, identities and communities. Yet a fifth was new social hierarchies, forms of inequality and relations of domination around the world and in the global system as a whole.

The scholarly literature on these phenomena has proliferated, as have specific studies of the impacts of globalization on particular countries and regions and on gender and ethnicity, not to mention much pop treatment of the subject. Recent research agendas have branched out into an enormous variety of topics, from transnational sexualities, to global tourism, changes in the state, the restructuring of work, transnational care-giving, globalization and crime, the global media and so on. This explosion of research points to the ubiquity of the effects of globalization. All disciplines and specializations in the academy, it seems, have become implicated in globalization studies, from ethnic, area and women's studies, to literature, the arts, language and cultural studies, the social sciences, history, law, business administration and even the natural and applied sciences.

The proliferating literature on globalization reflects the intellectual enormity of the task of researching and theorizing the breadth, depth and pace of changes underway in human society in the early twenty-first century. We find two broad categories of research: (1) those studying specific problems or issues as they relate to globalization; (2) those studying the concept of globalization itself – theorizing the very nature of the process. In a time when social relations and institutions are everywhere subject to rapid and dramatic change, and to the extent that this change is linked to globalization, theories of globalization are without doubt of major import to the contemporary world. How do we theorize this phenomenon which we will call globalization? What types of theories have been developed to explain twenty-first century social change? Are our existing theories adequate to capture this change, or do we need new theoretical models?

If it is true that globalization is one of the key concepts of the twenty-first century, it is also true that it is one of the most hotly debated and contested. There is no consensus on what has been going on in the world denoted by the term 'globalization'; competing definitions will give us distinct interpretations of social reality. Hence the very notion of globalization is problematic given the multitude of partial, divergent and often contradictory claims surrounding the concept. Considering the political implications of these claims it is clear that, at the least, globalization has become what we refer to as an essentially contested concept. The contending battleground of such concepts is a leading edge of political conflict since the meanings of such concepts are closely related to the problems they seek to discuss and what kind of social action people will engage in. Knowledge claims are not neutral. They are grounded in situated social and historical contexts, often in competing social interests. Nowhere is this clearer than with globalization theories.

We cannot here, given space constraints, take up the political and the normative dimensions of the globalization debate and the relationship of distinct theoretical discourses on globalization to these debates. Nonetheless, it would be impossible to speak of globalization without reference to the highly conflictive nature of the process. Diverse actors have associated globalization with expanding worldwide inequalities, new modes of exploitation and domination, displacement, marginalization, ecological holocaust and anti-globalization. Others have trumpeted the process as creating newfound prosperity, freedom, emancipation and democracy. These normative issues, whether or not they are foregrounded, will loom large in any survey of theories of globalization. How we define the process will very much depend on what theoretical perspectives we bring to bear on the definition. At the same time, our theories cannot but both shape and reflect normative and political signposts.

THE GLOBALIZATION DEBATE AND THEORETICAL DISCOURSES

While there is much disagreement among scholars on the meaning of globalization and on the theoretical tools that are best to understand it, we can identify a number of points with which, it is safe to say, most would agree. First, the pace of social change and transformation worldwide seems to have quickened dramatically in the latter decades of the twentieth century, with implications for many dimensions of social life and human culture. Second, this social change is related to increasing connectivity among peoples and countries worldwide, an objective dimension, together with an increased awareness worldwide of these interconnections, a subjective dimension. As well, most would agree that the effects of globalization – of those economic, social, political, cultural and ideological processes to which the term would allegedly refer – are ubiquitous, and that different dimensions of globalization (economic, political, cultural etc.) are interrelated, ergo, that globalization is multidimensional. At this point agreement ends and debates heat up. How different theoretical approaches address a set of basic assumptions – what we will call 'domain questions' – will tend to reveal the domain of each theory and the boundaries among distinct and often competing theories. Theories consist of particular ontological assumptions and epistemological principles, both of which are of concern in examining globalization theories.

Perhaps the most important 'domain question', and one that cuts to the underlying ontological issue in globalization studies, is 'when does globalization begin?' The rise of globalization studies has served to reassert the centrality of historical analysis and the ongoing reconfiguration of time and space to any understanding of human affairs. How we view the temporal dimension will shape – even determine – what we understand when we speak of globalization. Among globalization theories there are three broad approaches. In the first, it is a process that has been going on since the dawn of history, hence a 5,000–10,000 year time frame. In the second, it is a process coterminous with the spread and development of capitalism and modernity, hence a 500 year frame. In the third, it is a recent phenomenon associated with such processes as post-industrialization, postmodernization or the restructuring of capitalism, hence a 20–30 year frame.

A second 'domain question' is that of causal determination(s) in globalization. Is the core of the process economic, political or cultural? Is there an underlying material or an ideational determinacy? Are there multiple determinations, and how would they be ordered? Whether distinct globalization theories choose to give a causal priority or empirical emphasis to the material or the ideational will depend on the larger metatheoretical and even philosophical underpinnings of particular theories, but as well on normative and political considerations.

Other major domain questions are:

- Does globalization refer to a process (as I have been assuming here) or to a condition? Most theories would see it as a process of transformation, and some theorists therefore refer to globalization as a process and globality as a condition.
- How do modernity and postmodernity relate to globalization?
- What is the relationship between globalization and the nation-state? Is the nation-state being undermined? Has it retained its primacy? Or is it becoming transformed in new ways? Does globalization involve internationalization, seen as an increased intensity of exchanges among nation-states, or transnationalization, involving emerging structures, processes and phenomena that transcend the nation-state system?
- Relatedly, to what extent is the relationship between social structure and territoriality being redefined by globalization? Is there a deterritorialization of social

relations under globalization? What is the relationship between the local and the global? How are space and time being reconfigured?

How different theories approach these 'domain questions' will reveal something of the core ontological and epistemological claims of each theory. Recall that there is not a single 'theory of globalization' but many theoretical discourses. These tend to be grounded in broader theoretical traditions and perspectives, such as Marxism, Weberianism, functionalism, postmodernism, critical and feminist theory, and involve a number of distinct approaches to social inquiry, such as cultural studies, international relations, post-colonial studies, literature and so on. However, most theories draw on the distinctive contributions and traditions of multiple disciplines. Indeed, one of the most refreshing hallmarks of globalization studies is its interdisciplinary – nay, transdisciplinary – character; a renewed holistic approach to the study of social structure and change. The traditional borders between disciplines have become blurred in both theories and empirical studies on globalization.

Rather than propose a classification of globalization theories I identify here a variety of theoretical discourses that typically serve as heuristic tools in concrete globalization studies. The focus is on key theories and theorists that have already – or are likely to – become markers across social sciences disciplines and humanities for the field of globalization studies. What follows is not a comprehensive review of extant theories, which would be impossible here, but a limited selection intended to provide a view of the range of theoretical discourse on which scholars researching globalization are likely to draw.

A Sampling of Theories of Globalization

World-system theory

Some see the world-system paradigm as a 'precursor' to globalization theories, and indeed, as Arrighi has observed, 'world-systems analysis as a distinctive sociological paradigm emerged at least 15 years before the use of globalization as a signifier that blazed across the headlines and exploded as a subject of academic research and publication' (Arrighi 2005: 33). Yet what is distinctive to world-systems theory is not that it has been around longer than more recent globalization theories. Rather, this paradigm – and certainly its principal progenitor, Immanuel Wallerstein – tends to view globalization not as a recent phenomenon but as virtually synonymous with the birth and spread of world capitalism, *c*.1500.

World-systems theory shares with several other approaches to globalization a critique of capitalism as an expansionary system that has come to encompass the entire world over the past 500 years. As elaborated by Wallerstein, it is constituted on the proposition that the appropriate unit of analysis for macrosocial inquiry in the modern world is neither class, nor state/society, or country, but the larger historical system, in which these categories are located.

The capitalist world-economy emerged *c*.1500 in Europe and expanded outward over the next several centuries, absorbing in the process all existing mini-systems and world-empires, establishing market and production networks that eventually brought all peoples around the world into its logic and into a single worldwide structure. Hence, by the late nineteenth century there was but one historical system that had come to encompass the entire planet, the capitalist world-system, a truly 'global enterprise' (1974). It is in this sense that world-system theory can be seen as a theory of globalization even if its principal adherents reject the term globalization (see below).

A key structure of the capitalist world-system is the division of the world into three great regions, or geographically based and hierarchically organized tiers. The first is the core, or the powerful and developed centres of the system, originally comprised of Western Europe and later expanded to include North America and Japan. The second is the periphery, those regions that have been forcibly subordinated to the core through colonialism or other means, and in the formative years of the capitalist world-system would include Latin America, Africa, Asia, the Middle East and Eastern Europe. Third is the semi-periphery, comprised of those states and regions that were previously in the core and are moving down in this hierarchy, or those that were previously in the periphery and are moving up. Values flow from the periphery to the semi-periphery, and then to the core, as each region plays a functionally specific role within an international division of labour that reproduces this basic structure of exploitation and inequality.

Another key feature of this world-system is the centrality and immanence of the inter-state system and inter-state rivalry to the maintenance and reproduction of the world-system. The world-system paradigm does not see any transcendence of the nation-state system or the centrality of nation-states as the principal component units of a larger global system. Other structural constants in the world-system are cyclical rhythms of growth and crisis, several secular trends such as outward expansion, increasing industrialization and commodification, struggles among core powers for hegemony over the whole system and the oppositional struggles of 'anti-systemic forces'.

Some would consider the world-system approach not a theory of globalization but an alternative theory of world society. This, however, would depend on how we define the contested concept of globalization. If a bare-bones definition is intensified interconnections and interdependencies on a planetary scale and consciousness of them, then certainly world-system theory is a cohesive theory of globalization, organized around a 500 year time scale corresponding to the rise of a capitalist world-economy in Europe and its spread around the world, and must be included in any survey of globalization theories.

On the other hand, however, it is not self-identified as a theory of globalization, is not a theory of the worldwide social changes of the late twentieth and early twenty-first centuries, and there is no specific concept of the global in world-system literature. Wallerstein has himself been dismissive of the concept of globalization. 'The processes that are usually meant when we speak of globalization are not in fact new at all. They have existed for some 500 years' (2000: 250). Wallerstein has put forward an explanation of late twentieth/early twenty-first century change from the logic of world-system theory as a moment of transition in the system. In an essay titled 'Globalization or the Age of Transition?' (2000), he analyses the late twentieth and early twenty-first century world conjuncture as a 'moment of transformation' in the world-system, a 'transition in which the entire capitalist world-system will be transformed into something else' (2000: 250). In this analysis, the system has entered into a terminal crisis and will give way to some new, as of yet undetermined historical system by the year 2050. Wallerstein's thesis on the terminal crisis of the system can be said to provide an explanation for social change in the age of globalization consistent with his own world-system theory.

Theories of global capitalism

Another set of theories, what I catalogue here as a global capitalism school, shares with the world-systems paradigm the critique of capitalism, an emphasis on the long-term and large-scale nature of the processes that have culminated in globaliza-tion, and the centrality of global economic structures. Yet this group of theories differs from the world-system paradigm in several essential respects. In particular, these theories tend to see globalization as a novel stage in the evolving system of world capitalism (hence these theorists tend to speak of capitalist globalization), one with its own, qualitatively new features that distinguish it from earlier epochs. They focus on a new global production and financial system that is seen to supersede earlier national forms of capitalism, and emphasize the rise of processes that cannot be framed within the nation-state/inter-state system that informs world-system theory – and indeed, much traditional macrosocial theory.

Sklair (2000, 2002) has put forward a 'theory of the global system', at the core of which are 'transnational practices' (TNPs) as operational categories for the analysis of transnational phenomena. These TNPs originate with non-state actors and cross state borders. The model involves TNPs at three levels: the economic, whose agent is transnational capital; the political, whose agent is a transnational capitalist class (TCC); and the cultural-ideological, whose agent is cultural elites. Each practice, in turn, is primarily identified with a major institution. The transna-tional corporation is the most important institution for economic TNPs; the TCC for political TNPs; and the culture-ideology of consumerism for transnational cul-tural-ideological processes. Locating these practices in the field of a transnational global system, Sklair thus sets about to explain the dynamics of capitalist globaliza-tion from outside the logic of the nation-state system and critiques the 'state-centrism' of much extant theorizing. His theory involves the idea of the TCC as a new class that brings together several social groups who see their own interests in an expanding global capitalist system: the executives of transnational corporations; 'globalizing bureaucrats, politicians, and professionals', and 'consumerist elites' in the media and the commercial sector (Sklair 2000).

Robinson (2003, 2004) has advanced a related theory of global capitalism involving three planks: transnational production, transnational capitalists and a transnational state. An 'epochal shift' has taken place with the transition from a world economy to a global economy. In earlier epochs, each country developed a national economy that was linked to others through trade and finances in an integrated international market. The new transnational stage of world capitalism involves the globalization of the production process itself, which breaks down and functionally integrates what were previously national circuits into new global cir-cuits of production and accumulation. Transnational class formation takes place around these globalized circuits. Like Sklair, Robinson analyses the rise of a TCC as the class group that manages these globalized circuits. Transnationally oriented fractions achieved hegemony over local and national fractions of capital in the 1980s and 1990s in most countries of the world, capturing a majority of national state apparatuses, and advancing their project of capitalist globalization. Globalization creates new forms of transnational class relations across borders and new forms of class cleavages globally and within countries, regions, cities and local communities, in ways quite distinct from the old national class structures and international class conflicts and alliances.

However, in distinction to Sklair, for whom state structures play no role in the global system, Robinson theorizes an emergent transnational state (TNS) apparatus. A number of globalization theories see the rise of such supranational political and planning agencies such as the Trilateral Commission, the World Economic Forum, the Group of Seven and the World Trade Organization as signs of an incipient transnational or global governance structure (see, *inter alia*, Held et al. 1999). Robinson, however, wants to get beyond what he sees as a national-global duality in these approaches. This TNS is a loose network comprised of supranational political and economic institutions together with national state apparatuses that have been penetrated and transformed by transnational forces. National states as components of a larger TNS structure now tend to serve the interests of global over national accumulation processes. The supranational organizations are staffed by transnational functionaries who find their counterparts in transnational functionaries who staff transformed national states. These 'transnational state cadres' act as midwives of capitalist globalization. The nature of state practices in the emergent global system 'resides in the exercise of transnational economic and political authority through the TNS apparatus to reproduce the class relations embedded in the global valorization and accumulation of capital'.

Hardt and Negri's twin studies, *Empire* (2000) and *Multitude* (2004), have been referred to by some as a postmodern theory of globalization that combines Marx with Foucault. They take the global capitalism thesis a step further, proposing an empire of global capitalism that is fundamentally different from the imperialism of European domination and capitalist expansion of previous eras. This is a normalized and decentred empire – a new universal order that accepts no boundaries and limits, not only in the geographic, economic and political sense, but in terms of its penetration into the most remote recesses of social and cultural life, and indeed, even into the psyche and biology of the individual. While for Sklair and Robinson the TCC is the key agent of capitalist globalization, for Hardt and Negri there is no such identifiable agent. In more Foucauldian fashion, an amorphous empire seems to be a ubiquitous but faceless power structure that is everywhere yet centred nowhere in particular and squares off against 'the multitude', or collective agencies from below.

Other variants of the global capitalism thesis have been taken up by McMichael (2000), Ross and Trachte (1990) and Went (2002), among others. There is as well a considerable amount of theoretical work on globalization among international relations (IR) scholars, a subdiscipline that has come under special challenge by globalization given that it is centrally concerned – by definition – with the state system and the interstate system. Here there is a tension between those theories that retain a national/international approach and view the system of nation-states as an immutable structural feature of the larger world or inter-state system, and those that take transnational or global approaches that focus on how the system of nation-states and national economies are becoming transcended by transnational social forces and institutions grounded in a global system rather than the interstate system. Notable here is the 'neo-Gramscian school' in IR, so-called because these scholars have applied the ideas of Antonio Gramsci to attempt to explain changes in world power structures and processes from a global capitalism perspective. Scholars from the neo-Gramscian school have been closely identified with the works of Cox (see, esp., 1987), and have explored the rise of new global social forces and sets of trans-national class relations, the internationalization of the state, and transnational hegemony and counter-hegemony in global society.

THE NETWORK SOCIETY

Manuel Castells' groundbreaking trilogy, *The Rise of the Network Society* (1996, 1997, 1998), exemplifies a 'technologistic' approach to globalization. While his theory shares with world-system and global capitalism approaches an analysis of the capitalist system and its dynamics, it is not the logic of capitalist development but that of technological change that is seen to exercise underlying causal determi-nation in the myriad of processes referred to as globalization. Castells' approach has been closely associated with the notion of globalization as representing a new 'age of information'. In his construct, two analytically separate processes came together in the latter decades of the twentieth century to result in the rise of the network society. One was the development of new information technology (IT), in particular, computers and the Internet, representing a new technological paradigm and leading to a new 'mode of development' that Castells terms 'informationalism'. The other was capitalist retooling using the power of this technology and ushering in a new system of 'information capitalism', what Castells and others have alterna-tively referred to as the 'new economy'.

This new economy is: (1) informational, knowledge-based; (2) global, in that production is organized on a global scale; and (3) networked, in that productivity is generated through global networks of interaction. Castells' definition of the global economy is an 'economy with the capacity to work as a unit in real time, or to choose time, on a planetary scale', and involving global financial markets, the globalization of trade, the spread of international production networks and the selective globalization of science and technology. A key institution of this new economy is the 'networked enterprise', which Castells sees as the vanguard of a more general form of social organization, the network society itself. This involves a new organizational logic based on the network structure in interaction with the new technological paradigm. The network form of social organization is manifested in different forms in various cultural and institutional contexts.

Here Castells, along with global capitalism approaches, that of Harvey (see below), Lash and Urry (1987), Cox (1987) and others, draw on a number of strands of late twentieth-century political economy scholarship, especially that of post-Fordism and flexible accumulation, involving a breakdown of the old rigid, vertical corporate structures and the rise of new horizontal and flexible structures. In

Castells' view, 'the networked enterprise makes material the culture of the informational, global economy: it transforms signals into commodities by processing knowledge' (1996: 188). Castells goes on to argue that the image of giant transnational corporations (TNCs) as centralized structures driving the global economy is 'outdated' and 'should be replaced by the emergence of international networks of firms and of subunits of firms, as the basic organizational form of the informal, global economy' (1996: 206–7).

Castells sees a close linkage between culture and productive forces in this informational mode of development due to the centrality of the symbolic order, of sign production and of consumption to IT. Indeed, Castells' approach can be seen as much a cultural as an economic theory of globalization. Human society has moved from a verbal order in pre-literate societies to an alphabetic order and later an audiovisual system of symbols and perceptions. In the globalized age this gives way to the integration of various modes of communication into an interactive network involving the formation of hypertext and a meta-language integrating into a single system the written, oral and audiovisual (or text, image and sound) modalities of human communication. This interaction takes place along multiple points in a global network, fundamentally changing the character of communications. In turn, 'communication decisively shapes culture because we do not see . . . reality as it "is" but as our languages are'. He adds, 'we are not living in a global village, but in customized cottages, globally produced and locally distributed' (1996: 370).

The Internet, in this regard, constructs a new symbolic environment, global in its reach, which makes 'virtuality a reality'. One of Castells' core concepts that captures this image is the space of flows and timeless time. As a space of flows substitutes for the space of places, time becomes erased in the new communications systems, 'when past present and future can be programmed to interact with each other in the same message'. The space of flows and timeless time become 'the material foundations of a new culture' (1996: 406).

While the normative structure of world-system and global capitalism approaches is decidedly critical of what those theories conceive of as globalization, Castells is more upbeat on the possibilities opened up by the global network society. Nonetheless, a central theme is the division of the world into those areas and segments of population switched on to the new technological system and those switched off or marginalized, giving rise to the oft-cited digital divide.

THEORIES OF SPACE, PLACE AND GLOBALIZATION

This notion of ongoing and novel reconfigurations of time and social space is central to a number of globalization theories. It in turn points to the larger theoretical issue of the relationship of social structure to space, the notion of space as the material basis for social practices and the changing relationship under globalization between territoriality/geography, institutions and social structures. For Anthony Giddens, the conceptual essence of globalization is 'time-space distanciation'. Echoing a common denominator in much, if not all, globalization theories, Giddens defines time-space distanciation as 'the intensification of worldwide social relations which link distant localities in such a way that local happenings are shaped by events occurring many miles away and vice versa' – social relations are 'lifted out' from local contexts of interaction and restructured across time and space (1990: 64).

In a distinct variant of this spatio-temporal motif, David Harvey, in his now-classic 1990 study *The Condition of Postmodernity*, argues that globalization represents a new burst of 'time-space compression' produced by the very dynamics of capitalist development. While Harvey's concept is similar to that of Giddens, the former's involves a normative critique of the global capitalist order and its restructuring whereas the latter would seem to be almost celebratory. What Harvey means by time-space compression is the process whereby time is reorganized in such a way as to reduce the constraints of space, and vice versa.

Here Harvey is close to the global capitalism thesis (although he does not refer specifically to a new epoch in the history of world capitalism), and as well to world-system theory, in that a key causal determinant in the new burst of time-space compression that started in the late twentieth century was the cyclical crises of capitalism. In particular, the world economic crisis that began in the early 1970s led to the breakdown of the old Fordist-Keynesian model and the development of flexible accumulation models. Drawing on Marx's analysis of accumulation crises, Harvey shows how each major crisis in the historical development of capitalism has been resolved, in part, with new forms of social organization of capitalism made possible by new technologies and predicated on successive waves of time-space compression. And Harvey also makes reference to Marx's characterization of capitalist expansion as the 'annihilation of time through space'.

The matter of a transformation in the spatial dynamics of accumulation and in the institutional arrangements through which it takes place is taken up by Saskia Sassen, whose works have generated new imageries of a restructuring of space and place under globalization. Sassen's modern classic *The Global City* (1991) has had an exceptionally broad impact across the disciplines and left an indelible mark on the emergent field of globalization studies. Sassen's study is grounded in a larger body of literature on 'world cities' that views world-class cities as sites of major production, finances or coordinating of the world economy within an international division of labour, and more recent research on 'globalizing cities' (see, e.g., Marcuse and van Kempen 2000).

Sassen proposes that a new spatial order is emerging under globalization based on a network of global cities and led by New York, London and Tokyo. These global cities are sites of specialized services for transnationally mobile capital that is so central to the global economy. This global economy has involved the global decentralization of production simultaneous to the centralization of command and control of the global production system within global cities. Here Sassen draws on the basic insight from the sociology of organization that any increase in the complexity of social activity must involve a concomitant increase in the mechanisms of coordination. Global cities linked to one another become 'command posts' of an increasingly complex and globally fragmented production system. It is in these cities that the myriad of inputs, services and amenities are to be found that make possible centralized coordination. In Sassen's words, 'the combination of spatial dispersal and global integration has created a new strategic role for major cities' (1991: 3).

Sassen identifies four key functions of the global city: (1) they are highly concentrated command posts in the organization of the world economy; (2) they are key locations for finances and for specialized service firms providing 'producer services', which are professional and corporate services inputs for the leading global firms such as finances, insurance, real estate, accounting, advertising, engineering and architectural design; (3) they are sites for the production and innovation of these producer services and also headquarters for producer-service firms; (4) they are markets for the products and innovations produced and in these cities. Sassen documents how New York, London and Tokyo as the quintessential global cities have restructured from manufacturing centres to producer service centres, and how producer service activities become 'networked' across global cities.

The social order of the global city shatters the illusions of the affluent service economy proposed by such commentators as Bell (1976) and Toffler (1980). Producer service jobs are global economy jobs, yet they involve a new class and spatial polarization, involving new high-income sectors involved in professional work such as investment management, research and development, administration and personnel and so on, and enjoying affluent lifestyles made possible by the global economy. On the other side are low income groups providing low-skilled services such as clerical, janitorial, security and personal services. These low-income groups are largely constituted by transnational migrants drawn from Third World zones. In these global cities we see a concentration of new gendered and racialized transnational labour pools increasingly facing the casualization and informalization of work.

What this all represents is 'a redeployment of growth poles' in the global economy. Global cities are new surplus extracting mechanisms vis-à-vis transnational hinterlands. 'The spatial and social reorganization of production associated with dispersion makes possible access to peripheralized labor markets, whether abroad or at home, without undermining that peripheral condition' (Sassen 1991: 31). This new transnational structure creates new forms of articulation between different geographic regions and transforms their roles in the global economy. It involves as well a global hierarchy of cities. The stock markets of New York, London and Tokyo, for example, are linked to those of a large number of countries, among them Hong Kong, Mexico City, Sao Paolo and Johannesburg.

Global cities draw our attention to another leading motif in globalization theory, how to conceive of the local and the global. Roland Robertson's concept of glocalization suggests that the global is only manifest in the local. By glocalization, Robertson means that ideas about home, locality and community have been extensively spread around the world in recent years, so that the local has been globalized, and the stress upon the significance of the local or the communal can be viewed as one ingredient of the overall globalization process (Robertson 1995). For Appadurai, locality is less a physical than 'a phenomenological property of social life' (1990: 182) and involves in the age of globalization new translocalities, by which he means local communities located in particular nation-states but culturally and phenomenologically existing beyond the local and national context (such as tourist localities). For others, the local–global link means identifying how global processes have penetrated and restructured localities in new ways, organically linking local realities to global processes. Burawoy and his students have called for a global ethnography. Their diverse locally situated studies show how 'ethnography's concern with concrete, lived experience can sharpen the abstractions of globalization theories into more precise and meaningful conceptual tools' (Burawoy et al. 2000: xiv).

THEORIES OF TRANSNATIONALITY AND TRANSNATIONALISM

Although limited in the questions it can answer, the study of global cities gives us a glimpse of how transnationalized populations reorganize their spatial relations on a global scale, a topic taken up as well, and with quite a different perspective, by theories of transnationality and transnationalism. The former refers to the rise of new communities and the formation of new social identities and relations that cannot be defined through the traditional reference point of nation-states. The latter, closely associated, denotes a range of social, cultural and political practices and states brought about by the sheer increase in social connectivity across borders. Transnationalism is referred to more generally in the globalization literature as an umbrella concept encompassing a wide variety of transformative processes, practices and developments that take place simultaneously at a local and global level. Transnational processes and practices are defined broadly as the multiple ties and interactions – economic, political, social and cultural – that link people, communities and institutions across the borders of nation-states.

Within the field of immigration studies, transnationalism came to refer to the activities of immigrants to forge and sustain multi-stranded social relations that link their societies of origin and settlement as a single unified field of social action (Basch et al. 1994: 7). Innovations in transportation and communications have made possible a density and intensity of links not previously possible between the country of origin and of settlement. This, in turn, has allowed for these communities to live simultaneously in two or more worlds or to create and live in 'transnational spaces' to a degree not previously known. Recognizing this new reality, the scholarly literature undertook a paradigm shift from international migration to transnational migration, and began to refer to these communities as transnational communities. Such communities come in different varieties, including those formed by new immigrant groups migrating to First World countries, as well as those older diasporic populations whose status and attitude is continuously influenced by the accelerating pace of economic, cultural and institutional globalization.

Scholars such as Levitt (2001), Smith and Guarnizo (1998) and Portes and his colleagues (1999) point to the novel character of transnational links in the era of globalization. Transnational ties among recent immigrants are more intense than those of their historical counterparts due to the speed and relatively inexpensive character of travel and communications and that the impact of these ties is increased by the global and national context in which they occur (Levitt 2001; Portes 1995; Portes et al. 1999). Transnational migration theorists have in this regard questioned seemingly dichotomous and mutually exclusive categories, such as external vs internal, national vs international, sending vs receiving countries, sojourner vs settler, citizen vs non-citizen, and to look for continuities and overlaps between and among them. Scholars working within the framework of transnationalism generally see transnational links, activities and spaces as both an effect of globalization and a force that helps to shape, strengthen and fuel it. The immigrants and non-immigrants who create these links and spaces are seen not only as objects upon which globalization acts but also as subjects who help to shape its course. Another set of questions these theories take up is the extent to which, and in what ways, transnational practices increase the autonomy and power of the migrants and non-migrants engaged in them; to what extent transnational ties or spaces are liberating or to what extent they reinforce or challenge existing power structures.

The concepts of transnationality and transnationalism have increasingly been given a broader interpretation beyond immigration studies. In acknowledgment of the broad and expanding range of experiences that are truly transnational, scholars have argued that the transnational experience should be conceived as involving several layers and that transnationality should be understood as a form of experience that cannot be restricted to immigrant groups (Roudometof 2005).

The experience involves, for instance, the transnational mobility of more affluent sectors, such as professional and managerial groups. Transnationality must be seen as constructed through class and racial boundaries and as a gendered process. Transnational social spaces can extend into other spaces, including spaces of transnational sexuality, musical and youth subcultures, journalism, as well as a multitude of other identities, ranging from those based on gender to those based on race, religion or ethnicity. They also involve communities constructed by members of professional and non-governmental associations (Kennedy and Roudometof 2002). Members of cultural communities who live in different countries but remain connected to each other through their cultural taste or pastimes may also construct transnational communities. Transnational social spaces, hence, are constructed through the accelerated pace of transnational practices of actors worldwide. These practices become routine to social life and may involve transient as well as more structured and permanent interactions and practices that connect people and institutions from different countries across the globe.

Transnationalism/ality has also been central to theories of ethnic group formation and racialization in global society. These theories have focused on transnational immigrant labour pools and new axes of inequality based on citizenship and non-citizenship (see, e.g., Espiritu 2003). A popular motif in post-colonial theory is a view of globalization as a new phase in post-colonial relations (Wai 2002). Similarly, studies of transnationalism have emphasized the gendered nature of transnational communities, changing gender patterns in transnational migration and the impact of globalization and transnationalism on the family. There has been an explosion of research and theoretical reflection on women, gender and globalization. Predicated on the recognition that the varied processes associated with globalization are highly gendered and affect women and men differently, research has taken up such themes as young women workers in export-processing enclaves, the feminization of poverty and the rise of transnational feminisms.

Notable here is Parreñas' (2001) theory of the 'international division of reproductive labor'. Women from poor countries are relocating across nation-states in response to the high demand for low-wage domestic work in richer nations. A global South to global North flow of domestic workers has emerged, producing a global economy of care-giving work and a 'new world domestic order' in which reproductive activities themselves become transnationalized within extended and transnationally organized households, in broader transnational labour markets and in the global economy itself.

MODERNITY, POSTMODERNITY AND GLOBALIZATION

Another set of theoretical approaches to globalization refers to the process in terms of modernities and postmodernities. Some theories conclude we are living now in a postmodern world while others argue that globalization has simply radicalized or culminated the project of modernity. Robertson, Giddens and Meyer and his colleagues take this latter view. For Robertson, an early pioneer in globalization theory, the process represents the universalization of modernity. In his 1992 study, *Globalization: Social Theory and Global Culture*, Robertson provided perhaps the most widely accepted definition of globalization among scholars: 'Globalization as a concept refers both to the compression of the world and the intensification of consciousness of the world as a whole . . . both concrete global interdependence and consciousness of the global whole in the twentieth century' (Robertson 1992: 8). In what appears as a clear application of the Parsonian social system to the globe as a whole, the 'global field' is constituted by cultural, social and phenomenological linkages between the individual, each national society, the international system of societies and humankind in general, in such a way that the institutions of modernity become universal. But Robertson's particular theory is also centrally concerned with the subjective, cultural and phenomenological dimensions of globalization, to which I will return below.

For Giddens, who advances a similar construct, this universalization of modernity is central to the very concept of globalization. This process involves the universalization of the nation-state as the political form, the universalization of the capitalist system of commodity production, a Foucauldian surveillance by the modern state and the centralization of control of the means of violence within an industrialized military order. Here Giddens views globalization, defined earlier as 'time-space distanciation', as the outcome of the completion of modernization – he terms it 'late modernity' – on the basis of the nation-state as the universal political form organized along the four axes of capitalism, industrialism, surveillance and military power. Hence the title of his noted 1990 publication, [globalization constitutes] *The Consequences of Modernity*.

Meyer and his colleagues put forward an institutional and network analysis to globalization that can be viewed as a cultural as well as an institutional theory of globalization, and they have alternatively referred to their approach in terms of 'world polity' and of 'world society', as distinct from global society (for a synthesis, see Lechner and Boli 2005). Globalization is seen as the spread and ultimate universalization of sets of modern values, practices and institutions through 'isomorphic' processes that operate on a global scale. The growth of supranational institutional networks and of universal modern norms of organization bring about what they refer to as 'world society' (Boli and Thomas, 1999; Meyer et al. 1997). Educational institutions are singled out as central to the isomorphic transmission of culture and values that become global in scope.

For Albrow, in contrast, the transition from modern to postmodern society is the defining feature of globalization. A new 'global age' has come to supersede the age of modernity (Albrow 1997). Albrow argues that globalization signals the end of the 'modern age' and the dawn of a new historic epoch, the 'global age'. In Albrow's Weberian construct, the quintessence of the modern age was the nation-state, which was the primary source of authority, the centralized means of violence, and of identity among individuals, and hence the locus of social action. However, the contradictions of the modern age have resulted in the decentring of the nation-state, so that under globalization both individuals and institutional actors such as corporations relate directly to the globe, rendering the nation-state largely redundant. As the nation-state is replaced by the globe, the logic of the modern age becomes replaced by a new logic in which the globe becomes the primary source of identity and arena for social action.

Much of the literature on modernity, postmodernity and globalization exhibits certain continuity with an earlier generation of modernization theories associated with development sociology, so that globalization is insinuated to be a continuation at the global level of the processes of modernization that were formally studied and theorized at the nation-state level. Indeed, from this genealogical perspective, we could say that if mainstream modernization theory has metamorphosed into theories of global modernity and postmodernity, early radical theories of development have metamorphosed into theories of the world-system, global capitalism, time-space compression, global cities and so on. Nonetheless, another striking feature of the set of theories associating globalization with modernity and postmodernity is the continued centrality accorded to the nation-state and the inter-state system, in contrast to propositions on the transcendence of the nation-state that constitute a core motif of competing theories.

THEORIES OF GLOBAL CULTURE

Finally, a number of theories are centrally, if not primarily, concerned with the subjective dimension of globalization and tend to emphasize globalizing cultural forms and flows, belief systems and ideologies over the economic and/or the political. Such approaches distinctively problematize the existence of a 'global culture' and 'making the world a single place' – whether as a reality, a possibility or a fantasy. They emphasize the rapid growth of the mass media and resultant global cultural flows and images in recent decades, evoking the image famously put forth by Marshall McLuhan of 'the global village'. Cultural theories of globalization have focused on such phenomena as globalization and religion, nations and ethnicity, global consumerism, global communications and the globalization of tourism.

For Robertson (1992), the rise of global or planetary consciousness, meaning that individual phenomenologies will take as their reference point the entire world rather than local or national communities, is part of a very conceptual definition of globalization. Such a global consciousness means that the domain of reflexivity becomes the world as a whole. Hence 'the world has moved from being merely "in itself" to being "for itself"' (1992: 55). In Robertson's account, the gradual emergence of a global consciousness, an awareness of the world as a single place, signals a Durkheimian collective conscience that becomes now a global consciousness.

Cultural theories of globalization tend to line up along one of three positions (Tomlinson 1999; Nederveen Pieterse 2004). Homogenization theories see a global cultural convergence and would tend to highlight the rise of world beat, world cuisines, world tourism, uniform consumption patterns and cosmopolitanism. Heterogeneity approaches see continued cultural difference and highlight local cultural autonomy, cultural resistance to homogenization, cultural clashes and polarization, and distinct subjective experiences of globalization. Here we could also highlight the insights of post-colonial theories. Hybridization stresses new and constantly evolving cultural forms and identities produced by manifold transnational processes and the fusion of distinct cultural processes. These three theses certainly capture different dimensions of cultural globalization but there are very distinct ways of interpreting the process even within each thesis.

Ritzer (1993, 2002) coined the now popularized term 'McDonaldization' to describe the sociocultural processes by which the principles of the fast-food restaurant came to dominate more and more sectors of US and later world society. Ritzer, in this particular homogenization approach, suggests that Weber's process of rationalization became epitomized in the late twentieth century in the organization of McDonald's restaurants along seemingly efficient, predictable and standardized lines – an instrumental rationality (the most efficient means to a given end) – yet results in an ever deeper substantive irrationality, such as alienation, waste, low nutritional value and the risk of health problems, and so forth. This commodification and rationalization of social organization spreads throughout the gamut of social and cultural processes, giving us 'McJobs', 'McInformation', 'McUniversities', 'McCitizens' and so forth (Ritzer 2002; Gottdiener 2000). As McDonaldization spreads throughout the institutions of global society cultural diversity is undermined as uniform standards eclipse human creativity and dehumanize social relations.

Ritzer's McDonaldization thesis is part of a broader motif in critical approaches to the cultural homogenization thesis that emphasize 'coca-colonization', hyperconsumerism and a world of increasingly Westernized cultural uniformity (indeed, 'McWorld'). Ritzer has himself more recently extended the McDonaldization thesis with the notion of the 'globalization of nothing' (2004), by which he means culturally meaningful institutions, sites and practices locally controlled and rich in indigenous content – 'something' – are being replaced by (corporate driven) uniform social forms devoid of distinctive substance – 'nothing'.

Another recurrent theme among cultural theories of globalization is universalism and particularism. While some approaches see particularisms as being wiped out others see in cultural resistance, fundamentalism and so on, a rejection of uniformity or universalism. A key problematic in these theories becomes identity representation in the new global age.

Appadurai's thesis on the 'global cultural economy' refers to what he sees as the 'central problem of today's global interactions', the tension between cultural homogenization and cultural heterogenization (1990: 296). To illustrate this tension he identifies 'global cultural flows' that 'move in isomorphic paths'. These flows generate distinct images – sets of symbols, meanings, representations and values – that he refers to as 'scapes', or globalized mental pictures of the social world, perceived from the flows of cultural objects. These 'scapes' illustrate for Appadurai what he refers to as a disjunctive order, or a disjuncture between economy, culture and politics in the globalization age. Ethnoscapes are produced by the flows of people (immigrants, tourists, refugees, guest workers etc.). Technoscapes are produced from the flows of technologies, machinery and plant flows produced by TNCs and government agencies. Financescapes are produced by the rapid flows of capital, money in currency markets and stock exchanges. Mediascapes are produced by the flow of information and are repertoires of images, flows produced and distributed by newspapers, magazines, television and film. Finally, ideoscapes involve the distribution of political ideas and values linked to flows of images associated with state or counter-state movements, ideologies of freedom, welfare, right and so on. These different flows, in Appadurai's view, create genuinely transnational cultural spaces and practices not linked to any national society and may be novel or syncretic; hence a disjuncture between culture and the economy and culture and politics.

A Concluding Comment

As noted earlier, there are many theories I am unable to include in the preceding survey, intended only as a sample of the range of theoretical discourse on which scholars researching globalization may draw. These and other theories have informed empirical research into global processes, helped recast varied current social science agendas in light of globalization and provided paradigmatic points of reference for studying social change in the twenty-first century.

If we contemplate more broadly the monumental changes sweeping the planet in the new century we can truly appreciate the real and potential contribution of globalization theory. Clearly, future theoretical work into globalization would do well to theorize more systematically changes in the nature of social action and power relations in the globalization age, and how globalization may extend the 'limits of the possible'. Such urgent problems – indeed crises – as global terrorism, militarism, authoritarianism, ecological degradation and escalating social polarization make imperative the theoretical enterprise that has been the object of this chapter.

Acknowledgment

I would like to thank Christopher J. Kollmeyer and George Ritzer for their critical comments on an earlier draft of this chapter.

References

Albrow, M. 1997. *The Global Age*. Stanford, CA: Stanford University Press.
Appadurai, A. 1990. 'Disjuncture and difference in the global cultural economy'. In M. Featherstone (ed.), *Global Culture: Nationalism, Globalization and Modernity*, 295–310. Thousand Oaks, CA: Sage.

Appelbaum, R. and Robinson, W.I. 2005. *Critical Globalization Studies*. New York: Routledge.

Arrighi, G. 2005. 'Globalization in world-systems perspective'. In R. Appelbaum and W.I. Robinson (eds), *Critical Globalization Studies*, 33–44. New York: Routledge.

Basch, L., Schiller, N.G. and Blanc, C.S. 1994. *Nations Unbound: Transnational Projects, Postcolonial Predicaments, and Deterritorialized Nation-States*. New York: Gordon and Breach.

Bell, D. 1976. *The Coming of Post-Industrial Society*. New York: Basic Books.

Boli, J. and Thomas, G.M. 1999. *World Polity Formation since 1875: World Culture and International Non-Governmental Organizations*. Stanford, CA: Stanford University Press.

Burawoy, M., Blum, J.A., George, S. et al. 2000. *Global Ethnography: Forces, Connections, and Imaginations in a Postmodern World*. Berkeley: University of California Press.

Castells, M. 1996. *The Rise of the Network Society*. Vol. I of *The Information Age: Economy, Society, Culture*. Oxford: Blackwell.

Castells, M. 1997. *The Power of Identity*. Vol. II of *The Information Age: Economy, Society, Culture*. Oxford: Blackwell.

Castells, M. 1998. *End of Millennium*. Vol. III of *The Information Age: Economy, Society, Culture*. Oxford: Blackwell.

Cox, R.W. 1987. *Production, Power, and World Order: Social Forces in the Making of History*. New York: Columbia University Press.

Espiritu, Y.L. 2003. *Home Bound: Filipino American Lives across Cultures, Communities, and Countries*. Berkeley: University of California Press.

Giddens, A. 1990. *The Consequences of Modernity*. Cambridge: Polity Press.

Gottdiener, M. (ed.) 2000. *New Forms of Consumption: Consumers, Culture, and Commodification*. Lanham, MD: Rowman and Littlefield.

Hardt, M. and Negri, A. 2000. *Empire*. Cambridge, MA: Harvard University Press.

Hardt, M. and Negri, A. 2004. *Multitude: War and Democracy in the Age of Empire*. New York: Penguin.

Harvey, D. 1990. *The Condition of Post-Modernity*. London: Blackwell.

Held, D., McGrew, A., Goldblatt, D. and Perraton, J. 1999. *Global Transformations: Politics, Economics and Culture*. Stanford, CA: Stanford University Press.

Kennedy, P. and Roudometof, V. (eds.) 2002. *Communities across Borders: New Immigrants and Transnational Cultures*. London: Routledge.

Lash, S. and Urry, J. 1987. *The End of Organized Capitalism*. Cambridge: Polity Press.

Lechner, F.J. and Boli, J. 2005. *World Culture: Origins and Consequences*. New York: Blackwell.

Levitt, P. 2001. *The Transnational Village*. Berkeley: University of California Press.

McMichael, P. 2000. *Development and Social Change: A Global Perspective*, 2nd edn. Thousand Oaks, CA: Pine Forge.

Marcuse, P. and van Kempen, R. 2000. *Globalizing Cities: A New Spatial Order?* Oxford: Blackwell.

Meyer, J.W., Boli, J., Thomas, G.M. and Ramirez, F.O. 1997. 'World society and the nation-state', *American Sociological Review*, 103(1), 144–81.

Nederveen Pieterse, J. 2004. *Globalization and Culture: Global Melange*. Lanham, MD: Rowman and Littlefield.

Parreñas, R.S. 2001. *Servants of Globalization: Women, Migration, and Domestic Work*. Stanford, CA: Stanford University Press.

Portes, A. 1995. 'Transnational Communities: Their emergence and significance in the contemporary world-system', Working Papers No. 16, April, Department of Sociology, The Johns Hopkins University, Baltimore, MD.

Portes, A., Guarnizo, L.E. and Landolt, P. 1999. 'The study of transnationalism: Pitfalls and promise of an emergent research field', *Ethnic and Racial Studies*, 22 (2), 217–37.

Ritzer, G. 1993. *The McDonaldization of Society*. London: Sage.

Ritzer, G. (ed.). 2002. *McDonaldization: The Reader*. Thousand Oaks, CA: Pine Forge.

Ritzer, G. 2004. *The Globalization of Nothing*. Thousand Oaks, CA: Pine Forge.

Robertson, R. 1992. *Globalization: Social Theory and Global Culture*. Thousand Oaks, CA: Sage.

Robertson, R. 1995. 'Glocalization: Time-space and homogeneity-heterogeneity'. In M. Featherstone, S. Lash and R. Robertsom (eds.), *Global Modernities*, 25–44. London: Sage.

Robertson, R. 1998. 'The new global history: History in a global age', *Cultural Values*, 2 (2/3), 368–84.

Robinson, W.I. 2003. *Transnational Conflicts: Central America, Social Change, and Globalization*. London: Verso.

Robinson, W.I. 2004. *A Theory of Global Capitalism: Production, Class and State in a Transnational World*. Baltimore, MD: The Johns Hopkins University Press.

Ross, R.J.S. and Trachte, K.C. 1990. *Global Capitalism: The New Leviathan*. Albany: State University of New York Press.

Roudometof, V. 2005. 'Transnationalism and cosmopolitanism'. In R. Appelbaum and W.I. Robinson (eds.), *Critical Globalization Studies*, 65–74. New York: Routledge.

Sassen, S. 1991. *The Global City: New York, London, Tokyo*. Princeton, NJ: Princeton University Press.

Sklair, L. 2000. *The Transnational Capitalist Class*. London: Blackwell.

Sklair, L. 2002. *Globalization: Capitalism and Its Alternatives*. New York: Oxford University Press.

Smith, M.P. and Guarnizo, L.E. (eds.) 1998. *Transnationalism from Below*. Rutgers, NJ: Transaction.

Toffler, A. 1980. *The Third Wave*. New York: Bantam Books.

Tomlinson, J. 1999. *Globalization and Culture*. Chicago: University of Chicago Press.

Wai, C.Y. 2002. 'Postcolonial discourse in the age of globalization', *Social Analysis*, 46 (2), 148–58.

Wallerstein, I. 1974. *The Modern World System*, vol. I. New York: Academic Press.

Wallerstein, I. 2000. 'Globalization or the age of transition?' *International Sociology*, 15 (2), 249–65.

Went, R. 2002. *The Enigma of Globalization*. London: Routledge.

Chapter 7

Studying Globalization: Methodological Issues

Salvatore Babones

Introduction

Globalization means many things to many people, so many things that it hardly seems worth offering yet one more definition of the term. It would be difficult enough to pick among existing definitions, or even to list them: reviewing trends in 26 indicators of globalization, Guillen (2001) notes that not one has risen as quickly over the past 20 years as the number of academic publications on the topic. Happily for future writers of review articles, a search of the Sociological Abstracts database suggests that this trend has reversed: after peaking at 705 in 2002, the number of peer-reviewed publications returned from a keyword search on globalization declined to 601 in 2003 and 553 in 2004. Perhaps Chase-Dunn and Babones (2006) are right to caution that 'waves of globalization have been followed by waves of deglobalization in the past, and this is also an entirely plausible scenario for the future'. If academic interest is a leading indicator, this future may come sooner than any of us expect.

Whatever the trend, the sheer number of academic treatments of globalization eliminates the possibility of agreeing on a common definition for the term; a common definition of globalization may not even be desirable from the standpoint of advancing our theorizing on the subject (Smith 2001). Lack of consensus among theorists and practitioners, however, does create difficulties for the methodologist. Ideally, operational definitions of concepts should follow from theoretical definitions, and measurement choices should reflect operational definitions. Without agreement on theory, research tends to be driven by empiricism: concepts are defined to conform to the data that are conveniently available, or simply are not defined at all. The result is the existence of a wide variety of globalization indicators in the empirical literature, none of which can be judged theoretically superior to any other.

Lacking a commonly agreed theoretical definition, individual researchers can (and do) operationalize globalization as they see fit. Many operationalize globalization using country-level economic indicators, such as foreign trade as a proportion of total economic activity. Some take a qualitative case-study approach, operationalizing globalization at a much more local level. A few operationalize globalization temporally, as a sort of all-pervasive force in the world-economy that has existed since 1980 or so. Still others – one suspects the plurality or even the majority of the hundreds of articles mentioned above – use globalization more as a rhetorical backdrop than as a variable to be operationalized and measured.

While the formulation of a general theoretical framework for the study of globalization may be impractical, one broad guideline can be identified: empirical research on globalization should be conceived at a global level of analysis. Level of analysis refers to the scope at which research questions are posed. Even when the evidence adduced to demonstrate an effect of globalization is highly local, research questions must be asked at a global level if the study is to shed any light on globalization as such (Babones 2006). For example, when Macleod (1999) investigates the impact of individual people's integration into global business networks on gender roles in a small port city in the Canary Islands, the research question is clearly global in scope, despite the extremely local nature of the study.

Important as qualitative case studies are for advancing our understanding of how processes of globalization play out at the level of agency and action, it is difficult to generalize methodological principles about them. In scale they range from localized ethnographic studies like Macleod's to wide-ranging analyses of transnational social movements (Moghadam 1999). Units of analysis range from the individual person all the way up to the world-system; the methodological tools they employ are equally varied. Quantitative cross-national studies, on the other hand, are more uniform, and thus more tractable from a methodologist's perspective. They employ a relatively uniform bag of statistical tools to analyse data drawn from a small number of standard sources on similar panels of cases. Thus, with no prejudice to the qualitative case study approach, in what follows I focus on the methodology of quantitative cross-national studies of globalization, though where possible I also highlight opportunities for globally representative qualitative research.

The remainder of this chapter is organized into three sections. In the first section, I describe some of the most important standard data sources used in research on globalization, including sources for the study of economic globalization, cultural globalization and political globalization. In the second section, I discuss the use and misuse of common statistical tools for analysing cross-national panel data, focusing in particular on unintended consequences in various kinds of regression models. In the third section, I consider some more general questions about the nature of countries as cases. I conclude with a few straightforward guidelines for improving future research on globalization.

STANDARD DATA SOURCES

For strictly practical purposes, most cross-national research on globalization relies on published compilations of existing data: it is generally unrealistic for individual researchers to contemplate collecting data that is representative, or even broadly comprehensive, in covering the 200 or so countries of the world. As a result, a relatively small number of data sources have become standard data sources for research dealing with globalization. 'Generic' globalization can be subdivided into at least three narrower (but interlaced) processes of globalization: economic globalization, cultural globalization and political globalization (Evans 2005, cited in Lechner 2005). In this section, I examine in turn the standard data sources for studying each of these.

Economic globalization

Three variables have typically been used to operationalize globalization in broadly cross-national panel studies of economic globalization: foreign trade, foreign direct investment and foreign portfolio investment. Foreign trade as a proportion of GDP is the ratio of imports plus exports to total economic activity within a country; when a country is more closely tied into global trade networks, it is more exposed to pressures emanating from the world outside its borders. Foreign direct investment as a proportion of GDP (FDI) is the ratio of active foreign investment (investment that implies some level of management involvement, typically defined as at least 10 per cent of a company) to total economic activity; it tends to vary widely year by year. Foreign portfolio investment as a proportion of GDP (FPI) is the ratio of passive foreign investment (investment that is motivated by speculative gain, with no implications for management control) to total economic activity; it is even more variable than FDI.

In general, foreign trade is more an indicator of exposure to global economic forces, while foreign investment is more an indicator of economic sovereignty. Most empirical studies of globalization as such have operationalized levels of globalization using trade. For example, in their benchmark study tracing the trajectory of world trade over the past two centuries, Chase-Dunn et al. (2000) identify two peaks in the globalization of the world-economy (1880s, 1920s) that predate the current upsurge in world trade. The authors simply equate higher levels of foreign trade with greater globalization. Kim and Shin (2002) focus on the most recent wave of globalization, defining globalization in terms of increasing numbers of partners in foreign trade. Kaplinsky (2001), in a wide review of the costs and benefits of globalization, defines globalization exclusively in terms of the ratio of foreign trade to GDP. Occasional studies, however, also use FDI (Chase-Dunn 1999) or, less often, FPI (Reuveny and Li 2003) alongside foreign trade as indicators of globalization.

That such qualitatively different and only moderately correlated indicators as trade and investment are used interchangeably to operationalize globalization underscores the theoretical ambiguity of the term. In general, any variable that rose over the period 1980–2000 can be used – and probably has been used – as an indicator of globalization. Trade and investment are convenient indicators because they have good face validity (both represent connections between a country and the outside world) and the necessary data are widely available. Both, however, should be used with caution, as explained below.

FOREIGN TRADE

The most common indicator of a country's level of globalization used in the empirical literature is its ratio of foreign trade to GDP. Foreign trade is the sum of a country's imports and exports; GDP is discussed in detail below. Foreign trade as a proportion of GDP is most conveniently accessible from the World Bank's *World Development Indicators* (WDI) database, which is published annually in April. The WDI reports trade data from 1960 to the year 2 years preceding publication (i.e. WDI 2005 reports data for 1960–2003). Since these data are compiled from figures supplied by national statistical offices, there can be a lag in reporting of as long as 5 years. On the other hand, every year more countries report as statistics improve over time. The net result is that the maximum panel of countries for which data are available is usually for the year 5 or 6 years or so before the last reporting year. In the 2005 WDI, the maximum number of reporting countries is reached in 1997 (199 countries versus 151 for 2003, the most recent year), though the panel is close to this maximum as late as 2002 (183 countries).

As a general rule, one should use the most recent version of the WDI for data from any year 1960 to current, since data in the WDI are always subject to update. There is, however, one major exception to this rule: countries are dropped from WDI when they cease to exist, even for historical data. Thus, for trade figures for East Germany, West Germany, the USSR, united Yugoslavia etc., one must turn to older editions of the WDI; similarly, users should be aware that territorial discontinuities caused by war or separatism may be reflected in WDI data. For pre-1960 data, ad hoc sources, such as Mitchell (1992, 1993, 1995) must be used.

Foreign trade expressed as a proportion of GDP presents some odd qualities. First, though the net trade balance (exports minus imports) is properly a component of GDP, gross foreign trade is not. It is entirely possible for imports plus exports to total more than a country's total GDP; this is in fact the case for more than 50 countries today. Second, trade as a proportion of GDP has a moderate positive skew, as infinitely positive outliers are theoretically possible (trans-shipment ports such as Hong Kong and Malta score particularly high) but negative outliers are bounded by zero (trade is always positive). Third, small countries engage more (proportionally) in foreign trade than do large countries, simply because they are smaller units (much of what is counted as foreign trade for small countries is equivalent to inter-regional domestic trade in large countries). These complications suggest that foreign trade as a proportion of GDP should not be used to operationalize globalization without careful consideration.

The key to dealing with operationalization issues like these is to theorize what is meant by globalization. If globalization is theorized as the degree to which jobs in a country are exposed to the vagaries of supply and demand on world markets, then exports as a proportion of GDP might be a more appropriate operationalization of the concept than total trade. On the other hand, if globalization is the degree to which consumers are exposed to products from throughout the world, imports might be more appropriate. Imports and exports as proportions of GDP are highly correlated ($r \approx 0.78$ between countries, 2000), but it is not clear that they are always manifestations of the same latent concept. In some cases they probably are: if globalization is the degree to which members of a population have contact with the world outside their country, then trade as a proportion of GDP is probably an appropriate operationalization.

The skew in trade as a proportion of GDP can easily be handled by logging the data. For example, using 2000 WDI data, trade as a proportion of GDP has a positive skew of 1.5. The logged series shows a negative skew of less than 0.1. Few researchers bother to log trade data, but both the empirical and the methodological cases for logging are strong. The only question is whether it makes theoretical sense; if globalization is mainly conceived at an ordinal level, one should log the data to remove the skew. If, on the other hand, globalization is conceived at a ratio level, incorporating the implicit claim that each unit of trade as a proportion of GDP produces an equivalent effect in the dependent variable, then trade should not be logged. It is unusual, however, to find social science theories that are truly couched at a ratio level. In most cases, trade should probably be logged.

The solution to the small country problem is more complicated but no less necessary, again subject to theoretical judgment. In some senses, small countries like Belgium (trade as a proportion of GDP = 168 per cent in 2000) are far more exposed to the global economy than are large countries like France (56 per cent in 2000). On the other hand, much of that excess trade in Belgium is 'local' foreign trade with neighbouring countries, rather than 'global' overseas trade. Taking out the effects of country size would seem appropriate in most cases; as with logging trade to remove skew, it should probably be done in all cases except where an explicit theoretical argument is made not to do it. This can be done by regressing logged foreign trade as a proportion of GDP on logged population size, then using the residual to operationalize trade globalization.

Not only is foreign trade as a proportion of GDP correlated with population size, but that correlation changes over time. Using logged series for both foreign trade and population, the correlation has declined from $r = -0.73$ in 1980 to $r = -0.55$ in 2000 for a constant panel of 128 countries; thus, separate regression models must be estimated for each year in the study panel. This observed decline in the correlation of foreign trade with country size is presumably itself a product of globalization: as the world globalized between 1980 and 2000, the 'global' portion of total foreign trade was presumably expanding. This would tend to attenuate the correlation between foreign trade and country size, which originates in the 'local' portion of total trade.

For some study designs, aggregate trade data are insufficient, and trade flows must be differentiated by partner country. Country to country trade flows are reported by the International Monetary Fund (IMF) in its Direction of Trade Statistics (DOTS) database. The DOTS database reports monthly, quarterly and annual country to country trade flows for 186 countries for the period since 1980. Only the 60 or so largest countries report continuous monthly series, but annual series are available for all countries for most years. Limited pre-1980 data are reported separately in a DOTS historical compendium covering the years 1948–80.

The DOTS database is keyed by country and contains both import and export data for trade between the keyed country and every other country of the world. Since the underlying raw data originate in the individual countries' statistical offices, the exports recorded from any one country do not necessarily match the imports recorded by the other. Reported imports and exports between country pairs can also be misaligned because the IMF DOTS data have been converted to US dollars, while the underlying raw data are in national currency units. Since the DOTS data are reported in US dollars evaluated at market and official exchange rates, they must be paired with GDP per capita of the same character in order to compute ratios of imports and exports to GDP. These data can be found in the WDI, as described below.

An even more detailed source of trade data between pairs of countries is the United Nations (UN) COMTRADE database, which records each reporting country's imports and exports by industry classification, beginning in 1962. Over 120 countries, including most major trading countries, currently report trade data to COMTRADE. Industry-specific data are available at the five-digit Standard International Trade Classification (SITC) level, though not all countries report in such detail for all periods. As with the IMF DOTS database, data are keyed by reporting country, so figures reported by pairs of countries may not correspond. Also, as with the DOTS data, COMTRADE statistics should be paired with GDP evaluated at market and official exchange rates to compute ratios.

FOREIGN INVESTMENT

Like foreign trade, foreign investment (FDI or FPI) as a proportion of GDP is most conveniently accessible from the World Bank's World Development Indicators (WDI) database. As with trade, the WDI reports investment data with a nominal 2 year lag. In general, FDI data are not as well reported as trade data; only about 75 per cent as many countries report FDI figures as report trade figures. In general, the FDI reporting countries are a subset of the trade reporting countries; thus, adding trade to an analysis that already includes FDI results in little or no loss of cases, but adding FDI to a trade analysis can result in substantial loss of cases. This is surely one reason why FDI is less common in the empirical literature on globalization than is trade.

Though foreign direct investment as a proportion of GDP is sometimes used alongside trade as an indicator of globalization, it suffers from a similar lack of theorization. Certainly the aggregate of all global FDI flows is an indicator of the globalization of the world-economy; FDI (and FPI) flows have grown over the past 25 years in step with all other global financial markets. This does not imply, however, that an individual country's level of FDI as a proportion of GDP is a good general indicator of that country's level of globalization. It is probably appropriate to use FDI (or FPI) as an indicator only where the theoretical model is explicitly concerned with issues of economic control.

Like trade, FDI as a proportion of GDP is skewed to the right, though it is not highly correlated with population size. Correcting for the right skew is problematic, since FDI is technically a net measure and can take minor negative values (which cannot be logged). One strategy is to use the log of 1 plus FDI, throwing out as outliers any cases in which FDI net inflows are more than 1 per cent of GDP in the red. This gives a result for 2000 that is reasonably well behaved (skew = −0.33).

FDI also presents difficulties due to its high annual volatility. I analysed FDI volatility in a panel of 51 countries for which continuous FDI data are reported in the WDI database for the period 1980–2000. Since these are the countries with the best reporting records, any estimate of FDI volatility derived from them is likely to be conservative. I first found the residual of a linear regression of each country's FDI series on time to detrend the data. I then computed a coefficient of variation for each country by dividing the standard deviation of the detrended data by the mean of the raw data. The average coefficient of variation across 51 countries was 0.74. By comparison, repeating the exercise using trade data gave an average coefficient of variation of 0.12 ($n = 123$). Clearly, the high annual volatility in FDI flows calls into question the use of point estimates for magnitudes of FDI.

The obvious solution is to average FDI over periods of several years. This solution, however, creates its own problems. Averaging FDI over a period of Y years creates a variable that is arithmetically a multiple of $1/Y$ times the sum of FDI over Y years. This accumulation of foreign investment over a period of years is recognized as a distinct variable in the development literature, foreign capital penetration or PEN. A common operationalization of PEN is the ratio of the total accumulated stock of foreign investment in a country divided by that country's total GDP. Though PEN can be measured directly as foreign ownership interest in a country's economy at a given point in time, it is not analytically distinct from the sum of past years' flows of FDI. In fact, the correlation between foreign capital penetration in 2000 reported by the United Nations Conference on Trade and Development (UNCTAD) and the sum of FDI flows over the 10 years 1991–2000 reported in the WDI database is 0.75 for a panel of 99 countries for which full data are available. Considering the fact that the two figures are computed using completely distinct methods, the correspondence is remarkable.

In short, FDI as a proportion of GDP is probably best avoided as a measure of globalization. It is volatile, difficult to transform and, in most cases, poorly theorized. Foreign capital penetration, on the other hand, is a valuable indicator, though not properly an indicator of globalization. Further difficulties arising from the use of FDI in statistical models of globalization are discussed below in the section on statistical tools.

NATIONAL INCOME

National income is the total final value of all goods and services produced by an economy. The two most common measures of national income are gross domestic product (GDP) and gross national product (GNP), though other similar measures do exist. In broad terms, GDP is the total final value of goods and services produced within a country's borders, while GNP is the total final value of goods and services produced by the citizens of a country. The difference between the two is the net of factor payments (wages, profits, interest) made to resident foreigners and factor payments made by foreigners to citizens. The difference between the two is usually minor, but can exceed 10 per cent in extreme cases (such as countries with large overseas holdings or guest worker programmes).

GDP and GNP are often divided by population to create per capita measures of national income, which are used as proxies for countries' overall levels of development. These series exhibit a strong positive skew, so they are customarily logged before being used in statistical models. Aggregate GDP and GNP figures are also sometimes used as indicators of country size, though population is more common for this purpose. Again, when used as aggregates GDP and GNP should be logged to correct for extreme positive skew.

Whether expressed as GDP or GNP, national incomes must be converted to a common currency unit (usually US dollars) to facilitate comparisons across countries. A fierce methodological debate has raged in recent years over just how to accomplish this currency conversion, driven by the fact that our interpretation of inequality trends in the world-economy hinges on the currency conversion method chosen (see Babones and Turner 2004 for a summary of the arguments). Two basic options exist. Currencies can be converted to dollars using the combination of market and official exchange rates reported by multilateral agencies such as the IMF and the World Bank (F/X method), or currencies can be converted to dollars at the purchasing power parity level that would equalize the prices of goods across countries (PPP method). Each method has both advocates and opponents, but each also has appropriate uses, which I describe below.

The F/X method is most closely associated with the world-systems school in sociology (Korzeniewicz and Moran 2000), while the PPP method is most closely associated with social demographers (Firebaugh 2000). Dollar denominated national income figures resulting from F/X conversion factors better represent command over goods and services traded on world markets, while those resulting from PPP conversion factors better represent the physical standards of living obtaining within a country. In recent extended treatments of the topic of national income measurement, Korzeniewicz et al. (2004) repeatedly contrast the 'successes' of F/X methods with the 'failures' of PPP methods, while Firebaugh (2003) labels the F/X estimates 'implausible (p. 36) and 'dubious' (p. 38).

Perhaps the most balanced appraisal of the relative merits of F/X versus PPP based national income figures comes, ironically, from those very scholars who are most responsible for the creation of today's PPP figures. Summers and Heston (1991) emphasize that their PPP estimates are intended as a 'companion' to previously existing F/X methods, 'not at all a replacement' for them (p. 355). They explicitly conclude that 'a country's international transactions . . . are best compared with . . . other countries' transactions via exchange rates rather than PPPs' (p. 360). Following Summers and Heston's guidance, a reasonable solution to the F/X versus PPP controversy is to operationalize national income using F/X series where structural position in the world-economy is the main concern, and to operationalize national income using PPP series where the relative standard of living between countries is the main concern.

In general, the use of GDP per capita tends to be associated with PPP based currency conversions, while the use of GNP per capita tends to be associated with F/X based currency conversions. This makes some methodological sense, since PPP currency conversion factors are based on prices within a country, and thus cannot appropriately be applied to that portion of GNP that represents transfers from abroad. Both dollar denominated series (GDP-PPP and GNP-F/X) are reported in the World Bank's World Development Indicators. A cleaner but less up-to-date source of GDP-PPP data is the University of Pennsylvania Center for International Comparisons' Penn World Table.

Ultimately, the heated debate over the validity and reliability of GDP-PPP versus GNP-F/X national income figures is not very relevant to regression-based panel studies of globalization. While the choice of data series is of critical importance in describing the trajectory global inequality, it has very little effect on inferential statistics in regression models. This is because the correlation between logged GDP-PPP per capita and logged GNP-F/X per capita in any given year is in the order of $r = 0.97$ (based on series reported in the WDI).

Finally, it should be noted that the operationalization of GDP or GNP growth requires no currency conversion at all. Growth figures should be derived from national income reported in local currency units, adjusted for inflation. Using dollar-based figures to compute economic growth inappropriately incorporates currency effects into the resulting growth statistics. Unless this outcome is explicitly desired, currency conversions (and their associated debates) are best avoided.

Cultural globalization

Research on cultural globalization has a long pedigree, dating at least to the controversial 'modernization' literature of 40 years ago (e.g. Lerner 1958; Inkeles and Smith 1974). It was not until the 1980s, though, with the first wave of the World Values Survey (WVS), that cross-nationally comparable cultural data based on national probability samples became available. The WVS is a collaborative effort involving researchers in over 80 countries asking parallel questions on values and beliefs (plus basic demographics) in four waves spanning the two decades 1981–2001. Although precautions must be taken to establish the lexicon, contextual and conceptual equivalence of questions across so many cultures, the WVS is an invaluable one-of-a-kind resource. The latest wave, Wave 4 (1999–2001), contains data for over 160,000 individuals from 69 distinct countries and regions.

The key strength of the WVS is national probability sampling. Other surveys that might otherwise provide useful data on cultural globalization, from the early modernization literature to the latest National Institute on Aging National Character Survey (Terracciano et al. 2005), are limited by their samples of convenience. Their results can be considered no better than indicative.

Political globalization

A standard source of data used in studies of political globalization is the Europa World Year Book. The Europa yearbook reports annual relational data on the diplomatic representation of every country to and from every other country, as well as memberships in major multilateral institutions, signatories of major international treaties etc. Military data from the International Institute of Strategic Studies' (IISS) annual volume *The Military Balance* is often used to complement political data from the Europa yearbook. *The Military Balance* reports data on troop levels, military exchanges and the like. The IISS also maintains an Armed Conflict Database identifying and providing background statistics on substantially all armed conflicts ongoing throughout the world. For data on international terrorism, the US State Department's annual *Patterns of Global Terrorism* report is the standard source for historical data, but beginning with the 2005 report (on 2004 activity) the detailed data section of the report is classified. Hopefully these reports will once again be made public in the future on completion or after a reasonable time lag.

STATISTICAL TOOLS

In this section I review some common but sometimes quite subtle errors in interpreting the results of statistical analyses of country level panel data. Multiple linear regression, in which a single dependent variable is regressed on a vector of several independent variables, is a workhorse tool of globalization research. When the independent variables in a multiple linear regression model are uncorrelated with each other and only moderately correlated with the dependent variable, their coefficients can be interpreted relatively straightforwardly as the effects of the independent variables on the dependent variable. Unfortunately, in globalization research this benign scenario almost never comes to pass. Independent variables are often highly correlated with each other, and lagged versions of dependent variables are often themselves used as independent variables.

Making matters more confusing, multiple ratio variables in a regression equation often share the same numerator or denominator. For example, it would not be uncommon to find GDP, GDP/population, population, trade/GDP and investment/GDP together in a single regression equation. Of course, all of these variables trend over time, though at different rates in different countries. Underlying all of this might be a country level fixed or even variable effect. Throw in a few interaction terms, and it is clear that models like this must be interpreted with care, if they can be interpreted at all. Models like this are, however, quite common.

It has become commonplace to observe that the ease of use of statistical software has allowed the ability to run statistical models to far outstrip the ability to understand them. In my experience, the problem is usually not a lack of technical understanding of the mathematics that underlie the tools, but a lack of careful thought being put into understanding the meaning of coefficients, especially partial coefficients ('controlling for' other variables). Many times the risk is as simple as being seduced by the name of a variable; what could be more obvious than that the effect of the variable 'GDP per capita' is the effect of GDP per capita? As I demonstrate below, in many very common research designs it is not. In this section, I address several such situations in which the difficulty lies not in understanding the mathematics of the statistical models estimated but in understanding the substantive meaning of the results.

Difficulties interpreting multiple regression coefficients

Despite the fact that multiple linear regression has long been a basic tool of statistical analysis in the social sciences, and despite the fact that the mathematics underlying multiple linear regression are relatively accessible even to non-mathematicians, the behaviour of variables in multiple regression equations is still often the subject of serious controversy. Consider, for example, the now famous (or infamous) 'denominator effect' debate on the effects of foreign capital penetration on growth (Firebaugh 1992, 1996; Dixon and Boswell 1996a, 1996b). A total of 68 pages of one of sociology's top journals were devoted, fundamentally, to the question of how to interpret the coefficient for foreign capital penetration in a model of economic growth. Throughout this debate (which still ripples through the dependency literature; see Kentor and Boswell 2003), the mathematics and numerical results were never at issue; the debate was over what words should be attached to the agreed numbers.

Whatever the actual effect of foreign capital on economic growth, several methodological lessons can be learned from the debate, beyond the mere fact that ratio variables are tricky (Firebaugh and Gibbs 1985). First and foremost, one should take great care in interpreting models when the same variable appears in multiple places in a single regression equation. This caution applies equally when two different variables are so highly correlated as to be effectively indistinguishable. Second, as a corollary, the use of lagged dependent variables in regression models should be avoided. It is simpler – and more direct – to study change in the dependent variable instead. Third, another corollary, one should take great care in interpreting interaction effects. Interactions generally involve variables that appear elsewhere as main effects; main and interaction effects cannot be interpreted separately from one another.

The use of lagged dependent variables is particularly problematic. Do their coefficients represent 'stability effects', underscoring the fact that earlier values of dependent variables are often the best guides to predicting later values? Or do they simply represent change scores on the sly: a lagged coefficient of 1, when moved to the dependent side of the equation, becomes a change score. The answer is likely a combination of the two. For example, Reuveny and Li (2003) report a lagged dependent variable coefficient of 0.7 in a study of within-country income inequality. Moving a 'phantom' coefficient of 1.0 to the dependent variable side of the equation changes the dependent variable from inequality at time t to inequality growth over the period from $t - 1$ to t. The remaining coefficient for income inequality at time $t - 1$, -0.3, is consistent with a model of regression to the mean.

The use of multilevel models in globalization research

Since we are now in the midst of an 'age of globalization', every year that passes generates one more year of data for studying globalization. As the time period for which broadly cross-national data are available has lengthened, researchers have naturally sought to expand their panels longitudinally. Where researchers once studied outcomes for a single panel of countries over the full period for which data were available, they are now able to study multiple unbalanced panels over shorter periods. There has also been an explosion in multiple time point cross-sectional research, in which countries appear for each year or period for which data are available. Studies in which individual countries each appear multiple times almost always adopt a multilevel modelling approach, whether or not such an approach is called for.

There are two basic varieties of multilevel models: fixed effects models (FEMs) and random effects models (REMs). The fixed effects model as used in globalization research is a hybrid between a one-way analysis of variance (ANOVA) model (in which the country is the fixed factor) and a multiple linear regression model (in which all other independent variables are covariates); it is thus the equivalent of estimating a multiple linear regression with indicator variables representing countries. Each country's effect on the dependent variable is 'fixed' across all observations and the country mean is taken out of the analysis; in effect, the problem is reduced to estimating the relationships between the independent variables ('covariates') and the within-country variation of the dependent variable. Between-country variation in the dependent variable is ignored in estimating the effects of other independent variables in FEMs.

The random effects model is similar to the fixed effects model, but as the name implies the country effects are not fixed at a single value but instead are modelled as random variables with their own means and variances. The REM assumes that the array of unobserved factors unique to each country has the same expected impact on the dependent variable across all time points, but that there is some element of randomness in the actual impact recorded for any particular realization of the dependent variable. Because they allow some variability in the realized magnitude of country effects at multiple time periods, REMs allow independent variables to affect realizations of the dependent variable both within and between countries. The relative influence of between-country variation in estimating the effects of independent variables in REMs increases as the number of time points over which each country is observed declines.

Multilevel models were developed for use in experimental settings where the choice between FEMs and REMs is clear: when values of the treatment variable (analogous to the country in cross-national applications) are fixed by the experimenter, use FEMs; when values of the treatment variable are not under the control of the experimenter (and thus might be associated with other unobserved variables), use REMs. In experimental research, REMs are the more conservative choice of the two, since the main object of interest is the effectiveness of the treatment; REMs allow for the fact that part of the apparent effect of the treatment may be attributable to other unobserved variables. As the number of distinct observations for each treatment increases, treatment means become better defined, and the REM converges to a FEM.

In experimental research, the effects of covariates (other independent variables) are a distraction; in most statistical packages, they are not even included in the default output for multilevel models. In globalization research, of course, priorities are reversed, and the effects of the independent variables are of primary interest; the actual country effects are typically not even reported. The result of this flip in priorities is to make FEMs the more conservative approach; it is often difficult to 'achieve' statistically significant results with FEMs, especially when the number of time points observed per country is small. The temptation is strong to use REMs in these cases, but this often flies in the face of the rationale for using multilevel models in the first place. The motivation for using multilevel models in cross-national research is to control for time-invariant unmeasured variables at the country level (Firebaugh and Beck 1994). Where statistical power is more important than controlling for unmeasured variables, other strategies are more appropriate. Multilevel models should not be employed simply because multiple observations exist for each country in a study; this situation can be handled by allowing for the correlation of errors within countries.

Another situation where multilevel models are inappropriate occurs when the researcher wants to estimate the effects of time-invariant variables. For example, Alderson and Nielsen (1999) used multilevel models to study the effects of foreign capital penetration on within-country inequality. They chose an REM because they also wanted to include two time-invariant controls in their models; in an FEM, the effects of time-invariant variables cannot be estimated, since in FEMs all time-invariant covariates are incorporated into the country level fixed effects. Tellingly, the results of their REM were 'substantively identical' (p. 616) to those given by an FEM for their main variables of interest. Since the time-invariant variables were only used as controls, they were unnecessary to the model, and their absence in the FEM did not affect the performance of other variables. Where time-invariant variables are not merely controls but are in fact the main variables of interest, regression models incorporating correlations of errors by country are the better choice.

Where the object is to control for country level unmeasured variables, the experimental analogy provides a guide for deciding whether FEMs or REMs are more appropriate. In experimental research, REMs are used when unmeasured variables partially or wholly determine the values of the treatments for which the dependent variable is to be evaluated. For example, educational sociologists regularly use REMs to control for school effects in studying student performance: what school a child attends is the result of many unmeasurable factors beyond the researchers' control, factors that likely also effect student performance. It is difficult to imagine a scenario in cross-national research in which the assignment of cases to be subjected to country effects is due to unmeasurable factors that are systematically related to the dependent variable. Thus, FEMs are probably the methodologically appropriate choice in almost all cases. They are certainly the more conservative choice.

Multilevel models often strain statistical intuition to the breaking point, and thus there are many pitfalls to avoid in interpreting the coefficients of FEMs, never mind REMs. A particularly insidious pitfall for globalization researchers results from the fact that most variables associated with globalization exhibit strong secular trends. One example is GDP per capita; it consistently rises over time in almost all countries, though at very different rates. GDP per capita is near ubiquitous as a control variable; it is rarely the variable of interest, but it is present in almost every model of the effects of globalization. When used in country level FEMs, however, the statistical power of GDP per capita has nothing to do with level of development, since each country's mean level of GDP per capita is accounted for by its fixed effect; all that remains is each country's trend in GDP per capita over time. For the 24 historical members of the OECD over the period 1975–2000, these trends are correlated on average $r = 0.98$ with time. Practically speaking, GDP per capita operationalizes in fixed effects models as time, though time that ticks at a different rate in each country.

COUNTRIES AS CASES

Pragmatically, the unit of analysis in almost all globalization research is the country, since in today's world the country is the primary political unit (and thus the primary data collection unit). When countries representing more than 90 per cent of the world's population are included in a study, most scholars accept it as globally representative. It should be noted that this is not a sampling issue: in all cases involving country level data, the sampling ratio is 100 per cent. There is, however, an unavoidable gap between the target population (cases covering all people in all countries) and the sampling frame (those countries for which data are available). Unfortunately, data availability is not distributed at random with respect to variables of interest: small, poor and conflict-ridden countries are those most likely to be missing. Meeting a 90 per cent (or higher) world population threshold ensures that the study coverage is reasonably broad.

The political independence of a country, however, does not necessarily imply its statistical independence as a case that is free to vary independently of other countries. The classic formulation of the interdependence of societies is Galton's problem of cultural diffusion. Nineteenth-century geneticist Frances Galton questioned whether similar marriage customs arose independently in multiple societies or were adopted in each society through cultural diffusion from a single source. A modern variant of Galton's problem is at the heart of the debate between Wallerstein's (2004) world-systems and Meyer et al.'s (1997) world society approaches to studying globalization: is globalization at the country level best modelled as a similar response to common structural forces affecting all countries simultaneously (world-systems approach) or as a process of cultural diffusion in which practices that are associated with successful countries are emulated by countries that aspire to be successful (world society approach)?

Solutions to these modern variants of Galton's problem are not easy to come by. Naroll (1968) suggests that researchers compare cases for which diffusion would have been impossible, but this is difficult to apply in practice. Chase-Dunn (1989: 311) suggests diffusion be endogenized and itself studied as a system property. This is, however, virtually impossible to operationalize in a cross-national panel context. The world-systems–world society debate is probably more amenable to qualitative comparative case studies rather than to quantitative statistical models. When it comes to quantitative modelling, the truth is that we probably have fewer independent cases – a smaller N, so to speak – than we think we have.

The larger problem of the interdependence of cases is a hidden plague on all research that uses the country as the unit of analysis. The simple fact is that countries are not independent cases when it comes to the study of globalization. A basic assumption of regression analysis is that errors are uncorrelated across cases, but this assumption probably does not hold for neighbouring countries or those occupying similar structural positions in the world-economy. Of course, the use of country level fixed effects solves this problem, but creates others (as discussed above); also, fixed effects models are infeasible when data are available for only one or two time periods.

Environmental scientists have recently begun addressing problems of spatial autocorrelation using Bayesian statistical methods based on Markov random fields (see Rue 2005). In the Markov random field approach an underlying error structure is specified in which each country's error terms are assumed to be influenced by neighbouring countries' error terms. A graph is constructed in which each country is represented by a vertex which is connected to each neighbouring country by an edge; this graph forms an (irregular) lattice across which errors are allowed to 'flow': countries' errors are associated most strongly with their immediate neighbours' errors, but are also associated to their neighbours' neighbours' errors, and so on across the entire lattice.

Models using Markov random fields have begun to be adopted in the epidemiological literature, but have not yet appeared in the mainstream of political economics research; a seminal application in economic geography is Dezzani (2004). One factor holding back their use is the lack of well-developed tools for statistical inference: research to date has focused on using Markov random fields for estimation and prediction. Currently, only rather crude Monte Carlo techniques are available for computing confidence intervals for coefficients estimated using Markov random field models. This gap in inferential statistics is an area of active research in mathematical statistics, and is likely to be filled with time.

A complementary problem to the lack of independence of countries as units of analysis is the lack of independence between observations of the same country at different points in time, or temporal autocorrelation. A simple and direct fix for temporal autocorrelation in the dependent variable, which often leads to temporal autocorrelation of errors, is to take the first difference in the dependent variable, subtracting its value at time $t - 1$ from its value at time t. Differencing transforms the dependent variable from being the level of a phenomenon to being the degree of change in a phenomenon; special care must be taken in determining whether or not to difference independent variables as well (Firebaugh and Beck 1994). Thought should also be put into determining the appropriate period over which to take the difference, what Chase-Dunn (1989: 321–2) calls the 'width of a time point'. Too often in the economics literature annual first differences are applied mechanically to dependent variables without appropriate consideration of the implications this holds for the interpretation of the model or the roles of other variables in it.

An alternative to differencing is to explicitly model regression errors as autoregressive processes. Usually a first-order or AR(1) model, in which each country's error at time t is conditioned on its error at time $t - 1$, is sufficient, though more complicated error structures can be modelled. As with the treatment of spatial autocorrelation, so too with temporal autocorrelation the Bayesian Markov random field approach may ultimately become a standard tool. In addition to linking countries geographically to their neighbours, Markovian lattices can be used to link countries to themselves at previous and future time points. While these emerging techniques present intriguing possibilities for improving our understanding of globalization, they have not yet been tested in practice.

CONCLUSION

The foregoing discussion outlines many subtle and sometimes quite technical methodological issues to keep in mind when studying the causes or consequences of globalization. In the end, they are nothing more than special cases of much more general principles of sound methodology. Empirical research should be grounded in theory. Theoretical models should guide the formulation of statistical models. Operational definitions of variables should match their theoretical definitions. Partial regression coefficients should not be interpreted as simple regression coefficients. Occam's razor should be applied at all times.

What is distinct about broadly cross-national research on globalization is that for the most part we are all using the same data. Thus, methodological considerations come to the fore as they do in few other areas of social scientific research. Often, as in the international inequality debate, only the operationalization of a key variable stands between wildly opposing substantive conclusions; as a result, there is now an entire literature evaluating the appropriateness of different measures of national income for studying international inequality. Where research is less controversial – and the level of scrutiny is lower – methodological oversights can more easily go unnoticed.

Hopefully, future creators and consumers of globalization research will find the pointers given here useful in improving their own understandings of the complex methodological issues raised in the study of globalization. The literature on economic globalization is methodologically quite advanced; in many cases, the level of methodological sophistication may be said to have outstripped the ability of the data to support it. The research literatures on cultural and political globalization are not as extensive as that on economic globalization, but given that theory is well in advance of research in these areas the research literatures will likely catch up quickly. As all three research literatures become ever more sophisticated methodologically, it is well to remember that parsimony should be valued at a premium.

References

Alderson, A.S. and Nielsen, F. 1999. 'Income inequality, development, and dependence: A reconsideration', *American Sociological Review*, 64, 606–31.

Babones, S.J. 2006. 'Conducting global social research'. In C.K. Chase-Dunn and S.J. Babones (eds), *Global Social Change*, ch. 2. Baltimore, MD: The Johns Hopkins University Press.

Babones, S.J. and Turner, J.H. 2004. 'Global inequality'. In G. Ritzer (ed.), *Handbook of Social Problems*, 101–20. Thousand Oaks, CA: Sage.

Bornschier, V. and Chase-Dunn, C.K. 1985. *Transnational Corporations and Underdevelopment*. New York: Praeger Press.

Bornschier, V., Chase-Dunn, C.K. and Rubinson, R. 1978. 'Cross-national evidence of the effects of foreign investment and aid on economic growth and inequality: A survey of findings and a reanalysis', *American Journal of Sociology*, 84, 651–83.

Chase-Dunn, C.K. 1989. *Global Formation: Structures of the World-Economy*. Cambridge, MA: Basil Blackwell.

Chase-Dunn, C.K. 1999. 'Globalization: A world-systems perspective', *Journal of World-Systems Research*, 5, 187–215.

Chase-Dunn, C.K. and Babones, S.J. 2006. 'Global social change'. In C.K. Chase-Dunn and S.J. Babones (eds), *Global Social Change*, ch. 1. Baltimore, MD: The Johns Hopkins University Press.

Chase-Dunn, C., Kawano, Y. and Brewer, B.D. 2000. 'Trade globalization since 1795: Waves of integration in the world-system', *American Sociological Review*, 65, 77–95.

Dezzani, R. 2004. 'Spatial probability modeling of regional convergence and development'. Paper presented at the 2004 Annual Meeting of the Association of American Geographers, Philadelphia, PA.

Dixon, W.J. and Boswell, T. 1996a. 'Dependency, disarticulation, and denominator effects: Another look at foreign capital penetration', *American Journal of Sociology*, 102, 543–62.

Dixon, W.J. and Boswell, T. 1996b. 'Differential productivity, negative externalities, and foreign capital dependency: Reply to Firebaugh', *American Journal of Sociology*, 102, 576–84.

Evans, P. 2005. 'Counterhegemonic globalization: Transnational social movements in contemporary political economy'. In T. Janoski et al. (eds), *Handbook of Political Sociology: States, Civil Societies, and Globalization*, 655–70. New York: Cambridge University Press.

Firebaugh, G. 1992. 'Growth effects of foreign and domestic investment', *American Journal of Sociology*, 98, 105–30.

Firebaugh, G. 1996. 'Does foreign capital harm poor nations? New estimates based on Dixon and Boswell's measures of capital penetration', *American Journal of Sociology*, 102, 563–75.

Firebaugh, G. 2000. 'Observed trends in between-nation income inequality and two conjectures', *American Journal of Sociology*, 106, 215–21.

Firebaugh, G. 2003. *The New Geography of Global Income Inequality*. Cambridge, MA: Harvard University Press.

Firebaugh, G. and Beck, F.D. 1994. 'Does economic growth benefit the masses? Growth, dependence, and welfare in the Third World', *American Sociological Review*, 59, 631–53.

Firebaugh, G. and Gibbs, J.P. 1985. 'User's guide to ratio variables', *American Sociological Review*, 50, 713–22.

Guillen, M.F. 2001. 'Is globalization civilizing, destructive or feeble? A critique of five key debates in the social science literature', *Annual Review of Sociology*, 27, 235–60.

Inkeles, A. and Smith, D.H. 1974. *Becoming Modern: Individual Change in Six Developing Countries*. Cambridge, MA: Harvard University Press.

Kaplinsky, R. 2001. 'Is globalization all it is cracked up to be?' *Review of International Political Economy*, 8, 45–65.

Kentor, J. and Boswell, T. 2003. 'Foreign capital dependence and development: A new direction', *American Sociological Review*, 68, 301–13.

Kim, S. and Shin, E.H. 2002. 'A longitudinal analysis of globalization and regionalization in international trade: A social network approach', *Social Forces*, 81, 445–71.

Kohn, M.L. 1987. 'Cross-national research as an analytic strategy', *American Sociological Review*, 52, 713–31.

Korzeniewicz, R.P. and Moran, T.P. 2000. 'Measuring world income inequalities', *American Journal of Sociology*, 106, 209–14.

Korzeniewicz, R.P., Stach, A., Patil, V. and Moran, T.P. 2004. 'Measuring national income: A critical assessment', *Comparative Studies in Sociology and History*, 46, 535–86.

Lechner, F.J. 2005. 'Globalization and inequality: The "great reversal" and its implications'. Paper presented at the 100th Annual Meeting of the American Sociological Association, Philadelphia.

Lerner, D. 1958. *The Passing of Traditional Society: Modernizing the Middle East*. Glencoe, IL: Free Press.

Macleod, D.V.L. 1999. 'Tourism and the globalization of a Canary Island', *Journal of the Royal Anthropological Institute*, 5, 443–56.

Meyer, J.W., Boli, J., Thomas, G.M. and Ramirez, F. 1997. 'World society and the nation-state', *American Journal of Sociology*, 103, 144–81.

Mitchell, B.R. 1992. *International Historical Statistics: Europe 1750–1988*, 3rd edn. New York: Stockton Press.

Mitchell, B.R. 1993. *International Historical Statistics: The Americas 1750–1988*, 2nd edn. New York: Stockton Press.

Mitchell, B.R. 1995. *International Historical Statistics: Africa, Asia, and Oceania 1750–1988*, 2nd edn. New York: Stockton Press.

Moghadam, V.M. 1999. 'Gender and globalization: Female labor and women's mobilization', *Journal of World-Systems Research*, 5, 367–88.

Naroll, R. 1968. 'Some thoughts on comparative method in cultural anthropology'. In H.M. Blalock Jr and A.B. Blalock (eds), *Methodology in Social Research*, 236–77. New York: McGraw-Hill.

Reuveny, R. and Li, Q. 2003. 'Economic openness, democracy, and income inequality: An empirical analysis', *Comparative Political Studies*, 36, 575–601.

Rue, H. 2005. *Gaussian Markov Random Fields: Theory and Applications*. Boca Raton, FL: Chapman & Hall.

Smith, D.A. 2001. 'Editor's introduction – Globalization and social problems', *Social Problems*, 48, 429–34.

Summers, R. and Heston, A. 1991. 'The Penn World Table (Mark 5): An expanded set of international comparisons, 1950–1988', *Quarterly Journal of Economics*, 106, 327–68.

Terracciano, A., Abdel-Khalek, A.M., Ádám, N. et al. 2005. 'National character does not reflect mean personality trait levels in 49 cultures', *Science*, 310 (5745), 96–100.

Wallerstein, I. 2004. *World-Systems Analysis: An Introduction*. Durham, NC: Duke University Press.

Chapter 8

Cosmopolitanism: A Critical Theory for the Twenty-first Century

Ulrich Beck

In this chapter I want to outline an argument for cosmopolitanism as a new critical theory for the twenty-first century. Its main purpose is to undermine one of the most powerful beliefs of our time concerning society and politics. This belief is the notion that 'modern society' and 'modern politics' are to be understood as society and politics organized around the nation-state, equating society with the national imagination of society. There are two aspects to this body of beliefs: what I call the 'national perspective' (or 'national gaze') of social actors, and 'methodological nationalism' of scientific observers. This distinction between these two perspectives is important because there is *no* logical co-implication between them, only an interconnected genesis and history.

METHODOLOGICAL NATIONALISM AND ITS CRITIQUE

Methodological nationalism takes the following premises for granted: it equates societies with nation-state societies, and sees states and their governments as the cornerstones of social-scientific analysis. It assumes that humanity is naturally divided into a limited number of nations, which internally organize themselves as nation-states and externally set boundaries to distinguish themselves from other nation-states. And it goes further: this outer delimitation as well as the competition between nation-states represent the most fundamental category of political organization.

Much social science assumes the coincidence of social boundaries with state boundaries, believing that social action occurs primarily within, and only secondarily across, these divisions:

> [Like] stamp collecting . . . social scientists collected distinctive national social forms. Japanese industrial relations, German national character, the American constitution,

the British class system – not to mention the more exotic institutions of tribal societies – were the currency of social research. The core disciplines of the social sciences, whose intellectual traditions are reference points for each other and for other fields, were therefore *domesticated* – in the sense of being preoccupied not with Western and world civilization as wholes but with the 'domestic' forms of particular national societies. (Shaw 2000)[1]

Of course, from a sociological perspective the cosmopolitan question is not primarily the normative question of what a 'cosmopolitan society', 'cosmopolitan democracy', 'cosmopolitan state' or regime *ought* to be. The question is: Is there a clear sociological alternative to the national mystification of societies and political order? Is there an *actually existing* cosmopolitanism, a reality of (re)attachment, multiple belongings or belonging-at-a-distance? To belong or not to belong – *that* is the cosmopolitan question.

A sharp distinction should be made between *methodological* nationalism on the one hand and *normative* nationalism on the other. The former is linked to the social-scientific observer perspective, whereas the latter refers to the negotiation perspectives of political actors. In a normative sense, nationalism means that every nation has the right to self-determination within the frame of its cultural distinctiveness. Methodological nationalism assumes this normative claim as a socio-ontological given and simultaneously links it to the most important conflict and organization orientations of society and politics. These basic tenets have become the main perceptual grid of social science. Indeed, the social-scientific stance is rooted in the concept of nation-state. A nation-state outlook on society and politics, law, justice and history governs the sociological imagination. To some extent, much of social science is a prisoner of the nation-state.

These premises also structure empirical research, for example, in the choice of statistical indicators, which are almost always exclusively national. A refutation of methodological nationalism from a strictly empirical viewpoint is therefore difficult, well nigh impossible, because so many statistical categories and research procedures are based on it.

The comparative analyses of societies, international relations, political theory and a significant part of history and jurisprudence all essentially function on the basis of methodological nationalism. This is valid to the extent that the majority of positions in the contemporary social and political science debate over globalization can be systematically interpreted as transdisciplinary reflexes linked to methodological nationalism. It is therefore of historical importance for the future development of social science that this methodological nationalism, as well as the connected categories of perception and disciplinary organization, be theoretically, empirically and organizationally reassessed.

What body of belief am I talking about? Methodological nationalism includes the following principles: (a) The *subordination* of society to state, which implies (b) that there is no singular, but only the *plural* of socie*ties*,[2] and (c) a *territorial* notion of societies with state-constructed *boundaries*, that is, the territorial state as container of society. (d) There is a *circular determination* between state and society: the territorial nation-state is both the creator and guarantor of the individual citizenship rights and citizens organize themselves to influence and legitimate state actions. (e) Both states and societies are imagined and located within the *dichotomy of national and international*, which so far has been the foundation of the dominant ontology of politics and political theory. (f) The state as the guarantor of the social order provides the instruments and units for the collection of *statistics* about social and economic processes required by empirical social science. The categories of the state census are the main operational categories of empirical social science. This is even true for most 'global' data, which presuppose nation-state statistics and exclude transnational 'networks', 'flows' and 'scapes'. (g) In membership and statistical representation, methodological nationalism operates on the either-or principle, excluding the possibility of both-and. But the opposition – either 'us' or 'them', either 'in' or 'out' – does not capture the reality of blurring boundaries between political, moral and social communities and thus fails the ongoing experiment to create post-Westphelian transnational public spaces and citizens. Global transformations represent a meta-change that makes us displace *zombie-categories* by concepts of 'inner globalization' or 'cosmopolitization from within'. Zombie concepts are those that were appropriate to the period of methodological nationalism. They are not appropriate to the age of global ecological, economic and terrorist threats. There is coming into being a new system in which everyday practices involve an exceptional level of cosmopolitan interdependences. Thus, forced cosmopolitanism represents no longer just an idea of reason (*Vernunft*) but has invaded, however misformed, politics, society and everyday practices.

Before one can engage in a critique of methodological nationalism, there is an epistemologically prior step: recognizing what Max Weber called *kulturelle Wertbeziehungen*, cultural value relationships. Weber argued that these are not 'value judgments'; they are in fact necessary (there is no social science without cultural value relationships built into its point of view, questions and frames of reference) cultural as well as scientific precommitments which fundamentally structure social and social-scientific perceptions of reality. So the critique of methodological nationalism is about the rights and wrongs of a historically specific *national* value relationship which the classics build into the sociological imagination. How can we recognize, criticize and possibly replace it with an alternative 'post-national imagination'?

There is, however, a problem with the word 'methodological nationalism'. It can be thought of as a sort of prejudice, a 'belief' or 'attitude', and therefore something that can be eliminated from modern enlightened thought in the same way we eliminate other attitudes such as racism, sexism or religious bigotry. But the crucial point about methodological nationalism does not concern values and prejudices, but rather science, scholarship and expert opinion. Methodological nationalism refers to a set of beliefs about empirical reality: statements which mainstream social scientists, using highly sophisticated empirical research methods, accept as true, as propositions supported by 'the facts'. Methodological nationalism is therefore a very complex thing. We have to ask, on what ground do we reflect upon and criticize methodological nationalism? And is there an alternative?

Of course, the critique of methodological nationalism should not be mistaken for the thesis of the end of the nation-state. Just as when criticizing methodological individualism one does not necessarily promote the end of the individual, nation-states (as all investigations have shown) will continue to thrive or will be transformed into transnational states. What, then, is the main point of the critique of methodological nationalism? The decisive point is that *national organization as a structuring principle of societal and political action can no longer serve as a premise for the social-scientific observer perspective.* In order even to understand the trend toward renationalization or re-ethnification in the United States, Western or Eastern Europe, one needs a cosmopolitan perspective. But the dissolution of the national *Wertbeziehung* of the social sciences is not only an analytical and empirical challenge; it is at the same time a normative and political issue as well. In this sense, social science can only respond to the challenge of a global civil society if it manages to overcome methodological nationalism, to raise empirically and theoretically fundamental questions within specialized fields of research, and thus to elaborate the foundations of a *cosmopolitan* social and political science.

Cosmopolitan social science entails the systematic breaking up of the process through which the national perspective of politics and society as well as the methodological nationalism of political science, sociology, history and law confirm and strengthen each other in their definitions of reality. It thus also tackles (what had previously been *analytically* excluded as a sort of silent cartel of divided fundamental convictions) the various developmental versions of debounded politics and society, corresponding research questions and programmes, the strategic expansions of the national and international political field, as well as basic transformations in the domain of state, politics and society.

This paradigmatic reconstruction and redefinition of social science from a national to a cosmopolitan perspective can be understood as a 'positive problem shift' (Lakatos 1970), a broadening of horizons for social science research:

> When politics and society are de-bounded, the consequence is that the labels 'national' and 'international' can no longer be separated. Considering the fact that to an increasing extent governance 'takes place in debounded spaces,' the increasingly problematic distinction – but which is typical of the field – between 'domestic' and 'foreign' politics, as 'national governmental politics' and 'international relations,' becomes definitely obsolete. Thus it is not only a matter of integrating national explanation factors in the analysis of international political processes, or of re-evaluating the international determinants of national political processes, as was pursued in numerous approaches over the past years. Rather, it is a matter of questioning the very separation between 'inside' and 'outside.' (Grande and Risse 2000)

In sum, traditional conceptualizations of terms and the construction of borders between the 'national' and the 'international', domestic and foreign politics, or society and the state are less and less appropriate to tackling the challenges linked to the global age.

Let me point to one implication of this: the understanding of sovereignty in the national and cosmopolitan perspectives. From a national perspective, we find it easiest to think about globalization as a simple alternative to or negation of the modern state or system of states. This framing is often articulated as an opposition between *political realism* as an affirmation of the necessity of state interests and *political idealism*, which celebrates the potential of some kind of universality, some global or human community.

Table 8.1 Paradigmatic change from a national perspective to a cosmopolitan social science

		Political action	
		National perspective	*Cosmopolitan perspective*
Political science	*Methodological nationalism*	Nation-state centred understanding of society and politics in both political practice and political science.	Globalization seen from within the nation-state: under which conditions do actors change from a national to a cosmopolitan perspective? Actually existing cosmopolitanism.
	Methodological cosmopolitanism	Opening up of the nation-state centred society and politics, sociology and political science: new critical theory with a cosmopolitan intent; redefinition of basic notions and frames of references from a cosmopolitan perspective.	The cosmopolitan society and its enemies: what does a cosmopolitan society, state and regime mean?

The cosmopolitan perspective does not, like the national perspective, focus on the fall (or rise) of the nation-state in the global age. Instead, it is a new perspective on the whole global power game, redefining the state as one actor among others in a broader meta-game over the rules of world domestic politics (*Weltinnenpolitik*). The cosmopolitan perspective dismisses the either-or principle of realism: either the state exists, albeit only as an essential core, or it does not exist at all; either there is national sovereignty – a zero-sum game between national and international competence – or there is no sovereignty at all. From a cosmopolitan perspective, 'realism' is a kind of political *ir*realism because it neglects the possibility and reality of a second 'Great Transformation' of the global power game. We need to develop a concept of *cosmopolitan Realpolitik* to understand the positive-sum game of pooled sovereignties. In an era of global crises, national problems can only be solved through transnational/national cooperation and state networks (Beck 2005).

Thus, it becomes necessary to systematically raise the question of a paradigm shift characterized by the conceptual opposition of methodological nationalism and methodological cosmopolitanism (Beck 2000, 2002a, 2002b, 2006). The horizon opened up by this distinction reveals a new global configuration (see Table 8.1). Previously, the national cosmos could be decomposed into a clear distinction between inside and outside. Between the two, the nation-state governed and order was established. In the internal experiential space, work, politics, law, social inequality, justice and cultural identity were negotiated against the background of the nation, which was the guarantor of unitary collective action. In the external experiential field, the international realm, the corresponding concept of 'multiculturalism' developed. Multiculturalism, by means of delimitation from and exclusion of the foreign, mirrored and crystallized national self-image. The national/international distinction always represented more than a distinction, it actually functioned as a permanent self-fulfilling prophecy.

Against the background of cosmopolitan social science, it becomes suddenly obvious that it is neither possible to clearly distinguish between the national and the international, nor, in a similar way, to convincingly contrast homogeneous units. National spaces have become denationalized, so that the national is no longer national, just as the international is no longer international. This entails that the power stays of the nation-state are collapsing from both the inside and the outside, and that new realities are arising: a new mapping of space and time, new coordinates for the social and the political, which have to be theoretically and empirically researched and elaborated.[3]

However, the paradigmatic opposition between (inter)nationalism and cosmopolitanism does not establish a logical or temporal exclusivity, but an ambivalent transitional co-existence, a new concurrence of non-concurrents.

Social science must be re-established as a transnational science of the reality of denationalization, transnationalization and 're-ethnification' in a global age – and this on the levels of concepts, theories and methodologies as well as organizationally. This entails a re-examination of the fundamental concepts of 'modern society'. Household, family, class, social inequality, democracy, power, state, commerce, public, community, justice, law, history and politics must be released from the fetters of methodological nationalism, reconceptualized, and empirically established within the framework of a new cosmopolitan social and political science. So it would be hard to understate the scope of their task. But nevertheless it has to be taken up if the social sciences want to avoid becoming a museum of antiquated ideas (Beck and Willms 2003).

NEW CRITICAL THEORY OF SOCIAL INEQUALITIES FROM A COSMOPOLITAN PERSPECTIVE

I would now like to address a theme, as well as a research area, which is central but has until now received little attention from the cosmopolitan perspective, in order to both test and illustrate the relevance of the new critical theory and its empirical claims by using a concrete example: the sociology of social inequalities. The report on the financial situation of developing countries published in March 2002 by the World Bank can be read as an official accusation of 'Terre des Hommes' against the ignorance of wealthy countries. The falling prices of raw materials on the world market, commercial protectionism and the economic slump in industrialized states, and above all the decline of worldwide tourism after 11 September 2001 have all dramatically increased the destitution of the world's poorest regions. The world has become a dangerously unequal place – even for the rich in Western metropoles. For debt repayment alone, $200 billion per year move from the South to the North. In parallel, the private capital investment flows to the South have

Table 8.2 Sociology of social inequalities in the tension between the national and the cosmopolitan perspectives

	Matrix of social positions	
	Large (global) inequalities	Small (nation-state level) inequalities
National perspective	Irrelevant, inexistent	Merit system
Cosmopolitan perspective	Nation-state principle: exclusion of the excluded	Nation-state principles, which make global inequalities invisible

(Legitimization — row label at left)

shrunk for the fifth year in a row, settling below 1997 levels. While 1.2 billion people, almost a fifth of the world population, must make do with less than a dollar per day, state development aid has decreased 20 per cent since 1990. How can one explain the contradiction between the growing poverty of ever-increasing sections of the population and the growing ignorance about this problem?

In Germany, many members of the *Bundestag* (parliament) belong to the generation which 20 to 30 years ago pledged a form of 'international solidarity'; they were active in Third World initiatives or fought against poverty and for the needs of 'One World'. Now it appears that the policies of this generation have transformed Germany into one of the slowcoaches of development politics. Can this be explained by the inconsequence of politicians? Or is the neglect of global injustices structurally conditioned? Is there a principle that can account for how global inequalities grow while, from a sociological point of view, they are legitimized?

There are at least two possible answers to the question of what legitimates social inequality: the merit system (equal pay for equal work) and the nation-state principle. The first answer has been carefully elaborated and criticized; it derives from the self-understanding of the national perspective and is related to internal, intra-state inequalities. The second answer can be drawn from the frame of reference of the cosmopolitan perspective and is related to the 'legitimization' of much greater inequalities between states. Thus, the bigger blind spots – and sources of error – of methodological nationalism linked to research on inequality will only be recognizable by means of a systematic switch from the national to the cosmopolitan perspective. It is only within the framework of such a new critical theory of social inequality that the *fundamental asymmetry of inequality perception – as embedded in the national viewpoint as well as in the social-science perspective – can be unravelled.* This is to stress that the 'legitimatory system' of the nation-state rests on the fact that attention is exclusively focused on the inside, thereby banning global inequalities from the field of vision of the (relatively) privileged.

It makes sense to distinguish between *large* inequalities (which can further be divided into transnational, supranational, international and global inequalities) and *small* inequalities (see Table 8.2). The 'small' inequalities are those found within the nation-state. (Of course there are 'big inequalities' in a country like the United States, but there are even larger inequalities in the global society.) They appear large to the people or groups concerned for obvious reasons, but from a cosmopolitan perspective they are small, because they collapse under the projector beam of self-description, self-ascription and self-control. The merit system both points to intra-state inequalities and legitimizes them. The appropriate paradigm to describe this phenomenon is the written examination: people enter as equals but come out unequal (with differentiated positions in the hierarchy of credits). With the help of the merit system, for example, incomes can be both unequal and legitimate. In contrast, when we speak of the nation-state principle as a 'legitimization' of social inequalities, we point out that the nation-state perspective, engrossed in national inequalities, effaces global inequalities – a form of legitimization through neglect. Large inequalities are thus invisible from the national perspective; they can both grow and be 'legitimized' via a form of institutionalized irrelevance and unreality. How is this possible? Because the national perspective functions like a microscope. By focusing on small internal inequalities, the bigger global ones are left out. Thus, in this case, the thematization of small national inequalities legitimizes large inequalities.

The differentiation between 'large' and 'small' also refers to spaces of perception and population figures. The law of the nation-state exclusion of global inequalities is obviously also a case in point. The particularism of the nation-state does not necessarily exclude universal principles and perceptions. Nevertheless, it does appear that the nation-state perspective provides a 'liberation' from the misery of the world. It functions according to the model of *double exclusion*: it excludes the excluded. It is surprising that the large inequalities suffered by humanity can be continuously legitimized through a silent complicity between state authority and the state-obsessed social sciences, by means of a form of organized non-perception. Global inequalities have grown – from 1960 to 2000, the 70 per cent of the global income possessed by the richest 20 per cent of the world population increased to 90 per cent, whereas the 2.3 per cent of the poorest decreased to approximately 1 per cent. In the meantime, the unchanging nation-state viewpoint is confirmed behind its perceptual wall of predetermined irrelevance and unreality.

While the merit system enables a *positive* legitimization of small inequalities, the nation-state principle produces a *negative* 'legitimization' of large inequalities. 'Positive' legitimization means that the merit system validates a reflexive and reciprocal legitimization: social inequalities can in principle be tolerated by the underprivileged. In contrast, 'negative' represents the legitimization of the nation-state principle: it is characterized by *non*-reflexivity and *non*-reciprocity, entailing that it cannot be tolerated by the underprivileged and the excluded. The nation-state principle searches for the justification of global inequalities in the dark. It is based on non-reflection, not on reflection, as in the case of the merit system. Thus, negative legitimization through institutionalized silence or averted looks cannot be legitimized; it precludes the acceptance of those whose acceptance is most needed: the poor, the humiliated and the excluded. The nation-state does *not* legitimate global inequalities. Rather, the *non*-legitimized global inequalities are banned from the field of vision and *thereby* stabilized. Historically, this means that the European nation-state represents the institutionalized forgetting of colonialism and imperialism, both of which fostered its development. What then does this negative 'legitimization' through silence bring when faced with the growing permeability of boundaries? One can distinguish between four types of nation-state unreality construction.

First, I would like to mention the nation-state's fragmentation of accountability for global inequalities: as long as there is no global jurisdiction and reporting institution to survey global inequalities, these will remain disintegrated into a motley pattern of nation-state inequalities. Because there are approximately 200 states, there are approximately 200 different frames for small social inequalities. But the sum of these recorded infra-state inequalities does not correspond to the larger global inequalities. In particular, national self-ascription and the endogenous causal suppositions linked to it contradict the cosmopolitan viewpoint, which stresses the fact that transnational interdependences, power relations and their 'side effects', decision-making authorities and causalities also contribute to the explanation of inequalities within nation-states.

The *South Commission Report* (1990) argues that 'if humanity were a single nation-state, the current North–South split would transform it into a politically explosive, semi-feudal unit, the stability of which is threatened by internal conflicts' (quoted in Falk 1995: 50). This is both right and wrong: it points to the scale of global inequalities, but does not recognize that the nation-state world order structurally ignores, and therefore 'legitimizes' them.

The nation-state principle is the analytical key to understanding why the connection between globalization and poverty has been so seldom researched in the social sciences. As long as the national perspective reigns in political action as well as in social science analysis, poverty and wealth will continue to be localized in the national context as a matter of course. Even the possibility that the problematic consequences of globalization materialize in various historical contexts – in the shape of growing inequalities, declining incomes, overexploitation of natural resources and eroding democracies – remains *analytically* excluded. Thus, as far as social science inequality research is concerned, the principle of nation-state fragmentation is linked to a major source of error: the danger of a *misguided 'nation-state oriented' conclusion*. Global or transnational interdependences, processes, power relations and causalities simply fade away or are misinterpreted within the closed circle of a national perspective. The crucial point is that this mistake can be neither unravelled nor avoided using a national perspective; only a cosmopolitan outlook, only a cosmopolitan sociology which overcomes the national-universal imagination of mainstream sociology can provide a way out of the deadlock.

The second principle is that *the perception of social inequalities presupposes equality norms*. Within the nation-state perspective, stability rests on the validity of national equality norms, be they culturally, ethnically, legally or politically defined. The objectivity of global social inequalities is politically irrelevant as long as these inequalities remain in the shadow of institutionalized equality norms, like citizenship (Stichweh 2000). Therefore, to the extent that national equality norms are replaced by transnational or cosmopolitan ones, the necessity and urgency of politically legitimizing large existing inequalities increases. Within the national paradigm, what does this equality rest on in Western welfare states? It rests on the formal equality of the citizens: income differences between men and women, places of residence etc. do not endorse a differentiated citizen status. All the individuals of a nation have the same rights and duties; differentiated citizenship status is unacceptable. This legally sanctioned citizen equality corresponds to the guiding nation-state principle of cultural homogeneity (language, history, cultural traditions). The national principles of inclusion and exclusion thus determine and stabilize the perceptual boundaries of social inequalities.

This leads to a third principle, that of *the difficulty of comparing social inequalities between nation-states*. The 'functional capacity' of the nation-state and the national perspective to legitimize global inequalities also rests on the fact that politicizing comparisons can only be completed *infra*nationally and not *inter*nationally. Comparisons here again presuppose national equality norms. In that sense, income differences between, for example, Nigerians and Germans, South Americans and Finns, Russians and Chinese, Turks and Koreans – even in the case of similar qualifications and functions – can be very important. But the delegitimizing potential of these comparisons is only felt if they take place within a common perceptual framework of institutionalized equality. This can be achieved through belonging to a particular nation or belonging to a globally active corporation.

This leads to the interesting question of how far one can and will be able to legitimize the international wage differences within the European Union by means of the principle of incomparability. Another way of formulating the question could be how far – with growing European self-consciousness (and the institutionalization of European self-observation) – inequalities which were previously ignored because they were international will be perceived as *intra*national European inequalities and thus have to be legitimized. To the extent that these barriers enforcing the international incomparability of inequalities dissolve (for whatever reason), the states of the European Union – even when facing so-called 'fixed' inequality relations – will probably experience considerable turbulence.

Nevertheless, the role of the nation-state is not confined to a so-called legitimization function within the system of global inequalities. The fourth principle can be summed up as follows: the 'fading out phenomenon' legitimizes *in*action, or rather it legitimizes those actions which increase large inequalities because so-called '*external*' effects, from the national perspective, fall into a form of predetermined unreality or political irrelevance. Exclusively thematizing internal inequalities thus facilitates a global redistribution politics whereby risks are externalized, that is, imposed on weaker developing or emerging countries and regions, while profits are maximized within the rich countries of the West.

While Western politicians were busy extolling the fact that we had achieved a decade of unexpected peace and wealth, a growing number of countries were engulfed in debts, unemployment and the decline of health, social services and urgently needed infrastructures. What proves profitable for Western corporations – the strict enforcement of deregulation, privatization and flexibilization in developing countries – often proves a disaster for these countries. Just to cite an example: the World Bank, in its role as an extension of the G7 states, supported contracts with private energy suppliers in Indonesia and other countries. 'These contracts obliged the public sector to buy great quantities of electricity at very high prices.' The international corporations pocketed the profits while the risks were imposed on the 'anyway already' poor states:

> The US Ministry of Finance and the World Bank became renowned for precisely this type of private commercial activity. That is already bad enough. But when the corrupt governments of these emerging economies were overthrown (cf. e.g. Suharto

(Indonesia) in 1998 . . .), the US administration put the new governments under pressure to honour the contracts, instead of releasing them from their obligation to pay or at least renegotiating conditions. Indeed, there is a long list of unfair contracts, the honoring of which western governments achieved by exerting pressure through oppression. (Stieglitz 2002: 38ff.)

To sum up these principles: the nation-state world order fragments global inequalities, national equality norms exclude global inequalities and infranational inequality comparisons ensure international incomparability. The predetermined irrelevance of large inequalities enables powerful and wealthy nation-states to burden poor states with the risks entailed by their decisions. Additionally, these decisions are stabilized because the scope of action of these rich nation-states is confirmed and strengthened by the methodological nationalism of their social sciences. The inequality research based on this perspective greatly reinforces national myopia; it confines both itself and its object of research within the framework of a nation-state 'inborn science'. What is normally seen as problematic from a scientific point of view, that is, research on one's self, is extolled here as a methodological principle. At best, the autism entailed by the national perspective is extended into a comparative autism in international comparison. But this comparative methodological nationalism remains bound by methodological nationalism. The nation-state is a state of mind. Walls hindering perception are erected and fostered, and they are justified and cemented thanks to the knowledge produced by social science that bases itself on methodological nationalism.

However, this social and social-scientific creation, that is, the unreality of growing global inequalities, is becoming increasingly problematic.

The mistakes of the national perspective are recognizable to the extent that boundaries have become permeable and interdependences, which transcend all borders, are growing exponentially. One can illustrate this point by mentioning the obvious contradictions of restrictive immigration politics. On the one hand, the rich northern countries are currently plagued by a spectacular demographic regression, entailing the known consequences of ageing populations, jeopardizing pension and health systems, and bringing political conservatism. On the other hand, these very countries are busy building ramparts to ward off feared and real immigration flows from the poorer South. At the same time, military, economic and political interdependences are growing worldwide, which entail new flows of migrants and refugees. Every measure in this field is doomed: it leads to foreseeable side-effects and often proves utterly counterproductive. Thus, in the aftermath of the 11 September 2001 terrorist attacks, the political ambition of controlling migration flows, especially in the United States but also in Europe, has been strengthened and sharpened. But the associated reduction of civil liberties undermines the necessary readiness to authorize more immigration, which alone would enable the curbing of falling demographic curves and the rejuvenation of the population.

Additionally, the national perspective is thrown into question by the inner globalization of nation-states as experiential spaces. Human rights are increasingly detached from citizenship status and are no longer bound by national contexts. Good examples of this trend are international education curricula, the growing number of binational marriages, as well as increasing transnational work and private life connections. Finally, the national perspective is imperilled by the growing mobility of communication, information, cash flows, risks, products and services. Even indigenous groups who had remained immobile are being experientially trans-nationalized through mass-communication, publicity etc.[4] Moreover, supranational institutions such as the World Bank, UNESCO and various NGOs systematically provide data which make large inequalities visible worldwide, throwing the mechanisms of the national unreality-making process into question.[5] The mistakes of the national perspective are recognizable because of new and increasingly important ways of differentiating between inclusion and exclusion. Increasingly, mechanisms of inclusion and exclusion no longer follow the classifications into classes and strata which end at the national border – a feature typical of the nation-state. New patterns of inclusion and exclusion are developing along the lines of, for instance, (a) supranational trade agreements (European Union, NAFTA etc.), (b) diaspora cultures based on ascriptive characteristics (e.g. Paul Gilroy's 'Black Atlantic'), or (c) the conditions of everyday life in *global cities* (cf. the analyses of Saskia Sassen, Manuel Castells, Martin Albrow, John Eade, Michael Dürrschmidt and Rüdiger Korf). In these cases, the arguments with which the national perspective is defended also break down.

Garrét Hardin, in his book *Living on a Lifeboat* (1974), provided an early and famous defence of the national perspective and critique of the cosmopolitan outlook. He compared nation-states with diversely equipped lifeboats, arguing that every one of these boats is free to offer a seat to the many survivors who are struggling against the wild sea. But this possibility cannot be a duty, since the taking on of castaways disregards the very security regulations of the lifeboat, thus endangering all the passengers on board.

This 'lifeboat ethics' ('the-boat-is-full') argument, which is still very effective today, is especially inappropriate because the nation-state lifeboats suggested by the national perspective have become fewer and fewer. Current post- and transnational inequalities and their causes are misinterpreted. It is primarily therefore the uncovering of the national perspective's misdiagnosis – and not a moral critique – which constitutes the essence of the cosmopolitan outlook and substantiates its superiority.

The mistakes of methodological nationalism are also recognizable to the extent that the distinction between large and small inequalities – or, to express it differently, between the cosmopolitan and national perspectives – have themselves become questionable. We are increasingly confronted with an *internationalization of national models of inequalities*. Competition within and between national spaces increases along with the permeability of national boundaries. Correspondingly, globalization's winners and losers are increasingly distributed according to production sectors that are either shielded from the market or exposed to it. Last but not least, the nebulous concept of 'globalization' is often used in the *struggle between national and transnational elites*, who fight over positions and resources *within* national power spaces.

Finally, the view-obstructing walls are also disintegrating in relation to the international situation. At least since the terrorist attacks, it has become more difficult to exclude the excluded: the increasing poverty of the world population is also perceived as a problem of the wealthy Western countries, though the practical consequences of this remain to be defined. The danger of terrorism, which defies national borders, also abrogates the walls of nation-state vision, behind which global inequalities continue to grow menacingly.

There is no doubt that these developments overstrain nation-states. Not only do they not possess appropriate capabilities to intervene, they do not even possess the necessary observation capacities. Hence the central paradox of a new cosmopolitan orientation can be – self-critically, of course – justified. To the extent that the boundaries between large and small inequalities become more permeable and no longer correspond to national borders, the mental wall, the institutionalized non-perception of large inequalities, is further buttressed. Why? Because it is only thus that the growing asymmetry between intervention demands addressed to states and the actual intervention possibilities of these states can be bridged.

Conversely, it can be deduced that if the nation-state 'legitimizes' global inequalities according to the Brechtian principle 'because we don't see those who are in the dark', this legitimization breaks down with the 'cosmopolitization' of the state. The cosmopolitan state, which (however selectively) integrates cultural others, unleashes – even in the most optimal case of stable inequalities – an avalanche of legitimation problems as a side-effect. Why? For the simple reason that it abolishes the boundaries of the incomparability of social inequalities. With cosmopolitization, however, the seduction and possibilities of re-ethnification and renationalization of both society and politics increase. Precisely because boundaries are no longer fixed, the mental wall which hinders perception is cemented anew.

Can one or must one say now whether the nation-state principle is an achievement or a trap? Whatever the answer, it is clear that the non-reflective unity between the state and the social sciences' ability to make global inequalities invisible affects political and scientific actors in contrasting ways. Whether or not the national perspective can be attributed to the 'functional performance' of the nation-state, it perverts the social sciences, which are trapped in an increasingly obvious contradiction with their scientific mission and ethics. Indeed, they base themselves (often without noticing and unintentionally) on the generation of unreality within reality. The silence of social science concepts on the subject of global inequalities is a scandal.

In this new era, a new critical theory with a cosmopolitan intent plays a key role. It must break through the fixed walls of categories and research routines of the methodological nationalism used by social sciences, in order to, for example, shift the legitimatory role of the nation-state in the system of large equalities back into the field of vision. The established *infra*national maps of social inequalities are elegant, detailed and generally thought to be sufficient to politically manage the potential agitation of the more privileged part of the world population. But the dragons of large, unknown, completely inadequately researched inequalities are no longer just decorative motifs which adorn the borders. The nation-state belief and the national narratives which dominate both public commentaries and academic research can no longer be overlooked or ignored. At least since the 11 September terrorist attacks, it has become clear to many people that a glance through the perceptual wall which separates small inequalities from larger ones can resemble a look into the barrel of a gun.

Finally, the new critical theory is also a self-critical theory. The cosmopolitan viewpoint first of all detects, linked to various realities, the *chasms* that threaten the beginning of the twenty-first century. The new critical theory investigates the *contradictions, dilemmas, and unseen and unwanted (unintentional) side-effects* of a modernity which is becoming increasingly cosmopolitan and draws its critical power from the tension between political self-description and the observation of the social sciences. The main thesis is then that *the cosmopolitan perspective opens up negotiation spaces and strategies which the national viewpoint precludes.* This interpretation becomes more plausible when we consider that the negotiation space which the cosmopolitan viewpoint opens up contradicts the absence of alternatives, which, within the national viewpoint, is diagnosed both by political actors and the social sciences.

In this respect, one can differentiate between four large tasks, which remain to be substantiated by the new critical theory:

- revealing and naming the forms and strategies used to render cosmopolitan realities invisible;
- criticizing national circularity, that is, uncovering the fact that neither the nationalization nor the ethnification of negotiation perspectives can justify the methodological nationalism of the social sciences;
- overcoming the ahistorical self-perpetuation of the concepts and research routines of the social sciences by fostering the creation of alternative concepts and research strategies; and
- stimulating and contributing to the re-imagination of the political, that is, marking and experimenting with the difference between the national viewpoint of political actors and the cosmopolitan perspective of the political and social sciences.

In debates about globalization, the main point does not revolve around the meaning of the nation-state and how its sovereignty has been subordinated, but rather focuses on gaining a new cosmopolitan perspective on the global power field, pushing new actors and actor networks, power potentials, strategies and forms of organization of debounded politics into the field of vision. Thus, the cosmopolitan critique of the politics and political science centred on and buttressed by the nation-state from the standpoint of a new critical theory is empirically and politically central.

Notes

1 This and other arguments are developed extensively in my book *Power in the Global Age* (2005).
2 Excluding, for example, the opposite notion of Niklas Luhmann, who argues that there is only *one* society, 'world society'.
3 This is the research agenda of the 'Reflexive Modernization' Research Centre at Munich University; see Beck et al. (2003).
4 Cf. the empirical data in Beisheim and Zürn (1999); Held et al. (1999).
5 Institutions and organizations focusing on a form of 'cosmopolitan' social science research have a long history, and they have competed with the 'self-confirmation circle' of nation-state data and knowledge production. First of all, the scientific ethos has based itself on

the higher quality of nation-state data. In parallel, one witnesses, along with the feared 'cosmopolitan turn', the return of either metaphysics or non-scientific perspectives, and often both, into the centre of academic social science. Furthermore, methodological nationalism acquires its superiority from the prevalent conviction of philosophy and political theory that Western values – democracy, the rule of law, social justice – are only possible in the shapes and contexts provided by the nation-state. This leads to the conclusion that the cosmopolitan opening betrays and endangers the democratic ethos.

In both these scenarios, the major mistake is based on two kinds of neglect. On the one hand, the interpretations of the classical researchers and their nation-state premises have been dehistoricized and absolutized. Lauding the classical researchers masks mental sterility when it reduces one to copyist – a longstanding tendency. On the other hand, one reproduces the mistake (according to the old principle of 'es darf nicht sein, was nicht sein soll') of sacrificing scientific curiosity to institutionalized value convictions. Even the most rigorous data from the methodological point of view can be blind and lead to our being overwhelmed by the cosmopolitan reality.

References

Beck, U. 2000. 'The cosmopolitan perspective: Sociology of the second age of modernity', *The British Journal of Sociology*, 51(1), 79–107.

Beck, U. 2002a. 'The cosmopolitan society and its enemies', *Theory, Culture and Society*, 19(1–2), 17–45.

Beck, U. 2002b. 'The terrorist threat: World risk society revisited', *Theory, Culture and Society*, 19(4), 39–57.

Beck, U. 2005. *Power in the Global Age*. Cambridge: Polity Press.

Beck, U. 2006. *The Cosmopolitan Vision*. Cambridge: Polity Press.

Beck, U., Bonß, W. and Lau, C. 2003. 'The theory of reflexive modernization', *Theory, Culture and Society*, 20(2), 1–33.

Beck, U. and Willms, J. 2003. *Conversations with Ulrich Beck*. Cambridge: Polity Press.

Beisheim, M. and Zürn, M. 1999. *Im Zeitalter der Globalisierung? Thesen und Daten zur gesellschaftlichen und politischen Denationalisierung*. Baden-Baden: Nomos.

Falk, R. 1995. *Humane Governance*. Cambridge, MA: Polity Press.

Grande, E. and Risse, T. 2000. 'Bridging the Gap. Konzeptionelle Anforderungen an die politikwissenschaftliche Analyse von Globalisierungsprozessen', *Zeitschrift für Internationale Beziehung*, 2, 235–67.

Hardin, G. 1974. 'Living on a lifeboat', *Bioscience*, 24(10), 561–8.

Held, D., McGrew, A., Goldblatt, D. and Perraton, J. 1999. *Global Transformations: Politics, Economics, and Culture*. Cambridge: Polity Press.

Lakatos, I. 1970. 'Falsification and the methodology of scientific research programmes'. In I. Lakatos and A. Musgrave (eds), *Criticism and the Growth of Knowledge*. Cambridge: Cambridge University Press.

Shaw, M. 2000. *Theory of the Global State: Globality as Unfinished Revolution*. Cambridge, MA: Cambridge University Press.

Stichweh, R. 2000. *Die Weltgesellschaft. Soziologische Analysen*. Frankfurt am Main: Suhrkamp.

Stieglitz, J. 2002. *Globalization and its Discontents*. New York: W.W. Norton.

Part II

The Major Domains

Introduction to Part II

GEORGE RITZER

This is by far the largest section in the book and deals with the vast majority of major topics in the study of globalization. So many areas are involved in, and affected by, this process that it is impossible to cover all of them in one volume, but I feel confident that few, if any, significant issues have been omitted. While most topics are covered in one chapter, a few, especially economic aspects of globalization, are covered explicitly in several chapters and implicitly in many others.

While a beginning point for coverage of the major concerns in globalization studies is somewhat arbitrary, I have opted to begin with the global movement of people, especially in the form of migration (tourism would be another form of such movement).

Guhathakurta, Jacobson and DelSordi argue that our sense that we live in a global era of unprecedented international migration is incorrect. While international migration has ebbed and flowed over time, the current rate is unspectacular in comparison to at least some of the recent past. While the contemporary numbers may not be impressive, there are interesting and important changes in the nature of today's migrants. First, the proportion of international migrants from the developed world has declined. Second, there has been a large increase in the number of migrants from the developing world and a very significant proportion of them (70–90 per cent) are moving to North America.

Migrants from the less developed world to North America tend to be divided into two profoundly different groups. The first is the highly skilled, technically competent migrants, as well as students, who tend to be welcomed by host countries and to fare comparatively well there. On the other hand, there are the often unwelcome less skilled and unskilled, especially those who are illegal migrants, who are likely to exist at the margins of North American society (and other societies) and who are likely to fare poorly.

A combination of push and pull factors is usually used to explain migration. Among the push factors are the motivations of the migrants, contextual issues in the home country making it difficult or impossible for them to achieve their goals and major disruptions like war, famine, political persecution or an economic depression. Then there are such pull factors as a favourable immigration policy in the host country, formal and informal networks in such countries that cater to migrants, labour shortages and a similarity in language and culture between home and host country. To these traditional factors are added additional ones in the era of globalization. There is, for example, the global dispersion of information which makes it easier to find out about, and become comfortable with, a host country. Then there is the interaction of global–local networks, either through formal networks mediated by modern technologies like mobile phones and the Internet, or through more informal family and social networks that might well employ the same technologies. All of this makes it much easier to migrate and to be more comfortable in a new setting. The presence of diasporic communities in such settings makes it easier for migrants to find such things as housing and work. At the same time, remittances to the home country have become an increasingly significant factor in globalization and in the economies of many (home countries).

While we have seen some retrenchment in recent years, overall there has been at least a selective reduction in barriers to migration in many countries. This is driven by various factors, including labour shortages, an ageing population, the voracious needs of multinational corporations for workers and the possibility of new tax revenues to be derived from migrants and to be used to help support state welfare systems.

Migration has a variety of different effects on the countries of origin. We have already mentioned the remittances that can help bolster their economies. However, this can lead to increased inequality as those individuals and families who receive remittances grow better off than those who do not. The loss of human capital can have an adverse effect on the economy of sending nations, but it is also possible that it can make room for other people to become more skilled and/or for new types of skills to arise.

The changes in international migration have led to various legal changes including not only an increasing density of laws on this issue, but also more international (and national) laws. This has led to conflict between judicial decisions relating to migrants and legislative positions. This conflict is clear also in the case of terrorism where the United States is circumventing the judiciary through a variety of legislative mandates (e.g. the Patriot Act, see below).

Guhathakurta, Jacobson and DelSordi reject the 'end of globalization' argument based on the idea that we have achieved the free movement of labour. We are, in their view, far from such a state and this is traceable to the (questionable) essentializing idea that there is a human need to create barriers. However, whatever its merits, it is this view that leads them to argue that globalization is likely to continue well into the future, if not forever, because of the continuing need to overcome barriers that are, themselves, continuously being created.

In examining globalization and its relationship to agriculture, McMichael focuses on the global South and its four billion people which he sees as in the vortex of globalization. This is not the first time the global South has played a central role in global agriculture; for example, the British outsourced (see Ritzer and Lair) agricultural production to it (e.g. to India) during the height of their empire. However, contemporary globalization has profoundly affected and altered North–South relationships.

McMichael begins with the new relations of agricultural production. The crucial development here is the rise of global agribusiness dominated by the North in general, and the United States in particular. These new relations of agricultural production have come to be defined by the law of comparative advantage which in practice has come to mean that the global South produces non-traditional products (e.g. flowers, fruit, vegetables, shrimp) that it exports to the North. This means that Southern countries are consuming less of their own products, including those that have been the traditional staples of their diet. Instead, they are increasingly coming to consume cheap (sometimes cheaper) food imports from the North and these imports serve not only to replace traditional staples, but also to displace large numbers of local farmers. For example, thanks to NAFTA, the inexpensive and traditional white maize Mexican tortilla has tended to be replaced by yellow corn tortillas mass produced at triple the price by agribusiness in the American midwest. This constitutes a whole new relation of production that is leading to global changes in social class and dietary relationships.

McMichael places much of the responsibility (blame) for most of these changes on the United States and its agricultural model that emphasizes commercial mono-crops and capital/energy intensive agriculture that has transformed the rural landscape not only in the global South, but throughout much of the world. Indeed, Europe was one of the early targets of this transformation through the Marshall Plan. Later, agribusiness disseminated this model throughout the world. It was also fostered by the green revolution which, among other things, led to the decline of traditional mixed crops and their replacement by the domination of capital-intensive hybrids of wheat, corn and rice.

Also involved is the development and exportation of US-style consumption patterns, in this case of food, that has led to global convergence on a diet that includes a narrowing base of staple grains; increased consumption of animal protein, edible oils and salt and sugar; and a decline in dietary fibre. Such a diet has contributed, among other things, to a rise in such dietary diseases as diabetes and to a global epidemic of obesity (Hashemian and Yach). In fact, obesity has in recent years come to be as common throughout the world as malnutrition (about 1.3 million people are afflicted with each!).

Another US-based development – the supermarket revolution – has also played a key role here. It is has obviously centralized food processing and retailing, but it has also exerted increasing control over farmers, ranchers and so on. (The same could be said about the fast food chain revolution.) The latter, however, rarely have binding contracts, are rewarded only if they meet centrally defined quality standards and have tended to face declining prices for their products because virtually all of the power rests with the great supermarket chains. The creation of both public and private standards for things like food quality and packaging are central not only to increasing global inequality (the North tends to set the standards that the South must follow), but also to homogenization[1] of both food production (e.g. industrial agriculture, factory farms) and food consumption (less grain, more animal protein).

A second area of concern to McMichael is relations of social production, or how populations survive within international and national institutions that govern material and livelihood opportunities. Overall, a broad change is depicted from solutions of food security issues lodged in the local community to those solutions being handled by global processes of social reproduction. Most generally, commercial agriculture replaces local provisioning. Declining income in less developed rural areas leads people to need to supplement their incomes through off-farm sources such as working on neighbouring farms, taking jobs in rural industries/*maquilas* or relying on remittances from family members who have moved elsewhere, perhaps in the North.

These changes in the South have not eliminated poverty and hunger, but have led to a change from poverty/hunger amidst scarcity to poverty/hunger amidst abundance. Neoliberal philosophies and policies, including free trade, serve to advantage the global North and its enormous agribusinesses. In the meantime, rural economies everywhere are in depression and crisis with low prices, declining public supports, rural exodus, increases in rural suicides and so on. De-agrarianization and de-peasantization have been accompanied by the rise of rural industrialization, beginning with export-processing zones. Mexico's 1965 Border Industrial Program was key, leading to series of *maquiladores* designed to compete with the rising economies of East Asia. This sparked the revolutionary movement of low-wage manufacturing settings and jobs from the North to the South. In the early twenty-first century there are 70 million *maquila* jobs, but most workers take home only about a third of a living wage with the result that they are forced to supplement their incomes in various ways and, thereby, in a sense, subsidize the factories and their work. But the *maquilas*, themselves, are now being undercut by the increasing importance of low-wage Chinese manufacturing, making even those settings increasingly tenuous.

The third issue of concern to McMichael is relations of resistance. Here he details a wide range of consumer, farmer, farm worker and peasant movements. Also of importance are the Slow Food Movement, land rights activists, the occupation of land en masse, as well as the transnational peasant movement, *Via Campesina* involving farm organizations from 43 countries and millions of farm families. The latter does not reject modernity, but is seeking an alternative to it that involves credit, land, fair prices and rules of fair trade. Overall, perhaps a bit hyperbolically, McMichael finds the core of the new relations of resistance in the realm of food.

In spite of this generally bleak picture, McMichael holds out hope for the future. Agricultural life is resilient and capable of taking on new forms. At the same time, there are social and environmental limits to the corporate globalization of agriculture. Once these limits are reached it is possible to envision a new, robust form of agriculture dedicated to social and ecological sustainability. This holds out the promise (hope?) of a renewal and a revaluing of agrarian life.

This leads nicely into Yearley's chapter on the relationship between globalization and the environment. In his view, the environment is inherently, and has always been, global in that, for example, all share the atmosphere, are warmed by the sun and are connected by the oceans. In spite of this, early work on globalization tended to ignore the environment. However in the 1980s and 1990s the environmental movement made great progress and a number of notable problems, especially the depletion of the ozone layer and global climate change, brought the environment to the fore as a global issue and problem. In the case of the two issues singled out by Yearley, we all play a role in the creation of these problems and we all suffer their adverse consequences. In that sense they are clearly global in nature.

However, while reaffirming this view, Yearley also challenges it in various ways. First, not everyone or every part of the world is equally culpable – some (especially the most developed countries) contribute disproportionately to these and other environmental problems. Second, such problems do not affect everyone and all areas of the world in the same way. Third, there are global differences in the importance accorded to, and the dangers associated with, these problems (e.g. profound differences between the United States and Europe over genetically modified [GM] foodstuffs). In addition, there are other candidates for globally important environmental problems. And the causes of environmental problems change as, for example, the centre of manufacturing (with its associated pollutants) begins to move from, for example, the United States to China.

The free trade that is so central to globalization, as well as the global organizations (e.g. WTO) that support it, is seen as generally the enemy of the environment. Not only does such trade lead to the expansion of manufacturing (and those pollutants), but also to the view that regulations favoured by environmentalists are impediments to free trade and need to be softened or eliminated.

In effect, environmentalists offer an alternative model of globalization to the capitalists and the neoliberals (see Antonio, Part I). To environmentalists, it is environmental issues that are not only global in nature, but that also should be accorded priority over economic considerations. The alternative proposed by Yearley and others is *ecological modernization theory* which argues that economic and technological development and rising environmental standards can go hand-in-hand. Examples include the creation of low-odour paints and less environmentally destructive pesticides. Key here are environmental NGOs that put pressure on nation-states and other entities to move toward policies that are less slavishly devoted to economic development and more attuned to the environment, its protection and even its enhancement. In sum, globalization need not be a 'race to the bottom' ecologically and in many other senses, but can be a process that protects and enhances the environment as well as much else that is of importance to all of us and that all of us value greatly (or at least should).

Timberlake and Ma see cities as central to both scholarly and popular discourse on globalization from the beginning of interest in it as a topic and as a phenomenon. Cities were cosmopolitan (see Beck, Part I), and therefore inherently global, because they encompassed a range of cultures, ethnicities, languages and consumer products. Cities also exerted powerful influence (cultural, political and economic) over surrounding areas. The many city-based organizations were also linked, through elaborate networks, to organizations in other cities throughout the home country and the world. The system of national and global cities was hierarchical with substantial flows of people, information and objects moving both up and down the hierarchy.

The most important of the world's cities are *global cities* (Sassen 1991), with only New York, London and Tokyo usually included in that category. It is no coincidence that the world's most important stock exchanges are located in those cities. More generally, those cities tend to be chosen by many organizations as sites for key offices through which they exert great control over the world's political economy.

A somewhat larger group of cities (perhaps thirty, or so) can be classified as *world cities*. While the size of these cities is important, it is their national and international influence that is of greater importance. Among other things, world cities are homes to many TNC headquarters, major centres of political power, national trade centres, have concentrations of professional expertise, encompass research and education centres, are highly affluent and therefore offer easy access to consumer goods and culture.

The ideas of both global and world cities have, of course, spatial overtones and implications. Those spatial implications can, in turn, be linked to inequality and spatiality. For example, cities that are low in the hierarchy of world cities, or better yet that do not make the list, are likely to be far less well off economically than those at or near the top, to say nothing of the global cities. The key cities are much more tied into the world economy than the hinterlands with the result that the latter, more isolated from that economy, are likely to be less well-off than the cities. Furthermore, even the global cities are likely to have internal inequalities with the well-to-do living in elite areas of the cities, while the poor might live in inner-city ghettos (more the US pattern) or in suburban squatter housing (more the European and Latin American pattern).

Why are global/world cities still important in a flat world (Friedman 2005; see Antonio, this volume) of computer-enhanced telecommunications? Since everyone can, at least theoretically, have access to this system from anywhere, the world's great cities should cease to be so important. However, contradicting the flat world thesis, these cities remain important. In fact, beyond their continued centrality in the global economy, they tend to be the centres for the production of various aspects of the telecommunications industry, as well as the places where the most important innovations take place.

Increasingly, global/world cities can be seen, following Castells (1996), as key nodes in a variety of networks and flows. In fact, leaders in those cities compete to make their city a central node in one or more networks. For example, one type of flow is that of people, especially airline passengers, and it is relatively easy to quantify the number of passengers passing through the great airports of the world's major cities. All of this means that place remains important even in a world increasingly dominated by networks and flows.

Timberlake and Ma conclude that in many ways this global city network constitutes globalization. While it is clear that cities, especially global/world cities, are important in globalization, this seems like a bit of hyperbole, especially given the arguments made in many of the other chapters in the volume.

While the previous chapters in Part II have touched on economic matters as they relate to migration, agriculture, the environment and cities, economics takes centre stage in the next several chapters. We begin with the paper by Clegg and Carter which, while it deals generally with organizations, focuses mainly on those related to business. Globalization is undermining the Tayloristic/Fordist organizational forms (characterized by bureaucratization, industrialization and the strict subjugation and control of employees) that dominated much of the twentieth century and made much of the conquest of the globe possible. There is a new global world and business, in particular, is in the process of creating new organizational forms across vast expanses of space. In fact, Clegg and Carter regard this space as the last frontier of business. (While dramatic, one wonders why this would be the last frontier. For example, one could envision, adopting a Foucauldian perspective, organizations seeking ever-greater bio-physical control over human beings as yet another frontier to be conquered in the future).

Clegg and Carter are primarily concerned with the growth of a new global management ideas industry that is creating blueprints for organizational forms that are being used throughout the world. The following are the major forces in this new management ideas industry:

1 *Large IT firms.* The major information technology firms played a key role in both globalization (through their technology) and the development of new management ideas. They infiltrated organizations throughout the world, bringing with them not only their technology and systems, but most importantly for our purposes, ideas on how to manage organizations.

2 *Management consultants.* A key role was played here by the large accounting firms. They helped to produce, and were a significant part of, the rise of an audit culture in many places in the world. Such a culture emphasized such things as calculability and verification. This allowed accounting firms to proliferate and spread their influence widely. In addition, they used this point of entry to create and to sell all sorts of other management services and ideas to firms throughout the world. Most generally, such consultancies expanded because they were able to create anxiety among their client organizations and then to sell those organizations services designed to reduce that anxiety.

3 *MBAs.* MBAs, and the graduate programmes that create them, are increasingly common throughout the world. Like much else in globalization, they had their origins in the United States and represent the neo-colonial domination of an American educational model on a global scale. In fact, such programmes have become *the* global model of management education. In the process, they have served in various ways to rationalize or McDonaldize management globally. Examples include MBA-speak, the *de rigueur* use of PowerPoints in presentations, the creation of a homogenized body of management knowledge, all of which has been exacerbated by the growth of international credential bodies for MBA programmes. While MBAs and their programmes have been criticized for these and other reasons (the role of MBAs in recent accounting scandals and corporate collapses; their lack of professional ethics), globalization is seen as favouring the survival and further expansion of the MBA.

4 *Management gurus.* This is another American innovation and it remains an area dominated by Americans like Tom Peters (co-author of *In Search of Excellence* [Peters and Waterman 1988]). These people created simplified management ideas and published best-selling books devoted to them. The books have come to be widely sold and translated throughout the world and the gurus themselves are in great demand as highly paid speakers around the globe. In these and other ways gurus have produced and disseminated globally accepted ideas on basic management practices.

5   *Management fashions*. Gurus are major producers of ideas and imaginaries that
    have become fashionable in MBA programmes and with managers throughout
    the world. Like the gurus and others who create them, management fashions
    are usually American in origin. These fashions may be attractive because of their
    aesthetic (e.g. narratives on how effective they have been) and technical (tools
    and techniques) dimensions. Following the new institutional theory we have
    already encountered on several occasions in this volume, some fashions prolifer-
    ate because of isomorphism – best practices are copied (mimetic), regulations
    compel organizations to adopt them, and some fashions become normative.

Clegg and Carter offer various thoughts on the changing nature of work in global
organizations including downsizing, privatization, outsourcing (see Ritzer and Lair,
below), labour intensification, increased insecurity, decline of organized labour,
increased importance of some service workers – knowledge workers/symbolic analysts – but decline of others who hold McJobs in the service economy, such as those
in call centres. Among other things, such jobs are tightly scripted, exist in simple,
unambiguous environments, are associated with great pressure and monotony, have
exacting regulations about time and manner of work, involve panoptic surveillance,
have very high turnover and are supported by even lower-status grunge jobs manned
by contingent employees, illegal immigrants and those in the sex industry (see Farr,
below).

Clegg and Carter return to the issue of Americanization and argue (correctly, in
my view) that this process is not so much about the consumption of American
products (coke, Big Macs), but about more fundamental ways of engaging with
people and things that enable the global spread of a given way of doing business.
However, they are careful to reject a totalizing conception of Americanization,
arguing that there are other models (e.g. from Japan), a process of reverse colonization and the development of hybrid forms that are only in part a reflection of
Americanization.

Clegg and Carter close with several issues, especially the question of where innovations are apt to come from if all organizations around the world are following
the same model. Then there is the issue of various environmental impacts (e.g. global
warming), the causal roles played by various organizations and the question of
whether contemporary managers can respond adequately to these threats. While
these organizations and managers have great power, Clegg and Carter conclude
hopefully that such power, indeed all power, is assailable.

Dicken looks at the global economy and what he considers the misleading idea
that the transnational corporation (TNC) is the most powerful actor on the global
stage, overwhelming even the nation-state (see Thomas, this volume). Based on
ownership criteria, Dicken estimates that there are about 61,000 TNCs accounting,
among other things, for about a tenth of world gross domestic product. Of that
total number of TNCs, only a small number are what Dicken calls global corporations. (While he includes Toyota in this category, Dicken also includes two
companies that are in increasing financial difficulty – IBM and especially General
Motors. This leads one to question the whole notion of a global corporation or at
least the long-term viability of any such corporation.) But even these are not as

powerful global actors as many suppose, if for no other reason than more than half of their activities remain in their home countries.

TNCs are also not the force in the less developed world that many believe. The vast majority – 96 per cent – of TNCs in 2002 were from developed countries and more that two-thirds of the world's foreign direct investment (FDI) was directed towards developed countries. Even when it is aimed at less developed nations, it is heavily concentrated in a small number of countries, especially in East Asia and to a lesser extent in Latin America.

One way that it is clear that TNCs are growing is the fact that FDI has grown substantially in the last two decades. Such investments across borders involves one firm investing in another with the intention of gaining control of its operations, or the setting up of a branch (or subsidiary) operation in another country. (This contrasts with portfolio investment in which equity is purchased in another company purely for financial reasons and not to gain control over it.)

Dicken rejects the idea of a placeless corporation and argues that place and geography continue to matter. The cognitive, cultural, social, political and economic characteristics of the home base, the place of origin, play a dominant role in TNCs. As Dicken puts it, the *aroma of native land* continues to pervade a TNC, to leave a permanent imprint on its strategic behaviour, no matter how global it may become. We are not witnessing the convergence of business-organizational forms towards a single placeless type. It would be surprising for distinctive nationally based TNCs to be replaced by a standardized, homogenized form. He argues that TNCs interact with the place-specific characteristics of geographic areas in which they find themselves, leading to distinctive outcomes.

Dicken sees great differences in TNCs in their basic architecture (integrated network, multinational, international, global) and the location of their corporate headquarters (usually in the home country), their core research and development centres (also usually in the home country), their sales and marketing operations (usually dispersed) and their production operations (increasingly dispersed). TNCs are also always changing and confronting a variety of tensions that may change them, perhaps dramatically, including those with states, local communities, labour, consumers, civil society and various organizations. This, too, contributes to the great diversity among TNCs and to the point that a very few TNCs are in fact global and they come in a wide array of shapes and sizes.

Furthermore, contrary to the opinion of many, TNCs may not always have the advantage. Powerful adversaries include multi-scalar regulating systems (e.g. WTO), international institutes for technical standards (e.g. ISO) and the nation-state. The latter engages in complex bargaining processes with TNCs and their power in this process means that while TNCs are also powerful, they do not have absolute power. Overall, TNCs are not the unstoppable juggernauts that many of their critics, and critics of globalization, assume. What is needed is a more nuanced picture of TNCs and their role in globalization.

Ritzer and Lair deal with a more specific economic aspect of globalization, but one that despite great attention in the popular press and from journalists like Thomas Friedman (see Antonio, this volume) has received relatively little attention from scholars and little more than passing mention in some of the chapters in this volume. Ritzer and Lair seek to deal with this lacuna by analysing the role of economic outsourcing in globalization, but they go beyond that issue in various ways. For one thing, they argue that global outsourcing is not restricted to the economy and they illustrate that with a discussion of the outsourcing of healthcare and the military. For another, they seek to go beyond the macro-level of outsourcing to deal with it at the meso- and micro-levels. Inclusion of these levels makes for a more satisfying and complete sociology of outsourcing, although much of it may not relate directly to globalization. Nonetheless, globalization is often involved even at these levels as exemplified by the fact that the micro-level of the outsourcing of care for children or aged parents in developed countries is often to immigrants, legal or illegal, from less developed countries. This kind of outsourcing feeds into the global flow of migrants (see Guhathakurta et al., this volume), but also may be a significant pull factor in both forms of such global migration. These migrants can be seen as part of a global care chain (Hochschild n.d.) and those who care for children, as well as the children themselves, as part of the globalization of motherhood.

In the realm of globalization and outsourcing, it is clear that there is great need for conceptual clarification. The most general concept is *sourcing*, or the strategies for placement of goods or activities that are location, or source, sensitive. Under this heading, Ritzer and Lair begin with the forms that are most closely and impor- tantly associated with globalization, at least in the United States: *offshoring* and *offshore outsourcing*. Offshoring involves the movement of jobs and/or operations to foreign locations, albeit within the same TNC. Thus, offshoring does not involve outsourcing, but of course offshore outsourcing, by definition, does and it is that that is of great interest and concern to many observers. For example, a variety of Indian firms have become very important settings for the outsourcing of various kinds of work – the best known of which is that performed by call centres – from especially the United States and Great Britain (although offshore outsourcing is a two-way street and some such work is finding its way into these developed coun- tries). While blue-collar manufacturing work has long been outsourced, and the outsourcing of low-level service work is of more recent vintage, what is eye-catching is the increasing outsourcing of high-level white collar and service work such as IT, accounting, law, architecture, journalism and medicine. There are many advantages of offshore outsourcing to both outsourcers (e.g. 24/7 availability of workers) and outsourcees (e.g. job and wealth creation) and that is why it has grown so dramati- cally and is likely to continue to grow. However, there are many costs, especially in the country doing the outsourcing and most notably in job loss and destruction. It is the array of costs that has made offshore outsourcing a hot-button issue in the United States and other developed nations and has led to calls for the government to act to restrict it.

Near-shore offshoring involves outsourcing work to nearby neighbours such as, in the US case, Canada and Mexico. While there is relatively little concern over near-shore offshoring to Canada, racism seems to be one of the factors involved in the greater concern when Mexico is involved. *On-shore outsourcing* (or *domestic outsourcing*) is of importance, but it does not involve globalization and thus is of only conceptual importance as far as this volume is concerned. *Home-sourcing* can involve globalization when the homes to which the work is outsourced are in a foreign country.

In-sourcing, or the fact that all outsourcing, including offshore outsourcing, involves in-sourcing, is of concern in globalization in that work that is outsourced from one country is in-sourced in another. In the case of the United States (and other developed countries), the work – say call-centre work – that is outsourced to, say, India is simultaneously in-sourced by that country. It is also the case that while it is offshore outsourcing a great deal of work, the United States is also in-sourcing some work that had been performed in other countries.

The chapter then shifts to healthcare and the military and the discussion focuses specifically on offshore outsourcing in both domains. In healthcare some of the issues covered include outsourcing of advanced medical procedures to countries like India, of medical work such as the reading of X-rays, of the consumption of expensive pharmaceuticals to, in the case of the United States, Canada and Mexico (near-shore offshoring), and of the production of various pharmaceuticals, most notably flu vaccine. A similar set of points about the offshore outsourcing of war (which has a long history including the outsourcing by the British of fighting much of the Revolutionary War to paid mercenaries, the Hessians), but it boomed, at least in the case of the United States, following the end of the Cold War. A variety of for-profit private organizations have emerged to which various war functions are outsourced. Thus, so many aspects of the current US war in Iraq are outsourced that one wag joked that President George *Bush*'s 'coalition of the willing' might thus be more aptly described as the 'coalition of the billing'.

The theory that is employed to think about all of this sourcing is Joseph Schumpeter's (1950) *creative destruction*. It is argued that it is this theory that undergirds most thinking, at least by neoliberals, on this (and much else related to globalization). That is, it is recognized that much sourcing is destructive (although in-sourcing, in particular, shows its constructive side), but the overall view is that it is, at least in the long run, constructive, good for the economy and ultimately the capitalist system. The argument is made, however, that this is far too rosy a picture and that there are destructive sides to outsourcing that are just that, destructive, at least for the entities in question. For example, in the case of the United States, outsourcing can be seen as responsible for job loss, the hollowing out or complete destruction of businesses and industries, the evisceration of the military and healthcare system, and the emptying of many lives that were once filled with highly meaningful tasks like parenting.

The theory of creative destruction was invented before the current era of globalization and is ill-suited to deal with it. It is ill-equipped to deal with a situation in which, for example, the jobs lost in one country (perhaps only involving destruction there) are created in another. Schumpeter and followers of his theory always intertwine creativity and destruction, but in the global age (if not always) they clearly can be, and are, separated. Furthermore, the idea needs to be extended from its home in the macro-level economy to other social institutions (e.g. healthcare) and to other levels (meso-, micro-) of analysis. What such a change would mean, in the end, is the creation of a true sociology, not economics, of outsourcing as well as of creative destruction.

Goodman deals with another crucial aspect of the economy – consumption – and its relationship to globalization. However, Goodman focuses more on the cultural rather than economic aspects of consumption and thus his chapter constitutes a nice bridge to the following one by Tomlinson in which the focus shifts entirely to culture and globalization.

The central question raised by Goodman is: While it is clear that the globalization of consumption has cultural effects, does it produce a global culture? After much analysis, including a great effort to define what he means by culture (a system in which meaning is derived from one's place in it and a set of practices that constitute that system), Goodman concludes that to the degree that there is a global culture, it is a consumer culture and whether or not there is a global consumer culture, there is certainly a *Western* consumer culture.

Goodman takes on the oft-discussed issue, both in the globalization literature and in this volume, of cultural homogenization and heterogenization, arguing that it is the wrong issue because *all* cultures are characterized by *both*. Rather, he focuses on the type of evidence that would need to be collected in order to deal with the issue of the homogenization/heterogenization of global culture. Overall, he rejects the idea that the globalization of consumer culture involves the reproduction of identical cultural objects, but rather he sees it as constituting a framework for a new cultural understanding of intra- and inter-social differences. Overall, globalization, especially of consumer culture, makes people more different, but in a similar way. To put this slightly differently, people increasingly assert their differences in a common medium. Citing Levitt, Goodman talks of heteroconsumers, or those who become increasingly alike and indistinct from one another, and yet have simultaneously varied and multiple preferences. At a more macro level, global consumer culture often uses cultural differences as resources to sell similar products with the result that global diversity takes standardized forms. In the end, at least in the realm of consumer culture, what we have is a global system of common difference.

Goodman critically reviews several of the major theoretical approaches to global consumer culture including Sklair's thinking on the culture ideology of consumption (2002), Canclini on hybridization (1995), Barber on Jihad vs McWorld (1995) and Ritzer on McDonaldization (2004b) and the globalization of nothing (2004a). He concludes that we need such theories (and research), and improved ones, in order not only to allow us to understand global consumer culture, but also to point us in the direction of social action needed to deal with the problems it produces.

Tomlinson begins his analysis of global culture with his well-known definition of globalization that emphasizes global connectivity. While he recognizes the importance of economic issues in global connectivity, he feels that we must resist giving it causal primacy (many, including Hashemian and Yach, do) because economic processes are to some extent cultural and culture is not inert and simply acted on by the economic (and other things), but is itself active and transformative. Similarly, culture is both shaped by and shapes globalization.

Like Goodman, Tomlinson asks whether or not there is a global culture. While he sees many obvious examples in the global capitalist system and in environmental effects, there are also many global differences and countervailing trends. Globalization is uneven and neglects and even excludes some areas. Thus, globalization, to Tomlinson, is not quite global. However, he sees, and is critical of, a persistent view that there is a global culture formed, most generally by cultural imperialism emanating from the West, especially the United States. Involved in this is the simultaneous loss of distinct, non-Western cultural traditions. He sees this perspective as focusing on the superficial issue of the global distribution of cultural goods. (I am not so sure that they are superficial, but in any case my concern, and that of others [e.g. Bryman 2003; Ram 2004], is the global spread of systems, like those of McDonald's and Disney, and *not* their products.)

Central to Tomlinson's work is the issue of deterritorialization. The significance of the geographic location of culture is eroding; no longer is culture so tied to the constraints of local circumstances. In terms of his definition of globalization, this means that connectivity is reaching into local culture and the localities of everyday life. This transformation is both perplexing/disruptive and exhilarating/empowering (following Giddens 2000). Involved is the penetration of everyday life by distant forces and the dislodging of everyday meanings from the anchors of the local environment. In the long run, it may be that this weakening of traditional bonds between cultural experience and geographic territory will be the most far-reaching effect of cultural globalization. However, Tomlinson is careful to point out that this does not simply involve loss, but localities also thrive in globalization. Yet, he admits that the culture produced by locality (if such a narrow source of production was ever the case; see Caldwell and Lozada, Part III, for a critique of this view) is no longer the single most important factor in our lived reality. It has been attenuated by deterritorialization with the integration of distant events, processes and relationships into everyday lives. Tomlinson singles out the role of the media and communication technology for their role in deterritorialization, an issue that is focal to a later chapter by Kellner and Pierce. Tomlinson, as always, is very even-handed, arguing that while there might be negatives associated with all of this for, for example, emotions, social relations and cultural identity, there are also many positive potentialities including a new sensibility of cultural openness, human mutuality and global ethical responsibility (versus a view of ethics in a postmodern age which rejects such a totalizing ethic; see Bauman 1993).

Closely related in many ways to culture is the idea of ideology (for evidence on this connection, see definition of this term below), the focus of the next chapter by Steger. Like many (including Tomlinson), Steger feels that his primary concern in the study of globalization – in this case, ideology – has been marginalized because of the focal interest in the field in the economy (and technology). Steger defines ideology as a system of widely shared ideas, patterned beliefs, guiding norms and values, and ideals accepted as truth by some group. People are offered a more or less coherent picture of the world not only as it is, but as it ought to be. While ideology simplifies tremendous complexity, it is often distorted, as well. In addition to distortion, ideology also serves to legitimate and to integrate.

Steger's primary concern is with an ideology he calls globalism, or the hegemonic system of ideas that makes normative claims about a set of social processes called globalization. There are six core claims in globalism:

1   Globalization is about the liberalization and global integration of markets.
2   Globalization is inevitable, irreversible (this devalues human agency and is fundamentally illiberal).
3   Nobody is in charge of globalization (Friedman's [2005] 'electronic herd'); it, especially the market, is self-regulating; and it is not the arbitrary agent of any

single class, group or nation (although in the view of many, US militarism after 9/11 has put the lie to that assertion).

4 Globalization benefits everyone . . . in the long run. Among other things, it is self-correcting, will increase productivity and will move entire societies out of poverty.
5 Globalization furthers the spread of democracy in the world with market, freedom, free trade and democracy linked, even synonymous.
6 Globalization requires the global war on terrorism (but Steger wonders whether this constitutes a turn towards fascism). There is an obvious contradiction between US nationalism in that war and globalization and this leads to the question of whether globalization will be undermined by such contradictions. On the other hand, if globalism can combine such contradictions, that might give it an unprecedented level of ideological dominance.

Of course, there are counter-ideologies on globalization from both the right and the left. In the main, the right adopts particularist protectionism focusing on protecting the well-being of their citizens, while the left supports universalist protectionism involving reducing inequality (especially North–South), and protecting the environment, human and women's rights, and so on. The left is opposed to globalization from above (grobalization) and for globalization from below (glocalization or even localization).

In sum, Steger sees globalism as the dominant ideology of our times that sustains asymmetrical power relations and benefits some at the expense of others. There have been backlashes in the past against globalization that led to the rise of fascism and Nazism with the free market being reduced to an appendage of the state. It is clearly possible that such a reversal could occur again.

Kellner and Pierce turn to the media, which is integral to many of the immediately preceding concerns – ideology, culture and consumer culture. Much of current thinking on the relationship between globalization and the media has its roots in McLuhan's (1962) prescient ideas on the global village. Of course, this brings focal attention to the medium itself (although Marcuse 1964 argued that the problem was not such technologies as the media, but rather the way they were employed in capitalism) in the new media age where, famously, the medium is the message. This led to a new sense of the power of the media to shape both individual subjectivity and culture. Other theoretical perspectives of relevance to thinking about the globalization and the media are those of Baudrillard (signs, the code, hyperreality and global consumer culture [1983, 1998]), DeBord (spectacle, media spectacle, the globalization of such a spectacle and its production and reproduction of capitalism and consumer culture on a global scale [1984]), Hall (the importance of marginal voices, counter-hegemonic narratives [see Rojek 2003]) and the Frankfurt School (the media as a new source of capital realization, social control and its unprecedented influence on culture tending to foreclose the possibility of emancipatory action).

Kellner and Pierce link global media culture both to TNCs (versus Dicken's de-emphasis of them) and to globalization from above. The importance of the state is minimized (also contra Dicken) and seen as merely distributing cultural forms and commodities for the TNCs. While there are obvious American examples of powerful media conglomerates, Kellner and Pierce mention Brazil's Globo and Mexico's Televisa as examples of globalization from above in that they extend media and consumer culture into diverse communities, serve to blur national boundaries, and they have at least the potential not only to supplement, but replace, local culture (versus Tomlinson; Caldwell and Lozada, Part III). Yet, they do, of course, recognize the importance of the global–local struggle and the possibility that the local – especially when a number of local movements, perhaps across the globe, band together – can triumph over the global (globalization from below). In fact, new media, especially those associated with the Internet (e.g. blogs), make such opposition more likely and powerful. In this realm, Kellner and Pierce also mention anti-globalization movement websites (e.g. McSpotlight), Indymedia with hundreds of centres in many different countries, and the Live 8 concerts.

As suggested by DeBord, the media are increasingly characterized by global spectacles such as those associated with 9/11 and its aftermath, the invasion of Iraq, the famous subsequent toppling of the statue of Saddam Hussein and George Bush's appearance on an aircraft carrier announcing (prematurely) the end of hostilities in Iraq. However, these spectacles can cut both ways and serve not only to control people, but also to energize them (e.g. Al-Jazeera's use of many of the same spectacles to help create opposition to the Iraq war) and to make contradictions abundantly clear (as was the case when accelerating hostilities made it clear that Bush's pronouncements about the close of hostilities were simply untrue). The photos taken by soldiers themselves of the abuses at the Abu Ghraib prison escaped the filters of the mainstream media and made their way directly into people's homes via the Internet. Overall, Kellner and Pierce see these as positive developments and, indeed, argue that there are signs that the democratization of the media is underway.

Tumber and Webster take up similar issues in discussing the globalization of information and communication technology in the case of war (see also Schneider, Part III). They focus on information war which has two forms. The first, or hard, form involves the use of sophisticated weaponry (smart missiles; surveillance through, for example, drones; command and control mechanisms) based on advanced computer and communication technology. The second, or soft, form involves great emphasis on the media in wartime and involves thousands of reporters; heavy use of military public relations; exploding use of the Internet, blogs and indy websites; and increasing public involvement around the world through the viewing of war-related events in real time. But the lines between these two forms are blurring with, for example, some of the soft forms becoming weapons (e.g. Al-Jazeera's use of TV images of the horrors associated with US bombing in Iraq which helped fuel the opposition to the war).

Their view of information war is embedded in a modern grand narrative of the transition from industrial to information war. *Industrial war* was mostly between sovereign states, was chiefly fought over territory, involved the mobilization of a large portion of the population, involved large numbers of combatants and led to mass casualties, and the media were used to assist the war effort and were unable to see what was happening behind enemy lines. In *information war*, information permeates all aspects of the war, war is massively asymmetrical dominated by advanced nations and alliances (NATO), involves a small number of troops, many of the troops are knowledge warriors and wars are of short duration. In industrial war the population has direct experience with warfare, whereas in information war that experience is largely, if not totally, mediated.

The media have been long involved, and used, in war, but historically it has been in support of the homeland. Today, the functions of the media are more ambiguous and ambivalent. The increase in their number and diversity has led to increased uncertainty about the messages that are disseminated and received.

Overall, what we are witnessing is a globalization of the media as they relate to war and much else. This leads to a common symbolic environment around the world, although the messages may be received, understood and remembered differently.

The nation-state and its military try to control the war-related messages that do get out, but there is always seepage and most stories get out one way or another. This is aided by growing porosity of the nation-state as a result of e-mail, bloggers and so forth. As did Kellner and Pierce, Tumber and Webster illustrate this with the Abu Ghraib photos, but they add the case of the Baghdad Blogger who was in Baghdad during the early stages of the 2003 US attack and sent out messages that offered an alternative view of what was taking place there.

In the era of globalization with the declining importance of borders, some (e.g. Giddens) see the emergence of states without enemies. However, there are a long list of factors that continue to stimulate conflict between nation-states including increasing inequalities, competition, marketization, technological innovation and hostility towards and apprehension about the have-nots. In addition, there is globalization's stimulation of fundamentalists, or enemies without states (most notably, Al-Qaeda), who are oriented to resist, if not go to war with, the forces that benefit most from globalization and push it most actively and aggressively.

Tumber and Webster end on relatively positive notes emphasizing the fact that the number of democratic states in the world is increasing and that most of the world's states are now democracies. They also perceive an as-yet unfinished trend towards the development of global citizens. They also applaud the fact that nation-states are finding it increasingly difficult to hide human rights abuses; because of the media they are becoming everyone's business. Finally, they see an increasingly common perspective on the world around the globe and conclude that we should be grateful for the new reality.

Much of this, at least as it applies to war, has involved politics and it is to that topic specifically that the next two chapters are devoted. Delanty and Rumford's approach to politics in the global age emphasizes post- and transnational processes and an increased (political) consciousness of the compressed nature of space and time in the world today. Among the key issues today are the decline of the nation-state (a theme repeated many times in this volume – with some dissenters – and in the literature on globalization), the fact that transnational networks and flows are likely to lead to a different kind of politics and the processes of de- as well as re-territorialization. While all of this opens up new emancipatory possibilities, it also can lead to declines in autonomy and increasing fragmentation of the social world.

They see political globalization as involving the tensions between three processes that are interrelated products of globalization. First, there is global geopolitics no longer dominated by the United States and therefore with many centres of power, although contra other views, most of these centres are still seen by them as states. Second, there is a global normative culture (influenced by Meyer's views on the development of a global culture that is a reference point for all) involving such things as human rights, cosmopolitanism and environmentalism. Finally, there are polycentric global networks involving non-territorial politics from a multitude of sites and spaces (e.g. global civil society, INGOs).

In a positive sense, Delanty and Rumford adopt a view similar to that of Tumber and Webster on the worldwide spread of democracy based on parliamentary nation-states. More generally, they argue that democracy has become the universally accepted form of government. Therefore, far from undermining the democratic nation-state, globalization gives it worldwide acceptability. At the same time, they reject the idea that we are moving towards the emergence of a global polity, or a new global order of governance, but rather see a transnational world of political action.

Delanty and Rumford then examine four examples of social transformation from the perspective of the three dynamics mentioned above. First, there is the transformation of the nation-state, nationality and citizenship. They reject a number of extant views on the decline and disappearance of nation-states to argue that while nation states will continue to change, they will continue to be powerful, albeit in a globally connected world that they do not fully control. In terms of the transformation of nationality, they see two types of decoupling – of nationality and citizenship (migrants can better remain tied to their nation and even appeal to international law thereby reducing the linkage between nation and citizenship), and of nationhood and statehood (e.g. new nations [supported by global processes] within states, nationalistic movements within states, states transnationalized).

Second, there is the transformation of the public sphere and communication. While the national public sphere in developed countries has declined due, at least in part, to the rise of commercial mass media, it has increased in less developed societies and, more generally, in the form of global civil society. The global public has grown increasingly important on such issues as human rights, the environment, health and security. Political communication in the public sphere is increasingly framed by global issues. Global normative culture is playing an increasing role in shaping political communication and the politics emanating from it is increasingly confronting economic globalization and its negative consequences.

Third is the issue of the centrality of civil society, or the civil societalization of politics. Global civil society is characterized by INGO-led political campaigns, trans-border social movements, transnational advocacy networks, or to put it in other ways, it is the realm of civic activity that is global in scope, where trans-world issues are addressed, and in which actors organize in supra-national solidarity. Global civil society is not simply the sum of existing national civil societies; it is founded on a non-territorial imaginary. The global civil society is seen as leading to the construction of the mechanisms of polycentric government, the emergence of transnational movements and networks working to erode more territorial organizational forms, working to undermine the importance of the territorial state in favour of new networked forms of opposition, and encouraging individuals to see themselves less as national citizens and also as cosmopolitan citizens (see Beck, this volume) endowed with natural rights.

Fourth, there is the transformation of spaces and borders. We are witnessing the emergence of new political spaces and we need to rethink borders, especially the possibilities of bordering and re-bordering. In addition, it is increasingly possible to think of the globe as a single political space that can be the focus of political attachments and identities, communities of interest and a sphere of action. While Delanty and Rumford offer a generally positive view of global civil society, they recognize that it has a dark side in the form of terrorists and traffickers in drugs, the sex trade and so on.

Blackman deals more specifically with the issue of public policy which he defines as what governments do with their authority and their commitment of resources to what they see as public problems or challenges. Public policy is wide in scope, encompassing foreign policy, social policies, regulation of scientific activity and so on. Globalization is a new context for public policy that creates both new opportunities and new risks. Among the public policies that relate to globalization are regulation, fiscal measures, investment and spending decisions, and trade agreements.

For some governments, the issue is how to better benefit from globalization in general and global commerce in particular; while for others it is how to protect themselves from threats to indigenous economies and cultures. The key tension as far as Blackman is concerned is between trade liberalization and such social issues as inequality and exclusion. Thus, 80 per cent of the world's GNP goes to one billion people; the other five billion souls share the remaining 20 per cent. However, it is not clear that globalization is the source of this inequality (and other problems), especially since globalization has brought with it various advances (e.g. extreme poverty is in retreat being halved between 1981 and 2001, increasing democratization). Yet poverty and inequality continue on a massive scale and are deepening in large parts of the world.

Blackman's interest is in the roles that the nation-states can still perform (although they vary greatly in their capacities) in a globalized world, especially in the areas of education and training, research and development, and infrastructure. The globalized economy remains (and perhaps always will) an emergent product of the international order of states and smart state policies continue to make a huge difference for its citizens. Blackman accords great important to state spending on education in light of the growing importance of knowledge economies. Governments need to create the conditions not only to produce, but attract, knowledge workers. However, this means that inequality will grow within a given country unless measures are taken to better equalize incomes between those knowledge workers and those who are less well trained and educated.

In terms of global inequality, Blackman looks at impoverished Africa and argues that most nations there cannot transform their situation on their own. They need massive external support, more trade and debt cancellation; more aid is a necessary but not sufficient condition for greatly reducing inequality.

Blackman also takes on the neoliberal argument that a smaller state is the route to global success. Again the issue is how smart a state is, not how big or small it is. In addition, he defends the relatively large welfare state against neoliberal arguments that it crowds out private enterprise and that it creates dependency among service users and benefit claimants. He argues, however, that there is no evidence that the welfare state is bad for economic growth. Economic globalization may change the relationship between nation-states and public policy but it does not need to curtail welfare provisions. Welfare states need to search for ways (especially through education, training) to take advantage of globalization and to reduce their vulnerability to its negative characteristics. However, Blackman recognizes that the welfare state is threatened by ageing populations, increased healthcare costs and unemployment. The future is uncertain for those states with these characteristics and others such as shrinking labour forces and generous benefit systems.

The next several chapters deal with a diverse array of social institutions and their relationship to globalization. Beyer deals with religion and globalization and while it can be argued that religion globalized before anything else, Beyer complains that it has received little attention (except for Islam and fundamentalism) because of the argument (that occurs several times in this volume) that the predominant focus has been on economics and politics. While religion (like globalization) is a highly contested concept, he focuses on institutional religion and under that heading on three specific issues in terms of its relationship to globalization.

The first is the issue of the importance of religion in transnational migration; in the bringing of institutional religion to new locales. Migrants transplant religions into new places making those places more multi-religious. They also generate in those locales new and different versions of their religions and their versions are influenced and altered by local religions. This, in turn, can alter religion in the homeland. Thus, transnational migration globalizes religion spatially and contributes to the further pluralization of religion around the world.

Second is the spread of religious organizations and movements sometimes through migration, but also through independent missions. Here the Christian Church – through its missionaries – has been central in this as has Islam, which created the most global system prior to the modern era. Special attention must be given to European Christianity, especially the Roman Catholic Church. However, it is important to remember that there were not just outflows from Europe, but reverse- and cross-flows producing original variants on Christianity. Multi-directionality is especially important in the case of Christian Pentecostalism which began in the United States in the early twentieth century, but grew rapidly worldwide producing many variations and localized forms that are linked through publications, conferences, electronic media and travel. It is now the second largest Christian identification in the world. It is centred away from core nations in Africa, Latin America and parts of Asia. Many other religions have expanded globally, but special note must be made of Buddhism and Islam and their renewed expansion.

Third, there is the issue of the role of religion in global social and political movements. Religions are often a fertile source for visions of the good and proper society, what a nation and state are all about, what makes them distinct from others, and so on. They seek to put their ideas in effect in the state. Islam in the Iranian Revolution and the New Christian Right in the United States today are good examples of religious movements with national and global implications.

The fact that the religions discussed by Beyer can be traced back thousands of years is a reflection of the view held by some that globalization is far from a new process. However, in the last two centuries we have seen the emergence of a global system of several religions and they can be seen as, in the main, a modern phenomenon. Ancient or modern, religion is a critical part of the process of globalization.

In Manicas's view, there has been a phenomenal growth of education, especially higher education, in many countries and it can be attributed to globalization, although the initial impetus was from governments accepting the importance of economic growth and the idea that education was critical to that, including the development of a knowledge economy.

Manicas looks at a number of aspects of higher education in order to ascertain the degree to which they have become globalized. For example, the commitment to research had its origins in German universities, but in the early twentieth century the United States created a now globally accepted model of the research university. Public funding of universities in the United States is declining while in much of the rest of the world it remains high. Yet there are signs that this, too, will follow the US model and decline elsewhere in the world as the privatization of the university accelerates. For-profit universities are increasingly important in the United States (e.g. Phoenix University), but as a result of Americanization there are many more of them outside the United States. These changes, and others, have been made possible and expedited by new technologies that enable, among other things, distance learning.

Manicas fears that it may not be the best features of American higher education that are being globalized. For example, the model of American academic research that is emulated throughout the world is often narrow, dominated by replication rather than new research, and advances careers while being unclear as to whether it generates much in the way of new knowledge. Other aspects of American higher education – tenure with the relegation of a large part of teaching to teaching assistants, and department specialization that isolates faculties – are also globalized to mixed effect. Overall, it is not clear that the best features of American higher education are the ones that are being globalized.

Globally, higher education is increasingly influenced by markets, managerialism and the commodification of education and is increasingly run, albeit often poorly, like a business. However, Manicas argues that there is a place for business-like universities, but also needed is state support and rules.

Andrews and Grainger see sport as both a central element of the global popular and an important vehicle for institutionalizing the global condition (the Olympic Committee has more members than the UN!). At first, sport was clearly local, but by the early twentieth century a global sport system and imaginary had developed. In the second half of the twentieth century sport was increasingly colonized by capitalism. The Andrews–Grainger analysis is heavily informed by the global–local nexus and it goes to great lengths to argue that sport today is best seen as glocal (and not, in my terms, grobal, or as a romanticized local phenomenon). In fact, they distinguish two types of the glocal. The *organic glocal* is globalized, internationalized sport that has been incorporated into the local. The *strategic glocal* involves TNCs exploiting the local, through either interiorized glocal strategizing (global sport co-opting and exploiting sports' local dimension [this sounds very much like a form of grobalization]) or exteriorized glocal strategizing (importation and mobilization of sporting differences into the local market).

Andrews and Grainger further distinguish between glocal sport practices, spectacles and bodies. In terms of practices, there is the transformation of imposed, transplanted sporting practices into local contexts where they are transformed by the local. The way in which Indians came to transform the British-imposed cricket is an excellent example (Appadurai 1996). The way the Olympics reflects, especially in its televised versions, the local setting and nation in which it occurs is an example of a glocal spectacle. Finally, the glocal sport body is a function of the migration of athletes and the way stars from halfway around the world are integrated into local teams.

The same issues concern Caldwell and Lozada, although not through the lens of sport, but as anthropologists concerned with culture in general. They recognize that globalization does affect local communities in various ways, but it is moderated and modified by the active agency of people in local societies, their choice of particular lifestyles, their selective adoption of non-local cultural practices and the differential impact of the global depending on the social and economic resources of the actor in the local community.

The long history of work on economic and cultural imperialism worries about the identity crises that result from the erosion of cultural values, the disappearance of civic engagement, the commodification of social life and the loss of meaning in everyday life. As a result, local settings are seen as becoming no where, nowhere places, non-places, simulacra. Further, because of time-space compression (Harvey 1989), things move too quickly to be identified as local.

One of the ways Caldwell and Lozada respond to such criticisms is to argue that much of it is animated by the myth of the local. Among the components of that myth are the ideas that there exists a local untouched by modern conveniences of civilization; that possesses cultural practices that are unique, exotic, primitive and unchanging; that is small in scale; that is culturally and socio-economically homogeneous; and is idealized so that, as they used to say in the TV show *Cheers*, in the local 'everyone knows your name'.

They suggest that to avoid such negative views, it is better to see the local not so much as a thing to be discovered, but as a set of processes of social change. The issue, then, becomes how to best represent these processes. Anthropologists tend to see fragility, diversity and contradictions within these seemingly homogeneous communities. To them, the focus should be on the processes through which the local is generated; on location-work. In general, localism is a dynamic, interactive and continually renegotiated process.

After looking at four types of promising studies of, and routes into, the local, they conclude that locality is not lost in the tide of globalization. People are being affected by the challenges of globalization, but they are also creating those challenges, as well as both globalization and locality.

In the final chapter in Part II, Hashemian and Yach deal with the challenges and the opportunities of globalization for public health. Globalization has led to increased aggregate life expectancy, but it also has tended to widen global economic disparities. Poor nations tend to have poorer health as a result of limited access to health services, education, sanitation and adequate nutrition and housing. Conversely, poor health tends to limit economic growth in those nations mainly by adversely affecting productivity. Developing countries have a disproportionate share of mortality and morbidity, much of which could be prevented inexpensively and treated effectively if the money was available. Ninety per cent of the total burden of disease is concentrated in low and middle income countries which account for only 10 per cent of healthcare expenditures. Even though the United States spends the most on healthcare, it ranks significantly lower than other developed countries on a number of public health indicators. This, of course, is traceable to the wide disparities between whites and racial and ethnic minorities in the United States. Thus, for example, the infant mortality rate in the United States has been increasing and the rate for African Americans is twice that of whites. Generally, while wealth is important, once minimum per capita incomes are achieved, health comes to be affected by factors other than wealth.

Developing countries also suffer disproportionately from hunger and malnutrition. This is especially important for children because those who are underweight are, as adults, likely to be less physically and intellectually productive and to suffer more chronic illnesses and disabilities. This carries on intergenerationally as their ability to provide adequate nutrition for their children is compromised. To being underweight is now being added the increase in obesity among the poor in less developed countries.

Developing countries also suffer from the double burden of traditional problems such as malnutrition and infectious diseases as well as now the chronic diseases usually associated with developed nations. Of special importance from the point of view of globalization is the increasing global marketing of tobacco, alcohol, sugar and fat (the latter two especially aimed at children) and the consequent global spread of diseases associated with these products. Despite beliefs to the contrary, the vast majority of chronic diseases occur at younger ages and in low and middle income countries. Further, the rising cost of dealing with chronic diseases in developing countries will adversely affect their ability to deal with infectious diseases.

Then there is the increasing prevalence of borderless diseases, many of them relatively new, such as SARS, avian flu and HIV/AIDS. These spread readily throughout the globe and the response to them must be equally global. As I write, there is fear of a pandemic of avian flu and should it occur its spread will be faster and more extensive because of globalization. It is true that the ability to deal with such a pandemic is also enhanced by globalization (global monitoring and the ability to get health workers and pharmaceuticals to the site of an outbreak), but it appears at the moment that globalization is more likely to spread the disease than it is to help in preventing a pandemic.

There needs to be a new approach to global governance and health. The World Health Organization is no longer the major player it once was. Other organizations have become increasingly important (e.g. the Melinda and Bill Gates Foundation), but none is the unquestioned global leader. Until recently there has been no monitoring of these organizations. A concerted global approach (or approaches) is needed which operates under the assumption that health is a human right. It is clear that in the area of health, and much else, both the gains and the risks from globalization are great.

Note

1 This stands in contrast to the dominant view throughout this volume (although not mine) that it is heterogenization not homogenization that characterizes globalization.

References

Appadurai, A. 1996. *Modernity at Large: Cultural Dimension of Globalization*. Minneapolis: University of Minnesota Press.

Barber, B. 1995. *Jihad vs. McWorld*. New York: Times Books.

Baudrillard, J. 1998 [1970]. *The Consumer Society*. London: Sage.

Baudrillard, J. 1983. *Simulations*. New York: Semiotext(e).

Bauman, Z. 1993. *Postmodern Ethics*. Oxford: Basil Blackwell.

Bauman, Z. 1998. *Globalization: The Human Consequences*. New York: Columbia University Press.

Bryman, A. 2003. 'McDonald's as a Disneyized institution: Global implications', *American Behavioral Scientist*, 47, 157–64.

Canclini, G. 1995. *Hybrid Culture: Strategies for Entering and Leaving Modernity*. Minneapolis: University of Minnesota Press.

DeBord, G. 1994 [1967]. *The Society of the Spectacle*. New York: Zone Books.

Friedman, T. 2005. *The World Is Flat*. New York: Farrar, Strauss and Giroux.

Giddens, A. 2000. *Runaway World: How Globalization Is Reshaping our Lives*. New York: Routledge.

Harvey, D. 1989. *The Condition of Postmodernity*. Oxford: Blackwell.

Hochschild, A. n.d. 'The nanny chain', *The American Prospect*, 11 (4). Available at <http://www.prospect.org/print/V11/4/hochschild-a.html>, retrieved 1 January 2007.

McLuhan, M. 1962. *The Gutenberg Galaxy: The Making of Typographic Man*. Toronto: University of Toronto Press.

Marcuse, H. 1964. *One-Dimensional Man: Studies in the Ideology of Advanced Industrial Society*. London: Routledge.

Peters, T.J. and Waterman, R.H. 1988. *In Search of Excellence: Lessons from America's Best Run Companies*. New York: Warner Books.

Ram, U. 2004. 'Glocommodification: How the global consumes the local; McDonald's in Israel', *Current Sociology*, 52, 11–31.

Ritzer, G. 2004a. *The Globalization of Nothing*. Thousand Oaks, CA: Pine Forge Press.

Ritzer, G. 2004b. *The McDonaldization of Society*, rev. New Century edn. Thousand Oaks, CA: Pine Forge Press.

Rojek, C. 2003. *Stuart Hall*. Cambridge: Polity Press.

Sassen, S. 1991. *The Global City*. Princeton, NJ: Princeton University Press.

Schumpeter, J. 1950. *Capitalism, Socialism and Democracy*. 3rd edn. New York: Harper and Brothers.

Sklair, L. 2002. *Globalization: Capitalism and Its Alternatives*. New York: Oxford University Press.

Chapter 9

The End of Globalization?
The Implications of Migration
for State, Society and Economy

SUBHRAJIT GUHATHAKURTA, DAVID JACOBSON
AND NICHOLAS C. DELSORDI

GLOBALIZATION AND MIGRATION

Globalization is now a pervasive word that seems to underpin most discussions of cross-national flows of goods, services, capital, people, technology, ideas and culture. The term often alludes to an elusive superstructure that ties together far-flung regions of the world through a web of regulated as well as unregulated exchanges. The wide use and application of the term led to the warning by Held et al. (1999: 1): 'globalization is in danger of becoming, if it has not already become, the cliché of our times: the big idea which encompasses everything from global financial markets to the internet but which delivers little substantive insight into the contemporary human condition'. The processes and structures of globalization rest on a theoretically contested sphere, but there are enough common elements to enable meaningful dialogue. In other words, the neoclassical economist examining convergence or divergence of costs and prices across the globe, the sociologist interested in extra-territorially based social networks and the political scientist who is concerned about the changing nature of citizenship and human rights are all addressing globalization as a process where the increasing speed and volume of cross-national flows have more tightly integrated the social and economic fortunes in the impacted countries. Although increased mobility is the hallmark of globalization, labour mobility has lagged far behind the mobility in goods, services and technologies. In this chapter we examine the contradiction between market and political forces as they relate to international labour mobility. Specifically, we address four related questions: (1) How are migration flows and migrant types changing in the post-Cold War era? (2) How do globalizing forces regulate such migration flows? (3) What impacts do migrants have on the receiving as well as home countries? And (4) how do states and other institutions mediate social and political differences between migrant and native populations in a globalized world?

Given that globalization has a differential impact on different regions, the nature of migration flows would also be diverse and linked to the nature of interaction between the receiving and home countries. The movement of information technology (IT) professionals from India to OECD countries and the illegal agricultural labourers from Mexico to California are responding to an economic demand in the receiving region. However, the social and political impact of these two types of migrants is quite different. Indeed, no other aspect of globalization articulates the disjunction between market rationality and social stability more than migration. Regardless, there is a growing sense that globalization is an inexorable and irreversible force. Unfettered movement of people will perhaps be the final project of globalization and mark, borrowing from Fukuyama, 'the end of globalization'. The consequences of such a historic moment on the nature and function of nation-states would be breathtaking. From the current vantage point, some implications of a borderless world can be gauged by studying the growing number of *transnationals* who maintain 'a set of intense cross-border social relations that enable them to participate in the activities of daily life in two or more nations' (Portes 1996). This chapter also provides a brief review of the distinctive nature of transnational communities and the ensuing emergence of different sets of identities and political structures.

Migration facts

Our ability to quantify migration flows is limited by a number of data and definitional issues. A significant number of countries either do not collect such data or do not report migration statistics to international bodies. In addition, the term 'immigrant' is defined differently in different countries. For example, in the settlement countries (Australia, Canada, New Zealand and United States) an immigrant is a person who is 'foreign-born', while in many other countries (especially those within the European Union) an immigrant is considered to be a person of 'foreign nationality'.[1] In addition, few countries keep track of their expatriates and their whereabouts, which would offer an opportunity to reconcile the number of migrants reported by destination countries. Other confounding issues include variation in defining permanency of move, residency period required for migrant status, as well as the problem of tracking illegal immigrants. Regardless, given the high social and political significance of migrants in most countries, data on migration flows and migrant stock have been compiled by many scholars and international organizations (OECD; the World Bank; United Nations; the International Labour Organization (ILO); Zlotnik 1999; Castles and Miller 1998; Champion 1994; Stalker 2000, 2005). We have relied on these and other sources to report on some overarching trends in international migration with a focus on shifts that may have occurred in the post-Cold War era.

International migration has ebbed and flowed throughout history and the current rates of migration flows are unspectacular compared to similar rates in the past. In the period between the industrial revolution and World War I, around 60 million migrants from Europe went to the countries of the New World – Australia, Argentina, Brazil, Canada and the United States (Solimano 2001). By far the largest group at that time, about 75 per cent, went to the United States (Stalker 2005). This flow was somewhat contained in the United States through the Quota Act of 1921 and

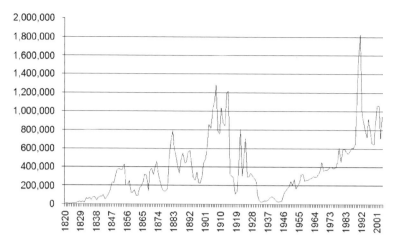

Figure 9.1 Immigration to the United States, 1820–2001
Source: US Department of Homeland Security, *Yearbook of Immigration Statistics 2004*.

the Immigration Restriction Act of 1924. Movement of population gained momentum again after World War II. After the War, about 15 million people, mostly Europeans, transferred from one country to another. This was aided by a postwar economic boom in the United States that created a demand for labour, which coincided with unpopular austerity policies in Europe. According to US data on immigration, the volume of immigrants increased every decade after 1940 (Solimano 2001). Currently the United States is accommodating about one million immigrants per year (see Figure 9.1).[2]

The growing numbers of immigrants are pushing up the total stock of foreign-born population in many countries. Most recent estimates available from the United Nations suggest that around 191 million people currently reside in a country other than their country of origin (United Nations General Assembly 2006). Contrary to popular perceptions, developing nations accommodate as much as 40 per cent of the global foreign-born population. According to recent OECD statistics, about 7.8 per cent of the population in 28 member countries is foreign-born (OECD 2005). In the United States, 13 out of every 100 people are born in another country. Of the total foreign-born population in all OECD countries, the largest group is from Europe, followed by Asia and Latin America. In the United States, however, Latin Americans comprise the largest foreign-born community, followed by Asians and then people from Caribbean nations.

Although the total volume of migration flows has not registered a substantial shift during the post-Cold War globalization era, the characteristics of migrants in this period are distinctively different from the past. In particular, the proportion of migrants from the developed world has declined together with large increases in the proportion of migrants from the developing world. About 50 per cent of all migrants to Australia and 70 to 90 per cent of all migrants to North America have come from developing countries during the past 15 years (OECD 2005; Champion 1994). The break-up of the Soviet Union and the removal of the Berlin Wall have reconfigured boundaries in Europe and unleashed a massive movement of people mostly within Europe but also to other parts of the world. Large movements of populations have been recorded between East and West Germany, from Poland to France, and from the former Soviet Union to Israel. Another significant group of Eastern Europeans has migrated to North America, mostly from Hungary and Poland. These are unprecedented flows based on past migration from Warsaw Pact countries, which amounted to less than 100,000 annually (Widgren 1989).

The characteristics of recent immigrants to the developed countries in North America, Western Europe and Australia also suggest a dualism in terms of occupational skills and human capital (Champion 1994; Borjas 1990). At one end of the spectrum is a growing demand for highly skilled and technically competent personnel, which is driving the flow of workers to these countries on special long-term visa status (many of them eventually emigrate permanently). In addition, the flow of students from other countries tends to boost the high skilled labour force of the receiving countries since many of them accept jobs and become residents of the countries in which they complete their education. Through a careful examination of data in the 1990 and 2000 Census of Population as well as in the 2004 Current Population Survey (CPS), Freeman (2005) reports that in 2000 the foreign-born made up 17 per cent of the bachelor's Science and Engineering (S&E) workforce, 29 per cent of master's S&E workers and 38 per cent of PhD S&E workers in the United States. These numbers not only indicate huge gains when compared to 1990 statistics but they also herald large shifts in the future, given the significant foreign-born cohort under the age of 45.

At the other end of the spectrum is a rising trend in illegal immigration and asylum seekers. As noted by Hatton and Williamson (2004), the number of refugees worldwide has jumped by a factor of four and asylum seekers by a factor of ten since the early 1970s. In the United States, the number of asylum seekers during 1991–2000 increased over 100 per cent compared to the previous decade (1981–1990) (USDOJ-INS 2003: Table 25). Estimates of the unauthorized resident population in the United States also grew 100 per cent from 1990 to 2000 (USDOJ-INS 2003). The flow of clandestine or illegal immigrants to Europe has been estimated to be as large as half a million a year by the International Center for Migration Policy Development (Coppel et al. 2001). The estimate of undocumented migrants in the beginning of 1999 was 270,000 in Japan and at least 53,000 in Australia.

Although the dualistic nature of migrant skills and aptitudes has an overarching impact on policy debates, this characterization hides significant variation by professions, type of work and geography. Mahroum (2000) identified five major groups within the high-skilled foreign-born workforce: (1) senior managers and executives; (2) engineers and technicians; (3) scientists; (4) entrepreneurs; and (5) students. The motivation, incentives and length of commitment to live and work in a foreign country vary considerably among the five major groups noted above. For example, senior managers and executives are usually associated with large multinational organizations and show high mobility across national boundaries. In addition, they are attracted to metropolitan areas that provide a high quality environment with significant cultural and entertainment amenities. In contrast, the low skilled workforce tends to flow towards established concentrations/enclaves of ethnic groups to which they belong. These ethnic enclaves provide support and information networks that mitigate risks and enhance opportunities for gainful employment.

Migration in the context of globalizing forces

Traditionally, the factors that regulated migration flows were conveniently categorized as 'push' and 'pull' factors. The 'push' factors were related to motivations of migrants and the contextual issues in home countries that made it potentially difficult for migrants to reach their goals. For example, the gap in relative expected incomes between the home and host countries is an important factor influencing the decision to migrate. More critical 'push' factors include wars, famines, political persecution and other economic disruptions. However, 'push' factors alone do not determine the actual migration movements. These movements, in the most part, flow to regions that offer some combination of a favourable immigration policy, established formal and informal networks that cater to specific migrants, labour shortages within the native-born in specific sectors and a similarity between linguistic/cultural elements in the home and host nations. The characteristics of the destination countries described above are some examples of the 'pull' (or demand) side factors affecting migration flows.

Within the context of globalization, the traditional 'push' and 'pull' factors have been amplified through both the global dispersion of information and increased global–local, or 'glocal', interactions. The dispersion of information is happening at several levels. International media, spearheaded by CNN, the BBC and others, are able to bring real-time news and information to most parts of the world. This is aided by other global forces that strive to continuously lower the costs of technology enabling wider groups of people greater access to information. International brands that splash across television screens and large signboards in remote corners of the world create a global consumer market, thereby homogenizing tastes, desires and incentives globally. The penetration of global brands in new territories often overwhelms local products, thereby dramatically transforming the local and regional economy, dislocating jobs and increasing the incentive for migration. In other cases, multinational industries absorb local brands and create strong glocal linkages to the region. In all such situations, the increased flow of goods, services, capital and information from one part of the globe to another also leads to increased flows of labour.

The intensity of global–local interactions is indeed mediated by advances in technology. As mentioned earlier, improved technologies both increase market penetration and reduce the costs of access to such globally procured information and products. The rapidity of technological diffusion is also allowing countries to 'leapfrog' technological frontiers and arrive quickly at the current international standard for that technology. A prime example of such leapfrogging is the increasing use of high-end mobile phones in developing countries. For instance, mobile subscribers in low-income countries registered an annual percentage growth rate of 117 per cent compared to a rate of 47 per cent for high-income countries during 1995–8 (ITU 1999). Consequently, the developing countries' share in the world mobile market increased from 5 per cent in 1990 to 20 per cent in 1999, and that of the Asia-Pacific region rose from 15 to 20 per cent during the same period (Wai 2001). More importantly, a large proportion of new mobile subscribers in developing countries are relatively poor people (*The Economist* 1999).

Potential migrants respond to increased flows of information from traditional media outlets as well as from their own family and social networks that are becoming more global in scope. The knowledge of diasporic communities in various parts of the world is becoming more personal given the closer interactions with members of the diaspora. The ease of movement between countries and the availability of cheap communication channels such as phone calls and emails have raised the intensity of contact. The high level of contact provides a powerful incentive to migrate given that the presence of such diasporic communities reduces search costs and improves the likelihood of finding gainful employment. The ethnic diaspora also impacts the home countries through investments and remittances. Through their investments in home countries, these diaspora provide a bridge between the lifestyles and consumption patterns in the source and destination countries. The conspicuous consumption of foreign-residents mostly in real estate but also in other high-price consumer items in places within the source country has a significant impact on the local economy. While there is a positive spillover effect of such spending, there are also costs such as the inflation of housing prices. Regardless, even well-settled individuals who were otherwise comfortable in their current surroundings in developing countries are tempted to migrate and become global consumers.

Recent immigration policies in many developed countries are selectively reducing barriers for some types of migrants; thereby abetting the 'pull' factors affecting migration flows to these countries. These policies are driven by several pressing issues in the OECD countries including labour shortages in some sectors, an ageing population profile and its impact on the welfare state, the needs of multinational companies and the demands of the increasingly multiethnic and multicultural polity. The flow of IT professionals to the United States in the 1990s, mostly in response to the sharp increase in demand for programmers to address the 'millennium bug', led to a fundamental shift in the perception and utility of a foreign-trained IT workforce. The cost and quality trade-offs of such a migrant workforce have been so profound that the industry cannot now compete globally without the benefits of global outsourcing (both offshore and in-shore). Other sectors of the economy in the United Staes that have become perennially dependent on foreign workers include the healthcare sector (nurses, doctors, radiologists etc.), and the education sector (school teachers, professors, research scientists, among other educators). Given the demographic profile of the country, the need for foreign workers in these sectors is expected to rise in the future. Consequently, immigration policies will continue to favour those migrants whose skills are in high demand in the host countries.

The welfare state in many OECD countries is heading towards a crisis, in part due to the low birth rates and increasing ratio of pensioners to total workforce. The scale of the problem as estimated by the OECD, in parallel with work at the European Commission, suggests that pension expenditures in relation to GDP in the European Union countries could rise on average by about 3 percentage points between now and 2050. Similar estimates also pointed to a gradual rise of total government health expenditures by more than 2 percentage points relative to GDP over the next 50 years (Visco 2001). Increasing the labour force with younger migrants who contribute to the social security system through taxes and other payments seems to be an attractive proposition for many European governments. However, the European governments are also striving to balance the long-term economic needs with the potential destabilizing effect of high rates of migration on society.

Among the OECD countries that have escaped the demographic shift up the age profile are countries like the United States, the United Kingdom and France that have slowly but steadily institutionalized a multicultural and multiethnic society. The evolution of such a multicultural society within liberal democracies is a continuing project, the ramifications of which are not well understood. Regardless, the process of societal change towards multiculturalism brings the perception of a globalized world closer to home, while, at the same time, it catalyses labour migration. In fact, the forces of multiculturalism, globalization and labour migration reinforce each other through a dynamic web of relationships that inexorably lead towards a more globalized world.

Migration impacts

What are the potential effects of migration, driven by globalization, on the international dimension of economic inequality? Neo-classical economic migration theory has consistently predicted that recent increases in international migration will, in the long run, lead to a convergence of wage levels across countries and, hence, between-nation inequality should continue to decrease. Castles (2002) argues conversely that developed and developing world disparities in income will continue to grow as they have throughout the past century. However, recent literature (see Firebaugh 2003) has found that (when controlling for population size) between-nation inequalities have actually declined in the last few decades, while within-nation inequality has increased (and particularly for core Western states). This recent inequality transition models neo-classical theories. However, older theories tended to stress that if wage convergence did occur, then there would be an ultimate decline in transnational migration (since both push and pull factors tend to rely on income and wage differences across borders, and these two factors would gradually fade away). However, while world inequality is on the decline, international migration continues to rise, which challenges older theoretical assertions.

At the regional or local level, migration effects are more robust, since recent immigrants tend to be regionally concentrated. Furthermore, studies that do not separate men and women in their analyses run the risk of generalizing their findings to all citizens, when in fact, evidence suggests that there are differential effects of wages when we bracket-out men and women. For example, Borjas (2004) found

A recent strand of literature has called attention to the possible effects of certain migrants on the wages and earnings potential of those who compete with these migrants in the labour market – low-skilled workers with high school or lower educational attainment. On the whole, it appears that the results are highly contingent upon the level of analysis. For example, at the national level, it seems that migration has only a negligible effect on wages (this is also the case for the effect of migration of local income inequality – also called earnings polarization). The effect of, say, women's entrance into the labour force, the massive entrance of baby boomers into the market during the 1960s and 1970s or the structural movement of the economy towards deindustrialization and growing service-orientation *may* be as strong or stronger than the effect of migration *itself* (Morris and Western 1999). Therefore the effect of low-skilled migration on the wages of low-skilled native workers is ambiguous at best at the level of the nation-state.

that for *men*, across the 1960–2000 period, increasing immigration has *indeed* harmed native workers' wages. However, Borjas also explains that, for example, the immigrant influx that entered between 1980 and 2000 lowered wages for native high-school dropouts by 7.4 per cent and by only 3.6 per cent for college graduates. More specifically, white native wages were lowered by 3.5 per cent overall, black native wages lowered by 4.5 per cent and, interestingly, native Hispanic wages lowered by a full 5 per cent. Studies looking at women only have found that in both 1980 and 1990, a higher percentage of Mexican immigrant women in US metropolitan areas tended to hurt Mexican immigrant women *themselves* more than any other social group. There was also evidence to suggest that 'where Mexican immigrant women go, higher earnings and wages for non-Hispanic white women have been evident' (Gonzalez Baker 1999: 266). Thus, the differential effects by gender are symptomatic of the larger issue that localized labour markets (as well as occupations and jobs) tend to be heavily segregated by sex.

While we must recognize the multitude of effects that the dual processes of globalization and migration have on receiving communities, we must not forget that transnational migration also has profound and lasting, albeit smaller, effects on the communities of origin. As Castles (1998) explains, *emigration* is one aspect of the dissolution of traditional economic and social structures resulting from globalization. He argues that entire countries may develop 'cultures of emigration' (such as in Italy or the Philippines). This not only has the potential to divide the sending community into segments that are more 'nationalist' or oriented towards sustaining the local, indigenous culture *and* those who are predestined (due to previous familial migrant legacies) to emigrate and thus hold negative sentiments towards the local social structure, but it also can create precarious situations for gender and family relations among those who *do* remain for a lifetime. For example, empirical studies of Mexican migrant communities have found that men often migrate in response to the economic necessities of marriage and children and the growing needs of a family. Women's migration, however, does not increase with the formation of a family, and the rate of movement among women remains quite low throughout the early familial years (Kanaiaupuni 2000: 1318).

What this means is that the pre-existing gender division of household labour (that already exists at an extreme level in the Mexican patriarchal culture) becomes further reinforced, as increasing amounts of women in heavy 'sending' communities bear a disproportionate amount of the labour in the 'private' sphere as men leave the community. Another issue for sending communities involves the expansion of economic 'remittances'. Increasingly, the progression of the technological means of transferring money has created a situation where many sending countries have been altered structurally. For example, in remitting earnings back home to family members, migrants also affect the local distribution of income, thereby changing the relative deprivation experienced by others (who do not migrate), which, in turn, affects their propensity to migrate. In the end, remittances not only create more polarization 'back home', they also tend to promote and expand already existing migrant networks, thus leaving the local structure altered economically, socially, as well as politically (in the sense that changes in the distribution of income tends to correlate with changes in electoral behaviour as well as the effectiveness of a democracy). After all, it is a consistent finding that a large middle class (which usually declines as income polarization grows) is vital to a nation, since it has been found to contribute not only to economic growth, but to social and political stability as well (Pressman 2001; Thurow 1984).

Another dimension of the impacts of migration for the source countries is the loss of human capital in the form of high-skilled and educated workers who contribute their talents to a foreign country. Often the welfare system in the source countries provides considerable scarce resources for the education of this workforce without reaping the direct benefits of this investment. However, it is now generally accepted that the net effect of high-skilled migration is positive for both the source and destination countries. While the developed (destination) countries are able to leverage their technical and research and development infrastructure through the efforts of a global pool of talented workers, the source countries also benefit from remittances, international networks and leadership in developing innovative sectors. Recent research has also pointed to a positive relationship between trade in goods and services between countries and the size of ethnic diasporas of the trading partners (Bardhan and Guhathakurta 2004). There is also significant evidence of reverse migration, where foreign-born residents return to their native countries, bringing with them their breadth of experience, talents, entrepreneurial zeal and capital. Hence, denying the well-educated workforce the ability to migrate would not only be, in the words of Adam Smith, 'an evident violation of natural liberty and justice', but also counterproductive for both the source and destination countries (Griswold 2003: 24).

Implications for national and supra-national institutions

Broad arguments emerged in the migration literature in the 1990s over the impact of various forms of migration, notably guest workers and undocumented or illegal immigration, on citizenship, human rights and the state.

One approach suggested that the scale and character of postwar immigration waves from the South to the North had fundamentally altered the nature of citizenship and the nation-state. Rights increasingly became predicated on residency, not citizenship status. States in an uneven, piecemeal fashion turned concomitantly to international human rights law and institutions (notably in Western Europe) to account for the large foreign or immigrant populations in their midst. This was accompanied by a shift in the perception of the nation-state as a political-cultural or ethnically homogeneous entity (at least in aspiration) to a state as a framework for accommodating varying versions of multiculturalism. The state did not necessarily 'weaken' in this context; indeed, as a bureaucratic entity the state could even loom larger, as it regulated and mediated the legal thicket generated by these changes. Even when movements sought to increase the importance of citizenship, such as in the case of Proposition 187 in California, the net effect was to induce growing dual citizenship thus undermining traditional notions of citizenship further.[3]

However, less noticed in this discussion were the institutional changes – and institutional (and associated normative) tensions – induced *within* the state.

Increased global flows of all kinds, from migration to trade, are matched by a growing density of law, domestically as well as internationally. This is akin to the growing role of law domestically – in its density, in its increased specialization in different issue areas, in the growth in size and numbers of different entities – in industrializing countries from the eighteenth through to the twentieth centuries. Indeed the increasing role of law is related to the growing salience of the state domestically. As the classical sociologist Émile Durkheim (1984) suggested, the number of social or economic relationships is proportional to the legal rules that enable them and, furthermore, if social life generally is to have any regularity, it becomes organized, and law is that organization in its most precise form. Encounters become much more multifaceted and nuanced and, as a consequence, demand increasing regulation and institutionalization to ensure predictability and continuity, be it from a social, political or economic perspective. Migration is of particular interest in this context because it creates immediate (in its root sense of 'unmediated') social, political and economic effects that are not experienced in, say, trade in oranges.

The difference with the industrializing states of past centuries, however, is that there is no central global government to step in and regulate this process, such as national governments did through anti-trust acts, welfare support and the general panoply of measures that followed industrialization in varying degrees cross-nationally. International regimes and legal instruments emerge, in areas from the World Trade Organization to human rights, but they are predicated on contractual relationships among states. So we have an increasingly dense web of legal relations, ties and regimes; one could even suggest that globalization (as a shorthand term for the web of global activities that parallel and transcend states) is rule-driven. There is no 'felt identity' on the global level, but law, in one sense, becomes the common (if contested) language (Jacobson 1998–9).[4]

In the absence of some form of world government, domestic judicial, quasi-judicial and administrative institutions and bodies (as well as regional institutions in the European Union) have taken an increasingly salient role. The growing density of rules needs interpretation, mediation and enforcement – and judicial and administrative entities take on that role. The state, through its judicial and administrative branches, mediates the impact of greater global flows and their domestic 'outcomes'. This has been particularly striking in the area of migration. States, faced with increasingly polycultural populations, which are similarly making claims on the basis of (transnational) human rights rhetoric, found themselves mediating myriad social claims. As national borders became lesser markers of communal solidarity, so internal, domestic social boundaries became accentuated, notably in the idiom of multiculturalism. Courts found themselves, and appropriated for themselves, doing what courts do – arbitrating the multiple claims and 'boundary crossings'.

The growing role of judicial and administrative bodies within the state is of course not a novel phenomenon. But now states are responding to international laws on human rights, the environment, intellectual property, among other areas. While courts had traditionally deferred to other branches of government in cross-border matters, this became much less the case, especially in Europe, and especially in areas like migration and human rights. Through the courts, individuals and advocacy groups could potentially help shape understandings of human rights. This process of the growing judicial and administrative role was not limited to court cases. International norms cascaded down, creating a tumult of domestic regulations not only in the public sphere but also in private and corporate institutions. Thus this process involves not just courts: it is explicit in public and private organizations' rules on 'diversity', and 'hostile work environments' (regarding both ethnic and gender issues). It is on this broader canvas that we must understand 'judicialization' and the remarkable expansion in administrative rules and cross-border human rights understanding.[5]

NATIONAL VOICES AND GLOBAL AGENTS

In this light, Jacobson and Ruffer (2003) suggested that the political rules of engagement have evolved and become contested, which in turn has created sharp institutional and normative divisions within, as well as across, states. It is a shift of particular consequence in the area of migrants and migrant populations. The shift is one towards 'judicial agency', driven in part by, and of particular importance in, contemporary polycultural environments. Increasingly dense webs of legal rights mediated by judicial and administrative bodies enable the individual to bypass traditional democratic forms of political mobilization. Through this new mode of political engagement, litigants challenge legislative and executive authority as they cross organizational and even national boundaries through a 'nesting process', seeking judicial ways through which they can restructure rules and norms over a range of issues. This development is particularly marked in the European Union.

Such agency is not expressed primarily at the international, regional or even the national level. Rather, the dense legal webbing enables human rights claims (for example, on religious or racial discrimination) at the lower-order organizational level – such as, notably, the workplace. In recent decades, in order to generate change at 'lower level' organizations, appeals have been made to the 'higher level' organizations (say, state or provincial courts, to change institutional patterns in the original organization). This results in a nesting effect, where people will go to a higher nested organization to appeal, judicially, for recourse. The effect is that relatively limited cases can have broad ripple effects, legally or socially.

But this sets up the institutional and normative clash we have alluded to: the politics of rights is not about the politics of consent as such, and agency, centred on the individual, is distinct from collective notions of national self-determination – or democratic notions of self-government. Judicial and administrative bodies, as opposed to the legislature and executive, are central in this process. Agency rests in the implicit or explicit philosophical belief that individuals should shape the circumstances in which they live. In contrast, 'collective authorship' rests in democratic concepts of freedom, lying in the public and civic realm, where citizens come together (through civic participation, including but not limited to, voting) to shape and form their nation. The implications of these differences for immigrants and in polyethnic polities are profound; they also set the grounding for the problems we face today with the acute danger of terrorism. Terrorism is in turn generally associated with individuals or groups that arise within populations that are potential migrants and asylees or, domestically, from within communities whose roots are immigrant. It is no surprise, then, that in Britain following the underground terrorist attacks, calls were made across the political spectrum to limit multiculturalism and stress once more assimilation into a common sense of being British.

It is also no surprise that we observe a pendulum-like shift back to executive and legislative branches. Since the 11 September 2001 terrorist attacks, governments worldwide have taken a series of actions, sometimes extra-legal, to circumvent agency and limit the use of the judiciary in the fight against terrorists, with particular import for the cross-border movement of people.

This institutional conflict was personified when Prime Minister Tony Blair attacked the judges who ruled, in December 2004, that the UK government had no right to detain foreign nationals who had claimed asylum in the United Kingdom, though it viewed them as dangerous to national security. The government had been, for legal reasons, unable to deport the suspected terrorists held at the Belmarsh penitentiary. The UK government was unwilling to release them and so held the men in 'three-walled prisons', meaning that they could leave the United Kingdom. The law lords argued that detaining suspected foreign terrorists without charge was incompatible with Article 5 of the European Convention of Human Rights. To Blair's consternation, Lord Hoffman stated that, 'the real threat to the life of the nation, in the sense of a people living in accordance with its traditional laws and political values, comes not from terrorism but from laws such as these'. In an editorial entitled, 'The judiciary should not patrol our borders', after the terrorist attacks on 7 and 14 July 2005, the London *Telegraph* (30 July 2005) described these words as 'absurd', and called for repealing the Human Rights Act, abrogating the European Convention of Human Rights from whence it was drawn, and for the United Kingdom to withdraw from the United Nations Convention on Refugees.

In this institutional opposition, the pendulum has swung; it may well swing much further.

End of globalization?

During the first great wave of globalization in the nineteenth century, about 10 per cent of the world's people lived outside their country of birth (Solimano 2001). That figure today is less than 3 per cent of the world population. If advances in technology, reduction in transportation costs or the gap in living standards between countries were the significant determining factors, we would have expected a sharp rise in labour mobility across the globe. The dominant reason for the decline in labour mobility since the first half of the twentieth century is the widespread controls on labour movement. Therefore, if something close to the free movement of labour is the final project of globalization, then the end of globalization is not only distant but also out-of-sight.

There are, however, signs of transformation in the structure and function of nation-states as a result of increasing integration of the global marketplace. The locus of power is shifting from states to multinational corporations who benefit from expanding markets in products, capital and labor. In addition, the increasing set of multilateral treaties and supra-national organizations that monitor them have circumscribed the sphere of influence of the nation-state. At the same time traditional sources of identity and belonging are being undermined and a postmodern, fragmented political landscape is emerging. We are witnessing a curious break in the political and economic futures where on the one hand new regions of the world are surging ahead economically together with a convergence of lifestyles, while on the other hand, increasing uncertainties about terrorism, rogue governments and global environmental catastrophes have eroded trust in the very institutions that are mediating the forces of globalization.

As national boundaries become increasingly porous, internal fortresses are growing that are both physical and ideological. The convergence of lifestyles between countries is continuing together with increasing inequality within countries. A new class system is emerging that is global, or even transnational in scope, but compressed in both time and space. The new class relates less to the immediate civic society and more to a global image defined by specific consumption as well as thought patterns. The expansion of mobility is therefore moving hand-in-hand with a suspicion, even fear, of the 'other', where the 'other' is made 'immediate' in time and space. According to Shamir, 'In this sense, the already familiar legal and constitutional debates concerning the adequate balance between human rights and, say, national security, are not mere replications of the tension between the global and the local. Rather, they should be understood as increasingly representing the tension between universal rights and universal fears, both operating at the global level, albeit materializing at concrete localities' (2005: 214).

Therefore, if globalization were only perceived as the reduction of barriers to mobility between nation-states and the conquest of geographic space, unfettered migration would perhaps constitute 'the end of globalization'. However, this would ignore the human need for defining identities and cultures that differentiate individuals and groups from 'others'. This imperative will give rise to new patterns of resistance and accommodation between different cultures, and between dominant and marginal groups, thereby establishing new mechanisms for inclusion, exclusion and group membership at different space-time scales. The mobility across these groups would then become the next project of globalization. In other words, like the elusive and unreachable 'end of history', globalization would persist as a continuous process, but contextualized in space and time.

Notes

1 Beginning in 2000, virtually all OECD countries have incorporated in their census a question on the country of birth of persons enumerated, as well as on their nationality. This should address some of the data compatibility issues about 'foreign-born' individuals.

2 This figure does not include illegal migrants.

3 See discussion in Castles (2002), Jacobson (1996) and Soysal (1994). A long literature followed debating this issue. See, for example, Joppke (1999).

4 Martin Shapiro (1993) has referred to this growing world legal density as the 'globalization of law'.

5 This section draws on Jacobson (1998–9).

References

Bardhan, A.D. and Guhathakurta, S. 2004. 'Globalization of sub-national regions: Exports and international social and business networks', *Journal of Contemporary Economic Policy*, 22, 225–36.

Borjas, G.J. 1990. *Friends or Strangers: The Impact of Immigration on the US Economy.* New York: Basic Books.

Borjas, G.J. 2004. 'Increasing the supply of labor through immigration: Measuring the impact on native-born workers', *Center for Immigration Studies*, May, 1–10.

Castles, S. 1998. 'Globalization and migration: Some pressing contradictions', *International Social Science Journal*, 50 (156), 179–86.

Castles, S. 2002. 'Migration and community formation under conditions of globalization', *International Migration Review*, 36 (4), 1143–68.

Castles, S. and Miller, M.J. 1998. *The Age of Migration*, 2nd edn. Basingstoke: Macmillan.

Champion, A.G. 1994. 'International migration and demographic change in the developed world', *Urban Studies*, 31 (4/5), 653–77.

Coppel, J., Dumont, J.C. and Visco, I. 2001. 'Trends in immigration and economic consequences', OECD Economics Department Working Paper No. 284. Available at <http://www.oecd.org/dataoecd/54/24/31829838.pdf>.

Durkheim, E. 1984. *The Division of Labor in Society*, trans. W.D. Halls. New York: Free Press.

Firebaugh, G. 2003. 'The causes of inequality transition'. In G. Firebaugh (ed.), *The New Geography of Global Income Inequality*. Cambridge, MA: Harvard University Press.

Freeman, R.B. 2005. 'Does globalization of scientific / engineering workforce threaten U.S. economic leadership?' National Bureau of Economic Research Working Paper No. 11457. Available at <http://www.nber.org/papers/w11457> accessed 9 August 2005.

Gonzalez Baker, S. 1999. 'Mexican-origin women in southwestern labor markets'. In I. Brown (ed.), *Latinas and African American Women at Work*. New York: Russell Sage.

Griswold, D.T. 2003. *Migration, Globalization and the Spirit of Peter Bauer*. Institute of Economic Affairs. Oxford: Blackwell Publishing, 20–6.

Hatton, T.J. and Williamson, J.G. 'Refugees, asylum seekers and policy in Europe', NBER Working Paper No. 10680, August 2004. Available at <http://papers.nber.org/papers/w10680.pdf> accessed 29 July 2005.

Held, D., McGrew, A., Goldblatt, D. and Perraton, J. (eds.) 1999. *Global Transformations: Politics, Economics, and Culture*. Cambridge: Polity Press.

ITU (International Telecommunications Union) 1999. *World Telecommunication Development Report: Mobile Cellular World Telecommunication Indicators*.

Jacobson, D. 1996. *Rights across Borders: Immigration and the Decline of Citizenship*. Baltimore, MD: The Johns Hopkins University Press.

Jacobson, D. 1998–9. 'New border customs: Migration and the changing role of the state', *UCLA Journal of International Law and Foreign Affairs*, 3 (Fall/Winter), 443–62.

Jacobson, D. and Ruffer, G. 2003. 'Courts across borders: The implications of judicial agency for human rights and democracy', *Human Rights Quarterly*, 25 (February), 74–93.

Joppke, C. 1999. *Immigration and the Nation-State: The United States, Germany, and Great Britain*. Oxford: Oxford University Press.

Kanaiaupuni, S.M. 2000. 'Reframing the migration question: An analysis of men, women and gender in Mexico', *Social Forces* 78 (4), 1311–47.

Mahroum, S. 2000. 'Highly skilled globetrotters: Mapping the international migration of human capital', *R & D Management*, 1, 23–31.

Massey, D.S., Arango, J., Hugo, G., Kouaouci, A., Pelligrino, A. and Taylor, J.E. 1994. 'An evaluation of international migration theory: The North American case', *Population Development Review*, 20 (4), 699–751.

Morris, M. and Western, B. 1999. 'Inequality in earnings at the close of the twentieth century', *Annual Review of Sociology*, 25, 623–57.

OECD (Organization for Economic Cooperation and Development) 2005. *Trends in International Migration 2004: SOPEMI*. Paris: OECD.

Office of Policy and Planning, US Immigration and Naturalization Service. 'Estimates of the unauthorized immigrant population residing in the United States: 1990 to 2000'. Available at <http://uscis.gov/graphics/shared/aboutus/statistics/Ill_Report_1211.pdf> accessed 29 July 2005.

Portes, A. 1996. 'Global villagers: The rise of transnational communities', *American Prospect*, 25, 74–7.

Pressman, S. 2001. 'The decline of the middle class: An international perspective', Luxembourg Income Study Working Paper No. 280. Maxwell School of Citizenship and Public Affairs, Syracuse University.

Shamir, R. 2005. 'Without borders? Notes on globalization as a mobility regime', *Sociological Theory*, 23 (2), 197–217.

Shapiro, M. 1993. 'The globalization of law', *Indiana Journal of Global Legal Studies*, 1 (1), 37.

Solimano, A. 2001. 'International migration and the global economic order: An overview', The World Bank Policy Research Working Paper No. 2720. Available at <http://wdsbeta.worldbank.org/external/default/WDSContentServer/IW3P/IB/2002/01/17/000094946_0112110518493/Rendered/PDF/multi0page.pdf> accessed 9 August 2005.

Soysal, Y. 1994. *The Limits of Citizenship: Migrants and Postnational Membership in Europe*. Chicago: University of Chicago Press.

Stalker, P. 2000. *Workers without Frontiers: The Impact of Globalization on International Migration*. Boulder, CO: Lynne Rienner.

Stalker, P. 2005. *Stalker's Guide to International Migration*. Available at <http://pstalker.com/migration/> accessed 9 August 2005.

The Economist 1999. *Survey: Telecommunications*, 9 October.

Thurow, L.C. 1984. 'The disappearance of the middle class', *The New York Times*, 5 February, f3.

United Nations General Assembly 2006. *International Migration and Development: Report of the Secretary-General*. Available at <http://daccessdds.un.org/doc/UNDOC/GEN/N06/353/54/PDF/N0635354.pdf> accessed 9 January 2007.

USDOJ-INS (US Department of Justice, Immigration and Naturalization Service) 2003. *2001 Statistical Yearbook of the Immigration and Naturalization Service*. Washington, DC: US Government Printing Office. Available at <http://dhs.gov/xlibrary/assets/statistics/yearbook/2001/yearbook2001.pdf>.

Visco, I. 2001. *Paying for Pensions: How Important is Economic Growth?* Paris: OECD. <http://www.oecd.org/dataoecd/31/0/2402444.pdf> accessed 7 August 2005.

Wai, T.C. 2001. 'WAPping into developing countries', <http://www.sibexlink.com.my/g15magazine/g15mag_vol3apr_infotech.html> accessed 10 July 2005.

Widgren, J. 1989. 'Asylum seekers in Europe in the context of South–North movements', *International Migration Review*, 23, 47–66.

Zlotnik, H. 1999. 'Trends of international migration since 1965: What existing data reveal', *International Migration*, 37 (1), 21–61.

Chapter 10

Globalization and the Agrarian World

PHILIP MCMICHAEL

INTRODUCTION

Over a century ago, Mahatma Gandhi posed the question: 'If it took Britain the exploitation of half the globe to be what it is today, how many globes would India need?' One might just as provocatively ask this question today, noting that the division of the world under colonialism continues to shape the uneven consumption of resources, and that it is now commonplace to substitute the United States for Britain and China for India.

The British 'workshop of the world' model depended on an unprecedented radical experiment of outsourcing its agriculture to the colonies. Today, while the United States and Europe, and to some extent Japan, continue to protect their intensive farm sectors, the model of agricultural outsourcing continues, and is expected to intensify with the rising costs of Northern farm subsidies. Meanwhile, the corporate reconstruction of food consumption relations on a world scale increasingly overrides customary (subsistence) food cultures in the global South, where the bulk of rural populations reside, and consume 60 per cent of the food they produce. For the roughly 4 billion of the world's population excluded from the global marketplace, to access land and resources means competing with the combined pressures of agro-exporting and the global supermarket revolution. To the extent that the agrarian South represents the vortex of globalization, it is the major focus of this chapter.

Pressure on resources of the agrarian South is a key dimension of contemporary globalization, with its roots in the imperial past. It represents a world in which those with power, whether military or monetary, have means to commandeer resources and transform rural landscapes. These new *relations of production*, converting agriculture to agribusiness, represent both obstacles and options for rural producers and labourers in the global South as 'non-traditional exports' (e.g. flowers, fruits and vegetables, shrimp), specialized commodity chains (e.g. feedstuffs and livestock) and domestically located retailers/processors enclose the agrarian world. Such developments are complemented by cheap food imports from the global North that displace local farmers and replace food staples lost through this process and agro-exporting.

While economic theory may refer to this bait and switch operation as the operation of the law of comparative advantage, the reality is a profound transformation of relations of consumption. Not only are producing regions exporting, rather than consuming, the products of their lands, but also staple foods are often displaced as small farmers yield to larger market forces. The classic example is the displacement of Mexico's inexpensive white maize tortillas by yellow corn tortillas manufactured at triple the price as a consequence of the torrent of corn imports from the US midwest via the North American Free Trade Agreement. That is, the changing geography of agriculture and food markets expresses a global re-composition of class and dietary relations.

A second dimension of globalization in the agrarian world involves transformation of the *relations of social reproduction*. In the context of the above shifts in relations of agricultural production, food security is converted from a local to a global process of social reproduction. New commercial agricultures displace local provisioning with staple foods in the global South, and producers enter global circuits whereby they source (and reproduce) distant consumers, and in turn rely on imported and/or inferior foods to replenish their own diets. Many rural households supplement their subsistence consumption with off-farm income, earned on neighbouring farms or plantations, in mushrooming rural industries/*maquilas*, and with remittances from family members engaged in migrant work.

Relations of resistance constitute the third dimension of globalization. Here, the politics of production and reproduction are expressed through movements to reclaim the agrarian world from its conversion to a site of profit. Landless peasants and workers combine with and complement eco-agriculturalists, seed savers, fair traders and food sovereignty movements, challenging the corporate and institutional mechanisms that impose monocultures and unequal market relations. The episteme of the global justice movement for diversity is very much 'agri-cultural': 'encompassing first world farmers seeking market protection, farmers resisting genetic engineering, indigenous sovereignty movements seeking to control land and practices, sustainable development, localist economic visions, and third world peasant movements reacting to the failures of urbanization and neoliberalism by insisting on rights to land and subsistence' (Starr 2001: 224). These relations reveal the world-historical antecedents of globalization in the twenty-first century agrarian world.

WORLD-HISTORICAL PERSPECTIVE ON THE AGRARIAN WORLD

The social impulse for protection against market privations perhaps defines the political history of modernity (Polanyi 1957). Today's global justice movements problematize modernity, in the name not just of current social pathologies, but also of the long-term sustainability of the social and natural world. Candido Grzybowsky, director of IBASE in Rio de Janeiro, observed of the landless-workers' movement in 2004:

The modernity of the MST consists in questioning us about . . . the past of our agrarian origins and about the future in the use of our natural resources, with the question of land at the center. . . . the landless, on occupying ranches, bring to the surface a fundamental question about the possibility of sustainable democratic development in Brazil. We are, of the large countries of the world, the least demographically dense, the most privileged in terms of natural resources – land, water, biodiversity – and at the same time, the most unequal and tragically, the most predatory. For how long, in the name of an even more narrow vision, will we be able to maintain the right to act on this part of Planet Earth in a way that is so socially and ecologically irresponsible? (Grzybowsky 2004)

This rendition of Brazil challenges 'globalization', and the modernity project, which linked the inevitability of progress to the necessity of science in the service of the industrial state, naming this phenomenon 'development'. Much of the global justice movement questions this paradigm with a different conception of modernity, revalorizing the Enlightenment principle of self-organization with social and ecological responsibility.

Brazil has emerged as the new agro-export powerhouse in the world economy. Exports of coffee, sugar, poultry, cacao, orange juice concentrate and soy and corn destined for livestock in the global North leave behind 44 million chronically hungry Brazilians. For Brazilian policy, 'the problem of agriculture is not about feeding the hungry, it is about profits and the national balance of trade. The potential for profitable agricultural expansion lies not in feeding the hungry but in better serving the markets of those with plenty to spend' (Wright and Wolford 2003: 279). But this observation applies universally, not just to Brazil. It refers to the paradox of 'abundance amidst scarcity' characterizing the food equation in this era of globalization.

The roots of this elemental inequality lie in empire, one legacy of which was to divide the world economically, with powerful cultural effects. European colonialism converted parts of the non-European world to export monocultures provisioning the West with various raw materials and foodstuffs. Such conversion reconstructed the dietary geography of the world, with a racialized legacy of under-consumption in the global South linked to over-consumption in the global North. While the under/over consumption relation obtains within all societies, this global dialectic has conditioned the politics and culture of globalization and agrarian relations.

Initially, the fruits of empire included those well-known 'articles of pleasure' – the stimulants, tobacco, coffee, tea and sugar. Sheller notes that despite the association of European exploration with precious metals, 'it was as much the desire to acquire new edible, pleasurable, and pharmaceutical substances, things that had direct and powerful effects on the bodies of those empowered to consume them' (2003: 77). She concludes: 'As Europeans became more and more attached to these goods, they were sucked into the vortex of slavery and its human-consuming economy' (Sheller 2003: 81). Sugar, originally a luxury for the European aristocracy, became a household commodity by the nineteenth century, and the object of intense imperial rivalry. Chronicling the commitment of imperial resources to securing the sugar colonies in the Caribbean, Mintz anticipates the role of imperial power today in managing the consumption relations of industrial capitalism.

The history of sugar follows a clear contour: 'A rarity in 1650, a luxury in 1750, sugar had been transformed into a virtual necessity by 1850 . . . The difference had to do with the ongoing development of an industrial economy and with the changing relationships between that economy and the overseas colonies.' The key to this relationship was: 'the provision of low-cost food substitutes, such as tobacco, tea, and sugar, for the metropolitan laboring classes. By positively affecting the worker's energy output and productivity, such substitutes figured importantly in balancing the accounts of capitalism' (Mintz 1985: 148–9).

In other words, a world food such as sugar was integral to the value calculus of capitalism, whereby an uneven but combined *global* labour force was constructed and provisioned through an elaborate imperial relation. The empire not only secured the sugar colonies as European supply zones, it also imported supplies of starch such as breadfruit from the South Pacific, and protein such as salted cod from the North Atlantic, to complement indigenous fruits sustaining the bodies of plantation workers. Meanwhile the white settlers of the Caribbean consumed a *creole* cuisine invented by African cooks, and the propertied classes in Europe dined on roast beef harvested from the growing cattle culture introduced by John Bull into the American plains. Empire's transformation of the agrarian world was irrevocably embedded in complex dietary relations.

Sugar and other stimulants supported the new schedules of industrial work and leisure, becoming generalized as both luxury and wage foods, and, indeed, 'refined sugar . . . became a symbol of the modern and industrial' (Mintz 1985: 193). Sugar's reconstruction of the modern diet linked the emerging food culture to the identification with empire: 'As the exemplar of luxuries turned into affordable proletarian goodies by dint of individual effort, sucrose was one of the people's opiates, and its consumption was a symbolic demonstration that the system that produced it was successful' (Mintz 1985: 174). A current analogue is the brisk and growing trade in foodstuffs, propelled by relatively affluent urban consumers desiring exotic, high-value and all-seasonal foods – sourced globally by transnational firms and retailers. A related and increasingly consequential analogue is the dietary transition in domestic food markets everywhere: a shift towards consumption of processed foods, expressing the embrace of modernity, and enabled by the global supermarket revolution.

The *conditions* of the empire's success in delivering the goods, through agro-exporting, has been likened by Davis (2001) to a holocaust. The last quarter of the nineteenth century saw a synchronization of El Niño famines, causing a devastating drought across the tropics, accompanied by a swathe of famine-induced deaths (30–60 million people) from India through northern China to Brazil. In India, British colonialism dismantled village grain reserve systems as grain was transformed into an export product. Transport systems, including the telegraph and its coordination of price hikes, regardless of local conditions, enabled merchants along the line to transfer grain inventories from the drought-stricken hinterland to hoarding centres. Through this device, India was 'force-marched into the world market', with grain exports rising from 3 to 10 million tons annually (equivalent to the annual nutrition of 25 million people), coinciding with the rough estimate of 12–29 million deaths during this period. Davis remarks, 'Londoners were in effect eating India's bread', and notes that 'the perverse consequence of a unitary market was to export famine, via price inflation, to the rural poor in grain-surplus districts' (2001: 7, 26, 285).

The response, across what came to be called the Third World, was an anti-imperial millenarianism that fuelled the decolonization movements of the twentieth century. Whereas Polanyi's account of the social regulation of the market described European modernity in the making, Davis completes the narrative by revealing 'the secret history of the nineteenth century' – documenting the profound impact of the gold standard on the non-European world. Modernity, for non-Europeans, involved the subjection of their material life to the price form – a lever by which necessities and new resources alike could be removed without evident force, and transported by price-making merchants to price-taking European consumers.

Modernity, in short, was double-edged, and the market remains one of the foundational elements of this paradox. Today, the World Trade Organization imposes the unitary market via its 1995 Agreement on Agriculture, which prioritizes a model of agro-exporting and food importing over domestic production that cannot compete in the world market. In India, for example, subsidies to small farmers have been withdrawn, and now target agribusinesses involved in export crops. That is, following the post-colonial project of self-sufficiency via the green revolution, Indian agriculture is once again undergoing conversion to serve the world market.

DEVELOPMENT AND THE RELATIONS OF AGRICULTURAL PRODUCTION

The immiseration of colonial peoples through such mechanisms inspired the mid-twentieth century project of development, elaborated in powerful corridors of post-World War II Washington, London and Paris, and at the Bretton Woods conference of 1944, creating the World Bank and its sister institution, the International Monetary Fund (IMF). This was the age of 'hunger amidst scarcity', and development discourses formed around the problematic of Third World poverty, as a political threat. President Truman's Four Point Declaration of 1948 noted: 'The economic life of the poor is primitive and stagnant . . . Their poverty is a handicap and a threat both to them and to more prosperous areas' (quoted in Escobar 1995: 3).

The post-World War II development project included a vision of the agrarian world as destined to disappear in a trope of industrial modernity, which would reshape agriculture as an industrial input and expel peasants into the manufacturing labour force. Contributing to the vision was the complementarity between US agribusiness and the disposal of its food surpluses, to subsidize industrialization in geo-politically strategic Third World states. This food export regime reshaped, indeed Westernized, social diets of newly urbanized consumers in industrializing regions of the Third World, at the same time as it undermined local farmers with low-priced staple foods (Friedmann 1982). The managed construction of the Third World consumer paralleled the decimation of peasant agriculture – each confirmed the simple truths of the development vision, that the Western consumption pattern was a universal desire and peasants were historical residuals, destined to disappear.

Post-colonial states implemented this development model in the name of modernity, commercializing public goods (land, forest, water, genetic resources, indigenous knowledge), and extending cash cropping systems to pay for rising imports of technology and luxury consumer goods. Subsistence cultures experienced sustained pressure from cheap food imports and expanding commodity relations, resulting in patterns of peasant dispossession (Araghi 1995). From 1950 to 1997, the world's rural population decreased by some 25 per cent. During the 1990s, the global urban population increased by 36 per cent, and by the early twenty-first century 63 per cent of the world's urban population dwells in, and on the margins of, sprawling cities of the global South – a 2003 UN report noted that slum-dwellers account for an average 43 per cent of the population of the global South (Vidal 2004b: 17).

Commercial mono-cropping transformed rural landscapes as the US model of capital/energy-intensive agriculture was universalized through the European Marshall Plan, agribusiness deployment of counterpart funds from the food aid programme and green revolution technologies (substituting dependence on capital-intensive hybrids of wheat, rice and corn staples for 'traditional' systems of mixed cropping). In addition, postwar American-style consumption transformed food from its nineteenth-century role of cheapening labour costs to its current role of extending the boundaries of profit, from fast food to the proliferation of processed food via the supermarket revolution. Globally, this appears in the convergence of (largely) urban diets on a narrowing base of staple grains, increasing consumption of animal protein, edible oils, salt and sugar, and declining dietary fibre, contributing to an increasing prevalence of non-communicable (dietary) diseases and obesity. And it gives rise to the notion of a 'global epidemic of malnutrition', in which the 1.2 billion underfed match the 1.2 billion overfed (Gardner and Halweil 2000).

The supermarket revolution centralizes food processing and retailing via continuing pressure on small or independent producers (Reardon et al. 2003). For example, the purchase of meat from small ranchers in the Amazon by local Brazilian slaughterhouses has been recently replaced by large commercial ranchers producing directly for supermarkets that service the Brazilian and global market. European supermarkets dominate the beef export market with extensive cattle ranching, and Europe and the Middle East account for 75 per cent of Brazil's beef exports. Supermarkets expanded their reach in Latin American countries during the 1990s from 15–30 per cent to 50–70 per cent of national retail sales. This growth rate exceeds that in the United States by five times, and is now accelerating throughout Asia. Transnational firms such as Ahold, Carrefour and Wal-Mart comprise 70–80 per cent of the top five supermarket chains in Latin America, centralizing procurement from farmers across the region (and their own processing plants), and, together with Nestlé and Quaker, are supplying regional consumer markets throughout the MERCUSOR trading bloc. In Guatemala, where supermarkets now control 35 per cent of food retailing, 'their sudden appearance has brought unanticipated and daunting challenges to millions of struggling, small farmers', lacking binding contractual agreements, rewarded only if they consistently meet new quality standards and facing declining prices as they constitute a virtually unlimited source for retailers (Dugger 2004).

Standards are now a significant new vector in the global food production complex. WTO regulation of trade relations is complemented by a far-reaching private regulation of production standards, regarding quality, food safety, packaging and convenience. It is integral to the centralization of retailing capital, and the dual imperatives of satisfying quality demands of relatively affluent consumers and replacing smallholding by global/factory farms in order to realize those standards. UK supermarkets, for instance, 'believe that concentrating their grower base will reduce their exposure to risk by giving them greater control over the production and distribution processes' (Dolan and Humphrey 2000: 167). As a new vector, the standards revolution expresses a transformation of the conventions of capitalism, whereby 'Good Agricultural Practices' underlie certification schemes within EUREP, an association of European supermarket chains concerned with regulating quality, safety, environment and labour standards surpassing publicly required standards (Busch and Bain 2004). But the standards revolution involves selective appropriation by food corporations of social movement demands for environmental, food safety, animal welfare and fair trade relations, with the potential of deepening social inequality globally (at the expense of peasants and poor consumers) as private regulation displaces public responsibilities (Friedmann 2005). Nevertheless, the new emphasis on quality has been regarded as 'one of the bright spots of African development. It has raised production standards in agriculture, created supporting industries, and provided considerable employment in rural areas' (Dolan and Humphrey 2000: 159).

Factory farming is the new model of development in the food sector – currently targeting Argentina, Brazil, China, India, Mexico, Pakistan, the Philippines, South Africa, Taiwan and Thailand. Asia, whose global consumer class outstrips that of North America and Europe combined, leads the livestock revolution, driven by an association of development with animal protein consumption. 'Beefing up' has been a long-standing legacy of the British empire, now reproduced through the corporate empire. Two-thirds of global meat consumption expansion is in the global South, sourced with soybeans from Brazil. As its middle class emerges, China has shifted from an originating exporter of soybeans to the world's largest importer of whole soybeans and oils – a dynamic converting Brazilian pastures to soyfields, and displacing cattle herds deeper into the Amazon.

The global livestock industry represents the contradictory legacy of the modern dietary transition for ecological and public health. Meat consumption in the global South outstrips that in the North, and has been referred to as a 'demand-led livestock revolution' in implicit reference to the deepening of the global market relations (Delgado et al. 1999). Expanding animal protein consumption is both an indicator of rising dietary standards, and an increasing source of non-communicable, dietary diseases, with rising obesity rates worldwide. But animal protein consumption also has substantial environmental impacts, alongside those of intensive agriculture. A recent report from the International Water Management Institute regarding the global water crisis notes that 'Western diets, which depend largely on meat, are already putting great pressures on the environment. Meat-eaters consume the equivalent of about 5,000 liters of water a day compared to the 1,000–2,000 liters used by people on vegetarian diets in developing countries' (quoted in Vidal 2004a: 31). The contributions of the global livestock industry to global warming, via carbon dioxide, nitrous oxide and methane, are significant:

Global warming is the inverse side of the Age of Progress. It represents the millions of tons of spent energy of the modern era. . . . Altered climates, shorter growing seasons, changing rainfall patterns, eroding rangeland, and spreading deserts may well sound the death knell for the cattle complex and the artificial protein ladder that has been erected to support a grain-fed beef culture. (Rifkin 1992: 229–30)

Climate change is a significant natural effect of globalization, and is already affecting the agrarian world. From the Peruvian Andes, where late blight (of the Irish potato famine) is creeping into high altitude potato fields for the first time in thousands of years, through the great plains of the United States and the North China Plain to the fields of southern Africa, patterns of rainfall and temperature are destabilizing agriculture. The Pentagon reported in 2004 that climate change could plunge the North into a mini-Ice Age, with a 'significant drop in the human carrying capacity of the Earth's environment' (Nierenberg and Halweil 2005: 71).

Rifkin's reference to the artificial protein ladder concerns the displacement of food, by feed, grains across the world, as access to the global market via ubiquitous food corporations allows more affluent consumers to bid away the staple foods of the world's poor. Thus the relationship identified by Gandhi above becomes a mechanism whereby the global North consumes the food and resources of the global South through the expansion of agribusiness and agro-exports. These resources include the stock of genetic diversity in the South.

Universalization of the Northern model of industrial agriculture through the twentieth century has resulted in the loss of 75 per cent of the genetic diversity of agricultural crops across the world. Green revolution crops (new, bioengineered varieties) now account for more than half of the South's rice culture. The adoption of transgenic technology substitutes monopoly for diversity, threatening ecological and social sustainability, and local food security. A century ago, hundreds of millions of the world's farmers controlled and reproduced their seed stocks, whereas today 'much of the seed stock has been bought up, engineered, and patented by global companies and kept in the form of intellectual property', converting farmers into consumers of genetically altered seeds (Rifkin 1998: 114).

The 'export of sustainability' from the South includes the relocation of intensive agriculture to the South, where relatively inexpensive land and labour combine with relatively lax environmental laws (Gupta 1998; Blank 1998). Relocation is partly related to Northern environmental degradation – in the United States, 2 million acres of farmland are lost annually to erosion, soil salinization and flooding or soil saturation by intensive agriculture, which consumes groundwater 160 per cent faster than it can be replenished. Relocation of food production resembles Britain's nineteenth-century decision, but it also follows the pattern of outsourcing manufacturing and services from the global North. It is a model replicated in China, where the recent acceleration of intensive agriculture has degraded soils from reduced crop rotation, erosion, over-fertilization and the loss of organic content of soils once nourished by manure-based farming. Over 2 million square kilometres of land turn to desert annually. During the 1990s, 20–30 million Chinese farmers were displaced by environmental degradation during the 1990s, with predictions of almost twice that number by 2025 (Economy 2004: 82).

As the Chinese case indicates, the elaboration of a global agro-food complex is not simply a proliferation of commodity flows. It involves a transformation, and integration, of conditions of social reproduction within and across national borders. In what follows we consider the impact of such a transformation on the agrarian world.

GLOBALIZATION AND THE RELATIONS OF SOCIAL REPRODUCTION

The relations of social reproduction concern how populations survive within international and national institutions that govern material and livelihood opportunities. The dominant theme of neoliberal globalization is the re-privatization of social reproduction. For our purposes, this is best captured in the changing discourse of food security, reframed in the WTO as food provisioning through the allocative efficiencies of a unitary global market. Since markets respond to (monetized) demand rather than need, this system reproduces hunger at the same time.

Across the broad transition from the development, to the globalization, project, hunger has been a global phenomenon, that is, '"Hunger amidst scarcity" has given way to "hunger amidst abundance"' (Araghi 2000: 155). Mid-twentieth century food security concerns were addressed through broad public programmes committed to poverty alleviation via social reproduction mechanisms of social welfare and development (including food aid), but twenty-first century food security concerns focus on private mechanisms, emphasizing consumer rights to corporate-managed delivery of goods and services. While the market is the designated vehicle and realm of social reproduction, its contradictory relations (cheap food for consumers vs displacement of rural cultures) mean that a large portion of the world's population is either reproducing the smaller, affluent proportion, or combining livelihood strategies on the margins of the market to reproduce themselves and their families.

These contradictory relations underlie the WTO's Agreement on Agriculture, a protocol at the centre of controversy over trade rules (McMichael 2005). This agreement governs agricultural policy among member states, outlawing artificial price support via trade restrictions, production controls and state trading boards. While countries of the global South are instructed to open their farm sectors, those of the global North have so far retained their huge subsidies. Such decoupling of subsidies from prices removes the price floor, establishing a *low* 'world price' for agricultural commodities, and favouring traders and processors in the global food industry at the expense of farmers everywhere.

The price depression is enabled by a WTO rule eliminating the right to a national strategy of self-sufficiency. The minimum market access rule guarantees the right to export, privileging Northern states and the global sourcing strategies of agribusiness. Sixty per cent of global food stocks are in corporate hands, six of which control 70 per cent of the world's grain trade. The United States accounts for 70 per cent of world corn exports, 70 per cent of which are controlled by two corporations, Cargill and Archer Daniel Midlands. At the 1999 WTO Ministerial in Seattle, a Honduran farmer observed: 'Today, we cannot sell our own farm products on the markets because of . . . imports . . . of cheap food produce from Europe, Canada and the US . . . Free trade is for multinationals; it is not for the small peasant farmers' (quoted in Madeley 2000: 81). Southern food dependency is the result: for example, after 9,000 years of food security, Mexico, the home of maize, was transformed by liberalization policies and NAFTA into a food deficit country, compelled to import yellow corn from the United States at the expense of almost 2 million *campesinos*. The chairman of Cargill observed: 'There is a mistaken belief that the greatest agricultural need in the developing world is to develop the capacity to grow food for local consumption. This is misguided. Countries should produce what they produce best – and trade' (quoted in Lynas 2001).

The corporate food regime displaces staple food crops by exports – whether dumped on the world market, or installed locally as the measure of (global) development. Small farmers face both obstacles and opportunities. With respect to obstacles, the privatization of food security via liberalization not only reduces farm supports (credit, subsidized inputs etc.), but also exposes small farmers to the competitive pressures of artificially cheapened world prices for agricultural commodities. Liberalization policies are rooted in IMF-World Bank structural adjustment measures, which have routinely required 'free markets' in grain – for example, in formerly self-sufficient countries like Malawi, Zimbabwe, Kenya, Rwanda and Somalia. Somalia's pastoral economy was decimated by a structural adjustment programme of duty-free imports of subsidized beef and dairy products from the European Union (Chossudovsky 2003). There is evidence, however, that the volatility of agro-exporting has encouraged farmers, close to dynamic urban markets, to shift into 'fast crop' production (fruits and vegetables) to regularize cash income as a matter of sustainability (Ponte 2002: 114).

Neo-liberal policies intensify de-peasantization. In Peru, for example, debt rescheduling in the 1990 'IMF Fujishock' introduced cheap corn imports, and inflated prices for fuel, farm inputs and agricultural credit, bankrupting small farmers and enriching agro-industrial concerns. New laws in 1991 privatizing and concentrating landownership fuelled export agriculture, polarizing the countryside, with peasants forced into coca cash-cropping, and/or providing a labour reserve for agro-export production (Chossudovsky 2003). Chile, an early laboratory for neoliberal policies, pioneered success in non-traditional exports from the 1970s, becoming the largest supplier of off-season fruits and vegetables to Europe and North America. Meanwhile, food cropping in beans, wheat and other staples has declined by more than a third, as corporate plantations have displaced local farmers into the casual labour force. Across Latin America, while 90 per cent of agricultural research was devoted to food crops in the 1980s, during the 1990s export crops commanded 80 per cent of research expenditures (Madeley 2000).

Agro-food export strategies typically divide between corporate plantations and smallholder contract farming. Research on Thai agro-exporting (chicken, shrimp, seafood and fresh fruit) documents limits on income generation and food security (Goss and Burch 2001), and research on contract farming for the international processing tomato industry confirms that long-term volatilities override short-term gains to producers (Pritchard and Burch 2003). But the *extant* producers are not the only ones affected. In the Philippines, the average shrimp farm provides 15 jobs on the farm and 50 security jobs around the farm, while shrimp culture displaces

50,000 people through loss of land, traditional fishing and agriculture. One Filipino fisherman observed: 'The shrimp live better than we do. They have electricity, but we don't. The shrimp have clean water, but we don't. The shrimp have lots of food, but we are hungry' (quoted in Tilford 2004: 93).

As agro-industrialization deepens under the spur of global markets and agribusiness, rural economies everywhere are experiencing depression or crisis. Low prices and shrinking public supports undermine the viability of farming as a livelihood as well as a way of life. In Brazil, price falls for staple crops like rice and beans have exacerbated rural exodus and rising urban unemployment. The extreme form of crisis is expressed in the rising incidence of farmer suicides around the world, following the spread of the neoliberal model and its subjection of farming to the price form, reflected in debt stress – from the United States in the 1980s, through the United Kingdom in the 1990s to India in the late 1990s, and now to China, where privatization of the rural collective has exposed farmers to the market. The Beijing Suicide Research and Prevention Centre reports the incidence of suicide in 2004 exceeded the global average: 'those who took their own lives were rural women who remained behind in villages as males in the family migrated to towns and cities in search of work' (Mohanty 2005: 267–8). In the dramatic collapse of the WTO Ministerial in Cancun in 2003 over agricultural subsidies, the ultimate symbol of this agrarian crisis was expressed in the suicide of a Korean farmer, Mr Kyung-Hae Lee, on the barricades.

Conservative FAO estimates are that, globally, liberalization has deprived 20–30 million people of their land. This outcome includes a characteristic process of 'semi-proletarianization', which has a long history but has been deepened by neoliberal policies. Research in Africa documents the impact of structural adjustment through the displacement of the stable servicing of peasants by parastatal marketing boards with private traders, who 'rarely provided the market efficiency that the [International Financial Institutions] had anticipated'. The impact has been either 'deagrarianization', with African peasants reallocating land and labour away from commercial agriculture, or 'de-peasantization': 'selling or renting their land to large-scale farmers and turning to agricultural wage labour or non-farm activities'. These processes are accelerated by real wage reductions associated with liberalization, undermining the off-farm income supplements necessary to sustain farms. Evidence from the late 1990s 'indicates that most households now have one or more non-agricultural income sources, and between 60 to 80 percent of their income derives from these sources' (Bryceson 2004: 618–19). Differentiated off-farm labour market conditions correlate with socio-economic differentials among peasants, the poorest households being the most heavily dependent on off-farm, informal piecework labour (Bernstein 2005; Bezner-Kerr 2005).

For Asia, between 30 and 40 per cent of rural household incomes are supplemented with off-farm sources, household well-being often best-served in contexts supporting women's ability to diversify out of farming (Kabeer and Tran 2002). And for Latin America, the large majority of the peasantry is semi-proletarianized (Kay 2000), with 'subfamily farmers . . . now increasingly complementing [60 per cent of] their incomes with rural non-agricultural employment' (Moyo and Yeros 2005: 28–9). For example, in the Mexican *agro-maquila* industry:

campesinos who are the salaried workforce in the growing agro-export economy no longer have access to land for their own subsistence, have been deprived of their small producer credits and food subsidies, and must piece together their survival often with a patchwork of part-time and seasonal waged work, informal sector jobs, and subsistence activities such as farming their own plots or making their own food. (Barndt 2002: 175)

Barndt's 'corporate tomato' research qualifies the notion of the rural family unit as the 'family wage economy', where family farm labour is supplemented by 'remittances from members who migrate, and migrating families often offer several family members as salaried workers to agribusiness' (2002: 182).

The corporate tomato is one of several fruits developed now for export to urban and overseas markets across Latin America, in which fruit and vegetables accounted for 27 per cent of its major agricultural exports (oilseeds at 32 per cent) in 2000. But in the Latin American countryside, in particular, 'agricultural production can no longer be privileged over other income earning/livelihood activities, and there is at the same time growing concern for landscape and environmental considerations and management of forests and water resources' (Long and Roberts 2005: 66). This has been termed the 'new rurality', in which urban residents make claims on and for the countryside, even as agro-industrialization intensifies. The commercial agricultural complex is fast-changing, using information technology and mobile phones to link to commodity markets, and seeking production niches in a volatile global marketplace – where retail markets include a proliferation of speciality products. An example of the latter is the market for corn-husks grown by Mexican *campesinos*, and packaged for *tamale* production in California, often provisioning the proliferating 'transnational communities' formed through labour migration to supplement the family wage economy (Long and Villarreal 1998).

The discourse of the 'new rurality' is related to the production of 'global food spaces', regions where agricultures are transformed by their articulation with the institutional and quality standards of the global market. Marsden's analysis of the 'new agrarian districts' of Brazil's São Francisco Valley, based in exports of mangoes, grapes, tomatoes and acerola (50 per cent overseas, with 25 per cent under contract with French retail giant, Carrefour, and 50 per cent to Brazilian cities, in the *Uvale* enterprise), focuses on the new forms of 'governance' of the food industry, requiring specific quality controls and design, as well as setting parameters for labour and environmental conditions (Marsden 2003: 30, 57). A successful producer in the shift from seller- to buyer-driven chains, characteristic of neo-liberal globalization, comments:

the market had changed and was demanding quality. We had to change too; more qualified people, new technologies at harvest and after harvest; packing houses, cooling chambers, packaging and wrapping papers.... We had to travel, to hire external experts, and to develop new systems of cutting and irrigation. There were changes in labour control and in the ways fertilization, pulverization and timing were done; the introduction of computer programming was also new. (Marsden 2003: 56)

This form of agro-industrialization, like earlier green revolution technologies, is beyond the resources of most farmers, who surrender their farms to their commercial neighbours or incoming entrepreneurial farmers, and may stay on as hired labour. But, given the new conditions of food governance, the character of rural labour is irrevocably changed. While there is always unskilled work, often assigned to ethnic and female minorities, the new agrarian regions become more selective in their employment practices, opening up the region to qualified newcomers:

> whereas the growth of the region was a result of the extensive use of labour, the actual conditions of production led by global standards of competitiveness pressed producers to restructure the organization of production by employing new labour-saving technologies and a more adaptable and qualified workforce. (Marsden 2003: 61)

In Kenya's export horticulture, growers rely on migrant female labour, with gains being realized through the 'comparative advantage of women's disadvantage' that characterizes the global horticulture labour force, in a context where retailers (with just-in-time inventories) organize global commodity chains (Dolan 2004). In Latin America, this 'comparative advantage' involves agribusinesses hiring women to combine high-quality labour with the lower costs associated with the flexible employment patterns of women, related to their primary responsibility to provision their household – in other words, capitalist social relations are not simply market relations, but implicate household relations also as part of their conditions of reproduction. That is: 'Agribusinesses use gender ideologies to erode stable employment and worker rights where women are concerned. Of equal significance, employing women provides the employer with a way of invoking institutions beyond the workplace to extend and reinforce labor discipline' (Collins 1995: 217). From the household angle, female migrant labour patterns are based in decisions 'nested within a wider household strategy to enhance security and well-being'. In Kenya, where 89.4 per cent of horticulture is destined for Europe (especially the United Kingdom), the shift away from smallholder-contract production to centralized employment on farms and in packhouses in the mid-1990s has depended on a migrant labour force, as women in particular migrate for short-term employment to help sustain the household (Dolan 2004).

The proliferation of new rural districts, as global food spaces supplying urban produce markets, is matched by an expansion of new urban centres in rural areas. One form is 'corporate urbanization' on new agricultural frontiers, notably in the soybean boom in Mato Grosso, Brazil. Here, the *Avanca Brasil*, a $40 billion state-supported project to open the Amazon for its timber and farmland, partners with global agribusiness such as Cargill, which has the contract to build a new port terminal in the Amazon delta, to connect the vast Mato Grosso soy fields with the insatiable appetite of the ballooning Chinese middle class (Vidal 2001). As a consequence, 'small and medium size towns arise to service the projects, such as the town of Campo Verde in Mato Grosso . . . with a population in the municipality that grew from nothing to 30,000 in fifteen years' (Long and Roberts 2005).

An alternative to opening forest land to development is the Chinese version, where farmers, designated as members of village collectives, have only leasehold rights to their land. Land seizures by city officials for lucrative development possibilities have confiscated land from as many as 70 million farmers over the last decade, driven by the possibility of earning 10 times more on land transaction fees than on farm taxes (Yardley 2004a). While local grain self-sufficiency was the standard under the Mao Zedong regime, the priority has shifted to exploiting water and land resources for urban development. The annual migration of 10 million peasants into cities has dramatically reduced arable land and domestic grain supplies, leading China to more than double its food imports, wheat from the United States, soybeans from Brazil and rice from south-east Asia.

China's de-peasantization is reflected in the dramatic transformation of rural landscapes, as industrial estates have mushroomed on former rice paddies. In Dongguan City (producing Reebok and Nike shoes), local farmers now live off factory rents, while tens of thousands of migrants from the hinterland swell the workforce, with Korean or Taiwanese managers (Chan 1996). Datang, a rice farming village in the late 1970s, with a cottage industry in socks, now produces nine billion socks annually:

> Signs of Datang's rise as a socks capital are everywhere. The center of town is filled with a huge government-financed marketplace for socks. The rice paddies have given way to rows of paved streets lined with cookie-cutter factories. Banners promoting socks are draped across buildings. (Barboza 2004: C3).

Renamed 'Socks City', Datang is one of many new coastal cities: south-east is Shenzhou, the world's necktie capital, west is Sweater City and Kid's Clothing City and to the south, in the low-rent district is Underwear City. In China, medium and small town and village enterprises account for over 140 million jobs, roughly one-third of the rural labour force (Eyferth et al. 2003).

Globalization intensifies rural industrialization, beginning with export-processing zones. From the 1960s, firms seeking lower wages were attracted by host governments seeking investment and foreign currency via specialized manufacturing export estates, with minimal customs controls, and exempt from labour regulations and domestic taxes. The Mexican government's Border Industrial Program (1965) established a string of *maquiladoras* to compete with East Asian export manufacturing, sparking a global trend of relocation of manufacturing from North to South via this model of low-wage assembly work.

As de-peasantization advances, states and provinces across the world have embraced the *maquila* model to provide off-farm employment. Between 1975 and 1995, 1,200,000 jobs in the global garment industry located in the newly created state of Bangladesh, alone, and by the start of the twenty-first century the world economy accounted for almost 30 million *maquila* jobs. From the 1970s, Mexico's *maquilas* spread inland, driven by firms intent upon improving their bargaining position with labour through subcontracting arrangements, beyond reducing wages. Most workers' take-home pay is one-third of a 'sustainable living wage', forcing them to rely on household and community networks to pool resources to make ends meet. Here local, and global, relations of social reproduction intersect: 'When branded marketers of apparel subcontract their production in the developing world, they tap the resources of these communities. By paying less than a living wage, they require them to supplement and subsidize the work that is done in the factory' (Collins 2003: 168–9).

While the development narrative represents rural industrialization as a first step on the ladder of economic success, the world-historical context through which agrarian regions are transformed is more complex. Differential conditions and class differentiation across the agrarian world make generalization impossible. Where rural industrialization is robust and cumulative, such as in parts of south-east Asia, 'peasants appear to have improved their socio-economic status even without a change in the distribution of agricultural land', or sometimes by pawning their land to invest in human capital, such as education for their children or in securing overseas employment (Aguilar 2005: 227–8). Global assembly work typically intensifies gender and ethnic inequalities in rural regions, often generating powerlessness among adolescents, and intergenerational tensions as young people are at once seduced by, and excluded from, symbols of modernity associated with off-farm work (Green 2003).

A recent study of rural industrialization, via the insertion of two of Mexico's rural areas, Yucatán and La Laguna, into the global garment industry in the context of a deteriorating agricultural economy, reveals the limits of the development narrative in this 'low road to competition'. Aside from the absence of technology transfer, global assembly work is increasingly tenuous, where Chinese labour costs (one-sixth of the Mexican wage) are now undermining the *maquilas* (Van Doren and Zárate-Hoyos 2003). The outcome, intensified labour migration, is often prefigured in gendered relations of social reproduction. For example, in the Los Amoles group of communities in the lowlands region of southern Mexico, while women manage subsistence farms as well as perform domestic assembly work for, or work in, nearby clothing *maquiladoras*, men migrate to the United States for short-term work, returning at agricultural harvest time (Gonzalez 2001).

The migrant labour phenomenon ultimately represents a global response to the changing requirements of social reproduction. In rural China, where the migrant labourer population is around 120 million, 'the only way to survive as a family is to not live as one. Migrant workers . . . are the mules driving the country's stunning economic growth. And the money they send home has become essential for jobless rural China' (Yardley 2004b: A1). Already in the mid-1990s, 37 million rural migrants remitted an average of 2,000 *yuan* to their villages, especially in richer provinces (Zhejiang, Fujian and Guangdong) on the coast (Eyferth et al. 2003).

Whether in China's vast territory, or on an international scale, the export of labour from rural communities has become a key livelihood strategy in the neoliberal era. Within the global South, under the pressures of structural adjustment in the 1980s, internal migration reached between 300 and 400 million people. Continuing into the twenty-first century, this pool of labour contributes to current levels of 150 million migrants leaving overburdened cities to find work in metropolitan regions of the global economy. Estimates suggest that roughly 100 million kinfolk depend on remittances of the global labour force. Mexico, a nation of 100 million, earns more than $9 billion a year in remittances – almost as much as India, with its population of 1 billion. And Latin America and the Caribbean received $25 billion in 2002 from remittances, which, along with foreign direct investment, are now more important sources of finances than private lending (McMichael 2004: 208). Sometimes these funds are channelled into public ventures to replace shrinking public largesse in the neoliberal era. Indonesian villages have used remittances to finance schools, roads and housing, and in Zacatecas, Mexico, remittances have financed new roads, schools, churches, water systems and parks.

The migrant labour performed, whether in fields, sweatshops, restaurants, care industry, transport, entertainment, sex tourism, building maintenance or burgeoning informal arenas of Northern economies, binds host and sending communities together in a tangle of circuits of social reproduction. These are circuits within which exile, opportunity, vulnerability, dependence and slavery combine distinct cultures of survival and exploitation. Where possible, 'transnational peasants' employ differential migration strategies. For example, peasants from the Andean region use migration 'not to escape their regions but to better position themselves structurally in a well-articulated, migrant export economy' (Kyle 2000: 197). Comparing two highland villages in Ecuador, Azuay and Octavalo, Kyle distinguishes between communities sending wage labour abroad, and 'merchant migrants' who commodify and market their own and others' indigenous culture (notably Andean music) in the global marketplace, concluding:

> Transnational migration may be fundamentally rooted in economic processes of capital accumulation (class) but is often impossible to disentangle from other important areas such as ethnic and gender discrimination (caste) and historical social norms and ideologies of the migrating group (culture) because all three have a synergistic or multiple conjunctural effect. (Kyle 2000: 198)

GLOBALIZATION AS RESISTANCE

Global power relations are inevitably infused with resistances, which take multiple forms affecting the agrarian world. These include consumer movements concerned with food safety and fair trade; farmer movements concerned with the impact of globalization on rural/urban distributive relations; farm-worker movements concerned with human rights, pesticide use and worker security; farmer/peasant movements concerned with protecting a way of life against agribusiness – such as seed savers, land rights claimants and community supported agricultures; and indigenous peasant movements struggling for regional and cultural (landed) autonomy – notably the neo-Zapatista movement in southern Mexico (Bartra and Otero 2005).

The broadest contours of these relations of resistance are perhaps captured in the elemental struggle between a centralized agro-industry with market coordinates, and a democratic and diversifying eco-agriculture with its coordinates in various forms of public sovereignty. In between are distributive movements like the rural Mexican Barzón movement of the 1990s, generating a 'debtors' insurgency contesting neoliberalism (Williams 2001); and the social experiment of 'fair trade', addressing the colonial legacy of tropical mono-crops, by reducing the psychic distance between producers and consumers, eliminating intermediaries and building social needs (education, health, environmental protections, job security, nondiscriminatory work conditions) into the price structure of the commodity (Raynolds 2000).

Parallel to global fair trade schemes for certification, civil society groups are exploring *domestic* fair trade schemes – such as Red Tomato, based in Massachusetts, which markets produce from Southern small farmers in New England, or Mexico's *Comercio Justo*, which markets coffee, cacao, honey, handicrafts and basic grains for small producers, within a set of fair trade standards based on international criteria, and with the goal of obtaining just prices for small producers as an alternative to export market dependence (Jaffee et al. 2004). Related efforts to protect Mexico's 'culture of maize' are underway in response to the neoliberal assault on peasant maize farming. However limited in scope, off-farm activities subsidize this culture – ranging from monetary remittances to creating new markets for locally grown maize varieties and other peasant products, such as amaranth, beans and honey: 'large numbers of urban denizens are now purchasing hand-made tortillas by the dozen . . . Similarly, coloured tortillas, *tamales* made from *criollo* maizes, *mole*, *pozole* and other traditional foods from Mexico's indigenous and peasant cultures command premium prices from peasant salespeople (mostly women) in many parts of the country' (Barkin 2002: 82–3).

The Slow Food movement, originating in Italy but now global, builds on similar principles to fair trade: localizing foodsheds, retaining local cuisines and protecting food heritage in general. The Slow Food Foundation for Biodiversity formed in Italy, 2003, to 'know, catalogue and safeguard small quality productions and to guarantee them and economic and commercial future'. In relation to this, COOP-Italia, a consortium with over 200 consumer cooperatives, coordinates production and sale of quality food products traceable to their socio-spatial origins, with the aim of protecting links between consumers and producers, within a broader ethical engagement that includes supporting fair trade initiatives, water provisioning in Africa and contesting diffusion of genetically modified organisms (Fonte 2006). Alternative Food Networks also contribute to the proliferation of new rural development practices, such as agro-tourism, energy production and landscape management. These developments, known as 'multi-functionality', have potential as a new Northern agricultural policy paradigm (Pretty 2002), once current WTO trade rules cease using multifunctionality as a façade for concealing subsidies at the expense of the 2.5 billion rural peoples in the South (Losch 2004).

On a broader scale, the proliferation of movements for land rights coincides with the privatization of agricultural resources, such as marketing boards, credit and collective lands, led by the World Bank's 'market-assisted reform programme'. This programme views land markets as a solution to poverty and rural development by facilitating titling and redistribution of land through land banks, releasing the 'social capital' of the rural poor through cooperative networks, subsidized with microfinance (cf. Woolcock and Narayan 2000). But land inflation is a typical outcome, and this is exacerbated by financial liberalization, which replaces public farm credit systems with individualized micro-credit markets, deepening patterns of indebtedness among rural households (Barros et al. 2003; Ramachandran and Swaminathan 2002). Privatization intensifies debt stress under conditions of highly unequal landholding patterns, and access to markets, resulting in individual acts of suicide or collective resistances.

Relations of resistance are embodied in a proliferating occupation of land *en masse*, as the material and political act of a 'new peasantry' (Petras 1997), committed to a relatively autonomous politics of 'agrarian citizenship' (Wittman 2005).

Such movements seek to reconstitute the rural as a civic base through which to critique conventional electoral politics and the development narrative. The most substantial movements are the Brazilian *Movimento dos Trabalhadores Rurais Sem Terra* (MST), which emerged in the 1980s, and the South African Landless People's Movement (2002). Land rights movements have formed alliances within the framework of the Landless People's Charter, adopted in Durban in 2001, and oriented to the shared goals of the global justice movement.

The core of the new relations of resistance, perhaps, centres on the food sovereignty movement. 'Food sovereignty' expresses a variety of agrarian relations that counterpoint corporate relations of production and consumption of food. It is a unifying concept emerging from the transnational peasant movement, *Via Campesina*, which introduced food sovereignty into public debate during the 1996 World Food Summit in Rome. While food sovereignty has multiple meanings depending on context, the movement is building an alternative, decentralized understanding of food security in which material want-satisfaction is not subordinated to the market, but embedded in ecological principles of community and environmental sustainability.

The *Via Campesina* includes 149 farm organizations representing millions of farming families from 56 countries (Desmarais 2007). Food sovereignty, in the *Via Campesina* vision, would subordinate trade relations to the question of access to credit, land and fair prices, to be set via rules of fair trade negotiated in UNCTAD and not at the WTO, with active participation of farmers' movements. This principle of self-organization would inform a distinctive vision of strategic diversity, sanctioned multilaterally. French farmer and member of *Via Campesina*, José Bové, observed: 'Why should the global market escape the rule of international law or human rights conventions passed by the United Nations?' (Bové and Dufour 2001: 165). But access to land is fundamental.

The MST, a member of *Via Campesina*, has settled over 400,000 families on 15 million acres of land seized by takeovers in Brazil over the past 18 years. The landless-workers' movement draws legitimacy from the Brazilian constitution's sanctioning of the confiscation of uncultivated private property. From 1985 to 1996, rural unemployment rose by 5.5 million, and from 1995 to 1999 a rural exodus of 4 million Brazilians occurred. While dispossessed farmers comprise 60 per cent of the movement's membership, it also includes unemployed workers and disillusioned civil servants. Land seizures are followed, gradually, by the formation of cooperatives, which involve social mobilization to transform a material act into a politics of social and ecological practice.

This 'peasant model' 'does not entail a rejection of modernity, technology and trade accompanied by a romanticized return to an archaic past steeped in rustic traditions [but is based on] ethics and values where culture and social justice count for something and concrete mechanisms are put in place to ensure a future without hunger' (Desmarais 2003: 110). The *Via Campesina* is developing alternative forms of modernity drawing on deeply rooted traditions. Its vision is for the right of peoples, communities and countries to define culturally, socially, economically and ecologically appropriate policies regarding agriculture, labour, fishing, food and land. While demanding guarantee of such rights through the state system, the substantive content of those rights is to be determined individually by communities and countries.

There are, of course, multiple examples of communities, and even governments, promoting conditions resembling food sovereignty. In Thailand, for example, farmers in the semi-arid north-east have been developing 'local wisdom networks', using the concept of 'learning alliances' to rehabilitate local ecological relations and promote health before wealth in agricultural practices. Since the 1997 financial crisis, these alliances have supported partnerships between farmer networks and the government, dedicated to improved water conservation, participatory technologies, community forest management and biodiversity promotion. The goal is to convert monoculture to integrated, diversified farming and community development, and to convert state agencies to a rural sustainability paradigm (Ruaysoongnern and de Vries 2005).

Resistance to the effects of corporate globalization ultimately concerns not only reintegrating social, agricultural and ecological relations into alternative models, but, in doing so, transforming *political* cultures of modernity that have been premised on the industrialization of rural economy and the redundancy of peasantries.

CONCLUSION

The dominant theme in this chapter concerns the social stakes involved in universalizing an industrial culture across the agrarian world. Industrial agriculture, in its most mature form in California, nevertheless depends on an endless stream of low-wage Mexican farm-workers and sharecroppers (Walker 2005). That is, agro-industrial production relies on global circuits of social reproduction, which in turn have become essential (through remittances) to the survival of 'peasant-based' rural cultures. As we have seen, the protocols of the WTO sanction the spread of corporate agriculture, a significant element of which involves a process of 'de-peasantization' as small farmers join the global labour force. In the Mexican case, NAFTA, the leading edge of these protocols, sanctions US corn dumping in the Mexican market, at the expense of maize producers, and generates the migrant labour force that reproduces Californian agriculture, among other parts of the US economy.

Thus the consequences are not an inevitable homogenization of the agrarian world. Certainly the social reproduction of an affluent global consumer class has woven a web of corporate relations that will remain as tight as the fossil-fuel energy system can bear into the foreseeable future. But in the disruptions to rural cultures across the world, there are a variety of alternatives forming, by necessity, to weather the agrarian crisis. As it has over the centuries, the agrarian world has often displayed resilience in the face of natural disasters, and the disruptive reach of empire. The world itself faces a serious threshold in the twenty-first century, whereby corporate globalization's pursuit of an all-embracing market culture is facing, and producing, social and environmental limits that can offer new spaces for a robust variety of agricultures dedicated to principles of social and ecological sustainability. These, in turn, promise to revalue the contribution of the agrarian world to life itself.

References

Aguilar, F.V. Jr. 2005. 'Rural land struggles in Asia: overview of selected contexts'. In S. Moyo and P. Yeros (eds), *Reclaiming the Land: The Resurgence of Rural Movements in Africa, Asia and Latin America*, 209–34. London: Zed.

Araghi, F. 1995. 'Global de-peasantisation, 1945–1990', *Sociological Quarterly*, 36 (2), 337–68.

Araghi, F. 2000. 'The great global enclosure of our times: peasants and the agrarian question at the end of the twentieth century'. In F. Magdoff, J.B. Foster and F.H. Buttel (eds), *Hungry for Profit: The Agribusiness Threat to Farmers, Food and the Environment*, 145–60. New York: Monthly Review Press.

Barboza, D. 2004. 'In roaring China, sweaters are west of socks city', *The New York Times*, 24 December, C1, C3.

Barkin, D. 2002. 'The reconstruction of a modern Mexican peasantry', *The Journal of Peasant Studies*, 30 (1), 73–90.

Barndt, D. 2002. *Tangled Routes: Women, Work and Globalization on the Tomato Trail*. Aurora, ON: Garamond Press.

Barros, F., Sauer, S. and Schwartzmann, S. (eds) 2003. *The Negative Impacts of World Bank Market Based Land Reform*. Brasilia: Rede Brasil.

Bartra, A. and Otero, G. 2005. 'Indian peasant movements in Mexico: The struggle for land, autonomy and democracy'. In S. Moyo and P. Yeros (eds), *Reclaiming the Land: The Resurgence of Rural Movements in Africa, Asia and Latin America*, 383–410. London: Zed Books.

Bernstein, H. 2005. 'Rural land and land conflicts in Sub-Saharan Africa'. In S. Moyo and P. Yeros (eds), *Reclaiming the Land: The Resurgence of Rural Movements in Africa, Asia and Latin America*, 67–101. London: Zed Books.

Bezner-Kerr, R. 2005. 'Informal labor and social relations in Northern Malawi: The theoretical challenges and implications of ganyu labor for food security', *Rural Sociology*, 70 (2), 167–87.

Blank, S.C. 1998. *The End of Agriculture in the American Portfolio*. Westport, CT: Quorum Books.

Bové, J. and Dufour, F. 2001. *The World Is Not for Sale*. London: Verso.

Bryceson, D. 2004. 'Agrarian vista or vortex? African rural livelihood policies', *Review of African Political Economy*, 102, 617–29.

Busch, L. and Bain, C. 2004. 'New! Improved? The transformation of the global agrifood system', *Rural Sociology*, 69 (3), 321–46.

Chan, A. 1996. 'Boot camp at the shoe factory', *Guardian Weekly*, 17 November, 20–1.

Chossudovsky, M. 2003. *The Globalization of Poverty and the New World Order*. Shanty Bay, ON: Global Outlook.

Collins, J. 1995. 'Gender and cheap labor in agriculture'. In P. McMichael (ed.), *Food and Agrarian Orders in the World-Economy*. Westport, CT: Greenwood Press.

Collins, J. 2003. *Threads: Gender, Labor and Power in the Global Apparel Industry*. Chicago: University of Chicago Press.

Davis, M. 2001. *Late Victorian Holocausts: El Niño Famines and the Making of the Third World*. London: Verso.

Delgado, C., Rosegrant, M., Steinfeld, H., Elui, S. and Courbois, C. 1999. *Livestock to 2020: The Next Food Revolution*. Washington, DC: IFPRI.

Desmarais, A.A. 2007. *La Via Campesina: Globalization and the Power of Peasants*. Point Black, NS and London: Fenwood Books & Pluto.

Dolan, C.S. 2004. 'On farm and packhouse: Employment at the bottom of a global value chain', *Rural Sociology*, 69 (1), 99–126.

Dolan, C. and Humphrey, J. 2000. 'Governance and trade in fresh vegetables: The impact of UK supermarkets on the African horticulture industry', *Journal of Development Studies*, 37, 147–76.

Dugger, C.W. 2004. 'Supermarket giants crush Central American farmers', *The New York Times*, 28 December, A1, A10.

Economy, E.C. 2004. *The River Runs Black: The Environmental Challenge to China's Future.* Ithaca, NY: Cornell University Press.

Escobar, A. 1995. *Encountering Development.* Princeton, NJ: Princeton University Press.

Eyferth, J., Ho, P. and Vermeer, E.B. 2003. 'Introduction: The opening up of China's countryside', *The Journal of Peasant Studies*, 30 (3–4) (April–July), 1–17.

Fonte, M. 2006 'Slow food's presidia: What do small producers do with big retailers?'. In T. Marsden and J. Murdoch (eds), *Between the Local and the Global: Confronting Complexity in the Contemporary Agri-food Sector*, 203–240. Amsterdam: Elsevier.

Friedmann, H. 1982. 'The political economy of food: The rise and fall of the postwar international food order', *American Journal of Sociology*, 88S, 248–86.

Friedmann, H. 2005. 'From colonialism to green capitalism: Social movements and emergence of food regimes'. In F.H. Buttel and P. McMichael (eds), *New Directions in the Sociology of Global Development*, 229–68. Oxfordshire: Elsevier.

Gardner, G. and Halweil, B. 2000. *Underfed and Overfed: The Global Epidemic of Malnutrition.* Washington, DC: Worldwatch Paper 150.

Gonzalez, L. 2001. 'Mexico/U.S. migration and gender relations: The Guanajuatense community in Mexico and the United States'. In R.M. Kelly, J.H. Bayes, M.E. Hawkesworth and B. Young (eds), *Gender, Globalization and Democratization*, 75–94. Lanham, MD: Rowman and Littlefield.

Goss, J. and Burch, D. 2001. 'From agricultural modernization to agro-food globalization: The waning of national development in Thailand', *Third World Quarterly*, 22 (6), 969–86.

Green, L. 2003. 'Notes on Mayan youth and rural industrialization in Guatemala', *Critique of Anthropology*, 23, 51–73.

Grzybowski, C. 2004. 'Taboo in the countryside, thank you MST', *Land Action Research Network*, 27 April. Available at <http://www.landaction.org/display.php?article>

Gupta, A. 1998. *Postcolonial Developments. Agriculture in the Making of Modern India.* Durham, NC: Duke University Press.

Jaffee, D., Kloppenburg, J.R. Jr and Monroy, M.B. 2004. 'Bringing the "moral charge" home: Fair trade within the North and within the South', *Rural Sociology*, 69 (2), 169–96.

Kabeer, N. and Tran, T.V.A. 2002. 'Leaving the rice fields, but not the countryside: Gender, livelihoods diversification, and pro-poor growth in rural Vietnam'. In S. Razavi (ed.), *Shifting Burdens: Gender and Agrarian Change under Neoliberalism.* Bloomfield, CT: Kumarian Press.

Kay, C. 2000. 'Latin America's agrarian transformation: Peasantization and proletarianization'. In D. Bryceson, C. Kay and J. Mooij (eds), *Disappearing Peasantries?* London: ITDG Publishing.

Kyle, D. 2000. *Transnational Peasants: Migrations, Networks, and Ethnicity in Andean Ecuador.* Baltimore, MD: The Johns Hopkins University Press.

Long, N. and Roberts, B. 2005. 'Changing rural scenarios and research agendas in Latin America in the new century'. In F.H. Buttel and P. McMichael (eds), *New Directions in the Sociology of Global Development*, 55–89. Oxfordshire: Elsevier.

Long, N. and Villarreal, M. 1998. 'Small product, big issues: Value contestations and cultural identities in cross-border commodity networks', *Development and Change*, 29 (4), 725–50.

Losch, B. 2004. 'Debating the multifunctionality of agriculture: From trade negotiations to development policies by the South', *Journal of Agrarian Change*, 4 (3), 336–60.

Lynas, M. 2001. 'Selling starvation', *Corporate Watch*, 7, Spring.

McMichael, P. 2004. *Development and Social Change: A Global Perspective*, 3rd edn. Thousand Oaks, CA: Pine Forge Press.

McMichael, P. 2005. 'Global development and the corporate food regime'. In F.H. Buttel and P. McMichael (eds), *New Directions in the Sociology of Global Development*, 269–303. Oxfordshire: Elsevier.

Madeley, J. 2000. *Hungry for Trade*. London: Zed Books.

Marsden, T.K. 2003. *The Condition of Rural Sustainability*. Wageningen: Van Gorcum.

Mintz, S. 1985. *Sweetness and Power: The Place of Sugar in Modern History*. New York: Vintage.

Mohanty, B.B. 2005. ' "We are like the living dead": Farmer suicides in Maharashtra, Western India', *The Journal of Peasant Studies*, 32 (2), 243–76.

Moyo, S. and Yeros, P. (eds.) 2005. *Reclaiming the Land: The Resurgence of Rural Movements in Africa, Asia and Latin America*. London: Zed Books.

Nierenberg, D. and Halweil, B. 2005. 'Cultivating food security'. In *State of the World 2005. Redefining Global Security*. Worldwatch Institute. New York: W.W. Norton.

Petras, J. 1997. 'Latin America: The resurgence of the left', *New Left Review*, 223, 17–47.

Polanyi, K. 1957. *The Great Transformation*. Boston: Beacon Press.

Ponte, S. 2002. *Farmers and Markets in Tanzania: How Policy Reforms Affect Rural Livelihoods in Africa*. Oxford: James Currey.

Pretty, J. 2002. *Agri-Culture: Reconnecting People, Land and Nature*. London: Earthscan.

Pritchard, B. and Burch, D. 2003. *Agro-Food Globalization in Perspective: International Restructuring in the Processing Tomato Industry*. Aldershot: Ashgate.

Ramachancran, V.K. and Swaminathan, M. 2002. 'Rural banking and landless labour households: Institutional reform and rural credit markets in India', *Journal of Agrarian Change*, 2 (4), 502–44.

Raynolds, L. 2000. 'Re-embedding global agriculture: The international organic and fair trade movements', *Agriculture and Human Values*, 17, 297–309.

Reardon, T., Timmer, C.P., Barrett, C.B. and Berdegue, J. 2003. 'The rise of supermarkets in Africa, Asia and Latin America', *American Journal of Agricultural Economics*, 85 (5), 1140–6.

Rifkin, J. 1992. *Beyond Beef: The Rise and Fall of the Cattle Culture*. New York: Penguin.

Rifkin, J. 1998. *The Biotech Century: Harnessing the Gene and Remaking the World*. New York: Tarcher/Putnam.

Ruaysoongnern, S. and de Vries, F.P. 2005. 'Learning alliances development for scaling up of multi-purpose farm ponds in a semi-arid region of the Mekong basin'. Paper presented at the Learning Alliances Conference, Delft, 6–10 June.

Sheller, M. 2003: *Consuming the Caribbean*. New York: Routledge.

Starr, A. 2001. *Naming the Enemy: Anti-Corporate Movements Confront Globalization*. London: Zed Books.

Tilford, D. 2004. 'Behind the scenes: Shrimp'. In *State of the World 2004*, 92–3. Washington, DC: WorldWatch Institute.

Van Doren, R. and Zárate-Hoyos, G.A. 2003. 'The insertion of rural areas into global markets: A comparison of garment production in Yucatán and La Laguna, Mexico', *Journal of Latin American Studies*, 36, 571–92.

Vidal, J. 2001. 'Brazil sets out on the road to oblivion', *Guardian Weekly*, 19–25 July, 20.

Vidal, J. 2004a. 'Meat-eaters devour world's water', *Guardian Weekly*, 3–9 September, 31.

Vidal, J. 2004b. 'Beyond the city limits', *Guardian Weekly*, 17–23 September, 17–18.

Walker, R.A. 2005. *The Conquest of Bread: 150 Years of Agribusiness in California*. New York: The New Press.

Williams, H.L. 2001. *Social Movements and Economic Transition: Markets and Distributive Conflict in Mexico*. Cambridge: Cambridge University Press.

Wittman, H. 2005. 'The social ecology of agrarian reform: The landless rural workers' movement and agrarian citizenship in Mato Grosso, Brazil'. Unpublished PhD dissertation, Development Sociology, Cornell University.

Woolcock, M. and Narayan, D. 2000. 'Social capital: Implications for development theory, research and policy', *World Bank Research Observer*, 15 (2), 225–49.

Wright, A. and Wolford, W. 2003. *To Inherit the Earth: The Landless Movement and the Struggle for a New Brazil*. Oakland: Food First Books.

Yardley, J. 2004a. 'Farmers being moved aside by China's real estate boom', *The New York Times*, 8 December, A1, A16.

Yardley, J. 2004b. 'Rural exodus for work fractures Chinese family', *The New York Times*, 21 December, A1, A12.

Chapter 11

Globalization and the Environment

Steve Yearley

INTRODUCTION: THE EARTH, THE GLOBE AND THE DISCOURSE OF THE GLOBAL ENVIRONMENT

At first sight, the environment and globalization seem to be very intimately connected since the environment is already global in very many ways. The atmosphere is shared by all; the sun's warmth heats everyone; the oceans of the world all connect, effectively giving us one global marine environment. One could say that, unlike the market or telecommunications or terrorism, the environment always has been global. In this context, to talk about the 'globalization of the environment', as though the environment had only recently gained a global dimension, appears peculiar. Accordingly, one key issue for social scientists interested in globalization processes and the environment is about the very conceptualization of the 'global environment': what does it mean to think of the environment 'globally'. In this chapter I shall review our understanding of globalization and the environment from three main perspectives. The first relates to the global environment itself and particularly to recent influences on the way that we think about issues at the level of the global environment. The second main perspective relates to institutions that affect the environment at a global level – specifically the interactions between environmental questions and bodies (particularly the World Trade Organization [WTO]) that aim to regulate global trade and to encourage world economic growth. Finally, I shall examine sociological arguments about the precise nature of globalization and their implications for environmental reform and for the prospects for the globalization of environmental protection. I shall begin with the first of these: the idea of the 'global environment' itself.

Ironically, the initial commentators on the trends towards globalization and on the need for a sociology of global phenomena, writing in the late 1980s and 1990s, tended to overlook the environment as an area of globalization. It was common for writers to concentrate on the worldwide spread of cultural products such as television programmes, popular music and sports, on the global reach of communications technologies, on international currency movements and the power of the world's financial markets, and on the global strategies of transnational firms but to omit the environment (see Yearley 1996: 2–15). The irony lies in the fact that the Earth and its environment can make some claim to utter, physical global-ness. By the middle 1990s it was apparent that, outside of sociology texts, the environmental movement had made solid progress in appropriating the imagery and language of the globe for itself. Environmental non-governmental organizations (NGOs) dominated the use of images of the Earth as a global entity for which we should have feelings of compassion and caring. The term 'Earth Day' had become synonymous with the movement. Groups could unselfconsciously call themselves Friends of the Earth or proclaim their orientation as EarthFirst! In most contexts, to hear the word 'Earth' led one to think straight away of the environment.

Furthermore, during the 1990s – in the wake of the 'Earth Summit' of 1992 in Rio de Janeiro – there emerged the language of 'global environmental problems'. The environmental movement and environmental policy prescriptions which had hitherto typically focused on national or regional needs were now re-thought as specifically global. On this view, you could not, for example, get rid of your industrial waste problems in Northern countries by displacing them to the South; this was environmental hypocrisy and was still injurious to the Earth. In any event, such practices were held likely to boomerang back (George 1992), for example by leading to pollution which could re-enter the North via agricultural exports (Yearley 1996: 76–7). Environmentalists encouraged us to think of the world as small, with nowhere so remote that problems there might not work their way back to us. Though well aware that poorer countries and poorer regions tended to suffer high levels of environmental problems, many environmentalists nonetheless felt that there was an important level of worldwide similarity in the ecological threat to humankind. The favoured image was of the human race adrift in space in a lonely lifeboat with both a moral and practical imperative to look to our common interests. In an age of globalization, many environmentalists felt their cause to be the exemplification of the new culture of global-ness.

Two important developments at the end of the 1980s and in the 1990s formed the decisive framework that shaped how these considerations played out. First, this period witnessed two celebrated candidates for global environmental problems: ozone depletion and global climate change. As described below, these cases appeared straightforwardly and intrinsically global and helped to make the globalization of the environment appear compelling and obvious. New institutions such as the Intergovernmental Panel on Climate Change (or IPCC, see the next section) were established to pursue the global interest in such global environmental protection matters. Second, and less noticed by environmentalists until the process was well underway, there was a growing trend towards the global liberalization of trade, also overseen by global institutions (the WTO and the International Monetary Fund [IMF] and meetings of the G7 and G8), that many have seen as inimical to environmental protection. Over the last decade, meetings of the latter organizations have given rise to fierce and determined protest by groups and movement activists associated with environmental protection and international fair trade. Nearly every form of environmental protection regulation looks like an impediment to trade, so the anxiety is that the WTO is on a mission of global deregulation, as will be discussed in the second perspective below. Viewed in this light, though global institutions are on the rise, they seem, in a paradoxical way, both to advance and to threaten the cause of environmental protection. In the twenty-first century it is now clear that the relationship between globalization and the environment is a complex one, full of strains and competing visions, and at times almost paradoxical.

THE 'GLOBAL-NESS' OF GLOBAL ENVIRONMENTAL PROBLEMS

In undertaking this review it will be beneficial to start by exploring the two canonical global environmental problems that lent such support to the straightforward idea that there is a worldwide interest in environmental reform. In the case of the ozone layer, there is a stratum in the atmosphere where oxygen molecules (made up of two oxygen atoms) are converted into ozone (composed of three) by incoming solar radiation. Ozone is an unstable compound and spontaneously turns back into molecular oxygen (every two molecules of ozone produce three of oxygen). For this reason, ozone is very uncommon close to the Earth's surface; any that forms rapidly reverts to oxygen. But in the ozone layer concentrations are much greater and reasonably stable: approximately the same amount of ozone is formed every minute as decomposes in that minute. The ozone layer is around 30 km up but is important to life on the Earth's surface precisely because the continuous formation of ozone absorbs a large share of the incoming radiation which would otherwise be harmful to people and other creatures. The ozone layer came under threat from manufactured chemicals, notably chlorofluorocarbons (CFCs). These chemicals, containing carbon, chlorine and fluorine, are not present in nature but are reasonably easily synthesized. They are non-poisonous and very stable and more or less inert. They were thus widely used in a variety of applications including refrigeration systems, fire extinguishers and 'clean room' air conditioning. When they were released into the atmosphere after use nobody assumed that they would have any harmful effects since they were non-toxic and unreactive. But it was precisely this unreactive nature that allowed these chemicals to persist in the atmosphere for years, even decades. And slowly, as they dispersed through the whole atmosphere, a proportion of these chemicals entered the ozone layer where incoming solar radiation was strong enough to encourage their breakdown in conjunction with the ozone gas in the layer. As it turned out, each molecule of the CFCs could consume numerous ozone molecules, thus shifting the balance in the ozone layer in favour of oxygen and against ozone. This process was more rapid at the South Pole in winter time when the surface of minute particles, condensed by the cold, offered a medium where these reactions could proceed more rapidly. Accordingly the depletion of the ozone was strongest around the poles and was so advanced over the Antarctic that commentators spoke of an ozone 'hole' that was first detected in the mid-1980s. The area of pronounced ozone thinning was huge – larger than the size of the entire United States – and it was subject to a certain amount of drifting and hence could unpredictably affect Australasia and the southernmost parts of South America.

The case of ozone depletion had two key attributes. First, the ozone layer lends itself to being considered in global terms. It is a hollow protective sphere encasing the whole world and protecting us from cancer-causing high-energy radiation. It is far above the Earth's surface and does not belong to anyone. The fact that many people had never known of its existence only added to its rarity and sense of indiscriminate worldwide beneficence. The second realization is that in the case of the ozone layer there is very little correlation between pollution and its impact. Emissions from vehicle exhausts, for example, cause pollution in the cities and around the highways where the cars are. The impact falls off rapidly with distance. But because the CFCs might circulate in the atmosphere for many years before working their harmful effects, there was no geographical connection at all between the source of the pollutant and its eventual impact. This meant both that my emissions could impact someone else anywhere on the globe and that no country could seek a solution to the problem by actions within that country alone. It made little sense, for example, for Australians, badly affected by the Antarctic 'hole', to change their practices unless everyone in the whole world changed too. This was a problem affecting a global resource that needed concerted international action.

The main debate about ozone depletion occurred in the second half of the 1980s and the framework of the UN-brokered agreement to phase out 'ozone-eating' substances was in place by the end of the decade (Benedick 1991: 213–69). There was a general air of optimism engendered by the rapidity of this international agreement even though, 15 years later on, there are still some problems. The replacement chemicals that have been substituted for the CFCs are still somewhat ozone depleting and there remain hundreds of thousands of tons of ozone-depleting chemicals in the atmosphere that were manufactured before the agreement came into force. Thus the ozone layer is likely to continue to be under threat for tens of years. The situation is also aggravated because there is an unknown amount of smuggling and illicit CFC use. Furthermore, additions to the list of substances that deplete the ozone layer are still being found (a recent concern relates to sulphur hexafluoride, a substance used extensively in electrical insulation). All the same, the ozone case suggested that effective and relatively rapid action could be taken to tackle global environmental problems and international attention switched to climate change shortly after the ozone case had been agreed, in part because of optimism induced by the success of the ozone talks.

The issue of climate change has received a great deal of publicity but it will be useful to review quickly its qualifications for global status. The 'greenhouse effect' is the reason why Earth is considerably warmer than the moon, even though both bodies are the same average distance from the sun. Each square metre of the surface of each receives about the same amount of heat from the sun but the heat-energy that the moon gets from the sun's rays is dissipated into space while the atmosphere forms an insulating layer around the Earth, causing the diffusion of heat energy to occur more slowly. Over millions of year both bodies have arrived at an equilibrium temperature with the average surface temperature on Earth around 15 °C and the moon's around −18 °C (Ross 1991: 75–7). Various components of the Earth's atmosphere are responsible for this greenhouse warming though carbon dioxide is one of the principal greenhouse gases. The claim is that, for many thousands of years, carbon dioxide levels have been low and reasonably constant but that they are now increasing enormously due to industrialization and the burning of fossil fuels. An increase in the concentration of this gas and others (for example, the CFCs are also highly effective greenhouse molecules) will intensify the insulating effect of the atmosphere and result in higher average temperatures. Thus human activity is forecast to cause the Earth to warm to 'unnatural' levels, leading not just to higher average temperatures but also to profound changes in the climate. Such predictions have been supported by the specially convened expert panel, the Intergovernmental Panel on Climate Change (IPCC), an unprecedented international working party on climate science (see Boehmer-Christiansen 2003).

The feature that makes this problem a global one is that carbon dioxide is inevitably emitted by all the people of the world, if only just through breathing, but more dramatically in so far as they burn fossil fuels or wood. But the greenhouse gases each of us emits do not affect us only. The carbon dioxide molecules we liberate stay in the atmosphere on average for around 6 years (Silvertown 1990: 78–82), meaning that they become dispersed around the globe. Inevitably, our individual emissions get mixed in with everyone else's. Thus, the greenhouse phenomenon appears to operate at a planetary level. Reducing my emissions is not generally likely to lessen the impact of global warming or climate change at my locale any more than at any other specific point on the globe. Furthermore, atmospheric warming is thought likely to induce physical and biological changes at a planetary level. For example, a warmer biosphere will lead to an expansion of the water in the oceans. Sea-level rise, perhaps by tens of centimetres, will occur all over the world's oceans. Similarly, changes in the weather system will have implications for climate across the whole world. On this view, we are all implicated in the cause. We are all likely to be affected by the consequences. And we cannot isolate our individual responsibility for the pollution because physical and biological systems lead to connections taking place across the planet. No polluter is an island.

THE PROBLEMATIC GLOBAL QUALIFICATIONS OF GLOBAL ENVIRONMENTAL PROBLEMS

The two canonical problems appeared to have a strong physical 'global-ness' to them. They seemed to make a compelling case for environmental protection to be a global obligation and something in humanity's common interests. In both cases, the global environment appeared to be a worldwide commons that was under collective threat. People could not solve the problems themselves since any one person's pollution could end up virtually anywhere on earth. Equally, one could not protect one's own local environment from the impact of the actions of others. Collective action was needed in order to tackle these problems. In the 1990s, environmental organizations and campaigners appeared happy to take this situation at face value (even while acknowledging in other contexts the persistence of major environmental differences between the rich North and the poor South), not least because it endorsed their universalistic view of the environmental agenda.

Convincing though this account appears for these two global issues, in assessing the globalization of environmentalism we need to examine – first – whether these problems are as fully global as they appear and – second – whether other environmental problems (including the contamination of the air with noxious chemicals including acid emissions, the fouling of rivers and lakes, pollution of the marine environment, loss of natural species, deforestation and the depletion of fish stocks, the rapid diminution of energy reserves and the wasteful use of mineral resources) are global in all the same senses. If this story is not the same for all supposedly global environmental threats we should also consider how the epithet 'global' has come to be so ubiquitous.

This topic can be clarified using the case of climate change. It is rather quickly evident that the global character of this issue is problematic. First, even if the problem is in some sense everyone's, it is not clear that everyone is similarly culpable. Until recently, the vast majority of additional carbon dioxide that had been introduced into the atmosphere came from the industrialized world, both the wealthy West and the former Soviet bloc. Under these circumstances, to say that the problem is everyone's is effectively a way for the wealthy countries to partially absolve themselves of responsibility for past emissions. It is to share out the responsibility for the impacts in a global way while reserving as private gains the wealth amassed during 200 years of industrial development. It was for more or less these reasons that the Kyoto Protocol, the first agreement for carbon dioxide emissions reduction targets (it followed from the work of the IPCC, was adopted in 1997 and finally entered into force in 2005) applied only to wealthy countries. Though President Bill Clinton was apparently sympathetic to this agreement, at least once it had been tailored somewhat to the USA's preferences, the US Senate refused to ratify it, apparently for fear of the economic harm it might do to the US economy (Hempel 2003: 312). His successor (from 2000), President George W. Bush, has consistently argued that the agreement would be unfair to the United States because high-emitting non-treaty countries (notably China and India) are exempted from its provisions. Such has been the growth of the Chinese economy that this claim, weak and tendentious-looking in 2000, has come to seem a little more plausible by the time of Bush's second term. To his supporters, this looks like a vindication of his approach, though critics point out that his stance has simply increased the net amount of greenhouse gas added to the atmosphere without bringing an international agreement any closer.

At the same time as there is unease about treating the source of climate change as a shared global burden, it is equally clear that there are differential impacts. High-altitude countries clearly have less to fear from sea-level rise than do low-lying ones. But even among lowland countries there is a great deal of disparity. A considerable amount of the Netherlands, for example, is below sea level or in principle in danger of inundation. But the wealthy Dutch, with many centuries of water management, canal building and dyke construction behind them, have much less to fear from sea-level rise than do the average citizens in coastal areas of Bangladesh or the Maldives.

There is furthermore the issue of the perceived importance of these global issues. It is easy to suppose that a global problem is also an urgent or pressing one. But even among the wealthy countries there was no consensus on the urgency of climate change. European countries were enthusiastic supporters of the Kyoto agreement while the United States regarded the possible harm to its economic growth prospects as more serious. Canada ratified the Kyoto Protocol while Australia, similar in many ways, has not. In many developing countries (which are exempted from the Kyoto Protocol at present) other environmental and development issues simply seem more pressing than global warming. Urban air pollution from vehicles, factories, power stations and even from cooking appliances is typically regarded as more important than the relatively remote issue of the enhanced greenhouse effect. Just because an issue is global, that does not mean that it is viewed as urgent or significant every-where. Thus it does not take much scrutiny before these global issues come to appear less universal than much environmental and scientific discourse would imply (Yearley 1997: 233–6).

Turning to the second point, about the global status of other environmental problems, it is clear that there are some other candidate global problems in approxi-mately the same sense. For example, in the last decade a lot of attention has been paid to 'POPs': persistent organic pollutants. These are chemicals, such as some weedkillers, some industrial substances and some unintended by-products of indus-trial activity (such as dioxins), that are resistant to breakdown and which may therefore circulate in the atmosphere for long periods and even become locally concentrated in unpredictable ways. Ecotoxicologists have also become interested in other long-lasting and slow-acting pollutants. Other problems, though not perhaps literally global, are definitely supranational. Perhaps the most famous of these is the so-called Asian Brown Cloud (ABC): a virtually constant, immense smog haze that moves slowly around above the Indian subcontinent and Indian Ocean countries. The cloud, fed by industrial and domestic emissions, reduces sunlight at the ground level, thus cooling the surface while heating the atmosphere (see Ramanathan et al. 2005). The ABC may be impacting agriculture and affecting the regional climate, making monsoons more erratic, for example. Nonetheless, a great deal of pollution and problems of environmental destruction are incontestably local and regional. Environmental problems associated with poverty are typically local. Their continued salience contradicts the idea that we are all in the same collective boat and has led spokespersons for developing-country environmentalism to argue that so-called global environmental problems typically coincide with the concerns of the wealthy North. Northern politicians and policy-makers typically control the application of the 'global' label (Yearley 2005: 46–52).

Finally in this section, it is increasingly evident that things other than explicit environmental policies affect how countries perform relative to the global environ-ment. For example, most Northern countries have greatly reduced their carbon dioxide emissions relating to industrial production since 1990. To some small extent this is due to explicit environmentally related objectives: because their manufacturing processes have become more efficient and less wasteful. But it is largely because so much manufacture has simply been taken over by China. During the 1970s and 1980s many commentators worried about the cynical export of polluting industries to developing countries with lower environmental standards (see Leonard 1988). Such practices were largely halted by international agreements on minimum ecologi-cal standards, but they have in any event simply been overtaken by the wholesale migration of manufacture away from Western Europe, North America and Japan. These days, the pollution associated with the manufactured goods Northern shop-pers consume is largely felt in, and for bureaucratic purposes ascribed to, China, India and so on. This indicates that the explicit goals of environmental policies may be swamped by the impacts of trade and industrial policies, especially in a globalized market. It is to the regulation of this world market that we turn in the next section.

GLOBAL FREE TRADE AND THE CONCEPTUALIZATION OF
ENVIRONMENTAL INTERESTS

As mentioned at the outset, the growth of international and UN bodies associated with tasks such as protecting the ozone layer and working out carbon dioxide reduction targets has been matched and exceeded by the growth of institutions committed to economic growth and specifically the promotion of free trade. Economists have maintained for at least a couple of centuries that there are economic benefits to free trade. In principle, if every country specializes in what they are economically best at and engages openly in trade, this will lead to the highest overall level of wealth. However, national governments have tended to extol the virtues of free trade whilst practising high levels of protectionism. Governments and nationally based industries are attracted to protectionism for a variety of reasons, for example to protect prestigious industries in the face of foreign competition or to defend what they see as strategically or socially necessary employment sectors such as farming. The United States, the European Union (EU) and Japan all protect their farming industries from cheaper food that would be available from lower-income countries and they have done this through a variety of techniques such as taxes on foreign goods and subsidies to their own producers. Exporters clearly dislike protectionism and governments are torn between promoting the interests of exporters, by pressing for freer trade, and the desire to exercise selective protectionism in their own domestic markets. The need for countries to reach some sort of accord on these matters led to the first steps towards an international framework for dealing with barriers to trade; this resulted in the establishing of GATT, the General Agreement on Tariffs and Trade, in 1947. GATT was subject to periodic review, aiming for a progressive smoothing out of obstructive trade barriers. Following a final lengthy set of negotiations (known as the 'Uruguay Round' since the first meeting was held in that country), GATT gave rise to the WTO, a formal body which national governments may join but only by surrendering a degree of sovereignty. Members of the WTO agree to be bound by the WTO's judgments and the WTO is able to impose financial punishments on members who do not comply with its rulings.

The reason this matters to the globalization of environmental concern is that by the time of the WTO's formation at the beginning of 1995, most leading governments had got rid of the crudest and most obvious forms of impediments to trade. They had eliminated arbitrary taxes and tariffs except in areas where these were still permitted (as in the defence of agriculture), but there was increasing concern about so-called technical barriers to trade (known in the business as 'TBTs'). A technical barrier to trade could be such a thing as peculiar and stringent requirements for car lights which made it hard for foreign vehicle companies to satisfy the regulatory authorities but which are well institutionalized among domestic manufacturers. The aim was to eliminate such barriers when they were without sound foundation but to allow them when they had a reasonable justification. The problem for environmentalists was that nearly all environmental regulations can be made to look like TBTs. When the US authorities first demanded that vehicles had catalytic converters to reduce noxious exhaust emissions this was more of a problem to importers who had to make cars specifically for the US market with catalysers in place than for the US industry that simply made all cars compatible with US regulations; it helped the environment and US car companies. And the second problem is that under the WTO rules, it is the WTO that finally decides on whether the environmental regulation is to be allowed or to be struck down as a TBT. Environmentalists saw that many environmental regulations would be subject to review and legally binding judgment by an organization that was constitutionally committed to free trade and not to environmental protection *per se*.

A series of cases indicates that these worries are not just abstract but operate in practice. A key instance was the so-called tuna-dolphin case, tackled by GATT in the run-up to the WTO's foundation. Shoppers in the United States consume a great deal of canned tuna and it became well known that the nets used to catch tuna tended also to kill dolphin which liked to swim above the schools of tuna. By the 1980s US fishers had changed their practices and the design of their nets in such a way as to reduce significantly the dolphin fatalities. But other countries' fishers whose catch was in part exported to the United States had not adopted the same approach. Hence it was claimed that Mexican and Venezuelan tuna, among others, was not comparably dolphin friendly and such tuna was embargoed in the United States. Mexico challenged the US ruling at the GATT, and the GATT arbitration panel supported the challenge. They argued essentially that the USA could not 'regulate how foreign nationals produce goods or raw material outside its legal jurisdiction' providing that the method does not affect the quality of the goods or raw material itself (Vogel 2003: 374). According to the GATT officials, because it was not US dolphins that were being harmed and because the quality of the tuna was unaffected, the United States had no grounds for discriminating against the methods that foreign fishers happened to choose. Environmentalists in the United States and elsewhere were incensed, even if the problem was in fact resolved by subsequent political compromises between the United States and Mexico which led to the adoption of something close to US standards by Latin American fishers in 1997 (Vogel 2003: 379). In this case, negotiations eventually led to higher standards being adopted. Still, this ruling set the pattern for environmentalists' opposition and made clear the two anxieties associated with the WTO: that the decision would be made on a legalistic basis by trade officials or lawyers and that, in some ways worse, the decision is legally binding. Prior to the 1997 agreement, fishers from Mexico and elsewhere who killed dolphin in the course of fishing for tuna had the legal right to export their tuna to the United States even though majority opinion in the United States and most legislators were against this practice.

Of course, the aim of the WTO is to achieve a uniform and (from a certain point of view) fair system of international trade. The WTO is not intended to undermine existing environmental agreements. For example, one could not use the WTO to challenge the treaty against ozone-depleting chemicals on the grounds that the treaty limited one's trade freedoms. Nonetheless, the WTO and associated institutions, such as the IMF, do tend to take the view that, essentially, progress amounts to a growth in economic activity (see Eckersley 2004). Such institutions would be in sympathy with the idea that, as a rule, the market is the best way to put a value on something that is desirable and that most goods are best handled through market mechanisms. They accept that some environmental regulations are necessary but see regulation more as a last resort than as a generally desirable thing. Only the truly indispensable regulations should be retained. Stung by accusations that it is an enemy to environmental protection the WTO makes the case on its website that it is thoroughly compatible with environmental protection: it points out that WTO regulations permit a variety of restrictions on free trade. For example, signatory governments can impose national standards designed to protect the safety of workers (and thus exclude certain products that other countries choose to accept) or they can elect to protect the environment through regulations about nature protection or energy conservation. The WTO asserts that it requires only that governments refrain from using such regulations to benefit their own nation's firms at the expense of other countries' traders (see http://www.wto.org/english/thewto_e/whatis_e/10mis_e/10m04_e.htm).

A change in outlook was reflected in a case that arose almost immediately after the WTO's foundation. The United States wished to protect sea turtles by fitting protective devices (known as 'TEDs', turtle exclusion devices) to shrimp nets to prevent turtles being accidentally caught up and killed. They then wished to prohibit imports from other countries' shrimp fishers who did not fit similar devices. India, Malaysia, Pakistan and Thailand, supported by other Pacific Rim countries and Australia, filed a complaint with the WTO. The parallels with the tuna-dolphin case were very clear and again the WTO initially ruled against the United States. However, as Vogel explains:

> in a significant concession to environmentalists, the WTO's appellate body's decision departed significantly from the language of the tuna-dolphin ruling. It stated that trade restrictions based on production methods *could* be used to protect the environment and to guard natural resources outside a nation's borders. This meant that the United States was permitted to exclude shrimp from vessels that had not installed appropriate turtle protection devices. However, it found the US embargo inconsistent with WTO rules on two grounds. First, the United States had insisted that its trading partners adopt regulations essentially identical to its own, and it had not applied the same turtle protection standard to each of its trading partners. Second, the appellate body faulted the United States for not having done enough to pursue bilateral or multilateral approaches before applying its own unilateral sanctions . . . In January 2000, the United States indicated that it had implemented the panel's decision. It had revised and clarified its guidelines for enforcing the US shrimp-turtle law, assuring all countries equal treatment; launched negotiations for the protection of sea turtles in the Indian Ocean region; and offered technical training to shrimp producers. In June 2001, a dispute settlement panel found that the revised US implementation of its sea turtle protection law to be fully consistent with WTO rules. This decision represents a significant change in the interpretation of WTO rules affecting environmental standards and should reduce future tensions between the WTO and US environmental policies. (Vogel 2003: 380–1, original emphasis)

In less than a decade, the WTO had clearly changed the priority accorded to environmental considerations and allowed a country to introduce a barrier to trade that was based on the need to protect endangered wild species even if those animals are living outside of that nation's boundaries.

However, this environmental trend in the WTO's approach is not a straightforward or uni-dimensional one as is revealed by the recent case of genetically modified

(GM) foodstuffs (in North America GM is often referred to as genetic engineering). The United States has been a big enthusiast for the new GM technology and particularly its use in producing new varieties of agricultural crops. In the United States, new varieties produced through genetic engineering, rather than through the various forms of conventional plant breeding, have been widely planted. The relevant authorities have judged these new crops to be acceptable at two levels. They are thought to be fit to eat and are judged to be safe enough to plant in the sense that they will not have seriously adverse effects on wildlife and biodiversity. GM crops have been very extensively planted in the United States and also in Canada and Argentina even though the big seed and agrochemical producers are mostly US based. By contrast, most European governments and the EU itself have been much less willing to embrace this new technology. There have been a few worries about the consequences of eating GM material but most concerns have focused on the environmental consequences of GM food production. In other words, environmentalists and state nature-conservation groups have feared that GM crops might have significant and detrimental effects on local wildlife (for more detail see Yearley 2005: 159–75). Effectively, most European countries have established a moratorium on the introduction of GM crops for cultivation and there are significant limitations on the import of GM foodstuffs, though some GM animal rations are imported (see Levidow 2001). The European authorities maintain that they are taking a precautionary approach to this new technology while US farmers and seed companies view Europe's activities as a form of protectionism. The issue here turns on how the risks are assessed, measured and weighed.

The US companies have urged that European resistance to GM imports should be combated by appeals to the WTO. A formal complaint was lodged in 2003 and the United States is hoping to use the WTO to force open European markets so that US farmers and US seed companies can export GM materials. The US argument is that there is no scientific evidence of harm arising from GM food and crops, since these products have all passed proper regulatory hurdles in the US system. Furthermore, on this view, labelling of GM produce in the European market (the procedure favoured in most EU member states as a possible compromise way forward) is discriminatory and an unfair trading practice since it draws consumers' attention to an aspect of the product which has no relation to its safety. The label 'warns' the customer of the GM content but, if that content is not dangerous, then all the label will do is penalize the United States and other GM-using suppliers. According to this way of seeing things, the WTO should outlaw this labelling practice as an unjustified impediment to trade. European consumer advocates argue, by contrast, that the US testing has not been precautionary enough and that properly scientific tests would require much more time and more diverse examinations than have been applied in routine US trials.

The distinctive difficulty in this case is that, by and large, the official expert scientific communities on opposing sides take diametrically opposing views. In the United States, the conceptualization of the issue is primarily this: all products have potential associated risks and the art of the policy maker is to ensure that an adequate assessment of risk is made. The Europeans are more inclined to argue that the very risk framework itself leaves something to be desired since the calculation of risk necessarily implies that risks can be quantified and agreed. In the case of

GM crops, so the argument goes, there is as yet no way of establishing the full range of possible risks so no 'scientific' risk assessment can be completed.

Within their separate jurisdictions, in Europe and the United States, each of these opposing views can be sensibly and more-or-less consistently maintained. However, the differing views appear to be tantamount to incommensurable paradigms for assessing the safety and suitability of GM crops. There is no higher level of scientific rationality or expertise to which appeal can be made to say which approach is correct, and of course the WTO does not have its own corps of 'super scientists' to resolve such issues. However, observers of the WTO fear that its dispute settlement procedures, although supposedly neutral and merely concerned with legal and administrative matters, tacitly favour the US paradigm since the WTO's approach to safety standards emphasizes the role of scientific proofs of safety and, in past rulings, 'scientific' has commonly been equated with US-style risk assessment (on this see Busch et al. 2004).

Although the GM case is currently mainly a bone of contention between wealthy Northern countries, other nations have got caught up in the struggle. Facing food shortages caused by drought, in 2002 Zambia was offered food aid by the United States which just happened to consist of genetically engineered cereals (see http://news.bbc.co.uk/1/hi/world/africa/2371675.stm). It seemed clear to many that the United States was using this case as a Trojan horse to encourage the uptake of GM foods. On the other hand, Zambians realized that there was a danger that their future exports to the EU would be threatened if they lost their GM-free status. The government thus equivocated over accepting the food aid.

In summary, it is clear that though not an environmental organization, the WTO has far-reaching implications for the environmental worldwide. Though not 'anti-environmental' in the way its more extreme critics paint it, the WTO and associated organizations strongly influence the global environment because the WTO's decisions are legally binding and because many of those decisions impact the environment while not being based primarily on environmental considerations.

GLOBALIZATION AND THE PLAY OF ENVIRONMENTAL STANDARDS

Campaigners who oppose the WTO and who protest at meetings of the IMF and G7 commonly equate globalization with the spread of neoliberal capitalism. Their worry is that there is a general trend towards deregulation and commodification which will result in globalization stifling, subverting and overruling attempts at environmental reform. But, as Nederveen Pieterse claims, it is analytically mistaken to reduce the whole of the phenomenon of globalization to the unregulated market (1995: 47). Globalization is a cultural phenomenon as well as an economic one. Reflecting on the arguments presented in this chapter to date, it is clear that they exemplify Nederveen Pieterse's assertion. Thus, the environmental movement's idea of a shared global environment, with worldwide environmental problems such as those threatening the ozone layer and the climate, is not at all reducible to the worldwide spread of capitalism. Indeed for many environmentalists, the idea of a common global interest in environmental protection posed a contrasting worldview to the capitalist one. They imagined a globalized world focused on environmental protection with economic considerations subordinated to ecological priorities. Similarly, the details of the WTO's operation in relation to TEDs show that it can reform its rules in an environmentally benign direction, even if its commitment to scientistic risk assessment in relation to GM products is viewed as problematic. To use a phrase no longer in vogue, the way that the WTO interprets its mission of global harmonization is 'relatively autonomous' in relation to the straightforward demands of the market. Logically, the WTO could grant higher priority to environmental considerations without relinquishing its global ambitions, even if observers think that such a shift in its priorities is decidedly unlikely.

A useful basis for building a connection between these phenomena and the sociological literature on globalization is offered to us by Mol (2001). The key point for Mol and other commentators, such as Vogel, is that the consequences of globalization are open ended. Vogel observes (citing Wheeler 2001) that as China, Mexico and Brazil 'became increasingly integrated into the global economy as both foreign investment and trade expanded' in the 1980s and 1990s, sample measures of urban air quality improved in all three countries (Vogel 2003: 386). Commercial globalization led to environmental improvement, not deterioration.

Mol seeks to anchor this point in the context of 'ecological modernization theory', the suggestion associated with authors such as Mol (1997), Spaargaren (1997) and Huber (1982) that, in specific ways, commercial development and rising environmental standards go hand-in-hand. In particular, such authors assert that in specific cases the theory of ecological modernization actually accounts for the way in which reforms have been instituted: '[the] theory has proved valuable in elucidating *how* the "environment" moves into the process of chemical production and consumption and transforms it' (1995: 391, original emphasis). Cases such as those of low-odour paints, or less and less environmentally damaging pesticides become paradigmatic for this analysis. There is, so to speak, a ratchet effect which drives environmental reform in a single direction and makes it more or less cumulative. Moreover, once one country establishes demonstrable environmental improvements through the pursuit of a policy, there is enormous pressure on others to follow. If limitations on acid emissions result in improved air quality or if one country reduces demands on landfill by obligatory recycling measures, others will (in some strong sense) have to follow. The 'betterness' of the new procedure is indubitable. Of course, this is not to imply that ecological modernization guarantees that enough reform can be achieved to avert major ecological problems. The claim is a weaker one than that, amounting to the idea that technological development, industrial policy and environmental improvement can pull in the same direction.

Mol has argued (2001) that there is now evidence for the worldwide applicability of ecological modernization. Of course, such modernization remains uneven and subject to setbacks, but he claims that 'Powerful, reflexive, countervailing powers are beginning to get a grip on the contradictory developments of environmental reform' (2001: 205). To support this case he uses evidence of the increasingly worldwide adoption of environmental standards. Like Vogel, he concludes that international competition in a globalized world does not necessarily lead to a 'race to the bottom'. Under some circumstances it may, but usually it does not. For Mol the key is to understand what globalization is: it is not just the free market and economic liberalism. Rather, it is a growth in the number and complexity of links between people and the introduction of novel limitations on the nation state. Thus environmental NGOs can use cross-national links and the availability of international environmental data to put new forms of pressure on national governments. As early as the 1980s, Greenpeace was using data about vehicle emissions in the United States to shame retailers in Europe where emission control technologies were not yet obligatory. Greenpeace even used Ford's slogan of the time – 'Ford gives you more' – to point out that, in Europe, Ford did indeed give consumers more: more pollution and more noxious emissions than in the United States. In this way, globalization opens new avenues for non-state actors and offers new opportunities for campaigning, for outreach and even for taking legal action on behalf of the environment. Mol is no doubt correct to argue that such developments allow a degree of freedom for environmental reform, even if studies conducted to date do not allow us to determine the environmental pros and cons of globalization. A great deal of work still needs to be done in this area though it is intriguing to note that in the recently established market for carbon dioxide emissions (set up in Europe following the Kyoto Protocol) the value of emissions permits has risen so quickly that carbon dioxide has, on occasions, become more valuable than the coal that gives rise to it (*The Economist* 376 (8434), 9 July 2005, 60–2).

CONCLUDING REMARKS

The environment is an exciting area for social scientific work on globalization because of the practical urgency of the issues and because of the conceptual richness of the topic. We have seen that, compared to other fields of globalization, the environment stands out because of the physical reality of aspects of its globalization, such as global warming, the worldwide diffusion of persistent pollutants and damage to the world's ozone layer. At the same time, we have noted the irony that the state of the world's environment is probably more influenced by trade and economic policies and actions than by explicitly environmental ones. Ideas, doctrines and institutions become global, and it turns out that these are as global and as important for the environment as physical globalization. The pressure for 'free trade' and its embodiment in the WTO has allowed a novel institutional actor to impact the global environment, in some cases even in the face of opposition from politicians and interest groups in the world's most powerful country. Furthermore, the current struggle at the WTO over the regulation of genetically modified organisms indicates how subtle and technical these issues of trade and safety can become. Finally, it is clear that the case of the global environment speaks to sociological arguments about the precise nature of globalization: the example of the global environment reaffirms the conclusion that it is mistaken to reduce the whole of the phenomenon of globalization to the worldwide spread of the unregulated market. Environmental globalization reveals something much more complex than a 'race to the bottom'; it shows also the rise of new opportunities and resources for myriad non-state actors.

References

Benedick, R.E. 1991. *Ozone Diplomacy: New Directions in Safeguarding the Planet*. London: Harvard University Press.

Boehmer-Christiansen, S. 2003. 'Science, equity, and the war against carbon', *Science, Technology and Human Values*, 28 (1), 69–92.

Busch, L., Grove-White, R., Jasanoff, S., Winickoff, D. and Wynne, B. 2004. 'Amicus Curiae Brief Submitted to the Dispute Settlement Panel of the World Trade Organization in the Case of "EC: Measures Affecting the Approval and Marketing of Biotech Products"', 30 April 2004.

Eckersley, R. 2004. 'The big chill: The WTO and multilateral environmental agreements', *Global Environmental Politics*, 4 (1), 24-50.

George, S. 1992. *The Debt Boomerang: How Third World Debt Harms Us All*. London: Pluto.

Hempel, L.C. 2003. 'Climate policy on the installment plan'. In N.J. Vig and M.E. Kraft (eds), *Environmental Policy: New Directions for the Twenty-First Century*, 299–323. Washington, DC: CQ Press.

Huber, J. 1982. *Die verlorene Unschuld der Ökologie: Neue Technologien und superindustrielle Entwicklung*. Frankfurt am Main: Fischer.

Leonard, J.H. 1988. *Pollution and the Struggle for the World Product*. Cambridge: Cambridge University Press.

Levidow, L. 2001. 'Precautionary uncertainty: Regulating GM crops in Europe', *Social Studies of Science*, 31 (6), 845–78.

Mol, A. 1995. *The Refinement of Production: Ecological Modernization Theory and the Chemical Industry*. Utrecht: International Books.

Mol, A. 1997. 'Ecological modernization: Industrial transformations and environmental reform'. In M. Redclift and G. Woodgate (eds), *The International Handbook of Environmental Sociology*, 138–49. Cheltenham: Edward Elgar.

Mol, A.P.J. 2001. *Globalization and Environmental Reform: The Ecological Modernization of the Global Economy*. Cambridge, MA: MIT Press.

Nederveen Pieterse, J. 1995. 'Globalization as hybridization'. In M. Featherstone, S. Lash and R. Robertson (eds), *Global Modernities*, 45–68. London: Sage.

Ramanathan, V., Chung, C., Kim, D., et al. 2005. 'Atmospheric brown clouds: Impacts on South Asian climate and hydrological cycle', *Proceedings of the National Academy of Sciences*, 102 (15), 5326–33.

Ross, S. 1991. 'Atmospheres and climatic change'. In P.M. Smith and K. Warr (eds), *Global Environmental Issues*, 72–120. London: Hodder and Stoughton.

Silvertown, J. 1990. 'Earth as an environment for life'. In J. Silvertown and P. Sarre (eds), *Environment and Society*, 48–87. London: Hodder and Stoughton.

Spaargaren, G. 1997. *The Ecological Modernization of Production and Consumption: Essays in Environmental Sociology*. Wageningen: University of Wageningen.

Vogel, D. 2003. 'International trade and environmental regulation'. In N.J. Vig and M.E. Kraft (eds), *Environmental Policy: New Directions for the Twenty-First Century*, 371–89. Washington, DC: CQ Press.

Wheeler, D. 2001. 'Racing to the bottom? Foreign investment and air pollution in developing countries', *Journal of Environment and Development*, 10 (1), 225–45.

Yearley, S. 1996. *Sociology, Environmentalism, Globalization*. London: Sage.

Yearley, S. 1997. 'Science and the environment'. In M. Redclift and G. Woodgate (eds), *The International Handbook of Environmental Sociology*, 227–36. Cheltenham: Edward Elgar.

Yearley, S. 2005. *Cultures of Environmentalism*. Basingstoke: Palgrave Macmillan.

Chapter 12

Cities and Globalization[1]

Michael Timberlake and Xiulian Ma

INTRODUCTION

From nearly the beginning of scholarly and popular discourse on globalization, writers on the subject have featured the world's large cities. There are at least three reasons for this. First, the great cities in the world are cosmopolitan places. They embody notions of globalization in the way visitors experience them. Usually various cultures from around the world are represented on the city streets, in the dress and ethnicity of the residents, in the array of cuisines available in restaurants and from street vendors, in the languages one hears spoken at cafes and in the wide array of consumer goods available in shops. Second, scholars who study cities and urbanization processes have long recognized that large cities command considerable influence over the regions surrounding them, constituting 'central places' in the immediate region. Such cities are frequently the sites of relatively greater economic opportunity than the surrounding region and, thus, attract migrants from rural areas and smaller towns. Large cities frequently exert considerable cultural and political sway as well as economic weight. Cities have such influence because they are administrative centres for organizations such as corporations, government bureaucracies and non-profit organizations whose dealings extend well beyond the city limits. In fact, these city-based organizations are usually part of larger networks of organizations and, therefore, they serve to link a given city to cities elsewhere in the world, forming networks of cities which may be regional, national, hemispheric or even global in their reach.

Finally, these 'systems of cities' are hierarchical. That is, some cities in these systems exert more influence than others. Indeed, there is a substantial record of scholarship showing that cities within a system of cities can be ranked along a continuum indicating the relative influence each exerts across the entire system. Pertinent to discussions of globalization, then, many scholars assume, and some have shown through their research, that there seems to be a global system of cities characterized by a few dominant cities at the 'top', whose influence is global, followed by increasingly less important cities, but all of which are involved in organizational networks which span regions of various size. Moreover, these networks are defined by the flows of people, information and things, such as commodities, among cities. Clearly, the global processes described throughout this volume encompass geographic places all over the world. Less obvious is that the very processes linking the world's great cities to one another *constitute* globalization in many important respects.

CITIES IN GLOBAL CONTEXT

Historical precedents

Cities are not autonomous social entities, isolated from their geographic and social surroundings – their 'hinterlands'. Cities emerge within, and are sustained by, their connections with their respective hinterlands. The growth in size and cultural significance of the world's great cities, as well as their decline, involves their relationships with broad geographical regions, their respective 'hinterlands'. For example, Rome in the third century AD was probably the largest city in the world as well as the one from which emanated vast political and cultural influence, stretching from the immediate hinterland on the Italian peninsula to the Caspian Sea to the east and Britannia to the north. On the other hand, at the beginning of the seventeenth century, Potosi, Bolivia was among the ten largest cities in the world (Demos 2003). While it was hardly a site of global power, it was the product of the Castilian quest for such power, a city built on a mountain of silver, growing to a population of more than 150,000 (at a time when London was home to 200,000), before losing its prominence as the silver was soon mined and shipped back to the coffers in Seville (e.g. Wallerstein 1976: ch. 1). By 1700 Potosi's population had declined by more than half. Both Rome and Potosi can be said to have been globally significant cities. Both were deeply embedded in political, cultural, economic and social networks spanning large sectors of the world's surface, indeed extending beneath that surface as well (with considerable consequences for a number of ecosystems as well as human misery). Clearly, however, the two cities were quite different in terms of their relationships to powerful social institutions. Rome was the seat of power for the Roman Empire, a city fed by Roman military conquest and concomitant territorial expansion. Potosi was the object of power within an empire, a city that fed the Spanish crown's appetite for precious metals which were then used to repay debt and extend the crown's global reach.

City formation

In order to better understand how global processes involve cities, it is helpful to think of the city as being constantly in change. This is not intuitive because most of us experience cities as masses of buildings and roads that we learn to recognize and to which we relate as we navigate around the city in which we live, or, with the aid of maps, the cities we visit. In important ways, the seeming concreteness of cities is an illusion. 'City formation' is a phrase that challenges us to think about cities as outcomes of activities, of social processes that preserve them or which quickly may change them. In the United States and elsewhere, 'urban sprawl' describes the ways in which the built up area of cities has expanded outward into what may once have been countryside. But even cities that appear stable over time do so because of constellations of processes that have preserved their outward appearance. City contractors re-pave streets, homeowners mow their lawns and paint their houses, city residents continue to work for a living, garbage is removed, water is piped in and so on. Trying to understand the qualities of a particular city and how they change (or not) turns our attention to the city's economic base, its migration history, its political role and myriad other ways in which it is and has been linked to processes operating at various geographic levels. The most compelling research on cities locates them historically in these webs of relationships. One early example is Pirenne's 1925 history of the emergence of the medieval city from feudalism in which he ties this development to the emergence of merchant capitalism in the interstices of the feudal political economy (Pirenne 1956). Another is Adna Weber's 1899 treatment of industrial cities of the nineteenth century (Weber 1963). More recently Paul Bairoch (1988) provides a comprehensive political economy of city formation from the first cities through contemporary cities.

William Cronon's treatment of Chicago's history in *Nature's Metropolis* (1991) provides a convincing, concrete description of these general points. In the first third of the nineteenth century, on the edge of Lake Michigan, land speculators built Chicago in a muddy swamp on land from which the US government had just finally evicted Native Americans. Banking on this site becoming the terminus of a canal, the investors, backed by finance capital from New York and elsewhere in the east, began building the Windy City. The canal never really played a role in Chicago's economic vitality, but once the stakeholders succeeded in siting the chief rail lines into the city, its economic significance seemed assured. Cronon describes Chicago's growth in relation to the opening of 'the west', first, as a source of natural resources (i.e. timber from Michigan and Wisconsin), and then agricultural products (grain and meat), which were processed in the city and shipped back east for consumption. He shows how a city growing to become one of the world's most important urban places was a process which involved it in a complex of regional and national networks of financial capital, transport, labour migration, commodity chains and ecosystems. Cronon acknowledges that Chicago is not unique in embodying these processes. 'Many of Chicago's characteristics apply just as easily to the other gateway cities . . . and one could write similar books for each of them as well. And the most general question of all – how a city's life and markets connect to the countryside around it – can be asked of every urban place that has ever existed, no matter how large or small . . . The city–country relations I have described in this book now involve the entire planet . . .' (Cronon 1991: 384–5).

Global social change theory and cities

Though among the most interesting and concrete treatments of a major city in its broader context, Cronon was hardly the first scholar to draw attention to the way in which cities are embedded in processes of large geographic scope. Over the last

25 years, social scientists who focus their research on cities have increasingly used theoretical assumptions developed in the study of large-scale social change more generally. Some time in the 1970s there was a revolution in the sociological study of 'development'. Throughout the 1950s and 1960s, at least in American sociology, the dominant view on how 'societies' changed focused on explanations nearly exclusively having to do with social factors *internal* to a particular country or region. Thus when asking why poor countries remain poor, the answers usually had to do with their traditional cultural values, their non-democratic forms of government and their non-capitalist economies, as examples. This way of thinking was applied to questions about cities and urbanization, particularly in low income countries. These countries seem to have 'pathological' forms of city growth. Their populations were too large relative to the job opportunities they offered. They grew too fast, and they had large numbers of recent rural migrants living in makeshift housing, and working in marginal jobs. In many of these countries, the largest city was far too large in population size relative to other cities in the country, a condition known as 'urban primacy'. The standard scholarly answers to why low income countries had these urban problems were based on a conventional set of assumptions and leading to the same sort of answers. For example, government policies favour cities relative to rural areas, disrupting labour market equilibrium in a way that artificially promotes rural to urban migration. This explained the high rates of rural to urban migration in the face of high urban unemployment rates. If market forces were allowed to operate, then the population would distribute itself in rural and urban areas in harmony with the opportunities that existed in each. Explanations that focused on internal factors within countries guided most scholarship on large-scale social change throughout the first three quarters of the twentieth century.

In the last part of the twentieth century, a growing body of theory and research exploring the relationships between local (e.g. national-level) social change and global processes challenged these internal-oriented explanations (cf. Chase-Dunn 1989). For example, Immanuel Wallerstein proposed that a 'world-system' emerged about 500 years ago. According to this view, many of the social change processes with which social scientists are concerned are, in large part, better understood as operating on the level of the world-system. More accurately (for Wallerstein), this is a *capitalist* world-system, and its basic logic involves competition among capitalist firms and nation-states who compete in markets and geopolitically for relative advantage over other capitalists (and 'their' states). An important historical feature of the world-system is that it expands. Over its 500 years, it has grown from a European-centred world-economy to one encompassing much of the globe and, at the same time, one in which the logic of global capitalism (and the associated tensions, or 'contradictions') has become ever more deeply institutionalized. The competitive nature of the system and the huge advantages that accrued to the successful capitalists and their states means that there are winners and losers. And since these winners and losers are nation-states and territorially based capitalist firms, one result is a geographical hierarchy – a system with a 'core' area where wealth is relatively concentrated and where there are strong states, a 'periphery' of relative disadvantage in terms of wealth and global political power, and a 'semi-periphery' lying between the core and periphery. Five hundred years ago, this capitalist world-system was confined to Europe for the most part, and huge areas of the world were not 'incorporated' into the system at all. However, its nature is to expand, and, as it has done so, external areas have been 'incorporated' into the system, usually as part of the periphery. Wallerstein and others argued that this world-system involves processes and institutional arrangements that reproduce 'underdevelopment' in some regions and relative affluence in others. Wallerstein's world-system perspective is but one of several theoretical approaches that have opened our eyes to the global dimensions of 'local' social change. The intellectual influence of these global perspectives is tremendous. No longer can research on cities be taken seriously if it is not sensitive to the broader global contexts in which cities are situated (cf. Chase-Dunn 1989; Timberlake 1985).

Beginning in the 1970s scholars began moving away from the urban ecology perspectives which had framed the research on urban change for a number of decades. Walton (1976) points out that a 'new urban sociology' emerged simultaneously in Europe and the United States under different rubrics: Marxist or neo-Marxist (France, Italy), structuralist (British) and political economy (North America). Together they constituted a general paradigm which, according to Walton, (1) provided a theoretical perspective that would explain the distinctive characteristics of urbanism and urbanization as a social process (i.e. 'city formation'), rather than looking at the city merely as a place-bound locus of human activity; (2) is heavily influenced by Marxist theory, emphasizing the materialist (e.g. economic) aspects of the relevant processes; (3) accounts for various urban forms by reference to changing modes of production and accumulation; and (4) is empirically grounded. Examples of prominent influences on this new urban sociology were Castells (1976a, 1976b), Lojkine (1972), Harvey (1973) and Molotch and Logan (1976), as well as Walton.

Walton also urged urban research to move its focus from the city as the unit of analysis to cross national exchange processes in which cities assume particular roles. He argued that cities are shaped by 'forces [that] operate cross nationally, . . . [thus] cities need to be studied from the standpoint of how they operate within and are shaped by international hierarchies linked by economic process' (1976: 307). Similarly, writing over 20 years ago, Timberlake wrote:

> The claim is not that world-system processes determine everything. Rather, the fundamental lesson is that social scientists can no longer study macrolevel social change without taking into account world-system processes. Specifically, processes such as urbanization can be more fully understood by beginning to examine the many ways in which they articulate with the broader currents of the world-economy that penetrate spatial barriers, transcend limited time boundaries, and influence social relations at many different levels. (Timberlake 1985: 3)

Thus, whether we are studying New York City or Seoul, we will want to know not only about the city's role in its national economy, about how it is managed and governed, about the living conditions and job opportunities it offers its residents, and about the cultural amenities available in it. We will also want to know about how it is 'plugged in' to the *global world economy*. What are the major firms operating in the city? What are the roles of these firms in the world economy? Where are their headquarters? Are there significant economic, political, social or cultural linkages between New York and other cities and between Seoul and other cities? What is the role of each city in the worldwide system of cities?

GLOBAL SYSTEMS OF CITIES

The world-system's city system (see Knox and Taylor 1995) is one of the building blocks of globalization, in other words. The various transactions and flows that criss-cross the globe with ever increasing rapidity are nearly always rooted in geographic space, at least in the beginning and in the end. Think of 'commodity chains', which describe the transformation of the goods we buy and use in our everyday lives, such as a pair of blue jeans. The cloth for the jeans is produced from cotton, a crop that might be sewn and harvested in the Mississippi Delta in the southern United States. Once the cotton boll is plucked from the cotton plant, workers and machines transform it through a series of processes from something very close to nature to a piece of clothing that has been woven from cotton, dyed, sewn, embellished with hardware such as zippers and buttons, shipped to a retail outlet, purchased by a consumer, worn by someone over the course of time and eventually discarded. Each step of this transformation process is space-bound. Workers use sewing machines and other technology in a 'cut and sew' factory in which the final product is produced. The factory may be located in a city in South-east Asia. Eventually the jeans are picked up off the shelf of a retail store in another city, perhaps a city in the United States, perhaps by you. While the example of blue jeans can be more easily envisioned, a similar process describes the production of many other goods and even the creation of knowledge that may be consumed in the form of services, such as the services a corporate attorney might render. Research reveals that it is in the world's great cities that we find the administrative headquarters of many of the firms which oversee and control many of these sorts of production processes.

In both academic and popular discourse today, 'global cities' is a term associated with only one end of this chain-of-command continuum. Global cities are the few cities in which are sited the organizations exerting pre-eminent control over the most important functions in the global political economy. Today we can deliberate about which functions these are and, therefore, which cities can be truly described as 'global cities', but we are indebted to the work of Saskia Sassen, who coined the term. For her, New York, London and Tokyo were the 'first' global cities, serving as the sites for the modern world economy's global control functions in banking and other financial services and law (Sassen 1991). It is no coincidence that these are the cities in which are located the three major stock exchanges.

World cities and global cities

Key concepts in the research on cities in globalization are those of 'world cities' and 'global cities'. However, these terms have not always been employed consistently. Sometimes they are used interchangeably, sometimes distinctions are drawn and sometimes these distinctions are switched, one to the other. Early on, Peter Hall, following Geddes, defined world cities as 'certain great cities in which a quite disproportionate part of the world's most important business is conducted' (1966: 1). A world city has several defining characteristics according to this work. In the first place, it is usually the major centre of political power. Secondly, it is the national centre of trade, serving as the great port, site of the great international airports, and the leading banking and finance centre of the country. The world city is a centre in which professional expertise of all kinds concentrates, and in turn, it is a locus in the processes of accumulating and disseminating new knowledge, through research and education.

Among the residents of the world city are a significant proportion of the most affluent members of the region. Thus, these cities offer easy access to luxury goods and services as well as plentiful entertainment and culture consumption opportunities. For Hall and most who followed him, world cities are centres of both political and economic power, and in turn, they are centres for culture, information, the wealthy, professionals and so on. Although population size can be an indicator of the world city, its national and international significance is the most important characteristic. Hall (1966) identified several world cities, from the relatively highly concentrated metropoli of London and Paris, to the polycentric metropoli, Randstad of the Netherlands and the Rhine-Ruhr urban agglomeration of Germany.

In contrast to Geddes' and Hall's richly descriptive conceptualization of world cities, Friedmann and Sassen theorize the term more succinctly. The work of each of these scholars situates the large cities relative to the contemporary world economy, which is explicitly capitalist and explicitly 'globalizing' in the current era. To different degrees, each is sensitive to the relationship of cities to the capitalist world-system. Both see such cities as nodes in regional and worldwide urban *hierarchies* corresponding to the 'new international division of labor'. Some criticize Sassen's 'take' on world cities as overly determined by economic considerations alone, ignoring, for example, the cultural dimensions of world cities. Friedmann and Sassen might counter by asking 'What is most essential?' Their answer would be 'economic relations', but there is an important social organization basis as well. Since transnational corporations are the main agents in the new international division of labour, cities are the places in which corporate power resides and is exercised. On one level, relations among world cities are a matter of purely global corporate geography. But their views are much more complex. Economic power is concentrated within firms but it is organized and articulated socially within complex organizations and the networks in which these organizations embed themselves.

As Friedmann points out, certain key cities are 'basing points' for transnational corporations and other organizations whose operations span vast stretches of the globe. When the main offices of such organizations are located in certain cities and branch offices in certain other cities, the resulting linkages between the control centres and the branches creates a hierarchy of cities, with some cities being more central in terms of exercising power over the others. In his seminal 1986 article Friedmann identified 30 world cities, using seven criteria of world 'cityness' including the extent to which a city is home to major financial institutions; headquarters for transnational corporations (TNCs); headquarters to international institutions; the rapidity with which the business service sector has grown; its importance as a manufacturing centre; the extent to which it serves as a major transportation node;

Box 12.1 Friedmann's 'World Cities', 1986 and 1995

1986
Core World Cities
- Primary: London, Paris, Rotterdam, Frankfurt, Zurich, New York, Los Angeles, Chicago, Tokyo
- Secondary: Brussels, Milan, Vienna, Madrid, Toronto, Miami, Houston, San Francisco, Sydney.

Periphery World Cities
- Primary: São Paulo, Singapore
- Secondary: Johannesburg, Buenos Aires, Rio De Janeiro, Mexico City, Hong Kong, Taipei, Manila, Bangkok, Seoul

1995
Global Financial Articulations: New York, London, Tokyo
Multinational Articulations: Miami, Los Angeles, Frankfurt, Amsterdam, Singapore
Important National Articulations: Paris, Zurich, Madrid, Mexico City, São Paulo, Seoul, Sidney
Subnational/Regional Articulations: Osaka-Kobe, San Francisco, Seattle, Houston, Chicago, Boston, Vancouver, Toronto, Montreal, Hong Kong, Milan, Lyon, Barcelona, Munich, Düsseldorf.

---

and its population size. He finds 'a distinctively linear character of the world city system which connects, along East–West axis, three distinct sub-systems' (1986: 72), including an Asian sub-system, a North American sub-system and a West European sub-system.

About a decade later, Friedmann had expanded his list of world cities and he had developed a different classification scheme to describe their hierarchy (1995). Moreover, he acknowledged that because the world economy is so dynamic, the hierarchical ordering of world cities is quite contingent and, therefore, subject to change from time to time (1995: 25). Nevertheless, he identifies 'the' 30 world cities of the day and orders them into four categories based on his estimate of the geographic scale and intensity of the global reach of the organizations sited in these cities. At the top are New York, London and Tokyo, which he classifies as 'global financial articulations'. Respectively, the other categories are 'multinational articulations', 'important national articulations' and 'subnational/regional articulations' (see Box 12.1). Friedmann also summarizes the state of knowledge at that time on world cities, arguing that we can identify five general areas of agreement. First, global cities 'serve as the organizing nodes of the global economic system'. Second, significant areas of the world are not articulated into the global capitalist system of accumulation and in these areas there are, essentially, 'subsistence economies'. Third, world cities are big, populous and characterized by frequent and dense social and economic interaction. Fourth, as we have seen, world cities are systematically and hierarchically arranged, and this arrangement, due to the competitive nature of global capitalism, is subject to rearrangement. Finally, the system that gives rise to this global hierarchy of world cities is one in which the interests of a particular social class are primarily represented. This is the 'transnational capitalist class', whose very dominance, wealth and power represents social polarization which can be extreme within global cities (1995: 26).

The theme of social polarization is one of the important ways in which Friedmann and other world city researchers make the connection between the large-scale processes which produce the global city hierarchy and the nature of social life within global cities. In 1986, Friedmann's answer to this implicit question was that a city's position in this global hierarchy influences its division of labour: the degree and nature of the divisions between the urban rich and poor, between urban immigrants and natives, and between dominant ethnic group members and members of subordinate ethnic groups. These divisions are manifest spatially in world cities, he argues. He points out that spatial polarization occurs at three levels. On the global level is the widening gap between a handful of rich countries and poor peripheral economies. On the regional scale, in semi-periphery and periphery countries, the income difference between rich and poor regions, or world cities and the rest of the national economy, is exacerbated by globalization. On the metropolitan level, 'it is the familiar story of spatially segregating poor inner-city ghettos, suburban squatter housing and ethnic working-class enclaves' (1986: 76).

Friedmann argues that this spatial polarization arises from three sorts of class polarization. The first is reflected in the huge wealth and income gaps between the transnational capitalists along with its cadre of highly paid professionals and low-skilled workers, reflecting the increasingly dichotomized labour force structure in global cities. Cities at and near the top of the global hierarchy have a larger proportion of professionals specializing in occupations associated with global control (e.g. financiers), and they are served by a vast army of low-skilled workers engaged in personal services (1986: 73). Second, world cities attract large-scale immigration from rural areas and from abroad, fuelling the size and competitiveness of the low wage labour force. We will return to the subject of social polarization and world cities below. However, we need to note that Friedmann departs from many global political economy scholars by arguing that the most severely deprived segments of the world's population are those who are excluded from 'the space of accumulation'. These population segments are not articulated, except very marginally, with the global city system in particular and global capitalism more generally, and they represent the third face of social polarization in world cities.

Sassen pries into the issue of globalization and cities by trying to solve a puzzle: In the era of globalized, computer-enhanced telecommunications in which people can communicate instantaneously, without the apparent 'friction of space', why do cities remain so important as, for example, sites of the headquarters of the world's biggest corporations? Why haven't cities declined in importance as homes to the world's most powerful people? Why do we continue to see centralization in the face of technological developments favouring – or at least permitting – spatial decentralization? In fact, this is the contradiction between continued geographic centralization of some key human activities in the face of decentralization of other activities and the capacity for even more widespread decentralization accompanying 'post-industrialization' and internationalization since the late 1970s. That is, TNCs have dispersed many economic activities that had once been geographically concentrated;

yet economic control continues to be concentrated spatially and organizationally. In solving this puzzle, Sassen identifies a new category of world cities, those few that are at the very top of the global hierarchy:

> it is precisely the combination of the global dispersal of economic activities *and* global integration – under conditions of continued concentration of economic ownership and control – that has contributed to a strategic role for certain major cities . . . [T]oday's global cities are (1) command points in the organization of the world economy; (2) key locations and marketplaces for the leading industries of the current period – finance and specialized services for firms; and (3) major sites of production for these industries, including the production of innovations in these industries. (Sassen 2000: 4)

She goes on to make the point that there are cities which perform similar functions on a smaller scale (in terms of geographic scope and economic power), and these are regional and national urban centres. Again, the result is networks of cities (see Sassen 2002). There are a score or more of very important world cities whose influence extends over broad international regions. Examples include Hong Kong (see Meyer 2000, 2002), Los Angeles and Chicago (Abu-Lughod 1999) and, increasingly, Shanghai (see Gu and Tang 2002).

POLARIZATION AND GLOBALIZATION

Regional polarization

According to Sassen (2000) these global cities are more integrated with the world economy than they are with their own national 'hinterlands'. This runs counter to the older urban ecology research which focused on national and subnational (regional) systems of cities. This earlier research indicated that within an economically vibrant regional economy towns and cities form a system of relatively dominant and subordinate population centres, each of which have somewhat specialized economic roles with respect to the region as a whole. They form a coherent 'system', in other words. Sassen indicates that under globalization, some cities are increasingly integrated into the global urban system while others are not. Those that are not becoming globally integrated are peripheral (being peripheralized) with respect to global processes. This means that within some nations there is growing territorial inequality, Sassen implies. Regional inequalities are growing.

Polarization within global cities

Another kind of social inequality is increasingly pronounced within global cities, according to Sassen (1991). Central to Sassen's thesis is that a major consequence of global city formation processes is social polarization. For example, she finds evidence of a growing income gap within global cities. 'The globalization of the economy has necessitated the development of centres of control, which has led to massive and parallel changes in the economic base, spatial organization and social structure in New York, London and Tokyo . . . [Sassen] finds that the reorganization of work and new types of employment have led to increased social polarization'

(Nørgaard 2003: 109). This is class inequality. New York, London and Tokyo are home to an increasingly affluent global capitalist class as well as their contingent of well-paid professionals who staff the top positions in the global producer services firms that are headquartered in these cities. However, these highly paid global corporate professionals have developed lifestyles that create demand for relatively low skilled, and low paid, service workers. These include restaurant workers, maids, security guards, custodial workers and others who engage in paid labour at the low end of the wage ladder. It is common for new immigrants to fill many of these positions. Moreover, increasingly absent are opportunities for employment in relatively well-paid working-class jobs that may have once been present in cities that had been manufacturing centres. Much of the work accomplished in these kinds of jobs has long since been outsourced and moved offshore where wages are lower. Even white-collar jobs requiring fairly high education have moved to lower wage regions of the world (e.g. call-in support technicians for US computer users are more likely to be reached in Hyderabad than Houston).

The result is income polarization: 'an expansion at the top and bottom of the occupational/income distribution at the expense of the middle' (Vaatovaara and Kortteinen 2003). This process is often accompanied by heightened spatial segregation of these two disparate groups. Again, to the extent immigrant groups play a role in the low wage sector, this may exacerbate race/ethnic residential segregation as well as class segregation in global cities, possibly leading to more social isolation from more affluent residents and from desirable urban amenities and services.

Sassen's internal polarization thesis has not gone unchallenged by scholars. Some see a brighter side of globalization, a 'rising tide lifting all boats'. What can be termed the 'professionalization thesis' is that globalization, and specifically global cities, manifest occupational upgrading. That is, more and more people are able to become professionals, resulting in a decrease in the size of the unskilled, low-income labour force. Nørgaard (2003) elaborates on this debate, suggesting that theories about the impact of globalization on local social stratification can be divided into two major camps. Nørgaard refers to these as the 'Whole Economy Approach' and the 'Individual in the Employment Place Approach'. Sassen and her ilk are categorized, according to Nørgaard, in the latter group. This camp stresses the importance of the 'shifts in the structure of occupations and their impact upon the individual's earnings' (Nørgaard 2003: 103). More precisely this group holds that the restructuring of the global economy has created a job squeeze, resulting in a reduction in the size of the middle class and a concomitant rise in both the high- and low-wage sectors. A graphical illustration of the resulting income distribution across a population would be shaped like an hourglass, wide at each end and pinched in the middle.

In contrast, the adherents of the Whole Economy Approach, represented by Hamnett (1996, 1994), for example, characterize the Individual in the Employment Place Approach as too narrow to describe the overall effects of globalization on the economy. They have found evidence pointing to the ascendance of a new professional and managerial class of workers (see, for instance, Bell 1973; Hamnett 1994), and upward mobility for virtually everyone involved in the global economy. The implied graphical representation of the occupational structure is egg-shaped, with a broad middle, and the ends tapering off at the high end of the income distribution.

A third paradigm, more contextual than the above two theses, is Wilson's Mismatch Theory. Burgers and Musterd (2002) describe this as the 'process of economic restructuring caused by increasing globalization . . . a post-industrial society needs more highly-educated workers. The labor market will therefore be subject to continuous upgrading' (2002: 404). Mismatch Theory differs from the Whole Economy Approach in one important respect: Wilson argues that inequality occurs when inner-city blacks in the United States are denied access to education, thus being barred from entry into professional jobs. In addition, they are confined to areas of inner cities that lack certain important elements of the infrastructure, not the least of which are living-wage jobs, which, he argues, have been outsourced to low income countries. Thus there are far too few moderately high-paying, unskilled industrial jobs in the city. Wilson (1987) calls the victims of this process the 'truly disadvantaged'. Unlike Sassen and others, Wilson argues that the middle class is expanding and it is primarily poor blacks in the United States who are unable to join its ranks. However, while there is considerable cross-national variation in the extent of race/ethnic segregation and how it is manifest across global cities in different countries, there is some comparative evidence indicating that residential segregation of ethnic immigrants is on the rise throughout much of Europe, and that it may indicate that the 'truly disadvantaged' can be found in world cities abroad as well as in the United States.

MAPPING THE WORLD-SYSTEM'S CITY SYSTEM

As we have seen, Friedmann and Sassen both frame much of their discussion of globalization and cities in terms of networks of urban places that are arranged hierarchically in terms of their relative importance as sites of corporate control. Other scholars have emphasized global networks as well. Taylor (2004) points out that this hierarchical thinking is inherited from the 'national urban hierarchy' school of the 1960s and 1970s to which Friedmann belonged, and subsequently modified for global city analysis by broadening to the global level the geographic scope at which the city network is defined.

Castells has referred to the 'network society' to describe such processes. Interdependence and integration make the globe 'smaller'. Castells (1996) describes globalization as a network society constituted across space as a myriad of linkages, connections and relations – a space of flows. Across the globe nearly every locality now is penetrated by extra-local forces to varying degrees in terms of intensity (of global interconnectedness), extensity (the extent of overlapping network flows), velocity (the rapidity of flows) and import propensity (degree of influence on local social relations).

This network society contains the space of flows. Our society is constructed around flows, Castells points out: flows of capital, flows of information, flows of technology, flows of organizational interaction, flows of images, sounds and symbols. The first layer of the space of flow, also the first layer of material support, is constituted by 'a circuit of electronic exchange'; the second layer is by 'its nodes and hubs'; the third, 'the spatial organization of the dominant, managerial elites' (Susser 2002: 344). In sum, the network, in Castells' view, is like vast nets cast over the whole globe. In the global space of flows within the network, information technology is its most basic material support, and the space of flows, in the last instance, is dominated by 'the meta-network of financial flows', controlled by managerial elites (Castells 1996: 472). Cities are the nodes and hubs of Castells' network society. As Castells points out:

> The space of flows is not placeless . . . this network links up specific places, with well-defined social, cultural, physical, and functional characteristics. Some places are exchangers, communication hubs playing a role of coordination for the smooth interaction of all the elements integrated into the network. Other places are the nodes of the networks; that is, the location of strategically important functions that build a series of locality-based activities and organizations around key functions in the network. Location in the nodes links up the locality with the whole network. Both nodes and hubs are hierarchically organized according to their relative weight in the network. But this hierarchy may change depending upon the evolution of activities processed through the network. (Susser 2002: 345)

Place-based stakeholders (capitalists, local governments etc.) seek to promote the cities in which they have decided to invest, using their resources and influence to help make 'their' cities become the nodes and hubs in the network of places. To the extent they are successful in this endeavour, they will remain able to accumulate and retain wealth and power through what flows through their cities, including goods, information, knowledge, money and cultural practices. On the other hand, stakeholders in less dominant global cities may compete in an effort to gain a larger share of global flows. They may invest in their cities' globally relevant infrastructure, such as information technology and transportation capacity (e.g. by building new airports), in an effort to make them more significant nodes in the global system of cities.

Smith and Timberlake (1995) described such a place-bound network in terms of the form and function of such flows. Material 'things', people and information flow across the network of places on the globe, involved in processes that may be of an economic nature, of political significance, of cultural import, or involve social reproduction. We have already evoked the notion of commodity chains to describe one kind of flow. Corporate control may be exerted across the network of places through a combination of business directives (intra-organizational communications) and investment transactions (capital flows). Migrants move from one place to another for work (economic) or to join family members who have migrated earlier (social reproduction). In principle, these flows can be mapped, and researchers have developed new representations of the world which are based on networks of cities rather than the more common images of international relations.

One common type of 'map' that is produced by this sort of research is one which focuses on the hierarchy of cities rather than their geographic locations. That is, using the notion of global city hierarchies in conjunction with global networks, this research focuses on the degree to which cities are central to the network flows. An early attempt at this was Smith and Timberlake's (1995) use of formal network analysis of the flows of airline passengers between 23 pairs of Friedmann's 30 'world cities'. They reasoned that cities that were relatively more important to the global

---

Box 12.2   Rankings of 23 of Friedmann's 30 world cities (from highest to lowest 'interconnectivity'), 1991

Group 1 (Highest level of interconnectivity): London, Paris, New York, Tokyo
Group 2: Hong Kong, Amsterdam, Singapore, Frankfurt, Los Angeles
Group 3: Chicago, Mexico City, Zurich
Group 4: Milan, Madrid, Miami
Group 5: San Francisco, Seoul, Houston
Group 6: Boston, Montreal, Sydney
Group 7 (Lowest levels of interconnectivity): São Paulo, Seattle

Source: Smith and Timberlake (1995).

---

network would have more passengers flying to and from them *and* from more other places in the network. For example, corporate managers still find the need for face-to-face communication (as Sassen contends), and they have to travel from the headquarter city to the branch offices in lesser cities in the network in order to conduct business. Likewise, headquarters needs to 'call in' its lieutenants from the field from time to time. Box 12.2 shows the hierarchical list of cities produced by this early attempt to use network analysis to map the global city system. Since then, Smith and Timberlake (1998, 2002) and Shin and Timberlake (2000) have produced similar maps using the same sort of air passenger flow data with larger numbers of cities – up to about 100.

Other examples of this kind of mapping include those by Peter Taylor and his associates (e.g. Taylor 2004; Derudder et al. 2003) and Alderson and Beckfield (2004). Rather than using true network flow data (such as airline passengers), each uses organizational linkages which are sensitive to the hierarchical relations inherent within business firms. The researchers identify the headquarter cities of large, economically powerful corporations and then, for each firm, they create a link to each other city in which those firms have offices. Cities with many headquarters for firms that have branch offices in other cities around the world are considered to be more significant in the global hierarchy of cities than those which tend to be only the locations of the branch offices and which have few linkages to other cities through these firms. While Taylor and his associates focus their data collection on the world's top service producer corporations (i.e. those in banking/finance, legal, advertising, accounting, following Sassen), Alderson and Beckfield used data on the *Fortune* 500 corporations, regardless of industry. Box 12.3 shows the hierarchical arrangements produced by some of these research efforts. Using data on telecommunications exchanges (e.g. Barnett 2001) and Internet linkages (e.g. Townsend 2001) are also promising ways to derive a map of the global web of place-based social relations that constitute the social geography of globalization.

There are important differences among these various empirically based estimates of the relative importance of the major cities of the world. But certain cities are among everybody's 'most global' of the world cities: London is nearly always at the top, followed closely by New York, Tokyo, Frankfurt, Paris and Amsterdam. Clearly the very top of the world city hierarchy is reserved for the major cities in the Western

---

Box 12.3 Recent empirically based estimates of the top world cities

Beaverstock, Taylor and Smith (1999; based cities' importance as sites for top service producer firms' organizational networks):

- *Alpha World Cities*: London, Paris, New York, Tokyo
- *Beta World Cities*: San Francisco, Sydney, Toronto, Zurich, Brussels, Madrid, Mexico City, São Paulo, Moscow, Seoul
- *Gamma World Cities*: Amsterdam, Boston, Caracas, Dallas, Düsseldorf, Geneva, Houston, Jakarta, Johannesburg, Melbourne, Osaka, Prague, Santiago, Taipei, Washington.

Smith and Timberlake (2001; based on cities' importance in air passenger networks): London, Frankfurt, Paris, New York, Amsterdam, Miami, Zurich, Los Angeles, Hong Kong, Singapore, Tokyo, Seoul, Bangkok, Madrid, Vienna, San Francisco, Chicago, Dubai, Osaka, Brussels, Milan, Copenhagen, Mexico City, Kuala Lumpur, Athens, Istanbul, Cairo, Manila, Buenos Aires, Sydney

Alderson and Beckfield (2004; based on cities' importance as sites for *Fortune* 500 corporations): Tokyo, New York, Paris, London, Düsseldorf, Amsterdam, Zurich, Munich, Osaka, San Francisco, Frankfurt, Vevey, Chicago, Stockholm, Dallas, Detroit, Utrecht, Toronto, Saint Louis, Basel, Philadelphia, Atlanta, Oslo, Beijing, Hamilton, Omaha, Houston, Ludwigshafen, Turin, Rome

---

'core' of the world-system. The studies that have examined change over time within the world city hierarchy show another very significant trend: major Asian cities of the semi-periphery have become increasingly important. Hong Kong, Bangkok and Singapore have long been among the top 30 or so world cities, but their positions have been consolidated and they have been joined by the likes of Seoul, Osaka and Kuala Lumpur. We suspect that Beijing and Shanghai will become increasing central world cities as China continues to integrate itself in global markets in a powerful way. On the other hand, major South American cities, such as Buenos Aires, have become less significant over time.

Taylor (2004) finds that the region has more significance for the global city system than the strata. He identifies seven regions: USA, Western Europe, Pacific Asia, Latin America, Eastern Europe and Afro-Asia, plus the old Commonwealth. He finds a strong regional tendency in the corporate geography using his data on linkages among producer service firms. He finds that, first, firms tend to locate more of their branches in their home region; second, sectors (e.g. banking, law, advertising, accounting) also tend to concentrate in certain regions. For example, firms in the banking/finance sector are over-represented in Pacific Asia, and management consultancy remains very US-based. He points out that these geographies can be traced back to the nature of the services being provided, the relative sizes of firms in sectors and the timing of when the sector started globalizing. Alderson and Beckfield (2004) define world cities in terms of the locations of the headquarters and subsidiaries of *Fortune*'s 500 top multinational firms in 2000, an operational definition more akin to Friedmann's. They find that the world city system comes close to approximating an idealized core/periphery structure (Borgatti and Everett 1999). Their global hierarchy of cities, overall, closely reflects the cities' locations in core versus non-core countries.

To be sure, there are very large cities that are not significant nodes in the 'space of flows' that constitutes globalization. Clearly there are other forces that contribute to urbanization than the global processes emphasized in this chapter. Dogan (2004) writes of giant cities, or 'megacities', some of which have a logic of their own apart from global processes. Regional dynamics, such as demographic patterns bearing on high rates of rural–urban migration and fertility, national politics (e.g. civil warfare that produces refugees) and national policies favouring cities over rural areas, contribute to city growth. The key global-level factor influencing many African cities, for example, may be that they are *not* connected to global flows discussed by Castells and others. They are peripheral to the global world-economy – peripheral literally as well as in the sense of not being in the core. Some of the research on global city hierarchies has also indicated that some cities have become more peripheral (e.g. Buenos Aires) and others more central to global networks (e.g. Shanghai).

CONCLUSION

Urbanization and city formation are processes which are closely connected to globalization for much of the world. In spite of the increasing technological capacity for human interaction to be freed from the constraints of place, humans continue to congregate in urban places, and cities remain key elements in many globalization processes. Many cities' histories can therefore be written in connection with their role in globalization processes. Today Asian investors and the Chinese state seem to be propelling Shanghai to global prominence as the key node in the booming Asian economy. Today, in the twenty-first century it is impossible to understand Shanghai's dynamic growth apart from the increasing involvement of China in globalization, just as it would misrepresent Chicago's rise to prominence in the nineteenth and early twentieth centuries apart from the integration of the central and western part of the United States into the national and world economy of the time. This is not to argue that nothing has changed. Today there is a relatively highly integrated global system in which many of the world's large cities are the key nodes. Cities are the places at which the very flows that constitute globalization are grounded and tied to place. These cities form a network that spans the globe, and, in many ways, this global city network constitutes globalization.

Note

1   The research was supported in part by a grant from the National Science Foundation (Collaborative Research Globalization and the Network of World Cities #0350078). Others contributing to the research at the University of Utah were Jessica Winitsky and Matthew Sanderson.

References

Abu-Lughod, J.L. 1999. *New York, Chicago, Los Angeles: America's Global Cities*. Minneapolis: University of Minnesota Press.

Alderson, A.S. and Beckfield, J. 2004. 'Power and position in the world city system', *American Journal of Sociology*, 109 (4), 811–51.

Bairoch, P. 1988. *Cities and Economic Development*. Chicago: University of Chicago Press.

Barnett, G. 2001. 'A longitudinal analysis of the international telecommunications network, 1978–1996', *American Behavioral Scientist*, 44 (10), 1638–55.

Beaverstock, J.V., Taylor, P.J. and Smith, R.G. 1999. 'A roster of world cities', *Cities*, 16, 445–58.

Bell, D. 1973. *The Coming of the Post-Industrial Society: A Venture in Social Forecasting*. New York: Basic Books.

Borgatti, S.P. and Everett, M.G. 1999. 'Models of core/periphery structures', *Social Networks*, 21, 375–95.

Burgers, J. and Musterd, S. 2002. 'Understanding urban inequality: A model based on existing theories and an empirical illustration', *International Journal of Urban and Regional Research*, 26 (2), 403–13.

Castells, M. 1976(a) [1968]. 'Is there an urban sociology?' In C.G. Pickvance (ed.), *Urban Sociology: Critical Essays*, 33–59. London: Tavistock.

Castells, M. 1976(b) [1969]. 'Theory and ideology in urban sociology'. In C.G. Pickvance (ed.), *Urban Sociology: Critical Essays*, 60–84. London: Tavistock.

Castells, M. 1996. *The Rise of the Network Society*. Vol. I of *The Information Age: Economy, Society and Culture*. Oxford: Blackwell.

Chase-Dunn, C. 1989. *Global Formation: Structures of the World-Economy*. New York: Basil Blackwell.

Cronon, W. 1991. *Nature's Metropolis: Chicago and the Great West*. New York: W.W. Norton.

Demos, J. 2003. 'High place: Potosi', *Common-place*, 3 (4) <http://www.common-place.org/vol-03/no-04/potosi/>.

Derudder, B., Taylor, P.J. and Catalano, G. 2003. 'Hierarchical tendencies and regional patterns in the world city network: A global urban analysis of 234 cities', *Regional Studies*, 37 (9), 875–86.

Dogan, M. 2004. 'Four hundred giant cities atop the world', *International Social Science Journal*, 56 (181), 347–60.

Friedmann, J. 1986. 'The world city hypothesis', *Development and Change*, 17, 69–84.

Friedmann, J. 1995. 'Where we stand: A decade of world city research'. In P.L. Knox and P.J. Taylor (eds), *World Cities in a World-System*, 21–47. Cambridge: Cambridge University Press.

Gu, F.R. and Tang, Z. 2002. 'Shanghai: Reconnecting to the global economy'. In S. Sassen (ed.), *Global Networks/ Linked Cities*, 273–308. New York: Routledge.

Hall, P. 1966. *The World Cities*. London: Weidenfeld & Nicolson.

Hamnett, C. 1996. 'Why Sassen is wrong: A response to Burgers', *Urban Studies*, 33 (1), 107–11.

Hamnett, C. 1994. 'Social polarization in global cities: Theory and evidence', *Urban Studies*, 31 (3), 401–25.

Harvey, D. 1973. *Social Justice and the City*. Baltimore, MD: The Johns Hopkins University Press.

Knox, P.L. and Taylor, P.J. 1995. *World Cities in a World-System*. Cambridge: Cambridge University Press.

Meyer, D. 2000. *Hong Kong as a Global Metropolis*. Cambridge: Cambridge University Press.

Meyer, D. 2002. 'Hong Kong: Global capital exchange'. In S. Sassen (ed.), *Global Networks, Linked Cities*, 249–71. London: Routledge.

Molotch, H. and Logan, J. 1976. 'The city as a growth machine: Toward a political economy of place', *American Journal of Sociology*, 82, 309–32.

Nørgaard, H. 2003. 'The global city thesis: Social polarization and changes in the distribution of wages', *Geografiska Annaler*: Series B, Human Geography, 85 (2), 103–19.

Pirenne, H. 1956. *Medieval Cities: Their Origins and the Revival of Trade*. Garden City, NY: Doubleday.

Sassen, S. 1991. *The Global City: London, New York, Tokyo*. Princeton, NJ: Princeton University Press.

Sassen, S. 2000. *Cities in a World Economy*, 2nd edn. Thousand Oaks, CA: Pine Forge Press.

Sassen, S. 2002. *Global Networks, Linked Cities*. London: Routledge.

Shin, K.H. and Timberlake, M. 2000. 'World cities in Asia: Cliques, centrality and connectedness', *Urban Studies*, 37, 2257–85.

Smith, D.A. and Timberlake, M. 1995. 'Conceptualizing and mapping the structure of world system's city system', *Urban Studies*, 32 (2), 287–302.

Smith, D.A. and Timberlake, M. 1998. 'Cities and the spatial articulation of the world economy through air travel'. In P. Ciccantell and S.G. Bunker (eds), *Space and Transport in the World-System*. Westport, CT: Greenwood Press.

Smith, D.A. and Timberlake, M. 2001. 'World city networks and hierarchies, 1977–1997', *American Behavioral Scientist*, 44 (10), 1656–78.

Smith, D.A. and Timberlake, M. 2002. 'Hierarchies of dominance among world cities: A network approach'. In S. Sassen (ed.), *Global Networks, Linked Cities*, 117–41. London: Routledge.

Smith, R.G. 2003. 'World city actor-networks', *Progress in Human Geography*, 27(1), 25–44.

Susser, I. 2002. *The Castells Reader on Cities and Social Theory*. Oxford: Blackwell.

Taylor, P. 2004. 'Regionality in the world city network', *International Social Science Journal*, 56 (181), 361–72.

Taylor, P., Catalono, G. and Walker, D.R.F. 2002. 'Exploratory analysis of the world city network', *Urban Studies*, 39 (13), 2377–94.

Timberlake, M. (ed.) 1985. *Urbanization in the World Economy*. Orlando, FL: Academic Press.

Townsend, A.M. 2001. 'Network cities and the global structure of the internet', *American Behavioral Scientist*, 44 (10), 1697–716.

Vaattovaara, M. and Kortteinen, M. 2003. 'Beyond polarization versus professionalism? A case study of the development of the Helsinki region, Finland', *Urban Studies*, 40(11), 2127–45.

Wallerstein, I. 1976. *Modern World-system: Capitalist Agriculture and the Origins of the European World-economy in the Sixteenth Century*. New York: Academic Press.

Walton, J. 1976. 'Political economy of world urban systems: Directions for comparative research'. In J. Walton and L. Masotti (eds), *The City in Comparative Perspective*. Beverley Hills, CA: Sage Publications.

Weber, A.F. 1963. *Growth of Cities in the Nineteenth Century: A Study in Statistics*. Ithaca, NY: Cornell University Press.

Wilson, W.J. 1987. *The Truly Disadvantaged*. Chicago: University of Chicago Press.

Chapter 13

The Sociology of Global Organizations

Stewart Clegg and Chris Carter

Defining Globalization

Globalization can be thought of as worldwide integration in virtually every sphere (B. Parker 2003: 234), achieved principally through markets. For some theorists this amounts to the financialization of the everyday (Martin 2002), while others see it in terms of the Americanization of the world (Ritzer 1993). While Goran Therborn (2000: 154, 149) has defined contemporary globalization in terms of a substitution of the global for the universal and of space for time, it is also necessary to consider that what is overwhelmingly being posited as the global is a production system of production in mass terms, which is American: American products, designs and politics dominate the global world – even when they are being manufactured by Japanese and Chinese companies. The US military dominates this world; it is the only global superpower. American consumption, especially of energy, dominates this world. If globalization is a process what is increasingly being globalized – globalizing – are North American values, products, force and debt. America is not only hugely globalized; it is also massively indebted, with much of that debt held in Japanese banks. Thus, from a rational actor perspective, debt is unlikely to throw the behemoth off course as it would not be in the interests of a world so dominated any more than it would be the nature of that which is globalizing. However, what is global floats on a sea of oil and other energy resources that, according to some analysts, are at a tipping point in terms of exploitable reserves and existing price mechanisms. Future reserves will only be had at historically much higher prices.

It is perhaps better to think in terms of globalizing as a process rather than a noun. In a seemingly inexorable fashion, increasing parts of the world's social and economic life are being linked through a multiplicity of processes and flows which are linked in circuits of organizational production and consumption. In place of all nations converging on one narrative of progress, based on Western, liberal democratic models and functionalist bureaucracies, there will be a plurality of possible ways of becoming modern. Businesses organized on a transnational basis are coordinated temporally by digital technology with dispersed branch offices coordinating production and marketing capacities (Hardt and Negri 2000). The organization of their forms across spatial relations remains the last frontier for business to exploit and conquer, given the virtual capillaries of instantaneous communication and trade embedded in the Internet (see Clarke and Clegg 1998). The Internet allows for far less centralized modes of organization – and, indeed, in the present state of anxiety in society about terrorist attacks, organizations are likely to adopt more distributed and network structures, with responsible autonomy in each of their nodal points – if only to be sure that the organization can survive a cataclysmic event such as 9/11. It is evident that organizations that have distributed systems and networked leadership will better survive catastrophe. After all, that is precisely what the Internet was designed to do. Hence, contemporary globalization is actually undermining the organizational forms that first made the conquest of the globe possible.

THE ANTECEDENTS OF GLOBAL ORGANIZATION

The earliest forms of global organization were religious and mercantile. In terms of religion, the Roman Catholic Church extended its sway over all of Europe from its formal adoption as the religion of the Roman Empire during the fourth century AD. The church was highly centralized and hierarchical in its organization, and, in its actions, highly political. It sought monopoly of spiritual power against both paganism and other religious faiths in those territories that came under its influence. The other form of early globalized organization was also monopolistic: this was the Dutch East India Company, founded in 1602 in Amsterdam. The Dutch East India Company very quickly became the wealthiest and largest mercantile organization the world had ever seen; by 1669 it had 150 merchant ships, 40 warships, 50,000 employees and a private army of 10,000 soldiers, and paid dividends of 40 per cent per annum.

These religious and mercantile auspices, although significant, were not, however, to be the basis of twentieth century organization. These earlier enterprises sought to standardize their organization through monopoly; by the twentieth century standards were to be set by more competitive pressures as organizational forms emerged that seemed to best fit the environment of the new age of industrial capitalism. Increasingly, organizations globalized around a norm informed by bureaucracy, industrialization and strict subjugation and control of employees.

Modern industrially based bureaucracies derived their organizing forms both from German developments in state organization and from US engineering achievements in the late nineteenth century steel industry. The former were codified by Max Weber (1978) as the 'ideal type of bureaucracy' while the latter were written up by Frederick Winslow Taylor, son of a wealthy Philadelphian family, as the *Principles of Scientific Management*. It was the convergence of these two forms that gave the twentieth century its dominant organizational story of a bureaucratic superstructure and a highly routinized and standardized substructure. It was in the United States, and then Germany, that the ingredients first came together. In the United States there were practical antecedents in the slave plantations in the antebellum states of the south (Cooke 2003), the military academy of West Point (Hoskin and MacVe 1988) and naval discipline (Clegg et al. 2006). In Germany, during the last quarter of the nineteenth century, the new chemical industry saw the fusion of bureaucratic control with disciplined processes.

The development of industrial discipline is best known through the ways in which Taylor's ideas heightened concern with surveillance, discipline and control of the body enshrined in what we now know as Scientific Management. Of course, Taylor was not operating in a vacuum but was at the hub of discussions – and practice – involving factory owners, supervisors and engineers. His own early experiments included using mathematical tables to work out the best way of using electrically powered lathes and redesigning shovels to enable men to move materials with greater efficiency (Jacques 1996: 105–6). Taylor took his homespun observations and discussions and codified, systematized and marketed them to have a far-reaching impact on society. As far as management thought is concerned Taylor marked the birth of modern management.

Taylor was convinced of the capacity of Scientific Management to deliver efficient organizations. As a corpus of ideas Scientific Management was of the zeitgeist and was to attract supporters ranging from American businessmen through to Soviet revolutionaries (Lenin is on record as a known admirer). What Taylor promulgated was an engineering theory of work (Shenhav 1999) which had as its central target the body of the worker (Miller and O'Leary 2002). As a factory insider possessing an intimate knowledge of the games that workers play, Taylor sought to eliminate possibilities for games that favoured worker interests through appropriating the skilled knowledge that existed in the head of the worker and placing it in the codified records of management. Taylor's system of management strove to find the 'One Best Way' of performing a particular task – once this had been discovered it was not to be deviated from.

Adding to the process of deskilling Taylor sought to separate those that were designing and planning the work from the factory workers who were executing the tasks. The corollary was that the jobs produced in the Taylorist factory were primarily of low skill and requiring little thought. The separation of the conception and execution of tasks stripped autonomy away from workers and made them interchangeable, something that was taken to new levels by Henry Ford. The vagaries of craft custom and lore no longer set the tempo of work, which was now the prerogative of management. Scientific Management and Ford's mass production system were essential to the rise of Industrial America. The ideas not only created the capacity for mass production but also, through the payment of higher wages, simultaneously created the consumer society that could consume the goods produced. It was an American story, even though, at its zenith in the 1920s, few American employers adopted the full panoply of techniques (Edwards 1979; Nelson 1975).

The take-up of the new ideas was patchy in Europe, in no small part due to the start-up costs of creating the organizational capabilities to accommodate the needs of a scientific management system (McKinlay 2006). The incomplete adoption of Taylorism was in part due to societal differences. In the melting pot of the northeast United States vast armies of immigrant labour were easily transformed into production line workers, while elsewhere in the UK, Germany and France, for instance, employers were more reluctant to impose Scientific Management. Specific societal differences – known in the literature as societal effects – came into play.

The 'societal effects' literature in organization theory highlights the existence of elective affinities between the organizational forms of a country and its broader cultural and social institutions (Sorge 1991). The explanation of West German engineering excellence is often attributed to the effectiveness of the vocational and educational training system, the systems of company ownership and the cultural importance of engineers (Lane 1989), for example. Equally, authors have pointed out the historical and cultural specificity that has shaped Japanese corporations that were much admired and fetishized in the West during the early 1990s (Kono and Clegg 2001). The work of Peter Clark (1987, 2000) goes some way to explaining differences between the United Kingdom and the United States in their manufacturing capacities. He suggests that particular home bases for organizations endow them with limited zones of manoeuvre. Clark builds an argument that had Henry Ford started out in the English West Midlands (the home of the now defunct Rover group) he would have failed. He suggests that the home base did not possess the supply networks, the infrastructure or the cultural capacity for mass production. Thus, it was no accident that Ford globalized a system of production and UK manufacturing did not: the latter lacked the capacities and capabilities to do so.

The era that Taylor and Ford ushered in can be said to have lasted until the 1980s; the characteristics were large-scale mass production, organized around long productions runs, economies of scale and hierarchical bureaucracies. It was a merger of Taylor at the base, Ford in the flows and integration of supplies, and Weber in the superstructure of control. As a system it was probably best analysed by Braverman (1974) in his account of the labour process under monopoly capitalism.

Initially, it was widely believed by strategy scholars that the rise of the multidivisional firm (MDF) superseded the classic bureaucracy (Chandler 1962). In practice, however, even though the MDF was capable of more flexible articulation across space, and became the ideal type of multinational organization for this reason, it merely reproduced performance-oriented bureaucracies at each of its divisional nodes while retaining certain core functions to the centre, such as financial controls. The framework for their organization corresponded to the first of what Bartlett and Ghoshal (1989) highlighted as three models for global management, the multinational model. The multinational model conceptualizes the organization as a portfolio of different businesses in different sectors and nations. The multinational is managed by a relatively straightforward set of financial controls. The component businesses in the portfolio are relatively autonomous in their activities.

More recently Alfred Chandler and Bruce Mazlish (2005) have edited a collection that chronicles the rise of multinationals in a set of terms that are somewhat broader than Chandler's (1962) early work. Their argument is that to conceive of multinationals as merely economic entities is to miss the point. Multinationals are the leviathan figures of our time, actively shaping the world in which we live. The reach of multinationals is now such that they interpenetrate every aspect of human life.

Two additional models for understanding global organization, in addition to the multinational model, are identified by Bartlett and Ghoshal (1989). The *international* model has a core market – normally its home one – upon which most energy is concentrated. Its operations in other markets are regarded as peripheral. The subsidiaries are tightly controlled from the centre. The *global* model concentrates on global markets and attempts to integrate operations between different markets.

Production is generally centralized and the different national organizations are used to distribute the products. What make global organizations possible are global management capabilities; these are forms of management that are capable of operating effectively in terms of action at a distance and in the abstract in ways that transcend the limitations of spatial distance and the constraints of temporal distance. While the potential for such control was always a part of the managerial project, it was as a result of the emergence of a global neoliberal economic agenda in the 1980s that it actually achieved dominance.

THE NEW MANAGERIAL REVOLUTIONARIES

The elections of Margaret Thatcher and Ronald Reagan to office are generally held to be hugely symbolic markers of a new era. In the well-documented restructuring that was to follow the manager was one of the social figurations elevated as a new moral ideal (see Macintyre 1981; Townley 2002). If Reagan and Thatcher were significant in political and social circles, management had its own watershed year in 1982 when former McKinsey consultants Tom Peters and Robert Waterman published *In Search of Excellence*. In many ways it was an attempt by America to counter the perceived Japanese challenge by demonstrating that there were equally robust indigenous ways of organizing available in the United Kingdom to those in Japan. Blockbusting their way up the bestseller lists a new genre of management writer was borne.

We will deal with the fuller significance of the Peters phenomenon later in this chapter but at this point content ourselves with the central theme of *In Search of Excellence*, namely that organizations had to change their corporate cultures to survive and be excellent. Profiling 'excellent companies' Peters and Waterman identified eight successful attributes of successful companies which were widely enacted by the millions of managers who read their book. If critics took pleasure in pointing out the questionable theoretical assertions, this was nothing on the empirical *schadenfreude* enjoyed a year or so later when the excellent companies started failing. Yet this turned out to be an irrelevant detail, for the corporate culture agenda had been set and organizations set about trying to transform themselves. In the years that followed initiatives such as total quality management (TQM) and business process re-engineering (BPR) followed. The consultative, participative approach at process improvement often ended in frustration as the recursive tendencies of organizations (Giddens 1984) often raised their bureaucratic head. BPR took an altogether more violent approach to the pre-existing context of an organization by seeking to 'obliterate' it and start again. It is perhaps unsurprising that BPR was often ruinous for the knowledge base of firms it sought to transform. Many times the things that made the organizations special, or indeed viable, were rationalized out of existence in a kind of Taylorization of all knowledge and work in the organization. But it did have significant effects in popularizing the idea that there were post-bureaucratic ways of organizing available, or that there were new organization forms with which it was possible to rethink the dominant bureaucratic models of the twentieth century. The reach of anti-bureaucratic managerialism has crossed sectors as well as nations. The New Public Management movement has travelled far from its origins in the British public sector to be applied across the public sector world, globally.

Post-bureaucracy has been an important theme in management thought in both private and public sectors over the last 20 years. In the management literature, bureaucracy and bureaucrats went from being a description of a mode of organizing to a pejorative term of abuse. In sociology, authors such as Bauman (1989) highlighted some of the terrible historical events made possible by bureaucracy. The more recent symbolic assault on bureaucracy has imbued the term with negative connotations. Paul du Gay (2002) has made a spirited defence of bureaucracy, arguing that attacks on bureaucracy ignore the positive connotations found in Weber's original conceptualization of the term. In particular, du Gay draws attention to the equality and impartiality that characterized the treatment of the individual in bureaucracy, as did Perrow (1986). The broad trend, however, has been to castigate bureaucracy and for organizations to attempt to escape their bureaucratic practices. From the late 1980s onwards these escape attempts were increasingly concentrated on a series of management fads that were marketed globally by international consultancies, such as McKinsey, who were the source of the cases originally used in the Peters and Waterman (1982) volume that may be said to have kicked off modern managerial concern with organization forms, which has seen waves of successive innovations wash over the global corporate scene.

THE SOCIOLOGICAL ORIGINS OF MANAGEMENT FORMS

The modernity of management?

Much is made of emphasizing the 'newness' of recent management ideas. Yet management academics have been quick to point out that many of these ideas are in fact remarkably similar to past initiatives. For instance, knowledge management, a managerial initiative that seeks to create competitive advantage for leveraging the organization's knowledge base in practice has more than a passing resemblance to Taylorism (Fuller 2002). Taylor sought to take the knowledge from the craft worker and place it in the hands of management; knowledge management seeks to codify tacit knowledge in the workplace. Tacit knowledge exists in the minds of employees and has to be taken out of mind and put into organization practice, independently of whosever's mind it may have first come from. Equally, other initiatives such as total quality management or business process re-engineering have a resonance with ideas that preceded them. Our argument is that the last 20 years have witnessed a dramatic shift in management ideas, one which clearly requires some justification.

We accept that many 'new' management ideas can in many ways be regarded as recycled management nostrums from the past. When Fuller (2002) makes the link between Taylorism and knowledge management we think he is right. Yet there is a crucial distinction not so much relating to the content of the ideas – though of course information technology now underpins most managerial initiatives – but the context in which the ideas are created. Over the last 25 years there has been an emergence of a powerful management ideas industry which has successfully packaged, communicated and sold discontinuous innovation as a cultural ideal and a desirable good (Townley 2002). A management-ideas industry has been fuelled by the rise of business schools, especially through the provision of MBA degrees, the growth in management consultancies and the emergence of self-styled management gurus. Taken together this amounts to an actor-network that has successfully packaged and commoditized managerial initiatives. These models of 'best practice' have been disseminated throughout the organizational world. We argue that this has been profoundly important in terms of creating blueprints of what organizations 'should' look like. Collectively the key players of the management ideas industry have helped produce management fashions.

Large IT firms

The major actors in the management ideas industry have been the major IT companies, such as SAP and Cap Gemini. The changes in IT have been one of the major enabling factors behind globalization. IT firms have played an important role in the development of the management ideas industry. Recent initiatives such as enterprise resource planning and knowledge management rely very heavily on IT practices. Matthias Kipping (2002) has argued that consultancies go through waves of development. According to his analysis large IT firms are riding the most recent wave and are becoming the dominant players in the consulting industry. We may think of them as the 'fifth column' of the management ideas industry: they penetrate businesses that need the technical capabilities that IT brings, but their entry becomes a beachhead for sustained attack by management ideas. The first of these are usually introduced by management consultants, often called in to try and make the IT systems that millions have been expended on work better, to live up to expectations.

Management consultancy

Large-scale management consultancy has grown exponentially and consultants have become major actors in the creation and transmission of management ideas. While many US consultancies had been in existence for much of the last century – coming out of the systematic management movement of Taylor's day – it is over the last 20 or so years that demand for their services has boomed. For instance, in 1980 the consulting sector did about $3 billion worth of business a year. By 2004 this had increased to a staggering $125 billion (Kennedy Information, 2004). Organizations such as McKinseys and the Boston Consulting Group have become high-status brands in their own right. Other consultancies emerged out of the large accountancy partnerships. Uniquely placed as the auditors to large firms, most large accountancy firms commercialized to the extent that their consultancy operations became at least as important as the core auditing business, which was notably the case with Arthur Andersen and their most infamous client, Enron.

What were the circumstances that led to the rise of management consultants? Andrew Sturdy has pointed out that management consultants simultaneously instil a sense of security and anxiety in their clients: security, because they imbue managers with a sense of certainty and control over the future or whatever organizational problem it is that the consulting is concerned with; anxiety, because the managers are in a sense emasculated – unable to manage without the guidance of consultants.

The role of the large accounting firms is pivotal to understanding the story of the rise of consultancies. By the mid 1980s the market for financial audit was mature and had stagnated. In any case, outside of a few accounting firms in a few geographical locations, competition between these firms was frowned upon and for the most part regarded as being somewhat aggressive and ungentlemanly. What the large accounting firms possessed was a monopoly over the provision of audits to large firms. The 'full professional jurisdiction' (Abbott 1988) was protected by law. The large accounting firms developed a number of capabilities, one of which was the ability to cultivate and sustain long-term relationships with clients. These connections were often cemented by their own accountants going to work in client firms after a number of years with the accounting partnership. Accounting partnerships also possessed highly sophisticated means of charging for audits and managing large-scale interventions into organizations. The shifting context of accounting firms in the 1980s allowed them to diversify outside of audit activities, though their clients were generally those that they also sold audit services too. Audit became the wedge that opened the corporate door to the on-selling of additional services. Hanlon (1994) has demonstrated the way in which the large accounting firms commercialized themselves – pursuing capital accumulation strategies. Equally, Greenwood et al. (1999) have written extensively on the unique characteristics of accounting firms that allowed them to globalize so successfully. Mike Power (1994) has argued that we increasingly live in an audit society, one in which the principles of verification and calculability underpin society. During this time accountants and management consultants have risen to powerful positions within civil society. In the UK, for instance, large accounting firms played an important role in drafting privatization and private finance initiatives. They were simultaneously to profit from the implementation of such policies. Government work, that was once the sole preserve of mandarins, is now often carried out by accountants and management consultants. What marks out a mandarin from a management consultant or an accountant is a different type of intellectual capital: the mandarin was most likely to be a classicist, schooled in a classical discipline, educated at a socially elite university and drawn from a wealthy family background. The moral sentiments of the knowledge born by a management consultant are more technocratic and democratic, and are likely to be premised on less concern with social origins, and education in a business school, usually in an MBA.

MBAs

Management education has penetrated the Anglo-American university system to a considerable degree. Andrew Sturdy (2006) reports that '25% of US university students currently major in business or management and in the UK, 30% of undergraduates study some management'. Equally, fast emerging economies such as China and India have embraced the MBA with great enthusiasm. A small number of business schools' MBAs are rich in symbolic capital, while some such as Harvard enjoy iconic status. Thus, from being, once upon a time, the province of an elite cadre of

American business aspirants, the MBA is now offered in ever-increasing volumes across the world, fast over-shadowing the traditional undergraduate domains of academic endeavour. In one sense, the growth of the MBA may be taken as a case-in-point of what some critical scholars have seen as the neo-colonial domination of an American educational model on a global scale (Miller and O'Leary 2002). Hence, the cultural logic of the MBA, from its beginning in the neo-classical architecture and green pastures of Harvard University, has developed in the latter part of the twentieth century to become *the* model of management education. As such it is the principal vehicle for the normalization of disciplined expectations in the managers of tomorrow, while offering practical opportunities for the consultants of today to enrol others who will soon be influential to their ideas and to expound them in settings that proffer great legitimacy and legitimation. The interconnections become almost seamless; the managers in training are normalized into the idea that consultancy is a solution provider; the consultancies gain exposure to attract the brightest and the best from the top MBAs. The MBA-speak of PowerPoints and spreadsheets prepares the student of today for the consulting and management presentations of tomorrow. Thus, the MBA acts as a rationalizing device. There is a canon of knowledge which has been increasingly homogenized, which is further exacerbated through international credentialing bodies such as the AASCB (Association for the Advancement of Collegiate Schools of Business) and EQUIS. Most particularly, the move towards centralized standardization has been achieved by the AACSB and its emergence as the peak standards making body. To have won membership of the AASCB has become an obligatory passage point for those business schools seeking global legitimacy. One consequence of the AACSB and its framing of the field is that, across the world, students will be tutored in similar lessons in strategy, finance, marketing, human resources and so forth.

One of the fascinating features of the MBA is its link with management practice. The promissory note of the MBA is to deliver more highly paid jobs to students. While there are a host of distance and part-time programmes available the costs of participating in a full-time programme are considerable. Students have to be fairly sure that their investment will be worthwhile by providing them with a degree of fluency in the cultural capital of managerialism: of course, whether being able to be a smooth conversationalist in a particular rhetoric makes better managers or not is an open question. What it certainly does do is to allow them to communicate with other managers in a global management. As Victorian administrators were schooled in studies of long dead languages and the histories of classical civilizations the managerial classes of today study a syllabus that is remarkably uniform in its content. The MBA curriculum and skills are fast becoming the Latin of the modern world.

The MBA also achieves the material production of ideational values. It acts as a vehicle for creating self-fulfilling prophecies. An illustration of this is the so-called flexibility debate that took place in the late 1980s in the UK. Atkinson (1984) outlined a model of the 'flexible firm' in which he argued that organizations were moving increasingly to employing a core workforce, enjoying secure employment and good working conditions, and a peripheral workforce that was much more casualized. Debates raged as to whether this was the case or not. Empiricists argued that Atkinson was overstating the shift and that employee relations were unchanged.

The model entered into the curriculum of many human resource management courses in many British business schools. The result was that managers learnt – and many are sure to have applied Atkinson's model – such that it did become part of the employment landscape. Similarly the influential research done on strategy by Michael Porter into regional clusters has had an important influence in regional policy whereby regional governments actively try to create a cluster.

The MBA has been thought of as the solution to the problem of making up managers (Watson 2004; du Gay and Salaman 1991). Managers would not be people with skills merely learnt on the job but they would have been prepared, vocationally, beforehand. They would be well-prepared receptacles for the received forms of calculation with which, globally, management makes its ready reckoning. From within business schools there have been rumblings of disquiet about the MBA. However, almost exactly a hundred years after its inception in the United States, the concept of the MBA has swapped sides, now being critically perceived as part of the problem rather than the solution. Some authors regard the MBA as neo-colonial domination of an American educational model on a global scale (Miller and O'Leary 2002). Henry Mintzberg's 'hard look at the soft practice of managing and management development' (2004; see also Bennis and O'Toole 2005) revealed in a popular tone what other scholars such as Parker and Jary (1995) and Sturdy and Yiannis (2000) theorized more critically earlier: the concept of the MBA is producing neither a humanistically educated workforce nor good managers.

The wave of accounting scandals and corporate collapses has led to further soul searching over the MBA. Enron were enthusiastic recruiters of MBAs (Cruver 2003). Cruver, a Texas A&M MBA graduate, chronicles his 18 months at Enron before the company collapsed. The enduring images are of highly motivated, bright MBA graduates not asking difficult questions, not raising concerns over dubious practice and generally being socialized into the macho, competitive 'win at all costs' culture of Enron. That these MBAs' professional education seeded ethical concerns so lightly is one thing but some writers such as the late Sumantra Ghoshal have argued that the MBA actually made crashes such as Enron possible. The lack of professional ethical formation of future managers makes them extremely plastic at the hands of those whose heroic leadership status in hot-shot organizations defines that which the young managers aspire to be. It institutionalizes the possibility of management's ethical failure as the norm to which recruits will be socialized. By contrast with professions such as medicine and law there is little attention paid to professional ethics and civic morals, other than those that emphasize winning at all costs, being a corporate game player and being the one who ends up with the most chips in the lottery of organizational life.

How has the MBA achieved the global significance that it has? In part this is an outcome that is dialectically related to globalization; globalizing processes encourage the employment and utilization of the technical knowledge associated with MBAs to maintain their momentum. However, it is also part of a wider social phenomenon, itself related to the emergence of a global management project. The phenomenon in question is the emergence of a huge commercial market in popular management books and a circuit of celebrity for those who write them. They are the gurus of the modern age, the 'management gurus'.

Management gurus

Earlier in this chapter we introduced Tom Peters. He is the most celebrated and, at the same time, infamous of the management gurus. Gurus are generally self-styled and known for their image and rhetoric intensity. Producing airport lounge best-sellers and conducting world lecture tours, gurus hawk their homespun nostrums throughout the corporate world. Analysts of gurus have argued – in a McLuhan fashion – that the medium is the message. Evangelical-style exhortations to change accompanied by convincing stories and snappy sound bites characterize the genre. The books follow a similar vein and, as we suggested above, are often taken to task for their theoretical and methodological failings. This is perhaps to miss the point. Even more managers are likely to listen to a guru presentation or perhaps read a guru book than are likely to attend business school (Clegg and Palmer 1996). Many of the gurus have enjoyed glittering corporate careers and their ideas on management are lent credibility by this corporate experience – such texts have elsewhere been characterized as 'karaoke texts', in a reference to their 'I did it my way' quality (Clegg and Palmer 1996).

MANAGEMENT FASHIONS

The four main actors of the management ideas industry have reshaped the corporate world. They have changed the linguistic and ideational context in which organizations operate by ushering in a new grammar for organizations. Most large organizations' managers today can talk about their 'strategy', articulate their 'mission', their 'values' and their 'corporate culture', as if they were talking about self-evident concepts. These are abstractions that the management ideas industry has made as real as writers such as J.M. Barrie were able to make Peter Pan, Wendy and the Lost Boys, for children. They are imaginaries, conjured up to be real, which is not to say that in the past organizations did not possess such attributes, but that there certainly was not a global managerial language articulating the same imaginaries in so many different boardrooms, on so many brochures and in so many websites. When every organization has a vision, a mission and a strategy the manager who dreams different dreams risks going naked to the market.

The management ideas industry has also given rise to management fashions. Eric Abrahamson has argued that management fashions possess both an aesthetic and technical dimension. The aesthetic dimension makes a robust argument in an 'attempt to convince fashion followers that a management technique is both rational and at the forefront of managerial progress' (Abrahamson 1996: 267). The new technique will be backed up by war stories that confirm its effectiveness and statistics demonstrating its worth to the organization. The careful styling and well-crafted success stories and plausible philosophical rationale for the adoption of such a technique constitute a rhetoric intensive manifesto of action for organizations. The technical dimension includes a number of tools and techniques that can be used to perform a particular initiative. For TQM this included brainstorming, process mapping techniques, cause and effect diagrams and so forth. The overarching characteristic of an initiative is that it is imperative for the success and indeed survival of the organization.

Fashions are instances of 'blackboxed' (Latour 1987) knowledge which, while usually American in origin, are footloose and suitably ambiguous to traverse sectors and nations. As part of their pressure for capital accumulation, actors within the management ideas industry are constantly seeking the next initiative that will sell well. The search for discontinuous innovation – necessary to maintain the portfolio of new products for a market that quickly tires of the same old recipes – involves careful market research into managerial anxieties and organizational issues. Thought leaders scan the management journals for ideas and potential gurus that can be translated into profitable business. Successful fashion innovators possess sufficient *habitus* to be able to construct managerial initiatives that capture the corporate zeitgeist.

While the management ideas industry supplies, commodifies and disseminates, what of organizations that have seemingly become dedicated followers of fashion? New institutional theory suggests that some initiatives are consumed for mimetic reasons which are the copying of 'best practices', regulative reasons where an organization is compelled to adopt an initiative, and normative reasons where the idea is held to be at the zenith of best practices. All of these forms of isomorphism have led – at the surface levels at least – to organizations increasingly coming to resemble each other.

WORK AND GLOBALIZATION

Over 30 years ago in his classic analysis of the US labour force, Harry Braverman noted the tendency for organizations to deskill their labour force. What does the experience of globalization mean for the experience of work? We will address a number of shifts that appear to have taken place in the labour force. In many of the change programmes of the last 20 years, one of the central targets has been labour. The downsizing that characterized the 1990s led to a 'gouging' (Littler and MacInnes 2004) of the workforce and a removal of swathes of middle management. The waves of privatization across the world were to have many effects on labour. One was to challenge seriously the power base of existing dominant groups. In the United Kingdom, there was an assault on state-sponsored professionals such as teachers, social workers and engineers in state utilities. The assault on the professions has led to some authors suggesting that the bell tolls a death knell or at least announces twilight time for some professions. It is quite clear that some professions have fared better than others. Groups such as lawyers, but particularly accountants, have profited hugely from the changes in the global economy. The shifts in the last 20 years have, according to Madelaine Bunting (2004), led to an 'overwork culture' which is ruining people's lives. Labour intensification and growing levels of insecurity are key motifs in the study of work under globalization.

The 1990s saw shifts in the labour market that for some have heralded a coming of knowledge work. There are of course important qualifications that need to be attached to such labels, yet it is the view of the authors that knowledge work is too important to be dismissed as the stuff of philosophical whim. Robert Reich (1991) observed it in terms of the rise of symbolic analysts, the elite of the international service class. Symbolic analysts are marked out by their symbols of success – the Porsches, the Rolexes and the Armani suits – and the nature of their work on the semiotics of money, images or words. Symbolic analysts include city analysts, corporate lawyers, advertising executives and management consultants. Symbolic analysis manipulates symbols to involve, identify and broker problems. It simplifies reality into abstract images by rearranging, juggling, experimenting, communicating and transforming these images, using analytical tools such as mathematical algorithms, legal arguments, financial analysis, scientific principles or psychological insights that persuade and somehow or other address conceptual puzzles. What mark such work as different are its linguistic and social accomplishments. In circumstances of high uncertainty and high ambiguity there is never one correct answer (Alvesson 2001). Instead, any number of plausible alternatives can be posed. It is work that places the persuasive abilities of the knowledge worker to the fore. Image intensity, the suit they wear, the briefcase they carry, the sleekness of their Power-Point presentation and the persuasiveness of their rhetoric are all as essential to the robustness of their argument as their mastery of the appropriate vocabulary. An essential part of a knowledge worker's repertoire is to appear to be an expert, which takes primacy over 'actually being an expert'. This is not to suggest that knowledge workers are charlatans, as Alvesson makes it clear that technical competence is taken for granted, but that the ability to persuade comes to the fore. These are the global workers, working for the Big Four accounting firms and other boutique equivalents. They often move between the great corporate capitals of the world creating genuinely global corporate elites. Such transience perhaps engenders networking skills and alters sensibilities around risk – two other important characteristics of the symbolic analyst.

The hours worked and the air-miles travelled by symbolic analysts, armed with their elite MBAs and their glittering symbols of success, have been the subject of analysis. Australian writers Trinca and Fox (2004) highlight how many knowledge workers have become hooked on work. They make the point that it is not just those motivated by material gain and the trappings of power but also 'cultural creatives', who often possess alternative value systems, who are also becoming addicted to work. Knowledge workers, whether through desire or compulsion, according to Trinca and Fox, are becoming addicted to work. In summary, they are the well-remunerated stressed out shifters and shapers of money, meanings and markets, doing deals, making business and moving from project to project, hooked on the experience. Work becomes one of the addictions of the global capitalist era for the creative class, along with other sources of intense nervous stimulation. The 'better than sex' argument is quite a challenge for conventional industrial sociology. For the past 30 years most of its arguments have engaged with theories developed in the Braverman tradition; undoubtedly these have the capacity to illuminate the nature of some contemporary work, even when they overstate the tendencies that they identify (see Clegg 1990 for a critical account). Yet the sociology of work needs to look beyond metaphors derived from the production line. So much of contemporary employment involves the manipulation of knowledge and symbols, and is, as we have argued, concerned more with identity work than manual labour and has an immaterial quality to it, rather than being based in material production. To understand the work of such people it will be necessary to engage with issues of identity, social capital and immaterial labour.

Symbolic analysts are, of course, the fortunate members of the global economy. Additionally there is a shadow group of workers in the symbolic sphere, workers who are tightly scripted, operating in simple and unambiguous environments. These workers work in call centres. Call centre work is characterized as pressured and at the same time monotonous. For some, call centres are the factories of the future. Call centre workers are under exacting targets to deal with a client's call in a particular time and manner. Much has been made of the panoptic surveillance regimes that call centre workers are subjected too. Yet the Orwellian dystopia of the controllable, governable worker seems to ignore that call centre workers do not occupy total institutions and their subjectivities draw on a range of different roles they may play in life. In the UK, call centres are notorious for their very high turnover rates, which is perhaps a good proxy for the extent to which workers resist buying into the logics they are subjected to. The last few years have seen call centres go global – especially to places such as Delhi and Bangalore. The Indian counterparts of a UK or US call centre worker will earn around a fraction of these employees, or, looked at another way, the organizational costs of highly routinized work that cannot be eliminated will be hugely reduced by shifting the service provision offshore. A customer service call placed in the United Kingdom or United States is likely to be routed a continent away.

The global symbolic analyst elites are supported by a vast number of workers doing casual, boring, dirty and exploitative jobs. Those who cook, wash, clean up, who pack and sell convenience foods, park and service cars, the people who attend to appearance, the body workers – the people that keep the symbolic analysts' image looking good.

There are also the grunge jobs – the semi-skilled workers who work in the lower reaches of the supply chains established by the global giants – which account for around 35 per cent of the jobs found in the US economy. It is a contingent, easily dismissed mass of people who can be used and laid off to absorb transaction costs and cushion demand for global corporations. These workers are the first to feel the chill of a cold economic wind – buffering the core contract employees. These workers are low skill, are often regarded by corporations as adding little value and are easily disposable but they are likely to have some form of social insurance and they do work in the formal economy. The second element in the composition of the grunge economy comprises an underclass of workers who are often illegal immigrants working sporadically in extreme conditions outside of the formal economy and the regulated labour market. Think of sweat shops in the garment industry or contract labour and seasonal employees in the agricultural sector. Many jobs are done in conditions of virtual slavery – with thousands of Eastern European women being trafficked across Europe to work in the sex industry. These are global supply chains that bring misery. Outside of the commercial centres of the West fashionable businesses source inputs from factories that operate in conditions that would be unacceptable in the West. The garment and footwear industry in global brands such as Nike, especially, have been singled out for adverse academic and political attention in these terms. A good guide to the concerns that have been articulated is to be found in the web pages maintained by David Boje (http://cbae.nmsu.edu/~dboje/nikerpts.html).

While capital has successfully globalized, labour unions have found things more difficult. Under assault in countries such as the United Kingdom, the last 20 years has seen the relations of power shift away from the traditionally powerful unions. In part, this has been due to legislative changes. It has also been due to the decline in some traditionally well-organized and militant industries such as steel and coal. What is notable, however, is that barring a few exceptions labour has found it difficult to organize globally. In no way has it matched the ingenuity of corporations in their accomplishment of globalization, although significant global campaigns have emerged from within the trade union movement and from the critics of globalization to confront the new global realities (Hogan and Greene 2002). However, trade unions remain, for the present, largely nationally institutionalized, and they do not afford much of a threat to existing organization of the relations of production, especially as their recruitment and penetration of the post-industrial services economy is far lower than was the case in the era of industrial labour and society. Also, they are increasingly irrelevant because their leadership is largely male and the domain of their traditional membership female. Thus, the biggest issues that unions face today on the membership front are low female and ethnic minority participation rates such that the people doing the representing rarely share either gender or ethnicity. There are cases of the use of the web by unions in concert with more traditional forms of mobilization (Carter et al. 2003). The emerging global system is far from complete and far from determined, but it is having a profound impact on social and working life in the regions included within and excluded from it.

GLOBAL PROTEST

Globalization is the perfidious issue of our times. Every time the G8 finance ministers meet – important architects of the global economic system – it is amidst the tightest security. It will be an event which will draw thousands of people to the streets to protest against the iniquities of global capitalism. The arguments against globalizations are complex and demonstrations invariably bring together a wide-ranging group of solutions as diverse as Trotskyite global revolution or a reassertion of key lessons from the Christian New Testament. The demonstrations are important symbols of democracy and have a carnivalesque quality to them. Yet it is difficult to see them being the source of an alternative to the current global order. Ironically, many of the iconic anti-globalization movements that are being held by their members to resemble increasingly the managerialist corporations that are so despised. The work of O'Doherty and Unerman (2005), for instance, charts the managerialization of Amnesty International.

In trying to inject greater transparency and accountability into global capital, we would disagree with Naomi Klein. Logos provide the ability to monitor and scrutinize global supply chains. Fairtrade movements provide similar possibilities. Corporate social responsibility is an initiative which has been trumpeted by oil companies and the like as a demonstration that they are taking their obligations seriously. While many such corporate endeavours may well be 'greenwash' and 'whitewash', activists can expose them as such and try to make corporate entities whose brand reputation is vital to their global dominance, especially in sophisticated liberal democratic markets, take some self-interest in improved practices. Thus, the ultimate aim of a great deal of activist pressure is improved self-management and self-regulation.

CONCLUSION

In this chapter we have discussed some of the central aspects of globalization from an organizational perspective. A key motor – we argue – has been what we have termed the management ideas industry that has led to a surface homogenization across the organizational world. The US dominance of managerialism has succeeded in setting the terms of debate and has established the language of engagement, which has penetrated most sectors and nations. Thus, to an extent, globalization does represent Americanization, albeit one that is distinct from the cultural imperialism often associated with critiques of such processes. It is not the consumption of Coca-Cola and fast food that drives this globalization, although it is often a secondary characteristic. More fundamental are the development of abstracted ways of engaging with people and things that enable a way of doing business to spread globally, whose genetic imprint is American and for which the majority of ideas production and dissemination is American. While this chapter has reviewed some of the key aspects of the globalization of organizations it should not be read as a totalizing Americanization of the organizational world. While the American model, for the time being at least, has seemingly triumphed there are likely to be other models that come to challenge it. Japanese industry was fetishized by Western observers in the late 1980s and early 1990s. When the Japanese economy encountered problems, Japanese modes of organizing were written off as quickly as they had once been embraced. Metaphorically speaking Japanization lies prostrate in the managerialist mausoleum, an object of historic curiosity rather than current interest. It remains to be seen whether interest in Japanese modes of organization will be reanimated as Japan's economy re-emerges from its current gloom (Kono and Clegg 2001).

The success of some models might owe much to unintended consequences, coming out of the attempt to managerialize according to a consultancy blueprint. Other models might emerge out of the fast developing, super economies of the near future such as China and India. We may see examples of reverse colonization, whereby ideas from the post-colonial world become standard organizing techniques in the West. Hybridity is likely to be the name of the game in the future. The management ideas industry certainly possesses the capacity to take ideas from anywhere in the world and turn them into management initiatives. Much of the managerialization of the last 20 years has focused on taking ideas of 'best practice' from the corporate world and applying them to the state or former state owned sector. The extent to which this trend will continue is an open question; will the appetite remain for private sector inspiration and consultant delivered change?

The sustainability of managerialism is open to question. If organizations increasingly follow one template and become more and more alike, where is a sense of difference or competitive advantage likely to come from? Similarly, much of the managerialization of organizations has been about modernization and, by implication, dissociation from the organization's past. What will future forms of managerialism look like when managerialism is seen as the problem rather than the solution?

Organization studies teaches us that power – however apparently unassailable – is always capable of being challenged and overturned. We remain alert to this possibility with global forms of organization, although it is difficult to see this coming out of global anti-capitalist protest movements. It seems increasingly clear that it is environmental issues that are shaping up to be the defining issue – and societal problem – of the age. It is less clear what global organizations, the management ideas industry and managerialism have to offer as a solution to this growing problem. However, it is also equally clear that their address will require a new form of global regulation that is unlikely to be delivered through the neoliberal agenda. Hence, we speculate that the next major shift in the development of globalizing capacities is likely to emerge from the ecological politics arising from globalization's unanticipated consequences, around issues such as global warming.

References

Abbott, A. 1988. *The System of Professions: An Essay on the Division of Expert Labour.* Chicago: Chicago University Press.

Abrahamson, E. 1996. 'Management fashion', *Academy of Management Review*, 21 (1), 254–85.

Alvesson, M. 2001. 'Knowledge work: Ambiguity, image and identity', *Human Relations*, 54 (7), 863–86.

Atkinson, P. 1984. 'Manpower strategies for flexible organizations', *Personnel Management*, August, 26–9.

Bartlett, C. and Ghoshal, S. 1989. *Managing across Borders: The Transnational Solution.* Boston, MA: Harvard Business School Press.

Bauman, Z. 1989. *Modernity and the Holocaust.* Oxford: Polity Press.

Bennis, W.G. and O'Toole, J. 2005. 'How business schools lost their way', *Harvard Business Review*, May, 96–104.

Braverman, H. 1974. *Labor and Monopoly Capitalism: The Degradation of Work in the Twentieth Century.* New York: Monthly Review Press.

Bunting, M. 2004. *Willing Slaves: How the Overwork Culture Is Ruling our Lives.* London: HarperCollins.

Carter, C., Clegg, S.R., Hogan, J. and Kornberger, M. 2003. 'The polyphonic spree: The case of the Liverpool dockers', *Industrial Relations*, 34 (4), 290–304.

Chandler, A.D. Jr. 1962. *Strategy and Structure.* Cambridge, MA: MIT Press.

Chandler, A.D., Jr and Mazlish, B. (eds) 2005. *Leviathans: Multinational Corporations and the New Global History.* Cambridge: Cambridge University Press.

Clark, P. 1987. *Anglo-American Innovation.* Berlin: De Gruyter.

Clark, P. 2000. *Organizations in Action.* London: Routledge.

Clarke, T. and Clegg, S.R. 1998. *Changing Paradigms: The Transformation of Management Knowledge in the 21st Century.* London: Harper Collins.

Clegg, S.R. 1990. *Modern Organizations.* London: Sage.

Clegg, S.R., Courpasson, D. and Phillips, N. 2006. *Power and Organization.* Thousand Oaks, CA: Sage.

Clegg, S.R. and Palmer, G. 1996. *The Politics of Management Knowledge.* London: Sage.

Cooke, B. 2003. 'The denial of slavery in management studies', *Journal of Management Studies*, 40 (8), 1895–918.

Cruver, B. 2003. *Enron: The Anatomy of Greed: The Unshredded Truth from an Enron Insider*. London: Arrow.

Du Gay, P. 2002. *In Praise of Bureaucracy*. London: Sage.

Du Gay, P. and Salaman, G. 1991. 'The cult[ure] of the customer', *Journal of Management Studies*, 29 (5), 615–33.

Edwards, R. 1979. *Contested Terrain: The Transformation of the Workplace in the Twentieth Century*. London: Heinemann.

Fuller, S. 2002. *Knowledge Management*. London: Butterworth Heinemann.

Giddens, A. 1984. *The Constitution of Society*. Cambridge: Polity Press.

Greenwood, R., Rose, T., Brown, J., Cooper, D. and Hinings, B. 1999. 'The global management of professional services: The example of accounting'. In S. Clegg, E. Ibarra-Colado and L. Bueno-Rodriquez (eds), *Global Management: Universal Theories and Local Realities*, 265–96. London: Sage.

Hanlon, G. 1994. *Commercialisation of the Service Class*. London: Macmillan.

Hardt, M. and Negri, A. 2000. *Empire*. Cambridge, MA: Harvard University Press.

Hogan, J. and Greene, A. 2002. 'E-collectivism: On-line action and on-line mobilisation'. In L. Holmes, D.M. Hosking and M. Grieco (eds), *Organising in the Information Age: Distributed Technology, Distributed Leadership, Distributed Identity, Distributed Discourse*. Aldershot: Ashgate.

Hoskin, K. and MacVe, R. 1988. 'The genesis of accountability: The West Point connections', *Accounting, Organizations and Society*, 13, 37–73.

Jacques, R. 1996. *Manufacturing the Employee*. London: Sage.

Kennedy Information. 2004. 'The global consulting marketplace 2004–2006' (online) <http://www.kennedyinfo.com/mc/mcindex>.

Kipping, M. 2002. 'Trapped in their wave: The evolution of management consultancies'. In T. Clark and R. Fincham (eds), *Critical Consulting: New Perspectives on the Management Advice Industry*, 28–49. Oxford: Blackwell.

Klein, N. 2000. *No Logo: Taking Aim at the Brand Bullies*. London: HarperCollins.

Kono, T. and Clegg, S.R. 2001. *Trends in Japanese Management*. London: Palgrave.

Lane, C. 1989. *Management and Labour in Europe*. Cheltenham: Edward Elgar.

Latour, B. 1987. *Science in Action: How to Follow Scientists and Engineers through Society*. Milton Keynes: Open University Press.

Littler C.R. and MacInnes, P. 2004. 'The paradox of managerial downsizing', *Organization Studies*, 25, 1159–84.

Macintyre, A. 1981. *After Virtue: A Study in Moral Theory*. London: Duckworth.

McKinlay, A. 2006. 'Labour process theory'. In C. Carter and S. Clegg (eds), *The Encyclopedia of the Sociology of Management*. Oxford: Blackwells.

Martin, R. 2002. *Financialization of Daily Life*. Philadelphia, PA: Temple University Press.

Miller, P. and O'Leary, T. 2002. 'Hierarchies and American ideals, 1900–1940'. In S.R. Clegg (ed.), *Central Currents in Organization Studies*. Vol. 1: *Frameworks and Applications*, 192–221. London: Sage; originally published in *Academy of Management Review* (1989) 14, 250–65.

Mintzberg, H. 2004. *Managers not MBAs: A Hard Look at the Soft Practice of Managing and Management Development*. San Francisco: Berrett-Koehler.

Nelson, D. 1975. *Managers and Workers: Origins of the New Factory System in the United States 1880–1920*. Madison: University of Wisconsin Press.

O'Doherty, B. and Unerman, J. 2005. 'Corporate social responsibility and the case of Amnesty International'. Paper presented at the 17th CSEAR conference, University of St Andrews, September.

Parker, B. 2003. 'The Disorganization of Inclusion: Globalization as Process'. In R. Westwood and S.R. Clegg (eds), *Debating Organizations: Point-Counterpoint in Organization Studies*, 234–51. Oxford: Blackwell.

Parker, M. 2003. *Against Management*. Cambridge: Polity Press.

Parker, M. and Jary, D. 1995. 'The McUniversity: Organisation, management and academic subjectivity', *Organization*, 2 (2), 319–38.

Perrow, C. 1986. *Complex Organizations: A Critical Essay*. New York: McGraw-Hill.

Peters, T. and Waterman, R. 1982. *In Search of Excellence*. New York: Harper & Row.

Power, M. 1994. *The Audit Society*. London: Demos.

Reich, R.B. 1991. *The Work of Nations*. New York: Vintage Books.

Ritzer, G. 1993. *The McDonaldization of Society*. Thousand Oaks, CA: Sage.

Shenhav, Y. 1999. *Manufacturing Rationality: The Engineering Foundations of the Managerial Revolution*. Oxford: Oxford University Press.

Sorge, A. 1991. 'Strategic fit and the societal effect: interpreting cross-national comparisons of technology, organization and human resources', *Organization Studies*, 12, 161–90.

Sturdy, A. 2006. 'Management education'. In C. Carter and S. Clegg (eds), *The Encyclopedia of the Sociology of Management*. Oxford: Blackwell.

Sturdy, A. and Yiannis, G. 2000. 'Missionaries, mercenaries or car salesmen? MBA teaching in Malaysia', *Journal of Management Studies*, 37 (7), 979.

Therborn, G. 2000. 'Globalizations: Dimensions, historical waves, regional effects, normative governance', *International Sociology*, 15 (2), 151–79.

Townley, B. 2002. 'Managing with modernity', *Organization*, 9 (44), 549–73.

Trinca, H. and Fox, C. 2004. *Better than Sex: How a Whole Generation Got Hooked on Work*. Melbourne: Random House.

Watson, T.J. 2004. 'Managers, managerialism and the tower of babble: Making sense of managerial pseudo-jargon', *International Journal for Sociology of Language*, 166, 67–82.

Weber, M. 1978. *Economy and Society: An Outline of Interpretative Sociology*. Berkeley: University of California Press.

Chapter 14

Economic Globalization: Corporations

PETER DICKEN

INTRODUCTION

Amidst the cacophony of opinions on economic globalization, there is a clear consensus that the business corporation – specifically the *transnational* corporation (TNC) – is *the* central actor: the primary shaper of the global economy. Indeed, there is a widely held view, on both the right and the left of the political spectrum, that we increasingly live in a world of global corporations, whose gargantuan footprints trample largely unhindered across national boundaries, emasculating the autonomy of nation-states. In reality, this is a highly misleading stereotype. The purpose of this chapter, therefore, is to provide a more nuanced depiction and explanation of the nature and significance of TNCs in the processes of economic globalization, an approach that is firmly grounded in the empirical reality of a highly differentiated geography whilst, at the same time, providing a theoretical basis for understanding what is, indeed, a highly complex phenomenon. The chapter focuses on five related issues: (1) the scale and geographical distribution of TNCs in the global economy; (2) why and how corporations engage in transnational activities; (3) the geographical embeddedness of transnational corporations; (4) the 'webs of enterprise' manifested in transnational production networks; (5) the power relationships between TNCs and other actors in the global economy.

THE SCALE AND GEOGRAPHICAL DISTRIBUTION OF TRANSNATIONAL CORPORATIONS

The development of companies with interests and activities located outside their home country was part and parcel of the early development of an international economy. Certainly, the chartered trading companies, which emerged in Europe from the fifteenth century onwards – such as the East India Company and the Hudson's Bay Company – played extremely important roles in the evolution of an increasingly interconnected political economy. As essentially colonial and merchant capitalists, they created vast business empires at a world scale. The main *raison d'être* of such firms was trade and exchange and, in that sense, they are clearly the ancestors of today's global trading and service companies.

However, the first firms to engage in *manufacturing production* outside their home country did not emerge until the second half of the nineteenth century. Nevertheless, by the eve of World War I, in 1914, considerable numbers of US, UK and some continental European manufacturing companies were becoming increasingly transnationalized (see Dunning 1993). Since then, and especially during the past 50 years, the number of TNCs in the world economy has grown exponentially.

The most comprehensive definition of a modern TNC, and the one that underpins the discussion in this chapter, is 'a firm which has the power to *coordinate* and *control* operations in more than one country, even if it does not own them'. Unfortunately, it is a definition that is impossible to quantify in aggregate terms because it involves a number of qualitative attributes concerned with the complex relationships between, and within, firms operating across national boundaries, for which no comprehensive data are available. Using a more restrictive definition, based on ownership criteria alone, UNCTAD (2004: 8) estimates that around 61,000 TNCs currently carry out international production in over 900,000 foreign affiliates. These operations represent roughly one-tenth of total world gross domestic product and generate one-third of total world exports. However, most of that activity is generated by a much smaller number of very large TNCs:

> the top 100 (less than 0.2% of the total number of TNCs worldwide) accounted for 14% of the sales of foreign affiliates worldwide, 12% of their assets and 13% of their employment in 2002. (UNCTAD 2004: 9)

These are what have come to be called *global* corporations, the allegedly 'placeless' giants whose operations span the globe and which owe no allegiance to any particular country or community. Firms like General Motors, Royal Dutch Shell, IBM, Toyota, Unilever and others, are often held up as being more powerful than many nation-states, although the commonly used device of comparing the relative sizes (and, by implication, the powers) of TNCs and nation-states is a highly misleading comparison, not least because it is based upon a fallacious statistical argument. Very few of even the 100 leading TNCs can be regarded as 'global' corporations in terms of their geographical extent. The vast majority of the world's leading 100 TNCs still retain more than half of their activities in their home country. In fact, TNCs come in all shapes and sizes, from the so-called global corporations operating in scores of countries to TNCs operating in only one or two countries outside their home base. What they all have in common is that they operate in different political, social and cultural environments.

In aggregate terms, TNC activity is conventionally measured using statistics on foreign direct investment (FDI). 'Direct' investment is an investment by one firm in another with the intention of gaining control over that firm's operations. 'Foreign' direct investment is simply direct investment that occurs across national boundaries, that is, when a firm from one country buys a controlling investment in a firm in another country or where a firm sets up a branch or a subsidiary operation in another country. It differs from 'portfolio' investment, which refers to the situation in which firms purchase equity in other companies purely for financial reasons and not to gain control. During the past two decades, in particular, FDI has grown at an accelerating pace (at least until the global economic slowdown of 2001). FDI growth has consistently outpaced growth of world trade – by a factor of between two and ten times over the 1986–2000 period – a clear indicator of the increasing significance of TNCs as the leading integrating force in the global economy.

The vast majority of the world's TNCs originate from the developed economies: 96 of the top 100 non-financial TNCs in the world in 2002. Although the share of world FDI originating from developing countries has increased, it remains small (around 10 per cent of the world total). At the same time, the bulk of the world's FDI is directed towards developed economies. Less than one-third of the world FDI total is in developing countries. Indeed, the vast majority of FDI consists of cross-investment between developed countries. Of course, there is significant – and growing – FDI in developing countries. But this is far less than popular opinion suggests and is, in any case, highly concentrated in a very small number of countries, primarily in East Asia and to a lesser extent in parts of Latin America. Nevertheless, the number of TNCs originating from the leading developing countries is undoubtedly growing. There is an increasing diversity of TNCs in the global economy.

Why (and How) Firms 'Transnationalize'

Motivations

The reasons why business firms extend their operations outside their home countries, and how they do that, are complex and highly contingent on particular circumstances. But, although there may appear to be a bewildering variety of reasons for TNC activity, we can boil these down to two broad categories (although the boundary between them is frequently blurred): *market-oriented* investment and *asset-oriented* investment.

MARKET-ORIENTED INVESTMENT

Despite recent developments in TNC activity, much of their investment continues to be market-oriented. There are several reasons why this is so. A firm may have reached saturation point in its domestic market (an issue clearly related to the overall size of the national market). Increasing profitability may well depend, therefore, on being able to expand its market beyond its home territory. It may have identified new markets that require a direct presence in order to serve them efficiently: for example, transportation costs may be excessive (although this is less and less the case in the case of many products) to make exports uneconomic. Access to the market may be restricted because of political regulatory structures (such as import tariffs). The idiosyncratic nature of a particular market may necessitate a direct presence in order to understand, and to cater to, such specific circumstances. Both for political, as well as cultural reasons, it may be desirable for a TNC to appear to be strongly embedded in a local market. In other words, both the size and the particular characteristics of markets continue to influence the locational decisions of TNCs.

ASSET-ORIENTED INVESTMENT

The geographical unevenness of markets is one major set of reasons why firms engage in transnational investment. The second set of reasons derives from the fact that the *assets* that firms need to produce and sell their products and services are also geographically very unevenly distributed and, therefore, may need to be exploited *in situ*. Traditionally, of course, it was the geographical localization of many natural resources that drove much of the early development of TNCs. It is no coincidence that many of the early leading TNCs were in the natural resource sectors, including energy and industrial resources as well as in agricultural products. Firms in the natural resource industries must, of necessity, locate at the source of supply, although it is often the case that subsequent processing of the resource takes place elsewhere, generally close to the market.

Natural resource-oriented investment has a very long history. However, developments in transportation and communications technologies, as well as in production process technologies, have increased the ability of firms to access other unevenly distributed assets on increasingly wide geographical scales. This is most notably the situation in the case of *human* resources or assets: the skills and knowledge embodied in people in specific local settings, with their particular assemblages of social and cultural institutions and practices. Such assets are, again, very unevenly distributed geographically. It is really only in the past 50 years or so that these kinds of assets have come to play a significant role in transnational investment.

Initially, it was the attraction of cheap – and usually unorganized – labour that was the primary attraction for firms in certain industries, such as textiles, garments, footwear, toys and consumer electronics. The so-called 'New International Division of Labour' that sprang into prominence in the literature of the 1970s and 1980s was based upon the claims that firms in the Western industrialized countries were fleeing the constraints of high-cost, militant labour to tap cheap and malleable labour in developing countries (see, for example, Fröbel et al., 1980). There is no doubt that some types of transnational investment have been – and remain – very sensitive to geographical variations in labour costs. TNCs do have the potential to shift at least some of their operations in response to changes in labour costs.

But it is not only labour *costs* that are the major driving force. Except in those industries where unskilled – and, therefore, cheap – labour is important, it is other attributes of *human capital* that have become more significant. In particular, it is increasingly the availability of well-educated, highly skilled and strongly motivated workers located in 'quality' communities that are exerting a very strong influence on TNCs. Of course, where these attributes are combined with relatively low costs then the attraction is much reinforced. Such circumstances underpin much of the current transnational investment in East Asia, in the emerging market economies of Eastern and Central Europe, and in some cities in India (for example, the much-quoted example of the IT cluster in Bangalore).

Modes

There are two major ways in which firms develop transnational activities: one is through what is known as 'greenfield' investment; the other is through engagement with other firms, through either merger and acquisition or some form of strategic collaboration.

Greenfield investment is simply the building of totally new facilities (an administrative office, a factory, a research and development facility, a sales and distribution centre and so on). By definition, it adds to the productive stock of both the firm itself and the country/community in which it occurs. For that reason, it is generally the type of investment most favoured by host countries. An especially important example was the series of new assembly and components plants constructed by the Japanese automobile firms – Nissan, Toyota, Honda and others – in North America and Europe (notably in the UK) in the 1980s and 1990s. However, greenfield investment is far from being the most common mode of overseas expansion. Building a totally new facility, especially one of a significant scale, is a risky venture. For that reason, a firm may well prefer to establish a presence in an overseas location through an involvement with an existing firm.

Many firms, especially US and UK firms (though not only these) have preferred to *merge* with, or to *acquire*, another firm to establish, or to expand, their presence in a particular overseas location. In fact, in recent years, most of the growth in world FDI has been driven by merger and acquisition (M&A), rather than by greenfield investment. This was especially the case during the second half of the 1990s, when a number of massive cross-border mergers occurred, including the UK telecommunications company Vodafone's acquisition of the US company AirTouch Communications for $60.3 billion, Daimler-Benz's acquisition of Chrysler, Wal-Mart's acquisition of Asda and Renault's purchase of a controlling share in Nissan (UNCTAD 2000). Indeed, it is significant that the slowdown in FDI growth after 2000 coincided with a massive reduction in M&A activity. M&A involves the transfer of equity between companies; in other words, it involves a shift in ownership and control of both firms' entire assets.

Another widely used mode of TNC expansion is to enter into a *strategic collaboration* with one or more other firms. Although collaborative ventures have been around for a very long time, what is new about their current manifestation is their scale, their proliferation and the fact that they have become central to many firms' transnational strategies. Most strikingly, most strategic alliances are between firms that are, otherwise, fierce competitors. In other words, they reflect a new form of business relationship, a 'new rivalry . . . in the way collaboration and competition interact' (Gomes-Casseres 1996: 2). Many companies are forming not just single alliances but *networks of alliances*, in which relationships between partner firms are increasingly multilateral, rather than bilateral, polygamous rather than monogamous. In effect, they are creating 'new constellations' of economic power and adding a new component – 'collective competition' – to the economic landscape. For example, the automobile industry is now made up of a complex spider's web of alliances between competing firms: GM has collaborative ventures with Toyota, Ford, Fiat, Renault amongst others; Ford with Mazda, VW, BMW, Nissan. International strategic alliances also proliferate in the semiconductor industry, for example, between Motorola/IBM/Siemens/Toshiba to develop new generations of memory chips; between STMicroelectronics/Philips/Motorola in a research and development alliance; between Fujitsu and AMD to develop the production of flash memory devices. Similar complex, international, relationships exist in virtually all significant economic sectors.

Unlike mergers and acquisitions, in which the identities of the merging partners are completely subsumed (in fact, if not always in name), strategic alliances are usually focused on a specific business problem. In an alliance, only some of the participants' business operations are involved; in every other respect the firms remain not only separate but also usually competitors. They are formal agreements between firms to pursue a specific strategic objective, to enable firms to achieve a specific goal that they believe cannot be achieved on their own: for example, to overcome problems of gaining access to particular markets; to share the risks of market entry; to share the costs, uncertainties and risks of research and development and of new product development; to gain access to technologies; to achieve economies of synergy, for example, by pooling resources and capabilities and rationalizing production.

Advocates of strategic alliances claim that by cooperating, firms can combine their capabilities in mutually beneficial ways. Critics point to the potential risk of losing key technologies to competitors. Nevertheless, the proliferation of such alliances has greatly increased the complexity and variety of TNC operations in the world economy.

A sequence of TNC development?

It has been conventional in the international business literature to argue that TNCs develop in a sequential manner, starting with achieving a position of strength in their domestic market and only after that has been achieved do they venture abroad. The sequence usually identified is as follows. First, overseas markets are served by direct exports, normally utilizing local independent sales agents. Second, as local demand grows, it may become desirable for the TNC to exert closer control over its foreign markets by setting up overseas sales outlets of its own. This may be achieved either by setting up an entirely new (greenfield) facility or by acquiring a local firm (possibly the previously used sales agent itself). Acquisition offers the attraction of an already functioning business compared with the more difficult, and possibly more risky, method of starting from scratch in an unfamiliar environment. Eventually, the time may come – though not inevitably – when the need is felt for an actual foreign production facility. Again, this may be achieved through either greenfield investment or acquisition.

There is substantial anecdotal evidence of such a developmental sequence, for example among US TNCs, especially during the early and middle decades of the twentieth century. US consumer products firms, such as the major food manufacturers Heinz and Kellogg, and personal products manufacturers, such as Procter and Gamble, moved cautiously and incrementally in their overseas expansion, initially targeting neighbouring Canada and serving other markets (including Europe) through exports and then local distributors, before establishing their own manufacturing facilities. Japanese firms investing in North America and Europe from the

1970s – including the automobile companies Honda, Nissan and Toyota, and the electronics companies Sony and Matsushita – showed similar tendencies. In the latter case, actual manufacturing operations came rather late, following a long period of development of Japanese service investments by the general trading companies, banks and other financial institutions, and by the sales and distribution functions of the manufacturing firms themselves.

However, there is nothing inevitable about such a sequence. The process may be interrupted or 'short-circuited' for a variety of reasons. More significantly, the emergence of a new generation of TNCs, particularly in the knowledge-intensive industries, has produced a developmental sequence in which firms are not necessarily large and/or with a dominant domestic market position before embarking on the establishment of overseas operations. In other words, there are firms often referred to as 'born globals', entrepreneurial ventures which operate beyond their home territory from the outset. Such firms have to rely on a variety of channels, notably the networks of other TNCs, as well as the Internet (Gabrielson and Kirpalani 2004). In other words, the nature of TNC networks in general is a critical influence on the potential for development of firms seeking to operate beyond their home territories.

GEOGRAPHY MATTERS: THE EMBEDDEDNESS OF TRANSNATIONAL CORPORATIONS

Contrary to much of the received wisdom on the global economy, place and geography still matter fundamentally in the ways in which firms are produced and in how they behave. All business firms, including the most geographically extensive TNCs, are 'produced' through an intricate process of embedding in which the cognitive, cultural, social, political and economic characteristics of the national home base play a dominant part. TNCs, therefore, are 'bearers' of such characteristics, which then interact with the place-specific characteristics of the countries and communities in which they operate to produce a set of distinctive outcomes.

The Russian painter Marc Chagall once observed that every painter is born somewhere, and even if later he responds to other surroundings, a certain essence, a certain aroma of his native land will always remain in his work. It seems to me that Chagall's observation is a better metaphor of the relationship between TNCs and place than many globalizers' visions of the 'placeless' corporation. It more sensitively captures the complexity of the embeddedness process in which both place of origin, and the other places in which TNCs operate, influence the ways in which such firms behave and how they, in turn, impact upon such places. Within this essentially dialectical relationship, however, the TNC's *place of origin* appears to remain the dominant influence.

A number of strands of empirical evidence support this assertion. For example, Doremus et al. (1998) argue, on the basis of their detailed empirical study of US, German and Japanese TNCs, that there appears to be

little blurring or convergence at the cores of firms based in Germany, Japan, or the United States . . . Durable national institutions and distinctive ideological traditions still seem to shape and channel crucial corporate decisions . . . the domestic structures within which a firm initially develops leave a permanent imprint on its strategic behavior. (Pauly and Reich 1997: 1, 4, 5, 24)

Empirical research in East Asia shows how Japanese and US electronics firms have distinctively different ways of organizing their regional production networks, differences that clearly reflect their different home characteristics. Within the Indonesian garment industry, East Asian firms tend to establish direct manufacturing operations whilst American and European firms tend to operate through networks of local agents and traders. Even countries with rather similar characteristics, such as South Korea and Taiwan, have produced distinctively different forms of business organization (Dicken 2003b).

Hence, despite the unquestioned geographical transformations of the world economy, driven at least in part by the expansionary activities of transnational corporations, we are not witnessing the convergence of business-organizational forms towards a single 'placeless' type. This is because, over time, and under specific circumstances, societies have tended to develop distinctive ways of organizing their economies, even within the broad, apparently unitary, ideology of capitalism. Not all capitalisms are the same; capitalism comes in many different varieties. Not only this, but such distinctive forms tend to persist over time, even though they may become modified 'at the margin' through interaction with other social systems of production:

> forms of economic coordination and governance *cannot* easily be transferred from one society to another, for they are embedded in social systems of production distinctive to their particular society . . . Economic performance is shaped by the entire social system of production in which firms are embedded and not simply by specific principles of management styles and work practices . . . institutions are embedded in a culture in which their logic is symbolically grounded, organizationally structured, technically and materially constrained, politically defended, and historically shaped by specific rules and norms.
>
> There are inherent obstacles to convergence among social systems of production of different societies, for where a system is at any one point in time is influenced by its initial state. Systems having quite different initial states are unlikely to converge with one another's institutional practices. Existing institutional arrangements block certain institutional innovations and facilitate others (Hollingsworth 1997: 266–8).

Such persistent differences help to explain why TNCs from different home countries are likely to continue to exist. However, this is not to claim that TNCs from a particular national origin are identical. This is self-evidently not the case. Within any national situation there will be distinctive corporate cultures, arising from the firm's own specific corporate history, which predispose it to behave strategically in particular ways. Neither does this imply that nationally embedded business organizations are unchanging. On the contrary, the very interconnectedness of the contemporary global economy means that influences are rapidly transmitted across boundaries. This will, inevitably, affect the way business organizations are configured and behave. There 'is essentially a process of co-evolution through which different business systems may converge in certain dimensions and diverge in other attributes' (Yeung 2000: 425).

For example, the distinctive Japanese business groups (*keiretsu*) have been at the centre of Japanese economic development during the post-World War II period. But the financial crisis in Japan that has persisted since the bursting of the 'bubble economy' at the end of the 1980s has put them under considerable pressure to change at least some of their practices. In particular, the recent influx of foreign capital to acquire significant, sometimes controlling, shares in some of these companies has had a catalytic effect. There are strong pressures, particularly from Western (notably US) finance capital, for the Japanese business groups to open up to outsiders, to reduce or eliminate the intricate cross-shareholding arrangements, and to become more like Western (i.e. US) firms with their emphasis on 'shareholder value' rather than the broader socially based 'stakeholder' interests intrinsic to Japanese companies. While, without doubt, some changes are occurring it would be a mistake to assume that Japanese firms will suddenly be transformed into US clones. The Japanese have a very long history of adapting to external influences by building structures and practices that remain distinctively Japanese.

Similarly, South Korean and other East Asian firms have come under enormous pressure to change some of their business practices in the aftermath of the region's financial crisis of the late 1990s. In Korea, the *chaebol* are being drastically restructured and the relationships with the state reduced. Among overseas Chinese businesses, the strong basis in family ownership and control is being challenged by both internal and external forces. Greater involvement in the global economy is forcing these firms to modify some of their practices (see Yeung 2000: 411–24). And yet it would be extremely surprising if the distinctive nature of nationally based TNCs were to be replaced by a standardized, homogeneous form. Diversity, not uniformity, therefore, related at least in part to the place-specific contexts in which firms evolve, continues to be the norm.

'WEBS OF ENTERPRISE': TRANSNATIONAL PRODUCTION NETWORKS

Although the focus of this chapter is on 'corporations', it is inadequate to conceive of such organizations as being, in some way, 'free-standing', clearly bounded, independent entities. On the contrary, all business firms are constituted as, and embedded within, highly complex and dynamic *networks* of production, distribution and consumption. Such networks have become increasingly extensive geographically and controlled – or, at least, coordinated – primarily by transnational corporations. TNCs, therefore, like firms in general, can best be considered as 'a dense network at the centre of a web of relationships' (Badaracco 1991: 314).

Precisely how a TNC's *internal* networks are configured, both organizationally and geographically, and how they are connected into the *external* networks of suppliers and customers varies considerably. Such variety arises primarily from such interrelated influences as:

- the firm's *specific history*, including characteristics derived from its *country of origin*;
- its *cultural and administrative heritage* in the form of accepted practices built up over a period of time, producing a particular 'strategic pre-disposition';
- the nature and complexity of the *industry environment(s)* in which the firm operates, including the nature of competition, technology, regulatory structures and so on.

By the very nature of their dispersed geographical spread across different political, cultural and social environments, TNCs are far more difficult to coordinate and control than firms whose activities are confined to a single national space. They require, in other words, a more sophisticated *organizational architecture*. Not surprisingly, certain organizational forms have come to dominate at different times. Table 14.1 shows the basic characteristics of four 'ideal-types' of TNC organization, each of which displays varying degrees of centralized or dispersed control and coordination. It is a typology that captures many of the attributes of different forms of TNCs' organizational architecture. Each of the ideal-types shown in Table 14.1 represents alternative ways of attempting to solve the basic organizational problem facing all TNCs operating in highly diverse and geographically dispersed locations. How best can they achieve an optimal balance between the advantages of centralized control and localized sensitivity, between economies of scale in production and responsiveness to local market conditions? How best can they benefit from the concentration of knowledge at the core of the firm as well as from the variety of local knowledges in the firm's dispersed operations? How, in other words, can they resolve the tension between global integration and local responsiveness which, as Prahalad and Doz (1987) show, is a very tricky problem indeed.

In addition to the question of a TNC's organizational architecture there is the related, though not identical, issue of the *geographical configuration* of its activities. Developments in transportation and communications technologies, as well as in production process technologies, have facilitated the transformation of the geographical extent over which a TNC can separate out its different functions as well as their precise geographical configuration. Because different functions – administration, R&D, production, marketing, sales – have different locational requirements, and because these requirements can be satisfied in different types of location, TNCs tend to develop distinctive spatial patterns for each function. Hence, their internal corporate division of labour is expressed in a distinctive external division of labour, although such patterns show enormous variation between different types of TNC and also between different industries.

However, a few generalizations can be made. Characteristically, the corporate headquarters of TNCs invariably remain in the firm's home country (often in the community in which the firm originated). Some kinds of headquarters functions may well be dispersed to key locations within the firm's transnational network, usually in key cities. These may, for example, be regional headquarters functions or possibly specialized control functions for specific lines of business. Core R&D facilities also still tend to remain in the home country although some kinds of R&D have become increasingly dispersed, particularly to tap into localized sources of scientific and technological expertise, both institutional (as in the case of universities or other

Table 14.1 Some ideal-types of TNC organization: basic characteristics

Characteristics	'Multinational'	'International'	'Global'	'Integrated network'
Structural configuration	Decentralized federation. Many key assets, responsibilities, decisions decentralized	Coordinated federation. many assets, responsibilities, resources, decisions decentralized but controlled by HQ	Centralized hub. Most strategic assets, resources, responsibilities and decisions centralized	Distributed network of specialized resources and capabilities
Administrative control	Informal HQ–subsidiary relationship; simple financial control	Formal management planning and control systems allow tighter HQ–subsidiary linkage	Tight central control of decisions, resources and information	Complex process of coordination and cooperation in an environment of shared decision making
Management attitude towards overseas operations	Overseas operations seen as portfolio of independent businesses	Overseas operations seen as appendages to a central domestic corporation	Overseas operations treated as 'delivery pipelines' to a unified global market	Overseas operations seen as an integral part of complex network of flows of components, products, resources, people, information among interdependent units
Role of overseas operations	Sensing and exploiting local opportunities	Adapting and leveraging parent company competencies	Implementing parent company strategies	Differentiated contributions by national units to integrated worldwide operations
Development and diffusion of knowledge	Knowledge developed and retained within each unit	Knowledge developed at the centre and transferred to overseas units	Knowledge developed and retained at the centre	Knowledge developed jointly and shared worldwide

Source: Dicken (2003a, Table 7.1). Based on material in Bartlett and Ghoshal (1998).

research institutions) and human (pools of key scientific and technical workers), or to adapt new products to local conditions. Conversely, sales and marketing functions tend to be dispersed to locations in key markets, while production functions are sensitive to the technical needs of the specific sector in question.

Compared with corporate headquarters and R&D facilities, there is no doubt that production activities have become more dispersed geographically in the search for key assets and/or proximity to markets. A number of geographical configurations of TNC production activities are apparent (Dicken 2003a: 246–50). One option is to concentrate production at a single location. Such globally concentrated production generates economies of scale in production but increases transportation costs and lessens the firm's knowledge of distant markets. A second option is to produce specifically for a local/national market. Here economies of scale are limited by the size of the market. A third option is to create a structure of specialized production for a regional market (such as the European Union). A fourth possibility is to segment the production process and to locate each part in different locations: a form of transnational vertical integration of production.

Of course, firms never work with a blank surface. They have to deal with a complex mix of facilities that have been built up, or acquired, over a period of time and whose structure, at any one time, may no longer be appropriate for changing circumstances. For that reason, TNCs are constantly engaged in processes of restructuring, reorganization and rationalization. TNC networks are always in a continuous state of flux. At any one time, some parts may be growing rapidly, others may be stagnating, others may be in decline. The functions performed by the component parts and the relationships between them will alter. Such restructuring and rationalization inevitably causes tensions between TNCs and other 'stakeholders', notably governments and labour.

Changes to a firm's geographical configuration often occur as a result of the firm's decision on what to produce for itself, in-house, and what to externalize to independent suppliers. The 'make or buy' decision has become particularly critical as competition has intensified and as firms strive to increase their efficiency to enhance or maintain profitability. TNCs, therefore, are highly dependent on other firms for many of their needs. The specific relationships between TNCs as customers and other firms (including other TNCs) as suppliers – both organizationally and geographically – are currently in a state of flux. Pressures on suppliers to deliver 'just-in-time', pressures on them to reduce prices, pressures on them to take on more responsibility and risk have come to characterize a number of global industries. Perhaps the best example is the automobile industry, but similar trends exist in most other industries.

The geographical extent of such transnational production networks is highly variable. In fact, few such networks can be described as being truly 'global'. A marked recent trend, however, is for such networks to have a strong *regional* dimension, that is, networks organized on a multinational scale of groups of contiguous markets (Rugman and Brain 2003). In some instances, such a tendency is reinforced by regional political structures – as in the cases of the EU or NAFTA – although this is not invariably the case. Simple geographical proximity is, itself, a powerful stimulus for integrating operations:

A regional strategy offers many of the efficiency advantages of globalization while more effectively responding to the organizational barriers it entails . . . From the perspective of a TNC, a regional strategy may represent an ideal solution to the competing pressures for organizational responsiveness and global integration (Morrison and Roth 1992: 45, 46).

Transnational production networks organized at the regional scale are evident in most parts of the world, but most especially in the three 'triad regions' of Europe, North America and East Asia. In North America, the establishment of the NAFTA is leading to a re-configuration of corporate activities (especially in Mexico) to meet the opportunities and constraints of the new regional system. In the garment industry, for example, firms like DuPont, Burlington Industries, VF Corporation have all reorganized the regional geography of some of their activities (Bair and Gereffi 2002). In Europe, the increasing integration of the EU has led to substantial reorganization of existing corporate networks and the establishment of pan-EU systems by existing and new TNCs. 'The EU can be seen as a gigantic international production complex made up of the networks of TNCs which straddle across national boundaries and form trade networks in their own right' (Amin 2000: 675). Ford was probably the first major US company to recognize the potential of regional production when it established a pan-European structure in 1967.

There is abundant evidence of US and Japanese TNCs – as well as many European firms themselves – creating regional networks within the EU (often incorporating the transitional economies of Eastern Europe as well, especially those that have recently become members of the EU). However, the process is a complicated one. On the one hand, supply-side forces are stimulating a pan-EU structure of operations to take advantage of scale efficiencies. On the other hand, demand-side forces are still articulated primarily at the country-specific level, where linguistic and cultural differences play a major role in the demands for goods and services. In effect, the strategic tensions between global integration and local responsiveness are played out at the EU regional level.

Although East Asia does not have the same kind of regional political framework as the EU or NAFTA, there is very strong evidence of the existence of regional production networks organized primarily by Japanese firms, although non-Asian as well as some other Asian firms (from Korea, Hong Kong and Taiwan, for example) also tend to organize their production networks regionally. Within East Asia, a clear intra-regional division of labour has developed consisting of four tiers of countries: Japan; the so-called 'four tigers' of Hong Kong, Korea, Singapore and Taiwan; the South-east Asian 'later industrializers' – Malaysia, Thailand, Indonesia, the Philippines; China, together with, at least potentially, countries such as Vietnam.

Asymmetries of power

Transnational corporations are, without doubt, one – arguably the most important – of the primary shapers of the contemporary global economy. There is no doubt, either, that their significance is increasing; more companies are becoming transnational at an earlier stage of their development. But TNCs are a far more diverse population than is often recognized. Not all are 'global' corporations. Indeed, very few are. TNCs come in a whole variety of shapes and sizes and there remain significant differences between TNCs from different countries of origin. Diversity, rather than uniformity, rules.

Both the organization and the geography of large TNCs, and of their transnational production networks, are immensely complex and dynamic. In a very real sense, the global economy can be pictured as intricately connected localized clusters of activity embedded in various ways into different forms of corporate network that, in turn, vary greatly in their geographical extent. Some TNCs are globally – or at least regionally – extensive, others are more restricted geographically. In all cases, however, firms in specific places – and, therefore, the places themselves – are increasingly connected into transnational networks.

Inevitably this creates tensions between TNCs and other significant actors in the global economy: states, local communities, labour, consumers, civil society organizations.

The basis of TNCs' power lies in their potential ability to take advantage of geographical differences in the availability and cost of resources and in state policies and to switch and re-switch operations between locations. However, this recognition of TNC power has led to some very shaky generalizations because it does not necessarily mean that TNCs *always* have the advantage. All transnational production networks are influenced by, and embedded within, *multi-scalar regulatory systems*. International regulatory bodies, such as the WTO – part of the 'confusion' of institutions that makes up the incoherent architecture of global governance – are immensely significant in influencing the geography of transnational production networks. International institutions establishing technical standards (like the ISO 9000, the international quality management standard, or the ISO 14000 international environmental standard), likewise, play a highly significant role. In some cases they make the operation of transnational networks more feasible through their introduction of codifiable standards. In other cases, they create problems of conformity to an international standard in specific places.

Among the multiplicity of regulatory institutions, and allowing for the proliferation of international and sub-national bodies, the *national state* remains especially important. *All* the elements in transnational production networks are regulated within some kind of political structure whose basic unit is the national state. International institutions exist only because they are sanctioned by national states; sub-national institutions are commonly subservient to the national level, although, of course, the situation is more complex in federal political systems.

As a result, TNCs and states are continuously engaged in intricately choreographed negotiating and bargaining processes. On the one hand, TNCs attempt to take advantage of national differences in regulatory regimes (such as taxation or performance requirements, like local content). On the other hand, states strive to minimize such 'regulatory arbitrage' and to entice mobile investment through competitive bidding against other states. The situation is especially complex because while states are essentially territorially fixed and clearly bounded geographically, a TNC's 'territory' is more fluid and flexible. Transnational production networks slice through national boundaries (although not necessarily as smoothly as some would claim). In the process parts of different national spaces become incorporated into transnational production networks (and vice versa).

There is, in other words, a *territorial asymmetry* between the continuous territories of states and the discontinuous territories of TNCs and this translates into complex bargaining processes in which, contrary to much conventional wisdom, there is no unambiguous and totally predictable outcome. TNCs do not always possess the power to get their own way, as some writers continue to assert. In the complex relationships between TNCs and states – as well as with other institutions – the outcome of a specific bargaining process is highly contingent. States still have significant power vis-à-vis TNCs, for example to control access to their territories and to define rules of operation. In collaboration with other states, that power is increased (the EU is an example of this). So, the claim that states are universally powerless in the face of the supposedly unstoppable juggernaut of the 'global corporation' is nonsense; the question is an empirical one.

Two examples drawn from the automobile industry illustrate this. In the early 1970s, Ford used its bargaining strength to gain highly preferential access to the Spanish market to produce its first small car (the Fiesta). It was able to do so because the Spanish state faced massive competition from other European countries for the investment (even though it emerged later that Ford wanted to go to Spain anyway). In contrast, the recent attempts by US and European auto firms to enter the Chinese market have been heavily circumscribed by the overwhelming desire of the firms to get into the rapidly growing Chinese market and the power of the Chinese state to control access to it.

As Stopford and Strange point out, 'governments as a group have indeed lost bargaining power to the [trans]nationals … [but] … one needs to separate the power to influence general policy from the power to insist on specific bargains' (Stopford and Strange 1991: 215–16). A similar, though rather weaker, argument can be made in the case of labour. Because of its strongly localized nature (especially compared with the spatial flexibility of TNCs), it is difficult for labour to bargain effectively with TNCs. As Harvey (1989, cited in Peck 2000: 141) notes, 'unlike other commodities, labour power has to go home every night'. One way in which labour (and also consumer and other) interests may be addressed is through international civil society organizations (CSOs), which have the potential to overcome the geographical constraints of localized labour and consumers, often through the 'virtual' medium of the Internet. So, while recognizing the undoubted power and influence of TNCs in the global economy, we need to avoid the simplistic view that TNCs always prevail. On the contrary, as a number of recent events demonstrate, TNCs may be constrained in their freedom of action. TNCs may be powerful – but they do not possess absolute power.

References

Amin, A. 2000. 'The European Union is more than a triad market for national economic spaces'. In G.L. Clark, M.P. Feldman and M.S. Gertler (eds), *The Oxford Handbook of Economic Geography*, 671–85. Oxford: Oxford University Press.

Badaracco, J.L. Jr. 1991. 'The boundaries of the firm'. In A. Etzioni and P.R. Lawrence (eds), *Socio-Economics: Towards a New Synthesis*, 293–327. Armonk, NY: M.E. Sharpe.

Bair, J. and Gereffi, G. 2002. 'NAFTA and the apparel commodity chain: Corporate strategies, interfirm networks, and industrial upgrading'. In G. Gereffi, D. Spener and J. Bair (eds), *Free Trade and Uneven Development: The North American Apparel Industry after NAFTA*, 23–50. Philadelphia: Temple University Press.

Bartlett, C.A. and Ghoshal, S. 1998. *Managing across Borders: The Transnational Solution*. New York: Random House.

Dicken, P. 2000. 'Places and flows: Situating international investment'. In G.L. Clark, M.P. Feldman and M.S. Gertler (eds), *The Oxford Handbook of Economic Geography*, 275–91. Oxford: Oxford University Press.

Dicken, P. 2003a. *Global Shift: Reshaping the Global Economic Map in the 21st Century*, 4th edn. London: Sage Publications; New York: Guilford Press.

Dicken, P. 2003b. ' "Placing" firms: Grounding the debate on the "global" corporation'. In J.A. Peck and H.W-C. Yeung (eds), *Remaking the Global Economy: Economic-Geographical Perspectives*, 27–44. London: Sage Publications.

Doremus, P.N., Keller, W.W., Pauly, L.W. and Reich, S. 1998. *The Myth of the Global Corporation*. Princeton, NJ: Princeton University Press.

Dunning, J.H. 1993. *Multinational Enterprises and the Global Economy*. Reading, MA: Addison Wesley.

Fröbel, F., Heinrichs, J. and Kreye, O. 1980. *The New International Division of Labour*. Cambridge: Cambridge University Press.

Gabrielson, M. and Kirpalani, V.H.M. 2004. 'Born globals: How to reach new business space rapidly', *International Business Review*, 13, 555–71.

Gomes-Casseres, B. 1996. *The Alliance Revolution: The New Shape of Business Rivalry*. Cambridge, MA: Harvard University Press.

Hollingsworth, J.R. 1997. 'Continuities and changes in social systems of production: The cases of Japan, Germany and the United States'. In J.R. Hollingsworth and R. Boyer (eds), *Contemporary Capitalism: The Embeddedness of Institutions*, 265–310. Cambridge: Cambridge University Press.

Morrison, A.J. and Roth, K. 1992. 'The regional solution: An alternative to globalization', *Transnational Corporations*, 1, 37–55.

Pauly, L.W. and Reich, S. 1997. 'National structures and multinational corporate behaviour: Enduring differences in the age of globalization', *International Organization*, 51, 1–30.

Peck, J.A. 2000. 'Places of work'. In E. Sheppard and T.J. Barnes (eds), *A Companion to Economic Geography*, 133–223. Oxford: Blackwell.

Prahalad, C.K. and Doz, Y. 1987. *The Multinational Mission*. New York: The Free Press.

Rugman, A.M. and Brain, C. 2003. 'Multinational enterprises are regional, not global', *Multinational Business Review*, 11, 3–12.

Stopford, J.M. and Strange, S. 1991. *Rival States, Rival Firms: Competition for World Market Shares*. Cambridge: Cambridge University Press.

UNCTAD 2000. *World Investment Report 2000: Cross-Border Mergers and Acquisitions and Development*. New York: United Nations.

UNCTAD 2004. *World Investment Report 2004: The Shift towards Services*. New York: United Nations.

Yeung, H.W-C. 2000. 'The dynamics of Asian business systems in a globalizing era', *Review of International Political Economy*, 7, 399–433.

Further reading

Dicken, P. 2007. *Global Shift: Mapping the Changing Contours of the World Economy*, 5th edn. London: Sage Publications; New York: Guilford Press.

Dunning, J.H. 1993. *Multinational Enterprises and the Global Economy*. Reading, MA: Addison Wesley.

UNCTAD (annual): *World Investment Report*. New York: United Nations.

Chapter 15

Outsourcing: Globalization and Beyond

GEORGE RITZER AND CRAIG LAIR

Outsourcing is clearly an important economic phenomenon and certainly a key aspect of globalization. When addressed in the globalization literature, most analysts connect outsourcing to various trends that have made the economy increasingly global. Thus, the issue of outsourcing is often connected to global commodity chains (Gereffi and Korzeniewicz 1994); global networks (Castells 1996); lean or flexible production practices (Harvey 1990; Inda and Rosaldo 2002: 6–7; Harrison 1994); the internationalization of production and the division of labour (Jameson 1991; Beck 2000; Robinson 2003) which some thinkers see as undermining local labour's power vis-à-vis global corporations (Smith 2005; Petras and Veltmeyer 2001; Rodrik 1997; Isaak 2005; Applebaum and Robinson 2005); and/or an increase in the level of international stratification (Held and McGrew 2002). While undoubtedly important, these analyses tend to confine themselves to macroeconomic issues, particularly the flow of jobs from some nations to others. Outsourcing, however, is increasingly being seen as something that has connections beyond the 'loss' of jobs and a focus on the economy more generally. For example, the *Wall Street Journal* on 14 November 2005 had a piece on how retirees are 'outsourcing' their 'golden years'[1] by spending them in foreign countries (e.g. in South and Latin America) where the cost of living is lower than that of the United States (Millman 2005), and two days later it had an article on plans by the Internal Revenue Service (IRS) to outsource tax-debt collection (Herman 2005). In a very different vein, Hochschild has explored how emotional labour (i.e. emotional tasks that have traditionally been, or have been conceived of as being, confined largely to the private sphere of home-life) has been 'outsourced' to commercial enterprises (e.g. the care of children being outsourced to daycare centres), as well as to individuals (frequently immigrants, sometimes in this country illegally) (Hochschild 2005). Indeed, the globalization literature has been surprisingly silent on *all* of the outsourcing that is occurring outside of the macro flows of jobs and industries between nation-states.

In light of this lacuna, the objective of this chapter is two-fold. First, we will highlight the importance of outsourcing as a key aspect of globalization. Secondly,

however, we will argue for the importance of a *sociological* understanding of outsourcing; that is, an understanding of outsourcing that, while it pays attention to
the economic aspects of outsourcing, is not limited to it. This will be done by focusing on two prominent areas where outsourcing is occurring in the social world that
are not matters exclusively of economics: healthcare and the military. In addition,
a sociological approach to outsourcing must not be satisfied with a traditional focus
on macro-level phenomena (be they in the economy, healthcare, the military or
elsewhere), but must also be extended to more meso- and micro-level phenomena.
Indeed, that is exactly what Hochschild's work suggests. These more micro-level
phenomena may or may not involve globalization, but in either case they must be
part of a more truly sociological approach to outsourcing (and globalization). That
globalization can be involved is indicated by, for example, the fact that the kind of
outsourcing (mainly in the United States) of concern to Hochschild, for example
the care of our children or aged parents, is likely in many cases to involve immigrants, legal or illegal, from less developed nations.

Also, since much of the economic/business accounts of outsourcing have been
either implicitly or explicitly influenced by Joseph Schumpeter's conception of creative destruction (Schumpeter 1947), the strengths and, in particular, the weaknesses
of this approach as it can be applied to outsourcing will be addressed as the
chapter proceeds as well as in the conclusion. To Schumpeter, a key dynamic in
the progressive development of capitalism, indeed the 'essential fact about capitalism' (1947: 83), is the destruction of outmoded businesses and the creation of newer,
more sophisticated and more profitable ones. In this way, capitalism continually
revolutionizes itself from within; that is, change is endogenous to it. This is a clearly
positive view of the evolution of capitalism as outmoded firms are pushed out of
the way to make room for the most recent developments. In fact, a uniformly positive view of creative destruction is found in almost all of the work on it from
Hinduism to Nietzsche to Sombart to Schumpeter and more recently to Cowen
(2002).

CONCEPTUAL CLARIFICATION

In order to address these issues we need to begin with the point that outsourcing is
only one example of a more general phenomenon that can be called *sourcing* and
that only some types of sourcing relate directly to globalization.[2] In this paper sourcing will be used as a general term to encompass a number of different strategies
dealing with the placement of certain goods or activities. In other words, it refers
to a number of strategies that are location, or source, sensitive. Of course, this sensitivity to the source of activities has, in large part, been spurred on by the increased
international nature of the economy and the increasingly global nature of commodity chains, though, as will be argued below, sourcing, and more specifically outsourcing, have a relevance beyond that of economics and commodity chains alone. Also,
it should be noted that while some sourcing strategies are not necessarily global in
nature (e.g. 'on-shoring'), the sensitivity to their location is in large part due to
a response to the increasingly global nature of many sourcing strategies. Thus,
our definition of sourcing encompasses other such source-sensitive strategies as

in-sourcing, home-sourcing, open-sourcing, offshoring, near-shoring and on-shoring (i.e. domestic outsourcing) (Friedman 2005: 38). One of the goals here will be to sort out the various types of sourcing and identify those that relate most directly to globalization. However, it will be noted that many of these conceptions are limited by being overly focused on economics, by being ethnocentric (i.e. having an unstated geographical preference contained within them) and/or by being focused on only one level of analysis (especially the macro level and therefore not being multidimensional). All of these limitations again point towards the need for a sociological conception of sourcing in general and outsourcing in particular.

CONCEPTUALIZING SOURCING, OUTSOURCING AND GLOBALIZATION

The discussions of, and concerns over, sourcing that are most closely and importantly associated with globalization, at least in the United States,[3] deal with *offshoring* and *offshore outsourcing*. The former refers to instances where 'a multinational company moves or expands some [or all] of its operations and jobs to overseas locations' (Hira and Hira 2005: 201). In other words, it is the movement of jobs and/or operations to 'foreign' locations; however, all of this movement takes place internally within a single company's structure. Thus, offshoring occurs when companies such as Ford expand their operations outside of the United States. Offshoring, however, is not the same as outsourcing and, in fact, offshoring does *not* involve outsourcing. The latter, as it is defined in the business literature, generally refers to instances where a company decides to buy goods or services, once performed in-house, from a supplier outside of the firm. In other words, it involves the transfer of the production of goods and/or the performance of services from one company to another, outside business. Thus, if an automobile company produces parts as part of its production process, but then decides to purchase them from an external supplier, this would be a case of outsourcing. It should be noted, however, that goods and/or services can be outsourced either domestically, to other nations on (or near) the same land mass (i.e. on-shore), or internationally across seas to still other nations (i.e. offshore). Thus, it is offshore outsourcing (or the outsourcing of goods and services offshore) that most Americans have in mind when they fear that jobs are being lost to foreign locations. However, what of work in Western Europe that is outsourced to Eastern Europe? Since no oceans are involved, the term offshoring would be inappropriate in this context.

There are many US-based examples of outsourcing. Illustrations include having those who live and work across the seas and are employed by other, indigenous companies manufacture components or the final products, do US tax returns, read X-rays taken in the United States, answer e-mail inquiries from Americans and even respond to phone questions from Americans, often in perfect English.[4] Offshoring can involve US firms opening factories and offices in other countries (e.g. Microsoft's campus in Hyderabad: Rai 2004c), but of greater interest is offshore outsourcing involving, for example, contracting for work to be done by independent offshore firms. Thus, for example, Wipro in Bangalore, India, has highly trained workers who write code, create software and maintain computer systems for a number of

US companies, such as Lehman Brothers, General Motors, Home Depot and Boeing. But the outsourcing of work to Wipro goes well beyond this since it also handles phone calls involving a major airline's baggage-claim services and frequent-flier programme, designs a top auto manufacturer's navigation system and even reads X-rays (Rai 2004a). It is really these kinds of offshore outsourcing that are of greatest concern, at least in the United States, in the era of globalization and when observers discuss and often lament the impact of outsourcing. It is in this realm, for example, that there is great fear over the loss of jobs and income to those in other countries. More generally, there is the fear that this augers badly for the future of the economic health of the United States. Thus, expressing this view in Schumpeter's terms, the United States is experiencing the destruction of jobs and industries with woefully little creation of new ones to compensate for the losses.

There is a long history of outsourcing blue-collar manufacturing jobs, but the amount and kind of such work that is being outsourced has grown dramatically in the recent past. For example, while European firms have long outsourced, and in some cases offshored, the mass production of mundane fashions like jeans and T-shirts to places in Western Europe and North Africa, we are now seeing high fashion designers from Italy (e.g. Valentino, Louis Vuitton, Gucci) outsourcing, including offshore outsourcing, the production of many of their smaller-batch and higher-priced products (Galloni et al. 2005) While a few very sophisticated goods made in even smaller volume (such as hand-woven leather bags) are likely to continue to be made in Italy by skilled craftspeople, most, if not all, of the rest is likely to be outsourced. What this will mean for the much-prized label 'Made in Italy' and the ability of products on which it is affixed to demand a price premium is open to question.

In more recent years we are also witnessing an increasing number of white-collar jobs being outsourced offshore. Spearheading the latter has been the offshoring of service work such as information technology (IT) jobs,[5] accounting, telemarketing and debt collection (*The Economist* 2004a). India's exports of software and back-office services rose 34.5 per cent, to $17.2 billion, in the year ended in March 2005, with another 30-plus per cent rise forecast for the next fiscal year. The industry's total revenue was $22 billion, with most of the business coming, not surprisingly, from the United States and the United Kingdom (Ray 2005b). In contrast to the United States, India is experiencing much 'creation' and very little 'destruction' in Schumpeter's terms. Bardhan and Kroll (2003) list the following as attributes of jobs most amenable to outsourcing in general (and offshore outsourcing, more specifically): no face-to-face contact with customers, high information content, the work is telecommutable and enabled by the Internet, high wage differences between nations outsourcing and receiving outsourced work, and low set-up barriers and social networking requirements (Bardhan and Kroll 2003: 4). However, abilities to transfer information and people rapidly through advances in information technology and transportation have opened the door to offshore outsourcing service jobs that do not fit Bardhan and Kroll's criteria. For example, some businesses use video technology to have their visitors greeted by a TV screen that transmits the image of a 'virtual receptionist' who is actually located in India (Realcomm Advisory 2004), while Northwest Airlines is seeking to increase its use of non-American workers on foreign flights since these workers, even while sharing the same space and performing the same duties as their American counterparts, are paid a fraction of the salary of US-based flight attendants (Carey 2005).

In addition, offshore outsourcing is now spreading into other surprising areas. While it was at one time dominated by IT tasks, offshore outsourcing is moving more in the direction of BPO (business-process [offshore] outsourcing), involving services such as finance and accounting, human resources, and design and engineering. While still dominated by IT, offshore outsourcing increasingly involves BPO (*The Economist* 2005). More specific examples include the creation of innovations in software processing that earn (US) patents (Rai 2003), the handling of e-loans (Rai 2004b), creating software architecture of early blueprints for programs (Lohr 2004), preparing tax returns (Browning 2004) and doing law (Bellman and Koppel 2005). The offshore outsourcing of legal work from the United States and the United Kingdom to India has been going on for some time, but in the past it was limited to basic operations such as word-processing and filing. It has now been extended to much more complex tasks such as patent applications, divorce papers and legal research (US companies that engage in this are often unwilling to admit to doing it). Indian lawyers are an attractive resource for US and UK firms because of their numbers (India produces over 200,000 law school graduates a year; five times the number produced in the United States), the Indian legal system, like the other two, is rooted in UK common law, Indian lawyers work for far less (perhaps 10 per cent of what lawyers in large US firms charge) and demand far less in terms of perks (e.g. they do not demand large offices and often work in a cubicle of their own or shoulder to shoulder in larger rooms). They are also attractive because they allow US and UK firms to hire fewer people (job destruction) and to concentrate on bigger issues and cases (creativity, at least in a sense). While the work being outsourced offshore is more sophisticated than in the past, it remains fairly routine. Thus, Indian lawyers might be hired to engage in such repetitive tasks as examining huge amounts of evidence or large quantities of documentation and to highlight what they consider important. This work is then scanned and e-mailed back to US or UK law firms. Time will tell whether even more sophisticated legal tasks will be outsourced in this way.

In another example of offshore outsourcing, not long ago Reuters announced a plan to hire six Indian journalists in Bangalore to do basic financial reporting on a large number of small and middle-sized US companies. Said Reuter's global managing editor: 'It's a place where you can get people who understand English, understand financial statements, understand journalism and who are educated to a very high standard and eager to do this kind of work' (Steinberg 2004). Indeed, increasingly the issue will not be so much what kind of work can be outsourced offshore, but is there any work that cannot be outsourced in this way?

India has been the leading recipient of offshore outsourced work, but other continents and nations are growing increasingly interested and involved. In other words, offshore outsourcing is progressively being globalized. According to one estimate, there are approximately 6 million call centre jobs in the world and slightly more than 50,000 of them are in the most developed countries in Africa (mostly in the north and in South Africa; the latter has over half of all call centre jobs on the continent). One Kenyan firm, KenCall, has up to 200 agents doing such things as calling Britons and asking them if they are interested in lower cost cell phone service,

phoning Americans and inquiring about their interest in refinancing home mort-
gages, and some Americans are unwittingly calling Kenya when they respond to
offers of job assistance (Lacey 2005). While call centre work is one of the least
lucrative forms of offshore outsourcing, it is seen as offering an entry to African
countries into more profitable forms of such work (e.g. that related to IT). The
attractions of various African countries include comparatively low pay and other
costs, availability of a highly educated workforce and the language (e.g. English in
Kenya and South Africa and French in Morocco and Tunisia).[6] Russia and other
Eastern European counties are also seeking to be a more important recipient of
offshore outsourced work (Arvedlund 2004).

However, it should be noted that offshore outsourcing is not simply a one-way
process as can be seen in the case of the outsourcing that has been occurring in
India. For example, some US (and other nation's) firms with subsidiaries in India
are selling them to Indian firms thereby increasing the amount of offshoring handled
by Indian companies. Also, big Indian firms (e.g. Wipro) are matching the actions
of US counterparts by expanding overseas, and therefore offshoring, through the
acquisition of companies in, for example, the United States and Australia.[7]
Thus, the nature of offshore outsourcing is changing dramatically (i.e. it is not a
simple flow from developed nations like the United States to developing nations
such as India) as it is simultaneously expanding at a rapid rate (Economist.com
2004).

Indeed, in some cases there has been a partial retrenchment in offshore outsourcing as more complex tasks that at one time were handled in this way are brought
back into the home company and country. This has occurred, for example, in call
centre operations dealing with computer-related questions. While the routine calls
of individual computer users can be handled offshore, the more complex needs of
corporate clients require the use of call centre operators in the home country,
perhaps even in the home company. Said an executive with a consulting firm: 'What
companies are finding is that offshore can be good for generic, commodity
services. . . . Corporate customers have problems very local to their applications and
very specific to their companies' (Flynn 2003). In a similar example, it was found
that it was difficult to offshore outsource phone queries from American teenagers
about their skateboards. It proved far better to use Americans to respond to such
calls involving such specialized and localized interests, jargon and so on.

Nevertheless, many see great merit in and advantages of offshore outsourcing.
Obviously, many business leaders are in favour of, and are taking the lead in, it
because they think it leads to both lower production costs (and therefore lower
prices and less likelihood of inflationary pressures) and greater profitability. Greater
profitability is seen as in the interest not only of those companies, but also of the
economy and ultimately the society as a whole.[8] It is even seen in the interest of
workers since greater profitability leads to new investments and new jobs, many in
the United States. Also, since goods that are outsourced offshore can now theoretically be produced much more inexpensively than before, the lower costs of those
goods will be beneficial to consumers (although, of course, that may be more than
offset by the fact that it might have been *their* jobs that were offshored).

Other possible advantages of offshore outsourcing include (Brady 2003):

- use of better educated personnel (those in the United States with a similar level of education would be loathe to accept most outsourced jobs, especially with the pay being offered);
- lower turnover rates than in comparable areas and jobs in the United States;
- 24/7 availability of workers, production and the provision of services;
- improved customer service leading to higher customer satisfaction;
- companies can focus on their core competencies while drawing on the resources of other companies that can concentrate on theirs;
- greater US access to foreign markets;
- greater demand for, and ability to afford, US products and services;
- lower taxes on profits earned by offshore subsidiaries handling outsourced work.

Beyond all of that, an increasing number of companies are undoubtedly coming to believe that they have no choice and that if they don't outsource work offshore, they will lose out to competitors who do. This is traceable to the basic operations of the capitalist system and the fact that those who don't cut costs and innovate tend to lose out to those who do. That is, those capitalist enterprises that do not engage in creative destruction will decline or even die.

One could also take a broader view towards offshore outsourcing and the gains from it. It could be argued that the United States (and the West) has for a century and more reaped an inordinate share of the wealth derived from the world capitalist system. With offshore outsourcing, as well as other changes in the capitalist system, long-impoverished nations like China and India are now moving in the direction of obtaining and enjoying a larger portion of that wealth. While this will undoubtedly mean some diminution in American wealth and its standard of living (and that of other developed nations), such a change is long overdue. Greater global equality in wealth and standard of living is not only in the interest of nations like China and India, but it could be argued that it is in everyone's interest. For one thing, greater global economic equality will likely lead to a more stable and secure world. For another, growing wealth in the Third World will greatly expand consumers and consumption and at least some of that increase will advantage American business, economy and society. It may even lead to new kinds of jobs in the United States. Thus, consistent with Schumpeter's general view, from this perspective creative destruction is good for all of those involved in capitalism.

Relatedly, it could be argued that offshore outsourcing is good for the United States in another way because it will force it to do something it has, at least histori-cally, done best – to innovate ('create') in order to find new sources of wealth and work (Florida 2004). The work that is being destroyed is of the more routine sort that is the result of past innovations. Having lost those jobs, and likely to lose more of them in the future, the United States will be forced to be creative (innovative) in order to find new sources of wealth and work. (However, as we have seen, there are limits to offshore outsourcing, especially in terms of services [e.g. fast food workers and security guards] that require a workers' physical presence.)

However, offshore outsourcing (and other forms of outsourcing) also creates problems for US capitalist firms and others engaged in it. While some US workers gain by being able to obtain new jobs created by offshore outsourcing, others have their jobs destroyed as a result of it. If they are able to find new jobs, they are likely to be lower-paying jobs. There are, of course, other costs involved in offshore outsourcing such as:

- a loss of control over activities that are basic to a company's success;
- a loss of control over intellectual property;
- a greater possibility of compromising the personal information of customers (e.g. tax or credit card information);
- a lack of knowledge (perhaps by design) of the pay, working conditions, work hours, use of child labour (even slavery) in the companies and nations that take on offshoring;
- public relations disasters resulting from revelations of the nature of pay and working conditions in such companies and nations;
- infrastructural problems that adversely affect the ability of offshore firms in developing countries to accomplish the required work including poor roads, inadequate bus service for employees, not enough overseas flights and a lack of hotel rooms for visitors from the company and country from which the work emanates, lack of adequate power, traffic tie-ups and high telecommunication fees (Rai 2005).

For these and other reasons offshore outsourcing has become a hot issue in the United States and other nations (e.g. the United Kingdom), with various efforts having emerged or been discussed to enact limitations on it. Many politicians have run on anti-offshore outsourcing platforms of one sort or another.

In spite of the problems, it would appear, at least from an economic point of view, that offshore outsourcing is a gain for the United States in general and affluent companies and consumers (although it is a mixed blessing for workers both in the United States and abroad). It may well be that it is US firms that own, in full or in part, firms in other countries doing the offshored work. It is also the case that the areas (e.g. Bangalore) and nations (e.g. India) that are growing more affluent because of this work grow increasingly interested in, and able to afford, US exports (everything from Microsoft programs to McDonald's Big Macs).

Whatever the balance, it is the costs, the destruction, rather than the gains from offshore outsourcing that have caught the public's, and therefore politicians', attention. There has been a considerable backlash against this with a number of state's passing bills to limit offshore outsourcing. Among the issues addressed by these bills are limiting offshore outsourcing jobs by firms receiving state assistance, restricting the offshore outsourcing of personal information and requiring that call centre operators in other countries disclose where they are in the world and reroute calls to US operators upon request (Hrivnak and Smith 2005). However, there are great risks and costs associated with such legislation such as higher costs to the states implementing them, a backlash among foreign providers of products and services to the United States and a decline in foreign investment in the USA.

But offshore outsourcing is not solely a US phenomenon as some of the more ethnocentric conceptions of it seem to imply (i.e. that only US jobs are offshore outsourced or that the 'out' of *out*sourcing refers to that of the United States); rather, it is a global phenomenon. Thus, the United States is not only far from the only nation to engage in offshore outsourcing, but it may even be the recipient of work offshored by companies in other nations. For example, on 1 September 2005, ABN Amro, a huge Dutch bank, announced that it was offshore outsourcing about 2,000 jobs at a cost of over $2 billion, but leading to an estimated savings of $315 million a year beginning in 2007 (Taylor 2005). Not surprisingly, a significant amount of that work went to Indian companies, Tata Consultancy Services, Ltd ($240 million) and Infosys Technologies Ltd ($140 million) (Bellman 2005). Said the Chief Executive Officer and President of Infosys, 'This is a landmark deal in terms of size as well as long-term commitment. . . . Our European business is really going gangbusters' (ibid.). However, the lion's share of the offshore outsourcing business ($1.5 billion; about 1,800 of ABN's jobs) went to IBM, a US-based corporation. Offshored to this array of companies were the maintenance of computers, software programs and the development of new software. What did ABN retain? Little more than testing new software on legacy systems and dealing with highly sensitive security matters. Why did they do it? It is estimated that savings could approach 40 per cent through offshore outsourcing to India *and* to the United States.

The global implications of offshore outsourcing (and offshoring more generally) are clear: by definition they imply that work activities are being transferred internationally. The same is true for another term closely related to the idea of offshore outsourcing (and also having global implications): *near-shore offshoring*. Near-shore offshoring, in the case of the United States, would involve outsourcing work to its closest neighbours – Canada (Austen 2004) and Mexico – which also happen not to exist across any seas. In reality, there is nothing conceptually distinct in the idea of near-shore offshoring vis-à-vis offshore outsourcing more generally (the former is an example of the latter) other than that it carries with it a specific geographical reference (i.e. that the offshore outsourcing that will take place will be in countries near to, or contiguous with, the United States). There are advantages to near-shore offshoring, especially in terms of work and jobs sent to Canada, in that there is the elimination of such potential problems as language, cultural and time zone differences. Another advantage is that shipping costs, in the case of production of material products, are lower. Near-shore offshoring carries the same dangers (e.g. job destruction in the United States) as offshore outsourcing more generally. However, in the case of Canada and Mexico, one hears fewer outcries about jobs being lost to Canada than to Mexico. This may be due to the fact that Canada is much smaller than Mexico, its living costs are far closer to the United States than is the case in Mexico, its cost advantages are consequently less and therefore it seems less likely to take away many jobs than Mexico, and so on. It may also be, however, that there is a measure of racism here as the Canadians are seen as much more like most US citizens (although the growth of the Hispanic population in the United States, especially in certain areas of the country, makes it increasingly like Mexico) than Mexicans. In fact, many of the fears associated with both near-shoring and offshoring may have a racial element to them (jobs lost to Indians or Chinese).

While offshore and near-shore outsourcing necessarily involve globalization, other forms of outsourcing are not as directly connected to globalization as these, at least on the surface. For example, it is also possible to outsource work *within* the same country as the company that is doing the outsourcing passes work on to companies within the same nation. The latter can be called *on-shore outsourcing* (or *domestic outsourcing*). There is little that is new here – companies have been 'sub-contracting'[9] within their own country for about as long as there have been companies. However, it is undoubtedly the case that there is now much more of this as a result of many of the same kinds of technological advances that have made so much offshore outsourcing possible. There is also probably little worry over on-shore outsourcing, at least at the national level (at least in the United States), since it constitutes economic shifts within a nation, rather than the shifting of work, and the attendant economic gains, to other countries. Nonetheless, creative destruction is involved since some areas and companies grow while others wither and die. Sub-contracting now requires a new label – on-shore outsourcing – and perhaps greater attention largely because of the enormous expansion of offshore outsourcing and the need to look at on-shore outsourcing in that context.

Take, for example, design work, where an increasing amount of complex, innovative, even creative work is being outsourced, including on-shore.[10] Thus, for example, instead of designing the next generation of a successful technology, one US company might on-shore that design work to another. Other companies might keep the design of the basic structure of what it produces in-house, but sub-contract the design of many of the peripheral components. Instead of operating from designs created by the home company, the companies that are handling the outsourcing of production are often handling the design themselves as well (Deutsch 2004).

However, even on-shore outsourcing is not without its problems. For example, American airlines are on-shore outsourcing all types of work and in the process moving in the direction of becoming 'virtual airlines'. Thus, the ticket agent (and the baggage handlers) that one encounters may not work for the airline but for a firm to which such work has been outsourced (and involves the destruction of jobs in the airline). Such employees are likely to have little commitment to the airline, to providing high-quality service even to highly valued frequent fliers, and may even refer passengers to a competing airline if they are dissatisfied with their options (Elliott 2005).

Home-sourcing, or performing tasks at home formerly performed in a work setting, can involve either on-shore or offshore outsourcing (and thereby globalization). That is, the home-based work can be performed in either the mother-country, or in another country to which the work is offshored. Technological advances, especially those that are computer-related, have made both types of home-sourcing more possible. Work at home, especially in less-developed countries, involves great savings in costs and therefore makes offshore (and on-shore) outsourcing more likely. People in India can answer phone calls (in excellent English) in their homes or they can prepare American tax returns on their home computers. While there is great concern over the economic costs to the United States about home-sourcing work to other countries, few of these concerns apply to home-sourcing in the United States. Also involving globalization in this realm is the fact that some jobs that had been offshore outsourced, especially relating to call centre work, are now, as pointed out above, returning to the United States; however, they are being handled in their homes by 'virtual agents' who are part of 'virtual call centers' (Mincer 2005).

All of the above – offshore and on-shore outsourcing, home-sourcing – can be seen as forms of sourcing in general and outsourcing in particular. As such, they can take two basic forms (Nikolova, forthcoming). The first is a long-term relationship between outsourcer and outsourcee that involves, among other things, an intensive relationship, one characterized by a high level of trust, refined forms of communication and a sharing of risks and rewards.[11] In such long-term relationships those involved can be seen as forming a network. The other type is a looser, more arm's-length relationship between outsourcer and outsourcee. Here, there is a less intense relationship, some diminution in the need for trust since relationships are likely to be more tenuous, less sophisticated forms of communication are needed and there is little sharing of risks and rewards. While both types of outsourcing have increased, it is probably the case that the latter has grown more than the former as the economy has globalized.

It is worth noting that outsourcing tasks to sites on the Internet can encompass one or even all of the types of outsourcing discussed above (Treaster 2001). This is because the locale to which work on the Internet is outsourced can be anywhere in the world. Thus, outsourcing to the Internet can involve offshore outsourcing, onshore outsourcing, home-sourcing and so on.[12]

However, the most important concept (outsourcing aside) in this arsenal of ideas, one that can be seen as a complement to the concept of outsourcing, is the idea of *in-sourcing* (Slaughter 2004). That is, at the same time that much has been outsourced, much else has been in-sourced. This term is employed by Friedman, but in a way very different from the way it is used here. In his conceptualization, in-sourcing involves one firm literally taking in another, or at least some of its functions. His example is UPS which, on the surface, seems to handle only the shipping of Toshiba computers in need of repairs, but in fact does those repairs itself. In a sense, Toshiba has taken in, 'in-sourced', UPS, at least as far as repair work is concerned. More generally, UPS engages in in-sourcing by literally entering other businesses, analysing the basic components of their work and then (re-)designing and managing those businesses' entire global supply chain. While useful, we think Friedman has a far too limited a sense of in-sourcing.

For example, while most of the concern in the United States is over offshore outsourcing, the fact is that the US is engaged in in-sourcing, as well. We already discussed the case of IBM gaining jobs as result of outsourcing by a Dutch bank. More importantly, foreign direct investment (FDI) in the United States is growing and producing in-sourced jobs. For example, there are the many companies in various industries, most notably the Asian automobile manufacturers (Toyota, Honda etc.) that have opened factories in the United States (Wriston 2004). Then there are European manufacturers who, because of the higher cost of manufacturing there, are outsourcing work to the United States. In fact, over 6 million Americans work for foreign companies that have outsourced work to the United States; work that has been in-sourced into the US (Nicklaus 2004). Thus, in-sourcing indicates that the global shifts currently affecting the United States are not simply destructive, but also lead to the creation of many new jobs.

While most of the attention in the United States is devoted to US companies that are outsourcing work, there are other companies and industries that are moving in the opposite direction. In fact, there are some who argue that outsourcing may have been a fad that many companies are now reversing by in-sourcing that which at one time they outsourced (e.g. data management, IT infrastructure, billing) (*Computing*

2005). Businesses that have outsourced work previously are deciding for one reason or another to bring it back into the company – to in-source it (*The Economist* 1996). An example is the credit card industry where most large companies are moving in the direction of in-sourcing various tasks that were at one time outsourced, often offshored, such as the processing of credit-card applications, issuing credit cards, authorizing transactions, detecting fraud and rendering statements (Marlin 2004).

Of course, all of those jobs that have been offshored by the United States are being in-sourced (or better, in-shored) by other nations (which, as a result, are enjoying far more creation than destruction). In fact, it is impossible to discuss outsourcing without consideration of its flipside, in-sourcing. One nation's or corporation's outsourcing is another's in-sourcing: 'Novartis, headquartered in Basel, Switzerland, is a global pharmaceutical leader. Recently, the company relocated its global research headquarters from Switzerland to Cambridge, Massachusetts. Depending on whether you are reading a newspaper in Basel or Boston, the move can illustrate either outsourcing or insourcing' (Slaughter 2004: 6).

While there are those who see nothing new about in-sourcing – it is seen as little more than a continuation of foreign investment in the United States – Slaughter argues that these investments are not only best seen in the context of this concept, but they are of great importance to the US economy. Among the major contributions are the creation of new jobs, but beyond job growth (and paying relatively high wages), in-sourcing companies contribute to the US economy by performing crucial tasks that increase the overall productivity of the economy, by investing large sums in the United States.

Of course, there is often a big difference between that which is being outsourced (especially offshore) and in-sourced. In the main, at least in the past, that which has been outsourced is that which a given entity is interested in divesting, perhaps even eager to divest, itself of. Thus, individuals, corporations and perhaps even nations are quite willing to outsource dangerous, dirty, low paying or otherwise undesirable tasks. Of course, this means that there are others at all of these levels who, because they are less well-off economically, are quite willing to in-source these tasks. However, what is of perhaps greatest interest here is the fact that outsourcers may increasingly find themselves in the position that they are being forced to outsource tasks that they might prefer to keep. For example, market demands may force corporations to outsource work (and lay off employees) that they might prefer to keep. If they insisted on keeping those tasks, their costs would undoubtedly be higher than those of competitors who outsourced them. As a result, business would be lost to those competitors. Thus, corporations are often forced to outsource work. More generally, this is almost always the case at the national level. That is, nations generally would prefer to keep all jobs and keep a larger portion of the population working. However, the nature of global competition forces nations to give up jobs that they would usually prefer to keep.

BEYOND ECONOMIC OUTSOURCING

The above focuses on outsourcing (especially offshore and on-shore outsourcing) and in-sourcing from the point of view of globalization and the economy. However, such sourcing is also occurring far beyond the economic domain, often in a global context. Thus, a general concern for out- and in-sourcing and globalization must include the economy, but also go beyond it. This can be seen in two cases – that of healthcare and of the military – although many others (e.g. the government) are also deeply involved in these processes.

A form of outsourcing, especially offshore outsourcing, that relates to the economy (especially work and jobs) only in part is that involving healthcare. For example, the high cost of certain medical procedures (say open heart surgery) in the United States (and other developed nations) is leading people to outsource (offshore) such procedures by having them performed outside the United States at a fraction of the cost. Thus, heart surgery that would cost $200,000 in the United States costs only $10,000 (including airfare) at New Delhi's Escort Heart Institute and Research Centre (in addition to India, Singapore and Thailand attract large numbers of foreign patients) (Batra 2004). In fact, so many health consumers, mostly in developed countries, are availing themselves of such opportunities that a new term – 'medical tourists' – has emerged to describe them. The Indian government, for its part, has responded with the creation of special one-year medical visas that can be extended for a second year (Shanker 2005).

Furthermore, the medical profession is outsourcing, often offshore, an increasing amount of its work. One example of this that has been going on for quite some time is the offshore outsourcing of the transcription of doctor's notes. Another is the coding of patients' conditions for billing purposes. Of course, much of the billing itself, as well as bill collection services, is being outsourced offshore. All of the latter are 'back office services' that are often outsourced offshore not only in medicine, but in many other sectors. However, other forms of offshore outsourcing are much more eye-catching and controversial. Among the most notable examples is in radiology where practitioners in many parts of the world are reading and interpreting test results (X-rays, CAT scans, MRIs) on a 24/7 basis thereby taking much work away from their US counterparts and even threatening the continued existence of that medical specialty in the United States (Pollack 2003). In Schumpeter's terms, radiology in the United States is being destroyed, while creativity is occurring in that medical specialty in many other parts of the world. (However, there do not seem to be enough American radiologists to handle the work and furthermore offshore outsourcing the reading of test results in the middle of the night [or on weekends] helps to make the work lives of American radiologists easier and, in any case, many do not want to work during those hours. In fact, some 'nighthawk' companies employing American radiologists have been opened in countries [e.g. Australia] where it is day time when it is the middle of the night in the United States.) The key here is that digitized results of such tests can be transported instantly around the world as can responses from radiologists from all parts of the world. The motivation is clear – American radiologists earn $250,000 or more a year whereas a comparable radiologist in a less developed country might earn a tenth of that. Similarly, some lab work, for example testing blood serum and images of tissue samples, is also now being outsourced. Beyond that, we may soon see a variety of other medical tasks being outsourced offshore including reading electrocardiograms, supervising the technologies (including monitoring devices and TV cameras) in intensive care units and perhaps even performing robotic surgery via video transmissions from the operating room. Thus, we can anticipate the destruction of many other medical specialties in the United States with simultaneous job creation in other parts of the world.

Another example, within the domain of health, is the fact that consumers, and even state governments, are outsourcing offshore the consumption of various prescription drugs in order to cut costs. Thus, instead of buying drugs at the local pharmacy, many Americans are travelling to other countries (most notably Canada and Mexico) to purchase medications and/or making such purchases over the Internet or by 'snail mail'. The pharmaceutical companies themselves are engaging in various forms of offshore outsourcing with the most interesting involving clinical trials for new drugs. While certainly a cost-saving measure, this clearly raises all sorts of ethical issues involved in trying out new drugs on those who are less well-off and live in less developed countries such as India (Ray 2005a). One other example in this domain was underscored by the de-licensing of the British producer of flu vaccines Chiron because its plant was contaminated. This served to reveal the fact that the United States is outsourcing offshore much of its vaccine production. Thus, in these, and many other ways, various aspects of healthcare are being outsourced offshore.

Similar points can be made about the offshore outsourcing of war (Shearer 1998). The recent explosion of this form of outsourcing in the United States is largely traceable to the end of the Cold War, the demise of the Soviet Union and the resulting downsizing of the US (and Russian) military. The downsized US military with decreasing budgets could no longer handle functions it once did and a large number of military personnel, especially high-ranking officers, were freed from military service and available to handle outsourced functions. The end of the Cold War also brought with it a rise of ethnic and regional conflicts around the world that, in the view of at least some, required outside intervention. Outsourcing war is nothing new (it has ancient roots and was most famously the case when the British hired thousands of Hessian troops to help prosecute the Revolutionary War in America and when in the early 1800s the East India Company employed an army of 150,000 soldiers on behalf of the British government). In the Middle Ages, prior to the rise of the modern nation-state, nearly all military force was contracted. What is unique about this today is the rise of companies/corporations (the best-known is Halliburton) to do this kind of work (and to reap the huge profits associated with it). Other unique characteristics today include the development of a vast open global market for such work, those who do it work for many employers simultaneously; they are frequently former military or law enforcement officers, and such employees move freely among firms handling such work around the world and may even freelance (Avant 2004). In the case of the military, it might be argued that what is of greatest importance today is the *privatization* of war (Holzner, forthcoming; Cardinali 2001). This, of course, is a form of outsourcing that involves private, usually for-profit, organizations.[13] While this, too, is not new (the United States engaged in some privatization in the Revolutionary War [e.g. hiring of drivers and teams of horses to transport troops]), it clearly has expanded enormously in recent years.[14]

There are three basic sectors of the 'private military industry' composed of 'private military firms' (PMFs), involved in the outsourcing of war (Singer 2005). The first are military provider firms that furnish tactical military aid, including combat services, to their clients who can be anywhere in the world. Second, there are 'military consulting firms' that generally employ retired military officers to provide strategic advice and training. One example is Military Professional Resources, Inc. (its motto is 'The Greatest Military Expertise in the World'), involved in training the military in selected African nations (Burton-Rose and Madsen 1999). Finally, there are 'military support firms' that furnish such things as logistics, intelligence and maintenance. Among the support functions that have been increasingly privatized are:

- food services;
- sanitation and showers;
- recreation;
- construction;
- laundry service;
- translation services;
- running base camps;
- security;
- communications;
- maintenance. (Cardinali 2001)

Such services allow the military of the client nation to focus on combat and they reduce the host government's need to recruit more troops or to call up reserves. Theoretically, the use of mercenaries (like the Hessians in the Revolutionary War) is outlawed by Article 47 the Geneva Convention, but the private military industry is able to circumvent this because it does not, or at least claims that it does not, engage in actual combat (Blondell 2004).

Many countries have become increasingly reliant on PMFs, or been the site of their activities. The United States is a heavy user of PMFs, most notably in the war in, and occupation of, Iraq. There are so many of these firms in Iraq doing so many different things that one wag quipped that 'President George Bush's "coalition of the willing" might thus be more aptly described as the "coalition of the billing"' (Singer 2005). For example, the gigantic launch pad for the US invasion of Iraq in Camp Doha, Kuwait was built, operated and guarded by a PMF. Others maintained and loaded the most sophisticated weapons systems. They even helped in the operation of various combat systems such as missile batteries and missile defence systems. After George W. Bush (falsely) announced the end of military operations in Iraq, the country was flooded with military contractors. The ambassador to Iraq was guarded by heavily armed private security people. Vinnell trained the new Iraqi army, Erinys protected oil pipelines and CACI interrogated prisoners (and was involved in the scandal at Abu Ghraib) (*The Nation* 2004). Many European nations have also become reliant on PMFs for, for example, the transportation of troops. A Ukrainian firm, using old Soviet jets, transported European troops to the war in Afghanistan at a cost of $100 million.

Then there is the offshore outsourcing of torture and other extreme measures, many examples of which have come to light in US actions post 9/11. These have generally involved abducting suspected Al-Qaeda members (for example, in Sweden) and transporting them to another country, often Egypt. Prevented from torturing such people themselves, the US offshores such actions (calling them, euphemistically, 'extraordinary rendition'), to countries like Egypt where there are fewer restrictions on, and qualms about, them. The goal is to get desired information without the United States having to dirty its own hands, at least directly, by engaging in behaviours that would be deemed not only reprehensible, but also illegal, if they were to occur on US soil. Of course, one might ask if they are any less reprehensible, and even illegal, simply because they have been outsourced (Mayer 2005).

Overall, one could conclude that the US military has undergone some measure of destruction with corresponding creativity occurring in private military firms to which work of various types has been outsourced.

TOWARDS A BROADER, MULTIDIMENSIONAL, SOCIOLOGICAL CONCEPTION OF OUTSOURCING

However, even the extensions discussed in the preceding sections do not begin to get at the breadth and degree of outsourcing that is increasingly characteristic of developed societies. All of the preceding examples operate at the same, more macroscopic, level of analysis as the outsourcing of work and jobs. In one sense, this more macro-focus serves to mask the more meso- and micro-levels of outsourcing. That is, for example, changes in the nature of the work process (the meso-level) and individual work lives (micro-level) are also clearly involved in the outsourcing of work, healthcare and war. Thus, the nature of radiology as well as the lives of many individual radiologists in the United States (and elsewhere) are being profoundly affected by the outsourcing and offshoring of many of their traditional tasks. The same can be said about the character of the US military and of individual work and careers within the military. In another sense, the focus on the macro-levels of outsourcing obscures the fact that there are all sorts of *other* examples of meso- and micro-level outsourcing.

This is illustrated by Arlie Hochschild's extension of the concept of outsourcing in some surprising directions in ongoing research (see also Sandholtz et al. 2004; Salmon 1996) on the outsourcing of emotional labour (Hochschild 2005). Hochschild is not concerned, at least focally, with economics or the other macro-domains of outsourcing discussed above. Indeed, what she does is to extend outsourcing from such more macroscopic levels to more meso- and micro-scopic levels such as the family and individuals in or out of families. Thus, at the micro-level we are talking about individuals outsourcing to others tasks and responsibilities that have traditionally been their near-exclusive concern and responsibility. Examples include having children raised in daycare centres (Eberstadt 2004) and by nannies; having aides and institutions care for ageing parents and having hospices care for them when they are dying; hiring wedding planners and photo assemblers to handle these most personal of events; and so on. To take a very recent example, shopping for beginning-of-school needs is an important *rite of passage* for children and their parents, but there is now an online company (ezschoolsupplies.com) that, with the cooperation and involvement of school coordinators and teachers, will do it for them; shopping for school supplies can now be outsourced. These are all important leads in the extension of the idea of outsourcing because they move the concept of outsourcing from its usual macro-domain in the global work world, military and healthcare etc., to the micro-level of emotional labour in everyday life.

We will not say more about this here, although it is worth noting that globalization is implicated even at such micro- (and meso-) levels. To take one example, many of those handling such outsourced tasks as nannies, or aides in old age centres, are immigrants, often illegal, from other parts of the world. They are, in terms of thinking on globalization, part of the human 'flows' analysed by Castells (1996) or Appadurai's (1996) ethnoscapes. Indeed, the care offered to US citizens – both young and old – by immigrants from around the world has prompted Hochschild to speak of 'a global care chain' (Hochschild 2000) extending from the Third World to the First, and for Parrenas (2001) to speak of the 'globalization of motherhood'.

CREATIVE DESTRUCTION AND OUTSOURCING

Creative destruction is clearly occurring to some degree in the realm of outsourcing in general and offshore outsourcing in particular. It could be argued, for example, that call centres or IT operations in less developed countries like India or the Philippines are able to do this type of work better, and certainly much more cheaply, than their counterparts in more developed nations. Thus the latter are disappearing, and deservedly so (at least from the point of view of Schumpeter and the theory of capitalism), in a process of creative destruction. Everyone is seen as being advantaged by this process: developed nations get cheaper, and perhaps even better, services and the less developed nations get jobs and industries that will allow them to advance economically. Furthermore, the notion of creative destruction suggests that while there might be short-run dislocations in developed nations as a result of such offshore outsourcing, it serves to clear away outmoded industries and to lay the groundwork there for new, more advanced and presumably more profitable ones.[15]

There are those, however, who are not nearly so sanguine about this process, especially those in developed countries who see mostly destruction in the loss of familiar suppliers of goods and services, to say nothing of factories, work and jobs.

However, this focus on industry does not go nearly far enough in getting at the not-so-creative destruction associated with outsourcing. Much more has been destroyed, hollowed out, emptied, by outsourcing when it is examined more broadly. For example, it could be argued that the US military has been hollowed out with many of its components downsized or destroyed by the outsourcing of many of the tasks it once performed. Similarly, restaurants are being emptied as more of the cooking is being done by companies like Sysco. Families are being eviscerated by take-out restaurants, daycare centres, nursing homes and ezschoolsupplies.com. Ultimately, it could be argued that our individual lives (as children, parents and so on) are being emptied of content, and perhaps even meaning, as more and more of the things we once did are being outsourced. Thus, it could be argued that Schumpeter's positive view of creative destruction is a product of his exclusive focus on capitalistic businesses and that a broader view permits us to better see its negative sides.[16]

Another limitation of Schumpeter's theory relates to the fact that Schumpeter could not have had the kind of perspective required in the early twenty-first century to deal with the issue of creative destruction on a global scale. It is far more difficult in the 'global age' (Albrow 1997) to be sanguine about the creative destruction associated with offshore outsourcing, especially from the point of view of the developed nations doing the outsourcing. It is mainly destruction (of jobs, factories and profit centres) that is taking place there, whereas the creation (of jobs, factories etc.) is taking place elsewhere in the world. Schumpeter's theory of creative destruction badly needs revision in light of these new global realities. That is, we need to specify where globally both creativity and destruction are taking place; some areas of the world are more defined by destruction and others by creativity.

This points to a broader problem in Schumpeter's thinking and the theory of creative destruction. That is, in Schumpeter's theory the two aspects of *creativity* and *destruction* are always intertwined so they both are assumed to occur together and in concert with one another. But what globalization and outsourcing make clear is that the two processes (and the ideas of them) can, and do, occur independently of one another. This is clearest globally where it is easy to see that, for example, outsourcing (especially offshoring) is leading mainly to destruction in some places (e.g. developed nations), at least in the short run, and to creativity in others (less developed nations). However, creativity and destruction are probably always distinct processes, at least to some degree. Thus, even if one focuses on only a given country, creativity in one area or domain is almost always associated with destruction in others. This conjoined pair of ideas (i.e. creation and destruction) needs to be deconstructed and the relationship of one to the other analysed more carefully, especially in a global context as it relates to outsourcing, especially when this outsourcing occurs offshore.

If we take an even broader view on this and think beyond the destruction (and construction) of firms and the economy in general, it could be argued that in its latest forms outsourcing, at least outside of the economy, involve little in the way of creativity and is primarily, if not exclusively, destructive (at least in the United States and other developed countries). That is, it could be argued that, among many other things, much of what we have known as the military, healthcare, restaurants, families and individuals is being eviscerated, or at least adversely affected, by the current forms of outsourcing. Outsourcing leaves emptiness in its wake and that emptiness is being manifest, albeit in many different ways, in the military, healthcare, restaurants, families and among individuals. Thus, when we broaden our perspective on outsourcing to take into consideration areas outside the economy, it seems clear that Schumpeter's perspective is far too limited and that creative destruction can be far more destructive than it is creative. In other words, we need not follow Schumpeter in *assuming* change is always and everywhere *both* creative and destructive.

Thus, in the end, we need to rethink Schumpeter's notion of 'creative destruction' in a new era in the history of capitalism defined by globalization and outsourcing, in-sourcing and other types of sourcing activities. More importantly, at least from a theoretical perspective, it becomes necessary to extend the idea of creative destruction from its home in the economy to these other institutions and levels of analysis.

That is, not only are they affected by creative destruction in the economy, but they are themselves, at least in part autonomously, undergoing their own forms of creative destruction. Thus, we need to examine creative destruction *within*, for example, the nation, the family and the individual. Furthermore, we need to be attuned to the *relationship* among and between creative destruction in all of these institutions and levels of analysis. In other words, we need a multi-levelled and multidimensioned analysis of creative destruction rather than Schumpeter's with its exclusive focus on the economy. Ultimately, this is a *sociology, rather than an economics*, of outsourcing.

Finally, we need to look at creative destruction not only in how it relates to outsourcing, especially offshore outsourcing, but also to the way all of this plays out in the process of globalization. Offshore outsourcing as well as other types of out- and in-sourcing clearly relate to globalization and all of this is analysable from a greatly modified theory of creative destruction. It is yet to be seen whether these processes, analysed in this new and expanded light, will, in the end, yield more creation or more destruction not only in the US, but also elsewhere in the world.

Notes

1   This chapter points to the fact that the concept of outsourcing may be used so broadly and widely that it has lost its meaning. Here retirees are seen as outsourcing simply because they are retiring to Latin American countries like Costa Rica rather than remaining within the United States.

2   'Sourcing' has another meaning in the business literature involving a search for lower procurement costs. It is sometimes called, in this context, 'strategic sourcing'.

3   To simplify this analysis we will usually focus on the United States as the nation doing the outsourcing, or in this case offshoring, although, as we will see, many other nations are outsourcing and the United States is also in-sourcing (to be discussed later).

4   While other countries engage in outsourcing (e.g. Germany, Japan), those in other countries (most notably India) that are the recipients of this work have a far greater capacity for English than any other language. Of course, since English is also the language of the United Kingdom, it is the European country most likely to be involved in such outsourcing.

5   Although this is growing more sophisticated as Indian firms are moving from things like software development to taking over the entire administration and maintenance of an outsourcing company's IT systems; see *The Economist* (2004b).

6   Vietnam is also growing increasingly important as a destination for outsourcing because of, among other things, the number of people who speak French there; see Bradsher (2004).

7   US (and other) firms are buying Indian firms that handle offshore outsourced work. This, of course, is offshoring, not offshore outsourcing.

8   A report by Baily and Farrell (2004) issued on behalf of the McKinsey Global Institute entitled 'Exploding the Myths about Offshoring' argues not only that for every corporate dollar spent offshore US companies save 58 cents, but that for each dollar spent abroad, a net value is yielded for the United States between $1.12 and $1.14. Thus, in the opinion of Baily and Farrell, offshore outsourcing is not only good for the companies that receive the outsourced work, but also for the economies of the countries that do the outsourcing.

9   A term whose popularity predates that of outsourcing, but often means much the same thing.

10 For examples of design work being outsourced both on- and off-shore, see Deutsch (2004).

11 Michael Piore and Charles Sabel talk about the possibility of such collaborative relations between sub-contractors in their *The Second Industrial Divide: Possibilities for Prosperity* (1984).

12 There is another type of sourcing that we will not deal with here. *Open-sourcing* relates specifically to computers and the idea that a computer code is, or can be, open to anyone to use and to alter and improve upon. While this makes computer-related work especially amenable to outsourcing, much else about such work leads in the direction of outsourcing (including offshore). For example, as computers continue to decline in cost, they become more affordable to those in Third World countries, including those to be used at home for home-sourcing. Perhaps the key point about open-sourcing is that the arrival of the computer and its spread throughout the world is not going to lead to the creation of as many US jobs as was once thought. After all, the decline of the manufacturing jobs associated with the 'rustbelt' was thought, at one time, to be more than compensated for by the rise in computer-related work. While that might have been true for a time in the United States, many of those jobs have fled, or are now being offshored, as a result of open-sourcing, rapidly declining cost of computer equipment, fibre-optic cable that speeds the transmission of all sorts of data around the world and so on.

13 This view of privatization stands in contrast to that of the Defense Department which sees it as usually involving the transfer of facilities, equipment and other government assets (see Cardinali 2001). The view here is outsourcing in the military can be either to other governments or governmental agencies or to private companies. The latter is what is thought of here as 'privatization'.

14 Among other things, this calls into question notions such as *national* defence.

15 Hira and Hira (2005: 5–6) criticize economists' use of an '*ideal* scenario when thinking about outsourcing'. This scenario, which shares many of the same tenets as that of creative destruction, holds that while some tasks will be outsourced to developing countries, new, presumably better, forms of work will inevitably be created to replace what has been lost. Hira and Hira criticize this model on two accounts: the first is that there is no guarantee that any new jobs created after outsourcing has occurred will absorb the workers who have lost their jobs; and secondly, there is no guarantee that the new jobs being created in developing nations will be better or more advanced than the ones that were lost to outsourcing.

16 It is true that the development of new businesses (say, call centres in India) leads to the destruction of older ones (their US counterparts). While this might be viewed as a loss to US capitalism (although many argue that it is a gain in the long run even there), it can be seen as an overall gain to global capitalism as less efficient and more costly firms in developed countries give way to more efficient and less costly ones in less developed nations. Thus, within the realm of capitalistic business, Schumpeter's theory of creative destruction continues to hold (see Foster and Kaplan 2001, for an application of this idea to the internal dynamics of corporations and companies).

References

Albrow, M. 1997. *The Global Age: State and Society Beyond Modernity*. Stanford, CA: University of Stanford Press.

Appadurai, A. 1996. *Modernity at Large: Cultural Dimensions of Globalization*. Minneapolis: University of Minnesota Press.

Applebaum, R.P. and Robinson, W.I. (eds) 2005. *Critical Globalization Studies*. New York: Routledge.

Arvedlund, E.D. 2004. 'Modest now, Russian outsourcing has big hopes', *The New York Times*, 15 December, W1ff.

Austen, I. 2004. 'Canada, the closer country for outsourcing work', *The New York Times*, 30 November, W1ff.

Avant, D. 2004. 'Mercenaries', *Foreign Policy*, 143, 20–8.

Baily, M. and Farrell, D. 2004. *Exploding the Myths about Offshoring*. McKinsey Global Institute, April.

Bardhan, A.D. and Kroll, C.A. 2003. 'The new wave of outsourcing', Berkeley, CA: Fisher Center for Real Estate and Urban Economics (Paper 1103).

Batra, N. 2004. 'Outsourcing healthcare and other American problems', *The Statesman*, 3 November.

Beck, U. 2000. *What Is Globalization?*, Malden, MA: Polity Press.

Bellman, E. 2005. 'Indian companies win big outsourcing jobs', *Wall Street Journal Online*, 1 September.

Bellman, E. and Koppel, N. 2005. 'Legal services enter outsourcing domain', *The Wall Street Journal*, 28 September, B1ff.

Blondell, A. 2004. 'Fuelling the fire', *New Internationalist*, May (367), 22.

Bradsher, K. 2004. 'Outsourcing finds Vietnam', *The New York Times*, 30 September, W1ff.

Brady, D. 2003. 'All the world's a call center', *Business Week*, 27 October, 43.

Browning, L. 2004. 'Outsourcing abroad applies to tax returns, too', *The New York Times*, 15 February, 3, 12ff.

Burton-Rose, D. and Madsen, W. 1999. 'Corporate soldiers: The U.S. government privatizes the use of force', *Multinational Monitor*, 17–19 March.

Cardinali, R. 2001. 'Does the future of military logistics lie in outsourcing and privatization? Accountants – the new gatekeepers of war-time operations', *Work Study*, 50, 105–11.

Carey, S. 2005. 'Northwest targets flight attendants for outsourcing: Ailing carrier seeks savings by pushing veteran staffers off prized overseas routes', *The Wall Street Journal*, 25 October, A1.

Castells, M. 1996. *The Rise of the Network Society*. Vol. I of *The Information Age: Economy, Society and Culture*. Malden, MA: Blackwell.

Computing. 2005. 'Outsourcing, the insourcing trend is bringing it all back home', 12 May, 29ff.

Cowen, T. 2002. *Creative Destruction: How Globalization Is Changing the World's Cultures*. Princeton, NJ: Princeton University Press.

Deutsch, C.H. 2004. 'Outsourcing design', *The New York Times*, 30 December, C1ff.

Eberstadt, M. 2004. *Home-Alone America: The Hidden Toll of Day Care*. New York: Sentinel.

Economist.com. 2004. 'Growing up: Outsourcing in India', 22 May.

Elliott, C. 2005. 'Bumping jobs', *The New York Times*, 7 June, C7.

Florida, R. 2004. *The Rise of the Creative Class: And How It's Transforming Work, Leisure, Community and Everyday Life*. New York: Basic Books.

Flynn, L.J. 2003. 'New economy: Companies sending work abroad are learning cultural sensitivity – to their American customers', *The New York Times*, 8 December, C4.

Foster, R. and Kaplan, S. 2001. *Creative Destruction: Why Companies That Are Built to Last Underperform the Market – And How to Successfully Transform Them*. New York: Currency.

Friedman, T. 2005. *The World Is Flat: A Brief History of the Twenty-First Century*. New York: Farrar, Strauss and Giroux.

Galloni, A., Rohwedder, C. and Agins, T. 2005. 'Breaking a taboo: High fashion starts making goods overseas', *The Wall Street Journal*, 27 September, A1ff.

Gereffi, G. and Korzeniewicz, M. 1994. *Commodity Chains and Global Capitalism*. Westport, CT: Greenwood Press.

Harrison, B. 1994. *Lean and Mean: Why Large Corporations Will Continue to Dominate the Global Economy*. New York: Guilford Press.

Harvey, D. 1990. *The Condition of Postmodernity: An Enquiry into the Origins of Cultural Change*. Malden, MA: Blackwell.

Held, D. and McGrew, A. 2002. *Globalization/Anti-Globalization*. Malden, MA: Blackwell.

Herman, T. 2005. 'IRS plans to begin outsourcing tax-debt collection next summer', *The Wall Street Journal*, 16 November, D2.

Hira, R. and Hira, A. 2005. *Outsourcing America: What's Behind Our National Crisis and How We Can Reclaim American Jobs*. New York: AMACOM.

Hochschild, A.R. 2000. 'The nanny chain', *The American Prospect*, 11 (4), 32–6.

Hochschild, A.R. 2005. ' "Rent a mom" and other services: markets, meanings and emotions', *International Journal of Work Organisation and Emotion*, 1, 74–86.

Holzner, B. (Forthcoming). 'Privatization'. In G. Ritzer (ed.), *Encyclopedia of Sociology*. Oxford: Blackwell.

Hrivnak, T. and Smith, A. 2005. 'View from here: Offshore backlash', *Legal Week*, 30 June.

Inda, J.X. and Rosaldo, R. 2002. *The Anthropology of Globalization: A Reader*. Malden, MA: Blackwell.

Isaak, R.A. 2005. *The Globalization Gap: How the Rich Get Richer and the Poor Get Left Further Behind*. Upper Saddle River, NJ: Financial Times Prentice Hall.

Jameson, F. 1991. *Postmodernism or, The Cultural Logic of Late Capitalism*. Durham, NC: Duke University Press.

Lacey, M. 2005. 'Accents of Africa: A new outsourcing frontier', *The New York Times*, 2 February, C1ff.

Lohr, S. 2004. 'Evidence of high-skill work going abroad', *The New York Times*, 16 June, C2.

Marlin, S. 2004. 'Outsourced functions move in-house – Insourcing credit-card processing can get banks closer to customers', *InformationWeek*, 19 July, 26.

Mayer, J. 2005. 'Outsourcing torture: The secret history of America's "extraordinary rendition" program', *The New Yorker*, 14 February, 106ff.

Millman, J. 2005. 'Developing nations lure retirees, raising idea of "outsourcing" boomers' golden years', *The Wall Street Journal*, 14 November, A2.

Mincer, J. 2005. 'Instead of offshore, call centers start to move to U.S. kitchens', *The Wall Street Journal*, 29 November, B6.

Nicklaus, D. 2004. 'Insourcing shows the flip side of jobs going overseas', *St. Louis Post-Dispatch*, 16 April, C1ff.

Nikolova, N. (Forthcoming). 'Out-sourcing'. In G. Ritzer (ed.), *Encyclopedia of Sociology*. Oxford: Blackwell.

Parrenas, R.S. 2001. *Servants of Globalization: Women, Migration and Domestic Work*. Stanford, CA: Stanford University Press.

Petras, J. and Veltmeyer, H. 2001. *Globalization Unmasked: Imperialism in the 21st Century*. New York: Zed Books.

Piore, M. and Sabel, C. 1984. *The Second Industrial Divide: Possibilities for Prosperity*. New York: Basic Books.

Pollack, A. 2003. 'Who's reading your X-ray?' *The New York Times*, 16 November, 3, 1ff.

Rai, S. 2003. 'In India, a high-tech outpost for U.S. patents', *The New York Times*, 13 December, C4ff.

Rai, S. 2004a. 'An outsourcing giant fights back', *The New York Times*, 21 March, 3, 1ff.

Rai, S. 2004b. 'Financial firms hasten their move to outsourcing', *The New York Times*, 18 August, W1.

Rai, S. 2004c. 'Microsoft expands operations in India', *The New York Times*, 16 November, W1ff.

Rai, S. 2005. 'Gridlock on India's new paths to prosperity', *The New York Times*, 12 February, C1ff.

Ray, S. 2005a. 'Drug companies cut costs with foreign clinical trials', *The New York Times*, 24 February, C4.

Ray, S. 2005b. 'World business briefing Asia: India: Outsourcing said to rise 34%', *The New York Times*, 3 June, C4.

Realcomm Advisory. 2004. 'Receptionists outsourced to India?', 17 November. Available at: <http://www.realcomm.com/advisory.asp?aid=124>.

Robinson, W.I. 2003. *Transnational Conflicts: Central America, Social Change, and Globalization*. New York: Verso.

Rodrik, D. 1997. *Has Globalization Gone Too Far?* Washington, DC: Institute for International Economics.

Salmon, J. 1996. 'For hire: Helpers for harried parenting', *Washington Post*, 17 September, A1.

Sandholtz, K., Derr, B., Buckner, K. and Carlson, D. 2004. 'Beyond juggling, rebalancing your busy life'. Available at: <http://businessknowhow.com>.

Schumpeter, J. 1947. *Capitalism, Socialism, and Democracy*, 2nd edn. New York: Harper and Brothers .

Shanker, J. 2005. 'India caters to foreign medical patients as health system sags', 24 November. Available at: <http://www.pharmacychoice.com/News/article.cfm?Article_ID=17336>.

Shearer, D. 1998. 'Outsourcing war', *Foreign Policy*, 112, 68–81.

Singer, P.W. 2005. 'Outsourcing war: Understanding the private military industry', *Foreign Affairs*, 84, 119–32.

Slaughter, M.J. 2004. Report prepared for the Organization for Foreign Investors.

Smith, N. 2005. *The Endgame of Globalization*. New York: Routledge.

Steinberg, J. 2004. 'Media talk: Reuters takes outsourcing to a new level with journalists', *The New York Times*, 9 February, C6.

Taylor, E. 2005. 'ABN Amro signs outsourcing deal', *Wall Street Journal Online*, 1 September.

The Economist. 1996. 'DIY in Germany', 2 March, 60.

The Economist. 2004a. 'The Indians are coming: America's debt-collection Industry', 30 October, 78.

The Economist. 2004b. 'The latest in remote control: Outsourcing to India', 11 September, 57ff.

The Economist. 2005. 'Time to bring it back home? Outsourcing', 5 March, 63.

The Nation. 2004. 'Outsourcing is hell', 7 June, 5ff.

Treaster, J.B. 2001. 'Business to business: Moving the accountants out of the building and onto the Web', *The New York Times*, 18 April, H1, 7ff.

Wriston, W. 2004. 'Ever heard of insourcing?' *The Wall Street Journal*, 24 March.

Chapter 16

Globalization and Consumer Culture

Douglas J. Goodman

The world is increasingly connected by global processes. More and more local practices are motivated by distant events and have antipodal consequences. Although many of these global processes are uneven, contingent and contradictory, the economic and political interconnections are indisputable; as are the mass migrations of people, goods and especially information. While none of this is absolutely new, the tempo has reached the point that the term 'globalization' seems warranted. Globalization undoubtedly has cultural effects, but the question still remains open as to whether this constitutes a global culture. The theme of this chapter is that to the extent that there is a global culture, it is a consumer culture.

The birth date of this globalization is still a point of contention, even in those rare instances where globalization's basic definition is agreed on. The debate continues as to the underlying cause of globalization: whether it is a result of modernity (Giddens 2000), capitalism (Wallerstein 1991), technological progress (Rosenau 2003) or political power (Gilpin 1987), to name a few of the usual suspects. In addition, its strength is still hotly disputed (Hirst and Thompson 1996). Nevertheless, all of these points can be left unresolved for this chapter. No matter its birth date, its cause or even whether it exists yet in any strong sense, we can still ask questions about the form that a global culture may take.

The literature on a global consumer culture is dispersed in a number of disciplines and difficult to summarize. Perhaps the greatest problem is the lack in consistency in the concept of culture. Consequently, to summarize what we know about global consumer culture first requires some ground clearing. We need to reconceptualize culture before we can look at the relation between globalization and consumer culture. Indeed, the idea of culture is so problematic that we require a theoretical analysis before we will be able to recognize the evidence for and against a global consumer culture. Following this reconceptualization will be a summary of the primary cultural attributes of globalization and an assessment as to whether they constitute a global consumer culture. Then we will look at four of the most important theoretical approaches to a global consumer culture.

IS THERE A GLOBAL CULTURE?

In 1990, the journal *Theory, Culture and Society* opened its special issue devoted to 'Global Culture' with the simple question: 'Is there a global culture?' The editor rejected the idea that there can be a global culture where culture denotes a homogeneous and integrated entity. 'The varieties of response to the globalization process clearly suggest that there is little prospect of a unified global culture, rather there are global cultures in the plural' (Featherstone 1990: 10).

The idea of a global culture can be traced back to McLuhan's (1964) divination of a 'global village'. However, as Geertz (2000: 247) notes, this global version 'is a poor sort of village . . . As it has neither solidarity nor tradition, neither edge nor focus, and lacks all wholeness'. Despite this lack of many of the characteristics that traditionally identified a culture, a number of scholars have argued that a global culture does exist. Jameson (1998: xii) sees global culture as an 'untotalized totality' with patterns of negative and positive symbolic exchanges. Appadurai (1996) pictures a deterritorialized global culture growing out of the relations between mass mediated cultural productions and migratory audiences. Robertson (1992) describes the emergence of a global 'human condition' that connects and relativizes individuals, nations and international systems. According to Waters, cultural exchanges must inevitably result in a global culture. Indeed, he argues that cultural globalization will lead economic and political globalization since, as Waters (1995: 3) pithily writes, 'material exchanges localize, political exchanges internationalize; and symbolic exchanges globalize'.

Nevertheless, although virtually all globalization scholars believe that modern culture can only be understood within a global setting, a number of them do not believe that the global setting constitutes a global culture. They admit that there is a growing flow of people, goods and media. There are increased interactions in cultural 'border zones', a reaching of the centre's cultural industries into the periphery and spreading interconnections between local culture and global economic and political forces. There are fragmenting cultures, pluralistic cultures and interconnecting cultures. These sceptics also recognize that some cultural consequences of globalization have a certain autonomy on the global level, but they argue that these fall short of constituting a global culture.

Many have rejected the idea of a global culture because of the lack of homogeneity. For example, Guillen (2001: 254), in a review of the globalization literature, concludes that 'no such thing as a global culture is emerging'. For Anthony Smith (1995), cultures emerge from and express the historical identity of the society. He argues that there is no global culture because there is no such shared global historical identity. 'Given the plurality of such experiences and identities, and given the historical depth of such memories, the project of a global culture, as opposed to global communications, must appear premature for some time to come' (Smith 1995: 180).

In the debate over the existence of a global culture, one can see a more fundamental disagreement as to what is meant by culture. For some, culture is a homogeneous set of values and internalized norms. For others, it is a shared set of symbolic resources. For yet others, it is a pattern of symbolic exchanges. Whether or not one believes that there is a global culture is closely related to the definition of culture.

Culture is a notoriously difficult term. Contributing to this difficulty is its use in diverse disciplines, of which the analysis of globalization is only one. To simply put 'global' in front of 'culture' without a careful discussion of its meaning only compounds the difficulty. Many who have weighed in on the issue of global culture have found the phrase so difficult that they have simply avoided defining it. Roland Robertson (1992: 33) should be commended for being one of the few who have explicitly stated this tactic. However, the strategy that will be followed here is closer to Raymond Williams' (1983: xvii), who suggests that the term 'culture' is a record of the 'important and continuing reactions to . . . changes in our social, economic and political life, and may be seen, in itself, as a special kind of map by means of which the nature of the changes can be explored'. Williams used the term 'culture' to map and explore social changes in the Industrial Revolution. I believe we will find its transformations equally useful for understanding globalization.

In the literature on globalization, we see two different meanings of culture: (1) the meaningful aspect of social behaviour; and (2) the beliefs and practices that make a group of people distinct.[1]

A typical definition for the first meaning of culture is given by Wuthnow (1987: 50), who describes culture as 'built into all social relations, constituting the underlying assumptions and expectations on which social interaction depends'. As Sewell (1999: 39) points out, this type of culture's pervasive nature makes it 'a theoretically defined category or aspect of social life that must be abstracted out from the complex reality of human existence'. This is what Kroeber and Kluckhohn (1952: 90) call 'culture' as opposed to 'a culture' and what Wallerstein (1990: 33) and Nederveen Pieterse (2004: 78) call 'culture two'. I will follow Friedman's (1994) terminology and call it *generic culture*.

Also following Friedman, I will use *differential culture* to identify the beliefs and practices that make a group of people distinct. This use of culture goes back to nineteenth-century romanticism and it has been one of the fundamental concepts of modern anthropology. Culture here refers to a local, relatively coherent, self-contained set of norms, presuppositions and practices that belongs to a localized social group and is passed on to the next generation. This is what Geertz (2000) and Benedict (1934) call 'configurational', and what Wallerstein (1990) and Nederveen Pieterse (2004) call 'culture one'. As we will see below, this use of culture has been subjected to extensive criticism, but even its harshest critics still see its value. 'There are times when we still need to be able to speak holistically of Japanese or Trobriand or Moroccan culture in the confidence that we are designating something real and differentially coherent' (Clifford 1988).

When asking whether global culture exists, the definition of culture that we use predetermines our answer. Under the first definition, if there is global social behaviour, then there must be a global culture. Conversely, if we use the second definition, the answer as to whether there is a global culture is just as trivially 'no', since there is no reference group in comparison to which a global 'tribe' could be seen as distinct. To ask in a non-trivial way whether there is a global culture necessitates an analysis of the basis of culture's meaning and its adaptation to the new social context of globalization, since one of the many changes associated with the globalization process may be a transformation in the meaning of culture. This is what Tomlinson (1997: 133) suggests when he writes that 'the globalization process is revealing both political and conceptual problems at the core of our assumptions about what a "culture" actually is'.

The necessity of rethinking culture is especially apparent in regard to differential culture. Globalization contradicts the idea of a culture tied to a particular locality and segregated from the cultures of other localities. However, for the most part, anthropology has already abandoned this meaning of culture, preferring to see culture as a process (Keesing 1994). Despite anthropology's current uneasiness with the term, culture is commonly used outside of anthropology to refer to differences between groups. Mazzarella (2004: 347) notes the irony that 'the culture concept's newfound popularity often displays the kind of essentialist or substantialist tendency that drove many anthropologists in the 1980s and 1990s to disown the concept or at least to insist on a radical revision of its analytical status'.

In fact, it is precisely this meaning of culture that is usually assumed in globalization studies. Even *au courant* concepts such as hybridity and glocalization (see below) still depend on the idea of differential cultures. Without bounded, essentialist differential cultures, there would be nothing to hybridize and no place for the translocal to be embedded. Frow (2000: 174) points out that models of globalization continue 'to assume (and to be nostalgic for) the level of the *national* culture, which it equates with the "local"'. If this is the definition of culture, then globalization will inevitably be seen as the spread of an invasive culture to the detriment of native cultures, in other words, as cultural imperialism.

Neither does generic culture provide an adequate conception for understanding global culture. Generic culture's focus on the meaning of social action is an important corrective to an overly positivistic social science, but it is hopelessly vague since there is nothing human that is not meaningful. As Keesing (1994: 73) observes, this meaning of culture 'includes too much and is too diffuse either to separate analytically the twisted threads of human experience or to interpret the designs into which they are woven'. It is precisely this meaning of culture that Herbert Marcuse (1968) critiqued as 'affirmative culture', which pretends to a false universality in its representation of all of humanity.

Towards a new definition of culture

The idea of a global culture requires a reconceptualization of culture. This reconceptualization can begin with an analysis of what culture's different definitions have in common. Both definitions of culture point not just to meaning, but to a system of meaning. Generic culture extends this system to a universalization of all human meaning. Differential culture refers to the system of meaning attached to a particular social group.

Culture is a system, precisely as the structuralists describe it, with elements that are interrelated in structures of hierarchy, opposition and equivalence along paradigmatic, syntagmatic, synchronic and diachronic axes. Meaning is not an attribute of an individual cultural element, rather the meaning of any element emerges from its place in the structural system. Calling culture a system implies coherence, but this need not suggest homogeneity. Cultures can be structures of difference. Even anthropology, which has been most vulnerable to the charge of assuming cultural homogeneity, has always assumed that culture consists of structures of difference. If men wear pants and women wear skirts, this is no less a culture than if everyone wears togas.

What is not so obvious from these definitions of culture is that culture implies not only a system, but also a set of practices that constitute this system. That culture comprises both system and practice is convincingly argued by William Sewell (1999). On the one hand, culture represents 'a realm of pure signification' characterized by 'internal coherence and deep logic' (1999: 44). On the other hand, culture is a 'sphere of practical activity shot through by willful action, power relations, struggle, contradictions and change'. Sewell points out that system and practice are complementary concepts:

> The employment of a symbol can be expected to accomplish a particular goal only because the symbols have more or less determinate meanings – meanings specified by their systematically structured relations to other symbols. Hence practice implies system. But it is equally true that the system has no existence apart from the succession of practices that instantiate, reproduce, or – most interestingly – transform it. (Sewell 1999: 47)

Culture, then, is an articulation of system and practice. This helps explain the diversity of culture's meanings. The complex of meanings reflect the tension between system and practice. However, Sewell does not seem to realize the full implications of this conception of culture. Sewell's discussion of cultural practices indicates that he understands practice only as the *use* of culture, not its *creation*. Humans are not seen as meaning-making beings, but only as meaning-manipulating beings. In Sewell's descriptions, meaning is made accidentally through transformations due to the 'uncertain consequences of practice'.

A definition of culture that is adequate for understanding global culture requires a recognition that practices create meanings. Furthermore, as Sewell rightly notes, meaning implies systematically structured relations. Consequently, meaning-creating practices necessarily create the system that is at the core of the definition of culture. An analysis of global culture requires first that we identify the practices that create it. This is a shift in focus that has already occurred in anthropology.

> Over the past two decades, a definite shift has occurred in the way anthropologists formulate their central concept of culture. Long-standing assumptions about shared systems of symbols and norms have not been abandoned, despite challenges to think of culture as an organization of non-shared, distributed meanings. But questions about social agents and agencies, rather than about the structural logic or functional coherence of normative and symbolic systems, now orient cultural inquiry. More and more often culture is treated as the changing outcome of 'practice' – interested activity not reducible to rational calculation. The production and reproduction of collectively held dispositions and understandings – the work of making culture – is taken to be problematic rather than automatic, the site of multiple contests informed by a diversity of historically specific actions and intentions. (Foster 1991: 235)

The focus should be on the practices that construct the cultural system rather than on the system's pure autonomous transcendence. This is often referred to as a constitutive approach to culture, and as Street (1994: 104) describes this approach, it 'entails a recognition that culture is constantly being forged by the activities of individuals and groups; that the culture has not a single cohesive form, but is ambiguous; and that part of the reason for this ambiguity is the competing inter-pretations and meanings which can be derived from the available cultural resources'. Raymond Williams, one of its seminal practitioners, summarizes this new approach to culture as characterized by the 'insistence that "cultural practice" and "cultural production" . . . are not simply derived from an otherwise constituted social order but are themselves major elements in its constitution. . . . culture is the signifying system through which necessarily (though among other means) a social order is communicated, reproduced, experienced and explored' (1983: 12). Eric Wolf points out that the advantage of this approach is that it avoids 'the mistake of granting these groups or cultures some "essential" existence', while it recognizes 'the linguis-tic and other strategies through which they [cultures] are negotiated and produced' (Wolf 1997: 167).

The anthropological conception of culture has been attacked for ignoring the heterogeneity and struggle of the culture. However, in the constitutive approach, the practices that are most constitutive of the culture are precisely those struggles. Illouz and John (2003) conclude that culture is not a deep core of norms nor a set of explicit symbols, instead it is a battlefield in which actors struggle over questions of collective identity. In particular, culture is related to those struggles that take for granted the goals of the struggle. In this sense, a culture can be categorized as what Bourdieu calls a field.

> It is one of the generic properties of fields that the struggle for specific stakes masks the objective collusion concerning the principles underlying the game. More precisely, the struggle tends constantly to produce and reproduce the game and its stakes repro-ducing, primarily in those who are directly involved, but not in them alone, the practi-cal commitment to the value of the game and its stakes which defines the recognition of its legitimacy. (Bourdieu 1991: 58)

Culture, then, is both a system and the practices that constitute that system. An analysis of global culture does not require the identification of homogeneity, shared values or social integration. Rather it requires the identification of a set of practices that constitute a cultural field within which struggle and contestation occurs.

Given this understanding of culture, we must now address two questions: (1) can there be such a thing as a consumer culture; (2) what characteristics might we look for to identify a *global* consumer culture?

As with global culture, the existence of a consumer culture can also be given a facile answer depending on the definition of culture. For some, consumption must be cultural because it is meaningful. For others, the term consumer culture is an oxymoron – what the masses consume cannot be a true culture. However, the ques-tion being asked here is whether consumption is a set of practices that construct a system of meaning. To understand the relation between practices of consumption and a consumer culture, we would need to look at more than the obvious processes and practices of exchange. All cultures have exchanged and consumed goods. We also need to look beyond an individual object's meaning. All cultures have found consumption meaningful. The question is whether consumption has the double attributes identified by Sewell as system and practice. Does consumption construct, on the one hand, a realm of pure signification characterized by internal coherence and deep logic, and on the other hand, a sphere of practical activity shot through by wilful action, power relations, struggle, contradictions and change? Furthermore, does consumption provide opportunities for meaning creation, and does it provide a field in which struggle occurs over taken-for-granted goals?

Whether or not there is a global consumer culture, it certainly seems obvious that Western societies have such a consumer culture. In Western societies, consumption has become a source of systemic meaning: as identity and social status; and consumption provides opportunities for meaning creation: as self-expression and lifestyle. Consumption has become the field in which struggles occur with the taken-for-granted assumption that all problems can be solved through more, or better, consumption.

ATTRIBUTES OF GLOBAL CULTURE

Having reconceptualized culture so that we can identify a consumer culture, we will summarize what scholars have discovered about globalization and analyse whether the cultural attributes of globalization constitute such a culture.

In the debate around global culture, analysts have focused on two seemingly paradoxical trends: homogeneity and heterogeneity. Those who argue for a global culture (especially as a form of imperialism) have pointed to homogenization, while those who argue against global culture have pointed to increased heterogeneity. However, with the understanding of culture outlined above, the presence of homogeneity or heterogeneity is irrelevant to the issue of the existence of a global culture. All cultures have both homogeneity and heterogeneity. The correct question is whether these characteristics can be understood as part of a cultural system deriving from a shared set of practices. Consequently, we need to examine the discussions of homogeneity or heterogeneity to analyse whether there is evidence that they constitute a system of meaning that derives from shared practices of consumption.

Within the limits of this chapter, I will not go so far as to argue that such a global culture has now emerged. Even if we are able to show that these processes are part of consumer culture, the extent of culture is still an open empirical question. The aim in this chapter is to clarify the type of evidence and where we need to look to determine if we have a global culture.

Homogenization

Homogenization refers to the trend towards sameness and the reduction in diversity of cultures around the world. Steger (2002: 36) cites Nike sneakers on Amazonian Indians, Texaco baseball caps on sub-Sahara youths and Chicago Bulls sweatshirts on Palestinians. In such descriptions it is easy to see a homogenized global culture of standardized tastes and desires. This homogenization is sometimes referred to as

Americanization, coca-colonization or McDonaldization. However, not all of these are equally satisfactory descriptors for this trend in global culture.

Americanization is the least satisfactory term. For one thing, many of the companies spreading this homogenized culture are not from the United States. There are Benetton, Prada, Bertelsmann and many other non-US producers of culture. Even such an icon of popular culture as Bazooka gum is not made in the United States. In fact, it is transnational companies, not any one country, that are the driving force behind homogenization. Even when the company is based in the United States, there is no reason to think that the company's and the country's interests coincide. For example, the United States may have an interest in the free distribution of movies that promote the American way of life, but that is hardly in the interests of companies that make the movies. Sklair calls the focus on Americanization a mystification:

> Capitalist consumerism is mystified by reference to Americanization, while Americanization, the method of the most successfully productive society in human history, gives its imprimateur to capitalist consumerism . . . to identify cultural and media imperialism with the United States, or even with US capitalism, is a profound and a profoundly mystifying error. It implies that if American influence could be excluded then cultural and media imperialism would end. This could only be true in a purely definitional sense. Americanization itself is a contingent form of a process that is necessary to global capitalism, the culture-ideology of consumerism. (Sklair 1991: 152–3)

To the extent that these transnational companies produce standardized, identical products for diverse global markets, this process might be called coca-colonization (Mlinar 1992). However, only a fraction of global products fit that model. Even Coca-Cola claims that, 'We are not a multi-national, we are a multi-local' (quoted in Morley, 1991: 15). As a marketing executive at Coca-Cola said, 'It would not be in our best interest to give consumers a position that they don't want. It's just completely counterintuitive. . . . Trying to change the nature of cultures is not part of our success criteria. I don't even understand what would be the motivation' (quoted in Hunter and Yates 2002: 351). And, although the Coca-Cola drink itself is standardized, the Coca-Cola company is 'going native' with a variety of locally tailored teas, fruit juices and energy drinks (Yoon 2001: 34).

A more fitting description of global homogenization is McDonaldization, but it is first necessary to clearly define what this term means. While coca-colonization refers to the spread of a standard product, McDonaldization does not simply mean the spread of a particular restaurant chain. Instead it is the spread of the processes of efficiency, calculability, predictability and control which McDonald's successfully introduced into consumption. The idea of McDonaldization is that these processes are coming to dominate more economic and cultural sectors as well as spreading globally.

Nevertheless, Ritzer (2000), the originator of the term, recognizes the many counter trends to McDonaldization, such as the small, non-McDonaldized businesses in apparent reaction against McDonaldization. In fact, alongside the expansion of McDonald's and their ilk is the continued growth of independent restaurants motivated, at least in part, by artisanship (Fine 1996). And, of wider significance, the strongest growth in retail sales has been at both the McDonaldized discount mega-stores (e.g. Walmart) and boutiques.

The argument can be made that this is not a trend with its anomalies or even a trend and its reaction, but rather two faces of an underlying process. This underlying process is related to the practices of consumer culture. Buying lunch at McDonald's and clothes at Walmart or dinner at the latest pan-Asian restaurant and clothes at the local boutique are not simply economic decisions, these are also cultural decisions involving a system of meaning. While it would be absurd to deny the economics involved, it would be equally wrong to deny the system of meaning involved. Even such seemingly insignificant decisions about where to eat lunch become symbolic resources in status struggles. And in such struggles, what is assumed by all competitors is that our status and identity are more tied up with the meal we buy than with the food that we grow or the meal we prepare ourselves.

To the extent that there is a homogenization of global culture, it is a peculiar homogenization. It is not the spread of American culture or a soft drink or even a rationalizing process. It is the spread of consumer culture. Global forces don't seem to be reproducing identical cultural objects. Instead they are producing a framework for a new understanding of intra- and inter-social differences. Identity and difference are being channelled into the field of consumer practices.

Heterogeneity

In contrast to global homogeneity, many scholars see increased heterogeneity. It is not simply that cultures continue to be diverse, but that globalization is increasing diversity among cultures and especially within cultures. With globalization, Western cultural objects are 'indigenized' and given new local meanings; cultures influence each other, creating new hybrids; Western culture itself becomes more influenced by peripheral cultures; and new transnational cultural groupings emerge.

> Rather than the emergence of a unified global culture there is a strong tendency for the process of globalization to provide a stage for global differences not only to open up a 'world showcase of cultures' in which the examples of the distant exotic are brought directly into the home, but to provide a field for a more discordant clashing of cultures. While cultural integration processes are taking place on a global level the situation is becoming increasingly pluralistic, or polytheistic, a world with many competing gods. (Featherstone 1996: 13)

One of the trends leading to greater heterogeneity has been called glocalization (Robertson 1995). This refers to the heterogeneous reception, appropriation and response to even the most standardized global products. There is even evidence that the great homogenizing forces of Coca-Cola (Miller 1998) and McDonald's (Caldwell 2004) contribute to heterogeneity through glocalization. Similarly, Albrow (1996: 148) has referred to a 'karaoke effect', in which an idiosyncratic local performance is made against a standardized background. In such cases, globalization's homogeneity is dispelled by the local's heterogenizing power. This is not a one-way process. Some of this glocalization and karaoke effect takes the form of what

Biltereyst and Meers (2000) call 'contra flows', in which cultural products move from peripheral to core countries.

In addition, heterogeneity is increased because of more contact and influence between cultures through global connections. The interpenetration of the global and the local as well as the interpenetration of globally connected locals has led to the proliferation of 'hybrid' forms. Some hybridization can be close to homogenization with only minimal blends of standardized products. But the hybridization of most interest to globalization scholars has to do with those cases where standard global categories, such as core/periphery, male/female, native/cosmopolitan, art/craft etc., are blurred and subverted. Nevertheless, hybrids are not a new consequence of globalization. All culture can be seen as hybrid. What globalization adds is an increased pace that makes it more difficult to hide culture's hybrid nature (Franco 1993: 136).

Not only is heterogeneity increasing because of glocalization and hybrids, but also because of the diverse and contradictory forces of globalization itself. Arjun Appadurai (1996) identifies at least five complex, overlapping and disjunctive dimensions of global cultural flows with no single organizing principle. These include: ethnoscapes, the cultural imaginary of mobile individuals; mediascapes, the world conjured in movies, television and other global media; technoscapes, the uneven distribution of technologies; financescapes, the disposition of global capital; and ideoscapes, the distribution of political ideas and values. These forces combine and disperse to increase heterogeneity, having their greatest effect on the cultural imagination.

A number of analysts have pointed not just to heterogeneity, but to polarization as an argument against a global culture. Nederveen Pieterse (2004) sees polarization as one of the three fundamental paradigms of globalization. Friedman (2002) argues that what we see is not a global culture, but the global fragmentation of cultures. This is, again, a misunderstanding of culture. Cultures can be fragmented and even polarized. What culture is not fragmentized and polarized along gender lines? The question to ask is whether this fragmentation and polarization constitutes a system of meaning, and, in particular, whether polarizing struggles occur within a field of taken-for-granted goals. If polarization is due simply to increased exposure to others, we should not call it a product of a global culture. However, a number of scholars have pointed to underlying cultural factors. Appadurai (1996) points to the increase in uncertainty as one of the factors leading to the global increase in ethnic violence. Identities that are no longer anchored in stable cultural traditions are more likely to become part of fundamentalist religious movements or ethnic-based extremism. This is precisely the argument that Samuel Huntington makes in *The Clash of Civilizations*.

There are a number of ways in which polarization can be seen as a product of a consumer culture. First, an identity connected to a consumer culture is much less stable and more uncertain than one connected to a local culture. Second, I argue below that global consumer culture emphasizes culture as a valuable resource even as it destabilizes culture as a source of traditions. This can lead to resistance in the name of culture that can easily become polarizing (Yúdice 2003: 6). Finally, Sklair points out that global consumer culture increases resentment because it cannot fulfil the promises that it makes to the world's poor:

> Once the culture-ideology of consumerism is adopted, poor people cannot cope eco-
> nomically, and a mode of resistance must develop. In the Muslim case this mostly
> manifests itself in religious extremism, whose target is as often Americanization as it
> is consumerism as such. (Sklair 1991: 158)

Heterogeneity and even polarization are not evidence against the existence of a
culture. Underlying the heterogeneity may be the double attributes of system and
practice. Polarization may be a manifestation of the strategic struggles that constitute a cultural field.

GLOBAL SYSTEMS OF COMMON DIFFERENCE

The question as to whether globalization increases cultural homogeneity by establishing common codes and practices or whether it increases a heterogeneity of newly
emerging differences seems now, to many analysts, to have been answered. Globalization does both. What appears to be a dichotomy is, in fact, complementary. To
the extent that a global culture is emerging, it does not appear to be eliminating
diversity, instead it is providing a common framework for heterogeneity. Globalization makes people more different but in a similar way. It creates a mixed system,
where people are homogenized into similar individuals, ethnicities and nations who
want different things:

> the apparent increasing global integration does not simply result in the elimination of
> cultural diversity, but, rather, provides the context for the production of new cultural
> forms which are marked by local specificity. If, in other words, the global is the site of
> the homogeneous (or the common) and the local the site of the diverse and the distinc-
> tive, then the latter can – in today's integrated world-system – only constitute and
> reconstitute itself in and through concrete reworkings and appropriations of the former.
> (Ang 1996: 155)

Ulf Hannerz (1990: 237) describes globalization as characterized by 'an organization of diversity rather than by a replication of uniformity'. Richard Wilk (1995)
calls it 'structures of common difference'. In his study of beauty pageants in Belize,
Wilk discovered that the migration of beauty pageants to the Caribbean could not
be said to have led to homogeneity since the participants strongly stressed their
national and individual differences. Nevertheless, Wilk argues that they have learned
to assert their distinctiveness through a common medium, the beauty pageants, and
their distinctiveness is therefore framed within global structures of common difference. 'The global stage', argues Wilk (1995: 111), 'does not consist of common
content, a lexicon of goods or knowledge. Instead it is a common set of formats
and structures that mediate between cultures; something more than a flow of things,
or of the meanings attached to things, or even the channels along which those things
and meanings flow.' Such formats and structures 'put diversity in a common frame,
and scale it along a limited number of dimensions, celebrating some kinds of difference and submerging others'. Thus, there is indeed greater heterogeneity, but it
is in the context of and, to a large extent, in response to the homogeneity of a
consumer culture. As Jonathan Friedman (1994: 211) points out, 'what appears

as disorganization and often real disorder is not any the less systemic and systematic'.

Consumer culture is one of the primary forces that both propels increased heterogeneity and channels it into common differences. A global consumer culture encourages glocalization, hybridization and diversity because the local provides a valuable resource for our supra-local exchanges and therefore leads to increased heterogeneity of content along with homogeneity of form. Robertson recognizes this:

> Global capitalism both promotes and is conditioned by cultural homogeneity and cultural heterogeneity. The production and consolidation of difference and variety is an essential ingredient of contemporary capitalism, which is, in any case, increasingly involved with a growing variety of micro-markets (national-cultural, racial and ethnic; general; social-stratificational; and so on). At the same time micromarketing takes place within the contexts of increasingly universal-global economic practices. (Robertson 1992: 173)

The connection between micro-marketing and global heterogeneity should not be a surprise since the very term glocalization, so pervasive in globalization scholarship, began as 'one of the main marketing buzzwords of the beginning of the nineties' (Tulloch 1991: 134). In addition, critics of the use of hybridity in postcolonial studies have strongly pointed out its connection to consumer capitalism (Ahmad 1995). Hutnyk (2000: 36) reminds us, 'Hybridity and difference sell; the market remains intact.'

Global culture seems to track the trend among global consumer goods that marketers have already recognized. Although there are some global brands, one business analyst observed that this 'does not mean that there is a global consumer for companies to target. International cultural differences are by no means disappearing and, in the late twentieth century, individualism is as strong a world force as internationalism. Consumer goods are becoming more, rather than less, focused on the individual' (Fitzgerald 1997: 742). Robertson (1992: 46) also makes this connection: 'global marketing requires, in principle, that each product or service requires calculated sensitivity to local circumstances, identities, practices and so on'. However, the individuals focused on by global marketing are, as one business leader put it, 'heteroconsumers'. 'People who've become increasingly alike and indistinct from one another, and yet have simultaneously varied and multiple preferences' (Levitt 1988: 8). Not only do traditions become glocalized as an 'invention of tradition' (Hobsbawm and Ranger 1983) to appeal to the consumer tastes of tourists, but identity itself becomes a form of consumption shaped by a global consumer culture.

> Every social and cultural movement is a consumer or at least must define itself in relation to the world of goods as a non-consumer. Consumption within the bounds of the world system is always a consumption of identity, canalized by a negotiation between self-definition and the array of possibilities offered by the capitalist market. (Friedman 1994: 104)

Even the resistance to global homogenization has assumed this same homogenization of form. The products of global consumer culture are resisted, but always through a form of consumption. Axford (1995: 160), for example, notes that, 'in France the relative artistic merits of the motion-picture version of *Germinal* versus those of *Robocop* have been thematized as a defence of indigenous national culture versus the shallowness and meretriciousness of Americanized global cultures'. We see a similar effect in the marketing of such soft drinks as Mecca Cola and Qibla Cola, which target the European Muslim community and position themselves as an expression of anti-Americanization (Hundley 2003). The idea is that individuals are to express their contempt for America and its associated consumer society through the consumption of products that are produced, packaged and marketed in a way that is deeply dependent on consumer culture. Likewise, Foster (2002) describes the people of Papua New Guinea as using consumption to create a local identity in opposition to the identity attached to global brands. In these and many other cases, the homogenization of consumer culture is resisted by consumption, itself a form of homogenization (Goodman 2004).

Our new definition of culture allows us to see that homogeneity and heterogeneity within consumer culture are not contradictory. Instead, these common differences constitute the system of global culture. Consumer practices create and reproduce this system. Consumption provides opportunities for meaningful expression as well as resources for identity and social position. In addition, consumption structures a cultural field within which struggle and contestation occurs.

COMMODIFICATION OF CULTURE

One of the most prominent features of global consumer culture is its propensity to transform other cultures into commodities or resources for commodities. Anthony Smith describes this relation between consumer commodities and culture:

> Standardized, commercialized mass commodities will nevertheless draw for their contents upon revivals of traditional, folk or national motifs and styles in fashions, furnishings, music and the arts, lined out of their original contexts and anaesthetized. So that a global culture would operate at several levels simultaneously: as a cornucopia of standardized commodities, as a patchwork of denationalized ethnic or folk motifs, as a series of generalized 'human values and interests', as a uniform 'scientific' discourse of meaning, and finally as the interdependent system of communications which forms the material base for all the other components and levels. (Smith 1990: 176)

Strangely, Smith uses this insight to argue against the existence of a global culture, which only underlines the importance of our reconceptualization of culture. For Smith (1990: 177), consumer culture cannot be a real culture because it is not attached to a locality and history and because it is a patchwork of decontextualized elements. Once we realize that all cultures are patchworks; that no culture is ever homogenous; and that many cultures have fabricated their history, then we must look elsewhere for evidence of culture. We can see indications of culture in Smith's description of the hierarchy of levels of meaning, interdependent system of communications and the standardized form of its diversity.

Cultural difference becomes a resource for consumer culture, which draws upon diverse cultures for its ever-changing, new-and-improved content. Yúdice

(2003: 3–4) notes that 'Culture is invested in, distributed in the most inclusive ways, used as an attraction for capital development and tourism, as the prime motor of the culture industries and as an inexhaustible kindling for new industries dependent on intellectual property.' Despite its appetite for diversity, consumer culture demands that this diversity take standardized forms and genres.

> What becomes increasingly 'globalized' is not so much concrete cultural contents (although global distribution does bring, say, the same movies to many dispersed locals), but, more importantly and more structurally, the parameters and infrastructure which determine the conditions of existence for local cultures. (Ang 1996: 153)

Taylor (2000) describes how exotic musical elements from diverse cultures are appropriated and used as background for television advertisements. Wood (2000) describes the transformation of the daily lives of Zapotec weavers as they adapt to the consumer demands of tourists and international art markets. Little (2000) illustrates how private households can be transformed into public stages to exhibit and perform Mayan culture for tourists. And even the history of colonial repression and tribal resistance becomes staged as a tourist attraction (Bruner and Kirshenblatt-Gimblett 1994). Not only do cultures provide resources for consumer forms, but the culture itself becomes a signifier for consumption. For example, Edmondson (1999) describes how the cosmetics company, L'Oreal, uses different cultures – Italian elegance, New York savvy and French beauty – to distinguish its different lines. In old theories of modernization and development, culture was what stood in the way of modernization. Now culture is seen as a resource, if not for accomplishing modernization, at least as a chit to be traded in a global system for more material needs.

These effects demonstrate the remarkable power of consumer culture and further indicate why a reconceptualization of culture is so necessary. Indeed, Daniel Miller (1995) argues that the limited definition of culture has prevented anthropologists from recognizing the importance of consumption:

> as long as there was an explicit or even implicit culture concept as a definitional premise of anthropology, then consumption not only did not, but in a profound sense could not, arise within the discipline. It lay too close to the usually unstated core justification for the project of anthropology as the establishment of an 'other' constituted by holistic and unfragmented culture against which modernity – that is the form of society from which the anthropologist had come, could be judged as loss. (Miller 1995: 265)

If culture is understood as homogeneity or essential difference, we miss the protean effects of consumer culture. Within the context of consumer culture, cultural elements represent an individual choice in a cultural supermarket to be mixed and matched to suit our individual style. These cultural resources and individual choices are connected in a global system of meaning that is created and reproduced through the practices of consumption. This global system of common difference must be the starting point for any understanding of the relation between globalization and consumer culture.

Theoretical Approaches to Global Consumer Culture

Globalization cannot be understood without the category of consumption. Practically every analysis of globalization has recognized consumption, but only a few have made consumption an explicit part of their theory. In the discussion above, I have drawn on some of the theories that have focused on the connection between consumer culture and globalization. It is also useful to summarize four of the most important theories.

Leslie Sklair (1991) was one of the first to propose a theory of globalization that put consumer culture at the centre. Sklair forcefully argued for the need of a transnational or global approach to replace a state-centred one. He proposed transnational practices as the proper focus for a sociology of the global system, categorizing those practices into three levels: the economic level represented by the transnational corporation; the political level represented by a transnational capitalist class; and the most innovative part of his theory, the culture-ideology of consumerism. It is consumerism that is 'the nuts and bolts and the glue that hold the system together' (1991: 95).

The culture-ideology of consumerism is characterized by a belief that 'the meaning of life is to be found in the things that we possess. To consume, therefore, is to be fully alive, and to remain fully alive we must continuously consume' (Sklair 1998: 197). Sklair's focus on consumerism as a culture moved the analysis away from the homogenization of products towards a focus on the spread of a cultural system of desires. Sklair was one of the first to realize that a global consumer culture depends on commodification and the particular thing that is commodified is irrelevant.

Within this culture, people see themselves and others primarily as consumers rather than as citizens, and political action is reduced to providing the resources for consumption. Nevertheless, consumer culture has tremendous political effects including, Sklair argued, the fall of the Soviet Union. Resisting globalization is much more difficult than resisting American homogenization. Because of globalization's dependence on consumer culture, the counter movement to globalization must reject consumerism, a difficult proposition to 'sell'.

A second theorist who has dealt with the relation between consumer culture and globalization is Néstor García Canclini. Mixing theory with ethnographic research, García Canclini has examined the effect that globalization has had on handicrafts and fiestas (1993) and on art, literature, music and urban culture (1995). García Canclini argues that globalization is not characterized by homogenization, but by fragmentation and recomposition into hybrid cultural forms. These hybrid forms help to subvert such accepted dichotomies as native/foreign, high/popular, art/craft and traditional/modern. García Canclini points to the deep effect of such hybrids. 'Just as our commodities are manufactured with diverse parts from foreign places, so is our culture and, to that extent, our identities' (2001).

García Canclini argues that 'consumption is good for thinking'. Consumption is one way for people to make sense of the world by wearing objects, displaying them in homes and communicating with them. Interpretive communities of consumers ('ensembles of people who share tastes and interpretive pacts in relation to certain commodities') are replacing old groupings based on nations. A culture ordered by consumption is necessarily a global culture, since consumption now involves global trade. Consequently, our social and individual identities are constructed in relation to global processes of consumption.

For García Canclini, the most important focus of research should be on the relation between citizens and consumers. In a global consumer culture, the two roles are intertwined, so that consumption 'to a certain extent constitutes a new mode of being citizens' (2001: 26). Consumption in a consumer culture is not just the satisfaction of individual need, but rather participation in a complex socio-cultural interaction that apportions resources and produces relations of solidarity and distinction. Certainly, consumer choice is not the same as democratic participation, but people increasingly see consumption as a replacement for citizenship. The problem is that this new mode of social choice is dominated by for-profit corporations and no new models of consumer involvement have emerged that would provide a satisfactory replacement for citizen participation. 'If consumption has become a site from which it is difficult to think, this is the result of its capitulation to a supposedly free, or better yet ferocious, game of market laws' (2001: 45). However, for García Canclini, the political effects of a global consumer society are not yet determined. Interpretative communities of consumers may provide the basis for a kind of citizen participation.

If García Canclini is still optimistic about an emerging global consumer culture, Benjamin Barber (1995) is less so. Barber recognizes the twin trends of homogeneity and heterogeneity in a globalizing world, but he sees little hope in either of them. He calls the homogenizing trend McWorld – a consumer oriented capitalist global culture. He calls the heterogenizing trend Jihad, and means by this the particularizing force of religious, ethnic and tribal separatism. Neither is good for democracy. McWorld weakens the nation-states which Barber argues are the only vehicles for democratic citizenship. Jihad is an exclusionary and reactionary development with fanatical authoritarian tendencies.

McWorld once held the promise of undermining political extremism by spreading democratic ideals and making isolation impossible. Barber admits that McWorld has indeed eliminated isolationism, as well as spread economic and political stability, but it has also spread an inescapable message of 'secularism, passivity, consumerism, vicariousness, impulse buying, and an accelerated pace of life' (1995: 60). It has replaced nations with 'one homogenous global theme park, one McWorld tied together by communications, information, entertainment, and commerce' (1995: 4). But the consumer freedoms promised by McWorld are not the same as democratic ideals. The response of markets to individual consumer choices cannot take into account social needs. To make matters worse, the reigning neoliberal, laissez-faire ideology of McWorld paints any attempt by nations to defend themselves from the excesses of McWorld as anti-democratic.

Barber argues that McWorld cannot fulfil democratic ideals, but it often does not even deliver its promised consumer paradise:

> With a few global conglomerates controlling what is created, who distributes it, where it is shown, and how it is subsequently licensed for further use, the very idea of a genuinely competitive market in ideas or images disappears and the singular virtue that

markets indisputably have over democratic command structures – the virtue of that cohort of values associated with pluralism and variety, contingency and accident, diversity and spontaneity – is vitiated. (Barber 1995: 89)

What Barber calls 'Jihad' is a backlash against McWorld. By Jihad, he does not mean to indicate only, or even primarily, the Islamic reaction, but any of the 'communities of blood rooted in exclusion and hatred'. Jihad begins by promising the soul that is missing in McWorld, but ends up promoting intolerance and hatred.

Although McWorld and Jihad are in seeming opposition, Barber argues that the two forces are complementary. McWorld and Jihad feed off one another. McWorld opposes the state in favour of the global and Jihad opposes the state in favour of the tribal. Both are opposed to the democratic participation of citizens. McWorld needs Jihad to provide the sense of belonging and identity that is missing in the global market. Jihad needs McWorld's technological advances to be able to organize. This is why Barber argues that it is not really Jihad vs McWorld, but Jihad *and* McWorld or even Jihad *through* McWorld.

Unlike García Canclini, Barber sees consumers and citizens as innately in conflict. 'Capitalism seeks consumers susceptible to the shaping of their needs and the manipulation of their wants, while democracy needs citizens autonomous in their thoughts and independent in their deliberative judgments' (1995: 15). This is what makes Barber's analysis so pessimistic and his suggested alternatives so unrealistic.

Neither as optimistic as García Canclini nor as pessimistic as Barber, George Ritzer's (2004) theory reveals both threatening and promising trends in globalization. Ritzer dissects the categories of homogeneity and heterogeneity into two sets of oppositions: nothing vs something and glocalization vs grobalization. 'Nothing' refers to those things that are the true products of homogenization. It is not American culture that is being disseminated, but a nothing culture of centrally conceived and controlled forms devoid of any distinctive substantive content. Something is just the opposite: those distinctive things that are conceived and controlled locally.

Usefully, Ritzer separates the things themselves from the processes of globalization. Glocalization we already know, but Ritzer introduces another, and in many ways opposed, process: grobalization. In contrast to the power of the local in glocalization, Ritzer recognizes the power of capitalist enterprises to impose their cultural objects on the local. Using these terms, we can see that what has been called homogenization in the globalization literature is the grobalization of nothing: the profit-driven spread of a centrally conceived and controlled standardized culture. Whereas, what has been called heterogeneity is the glocalization of something.

Ritzer accepts the inevitability of globalization, but he sees its human impact as still undetermined. He discusses positive and negative consequences of the grobalization of nothing, as well as the possibilities for new forms of heterogeneity. For the latter, glocalization may increase, or there is the possibility that profit-driven businesses will be induced to distribute indigenously conceived and controlled objects with distinctive cultural properties. In any case, the future, according to Ritzer, belongs to the consumer, although he doubts that any of us will be happy with the world that our consumption is creating. There is no place in Ritzer's theory for

Barber's oppositional citizen or even for García Canclini's explorations of the new possibilities for citizenship through consumption.

Each of these theorists provides a new perspective on a global consumer culture. They also provide the sensitizing concepts that will guide further research. The culture-ideology of consumerism, hybridity, McWorld and grobalization are as much conceptual tools as they are empirical facts. And, indeed, this is equally true of global consumer culture. The way in which we understand the history of globalization, its current state and its feared or welcome future depends as much on our theoretical framework as on the facts on the ground. This realization should not lead to nihilistic scepticism, but to a recognition of the power of theories to revision our history, reframe the present and open up new alternatives for the future.

CONCLUSION

None of the above is an argument that there is now a global consumer culture. It may exist, but that is a question that requires a great deal more research. Instead, this chapter means to clear away some of the conceptual difficulties that hinder our ability to determine whether there is a global consumer culture. It is useless to sit in our armchairs and theorize about the state of the world. But it is equally useless to look for evidence of a global consumer culture, when we don't know the meaning of the phrase. The theoretical argument here is that to the extent that there is a global culture, it will be a consumer culture. This theory is meant to direct the empirical investigation to the underlying practices that would give rise to such a culture.

Nevertheless, it is clear that the extent of a consumer culture will always be limited. Consumption requires money and in the current state of the world and for the foreseeable future much of humanity will not have the money to actively participate in a global consumer culture. This, of course, does not mean that the poor will be absolutely barred from participation, but it will be as spectators who are invited to admire the seductive goods through the window of a locked door. And, indeed, this may be one of the primary sources of the Jihad that Barber warns of.

It will also take more research to understand the consequence of a global consumer culture. Many intellectuals assume it will be deleterious, but we mostly rail from within the belly of the beast. It could be nothing more than the complaint of a tourist that the picturesque poverty has been replaced by a Western-style prosperity. We should not forget the benefits of a consumer culture. Rational people want material goods and there is nothing ignoble about that. Societies driven by consumption have fed more people, clothed more people and housed more people than any in history. But neither should we ignore the disadvantages of a consumer society. The freedom of the individual consumer has limited the freedom of the community. The societies that have fed, clothed and housed people have also damaged the environment and created more trash than any others in history.

If we wish to place limits on a global consumer culture, it will take, not just more empirical research, but the development of better theories. A culture's dependence on everyday practices and its implicit, taken-for-granted core demands a theory that will analytically separate what is practically conjoined, that will make explicit what is implicit and that will provide alternatives for what seems natural or inevitable. The theories that we have looked at here have pointed us to the sites for empirical research. It is likely that further theories will point us to sites for social action.

Note

1 There is a third meaning of culture which is the set of symbolic objects produced by explicitly cultural industries (Goodman 2005). While this definition has provided a productive framework for work in the sociology of culture, especially the 'production of culture' approach, it has had little or no impact on the study of global culture.

References

Ahmad, A. 1995. 'The politics of literary postcoloniality', *Race and Class*, 36, 1–20.

Albrow, M. 1996. *The Global Age: State and Society Beyond Modernity*. Stanford, CA: Stanford University Press.

Ang, I. 1996. *Living Room Wars: Rethinking Media Audiences for a Postmodern World*. New York: Routledge.

Appadurai, A. 1996. *Modernity at Large: Cultural Dimensions of Globalization*. Minneapolis: University of Minnesota Press.

Axford, B. 1995. *The Global System: Economics, Politics and Culture*. Cambridge: Polity Press.

Barber, B. 1995. *Jihad vs. McWorld*. New York: Times Books.

Benedict, R. 1934. *Patterns of Culture*. New York: Houghton Mifflin.

Berger P. 1997. 'The four faces of global culture', *National Interest*, 49, 23–9.

Biltereyst, D. and Meers, P. 2000. 'The international telenovela debate and the contra-flow argument: A reappraisal', *Media, Culture & Society*, 22, 393–413.

Bourdieu, P. 1991. *Language and Symbolic Power*. Cambridge, MA: Harvard University Press.

Bruner, E. and Kirshenblatt-Gimblett, B. 1994. 'Maasai on the lawn: Tourist realism in East Africa', *Cultural Anthropology*, 9, 435–70.

Caldwell, M. 2004. 'Domesticating the French Fry: McDonald's and consumerism in Moscow', *Journal of Consumer Culture*, 4, 5–26.

Clifford, J. 1988. *The Predicament of Culture: Twentieth-Century Ethnography, Literature, and Art*. Cambridge, MA: Harvard University Press.

Crane, D. 1992. *The Production of Culture: Media and the Urban Arts*. Newbury Park, CA: Sage.

Edmondson, G. 1999. 'The beauty of global branding', *Business Week*, 28 June, 70–5.

Featherstone, M. 1990. 'Global culture: An introduction'. In M. Featherstone (ed.), *Global Culture: Nationalism, Globalization and Modernity*, 3–14. London: Sage.

Featherstone, M. 1996. *Undoing Culture: Globalization, Postmodernism and Identity*. London: Sage.

Fine, G.A. 1996. *Kitchens: The Culture of Restaurant Work*. Berkeley: University of California Press.

Fitzgerald, N. 1997. 'Harnessing the potential of globalization for the consumer and citizen', *International Affairs*, 73, 739–46.

Foster, R. 1991. 'Making national cultures in the global ecumene', *Annual Review of Anthropology*, 20, 235–60.

Foster, R. 2002. *Materializing the Nation: Commodities, Consumption, and Media in Papua New Guinea*. Bloomington: Indiana University Press.

Franco, J. 1993. 'Border patrol', *Travesia*, 3, 134–42.

Friedman, J. 1994. *Cultural Identity and Global Process*. London: Sage.

Friedman J. 2002. 'Champagne liberals and the new "dangerous classes": Reconfigurations of class, identity, and cultural production in the contemporary global system', *Social Analysis*, 46, 33–57.

Frow, J. 2000. 'Public domain and the new world order in knowledge', *Social Semiotics*, 10, 173–85.

García Canclini, N. 1993. *Transforming Modernity: Popular Culture in Mexico*. Minneapolis: University of Minnesota Press.

García Canclini, N. 1995. *Hybrid Cultures: Strategies for Entering and Leaving Modernity*. Minneapolis: University of Minnesota Press.

García Canclini, N. 2001. *Consumers and Citizens: Globalization and Multicultural Conflicts*. Minneapolis: University of Minnesota Press.

Geertz, C. 2000. *Available Light: Anthropological Reflections on Philosophical Topics*. Princeton, NJ: Princeton University Press.

Giddens, A. 2000. *Runaway World: How Globalization Is Reshaping our Lives*. New York: Routledge.

Gilpin, R. 1987. *The Political Economy of International Relations*. Princeton, NJ: Princeton University Press.

Goodman, D. 2004. 'Consumption as a social problem'. In G. Ritzer (ed.), *International Handbook of Social Problems*, 226–45. London: Sage.

Goodman, D. 2005. 'Culture as an autopoietic system'. Paper presented at the annual meeting of the American Sociological Association.

Guillen, M. 2001. 'Is globalization civilizing, destructive or feeble? A critique of five key debates in the social science literature', *Annual Review of Sociology*, 27, 235–60.

Hannerz, U. 1990. 'Cosmopolitans and locals in world culture'. In M. Featherstone (ed.), *Global Culture: Nationalism, Globalization and Modernity*, 237–51. London: Sage.

Hannerz, U. 1992. *Cultural Complexity: Studies in the Social Organization of Meaning*. New York: Columbia University Press.

Hannerz, U. 1996. *Transnational Connections: Culture, People, Places*. London: Routledge.

Hirst, P. and Thompson, G. 1996. *Globalization in Question*. Cambridge: Polity Press.

Hobsbawm, E. and Ranger, T. 1983. *The Invention of Tradition*. Cambridge: Cambridge University Press,

Holton, R. 2000. 'Globalization's cultural consequences', *Annals, AAPSS*, 570, 140–52.

Hundley, T. 2003. 'Foreign cola knockoffs offer anti-American political flavor', *Chicago Tribune*, 2 February, B1.

Hunter, J. and Yates, J. 2002. 'The world of American globalizers'. In P.L. Berger and S.P. Huntington (eds), *Many Globalizations: Cultural Diversity in the Contemporary World*, 323–57. Oxford: Oxford University Press.

Hutnyk, J. 2000. *Critique of Exotica: Music, Politics and the Culture Industry*. London: Pluto Press.

Illouz, E. and John, N. 2003. 'Global habitus, local stratification, and symbolic struggles over identity: The case of McDonald's Israel', *American Behavioral Scientist*, 47, 201–29.

Jameson, F. 1998. 'Preface'. In F. Jameson and M. Miyoshi (eds), *The Cultures of Globalization*, xi–xvii. Durham, NC: Duke University Press.

Keesing, R. 1994. 'Theories of culture revisited'. In R. Borofsky (ed.), *Assessing Cultural Anthropology*, 301–10. New York: McGraw-Hill.

Kroeber, A.L. and Kluckhohn, C. 1952. *Culture: A Critical Review of Concepts and Definitions*. New York: Meridian Books.

Levitt, T. 1988. 'The pluralization of consumption', *Harvard Business Review*, 2, 7–8.

Little, W. 2000. 'Home as a place of exhibition and performance: Mayan household transformations in Guatemala', *Ethnology*, 39, l63–81.

McLuhan, M. 1964. *Understanding Media: The Extensions of Man*. New York: McGraw-Hill.

Marcuse, H. 1968. 'The affirmative character of culture'. In J.J. Shapiro (trans.), *Negations: Essays in Critical Theory*, 88–133. Boston: Beacon Press.

Mazzarella, W. 2004. 'Culture, globalization, mediation', *Annual Review of Anthropology*, 33, 345–67.

Merton, R.K. 1949. *Social Theory and Social Structure*. Glencoe, IL: The Free Press.

Miller, D. 1995. 'Consumption studies as the transformation of anthropology'. In D. Miller (ed.), *Acknowledging Consumption: A Review of New Studies*, 264–95. New York: Routledge.

Miller, D. 1998. 'Coca-Cola: A black sweet drink from Trinidad'. In D. Miller (ed.), *Material Cultures: Why Some Things Matter*, 169–87. Chicago: University of Chicago Press.

Mlinar, Z. 1992. 'Individuation and globalization: The transformation of territorial social organization'. In Z. Mlinar (ed.), *Globalisation and Territorial Identities*, 15–34. Aldershot: Avebury.

Morley, H.D. 1991. 'Where the global meets the local: Notes from the sitting room', *Screen*, 32, 1–23.

Nederveen Pieterse, J. 1995. 'Globalization as hybridization'. In M. Featherstone et al. (eds), *Global Modernities*, 45–68. London: Sage.

Nederveen Pieterse, J. 2004. *Globalization and Culture: Global Mélange*. Lanham, MD: Rowman and Littlefield.

Ritzer, G. 2000. *The McDonaldization of Society*. Thousand Oaks, CA: Pine Forge Press.

Ritzer, G. 2004. *The Globalization of Nothing*. Thousand Oaks, CA: Pine Forge Press.

Robertson, R. 1992. *Globalization: Social Theory and Global Culture*. London: Sage.

Robertson, R. 1995. 'Glocalization: Time-space and homogeneity-heterogeneity'. In M. Featherstone et al. (eds), *Global Modernities*, 25-44. London: Sage.

Rosenau, J. 2003. *Distant Proximities: Dynamics beyond Globalization*. Princeton, NJ: Princeton University Press.

Sewell, W. 1999. 'The concept(s) of culture'. In V. Bonnell and L. Hunt (eds), *Beyond the Cultural Turn*, 35–61. Berkeley: University of California Press.

Sklair, L. 1991. *Sociology of the Global System*. Baltimore, MD: The Johns Hopkins University Press.

Sklair, L. 1998. 'Social movements and global capitalism'. In F. Jameson and M. Miyoshi (eds), *The Cultures of Globalization*, 291–311. Durham, NC: Duke University Press.

Smith, A. 1990. 'Towards a global culture'. In M. Featherstone (ed.), *Global Culture: Nationalism, Globalization and Modernity*, 171–92. London: Sage.

Smith, A. 1995. *Nations and Nationalism in a Global Era*. Cambridge: Polity Press.

Steger, M. 2002. *Globalism: The New Market Ideology*. Lanham, MD: Rowman & Littlefield.

Street, J. 1994. 'Political culture: From civic culture to mass culture', *British Journal of Political Science*, 24, 95–113.

Swidler, A. 1986. 'Culture in action: Symbols and strategies', *American Sociological Review*, 51, 273–86.

Taylor, T. 2000. 'World music in television ads', *American Music*, 18, 162–92.

Tomlinson, J. 1991. *Cultural Imperialism: A Critical Introduction*. Baltimore, MD: The Johns Hopkins University Press.

Tomlinson, J. 1997. 'Internationalism, globalization and cultural imperialism'. In K. Thompson (ed.), *Media and Cultural Regulation*, 117–62. London: Sage.

Tulloch, S. (compiler). 1991. *The Oxford Dictionary of New Words*. Oxford: Oxford University Press.

Wallerstein, I. 1990. 'Culture as the ideological battleground of the modern world-system'. In M. Featherstone (ed.), *Global Culture: Nationalism, Globalization and Modernity*, 31–56. London: Sage.

Wallerstein, I. 1991. *Geopolitics and Geoculture*. Cambridge: Cambridge University Press.

Waters, M. 1995. *Globalization*. New York: Routledge.

Webner, P. 1997 'Introduction'. In P. Werbner and T. Modood (eds), *Debating Cultural Hybridity*, 1–26. London: Zed Books.

Wilk, R. 1995. 'Learning to be local in Belize'. In D. Miller (ed.), *Worlds Apart: Modernity through the Prism*, 110–33. New York: Routledge.

Williams, R. 1983. *Culture and Society: 1780–1950*. New York: Columbia University Press.

Wolf, E. 1997. *Europe and the People without History*. Berkeley: University of California Press.

Wolff, J. 1997. 'The global and the specific'. In A.D. King (ed.), *Culture, Globalization and the World-System: Contemporary Conditions for the Representation of Identity*, 161–74. Minneapolis: University of Minnesota Press.

Wood, W.W. 2000. 'Flexible production, households, and fieldwork: Multi-sited Zapotec weavers in the era of late capitalism', *Ethnology*, 39, 133–48.

Wuthnow, R. 1987. *Meaning and Moral Order: Explorations in Cultural Analysis*. Berkeley: University of California Press.

Yoon, S.-K. 2001. 'Working up a thirst to quench Asia', *Far Eastern Economic Review*, 164, 34–6.

Yúdice, G. 2003. *The Expediency of Culture: Uses of Culture in the Global Era*. Durham, NC: Duke University Press.

Further reading

Featherstone, M. 1990. 'Global culture: An introduction'. In M. Featherstone (ed.), *Global Culture: Nationalism, Globalization and Modernity*, 3–14. London: Sage.

García Canclini, N. 2001. *Consumers and Citizens: Globalization and Multicultural Conflicts*. Minneapolis: University of Minnesota Press.

Goodman, D. 2004. 'Consumption as a social problem'. In G. Ritzer (ed.), *International Handbook of Social Problems*, 226–45. London: Sage.

Nederveen Pieterse, J. 1995. 'Globalization as hybridization'. In M. Featherstone et al. (eds), *Global Modernities*, 45–68. London: Sage.

Wilk, R. 1995. 'Learning to be local in Belize'. In D. Miller (ed.), *Worlds Apart: Modernity through the Prism*, 110–33. New York: Routledge.

Chapter 17

Cultural Globalization

JOHN TOMLINSON

THE RELATIONSHIP BETWEEN GLOBALIZATION AND CULTURE

It may seem a rather obvious point to begin with, but to understand the meaning and character of 'cultural globalization' we first have to understand some defining features of the two constituent terms. So let's begin with globalization.

Virtually every serious scholar today would accept the broad general proposition that globalization is a *multidimensional* process, taking place simultaneously within the spheres of the economy, of politics, of technological developments – particularly media and communications technologies – of environmental change and of culture. One simple way of defining globalization, without giving precedence or causal primacy to any one of these dimensions, is to say that it is a complex, accelerating, integrating process of *global connectivity*. Understood in this rather abstract, general way, globalization refers to the rapidly developing and ever-densening network of interconnections and interdependencies that characterize material, social, economic and cultural life in the modern world. At its most basic, globalization is quite simply a description of these networks and of their implications: of the 'flows' around them – and across international boundaries – of virtually everything that characterizes modern life: flows of capital, commodities, people, knowledge, information and ideas, crime, pollution, diseases, fashions, beliefs, images and so forth.

This increasing connectivity is, in many ways, an obvious aspect of our lives. It is something we can all of us – at least if we live in the more developed parts of the world – recognize in everyday routine actions and experiences. Connectivity pretty much defines our use of communications technologies – mobile phones, computers, e-mail, the Internet – but it is also characteristic of the urban environments most of us inhabit and it increasingly influences the way we earn our living, the styles of food we eat, the music, cinema and television that forms our entertainment, and our experience of mobility and travel. It also forms the backdrop to all manner of social and material anxieties and perplexities that characterize everyday modern life: from the shadow cast by terrorist attacks to worries over global warming, influenza pandemics or how fluctuations in the global economy are likely to affect our job security, our taxes or the interest payments on our home loans. In all these ways, it is quite clear that we are living in a much more globally connected world today than even 20 years ago, and in longer historical terms the level of global inter-dependence is without precedent.

So understanding globalization as a generalized process of increasing connected-ness helps us to keep in mind the multidimensional *complexity* of the process. But there nonetheless remain a good many tacit assumptions as to the relative impor-tance of each of these dimensions. And it is clear that chief amongst these assump-tions is that it is the *economic* sphere, the institution of the global capitalist market, that is the crucial element, the *sine qua non* of global connectivity. This is the dimen-sion that dominates the imagination and the language of corporate business, of politicians and of anti-globalization activists alike; it is the easy shorthand of the media discourse which forms most ordinary people's immediate understanding of what globalization is all about.

There is no escaping the global dominance of the capitalist system and there is little to be gained by cultural analysts from understating its huge significance. But, having said this, we must resist the temptation to attribute it with causal primacy in the globalization process. There are several reasons for this, but here I will only mention two. First, because we are not dealing with straightforward empirical judg-ments about what specific practices drive everything else, but also with questions of the constitution of analytical categories: to what extent are economic practices also, intrinsically, *cultural* ones? Plausible answers to this question range between 'some-what' and 'entirely'. What is *not* plausible – despite the constant rhetorical gestures of politicians towards the 'hard economic realities' – is the assumption that the realm of the economic is that of a machine-like system operating independent of the wishes, desires and aspirations of human agents, and thus entirely outside of the influence of culture. So the first reason to resist the temptation to economic reductionism is that it operates on an unrealistically narrow conception of the economic.

The second reason is that it distorts our understanding of the sphere of culture. Common expressions like 'the *impact* of globalization on culture' or 'the cultural *consequences* of globalization' contain a tacit assumption that globalization is a process which somehow has its sources and its terrain of operation *outside* of culture. One major reason why it seems natural to speak of globalization's 'impact' on culture is that global market processes – particularly the distribution of iconic consumer goods – are relatively easy to understand as having a potential influence on people's cultural experience. This, indeed, is at the core of the interpretation of cultural globalization as 'cultural imperialism', 'Americanization' or 'Westerniza-tion', or as the spread of a global capitalist-consumerist monoculture (Tomlinson 1991, 1999). In all such readings 'culture' seems to be a peculiarly inert category: something that people experience or imbibe but do not themselves produce or shape. Much has been written from the semiotic-hermeneutic perspective of cultural analy-sis in response to this deep misconception, demonstrating the active, transformative nature of the appropriation of cultural goods (Morley 1992; Thompson 1995; Lull 2000). But despite this critique, the idea of culture as being intrinsically *constitutive* of globalization – as being a dimension which has consequences for other domains – remains relatively obscure.

To clarify this, we have to probe a little more into the peculiarly complicated and often elusive concept of culture. 'Culture is not a power, something to which social events can be causally attributed' says Clifford Geertz (1973: 14) and this is surely right to the extent that we should think of cultural processes *primarily* as oriented towards the construction of socially shared meanings. If we were to ask the stark functional question, 'what is culture *for?*', the most satisfying answer is that it is to generate *meaning* in life. The need for 'meaning' is at the deep centre of the human condition, it is the cognitive-existential equivalent of the material needs for shelter and sustenance. Indeed it may be considered more than these, since people, in certain conditions, are willing to sacrifice these other needs to their convictions about the purpose and the good ends of existence. The shared stories – the 'narratives' – by which we render our existence meaningful, then, are, as it were, *ends in themselves* for culture. And this has, quite justly, shaped the way in which culture has been typically studied: as lived experience, as representation, as text and as context.

The notion of 'causality' sits awkwardly with this conceptualization. However, this does not mean to say that culture is not *consequential*. It is certainly so in that the practices and processes of meaning construction inform, inspire and direct individual and collective actions which are *themselves* consequential. Culture is thus not only 'a context in which [events] may be meaningfully interpreted' (Geertz 1973), it is *the* primordial context in which human agency arises and takes place. Cultural signification and interpretation constantly motivate and orient people, individually and collectively, towards particular choices and actions. Actions which may seem to be fairly instrumental ones, following a logic of practical or economic necessity, are nonetheless always undertaken within that set of self-understandings, plans, hopes or aspirations which we can think of as the constitutive elements of the individual's cultural 'lifeworld'. Even the most basic instrumental actions of satisfying bodily needs are not in this sense outside of culture: in certain circumstances – slimming, eating 'disorders' such as anorexia nervosa, religious fasting, political hunger strikes – the decision to eat or to starve is a *cultural* decision.

One useful way to think about the consequentiality of culture for globalization, then, is to grasp how culturally informed 'local' actions can have globalizing consequences. The 'moment of culture' in the shopping decisions of young people on Saturday afternoons – to buy this or that brand of jeans or training shoes or mobile phone – is one of self-representation, against a background narrative of appropriate cultural style: How do I want to be perceived? What cultural images do I want to conform to or contrast with? What do I value? What do I desire? These are not banal questions, even though we may judge consumerism incapable of providing satisfying answers. But neither are they questions that remain locked within the subjectivities of human beings. The answers to them are, as it were, *performative*. Consumer activity is, in micro, constitutive of the whole complex network of global market connectivity, having consequences not only for the employment of workers in distant parts of the world but, in respect of the natural resources consumed and the industrial processes entailed in their production, for the ecological fate of the planet. To borrow a term from Anthony Giddens (1990), cultural globalization involves the increasing 'reflexivity' of modern life: the systemic integration of myriad small individual actions into the workings of the social institutions which appear autonomously to govern our lives.

This is enough of a theoretical preamble. What I have emphasized here – because it is so fundamental to understanding the agenda of globalization from a cultural perspective – is that culture is a dimension in which globalization both has its effects and *simultaneously* is generated and shaped.

But now, moving to more concrete issues, we need to ask: what sort of shape is emerging?

A GLOBAL CULTURE?

One common speculation about the globalization process is that it will lead to a single global culture. This is only a speculation, but the reason it seems possible is that we can see the 'unifying' effects of connectivity in other spheres – particularly in the economic sphere where the tightly integrated system of the global market provides the model. And indeed, globalization in some of its aspects does have this general unifying character. Whereas it was in the past possible to understand social and economic processes and practices as a set of local, relatively 'independent' phenomena, globalization makes the world in many respects, to quote Roland Robertson (1992), a 'single place'. Obvious examples of this are the way in which nation-states are locked into a complex global capitalistic system which restricts their autonomy independently to order their economic affairs, or the now evident tendency for environmental effects of local industrial processes – for instance CFC emissions – rapidly to become global problems.

However, increasing global connectivity by no means *necessarily* implies that the world is becoming, in the widest sense, either economically or politically 'unified'. Despite its reach, few would dare to claim that the effects of globalization currently extend in any profound way to every single person or place on the planet, and speculation on its spread must surely be tempered by the many countervailing trends towards social, political and indeed cultural *division* that we see around us. This is a point that is frequently made in the field of development studies: what used to be called the 'Third World' clearly does not partake of the globalized economy or of globalized communications *in the same way* as the developed world. An overarching global economic system, it is true to say, is deeply influential in determining the fate of countries in Africa. But this is a far cry from saying that Africa is part of a single, unified world of economic prosperity and social and technological development. So we have to *qualify* the idea of globalization by saying that it is an *uneven* process – with areas of concentration and density of flow and other areas of neglect or even perhaps exclusion (Massey 1994). To this extent, globalization, it seems, is not quite global!

Despite all this, there persists, at least amongst some Western critics, a tendency to imagine globalization pushing us towards an all-encompassing 'global culture'. The most common way in which this is conceived is in the assumption that I mentioned earlier, that cultural globalization implies a form of cultural imperialism: the spread of Western capitalist – particularly American – culture to every part of the globe, and the consequent threat of a loss of distinct non-Western cultural traditions. What is feared here is the total domination of world cultures through the unopposed advance of iconic brands such as Disney, Coca-Cola, Marlboro,

Microsoft, Google, McDonald's, CNN, Nike and Starbucks. Globally marketed formulaic Hollywood movies, Western popular music genres and television formats appear to many as what the filmmaker Bernado Bertolucci once referred to as 'a kind of totalitarianism of culture'.

Much has been written in criticism of this anxiety and I don't want either to review or to add to this particular debate here. I will simply observe that the issue is incapable of resolution if we restrict analysis to the rather superficial issue of the global distribution of cultural goods. What is at stake for cultural analysis is not the (undoubted) capacity of Western corporations to command wide markets for their products around the world, but rather, the deeper cultural implications of this capacity. We have to be careful not to confuse mere cultural goods with the *practice* of culture itself – which involves the interpretation and the appropriation of meanings in relation to such goods. Eating McDonald's hamburgers, smoking Marlboro cigarettes, drinking Coke and playing computer games may be bad for you in all sorts of ways. But they do not in themselves provide much solid evidence of a capitulation to deeper Western cultural values.

Indeed, one of the inescapable implications of the current wave of anti-Western feeling in large parts of the Muslim world is precisely the demonstration of the resilience of cultural *opposition* to (certain, not all, of) these values. Just as we have witnessed a ratcheting up, since the events of 11 September 2001 and then the invasion of Iraq, in the neo-conservative rhetoric of a self-conscious project of US cultural-political global hegemony, there has been inescapable evidence – some of it violent, bloody and destructive, but much of it peaceful – of a rejection of this project. Without being drawn too deeply into these perplexing issues, we can at least see that the vision of Western liberal-capitalist consumer culture sweeping all before it is severely chastened by this cultural opposition. What the connectivity of globalization is doing is bringing quite disparate cultures into closer contact – by no means inevitably as a 'clash of civilizations' (Huntington 1996) – but certainly involving contending definitions of what the good, the virtuous and the dignified life involves. What globalization is clearly *not* doing, however, if it is doing this, is effortlessly installing Western culture as global culture.

A different way of approaching these issues is to view contemporary globalization in the context of a much longer historical context in which societies and cultures have imagined the world as a single place, with their own culture at the centre of it. This sort of imagination has been a consistent feature of the founding narratives of cultural collectivities – particularly of faith communities – and we can learn something appropriate to the contemporary situation from a brief consideration of a couple of historical examples.

The first comes from long before the current phase of globalizing modernity, in fact from thirteenth-century Europe. It is not a conventional cultural text, or a body of ideas associated with a particular thinker. It is a much more direct representation of the world: a map.

The Ebstorf Mappa Mundi, made in *c*.1284, is attributed to the English cartographer Gervase of Tilbury. It is typical of early medieval European world maps, in being a mixture of eo-topography and theology. The sources of this cartographic imagination are complex, with influences from Aristotelian notions of form, and from the more directly topographical style of Roman imperial maps. The map shows the world as round and with some recognizable features of the known physical world (that is, Europe) but without the familiar pattern of continents divided by oceans. Instead the land mass is roughly divided into three parts by rivers, and set within an encircling sea. But what is most striking is the complete domination of the representation by elements of Christian theology. Jerusalem – the Holy City – is placed at the centre, whilst the orientation of the map places the east at the top where is also depicted the Garden of Eden – scene of the Christian God's creation of mankind. The tripartite division of the map is inspired by the biblical story of the repopulation of the earth after the Deluge by Noah's three sons Ham, Shem and Japheth. All of these elements obviously reinforce Christian myths of origin, and in so doing represent the world as *unified* within the faith of Christianity. However, most striking of all is the binding force of the figure of the crucified Christ – seen in the mappa mundi only in the head, hands and feet – literally embracing the world – giving it life – from the cross.

Here, then, we find a very early, pre-modern example of an imagined theologi-cally revealed 'globalism'. We may, of course, from our vantage point in history, smile indulgently on the rudimentary nature of the topography. Or, taking a more sophisticated perspective, we can understand it, within its historical-cultural context, as a different *order* of representation in which the sacred and the empirical are not so easily disentangled. But what we cannot mistake, given our modern relativizing sensibilities, is the entirely spurious nature of its universal pretensions. This is not *the world*, but *a world*: the imagined world of 'Christendom'.

The interesting point, however, is that this universalizing discourse has by no means disappeared with the sophistications of cultural modernity. Just as the medi-eval cartographer ignored (or in some cases, more precisely, was ignorant of) the rival claims of the non-Christian world – of the Islamic Ummah, of Buddhism or Confucianism for instance – so, many contemporary universalizing narratives seem to work by ignoring or, worse, denigrating cultural difference.

Some believe that this is peculiarly emphasized within the tradition of Christian-ity. Slavoj Žižek for instance argues:

> In other 'particularistic' religions (and even in Islam, in spite of its global expansion-ism), there is at least a place for others, they are tolerated, even if they are condescend-ingly looked upon. The Christian motto, 'all men are brothers', however, means also that, 'Those who are not my brothers are not men'. Christians usually praise themselves for overcoming the Jewish exclusivist notion of the Chosen People and encompassing all of humanity – the catch here is that, in their very insistence that they are the 'Chosen People' with the privileged direct link to God, Jews accept the humanity of the other people who celebrate their false gods, while Christian universalism tendentially excludes non-believers from the very universality of mankind. (Žižek 2001: 144)

Though Žižek may have a point here – at least at the level of Christian dogma – it would be foolish, of course, to suppose that the *practice* of all Christians is so exclusive. For on the liberal wing of Christian ecumenism there are clearly deep inclusivist sensibilities which shade into forms of internationalism sometimes barely distinguishable from secular humanism in their implicit terms of membership. Moreover, as Terry Eagleton reminds us, many other cultures, besides Christian ones, have denied the status of 'human beings' to strangers and so, 'One should not be ethnocentric about ethnocentricity' (Eagleton 2000: 57).

But the point I want to press is that this tendency towards unwarranted universalizing – what we might call particular cultures *masquerading* as universal ones – is not restricted either to religious worldviews or to 'pre-modern' cultures, but can be seen at the core of European Enlightenment rationality. From this source, it preserves the imagined projection of 'our world' into 'the world' as a core feature of Western cultural modernity. This privileging of the European cultural experience – along with its particular version of rationality and its cultural and political values – can be seen in 'cosmopolitan' thinkers from Kant onwards. It is Kant, indeed, who in his famous seminal text on cosmopolitanism not only looks back for his model to classical Greece and Rome, but forwards, speculatively, to a time when the continent of Europe, 'will probably legislate . . . for all the others' (Kant (1784) 'The idea of a universal history from a cosmopolitan point of view' – quoted in Derrida 2002: 7). But for my second example of a global imagination, I want to take a European thinker who, though taking something from the Kantian tradition, is arguably a more influential cosmopolitan and one closer, culturally, to our times.

Karl Marx's depiction of a future communist society provides what is perhaps the most vivid imagination of a global culture to be found in either nineteenth- or twentieth-century social thought. In the *Communist Manifesto* Marx and Engels present a bold vision of a future world in which the divisions of nations have disappeared, along with all other 'local' attachments, including those of religious belief. Communist society is a world with a universal language, a world literature and integrated cosmopolitan cultural tastes. In fact, Marx and Engels write in a way that seems to anticipate some defining features of the current globalization process:

> In the place of the old wants satisfied by the productions of the country, we find new wants, requiring for their satisfaction the products of distant lands and climes. In the place of the old local and national seclusion and self-sufficiency we have intercourse in every direction, universal interdependence of nations. . . . The intellectual creations of individual nations become common property. National one-sidedness and narrow-mindedness become more and more impossible and from the numerous national and local literatures there arises a world literature. (Marx and Engels 1969: 52–3)

But Marx combines this vision with a deeply Eurocentric attitude to other cultures. He welcomes the way in which the bourgeois era is sweeping away pre-modern 'civilizations', preparing the way for the coming socialist revolution and the communist era which, he insists, 'can only have a "world-historical" existence'. To achieve this radically cosmopolitan end, Marx is quite happy to see the destruction of non-European cultures. The *Manifesto* continues:

> The bourgeoisie, by the rapid improvement of all instruments of production, by the immensely facilitated means of communication, draws all, even the most barbarian, nations into civilization. The cheap prices of its commodities are the heavy artillery with which it batters down all Chinese walls, with which it forces the barbarians' intensely obstinate hatred of foreigners to capitulate. (1969: 53)

For the fact is that Marx was a convinced internationalist who despised national sentiments as reactionary forces in all societies, set against the cosmopolitan interests of the proletariat – the true and only 'workers of the world'. But, for all his many progressive views and the brilliance and percipience of his political-economy, his view of culture was firmly rooted in a European tradition which – following Kant, Hegel and others – unquestioningly took its *own* experience as the pattern for universal experience. Indeed, it might be argued that it was this Eurocentric cast of Marx's thought which led him to underestimate the enduring power and significance of ethnic and religious attachments (or their transformation into nationalism) in modernity. Marx's universalizing modernism was, in a curious way, as blind to cultural difference as the universalizing Christianity of the medieval mapmaker.

Marx's views, formed in the mid-nineteenth century, a similarly turbulent and dynamic period of global capitalist expansion to our own, remain relevant today – though not in the form that he might have imagined. For what he saw as an ultimately benign aspect of the progress of transnational capitalism – which he argues 'must nestle everywhere, settle everywhere, establish connections everywhere' – as an agent of historical change, appears to today's cultural critics as precisely the reverse. By contrast with contemporary neo-Marxists, who, in the main, tend towards the pessimistic, Marx appears as cheerfully optimistic about the prospects for globality – and unabashed in his Eurocentrism.

True, such sentiments could scarcely flourish in today's liberal intellectual culture, sharply attuned as it is to the claims of cultural difference. But still we can take a lesson from Marx's example, and it is that the ethnocentric tendency towards universalizing projections of a global culture can coexist with otherwise rational progressive humanistic visions. This certainly remains true today: and it is there not just in the rhetoric of national political leaders, but in the constituencies to which this rhetoric appeals. To take one's own culture as the 'obvious' model for the one, true, enlightened, rational and good is as common as it is understandable. Relativizing this model requires much more difficult acts of hermeneutic distancing and of intellectual and affective imagination.

But this is precisely what we need to do if we are to avoid the sort of violent contestation of worldviews that looks so threatening in our present world. Making cosmopolitanism – in the rather simple, literal sense of 'world citizenship' – work in a way that does not impose any *one* particular, culturally inflected model is perhaps the most immediate cultural challenge that globalization faces us with. I will return to this issue in the last part of this chapter. But, before that, we can turn to another aspect of globalization – which might just offer a little more cause for optimism in the face of this challenge.

DETERRITORIALIZATION

One clear implication of the discussion in the previous section is that both utopian and dystopian speculations about a single integrated global culture are not only generally ethnocentric in their origins, they are – in part because of this – rather poor predictions of actual cultural development. But there is another, more promising, way of approaching cultural globalization. This is not via the macro analysis of 'globality', but precisely in the opposite way, by understanding the effects of globalization as they are felt within particular *localities*.

The vast majority of us live local lives, but globalization is rapidly changing our experience of this 'locality' and one way of grasping this change is in the idea of 'deterritorialization'. As Nestor García Canclini describes it, the idea of deterritorialization implies 'the loss of the "natural" relation of culture to geographical and social territories' (García Canclini 1995: 229). Deterritorialization, then, means that the significance of the geographical location of a culture – not only the physical, environmental and climatic location, but all the self-definitions, ethnic boundaries and delimiting practices that have accrued around this – is eroding. No longer is culture so 'tied' to the constraints of local circumstances.

In fact the idea of deterritorialization has fairly radical theoretical implications for traditional ways of understanding culture. Culture has long held connotations tying it to the idea of a fixed locality. The idea of 'a culture' implicitly connects meaning construction with particularity and location: with 'territory'. Indeed, in the mainstream sociological treatment of culture, particularly in the functionalist tradition where collective meaning construction is seen largely as serving the purposes of social integration, there has been a tacit assumption that culture is a spatially bounded entity, somehow paralleling the bounded, integrated entity of the 'society' (Mann 1986). But the complex connectivity of globalization threatens to undermine such conceptualizations, not only because the multiform *penetration* of localities disrupts this binding of meanings to place, but also because it challenges the rather insular thinking through which culture and fixity of location are originally paired.

If globalization, in its rawest description, is the spread of complex social-economic connections across distance, then deterritorialization refers to the *reach* of this connectivity into the localities in which everyday life is conducted and experienced. This is at the same time a perplexing and disruptive, and an exhilarating and empowering phenomenon, involving the simultaneous penetration of our local worlds by distant forces, and the dislodging of everyday meanings from their 'anchors' in the local environment.

It may well be that, in the long run, this 'weakening' of the traditional ties between cultural experience and geographical territory will prove to be the most far-reaching effect of cultural globalization. But we should be clear about precisely what this entails. Deterritorialization is *not* simply the *loss* of the experience of a local culture: it is not as though localities, and the particularities, nuances and differences they generate, suddenly and entirely disappear. Localities, on the contrary, thrive in globalization – this is the source of that often noted paradox that globalization tends to produce intensities in ethnic identification – even to the point of the violent contesting of local territory along ethnic lines (Kaldor 1999). In less extreme terms, a moment's thought about the places we live in reminds us that, despite the forces of globalization, they all retain a high degree of cultural distinctiveness. This applies not only to remote and 'exotic' corners and backwaters of the world, untouched by the flows of global modernity, but to capital cities and great metropolitan centres – the most concentrated locations of global connectivity. London clearly has its own cultural 'feel' which is quite different from Madrid, New York, Tokyo or Beijing.

So what is different? The difference that deterritorialization makes is that the culture produced by locality is no longer – as it may well have been in the past – the single most important factor in our lived reality. Deterritorialization refers to the integration of *distant* events, processes and relationships into our everyday lives and it is this *added* dimension of experience that accounts for the attenuation of the hold that local particularities have on modern cultures.

This 'deterritorializing' aspect of globalization is felt in very ordinary everyday practices: as we push our trolleys around the aisles of 'global foods' in local super-markets; as we choose between eating in Italian, Mexican, Thai, Indian or Japanese restaurants; as we settle down in our living rooms to watch an American soap opera or the news coverage of a distant political event; as we casually phone friends on other continents, aware of their 'distance' only in terms of a time difference; as we routinely log on to *Google* for information rather than walking down to the local public library. These activities are now so taken-for-granted in the affluent, devel-oped parts of the world, that they seem almost too trivial to consider as signalling deep cultural transformations. Yet they do. It is through such changes that globali-zation reaches deep into our individual cultural 'worlds', the implicit sense we all have of our relevant environment, our understanding of what *counts* as home and abroad, our horizon of cultural and moral relevance, even our sense of cultural and national identity (Tomlinson 1999: 113f; 2003).

The phenomenon of deterritorialization arises from a complex set of economic, political and technological factors and in fact, like globalization itself, it is not a phenomenon which can usefully be tied down to one dimension of analysis. But, having said this, there is one factor which *is* worth singling out for closer scrutiny, since it opens out on to areas of connectivity that are historically unprecedented and which may justifiably be said to define the tenor of our times. This is our increasing routine dependence on electronic media and communications technolo-gies and systems.

What we can call the 'telemediatization' of culture is a key distinction in twenty-first century life. Often this distinction is grasped as a peculiar form of *mobility* that does not involve actual physical movement. Typically, the use of the Internet, and even to some degree of television, is described as a form of 'virtual travel' and popular expressions often employ metaphors of mobility (surfing, channel hopping, navigating and so on). Whilst there is some force in these metaphors, it seems to me more useful to think of telemediatization as a historically novel form in which experience is made 'present' to human beings: as, indeed, a distinctive *mode* of deterritorialization. Telemediatized practices – watching television or typing, scroll-ing, clicking and browsing at the computer screen or talking, texting or sending and receiving pictures on a mobile phone – should be regarded as unique modes of cul-tural activity and perception. Although they are now so much a taken-for-granted aspect of everyday life in developed societies we should remember that none of these activities and experiences have any counterpart beyond the last few decades of world history. Our use of media and communications technologies thus helps to define what it is to exist as a social being in the modern world.

It seems to me, then, that one of the main challenges of global cultural analysis is to come to terms with the way in which telemediatization is shaping our lives – and, indeed, our values. Just to pick out one significant theme, there is now a widespread assumption that the *speed* of electronic communication is an undisputed good – and that modern social life as it were, has its inevitable 'pace' set by this technology. This is not, of course, an idea that has stolen upon us all at once: we can trace a trajectory of increasing acceleration in media technologies, from the telegraph through the telephone and radio and television broadcasting systems, up to the convergences between mobile phones, the Internet and a complex network of databases, tracking and delivery systems which is on the near technological horizon. But the cultural assumption that runs though these technological developments is in fact relatively historically novel: it is that communication is to be valued not only in terms of clarity, intelligibility, truthfulness and improved mutuality of understanding: it is to be valued, increasingly, in terms of *speed* of delivery.

If we add to these technological developments innovations in media institutions themselves – for instance 24-hour television, online news services, multimedia delivery systems via domestic broadband provision – there emerges a sense of what we could call the increasing 'immediacy' of modern global culture. The most direct impact of this is probably felt in changes in consumption practices (television or online shopping), entertainment (the downloading and retrieval of music via MP3 devices like the, now almost culturally iconic, *iPod*) or simply the possibility of immediate access to other people (mobile phone conversation or 'texting') – the last of which may, without exaggeration, be thought of as a defining feature of contemporary youth culture. And there are wider implications: for example in the political process, where the discourse of politicians is increasingly finely tuned to the demands of a media demanding instant responses on all issues, where political parties during elections even issue 'pre-emptive' policy statements and where global financial markets instantly react to political events – or merely to nuances in the words of political leaders.

But the larger cultural question – as yet scarcely addressed – is what all this speed and 'instant access' means in the longer term for our emotions, our social relations and our cultural values, for example, the value of patience. I do not want to suggest that global 'immediacy' will necessarily prove to be bad for us. But it is undoubtedly a dimension of cultural power in itself, to be reckoned alongside the power of the marketplace, or of political ideologies. And it is producing a definite shift in the way in which people make sense of the world. The agenda of global cultural analysis, then, certainly includes understanding the 'runaway' speed of modern media technologies and systems – and probably extends to the devising of viable strategies for their regulation.

But returning to the general theme of deterritorialization, I want to suggest, as I hinted at earlier, that there is at least the germ of optimism in this process for the broader cultural-political challenges that global connectivity poses. Deterritorialization not only disturbs and transforms local experience, it potentially offers people wider cultural horizons. In various ways – through increased travel and mobility, the use of new communications technologies and the experience of a globalized media – people effortlessly integrate local and 'global' cultural data in their consciousness. Thus, what happens in distant parts of the world, though still perhaps not so vivid as events in our neighbourhood, nonetheless has an increasing significance in our lives – particularly since it may have readily traceable consequences for us. The positive potential of deterritorialization, then, is that, in changing our experience of local life, it may promote a new sensibility of cultural openness, human mutuality and global ethical responsibility. In the final part of this chapter, I shall develop these thoughts via a brief consideration of the fate of cultural identity in a globalizing world.

COSMOPOLITANISM AND CULTURAL IDENTITY

As I suggested in discussion of the prospects for a global culture, the idea of a progressive, cosmopolitan cultural politics deserves to be taken seriously. This does not necessarily mean endorsing grand projects for 'global governance'; rather it means trying to clarify, and ultimately to reconcile, the attachments and the values of cultural difference with those of an emergent wider global-human 'community'. This is a dilemma. On the one hand there are the attractions of what we might think of as a 'benign' form of universalism, preserving some key ideas of human mutuality and underlying the broad discourse of human rights and the hope of wider horizons of global solidarity. But on the other, the equally attractive principles of respect for the integrity of local context and practices, cultural autonomy, cultural identity and 'sovereignty'. At the heart of the cultural-political problems posed by contemporary globalization, lies what Amanda Anderson (1998) has described as the 'divided legacies of modernity': two sets of strong rational principles pulling in different directions. Universal human rights or cultural difference? We don't really know which flag to stand beside because in most cases there seem good reasons to stand beside both (Tomlinson 2002; Walzer 1994).

I do not suppose there is any easy solution to this dilemma, but in the short space available I want to suggest that we may get some way along the road by addressing another rather vexed issue in cultural politics, that is, the question of the formation of 'cultural identity'.

Considered formally, rather than psychologically, 'identities' are aspects of the differentiating, institutionalizing and socially regulating nature of modern life. Modernity, indeed, might be considered, at a level of abstraction above that of a determinant set of social institutions (capitalism, technology and industrialism, urbanism, the nation-state system) as the very tendency to form institutions and to generate regulators of social-economic-cultural behaviour. Considered in this way, cultural identities are specifically *modern* entities – ways of categorizing, organizing and regulating the cultural practices, representations and imaginings by which we grasp our existential condition, our personal relations and our attachment to a place or a community.

This essentially modern, 'regulatory' category of cultural identity, then, consists in self and communal definitions based around specific, usually politically inflected, differentiations: gender, sexuality, class, religion, race and ethnicity, nationality. Some of these differentiations of course existed before the coming of modernity, some – like nationality – are more or less modern imaginings. But the relevance of modernity here is not so much in the nature and substance – the contents – of identifications, as in the fact they are formally and publicly recognized, named and regulated. Modern societies orchestrate existential experience according to tacit but nonetheless well-policed boundaries. We 'live' our gender, our sexuality, our nationality and so forth within institutional regimes of discursively organized belongings. What could be much more amorphous, contingent, particular and tacit senses of belonging become structured into an array – a portfolio – of identities, each with implications for our material and psychological well-being, each, thus, with its own 'politics'. As globalization distributes the institutional features of modernity across all cultures, it therefore generates these institutionalized forms of cultural belonging – in some cases where they have not before played any role in cultural life.

One rather interesting interpretation of the impact of globalization to flow from this is that, far from destroying it – as many suppose – globalization has been perhaps the most significant force in *creating and proliferating* cultural identity (Tomlinson 2003). Those who regard globalization as a *threat* to cultural identity tend to imagine identity quite differently. Rather than noticing its institutional features, they tend to see identity as something like an existential 'possession', an inheritance, a benefit of traditional long dwelling, of continuity with the past. Identity, according to this common view, is more than just a description of the experience of cultural belonging, it is a sort of collective treasure of local communities. Moreover, whilst long ensuring the culturally sustaining connections between geographical place and human experience, identity, according to this view, is suddenly discovered to be fragile, in need of protection and preservation, a treasure that can be lost. This is the story which implicates globalization – and specifically deterritorialization – in the destruction of local identities.

However, the crucial mistake of those who regard globalization as a *threat* to cultural identity is to confuse this Western-modern form of cultural imagination with a universal of human experience. All cultures construct meaning via practices of collective symbolization: this is probably as close to a cultural universal as we can get. But by no means all historical cultures have 'constructed' identity in the regulated institutional forms that are now dominant in the modern West (Morley 2000).

Let us now try to connect these thoughts about the institutionalization of identity with the issue of cosmopolitanism. The way we can do this is to understand the cosmopolitan disposition – the sympathy with a globally encompassing humanism and with rights and obligations belonging to this – as belonging to a specific identity position.

Whatever the composition, or the historical/territorial origins of the discourse of human rights – a discourse *encompassing* for the most part, rather than contesting other forms of universalism – it owes most to its modern institutional form. 'Humanity' – in its juridical form of an owner of rights or a victim of persecution or exploitation – is, in effect, a specific modern identity position which is universal by definition, but which remains compatible with a huge range of cultural variation, by dint of its precise context of invocation. Human rights can be invoked to defend cultural difference in just the same way that they can be used to argue for universal standards of justice, or equality of provision in healthcare, education and so forth.

To be, without contradiction, 'human' in its rich pluralist acceptation of preserving cultural difference, and 'human' in juridical-universalizing terms, is a trick brought off precisely by the institutionalized framing of *repertoires* of identity typical of modernity. The key here is the pluralism of identity positions. In the midst of the proliferation of localisms and sharpened identity discriminations, globalization also – formally, adroitly and without any recourse to particular cultural traditions – generates a flexible category of cosmopolitan belonging.

But how does this understanding help with the dilemma of whether to endorse universalism or the politics of difference? Well let's not pretend that it magics away all of the conceptual tensions, or the real political problems around putative regimes of global governance predicated on universal human rights. What we put inside the box labelled 'human rights' will still be a matter of contention. However, thinking about these issues in terms of identity positions does, perhaps, soften some of the starker intractabilities. Just as it is possible, without contradiction, to hold a repertoire of identities – to be at the same time female, Chinese, a Beijinger, a political dissident, a patriot, a Buddhist and an admirer of Western liberalism – so it is possible to hold rights which are, as it were, *transferable* across different contexts. To this extent, the appeal to human universalism is itself dependent on context: it can be invoked in situations where more particular local communal attachments can be reasonably judged to be repressive. But it does not need to be considered as the card which trumps all 'lesser' rights and duties. Identities we know are constructs not possessions. Despite the historical tendency for cultures and nations to claim universality as their possession, the appeal to the universal can perhaps be made to work in a cosmopolitan world order as a *construct*: as one way, amongst others, of understanding our human condition and of relating in dialogue with others. What is clear, finally, is that, faced with a future world of what Clifford Geertz has called 'pressed-together dissimilarities variously arranged, rather than all-of-a-piece nation-states grouped into blocs and superblocs' (Geertz 2000: 226), we urgently need to come up with much more nimble and flexible cultural concepts than we so far possess.

References

Anderson, A. 1998. 'Cosmopolitanism, universalism and the divided legacies of modernity'. In P. Cheah and B. Robbins (eds), *Cosmopolitics: Thinking and Feeling beyond the Nation*, 265–89. Minneapolis: University of Minnesota Press.

Derrida, J. 2002. *Ethics, Institutions and the Right to Philosophy*. Lanham, MD: Rowman and Littlefield.

Eagleton, T. 2000. *The Idea of Culture*. Oxford: Blackwell.

García Canclini, N. 1995. *Hybrid Cultures: Strategies for Entering and Leaving Modernity*. Minneapolis: University of Minnesota Press.

Geertz, C. 1973. *The Interpretation of Cultures*. New York: Basic Books.

Geertz, C. 2000. *Available Light: Anthropological Reflections on Philosophical Topics*. Princeton, NJ: Princeton University Press

Giddens, A. 1990. *The Consequences of Modernity*. Cambridge: Polity Press.

Huntington, S.P. 1996. *The Clash of Civilizations and the Remaking of World Order*. New York: Simon and Schuster.

Kaldor, M. 1999: *New and Old Wars*. Cambridge: Polity Press.

Lull, J. 2000. *Media, Communication, Culture: A Global Approach*. Cambridge: Polity Press.

Mann, M. 1986. *The Sources of Social Power, Vol. 1*. Cambridge: Cambridge University Press.

Marx, K. and Engels, F. 1969. 'Manifesto of the Communist Party'. In L.S. Feuer (ed.), *Marx and Engels: Basic Writings on Politics and Philosophy*, 43–82. London: Fontana.

Massey, D. 1994. *Space, Place and Gender*. Cambridge: Polity Press.

Morley, D. 1992. *Television Audiences and Cultural Studies*. London: Routledge.

Morley, D. 2000. *Home Territories: Media, Mobility and Identity*. London: Routledge.

Robertson, R. 1992. *Globalization: Social Theory and Global Culture*. London: Sage.

Thompson, J. B. 1995. *The Media and Modernity*. Cambridge: Polity Press.

Tomlinson, J. 1991. *Cultural Imperialism: A Critical Introduction*. London: Continuum.

Tomlinson, J. 1999. *Globalization and Culture*. Cambridge: Polity Press.

Tomlinson, J. 2002. 'Interests and identities in cosmopolitan politics'. In S. Vertovek and R. Cohen (eds), *Conceiving Cosmopolitanism*, 240–53. Oxford: Oxford University Press.

Tomlinson, J. 2003. 'Globalization and cultural identity'. In D. Held et al. (eds), *The Global Transformations Reader*, 2nd edn, 269–78. Cambridge: Polity Press.

Walzer, M. 1994. *Thick and Thin: Moral Argument at Home and Abroad*. Notre Dame, IN: University of Notre Dame Press.

Žižek, S. 2001. *On Belief*. London: Routledge.

Chapter 18

Globalization and Ideology

MANFRED B. STEGER

INTRODUCTION: THE IDEOLOGICAL DIMENSION OF GLOBALIZATION

From its beginnings in the late 1980s, the fledgling field of global[ization] studies has been dominated by accounts focusing primarily on the economic and technological aspects of the phenomenon. To be sure, a proper recognition of the crucial role of integrating markets and new information technologies should be part of any comprehensive understanding of globalization, but it is equally important to avoid the trap of technological and economic reductionism. As Malcolm Waters (2001) observes, the increasingly symbolically mediated and reflexive character of today's economic exchanges suggests that both the cultural and political arenas are becoming more activated and energetic. And yet, despite the burgeoning recent literature on crucial cultural and political aspects of globalization, researchers have paid insufficient attention to the global circulation of ideas and their impact on the rapid extension of social interactions and interdependencies across time and space. Save for a few notable exceptions (Mittelman 2004; Rupert 2000; Sklair 2002; Steger 2003, 2005), globalization scholars have been surprisingly reluctant to enter the misty realm of ideology. Bucking the trend, this chapter explores the ideological dimension of globalization with particular attention to its important discursive features.

Following Michael Freeden's (1996, 2003) and Lyman Tower Sargent's (2003) suggestion that political belief systems serve as cognitive maps that chart crucial dimensions of the political world, I define 'ideology' as a system of widely shared ideas, patterned beliefs, guiding norms and values, and ideals accepted as truth by some group. Ideologies offer individuals a more or less coherent picture of the world not only as it is, but also as it ought to be. In doing so, they help organize the tremendous complexity of human experience into fairly simple, but frequently distorted, images and slogans that serve as guide and compass for social and political action. Each ideology is structured around core claims which set it apart from other ideologies and endow it with a specific conceptual form or 'morphology'. As Freeden (1996: 77) puts it, 'Central to any analysis of ideologies is the proposition that they are characterized by a morphology that displays core, adjacent, and peripheral concepts'. What makes an ideology 'political' is that its claims select, privilege and constrict social meanings related to the exercise of power in society. Ideologies speak to their audiences in stories and narratives whose claims persuade, praise, cajole, convince, condemn and distinguish 'truths' from 'falsehoods'. Ideologies enable people to act, while at the same time constraining their actions by binding them to a particular set of ideas, norms and values.

The term 'ideology' was first coined by Antoine Destutt de Tracy in the late eighteenth century. The Enlightenment thinker sought to establish a positivistic 'science of ideas' employing the empirical tools of natural science to map systems of thought. In the Napoleonic era, however, 'ideology' acquired the pejorative meaning of 'falsehood' or 'deliberate distortion' that it has retained in public discourse until our time. French philosopher Paul Ricoeur (1986) identified the historical elements and functions of ideology. Drawing on the insights of the Marxist tradition, he characterized the first functional level of ideology as *distortion*, that is, the production of contorted images of social reality. Most importantly, the process of distortion hides the contrast between things as they may be envisioned in theory and things as they play themselves out on the plane of material reality. Indeed, all ideologies assemble a picture of the world based on a peculiar mixture that both represents and distorts social processes. Yet, Ricoeur disagreed with Karl Marx's notion that distortion explains all there is to ideology (Tucker 1978). For the French philosopher, distortion was merely one of the three main functions of ideology, representing the surface level of a phenomenon that contains two more functions at progressively deeper levels.

Inspired by the writings of Max Weber (Gerth and Mills, 1946) and Karl Mannheim (1936), Ricoeur identified *legitimation* as the second functional level of ideology. Two main factors were involved here: the claim to legitimacy made by the ruling authority, and the belief in the authority's legitimacy granted by its subjects. Accepting large parts of Weber's explanation of social action, Ricoeur highlighted ideology's function of mediating the gap between belief and claim. For Mannheim, it was the task of the intelligentsia capable of rising above their class and historical context to provide objective explanations of the discrepancy between the popular belief in the legitimacy of the ruling class and the authority's claim to the right to rule.

Ricoeur's analysis was completed in his description of *integration*, the third functional level of ideology. Drawing on the writings of the American anthropologist Clifford Geertz (1973), who emphasized the symbolic structure of social action, Ricoeur claimed that, on the deepest level, ideology plays a mediating or integrative role. It provides society with stability as it creates, preserves and protects the social identity of persons and groups. In its constructive function, ideology supplies the symbols, norms and images that go into the process of assembling and holding together individual and collective identity. Thus, ideology assumes a conservative function in both senses of that word. It preserves identity, but it also wants to conserve what exists. Such rigid forms of resistance to change contribute to turning beliefs and ideas into a dogmatic defence of dominant power structures. Suggesting that subordinate groups often give their spontaneous consent to the social logic of domination that is embedded in a 'hegemonic' ideology, the Italian Marxist philosopher Antonio Gramsci (1971), too, emphasized the integrative role of ideology. He noted that dominant groups frequently succeeded in enticing the working class into embracing a collective identity that ran contrary to their interests, allowing power elites to maintain a favourable social order without having to resort to open coercion.

In this chapter, I contend that 'globalism' is a hegemonic system of ideas that makes normative claims about a set of social processes called 'globalization'. It seeks to limit public discussion on the meaning and character of globalization to an agenda of 'things to discuss' that supports particular political objectives. In other words, like all social processes, globalization contains an ideological dimension filled with a range of norms, claims, beliefs and narratives about the phenomena itself. After all, it is chiefly the *normative* question of whether globalization ought to be considered a 'good' or a 'bad' phenomenon that has spawned heated debates in classrooms, boardrooms and on the streets.

In this chapter, I suggest that globalism consists of a *set of six core claims* that play crucial semantic and political roles. With regard to semantics, I argue that these claims absorb and rearrange bits and pieces of several established ideologies and integrate them with new concepts into a powerful political belief system whose role consists chiefly of preserving and enhancing asymmetrical power structures that benefit particular social groups wedded to the tenets of neoliberalism. I end the chapter with a short discussion of counter-ideologies from the political Left and Right and a brief speculation on the future of globalism.

GLOBALIZATION AND THE SIX CORE CLAIMS OF GLOBALISM

Denoting the rapid extension of social interdependencies across time and space, the term 'globalization' gained in currency in the late 1980s. In part, its conceptual unwieldiness arose from the fact that global flows occur in different physical and mental dimensions, usefully divided by Arjun Appadurai into 'ethnoscapes', 'technoscapes', 'mediascapes', 'financescapes' and 'ideoscapes'. The persistence of academic divisions on the subject notwithstanding, the term was associated with specific meanings in public discourse during the 1990s. With the collapse of Soviet-style communism in Eastern Europe, loosely affiliated power elites concentrated in the global North stepped up their ongoing efforts to sell their version of 'globalization' to the public. These power elites consisted chiefly of corporate managers, executives of large transnational corporations, corporate lobbyists, high-level military officers, prominent journalists and public-relations specialists, intellectuals writing to a large public audience, state bureaucrats and influential politicians. By the mid-1990s, large segments of the population in both the global North and South had accepted globalism's core claims, thus internalizing large parts of its overarching neoliberal framework that advocated the deregulation of markets, the liberalization of trade, the privatization of state-owned enterprises and, after 9/11, the qualified support of the global War on Terror under US leadership. Indeed, the comprehensive

University of Maryland Poll (2004) conducted in 19 countries on four continents found that even after 5 years of massive, worldwide demonstrations against neoliberal globalization, 55 per cent of the respondents believed that globalization was positive for them and their families, while only 25 per cent said that it was negative.

Seeking to make a persuasive case for a new global order based on their beliefs and values, these neoliberal power elites constructed and disseminated narratives and images that associated the concept of globalization with inexorably expanding free markets. Their efforts at decontesting the master concept 'globalization' went hand in hand with the rise of globalism. Ideological 'decontestation' is a crucial process in the formation of thought systems because it fixes the meanings of the core concepts by arranging them in a pattern or configuration that links them with other concepts in a meaningful way. As Michael Freeden (2003: 54–5) puts it,

> An ideology attempts to end the inevitable contention over concepts by *decontesting* them, by removing their meanings from contest. 'This is what justice means,' announces one ideology, and 'that is what democracy entails.' By trying to convince us that they are right and that they speak the truth, ideologies become devices for coping with the interdeterminacy of meaning.... That is their semantic role. [But] [i]deologies also need to decontest the concepts they use because they are instruments for fashioning collective decisions. That is their political role.

Effective ideological decontestation structures – I refer to them as 'ideological claims' – can thus be pictured as simple semantic chains whose conceptual links convey authoritative meanings that facilitate collective decision-making. Their interconnected semantic and political roles suggest that control over political language translates directly into political power, that is, the power of deciding 'who gets what, when, and how' (Lasswell 1958).

Claim 1: Globalization is about the liberalization and global integration of markets

Examining the utterances, speeches and writings of influential advocates of globalism, my previous work on the subject suggests that 'globalization' and 'market' constitute its twin core concepts. 'Market', of course, also plays an important role in two established ideologies: the libertarian variant of liberalism (often referred to as 'neoliberalism') inspired by the ideas of Herbert Spencer, Friedrich Hayek and Milton Friedman, and the late twentieth-century brand of Anglo-American conservatism ('neoconservatism') associated with the views of Keith Joseph, Margaret Thatcher and Ronald Reagan. While globalism borrows heavily from both ideologies, it would be a mistake to reduce it to either. Moreover, neoliberalism and neoconservativism should not be seen as ideological opposites, for their similarities sometimes outweigh their differences. In general, neoconservatives agree with neoliberals on the importance of 'free markets' and 'free trade', but they are much more inclined than the latter to combine their hands-off attitude towards big business with intrusive government action for the regulation of the ordinary citizenry in the name of public security and traditional values. In foreign affairs, neoconservatives advocate a more assertive and expansive use of both economic and military power, although they often embrace the liberal ideal of promoting 'freedom' and 'democracy' around the world.

Embracing the classical liberal idea of the self-regulating market, Claim 1 seeks to establish beyond dispute 'what globalization means', that is, to offer an authoritative definition of globalization designed for broad public consumption. It does so by interlocking its two core concepts and then linking them to the adjacent ideas of 'liberty' and 'integration'. For example, an explanation offered in a *BusinessWeek* article (13 December 1999) illustrates this process: 'Globalization is about the triumph of markets over governments. Both proponents and opponents of globalization agree that the driving force today is markets, which are suborning the role of government.' The same claim is made over and over again by Thomas Friedman (1999) whose best-selling book on globalization provides the dominant perspective on globalization in the United States. At one point in his narrative, the award-winning *New York Times* columnist insists that everybody ought to accept the following 'truth' about globalization: 'The driving idea behind globalization is free-market capitalism – the more you let market forces rule and the more you open your economy to free trade and competition, the more efficient your economy will be. Globalization means the spread of free-market capitalism to virtually every country in the world' (1999: 9).

By forging a close semantic link between 'globalization' and 'market', globalists like Friedman seek to create the impression that globalization represents primarily an economic phenomenon. Thus unburdened by the complexity of its additional non-economic dimensions, 'globalization' acquires the necessary simplicity and focus to convey its central normative message contained in further semantic connections to the adjacent concepts 'liberalization' and 'integration': the 'liberation' of markets from state control is a good thing. Conversely, the notion of 'integrating markets' is draped in the mantle of all-embracing liberty, hence the frequent formulation of Claim 1 as a global imperative anchored in universal reason. Thus decontested as an economic project advancing human freedom in general, globalization must be applied to all countries, regardless of the political and cultural preferences expressed by local citizens. As President George W. Bush notes in the *National Security Strategy of the United States of America* (2002), 'Policies that further strengthen market incentives and market institutions are relevant for all economies – industrialized countries, emerging markets, and the developing world.'

Claim 2: Globalization is inevitable and irreversible

The second mode of decontesting 'globalization' turns on the adjacent concept of 'inevitability'. In the last decade, the public discourse on globalization describing its projected path was saturated with adjectives like 'irresistible', 'inevitable', 'inexorable' and 'irreversible'. For example, in a major speech on US foreign policy, President Bill Clinton (1999) told his audience: 'Today we must embrace the inexorable logic of globalization. . . . Globalization is irreversible. Protectionism will only make things worse.' Frederick Smith (1999), chairman and CEO of FedEx Corporation, proclaimed that 'Globalization is inevitable and inexorable and it is accelerating. . . . Globalization is happening, it's going to happen. It does not matter whether you like it or not, it's happening, it's going to happen.' Neoliberal power elites in the global South often faithfully echoed the determinist language of globalism. For example, Manuel Villar (1998), the Philippines Speaker of the House of Representatives, insisted that, 'We cannot simply wish away the process of globalization. It is a reality of a modern world. The process is irreversible.'

At first glance, the attempt to decontest globalization in such determinist terms seems to be a poor strategy for a rising thought system that borrows heavily from neoliberalism and neoconservatism. After all, throughout the twentieth century, both liberals and conservatives criticized Marxist socialism for its devaluation of human agency and its contempt for individualism. However, there is a political reason why globalism puts a fundamental illiberal idea in close proximity to its core concepts. Presenting globalization as some sort of natural force, like the weather or gravity, makes it easier for globalists to convince people that they have to adapt to the discipline of the market if they are to survive and prosper. Thus suppressing alternative discourses about globalization, Claim 2 inhibits the formation of political dissent.

In the immediate aftermath of 9/11, however, Claim 2 came under sustained criticism by commentators who read the Al-Qaeda attacks as exposing the 'dark side of globalization'. Some proclaimed the imminent 'collapse of globalism', worrying that the terrorist attacks would usher in a new age of cultural particularism and economic protectionism. For example, noted neoliberal economists like Robert J. Samuelson (2003) argued that previous globalization processes had been stopped by similar cataclysmic events like the assassination of the Austrian Archduke Franz Ferdinand in Sarajevo. And yet, the unfolding War on Terror allowed for the semantic intermingling of military and economic inevitability. For example, Christopher Shays (2003), Republican Congressman from Connecticut and Chair of the House Subcommittee on National Security, argued that the 'toxic zeal' of the terrorists would eventually be defeated by the combination of military and market forces – 'the relentless inevitability of free peoples pursuing their own enlightened self-interest in common cause'. Thus, globalism's ability to adapt to the new realities of the post-9/11 world gives ample proof of its responsiveness to a broad range of political issues.

Claim 3: Nobody is in charge of globalization

The third mode of decontesting globalization hinges on the classical liberal concept of the 'self-regulating market'. The semantic link between 'globalization-market' and the adjacent idea of 'leaderlessness' is simple: if the undisturbed workings of the market indeed preordain a certain course of history, then globalization does not reflect the arbitrary agenda of a particular social class or group. In other words, globalists are not 'in charge' in the sense of imposing their own political agenda on people. Rather, they merely carry out the unalterable imperatives of a transcendental force much larger than narrow partisan interests.

For example, Robert Hormats (1998), vice chairman of Goldman Sachs International, emphasized that, 'The great beauty of globalization is that no one is in control. The great beauty of globalization is that it is not controlled by any individual, any government, any institution.' Likewise, Thomas Friedman (1999:

112–13) alleged that 'the most basic truth about globalization is this: No one is in charge. . . . But the global marketplace today is an Electronic Herd of often anonymous stock, bond and currency traders and multinational investors, connected by screens and networks.'

After 9/11, however, it became increasingly difficult for globalists to maintain this claim. While a number of corporate leaders still reflexively referred to the 'self-regulating market', it became obvious that the survival of globalization – conceived as the liberalization and global integration of markets – depended on the US government wielding its power. Having concealed their country's imperial ambitions behind the soft language of market globalism during the 1990s, many American globalists took off their gloves after 9/11, exposing the iron fists of an irate giant. The attacks changed the terms of the dominant discourse in that it enabled certain groups within the globalist camp to put their geopolitical ambitions explicitly before a public shocked by 'terrorism'. Indeed, their open advocacy of American global leadership spawned raging debates around the world over whether or not the United States actually constituted an 'empire'.

However, the replacement of Claim 3 with a more aggressive pronouncement of global Anglo-American leadership should not be read as a sign of globalism's ideological weakness. Rather, it reflected its ideational flexibility and growing ability to respond to a new set of political issues. Indeed, like all full-fledged political belief systems, globalism is broad enough to contain the more economistic variant of the 1990s as well as its more militaristic post-9/11 manifestation.

Claim 4: Globalization benefits everyone (. . . in the long run)

This decontestation chain lies at the heart of globalism because it provides an affirmative answer to the crucial normative question of whether globalization represents a 'good' phenomenon. The adjacent idea of 'benefits for everyone' is usually unpacked in material terms such as 'economic growth' and 'prosperity'. However, when linked to globalism's peripheral concept, 'progress', the idea of 'benefits for everyone' not only taps into liberalism's progressive worldview, but also draws on the powerful socialist vision of establishing an economic paradise on earth – albeit in the capitalist form of a worldwide consumerist utopia. Thus, Claim 4 represents another bold example of combining elements from seemingly incompatible ideologies under the master concept 'globalization'.

At the G7 Summit in Lyons, France, the heads of state and government of the world's seven most powerful industrialized nations issued a joint *Economic Communiqué* (1996) that exemplifies the principal meanings of this claim:

Economic growth and progress in today's interdependent world is bound up with the process of globalization. Globalization provides great opportunities for the future, not only for our countries, but for all others too. Its many positive aspects include an unprecedented expansion of investment and trade; the opening up to international trade of the world's most populous regions and opportunities for more developing countries to improve their standards of living; the increasingly rapid dissemination of information, technological innovation, and the proliferation of skilled jobs.

Even those globalists who concede the strong possibility of unequal global distribution patterns nonetheless insist that the market itself will eventually correct these 'irregularities'. As John Meehan (1997), chairman of the US Public Securities Association, puts it, 'episodic dislocations' such as mass unemployment and reduced social services might be 'necessary in the short run' but 'in the long run' they will give way to 'quantum leaps in productivity'.

The Al-Qaeda attacks only seem to have added to the fervour with which globalists speak of the supposed benefits accruing from the liberalization and global integration of markets. Asserting that the benefits of globalization must be defended at all costs, President Bush stated in his *National Security Strategy* (2002) that, 'Free trade and free markets have proven their ability to lift whole societies out of poverty – so the United States will work with individual nations, entire regions, and the entire global trading community to build a world that trades in freedom and therefore grows in prosperity.'

Claim 5: Globalization furthers the spread of democracy in the world

The fifth decontestation chain links 'globalization' and 'market' to the adjacent concept of 'democracy', which also plays a significant role in liberalism, conservatism and socialism. Globalists typically decontest 'democracy' through its proximity to 'market' and the making of economic choices – a theme developed through the 1980s in the peculiar variant of conservatism that Freeden (1996: 392) calls 'Thatcherism'. Indeed, a careful discourse analysis of relevant texts reveals that globalists tend to treat *freedom, free markets, free trade* and *democracy* as synonymous terms.

Francis Fukuyama (2000), for example, asserted that there exists a 'clear correlation' between a country's level of economic development and successful democracy. While globalization and capital development do not automatically produce democracies, 'the level of economic development resulting from globalization is conducive to the creation of complex civil societies with a powerful middle class. It is this class and societal structure that facilitates democracy.' Praising Eastern Europe's economic transition towards capitalism, then First Lady Hillary Rodham Clinton (1999) told her Polish audience that the emergence of new businesses and shopping centres in former communist countries should be seen as the 'backbone of democracy'.

After 9/11, Claim 5 became firmly linked to the Bush administration's neoconservative security agenda. The President (2002) did not mince words in his *New York Times* op-ed piece a year after the attacks: 'As we preserve the peace, America also has an opportunity to extend the benefits of freedom and progress to nations that lack them. We seek a peace where repression, resentment and poverty are replaced with the hope of democracy, development, free markets and free trade.' Fourteen months later, Bush (2003) reaffirmed his government's unwavering 'commitment to the global expansion of democracy' as the 'Third Pillar' of the United States' 'peace and security vision for the world'.

This idea of securing global economic integration through a US-led military drive for 'democratization' around the globe became especially prominent in the corporate scramble for Iraq following the official 'end of major combat operations' on

1 May 2003. Already during the first days of the Iraq War, in late March 2003, globalists had suggested that Iraq be subjected to a radical economic treatment. For example, Robert McFarlane, former National Security Adviser to President Reagan and current chairman of the Washington DC-based corporation Energy & Communication Solutions, LLC, together with Michael Bleyzer, CEO and president of SigmaBleyzer, an international equity fund management company, co-authored a prominent piece in *The Wall Street Journal* bearing the suggestive title, 'Taking Iraq Private' (2003). Calling on 'major U.S. corporations, jointly with other multinationals', to 'lead the effort to create capital-friendly environments in developing countries', the globalist duo praised the military operations in Iraq as an indispensable tool in establishing the 'political, economic and social stability' necessary for 'building the basic institutions that make democracy possible'. In their conclusion, the two men reminded their readers that 'the U.S. must demonstrate that it is not only the most powerful military power on the planet, but also the foremost market economy in the world, capable of leading a greater number of developing nations to a more prosperous and stable future'.

In what amounted to another clear demonstration of their political resonance, these globalist ideas translated almost immediately into collective decisions. For example, Ambassador Paul Bremer, the US head of the Coalition Provisional Authority, pressured the Governing Council to let Order 39 take effect, permitting complete foreign ownership of Iraqi companies and assets (apart from natural resources) that had hitherto been publicly owned, total remittance of profits and some of the lowest corporate tax rates in the world. Likewise, in his speeches at economic conferences on the Middle East attended by hundreds of American and Arab-American business executives, Secretary of State Colin Powell (Olivastro 2002) announced the development of a US–Middle East Free Trade Area (MEFTA) within a decade. Linked to the administration's 2002 'US–Middle East Partnership Initiative', the new project also included programmes to send Arab college students to work as interns in US corporations.

Claim 6: Globalization requires a global war on terror

Like the previous claims, this final decontestation chain attests to globalism's political responsiveness and conceptual flexibility. It combines the idea of economic globalization with openly militaristic and nationalistic ideas associated with the US-led global War on Terror. At the same time, however, Claim 6 possesses a somewhat paradoxical character. If global terror were no longer a major issue, it would disappear without causing globalism to collapse. In that case, it seems that Claim 6 is a contingent one and thus *less important* than the previous five. On the other hand, if the global War on Terror turns out to be a lengthy and intense engagement – as suggested by the current American political leadership – then it would become actually *more important* over time. No wonder, then, that commentators like Richard Falk (2003) who favour the second option have claimed to detect a dangerous turn of globalism towards fascism.

To be sure, throughout the 1990s there had been sinister warnings on the part of prominent cultural and social theorists that globalization was actually 'Americanization' (Latouche 1996) or 'McDonaldization' (Ritzer 1993) in universalist disguise. But US unilaterism and belligerence in the wake of 9/11 appeared to be a much more serious manifestation of the same phenomenon. In fact, the problem of globalism's turn towards nationalism was as much conceptual as political. After all, decontesting globalization through its proximity to the idea of a necessary 'global War on Terror' created obvious logical contradictions: the Anglo-American nationalist undertones emanating from the global War on Terror contradicted globalization's alleged universalism.

Instructive examples of the logical inconsistencies inherent in Claim 6 abound. Take, for instance, Thomas Barnett's best-selling book, *The Pentagon's New Map* (2004). The author, a professor of military strategy at the US Naval War College, also serves as the assistant for strategic futures in the Pentagon's Office of Force Transformations. In this capacity, Barnett has been giving his briefings regularly to the US Secretary of Defense, the intelligence community and high-ranking officers from all branches of the US armed forces.

Barnett (2004) argues that the Iraq War marks the moment when Washington takes real ownership of strategic security in the age of globalization. He breaks the globe down into three distinct regions. The first is characterized by 'globalization thick with network connectivity, financial transactions, liberal media flows, and collective security', yielding nations featuring stable democratic governments, transparency, rising standards of living and more deaths by suicide than by murder (North America, most of Europe, Australia, New Zealand and a small part of Latin America). He calls these regions of the world the 'Functioning Core' or 'Core'. Conversely, areas where 'globalization is thinning or just plain absent' constitute a region plagued by repressive political regimes, regulated markets, mass murder and widespread poverty and disease (the Caribbean Rim, virtually all of Africa, the Balkans, the Caucasus, Central Asia, China, the Middle East and much of Southeast Asia). The breeding ground of 'global terrorists', Barnett refers to this region as the 'Non-Integrating Gap' or 'Gap'. Between these two regions, one finds 'seam states' that 'lie along the Gap's bloody boundaries' (Mexico, Brazil, South Africa, Morocco, Algeria, Greece, Turkey, Pakistan, Thailand, Malaysia, the Philippines and Indonesia).

For Barnett, the importance of 9/11 is that the attacks forced the United States and its allies to make a long-term military commitment to 'deal with the entire Gap as a strategic threat environment'. In other words, the desired spread of globalization requires a War on Terror. Its three main objectives are: '1) Increase the Core's immune system capabilities for responding to September 11-like system perturbations; 2) Work on the seam states to firewall the Core from the Gap's worst exports, such as terror, drugs, and pandemics; and, most important, 3) Shrink the Gap . . . . The Middle East is the perfect place to start.' Barnett (2004) emphasizes that 'We ignore the Gap's existence at our own peril, because it will not go away until we as a nation respond to the challenge of making globalization truly global.'

This celebration of globalization in US nationalist terminology invites the kind of conceptual contradiction that may eventually prove to be fatal to globalism. On the other hand, if the political issues of our time indeed call for an ideology that boldly arranges seemingly conflicting pieces of various conventional political belief systems around the novel concept 'globalization', then globalism might actually achieve a level of ideological dominance unprecedented in history.

COUNTER-IDEOLOGIES FROM THE POLITICAL RIGHT AND LEFT

As the twentieth century was drawing to a close, more and more ordinary people became aware of the discrepancy between the ideological claims of globalism and their actual everyday experience of falling living standards and rapid cultural change. As a result, disparate anti-globalist arguments gelled into a coherent 'counter-ideology', which received more play in the public discourse on globalization. The formation and circulation of this oppositional ideology was aided by a heightened awareness of how extreme corporate profit strategies were leading to widening global disparities in wealth and well-being. Starting in the 1999 anti-WTO protest in Seattle, the contest between globalism and its ideological challengers erupted in street confrontations in many cities around the world.

One sentiment shared by these diverse groups opposed to globalism is their conviction that they must protect themselves and others from the negative consequences of globalization. In this regard, anti-globalist ideology amounts to 'protectionism' of some kind. However, as Robin Broad (2002) and David Held (2002) have suggested, anti-globalist groups pursue a wide range of goals and use different means to advance their political agendas. For example, they differ widely in their respective assessments of the constitutive features of globalization and its causes. Anti-globalist counter-ideologies come in two principal variants: particularist protectionists and universalist protectionists.

Particularist protectionists include groups on the political Right who blame globalization for most of the economic, political and cultural ills afflicting their home countries or regions. Threatened by the slow erosion of old social patterns, particularist protectionists denounce free trade, the power of global investors, the neoliberal agenda of multinational corporations and the 'Americanization of the world' as practices that have contributed to falling living standards and/or moral decline. Fearing the loss of national self-determination and the destruction of their cultures, they pledge to protect their traditional ways of life from those 'foreign elements' they consider responsible for unleashing the forces of globalization. Particularist protectionists are more concerned with the well-being of their own citizens than with the construction of a more equitable international order based on global solidarity.

In the United States, the former Republican Party and Reform Party Presidential candidate Patrick Buchanan, the popular CNN show host Lou Dobbs and other economic and cultural nationalists represent this position. In Europe, national-populist parties such as Jörg Haider's Austrian Freedom Party, Jean-Marie Le Pen's French National Front, Gerhard Frey's German People's Union or Gianfranco Fini's Italian National Alliance have expressed their opposition to 'American-style globalization' and its alleged tendency to produce a multicultural 'New World Order'. Their resistance to globalization has even increased in the face of US unilateralism after 9/11. In the global South, one finds similar voices on the right that blame globalization and the global expansion of US economic and military power for triggering economic crisis and cultural decay, and undermining regional autonomy. Osama bin Laden's radical Islamism and Hugo Chávez's Venezuelan brand of national populism represent extreme examples of particularist protectionism.

Universalist protectionists can be found in political parties on the Left dedicated to establishing a more equitable relationship between the global North and South. This camp also includes a growing number of progressive INGOs (international non-governmental organizations) like ATTAC (Association for the Taxation of Financial Transaction for the Benefit of Citizens), the International Forum on Globalization, Global Exchange, and Focus on the Global South, and transnational networks like the WEF (World Economic Forum) concerned with the protection of the environment, fair trade and international labour issues, human rights and women's issues. Challenging the central claims of globalism, these members of an emerging 'global civil society' point to the possibility of constructing a new international economic and political framework based on a global redistribution of wealth and power.

Universalist protectionists claim to be guided by the ideals of equality and social justice for all people in the world, not just the citizens of their own countries. They accuse globalist elites of pushing neoliberal policies that are leading to greater global inequality, high levels of unemployment, environmental degradation and the demise of social welfare. Calling for a 'globalization from below' that would empower the marginalized and poor, they seek to transform current corporate strategies of subjecting the world by a 'globalization from above'.

In the United States, the consumer advocate and 2000 Green Party presidential candidate and 2004 Independent presidential candidate Ralph Nader has emerged as the leading critic of the neoliberal corporate agenda. In particular, Nader argues that economic globalization has undermined the democratic accountability of transnational corporations. He also denounces the WTO, IMF and World Bank as undemocratic institutions that engage in imperialist forms of exploitation. In Europe, prominent public intellectuals as well as spokespersons for established Green parties have long suggested that unfettered economic globalization has resulted in serious ecological problems such as global warming, the mass extinction of species, the depletion of the earth's ozone layer and the pollution of oceans and rivers. In the global South, democratic-popular movements of resistance against neoliberal policies such as the Zapatista rebellion in Mexico or the Chipko movement in India have received some attention even in Western media. Many of these Third World social movements have forged close links to other anti-globalist INGOs. Such transnational alliances seek to draw people's attention to the deleterious effects of economic globalization, especially on the Southern Hemisphere. After 11 September, many of these organizations combined their anti-globalist positions with a strong anti-war stance, resulting in massive, worldwide demonstrations against the 2003 US-led war in Iraq.

THE FUTURE OF GLOBALISM

In this chapter, I have argued that globalism has emerged as the dominant ideology of our time. Its six core claims attest to the conceptual sophistication of the new political belief system and its ability to respond to a broad range of social issues. Absorbing miscellaneous ideational elements of established ideologies and realigning them around its core concepts 'globalization' and 'market', globalism sustains asymmetrical power structures in society that benefit a loose, heterogeneous and often disagreeing global alliance of social forces I have referred to as 'globalists'. Having come under attack by anti-globalist counter-ideologies on the political Right and Left, globalism has taken an ideological turn towards militarism and a US empire, especially after the cataclysmic events of 11 September 2001.

On first thought, it seems highly implausible that even an expanding 'war on terrorism' could stop, or slow down, such a powerful set of social processes as globalization. Yet, there are already some early warning signs. More intense border controls and security measures at the world's major air and seaports have made travel and international trade more cumbersome. Calls for tightening national borders and maintaining sharp cultural divisions can be heard more frequently in public discourse. Belligerent patriotic sentiments are on display all over the world.

A close look at modern history reveals that large-scale violent confrontations were capable of stopping and even reversing previous globalization trends. For example, sustained efforts to engineer a single global market under the auspices of the British Empire resulted in a severe backlash against globalization that culminated in the outbreak of World War I. In an important study on this subject, the political economist Karl Polanyi (2001) located the origins of the social crises that gripped the world during the first half of the twentieth century in ill-conceived efforts to liberalize and globalize markets. Commercial interests came to dominate society by means of a ruthless market logic that effectively disconnected people's economic activities from their social relations. As large segments of the population found themselves without an adequate system of social security and communal support, they resorted to radical measures to protect themselves against market globalization. After a prolonged period of severe economic dislocations following the end of the Great War, the particularist-protectionist impulse experienced its most extreme manifestations in Italian fascism and German National Socialism. In the end, the liberal-globalist dream of subordinating the whole world to the requirements of the free market had generated an equally extreme countermovement that turned markets into mere appendices of the totalitarian state.

The applicability of Polanyi's analysis to the current situation seems obvious. Like its nineteenth-century predecessor, today's version of globalism also represents a gigantic experiment in unleashing economic deregulation and a culture of consumerism on the entire world. But, as we have seen above, some anti-globalist forces of the twenty-first century seem to be capable of attracting millions of disaffected globalization losers who are willing to employ violent means in order to achieve their political ends. Hence, it is quite conceivable that the Al-Qaeda attacks on the World Trade Center and the Pentagon were only the opening salvos of a widening global war waged by the US government and its allies against a growing list of terrorist organizations and their supporters around the world.

On the other hand, it is also possible that the ongoing efforts to contain these violent forces of particularist protectionism might actually increase international cooperation and encourage the forging of new global alliances. In order to eradicate the primary social causes of terrorism, the global North might be willing to replace the dominant neoliberal version of globalization with a substantive reform agenda designed to reduce the existing disparities in global wealth and well-being. Unfortunately, despite their encouraging reassurances to put a 'human face' on their predatory version of globalization, many globalists have remained within the para-meters of their corporate agenda. If implemented at all, their proposed 'reforms' have remained largely symbolic in character. In order to prevent a further escalation of the ideological confrontation between globalism and its opponents, world leaders and concerned citizens must make serious attempts to build comprehensive networks of solidarity around the world. Most importantly, such transformative social processes must challenge current economic, political and cultural structures of global apartheid that divides the world into a privileged North and a disadvantaged South.

Let me end this chapter with a brief note on method. No serious analyst of glo-balism would wish to disavow the importance of conceptual precision and clarity, but the impulse to separate the social-scientific study of globalization from ideologi-cal and normative matters often serves to further perpetuate stale disputes over definitions and methodological differences. Any overly objectivist approach to glo-balization is bound to overlook the insight that all social scientific concepts are simultaneously analytical and normative. This dual status of concepts means that they never merely describe that to which they refer but are also necessarily engaged in a normative process of meaning construction. The scholarly suspicion of ideologi-cal 'contamination' derives partly from the historic mission of academic institutions. Like their nineteenth-century predecessor, today's universities subscribe to the belief that the world is, in principle, knowable and controllable through a balanced opera-tion of human rationality. This means that scholars are encouraged to conduct their research within established parameters of objectivity and neutrality in order to reach a clear understanding of the phenomenon in question. Matters of ideology – par-ticularly one's own political and moral preferences – are seen as compromising the scientific integrity of the research project. Therefore, the normative dimension of ideology is often excluded from academic attempts to understand globalization.

However, this argument misses the dynamics of globalization as a public dis-course. The public debate over globalization that occurs largely outside the walls of academia represents an important aspect of the phenomenon itself. If the researcher wants to understand the material and ideal stakes raised in the debate, then public judgments regarding the meanings and likely consequences of globalization repre-sent an important subject of study. Thus, the researcher must enter the value-laden arena of ideology. This chapter reflects my view that it is impossible for globaliza-tion scholars to interpret the public discourse on the subject apart from their own ideological and political framework. In spite of the obvious dangers inherent in this move, the inclusion of one's own beliefs and values does not necessarily invalidate one's research project. As the German philosopher Hans-Georg Gadamer (1975) has pointed out, the motivations and prejudices of the interpreter condition every act of understanding. Thus, my study of globalization as a real-life phenomenon is inextricably linked to a critical investigation of the ideological project that I have called 'globalism'.

References

Appadurai, A. 1996. *Modernity at Large: Cultural Dimensions of Globalization*. Minneapo-
    lis: University of Minnesota Press.

Barnett, T.P.M. 2004. *The Pentagon's New Map: War and Peace in the 21st Century*. New York: Putnam.

Bush, G.W. 2002. 'Securing freedom's triumph', *New York Times*, 11 September.

Bush, G.W. 2003. 'Transcript of his Address in London on Iraq and the Middle East', *New York Times*, 19 November.

Broad, R. (ed.) 2002. *Global Backlash: Citizen Initiatives for a Just World Economy*. Lanham, MD: Rowman and Littlefield.

Clinton, H.R. 1999. 'Growth of democracy in Eastern Europe', Speech in Warsaw, 5 October, <http:/www.whitehouse.gov/WH/EOP/FirstLady/html/generalspeeches/1999/19991005.html>.

Clinton, W.J. 1999. 'Remarks by the President on foreign policy', San Francisco, 26 February, <http://www.pub.whitehouse.gov/urires/12R?urn:pdi://oma.eop.gove.us/1999/3/1/3.text.1.html>.

Economic Communiqué. 1996. G7 Summit, Lyons, 28 June, <http:// library.utoronto.ca/www/g7/96ecopre.html>.

Falk, R. 2003. 'Will the empire be fascist?', The Transnational Foundation for Peace and Future Research Forum, 24 March, <http://www.transnational.org/forum/meet/2003/Falk_FascistEmpire.html>.

Freeden, M. 1996. *Ideologies and Political Theory: A Conceptual Approach*. Oxford: Oxford University Press.

Freeden, M. 2003. *Ideology: A Very Short Introduction*. Oxford: Oxford University Press.

Friedman, T. 1999. *The Lexus and the Olive Tree: Understanding Globalization*. New York: Farrar, Strauss and Giroux.

Fukuyama, F. 2000. 'Economic Globalization and Culture: A Discussion with Dr. Francis Fukuyama', <http://www.ml.com/woml/forum/global2.html>.

Gadamer, H.G. 1975. *Truth and Method*. New York: Seabury Press.

Geertz, C. 1973. *The Interpretation of Cultures*. New York: Basic Books.

Gerth H.H. and Mills, C.W. 1946. *From Max Weber: Essays in Sociology*. New York: Oxford University Press.

Gramsci, A. 1971. *Selections from the Prison Notebooks*. New York: International Publishers.

Held, D. 2002. *Globalization/Anti-Globalization*. Cambridge: Polity Press.

Hormats, R. 1998. 'PBS interview with Danny Schechter', <http://pbs.org/globalization/hormats1.html>.

Lasswell, H.D. 1958. *Politics: Who Gets What, When and How*. New York: Meridian Books.

Latouche, S. 1996. *The Westernization of the World*. Cambridge: Polity Press.

McFarlane, R. and Bleyzer, M. 2003. 'Taking Iraq private', *The Wall Street Journal*, 27 March.

Mannheim, K. 1936. *Ideology and Utopia: An Introduction to the Sociology of Knowledge*. Reprint. London: Routledge.

Meehan, J.J. 1997. 'Globalization and technology at work in the bond markets', Speech given in Phoenix, AZ, 1 March, <http://www.bondmarkets.com/news/Meehanspeechfinal.html>.

Mittelman, J.H. 2004. *Whither Globalization? The Vortex of Knowledge and Ideology*. London: Routledge.

National Security Strategy of the United States. 2002. <http://www.whitehouse.gov/nsc/print/nssall.html>.

Olivastro, A. 2002. 'Powell announces U.S.-Middle East Partnership Initiative', The Heritage Foundation, 12 December, <http://www.heritage.org/research/middleeast/wm179.cfm>.

Polanyi, K. 2001 [1944]. *The Great Transformation: The Political and Economic Origins of Our Time*. Boston, MA: Beacon Press.

Ricoeur, P. 1986. *Lectures on Ideology and Utopia*. New York: Columbia University Press.

Ritzer, G. 1993. *The McDonaldization of Society: An Investigation into the Changing Character of Contemporary Social Life*. Thousand Oaks, CA: Pine Forge Press.

Rupert, M. 2000. *Ideologies of Globalization: Contending Visions of a New World Order*. London: Routledge.

Samuelson, R.J. 2003. 'Globalization goes to war', *Newsweek*, 24 February.

Sargent, L.T. 2003. *Contemporary Political Ideologies*, 12th edn. Belmont, CA: Wadsworth/Thomson.

Shays, C. 2003. 'Free markets and fighting terrorism', *Washington Times*, 10 June.

Sklair, L. 2002. *Globalization: Capitalism and Its Alternatives*, 3rd edn. Oxford: Oxford University Press.

Smith, F.W. 1999. 'International finance experts preview upcoming global economic forum', 1 April, <http://www.econstrat.org/pctranscript.html>.

Steger, M.B. 2005. *Globalism: Market Ideology Meets Terrorism*, 2nd edn. Lanham, MD: Rowman and Littlefield.

Steger, M.B. 2003. *Globalization: A Very Short Introduction*. Oxford: Oxford University Press.

Tucker, R.C. 1978. *The Marx-Engels Reader*, 2nd edn. New York: W.W. Norton.

Villar, M. Jr. 1998. 'High-level dialogue on the theme of the social and economic impact of globalization and interdependence and their policy implications', New York, 17 September, <http://www.un.int/philippines/ villar.html>.

Waters, M. 2001. *Globalization*, 2nd edn. London: Routledge.

Further reading

On ideology

Ball, T. and Dagger, R. 2004. *Political Ideologies and the Democratic Ideal*, 5th edn. New York: Pearson/Longman.

Festenstein, M. and Kenny, M. (eds) 2005. *Political Ideologies: A Reader and Guide*. Oxford: Oxford University Press.

Hawkes, D. 2003. *Ideology*, 2nd edn. London: Routledge.

On ideology and globalization

Bourdieu, P. 1998. *Acts of Resistance: Against the Tyranny of the Market*. New York: New Press.

Mittelman, J.T. 2000. *The Globalization Syndrome: Transformation and Resistance*. Princeton, NJ: Princeton University Press.

Steger, M.B. (ed.) 2004. *Rethinking Globalism*. Lanham, MD: Rowman and Littlefield.

On anti-globalist ideologies

Barber, B.R. 1996. *Jihad vs. McWorld*. New York: Ballantine.

Brecher, J., Costello, T. and Smith, B. 2000. *Globalization from Below: The Power of Solidarity*. Cambridge, MA: South End Press.

Klein, N. 2002. *Fences and Windows: Dispatches from the Frontline of the Globalization Debate*. New York: Picador.

Chapter 19

Media and Globalization

DOUGLAS KELLNER AND CLAYTON PIERCE

The concept of globalization has its origin in the *philosophes* of the modern period, such as Condorcet who envisaged a universal and cosmopolitan global society. An early modern theory of globalization can be found in Adam Smith's *Wealth of Nations* (1994) where he famously introduced his concept of the 'invisible hand' of the market. Smith postulated that the individual interests of 'economic man' ought to be mediated through multinational trade and the market throughout Europe and the burgeoning colonial world.

The liberal ethos of Smith's market theory was one of the first enlightenment constructions of the concept of globalization; linking the advancement of both the nation state and the individual within modern society to the caprice of a laissez-faire political economy. Later in the modern period, Karl Marx and Friedrich Engels would articulate a critical theory of globalization that interpreted Smith's and other political economists' (such as David Ricardo) liberal market logic as the ideology of bourgeois imperialism where '[t]he need of a constantly expanding market for its products chases the bourgeoisie over the whole surface of the globe. It must nestle everywhere, settle everywhere, establish connexions everywhere' (Marx and Engels 1978: 476).

Marx and Engels did not theorize globalization one-dimensionally however; instead they interpreted the imperial tendency of the capitalist project to expand markets and modes of production as a dialectic phenomenon bringing about positive and negative effects. For them, nineteenth-century industrial capitalism was bringing the world closer together in ways never before imagined. Marx and Engels envisaged modern technologies such as railroads, the industrialization of the factory, rapid new communication systems such as the telegraph and postal system, and bureaucratic infrastructure from military colonial projects as producing forms of further subjugation as well as potential universal emancipation.

Similarly, proliferating print media, especially the press, called the Fourth Estate in the French Revolution, for both Marx and Engels was also important for the establishment of a democratic public body that could produce the conditions for revolutionary social change. Yet, print media in the mid to late nineteenth century largely was controlled by the bourgeoisie, marginalizing the revolutionary and critical views of the working class movement to counter-hegemonic publications such as Marx and Engels' famous manifesto of the communist party and socialist and other radical newspapers, journals and pamphlets. This decline in the public sphere, as Jürgen Habermas theorized, had been under way since the passing of the bourgeois public sphere of the English, US and French Revolutionary periods (Habermas 1986).

In its ideal form in the late eighteenth century, the public sphere was alive with democratic participation, thus reaching its historical apogee where forms of critical media found their expression in newspapers, journals, salons and public halls of debate. While Habermas' ideal formulation of the public sphere certainly has its limitations, it nonetheless emphasizes the importance of media as a central component for a robust democracy. The concept of the public sphere, therefore, serves as a useful tool in theorizing the role of media in society and a global world because it highlights its mediating function between the public and the systemic interests of capitalist society. As such, today's global public sphere(s) are filled with contradiction and ambiguity, as critical media and resistant social movements confront wealth and power.

Contemporary public sphere(s) are now characterized by some as the 'information society' where globalization involves capitalist markets and sets of social relations, flows of commodities, capital, technology, ideas, forms of culture and people across national boundaries via a globally networked society (Castells 2000; Held et al. 1999). Emphasis on the information and network society, however, can lose sight of how the restructuring of capitalism is taking place in the global age by putting less importance on the way in which technology has enabled the emergence of a networked global capitalist economy. Discussions on globalization and media, therefore, that centre on technological or economic determinism fail to articulate the formative role that capitalist logic plays in determining the qualitative character of technology within information and network society. The reductionist and determinist positions on globalization and media, then, can be categorized as either positive and celebratory globophilia or negative and rejective globophobia (see Kellner 2002).

Many contemporary debates on globalization and media are structured in the logic of either/or, advancing either legitimizing or rejective positions on globalization and media. On the one hand, proponents of globalization espouse celebratory claims of the virtues of a globally connected world and a unified market that usually culminates into some variation of an end of history thesis (Bell 1976; Fukuyama 1992; Gates 1995; Friedman 1999, 2006). Bill Gates (1995) for example, champions technological advancements as a panacea for many social and political problems – envisaging a streamlining of business and public institutions such as schools and corporations through the wonders of technological advancement.

On the other hand, many theorists argue that the negative aspects of globalization and media result in a homogenizing process that only strengthens the dominance of the global market through transnational corporate entities and governmental agencies such as the World Bank, World Trade Organization and the International Monetary Fund (Wallerstein 2004; Robins and Webster 1999; McChesney 2000), and homogenizing global corporations such as McDonald's, CNN, MTV, Microsoft and Nike (Kellner 2003a). These positions view globalization and global media primarily as a homogenizing phenomenon that generates facsimile global consumer cultures everywhere while destroying traditional ones in its wake. The hegemonic effect described by this position emphasizes how the same commodities have become ubiquitous while manifestations of technology, architecture, city planning and uniform infrastructure shape societies the world over. The critical version of globalization focuses on how the lengthening reach of transnational corporations produces a hegemonic form of globalization as they represent the standardization or 'Americanization' of cultures and societies to diverse locations across the world.

This view of globalization and media, however, is contested by arguments that contemporary global capitalism circulates difference, heterogeneity, hybridity and more pluralistic forms of culture. Canclini (1995) shows how Latin American cultures and media combine traditional national forms with more global ones, while the authors of *Golden Arches East* (Watson et al. 1997) show how different Asian cultures appropriate and reproduce products, forms and consumption of McDonald's according to local conditions.

Both the triumphalist and phobic analysis of globalization, however, often fall into a position of either blind enthusiasm and/or rejectionism. Therefore, in order to avoid reproducing a celebratory globophilia or a condemnatory globophobia, a dialectical analysis of media and globalization, by contrast, will allow for a more nuanced interpretation that illuminates both the damaging and liberatory potential of globalization and media in the present historical moment. A dialectic analysis, in other words, not only provides an articulation of oppressive forms of media and globalization, but also identifies how hegemonic forms of media and globalization have the potential to be turned against themselves, and how oppositional social movements can develop their own democratic media and democratize existing media. Articulating a dialectical analysis must first begin, however, by assessing theories of media in a global context.

THEORIZING GLOBAL MEDIA

Canadian scholar Marshall McLuhan was one of the first to theorize the emerging global character of communications media. His groundbreaking study *Understanding Media* (1994) articulated the profound changes that ever-proliferating media were having on everyday life and Western civilization as a whole. For McLuhan, new media were producing more fragmentary, non-rational and aestheticized subjects, immersed in the sights, sounds and spectacle of media such as film, radio, television and advertising. It was in the proliferating media culture of the emergent 'global village' where McLuhan brought attention to the technological medium itself, claiming that in the new media age 'the medium is the message'. His emphasis on communications media as transforming the way individuals come to understand and interpret the world opened up new perceptions of the power of images and sounds that are in constant circulation in the media age. McLuhan was thus one of the first theorists of media to appraise the powerful effects of mass media on subjectivity and culture. While his pioneering insights elucidated new forms of life in a highly technologically mediated society, McLuhan, however, ultimately failed to link the global proliferation of media to its structural and institutional origins.

Similarly, for postmodern theorists of globalization and media such as Jean Baudrillard (1975, 1983), the fetishization of media symbols and images in global consumer culture creates a unique experience of hyperreality where the time-space continuum is compressed through the mass dissemination of media and the commodities. For Baudrillard, commodities form a system of hierarchically organized goods and services that serve as signs pointing to one's standing within the system. According to Baudrillard, consumers have a sense of the codes of consumption whereby certain cars, clothes and other goods signify relative standing in the hierarchy of consumption. Thus luxury objects have more prestigious signification, are desired, and therefore provide seductive social gratifications. On this analysis, needs, use values and consumer practices are all socially constructed and integrate individuals into global consumer society.

While Baudrillard's account lacks a critique of the political economy of media and global consumer society, it nonetheless advances our understanding of the connection between media and global consumer culture by stressing how uses, wants, needs and sign values of commodities are all socially constructed, as part of a system of production and consumption. The emerging global character and rapid movement of signs and cultural symbols through multinational corporate channels form a new reality where the expanding globalization of media reduces society to what Guy Debord (1967) called 'the society of the spectacle'. Spectacles, which are technologically mediated forms of the media and consumer society, reproduce consumer capitalism on a global scale (Kellner 2003a). Thus, in the post-World War II conjuncture, the spectacle became globalized as corporations such as Coca-Cola and Pepsi, sundry national automobile corporations, IBM and the nascent computer industry, and subsequently McDonald's, Nike, forms of media culture, celebrities, Microsoft and a cornucopia of global products, circulated throughout the world. With increasingly complex forms of media, global culture and media were producing and disseminating the values, attitudes and the rationality of a capitalist consumer culture at unprecedented levels.

By contrast to Baudrillard and Debord, Stuart Hall views the spread of information and communication technologies as not necessarily translating into domination and subjugation to a global market and spectacle. Hall's (1980) writing on the 'Global Postmodern', for instance, articulates a hybrid theory of globalization and media as opposed to a homogenized and deterministic one. For Hall, the global postmodern signifies an ambiguous opening to difference and to the margins which can lead to a decentring of the Western narrative. His theory of the postmodern global, therefore, involves a pluralizing of culture, openings to the margins, and to voices excluded from the narratives of Western culture, while circulating a whole world of cultural difference and heterogeneity. While Hall's hybrid analysis of globalization valorizes the potential for plurality and counter-hegemonic narratives, it also de-emphasizes the negative effects of media and globalization.

In contrast to Hall's interpretation of the impact of globalization and media, Frankfurt School theorists Max Horkheimer and Theodor Adorno's seminal essay on the 'Culture Industry' accentuates how media technologies, such as film, television, radio, newspapers and magazines, represent powerful new sources for capital's realization in a new form of social control (Horkheimer and Adorno 2002). For Horkheimer and Adorno, the harnessing of media and communication technologies allow the forces of capital an unprecedented influence on forms of culture in advanced society, whereby media and information technologies under the tutelage of capital serve as a tool of administration that utilizes the sphere of culture to shape individuals and society into its own image. The culture industry for Horkheimer and Adorno forecloses emancipatory possibilities and produces instead the conditions for systematic domination and control. The negative dimension of the dialectic of the proliferation of media and communication technologies under Horkheimer and Adorno's analysis is given stark relief; yet it was another Frankfurt theorist who further developed a dialectic analysis of technology in advanced society.

Herbert Marcuse's critical theory of technology illuminates both the contradictions and potential of technological society and culture. In his critical theory of technology Marcuse provides a systematic treatment of technology and technique within the framework of capitalist society that emphasizes not only how technology is shaped, but also how individual needs, cultural expressions and ways of relating to technology are also produced. As such, Marcuse's dialectic of technology avoids technological or economic determinism by recognizing the potential for alternative expressions of technology and human relations with technology that are set within the present historical context. A critical and dialectical analysis of technology, such as the one articulated by Marcuse, elucidates both the potential and the contradictions of media and information and communication technology in the global age.

Thus, one of the major strengths of a critical theory of globalization, the media and technology is that it moves beyond both a blinding technological enthusiasm and the condemnatory deterministic model that perceives media and technology as antithetical to emancipatory political and social possibilities. But perhaps most importantly, the democratic potential of media and technology is drawn out in a dialectic analysis of the globalization of media and information and communication technologies. In other words, a systemic analysis best illuminates global media in the contemporary historical moment where the structural organization of media outlets spread both corporate domination and ideology, as well as their democratic potential.

GLOBAL MEDIA CULTURE

During the twentieth century, broadcast media tended to be dominated in most countries by the nation-state and transmitted national culture, with the important exception of the United States which developed a commercial broadcasting media from the beginning (Kellner 1990). During the 1980s, the rise of neoliberal politics and satellite and cable technology rapidly disseminated privatized media that soon led to the proliferation of global media culture, the decline of public service broadcasting and growing power of regional and global media conglomerates.

There is little doubt that from the perspective of political economy, global media outlets are overwhelmingly shaped and determined by transnational corporate interests. Megamergers over the last decade have produced massive, large-scale communication conglomerates such as AOL/Time Warner, Disney, News Corporation,

Viacom, Bertelsmann, AT&T, Viacom and others. The superstructure created by this global media oligopoly is an example of 'globalization from above' where the flow of information, images, cultural artefacts and entertainment is distributed from a uniform and increasingly unregulated source. The nation-state loses power as the distributor of cultural forms and commodities to transnational corporations where the reproduction of consumer culture attitudes and lifestyles has become one of the consequences of the 'globalization from above' model.

George Ritzer's 'McDonaldization' thesis provides a strong example of this phenomenon where US consumer culture icons and production process and consumption patterns are delivered to different contexts via the corporate franchise, such as McDonald's fast food restaurants (Ritzer 1996). In addition to consumer culture lifestyle, however, Ritzer argues that modern processes of rationalization, streamlined production and delivery practices, and uniform relations of exchange are all established and diffused through the franchise model, albeit in a variety of culturally variant forms. The McDonaldization process thus highlights another facet of globalization where iconic corporate entities not only colonize new markets, but also introduce a system of productions and consumption processes that reproduce global capitalist society.

Part of circulating a consumer culture throughout the world requires the ability to reach diverse markets with effective consumer messages and values. Brazil's Globo and Mexico's Televisa, for example, are two of Latin America's largest media conglomerates that disseminate both a consumer and entertainment culture across Latin America as well as to the rest of the Spanish-speaking globe that does not limit the market to national boundaries. In the examples of Globo and Televisa, the role of the nation-state, understood as the sole source of media and market regulation and distribution, has changed with the rise of the global and regional market which now almost effortlessly extends beyond the geographical boundaries of the state. Accompanying the 'globalization from above' model, therefore, is the extension of a consumer and media culture into diverse communities, blurring national boundaries while also creating the potential to either supplement and/or overtake local forms of media.

This new 'communications geography' described above, Morley and Robins argue (1995), has reconfigured how information, cultural images and commodities flow between nations and geographic boundaries. The transnational system of delivery by media conglomerates creates a unique media landscape where the articulation of global and local identities through media takes on great importance. Thus, through the emergent spatial environment of images and cultural representations a condition is formed where defining local or regional identities within global forces are of serious consequence. Taking the European context, for example, under the influence of entities such as the European Union and concomitantly the pan-European market, a European identity is produced and channelled through a uniform and economically 'stabilizing' media. As a result, local and regional cultures throughout Europe find themselves contesting the constructed pan-Euro image in order to retain their unique expressions of cultural identity. As the globally produced Euro-identity excludes many cultural articulations, the role of locally produced media, therefore, must shift in order to provide diverse cultures across Europe a space in which to articulate their own version of culture and the glocal. This tension between globalism and localism exemplifies for Morley and Robins the new spatial dynamics of globalized media and the diminished role of the nation-state. Resistance to forms of homogenization and the imposed cultural and market values indeed requires access and control of local and regional media outlets. Contestation to the expansion of markets and consumer culture into the four corners of the globe allows for a space of resistance and cultural autonomy in an increasingly predatory form of globalization.

GLOBALIZATION FROM BELOW AND RESISTANCE

While the negative aspects of corporate globalization certainly seem to be expanding, the conflicts it produces may be providing resistance to the 'globalization from above' model. The possibility for 'globalization from below' has begun to manifest itself through transnational alliances between groups that are struggling for better wages and working conditions, social and political justice, environmental protection and more democracy, freedom and social justice worldwide. The globalization from below model puts a renewed emphasis on local and grassroots struggle that have put dominant economic forces on the defensive in their own backyard – often disseminating media and messages over the Internet that have called attention to oppressive and destructive corporate policies on the local level, putting national and even transnational pressure upon major corporations for reform. Moreover, proliferating oppositional media make possible a greater circulation of struggles and the possibilities of novel alliances and solidarities that can connect resistant forces who oppose capitalist and corporate-state elite forms of globalization from above (for a survey of global forms of democratizing media, see the studies in Hackett and Zhao 2005).

A model of globalization from below is also articulated in Hardt and Negri's (2000, 2004) theory of globalization where they argue that autonomous grassroots movements in coalition with other social and political movements form a 'Multitude' to contest what they have termed 'Empire'. The emerging global 'Empire', for Hardt and Negri, produces evolving forms of sovereignty, economy, culture, and political struggle and resistance of the 'Multitude' that unleash an unforeseeable and unpredictable flow of novelty, flow and upheavals. From their perspective, resistance to 'Empire' will be a shifting and constantly transformative movement from below.

One of the most famous contemporary examples of the politicization of local and global media and communication and information technologies for radical social movements, and globalization from below, comes from the Zapatista indigenous movement in Chiapas, Mexico. Multiple sites on the Internet serve as a forum for the movement's communication and information as well as for individuals and groups who are sympathetic and supportive of the EZLN's grassroots political movement. The EZLN's Radio Insurgente is also accessible from the Internet where broadcasts of local programmes over FM and shortwave radio are able to reach a global audience. Other examples of 'globalization from below' come from a cornucopia of anti-corporate globalization movement websites that seek to organize as well as disseminate information and events at the local as well as the national levels such as those that took place in Seattle in 1999 and Cancun, Mexico in 2003 (Kahn and Kellner 2003).

As a result of such recent anti-capitalist globalization events, many activists were energized by the new alliances, solidarities and militancy, which have led to a continued cultivation of an anti-globalization movement that can be seen in the progeny generated by this enthusiasm: the Internet organization Indymedia (see www.indymedia.org). Indymedia is a locally produced and community-based operation that has evolved into an expanding international network that encompasses hundreds of like centres in numerous countries across the globe that focus on providing a space for local issues and community concerns over the Internet. The creation of Indymedia was linked to its organic connection to the anti-globalization movement which utilized the Internet as a space in which to continue dissent and the distribution of alternative forms of media as well as to organize for future political events and protests (see Morris 2004).

The Seattle demonstrations inspired not only new media organizations, but also other anti-corporate globalization movements as it was followed by April 2000 with struggles in Washington DC to protest the World Bank and IMF, later in the year against capitalist globalization in Prague and Melbourne, and in April 2001, an extremely large and militant protest erupted against the Free Trade Area of the Americas summit in Quebec City, followed by a powerful demonstration in Genoa in July 2001 against the G8 summit meeting. It was apparent that a new worldwide movement was in the making capable of uniting diverse opponents of capitalist globalization throughout the world. The anti-corporate globalization movement, as exemplified in the above protests, favoured globalization from below, which would protect the environment, labour rights, national cultures, democratization and other goods from the ravages of an uncontrolled capitalist globalization (see Falk 1999; Brecher et al. 2000).

More recently, the Live 8 concerts, coordinated to take place simultaneously with the G8 summit in the summer of 2005, utilized multimedia technologies, the Internet and other communication and information technologies to link up multiple cities across the globe in an effort to influence the world's wealthiest nations to put an end to world poverty and call attention to the plight and suffering of the people on the African continent. The merging of the entertainment world, information and communication technologies, and mainstream media culminated in a media megaspectacle where U2's Bono became the spokesman for a political movement to raise consciousness about the poverty epidemic on the African continent.

The Live 8 media spectacle exemplifies the phenomenon of global media spectacle where multi-millions are spent on the creation of a megaspectacle; ironically, the enormous amount of resources spent on Live 8 might have been better allocated if it would have instead directly gone towards obtaining sustenance for the millions of people that the concerts purportedly were speaking for. Indeed, the Live 8 megaspectacle highlights the logic of the spectacle where form disproportionately outweighs content, where transnational media conglomerates and the entertainment industry gain hefty profits and prestige all while under the pretence of 'consciousness raising'. The Live 8 example puts into stark relief the limitation of politics at the level of spectacle: progressive and transformative political content must come from a reconfiguration of media instead of relying on its existing inequitable and profit oriented form. In the age of media spectacle, one that is marked by a diversity of spectacles in the field of politics, culture, entertainment and every realm of social life, the distortion of reality has become the norm, pushing democracy in the United States and around the world further into crisis (Kellner 2003a and 2005).

GLOBAL MEDIA SPECTACLES

The contemporary moment's fluid media landscape reflects the incredible velocity at which major political and social events move through information and communication technologies, saturating public spheres across the world. Global media spectacles such as the 2000 US presidential election, the 11 September terror attacks, and the Afghanistan and the Iraq Wars have signalled a qualitative shift in our media driven society where politics and media have seamlessly merged into one. Add to this the breakneck pace at which images, sounds and filmed events circulate around the globe and it becomes clear that discerning reality in the global media landscape is much more difficult than ever before. Presidential elections, war, entertainment and consumer culture all travel at an amazing rate that produces the conditions in which the concrete referent is no longer required to attribute meaning to its spectacle form – blurring the boundaries of each.

The media spectacle of 11 September and its aftermath would mark a new era of global relations between nations and highly focused media coverage of a variety of 'Terror Wars' (Kellner 2005). In the heightened atmosphere of terror and anti-terrorist activity, global media images have become the face in which the world perceives the 'war on terror' and varied insurgencies and military action across the globe. The contesting images construct and deliver to US audiences messages such as the Bush administration promoting 'enduring freedom' and 'the spread of democracy', or from the perspective of Al-Jazeera and other Arab networks, as well as some European networks, conflicting views of a violent US and UK occupation of Iraq. In this atmosphere, getting one's political message across has taken on new gravity. Control and construction of information of the ongoing Iraq War, resistance to US military occupation and political justification for the intervention are structured by what images and events the various global, national or local media portray. In the United States, images of the toppling of a Saddam Hussein statue in Baghdad to the image of a triumphant US president upon an aircraft carrier communicate a strong and defiant resolve from one nation's leader. Yet, the political landscape in which such spectacles work in favour of specific political interests generates a space where contradictions and contestation can also come into plain view, such as the mocking of Bush's claim of 'mission accomplished' in Iraq.

Take, for instance, the construction of the images of torture and abuse from Abu Ghraib prison where digital pictures of detainees in barbaric and humiliating poses saturated the global media terrain. From the repetitive stream of images of Iraqi prisoner abuse by US soldiers and the quest to pin responsibility on the soldiers themselves and/or higher US military and political authorities, an intense media spectacle unfolded (Kellner 2005). The novelty of the Abu Ghraib media event, however, came from the fact that the origin of the digital images came from technologies carried and employed by the US soldiers themselves. Digital cameras and digital recorders allowed US soldiers in charge of detaining the Iraqi prisoners to be able to document the cruel and unusual punishment as though it were reality television. As the images quickly spread over the Internet, the global media landscape began to explode with graphic and shocking pictures and outrage. The amount of time that elapsed from the event itself to its reception in the public viewing audience was quite striking, revealing how new media technologies have altered traditional channels of news and information and how they flow between events and audiences. With the example of Abu Ghraib, therefore, it was the media and communication technologies that enabled contradictory information into the public sphere, escaping mainstream filters that may or may not have sanitized these particular images as well as their political consequences.

Similarly, the July 2005 London terror bombings also became a global media spectacle that utilized new technologies such as digital video phones to capture the immediate aftermath of train and bus bombings in the middle of London's morning commute. The spectacle of the London bombings showed vulnerabilities to terrorism in major Western cities and produced weeks of global media spectacle with further terror threats and an intense manhunt for the guilty parties. Media coverage of the London bombings focused dominantly on the victims and culprits – detaching the event from the UK's participation in the Iraq War and policies and treatment of discontented Muslim citizens within England. The US media framed the event as an isolated terrorist act perpetrated by misguided and malevolent domestic terrorists, whereas more critical global media framed it in terms of a price paid by the United Kingdom for its role in the invasion and occupation of Iraq.

The Abu Ghraib and London bombing spectacles point to the powerful role that information and communication technologies have in the global media landscape. In both cases, it was new technologies that allowed these events to surface in such a short amount of time. The rise of alternative media sources over the Internet such as blogs and other independent media sources found, such as Indymedia and Free Speech TV, could be signalling a departure from our reliance for information and news from traditional mainstream corporate media outlets.

The emergent presence of such alternative media outlets was felt during the 2004 presidential election in the United States where alternative media sources began to take on a degree of legitimacy (see Kellner 2005). Over the duration of the 2004 presidential campaigns, blog 'watches' become a part of corporate media programming as segments of network news programmes on CNN, MSNBC, MTV and other major networks devoted daily time to getting a sense of the blogsphere and what it was producing through various stories being transmitted over the Internet. It appeared during the US presidential elections of 2004 and Congressional elections of 2006 that coverage of the political pulse of the nation had at least been partially diverted to the Internet allowing a plethora of blogs from both the left and the right to disseminate voices and views that otherwise would not have been heard. However, it remains to be seen how new forms of media such as blogs will continue to have an effect in the public sphere which could decline into a fragmentary babble of views, positions and rhetoric that fail to articulate with on-the-ground political and social movements. Nevertheless, the accessibility and relatively user-friendly quality of Internet media sources offer the potential for a democratic reconfiguration and redistribution of traditional sources of news and information on a global scale.

In 2005, however, global media spectacles centred on a series of devastating natural disasters. During January 2005, dramatic images and stories of the Asian tsunami saturated the media and seduced a fascinated audience with the power and fury of Mother Nature with image after image of gigantic waves crashing with violent and tremendous force onto unsuspecting beaches and towns. The Asian tsunami global spectacle was characterized by images of devastation and death that covered headlines across the globe and propelled every major media network with horrific and dramatic content for the viewing audience. This was the first time that dead bodies were exhibited in such profusion on television as the death tolls and piles of drowned corpses drove the global spectacle of one of the worst natural disasters in history.

In late summer 2005, the global village experienced a spectacle of immense devastation and death from Hurricane Katrina. Global media, in the Hurricane Katrina example and the Asian tsunami, feed on images and stories of misery, despair, death and utter loss. Footage of dead bodies hanging from trees and floating in the flooded and abandoned streets of New Orleans marks the global media spectacle of the destruction of one of the United States' most historic cities. The old principle of local news – 'if it bleeds, it leads' – is now becoming a watchword of global media spectacles as it seems that the events themselves lose gravity in the wake of the media feeding frenzy that immediately ensues, constructing the horror of disaster and devastation into consumable mini-dramas interlaced with political talking heads who give some semblance of authority and direction in a time of extreme destruction and chaos.

Throughout the world, there were criticisms of the Bush administration's inadequate response to the disaster, claims that it revealed their distorted priorities and even racism, and that the spectacle of disaster revealed the growing discrepancies between haves and have nots in the United States. In the United States, there was sustained criticism of the Bush administration and serious critiques of Bush himself by appalled reporters experiencing the disaster first-hand and commentators appalled by the extent of the disaster and paucity of the US government response. Thus, spectacle of disasters can produce critical political discourse as well as allow governments to engage in propaganda and to push through their agendas, as the Bush administration manipulated the 9/11 tragedy (see Kellner 2003b).

With the global proliferation of novel forms of media and information and communication technologies our increasingly 'wired' world indeed requires new tools for understanding media and its relationship to the process of globalization. Undoubtedly, globalization from above has made its mark across the globe and continues to reproduce oppressive and anti-democratic uses of media and social relations. By approaching media in the global terrain, however, from a dialectic framework, a space for the articulation of resistive movements to dominant models of media can occur, opening up the possibility for democratic and autonomous uses of media and technology in both the local and global contexts. Resistance to globalization from above, therefore, may very well rest in a community's ability to produce and disseminate alternative forms of media and culture that are linked to transformative social and political movements that seek to change existing structures of production and distribution from the media to the economy. This emerging trend in the way media and information and communication technologies are used illuminates novel practices and reconfigurations of media and technology where the democratization of media can and has begun. In addition, vigilance to forms of corporate media and the triumph of spectacle must come from social and cultural referents that can generate democratic forces from their particular historical condition.

References

Baudrillard, J. 1975. *For a Critique of the Political Economy of the Sign*. St Louis: Telos Press.

Baudrillard, J. 1983. *Simulations*. New York: Semiotext{e}.

Bell, D. 1976. *The Coming of Post-Industrial Society*. New York: Basic Books.

Best, S. and Kellner, D. 2001. *The Postmodern Adventure*. London: Guilford Press.

Brecher, J., Costello, T. and Smith, B. 2000. *Globalization from Below*. Boston: South End Press.

Canclini, N.G. 1995. *Hybrid Cultures: Strategies for Entering and Leaving Modernity*. Minneapolis: University of Minnesota Press.

Castells, M. 2000. *The Rise of the Network Society*. Vol. I of *The Information Age: Economy, Society and Culture*, 2nd edn. Oxford: Blackwell.

Debord, G. 1967. *Society of the Spectacle*. Detroit: Black and Red.

Falk, R. 1999. *Predatory Globalization*. Cambridge: Polity Press; Palo Alto, CA: Stanford University Press.

Friedman, T. 1999. *The Lexus and the Olive Tree*. New York: Farrar, Straus and Giroux.

Friedman, T. 2006. *The World is Flat*. New York: Farrar, Straus and Giroux.

Fukuyama, F. 1992. *The End of History and the Last Man*. New York: Free Press.

Gates, B. 1995. *The Road Ahead*. New York: Viking Press.

Habermas, J. 1986. *The Structural Transformation of the Bourgeois Public Sphere*. Translated by T. Burger. Cambridge, MA: MIT Press.

Hackett, R.A. and Zhao, Y. (eds) 2005. *Democratizing Global Media*. New York: Rowman and Littlefield.

Hall, S. 1980. 'Encoding/decoding'. In S. Hall, D. Hobson, A. Lowe and P. Willis (eds), *Culture, Media, Language*, 128–38. London: Hutchinson.

Hardt, M. and Negri, A. 2000. *Empire*. Cambridge, MA: Harvard University Press.

Hardt, M. and Negri, A. 2004. *Multitude*. New York: Penguin Press.

Held, D., McGrew, A., Goldblatt, D. and Perratton, J. 1999. *Global Transformations*. Cambridge: Polity Press; Palo Alto, CA: Stanford University Press.

Horkheimer, M. and Adorno, T.W. 2002. *Dialectic of Enlightenment*. Translated by E. Jephcott. Stanford, CA: Stanford University Press.

Kahn, R. and Kellner, D. 2003. 'New media, Internet activism, and blogging'. In D. Muggleton (ed.), *The Post-Subcultures Reader*, 299–314. London: Berg.

Kellner, D. 1990. *Television and the Crisis of Democracy*. Boulder, CO: Westview Press.

Kellner, D. 2001. *Grand Theft 2000*. Lanham, MD: Rowman and Littlefield.

Kellner, D. 2002. 'Theorizing globalization', *Sociological Theory*, 20 (3), 285–305.

Kellner, D. 2003a. *Media Spectacle*. London: Routledge.

Kellner, D. 2003b. *From 9/11 to Terror War: Dangers of the Bush Legacy*. Lanham, MD: Rowman and Littlefield.

Kellner, D. 2005. *Media Spectacle and the Crisis of Democracy*. Boulder, CO: Paradigm Publishers.

Marcuse, H. 1991. *One-Dimensional Man: Studies in the Ideology of Advanced Industrial Society*. Boston: Beacon Press.

Marx, K. and Engels, F. 1978. 'The Communist Manifesto'. In R.C. Tucker (ed.), *The Marx-Engels Reader*, 469–501. New York: W.W. Norton.

McChesney, R. 2000. *Rich Media, Poor Democracy*. New York: New Press.

McLuhan, M. 1994. *Understanding Media: The Extensions of Man*. Cambridge, MA: MIT Press.

Morley, D. and Robins, K. 1995. *Spaces of Identity: Global Media, Electronic Landscapes and Cultural Boundaries*. New York: Routledge.

Morris, D. 2004. 'Globalization and media democracy: The case of Indymedia'. In D. Schuler and P. Day (eds), *Shaping the Network Society: The New Role of Civil Society in Cyberspace*, 325–52. Cambridge, MA: MIT Press.

Ritzer, G. 1996. *The McDonaldization of Society*. Thousand Oaks, CA: Pine Forge Press.

Ritzer, G. 2004. *The Globalization of Nothing*. Thousand Oaks, CA: Pine Forge Press.

Robins, K. and Webster, F. 1999. *Times of Technoculture*. London: Routledge.

Smith, A. 1994. *The Wealth of Nations*. New York: Random House.

Steger, M. 2002. *Globalism: The New Market Ideology*. New York: Rowman and Littlefield.

Wallerstein, I. 2004. *World Systems Analysis: An Introduction*. Durham, NC: Duke University Press.

Watson, J.L. (ed.) 1998. *Golden Arches East: McDonald's in East Asia*. Palo Alto, CA: Stanford University Press.

Chapter 20

Globalization and Information and Communications Technologies: The Case of War

HOWARD TUMBER AND FRANK WEBSTER

INTRODUCTION

Without information and communications technologies (ICTs) it is hard to conceive of the scale and scope of contemporary globalization: its reach, its immediacy, the volumes of information made available and exchanged as matters of routine. We could not be where we are without computers, satellites and associated technologies. Because of this it is tempting to offer here a technocentric account of the globalization process wherein technical advances are regarded as its creator and dynamo.

This would be mistaken for at least two reasons. First, because such technocentrism suffers from being technologically determinist, from the folly of supposing that technologies have social effects while themselves are untouched by social forces. Second, in prioritizing technology, a technocentric approach oversimplifies change, failing to acknowledge the multifarious influences on and directions of globalization (Webster and Erickson 2004; Veseth 2005). To address these errors, and to allow us to explore the complexities of the connections between ICTs and globalization, we focus here on contemporary war. In what follows we shall explore connections between globalization and ICTs as they are manifested in Information War (or what might be conceived as war in a globalized world). It is salutary to examine war for another reason as well: so much commentary on globalization stresses the positive elements of economic integration, cultural exchange and affordable travel that it is a jolt to be reminded that armed conflict has closely accompanied the globalization process.

Information War is much more than a matter of technology, though ICTs do play a prominent part and are amongst the most frequent phenomena observed by commentators. Information War has two key dimensions: first, advanced weaponry that incorporates best-available computer communications technologies and, second, an enormous emphasis on media. The weaponry is saturated with ICTs while the media concern massively promotes the role of information and communications. Information War weaponry is exemplified by smart missiles, by hugely expensive and virtuoso air power, by myriad forms of surveillance that involve satellites, intercepts and sensors, and by command and control systems of staggering sophistication; Information War media is manifest in the presence of hundreds, sometimes thousands, of reporters generating enormous piles of words and images, in the burgeoning growth of military public relations personnel, in Internet blogs from sites of conflict, in indy websites that challenge more mainstream media coverage and in the growth of publics watching, in real time and round the globe, the workings out of the most recent wars. Joseph Nye (2002) distinguishes these in terms of them being 'hard' and 'soft': Information War weapons are hard in that they disable and destroy identified enemies with unprecedented force and efficacy; Information War media is soft in that it deals with symbols that require interpretation and analysis. Boundaries between the two are sure to be blurred: ICTs radically influence the ecology of media and Psych Ops (the attempt to win hearts and minds, at home and abroad) is an integral element of armed forces. It should not be imagined that the 'hard' can do without the 'soft', even if it generally takes precedence in the short term.

Media have long played a vital role in war. As a rule they have been harnessed to the war effort to support the motherland. However, in circumstances of Information War media play a more ambiguous and ambivalent part. How could it be otherwise when, for instance, journalists may file stories from the remotest regions provided they have their satellite video phones, when the Internet means that the accounts they file are available for feedback almost immediately to the subjects upon whom they report, or when it is common to find correspondents reporting from locations on the receiving end of incoming missiles from 'their' side? In addition, there is such an increase in media coverage of conflict zones, such a convergence of media practitioners from around the world on particular trouble spots, and such a diversity of reporters and their organizations, that it cannot be surprising that there is considerable uncertainty about the messages generated on rolling news services, on weblogs, e-mails and the Internet.

GLOBALIZATION AND MEDIA

Globalization of media helps bring into being a common symbolic environment across the world (Tomlinson 1999). We may conceive now of large majorities sharing a symbolic sphere which achieves ready recognition irrespective of location: images of city scapes such as New York, San Francisco and Washington, key sites such as the Taj Mahal, the Wailing Wall and the Vatican, politicians like George W. Bush, Vladimir Putin and Silvio Berlusconi, etc. How these symbols are received and understood, indeed how long they are remembered, are of course different and complicated matters, but the fact remains that these exemplify a worldwide symbolic environment.

The media explosion of recent decades, across the world, has led to there being staggering amounts of information available – anywhere, anytime we have 24-hour news services, entertainment programmes, radio talk shows, Internet access, cable and satellite stations. This is inflected, to be sure, but there is such a vast quantity of information, in so many different outlets, coming with such velocity, that it is beyond the control of even majority suppliers.

Thus, while we can agree that the media are mostly owned and supplied by Western organizations, and that they offer predominantly Western ways of seeing, there are many instances of countervailing messages being put out, sent in and received. Al-Jazeera, for instance, is a small organization that competes for attention with major news outfits such as CNN and the BBC. Nonetheless, audiences with appropriate connections receive it across the world (Miles 2005). Not surprisingly, perhaps, its major audiences are in the Arabic countries (where it claims to be viewed by upwards of 35 million people), but English language versions are readily available virtually anywhere. In short, whatever its overall limits, from today's media its audiences can glean information about issues and events that is often counter to what one might presume is a 'Western interest' and, in turn, metropolitan viewers and listeners get access to information about events and issues, places and people, of which they are otherwise ignorant. To this extent, albeit imperfectly, the global media environment contains elements of what one may conceive of as a 'transnational public sphere' where information – even discussion and debate between strangers – may be exchanged (Calhoun 2004).

MEDIA, GLOBALIZATION AND WAR REPORTING

News media are drawn to cover war for several reasons. One is the obvious appeal of newsmakers towards the drama of conflict. The enormously high stakes ensure that it is a priority for most news media. When war erupts, or when it is sensed that war is about to break out, then nowadays the world's media swarm to the trouble spot. The bigger the conflict, the more consequential the fighting and the more involved are major powers (or those with access to nuclear weapons such as Israel, Pakistan and India) then the more media will attend. When one notes that an estimated two thousand journalists converged on the Balkans in 1999 during the Kosovan conflagration when NATO forces went into action against Serbia, then one may appreciate the scale of media attention. Not far short of double that number of journalists set off for Iraq in 2003 when the United States and its 'coalition of the willing' moved to overthrow Saddam Hussein. More than 700 went directly with the military forces as 'embeds', but the majority were there as freelancers, stringers or with media organizations but unattached to armed units. Many of these journalists are 'parachuted' in from metropolitan centres during notably serious conflicts, adding gravitas by their presence, edging local journalists aside, but giving more weight and urgency to the images and texts that flow from the trouble spot.

The output of journalists in these circumstances can be prodigious, whether in reports to newspapers, in photographs or video film, or in contributions to the weblogs that sprang up during the conflict. A good deal would of course have been filed in particular languages for particular places, but still much will emerge into a wider public realm since media personnel famously read and watch other media output and raid it unabashedly, and there are also other ways in which news gets circulated (e.g. academic and agitational networks which cull, translate and high-light pertinent items for diverse audiences and interests). Globalization ensures that this happens across great distances, in great volume, in great quantity and at times almost ceaselessly.

Undoubtedly, many of the journalists will be positioned with the military forces, and most there are restricted in what they can and perhaps are willing to report. Embeds, for instance, by and large provided stories supportive of the invading forces during the Iraq War, seeing the battles through the eyes of the military. Yet such is the volume of reportage, so diverse and so numerous are the correspondents who come from so many points of origin that in the ensuing 'information blizzard' (Keane 1998) that accompanies large-scale armed conflicts, it is to be expected that many reports that are not 'on message' get through. So Iraq video footage of dead American and British soldiers, first shown on Al-Jazeera, was quickly available. Moreover, film of civilian casualties and of stretched hospital staff desperately trying to cope with the injured, anathema to the invading forces, was highlighted by some journalists and widely circulated. The very presence of so many and so disparate journalists drawn to war situations, the sheer volume of reportage and the unman-ageable character of so many aspects of war, means that undesirable stories will get through, whatever the military authorities and politicians strive to do.

A second feature of media and war is the combination – one might say the paradox – of the journalists' search to 'tell it like it is' and what one may describe as their cultivated cynicism. Amongst the most revered journalists covering war are those with reputations for seeking 'truth', however much that might displease pow-erful interests. One thinks here, for instance, of James Cameron's reportage for *Picture Post* of ill-treatment of prisoners from Korea in the 1950s, of Seymour Hersh's exposure of the My Lai massacre in Vietnam in the late 1960s (and of Abu Ghraib prison abuses 40 years on [Hersh 2005]), of Maggie O'Kane's despatches from the Balkans in the 1990s, of John Simpson's defiantly independent reports from Baghdad (where he was wounded and one of his team killed in 2003) for the BBC and so on.

One should remember here that a good number of journalists are injured and even killed when reporting from war zones. To operate in such places generally requires an ethical calling. There are plenty of other ways in which a journalist may make his or her living, even if they remain within the business. Wars are inherently hazardous locations, so it is not surprising to see those who report from them described as 'an unacknowledged aristocracy of journalism' (Marr 2004: 327). The Committee to Protect Journalists (www.cpj.org) lists some 300 journalists killed in conflict zones (excluding those who died in accidents) over the past decade. In Afghanistan late in 2001 eight journalists were killed, actually more than US troops in action, and over three dozen have died in Iraq during the year following the 2003 war. Behind the deaths are many more instances of shrapnel wounds, threats and frightening episodes in places as varied as Israel and Sierra Leone.[1] War reporting undoubtedly has its rewards, but it requires an ethical calling from journalists pre-pared to risk life and limb.

The cynicism of journalists covering war comes from several sources, not least the experiences of the reporters in conflict situations, where they are likely to receive sharply conflicting accounts of events. A particular cause is the efforts of combatants to *perception manage*. Notably since the Vietnam War and the defeat there of the United States, the notion that it was an uncontrolled media that led to US withdrawal gained ground amongst powerful figures in political and especially military circles. The conviction that media were important to war, but not to be trusted, has informed military and political 'planning for war' ever since. So self-conscious and developed is this process of perception management that one might believe that the outcome in terms of media coverage is ordained – a one-way flood of items gathered away from the battlefield, at locations chosen by the military, and from handouts issued by the Defence Department. In certain circumstances, this may be the case – coverage from the Falklands, far away in the South Atlantic, accessible only by military transport, and with the media reliant on military technologies to get their messages through is one such example (Morrison and Tumber 1988). As regards the embeds in Iraq during 2003–4, it appears too that most reportage they offered was anodyne, supportive derring-do accounts from the units they were with, and it did little to inform the public of either the course or consequences of the war because what was reported tended to be localized and particular to a specific military unit, even if on occasion it could capture its chaos and confusion.

Journalists by and large went along with the policy because it was regarded as superior to the alternative (being excluded from the action). Sharing the conditions of the soldiers, an understandable empathy with their 'boys' quickly developed, but, as a TV news editor advised his embedded correspondents: 'you can't be friends with these people . . . they'll be nice people and you'll get to know them and like them, but . . . the journalist's duty is to betray'. What these efforts to manage war coverage by those who wage it have done for journalists is to bolster their scepticism. Journalists who did participate as embeds were aware of restrictions being imposed on them, as they were conscious of the military's desire to have them be extensions of the war effort.

It makes a cynical profession still more cynical when it notes the attempts of the military and official spokespeople to ensure that the media are 'on side', a feeling evident in the frustration expressed to us by a reporter for the conservative *Daily Mail* when she contrasted what she learned from talking to people whom she encountered in the streets after the fall of Baghdad with 'ludicrous press conferences' where journalists were 'hearing lies from the military'. This bolsters journalists' disposition to treat *all* sources sceptically, an important factor in what and how they report from the war zone.

Recent history, moreover, has weakened any sense journalists might have that they are reporting for their side, that they are *de facto* extensions of the military effort. If, for instance, journalists are foreign nationals, then it is likely that moral claims from the military for allegiance to their own country's soldiery will be weakened. When one adds that journalists now converge on trouble spots from around the globe, then one appreciates how difficult control becomes – it may just have been possible for British military forces in Northern Ireland to appeal to the shared nationality of British reporters to self-censor their stories (Curtis 1984), but just what strength has this when applied to a journalist from Australia or Sweden?

These factors – pervasive media availability, the attraction of news agencies to war situations, professional ethics amongst journalists and their entrenched scepticism – mean that, however urgent and sustained the efforts to control and contain coverage made by combatants, there will always be 'seepage' in what gets out. What gets covered, and how it gets covered, are thus necessarily variable and hard to control with precision.

We would draw attention here to a countervailing pressure that can tell on military forces that would like to determine news about their actions. These attempt a range of strategies to ensure that they get appropriate and acceptable messages reported about their activities, from long-term cultivation of contacts in the media, granting privileged access to favoured reporters, to aggressive physical threats towards journalists who get too close to situations the military does not want them to see. Journalists frequently comment on these strategies and they are acutely sensitive towards them. One option available to the military is exclusion of reporters from the battle scene. This may be tried, but it contains a fatal flaw. Today wars are almost invariably waged on grounds of the moral and practical superiority of democratic societies, a key element of which is that there is a free press and that citizens have a right to know what is being done in their name. When military forces exclude the media then this flies in the face of democratic principles and threatens the war's claims to legitimacy. More than that, it is met usually by accusations of military wrongdoing and is vulnerable to having damaging allegations being reported, on grounds that there must be something bad going on if the media is excluded. For instance, in April 2002 the Israeli Defence Force (IDF) denied access to journalists when it entered Palestinian areas of Jenin and Nablus. The IDF said that it was only in pursuit of terrorists, but the massive military forces and the banning of reporters from the scene led to rumours and accusations of a massacre of defenceless people taking place (it transpired that a massacre did not take place, but since journalists were not there to witness the fighting then such charges were given credence), of streets being pulverized with crippled people and children still indoors and arbitrary killing of Palestinians. This exclusion of journalists resulted in the sharpest criticism of the Israeli state since its establishment in the late 1940s. Consider, too, the salutary case of the military forces' exclusion of selected journalists from Iraq in the summer of 2004. An uprising in the city of Najaf, led by fighters loyal to the cleric Muqtada Sadr, resulted in fierce battles there. Because Najaf is the home of a holy Shia Muslim shrine, any attack on militants positioned round it was immensely sensitive, yet the rebellion had to be confronted if the occupation forces and the provisional government were to maintain authority. A response from the then provisional government of Iyad Allawi, prompted by the United States whose air power and weapons were spearheading the attack, was to ban Al-Jazeera from the country and all journalists from Najaf itself, apart from those embedded with US forces. The banned journalists (mostly Arab television crews, but others from UK newspapers such as the *Daily Telegraph* and *The Times*) were threatened with death and several came under machine gun fire. Pointedly, reportage from Iraq was then framed in terms of this prohibition of journalists being indicative of the failure of a major reason for the invasion itself. The clampdown on journalists was an assault on democracy, the very thing the Americans and their allies had pledged to establish in Iraq. As the front page of *The Independent* newspaper put it, such prohibition of the media was 'reminiscent in its own way of the Saddam Hussein regime' (16 August 2004). The presence of journalists is doubtless a nuisance to fighting men, but exclusion of them readily undermines the legitimacy of the military involvement itself.

THE POROSITY OF THE NATION-STATE

Globalization also means that nation-states are increasingly 'porous', being less able to contain the information that people within receive and give out. On one level, this is a matter of technological change – cable and satellite televisions, computer communications facilities and above all the Internet mean that it is difficult for nations to restrict what their inhabitants watch and send because technologies thwart attempts to do so. The emergence of bloggers (online diarists and commentators) from within war zones, even the exchange of e-mail between individuals across countries in conflict, may allow different perspectives on war. For instance, during the NATO bombing of Serbia in 1999 people in the United Kingdom could receive e-mail accounts of poundings from Belgrade, while throughout the assault on Iraq in 2003 Salam Pax (the 'Baghdad Blogger') recorded what it was like to be on the receiving end of bombing (http://dear_raed.blogspot.com). During the same war milblogs (military weblogs) emerged, soldiers recounting in bald language their experiences from the front. At another level, there is a worldwide decline of deference, an increased unwillingness to know one's place and not question what one's leaders do, which stimulates the development of information that is challenging. One dimension of this tendency, to which we return below, is the global development of democracy, the human rights demands that accompany it and the spread of non-government organizations that work for its development.

Consider here the series of photographs of Iraqi prisoners being abused and humiliated in the Abu Ghraib prison late in April 2004. These images of hooded prisoners, of a man stretched out in a crucifixion-like pose while his hands are connected to electric wires, of leering US guards, of naked Iraqis in sexually demeaning poses, of mocking female military police smirking at Iraqis' genitals, were taken with digital cameras. These were numbered in the hundreds of exposures, and are readily transmittable through wireless connections to friends, associates and even media organizations. The miniature format of these cameras, and the ease with which large numbers of images can be electronically disseminated, means that, however hard authorities try to control information flows, the likelihood is that some will get through that thwarts this ambition. Once the Abu Ghraib pictures got into the media, there was an escalation of negative stories, hence the treatment of terrorist suspects held at Guantanamo Bay was revisited, Senate and House Hearings were instigated, suspicions of US behaviour by the International Red Cross and Amnesty International were publicized and questions rose about the legitimacy of the entire Iraq operation (Hersh 2004). The photographs became 'the *image* of the war', anguished the *Washington Post* and the photograph of the hooded man with outstretched arms connected to electric wires was reproduced worldwide as 'this war's new mascot' (5 May 2004).

Again, there is now the presence of, and ready access of others via cable and Internet facilities to, alternative sources of news, stories and images. Though not many viewers in one nation will tune in to other countries' news programmes, the facility is available and interested people do watch – diasporic minorities, for instance, are amongst the keenest viewers of satellite television services from their home countries, and the *Guardian* newspaper, a left-of-centre UK broadsheet, has over 4 million users of its website in the United States where it would be considered left wing (Teather 2004). Amongst other close watchers are media organizations on the look out for information that may be newsworthy. An example here is the easy, direct and real time access, inside the United States, to BBC World News on cable, and, still more wide-ranging, print coverage from war zones on the Internet where a search on Google, or the Google News site itself, reveals information from varied sources. Another instance is the presence of Arab News agencies, notably Al-Jazeera since the mid 1990s, as news gatherers and as disseminators. After 9/11 Al-Jazeera gained several video messages from Osama bin Laden that it promptly showed on its news television. These reports were picked up in Western media because they were so obviously newsworthy, where however much they were edited and inflected, nothing could take away the fact that in front of viewers' eyes was the West's number one enemy palpably alive, unrepentant and continuing to threaten courtesy of a media outlet beyond the control of those in pursuit of Al-Qaeda's best-known member. During the Iraq War of 2003, and throughout the continuing civil unrest, Al-Jazeera, though attacked ideologically and militarily by the US forces (in 2001 Al-Jazeera offices were blown up in Kabul during the invasion of Afghanistan and in 2003 the act was repeated and reporter Tariq Ayoub was killed on camera), produced numerous reports and pictures at odds with what was being shown by the likes of CNN and NBC. Early on, for instance, the claim by UK forces that there was an uprising against Saddam Hussein from Shi'ites in Basra, widely reported in the United Kingdom, was flatly (and correctly) rejected by Al-Jazeera correspondents inside the town. Later Al-Jazeera showed pictures of the bodies of American and British troops killed in action and it also displayed coalition prisoners seized by the Iraqi forces. These were widely viewed on Arabic (and other) television channels. Moreover, though they were not shown in either the United States or the United Kingdom, knowledge of their display in itself was a story, as were the expressions of outrage of the UK Prime Minister and his US allies. Further, the images remained accessible to anyone wishing to look on the Internet at Al-Jazeera (and other) sites where they were presented in English. Try, as combatants do, to restrict what viewers see of war to what favours them, there are limits to what can be done to control reportage in today's high-tech globalized world.

STATES WITHOUT ENEMIES, ENEMIES WITHOUT STATES

Globalization announces the declining significance of territorial boundaries between nations. An effect is stimulation of what Anthony Giddens has termed 'states without enemies' (Giddens 1994: 235). The reasoning goes that, if there is large-scale cross-over of ownership of capital across frontiers, real-time decision-making across borders, high levels of business and tourist migration, and increasingly open markets, then there is a declining propensity for nations to go to war with one another over territory. One might suppose that this heralds an era of world peace, but there are more negative effects of globalization that stoke conflict. There is a toxic mix of increased inequalities on a global scale and further destabilization caused by heightened competition, marketization and technical innovation. Those with access to capital and possessed of high-level education may thrive in this flexible world, but the uprooted and marginal can find it deeply disconcerting. The globalization which demands of people that they change their ways as a matter of routine, that they abandon their cultures and take on more cosmopolitan forms and that they be willing to adapt to market behaviours which insist on the primacy of money in relations may be met by those least well situated to gain with hostility and apprehension.

This is fertile ground for the strengthening of fundamentalism, the expression of certainty in an uncertain world: an insistence that some things are *not* subject to change or challenge, that there are absolutes of morality, behaviour and belief. Fundamentalism of course is conditioned by a range of factors, from personality types to political circumstances, from geographical location to the particular events. But the destabilization that is integral to today's globalized market system is of major consequence, setting the preconditions for fundamentalism's emergence (Bauman 1998). It may take many forms, from born-again religion to neo-fascism, literal readings of the Bible to fervent Communism, from an escape into asceticism to embrace of deep ecology – and it may also find outlets in zealotry which can feed into terrorist organization and action. In these circumstances we may witness the emergence of what Giddens (1994) terms 'enemies without states', where fundamentalists resist the 'Great Satan' of globalized and secular capitalism in the name of absolutist creed that may even disregard national borders. This is the milieu in which Al-Qaeda and the Osama bin Laden network is situated (Burke 2003). It reveals an enemy of globalization and market society of which, after 11 September 2001, we are well aware, one prepared use the most advanced technologies to wreak destruction in the name of upholding primitive certainties. Since Al-Qaeda declared its jihad against 'Jews and Crusaders' in 1998 it has been responsible for more than 30 terrorist attacks in over 16 countries, claiming over 5,000 lives (mostly of Muslims) and very many more injuries. Members flew fully fuelled Boeing 757 and 767 aeroplanes into the World Trade Center and the Pentagon late in 2001 murdering 3,000 people. Others – probably loosely affiliated and inspired by Al-Qaeda – killed hundreds of mainly Australian tourists in Bali in 2003, massacred over 200 civilians in Madrid when commuter trains were blown up on 11 March 2004 and exploded bombs on the London underground on 7 July 2005 that caused over 50 fatalities. There is great apprehension that they might be able to gain access to weapons of mass destruction (WMDs) since few doubt that they will be used if the opportunity arises. This is a deterritorialized and networked enemy that poses serious problems for the state's conduct of war that, traditionally, has been conducted against other nations in the name of defence of one's own country.

Elsewhere, and more commonly, we find instances of fundamentalist creeds that urge 'ethnic cleansing' of 'aliens' in the name of a mythic nation in which everyone shared and upheld certain tenets. This form of terrorism, one that aims for establishment of its own nation, remains the most prevalent and it has close connections with the growth of nation-states in general (Mann 2005). It has been evident in recent decades in places as diverse as Northern Ireland, Corsica, Spain, Chechnya, Turkey, Rwanda, the Balkans and Palestine. It can be appallingly costly in terms of loss of life (from the massacre of over 300 schoolchildren in Beslan during September 2004 to the genocide of Muslim males at Srebrenica in July 1995), but it represents primary concern to establish a national territory.

This yearning for a place of one's own, generally ethnically conceived, as a haven for those who share a common descent and culture has roots in the building of the nation-state (almost all European Union countries remain over 80 per cent ethnically homogeneous to this day, and most cleansed themselves of minorities generations ago – notoriously and savagely of Jews, but also of Armenians, Slavs, Catholics, Muslims etc.) and it remains an extremely powerful force in the world. Globalization certainly influences the aspirations of these local struggles, but their locus in particular places should not be underestimated. Nor should the appeal of ethno-nationalism to the weaker and more vulnerable sections of society, those provincials ill-equipped to meet the challenges (and opportunities) of a globalized world as the enthusiastic and advantaged cosmopolitans do (Lasch 1995). By the same token, it can be an egregious mistake to categorize this sort of terrorism as the same as the international terror of Al-Qaeda (Mann 2003).

FROM INDUSTRIAL TO INFORMATION WAR

We may better appreciate these circumstances by distinguishing between Industrial and Information War. Briefly, Industrial War was conducted, for the most part, between sovereign nation-states and chiefly concerned disputes over territory. Such warfare reached its apogee during the twentieth century. It involved the mobilization of large elements of populations to support the war effort. This led to participation, by historical standards, of huge numbers of combatants, something generally involving the conscription of a majority of males between the ages of 18 and about 34. Concomitantly, when these massed forces were put into action, mass casualties were sustained. In addition, media were harnessed to assist the war effort by laying emphasis on the national interest in moral and material terms, hence nurturing strong media commitment in support of the fighting forces and using, where necessary, national powers to direct information. By and large it was not difficult to ensure that media gave strong support to the war effort of their own nations. They had a moral affiliation that disposed them to be sympathetic, they were unable to witness what was happening in the enemy camp and there was always the recourse to censorship should it be required.

Information war

Over the past generation or so we have been seeing the unravelling of Industrial War. There is a tendency to conceive its replacement only in technological terms, as the pervasive application of ICTs that expresses a Revolution in Military Affairs (RMA) (Cohen 1996). This evokes radical changes in military technologies, from the 'digital soldier' to the latest technologies involving drones, satellites and computer-drenched weapons of bewildering complexity. Enormous advances in technologies have been made, notably in aeronautics and electronics-rich weaponry, though applications from computer communications have also come at an unprecedented rate since the late 1980s.

Information can now permeate all dimensions of war, whether as satellites that surveille the enemy and make pinpoint accuracy possible, as computers and their programmes which record and assess military and material requirements rapidly and across vast distances, or as smart weapons that 'fire and forget', finding their way to targets on which they have been fixed. Information is now everywhere, integral to and incorporated into weaponry and decision-making. Central are developments in command, control, communications and intelligence (C3I) technologies, the pursuit of a first-rate system of one's own and identification of vulnerable points in the enemies' C3I capability. Ultra-sophisticated C3I networks can provide an enormous 'information advantage' in warfare, locating enemies, disrupting their operations and attacking with high-powered but precise missiles. Awesomely complex information intercept, analysis and communications systems are institutionalized in the US's National Security Agency (NSA) and the UK's Government Communications Headquarters (GCHQ) (Bamford 2001), while the jamming or deceiving of enemy radar and the disruption of command and control networks is a vital tool for well-equipped armies, navies and air forces (Berkowitz 2003). Operating with immediacy, across the globe, is a requisite of the US military since it has several hundred bases outside the homeland that must be coordinated and controlled (Johnson 2004). Information War is, of course, massively asymmetrical, the province largely of the advanced nations and NATO.

Information War relies on relatively small numbers of professional soldiers, pilots and support teams. This represents a shift in the military towards what have been called 'knowledge warriors' (Toffler and Toffler 1993), a term which underscores the centrality of personnel adept, not in close combat or even in riflemanship, but in handling complex and highly computerized tools such as advanced fighter aircraft, surveillance systems and guidance technologies.

This changing character of the military machine is consonant with what have been described as 'post-military societies' (Shaw 1991) where war-fighting institutions have moved to the margins of society and have taken on more specialized and technically demanding roles. This is also associated with what Edward Luttwak (1996) has called a 'post-heroic' military policy where one's own side brings to bear overwhelming force on an enemy chiefly through bombing while few, if any, casualties are risked from one's own side. The prominent role of knowledge warriors in Information War means that the possessor of appropriate capability will always prevail over an identified enemy that is forced to rely on the commitment, training and even experience of its soldiers (though defeated enemies generally face occupation, at which stage troops become important on the ground and thereby vulnerable to attack by sabotage, ambush and other forms of resistance).

Information War is of short duration, the United States (or NATO and/or UN approved forces) quickly victorious by virtue of the overwhelming superiority of its resources. So long as an enemy can be identified, isolated and located, then such is the asymmetry of Information War that it will be destroyed in quick time. The Gulf War of 1991, the Balkans War of 1999, the Afghanistan battles of 2001 and the 2003 Iraq War, each of which lasted between just 4 and 11 weeks, exemplify this.

Experiences of war

The removal of the civilian population to the margins of the day-to-day conduct of Information War, and the reliance on knowledge warriors, has profound implications for the experiences of war. On the one hand, without mass mobilization, the general population has little direct involvement with Information War, even when this is undertaken in its name. In former days, mass mobilization for war meant that soldiers and sailors were routinely seen on the streets. In the epoch of Information War few of us encounter the fighting forces, so there are no means by which we may get direct knowledge of what it was like to be at war. On the other hand, the general population has a very much expanded second-hand experience of war, in the particular sense of massively increased media coverage of conflicts. When war is in the offing media give saturation cover, round-the-clock reportage directly from the scene. That is, while in Information War the fighting units are at the margins of society, media coverage is massive and it is a most important and intrusive dimension of the wider public's experiences of war.

It follows that those who wage Information War devote great attention to 'perception management' of the population at home and, indeed, round the world. This is especially pressing in democratic nations where public opinion can be a vital factor in the war since this may impinge on the fighting capability of their forces. Anti-war protesters in Western societies popularly carry posters claiming 'Not in My Name', a vivid illustration of the key role of public opinion in both initiating and sustaining Information War efforts.

Acute concern about domestic public opinion especially impels military leaders into careful rehearsals and management of information from and about the war, though at the same time assiduous efforts must be made to avoid the charge of censorship, since this flies in the face of democratic states having a free media and undermines the persuasiveness of what does get reported. Perception management must therefore work to combine ways of ensuring a continuous stream of media coverage that is positive and yet ostensibly freely gathered by independent news agencies.

However assiduously practised, it is difficult to get the media to report just what the military and its political leaders would most like. We have suggested reasons why this should be so: professionalized and diverse reporters, the relative ease of communication from the war zone due to satellite technology and the Internet, the rather chaotic circumstances of 'information blizzard' and so on. Illustrations of reports and images that cause headaches for perception managers are easy to find, particularly where conflict continues after initial military triumph. It can be a photograph of a distressed child, reports of discontent amongst combatants, the killing of an innocent bystander by our side or tales of abuse of prisoners by their guards.

Rather than revisit such cases, we will make here some observations about the spate of video beheadings that became available in the spring and summer of 2004, because these show how difficult perception management has become. Al-Qaeda or associated groups such as one led by Abu Musab al-Zarqawi seemingly produce the videos. The content varies, but they typically show a victim, dressed in an orange jump suit, seated and bound in front of four or five standing men whose faces are covered. One of these reads out a statement denouncing the West, then the prisoner is killed by having his head cut off with a large knife while the men chant glorifying Jihad ('Allahu Akbar'). The severed head is then held aloft, to the camera, for display.

Though there are reports of such videos being made by Chechnyan rebels against Russian occupiers, they came to prominence with the gruesome torture and killing of Daniel Pearl, an American journalist on the *Wall Street Journal*, in Pakistan during 2002. They have since been made intermittently elsewhere, especially in Iraq, where the beheading of Nick Berg in May 2004 commenced a spate of such video productions that has included as victims several nationals who have found employment as contractors in Iraq or in other Arabic counties.

These are terrifying forms of video. They are real and real-time executions, made with a macabre amateurism, but with horrendous screams and involuntary body noises as throats are sawn and heads cut off. In an epoch accustomed to ostensibly graphic murders in a range of movies and television programmes, these videos are disturbing in altogether different ways. They are unmistakably real, impossible to confuse with the most 'realistic' scenes from any movie; they are pitiless (a human being is murdered before one's eyes), and there is palpable agony on display as a defenceless person's life is extinguished in a particularly barbarous way. They are highly newsworthy for precisely these reasons.

The executioners make these videos available to Arabic news agencies such as Al-Jazeera and they also mount them directly on militant Islamic websites. From these places Western and other media take them up. For reasons of ideology as well as respect for the victims the videos are edited and framed in ways the killers would not approve. For instance, major UK and US television networks use stills rather than video footage and the sounds are removed. Even so, they are not what perception managers from the military and government sides would like to have shown, since such videos compel attention and inevitably raise questions about the purpose of involvement in the war. Often other videos that show the victim desperately pleading for his life, appealing to politicians to save him by doing what the terrorists demand, precede the videos of the beheadings. These will spark a round of news reports that seek out government opinions, testing for vacillation and looking for signs of negotiation taking place. There will also be stories of anguished family and anxious friends, fearful for the prisoner who has been given a limited time to live. This is not at all the sort of coverage that perception managers would desire.

HUMAN RIGHTS, DEMOCRATIZATION AND MEDIA

Combatants desire to have media on board, so that what they do in war is presented in ways that are acceptable to the wider public. This is an obvious but vital point: combatants want to win wars at the least cost to themselves and with maximum public approval, and if this runs against correspondents' professional ideals then, in the view of those doing the fighting, the media must fall into line. However, as we have shown, perception management is difficult to successfully achieve, chiefly because strict control of the media in an era of globalization is, to say the least, problematic when there are thousands of reporters present, when many journalists consider their role to be primarily an investigative one, when domestic dissent is sure to get at least some coverage in democratic regimes and where technologies, from video cameras to the Internet, mean that images, reports and opinions are relatively easily gathered and transmitted.

But the media are needed for more than reporting acceptable news from battlefields and cognate areas. They are also central players in justifying war itself, again this especially so in democracies. The public may only be spectators in Information War, but interventions need to be legitimated and, in today's world, this is considerably more difficult than in the period of Industrial War. On the one hand, this legitimation is important because withdrawal of public support means that the fighting forces are weakened in their efforts. On the other hand, this need to gain public support in democratic societies is a key point of entry for consideration of 'human rights regimes'. And this is, necessarily, something in which media are involved, not merely as conduits for opinions of military or government leaders, but as agencies that examine and explore the democratic bases for interventions from outside. This was a distinguishing feature of media during the Iraq War of 1991, the Kosovan War of 1999 and the Afghanistan intervention of 2001. It was noticeably under-employed during the Iraq invasion of 2003 where major themes were the 'war against terrorism' and the alleged threat of WMD, though since the fall of Baghdad there has been much made of liberating Iraq and building democracy in that country, especially following the elections held there early in 2005.

Much of the foregoing analysis might suggest that media come to play a role in Information War only after open conflict has commenced. But media are usually present well before this stage and can play a key role in 'shaming' regimes by exposing poor human rights records and in instigating intervention in certain areas. It seems to us that there has developed an increased sensitivity towards, and awareness of, human rights and their abuses around the world (Robertson 1999). Globalized media can play a significant part in this, even if that involves little more than bringing issues to public attention (Sieb 2002).

The spread of concern for human rights is connected to a wide range of factors, though always media are intimately and integrally implicated: the spread of news reportage and television documentaries are crucial, but so too is the massive extension of foreign travel, as well as transnational organizations and social movements such as Amnesty International, the Red Cross and Médecins Sans Frontiers (Brysk 2002). These do not act with a single purpose, and neither do they develop or transmit messages of a uniform kind, but they do help engender a sentiment that human beings have universal rights – of freedom from persecution and torture, of the inviolability of the individual, of religious toleration, of self-determination, of access to resources such as food and water, and so on. They may also stimulate processes of democratization that, if imprecise, evoke notions of a vibrant civil society, contending political parties, free and fair elections, a free press, impartial civil servants, and legitimate legal authorities and due process (Held 1996). It has to be conceded that in practice things are variable, but it does not necessarily weaken the commitment, which can, in appropriate circumstances, lead to calls that 'something should be done' – whether about starving children, victims of disasters or even oppressive military aggressors (Norris 1999).

One of the more heartening features of the last 30 years or so has been the growth of democratic states, defined minimally as those allowing elections between competing parties. In the early 1970s, for instance, in Europe itself Spain, Greece and Portugal were ruled by militarized autocracies and the east of the continent was under Communist dictatorship. Today, all of Europe is democratic, the three nations mentioned above are thriving members of the European Union and all the former Soviet satellites are free. Even Russia, if imperfectly so, is a much more open society. Across the world, the majority of states are democracies today, 30 per cent of them becoming so only in recent decades (Diamond 2003). Furthermore, the extension of democracy, and of democracy as a human right, finds expression increasingly in international law, treaties and discourses.

Connected processes of accelerated globalization (which itself plays a key role in heightening awareness of human rights) and the collapse of communism have weakened nation-states and encouraged a more global orientation in which universal rights are more important than hitherto. There has been a perceptible 'alteration in the weight granted . . . to claims made on behalf of the state system and . . . to those made on behalf of an alternative organising principle of world order, in which unqualified state sovereignty no longer reigns supreme' (Held et al. 1999: 69). Martin Shaw (2000) is surely right to identify 'globality' as a distinguishing feature of our age, one where there is increasingly a 'common consciousness of human society on a world scale' (2000: 11–12). Because of this we may conceive now of 'global citizens', such that while the world may more and more be regarded as a single market, so too may it be seen as a society with rudimentary but common expectations of behaviour. Such universalism is far from achieved, but the trend towards it represents a significant break with established practices where emphasis has been placed on the territorial integrity of nations (Wheeler 2000). Appalling things might be happening to citizens inside a nation, but to date it has been virtually impossible to envisage other governments, so long as their own borders and/or interests were not threatened, intervening out of concern for victims within another's sovereign territory. It remains exceedingly difficult, but nowadays it is at least imaginable.

The abject circumstances of the Jews, persecuted for centuries but especially so over an intense period inside Nazi Germany and during the war the Third Reich precipitated, seems to us an especially clear instance of the former extreme unwillingness for outsider nations to become involved in others' internal affairs until their own borders (or that of their allies) were threatened. It must be remembered that total war was waged to counter German territorial aggression rather than to resist the genocidal policies that were being implemented inside the Axis nations – telling evidence for which is the well-documented reluctance of the Allies to give sanctuary to large numbers of Jewish refugees before and during the War, as well as the refusal to bomb extermination camps though the 'final solution' policy was known by the early 1940s and millions of Jews had already been murdered (Wasserstein 1979; London 2000). While 6 million of 8 million European Jews were murdered, prevention of their destruction was not a priority for the alliance of nations that took part in World War II. World War II was an anti-fascist campaign, but it was entered into because the Nazis and Axis countries invaded territory and/or acted aggressively towards the allies by seizing Polish territory. The Jewish anguish scarcely registered in most countries at war. In fact, German protestations in the early 1940s, that everything was the fault of the Jews so that Aryan nations such as Britain and Germany should not be fighting amongst themselves, were stifled in the United Kingdom for fear that this would resonate with domestic anti-Semitism and weaken the war effort, a concern given credence by the casual anti-Semitism recorded by Mass Observation diarists of the time (Garfield 2004). The word 'Holocaust' was not recognized until the late 1960s (Novick 2000). The Final Solution was never a central concern of the Allied forces or its publics. That World War II has come to be seen in some quarters as one to save the Jews is an interpretation that only began to be heard a generation after its end.

Václav Havel (1999) articulated the changing situation when he voiced support for the NATO engagement in Kosovo on the grounds that 'the notion that it is none of our business what happens in another country and whether human rights are violated in that country . . . should . . . vanish down the trapdoor of history'. One cannot be blind to the fact that nation-states remain important and that *realpolitik* concerns will continue to tell when it comes to questions of intervention of forces from outside (Hirst 2001). Nonetheless, it is the case now that Information War must be concerned with much more than strategic or territorial interest. And a key feature of their new situation is the spread of a universalism which denies the right of nations to do as they will inside their own borders and media coverage (as well as other agencies and actors) of events and issues which ensure that nations cannot easily hide from outside scrutiny. Globalization has brought about economic relationships in which the unit idea is operation across the planet in real time. This has engendered massive dynamism and growth (Wolf 2005); it has also, fitfully and unevenly, encouraged the spread of a common way of seeing our fellow inhabitants on this globe. For this we should be grateful.

Acknowledgment

The authors acknowledge the support of the ESRC (Economic and Social Research Council), reference RES-223-25-0033, *Journalists under Fire: Information War and Journalistic Practices*.

Note

1   Indeed, there is a stage at which dangers to life are so acute that reporting becomes impossible for even the most dedicated journalist. As the conflict developed in Iraq late in 2004, and with this Western journalists found themselves targeted (some 20 were killed by insurgents), so did it risk 'becoming a story too dangerous to cover' (Beaumont 2004). Those remaining in Iraq were pushed increasingly into the fortified Green Zone which meant that reportage – for instance of the massive US assault on Falluja in November 2004 – was severely circumscribed, presented on the terms of the US forces, so precise figures on death and injury of American forces were available, but nothing of Iraqi casualties or the degree of damage to a city once populated by over 200,000 people.

References

Bamford, J. 2001. *Body of Secrets: Anatomy of the Ultra-Secret National Security Agency.* New York: Doubleday.

Bauman, Z. 1998. *Globalization: The Human Consequences.* Cambridge: Polity Press.

Beaumont, P. 2004. 'Fear drives reporters to rooftops', *Observer*, 24 October, 6.

Berkowitz, B. 2003. *The New Face of War.* New York: Free Press.

Brysk, A. (ed.) 2002. *Globalization and Human Rights.* Berkeley: University of California Press.

Burke, J. 2003. *Al Qaeda: The True Story of Radical Islam.* London: I.B. Tauris.

Calhoun, C. 2004. 'Information technology and the international public sphere'. In D. Schuler and P. Day (eds), *Shaping the Network Society*, 229–52. Cambridge, MA: MIT Press.

Cohen, E.A. 1996. 'A revolution in warfare', *Foreign Affairs*, 75 (2), March–April, 37–54.

Curtis, L. 1984. *Ireland: The Propaganda War.* London: Pluto.

Diamond, L. 2003. 'Universal democracy?', *Policy Review*, 119, 1–28.

Garfield, S. 2004. *Our Hidden Lives: The Remarkable Dairies of Post-War Britain.* London: Ebury Press.

Giddens, A. 1994. *Beyond Left and Right.* Cambridge: Polity Press.

Havel, V. 1999. 'Kosovo and the end of the nation-state', *New York Review of Books*, 29 April.

Held, D. 1996. *Models of Democracy*, 2nd edn. Cambridge: Polity Press.

Held, D., McGrew, A., Goldblatt, D. and Perraton, J. 1999. *Global Transformations.* Cambridge: Polity Press.

Hersh, S.M. 2004. 'Torture at Abu Ghraib', *New Yorker*, 10 May.

Hersh, S.M. 2005. *Chain of Command.* London: Penguin.

Hirst, P. 2001. *War and Power in the 21st Century.* Cambridge: Polity Press.

Johnson, C. 2004. *The Sorrows of Empire: Militarism, Secrecy, and the End of the Republic.* New York: Metropolitan Books.

Keane, J. 1998. *Civil Society: Old Images, New Visions.* Cambridge: Polity Press.

Lasch, C. 1995. *The Revolt of the Elites.* New York: Norton.

London, L. 2000. *Whitehall and the Jews, 1933–48: British Immigration Policy and the Holocaust.* Cambridge: Cambridge University Press.

Luttwak, E. 1996. 'A post-heroic military policy', *Foreign Affairs*, 75 (4), July/August, 33–44.

Mann, M. 2003. *Incoherent Empire.* London: Verso.

Mann, M. 2005. *Dark Side of Democracy.* Cambridge: Cambridge University Press.

Marr, A. 2004. *My Trade: A Short History of British Journalism.* London: Macmillan.

Miles, H. 2005. *Al-Jazeera: The Inside Story of the Arab News Channel that is Challenging the West.* New York: Grove Press.

Morrison, D. and Tumber, H. 1988. *Journalists at War: The Dynamics of Newsreporting during the Falklands.* London: Constable.

Norris, P. (ed.) 1999. *Critical Citizens: Global Support for Democratic Government.* Oxford: Oxford University Press.

Novick, P. 2000. *The Holocaust and Collective Memory.* London: Bloomsbury.

Nye, J.S. Jr. 2002. *The Paradox of American Power.* New York: Oxford University Press.

Robertson, G. 1999. *Crimes against Humanity: The Struggle for Global Justice.* Harmondsworth: Penguin.

Shaw, M. 1991. *Post-Military Society: Militarism, Demilitarization and War at the End of the Twentieth Century.* Cambridge: Polity Press.

Shaw, M. 2000. *Theory of the Global State: Globality as an Unfinished Revolution*. Cambridge: Cambridge University Press.

Sieb, P. 2002. *The Global Journalist: News and Conscience in a World of Conflict*. New York: Rowman and Littlefield.

Teather, D. 2004. 'The war on bias', *Guardian*, 23 August.

Toffler, A. and Toffler, H. 1993. *War and Anti-War*. Boston: Little, Brown.

Tomlinson, J. 1999. *Globalization and Culture*. Cambridge: Polity Press.

Tumber, H. and Palmer, J. 2004. *Media at War: The Iraq Crisis*. London: Sage.

Veseth, M. 2005. *Globaloney: Unravelling the Myths of Globalization*. New York: Rowman and Littlefield.

Wasserstein, B. 1979. *Britain and the Jews of Europe, 1939–1945*. Oxford: Oxford University Press.

Webster, F. and Erickson, M. 2004. 'Technology and social problems'. In G. Ritzer (ed.), *Handbook of Social Problems: A Comparative International Perspective*, 416–32. Thousand Oaks, CA: Sage.

Wheeler, N. 2000. *Saving Strangers*. Oxford: Oxford University Press.

Wolf, M. 2005. *Why Globalization Works*. New Haven, CT: Yale University Press.

Chapter 21

Political Globalization

Gerard Delanty and Chris Rumford

Introduction

The concept of globalization as used in this chapter refers to the multidimensional, accelerated and interconnected organization of space and time across national borders. Specifically with respect to political globalization it concerns an approach to the social world that stresses postnational and transnational processes as well as a consciousness of the compressed nature of space and time. Political globalization has been much discussed in the globalization literature where the emphasis has been on the decline of the nation-state under the impact of global forces, which have created different kinds of politics arising from, on the one hand, the development of transnational networks and flows, and, on the other, processes of de- and re-territorialization. For some, processes of political globalization open up new emancipatory possibilities, while for others globalization leads to a loss of autonomy and the fragmentation of the social world. The approach to political globalization adopted in this chapter highlights the multifaced nature of globalization, which is best seen as a relational dynamic rather than a new kind of reality. Political globalization, we argue, can be understood as a tension between three processes which interact to produce the complex field of global politics: global geopolitics, global normative culture and polycentric networks.

There can be little doubt that one of the most pervasive forms of political globalization is the worldwide spread of democracy based on the parliamentary nation-state. Democratic government exists in some form in most parts of the world and where it does not, as in China, there is a considerable demand for it by democratic movements. This is a territorially based kind of globalization and largely confined to the political form of the nation-state. It takes traditional forms as well as constituting a new kind of global geopolitics. Since the collapse of the Soviet Union and the end of the communist regimes in Europe after 1991, democracy has become the universally acceptable form of government. In this sense then, globalization does not undermine the democratic nation-state but gives it worldwide acceptability. The famous thesis of the 'end of history' misinterpreted this to be the end of ideology, since the spread of liberal democracy did not lead to the end of ideology but to the proliferation of more and different kinds of ideology. The democratic nation-state in many parts of the world has given rise to very different kinds of political cultures. The globalization of democratic politics has been the basis of the so-called 'new world order' that has been associated with the bid for worldwide supremacy by the United States and the legitimation of global wars, from the Gulf War to the invasion of Afghanistan and Iraq. Despite the rise of the United States as a global power, global geopolitics is not, as it is often portrayed to be, a *Pax Americana*, or what Carl Schmitt called a new 'Nomos of the Earth', a Western world order (Schmitt 2003). The United States will not be able to establish global supremacy and will be challenged by many centres of power – centres that are mostly states. Thus, the first dimension of political globalization is the geopolitics of global power.

A second dimension of political globalization refers to the rise of a global normative culture. This is independent of geopolitics and is largely legal but diffused in global political communication. One of the main expressions of this is human rights, which lies at the centre of a global cosmopolitanism, but it also includes environmental concerns, which are now global. It is also a dimension of globalization that is not specifically Western. As a result of global communication and popular culture etc., political communication is now also global in scope, no longer confined to national borders. National politics is increasingly framed in terms of global discourses. Coupled with the global diffusion of democracy, political communication has become the basis of a global normative culture that has arisen as much in opposition to geopolitics as in support of it. Central to this are the rights of the individual but also included are environmental concerns such as sustainable development. The sovereignty of the state has been challenged by the rights of the individual leading to tensions between peoplehood and personhood. States were once the main agents of global norms, but today a global normative culture has come into existence beyond the state system and exists in a relation of tension with states. This global normative culture provides normative reference points for states and an orientation for political actors. As John Meyer and his colleagues have argued, for the first time in history there is now a global culture which provides a frame of reference for all societies (Meyer et al. 1997, 2004; Boli and Lechner 2005). For politics this means that political struggles and legitimation are ever more connected to global issues. It means that counterpublics as well as states will be shaped by it.

While globalization requires the existence of global players such as powerful states to diffuse and implement a global geopolitics, there is another dimension of globalization that is less related to states and which is not reducible to global normative culture. This may be termed polycentric networks, that is, forms of non-territorial politics which emanate from a multiplicity of sites and which cannot be reduced to a single centre. These processes of political globalization are associated with networks and flows, new sources of mobility and communication, and denote new relationships between the individual, state and society. Importantly, polycentric networks are associated with emerging forms of global governance. Whilst the global political order represented by the United Nations is largely based on nation-states, it is possible to speak of a different kind of global political order that can be associated with the notion of global civil society (see Kaldor 2003; Keane 2003).

The concept of civil society is much contested and for present purposes it simply refers to the political domain between the state and the market where informal politics takes place. In global terms this corresponds to new spaces beyond the state and the inter-governmental domain and which are independent of global capitalism. A global civil society has come into existence around international non-governmental organizations (INGOs), various grass-roots organizations and social movements of all kinds ranging from globally organized anti-capitalist protests and global civil society movements such as the World Social Form, anti-sweat shop movements to terrorist movements. One of the distinctive features of global civil society is that it does not have one space but many; it is polycentric and not based on any single principle of organization other than the fact that it is globally organized through loosely structured horizontal coalitions and networks of activists.

It must be stressed that these three dimensions of globalization do not exist separately from each other, for all are products of globalization and are interrelated. Global civil society, for example, is not separate from geopolitics, but occupies a separate space beyond the state and global market. It exists alongside the state and has been consequential in influencing global geopolitics in the direction of multilateralism and global solidarity. Geopolitics exists under the condition of what Hardt and Negri (2000: xii) call 'Empire': 'a decentred and deterritorializing apparatus of rule that progressively incorporates the entire global realm within its open, expanding frontiers'. Global normative culture exists alongside these movements, which Hardt and Negri characterize in terms of Empire versus the Multitude, providing them with a communicative frame of reference with which global politics is increasingly having to define itself. Political globalization generates a complex web of conflicts, dislocations, fluid political forms. In the view of many scholars these dimensions or processes of globalization, in particular, the latter two, all amount to a global polity (e.g. Held 1995). The argument in this chapter questions this assumption: political globalization is not leading in the direction of a new global order of governance or world society but to transnational political action which challenges neoliberal politics. The logic of globalization bears out the central logic of political modernity in expressing the inner conflict within the political frame of autonomy versus fragmentation: globalization can enhance democracy but it can also fragment democracy by shifting autonomy to capitalism.

The three dynamics of political globalization will be examined in this chapter around four examples of social transformation: the transformation of nationality and citizenship, the public sphere and political communication, civil society, and space and borders.

THE TRANSFORMATION OF THE NATION-STATE, NATIONALITY AND CITIZENSHIP

The notion of the decline of the nation-state in a post-statist world of governance without government – or in a 'new medievalism' of regional economies (Ohmae 1996) – should be replaced by the idea of the continued transformation of the nation-state. The idea of a zero-sum situation of states disappearing in a global world of markets or replaced by global structures of governance, on the one side, or as in the neo-realist scenario the survival of the so-called Westphalian state as a sovereign actor must be rejected. States continue to be powerful actors but exist in a more globally connected world that they do not fully control (see Sorensen 2004). The following arguments have been given with respect to the transformation of the nation-state under the conditions of largely economic globalization. According to Susan Strange (1996), in the most well-known formulation of this position, states have been usurped by global markets. With the transition from a world economy dominated by national economies to a global economy new economic forces come into play challenging the power of the nation-state. Instead of struggling to gain territorial power over other states most states are struggling to control firms that have become rivals to states. The result is that states have to share sovereignty with other global players. In other approaches, where the emphasis is more on the impact of global civil society the argument is that the nation-state must share sovereignty with non-governmental actors, leading to multi-governance. It is clear that in all these accounts the state is only one source of political power. Much of this revolves around the question of whether states are getting weaker or stronger as a result of global forces. In the case of Europeanization, which is a major area for the application of many of these arguments, at least two positions have emerged: the thesis that transnationalization enhances the power of the nation-state and the thesis of the rise of the regulatory state. According to Alan Milward (1993), European integration, as a movement that has led to the progressive erosion of national sovereignty, has paradoxically rescued the nation-state rather than undermined it. The movement towards transnational authority allows a more functional state system to operate since it is only those functions – for instance, regulation of finance markets and cross-border trade – that the solitary state is less well equipped to perform that are transferred upwards to the transnational level. But the result is an unavoidable loss of sovereignty, which does not necessarily translate into a loss of autonomy. According to Majone (1996) the transnationalization of the state in Europe is best seen in terms of a regulatory kind of governance rather than the creation of a new state system that challenges the nation-state. The European Union possesses a large number of independent regulatory authorities, working in fields such as the environment, drugs and drug addiction, vocational training, health and safety at work, the internal market, racism and xenophobia, food safety, aviation safety. States have always had regulatory functions; what is different today is simply these functions are being performed at a transnational level through cooperation with other states. According to Robinson (2001) a transnational state has come into existence. This is a multilayered and multicentred linking together on a transnational level of many of the functions of statehood. The nation-state does not 'wither away' but becomes transformed by becoming a functional component of this transnational apparatus and a major agent of global capitalism. In this analysis, globalization reconfigures the state around global capitalism, making it impossible for nation-states to be independent.

It is evident that what is being discussed here is a transformation of the nation-state rather than its demise. Moreover the European examples detract attention from the world context where the experience has been that the nation-state continues to be the principal political form of societal organization. Throughout Asia, Africa, Central and South America, nation-states are on the whole the main expressions of political mobilization and identity. Globalization has enhanced not undermined them. The two most powerful actors in the world today, the United States and China, are nation-states. Europe and the movement towards the transnationalization of the nation-state, is undoubtedly an exception. However, even in Europe, since the most recent enlargement of the European Union, it is arguably the case that the introduction of several new countries in central and eastern Europe will enhance rather than undermine the nation-state for the simple reason that for most of these countries entry into the European transnational order is a means of asserting rather than relinquishing national sovereignty. One only has to consider the result of the French constitutional referendum on the ratification of the European constitution in 2005 to see how consequential national publics can be. However, the aspiration to national autonomy cannot hide the general movement towards the transnationalization of the state and the even more extensive movement towards a geopolitics of global power in which a global state is emerging around the global military-political unification of much of the world. As Martin Shaw has argued, after 1989 and the removal of the Iron Curtain, the bifurcation of global space ceased with the result that the Western state system has become a global power (Shaw 1997). In other words the state has become more diffuse; it is less easily defined in terms of territory or in terms of political community.

A distinction needs to be made between states and nation-states. While most states are nation-states there is an important distinction which is particularly important in the context of political globalization. States, to follow Weber's definition, are centres of the monopoly of legitimate violence in a given territory while nation-states refer to the coincidence of the state with a defined political community. It is clearly the case that states are changing in response to globalization, as discussed in the foregoing. States are more flexible in responding to globalization than nations with the result that globalization has exercised tremendous pressure on nation-states, that is, on the relationship between political community and the exercise of legitimate violence. The resulting crisis of the nation-state is apparent in the transformation of nationality. Two kinds of decoupling processes are evident: the decoupling of nationality and citizenship and the decoupling of nationhood and statehood.

The decoupling of nationality and citizenship can be attributed to the impact of global normative culture, which has led to a blurring of the boundary between national and international law. Especially in the countries of the European Union, it is now more difficult for states to resist international law, which has become progressively incorporated into national law. The result of this is that migrants can make direct appeal to international law. International legal tribunals are playing a growing role in national politics. The rights of citizenship no longer perfectly mirror the rights of nationality despite the efforts of states to create lines of exclusion based on nationality (Jacobson 1996). The erosion of sovereignty has made a huge impact on nationality (Sassen 1997). In a similar way nationhood and statehood have experienced new lines of tension. There are many examples of the state disconnecting from the nation – France under Chirac is a striking example – with the result that nationhood takes on new and recalcitrant forms as reflected in the rise of the extreme right (see Delanty and O'Mahony, 2002). The transnationalization of the state in the countries of the European Union has undermined the nation-state leading to the rise of new nationalist movements (see Holmes 2005). The rise of nationalism since the early 1990s in Europe, which coincided with the fall of communism and the enhanced momentum towards European integration, created the conditions for a new kind of populist nationalism that has as its central animus the claim to protect the nation from globalization of all kinds, ranging from the transnationalization of the state to global migration and global markets. The nation-state has thus become bifurcated: nation and state have become divorced, each following different logics. The state has become in part transnationalized, while the nation – seemingly in the view of many national publics – abandoned by the state has taken new forms and which can often be enhanced by globalization. A striking example, once again, was in 2005 the French electorate's rejection of the European constitution. Thus many nations are now more shaped by globalization. In any case it is evident that due to the conditions of globalization the nation-state has become dislocated from the state. The political community of the nation does not exercise sovereignty over the state and the state has lost much of its sovereignty.

As Saskia Sassen (2002) and others have argued, a further dimension to the global transformation of the nation-state is the rise of subnational politics. Global cities, for example, are products of the de-nationalization of the nation-state and the rise of non-territorial politics.

THE TRANSFORMATION OF THE PUBLIC SPHERE AND COMMUNICATION

Communication is central to politics. Nation-states have been based on centralized systems of communication ranging from national systems of education and science, national newspapers and media such as TV as well as national commemorations and popular culture in which national narratives and collective identities were codified, reproduced and legitimated. Most nation-states have been based on a national language, which was increasingly standardized over time. In addition, political parties have been at the centre of large-scale apparatuses of political communication which they have used for social influence. If the Enlightenment public was based on alleged free discussion, the public today is based on professional political communication and mass persuasion through systematic advertising and lobbying: for Mayhew this amounts to a 'new public' (Mayhew 1997). However, as argued by Habermas (1989), communication is an open site of political and cultural contestation and is never fully institutionalized by the state or entirely controlled by elites and their organs of political communication. The public sphere is the site of politics; it is not merely a spatial location but a process of discursive contestation (see Calhoun 1992; Crossley and Roberts 2004).

Until now this has been mostly conceived of as a national public sphere. Most of the examples taken by Habermas relate to national public spheres. Moreover the idea of the public sphere was theorized in terms of decline as a result of the rise of the commercial mass media. Habermas's (1996) theory of discursive democracy revitalized the theory of the public sphere – which was in the meanwhile being complemented by alternative conceptions of the public sphere, including the notion of the 'proletarian public sphere', as opposed to the bourgeois public sphere

(Negt and Kluge 1993). This model remains largely based on national societies. The new social theory of the public sphere has now moved into a wider view of the public sphere as cosmopolitan, with recent contributions noting the existence of non-Western public spheres (Hoexter et al. 2002) and global public spheres constituted by global civil society and cosmopolitan trends (see Eder 2005; Kögler 2005; Strydom 2002).

While debates continue on the question of the global public sphere as a transnational space, what is more important is the emergence of a global public discourse, which is less a spatially defined entity than a manifestation of discourse (Delanty 2006). The public sphere is now pervaded by what can be called a global public. By this is not meant a specific public but the global context in which communication is filtered. The global public is the always ever present sphere of discourse that contextualizes political communication and public discourse today. The role of the public in this is of course also well documented, as is evidenced by the significance which is now attached to the public sphere, and which must be conceived as having a cosmopolitan dimension. The discursive construction of the social world takes place within the wider context of global communication in which the global public plays a key role. The global public has a major resonance in all of communication in the sense that it structures and contextualizes much of public discourse, as examples ranging from human rights, environmental concerns, health and security illustrate.

The global is not outside the social world but is inside it in numerous ways. So it is possible to see political communication in the public sphere as increasingly framed by global issues. In terms of the three-fold conceptualization of globalization discussed earlier, it may be suggested that global normative culture is playing a leading role in shaping political communication. This is due not least to global civil society which has greatly amplified global normative culture. However, global normative culture is diffused in many ways within public spheres and is carried by many different kinds of social agents, including states. Political globalization is most visible in terms of changes in political communication and in the wider transformation of the public sphere. It is possible to speak of a communicative kind of political globalization confronting economic globalization. This is different from global geopolitics, which as argued earlier has led to a transnationalization of the state in line with the rise of a global economy.

THE CENTRALITY OF CIVIL SOCIETY

We have seen how political globalization is associated with the changing relationships between state, society and the individual, and the new transnational or global communities, networks and publics which have come into existence and which are in turn driving new forms of politics. Central to understanding these developments is the idea of civil society which perhaps more than any other development has come to symbolize the political potential of globalization, and signals the onset of globalization from below. Before looking at the emerging reality of global civil society it is necessary to give consideration to a related development which we can term the 'civil societalization' of politics, a development stimulated, on the one hand, by the spread of governance practices which coordinate policy both beyond the nation-state and in partnership with a range of social actors not traditionally involved in the mechanisms of government, and, on the other, by shifts in the scale of the local, with social movements and grass-roots politics increasingly coordinated across national boundaries (Tarrow and McAdam 2005). The 'civil societalization' of politics both reinforces the idea that politics is increasingly informed by a normative global culture and points to the transformation of the nation-state as a site of political struggle. In other words, the 'civil societalization' of politics signifies a commonality of political forms which link the local and the global, the national and the transnational, and mobilizes a range of actors around common political codes: competitiveness, sustainability, personhood rights and social justice. 'Civil societalization' has also resulted from the erosion of the state/society distinction inspired by the 'governance turn', the concomitant transformation in the institutionalization of social and political cleavages, and the increasing connectivity between global and local political forms. Significantly, 'civil societalization' has permeated international relations, and nation-states increasingly choose to mobilize actors in global civil society (for example, the US-sponsored and transnationally organized NGOs and youth movements mobilizing for Westernization in the Ukraine), and contest politics in the global public sphere (the legitimation bestowed on Turkey's Kemalist elites resulting from the decision of the Council of Europe to uphold a ban on an Islamicist political party in Turkey, for example).

When considering the importance of global civil society to contemporary thinking about political globalization it is sometimes difficult to separate the facts from the rhetoric: the hopes and aspirations contained in the idea of global civil society often lead to inflated claims as to its importance. For example, Mary Robinson, former UN High Commissioner for Human Rights, claimed that 'there are still two super-powers left on the planet: the United States and global civil society' (Robinson 2003). This reflects the fact that, for many, the importance of civil society to political globalization lies in its potential to organize resistance to the global hegemony of capitalism and/or the United States.

Global civil society holds the promise of resolving contradictory tendencies which have become central to the experience of globality. The first contradiction is that between the tendency of globalization to homogenize and the increasing emphasis on and respect for difference. The second is the contradiction within the individuating power of globalization, which works to fragment, while at the same time allowing for the construction of new types of autonomy represented by new communities of interest, networked polities and collective identities. This in turn reveals a very interesting tension between accounts of nationally constituted civil societies and a global civil society which is a main driver of political globalization. This is because civil society, depending on how it is defined, covers a very broad field of political activity, including democratic contestation within national and sub-national systems, transnational social movements and political contention, and activism which encircles the globe or addresses global issues. In respect of national polities, Keane defines civil society as 'the realm of social (privately owned, market-directed, voluntarily run or friendship-based) activities which are legally recognized and guaranteed by the state' (Keane 1988: 3). The idea of civil society resonates most strongly with the democratic need for checks and balances, in particular the need to ensure that the state does not become too intrusive or controlling: totalitarianism implies the elimination of civil society. Thus for Krishan Kumar, the popularity and importance of the idea of civil society is that it promises to combine democratic pluralism with state regulation and guidance (Kumar 1993: 375).

Of course, global civil society is not defined in relation to a state. Although there is no simple consensus on the nature and dynamics of global civil society, we can say that it commonly refers to a complex of NGO-led political campaigns, transborder social movements and transnational advocacy networks which have developed global reach and/or address issues of global concern, and which are seen as a force for good (measured in terms of enhanced accountability, democracy and individual freedom, or more commonly human rights) and work to challenge the institutionalization of the hegemony of nation-states and/or global capitalism. Scholte (2002: 285) defines global civil society as a realm of civic activity which is global in organizational scope, where trans-world issues are addressed, trans-border communications are established, and in which actors organize on the basis of supra-territorial solidarity. On this basis, global civil society comprises organizations such as Greenpeace, Médecins sans Frontiers, the international women's movement and the World Social Forum. The tension between national and global civil societies is an enduring feature of the literature: they have emerged out of different traditions of political theorizing and are often conceptualized in very different terms. For example, in the classical liberal tradition market relations are seen as natural while civil society is man-made (constructed as a consequence of the need to escape the constant threats of the state of nature). In contemporary cosmopolitan thinking global civil society is often seen as a natural realm (governed by natural law and presumptions of inherent human rights) while markets are artificial and man-made.

In one sense, the globalization of civil society follows the same pattern as for democracy, the nation-state and citizenship: globalization has resulted in the universalization of territorial norms and practices. At the same time as national norms have become generalized the increasing transnational connectivity of social movements and activists' networks coupled with the globalization of environmental, personhood and identity politics have worked to remove borders from civil society activity and create new constituencies of interest and new communities of fate. In short, the growth of global civil society is the result of increasing opportunities for interaction between domestic and international politics. These developments raise interesting questions of chronology, the conventional assumption being civil society preceded global civil society. However, it is not adequate to view global civil society as an aggregate of previously existing national civil societies: global civil society is founded upon a non-territorial political imaginary. Opinion is very much divided along the lines of whether civil society should be seen as a cohesive political realm, or whether it is better understood as a convenient umbrella term for a range of social movements and new social movements (NSMs). These issues have further added to the lack of consensus regarding what constitutes global civil society, its relationship with citizenship and democracy, and the extent to which it can exist independently of any state architecture. There is an irony here; the term civil society or transnational civil society is not always used by those commentators who map its development and plot its dynamics (Della Porta and Tarrow 2005), while its existence is concretized by those who criticize it as ineffectual (Halperin and Laxer 2003).

The centrality of global civil society to political globalization inheres in its location at the confluence of processes leading to the construction of mechanisms of
polycentric governance (Scholte 2004) and the emergence of transnational movements and networks which are working to erode more territorial organizational
forms. Moreover, global civil society works to undermine the importance of the
territorial state in favour of new forms of networked opposition – Castells' interpretation of the Zapatista rebels in Mexico as the world's 'first informational
guerrilla movement' (Castells 1997) – or encourages individuals to see themselves
less exclusively as national citizens but also as cosmopolitan individuals endowed
with natural rights.

THE TRANSFORMATION OF SPACES AND BORDERS

The image of a 'borderless world' has long been associated with thinking about
globalization. The power of global processes to transcend national borders, annihi-
late distance and unite through global catastrophe has provided the globalization
literature with a range of powerful metaphors: the 'global village'; 'world polity';
'fragile earth'. It has also led to an interesting paradox. We are increasingly conscious of the shrinking dimensions or compression of an increasingly interconnected
world and the way in which this renders the globe meaningful and brings it within
the grasp of all individuals. At the same time the frictionless flows and untrammelled
mobilities constitutive of globalization are commonly held to represent a threat to
the nation-state, as a result of which economic and political processes are taken
beyond the reach of democratically elected polities, and the individuals that constitute them.

It would be too simple to reduce the spatial dynamics of political globalization
to a conflict between the flows and mobilities associated with global processes and
the spaces and borders of existing political realms. However, there exist interpretations of global transformation which focus on the emergence of multiple and
mutually dependent 'levels' of political organization – local, regional, national,
supra or transnational, global: globalization as a continuum with the local at one
end and the global at the other (Held et al. 1999). This serves to both relativize the
nation-state and at the same time render it 'as the normal, abiding state of society
and the transnational as new and something derived from globalization' (Albrow
1998). Moving beyond the 'national scheme of things' we are required to confront
the need to rethink space and borders in the global knowledge economy and the
networked society. If we view globalization as social transformation, that is to say
a transformation in the very nature of society, its relation to the state and citizens,
then we must rethink the nature and meaning of political spaces and borders. In
short, the rescaling of politics as a consequence of globalization has caused a major
reassessment of the role and meaning of borders and spaces in the construction of
polities.

Awareness of the transformative potential of globalization has encouraged a
'spatial turn' in the social and political sciences (Castells 2000a, 2000b; Thrift
1996). The idea of a spatial turn denotes an increasing interest in the processes by
which social space is constructed and the way space is constitutive of social and

political relations, not merely the pre-given environment within which social conflicts, institutionalization, governance and social transformations are played out.
This thinking has been stimulated on the one hand by the blurring of boundaries
between and within existing territorial entities fostered by processes of political,
economic and social globalization, and, on the other, by the rise of political forms
which are neither territorially based nor possessing a single centre or origin, such
as global civil society.

The relationship between globalization and new political spaces and borders
revolves around two key spatial dynamics. The first is associated with the work of
Castells (2000a) who holds that the network society is constituted by the space
of flows which exists in tension with a space of places. The space of flows refers to
'social practices without geographical contiguity' (Castells 2000b: 14), a world of
mobility and networked connections, while the space of places refers to a territorially defined form of spatial organization (the nation-state). For Castells, the advent
of network society signals the decline of industrial society, the former relying on a
space of flows, the latter on a space of places. The second dynamic is best represented by Beck's (2002) idea of 'cosmopolitanization' or 'globalization from within
societies'. Beck emphasizes that the nature of state and society is undergoing change
as a result of globalization and that inside/outside, and domestic/foreign assume
new meanings. For Beck, much more than for Castells, the relationship between
spaces and borders is central to understanding political globalization.

These dynamics have given rise to two central themes in the study of political
globalization. First, the emergence of new political spaces and the opportunities for
bordering/re-bordering which accompany them. Second, an increased emphasis on
mobilities, flows and networks, which either work to connect existing places in
novel ways or themselves represent emerging spatial forms. Spaces and borders do
not have to be conceived as unitary and exclusive; they can be plural, overlapping
and experiential. Importantly, the nation-state no longer dominates the spatial
imagination and global spaces abound. The globe can be experienced as a single
political space which can be the focus of political attachments and identities, communities of interest, and can form a sphere of action. For many, the world is a single
place and political activity and individual consciousness increasingly reflect this,
whether couched in terms of the threat of global warming, the goal of sustainable
development or the equity of fair trade. Globalization has also generated new roles
for sub-national regions and allowed for their greater interconnectivity and trans-
border networking, intensified opportunities for 'world cities' and generated an
awareness of cosmopolitan spaces created by belonging to a multiplicity of communities and the 'inner mobilities' associated with an increasingly networked
world.

The focus on new spaces and new forms of connectivity has led to a realization
that space is constitutive of social and political relations, not simply a 'given' which
comes with the territory. The management of space is no longer seen as an essential
component of polity-building. In modernity, mastery over space – through bordering
mechanisms, infrastructural networks and institutions of state – was central to the
construction of political community. The domestication of territory and place, and
the diminution of space as a physical barrier to the development of cohesive community, was central to the project of governing the nation-state. One important

consequence of this shift to spaces of flows is that mobility is increasingly seen as independent of space: postnational and cosmopolitan notions of mobility emphasize the ways in which we regularly move between communities, identities and roles, and across borders in ways that cannot be mapped onto geographical space.

On the model of the nation-state, borders are seen as mechanisms of state working to create governable territory. Although they still perform this function for the nation-state they also work in other ways, and in the global context have become multiple, relational and deterritorialized. As Balibar (1998: 220) points out, under conditions of globalization the quantitative relation between borders and territory has been inverted. There are two dimensions to this: (1) borders are to be found everywhere, existing both within and between polities; (2) borders have become important spaces in their own right and often take the form of zones of transition or borderlands. Borderlands are zones of interpenetration which 'cut across discontinuous systems' in Sassen's (2002) terms. In doing so they transform relations between inside and outside, us and them, in the way Beck describes. What this means is that the idea of a 'borderless world', once seen as emblematic of globalization, is now revealed as a chimera. Borders are back, and processes of rebordering have emerged alongside debordering, generated by new types of security concerns, the policing of immigration and the surveillance of mobility (Andreas and Snyder 2000). Rebordering should not be taken to imply that existing patterns of territorial borders are simply reproduced; borders do not necessarily map directly onto territory and states and they are becoming 'dispersed' throughout society (Balibar 2004).

CONCLUSION

Against the background of the shifts outlined in this chapter, away from a state-centric world towards polycentric networks of governance and the development of a global political culture which works, in part, to hold the nation-state in stasis, the central question generated by political globalization is the degree to which the fragmentation of the social world leads to a loss of political autonomy. The three processes outlined here – the universalization of nationally contained models of democracy, the onset of a global normative culture and the 'civil societalization' of governance structures – exist in complex and sometimes contradictory relationships. To conclude, we can point to three dilemmas to which these complex relationships give rise and the implications for the tension between autonomy and fragmentation.

First, the globalization of the nation-state, and its model of political membership and institutionalized governance, has given form to the universal aspiration for democracy. On this reading, the nation-state is an important vehicle for political autonomy, via the sovereignty of peoplehood, and democracy is an important badge of membership in a world community of nation-states. At the same time, criticisms of democracy provide a nucleus around which many forms of contentious politics coalesce. Democracy is both universally desired and universally distrusted; for being elitist, authoritarian, formal rather than substantive, imported and inauthentic etc. Wherever democracy exists, democratic deficits are being discovered.

Second, global normative culture, which has been disseminated by INGOs over a long period of time and has scripted the development of the nation-state as a global form, has also acted as a vector for global norms of personhood positing a world of individuals sustained by human rights law. At the same time as working to individuate and fragment, these processes also open up the possibilities of new cosmopolitan collectivities created in the recognition that the needs of humanity are prior to those of democracy, and new communities of fate emerging from the recognition that we live in a 'world risk society' (Beck 1999).

Third, polycentric networks, and in particular the development of global civil society, create new opportunities for autonomy and the recognition of a range of new actors and new modes of governance, but, at the same time, can create new instabilities and dangers. Global civil society actors do not necessarily work for peace, freedom and democratization; the so-called 'dark-side' of civil society (Rumford 2001). The autonomy possessed by civil society actors and the ways in which they lack accountability and democratic credentials, and tend in any case to be self-appointed spokespersons for the causes they espouse, creates new political spaces and transnational networks which can easily be appropriated by terrorists, traffickers in drugs and people, and organized crime in such a way as to undermine a nascent world polity.

Political globalization has resulted in a new set of tensions around which politics is now structured. Whereas key political conflicts were previously centred on class divisions, state versus civil society, cleavages between traditional and industrial economies or resistance to imperial rule, supplementary contestations have arisen around a changed set of concerns: the right to difference, individual versus community, liberal democracy versus cosmopolitanism. Indeed, political globalization has worked to create the possibility for a proliferation of sites of political conflict around an expanded set of concerns: governance, identity, mobilities and community prominent amongst them.

References

Albrow, M. 1998. 'Frames and transformations in transnational studies, transnational communities', Working Paper 98-02, Institute of Social and Cultural Anthropology, Oxford University.

Andreas, P. and Snyder, T. (eds) 2000. *The Wall around the West: State Borders and Immigration Controls in North America and Europe*. Lanham, MD: Rowman and Littlefield.

Balibar, E. 2004. 'The borders of Europe'. In P. Cheah and B. Robbins (eds), *Cosmopolitics: Thinking and Feeling about the Nation*. Minneapolis: Minnesota University Press.

Beck, U. 1999. *World Risk Society*. Cambridge: Polity Press.

Beck, U. 2002. 'The cosmopolitan society and its enemies', *Theory, Culture and Society*, 19 (1–2), 17–44.

Boli, J. and Lechner, F. 2005. *World Culture: Origins and Consequences*. Oxford: Blackwell.

Calhoun, C. (ed.) 1992. *Habermas and the Public Sphere*. Cambridge, MA: MIT Press.

Castells, M. 1997. *The Power of Identity*. Vol. 2 of *The Information Age: Economy, Society and Culture*. Oxford: Blackwell.

Castells, M. 2000a. *The Rise of the Network Society*. Vol. 1 of *The Information Age: Economy, Society and Culture*, 2nd edn. Oxford: Blackwell.

Castells, M. 2000b. 'Materials for an exploratory theory of the network society', *British Journal of Sociology*, 51 (1), 5–24.

Crossley, N. and Roberts, J.M. (eds.) 2004. *After Habermas: New Perspectives on the Public Sphere*. Oxford: Blackwell.

Delanty, G. 2006. 'Cosmopolitanism in contemporary social theory: Theoretical considerations and methodological implications', *British Journal of Sociology*, 57 (1), 25–47.

Delanty, G. and O'Mahony, P. 2002. *Nationalism and Social Theory*. London: Sage.

Della Porta, D. and Tarrow, S. 2005. *Transnational Protest and Global Activism*. Lanham, MD: Rowman and Littlefield.

Eder, K. 2005. 'Making sense of the public sphere'. In G. Delanty (ed.), *Handbook of Contemporary European Social Theory*. London: Routledge.

Habermas, J. 1989. *The Structural Transformation of the Public Sphere*. Cambridge: Polity Press.

Habermas, J. 1996. *Between Facts and Norms: Contributions to a Discourse Theory of Law and Democracy*. Cambridge: Polity Press.

Halperin, S. and Laxer, G. 2003. 'Effective resistance to corporate globalization', In G. Laxer and S. Halperin (eds), *Global Civil Society and its Limits*. Basingstoke: Palgrave.

Hardt, M. and Negri, A. 2000. *Empire*. Cambridge, MA: Harvard University Press.

Held, D. 1995. *Democracy and the Global Order*. Cambridge: Polity Press.

Held, D., McGrew, A., Goldblatt, D. and Perraton, J. 1999. *Global Transformations: Politics, Economics and Culture*. Cambridge: Polity Press.

Hoexter, M., Eisenstadt, S.N. and Levtzion, N. (eds) 2002. *The Public Sphere in Muslim Societies*. New York: State University of New York Press.

Holmes, S. 2005. 'Nationalism in Europe'. In G. Delanty and K. Kumar (eds), *Handbook of Nations and Nationalism*. London: Sage.

Jacobson, D. 1996. *Rights across Borders: Immigration and the Decline of Citizenship*. Baltimore, MD: The Johns Hopkins University Press.

Kaldor, M. 2003. *Global Civil Society*. Cambridge: Polity Press.

Keane, J. 1988. *Democracy and Civil Society*. London: Verso.

Keane, J. 2003. *Global Civil Society*. Cambridge: Polity Press.

Kögler, H.-H. 2005. 'Constructing a cosmopolitan public sphere: Hermeneutic capabilities and universal values', *European Journal of Social Theory*, 8 (4), 297–320.

Kumar, K. 1993. 'Civil society: An inquiry into the usefulness of an historical term', *British Journal of Sociology*, 44, 375–96.

Majone, G. 1996. *Regulating Europe*. London: Routledge.

Mayhew, L. 1997. *The New Public: Professional Communication and the Means of Social Influence*. Cambridge: Cambridge University Press.

Meyer, J.W., Boli, J., Thomas, G.M. and Ramirez, F.O. 1997. 'World society and the nation-state', *The American Journal of Sociology*, 103 (1), 104–81.

Meyer, J.W., Boli, J., Thomas, G.M. and Ramirez, F.O. 2004. 'World society and the nation-state'. In F.J. Lechner and J. Boli (eds), *The Globalization Reader*, 2nd edn. Oxford: Blackwell.

Milward, A. 1993. *The European Rescue of the Nation-State*. London: Routledge.

Negt, O. and Kluge, A. 1993. *Public Sphere and Experience*. Minneapolis: University of Minnesota Press.

Ohmae, K. 1996. *The End of the Nation-State: The Rise of Regional Economies*. London: HarperCollins.

Robinson, M. 2003. 'Good governance: The key to sustainable development', Speech given at 'The Global Development Challenge' conference, Dublin, 10 July.

Robinson, W. 2001. 'Social theory and globalization: The rise of the transnational state', *Theory and Society*, 30, 157–200.

Rumford, C. 2001. 'Confronting "uncivil society" and the "dark side of globalization": Are sociological concepts up to the task?', *Sociological Research Online*, 6 (3).

Sassen, S. 1997. *Losing Control? Sovereignty in an Age of Globalization*. New York: Columbia University Press.

Sassen, S. 2002. *Global Networks/Linked Cities*. London: Routledge.

Schmitt, C. 2003. *Nomos of the Earth in the International Law of Jus Publicum Europaeum*. New York: Telos Press.

Scholte, J.A. 2000. *Globalization: A Critical Introduction*. Basingstoke: Palgrave Macmillan.

Scholte, J.A. 2002. 'Global civil society'. In R. Robertson and K. White (eds), *Globalization: Critical Concepts in Sociology*. Vol. 3: *Global Membership and Participation*. London: Routledge.

Scholte, J.A. 2004. 'Globalization and governance: From statism to polycentricity', GSGR Working Paper No. 130/04; <http://www.csgr.org>.

Shaw, M. 1997. 'The state of globalization: Towards a theory of state transformation', *Review of International Political Economy*, 4 (3), 497–13.

Sorensen, G. 2004. *The Transformation of the State*. London: Palgrave.

Strange, S. 1996. *The Retreat of the State: The Diffusion of Power in the World Economy*. Cambridge: Cambridge University Press.

Strydom, P. 2002. *Risk, Environment and Society*. Buckingham: Open University Press.

Tarrow, S. and McAdam, D. 2005. 'Scale shift in transnational contention'. In D. Della Porta and S. Tarrow (eds), *Transnational Protest and Global Activism*. Lanham, MD: Rowman and Littlefield.

Thrift, N. 1996. *Spatial Formations*. London: Sage.

Chapter 22

Globalization and Public Policy

TIM BLACKMAN

Public policy is what governments do with the authority they have; their commitment of resources to what they see as public problems or challenges (Colebatch 1998; Dearlove 1973). The scope is enormous, from defence and foreign policy, to social policies for healthcare, education or tackling crime, to policies for science and technology, and the regulation of a range of activities from advertising to scientific experimentation. Globalization is creating a new environment for these concerns and activities; one in which interconnectedness is of fundamental importance, both as a source of opportunity and as a source of risk.

For there to be a policy there needs to be a problem, but how something gets to be recognized as a problem depends on societal values, dominant ideologies and ideas and political interests (Dorey 2005). Whether globalization is a problem is hotly contested, just as any solution depends on what sort of problem globalization may be. Public policy makes sense of globalization in a particular way, framing the action that follows, whether through regulation, fiscal measures, investment and spending decisions or trade agreements. If there is a thread that can be traced through the policy process of a government as it engages with an issue like globalization it is coherence around values. Policy decisions mobilize some values and exclude others, validate some actions and invalidate others, and include some interests while excluding others. This is rarely a rational process but one of complex interactions and overlapping interests.

Globalization, for example, is not 'out there' but has key features that are actively constructed by and between governments, as well as by companies and through the global networks of immigrants and diaspora, of cyberspace or of the international drugs trade (Amin 2002, 2004). How governments exercise their relative power to frame a phenomenon like globalization makes it easier for some, and more difficult for others, to participate in the process (Colebatch 1998). For a growing number of governments the problem is how to keep benefiting from the expanding commerce generated by economic globalization. For others, this expansion is not a benefit but a threat, whether to indigenous cultures drowned by the products of homogenizing global companies and 'Americanization', or to their very economic survival as their share of world trade declines. While public policy spans a huge range of governmental activities, it is social policy that faces the severest test from economic globalization. In particular, the values of a global 'social agenda', and concern with inequality and exclusion, forcibly promoted by the Live 8 concerts at the time of the G8 summit in July 2005, seem increasingly at odds with the trade liberalization promoted by Western development organizations as the path of economic and social progress for the developing world.

The world, according to a recent United Nations report, faces an 'inequality predicament' (United Nations 2005). This, the report argues, is a result of asymmetric globalization whereby the social agenda is marginalized by a preoccupation with economic growth. Eighty per cent of the world's gross domestic product (GDP) belongs to one billion people living in the developed world; the five billion people living in developing countries have to make do with the other 20 per cent. This situation is getting worse not better. But whether economic globalization is the problem is not clear. Extreme poverty is in retreat and halved between 1981 and 2001. Among developed countries unemployment has fallen in recent years. There have been advances in rights for indigenous peoples and people with disabilities, and over the last century as a whole there has been a large increase in the number of democratic states. In the round, the world has never been better off in material terms, and ever-increasing levels of technical, scientific and medical expertise are bringing huge benefits for billions of people. Yet poverty and inequality continue to exist on a massive scale and are deepening in large parts of the world.

This chapter considers the role of public policy in these circumstances, as pursued by nation-states but also through international bodies such as the European Union (EU) and the World Trade Organization (WTO). The focus of the discussion is on how public policies aim both to realize the opportunities created by economic globalization and to minimize the risks, with 'knowledge economies' being where many states have set their sights. This is considered in terms of the effects of both globalization and these policies on inequality between and within countries. There is still considerable diversity across countries in these respects despite three decades of dramatic globalization of capital flows and trade, reflecting different national norms and initial conditions. There are also many problems and tensions, to which economic growth is commonly regarded as a key solution, but which presents the world with challenges such as climate change and individual countries with issues such as the shrinkage of their labour forces with ageing.

While the nature and extent of globalization is still contested, it is clear that over the past two to three decades all but a few countries around the world have pursued policies to reduce the barriers that impede international trade and capital movements. National economies have been opened up to create an unprecedented level of global integration compared to the sheltered economies that gave the nation-state its rationale as a supreme agent of economic and public policy during most of the modern era. The agency of the nation-state is often questioned in this context, an issue that began with the post-1945 expansion of global production systems by multinational companies. This is often held to have created a world in the image of these powerful agents of globalization as the international division of labour has come to reflect their own corporate hierarchies of decision-making, apparently disempowering all but the most powerful nation-states (Hymer 1972; Nash 2000). In this environment, the worst location to occupy is that of an economic hinterland beyond the world cities and regional capitals where most value added is created.

Global flows of trade and private capital grew at an astonishing rate during the 1980s and 1990s, and far faster than the growth in world GDP (Brune and Garrett 2005). This has not, however, made nation-states irrelevant to the economic futures of their populations because there is an imperative to invest heavily in education and training, research and development and infrastructure to position open economies advantageously in these global flows. This is a role for the nation-state although, as we shall consider below, by no means all states command the resources necessary to do this at a level that can sustain their share of world trade or prevent a widening gap with richer countries.

The continuing agency of nation-states is apparent not just because of the importance of smart policies that can win competitive advantage in the global economy, but also because the globalized economy is itself the emergent product of an international order, the basic constitutive parts of which are nation-states (Axford 1995). European integration, for example, has been catalysed by economic globalization but the EU is a creation of democratic nation-states and not globalization, as the fate of the EU's new draft constitution starkly illustrates (http://europa.eu.int/constitution/). The draft emerged as a compromise between big and small states and between deregulated and regulated markets. It is designed to continue the process of Europeanization but has met with popular opposition, with critical rejections by referenda in France and the Netherlands because of its perceived threat to 'social Europe' and the jobs of workers in high wage economies that already have high unemployment. These referenda rejections mean that the constitution cannot be adopted and have plunged the EU into a heated debate about the future of social Europe and its spending priorities.

Europeanization has been a process of both facilitating economic globalization by opening member states up to global markets and competition, and protecting them from it through monetary union and the single market. The controversy over the new constitution is largely because by extending the single market to low wage economies this protective aspect is weakened. The EU has a significant social dimension reflected in a range of policies and measures designed to achieve economic and social cohesion, leading Graziano (2003: 174) to the conclusion that Europeanization has the character of a market-correcting antidote to globalization. The debate in Europe is therefore not so much about whether there should be a social Europe as whether the current model is working in the new global environment, especially given EU unemployment is now standing at 20 million.

Even within the EU, however, national policy regimes remain distinctive in mediating globalization processes. There is still space for countries to choose their trajectories of social and economic development, but these choices are made in an environment where the interconnectedness of the national and global mean that calculations of risk and opportunity have to be done in a global framework. This is engendering new approaches to policy-making characterized by flexible adaptation in an environment of complexity (Geyer 2003). Complexity emerges when the degree of interaction and feedback in an environment makes prediction impossible beyond broad qualitative states, and even these may transform, given enough change in a key parameter governing a particular state.

The uneven development of the world economic environment can be thought of as a landscape of peaks and valleys, and its state as its degree of ruggedness. This ruggedness can to some extent be tuned up or down by national or pan-national interventions. The EU is an example of tuning the landscape to a smoother topography with its structural programmes for economic and social cohesion (although many developing countries argue that the EU plateau leaves them excluded at the base of the sharp tariff precipice that surrounds it for many of their products). The valleys of this landscape are the economic hinterlands of the developing countries of the South or the depressed old industrial areas of the North. Nation-states are increasingly using their policy systems to move their economies uphill to the peaks, and the 'attractor' at this altitude is the knowledge economy.

GLOBALIZATION AND KNOWLEDGE ECONOMIES

It is has become accepted wisdom among developed countries that, as less skilled jobs move to the developing world to benefit from cheaper labour costs, their futures lie in becoming knowledge economies that generate wealth from a range of activities that are up the value chain from routine manufacturing. This exploits their existing competitive advantage, given the large tax resources that they have available to invest in education and research and development.

The current dominance of a few large developed economies is apparent in this respect when we look at patent ownership. Taking this as an indicator of economically significant research and development, patent ownership is currently concentrated in Japan, the United States and the large European economies (United Nations 2004). However, the rate at which patents are granted per head of population reveals a different picture. In 2001, the countries with high rates – of more than 100 patents granted per thousand population – were the wealthy, small European economies where international trade accounts for a high proportion of GDP: Denmark, Finland, Sweden, Switzerland, Ireland, Belgium and the Netherlands. These might indeed be regarded as knowledge economies, a position attained through explicit policy measures taken by their governments. One of the most significant in this respect is their level of spending on education.

Figure 22.1 shows a graph of the latest data available from the 2004 UN *Statistical Yearbook* for public spending per head on education, plotted against patent applications (United Nations 2004). While high education spending appears not to be a sufficient condition for high rates of technological innovation, as indicated by patents granted, the graph suggests that it may be a necessary condition. There is also a significant linear relationship: as education spending per capita increases, the rate of patents granted also increases. This is, though, by no means a perfect relationship. There is, for example, a wide gap between the rate of patents granted for Belgium and rate for the United States despite similar levels of spending on education.

Also of note in Figure 22.1 is the cluster of points at the extreme bottom left-hand corner of the graph. These are countries of the developing world and Eastern

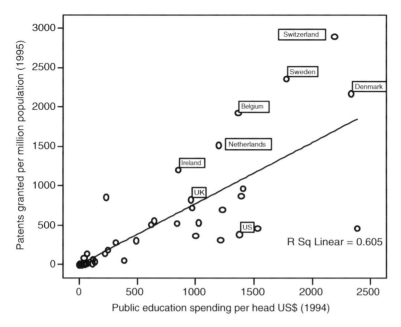

Figure 22.1 The relationship between education spending and patents

Europe that are in the economic hinterlands of the international division of labour. The issue for these countries is being locked into this state; even with stable political conditions their opportunities in the globalized economy are largely confined to capturing routine manufacturing jobs on the basis of their competitive advantage of low labour costs. This competition is often still regarded as a threat among developed countries. The loss of routine manufacturing jobs can be a sensitive political issue for their governments, despite their manufacturing output often increasing significantly because of substantially higher productivity from a much smaller manufacturing workforce. What appears to be deindustrialization is more typically a slower rate of growth in manufacturing output compared to the faster growth of services in developed economies.

The expanding service industries of developed countries can actually have a strong interest in manufacturing moving abroad to low cost locations, not least to support further expansion of service employment at home. The recent crisis of blocked clothing imports from China to the EU is a prime example. Following the scrapping of global textile quotas in January 2005, the EU capped the growth of imports from China's huge low-cost textile producers to give European producers time to adjust to the new competition. However, orders by EU retailers exceeded the quotas, resulting in clothing imports piling up at European ports. The crisis split EU governments, with the Netherlands, Denmark, Sweden and Finland warning of job losses among retailers unless the EU eases import curbs, while France, Italy and Spain continue to press for controls to protect their large textile industries. EU retailers benefit from sourcing cheap clothes from China and now employ a workforce twice the size of that of the EU's textile and garment manufacturers, so tighter quotas on Chinese textile imports could threaten many more European jobs than would be protected.

If some countries are making it to the peaks of the knowledge economy, where rewards from the value added created by design, marketing, retailing and other business and financial services far outstrip those of routine manufacturing, then are we seeing a growth of inequality? This question has two dimensions because in the global landscape it is possible for workers in the same country to occupy either the valleys or peaks of the world economy, as well as for national economies to be, on the whole, at a higher or lower altitude in this landscape. The inequality issue is one of inequality within countries and inequality between countries, both driven to a substantial extent by the higher incomes that highly skilled workers and managers can now command relative to less skilled workers.

Globalization is taking the form of competition by low wage countries with high wage countries that therefore move uphill through technological investment to the knowledge economy attractor. Because this increases demand and pay for highly skilled personnel, while reducing demand for less skilled workers, the process is often held responsible for the rising income inequality documented for most OECD countries during the 1980s and 1990s (Bjorvatn and Cappelen 2004). Countries cannot respond, it is also often argued, by taxing very highly paid personnel more heavily to narrow the widening pay gap through redistribution because these personnel are internationally mobile and could relocate to where taxes are not being increased. Therefore governments tend to settle for expanding their number by creating conditions that produce and attract knowledge workers, with their higher incomes boosting tax revenues even with tax cuts. The implications for income inequality, however, are that it will continue to grow unless measures are taken to equalize pre-tax incomes – one reason why some governments regard mass upskilling and higher education to be as much a social policy as an economic policy.

GLOBALIZATION AND INEQUALITY

International trade as a percentage of GDP varies significantly from country to country, but it is globalization as a process that is having most impact depending on whether a country's share of growing world trade is rising or falling. Parts of the Middle East and sub-Saharan Africa stand out for their declining share of trade growth (Sindzingre 2005). An important reason why these states are in such a disadvantaged position in the global economy is their initial condition when countries around the world began to open up their economies. Critical obstacles have been problems of land distribution, low levels of education, poor infrastructure and weak domestic financial and political institutions. When these obstacles are largely absent countries of the South have experienced impressive benefits from globalization, with China and India being notable examples where the gap in GDP with the developed world is narrowing because of their phenomenal growth rates. They are, however, exceptions (although very significant exceptions given the size of their populations) to a pattern of polarization between the increasingly rich OECD countries and the rest of the world, notably an increasingly poor Africa.

It is now widely agreed that the poor African states cannot transform their situation without external support on a massive scale; trade alone is insufficient (Commission for Africa 2005). Debt cancellation and more aid for investment in water supplies and tackling the devastating human and economic costs of AIDS and HIV are necessary but not sufficient. The Commission for Africa (2005) identifies over $1 trillion of investment and aid received by the sub-Saharan countries over the past 50 years, but many still experienced falls in their GDP. Institutional reform is also needed, especially tackling corruption, but this has sparked disagreement about how debt cancellation can be squared with good governance. Japan in particular – the second largest relief donor in the world – holds that cancelling debt promotes economic 'frivolity' (English 2005). Scale is also an issue: the G8 and the EU nation-states are urging moving up a level so that there is a Pan-African organization of development programmes and responses to the intrinsically cross-national problems of the AIDS crisis, famine and migration.

A key issue for Africa is the risk of opening up national economies when they are still very dependent on commodities markets dominated by a few multinational companies and terms of trade that are loaded against them. The EU and G8 nations are often accused of double standards in this respect because they continue to operate protectionist strategies and subsidies that manage their integration into the global economy selectively; the protected and highly subsidized agricultural sectors of France and the United States being particularly relevant to this claim. Integrating the sub-Saharan states into the global economy with the aim of them achieving a trajectory of sustainable economic growth by sharing in world trade is a major challenge. It confronts deep-seated vested interests among their ruling elites and the warlords in the conflict zones of some of these states, and among governments in Europe and North America facing protectionist political demands from farmers.

Does opening up economies to international markets, however, only serve to widen income inequalities between countries? There is in fact little evidence that economic globalization over the past two or three decades has substantially worsened or improved levels of income inequality between countries, largely because the outcomes are mixed (Brune and Garrett 2005). This points to the importance of national context but in interaction with global conditions, including the problem of unfair terms of trade already noted. The nation-state matters not just in terms of the success of domestic policy-making in positioning the national economy in the global landscape of peaks and valleys, but also domestically because national distributions of income should be considered as well as average differences between countries. The United States may be a richer country than Sweden but the poor are much worse off. While Sweden's GDP per head is little more than two-thirds of that of the United States, the poorest 20 per cent of Swedish households are 40 per cent better off than the poorest 20 per cent of US households because income is more evenly distributed (Jackson and Segal 2004). Across the EU, the overall poverty rate of 15 per cent would rise to 40 per cent without income transfers through tax and spend cash benefits.

The public policies of nation-states create a very mixed picture of changes in income as the globalization process continues, and not just because different social policies leave populations more or less exposed to global market forces. It is likely that the success of national policies for education and skills, for research and development, and to create and protect intellectual property will increasingly matter to standards of living. But while there is an incentive for developed countries to maintain their competitive advantage with high levels of spending on their human capital and infrastructure, this is far less the case for social security transfers such as pensions. Given the ageing of their populations, and the size of their grey votes, the stage is set for an intensification of conflicts over the composition of social spending and welfare reform that are already very evident in many OECD countries.

How reform occurs, however, depends on how labour, capital and the state work together. Ellison (2005), for example, discusses how Denmark and the Netherlands have adopted new 'competitive corporatist' arrangements that lead to incremental reforms, while in Germany and France governments face hostility from well-organized unions, leading to uneven case-by-case reform as changes are won or lost. In general, however, it still appears that developed countries with strong labour movements are more likely to maintain welfare regimes that curtail the extent of income inequality evident in others.

If we take the example of the United Kingdom, organized labour was weakened by unemployment, restructuring and anti-union legislation during the 1979–97 Conservative governments. Although the Labour government elected in 1997 restored some trade union rights, its approach has been cautious because of a pro-globalization belief in the need for labour market flexibility to underpin economic growth. Prime Minister Tony Blair has sought vindication for this position in terms of a healthy growth in real incomes, averaging 2.3 per cent a year over the period 1996/7 to 2003/4, and a Labour government was returned for an unprecedented third term in May 2005, with substantial trade union backing. New Labour social policy has been aimed at improving low incomes for working families and pensioners rather than narrowing the gap between rich and poor, but the policy measures have in effect been mildly and progressively redistributive (Adam et al. 2005).

The fact that redistribution has occurred at all in the United Kingdom is noteworthy given that it is difficult to tackle relative deprivation when average incomes are rising significantly – an aspect of the tendency for economic globalization to widen income inequality. But income inequality would undoubtedly have risen sharply with the same growth in average incomes and no redistribution. UK New Labour governments have had to run fast just to achieve a slow walking pace of redistribution. Under the previous Conservative administrations of Prime Minister John Major, from 1990 to 1996/7, income redistribution was actually more progressive than under New Labour (following the explosion in income inequality that occurred earlier under Margaret Thatcher) but the average annual rate of growth in median incomes was only 0.8 per cent.

There is evidence that the world's developed welfare states will find it increasingly difficult to win public support for levels of redistributive taxation that keep up with the continuing pulling away of high earners in the income distribution (Bjorvatn and Cappelen 2004). There is a convincing argument to be made that the growing income inequality discernible within many OECD countries during the 1980s and 1990s will intensify, and may be a consequence of economic globalization as their lower skilled workers become less valued and their higher skilled more so. But it is difficult to pin this on globalization alone given the influence of other factors such as technological development (Brune and Garrett 2005). Nevertheless, there are potent mixes of factors building up for developed welfare states. To the dynamic of widening income distributions, for example, can be added the economic pressures of ageing populations and declining fertility. Economic growth is widely seen as a way out of these pressures, but often with a neoliberal drift towards privatization and conditionality in the provision of welfare services and benefits.

It is beyond the scope of this chapter to consider in detail the consequences of growth being an imperative for all national economies. There is little doubt that many less developed countries need growth, but in developed countries there are already arguments being made that further growth in GDP per head is unlikely to add to such a basic human aspiration as happiness. It may actually undermine the security of income and work, and the quality and stability of family and friendship relationships, that human beings need most to be happy (Layard 2005). Growth could also be destroying the natural resources and systems on which any economic activity and human life depend unless huge strides are made to achieve environmentally sustainable development (Hamilton 2003).

GLOBALIZATION AND THE STATE

What governments do makes a difference in the globalized economy. The neoliberal discourse that links globalization and its benefits to small government is just that: a discourse that reflects the power and interests of those for whom small government is advantageous. This is never likely to be true for most people because of the need for smart public policies that have real impact across key sectors of education, research and development, health and infrastructure, and because democracies are unlikely to tolerate the extent of income inequality that globalization will fuel without state intervention. Thus, across the OECD, as GDP per capita has risen so has per capita social expenditure (OECD 2005).

This is not, however, to deny concerns about big government and particularly the public choice criticism that managers and professionals may well run public services in their interests rather than those of the public without means of encouraging efficiency and responsiveness to users (Boyne et al. 2003). It is necessary, though, to distinguish between economic globalization, which makes no demand on states to reduce government even though some interventions will be smarter than others in this environment, and the ideological position that responsibility for welfare should be shifted away from a collective commitment achieved through state intervention to an individual responsibility met by markets.

One reason why economic globalization is regarded as a threat to welfare states is the continuing pressure exercised by the WTO to open up markets in public services, with welfare states becoming barriers to trade under this logic. Potentially, WTO member states that make public subsidies to services such as healthcare and education could find these ruled to be trade distortive unless available to foreign as well as domestic providers. However, the extent to which this will really change welfare states from the viewpoint of their users is unclear.

In the United Kingdom, increasing use is being made of private healthcare services, often provided by multinational companies, to increase the capacity of the National Health Service. While representing a form of privatization, NHS patients benefit from faster treatment which is still provided free at the point of use according to established NHS principles. In fact, private hospitals are concerned that the NHS improvements in waiting times for treatment could crowd out their own business, which is substantially based on paying for faster treatment with private health insurance. Also, the use of private healthcare providers in this way is driven by public choice theory and a view among government that the NHS is still too dominated by the interests of healthcare providers rather than users. Nevertheless, the WTO's top-down imposition of an approach that regards all human services as commodities subject to world trade rules is likely to become a more intense political issue.

Many countries have opposed expanding WTO rules to human services and negotiations continue on what services are included or 'committed'. For example, the EU has requested that the United States facilitates access for foreign companies to its water and sanitation systems and deregulates the retail distribution of alcohol (Shaffer et al. 2005). However, the EU has refused to commit any more of its own human services, creating a stark contrast with the United States in the area of healthcare where hospitals and health insurance are committed under WTO rules.

The WTO is not all about free trade. The approach to intellectual property rights negotiated through what is known as the TRIPS agreement is highly protectionist on the basis of an argument that this is needed in order to incentivize innovation, given the high costs of research and development. This has been widely criticized for protecting the profits of multinational companies based in the North and has been most controversial with regard to denying lower cost medications to developing countries because the agreement bans competition from generic alternatives to patented drugs. In the face of opposition particularly from the United States, progress has been made with easing these restrictions with various approved exceptions, led by a coordinated international campaign to increase the availability of drugs for AIDS in Africa (Commission for Africa 2005). But much still remains to be done to improve access to medications in the South.

The WTO's advocacy of global trade is not unopposed and has been successfully resisted in specific cases, but overall it plays well with consumers in developed countries whose experience of globalization is often one of the greater freedoms that come from being able to buy goods from across the world, travel and holiday abroad, communicate globally and enjoy world sport and world music. The extent to which this greater freedom and choice is real is often questioned, most notably by Ritzer's McDonaldization thesis (Ritzer 2004). But the ideology of choice is a powerful one, including challenging welfare states that provide services according to need but with little choice of provider; a situation that raises issues about the solidaristic principle of developed welfare states given the risk of middle-class exit from their services in favour of market provision, and therefore pressure for tax cuts.

Developed welfare states, then, are under pressure to justify state intervention that crowds out the market. Social expenditure as a percentage of GDP reaches 25–30 per cent among the developed welfare states of countries such as Sweden, France and Italy, compared to less than 20 per cent in Australia, Japan or Ireland, despite very similar GDPs per capita (OECD 2005). Arguments in favour have to appeal beyond individual consumerism and personal responsibility to making a link between the societal outcomes of public policy and their implications for the individual.

The trends towards greater individualization in late modern societies certainly needs to be recognized, and has brought positive benefits in spheres such as women's pension entitlements and a recognition of the role of care services in gender equality, but there is also a political task to connect individuals' interests with collective action through democratic states that shape the nature of their societies. For example, in the United Kingdom the chances of an adult son's income being determined by the income of his father is three times higher than in Sweden, where the more egalitarian distribution of income creates more opportunity rather than less for social mobility (Jackson and Segal 2004). This intergenerational income elasticity is broadly similar for the United States and the United Kingdom: both societies regard themselves as meritocracies, but their marked inequalities of income and wealth not only reduce the chances of rewards being distributed according to merit but also extend into extremes that are difficult to justify with any distributive principle based on merit.

The neoliberal discourse of globalization is anti-big government and, in particular, opposes the principle of the welfare state. The welfare state is criticized for being an impediment to economic growth by crowding out private enterprise and creating dependency among service users and benefit claimants. There is, however, no evidence that welfare states are bad for economic growth. It is true that some policies are likely to be better than others in terms of effects such as incentivizing investment or maximizing employment, but these objectives can be served without contradicting welfare state principles of redistribution and providing publicly funded services according to need.

What evidence there is about the effects of welfare states points to their significance in reducing poverty, especially with regard to income transfers. Neoliberals regard income transfers as an infringement of the individual's right to be taxed as little as possible, and of an individual's responsibility to better themselves. But a society of wide inequalities in income and wealth is unlikely to be a society where either rights or responsibilities are widely shared and respected. A telling relationship in this respect is that between the rate at which countries imprison people and their level of income inequality. Figure 22.2 shows the general tendency for the rate of imprisonment among OECD countries to rise as the level of wage inequality increases, with the latter based on wage inequality data computed by the University of Texas Inequality Project (http://utip.gov.utexas.edu/). The wage inequality measure explains 15 per cent of the variation in imprisonment rates. The United States is a striking outlier: even with marked income inequality its imprisonment rate is exceptionally high.

CONCLUSION

Economic globalization is recasting the roles of the nation-state and public policy, not curtailing them. On the one hand there is a search for policies and institutional infrastructure that can take advantage of the perceived benefits of globalization. Primary among these benefits is the growth in world trade and prominent among national policy responses is investment in higher levels of education and training, given the promise of increased returns to well-educated and trained populations in the global international division of labour. On the other hand there is a search for means to reduce the vulnerability of national societies to a perception of new risks from global phenomena that are cross-national rather than national in scale, including companies in high wage economies outsourcing jobs to low wage countries, the

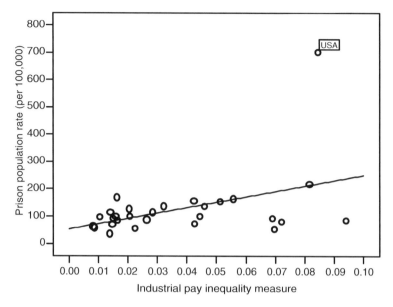

Figure 22.2 Income inequality and prison population rate, OECD countries
Notes: Prison population rates relate to dates between 1999 and 2003. Wage inequality data relates to dates between 1992 and 1999.
Source: Home Office (2003); http://utip.gov.utexas.edu/

in-migration of cheaper labour both legally and illegally, international terrorism and climate change.

It is also the case that the shrinkage of time and space in a globalized world where people, money, goods and media images move rapidly across national frontiers has redefined the parameters of familiar policy problems from crime prevention to public health (George and Page 2004). The pattern of national and international responses to all these issues is very varied. In some cases international agencies have become more engaged with problems that threaten to overwhelm individual states, such as the role of the United Nations in working with African governments to control AIDS, while in others international agencies are bypassed, most notably in the decision of the US and UK governments to intervene militarily in Iraq in the 'war against global terror'. Globalization is essentially a paradoxical phenomenon and this is no less true of the way public policy is responding; integration and harmonization are evident in some spheres but in others globalization creates space for difference and division.

Although there are features of the contemporary experience of globalization that are not new, it is widely recognized that the dramatic compression of time and space on such a scale and across so many facets of human enterprise is new. Technological advances have made this possible, but they are not the driver. Technology has been put to the service of those with the power and motives to exploit its capacity to shrink the world. The prime movers in this respect are the multinational corporations (MNCs) of the North, now with the agency to organize markets globally in the pursuit of profit, facilitated by the economic and military power of their governments.

Yet to suggest that globalization is imposed by the strong on the weak is to represent the phenomenon from one partial standpoint. Although economic globalization was identified a century ago by Trotsky as a driver of widening income and wealth inequalities, and his law of combined and uneven development seems even more true today than in 1900, in current times economic globalization cannot be regarded as a project of the capitalist class alone. Most governments welcome rising international capital mobility as an engine of economic growth that can raise living standards. However, they take different positions on how investment is regulated and how income and wealth are distributed, and this mediation between national and international conditions makes a significant difference to national outcomes such as the equity of income distributions, health inequalities and social cohesion. This can be considered in terms of the different choices that countries make about their welfare states.

Governments may also use the possibilities opened up by globalization to achieve domestic results for their welfare states. The declining ratio of working age populations to older people in many countries is a case in point. This is a more pressing issue in some countries than others: in Japan, Spain, Poland and the Czech and Slovak Republics old age dependency ratios are likely to triple over the period 2000–50, presenting a very different landscape for social policy and tax systems (OECD 2005). This is not just a consequence of ageing but also of low fertility as women's roles and aspirations, especially in relation to paid work, change across the OECD. A response to the threat to domestic economic growth, the funding of pension systems and the rising cost of health and social care posed by a deteriorating old age dependency ratio is to cushion this with higher inflows of foreign workers.

In an exhaustive survey of 'states in the global economy', Weiss (2003) concludes that across taxation and social spending there is little evidence that the capacity of states to act in these spheres has been reduced by economic globalization. Among developed democracies, greater trade openness has generally been associated with a growth in government spending. This has meant increased taxation of companies and individuals, often helped by using a wider range of taxes, and with corporate taxation still low compared with personal taxes. Domestic factors remain significant regarding how personal taxation is distributed in any one country, with the strength of organized labour and its political power still important in influencing where the tax burden falls.

Weiss draws the same conclusions about the pattern of social spending and the extent of neoliberal reforms of public services. Domestic politics still make a big difference, with these in turn heavily influenced by the still remarkably different social norms of individual countries. In economic and financial policy, Weiss finds too that there has been no retreat from state intervention, with states adapting their policy tools to emerging circumstances that they themselves create, such as the WTO's market-opening measures. Ellison (2005) comes to a similar conclusion: there is little evidence of interest, tax or exchange rate convergence across countries.

This adaptation is nicely illustrated by the rise of derivatives markets. These are an example of how globalization has created an environment in which innovations take place to manage the new risks that emerge while retaining the perceived benefits. More open markets expose companies and governments to a risk of damaging volatility in foreign exchange and interest rates, and derivatives markets are an innovation to hedge this risk. Both governments and corporations use derivatives to re-establish some certainty in a world that otherwise would be more risky, and in the process have created new markets that are global in scope. These in turn have brought new risks that have engendered new policy innovations to manage them (Coleman 2003).

While there remains significant space in which governments can develop their public policies according to domestic rather than global imperatives, globalization does frame what governments can do. Weiss (2003) argues that the vulnerabilities of nation-states in the global economy do present their governments with new challenges, but they respond influenced by national norms: social partnership in Sweden, economic nationalism in Japan, Korea or Taiwan, and *étatisme* in France for example. She also suggests that global economic interdependence is transforming how governments act. In particular, governments are managing specific areas of major risk by partnering with domestic business and labour organizations as well as with international bodies to arrive at joint approaches to these risks. Governments set the goals in this scenario but their transformational capacity operates through these alliances and networks.

Swank (2002) comes to similar conclusions about the absence of any necessary connection between globalization and the domestic policies of nation-states, although he focuses solely on developed welfare states. Given that many of the public services reform measures pursued by the states considered by Swank include cuts in benefits and eligibility, cost controls and privatizations, it is not surprising that these measures have been linked to the globalization imperative of opening up markets. But these reforms have sat alongside expansions of some social programmes, with benefits and entitlements becoming more generous in some areas. The large Nordic welfare states, for example, remain intact and the UK's welfare state expansion under New Labour has already been noted.

However, while the growth of global capital mobility cannot explain the spread of neoliberal welfare reforms, there are clearly other factors that have promoted them, including ageing, increasing healthcare costs, and unemployment and associated fiscal imbalances. Swank found an interaction between governments facing large budget deficits and international capital mobility that was associated with cutting back social expenditure, but he emphasizes that this retrenchment has been relatively modest. In general, welfare regimes are pretty much 'locked in' by the norms and institutions of their states. The future, though, presents many uncertainties, especially for those states facing a relative shrinkage of their labour force but with generous benefits for those outside it.

References

Adam, S., Brewer, M. and Wakefield, M. 2005. *Tax and Benefit Changes: Who Wins and Who Loses?* London: The Institute for Fiscal Studies.

Amin, A. 2002. 'Spatialities of globalisation', *Environment and Planning A*, 34, 385–99.

Amin, A. 2004. 'Regulating economic globalization', *Transactions of the Institute of British Geographers*, 29 (2), 217–33.

Axford, B. 1995. *The Global System: Economics, Politics and Culture*. Cambridge: Polity Press.

Bjorvatn, K. and Cappelen, A.W. 2004. 'Globalisation, inequality and redistribution', CeGE Discussion Paper 33, Georg-August-Universität Göttingen.

Boyne, G.A., Farrell, C., Law, J., Powell, M. and Walker, R.M. 2003. *Evaluating Public Management Reforms*. Buckingham: Open University Press.

Brune, N. and Garrett, G. 2005. 'The Globalization Rorschach Test: International economic integration, inequality, and the role of government', *Annual Review of Political Science*, 8, 399–423.

Colebatch, H.K. 1998. *Policy*. Buckingham: Open University Press.

Coleman, W.D. 2003. 'Governing global finance: Financial derivatives, liberal states, and transformative capacity'. In L. Weiss (ed.), *States in the Global Economy*. Cambridge: Cambridge University Press.

Commission for Africa 2005. *Our Common Interest: Report for the Commission for Africa*, <http://www.commissionforafrica.org/english/report/thereport/english/11-03-05_cr_report.pdf>.

Dearlove, J. 1973. *The Politics of Policy in Local Government*. Cambridge: Cambridge University Press.

Dorey, P. 2005. *Policy Making in Britain*. London: Sage.

Ellison, N. 2005. *The Transformation of Welfare States?* London: Routledge.

English, A. 2005. 'A New Marshall Plan?', *Policy World: Newsletter of the Social Policy Association*, Spring, 8–9.

George, V. and Page, R.M. 2004. *Global Social Problems*. Cambridge: Polity Press.

Geyer, R.R. 2003. 'Globalization, Europeanization, complexity, and the future of Scandinavian exceptionalism', *Governance: An International Journal of Policy, Administration, and Institutions*, 16 (4), 559–76.

Graziano, P. 2003. 'Europeanization or globalization? A framework for empirical research (with some evidence from the Italian case)', *Global Social Policy*, 3 (2), 173–94.

Hamilton, C. 2003. *Growth Fetish*. London: Pluto Press.

Home Office 2003. *World Prison Population List*, 5th edn, Findings 234. London: Home Office.

Hymer, S.H. 1972. 'The multinational company and the law of uneven development'. In J.N. Bhagwati (ed.), *Economics and World Order*. London: Macmillan.

Jackson, B. and Segal, P. 2004. *Why Inequality Matters*. London: Catalyst.

Layard, R. 2005. *Happiness: Lessons from a New Science*. London: Penguin.

Nash, K. 2000. *Contemporary Political Sociology: Globalization, Politics and Power*. Oxford: Blackwell.

OECD (Organisation for Economic Co-operation and Development) 2005. *Society at a Glance: OECD Social Indicators*. Paris: OECD.

Ritzer, G. 2004. *The McDonaldization of Society*. Thousand Oaks, CA: Pine Forge Press.

Shaffer, E.R., Waitzkin, H., Brenner, J. and Jasso-Aguilar, R. 2005. 'Global trade and public health', *American Journal of Public Health*, 95 (1), 23–33.

Sindzingre, A. 2005. 'Reforms, structure or institutions? Assessing the determinants of growth in low income countries', *Third World Quarterly*, 26 (2), 281–305.

Swank, D. 2002. *Global Capital, Political Institutions, and Policy Change in Developed Welfare States*. Cambridge: Cambridge University Press.

United Nations 2004. *Statistical Yearbook*, 48th issue, CD-ROM version, United Nations Publications.

United Nations 2005. *Report on the World Social Situation 2005: The Inequality Predicament*. New York: United Nations.

Weiss, L. (ed.) 2003. *States in the Global Economy*. Cambridge: Cambridge University Press.

Chapter 23

Religion and Globalization

PETER BEYER

THE CATEGORIES OF GLOBALIZATION AND RELIGION

Any discussion of the relation of globalization and religion must begin with a look at what these words actually mean. Like so many key orienting concepts in human discourse, they carry a variety of meanings in today's world. This variation, in turn, points to their status as categories of contestation, as ideas that matter because we use them not only to make sense of our world, but also to struggle for power. In seeking to understand what the two have to do with one another, one can begin by noting that *globalization* is a very new word, but it refers to developments that in many senses have been going on for a very long time; whereas *religion* is a very old word in many languages,[1] but it has in comparatively recent times acquired important new meanings that have everything to do with what we now call globalization. The central aim of this chapter is to show how this newer sense of religion has been and still is a significant aspect of globalization; the contestation around globalization and religion is symptomatic of how they are related.

It was only in the early to mid-1980s that scholars in the social sciences started using the neologism, globalization (see Levitt 1983; Robertson and Chirico 1985). The first sociologist to do so consistently was Roland Robertson (Robertson 1992; Robertson and Lechner 1985), even though the idea of a globally extended social system to which it primarily refers is somewhat older (see e.g. Luhmann 1971; Moore 1966; Nettl and Robertson 1968; Wallerstein 1974). Since the late 1980s, globalization has become a highly charged and popular word that has acquired diverse meanings along the way. The most widespread of these refers primarily to very recent or modern developments in global capitalism, especially the interconnectedness of markets and investment as well as the global operations of many transnational corporations. The core idea is that this economic system has become truly worldwide, that it has an increasingly determinative influence in all people's lives, for good or for ill (Beck 2000; Germain 2000; Wallerstein 1979). Often in connection with this economic sense of globalization, other meanings emphasize the international political system of states, the recent intensification of the worldwide network of communications and mass media, the global spread of iconic mass consumer products like Coca-Cola and McDonald's or popular culture trends like Rap music and Chinese food (Crane 2002; Defarges 2002; Jameson and Miyoshi 1998; McGrew et al. 1992; A.D. Smith 1991). Various additional transnational structures and phenomena ranging from non-governmental organizations and crime syndicates, to global migration, tourism and sport also enter into the picture. Some observers, subsuming the latter, argue for the existence of a transnational civil society, in effect a globalized social structure that parallels economy and the state system while not being identical with them (Braman and Sreberny-Mohammedi 1996; Florini 2000). Many of these perspectives also understand globalization in terms of a sometimes contradictory, sometimes complementary relation between local and global forces (Appadurai 1996; Bauman 1998; Nederveen Pieterse 2003; Tomlinson 1999). The world is not just becoming a more homogeneous place. For some observers, resistance to these processes or their variegated adaptation in diverse regions is as constitutive of globalization as capitalism and international relations. In comparatively little of the by now vast literature on globalization, however, has there thus far been much discussion of the role of religion, the only real exception being analyses of Islamicist and other religious militancy under such headings as 'fundamentalism' (Marty and Appleby 1991–5). This lack of attention itself is an indicator of just how dominant economic and political understandings of globalization have been thus far.

There is currently no general agreement on what religion means and what should count under this heading. Most understandings include some reference to supra-empirical beings or transcendent dimensions beyond the everyday world of the five senses; or to a foundational way of conducting one's life and orienting oneself in the world (Clarke and Byrne 1993; O'Toole 1984; Paden 1992; Segal 1992). These commonalities are, however, quite vague, allowing the inclusion or exclusion of virtually anything and really begging the question itself. Alongside the considerable range of such abstract meanings it is nonetheless remarkable that, when it comes to specific *religions* as opposed to *religion* more generally, the field narrows significantly. A clearly limited set of institutionalized religions is accorded broad recognition as religion(s) in virtually every corner of the globe and seemingly by most people. The most consistent members of this set are the Christian, Muslim, Buddhist and Hindu religions (Beyer 2001). To these, different people and different regions, often with few exceptions, add a variable list of others religions, such as Judaism, Sikhism, Jainism, Zoroastrianism, Daoism, Shinto, Cao Dai, Won Buddhism, Candomblé, Voudou and African Traditional Religion (ATR). Some of these are regional in character; with others their status as religions is sometimes questioned. Beyond these we find that range of other, less institutional phenomena ranging from morality and fundamental worldviews to ecstatic experiences and anything that is deemed to offer access to transcendence of the everyday. That is the religious or sometimes, to distinguish it from the institutional, the spiritual. Moreover, as with globalization, religion and all the religions are often highly contested categories, especially with respect to what does or does not belong to a particular religion, the relation among religions and what role religion should play in social life. If nothing else, such conflict over religion shows that it has some importance as a field of human endeavour and understanding under conditions of globalization.

GLOBAL RELIGIOUS INSTITUTIONS

Sociological discussion about the relation of religion and globalization has for the most part focused on institutional religion, although certain perspectives argue that, in some areas of the globe, highly individualistic and non-institutional forms under headings like spirituality are becoming increasingly dominant (see, e.g., Heelas et al. 2005; Inglehart 1997; Roof 1999). The use of terms like spirituality, however, already indicates that the phenomena under scrutiny are different, that they in some senses look like what we understand as religion, but are not quite the same thing. The distinction is instructive in the present context because it again points to the question of what counts as religion in global society. Specifically it implies questions about how religion is globally institutionalized, what variety of forms it does or does not take, and how important or unimportant these forms are. In tune with most of the literature, therefore, this chapter focuses on what, globally speaking, operates as institutional religion, what forms it takes and in that context how and in what sense one can speak of religion globally.

Three sorts of institutional manifestation have received the most attention with respect to at least the global spread of contemporary religion. First, there is the importance of religion in the context of *transnational migration*. When people move around the globe, they accidentally or deliberately carry their religious expressions with them, institutionalizing them in regions where before they may have been a negligible presence. Second, a great variety of *religious organizations and movements* have spread around the world, sometimes in the context of migrations, but also for their own independent, 'mission' reasons. These organizations and movements have local origins, but take advantage of global communicative possibilities to move well beyond them. Third, there is the role that religions have played in *social and political movements* that respond specifically to the globalized context. These need not be geographically global but are often global in their effects. These three modes of religious globalization are, of course, interrelated. They will serve as an introduction to the current literature, and then, in a subsequent section, provide the material and context for taking a more general look at the global nature of religion, institutional religion in particular.

Religion and transnational migration

Human migration in the contemporary world is of several varieties. People move from rural to urban areas, from one part of a country to another, from one country to a neighbouring country, or to another part of the world entirely. It is the last sort that concerns us particularly because of the global social relations that it engenders. The reasons for such transnational migration, as for all migration, are varied. Often the migrants seek to escape poverty, war or political insecurity in their places of origin; sometimes they take advantage of opportunities that arise or seek new ones; and sometimes they form chains of migration, later migrants following in the footsteps of earlier ones because these latter have established the possibility. One of the important characteristics of this transnational migration in today's global society is that very little of it takes place in the form either of 'conquest' or of settling supposedly unoccupied 'frontier' territory. Part of the global condition is that there is very little habitable territory left for new human settlement, and all the habitable territory is both included within the precise borders of one of the sovereign states that participate in the global political system and already recognized as inhabited. It is legitimately occupied and already ruled. Contemporary global migration therefore brings with it perceived problems that reflect this peculiar context: the migrants have to face a situation of adaptation to a 'host society' and the latter has to adapt to them. Much of the current literature on transnational migration focuses on the various issues that arise as migrants adapt to a new environment. These issues include the possibility of marginalization within that society, questions of personal and cultural identity, differences among first generation migrants and their locally born children, relations between migrant communities and those in the places of origin, and links among diverse diaspora locations of the same cultural group (Castles 2000; Friedman and Randeria 2004; Papastergiadis 2000). The other side of the equation, however, is how the various hosts of these migrants respond. While usually not faced with the same issues, the new arrivals often challenge the self-definitions of the hosts and make claims on the power resources within that society. They constitute one variety of 'deterritorialization' in global society, the condition in which place and distance matter less because what is 'there' is also 'here' (Giddens 1990; Hannerz 1996).

As is the case with globalization literature generally, much of that which focuses on transnational migration also ignores the subject of religion. Other dimensions, especially issues of economic integration, societal marginalization and ethno-cultural identity or conflict, are more major topics of attention. In itself, this skewing is somewhat surprising given how frequently and consistently religious institutions are among the first that migrant communities will attempt to recreate in their new homes, and the fact that these are among the few institutions whose resources they can quickly control. Migrant communities establish these churches, temples and mosques for expressly religious purposes, but they most often also serve a host of other functions including as places of cultural familiarity, social service providers, educational and recreational centres, resources for community and political mobilization, and simply as visible manifestations of a migrant community's arrival and claim to belong. Less surprising, therefore, is that a sizeable literature on precisely these institutions has begun to emerge, especially since the mid-1990s, literature that increasingly incorporates an explicitly global perspective, particularly as concerns the ongoing transnational linkages between migrant groups with home-countries and other diaspora communities (Baumann 2000; Bilimoria 1996; Bouma 1997; Bramadat and Seljak 2005; Ebaugh and Chafetz 2000; Haddad and Smith 2002; Vásquez and Marquardt 2003; Vertovec and Rogers 1998; Warner and Wittner 1998).

Migration across large distances is of course not a unique feature of more recent times. It is rather a constant of human history. One of the more significant ways in which contemporary transnational migration differs from those many earlier instances, however, is in the regularity, density and importance of ties that migrants maintain with places of origin and, indeed, with many other parts of the world. That is not something peculiar to migrants; it is yet another manifestation of how the contemporary social world is communicatively tied together. Distance does not cut off the way it used to, even less than it did fifty or a hundred years ago when many of the communicative links that constitute and propel globalization, like ships, railroads, mail, telephone, telegraph and even air travel, were already to some degree in place. Migrants take advantage of increasingly more available and efficient (that is, cheaper and better) forms of these, along with newer technologies like satellite communication and the Internet; and one of the more important social forms that travels along and constitutes these networks is religion. From transporting building materials, sacred objects and religious experts around the world, to pilgrimages and religious gatherings (e.g. *hajj*, *kumbh mela*, the election of a new pope), to prayer and *puja* in cyberspace, to consulting one's favourite source of religious advice on the Internet, not to mention sending money to build/maintain temples and churches 'back home', transnational migrants help to tie the world together, to make it socially a single place through religious communication as well as various other types.

The larger part of the literature on transnational migration, including on the role of religion in that context, focuses on migrants who move from non-Western regions of the world to the West. To some extent this emphasis reflects the relatively high volume of such migration; to some extent it undoubtedly has to do with the fact that the greater portion of the world's social scientists live or work in the West. It is, however, important to keep in mind that such migration also follows different routes. People from South-east Asia migrate to Middle Eastern countries; Brazilians migrate to Japan; Africans to Latin America. They also carry their religions with them. What the literature on Western regions has found about the religious establishments of migrants there does, however, notwithstanding also salient differences, apply to these instances as well (Buijs and Rath 2003; Cesari 1994; Coward et al. 2000; Ebaugh and Chafetz 2002; Hopkins et al. 2001; Kumar 2000; Levitt 2001).

As concerns those transnational migrants who settle in the West, a great deal of attention has been paid to 'recent immigrants' in the United States and Western Europe, and also proportionately to their small populations, quite a bit in Australia or Canada (Adogame 2000; Burghart 1987; Dessai 1993; Guest 2003; Jonker 2002; Khosrokhavar 1997; Leonard 2003; McLellan 1999; Min and Kim 2002; Prebish and Baumann 2002; Saint-Blancat 1997; Waugh et al. 1991; Williams 1988; Yoo 1999). Although the typical religious institutions created by migrants in these regions vary to some degree according to country of settlement, there is also a high level of similarity from one country to the other. Most typical, as already noted, are those religious establishments that serve more than religious purposes for their respective communities. Latin American Christian migrants in the United States use their churches as social service centres and as hubs for communication (including travel) with the communities and congregations in the home countries. Hindu temples in Great Britain and Sikh Gurdwaras in Canada serve similar functions. Mosques in places as diverse as Houston, Helsinki, Cologne, Melbourne or Ottawa provide a prime focus for their respective and usually multinational Muslim migrant communities. What is nonetheless striking, and highly relevant in the globalizing context, is also the variation present in these institutions, both in the country of settlement and in comparison with the religious institutions of the places of origin. Hindu temples in Canada come in a variety of forms, from those that combine, for instance, northern Vaishnavite and southern Shaivite traditions in the same establishment, to those that manifest only a Vaishnavite version, but one that is typical of the Trinidadian Hindus that founded it; or only a Shaivite version, but one that reflects the Sri Lankan Tamil Hindus that dominate it (Sekar 2001). Similarly, mosques in the United States may include in their congregations Muslims from various regions of the world, including a significant proportion of decidedly non-migrant African-American Muslims; or they may be the religious and cultural expression of Muslims mostly from one region like South Asia or West Africa (Haddad and Esposito 1998). What is therefore highly significant about these diaspora religious institutions is not just that they transplant religions associated primarily with certain regions of the world into virtually all other regions, such that previously more religiously homogeneous regions become increasingly multi-religious. Of equal importance is that they generate different and new versions of these religions, ones which through the transnational linkages that their respective communities maintain can have an influence both on each other and on the 'original' versions in the traditional 'homelands' (Beyer 1998a). Thus, among the examples just cited, combination Shaivite and Vaishnavite temples in India are rare; Trinidadian Vaishnavism would not be possible in Canada if it had not been created as a result of previous Hindu migration to the Caribbean; and the construction of a specifically African-American Islam has been largely made possible through the substantial transnational linkages among Muslims and by the presence of significant numbers of 'orthodox' Muslims as migrant communities in the United States. Thus not only does transnational migration have the effect of globalizing religions spatially, but just as importantly it contributes to the further pluralization or multiple particularization of universal religions in every part of the globe.

Globalization of religious movements and organizations

The religious establishments founded by migrant communities are far from the only way that religious institutions have created a worldwide presence. In fact, the spread of religious ideologies, institutions and specialists has been a major factor in the historical establishment of the contemporary globalized situation, as well as in the creation of different sub-global but still vast civilizations of the past. The part that the Christian Church played in medieval European civilization after the fall of the Roman Empire is one instance. Even more impressive is the role of Islam in the creation of empires from North Africa to central and south Asia after the sixth century CE. At its height, Islamic civilization extended from South-east Asia to central Africa, structuring the most global of all social systems before the modern era. The trading links created by Muslim merchants, the networks of Sufi brotherhoods, the system of Islamic centres of learning, Muslim pilgrimage, as well as Islamic political empires informed by Islamic legal systems, were all vital social structures in this regard. In the development of modern globalization, however,

Christian missionary movements have played a critical role up until at least the middle of the twentieth century. Although a good part of this expansion was for the purpose of converting hitherto non-Christian populations around the world, it was also an aspect of earlier waves of transnational migration by settler Europeans, especially in North and South America, southern Africa and Australasia. As a consequence of this combination of missionary impulse with Christian migration, by the beginning of the twentieth century, if not before, Christianity became the first truly worldwide religion, as globally extended as the system of political states and the capitalist economy. Indeed, this diffusion of Christianity was an integral dimension of the global expansion of European power between the sixteenth and twentieth centuries. Its churches, religious orders, other organizations and movements today make up a complex and worldwide network of non-governmental organizations and transnational social movements. The largest Christian variant by far is the Roman Catholic Church, but various Protestant and Eastern Orthodox Churches are almost as widespread. That said, much as with transnational migration, just as constitutive of this globalization of Christianity as the outflows from Europe to the rest of the world are the 'reverse flows' back to the original sending regions, 'cross-flows' between non-Western Christian centres and, in those contexts, the production of original variants of the Christian religion.

The linkages that Christian institutions establish have in fact long since ceased to be unidirectional. One important example is Christian Pentecostalism. Although the prevailing narrative of this movement has it beginning in early twentieth-century United States, similar developments were occurring at roughly the same time not only in Europe and Canada, but also as far away as India and sub-Saharan Africa (Hollenweger 1972; Wilkinson 2006). The American developments came to serve more as a focus of self-identity than as a movement that began in one place and then sent its emissaries to various others. People in different places heard about it, read about it, perhaps even visited the American venues; but then they took the idea for their own countries and began the movement anew there, sometimes on the basis of local quasi-Pentecostal precedents. Pentecostalism therefore grew worldwide as a series of variations on a common theme. It has its large organizations like the American Assemblies of God, but for the most part consists of independent churches founded locally. It has in this way become the second largest Christian identification in the world, after Roman Catholicism (which includes its own Pentecostals known as Charismatics), with hundreds of millions of adherents distributed across virtually every region of the globe (Cox 1995; Dempster et al. 1999; Martin 2002). Its highly diverse and localized forms maintain a wide variety of links with one another through publications, conferences, electronic media and travel (Coleman 2000). Like many of the more tightly organized Christian denominations such as the Anglican and Seventh-day Adventist churches, Pentecostalism's demographic centre of gravity is not or no longer in Western countries but rather in Africa, Latin America and parts of Asia. Indeed, one of the general peculiarities of global religious organizations and movements in comparison with other institutional domains is that the bulk of religious action occurs away from the economic, political, media and scientific core of the global social system. While this fact is perhaps more obvious in the case of religions such as Hinduism, Islam and Buddhism, it is only somewhat less the case for Christianity. This different distribution manifests itself in a variety of ways, including that missionary activity, such a critical element in the initial global expansion of Western influence, now takes a number of different directions, with South Korean and Latin American Christian missionaries in Africa, or African Christians seeking to 'return the favour' by re-evangelizing Western Europe and North America (Adogame 2000; Lanternari 1998).

Of the other major world religions Buddhism and Islam, as noted, like Christianity, also have a long history of 'transnational' expansion, having in their own way been instrumental in the establishment or characterization of vast but sub-global civilizational complexes before the modern periods. Both traditions have taken advantage of contemporary, much more intensive and extensive globalization to engage in a renewed and now global expansion, often in the context of trans-national migration, but also beyond this particular mode. Buddhism, perhaps more than other non-Christian religions, has thus far been the most successful in attracting adherents from populations not traditionally Buddhist in North America and Western Europe (Prebish and Tanaka 1998; Prebish and Baumann 2002). Although the numbers of such new followers are not great in comparison with the global Buddhist population, it is significant that in many cases, the Western converts have formed their own organizations largely independent of Buddhist forms from the 'sending' countries like Tibet and Japan. To be sure, much of this Western Buddhism has depended on the 'missionary' activity of Buddhist masters and leaders from traditionally Buddhist Asian countries, like the Vietnamese Thich Nhat Hanh, and some Asian movements such as Soka Gakkai International have had success in attracting converts from around the world, including in non-migrant populations in the West. Yet the adherents and by now much of the leadership of most of these Western organizations consists of Westerners, and the particular versions of Buddhism practised in these organizations are in most cases quite different when compared to the typical practice in Asian countries. As with various forms of Christianity in the non-West, the Buddhism of Western converts has spawned new Buddhist variations in their own way just as legitimate or authentic as those of the older Buddhist regions. In terms of raw numbers, however, most of Buddhism in the West is the Buddhism of relatively recent (above all late twentieth century) migrants. These too have their typical organizations, most often very local temple organizations, but sometimes also transnational organizations with a predominantly migrant membership such as the Chinese Fo Guang Shan/Buddha Light International or the True Buddha School.

Muslim movements, organizations and leaders have likewise established and expanded their presence in various global regions beyond their historical heartlands, such as, for instance, the West African Murid Sufi order or the South Asian Islamic Tablighi Jamaat. Although these and a number of others are predominantly the expression of migrant Muslims and their second generation offspring, that does not translate into a minimal presence of Islam in these new regions. Even before the twentieth century, Islam was already quite globally spread, being a dominant or at least significant presence from northern and western Africa through the southern half of the Asian continent into western China all the way to the Indonesian archipelago. With such a correspondingly large number of adherents, migration to other regions like North America, Europe and Australia, while small in percentage terms, has had the effect of making Islam the second largest religion, after Christianity, in several of these territories. Moreover, in at least one country in these new regions, the United States, Islam has attracted a significant number of converts from indigenous populations, notably African-American Muslims who probably constitute more than one-third of all Muslims in that country (Haddad and Esposito 1998; Leonard 2003). While this Islam has deeper historical roots than the context of late twentieth-century migration, it serves as an example of how today, as in the past, population migration brings in its wake not only the geographical spread of existing forms of a religion, but also the production of new regionally indigenous variations which add to the global mosaic of that religion. Migration and mission are very often related, even though they are not always identical.

To the examples of Buddhism and Islam, one could add a similar story of global spread of other religions in the form of their organizations and movements. In certain cases, the distinction between migration and mission is quite fluid. One thinks, for instance, of the spread of Rastafarianism from Jamaica to North America and Great Britain; of the nearly global extension of Judaism over the past two centuries; or of the expansion of Sikhism from its Punjabi heartland to the various corners of the former British empire from Malaysia to South Africa to Canada. In other cases, especially of relatively newer religions like Mormonism (if it is not to count as a version of Christianity) or Baha'i, the global expansion has been almost exclusively through mission, through the expansion of the organized forms of these religions.

Religio-political movements in global society

Although these explicitly religious institutions are the foundation of religion's global social presence, it is the implication of religion in other social, but especially political, movements that has thus far received the most attention in social-scientific literature. It is no mere coincidence that the political impact of religion in developments ranging from the Islamic revolution in Iran and the New Christian Right in the United States to the Hindu nationalism of the Bharatiya Janata Party in India and the religiously defined cleavages of Orthodox, Catholic and Muslim in the former Yugoslavia appeared on the global scene at roughly the same time as the notion of globalization (Jaffrelot 1996; Keddie 2003; Roudometof 2001; Wilcox 2000). The often invidious term 'fundamentalism' has gained a corresponding currency, referring to religious movements like these, ones that advocate the public enforcement of religious precepts or the exclusive religious identification of state collectivities. Characteristic of such movements is that they seek to enforce highly particular and frequently absolutist visions of the world in their countries, but with explicit reference to the globalizing context which they deem to be a prime threat under such epithets as 'global arrogance' (Iran) or 'one-worldism' (United States). The religious visions that inform them are the basis for this combination of a claim to universal validity with being centred in a particular part of the world among a particular people (Juergensmeyer 1993; Lawrence 1989; Marty and Appleby 1991–5; Riesebrodt 1993). Thus does religion serve as a globally present way of making cultural difference a prime structural feature of a globalized world that also relativizes all such differences by incorporating everyone in a single social system. This explains why these movements, with few exceptions such as the transnational Islamicist militancy dubbed 'Al-Qaeda', have as their prime goal the control or creation of particular states, including above all their legal and educational systems.

Although the various major religions are each concentrated in certain regions of global society and not others, the boundaries among them are neither clear nor very precise. The historical and contemporary global spread of these religions discussed in the previous sections makes this situation even more nebulous. In this respect, religions resemble a great deal what we call cultures: relatively clear group identities whose physical boundaries are not precise. By contrast, one of the more peculiar features of the modern political state is in fact its precise boundaries, exact lines of geographic demarcation rendered critical by the fact that beyond them is not simply a frontier zone or no-man's land, but other homologous states which share those boundaries. The surveillance and regulatory mechanisms of those states for the most part correspond to those precise boundaries; and it is the relations among those states, including the way that they share a roughly common model of how to structure themselves (Meyer et al. 1997), that constitutes the global political system. Yet the societies based in those states are also different; the state-centred societal model expects them to be different and to express that difference in the form of concrete national self-understandings or identities, enacted policies and cultural patterns. These, in turn, are not just given. They are the subject of a constant, and frequently contested, debate. Religions, with their universalist and absolute claims, offer fertile ground in which to build such visions of the good and proper society, of what the nation and its state are all about and what makes them distinct from the others. Such religious nationalism can be positively oriented towards its neighbours, as in the role of Buddhism in the prevailing national identity of Thailand, the role of Roman Catholic Christianity in Argentina or, more ambiguously, Shinto in Japan. Or it can be oriented in opposition to much or all of the rest of the world's states, as is the case with the various religio-political movements dubbed 'fundamentalist' like the American Christian Right, Hindu nationalism in India or Islamic nationalism in Iran. In some of these instances, the relation between the state, the vision of the national society within that state and the religion is quite close. The Shinto (especially before 1945) and the Hindu examples are cases in point (Gold 1991; Hardacre 1989; Van der Veer 1994). In others, the contention is that the nation-state in question is but one example among several where the respective religion plays this identifying role. Thailand, Sweden or Argentina would fit here. In still others, the claim is that the state and nation is the centre of a broader claim to (eventual) worldwide validity and even dominance, the American Christian Right and Iranian Islamicists serving as examples (Arjomand 1988; Bakhash 1990; Beyer 1994; Bruce 1988). In all cases, however, the state provides the geographically delimited territory in which an attempt can be made to put the religious vision into effect. This use of religious resources to further both the state and religion raises a great many questions. Among these is that of exactly what religion is in contemporary global society that it can be at one and the same time integrated into national cultural visions and yet also be something beyond these. It brings us back to the key organizing question of this chapter, namely what it is that counts as religion in this society and why and how this situation has come about.

RELIGION AND RELIGIONS AS GLOBAL SYSTEM

As noted at the outset, although sociologists and other observers do not agree as to the exact meaning of religion, there does seem to be a general and globally spread understanding about the existence of certain religions, especially but not exclusively those, like Christianity, Islam, Buddhism and Hinduism, that have just been the focus of discussion. To be sure, an important literature, predominantly originating in the discipline of religious studies, criticizes precisely this notion as well. One perspective insists that religion is at best an abstract and analytic term, but not something distinct and 'real' that is actually out there in the world (Smith 1988). A prime argument in support of this position is how the very idea of these distinct religions, and indeed of religion as a differentiated domain of social life, is for the most part so demonstrably a product of relatively recent history (W.C. Smith 1991) and so clearly implicated in the concomitant spread of Christian and European influence around the world (Chidester 1996; McCutcheon 1997; Peterson and Walhof 2002). Following this argument, religion and the religions are decidedly Eurocentric notions that fail precisely in that they are not globally applicable or relevant. Another related position has it that the idea of 'the religions' is empirically too narrow, that what is meant by them does not cover enough of what is manifestly religious using slightly different notions of religion. While both these lines of argument have a certain cogency, they also tend to beg the question of how and why something so supposedly illusory or inappropriate seems nonetheless to have achieved such broad acceptance as almost self-evident social realities. To address the validity of such critiques and also account for this reality, a further approach to the relation of religion and globalization focuses on the degree to which both modern institutional forms and modern understandings of religion are themselves outcomes of globalization. This approach accepts that the modern sense of religion as a differentiated domain manifested through distinct and plural religions is indeed a relatively recent social construction, one that was deeply implicated in the process of global European expansion of the last few centuries and that is today still highly contested. From this perspective, religion and the religions are similar to the ideas of nation and the nations: a set of words that have a long history but that have acquired new meanings in the context of modern globalization, meanings that have been today institutionalized in globalized structures.

As noted, a variable set of religions has an institutional presence and broad legitimacy in virtually every region of the globe. While the idea that religion manifests itself through a series of distinct religions may seem self-evident today, that notion is in fact historically of quite recent provenance. In Europe, where this understanding first gained purchase, it dates back at the earliest to the seventeenth century. Before this time Europeans understood religion, like people in other parts of the world, as the quality of piety and devotion, as the orientations and behaviours of human beings with respect to God, the gods or similar spiritual realities (Despland 1979; Harrison 1990; W.C. Smith 1991). Like the related idea of virtue, religion was something that manifested itself in diverse ways and of which one could have more or less; but it was not a separable or differentiable domain of life. The transition to the modern understanding accomplished precisely this separation:

a religion came to be seen as something to which one could belong, or not. As such, the new idea referred to a distinct domain of life, but it was also inherently plural. There was religion, but only as the religions. As Europeans expanded their influence around the world now armed with this notion, they 'discovered' other such religions, notably Hinduism, Buddhism and Confucianism, but also, over time, others (Almond 1988; Frykenberg 1989; Jensen 1997). The globalization of this idea was, however, not accomplished simply through this European colonialist projection. In some instances, such as Buddhism and Hinduism, local elites and eventually masses came to accept the idea and undertook to reconstruct their own traditions as one or more of these religions. In other cases, especially Confucianism, the relevant local people by and large refused such reconstruction or accepted it only very partially, with the result that today Confucianism is not one of the religions – at least not according to its supposed adherents – and Daoism or Shinto are only very ambiguously so. Thus emerged over especially the last two centuries a kind of global system of these religions, contested and variable in its institutionalization, but also parallel to and in distinction from 'secular' globalizing systems like the capitalist economy or the system of sovereign states. The development of this system is entirely coterminous with and a critical aspect of the historical process of modern globalization (Beyer 1998b, 2006).

The emergence of this system of institutional religions is not only recent. It is also quite selective; not every possible religion, not everything possibly religious counts. Symptomatic of both aspects are those ongoing and recent debates among scholars of religion concerning the meaning of the concept and its supposed Eurocentrism, the contestations surrounding what belongs or does not belong to a certain religion or which religions are to be recognized as genuine religions, and the salience of distinctions between such recognized religions and other, similar but also different, phenomena that appear under labels like spirituality or culture. Controversies such as what constitutes authentic/orthodox Islam, whether Scientology is a real religion, whether Mormonism is a version of Christianity or I-Kuan Tao a version of Daoism and whether 'New Age' practitioners are actually engaged in religion are not just the material of academic discussions. They are part of wider and global social processes that evidence both the fact that these distinctions are socially consequential – it often matters how they are decided – and that what counts as religion is as selective as what counts as economic production, scientific truth or political regulation. Thus is religion and the religions in global society as peculiar to the modern era as commodity capitalism, empirical science and the worldwide system of nation-states. And just as anti-globalization movements are themselves important manifestations of that which they oppose, so too is controversy around the idea of religion and the religions symptomatic of the social and cultural reality which it contests.

CONCLUSION

One of the more remarkable features of the religio-political movements that have garnered so much worldwide attention since the Iranian Revolution of 1979 is that all of them draw their religious components from one of the more or less globally structured and recognized 'world' religions. These movements are Islamic, Christian, Hindu, Jewish, Buddhist or Sikh, not some more nebulous form of religiosity. The religious institutions established by migrants in their new places of settlement also appear to be, with few exceptions, expressions of these same religions. Moreover, it is arguable that one of the most important ways for new religious movements to be recognized as religions is through the formation of distinct religious organizations and movements, with at least regional but preferably more or less global extent. It is to 'look like' the other religions. What establishes this role and importance of the religions is not, however, some inherent feature that they all share, unless it is the very fact of recognition and self-description as one of the religions. Put somewhat differently, the global institutionalization of religion *as these religions*, contested, fluctuating, selective and somewhat arbitrary as it is, has proceeded to such a point that, globally, we recognize as religion and as religious those things that belong to or are expressions of these religions. Other social manifestations are religious only in comparison. It is therefore not surprising that the religio-political movements and the migrant institutions are expressions of this narrow set of religions: that is what we are looking for, that is how we identify them as religious.

Within the scientific disciplines of the social sciences and the humanities, the explicit study of these religions and of religion more broadly in the context of globalization is only in its beginnings. The relative neglect of this topic may be due to the fact that religions usually ground themselves in tradition as opposed to contemporary developments, to the close relation between religion and local and regional culture, and perhaps to the lingering effect of secularization perspectives which have led many social scientists to expect religion to be irrelevant in the modern world. Be that as it may, a now rapidly growing literature that sees religion as an important player in today's global context heralds a much needed new direction in this regard. Religion is not just incidentally global in extent, an accident of the globalization of more powerful structures like mass media, capitalism and the modern state. Rather the formation and global spread of religion in general, and the religions in particular, is a critical expression of the historical process of globalization. Indeed, given the more than two-thousand year history that today's religions claim, it is an indicator of just how long the process of globalization itself has been going on.

Note

1   Certainly in most Western languages, but also as various cognate terms in other languages such as *din* in Arabic, *dharma* in South Asian languages, *agama* in Indonesian and Malay, and in at least the root portions of East Asian neologisms like the Japanese *shukyo* (*kyo*), Chinese *zongjiao* (*jiao*) or Korean *jonggyo* (*gyo*). These latter, in their very combination of old and new, make visible a transition that is less obvious in the former where new meanings have been given or added to old words (see Beyer 2003, 2004).

References

Adogame, A. 2000. 'Mission from Africa: The case of the Celestial Church of Christ in Europe', *Zeitschrift für Missionswissenschaft und Religionswissenschaft*, 84, 29–44.

Almond, P.C. 1988. *The British Discovery of Buddhism*. Cambridge: Cambridge University Press.

Appadurai, A. 1996. *Modernity at Large: Cultural Dimensions of Globalization*. Minneapolis: University of Minnesota Press.

Arjomand, S.A. 1988. *The Turban for the Crown: The Islamic Revolution in Iran*. New York: Oxford University Press.

Bakhash, S. 1990. *The Reign of the Ayatollahs: Iran and the Islamic Revolution*, revised edn. New York: Basic Books.

Bauman, Z. 1998. *Globalization: The Human Consequences*. London: Polity.

Baumann, M. 2000. *Migration – Religion – Integration: Buddhistische Vietnamesen und hinduistische Tamilen in Deutschland*. Marburg: Diagonal Verlag.

Beck, U. 2000. *What Is Globalization?* Translated by P. Camiller. London: Polity.

Beyer, P. 1994. *Religion and Globalization*. London: Sage.

Beyer, P. 1998a. 'The city and beyond as dialogue: Negotiating religious authenticity in global society', *Social Compass*, 45, 61–73.

Beyer, P. 1998b. 'The religious system of global society: A sociological analysis of an emerging reality', *Numen*, 45, 1–29.

Beyer, P. 2001. 'What counts as religion in global society? From practice to theory'. In P. Beyer (ed.), *Religion in the Process of Globalization / Religion im Prozeß der Globalisierung*, 125–50. Würzburg: Ergon Verlag.

Beyer, P. 2003. 'Defining religion in cross-national perspective: Identity and difference in official conceptions'. In A.L. Greil and D. Bromley (eds), *Defining Religion: Investigating the Boundaries between Sacred and Secular*, 163–88. London: Elsevier Scientific.

Beyer, P. 2004. 'Introduction: Controlling the power of faiths'. In S. Stålsett and O. Leirvik (eds), *The Power of Faiths in Global Politics*, 19–32. Oslo: Novus.

Beyer, P. 2006. *The Religious System of Global Society*. London: Routledge.

Bilimoria, P. 1996. *The Hindus and Sikhs in Australia: Religious Community Profile*. Canberra: Bureau of Immigration, Multicultural and Population Research.

Bouma, G.D. 1997. 'The settlement of Islam in Australia', *Social Compass*, 41, 71–82.

Bramadat, P. and Seljak, D. (eds) 2005. *Religion and Ethnicity in Canada*. Toronto: Pearson Longman.

Braman, S. and Sreberny-Mohammedi, A. (eds) 1996. *Globalization, Communication and Transnational Civil Society*. Cresskill, NJ: Hampton Press.

Bruce, S. 1988. *The Rise and Fall of the New Christian Right: Conservative Protestant Politics in America 1978–1988*. Oxford: Clarendon.

Buijs, F.J. and Rath, J. 2003. 'Muslims in Europe: The state of research', Amsterdam: University of Amsterdam, Department of Political Science/IMES.

Burghart, R. (ed.) 1987. *Hinduism in Great Britain: The Perpetuation of Religion in an Alien Cultural Milieu*. London: Tavistock.

Castles, S. 2000. *Ethnicity and Globalization: From Migrant Worker to Transnational Citizen*. London: Sage.

Cesari, J. 1994. *Être musulman en France: associations, militants et mosquées*. Paris: Karthala.

Chidester, D. 1996. *Savage Systems: Colonialism and Comparative Religion in Southern Africa*. Charlottesville: University Press of Virginia.

Clarke, P.B. and Byrne, P. 1993. *Religion Defined and Explained*. London: St Martin's Press.

Coleman, S. 2000. *The Globalisation of Charismatic Christianity: Spreading the Gospel of Prosperity*. Cambridge: Cambridge University Press.

Coward, H., Hinnells, J.R. and Williams, R.B. (eds) 2000. *The South Asian Religious Diaspora in Britain, Canada, and the United States*. Albany, NY: SUNY Press.

Cox, H. 1995. *Fire from Heaven: The Rise of Pentecostal Spirituality and the Reshaping of Religion in the Twenty-First Century*. Reading, MA: Perseus Books.

Crane, D., Kawashima, N. and Kawasaki, K. (eds) 2002. *Global Culture: Media, Arts, Policy, and Globalization*. New York: Routledge.

Defarges, P.M. 2002. *La mondialisation*. Paris: Presses universitaires de France.

Dempster, M.W., Klaus, B.D. and Petersen, D. (eds) 1999. *The Globalization of Pentecostalism: A Religion Made to Travel*. Oxford: Regnum Books International.

Despland, M. 1979. *La religion en occident: Evolution des idées ed du vécu*. Montreal: Fides.

Dessai, E. 1993. *Hindus in Deutschland*. Moers: Aragon.

Ebaugh, H.R. and Chafetz, J.S. (eds) 2000. *Religion and the New Immigrants: Continuities and Adaptations in Immigrant Congregations*. Walnut Creek, CA: AltaMira.

Ebaugh, H.R. and Chafetz, J.S. (eds) 2002. *Religion across Borders: Transnational Migrant Networks*. Walnut Creek, CA: Altamira Press.

Florini, A.M. (ed.) 2000. *The Third Force: The Rise of Transnational Civil Society*. Washington: Carnegie Endowment for International Peace.

Friedman, J. and Randeria, S. (eds) 2004. *Worlds on the Move: Globalisation, Migration and Cultural Security*. London: I.B. Tauris.

Frykenberg, R.E. 1989. 'The emergence of modern "Hinduism" as a concept and as an institution: A reappraisal with special reference to South India'. In G.D. Sontheimer and H. Kulke (eds), *Hinduism Reconsidered*, 29–49. Delhi: Manohar.

Germain, R.D. (ed.) 2000. *Globalization and Its Critics: Perspectives from Political Economy*. London: Macmillan.

Giddens, A. 1990. *The Consequences of Modernity*. Stanford, CA: Stanford University Press.

Gold, D. 1991. 'Organized Hinduisms: From Vedic tradition to Hindu nation'. In M. Marty and R. Appleby (eds), *Fundamentalisms Observed*, 531–93. Chicago: University of Chicago Press.

Guest, K.J. 2003. *God in Chinatown: Religion and Survival in New York's Evolving Immigrant Community*. New York: New York University Press:

Haddad, Y.Y. and Esposito, J.L. (eds) 1998. *Muslims on the Americanization Path?* Atlanta, GA: Scholars Press.

Haddad, Y.Y. and Smith, J.I. (eds) 2002. *Muslim Minorities in the West: Visible and Invisible*. Walnut Creek, CA: Altamira Press.

Hannerz, U. 1996. *Transnational Connections: Culture, People, Places*. London: Routledge.

Hardacre, H. 1989. *Shinto and the State, 1868–1988*. Princeton, NJ: Princeton University Press.

Harrison, P. 1990. *'Religion' and the Religions in the English Enlightenment*. Cambridge: Cambridge University Press.

Heelas, P., Woodhead, L., Seel, B., Szerszynski, B. and Tusting, K. 2005. *The Spiritual Revolution: Why Religion Is Giving Way to Spirituality*. Oxford: Blackwell.

Hollenweger, W.J. 1972. *The Pentecostals*. Translated by R.A. Wilson. London: SCM Press.

Hopkins, D.N., Lorentzen, L.A., Mendieta, E. and Batstone, D. (eds) 2001. *Religions/Globalizations: Theories and Cases*. Durham, NC: Duke University Press.

Inglehart, R. 1997. *Modernization and Postmodernization: Cultural, Economic, and Political Change in 43 Societies*. Princeton, NJ: Princeton University Press.

Jaffrelot, C. 1996. *The Hindu Nationalist Movement in India*. New York: Columbia University Press.

Jameson, F. and Miyoshi, M. (eds) 1998. *The Cultures of Globalization*. Durham, NC: Duke University Press.

Jensen, L.M. 1997. *Manufacturing Confucianism: Chinese Traditions and Universal Civilization*. Durham, NC: Duke University Press.

Jonker, G. 2002. *Eine Wellenlänge zu Gott: Der 'Verband der Islamischen Kulturzentren' in Europa*. Bielelfeld, Germany: Transcript.

Juergensmeyer, M. 1993. *The New Cold War? Religious Nationalism Confronts the Secular State*. Berkeley: University of California Press.

Keddie, N.R. 2003. *Modern Iran: Roots and Results of Revolution*. New Haven, CT: Yale University Press.

Khosrokhavar, F. 1997. *L'Islam des jeunes*. Paris: Flammarion.

Kumar, P. 2000. *Hindus in South Africa: Their Traditions and Beliefs*. Durban, SA: University of Durban-Westville.

Lanternari, V. 1998. 'From Africa to Italy: The exorcistic-therapeutic cult of Emmanuel Milingo'. In P.B. Clarke (ed.), *New Trends and Developments in African Religions*, 263–83. Westport, CT: Greenwood.

Lawrence, B.B. 1989. *Defenders of God: The Fundamentalist Revolt against the Modern Age*. San Francisco: Harper & Row.

Leonard, K. 2003. *Muslims in the United States: The State of Research*. New York: Russell Sage Foundation.

Levitt, P. 2001. *The Transnational Villagers*. Berkeley: University of California Press.

Levitt, T. 1983. 'The globalization of markets', *Harvard Business Review*, 61, 92–102.

Luhmann, N. 1971. 'Die Weltgesellschaft', *Archiv für Rechts- und Sozialphilosophie*, 57, 1–35.

McCutcheon, R.T. 1997. *Manufacturing Religion: The Discourse on Sui Generis Religion and the Politics of Nostalgia*. Oxford: Oxford University Press.

McGrew, A., Lewis, P. et al. 1992. *Global Politics: Globalization and the Nation-State*. Cambridge: Polity Press.

McLellan, J. 1999. *Many Petals of the Lotus: Five Asian Buddhist Communities in Toronto*. Toronto: University of Toronto Press.

Martin, D. 2002. *Pentecostalism: The World their Parish*. Oxford: Blackwell.

Marty, M.E. and Appleby, R.S. (eds) 1991–5. *The Fundamentalism Project*, 5 vols. Chicago: University of Chicago Press.

Meyer, J.W., Boli, J., Thomas, G.M. and Ramirez, F.O. 1997. 'World society and the nation-state', *American Journal of Sociology*, 103 (1), 144–81.

Min, P.G. and Kim, J.H. (eds.) 2002. *Religions in Asian America: Building Faith Communities*. Walnut Creek, CA: Altamira Press.

Moore, W.E. 1966. 'Global sociology: The world as a singular system', *American Journal of Sociology*, 71, 475–82.

Nederveen Pieterse, J. 2003. *Globalization and Culture: Global Melange*. Lanham, MD: Rowman & Littlefield.

Nettl, J.P. and Robertson, R. 1968. *International Systems and the Modernization of Societies: The Formation of National Goals and Attitudes*. New York: Basic Books.

O'Toole, R. 1984. *Religion: Classical Sociological Approaches*. Toronto: McGraw-Hill Ryerson.

Paden, W.E. 1992. *Interpreting the Sacred: Ways of Viewing Religion*. Boston: Beacon Press.

Papastergiadis, N. 2000. *The Turbulence of Migration: Globalization, Deterritorialization, and Hybridity*. Cambridge: Polity Press; Malden, MA: Blackwell.

Peterson, D. and Walhof, D. (ed.) 2002. *The Invention of Religion: Rethinking Belief in Politics and History*. New Brunswick, NJ: Rutgers University Press.

Prebish, C.S. and Baumann, M. (eds) 2002. *Westward Dharma: Buddhism beyond Asia*. Berkeley, CA: University of California Press.

Prebish, C.S. and Tanaka, K.K. (eds) 1998. *The Faces of Buddhism in America*. Berkeley, CA: University of California Press.

Riesebrodt, M. 1993. *Pious Passion: The Emergence of Modern Fundamentalism in the United States and Iran*. Translated by Don Reneau. Berkeley, CA: University of California Press.

Robertson, R. 1992. *Globalization: Social Theory and Global Culture*. London: Sage.

Robertson, R. and Chirico, J. 1985. 'Humanity, globalization, worldwide religious resurgence: A theoretical exploration', *Sociological Analysis*, 46, 219–42.

Robertson, R. and Lechner, F. 1985. 'Modernization, globalization, and the problem of culture in world-system theory', *Theory, Culture and Society*, 2 (3), 103–17.

Roof, W.C. 1999. *Spiritual Marketplace: Baby Boomers and the Remaking of American Religion*. Princeton, NJ: Princeton University Press.

Roudometof, V. 2001. *Nationalism, Globalization, and Orthodoxy: The Social Origins of Ethnic Conflict in the Balkans*. Westport, CT: Greenwood Press.

Saint-Blancat, C. 1997. *L'islam de la diaspora*. Paris: Bayard.

Segal, R.A. 1992. *Explaining and Interpreting Religion: Essays on the Issue*. New York: Peter Lang.

Sekar, R. 2001. 'Global reconstruction of Hinduism: A case study of Sri Lankan Tamils in Canada'. PhD dissertation, University of Ottawa, Ottawa.

Smith, A.D. 1991. *The Age of the Behemoths: The Globalization of Mass Media Firms*. New York: Priority Press.

Smith, J.Z. 1988. '"Religion" and "Religious Studies": No Difference at All', *Soundings*, 71, 231–44.

Smith, W.C. 1991. *The Meaning and End of Religion*. Foreword by John Hick. Minneapolis, MN: Fortress Press.

Tomlinson, J. 1999. *Globalization and Culture*. Chicago: University of Chicago Press.

Van der Veer, P. 1994. *Religious Nationalism: Hindus and Muslims in India*. Berkeley: University of California Press.

Vásquez, M.A. and Marquardt, M.F. 2003. *Globalizing the Sacred: Religion across the Americas*. New Brunswick, NJ: Rutgers University Press.

Vertovec, S. and Rogers, A. (eds) 1998. *Muslim European Youth: Reproducing Ethnicity, Religion, Cutlure*. Aldershot: Ashgate.

Wallerstein, I. 1974. *The Modern World-System: Capitalist Agriculture and the Origins of the European World-Economy in the Sixteenth Century*. New York: Academic Press.

Wallerstein, I. 1979. *The Capitalist World-Economy*. Cambridge: Cambridge University Press.

Warner, S. and Wittner, J.G. (eds) 1998. *Gatherings in Diaspora: Religious Communities and the New Immigration*. Philadelphia: Temple University Press.

Waugh, E.H., Abu-Laban, S.M. and Qureshi, R.B. (eds) 1991. *Muslim Families in North America*. Edmonton: University of Alberta Press.

Wilcox, C. 2000. *Onward Christian Soldiers: The Religious Right in American Politics*, 2nd edn. Boulder, CO: Westview Press.

Wilkinson, M. 2006. *The Spirit Said Go: Pentecostal Immigrants in Canada*. New York: Peter Lang.

Williams, R.B. 1988. *Religions of Immigrants from India and Pakistan: New Threads in the American Tapestry*. New York: Cambridge University Press.

Yoo, D.K. (ed.) 1999. *New Spiritual Homes: Religion and Asian Americans*. Honolulu: University of Hawaii Press.

Chapter 24

Globalization and Higher Education

PETER MANICAS

INTRODUCTION

Like 'globalization', 'higher education' is a high abstraction. Accordingly, it is easy to slip into the assumption that arrangements in higher education globally are pretty much the same as arrangements in the United States. But differences in the histories and political economies of the nations of the world have resulted in differences in the situation of higher education across the globe. This regards not only questions of access, funding, organization, programmes and institutional variety, but questions of needs and goals.

Moreover, even if one restricts one's sight to higher education in one country, for example, the United States, there are huge differences between public and private institutions, Research I Universities/Liberal Arts colleges, four-year colleges/Community colleges, non-profit/for profit, proprietary schools (which offer training in trades and regulated industries, e.g. auto-mechanics, tourism), online universities, corporate universities (for example, Sun Microsystems University, the University of Toyota) and finally, 'diploma mills', digital and otherwise.

Similarly, while it is clear that 'globalization' is a real phenomenon, one can easily fail to acknowledge its complex and multidimensional character. Depending upon how it is characterized, globalization takes on enormous ideological freight. One popular view, well articulated by Thomas Friedman (1999), holds that 'globalization involves the inexorable integration of markets, nation-states and technologies to a degree never witnessed before'. Friedman (2005) has more recently coupled this idea with an idea directly relevant to higher education, the idea that 'the earth is flat'. He quotes the co-founder of Netscape: 'Today, the most profound thing to me is the fact that a 14-year-old in Romania or Bangalore or the Soviet Union or Vietnam has all the information, all the tools, all the software easily available to apply knowledge however they want.' Reducing this process to economics and technology is one thing; whether indeed, the process is 'inexorable' is another, and finally, whether 'the world is flat' in Friedman's sense is still another highly contestable idea. Here we might notice that politics is and will remain a critical difference in outcomes – educational and otherwise. All of these layered dimensions have a bearing on higher education, some directly, some indirectly. But four additional problems need to be noticed here.

First, some of the processes and tendencies currently occurring in higher education at some places, at least, might well have occurred in the absence of the post-World War II phenomenon now titled 'globalization'. Second, there are reinforcing, overlapping and sometimes contradictory features of this process. Capitalism is surely a critical dynamic but as Ritzer (2004) notes, 'McDonaldization's' commitment to efficiency, calculability, predictability and control is a development of the 'rationalizing' process which Weber rightly associated with capitalism and modernity. Similarly, 'Americanization' is an obvious subprocess of globalization, since not only are US corporations still dominant forces in the global political economy, but a host of cultural features, many propelled by new technologies of mass communication, and many particularly pertinent to higher education, are American.

Third, different kinds of institutions in different places will react to these processes in different ways (Wagner 2004). As Ritzer argues, 'although all nations are likely to be affected by the spread of capitalism and rationalization, they are likely to integrate both with local realities to produce distinctly glocal phenomena' (Ritzer 2004). (For Ritzer, 'glocalization' is the opposite on a continuum to 'grobalization'.) Finally, there are causal relations between the many various facets of concern in higher education: policy, including goals, funding, access, institutional variety, organization, including administration and the nature of the work force, and programmes.

The most critical fact regarding higher education in the recent past is its phenomenal global post-World War II growth. Thus, to take but a few examples, as recently as 1980 there were some 32,000 degree-granting institutions in the United States; in 2004, there were 42,000 with a total enrolment of over 16 million. Since Indian Independence, the number of primary schools tripled (even while illiteracy remains high at 44 per cent), higher secondary schools increased by 18 times and the number of colleges for general education increased by 24 times. In 1950, India had 370 colleges and 27 universities; in 2002 there were 8,737 colleges and 272 universities. There are now in India some 320 universities and 16,000 colleges instructing some 9.3 million students (www.ugc.ac.in). China shows a similar trajectory. From 1978 to 1994, Chinese institutions of higher education went from 598 to 1,080. In 2003 there were 1,396 institutions of higher education and more than 1,000 'private' colleges with a total of over 16 million students (Lin 1999). From 1960, enrolments increased by 10 per cent in Indonesia, 19 per cent in Thailand, 20 per cent in Hong Kong and 51 per cent in the Republic of Korea. Indeed, 'half of the students in higher education live in developing countries' (World Bank 1997). By some estimates, the 65 million students enrolled in colleges and universities in 1991 will grow to 97 million by 2015 (Austin and Chapman 2002). A study by Merrill Lynch reported that the higher-education market outside the United States is worth $111 billion annually (*Chronicle of Higher Education*, 8 June 2002).

While this growth surely can be attributed, broadly, to globalization processes, the initial impetus for it was provided by governments committed to policies of economic growth and to the idea that education was a critical factor in this, including but certainly not reducible to the so-called 'knowledge economy' (Neef 1998). These ideas, while contestable, are thoroughly taken for granted by nearly everybody. To be sure, decisions regarding higher education made by governments, both in the advanced and less advanced capitalist and in the socialist societies, were made against the background, and in response to, several global dynamics in the post-World War II period. We can only note here the importance of the dynamics of capitalism, which among other consequences, spurred huge technological changes and revolutionary shifts in production arrangements, the dynamics of independence movements and efforts to 'catch up', and the political dynamics of the Cold War.

This growth was accompanied by a number of important shifts conveniently identified by critics of the effects of globalization on higher education. These include: privatization, managerialism, the reduction of its 'products' to 'commodities', a single-minded commitment to efficiency and submission of allocation decisions to the logic of the market (Currie 2004; Margolis 2004; Hayes and Wynyard 2002).

PRIVATIZATION OF HIGHER EDUCATION

There are, broadly, four sources of funds for sustaining an institution of higher education: public funds, tuition, endowments and funds generated by scientific research. As Johnston (2001) writes: 'Higher education is experiencing a worldwide shift of cost burden from governments to parents and students.' As with growth, this too reflects a globalization process. There are, nonetheless, significant differences across the globe. Most notable here is the fact that 'private' institutions of higher education are of critical importance *only* in the United States and Japan. That is, higher education in most of the world, until the recent past, was supported by public funds. Given that the US system is now taken by many to be the model for 'world class' institutions of higher learning, a good deal of what is happening globally looks like 'Americanization', often justified in terms of the free market, neoliberal, ideology of globalization (Steger 2005).

To give some order to our account, we begin with a consideration of these sources of funding, beginning with endowments, a nearly unique entirely 'private' US source of funding, state-supported research funding and proprietary research funding, the 'commercialization' of research. We then consider recent global changes in public funding and in tuition and suggest an explanation for this.

Endowments

The elite universities of the United States, some public, but mostly private, have huge endowments. Harvard's endowment at the end of the 2004 fiscal year was a remarkable $22.6 billion (*New York Times*, 22 May 2005) – easily more than the GNPs of most nations of the world. Only three public institutions are in the top 20: the University of Texas system (with an endowment of $5,043,333,000), the Texas A&M system and the University of California. Having a large endowment, of course, gives these institutions considerable autonomy. While both in the United States and globally, these institutions are standard setters, their uniqueness makes them poor exemplars. Indeed, the importance of the endowment for *public* four-year institutions is indicated by the fact that but 0.9 per cent of their current funds revenues were from their endowment. And over 80 per cent of students in the United States are enrolled in two or four-year *public* institutions (*Chronicle of Higher Education*, 2004–5 Almanac).

Research

Prominently led by state-funded 'institutes' in Germany, 'research' has been a fundamental part of the modern university since its creation late in the nineteenth century (Wittrock 1993). In the first two decades of the twentieth century, the new universities in the United States established the current globally taken-for-granted idea of social science *disciplines* that had as a goal of research the 'solution' of social problems (Manicas 1987). But what may be termed the 'commercialization' of research is relatively recent, dating perhaps from the 1930s (Shapin 2003). A very large impetus for 'entrepreneurial' efforts by faculty and an accelerated blurring of 'science' and 'industry' was the Bayh–Dole Act of 1980 which was motivated by concerns for national commercial competitiveness. The Act allowed (or indeed, mandated) US universities to patent the fruits of research. 'Technology transfer' offices proliferated.

Taken together, in the United States, government and private contracts for research represent some 20.3 per cent of current funds revenues for public four-year institutions. For private, non-profit four-year institutions, the total is a remarkable 31.5 per cent. Thus, in 2001, Johns Hopkins showed over $1 billion in federal research and development expenditures, of which over $283 million were defence related. (*Chronicle*, 2004–5 Almanac). Although US institutions have set the pace, others are definitely moving in this direction. For example, according to Shapin (2003), total licensing revenues at Cambridge University exceeded £1 million for the first time in 2001.

To be sure, there are obvious problems with the 'commodification' of the 'products' of research, not least the trade-off between the effort to advance science and technology and the loss of autonomy of researchers whose work inevitably will reflect the interests of their sponsors. And, if only marketable products are created, what of attention to 'public goods' which have little or no market value (Shapin 2003)?

Almost certainly, the Cold War and then globalization has powerfully reinforced this development in the United States, and increasingly elsewhere. The institutions of higher education were never ivory towers single-mindedly devoted to truth for its own sake, but the pressure to generate research monies – from whatever source – has challenged faculties and administrations in new ways. It is now commonplace for the classics faculty to be told that their computers were paid for by overhead funds from contracts generated by faculty in the physics or biology departments.

Public funding

The opposite of 'privatization' is public funding, the dominant source, until recently, of funds for all 'public' institutions of higher education, in the United States and elsewhere. In the United States, state support peaked in 1979 at 62 per cent and has declined steadily ever since. At the beginning of its most recent spiral, in 2001, it was 31.9 per cent (*Chronicle*, Almanac). 'We used to be state-supported, then we became state-assisted, and now we are state-located.' European institutions of higher education still get the majority of support, as much as 90 per cent, from public funds (Slaughter and Leslie 1997). For a variety of historical reasons, public funding was also the rule in most of the rest of the world.

In today's global political economy, governments are over-burdened in seeking to support a wide variety of infrastructures. In the United States, these include prisons, the state's share of medical costs for the elderly and indigent, and a host of other 'public services' including, obviously, public institutions of higher education. In Europe, efforts to sustain even modest 'welfare' policies are under attack (Judt 2005). In the poorer countries, of course, since all their needs are great, there is the complex problem of deciding what portion of public revenues should be used to support education, both lower and higher (Garnier 2004). It has been argued that while the advanced nations provide a considerably larger share of their large GNPs to education than do the poorer countries, poorer nations need to spend more (Fleisher 2002).

Certainly, globalization processes have reinforced the difficulties faced by governments. Of particular importance is the set of beliefs about globalization which has been used to legitimate decisions by governments to privatize. Once 'free market' fundamentalism captures the ideological territory, privatization becomes not only reasonable but essential. Nevertheless, these governments have made choices. While there is disagreement on what is to be counted as a pertinent expenditure, one study argues that California annually spends $5.6 billion on prisons and $4.3 billion on higher education (Prison Activist Resource Center).

Tuition

A key mechanism of privatization is the shift to tuition as a source of revenue. It is a rapidly growing source of income for *all* institutions, both public and private, but despite recent tendencies, still a relatively smaller ratio in most nations, excepting the United States and Japan. The United Kingdom, with a strong traditional commitment to free tuition for higher education, introduced limited tuition fees in 1998. Prime Minister Tony Blair pushed to allow UK universities to triple their annual tuition fees, to £3,000 a year, or $5,300, starting in 2006 (*New York Times*, 25 December 2003). This compares with tuition in US public institutions, but is much less on average than tuition at US private colleges and universities – a fact of some importance as regards access and affordability. In 1998, cash-strapped German universities abandoned free tuition for students. But Germany's highest court ruled early in 2005) that a ban on tuition imposed by the Social Democratic leadership of the federal government was unconstitutional (*Chronicle*, 4 February 2005), a victory for the German conservatives. In France, undergraduates pay from €280 to €350 a year, or $350 to $435, an obviously nominal fee. Fearing changes that 'would lead to competition between universities and pave the way for increased privatization and higher tuition fees', students in France took to the streets to protest (*New York Times*, 25 December 2003).

But the most radical changes are occurring in China and India where it is clear that increased integration into the global political economy has been the significant dynamic. We need to distinguish two sorts of changes, both representing privatization. One regards the fairly recent imposition of tuitions in state institutions; the other is the creation of 'private' institutions, paralleling US 'for-profits'.

Tuition costs in institutions of higher education in the developing world are not in themselves helpful since the question of importance is affordability: the extent to which people have the resources to pay for higher education. The much more remarkable development is the growth in Asia and elsewhere of self-supporting 'private' institutions, comparable to US 'for-profits'. Indeed, along with a host of features characteristic of the US system, including disciplinary divisions, the commercialization of research and the changes, in Europe, in the credentialing of faculty, this development distinctly represents 'Americanization'. To understand what is happening in China and India and to round out the US picture, we need to consider the 'for-profits'.

THE FOR-PROFITS

As Ruch (2001) points out, the essential difference in the United States between private non-profits, for example, Yale, and private for-profits, for example, Phoenix, is that their tax liability differs both as a source of revenue and as a form of expenditure. The main shared feature is the relative absence of public funds. Lacking endowments, however, the for-profits operate like businesses with close attention to the bottom line. Similarly, we tend to think of the for-profits as uniquely American and committed to the use of online pedagogies. Neither assumption is true. There are now many more for-profits outside the United States than in the United States, and, for good reasons (below), few for-profits extensively employ sophisticated online technologies.

In the United States, in 1991, there was one for-profit, degree granting, accredited institution listed on US stock exchanges, DeVry, Inc. By 1999, there were 40 (Ruch 2001). Generating some $16.5 billion in revenues, for-profit revenues increased by 20 per cent in 2001 over the previous year. 'According to analysts, enrollment growth at the seven biggest for-profit companies has outpaced overall enrollment growth in higher education for at least the last half-dozen years. Projections for next year show that trend will continue' (*Chronicle*, 19 December 2003). Indeed, the for-profit higher education industry is now valued at $15.4 billion with some 8 per cent of the 20 million students enrolled in 6,000 degree granting institutions in the United States (*Chronicle*, 7 January 2005). There is every expectation that this growth will continue.

Much of the success of these institutions depends on their willingness and ability to accommodate the special needs of non-traditionals, and on their niche programmes – 'degrees with real-world relevance' – which include information technology, international business, criminal justice and homeland security. The pattern is being reproduced around the globe. Of course, these institutions will need to prove that they can do what they promise, but what they promise is clear enough: rather than hard-to-measure values like 'becoming a well-rounded person' or 'a liberal education', students are promised what they came for, completing the programme and getting a better job. The US for-profits are highly conscious of placement rates. For example, they range from 96 per cent at De Vry to 76 per cent at Strayer. Similarly, the return on educational investment (ROEI) is higher than for the average BA: 28 per cent as compared to 18.7 per cent (Ruch 2001; Thomas 2004).

But the most remarkable shift towards the American system is occurring in China and India (Adamson and Agelasto 1998; Altbach 1999; Mauch and McMullin 2000). Following the US model, in China and India the shift to 'private' institutions includes primary and secondary education as well as higher education. Thus,

> the first private school to thrust private education into the spotlight was the Guangya Primary School, set up in August 1992 in the city of Chengdu in Sichuan province. Dubbed the 'first school for [training] aristocrats in China,' it caught national and international attention for its high tuition and fees, promise of high teaching quality, and superior learning conditions (such as computers, color TVs, and pianos installed in air-conditioned classrooms). Other features of the school, such as small class size, comfortable living conditions, foreign teachers teaching all subjects in English, and standard running tracks, also aroused much curiosity. (Lin 1999)

By 1994, China had 60,000 private, non-governmental schools and other types of unofficial educational institutions. Among them, 16,800 were kindergartens, 4,030 were primary schools, 851 were secondary schools and more than 800 were institutions of higher learning (Lin 1999). The development in India is more recent (Suri 2004). In both places the problems are obvious enough and include questions about the quality of such institutions, problems of access and affordability and problems with the ideology of 'privatization' and 'markets'. In India, a government-established Task Force (February 2003) considered measures to stop 'commercialization of education'. More recently, India's Supreme Court quashed a provision that allowed the establishment of private universities (Neelakantan, 2005a). The outcome is not yet clear.

In both China and India, the leading institutions remain the publicly funded state institutions. Currently, while tuition and fees are very low and loans are available, affordability is a serious problem. *But the effective demand is there*: as in the United States, education has become sufficiently profitable to propel educational entrepreneurs, including foreign investors. It has been estimated that by 2003, there were 746 'China-Foreign Cooperative' schools operating in China (Wang 2004).

ACCESS AND AFFORDABILITY: AN EMERGING GLOBAL MIDDLE CLASS?

A recent study restricted its concerns to 15 'of the world's most developed societies' (*Chronicle*, 22 April 2005). The nations included were Australia, Austria, Belgium, Britain, Canada, Finland, France, Germany, Ireland, Italy, Japan, the Netherlands, New Zealand, Sweden and the United States. There were no surprises. Sweden has the most affordable higher-education system, Japan with its high percentage of private schools, the least affordable, with the United States next to last. With evidently the least differences in participation by class indicators, the Netherlands is the most accessible. The United States places fourth for accessibility, 'with nearly a third of adults between the ages of 25 and 34 having paid the price to complete a college degree'.

But the real problem is not among the world's most developed societies but among the world's *least* developed nations, with nations like India and China somewhere in the middle. And the problem has been created largely by processes of globalization. While the process began earlier, we now have a global political economy which is rapidly eliminating all pre-capitalist modes of production. This means that the sons and daughters of subsistence farmers will either find employment in market-based modern economic activities or they will struggle in sweat shops or in the rapidly increasing informal economy (M. Davis 2004). With global inequalities in nations increasing, it is not easy to be optimistic on this score.

Primary education remains critical, but those who gain post-secondary education are potential players in an emerging global middle class. In a sense, young people all over the world now find themselves increasingly in the situation of young people in the advanced societies. But they are only *potential* players since their opportunities will depend critically on the character of development in these countries. In this regard, there are huge differences between India, China, the nations of South-east Asia, Russia, the Middle East, South America and Africa. Indeed, an increasingly difficult problem is the absence of good jobs for well-educated youth, perhaps especially in Egypt and the Middle East. A move to a radical politics is often the response (Kepel 2003). In India, there are 5.3 million unemployed university graduates, and in Kerala, with its high literacy, 'it is not uncommon to find bus drivers who are engineers or who hold multiple master's degrees or law degrees' (Neelakantan 2005b). China most certainly will produce increasingly large numbers of well-educated persons and, like India, it will increasingly become an important player in the global political economy. Most of the nations of Africa, tragically, remain in a poverty quagmire.

On the other hand, it would be a mistake to suppose, as suggested by Friedman's idea of the 'flattening earth', that the well educated of the advanced industrial societies will be replaced by well-educated elites in the developing world or that in the foreseeable future, the United States will become a minor player in the global political economy. Neither is likely.

To be sure, current 'information' technology has joined with what has been called 'flexible accumulation' (Harvey 1987), making it possible, among other things, that 'intellectual work, intellectual capital, could be delivered from anywhere. It could be disaggregated, delivered, distributed, produced and put back together again – and this gave a whole new degree of freedom to the way we do work, especially work of an intellectual nature.' Friedman continues: 'And what you are seeing in Bangalore today is really the culmination of all these things coming together.' This suggests Robert Reich's enthusiasm for what he called 'symbolic analysts'. But both ideas overlook obvious objections.

First, we are speaking about a tiny minority of workers in the global political economy. Most work is not 'intellectual' and it will not become so. The next 'napster' may well 'come out of left field', but this does little for the overwhelming majority of workers, well-educated or not. Indeed, worldwide, human labour is trafficked in conditions barely seen since the nineteenth century, including not merely terrible working conditions and long hours, but exploitation of women and children – including sex workers who are made vulnerable to HIV/AIDs. Second, as wages rise, the 'outsourced' white-collar employees in the developing countries will lose whatever initial advantages they have over those in the dominant corporations of the advanced industrial nations. Third, most of the work done by even the technologically sophisticated will remain low-paid and mostly uninteresting. Historically, while technological innovations in manufacturing did require that new skills be learned, overall, the result was a deskilling of workers (Granovetter and Tilly 1988).

Indeed, if construed instrumentally, education is a perfect case for what Hirsch (1976) has called the 'adding up' problem in which 'opportunities for economic advance, as they present themselves serially to one person after another, do not constitute equivalent opportunities for economic advance by all. What each one can achieve, all cannot.' For each of us the scramble for education is rational since individually we never confront 'the distinction between what is available as a result of getting ahead of others and what is available from a general advance shared by all'. Wider participation affects not only what one gets from winning the game, but the nature of the game itself. If the goal of a bachelor's degree is a better job and better income, then while getting a bachelor's degree remains rational, the consequence is the diminishing value of the degree – especially if the skills and knowledge represented by the credential are lacking. As Thomas concludes: 'for most, the new economy has helped make the college degree a necessity for maintaining one's rung on the socio-economic ladder. Career options for those without college credentials are increasingly bleak' (Thomas 2004).

But as elsewhere, enormous differences in access and affordability continue to make educational opportunity an increasingly unequal affair. While the United States was an early leader in efforts at mass education, even in the United States, there are huge advantages to completing work at an elite college or university, and access is very much structured by socio-economic status. Indeed, there is no nation in the world, excepting perhaps Cuba, that is anywhere near to achieving equality of opportunity, a mythical idea imported globally by a misunderstanding of the US educational system.

GLOBALIZATION AND THE NEW TECHNOLOGIES FOR EDUCATION

It has been widely assumed that the new Internet technologies, a visible feature of globalization, would, of themselves, create a revolution in higher education. We need to notice, first, that there are a wide variety of 'distance learning' forms, which range from traditional correspondence courses, to the use of TV, both interactive and not, to the use of new online technologies. The Chinese, for example, have an extensive system of RTVUs (Radio and Television Universities) which serve to deliver credit and non-credit courses aimed at developing various technical competences. But for a variety of reasons, 'e-learning' in China, as elsewhere, remains marginal.

In the United States, the for-profits have attracted students who otherwise might not have been in higher education – in part because community colleges and four-year institutions have generally not addressed their needs (Ruch 2004). But by offering online courses and programmes, especially in high-demand vocationally oriented areas, some large four-year public institutions have done very well in this. These include the University of Illinois, Pennsylvania State University and the University of Maryland. Indeed, perhaps contrary to generally held belief, the large public institutions, including both two-year and four-year institutions, dominate online education. In Autumn 2003, 1.9 million students were studying online with only 200,000 online students in private for-profits (Allen and Seaman 2004).

While the quality of pedagogy of online teaching remains contested, there is good evidence that it is at least as good and probably better than much face-to-face instruction – especially given the often large numbers of students in large lecture sections (Odin 2004). Despite problems and faculty resistance, effective assessment remains a crying need, not merely the assessment of online teaching outcomes, but more generally the assessment of the too often unclear goals of all sorts of education. Assessment has recently become a major requirement of accrediting agencies. This is often taken to be a symptom of 'McDonaldization', but of course, it is also a consequence of pressures from bill-paying parents and governments with shrinking budgets to get the most from their dollars.

But good online pedagogy needs to be learned and it is not a cost-saving approach (Odin 2004). Student opinion regarding its use is mixed, at best: 40.7 per cent of schools offering online courses found that 'students are at least as satisfied' with their online courses, with 56.2 per cent neutral (Allen and Seaman 2004). Only 28.0 per cent of students in private non-profits agreed that their online work was 'at least as good', suggesting that market-sensitivity, coupled with a realistic assessment of the costs of effective online teaching, may explain the more limited use of online teaching in the for-profits. Similarly, unlike Research I institutions, there are no teaching assistants (TAs) and generally no large lecture halls. This helps also to explain generally smaller classes for the for-profits in the United States. Given that they are not a panacea for mass education, the future of the use of online technologies remains contested (*New York Times*, 25 April 2004).

THE INSTRUMENTALIZATION OF THE CURRICULUM

Despite obvious changes in the character of student bodies, both in the United States and elsewhere, for many there is continuing nostalgia for the idea of a university where the *ars liberalis* were sharply distinguished from the *artes serviles,* where intellectually well-motivated students and an autonomous faculty could learn together and reflect on the meaning of life. It is surely contestable whether this was ever the case, even when universities served but a tiny percentage of well-to-do male students. It is certainly not the case today. If in the United States, roughly 84 per cent of incoming students in 1966 indicated that their primary goal was 'to develop a meaningful philosophy of life' and 44 per cent identified 'to be very well-off financially', in 1990 these numbers were reversed (Thomas 2004). Evidence suggests that globalized 'consumerism' makes economic motives even more pronounced elsewhere. Thus, in Kerala, India, applications for higher education have been falling. Neelakantan (2005b) quotes a 22-year-old shopkeeper very much interested in making money: ' . . . college is cheap enough, but it is no use . . . Better that I started a business early and started to make money than do a useless degree.' An Indian social scientist explains: 'College education is neither job-oriented nor research-oriented . . . It has created a false notion of knowledge and ego in people's minds' (Neelakantan 2005b).

The histories of India and of China almost certainly bear on attitudes regarding the 'status' of those who attain higher education, from producing *babus*, a pejorative term used to describe a class of clerks and petty bureaucrats, developed by British colonialists (Neelakantan 2005b), to producing a 'mandarin' class of 'globalized political elites' (Hao 2004). But while everyone would seem to agree that 'basic skills' and 'knowledge' are critical, it is not clear what this means in practice. For example, we very often hear that US graduates lack linguistic and mathematical competence or a basic familiarity with history, and that in the current competitive global environment, this predicts disaster (Friedman 2005; *New York Times*, 7 December 2004). But, typically, efforts at seeking consensus on measures of competence and on what should be taught run head-on into philosophical differences regarding the very idea of 'knowledge' and how it is be measured, with a loss of confidence in what constitutes a basic 'core', with a perfectly reasonable shifting of blame to primary and secondary education, and, as important, with no clarity regarding the goals of higher education (below).

MANAGERIALISM AND MARKETS

There is considerable difference globally in the degree and kind of control exerted by governments, generally through ministries of education (Wagner 2004). More or less centralized authorities can more easily define national goals, for example, to produce large numbers of scientists or engineers, as in China. Similarly, 'private' institutions have greater freedom, including efforts to resist critical aspects of globalization processes, for example, as in 'Wahibism' – the creation of International Islamic Universities (Inayatulla 2004).

But even where educational institutions have relative autonomy, for example, the Oxford system of colleges, it is no longer possible to make decisions about programmes, curriculum, student services, staffing needs etc., without attention to costs. Nor is the role of 'stakeholders' – the Ministry of Education, the Regents, the Chancellor, the faculty, taxpayers *or* the students – any longer clear.

Managerialism and a market orientation emerge as responses. The for-profits exemplify both. On the one hand, with clear goals, 'managers' can manage and faculty can teach. Similarly where there is a clear 'product', outcomes can be assessed and the institution can reproduce itself only if people will pay the price for securing the 'product'. But such is not the case as regards most institutions of higher education. Indeed, the worry is that globalization guarantees that in the near future this will be the case.

For most of these institutions, while 'faculty governance' has been an ideal, the degree and kind of faculty 'governance' has been institutionally variable, both historically, and between, for example, traditional Asian, European and American systems (Wittrock 1993). But if the increased tendency towards managerialism owes partly to globalization processes, it owes partly at least to decisions by faculty. One study (Minor 2004) showed that just 19 per cent of faculty in US doctoral universities had a high level of interest in governance matters. Typical responses were that their faculty senate is 'a waste of time': much time is spent, and given the highly bureaucratic structures of governance, all that is accomplished is the legitimation of decisions by administrators who are either beholden to powerful interests, official and otherwise, or take the path of least resistance.

Similarly, it is hardly clear that under present global circumstances, 'markets' should play no role in higher education. But we need to be especially clear about what this means. As Smith (2004) argues, 'there clearly needs to be greater reliance upon market-related factors, but these factors need to be filtered and structured through a governing set of educational principles and goals, which in turn need to be subject to constant review'. Indeed, since World War II the modern university has tried to adjust to a host of demands, demands which, indeed, are not necessarily compatible.

Consider: Is higher education primarily aimed at graduate, including professional education, or at undergraduate education? Is it aimed at liberalizing the young mind, developing skills for employment, promoting a national identity, or developing political elites or democratic citizenship? What are the goals in terms of access, or the priorities regarding the creation of new knowledge against an interest in its dissemination, in economic development and in service to the community or to the individual?

Perhaps because demands imposed on institutions of higher learning by globalization processes are both urgent and often conflicting, there has been little discussion about either goals or the appropriate means to attain them – except perhaps where the urgency is more obvious, again, for example, as in China. In contrast to the United States, for example, one senses an absence of nostalgia for the ideals of the 'traditional' university. Indeed, in the United States and Europe, the debate over goals has hardly started (May 2005). The upshot is an unreflexive reproduction of long-established classroom habits, across the board cuts and, overall, an impoverished effort to be all things to all people. Karelis (2004) offers a telling story. As Director of the Fund for the Improvement of Postsecondary Education, he travelled the United States talking to groups of undergraduates. Rarely could he find a student who could even parrot the goals and rationale of their general education requirement; still less, could he find one who could speak intelligently about it. As a consequence of their disdain for market logic, Karelis remarks, rightly, that faculties have simply fallen down on the job of creating an *informed* market for higher education.

But there is no requirement that all the many different *kinds* of institutions of higher education should all serve the same goals, or that there are not ways to both preserve what is valuable about 'liberal education' and still make institutions more flexible in meeting both 'national' needs and the needs and demands of students.

HIGHER EDUCATION AS A BUSINESS

A good deal of the foregoing could be summarized by saying that globalization is increasingly and everywhere making the university a 'business'. But this misses the main problem: it is not merely that the modern university is now increasingly being run as a business but that it is usually a poorly run business. This is best seen in the American system – often taken, as noted, as the model to be realized. While American institutions of higher education have many virtues, they also display 'a luxury of inefficiency' which, under conditions of globalization, they cannot afford. Thus, there is a high-priced, bloated administration, there is insufficient accountability and within the institution, too little transparency, costs are not seen as opportunity costs, almost no attention is paid to demand and there is too little attention paid to the 'product', in part because, as noted, it is not clear what the product is. Thus, there is waste, no consensus on priorities, programmes are invulnerable to assessment, students are run through bureaucratic mazes and poorly advised; graduate requirements are merely squares to be filled, professors who win teaching awards are not awarded tenure.

Examples of 'the luxury of inefficiency' are not hard to find. In the United States, one regards the place of athletics in the institution. Thus, most NCAA division one institutions, public and private, lose money on what are admittedly, quasi-professional athletic programmes. These losses are not always transparent (as a function of accounting mystification), and programmes are justified as necessary to sustain alumni support for the endowment. But as noticed, except for the handful of high prestige privates, endowments contribute preciously little to revenues.

Another far more sensitive issue among faculty regards 'research' as a condition for promotion and tenure. Given the replication, narrowness of concern and structure of review, it is hardly clear that research across the curriculum, funded and especially unfunded, produces much in the way of either new knowledge or better teaching – especially in the social sciences and humanities (Manicas 2003). To take one example: economics is often considered the most sophisticated of the social sciences and an indispensable asset to policy formation. But according to one study, 'a majority of AEA members' who responded to a survey conducted by William Davis (2004), admitted, 'at least privately, that academic research mainly benefits academic researchers who use it to advance their own careers and that journal articles have little impact on our understanding of the real world and the practice of public policy'.

But putting aside the genuine problem of determining what counts as 'good research', institutional imperatives shape the activities of even the best intentioned faculty. It begins with the reward system of faculty, starting with the socialization built into the constraints on the goals of the PhD as the condition for employment. One hundred years ago, William James complained of the 'PhD octopus'. What would he say now? It includes the tenure system, which, whatever its value as regards academic freedom – and this is not obvious (Ruch 2001) – permits irresponsibility (Coleman 1973), and has led to the creation of two classes of faculty. In his 1991 report, Harvard's Dean, Henry Rosovsky, noted that the senior faculty too often act as if they were in business for themselves, 'making their own rules'.

Alongside them is the junior faculty struggling to publish, and exploited part-timers who, teaching six courses at four institutions to keep a roof over their heads, have little time to do anything but to work on their dissertations and stay one day ahead of the awful textbooks. Remarkably, part-timers now do some 44 per cent of *all* the teaching. And it includes departmental specialization which serves very well to isolate faculties not only from the concerns of students but from one another *and* the larger community (Manicas 2003; Karelis 2004).

The American model of higher education surely has much in its favour, but globalization has produced anxiety about its future in part because it is forcing governments and faculties to confront some serious yet largely unacknowledged problems. Nor is it obvious that its better features can be replicated elsewhere, even if there is the will to do so.

THE IDEOLOGY OF GLOBALIZATION AND HIGHER EDUCATION

The critics of the effects of globalization on higher education have focused on privatization, managerialism and the reduction of its products to commodities. It is fair to say that these are globalization tendencies, but it is much less clear whether the critics – like those who see this as both inevitable and desirable, have not succumbed to a distorted picture of both globalization and its effects on the institutions of education.

A central feature of this ideology regards the idea that globalization is about the inevitable liberalization and global integration of markets (Steger 2005). On this view, the integration is inescapable, but since markets are 'efficient' only when they are 'free', standing in the way of 'liberalizing' them is destructive. This ideology is accepted as fact by large numbers of decision-makers everywhere. It is used by governments to justify 'privatization', by administrators to justify the 'commercialization of research', by educational entrepreneurs who market their 'products' as they would market television sets and perhaps, as important, it is assumed by faculty who strenuously oppose its application to their idea of an autonomous university, dedicated to the knowledge and learning for its own sake.

Remarkably, 'free market' ideology fails to notice that there can be no markets without a state-enforced body of rules. Thus, property rights are surely critical as regards exchange. Indeed, Coase (1995) argued that 'rights to perform certain actions are what is traded'. As a result, 'the legal system will have a profound effect on the working of the economic system and may in certain respects be said to control it'. And as the Chinese, Indians and Russians are discovering, there are a host of ways to constitute a market. The question, then, is not whether the state *should* act in *constituting* markets; the question rather is, what is the character and what are the consequences of widely varying forms of that constitution, of who benefits and who (and what) does not? For many people today, 'a free market' is a market constituted so that *entrepreneurial* actors are not hindered by laws or regulations aimed to protect employees, consumers, the environment or public goods – including education. It is not that 'free market ideology' fails to have application to educational matters, but that it fails to have application in *any* context. Governments have critical roles to play and while markets have distinct virtues (Manicas 2006), no government in any society can today justify a 'free market' which generates nine-teenth-century conditions of work and the destruction of the natural environment, a condition that would make unnecessary all worry about education or any-thing else!

Similarly, it is true and important that students are not (merely) 'customers' and that the 'products' of the university are not reducible to commodities. But this means that the production and distribution of its 'products' needs to be constrained by clarity regarding its goals. We need to be clearer about this and to make up our minds, if, indeed, we are to be in a position to shape the future of education in an increasingly globalized world (Delanty 2004).

References

Adamson, B. and Agelasto, M. (eds) 1998. *Higher Education in Post-Mao China*. Hong Kong: Hong Kong University Press.

Allen, E. and Seaman, J. 2004. *Entering the Mainstream: The Quality and Extent of Online Education in the United States, 2003–2004*. Needham: Centre for Online Education at Olin; Wellesley, MA: Babson College.

Altbach, P.G. (ed.) 1999. *Private Prometheus: Private Higher Education and Development in the 21st Century*. Westport, CT: Greenwood Press.

Austin, A.E. and Chapman, D.W. (eds) 2002. *Higher Education in the Developing World*. Westport, CT: Greenwood Press.

China Education and Research Network. <www.edu.cn/HomePage/English>.

Coase, R.H. 1995. 'The institutional structure of production'. In R.H. Coase, *Essays on Economics and Economists*. Chicago: University of Chicago Press.

Coleman, J.S. 1973. 'The university and society's new demands upon it'. In *Content and Context: A Report Prepared by the Carnegie Commission on Higher Education*. New York: McGraw-Hill.

Currie, J. 2004. 'The neo-liberal paradigm and higher education: A critique'. In J. Odin and P.T. Manicas (eds), *Globalization and Higher Education*. Honolulu: University of Hawaii Press.

Davis, M. 2004. 'Planet of slums', *New Left Review*, 26, 5–34.

Davis, W.L. 2004. 'Preference falsification in the economics profession', *Economic Journal Watch*, 1, 359–68.

Delanty, G. 2004. 'Does the university have a future? In J. Odin and P.T. Manicas (eds), *Globalization and Higher Education*. Honolulu: University of Hawaii Press.

Department of Education, Government of India. <http://www.education.nic.in/>.

Fleisher, B.M. 2002. 'Higher education in China: A growth paradox?' <http://economics.sbs. ohio-state.edu/Fleisher/working_papers/>.

Friedman, T.L. 1999. *The Lexus and the Olive Tree*. New York: Farrar, Strauss and Giroux.

Friedman, T.L. 2005. *The World Is Flat: A Brief History of the 21st Century*. New York: Farrar, Strauss and Giroux.

Garnier, L. 2004. 'Knowledge and higher education in Latin America: Incommodious commodities'. In J. Odin and P.T. Manicas (eds), *Globalization and Higher Education*. Honolulu: University of Hawaii Press.

Granoveter, M. and Tilly, C. 1988. 'Inequality and labor process'. In N. Smelzer (ed.), *Handbook of Sociology*. Beverly Hills, CA: Sage.

Hao, S. 2004. 'Interaction of global politics and higher education'. In J. Odin and P.T. Manicas (eds), *Globalization and Higher Education*. Honolulu: University of Hawaii Press.

Harvey, D. 1987. *The Condition of Post-Modernity*. Oxford: Basil Blackwell.

Hayes, D. and Wynyard, R. (eds) 2002. *The McDonaldization of Higher Education*. Westport, CT: Bergin and Harvey.

Hirsch, F. 1976. *Social Limits to Growth*. Cambridge, MA: Harvard University Press.

Inayatulla, S. 2004. 'Corporate, technological, and democratic challenges: Mapping the political economy of university futures'. In J. Odin and P.T. Manicas (eds), *Globalization and Higher Education*. Honolulu: University of Hawaii Press.

Johnston, B. 2001. *CCGSE Newsletter*, Center for Comparative and Global Studies in Education, 4 (1).

Judt, T. 2005. 'Europe vs. America', *The New York Review of Books*, 52 (2) (online).

Karelis, C. 2004. 'The used car dealership and the church: On resolving the identity of the university'. In J. Odin and P.T. Manicas (eds), *Globalization and Higher Education*. Honolulu: University of Hawaii Press.

Kepel, G. 2003. *Jihad: The Trial of Political Islam*. Cambridge, MA: Harvard University Press.

Lin, J. 1999. *Social Transformation and Private Education in China*. New York: Praeger.

Manicas, P.T. 1987. *A History and Philosophy of the Social Sciences*. Oxford: Basil Blackwell.

Manicas, P.T. 2003. 'The social sciences: Who needs 'em?' *Futures*, 35, 609–18.

Manicas, P.T. 2006. *A Realist Philosophy of Social Science: Explanation and Understanding*. Cambridge: Cambridge University Press.

Margolis, M. 2004. 'The withering away of the professoriate: Corporate universities and the Internet'. In J. Odin and P.T. Manicas (eds), *Globalization and Higher Education*. Honolulu: University of Hawaii Press.

May, T. 2005. 'Transformation in academic production: Content, context and consequence', *European Journal of Social Theory*, 8 (2), 193–209.

Mauch, J.E. and McMullin, M.S. 2000. *The Emerging Markets and Higher Education: Development and Sustainability*. Falmer: Routledge.

Minor, J.T. 2004. 'Four challenges facing faculty senates', *Thought and Action*, 20 (1), 125–40.

Neef, D. (ed.) 1998. *The Knowledge Economy*. Boston: Butterworth-Heinemann.

Neelakantan, S. 2005a. 'India's Supreme Court rules against private colleges', *Chronicle of Higher Education*, 51 (25), A25–7.

Neelakantan, S. 2005b. 'Higher education proves no match for India's booming economy,' *Chronicle of Higher Education*, 51 (39), A32–9.

Odin, J. 2004. 'New technologies and the reconstitution of the university'. In J. Odin and P.T. Manicas (eds), *Globalization and Higher Education*. Honolulu: University of Hawaii Press.

Odin, J. and Manicas, P.T. (eds) 2004. *Globalization and Higher Education*. Honolulu: University of Hawaii Press.

Prison Activist Resource Center. <http://www.prisonactivist.org/crisis/prison-industrial.html>.

Ritzer, G. 2000. *The McDonaldization of Society*. Thousand Oaks, CA: Sage.

Ritzer, G. 2004. *The Globalization of Nothing*. Thousand Oaks, CA: Pine Forge Press.

Ruch, R. 2001. *Higher Ed, Inc.: The Rise of the For-Profit University*. Baltimore, MD: The Johns Hopkins University Press.

Ruch, R. 2004. 'Lessons from the non-profit side'. In J. Odin and P.T. Manicas (eds), *Globalization and Higher Education*. Honolulu: University of Hawaii Press.

Shapin, S. 2003. 'Ivory trade', *London Review of Books*, 25 (17) (online).

Slaughter, S. and Leslie, L.L. 1997. *Academic Capitalism*. Baltimore, MD: The Johns Hopkins University Press.

Smith, C. 2004. 'Globalization, higher education and markets'. In J. Odin and P.T. Manicas (eds), *Globalization and Higher Education*. Honolulu: University of Hawaii Press.

Steger, M. 2005. *Globalism: Market Ideology Meets Terrorism*, 2nd edn. Lanham, MD: Rowman and Littlefield.

Suri, S.N. 2004. 'Private universities: New paradigm in university education in India', <http://www.imuakingston2003.org.jm/downloads/downloads_content1.htm>.

Thomas, S. 2004. 'Globalization, college participation and socioeconomic mobility'. In J. Odin and P.T. Manicas (eds), *Globalization and Higher Education*. Honolulu: University of Hawaii Press.

Wagner, P. 2004. 'Higher education in an era of globalization: What is at stake'. In J. Odin and P.T. Manicas (eds), *Globalization and Higher Education*. Honolulu: University of Hawaii Press.

Wang, W. 2004. 'Development of China's private education and prospect for international cooperation in education', <http://www.acpet.edu.au/_data/page/113/Professor_Wang.pdf>.

Wittrock, B. 1993. 'The modern university: The three transformations'. In B. Wittrock and S. Rothblatt (eds), *The European and American University Since 1800*. Cambridge: Cambridge University Press.

World Bank 1997. *China: Higher Education Reform*. World Bank Country Study.

Chapter 25

Sport and Globalization

DAVID L. ANDREWS AND ANDREW D. GRAINGER

As evidenced by the seemingly near-universal popularity of particular practices, spectacles and bodies, sport (the socially regulated expression of physical culture) and globalization (the process of spatial and temporal inter-connectivity) are emblematic features of the contemporary age (Bairner 2001). Moreover, the multi-faceted inter-penetration of sport and globalization – the one being realized, and modified, by the other and vice versa – speaks to the conclusive collapse of rigid superstructural demarcations so symptomatic of late twentieth/early twenty-first century capitalism (Jameson 1991, 1998). Within this moment, sport is simultaneously a central element of the 'global popular' (Kellner 2003), and a vehicle for institutionalizing the global condition (interestingly, the membership of the United Nations [191 member states] is less than that of the Olympic Movement [202 national Olympic committee members], and the *Fédération Internationale de Football Association* [FIFA; 204 member national federations]). As such, sport cannot be simply ignored, or summarily dismissed, by the sociological mainstream for being little more than a diversion from the most pressing social issues of the day. It is, as we intend to demonstrate in this chapter, an important empirical window into such concerns, specifically that of globalization.

Sport's innate visceral appeal and resonance have rendered it the 'most universal aspect of popular culture' (Miller et al. 2001: 1). Indeed, one is hard-pressed to invoke a social formation, historical or contemporary, devoid of some form of competitively based, popular physical culture. The pre-modern sporting landscape was, however, characterized by a compendium of localized game forms that, while displaying significant commonalities, were generally unable to travel beyond their place of origin and practice (not unlike the participant populace), and thereby lacked a broader coherence and influence. Prompted by the patrician-industrial power bloc's perceived need to regulate popular physical culture to the demands and discipline of the urban industrial capitalist order, modern sport forms (originally codified by the public school elite looking to further their sporting experiences in the adult world) were encouraged and popularized in the shadows of nineteenth-century Britain's satanic mills (Miller and McHoul, 1998). Intensifying commercial, cultural and military interdependencies within Western Europe, and between Western Europe and the rest of the world, resulted in the subsequent diffusion and institutionalization of these proto-modern sport forms around the globe. In an era within which modernizing nations turned to sport as a source of self-identification, the subsequent establishment of international governing bodies allowed for the global standardization of sport, and facilitated the establishment of truly international competition through which the national could be corporeally constituted (Hobsbawm 1983, 1990). Thus, by the early decades of the twentieth century – and as facilitated through the establishment of major international sporting bodies such as the International Olympic Committee (1894), and FIFA (1904) – a global sport system and imaginary had been firmly established. Sport, as ever a local convention, was now also an elemental actor on the global stage.

In the second half of the twentieth century, the global sport landscape (at both the international and national levels) became systematically colonized (initially in the United States and Canada, subsequently in Western Europe, Japan, Australasia and beyond) by an emergent strain of capitalism (what Jameson [1991] referred to as 'late capitalism') prefigured on the aggressive exploitation of culture as a pivotal source, and process, of capital accumulation. Sport may previously have been a 'semiautonomous sphere' of culture: somewhat implicated in the capitalist order, though rarely explicitly (Jameson 1991: 48). However, sport's appropriation by the forces of late capitalism placed the economic (profit maximization) ahead of the sporting (utility maximization), to the extent that many may lament, but few could argue against the fact that contemporary sport is, fundamentally, a vehicle for capital accumulation (Walsh and Giulianotti 2001). Virtually all aspects of the global sport infrastructure (governing bodies, leagues, tournaments, teams and individual athletes) are now un-selfconsciously driven and defined by the interrelated processes of: corporatization (the management and marketing of sporting entities according to profit motives); spectacularization (the primacy of producing of entertainment-driven [mediated] experiences); and commodification (the generation of multiple sport-related revenue streams). While there may be alternatives (premeditated or otherwise) to this corporate (Andrews 2001b), prolympic (Donnelly 1996a) or achievement (Maguire 1999) sport model, these are few and far between, and do not challenge its global hegemony. Thus, in Fukuyama's (1989) terms, there is perceived to be no 'viable alernative' to what is, fundamentally, a corporate capitalist iteration of sport.

Having highlighted the globally normalized understanding of sport as a commercially managed and exploited cultural commodity, it would appear that we are about to embark on an explication of sport as a virulent agent of global cultural homogenization. This is neither our interest nor intention. The pervasiveness of the corporate sport model has resulted in a considerable degree of uniformity with regard to, in the general sense, sport's institutional impetus and infrastructure. From certain vantage points, sport cultures located around the world would appear to be subject to revision by the conforming forces of 'grobalization' (Ritzer 2004a), whose overdetermining quest for capital accumulation threatens, in the name of market expansion and rationalization, local sporting forms 'generally indigenously conceived, controlled, and comparatively rich in distinctive substantive content' (Ritzer

2004a: 7). The anticipated corollary of this sporting grobalization would seem to be a global culture of sporting 'nothingness', wherein a narrow economy of centrally conceived and administered, geographically and historically abstract, and corporeally dehumanizing and disenchanting forms has come to define the sporting landscape (Ritzer 2004a). Despite the seeming inevitability of this march towards sporting McDonaldization (Ritzer 2004b), at the present time, even the most arresting exemplars of proto-grobal sport operate and exist in a mutually constitutive relation to the senses and sensibilities of the local. Thus, a reassuring unevenness (Maguire 2000) persists regarding the localized engagement and experience of corporate sport forms (practices, spectacles and bodies), which continue to invoke particular geographically and historically grounded differences, in a manner which provides a context for the creative expression of human labour, and the resultant excitement and enchantment of an expectant populace. In other words, even within the throes of a truly globalized sport order, it is still possible to experience palpable expressions of locally differentiated and differentiating forms of sporting 'somethingness' (Ritzer 2004a). Therefore, within this discussion, and following Appadurai (1990), Dirlik (1996), Hall (1991), Morley and Robins (1995) and Robertson (1995), amongst others, our aim is to elucidate the global–local interconnections, and disconnections, operating within contemporary sport culture. Differently put, we seek to critically explicate the global in the sporting local *and* the local in the sporting global.

THEORIZING GLOCAL SPORT

There have been numerous noteworthy contributions towards generating a theoretically based understanding of the relationship between sport and globalization which, in combination, offer important insights into global–local forces, relations and experiences, as manifest in and through contemporary sport cultures. However, rather than attempting to incorporate them all into this necessarily succinct overview, we have instead chosen to discuss representative works which signpost the broader trends and shifts within this ongoing theoretical debate. Furthermore, many of the works that could have been included herein will be discussed in later sections, where the more discrete elements of global–local sporting cultures (practices, spectacles and bodies) will be dissected.

Acknowledging the impossibility of singular points of origin, the globalization of sport debate was arguably ignited by Maguire's (1990) figurational analysis of American football's (and particularly the NFL's) concerted incursion onto the British sporting landscape during the 1980s. Couching his analysis within the established and emotive Americanization of culture debate, Maguire highlighted, in vivid diagrammatic form, the complex network of interdependencies (for instance, those linking corporate commercial, mass media and sport organization contingencies) responsible for what he described as American football's 'fairly significant' impact on British society at this time (Maguire 1990: 233). In hindsight, Maguire may have over-estimated the position of American football within British sporting culture. Nonetheless, and significantly, he explicated how within a context of increased scale and scope of global interconnectivity, sporting development necessarily involves a constitutive interplay between the global and the local. Distancing his work from the pitfalls of a 'crude Americanization thesis', Maguire (1990: 231) advocated a qualified understanding of cultural imperialism as a means of explaining this pheno-menon: American football's increased presence being attributable to a complex mix of marketing and media strategizing, which resonated with the market-driven, entrepreneurial and individualistic sensibilities of the Thatcherite Britain during the 1980s. Thus, Maguire embarked on a extensive, insightful and influential explica-tion of global–local sporting interdependencies, from an avowedly figurational perspective, which instructively highlighted the long-term, multidirectional and multicausal elements, as well as both the intended and unintended outcomes, of sporting globalization (cf. Maguire 1999, 2000).

Somewhat prompted by an implied critique of Maguire's perceived focus on Americanization, McKay and Miller (1991) explained the commercial corporatiza-tion of Australian sport through recourse to Jameson's (1991) cultural logics of late capitalism, and specifically their relationship to the global spread of post-Fordism and consumerism, 'all of which transcend the confines of the United States'. This point was furthered through Houlihan's explicit centring of the globalization process within sociological debates relating to sporting transformation. He thereby sub-limated the inadequacies of Americanization and cultural imperialist theses by incorporating their partial insights into a greater interpretative whole: that of a more complex and fluid understanding of sporting globalization. Moreover, and intended to bring about some 'consensus' regarding the 'nature and significance' of the glo-balization process as it pertains to sport, Houlihan (1994: 357) advanced a typologi-cal schematic incorporating six patterns of sporting globalization, which highlighted the differential exposure to, and reception of, globalizing sport forms within con-trasting local cultural contexts. He thus demonstrated how globalization is anything but a 'unidimensional and unidirectional' phenomenon; its relationship to, and influence upon, local sport cultures being equally dialectic and diverse (Houlihan 1994: 372).

Donnelly (1996b) provided a comprehensive summation of the sport and glo-balization *oeuvre* up to that point, and stressed the need to reassert the 'articulation between the local and the global'. His aim was to encourage researchers to navigate a mid-way course between the *Scylla* of romanticized accounts of the resistant capacities of local sport cultures, and the *Charybdis* of pessimistic commentaries of globally determined corporate sport locals. In a time of accelerated and intensified global flows (of people, images, capital, ideologies, practices, languages, pollutants, crime and design etc.) – Tomlinson's condition of 'complex connectivity' (1999) – the global and the local cannot be viewed as in any way discrete or autonomous entities. Rather, as Morley and Robins outlined, contemporary processes of globali-zation are 'about the achievement of a new global–local nexus, about new and intricate relations between global space and local space' (Morley and Robins 1995: 116). Hence, and paraphrasing Morley and Robins (1995: 117), the sporting global (the organization and credo of the modern sport system) and the sporting local (the lived experience of sport) can only be viewed as fluid and relational spaces consti-tuted through their non-necessary (in terms of intentions and outcomes) interactions with each other.

Within their broad ranging examination of sport as a 'principal front' of globali-zation, Miller et al. (2001) provide countless examples of the interconnected, yet productive, tensions between global corporate capital and local sport cultures. The thematic sections of the chapter that follow this conceptual overview similarly illustrate the tensions being played out, within various facets of contemporary sport culture (practices, spectacles and bodies), between global and local imperatives. Robertson's (1995) compelling concept of glocalization proves particularly instructive in this regard. Prefigured on an understanding of globalization as constituting, and being constituted by, the necessary interplay between the global and the local, Robertson advanced an understanding that positioned homogenization and heterogenization, universalism and particularism, sameness and difference, and the global and the local, as 'complementary and interpenetrative'. The process of glocalization thereby pivots on the concept of relationality, as understood in the global's complicity in the 'creation and incorporation' of the local, and vice versa (1995).

Informed by Robertson (1995), it is possible to conceptualize two forms of glocalization operating upon, and through, contemporary sport culture: organic and strategic glocalization (these labels being relational rather than discrete: organic glocalization frequently being subject to strategic co-optation, while the products of strategic glocalization can become incorporated as organic cultural forms). Simply put, *organic sporting glocalization* speaks to the process whereby either globalized or internationalized sport practices (depending on their spatial reach) become incorporated into local (communal, regional, but primarily national) sporting cultures and experienced as authentic or natural (hence organic) signs of cultural collectivity. In a general sense, organic glocalization is associated with local responses to the sporting flows that accompanied broader forces of social transformation (colonization, modernization, urban industrialization etc.). *Strategic sporting glocalization* is a more recent phenomenon derived from changes in the spatial ambition, organization and imagination of late capitalism (Jameson 1991) associated with the advent of transnational as the dominating logic of economic expansion and the transnational corporation as the 'locus of economic activity' (Dirlik 1996: 29; Morley and Robins 1995). Rather than treating, and hoping to realize, the world market as a single, un-differentiated entity (as in previous stages of development in the global economy), transnational capitalism has become increasingly concerned with commercially exploiting (through negotiated incorporation and commodified reflection) the local differences its international antecedent previously sought to overcome (Hall 1997: 32). Broadly speaking, this is achieved in two ways.

First, *interiorized glocal strategizing* refers to the manner in which global capital has aggressively co-opted local sport cultures and sensibilities into its expansive regime of flexible accumulation (Harvey 1989); not for global dissemination *per se*, rather for local market accommodation, and incorporation, as a constituent element of the broader transnationalist project. Thus, the architecture and convictions of the hegemonic corporate sport model (Andrews 1999) has become truly globalized (or grobalization in Ritzer's terms, and as operationalized by the expanding geographies of, amongst other entities: commercially driven sport organizations and governing bodies; professional sport leagues and tournaments; sport management companies; media and entertainment corporations; sporting goods manufacturers; and allied corporate sponsors), while its manifestations are expressly localized. *Pace* Rowe (2003), interiorized glocal strategizing acknowledges, and seeks to capitalize upon, local sporting practices' enduring ability to stimulate popular consciousness and behaviour. While this may preclude the realization of a post-particular form of globalization, sport's steadfastly local demeanour has been exploited by global capital's strategic incursion into the commercial management and production of locally inflected and resonant versions of corporate sport (the various components of which are constituted through the secular trinity of sporting corporatization, spectacularization and commodification). The result being the production of a global economy of sporting locals in which, despite their contrived appeals to indigenous sporting and cultural authenticity, can be considered little more, or indeed less, than a '*particular version* of a very general phenomenon' (Robertson 1995: 40).

Secondly, *exteriorized glocal strategizing* involves the importation and mobilization of – what are commonly perceived to be externally derived expressions of – sporting difference into a local market. Here, for those sport consumers looking to express their alterity from the cultural mainstream, the aim is to provide the opportunity to consume the sporting Other. For instance, far from seeking to realize a sporting monoculture, the exportation of American sport forms – even more than the American film and music genres that have become the cultural vernacular of the global popular (Kellner 2003) – represent a source of identity rooted in difference and opposition for, predominantly, youth and young adults located in disparate national settings (Andrews et al. 1996). The complicating factor being, the sense of sporting and aesthetic American Otherness communicated in, and through, these exports is by no means uniform in its cultural significance, nor in the manner in that it is consumed at the local level. As Van Elteren noted, there are 'multifarious, and often complex ways in which US popular culture forms [and indeed the very idea of America itself] are mediated and received abroad among various audiences and in diverse local contexts' (Van Elteren 1996).

Sporting glocalization, whether organic or strategic (exteriorized or interiorized), illustrates the fact that today's sporting locals can only exist and operate within the structures and logics of the global. As such, the cultural economy of sport vindicates Featherstone's assertion that 'globalization and localization are inextricably bound together in the current moment' (1996: 47). This necessary inter-relationship will be empirically interrogated within the rest of this discussion, wherein we explicate the global–local derivatives and implications of various sport practices, spectacles and bodies, all of which combine to form the global infrastructure, and inform the local experience, of corporate sport.

GLOCAL SPORT PRACTICES

Once characterized by a patchwork of locally bound, traditional forms, sport's pre-modern diversity has collapsed into a relatively small number of highly regulated, standardized and bureaucratized sport practices that now dominate and define the global sporting landscape (Maguire 1999). The reasons for this sporting consolidation are manifold, yet primarily need to be understood in relation to the sweeping social transformations in Western Europe in the period after 1700, that resulted in the establishment of an increasingly industrialized, urbanized and Westernized world order.

Despite its global omnipresence, it should not be forgotten that contemporary sport is the regulated embodiment and affirming expression of the distinctly modern Western (and specifically North Atlantic) values of competition, progress and achievement; values which, unsurprisingly, simultaneously underpin the liberal democratic, urban industrialist and market capitalist forces that spawned the modern societies from whence modern sport forms, and the modern sport order, emerged. As numerous social commentators have observed, modern sport practices and institutions – and indeed, the very ethos of modern sport – originated within eighteenth and nineteenth century Britain (cf. Van Bottenburg 2001; Elias and Dunning 1986; Guttmann 1978; Holt 1989a). There was nothing particularly remarkable about the physical culture of pre-industrial Britain that foretold the genesis of modern sport at this time. For instance, rudimentary stick and ball games and kicking games (the respective origins of cricket and association football which provide the focus for this section) were popular pastimes within a variety of social contexts across historical and spatial divides. However, due to its position at the forefront of the transformative processes of urbanization and industrialization, the social, political and economic exigencies of the time resulted in many traditional sport forms first being standardized, regulated and bureaucratized in Britain during the social tumult of the nineteenth century; thereby providing modern sport with peculiarly British origins. It was, as Van Bottenburg (2001: 197) noted, 'the mother country of modern sports'.

The subsequent global diffusion of modern sport forms first institutionalized within the British context (i.e. association football, boxing, cricket, field hockey, golf, horse racing, rugby, rowing, track and field, and tennis) was closely connected to the development of more complex chains of global interdependency (Maguire 1999) that arose from the intensifying imperially and commercially inspired relationships created between Britain and the rest of the world. Thus, Britain's imperial and commercial hegemony during the nineteenth century facilitated the global spread and legitimation of the modern sport forms developed within the British context. This resulted in the relatively rapid establishment of a global sporting hegemony through which many traditional pastimes became either subsumed within, or largely expunged in the face of, the unrelenting march of the modern sport order. However, the patterns of sporting diffusion were certainly not globally uniform. For instance, cricket's elite social habitus made it an important vehicle for the advancement of the British imperial project. It was used as a vehicle for embodying and imposing the physical and cultural superiority of the colonizer over the colonized: '"Playing the game" was a combined physical and moral activity, and exercise in the art of being "British"' (Holt 1989b: 236). Whereas, by the later decades of the nineteenth century, the working class demeanour of association football (it had by that time outgrown its patrician beginnings) meant 'Trade connections, rather than imperial links, were the most propitious outlets' (Giulianotti 1999: 6) in the export of the game to the rest of the world. Thus, the sizeable British working class diaspora of manual labourers, combined with the influence of ex-patriot artisans, teachers and cosmopolitans (Giulianotti 1999), helped establish the game wherever their roving employment took them. Pointing to these broader social, political and economic vectors responsible for the 'differential popularization' of sports around the globe, Van Bottenburg (2001: 176) noted: 'Worldwide it may be said that in countries with which Britain had close trade relations, soccer is far more popular than other sports, whereas cricket, field hockey, and rugby have done particularly well in countries over which Britain had political and military domination.'

Once exported around the globe along either imperial and/or commercial networks, in many if not all settings (cf. Kaufman and Patterson 2005), the rapid popularization of these sports resulted in them becoming understood and experienced as emotive and expressive embodiments of locality. Thus, in particular national contexts (depending on local social and sporting histories and landscapes, and the nature of the interdependency with Britain), cricket or football were incorporated into the local with such enthusiasm that they were able to conclusively circumvent their British provenance. Such *organic sporting glocalization* (the indigenization of globalized/ internationalized sport forms) was particularly evident during the four decades leading up to the beginning of World War I; a period in which sport became a 'crucible of nation' (Miller 2001: 29) in the truest sense of the term. Within a historical moment in which social elites were seeking to establish precisely what it meant (in economic, political, legal and cultural terms) to be a modern nation, sport played an important role in the attendant development of 'new devices to ensure or express social cohesion and identity and to structure social relations' (Hobsbawn 1983: 263). Institutionalized both 'officially and unofficially' (Hobsbawn 1983: 263) into the life of the nation, sport thus became an important feature of the invented national traditions, and sense of nation, deemed important as internal and external demonstrations of modern nationhood.

The transformation of an imposed or transplanted sporting practice into a local context is vividly illustrated in C.L.R. James' (1963) classic account of cricket in the West Indies. At one moment a symbol of British colonialism, James illustrated how cricket's enthusiastic and creative appropriation by the West Indies' populace rendered it an emotive and embodied expression of self-identification and – ironically but not surprisingly – cultural resistance over whence the game originated (see also Beckles 1998). A similar scenario was also enacted in India, where cricket's position and influence as a central part of the 'colonial ecumene' became so eroded that the very 'idea of the [*independent*] Indian nation emerged as a salient cricketing entity' (Appadurai 1996: 91, 97, italics added). In the late nineteenth and early twentieth centuries, the colonial rulers of 'British' India used cricket as a mechanism for constituting communal groupings (organizing teams along religious and ethnic divides), in a manner which prohibited the development of a more collectively encompassing, and difference transcending, sense of Indianness, and of the Indian nation as a whole. However, cricket's growing popularity, and its rapid vernacularization – initially through the English language broadcasts of All-India Radio, and later through blanket coverage from all popular media channels – led to the game becoming an important source of collective identification with the political and popular movement towards realizing the goals of Indian nationalism. Through 'experiential' (the widespread practice of the game) and 'pedagogical' (the mass mediation of the game) impulses, cricket within post-1947 India became a 'critical instrument of subjectivity in the process of decolonization' which, simultaneously, realized the 'unyoking of cricket from its Victorian value framework' and the dismantling of any residues of colonial power and authority exercised through the game. As Appadurai (1996: 105, 110) wryly noted, the empire had struck back.

Football's global diffusion having been significantly more widespread than that of cricket (it not being primarily restricted to those nations with British colonial connections), there are countless examples where football – generally understood to be 'a world game' (Dunning 1999) and/or the 'global game' (Giulianotti 1999) – has assumed the mantle of the national sport (cf. Armstrong and Giulianotti 1997), and one striking example where it has not (Markovits and Hellerman 2001; Sugden 1994). As Hobsbawm famously noted, in understandably ambiguous terms (there being a plethora of *football nations* after all): 'The imagined community of millions seems more real as a team of eleven named people. The individual, even the one who only cheers, becomes a symbol of his nation himself' (1990: 143). The global game is thus perhaps better understood as the (organically) glocal game; simultaneously existing and operating as a source of collective identity and pride for the national populaces, in numerous locations, at one and the same time. In doing so, football serves as a source of the 'vitality of specific local cultures in relation to globalization' (Giulianotti 2005: 204).

GLOCAL SPORT SPECTACLES

The essence of the late capitalist condition lies in an accentuation of the constitutive interrelationship between culture and the mechanisms of capital accumulation. The mass media has played an important role realizing this state in which 'economics has come to overlap with culture . . . everything . . . has . . . become cultural; and culture has equally become economic' (Jameson 1998: 73). Specifically, the commercial media has become both a core product (the centrality of mediated products and services within the consumer economy) and, equally importantly, a core process (marketing and advertising media stimulating, and to a large degree constituting, the consumer market) leading, almost unavoidably, to the 'institutional alignment of sports and media in the context of late capitalism' (Real 1998). Within this moment, sports merge into 'media spectacle, collapse boundaries between professional achievement and commercialization, and attest to the commodification of all aspects of life in the media and consumer society' (Kellner 2003: 66). As a result, sport has irrevocably morphed into a culture industry (Andrews 2001a), in that its unquestioned focus is now on the production and delivery of entertaining mediated products and experiences designed to maximize profit. Mediated sport spectacles now constitute the integrative heart of corporate sport's entertainment economy, and it is consumers of media content (the sport spectacles delivered and discussed via television, video, radio, magazine and web platforms), as opposed to event attendees, through which corporate sporting entities primarily attempt to penetrate the consciousnesses of, and seek to extrude capital from, the viewing/consuming global masses.

Williams (1994: 377) has charged sport (specifically what he termed 'sporting "muzak"') as being a major contributor to the 'flattening out of difference in postorganized capitalism' through the indiscriminate global dissemination of sports 'taken from localized cultural contexts'. Countering this position, due to the manner in which global spectacles are produced and consumed at the local, it is possible to argue that the economy of globally mediated sport spectacles actually contributes to the 'constant reinvention of particularity' associated with the process of glocality (Giulianotti 2005: 204). There are a number of 'global sport spectacles' (Tomlinson 2005: 59) that, superficially, would seem to unite the world's populace in acclamation for sport in general (i.e. the Olympic Games or the Commonwealth Games), or for a particular sport (i.e. the FIFA men's World Cup or the IAAF World Championships), or for a particular nation (the NFL Super Bowl). However, such institutionalized and spectacularized paeans to sporting universalism are misleading and inaccurate (cf. Martin and Reeves 2001), as will be demonstrated through reference to the glocalizing Olympic Games.

The global penetration of Olympic Games television coverage is remarkable, with worldwide audience figures for the 2004 Athens Olympics approaching 3.5 billion individual viewers; meaning approximately 60 per cent of the world's population watched an Olympic broadcast at least once (Wilson 2004). However, the global commonality nurtured by these sporting 'mega-events' (Roche 2000) is more a spectacular unity-in-difference than a serious contribution to global homogenization. Rather than transcending them as was the original, if naive intent (Guttmann 2002), today's staged presentations, and mediated representations, of the Olympic Games have consistently been forums for the accommodation and advancement of highly nationalized interests and concerns. As Tomlinson noted, illustrating the implicit strategic glocalization of the modern Olympic phenomenon in its late capitalist incarnation, 'the allegedly pure Olympic ideal has always been moulded into the image of the time and place of the particular Olympiad or Games' (Tomlinson 1996: 599).

Global in reach and philosophy, the Olympic Games are inveterately local in performance. Nowhere is this glocality better exhibited than in the highly choreographed spectacle of the game's opening ceremonies (Hogan 2003; Tomlinson 1996, 2005). Although making perfunctory reference to the modern Olympic's internationalist origins through a 'quota of Olympic-style spirit – youth, universalism, peace, and the like' (Tomlinson 2005: 11), the interpretative programmes within opening ceremonies, and indeed the structure and delivery of the games as a whole, speak to the 'staging of the nation' for internal and external audiences (Hogan 2003). The former motivated by a need to advance historical, contemporaneous and aspirational senses of self for an expectant, and potentially politically malleable, home audience (Silk 2002). The latter prompted by the need to spectacularize, through 'place marketing' strategies, urban/national space as a mechanism for stimulating tourism and other forms of global capital investment (Whitson and Macintosh 1993, 1996; Wilson 1996), within what is a 'period of intense interurban competition and urban entrepreneurialism' (Waitt 1999: 1061).

Despite being at the forefront of a 'worldwide sport culture given an unprecedented profile in the mediated global culture' (Tomlinson 2005: 36), even in terms of regular Olympic television broadcasts, local cultural proclivities often impinge upon the mediated global spectacle. Most of the television coverage of such events is selected from the international feeds of the host broadcaster. Those nations with sufficient economic and technological resources are able to locally embellish the generic coverage – much of which is bound up with the host's 'presentation of self' to the global (tourist and commercial) marketplace (Silk 2001: 297) – through preferred event and athlete selection, customized commentary, expert analysis and feature segments. The largest client broadcasters also utilize their own 'unilateral' cameras in order to better address the Olympic preferences of their national viewership (MacNeill 1996; Silk 2001; Silk and Amis 2000). In MacNeill's (1996) terms, this demonstrates how realizing a spectacle of accumulation (based on revenues tied to viewership) is significantly related to it also being a spectacle of legitimation (corroborates normalized discourses pertaining to sport, the nation and their relation). Hence, global coverage of the Olympic Games results in myriad different local representations of the Olympic spectacle, linked to a concomitant multiplicity in terms of the different ways the Olympics are lived at the local level (Bernstein 2000; Knight et al. 2005). Depending on the venue, partner broadcasters also frequently look to incorporate and mobilize difference within their coverage through recourse to the Otherness (social, cultural, historical, political and/or geographic) of the host location. Such broadcasts of sport spectacles thus adopt both interiorized and exteriorized forms of strategic glocalization, in that they simultaneously seek to customize coverage to internal local markets, while embellishing it through recourse to aspects of external local difference (Silk 2001).

Looking at this issue from a different institutional vantage point, sport is a significant component of television programming schedules around the world. This can be attributed to sport's unique and seductive qualities as a form of visceral, embodied and competitively based popular televisual entertainment: all of which contribute to its capacity for attracting high concentrations of 18–34-year-old male consumers, the demographic traditionally most prized by corporate advertisers. It is precisely these properties and opportunities which News Corporation International and other media concerns have sought to capitalize upon within their sport strategizing (Harvey et al. 2001; Law et al. 2002). Certainly, sport programming – what long-time Chairman and CEO Rupert Murdoch has described as the 'universal language of entertainment' (Murdoch 1998) – is at the core of News Corporation's global multimedia empire, incorporating nine media formats, spanning six continents and purportedly reaching two-thirds of the world's population (Herman and McChesney 1997). At the heart of Murdoch's corporate media philosophy is the steadfast belief that 'sports programming commands unparalleled viewer loyalty in all markets' (Murdoch 1996), and can therefore be used as a 'battering ram' to penetrate local media markets more effectively, and indeed more rapidly, than any other entertainment genre. This point has been corroborated by Peter Chernin, News Corporation President and COO, when identifying movies and live sport programming as the pivotal elements in their 'worldwide TV ventures . . . And sports is the more important' (quoted in Bruck 1997: 826). Certainly, News Corporation is liable to charges of advancing globally uniform processes and technologies regarding the use of sport to facilitate the penetration of national television markets. Unlike another of their global programming staples – high profile movies and television programmes emanating from the United States' highly developed media entertainment industry – News Corporation's relationship with sport is based on the aggressive incorporation of local sport programming into the schedules of its nascent national television outlets (i.e. the NFL on Fox Television in the USA, English Premier League Football on BSkyB in the UK and National Rugby League on Foxtel in Australia). As Murdoch himself outlined: 'You would be very wrong to forget that what people want to watch in their own country is basically local programming, local language, local culture . . . I learned that many, many years ago in Australia, when I was loading up . . . with good American programs and we'd get beat with second-rate Australian ones' (quoted in Schmidt 2001: 79). News Corporation thus adopts an interiorized glocal strategy with regard to sport spectacles, in that it looks to operate seamlessly within the language of the sporting local, simultaneously, in multiple national broadcasting locations. So, the rise of a global media oligarchy has had the effect of embracing and nurturing the sporting particularism of local media environments.

GLOCAL SPORT BODIES

As Hargreaves reminded us, 'it is the body that constitutes the most striking symbol, as well as constituting the material core of sporting activity' (Hargreaves 1987: 141). Evidently, the body is implicated in a number of different ways within globalizing sport culture: not the least of which being the manner in which the bodies of workers in developing nations are routinely exploited in order to produce the sporting goods and apparel, which strategically adorn the bodies of corporate sport's celebrity endorsers, and those of the globe's consuming masses. This interconnection between disparately located, and differentially empowered, bodies materializes 'a perversely postmodern irony that a First-World company exploits workers in the Third World, while deploying images of black men to embody freedom and individualism' (Miller et al. 2001: 58). The inhuman plight of the developing world's exploited labour force is not the focus of the present discussion (see Boje 1998; Enloe 1995; Ross 2004; Sage 1999; Stabile 2000); rather, we turn our attention to the materially and symbolically trafficked bodies of athletes, and their relationship to forces and experiences of glocalization.

The expanded channels of official and unofficial migration created by the post-industrial, developed world's need to bolster its menial and servile labour, offer an interesting correlative to corporate sport's scouring of the world for superior athletic talent. The ensuing establishment of talent pipelines provides the athletic raw materials required to enhance, or at the very least maintain, the marketability of the corporate sport product. So, in the sport economy, as in the broader economic formation, 'the core states dominate and control the exploitation of resources and production' (Maguire 1999: 19). That having been said, it would be wrong to assume a unidimensionality of athletic labour migrancy, for there are various iterations of, and motivations for, the sport migrant experience, the variations of which depend on the sporting migrant's range of movement, length of stay in any one given place and level of remuneration (Bale and Sang 1994; Magee and Sugden 2002; Maguire 2004; Maguire and Stead 1998).

Once largely demarcated along national boundary lines (the odd sport migrant being the exception that proved the homespun rule), the multinational composition of playing rosters has become a defining feature of many nationally based professional sport leagues and teams. In some instances, the proliferation of a class of globally mobile athletic migrants has led to a re-structuring and/or re-evaluation of local sport cultures in both host and donor settings. For instance, the multinationalization of NBA player personnel – during the 2004–5 season, the NBA featured

77 'international' players drawn from 34 different nations – has transformed the manner in which the league presents itself to the global market (Andrews 2003). The initial phase in the process of globalizing the NBA spectacle centred on selling the league as an explicitly American entertainment product, with high profile players (mostly African American) being used as the embodiments of what it meant to be American in sporting and cultural terms (something less comfortably realized on US soil). Prompted by the emergence of players such as Tony Parker (France), Dirk Nowitzki (Germany) and Pau Gasol (Spain) plying their trade to such effect in the NBA, the league began marketing itself differently to those who follow their local NBA heroes from afar (Fisher 2003). The NBA spectacle now exists and operates in numerous national locations at one and the same time, albeit customized – through media and commercial relationships with locally based broadcasters and sponsors – according to the player-oriented interests and expectations of local audiences. In this way, the NBA has moved from being an exclusively externalized form of glocal strategizing (the selling of the NBA through its explicit Americanness) to one that, in specific settings, additionally engages internalized forms of glocal strategizing (the mobilization of local affinity for specific NBA players).

Professional basketball is also an interesting exemplar of sporting glocalization since, like ice hockey (cf. Kivinen et al. 2001; Maguire 1996) and football (cf. Magee and Sugden 2002; Maguire and Stead 1998; Stead and Maguire 2000), a complex international hierarchy of professional leagues exists, resulting in multidirectional player movement. Not only do elite foreign players migrate from lesser leagues to the NBA and its feeder and developmental leagues, American players of not sufficient ability to play professionally in the USA have the opportunity, depending on their talent level, to make the reverse journey (Maguire 1994). Even so, at times, this seemingly benign sporting diaspora brings global and local issues and identities into sharp relief (Carrington et al. 2001). For example, local responses to American basketball migrants evoke a paradoxical mix of civic resentment for inhibiting the development of local talent, coupled with a tacit gratitude for the abilities they bring to the team (Falcous and Maguire 2005a, 2005b).

The athletic labour migration situation is considerably more exploitative in cases where the balance, in economic and political as much as sporting terms, between the donor and host countries is more unequal. This is frequently the case where developed nations mine developing or under-developed nations for their athletic talent, with little or no interest in the sporting and, more importantly, the social and economic consequences of such actions. Indeed, this problem is so significant that in December 2003, FIFA President Sepp Blatter, not renowned for his political incisiveness, made the following statement in a column that appeared in the *Financial Times*:

> I find it unhealthy, if not despicable, for rich clubs to send scouts shopping in Africa, South America and Asia to 'buy' the most promising players there . . . This leaves those who trained them in their early years with nothing but cash for their trouble . . . Dignity and integrity tend to fall by the wayside in what has become a glorified body market . . . Europe's leading clubs conduct themselves increasingly as neo-colonialists who don't give a damn about heritage and culture, but engage in social and economic rape by robbing the developing world of its best players. (Quoted in Anon 2003)

While the 'host' European football clubs – and, for that matter, Major League Baseball teams (Arbena 1994; Klein 1991) and National Collegiate Athletic Association (NCAA) sport programmes (Bale and Sang 1996) – benefit from this form of corporeal neo-colonialism in their ability to draw from a larger talent pool, and even market their sporting products to local diasporic communities, the situation in the donor countries is less positive. The exploitation of athletic talent in developing nations by sporting institutions from the developed world hinders the growth of national communities in sporting, social and economic terms. In the first instance, such drains on athletic talent lead to the 'de-skilling' of the sport in the donor countries (Maguire et al. 2002) which, in the Latin American context, leads to 'a sense of loss, a feeling that the home country is being robbed of its own human and recreational resources' (Arbena 1994: 103). Moreover, among many individuals and families within donor countries, such sporting neo-colonialism creates a sense of unrealistic opportunity through professional sport, and an ultimately unfulfilled dependency on the host nation, which when magnified across the local populace, can seriously impinge upon social and economic development in the local setting. In this way, the broader economic relations and inequities between the 'west and the rest' (Hall 1992) are replicated within the sporting context.

With regard to the global flow of symbolic bodies, within the context of a late capitalist order dominated by the hyper-individualizing medium that is television (Andrews and Jackson 2001), it is little wonder that the celebritization of culture in general has similarly been replicated in sport which has, not unreasonably, been described as 'basically media-driven celebrity entertainment' (Pierce 1995: 185). Sport's position as an agent and expression of celebritization can be attributed to the embodied nature of sport performance, which encourages a focus on individuals and attracts the televisual gaze required for their mass circulation. Thus, within the popular media, 'These sports celebrities . . . [such as Pete Sampras, Magic Johnson, Martina Hingis, Lindsey Davenport, Tiger Woods, Michael Owen and David Beckham] . . . are typically portrayed as superlatively talented and hard-working individuals who contribute to the pre-eminence of the dual ethic of individualism and personal competitiveness in society' (Rojek 2001: 37). The lure of sport's public figures has seen them sucked into the vortex of promotional culture (Wernick 1991) as seductive conduits allowing more prosaic commercial forms to engage mass markets. Hence, certain athletes have become truly 'international figures, marketed in global advertising campaigns, films, music, and other venues of media culture' (Kellner 2001: 42); however the list of truly global celebrities is relatively small, including such individuals as Michael Jordan, Muhammad Ali, Tiger Woods and perhaps David Beckham. Like the Martina Hingis described by Giardina (2001), these global sport icons are the product of, and have the potential to project, 'polymorphous media representations' according to the context in which they are being consumed. They are thus exemplars of exteriorized glocal strategizing in that their 'transnational celebrity' renders them 'flexible citizens' able to successfully negotiate and transcend the 'borders of the global market' (Giardina 2001: 201).

In addition to the exteriorized glocalizing capacities of sport celebrities, they probably exist and operate more abundantly through more interiorizing iterations. The structural and symbolic importance of the sport celebrity within the corporate sport model is widely accepted as both an important feature of sport's spectacularization and commodification, and an important conduit for other corporate interests looking to capitalize upon sports popular appeal (Amis and Cornwell 2005). Hence, transnational sport corporations such as Nike, Adidas and Reebok, and equally non-sport transnationals such as Ford, McDonald's and Coca-Cola (Silk and Andrews 2001, 2005), have, within various national cultural settings, used locally resonant sport celebrities as a means of incorporating 'localities into the imperatives of the global' (Dirlik 1996: 34). Of course, this marketing strategy is not without its problems:

> rather than romanticize or celebrate the sophistication of such campaigns, it is impor-
> tant to outline that these campaigns point to the ways in which transnational corpora-
> tions are providing commercially inspired representations of locality. In this case, Nike
> have done little more than select celebrities who represent a superficial and depthless
> caricature of national cultural differences, sensibilities, and experiences – modern
> nation-statehood effectively being replaced by late capitalist corporate-nationhood.
> (Silk and Andrews 2001: 198)

The role of sport celebrities as potentially potent sources of 'representative sub-jectivity' pertaining to the 'collective configurations' through which individuals fashion their very existence (social class, gender, sexuality, race, ethnicity, age, nationality) is troubling enough (Marshall 1997: xi, xii). However, this becomes even more problematic when the local is imagined and authenticated through an external and commercially inspired locus of control, which produces little more than 'generalized recipes of locality' (Robertson 1995). However, such, perhaps, is the corollary of sporting glocality.

CONCLUSION

Making something of a departure from some of his earlier contributions (Rowe 1996a, 1996b), and perhaps prompted by a perceived need to stimulate debate within what was threatening to become an all-too-predictable intellectual forum, Rowe (2003) provocatively contested sport's ability to 'resonate at the global level' and argued that sport may, in fact, 'be unsuited to carriage of the project of globaliza-tion in its fullest sense'. Rowe's position was prefigured on sport's importance as an emotive marker of local (communal, regional, national) belonging and identification. Specifically sport's 'constant evocation of the nation as its anchor point and rallying cry' evidences its 'affective power', making it impossible for sport to be 'reconfigured as postnational and subsequently stripped of its "productive" capacity to promote forms of identity' (Rowe 2003). Sport's symbiotic relationship with nationally con-toured forms of identity makes it antithetical to the process of globalization, and to be leading to the emergence of supra-national social systems and institutions that transcend the local in establishing a post-particular global order. This discussion will have provided an alternative to Rowe's (2003) dichotomizing of the global and the local. Our aim has been to point out the constitutive inter-relationship between globality and locality, as illustrated within the various iterations and expressions of sporting glocality. In doing so, we hope to have provided another conceptual platform from which it becomes possible to delve further into the contested structures and experiences of sport within the glocal age.

References

Amis, J. and Cornwell, T.B. (eds) 2005. *Global Sport Sponsorship*. Oxford: Berg.

Andrews, D.L. 1999. 'Dead or alive? Sports history in the late capitalist moment', *Sporting Traditions: Journal of the Australian Society for Sports History*, 16 (1), 73–85.

Andrews, D.L. 2001a. 'Sport'. In R. Maxwell (ed.), *Culture Works: The Political Economy of Culture*, 131–62. Minneapolis: University of Minnesota Press.

Andrews, D.L. (ed.) 2001b. *Michael Jordan Inc.: Corporate Sport, Media Culture, and Late Modern America*. Albany, NY: State University of New York Press.

Andrews, D.L. 2003. 'A propos de la NBA'. In F. Archambault, L. Artiaga and P.-Y. Frey (eds), *L'aventure des «grands» hommes. Etudes sur l'histoire du basket-ball*, 271–92. Limoges, France: University of Limoges Press.

Andrews, D.L., Carrington, B., Jackson, S. and Mazur, Z. 1996. 'Jordanscapes: A preliminary analysis of the global popular', *Sociology of Sport Journal*, 13 (4), 428–57.

Andrews, D.L. and Jackson, S.J. 2001. 'Introduction: Sport celebrities, public culture, and private experience'. In D.L. Andrews and S.J. Jackson (eds), *Sport Stars: The Cultural Politics of Sport Celebrity*, 1–19. London: Routledge.

Anon. 2003. 'Blatter condemns European clubs', from <http://news.bbc.co.uk/sport2/hi/football/africa/3326971.stm>.

Appadurai, A. 1990. 'Disjuncture and difference in the global cultural economy', *Theory, Culture and Society*, 7 (2–3), 295–310.

Appadurai, A. 1996. *Modernity at Large: Cultural Dimensions of Globalization*. Minneapolis: University of Minnesota Press.

Arbena, J.L. 1994. 'Dimensions of international talent migration in Latin American sports'. In J. Bale and J.A. Maguire (eds), *The Global Sports Arena: Athletic Talent Migration in an Interdependent World*, 99–111. London: Frank Cass.

Armstrong, G. and Giulianotti, R. 1997. *Entering the Field: Studies in World Football*. Oxford: Berg.

Bairner, A. 2001. *Sport, Nationalism, and Globalization: European and North American Perspectives*. Albany: State University of New York Press.

Bale, J. and Sang, J. 1994. 'Out of Africa: The "development" of Kenyan athletics, talent migration and the global sports system'. In J. Bale and J.A. Maguire (eds), *The Global Sports Arena: Athletic Talent Migration in an Interdependent World*, 206–25. London: Frank Cass.

Bale, J. and Sang, J. 1996. *Kenyan Running: Movement Culture, Geography and Global Change*. London: Frank Cass.

Beckles, H. 1998. *The Development of West Indies Cricket*. Vol. 1: *The Age of Globalization*. Jamaica: University of the West Indies Press; London: Pluto Press.

Bernstein, A. 2000. ' "Things you can see from there you can't see from here": Globalization, media, and the Olympics', *Journal of Sport and Social Issues*, 24 (4), 351–69.

Boje, D.M. 1998. 'Nike, Greek goddess of victory or cruelty? Women's stories of Asian factory life', *Journal of Organizational Change Management*, 11 (6), 461–80.

Bruck, C. 1997. 'The big hitter', *The New Yorker*, 8 December, 82–93.

Carrington, B., Andrews, D.L., Jackson, S.J. and Mazur, Z. 2001. 'The global Jordanscape'. In D.L. Andrews (ed.), *Michael Jordan Inc.: Corporate Sport, Media Culture, and Late Modern America*, 177–216. Albany: State University of New York Press.

Dirlik, A. 1996. 'The global in the local'. In R. Wilson and W. Dissanayake (eds), *Global Local: Cultural Production and the Transnational Imaginary*, 21–45. Durham, NC: Duke University Press.

Donnelly, P. 1996a. 'Prolympism: Sport monoculture as crisis and opportunity', *Quest*, 48, 25–42.

Donnelly, P. 1996b. 'The local and the global: Globalization in the sociology of sport', *Journal of Sport and Social Issues*, 20 (3), 239–57.

Dunning, E. 1999. *Sport Matters: Sociological Studies of Sport, Violence and Civilization*. London: Routledge.

Elias, N. and Dunning, E. 1986. *Quest for Excitement: Sport and Leisure in the Civilizing Process*. Oxford: Basil Blackwell.

Enloe, C. 1995. 'The globetrotting sneaker', *Ms*, March/April, 10–15.

Falcous, M. and Maguire, J. 2005a. 'Globetrotters and local heroes? Labour migration, basketball, and local identities', *Sociology of Sport Journal*, 22, 137–57.

Falcous, M. and Maguire, J. 2005b. 'Making it local? National Basketball Association expansion and English basketball subcultures'. In M.L. Silk, D.L. Andrews and C.L. Cole (eds), *Sport and Corporate Nationalisms*, 13–34. Oxford: Berg.

Featherstone, M. 1996. 'Localism, globalism, and cultural identity'. In R. Wilson and W. Dissanayake (eds), *Global Local: Cultural Production and the Transnational Imaginary*, 46–77. Durham,NC: Duke University Press.

Fisher, E. 2003. 'Going global: Major league sports poised to expand to overseas markets', *Washington Times*, Sport, 5 January, 1.

Fukuyama, F. 1989. 'The end of history?' *The National Interest*, 16, 3–18.

Giardina, M.D. 2001. 'Global Hingis: Flexible citizenship and the transnational celebrity'. In D.L. Andrews and S.J. Jackson (eds), *Sport Stars: The Cultural Politics of Sporting Celebrity*, 201–30. London: Routledge.

Giulianotti, R. 1999. *Football: A Sociology of the Global Game*. Cambridge: Polity Press.

Giulianotti, R. 2005. *Sport: A Critical Sociology*. Cambridge: Polity Press.

Guttmann, A. 1978. *From Ritual to Record: The Nature of Modern Sports*. New York: Columbia University Press.

Guttmann, A. 2002. *The Olympics: A History of the Modern Games*. Urbana: University of Illinois Press.

Hall, S. 1991. 'The local and the global: Globalization and ethnicity'. In A.D. King (ed.), *Culture, Globalization and the World-system*, 41–68. Basingstoke: Macmillan

Hall, S. 1992. 'The west and the rest: Discourse and power'. In S. Hall and B. Gieben (eds), *Formations of Modernity*, 275–320. Cambridge: Polity Press.

Hall, S. 1997. 'The local and the global: Globalization and ethnicity'. In A.D. King (ed.), *Culture, Globalization and the World-system*, 19–39. Minneapolis: University of Minneapolis Press.

Hargreaves, J. 1987. 'The body, sport and power relations'. In J. Horne, D. Jary and A. Tomlinson (eds), *Sport, Leisure and Social Relations*, 139–59. London: Routledge & Kegan Paul.

Harvey, D. 1989. *The Condition of Postmodernity: An Enquiry into the Origins of Cultural Change*. Oxford: Blackwell.

Harvey, J., Law, A. and Cantelon, M. 2001. 'North American professional team sport franchise ownership patterns and global entertainment conglomerates', *Sociology of Sport Journal*, 18 (4), 435–57.

Herman, E. and McChesney, R.W. 1997. *The Global Media: The New Missionaries of Corporate Capitalism*. London: Cassell.

Hobsbawn, E.J. 1983. 'Mass-producing traditions: Europe, 1870–1914'. In E.J. Hosbawn and T. Ranger (eds), *The Invention of Tradition*, 263–307. Cambridge: Cambridge University Press.

Hobsbawm, E.J. 1990. *Nations and Nationalism since 1870: Programme, Myth, Reality.* Cambridge: Cambridge University Press.

Hogan, J. 2003. 'Staging the nation: Gendered and ethnicized discourses of national identity in Olympic opening ceremonies', *Journal of Sport and Social Issues*, 27 (2), 100–23.

Holt, R.J. 1989a. 'Empire and nation'. In *Sport and the British: A Modern History*, 203–36. Oxford: Clarendon Press.

Holt, R.J. 1989b. *Sport and the British: A Modern History.* Oxford: Clarendon Press.

Houlihan, B. 1994. 'Homogenization, Americanization, and creolization of sport: Varieties of globalization', *Sociology of Sport Journal*, 11 (4), 356–75.

James, C.L.R. 1963. *Beyond a Boundary.* London: Stanley Paul.

Jameson, F. 1991. *Postmodernism, or, the Cultural Logic of Late Capitalism.* Durham, NC: Duke University Press.

Jameson, F. 1998. *The Cultural Turn: Selected Writings on the Postmodern 1983–1998.* London: Verso.

Kaufman, J. and Patterson, O. 2005. 'Cross-national cultural diffusion: The global spread of cricket', *American Sociological Review*, 70 (February), 82–110.

Kellner, D. 2001. 'The sports spectacle, Michael Jordan, and Nike: Unholy alliance?' In D.L. Andrews (ed.), *Michael Jordan Inc.: Corporate Sport, Media Culture, and Late Modern America*, 37–64. Albany, NY: State University of New York Press.

Kellner, D. 2003. *Media Spectacle.* London: Routledge.

Kivinen, O., Mesikammen, J. and Metsa-Tokila, T. 2001. 'A case study of cultural diffusion: British ice hockey and American influences in Europe'. *Culture, Sport, Society*, 4 (1), 49–62.

Klein, A.M. 1991. *Sugarball: The American Game, the Dominican Dream.* New Haven, CT: Yale University Press.

Knight, G., MacNeill, M. and Donnelly, P. 2005. 'The disappointment games: Narratives of Olympic failure in Canada and New Zealand', *International Review for the Sociology of Sport*, 40 (1), 25–51.

Law, A., Harvey, J. and Kemp, S. 2002. 'The global sport mass media oligopoly: The three usual suspects and more', *International Review for the Sociology of Sport*, 37 (3/4), 279–302.

McKay, J. and Miller, T. 1991. 'From old boys to men and women of the corporation: The Americanization and commodification of Australian sport', *Sociology of Sport Journal*, 8 (1), 86–94.

MacNeill, M. 1996. 'Networks: Producing Olympic ice hockey for a national television audience', *Sociology of Sport Journal*, 13 (2), 103–24.

Magee, J. and Sugden, J. 2002. ' "The world at their feet": Professional football and international labour migration', *Journal of Sport and Social Issues*, 26 (4), 421–37.

Maguire, J.A. 1990. 'More than a sporting touchdown: The making of American football in England 1982–1990', *Sociology of Sport Journal*, 7 (3), 213–37.

Maguire, J. 1994. 'American labour migrants, globalization and the making of English basketball'. In J. Bale and J.A. Maguire (eds), *The Global Sports Arena: Athletic Talent Migration in an Interdependent World*, 226–55. London: Frank Cass.

Maguire, J.A. 1996. 'Blade runners: Canadian migrants, ice hockey, and the global sports process', *Journal of Sport & Social Issues*, 20 (3), 335–60.

Maguire, J.A. 1999. *Global Sport: Identities, Societies, Civilization.* Cambridge: Polity Press.

Maguire, J.A. 2000. 'Sport and globalization'. In J. Coakley and E. Dunning (eds), *Handbook of Sports Studies*, 356–69. London: Sage.

Maguire, J. 2004. 'Sport labor migration research revisited', *Journal of Sport and Social Issues*, 28 (4), 477–82.

Maguire, J., Jarvie, G., Mansfield, L. and Bradley, J. 2002. *Sport Worlds: A Sociological Perspective*. Champaign, IL: Human Kinetics.

Maguire, J.A. and Stead, D. 1998. 'Border crossings: Soccer labour migration and the European Union', *International Review for the Sociology of Sport*, 33 (1), 59–74.

Markovits, A.S. and Hellerman, S.L. 2001. *Offside: Soccer and American Exceptionalism*. Princeton, NJ: Princeton University Press.

Marshall, P.D. 1997. *Celebrity and Power: Fame in Contemporary Culture*. Minneapolis: University of Minnesota Press.

Martin, C.R. and Reeves, J.L. 2001. 'The whole world isn't watching (but we thought they were): The Super Bowl and United States solipsism', *Culture, Sport, Society*, 4 (2), 213–36.

Miller, T. 2001. *Sportsex*. Philadelphia: Temple University Press.

Miller, T., Lawrence, G., McKay, J. and Rowe, D. 2001. *Globalization and Sport: Playing the World*. London: Sage.

Miller, T. and McHoul, A. 1998. *Popular Culture and Everyday Life*. London: Sage.

Morley, D. and Robins, K. 1995. *Spaces of Identity: Global Media, Electronic Landscapes and Cultural Boundaries*. London: Routledge.

Murdoch, R. 1996. *Annual Report: Chief Executive's Review*. Retrieved 12 June 2001 from <http://www.newscorp.com/report1996/letter.htm>.

Murdoch, R. 1998. *Annual Report: Chief Executive's Review*. Retrieved 12 June 2001 from <http://www.newscorp.com/report98/cer.html>.

Pierce, C.P. 1995. 'Master of the universe', GQ, April, 180–7.

Real, M.R. 1998. 'MediaSport: Technology and the commodification of postmodern sport'. In L.A. Wenner (ed.), *Mediasport*, 14–26. London: Routledge.

Ritzer, G. 2004a. *The Globalization of Nothing*. Thousand Oaks, CA: Pine Forge Press.

Ritzer, G. 2004b. *The McDonaldization of Society*, revised New Century edn. London: Sage.

Robertson, R. 1995. 'Glocalization: Time-space and homogeneity-heterogeneity'. In M. Featherstone, S. Lash and R. Robertson (eds), *Global Modernities*, 25–44. London: Sage.

Roche, M. 2000. *Mega-events and Modernity: Olympics, Expos and the Growth of Global Culture*. London: Routledge.

Rojek, C. 2001. *Celebrity*. London: Reaktion Books.

Ross, A. 2004. 'Trouble at the mill: Nike, United and the Asian garment trade'. In D.L. Andrews (ed.), *Manchester United: A Thematic Study*, 87–100. London: Routledge.

Rowe, D. 1996a. 'Editorial: Sport, globalization and the media', *Media, Culture and Society*, 18 (4), 523-526.

Rowe, D. 1996b. 'The global love-match: Sport and television', *Media, Culture and Society*, 18 (4), 565-582.

Rowe, D. 2003. 'Sport and the repudation of the global', *International Review for the Sociology of Sport*, 38 (3), 281–94.

Sage, G.H. 1999. 'Justice do it! The Nike transnational advocacy network: Organization, collective actions, and outcomes', *Sociology of Sport Journal*, 16 (3), 206–35.

Schmidt, R. 2001. 'Murdoch reaches for the sky', *Brill's Content*, June, 74–9, 126–9.

Silk, M. 2001. 'Together we're one? The "place" of the nation in media representations of the 1998 Kuala Lumpur Commonwealth Games', *Sociology of Sport Journal*, 18 (3), 277–301.

Silk, M. 2002. '"Bangsa Malaysia": Global sport, the city and the mediated refurbishment of local identities', *Media, Culture and Society*, 24 (6), 775–94.

Silk, M.L. and Amis, J. 2000. 'Institutional pressures and the production of televised sport', *Journal of Sport Management*, 14 (4), 267–92.

Silk, M. and Andrews, D.L. 2001. 'Beyond a boundary? Sport, transnational advertising, and the reimagining of national culture', *Journal of Sport and Social Issues*, 25 (2), 180–201.

Silk, M.L. and Andrews, D.L. 2005. 'The spatial logics of global sponsorship: Corporate capital, cola wars and cricket'. In J. Amis and T.B. Cornwell (eds), *Global Sport Sponsorship*, 67–88. Oxford: Berg.

Stabile, C.A. 2000. 'Nike, social responsibility, and the hidden abode of production', *Critical Studies in Media Communication*, 17 (2), 186–204.

Stead, D. and Maguire, J.A. 2000. '"Rite de passage" or Passage to riches? The motivation and objectives of Nordic/Scandinavian players in English league soccer', *Journal of Sport and Social Issues*, 24 (1), 36–60.

Sugden, J. 1994. 'USA and the World Cup: American nativism and the rejection of the people's game'. In J. Sugden and A. Tomlinson (eds), *Hosts and Champions: Soccer Cultures, National Identities and the USA World Cup*, 219–52. Aldershot: Arena.

Tomlinson, A. 1996. 'Olympic spectacle: Opening ceremonies and some paradoxes of globalization', *Media, Culture and Society*, 18 (4), 583–602.

Tomlinson, A. 2005. *Sport and Leisure Cultures*. Minneapolis: University of Minnesota Press.

Tomlinson, J. 1999. *Globalization and Culture*. Cambridge: Polity Press.

Van Bottenburg, M. 2001. *Global Games*. Translated by B. Jackson. Urbana: University of Illinois Press.

Van Elteren, M. 1996. 'Conceptualising the impact of US popular culture globally', *Journal of Popular Culture*, 30 (1), 47–89.

Waitt, G. 1999. 'Playing games with Sydney: Marketing Sydney for the 2000 Olympics', *Urban Studies*, 36 (7), 1055–77.

Walsh, A.J. and Giulianotti, R. 2001. 'This sporting mammon: A normative critique of the commodification of sport', *Journal of the Philosophy of Sport*, XXVIII, 53–77.

Wernick, A. 1991. *Promotional Culture: Advertising, Ideology and Symbolic Expression*. London: Sage.

Whitson, D. and Macintosh, D. 1993. 'Becoming a world-class city: Hallmark events and sport franchises in the growth strategies of western Canadian cities', *Sociology of Sport Journal*, 10 (3), 221–40.

Whitson, D. and Macintosh, D. 1996. 'The global circus: International sport, tourism, and the marketing of cities', *Journal of Sport and Social Issues*, 20 (3), 278–95.

Williams, J. 1994. 'The local and the global in English soccer and the rise of satellite television', *Sociology of Sport Journal*, 11 (4), 376–97.

Wilson, H. 1996. 'What is an Olympic city? Visions of Sydney 2000', *Media, Culture and Society*, 18 (4), 603–18.

Wilson, S. 2004. 'Athens Olympics draws record TV audiences', *USA Today*, 12 October.

Chapter 26

The Fate of the Local

Melissa L. Caldwell and Eriberto P. Lozada Jr

UNDERSTANDING LOCALITY

Discussions about global processes are typically grounded in two key premises. First, globalization is an evolutionary process that is unavoidably and irrevocably changing the world. Second, the homogenizing and unifying aspects of the globalization process are eliminating local cultures and replacing them with a generic, uniform global culture. Among critics of globalization, one of the most prominent suggestions for defeating globalization – or at the very least stemming its tide – is an imperative to locate, rescue and preserve local cultures. Often combined with anti-capitalism movements such as the protests that accompany World Trade Organization meetings, these efforts to sustain the local are often framed as efforts to protect local, small-scale communities that are in danger of losing their unique lifestyles and independence to the forces of global imperialism. As Anthony Giddens has described it, today's global world is a 'runaway world' that is increasingly out of our control (2000: 20). From the local perspective, however, none of these premises completely explain how globalization transforms local communities and their culture. Globalization does indeed greatly impact the way people in local communities relate to each other, and the cultural practices that they follow, but it often does so with the active agency of people in local societies who choose particular life strategies, selectively adopt non-local cultural practices and desire commodities that are exchanged in the expanding global market. Moreover, people in local communities throughout the world are transformed by globalization unequally; those with more economic and social resources can exercise their agency more profoundly than others.

Our task in this chapter is to explore how accounts of globalization have grappled with the question of the local. That is, to what extent do scholars acknowledge the local in their accounts of globalization? When they do recognize the local, what does this local look like? To what extent do perspectives on the local adequately account for changes? Can the local ever change, or is it forever doomed to one of two fates: disappearance or preservation in analytical formaldehyde?

Loss of the Local

Although globalization is generally recognized as a feature of the late twentieth century, global interconnections between different local communities have in fact long existed throughout history. Archaeological excavations and historical documents attest to the dispersal of social and material artefacts from far-flung cultures throughout the world (Wolf 1982; Mintz 1985). Ancient trade routes linking Asia, Africa, Oceania and eventually Europe and the New World facilitated the movement of people, goods and cultural practices across the globe. Similarly, although concerns with the disappearance of the local are most recognizable to studies of globalization from the past 20 years, this, too, is not a recent development. Already in the eighteenth and nineteenth centuries, social theorists like Karl Marx were ruminating on the implications of global trade and industrialization for local communities. Marx anticipated the positive potential of international commerce and technological innovation for the improvement of living standards, labour relations and international cooperation. But at the same time, he raised questions about the consequences for local communities who suddenly found themselves caught up in political, economic and social forces that drew them into relationships with other cultural systems and societies. On the one hand, Marx's vision for social change was predicated on a global community of workers who, united, could change global political structures. But on the other hand, when Marx cast his gaze to the effects of political and economic globalization on specific communities, he voiced concerns about the ability of cultural traditions to withstand these forces. For the specific case of the British colonialist project in India, Marx writes 'England has broken down the entire framework of Indian society, without any symptoms of reconstitution yet appearing. This loss of his old world, with no gain of a new one, imparts a particular kind of melancholy to the present misery of the Hindoo, and separates Hindostan, ruled by Britain, from all its ancient traditions, and from the whole of its past history' (Marx 1978: 654–5). Marx's despondency at the loss of cultural specificity in the late nineteenth century foreshadows later critiques of global capitalism in the late twentieth century.

What makes globalization the dominant concern in the twenty-first century is that the degree of rapidity, influence and reach of transnational flows is changing the very fabric of everyday life in profound ways. Consequently, one of the most prevalent and recurring fears articulated by globalization foes among academics and the general public is that local communities and cultures are being displaced, destroyed and eliminated by global forces at a greater rate and to a greater extent than ever before. Contemporary social analysts link these developments with a host of social pathologies: identity crises brought about by the erosion of the cultural values on which individual societies are based (Friedman 1991; Huntington 2004; King and Craig 2002); the disappearance of civic engagement (Putnam 2000); the commodification of social life (Barber 1995); and the loss of meaning in everyday life (Ritzer 2004).

For the specific issue of 'the local', social analysts have observed that global processes have uprooted communities and lifestyles from their historical, geographical and cultural origins (Featherstone 1995; Giddens 1990). At the same time, physical spaces themselves are transformed as interconnections of diverse localities in the postmodern capitalist production process have made local boundaries more porous, segmenting local communities along geographical lines that are not contiguous (Harvey 1990). It is, as Clifford writes, a struggle to 'define the local, as a distinctive community, in historical contexts of displacement' (Clifford 1994: 308). Anthony Giddens writes that places are no longer real but have 'become phantasmagoric' (Giddens 1990: 140). Benjamin Barber observes that there is no longer any 'there' there: 'You are nowhere. You are everywhere. Inhabiting an abstraction. Lost in cyberspace' (Barber 1995: 99). In a similar perspective, Mike Featherstone has written that 'Localism and a sense of place give way to the anonymity of "no place spaces", or simulated environments in which we are unable to feel an adequate sense of being at home' (1995: 102). In this perspective, local spaces take on the feel of the surreal – they are simulacra of reality and not necessarily reality themselves (see also Stewart 1988).

At the same time, globalization also speeds up the tempos of daily life. Advances in telephone and media technology have helped make the world smaller and more instantaneous. During the Gulf War in the early 1990s, CNN led the way in bringing news to people's living rooms. More than that, CNN's live format meant that viewers could watch events unfold in real time. High speed transportation systems mean that tuna caught off the coast of Maine can be eaten in a Tokyo restaurant within a matter of hours (Bestor 2004). Advances in telephone technology make it possible to 'reach out and touch someone' anytime, anywhere in the world. GSM (the Global System for Mobile Communications) means that people can travel the world with the same phone number and not be physically located in one single place. High speed communications systems enable software employees who are physically located in Ireland, India and the United States to work collaboratively at the same time as if they were in cubicles next to each other (Riain 2000); in fact, this chapter was written by two authors who were on two different continents at the time (one was in China while the other was in the United States, on her way to Russia). The next time you visit the drive-through at your favourite restaurant, your order may be taken by an employee working half-way around the world.[1] Rapid transnational flows of media and information through the Internet and satellites have created what Arjun Appadurai has referred to as a 'mediascape' that is crucial to the work of the imagination that structures social relations and generates possibilities. As a result, people's experiences of both time and space have become volatile – subject to rapid and intense change, dislocation and disjuncture that Harvey refers to as 'the postmodern condition'.

New technologies that facilitate processes of 'time-space compression' (Harvey 1990) make the world feel smaller and more intimate (Robertson 1992; Tomlinson 1999), which in turn affects how people identify themselves and their attachments to local communities. In particular, the speed with which daily life moves throughout the world, and the increasing rates of mobility among many sectors of the world's population (students, workers, tourists and lovers, among many others), complicates efforts to find anyone and anything standing still long enough to qualify

as local. Reflecting on more than 30 years of research following the global movement of residents from San Tin, a village in the Hong Kong New Territories, James
Watson writes: 'Diasporics are moving targets. What they are today, they will not
be tomorrow. How can one possibly write an adequate ethnography of a group that
is always and inevitably in the process of transformation?' (Watson 2004: 894).
This global movement of people has led to a wide literature on diasporas – also
referred to in more specific terms as transnational migrants, displaced persons,
depending on the specific definitions and categories used (see for example Ong 1999;
Guest 2003; Small 1997; Levitt 2001; Basch et al. 1994), where the definition of
diaspora has been widely contested (Ho 2004; Clifford 1994). Families and communities themselves are becoming virtual. Such experiences have made local
communities and particular cultural practices not so much disappear as take
different form.

LIFESAVING 101: RESCUING THE LOCAL

Rescuing 'the local' first requires defining it, a challenging task given analysts' inability to settle on common qualities or perspectives.[2] Among anti-globalization purists,
'the local' is shorthand for communities untouched by the modern conveniences of
civilization and who engage in cultural practices that are unique, static and exotic
– or better yet, primitive. In this fantasy, local communities are small-scale, culturally and socio-economically homogeneous, idealized places where 'everybody knows
your name'. This is the perspective driving heritage recuperation programmes such
as the Slow Food Movement, with its mission to respond to the presumed homogenization inherent in fast food by preserving indigenous culinary traditions and
lifestyles (Petrini 2001).[3] Yet this vision of pristine, traditional societies is in fact a
myth, debunked perhaps most vividly in Gary Larson's cartoon of native tribesmen
frantically hiding their electronics and home appliances in anticipation of the arrival
of the anthropologists.

Not only does attention to the constructedness of the local illuminate the contingent nature of what qualifies as 'local', but it also acknowledges the shifting sands
of the politics of globalization studies more generally. To recognize the dynamic
interplay between the global and the local as a process by which the global becomes
integrated into the cultural particularities of local life, Robertson proposes the term
'glocal' (1992: 173). Friedman displays a similar approach to the interplay of the
two registers but prefers terms like 'creolization' that emphasize the hybrid nature
of these dynamic creations (Friedman 1994: 208). Giddens, meanwhile, refers to
cultural particularities as 'local nationalisms' in distinction from global forces (2000:
31), a move that reifies both the national and the global. Yet another approach
characterizes the local as that which is familiar or comfortable (Featherstone 1995;
Lozada 2001; Wilk 2002). What links these various definitions together is the recognition that 'the local' is not so much a thing to be discovered as it is a process
of social change. And the struggles over definition that emerge are in fact struggles
over how to capture and represent these processes.

Fieldworking ethnographers who are based in specific local communities for long
periods of time have been uniquely positioned to document the social structures and

cultural practices that *define* locality. In such ethnographic studies, cultural change does not necessarily suggest the loss of cultural uniqueness or long-standing traditions. Instead, what anthropologists have carefully and consistently documented for local communities within different societies throughout the world has been that diversity and contradictions exist *within* seemingly homogeneous localities. For example, Hannerz (1992, 1996) examines the medium for transnational cultural flows, embodied in his social category of cosmopolitans (mediators who straddle the global and the local), in the formation of creole cultures, or unique non-territorially defined cultural systems (1992: 264–5). While 'locals' are rooted in a culture that is more geographically bound, cosmopolitans interact with global cultural centres and serve as the primary mediators in the creation of creole cultures. From Hannerz's model, *mobility* has become the means of stratification; while both locals and cosmopolitans share creole cultures, Hannerz highlights how they are shared unequally. Mobility gives cosmopolitans a wider array of social, economic and political resources and a more diverse range of strategies from which to improve their standing in local communities.

Arjun Appadurai goes further in his model of globalization, claiming that all aspects of everyday life must be understood from the perspective of maintaining a sense of locality. Appadurai asserts that 'locality is an inherently fragile achievement' (1996: 179). His model of transnationalism reveals these connections as the focus for anthropologists in the field, through his explication of *neighbourhoods* – 'situated communities characterized by their actuality, whether spatial or virtual, and their potential for social reproduction' (1996: 179). Globalization shapes the structures and practices of neighbourhoods through five dimensions: (1) ethnoscape (the transnational movement of people); (2) technoscape (the global transfer of technologies that are shaped by both the generalities of the market and the specificity of transnational social networks); (3) financescape (the flow of global capital); (4) mediascape (the global production, distribution and consumption of media); and (5) ideoscape (the transnational flow of ideologies and counter-ideologies) (Appadurai 1996: 33–6). The key element in Appadurai's model, however, is that such large-scale structures and practices take place in very specific local communities – globalization becomes situated in localities: a 'frame or setting within which various kinds of human action . . . can be initiated and conducted meaningfully' (Appadurai 1996: 184).

The very issue of identifying meaningful localities is one of the hallmarks of anthropological fieldwork, which relies on anthropologists embedding themselves in a local community for long-term participant-observation research. Even before globalization was seen as a principal factor structuring everyday life, anthropologists such as E.E. Evans-Pritchard (whose classic studies of the Nuer in what is now southern Sudan) grappled with the problem of the locality as he describes the 'nuerosis' (1940: 12–13) he encountered in his ethnological inquiry. He found that lineage, age-set and geographic social systems create shifting social boundaries through a process of fission and fusion based on the specifics of the particular social issue, a process that can be understood by the idea that the 'enemy of my enemy is my friend'. His model of segmentary political systems, moreover, reflects this Nuer grappling with the problem of the local. In many ways, this classic ethnography foreshadows postmodern ideas of the compression of time and space (cf.

Evans-Pritchard 1940: 94–138 with Harvey 1990), where what is considered local politically is not bound by geographical space but by social space. As a result, contradictory claims in defining what is a locality (such as those definitions generated by political entities such as states versus those generated by kinship groups, age or interest cohorts, businesses) is one of the first things faced by the anthropological fieldworker.

More recently, Akhil Gupta and James Ferguson highlight this problem as a contradiction in their analysis of the impact of a fieldwork-based methodology on anthropological knowledge: 'On the one hand, anthropology appears determined to give up its old ideas of territorially fixed communities and stable, localized cultures, and to apprehend an interconnected world in which people, objects, and ideas are rapidly shifting and refuse to stay in place. At the same time, though, in a defensive response to challenges to its "turf" from other disciplines, anthropology has come to lean more heavily than ever on a methodological commitment to spend long periods in one localized setting' (Gupta and Ferguson 1997: 4). Gupta and Ferguson's solution is not to take for granted definitions of the local, but instead to focus on the idea of location – examining the processes by which the local is generated. This is especially relevant in an age of globalization, where such 'location-work', as Gupta and Ferguson call this examination, is faced not only by professional social analysts, but also by everyday people in everyday life.

Despite our best efforts to 'find' something that we can call 'the local', the reality is that in some cases, it is the researcher who in fact represents the most stable and continuous presence in and for local communities. In revisiting his former field site in San Tin (2004), James Watson discovered that by recording and writing about this community's history and genealogies (1975), he has become the authoritative source for third- and fourth-generation non-Cantonese-speaking diasporics who want to get in touch with their cultural heritage. Since her 1997–8 fieldwork in a transnational Protestant community in Moscow, Melissa Caldwell has watched as most of her informants have moved away, died or disappeared as the programme has changed its focus and location (2005b). In other words, concerns with the status of the local in fact reflect the particular interests, values, beliefs and preferences of particular social actors – both locals and their observers – at a given moment in time. Thus, what may be more important is to ask the question, 'Local for whom?'

Collectively, these approaches reveal just how ambiguous 'the local' is and how attempts to define and recover 'the local' are in fact more focused on recovering and fetishizing the idea of 'the local' (Appadurai 1990: 307).[4] In contrast to approaches that bemoan the loss of the local, 'local life' remains the reality of everyday life, albeit perhaps in a slightly different form (Giddens 1991; Inda and Rosaldo 2002; Tomlinson 1999). Tomlinson reminds us that 'globalization disturbs the way we conceptualize "culture"' (1999: 27), but culture itself does not disappear. Although globalization is increasingly colonizing the local, this process involves changing the nature of localities themselves, so that 'the journey into locality then is a journey into the challenging reality of cultural difference' (Tomlinson 1999: 8). This emphasis on the dynamic nature of locality resonates with Miller's suggestion that analytical perspectives that search for the local are in fact proposing a reality that may not in fact exist (Miller 1995). To circumvent issues about the authenticity of local cultures, Miller proposes to shift analyses towards emphases on 'the construction of local culture' (Miller 1995: 11), which will reframe locality as a dynamic, interactive and continually renegotiated process (see also Ekholm-Friedman and Friedman 1995; Wilk 1999, 2002).

INTERVENTIONS INTO STUDIES OF THE LOCAL

As we have suggested, rethinking the nature of 'the local' through the prism of dynamic change requires new points of departure. In the following section, we outline four areas that, in our opinion, demonstrate theoretically innovative and ethnographically promising approaches to the study of the local.

Perhaps the first and most well-established intervention into studies of the local comes from research on specifics of the *circulation* that comprises globalization (Tsing 2000) in studies of global commodity chains. This approach follows things, people and ideas as they move from place to place and charts the relationships created by these movements and the ways in which individual encounters affect the meanings of the entities moving through these networks (e.g. Bestor 2004; Freidberg 2004; Gereffi and Korzeniewicz 1994). By considering the relationships that exist between partners in these chains, this approach accommodates multiple and shifting locales as well as subjects who may otherwise not 'fit' easily into territory-based identity classes. The flexibility of commodity chain approaches also pushes us beyond the directionally based models of core versus periphery, West versus Rest and insider versus outsider that remain pervasive in anti-globalization perspectives.

A second productive avenue of inquiry in recent ethnographies focuses on virtual communities, such as those that rely on the Internet (online gaming groups, listserves, forums etc.) (Miller and Slater 2000; Hakken 1999; Lozada 1999; Rai 1995; Escobar 1994). Instead of finding a new exotica created by computer-mediated communications, researchers have found that the Internet is in many ways replicating – rather than erasing – traditional social relationships, but in ways that compress time and space. Miller and Slater discuss in their ethnographic study of the production and consumption of the Internet in Trinidad how virtual communities are in fact structured by older communities: 'Not only were older identities such as religion, nation, and family embraced online, but the Internet could be seen by many as *primarily* a means of repairing those allegiances' (Miller and Slater 2000: 18). Similarly, in a study of Internet marriage services and 'mail-order brides', Constable (2003) finds that Chinese and Filipino women (and American men) value their e-mail and Internet forum communication with others and the online relationships as 'real' relationships. Relationships that are established over the Internet frequently lead to face-to-face contacts and marriage.

Although communities in an age of globalization are increasingly deterritorialized in ways that may appear to weaken bonds of locality, people are adapting and reconfiguring traditional structures and practices to maintain coherence. In his ethnographic study of a southern Chinese village in Guangdong, Lozada (2001) argues that this community must be seen as a transnational village. There are three characteristics of this Chinese village that makes it a deterritorialized community. First,

its very existence was a result of China's penetration by the prototypical transnational organization, the Roman Catholic Church. Second, the villagers are part of
a global diaspora, the Hakka; the movement of villagers in and out of the physical
space has historically and in the present been a part of this community's social
reality. Third, because of the demands of transnational capitalism, young adults
from the village almost all work and study far from home. Even with these potentially fragmenting processes, where spatial disjunctions are created through the
scattering of community members, the village still maintains its coherence as a community because of a multiplicity of communication and exchanges and through
participation in key rituals (calendrical Catholic, life-cycle and other cultural rituals).
Villagers maintain locality through a variety of mechanisms – a locality that must
be seen not as a physical property (an accident of geography or the design of the
nation-state), but as a social process, ongoing and in flux.

The effects of changing social structures reverberate in the identities and roles
that people make for themselves at the most intimate levels of gender and family.
Olwig describes a transnational African-Caribbean village, where immigration has
resulted in a deterritorialized community focused on the spatial site of the home
village though the maintenance of a 'family home' in Nevis and the steady flow of
remittances, no matter where in the world migrants actually live and work. Such
practices, maintained over generations of migrants, emphasize their continued presence and rootedness in local island communities, no matter where they are located.
These cultural practices of rootedness resolve the contradiction of being socially
present in multiple, specific localities – a condition that Olwig refers to as *translocal*
(1997: 33) – and of a local community's dependence upon social and economic
resources that are far from their geographic location. In her study of female Indian
labour migrants from the state of Kerala to the United States, Sheba George documents radical changes in Indian families who formerly found single, wage-earning
women dangerous but now find themselves dependent on daughters and wives who
immigrate as nurses to the United States (George 2000).

Research on international adoptions and child sponsorship programmes offer
critical insight into how changing notions of the family and personal identities
are also intertwined with changing definitions of race, ethnicity and nationality
(Anagnost 2000; Frechette 2004; Tunina and Stryker 2001; Volkman 2003).
Volkman describes how her Chinese-born daughter rates the Asianness of her
American classmates on the basis of whether they were adopted or not. Writing on
the related subject of child sponsorship projects in Africa, Erica Bornstein argues
that transnational remittances transform anonymous interactions between adult
donors and child recipients into familial relationships, even though the parties are
separated by continents located on opposite sides of the world and will never meet.
It is the sending and receiving of remittances and letters that creates 'relationships
of belonging' that are every bit as real and substantial as those existing in biological,
face-to-face families (Bornstein 2001: 614). One child related that she liked exchang-
ing letters with her sponsor because 'I am feeling like I am becoming part of their
family' (Bornstein 2001: 614). Nancy Scheper-Hughes's work on global organ
trafficking shows similar findings in terms of how human bodies are themselves
the means by which intimate social formations are being transformed (2000). The
process of removing body parts from citizens of one nation and implanting them in

citizens of other countries evokes critical debates about what constitutes local identities. Katherine Verdery's study of dead body politics in post-communist Europe illustrates the power – and danger – of bodies that are dug up from their burial spots, transported across regional and national borders, and reburied in new locations (Verdery 1999).

As all of these studies illustrate clearly, persons, their bodies and their body parts do not necessarily belong to a specific locale but can be transported – both virtually and actually – across regional, national and international borders and integrated into new locales. In this sense, origins are less important than destinations in the constitution of local communities and families. In the end, what studies of virtual communities and persons illuminate is the extent to which *all* social groups and identities are in essence 'virtual'. In other words, families, villages, towns, counties and nation-states are all imagined communities (Anderson 1983), even though the social and political technologies[5] of administration and control make communities seem real and natural (Aretxaga 2003; Trouillot 2001).

How globalization is transforming cultural systems of meaning in ways that paradoxically do not obliterate and may even reinforce local systems of meaning offers a third promising set of topics. In particular, although global aspects of religion have long attracted academic attention – in studies of the global spread of religion,[6] the transnational organization of religion (Eickelman and Piscatori 1996), syncretism (Worsley 1970; Watanabe 1990) and in inter-religious dialogue (Eck 1997), among other topics – the events of 11 September 2001 have made the study of religious globalization especially urgent. National security concerns, international relations and religiously inspired terrorism and conflict are all outgrowths of the globalization of religion. Studies of these issues highlight how religions that have been seen as a major component of local identity are being challenged by globalization. As Barber notes, 'What ends as Jihad may begin as a simple search for a local identity, some set of common personal attributes to hold out against the numbing and neutering uniformities of industrial modernization and the colonizing culture of McWorld' (Barber 1995). Although a 'clash of civilizations' grounded on competing systems of meaning is not necessarily inevitable, what comes through in these studies is that transnational religious systems are also transformed through a process of localization, creating a sense of locality through contextually driven systems of meaning.

In many respects, transnational religion provides an alternative basis for local *authority* that competes with the dominant nation-state political system and the hierarchies of global capitalism. As Ho points out in his study of the Hadrami diaspora and the spread of Islam in South and South-east Asia, the Islamic public display of authority and the conflict between diaspora and empire in the recent political conflict between the United States and bin Laden has historical and symbolic roots in the dissolution of the Muslim Caliphate (Ho 2004). Global Islam is not the only world religious tradition to provide competing authority to the Westphalian state, however. Other studies of transnational grass-roots movements of Pentecostals (Meyer 2004; Brodwin 2003), Catholic liberation theology in Latin America (Nagle 1997) and the spread of religious traditions from the periphery to the centre (as in the case of Falungong or Vodou, see Chen 2003 and McCarthy

Brown 2001) show that this resurgence of religion is a wider response by different local communities to global challenges.

Other studies of transnational religion shed light on how global processes are not only introduced and integrated successfully into local communities, but also stabilize local social systems. In her work on Chinese Muslims, Maris Gillette documents how the introduction of Western snack foods in China gave Muslim and non-Muslim Chinese a medium through which they could give and accept hospitality – and social relations – with each other (Gillette 2000). For the case of Russia, Melissa Caldwell writes that Muscovites have responded to the influx of transnational religious groups in Russia by forcing religious leaders to refashion the services they provide to focus less on theology and more on the provision of social services and personal networks (Caldwell 2004, 2005a). What Caldwell has found is that as global religions are made locally meaningful in Russia, they have emerged as partners (albeit uneasily in some cases) to the Russian state.

Finally, a fourth point of departure for critically exploring the local has emerged in recent studies of leisure and entertainment. While movies, television, music and other forms of entertainment are often cited as proof of the homogenizing influences of globalization (Hannerz 1996; Kearney 1995), these studies have found that people often use these globalized cultural artefacts to strengthen ideas of locality and for social purposes that make sense only in the local. One example of this is Richard Wilk's study of temporality in the consumption of television in Belize, where he finds that working-class people use the immediacy of satellite television to challenge the cosmopolitan claims of Belizean elites (Wilk 1995). In contrast, Lila Abu-Lughod (1993) finds that the state control over Egyptian television is used by the elite to push a national agenda that itself is struggling with its own modern Islamic identity. Television advertisements, as well as the television programmes themselves, have also shown their grounding in specific localities – even as they push global products (McCreery 1997; Mazzarella 2003). Similarly, in the realm of music in Tanzania, Kelly Askew (2003) finds that music – both *ngoma* ('traditional dance')[7] and *dansi* (globally influenced 'urban jazz') – is central to, not an outcome of, local Tanzanian politics. In film, the global spread of non-Western films is rooted in local understandings of particular places such as Hong Kong and India, not solely in dialectical opposition to Hollywood – which itself is an occidental gloss (Wong and McDonogh 2001; Tyrrell 1999; Ginsburg 1994).

In this vein, sport is especially illustrative of a re-defining of the local, since it is not only images and ideas that are on the move, but also human bodies. As a key cultural arena in which multiple identities are created, performed and essentialized (Messner 2002), sports serve as a boundary-maintenance mechanism (Barth 1969), providing people with bodily means to differentiate themselves from others latitudinally or hierarchically (MacClancy 1996). The connection between sports and identity is most visible in the areas of ethnicity and nationalism (Klein 2000; Morris 2000), especially in the spectacle of the Olympic Games (Fan 1998; Girginov 1998; MacAloon 1981). Joseph Alter, for example, demonstrates how Indian wrestling spreads an ideology that on the one hand is critical of the Hindu caste system through its interpretation of the body, but on the other hand is critical of the conditions of the modern Indian state (Alter 1992). As a result, the successes and failures of individual athletes in competition are social projections of regional and national pride (see also Brownell 1995; Stokes 1996) and can help integrate diverse societies through an imagined community generated by athletes and teams that physically represent the nation (Elling et al. 2001).

Locality is redefining itself in the realm of sports, now that the players who make up 'the home team' are from elsewhere and their careers on the team are ephemeral. Sports today is deterritorialized, marked by the transnational movement of athletes and sports and the global commodification of sports by transnational corporations such as Nike (Jackson and Andrews 1999; Korzeniewicz 2000).[8] Kendall Blanchard suggests that organized sports, as the 'New American Religion' (Sands 1999: xi), are heavily exported by the United States to other countries as part of the politicization of popular culture inherent in globalization (Nye 2002; Wang 2001; Fukuyama 1995), and need to be explored as part of what social analysts refer to as 'transnational civil society' (Florini 2000).

While sport affirms or establishes new social identities within a particular social community and connects people intergenerationally within ethnic communities, it can also demarcate differences that socially inscribe ethnic or foreign others (Shukert 2002; Bairner 2003). Nation-states are heavily involved in the use of sports for unifying diverse cultures and communities (Scherer 2001; Alter 2000), and through patronage transform sports into a political arena (Silverstein 2000; Moore 2000; Appadurai 1996). While the nation-state serves as an important patron of sports and other forms of popular culture, there are a number of other civil society organizations (including transnational business corporations, religious organizations and other civic associations) that at times compete with the state to promote their own ideologies and interests. As a result, global sport becomes local sport; while local sports, through the connections established, become global in the persons of athletes, commodities and organizations.

CONCLUDING THOUGHTS: THINKING WITH LOCALIZATION

Our goal in this chapter has been to explore how globalization studies have dealt with the issue of the local and to identify several promising trajectories for future research. Ultimately what guides our perspective is the idea that 'the local' is in fact a vantage point from which to get at larger questions about the nature of change, social relationships, social structures, cultural practices, authenticity and tradition, among many others. In this sense, we see studies of the local as returning to fundamental issues in social analysis.

While the realities of global capitalism cannot be dismissed, neither can the untested promises of globalization be accepted. The power of the structures that promote and sustain global capitalism ultimately lies in the *belief* that people have in them, as analysts of the most recent global currency crisis demonstrate (the Asian Financial Crisis of 1997–8; see Yergin and Stanislaw 2002; Woo et al. 2000). Given the very real constraints and influence of global capitalism, it is easy to forget, as Jameson notes, that the rules of the global game are *cultural*, and that people's ability to navigate the waters of globalization is *social*:

In this respect, Gray's account of the resistance to the global free market is finally not cultural, despite his repeated use of the word, but ultimately social in nature: the various 'cultures' are crucially characterized as able to draw upon distinct kinds of social resources – collectives, communities, familial relationships – over and against what the free market brings. (Jameson 2000: 56)

The social resources that Jameson points to – communities, families and other social groups – continue to be relevant despite the pressures of mobility. As a result, locality is not lost in the tide of globalization, as we have described above in the summaries of numerous studies on the impact of globalization in various local communities; locality is instead transformed, changed, but reconstituted nonetheless.

This transformed locality does not look like our imagined past of small towns where everybody knows your name. Perhaps our own nostalgic memory of locality is itself cloudy, forgetting the inequality that kept people apart, the mobility that (while more limited in scale) has always been a part of communities and the indispensable interconnections between local communities that today, in an era of globalization, have become even more necessary. As social analysts, we have to be more conscious of this shifting terrain of locality.

Calls for 'localization' to combat 'globalization' (see the essays in Hines 2000)[9] are not necessarily the solution to the well-documented problems created by global capitalism. The focus on localization that we have suggested is not a dismissal of globalization. What we would suggest instead is what Michael Herzfeld (2001) has called 'the militant middle-ground' – a position that, in this case, does not dismiss either the global or the local, but instead looks carefully at how the global transforms the local and, correspondingly, how the local transforms the global. The local is neither disappearing nor is it solely being analytically preserved. Instead, people in different areas of the world, within different social contexts and historical experiences, are recasting the way that they relate to other people as they face (or create) the challenges presented by globalization.

Notes

1 McDonald's is currently testing this off-site order processing at experimental locations in the United States; Chinese fast food companies have also picked up on this new technology, and have similarly created off-site order centres that are connected to restaurants by computers.
2 See also Bestor (2004) and Watson (1997).
3 For additional reading on this topic, see Leitch (2003) and the articles in Wilk (2006).
4 Appadurai writes that in studies of global economic systems, 'The locality . . . becomes a fetish which disguises the globally dispersed forces that actually drive the production process' (Appadurai 1990: 307).
5 Aretxaga describes such social and political technologies in her definition of the state as 'phenomenological reality . . . produced through discourses and practices of power, produced in local encounters at the everyday level, and produced through the discourses of public culture . . . an open field with multiple boundaries and no institutional or geographical fixity' (2003: 398). Sassen (1996) also addresses these technologies as part of her analysis of sovereignty.

6 Such studies focus on Christian missionaries, Marian devotion, Sufi saints, Buddhist pilgrimages, religion-based social justice activities etc.; see for example Hutchinson (1987), Turner and Turner (1978), Naquin and Yu (1992), Huang and Weller (1998) and Caldwell (2004).

7 In this study, Askew specifically questions this gloss which puts into opposition *ngoma* and *dansi*, as part of her critique of the lingering effects of such binary oppositions as traditional and modern in contemporary social thought.

8 While changing money in a Japanese bank in 2002, Melissa Caldwell discovered that her inability to speak Japanese and the bank manager's limited English did not prevent them from having a lively discussion about the Boston Red Sox and Japanese athletes who had played for American Major League Baseball teams.

9 In brief, such localization manifestos as in Hines (2000) emphasize greater local community and national control of the economy, a focus on building more self-sustainable communities (instead of interdependent communities).

References

Abu-Lughod, L. 1993. 'Islam and public culture: The politics of Egyptian television serials', *Middle East Report*, 180, 25–30.

Alter, J. 1992. *The Wrestler's Body: Identity and Ideology in North India*. Berkeley: University of California Press.

Alter, J. 2000. 'Kabaddi, a national sport of India: The internationalism of nationalism and the foreignness of Indianness'. In N. Dyck (ed.), *Games, Sports, and Cultures*, 81–116. Oxford: Berg.

Anagnost, A. 2000. 'Scenes of misrecognition: Maternal citizenship in the age of transnational adoption', *Positions: East Asia Cultures Critique*, 8 (2), 389–421.

Anderson, B.R. 1983. *Imagined Communities: Reflections on the Origin and Spread of Nationalism*. London: Verso.

Appadurai, A. 1990. 'Disjuncture and difference in the global cultural economy', *Theory, Culture and Society*, 7, 295–310.

Appadurai, A. 1996. *Modernity at Large: Cultural Dimensions of Globalization*. Minneapolis: University of Minnesota Press.

Aretxaga, B. 2003. 'Maddening states', *Annual Review of Anthropology*, 32, 393–410.

Askew, K. 2003. 'As Plato duly warned: Music, politics, and social change in coastal East Africa', *Anthropological Quarterly*, 76 (4), 609–37.

Bairner, A. 2003. 'On thin ice? The Odyssey, the Giants, and the sporting transformation of Belfast', *American Behavioral Scientist*, 46 (11), 1519–32.

Barber, B.R. 1995. *Jihad vs. McWorld: How Globalism and Tribalism are Reshaping the World*. New York: Ballantine Books.

Barth, F. 1969. 'Introduction'. In F. Barth (ed.), *Ethnic Groups and Boundaries*, 9–38. Boston: Little and Brown.

Basch, L., Schiller, N.G. and Blanc, C.S. 1994. *Nations Unbound: Transnational Projects, Postcolonial Predicaments, and Deterritorialized Nation-States*. Basel: Gordon and Breach Publishers.

Bestor, T.C. 2004. *Tsukiji: The Fish Market at the Center of the World*. Berkeley, CA: University of California Press.

Bornstein, E. 2001. 'Child sponsorship, evangelism, and belonging in the work of world vision Zimbabwe', *American Ethnologist*, 28 (3), 595–622.

Brodwin, P. 2003. 'Pentecostalism in translation: Religion and the production of community in the Haitian diaspora', *American Ethnologist*, 30 (1), 85–101.

Brownell, S. 1995. *Training the Body for China: Sports in the Moral Order of the People's Republic*. Chicago: University of Chicago Press.

Caldwell, M.L. 2004. *Not by Bread Alone: Social Support in the New Russia*. Berkeley: University of California Press.

Caldwell, M.L. 2005a. 'A new age for religion in Russia's New Consumer Age', *Religion, State, and Society*, 33 (1), 43–58.

Caldwell, M.L. 2005b. 'Newness and loss in Moscow: Rethinking transformation in the postsocialist field', *The Journal of the Society for the Anthropology of Europe*, 5 (1), 2–7.

Caldwell, M.L. 2006. 'Tasting the worlds of yesterday and today: Culinary tourism and nostalgia foods in Post-Soviet Russia'. In R. Wilk (ed.), *Fast Food/Slow Food: The Political Economy of the Global Food System*, 97–112. Lanham, MD: Altamira Press.

Chen, N.N. 2003. *Breathing Spaces: Qigong, Psychiatry, and Healing in China*. New York: Columbia University Press.

Clifford, J. 1994. 'Diasporas', *Cultural Anthropology*, 9 (3), 302–38.

Clifford, J. 1997. 'Spatial practices: Fieldwork, travel, and the disciplining of anthropology'. In A. Gupta and J. Ferguson (eds), *Anthropological Locations: Boundaries and Grounds of a Field Science*, 185–222. Berkeley: University of California Press.

Constable, N. 2003. *Romance on a Global Stage: Pen Pals, Virtual Ethnography, and 'Mail Order' Marriages*. Berkeley: University of California Press.

De Certeau, M. 1984. *The Practice of Everyday Life*. Berkeley: University of California Press.

Eck, D. 1997. *On Common Ground: World Religions in America*. Multimedia CD. New York: Columbia University Press.

Eickelman, D.F. and Piscatori, J. 1996. *Muslim Politics*. Princeton, NJ: Princeton University Press.

Ekholm-Friedman, K. and Friedman, J. 1995. 'Global complexity and the simplicity of everyday life'. In D. Miller (ed.), *Worlds Apart: Modernity Through the Prism of the Local*, 134–68. London: Routledge.

Elling, A., De Knop, P. and Knoppers, A. 2001. 'The social integrative meaning of sport: A critical and comparative analysis of policy and practice in the Netherlands', *Sociology of Sport Journal*, 18, 414–34.

Escobar, A. 1994. 'Welcome to Cyberia: Notes on the anthropology of cyberculture', *Current Anthropology*, 35 (4), 211–31.

Evans-Pritchard, E.E. 1940. *The Nuer: A Description of the Modes of Livelihood and Political Institutions of a Nilotic People*. Oxford: Clarendon Press.

Fan, H. 1998. 'The Olympic Movement in China: Ideals, realities, and ambitions', *Culture, Sport, Society*, 1 (1), 149–68.

Featherstone, M. 1995. *Undoing Culture: Globalization, Postmodernism and Identity*. London: Sage Publications.

Florini, A.M. (ed.) 2000. *The Third Force: The Rise of Transnational Civil Society*. Tokyo and Washington: Japan Center for International Exchange and the Carnegie Endowment for International Peace.

Frechette, A. 2004. 'Sexuality, the media, and intercountry adoption: Recent changes in China–U.S. adoption policy', *Asian Anthropology*, 3, 129–51.

Freidberg, S. 2004. *Green Beans and Food Scares: Culture and Commerce in an Anxious Age*. Oxford: Oxford University Press.

Friedman, J. 1991. 'Narcissism, roots and postmodernity: The constitution of selfhood in the global crisis'. In S. Lash and J. Friedman (eds), *Modernity and Identity*, 331–66. Oxford: Blackwell.

Friedman, J. 1994. *Cultural Identity and Global Process*. London: Sage.

Fukuyama, F. 1995. 'The primacy of culture', *Journal of Democracy*, 6 (1), 7–14.

George, S. 2000. ' "Dirty nurses" and "men who play": Gender and class in transnational migration'. In M. Burawoy et al. (eds), *Global Ethnography: Forces, Connections, and Imaginations in a Postmodern World*, 144–74. Berkeley: University of California Press.

Gereffi, G. and Korzeniewicz, M. 1994. *Commodity Chains and Global Capitalism*. Westport, CT: Praeger.

Giddens, A. 1990. *The Consequences of Modernity*. Stanford, CA: Stanford University Press.

Giddens, A. 1991. *Modernity and Self-Identity*. Stanford, CA: Stanford University Press.

Giddens, A. 2000. *Runaway World: How Globalization Is Reshaping Our Lives*. New York: Routledge Press.

Gillette, M.B. 2000. *Between Mecca and Beijing: Modernization and Consumption among Urban Chinese Muslims*. Stanford, CA: Stanford University Press.

Ginsburg, F. 1994. 'Some thoughts on culture/media', *Visual Anthropology Review*, 10 (1), 136–41.

Girginov, V. 1998. 'Capitalist philosophy and communist practice: The transformation of Eastern European sport and the International Olympic Committee', *Culture, Sport, Society*, 1 (1), 118–48.

Guest, K. 2003. *God in Chinatown: Religion and Survival in New York's Evolving Immigrant Community*. New York: New York University Press.

Gupta, A. and Ferguson, J. 1997. 'Discipline and practice: "The field" as site, method, and location in anthropology'. In A. Gupta and J. Ferguson (eds), *Anthropological Locations: Boundaries and Grounds of a Field Science*, 1–46. Berkeley: University of California Press.

Haas, P. 1992. 'Introduction: Epistemic communities and international policy coordination', *International Organization*, 46 (1), 1–35.

Hakken, D. 1999. *Cyborgs@Cyberspace? An Ethnographer Looks to the Future*. New York: Routledge.

Harvey, D. 1990. *The Condition of Postmodernity: An Enquiry into the Origins of Cultural Change*. Cambridge, MA: Blackwell.

Hannerz, U. 1992. *Cultural Complexity: Studies in the Social Organization of Meaning*. New York: Columbia University Press.

Hannerz, U. 1996. *Transnational Connections: Culture, People, Places*. London: Routledge.

Herzfeld, M. 2001. *Anthropology: Theoretical Practice in Culture and Society*. Malden, MA: Blackwell.

Hines, C. (ed.) 2000. *Localization: A Global Manifesto*. London: Earthscan Publishing.

Ho, E. 2004. 'Empire through diasporic eyes: A view from the other boat', *Comparative Studies in Society and History*, 46 (2), 210–46.

Huang, J. and Weller, R. 1998. 'Merit and mothering: Women and social welfare in Taiwanese Buddhism', *Journal of Asian Studies*, 57 (2), 379–96.

Huntington, S. 2004. *Who Are We? The Challenges to America's National Identity*. New York: Simon & Schuster.

Hutchinson, W.R. 1987. *Errand to the World: American Protestant Thought and Foreign Missions*. Chicago: University of Chicago Press.

Ikels, C. 1996. *The Return of the God of Wealth: The Transition to a Market Economy in Urban China*. Stanford, CA: Stanford University Press.

Inda, J.X. and Rosaldo, R. 2002. 'Introduction: A world in motion'. In J.X. Inda and R. Rosaldo (eds), *The Anthropology of Globalization: A Reader*, 1–34. Malden, MA: Blackwell.

Jackson, S. and Andrews, D. 1999. 'The globalist of them all: The "everywhere man" Michael Jordan and American popular culture in postcolonial New Zealand'. In R.R. Sands (ed.), *Anthropology, Sport, and Culture*, 99–117. Westport, CT: Bergin and Garvey.

Jameson, F. 2000. 'Globalization and political strategy', *New Left Review*, 4 (July/August), 49–68.

Kearney, M. 1995. 'The local and the global: The anthropology of globalization and transnationalism', *Annual Review of Anthropology*, 24, 547–65.

King, R., and Craig, T.J. 2002. 'Asia and global popular culture: The view from He Yong garbage dump'. In T.J. Craig and R. King (eds), *Global Goes Local: Popular Culture in Asia*, 3–11. Vancouver: University of British Columbia Press.

Klein, A. 1997. *Baseball on the Border: A Tale of Two Laredos*. Princeton, NJ: Princeton University Press.

Klein, A. 2000. 'Latinizing Fenway Park: A cultural critique of the Boston Red Sox, their fans, and the media', *Sociology of Sport Journal*, 17, 403–22.

Korzeniewicz, M. 2000. 'Commodity chains and marketing strategies: Nike and the global athletic footwear industry'. In F.J. Lechner and J. Boli (eds), *The Globalization Reader*, 155–66. Oxford: Blackwell.

Leitch, A. 2003. 'Slow food and the politics of pork fat: Italian food and European identity', *Ethnos*, 68 (4), 437–62.

Levitt, P. 2001. *The Transnational Villagers*. Berkeley: University of California Press.

Levitt, P. and Schiller, N.G. 2004. 'Conceptualizing simultaneity: A transnational social field perspective on society', *International Migration Review*, 38 (3), 1002–39.

Linger, D.T. 2001. *No One Home: Brazilian Selves Remade in Japan*. Stanford, CA: Stanford University Press.

Lozada, E.P. 1999. 'A hakka community in cyberspace: Diasporic ethnicity and the Internet'. In S. Cheung (ed.), *On the South China Track*, 148–82. Hong Kong: Chinese University of Hong Kong Press.

Lozada, E.P. 2001. *God Aboveground: Catholic Church, Postsocialist State, and Transnational Processes in a Chinese Village*. Stanford, CA: Stanford University Press.

MacAloon, J.J. 1981. *This Great Symbol: Pierre de Coubertin and the Origins of the Modern Olympic Games*. Chicago: University of Chicago Press.

McCarthy Brown, K. 2001. *Mama Lola: A Vodou Priestess in Brooklyn*. Berkeley: University of California Press.

MacClancy, J. 1996. 'Sport, identity, and ethnicity'. In J. MacClancy (ed.), *Sport, Identity, and Ethnicity*, 1–20. Oxford: Berg.

McCreery, J. 1997. 'Finding meaning in the muddle: Adapting global strategies to advertising in Japan', *City and Society*, 9 (1), 241–54.

Mankekar, P. 2002. '"India shopping": Indian grocery stores and transnational configurations of belonging', *Ethnos*, 67 (1), 75–98.

Marx, K. 1978. 'On imperialism in India'. In R.C. Tucker (ed.), *The Marx-Engels Reader*, 653–64. New York: W.W. Norton.

Mazzarella, W. 2003. '"Very Bombay": Contending with the global in an Indian advertising agency', *Cultural Anthropology*, 18 (1), 33–71.

Meyer, B. 2004. '"Praise the Lord": Popular cinema and Pentecostalite style in Ghana's new public sphere', *American Ethnologist*, 31 (1), 92–110.

Messner, M.A. 2002. *Taking the Field: Women, Men, and Sports*. Minneapolis: University of Minnesota Press.

Miller, D. 1995. *Acknowledging Consumption*. London: Routledge.

Miller, D. and Slater, D. 2000. *The Internet: An Ethnographic Approach*. Oxford: Berg.

Mintz, S. 1985. *Sweetness and Power: The Place of Sugar in Modern History*. New York: Viking.

Moore, P. 2000. 'Soccer and the politics of culture in Western Australia'. In N. Dyck (ed.), *Games, Sports, and Cultures*, 117–34. Oxford: Berg.

Morris, A. 2000. ' "To make the four hundred million move": The Late Qing Dynasty origins of modern Chinese sport and physical culture', *Comparative Studies in Society and History*, 42 (4), 876–906.

Nagle, R. 1997. *Claiming the Virgin: The Broken Promise of Liberation Theology*. New York: Routledge.

Naquin, S. and Yu, C.-F. 1992. *Pilgrims and Sacred Sites in China*. Berkeley: University of California Press.

Nye, J.S. 2002. *The Paradox of American Power: Why the World's Only Superpower Can't Go It Alone*. Oxford: Oxford University Press.

Olwig, K.F. 1997. 'Cultural sites: Sustaining a home in a deterritorialized world'. In K.F. Olwig and K. Hastrup (eds), *Siting Culture: the Shifting Anthropological Object*, 17–38. London: Routledge.

Ong, A. 1999. *Flexible Citizenship: The Cultural Logics of Transnationality*. Durham, NC: Duke University Press.

Petrini, C. 2001. *Slow Food: Collected Thoughts on Taste, Tradition, and the Honest Pleasures of Food*. White River Junction: Chelsea Green.

Putnam, R.D. 2000. *Bowling Alone: The Collapse and Revival of American Community*. New York: Simon & Schuster.

Rai, A. 1995. 'India on-line: Electronic bulletin boards and the construction of a diasporic Hindu identity', *Diaspora*, 4 (1), 31–58.

Riain, S.Ó. 2000. 'Net-working for a living: Irish software developers in the global workplace'. In M. Burawoy et al. (eds), *Global Ethnography: Forces, Connections, and Imaginations in a Postmodern World*, 175–202. Berkeley: University of California Press.

Ritzer, G. 2004. *The Globalization of Nothing*. Thousand Oaks, CA: Pine Forge Press.

Robertson, R. 1992. *Globalization, Social Theory and Global Culture*. London: Sage Publications.

Rudolph, S.H. and Piscatori, J. (eds) 1997. *Transnational Religion and Fading States*. Boulder, CO: Westview Press.

Sands, R.R. 1999. 'Anthropology and sport'. In R.R. Sands (ed.), *Anthropology, Sport, and Culture*, 3–13. Westport, CO: Bergin and Garvey.

Sassen, S. 1996. *Losing Control? Sovereignty in an Age of Globalization*. New York: Columbia University Press.

Scheper-Hughes, N. 2000. 'The global traffic in human organs', *Current Anthropology*, 41 (2), 191–224.

Scherer, J. 2001. 'Globalization and the construction of local particularities: A case study of the Winnipeg Jets', *Sociology of Sport Journal*, 18, 205–30.

Shukert, D. 2002. 'Culture, nationalism, and "saving face": Sport and discrimination in modern Japan', *Culture, Sport, Society*, 5 (1), 71–85.

Silverstein, P.A. 2000. 'Sporting faith: Islam, soccer, and the French nation-state', *Social Text*, 18 (4), 25–53.

Small, C. 1997. *Voyages: From Tongan Villages to American Suburbs*. Ithaca, NY: Cornell University Press.

Stewart, K. 1988. 'Nostalgia – a polemic', *Cultural Anthropology*, 3 (3), 227–41.

Stokes, M. 1996. ' "Strong as a Turk": Power, performance, and representation in Turkish wrestling'. In J. MacClancy (ed.), *Sport, Identity, and Ethnicity*, 21–41. Oxford: Berg.

Tomlinson, J. 1999. *Globalization and Culture*. Chicago: University of Chicago Press.

Trouillot, M.-R. 2001. 'The anthropology of the state in the age of globalization: Close encounters of the deceptive kind', *Current Anthropology*, 42 (1), 125–38.

Tsing, A. 2000. 'The global situation', *Cultural Anthropology*, 15 (3), 327–60.

Tunina, O. and Stryker, R. 2001. 'When local myths meet global reality: Preparing Russia's abandoned children for international adoption', *Kroeber Anthropological Society Papers*, 86, 143–9.

Turner, V.W. and Turner, E. 1978. *Image and Pilgrimage in Christian Culture: Anthropological Perspectives*. New York: Columbia University Press.

Tyrrell, H. 1999. 'Bollywood, versus Hollywood: Battle of the dream factories'. In T. Skelton and T. Allen (eds), *Culture and Global Change*, 260–73. London: Routledge.

Verdery, K. 1999. *The Political Lives of Dead Bodies: Reburial and Postsocialist Change*. New York: Columbia University Press.

Volkman, T.A. 2003. 'Embodying Chinese culture: Transnational adoption in North America'. *Social Text*, 21 (1), 29–55.

Wang, J. 2001. 'Culture as leisure and culture as capital', *Positions*, 9 (1), 69–104.

Watanabe, J.M. 1990. 'From Saints to Shibboleths: Image, structure, and identity in Maya religious syncretism', *American Ethnologist*, 17 (1), 131–50.

Watson, J.L. 1975. *Emigration and the Chinese Lineage: The Mans in Hong Kong and London*. Berkeley: University of California Press.

Watson, J.L. 1997. 'Introduction: Transnationalism, localization, and fast foods in East Asia'. In J.L. Watson (ed.), *Golden Arches East: McDonald's in East Asia*, 1–38. Stanford, CA: Stanford University Press.

Watson, J.L. 2004. 'Presidential address: Virtual kinship, real estate, and diaspora formation – the man lineage revisited', *Journal of Asian Studies*, 63 (4), 893–910.

Wilk, R. 1999. '"Real Belizean Food": Building local identity in the transnational Caribbean', *American Anthropologist*, 101 (2), 244–55.

Wilk, R. 2002. 'Food and nationalism: The origins of "Belizean Food"'. In W. Belasco and P. Scranton (eds), *Food Nations: Selling Taste in Consumer Societies*, 67–89. New York: Routledge.

Wilk, R. 1995. 'Consumer goods as dialogue about development: Colonial time and television time in Belize'. In J. Friedman (ed.), *Consumption and Identity*, 97–118. London: Routledge.

Wilk, R. (ed.) 2006. *Fast Food/Slow Food: The Political Economy of the Global Food System*. Lanham, MD: Altamira Press.

Wolf, E. 1982. *Europe and the People Without History*. Berkeley: University of California Press.

Wong, C.H.-Y. and McDonogh, G.W. 2001. 'The mediated metropolis: Anthropological issues in cities and mass communication', *American Anthropologist*, 103 (1), 96–111.

Woo, W.T., Sachs, J.D. and Schwab, K. 2000. *The Asian Financial Crisis: Lessons for a Resilient Asia*. Cambridge, MA: MIT Press.

Worsley, P. 1970. *The Trumpet Shall Sound: A Study of 'Cargo Cults' in Melanesia*. London: Paladin.

Yergin, D. and Stanislaw, J. 2002. *The Commanding Heights: The Battle for the World Economy*. New York: Free Press.

Chapter 27

Public Health in a Globalizing World: Challenges and Opportunities

FARNOOSH HASHEMIAN AND DEREK YACH

There is a rapidly growing body of literature on the topic of globalization and its implications for human health. The impetus of this chapter was to provide an overview on current debates in global health and to contribute to a fuller understanding of the challenges and opportunities of globalization on health. This chapter describes the important features of the globalization process that are linked to population health. The present framework is developed in the following steps: the concept of globalization and a conceptual model for globalization and population health; global economic and health inequities; the impact of globalization on human nutrition; changes in patterns of disease; human mobility and knowledge disparities; human security; and finally there is a discussion on global governance of health.

Globalization can be defined as an array of processes that are modifying the nature of humans' interactions across spatial, temporal and cognitive boundaries (Lee 2002). According to McBride and Wiseman (2000) globalization 'involves a range of contradictory and contested processes which provide new possibilities as well as threats to communities concerned with promoting relationships of diversity, solidarity and sustainability'.

Globalization has an impact on four key areas of public health: in reshaping the broad determinants of health, health status and outcomes, and healthcare financing and service provision (Lee and Yack 2007). In the last few years there has been a growing body of literature on the importance of globalization for health. In this regard, several researchers have developed frameworks that delineate the pathways between globalization and health. One of the most comprehensive frameworks provided by David Woodward and colleagues at the World Health Organization (WHO) illustrates a conceptual framework for systematically analysing and assessing the health effects of globalization (Figure 27.1). Woodward et al. (2001) contend that economic globalization has been the fundamental driving force behind the overall process of globalization over the last two decades.

Based on their model several driving and constraining forces influence economic globalization; including technological advances, political powers, economic

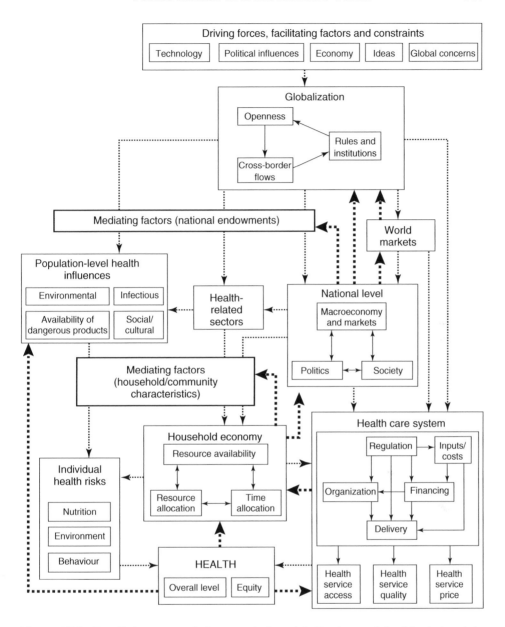

Figure 27.1 Detailed conceptual framework for globalization and health designed by Woodward et al. (1999)
Source: Woodward et al. (2001).

pressures, changing ideas and increasing social and environmental concerns. Further, this framework highlights five main pathways from globalization to health which have a circular relationship. The three direct channels are the effect of globalization on health systems and policies; through world markets; and the effects on population level health influences. Examples of these direct influences are the regulation of the General Agreement on Trade in Services (GATS), the effects of the Agreement on Trade-Related Aspects of Intellectual Property Rights (TRIPs) on pharmaceutical prices and mutual vulnerability to international transfer of risks such as infectious diseases, unregulated distribution of drugs or unhealthy lifestyles marketing. In their framework Woodward et al. speculate that the indirect influences of globalization operate through national economies and policies on the health sector and population risks. These indirect influences include the effects of globalization on fiscal constraints, on the availability of resources for public expenditure, on health and on livelihoods and income distribution. Woodward and his colleagues hope that this framework would serve as a basis for synthesizing existing relevant research, identifying gaps in knowledge and ultimately developing national and international policies that would benefit health.

GLOBAL INCOME AND HEALTH DISPARITIES

Economic growth and the dissemination of technology innovations and human rights values have enhanced life expectancy and quality of living worldwide. Increased literacy rates, socio-economic change, improved nutrition, infectious diseases control and public health initiatives have all contributed to the improvement of basic health indices. Nevertheless, the opportunities and rewards of globalization has spread unequally and exacerbated the economic and health disparities within and across nations. In fact, OECD countries, which comprise 19 per cent of the global population, enjoy 71 per cent of global trade in goods and services, 58 per cent of foreign direct investment and 91 per cent of all Internet users (UNDP 1999).

Patterns of global inequalities suggest that the division between developing and developed countries have endured and potentially worsened over the last 15 years. The Human Development Index (HDI) is a standard means of measuring human well-being and covers income, education and health. Based on the 2005 UNDP report, albeit showing overall progress in HDI across all developing regions, many countries suffer unprecedented reversals in measurements for income, education and health. According to this report, 18 countries from sub-Saharan Africa and the former Soviet Union region with a combined population of 460 million people had a lower HDI score in 2003 than in 1990. This reversal in sub-Saharan Africa is a production of economic stagnation, slow progress in education and the spread of infectious diseases, especially HIV/AIDS. The economic disruption that followed the fall of the Soviet Union and the catastrophic drop in life expectancy and high incidence of chronic diseases are the two drivers for HDI ranking decline in the former Soviet Union region (UNDP 2005).

Global forces have been associated with increased life expectancies on the aggregate but have tended to widen economic disparities. It is estimated that today approximately 75 per cent of the world's wealth is owned by just 25 per cent of the world's population. This profound division of wealth cannot merely be understood by differences between countries. Concentrated pockets of wealth and poverty exist in both industrialized and developing nations. Brazil is currently experiencing one of the largest income gaps in South America, where the per capita income of the most affluent 10 per cent of the population is 32 times that of the poorest 40 per cent (UNDP 2005). Further, evidence shows that poverty and enormous disparity of wealth in the United States is increasing (DeNavas et al. 2004). During the past three decades while the wages of low-skilled workers have been stagnant, income of the richest 1 per cent of Americans has nearly doubled from about 8 per cent in the late 1970s to about 15 per cent today (DeNavas et al. 2004). Moreover, public health indicators in the United States are significantly below those for other developed countries despite the fact that the United States has virtually the highest GDP per capita and highest healthcare spending in the world. Wide racial and ethnic disparities in income, education, health insurance and access to care explain poorer health outcomes in the United States compared to other industrialized countries. More striking is the fact that the infant mortality rate has been rising in the United States for the past 5 years. This rate is twice among African Americans compared to whites and the infant death rate among African Americans in Washington DC is higher than in the Indian state of Kerala (UNDP 2005).

The relationship between good health and economic prosperity is almost certainly bidirectional (Wagstaff 2002). Poverty affects health by limiting access to health services, education, sanitation and adequate nutrition and housing, but poor health also adversely impacts sustained economic growth through reduction in worker productivity, annual incomes of society, the lifetime incomes of individuals and prospects for foreign direct investments. However, the relationships between economic growth and health are complex. Once minimum per capita incomes have been achieved, human health appears to be determined by other factors than national wealth (Hales et al. 1999). For instance, Anand and Ravallion (1993) on the basis of inter-country comparisons found that life expectancy has a significant positive correlation with GNP per head, but that this relationship works mainly through the impact of GNP on reduction of income poverty and through the increase in government expenditure on healthcare. The success of nations such as Sri Lanka, China, Costa Rica and the state of Kerela in India in increasing survival chances and longevity of their populations illustrates that poor countries can achieve improvements in healthcare and life expectancy with more public-oriented policies and strategies in health and basic education (Sen 1999; UNDP 1999).

Developing nations share a disproportionate burden of mortality and morbidity, much of which can be inexpensively prevented or treated. Of the total global burden of disease, 90 per cent is concentrated in low and middle-income countries, where only 10 per cent of healthcare expenditure is spent (Murray and Lopez 1997a). The average life expectancy gap between a low-income country and a high-income country is still 19 years. Health and education provision has improved in the developing countries that have been more actively involved in the globalization process; in Brazil, Egypt and Malaysia, for example, infant mortality was reduced by an average of more than 30 per cent during the 1990s, compared with an average decline of 12 per cent for all developing countries. However, in the least-developed countries (with a combined population of 2 billion), overall economic growth has declined and poverty has been rising, which are critical considerations in the context of public health and global development.

Overcoming the immense economic and health disparities is the greatest challenge of our time. Practical solutions exist (Sacks 2005); the first step is to create a climate of unacceptability for the global inequalities.

GLOBALIZATION, NUTRITION, AND FOOD SECURITY
AND SAFETY

The phenomenon of globalization is having a major impact on food systems and human nutrition around the world. Trade, marketing, media, urbanization, global disparities and increasing technologies can play either a positive or a negative role in food security and safety. These issues are expanded upon here.

Hunger and malnutrition are part of the daily struggle of more than 850 million people – one-sixth of the developing world's population. Food security has three important dimensions: adequate availability of food supplies; assured access to sufficient food for all individuals; and its proper utilization to provide a proper and balanced diet (FAO/WHO 1992). Although there has been a slow decline in the number of people with insufficient food, in the worst-affected regions – sub-Saharan Africa and southern Asia – the number of hungry people has increased by tens of millions (UN 2005). Food security has been defined as access by all people at all times to the food needed for a healthy life. Growing populations, poor agricultural productivity and conflicts have been the main reasons for food shortages in these regions. In Africa alone, hunger kills more than all the continent's infectious diseases – HIV and AIDS, malaria and tuberculosis (TB) – combined (Commission for Africa 2005). Over 150 million children under age five in the developing world are underweight, including almost half the children in southern Asia and one of three children in sub-Saharan Africa. Childhood underweight is internationally recognized as an important public health problem and its devastating effects on human performance, health and survival are well established. Adults who survive malnutrition as children are less physically and intellectually productive and suffer from more chronic illness and disability (Murray and Lopez 1997b). Further, their ability to be productive and assure good nutrition for their children could be compromised, perpetuating a vicious cycle.

Scientific evidence demonstrates a compelling link between generational and intergenerational nutritional status at different stages of the life-cycle. Low birth weight babies face increased risk of dying in infancy, of stunted physical and cognitive growth during childhood, of reduced livelihood capacity and earnings as adults, of being parents to infants with intrauterine growth retardation and low birth weight, and of increased risk of chronic disease in later life (UN Standing Committee on Nutrition 2000). Such life-cycle and intergenerational links pose a tremendous need for the formulation of sustained and long-term policies and programmes.

According to the UN World Food Programme, only 8 per cent of hunger victims die in dramatic, high-profile emergencies. Despite available early warnings systems in place that could avert food crises in the world, evidence shows that international donor response only gains momentum when the nutrition condition becomes a crisis and after the media sheds light on the images of malnourished children. For example, millions of people that were affected by chronic malnutrition in Niger since 1998, had to wait for heavy and sensational media attention to arrive. Moreover, in industrialized countries aid policies to combat famine and hunger have benefited donors' business interests rather than delivering aid in an efficient and effective manner. For example, a recent paper, *US Food AID: Time to Get it Right* (Murphy and McAfee 2005), finds that US expenditures (the world's biggest food donor) in combating famine and hunger are highly inefficient. Based on this report, the majority of aid money is spent in buying crops from US farmers and shipping them to famine-affected countries. Strikingly, only one dollar's worth of food from every two dollars spent actually reaches a recipient. Wealthy countries have taken action to make the systems of food aid cost-effective. For instance, in the United States, although currently road-blocked by Congress, the Bush Administration is supporting a provision to food aid policies to 'un-tie' the US food aid (Dugger 2005).

Halving poverty and hunger by 2015 is the main aim of the Millennium Development Goals. Evidence shows that rapid progress towards massive and sustainable hunger reductions can be made by applying a 'Twin-Track Strategy' (FAO 2004) that confronts both causes and consequences of extreme poverty and hunger. This approach combines agricultural production and overall rural development promotion with enhancing direct and immediate access to food for vulnerable populations.

One of the most important aspects of globalization with implications for nutrition and food security is trade. As argued by many scholars, and described below, increasing trade plays a major role in the rapid shift of dietary and activity patterns and food intake, resulting in a growing epidemic of chronic diseases (Beaglehole and Yach 2003). In many developing countries, an increasing coexistence of under-nutrition and over-nutrition has created a 'double nutritional burden'.

There has been increasing research on assessing the important health effects of being chronically energy deficient (CED) or overweight (body mass index [BMI] values below 18.5 kg/m^2 and above 25 kg/m^2 respectively). In developing countries, evidence shows that individuals with a BMI below 18.5 kg/m^2 have a higher risk for mortality and morbidity. A recent study among Nigerian men and women has shown that mortality rates among CED individuals who are mildly, moderately and severely underweight are respectively 40, 140 and 150 per cent greater than rates among non-CED individuals (Rotimi et al. 1999). At the other end of the spectrum, being overweight is associated with an increased prevalence of cardiovascular risk factors such as hypertension, high blood lipid concentrations and diabetes mellitus (Seidell 2005). Studies show that risk of mortality and morbidity increases for both men and women who have a high BMI (Anonymous 2000; Stevens et al. 1998). Further, ample studies have documented that in Latin America, North Africa and the Middle East, and South-east Asia, more adults are overweight than underweight (Monteiro et al. 2000b; Popkin and Doak 1998). The ratio of under-nutrition to over-nutrition in a population has shifted dramatically in the past several decades in many countries (Monteiro et al. 2000a). Research from Latin America, China and India has shown that the burden of obesity is becoming greater among the poorest segments of the population (Monteiro et al. 2000b). A Brazilian study concluded that obesity and related chronic diseases are likely to increase in countries where maternal and child malnutrition coexists with urbanization and economic growth.

In fact, there is strong evidence that correlates foetal under-nutrition with chronic diseases in adulthood independent of adult risk factors such as social class and unhealthy lifestyles. Research shows that obesity, type-2 diabetes and hypertension in young adults, especially in low-middle income countries, are associated with lower birth weights and childhood stunting (Schroeder et al. 1999). David Barker and his colleagues at the University of Southampton explain this phenomenon in the Foetal Origins of Disease Hypothesis (Lynch and Smith 2005). The Barker Hypothesis suggests that foetal under-nutrition at critical periods of development *in utero* and during infancy leads to permanent changes in body structure and metabolism. It has been argued that these changes are adaptations for foetal survival in an inadequate nutritional environment, and that these changes persist postnatally, contributing to adult chronic disease when the individual is exposed to nutrimental affluence lifestyle shifts.

The impact of certain aspects of globalization, especially trade, has been thoroughly discussed by Diaz-Bonilla and his colleagues (2001). Trade is an essential component in reducing food insecurity and human under-nutrition by fostering economic growth and by increasing exports of agricultural and food products. This is particularly important since most of the world's food insecure rely on agricultural commodities for income. However, the expansion of trade in goods and services, along with technological advances and export subsidies in industrialized countries, have depressed world prices and resulted in sharp reductions from 20 per cent to about 6 per cent of exports in food income for all developing countries (see Lee and Yach 2007). This is an especially important issue for the poorer countries since agriculture accounts for 70 per cent of employment and generates over one-third of the gross domestic product. Elimination of subsidies and protectionism in industrialized countries along with fair access to the rich countries' markets would lead to economic gains for developing countries (FAO 2003).

Another aspect of globalization related to increasing trade is the development of uniform regulations for food safety across countries that influence production, processing, transportation and preparation of food products. Poor food safety control in international trade has raised important public health concerns. Food safety has been a long-term concern in the developing countries, where almost 2 million children die every year from diarrhoea, most of it caused by microbiologically contaminated food and water. In industrialized countries increasing episodes of food poisoning associated with the distribution and use of farm products have led to growing concerns for food safety (Diaz-Bonilla et al. 2001). For example, bovine spongiform encephalopathy (BSE) and other food-borne infections are becoming increasing threats to the food industry in many countries. As food safety concerns heighten, the use of food safety as a trade restriction against products from developing countries may become a more pressing concern. Exports of food commodities from developing countries now need to ensure the quality and safety requirements of importing countries and the demanding food safety standards of the Codex Alimentarius Commission (CAC) (Kaferstein et al. 1997). CAC objectives are to ensure the quality and safety of the world's food supply and fair practice in food trade. However, in developing countries food safety concerns are not as prominent as developed nations and farmers may not be able to meet the standards because they lack adequate institutions and infrastructure. Therefore, elevating standards of food safety may mean a trade-off between food safety and food security in developing countries.

DISEASES OF GLOBALIZATION[1]

Globalization has contributed to the rise in chronic diseases rates and risks in many complex ways. Changes in lifestyles of populations due to urbanization, globalization, nutrition transition and economic development have a direct and rapid impact on the health of individuals and communities.

The term 'health transition', which encompasses demographic and epidemiological transitions, has been employed to describe the recent social, behavioural and cultural changes that accompany mortality decline and improved health in populations (Caldwell 1993). The demographic transition describes the change from high fertility and mortality rates to low fertility and mortality rates that occurs as part of the economic development of a country from an agricultural to a manufacturing economy (Montgomery 2005). Further, the rapidly changing age structures of many populations and progress in medical sciences have brought a general improvement in health and a shift in causes of death from infectious diseases to chronic diseases such as cancer, heart disease and diabetes (Omran 1971). The current health transition is imposing a double burden of disease, disability and premature death on developing countries afflicted by both old-world problems of under-nutrition and infectious diseases and the new-world challenges of chronic diseases (WHO 2002). For example, in many low and middle income countries, ischaemic heart disease and cerebrovascular disease are among the leading three or four causes of death along with infectious diseases (Leeder et al. 2003). Further, approximately 171 million people are affected by diabetes, of which two-thirds live in the developing world (Marshall 2004).

The current burden of chronic diseases reflects the cumulative exposure to past risks to health. The future burden of disease will be determined by current population exposures to the major risk factors such as tobacco, diet/nutrition, physical activity and alcohol. According to Yach and Beaglehole (2004) the increase in worldwide production, promotion and marketing of tobacco, alcohol and other products with adverse effects on population health status has globalized chronic diseases risks. Further, they indicate that a significant portion of all global marketing of high sugar and high fat fast foods, cigarettes and alcoholic beverages is now targeted at children under the age of 14 in order to foster brand-loyalty among pre-teens and teenagers. The projections show that if investments in primary and secondary preventions of chronic diseases are not scaled up; 5 million people in 2020 in developing countries would face death, a year in which the number of deaths from infectious diseases and related conditions would equal the number of deaths due to chronic diseases (Leeder et al. 2003).

Yach and Beaglehole (2004) argue that 'policy makers and the donor community have neglected the rapidly growing burden of chronic diseases' even though they are the major cause of death and ill-health in most of the developing as well as the developed countries of the world. The 2001 global assessment of national capacity of the 167 countries for prevention and control of chronic diseases found that a substantial proportion of countries have no policies or plans to combat non-communicable diseases (NCDs)/cardiovascular diseases (CVDs) despite the growing

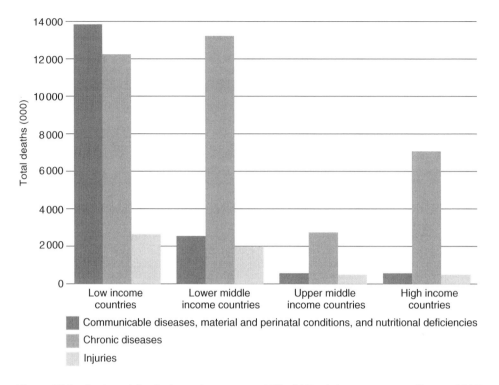

Figure 27.2 Projected deaths by major cause and World Bank income group, all ages, 2005
Source: WHO (2005a).

epidemic of chronic diseases (Alwan et al. 2001). In fact, less than half of these countries reported having no surveillance systems for the major NCDs. These findings are the reflection of the fact that NCD is still given low priority in national health policy planning.

The global health agenda is still dominated by the traditional perception that infectious diseases need to be tackled before chronic diseases. Strong beliefs persist that chronic diseases are diseases of wealthy nations, ageing populations and 'lifestyle', which was chosen by the individual's decisions (WHO 2003a).

The reality is quite different. Despite the common belief that chronic diseases mainly affect high-income countries, the 2005 WHO report 'Preventing Chronic Diseases: A Vital Investment' demonstrates that currently, 80 per cent of chronic disease-related deaths occur in low and middle income countries (see Figure 27.2). Other evidence shows that the probability of a man or woman dying from a chronic disease is higher in sub-Saharan Africa and other developing regions than in developed countries (Murray and Lopez 1997a). Furthermore, in low and middle-income countries, the incidence of and death from chronic diseases occur at younger ages compared to high-income countries. Most important risks of chronic diseases are a function of behaviour, culture, consumption, trade and economic policy (Leeder et al. 2003). Epidemics of chronic diseases will increasingly burden the poor (Yach and Hawkes 2004), and more importantly, the rising costs of clinical care for those with chronic diseases will adversely affect the ability of less-developed countries to deal with the unfinished agenda of infectious diseases. The shift from acute infectious diseases towards chronic illnesses entailed a change in focus from the transmission of pathogens to concerns about lifestyles, health-related behaviours and preventative healthcare.

As a consequence of the epidemiological transitions, health systems led by primary care are now required that can provide a life-span approach to health promotion and disease prevention for all common diseases, irrespective of their origin. A healthcare system based on primary healthcare will address both sides of the burden and will be in consonance with the Alma-Ata principles[2] of equity, universal access, community participation and intersectoral approaches to health improvement.

In order to improve health globally more emphasis is needed on defining and assessing risks and implementing prevention intervention for chronic diseases.

If prevention and control interventions for chronic diseases are not developed, an estimated 388 million people will die in the next 10 years (WHO 2005a). Increasing scientific evidence indicates that prevention of chronic diseases is possible in a cost-effective manner when sustained actions are directed at both individual and institutional levels (WHO 2005a). It is estimated that cost-effective and inexpensive prevention, such as healthy diet, regular physical activity and avoidance of tobacco use, could avoid 80 per cent of heart disease, stroke and type-2 diabetes and 40 per cent of cancer. The developing world needs to give greater emphasis to prevention of the adverse health consequences of the shifting of lifestyles. Further, implementing established global and local norms on control of tobacco products (as spelt out in the WHO Framework Convention for Tobacco Control, 2003c), prevention of alcohol abuse, regulating nutrition policy and policies to promote physical activity will significantly enhance the global governance of chronic disease control.

BORDERLESS DISEASES

A considerable body of literature has evaluated the implications of globalization on infectious diseases risk. According to WHO estimates, infectious diseases are responsible for the death of over 14 million people every year, with the vast majority of them occurring in developing economies. The causes range from poor sanitary and nutrition conditions to lack of public health infrastructure and financial means for pharmaceutical drugs.

The increase in human mobility has facilitated transmission of knowledge, ideas and values, but also microbiological agents. Based on the WHO report, 35 new and enhanced microbial diseases have been recorded in the last 20 years (WHO 2003b). According to the 2003 US Institute of Medicine (IOM) report a complex combination of factors such as breakdown of public health measures, global climate change, human demographic and behaviour, global mobility, war and famine, lack of political will and poverty have contributed to the rapid emergence and spread of infectious diseases.

The recent Severe Acute Respiratory Syndrome (SARS) and threat of Highly Pathogenic Avian Influenza virus (HPAI) outbreaks demonstrate the potential of rapid spread of the new infectious diseases and a looming threat for a global pandemic. Although the outbreak of SARS did not cause a significant disease burden in the short term, it demonstrated the emergency management capacity of public health systems worldwide. SARS showed the crucial role of WHO in governing global health and the incompetency of the International Health Regulations, as well as the national public health systems of the affected countries (Lee and Yach 2007).

The recent ability of avian influenza virus strains to 'jump species' and produce fatal diseases in humans has produced worldwide concern. Since the first outbreak in North Korea in 1997, avian flu has infected 91 people and killed 42 of them (WHO 2005b). If this virus develops the capacity to be transmitted from human to human, a pandemic of the magnitude of the 1918 Spanish flu, which killed 50 million people in 18 months, could occur (WHO 2005c). Emergence of the avian flu may necessitate significant restructuring of poultry production and could have a severe financial impact on the affected countries, an estimated cost as high as $30 billion (BBC 2005). Several measures can reduce the global public health risks that could arise from large outbreaks of avian flu in birds. An immediate response in halting the spread of epidemic in the poultry population can reduce opportunities for human exposure to the virus. Further, workers in poultry productions must be protected by appropriate prevention measures (WHO 2005c).

Over the last 20 years, new and re-emerging diseases such as HIV/AIDS and TB have contributed to a significant burden of infectious diseases worldwide. Today, *M. tuberculosis* infects one-third of the world's population, causing 1.84 million deaths in 2000. Further, the epidemic of HIV/AIDS has posed immense challenges for controlling TB worldwide. It is estimated that one-third of the 40 million people living with HIV/AIDS worldwide are co-infected with TB. People with HIV are up to 50 times more likely to develop TB in a given year than HIV-negative people (Corbett et al. 2003). The WHO response to the lethal combination of HIV and TB was forming the 'Two diseases, one patient' strategy. The integrated TB and HIV care objectives are to create collaborations between TB/HIV programmes, to reduce the burden of TB among people living with HIV/AIDS and to reduce the burden of HIV among TB patients.

The magnitude of the global HIV/AIDS epidemic is staggering (UNAIDS/WHO 2004). Globally an estimated 39.4 million people are living with HIV, including the 4.9 million people who acquired the virus in 2004. The global AIDS epidemic killed 3.1 million people, with over 2 million of them living in sub-Saharan Africa in the past year. The epidemic has a young woman's face, as it disproportionately affects women and girls in increasing numbers. Women and girls make up almost 57 per cent of all people infected with HIV in sub-Saharan Africa, where a striking 76 per cent of young people living with HIV are female. The vulnerability of women and girls to HIV infection stems not simply from biological factors, but from pervasive societal disempowerment and structural violence.

Only strategies that integrate HIV/AIDS response as part of the delivery of health, education and social protection systems, and take gender and power relationships into account will be able to combat the global scourge of HIV (Commission for Africa 2005).

An issue of global health concern is the emergence of antibiotic resistance as a key challenge to infectious diseases control efforts. Most resistant strains of infectious diseases emerge in areas with high poverty rates, low surveillance capacity, poor access to consistent treatment due to limited medical services, and political unrest. Emergence of multidrug-resistant tuberculosis and resistance among common pathogens in developing countries (e.g. malaria, pneumonia, salmonella and leishmaniasis) threatens to undermine many healthcare advances (WHO 2001). Moreover, it has posed a threat to security and political stability of some regions (this issue has been stressed by a report from the US Central Intelligence Agency [CIA 2005]).

In a borderless world, the emergence and re-emergence of infectious diseases pose a threat to individual, national and global security. Evidently, an effective response to the international mutual vulnerability must be a global one.

MIGRATION AND GLOBAL RACE FOR KNOWLEDGE

Advancement of information and communication technology has played a leading role in accelerating the processes of globalization and changing economies and societies. The production, dissemination and use of knowledge have become a vital source for enhancing economic growth, job creation, evidence-based policy development and welfare (OECD 1996). Thus, knowledge and the dissemination of information is a crucial factor for sustainable development in today's global economy. However, the growing disparities between the world's rich and poor are reflected in the gap between people with access to information and those without. The striking disparities in science and technology capacity between rich and poor countries, in terms of both input and output, stem from poor status of higher education systems, lack of access to communication technology and progress in science, brain drain and migration, and lack of investments for R&Ds in developing countries.

Global R&D challenges

The rapid pace of communication technology development has changed the speed in the production, use and distribution of knowledge – but divided the world into the connected and the isolated. According to the World Bank report, there is one Internet user per 5,000 people in Africa compared to one user per six people in Europe and North America. Moreover, of the 80 per cent of the world's population who live in the developing nations, only 5 per cent have access to the digital world (World Bank 2002).

Another crucial factor in impeding science and information progress in developing countries is the inadequate government support for R&D. It was estimated that in 1996, OECD member countries accounted for 85 per cent of total investment in R&D. China, India, Brazil and the newly industrialized countries of East Asia represented 11 per cent. However, this rate was only 4 per cent for the rest of the world. According to a World Bank report that ranks countries' science and technology capacity according to their national investment and productivity, 80 nations fall well below the international average, and are categorized as 'scientifically lagging countries'. These countries usually lack 'enabling conditions' within their political, economic and scientific systems and infrastructure. As a result, they are currently inept in generating new knowledge, or attracting scientific and technical knowledge flow from international resources (Wagner et al. 2001).

Education is a key determinant for closing the gap between the developing and the developed world and human development. Despite the rapid growth of literacy rates and tertiary education enrolments in most developing countries over the past decade, the enrolment gap in relation to OECD countries has not decreased. Africa is still experiencing the highest illiteracy rates and lowest gross enrolment rates (GER) in the tertiary education in the world, with 39 per cent of the population (179 million adults) lacking basic literacy skills and average tertiary enrolment of 4.8 per cent for men and about half of that for women (World Bank 2002). Ironically, the nations that face the most development challenges have the least education system capacity for confronting them.

Most universities in developing nations suffer from decline of the quality of education and research in public tertiary education institutions. Overcrowded and deteriorating physical facilities, obsolete library resources, insufficient instructional materials, unqualified teaching staff and an absence of systematic performance evaluation has crippled the higher education systems. In many poor countries especially in sub-Saharan Africa, the HIV/AIDS epidemic also creates challenges for higher education by infecting instructors and students and by increasing costs. For example, at the University of Nairobi, an estimated 30 per cent of the 20,000 students are HIV positive and Copperbelt University in Zambia lost approximately 20 staff members in 2001 alone. Further brain drain has diminished the capacity of the universities to play their essential role in meeting the development needs of nations. For instance, it is estimated that as many as 30,000 Africans holding PhD degrees are living outside the continent (World Bank 2002).

Global health research

There is a substantial need in investment for health information systems and research in developing nations. Worldwide data show that there is an enormous discrepancy between the allocation of health research funding and global health priorities. The imbalance has been known as 'the 10/90 gap', in which of the US$73 billion invested annually in global health research by the public and private sectors, less than 10 per cent is devoted to research into the health problems that account for 90 per cent of the global disease burden (Global Forum for Research 2004).

One of the most cost-effective and achievable strategies for sustainable improvements in healthcare in developing countries is to provide access to reliable information and improve surveillance systems (Pakenham-Walsh 1997). However, the inability of country health information systems to generate the data needed to underpin evidence-based decision-making poses a serious obstacle to public health in many developing countries. Strengthening the evidence-based policy-making in developing countries has become particularly crucial because of the need for tracking progress towards the Millennium Development Goals – especially Poverty Reduction goals, prioritizing complex health needs of populations and designing an equity-based health system. Further, evidence-based policy-making is the only way of applying public policy decisions that are characterized by transparency and accountability. At the global level there has been an increased attention to systems that develop timely, accurate and effective health data for developing countries. In recent years many global health initiatives have focused on neglected areas of research and the promotion of a culture of evidence-based policy process by building the statistical capacity, such as the Global Forum for Health Research, the Global Alliance for Vaccines and Immunizations, Ellison Institute for World Health, WHO STEPwise approach to surveillance, Global Youth Tobacco Surveillance System, Paris 21 and The Health Metrics Network.

Analysts report that scientific collaborations have a positive impact on enhancing research capacity in less advantaged countries. Partnerships with complementary research interests, mutual respect for countries' priorities and values, and transparency of activities will strengthen and sustain capacity development (Anthony and Alimuddin 2000). A key imperative to strengthening health information systems in low- and middle-income countries is to include links with other social and economic sectors by collecting systematic information on socio-economic, demographic, environmental and behavioural determinants of health. Further, health research must produce information on the performance of the health system, health inequalities and prevention and efficient and effective delivery of healthcare in a country-specific context and in resource poor settings.

Global forces and migration

Globalization, low transportation costs and the opening of political borders have facilitated increased movements of skilled people. It is estimated that almost 175 million people were living outside their country of birth in 2000, more than double since 1965. The direction of migration might occur from rural to urban areas, or between two industrialized countries, or from poorer to richer countries. There are several *push and pull* factors that motivate human mobility: political climate, human rights abuses, low standard of living, violence and increasing demands for health and care services in high-income countries (Stilwell et al. 2003).

Trends in the migration of healthcare workers suggest an emerging global marketplace for such labour. Health services in many industrial countries depend on the overseas-trained staff. Available data shows that at least 11,000 sub-Saharan African physicians are practising in the United Kingdom, United States and Canada (Hagopian et al. 2005). Increased migration of health professionals devastates the fragile health systems in poor countries and has a negative development impact where educational systems are not capable of regenerating the same skilled force. For example, of all medical graduates of the Medical School in Jos, Nigeria in 1998, 80 per cent had left the country by the end of 2000. Further, the individuals who choose to move are often highly skilled with strong leadership qualities, adding to the dwindling infrastructure and capacity.

The detrimental impact of international recruitment on low income, staff-short health systems and the populations that rely upon them requires development of a new migration regime. The current policies such as The Code of Practice in the United Kingdom or the coercive measures in some developing countries are ineffective in mitigating the effect of migration for developing countries (Save the Children 2005). A human rights framework provides an explicit way to examine the right of health workers to migrate in seeking a better life *and* articulates the migration consequences on the right to health of health system users in the country of origin (Bueno de Mesquita and Gordon 2005). Such a framework entails an integrated approach that combines preventative and mitigating responses that address the causes and consequences of the migration; and ensures that enhancements in the right to health are achieved without limiting rights to freedom of movement and rights in work. Most importantly, effective strategies to combat the negative impacts of international health worker migration require cooperation and collaboration from sources in destination countries, as well as international donors and the private sector.

GLOBALIZATION AND SECURITY

Efforts to eradicate poverty and hunger are frequently set back by conflict and natural disasters. World military expenditures have fallen 6 per cent in constant dollars between the peak of the Cold War in 1987 and 2000 (Stockholm International Peace Research Institute 2002). However, due to a substantial increase in US military spending after 11 September 2001 world military expenditure is likely to rise significantly in the coming years. Further, the resources for military programmes are four times greater than all public expenditures for health and education of over 4 billion people in the developing world (Sivard 1996). The developed world, as major arms producers, promotes and profits from the arms trade. War is in contrast to human health, environment protection and development. In addition to the direct impact of war on mortality and morbidity, the costs of preparation for war, constraining resources, and pollution caused by the production, testing, stockpiling and even destruction of arms has had destructive effects on the social and economic life of civilians, especially those who are impoverished. Current patterns of violent conflict worldwide indicate that over 90 per cent of all casualties are civilian (Ahlström 1991) and the impact of war extends well beyond the period of active warfare through war-related famine and disease due to destruction of agriculture and overall economic systems. For example, the conflict in the Democratic Republic of Congo is estimated to have caused nearly 4 million deaths, the vast majority from malnutrition and disease (International Rescue Committee 2004). Economic growth and violent conflict are mutually reinforcing. Cross-country econometric research suggests that countries with a per capita income of $600 are half as likely to experience civil conflict as countries with a per capita income of $250. Conflict reduces physical and human capital, the labour force and the prospects for investments; which in turn reinforces the conditions for poverty and low growth (Humphreys 2003).

Forces of globalization including advancement of technologies and communication, the growing number of weak states, transparent borders and the growing importance of non-military aspects of state security are shaping the new global security system (Stockholm International Peace Research Institute 2002). However, the struggle for global peace and security mostly focuses on military strategies, rather than human development and security. The recently released report of the Commission on Human Security (2003) identifies ten distinct but interrelated policy issues for human security, including promotion of public health. According to this report health challenges related to human security are global infectious diseases, poverty-related threats, and violence and crises. This report argues that protecting human security means protecting people through human development and human rights. In an interconnected world, a collective approach for the enhancement of human development, peace and prosperity will inevitably reach all humanity.

GLOBAL GOVERNANCE OF HEALTH

Mutual vulnerability of all nations to global problems such as climate change, environmental health issues, cross-border spread of disease and risks, illicit drugs trade, migration, violent conflict, political instability and human security has blurred the traditional distinction between national and international health. Although the responsibility of providing health remains within national governments, the social, economic and environmental determinants of health are increasingly shaped by global forces. Mutual vulnerability demands a multilateral approach to promotion of public health and other global goods for all populations. In a borderless world, eradication of poverty and global disparities and promotion of health and development becomes a matter of enlightened self-interest.

Globalization carries potentially enormous opportunities, as a result of sharing ideas, values, life-saving technologies and efficient production of goods and services. Yet, only if the benefits of globalization reach the poor and the neglected continent of Africa could it truly serve humanity. Therefore it is essential that international rules and institutional arrangements fully reflect the needs of disadvantaged populations. It also requires removal of major obstacles to development (debt, aid and protectionism trade) in the international economy (see Box 27.1).

To address the new challenges of globalization, a new approach to governance is needed. The WHO is no longer the major source of knowledge about global health issues and its budget is a fraction that of the total investment in global health. Over the last 5 years, the dramatic growth of number of players in the domain of health has led to 'pluralism in international health' (Ruger and Yach 2005). Health has become a hot topic in the G8 summits, the World Economic Forum, the World Bank and the IMF. Also the proliferation of private and not-for-profit sectors such as the Global Fund to Fight AIDS, TB and Malaria, the Bill and Melinda Gates Foundation, and the pharmaceutical industry have a powerful influence on international health policy and practice. Further, public–private partnerships, health research networks and international NGOs play a major role in the domain of international health.

Each of these institutions exerts independent influence on countries and with different governing boards and procedures they run the risk of making it tough for countries to develop coherent plans. Yet they represent a much needed injection of billions of dollars into global health. If a new approach to governance that takes account of these new players and sources of funding is developed, the prospects for improved health for all may well increase.

Global health actors influence the lives and welfare of billions of people, yet until the launch of a recent global campaign – The People's Health Movement (PHM

Box 27.1 *Our Common Interest*: **Report for the Commission for Africa (2005)**

The Commission for Africa was initiated in 2004 to put Africa on the global agenda and was designed to end Africa's status as the only part of the world continuing to stagnate in poverty and conflict. The Commission consists of 17 global members within the public, private and social sectors. The Commission's Report, 'Our Common Interest', is based on an 'investigation' into poverty in Africa, an 'argument' about its mitigation and an 'analysis' of the evidence that has been collected. Through this report, the Commission aims for greater commitment and faster action by the international community to achieve the Millennium Development Goals Africa-wide by 2015, by 'investing in the African people'. To help accomplish this, the Commission aims to create a 'new vision' of Africa that is 'strong and prosperous', to shift Africa away from its current global image as a destitute continent with only unattractive investment opportunities to offer the rest of the world.

In preparing its report, the Commission sought contributions from multiple domains, including governments, civil society, academia, and the public and private sectors. The Commission's investigations have taken place in 49 African nations, in all G8 nations and also in China, India and Europe. The report itself attempts to target the 'decision makers in Africa', the 'rich and powerful nations' (particularly the G8 and EU member states) and the larger 'international community'.

In this report, problems have been 'diagnosed' and 'categorized' into those 'internally' and 'externally exacerbating factors', and those 'natural disadvantages' that have had an impact on Africa. Exacerbating problems within Africa are reported as being due to corruption, incompetence and the conflicts that have been occurring within the continent. The external exacerbating factors are considered to stem from the developed world's use of 'skewed' Western trade policies, bad foreign debt policies and certain 'inappropriate' foreign aid policies. Natural disadvantages are considered as those relating to the climate, as well as to 'a changing global economy' and to 'politics'. The main areas considered important and in need of focus are trade, aid and debt relief, governance and corruption, healthcare, peace and security, and climate change (refer to Exhibit 1 for some of the specific examples that are cited in the report). According to the Commission, improved governance internally and enhanced cultural awareness externally are the essential components of a viable strategy for poverty mitigation at the scale that is now required. 'Development' is described in this report as 'a culturally sensitive term', which 'through the eyes of the African' translates to mean 'positive wellbeing, happiness, and community membership', the need for development to be relevant to African and not Western ideas is also underscored. Finally, 'social networks' are also referred to as a powerful tool for achieving positive results in a successful way. By highlighting the key areas for reform including health, education conflict resolution and infrastructure, the Commission outlines a new compact with Africa whereby development partners make additional resources available while African countries commit to improve standards of governance and focus their efforts on poverty reduction. This report urges the world to act in solidarity now and overcome poverty, despair and death in Africa. As this report states: 'It is in our common interest and moral duty to make the world a more prosperous and secure place.'

Exhibit one:

Topic	Arguments for Focus – Causes/ Effect of Problems	Suggested/Needed Actions
Trade	**Dramatic fall of share of world trade in Africa, caused by:** 1. Superimposed trade barriers. 2. Poor production/supply of goods. In 1980 to 2002 African world trade fell from 6% to 2%, while much of the world experienced economic growth. Only if sub-Saharan Africa could increase its share of world exports by just one percent, it would generate over US$70 billion.	1. Increasing capacity to trade by investment in infrastructure & trade facilitation. 2. Removing the trade barriers and ending developed countries' protectionism by successful completion of the WTO Doha Round in specific time bounds. 3. Providing transitional support as global trade barriers are removed
Aid and debt relief	**Inadequacies of the system of aid & development, caused by:** 1. Unpredictable aid that underscores long-term commitment and infrastructure investment. 2. Different bureaucratic requirements among donors. 3. Tied aid: scarce funds are spend on high-cost inputs 4. Unsystematic responses to single disease 5. Priorities of donors not nations	1. Doubling aid levels over the next three to five years. 2. Increasing financing to 0.7% GDP investment by rich nations. 3. Adding another ONE to the 'Three-Ones' approach by UNAIDS (one coordinating agency, one strategy and one monitoring framework): a single pooled fund in each country. 4. Endorse 100% debt cancellation for poor countries in sub-Saharan Africa – nearly half of all aid money to Africa has returned to the developed world in debt repayments. 5. Integrating responses to the burden of disease though health systems rather than single disease response. 6. Improving the quality of aid by: strengthening the processes of accountability to citizens in aid-recipient countries; harmonization/alignment with countries priorities; higher share of aid in the form of grants; long-term predictability and flexibly in aid flows.

Continued

| Governance | **Weakness in governance and capacity, caused by:** extensive 'internal' corruption within governments, corporations ('signature bonuses'), and at the grass roots level (bribes); and poor human development. | 1. Building effective states by donors' support for national strategy for building capacity, infrastructure and human capital.
2. Improve government accountability by increasing transparency of revenues and budgets; and strengthening parliaments, the media and the justice system.
3. Increase investments in human development and inclusion.
4. Develop legal mechanisms for multinational accountability levels for foreign investors; and corporate social responsibility. |

Source: *Our Common Interest*, Report of the Commission for Africa (2005).

2005) – there were no independent reports to monitor the performance of global health players and to hold them accountable to the world's population. In July 2005 the PHM initiated the Global Health Watch, which is the first 'alternative world health report', written from the perspective of civil society and global health activists (Global Health Watch 2005). This report scrutinizes the conduct, commitment and approaches of global health institutions, governments and transnational corporations. According to this report, WHO in particular faces leadership and governance problems such as insufficient financial resources, internal mismanagement and distorted priorities, 'vertical' and single diseases approaches, the power influences of rich nations and most importantly lack of political will and strength to tackle the global drivers of poverty and health inequity. This report proposes specific recommendations for a stronger WHO, with democratization of its governmental body, with increasing funding and with changing the management and leadership culture of the institution. It also advocates for comprehensive primary healthcare for all (as envisioned in the Alma Ata Declaration) and proposes the promotion of health as a fundamental human right, to be the basis for healthcare policy and to be respected by all national governments and intergovernmental organizations.

Tackling the complex challenges of globalization requires international cooperation among states and other global players. Therefore, international law as a mechanism for international cooperation could play a crucial role in responding to threats and opportunities of globalization. For the first time in the 50-year history of the organization, WHO exercised its constitutional treaty-making powers in developing the Framework Convention for Tobacco Control (WHO 2003c). The FCTC confronts compound issues such as liberalization of international trade, the enormous influence and wealth of tobacco industries, the dependence of economies of some developing countries on tobacco products and issues of cigarette taxes, policies, advertisements and rules on labelling and packaging.

In contemporary public health, effective actions against mutual vulnerability must employ international norms and standards. Further, in order to take advantage of the international mechanisms for the promotion of global health, public health capacities in trade, political science and international laws must be effectively strengthened.

CONCLUSION

The benefits of globalization for health are potentially enormous, as a consequence of sharing values, knowledge, technology advances and offering better prospects for economic growth and trade. However, these opportunities have not yet reached hundreds of millions of the world's poor. Further, globalization introduces new international challenges to health as national borders become transparent and vulnerable to environmental degradation, terrorism, spread of diseases and unhealthy behaviour, and armed conflict. Moreover, global forces have profoundly accelerated the health and wealth divisions within and across countries. In an increasingly interdependent world, mutual vulnerability provides a potential of self-interest for all nations to systematically enhance global public health and equitable economic growth.

Notes

1 McMurray and Smith (2001) referred to the rising incidence of chronic diseases as a result of shifting in lifestyle changes as 'diseases of globalization'.
2 Declaration of Alma-Ata, World Health Organization, International Conference on Primary Health Care, Alma-Ata, USSR, 6–12 September 1978. The Alma-Ata Declaration strongly affirmed health as a fundamental human right and called for a comprehensive approach to improvement of health whereby primary healthcare was seen as 'the key to achieving an acceptable level of health throughout the world in the foreseeable future as a part of social development and in the spirit of social justice'.

References

Ahlström, C. 1991. 'Casualties of conflict: Report for the World Campaign for the Protection of Victims of War', Department of Peace and Conflict Research, Uppsala, Sweden. Cited in B.S. Levy and V.W. Sidel (eds), *War and Public Health*, 31. New York: Oxford University Press.

Alwan, A., Maclean, D. and Mandil, A. 2001. *Assessment of National Capacity for Noncommunicable Disease Prevention and Control*. Geneva: WHO.

Anand, S. and Ravallion, M. 1993. 'Human development in poor countries: On the role of private incomes and public services', *Journal of Economic Literature*, 7 (1), 133–50.

Anonymous. 2000. 'Overweight, obesity, and health risk: National Task Force on the Prevention and Treatment of Obesity', *Archives of Internal Medicine*, 160 (7), 898–904.

Anthony, C. and Alimuddin, Z. 2000. 'Moving to research partnerships in developing countries', *British Medical Journal*, 321, 827–9.

BBC. 2005. 'Avian flu could cripple economy', BBC report, 20 August. Available at <http://news.bbc.co.uk/1/hi/business/4184948.stm> accessed September 2005.

Beaglehole, R. and Yach, D. 2003. 'Globalisation and the prevention and control of non-communicable disease: The neglected chronic diseases of adults', *Lancet*, 362 (9387), 903–8.

Bueno de Mesquita, J. and Gordon, M. 2005. 'Human rights analysis of health worker migration'. Health Charity Medact. Available at <http://www.medact.org/content/Skills%20drain/Bueno%20de%20Mesquita%20and%20Gordon.pdf> accessed September 2005.

Caldwell, J.C. 1993. 'Health transition: The cultural, social and behavioural determinants of health in the Third World', *Social Science & Medicine*, 36 (2), 125–35.

CIA (Central Intelligence Agency) 2005. 'The global infectious disease threat and its implications for the United States'. Available at <http://www.cia.gov/cia/reports/nie/report/nie99-17d.html> accessed September 2005.

Commission for Africa. 2005. *Our Common Interest*. Report of the Commission for Africa.

Commission on Human Security. 2003. *Report for Commission on Human Security: Human Security Now*. United Nations Publications.

Corbett, E.L., Watt, C.J., Walker, N., Maher, D., Williams, B.G., Raviglione, M.C. and Dye, C. 2003. 'The growing burden of tuberculosis: Global trends and interactions with the HIV epidemic', *Archives of Internal Medicine*, 163 (9), 1009–21.

DeNavas-Walt, C., Proctor, B.D. and Mills, R.J. 2004. *Income, Poverty, and Health Insurance Coverage in the United States*. Washington DC: US Census Bureau.

Diaz-Bonilla, E., Babinard, J. and Pinstrup-Andersen, P. 2001. 'Globalization and health: A survey of opportunities and risks for the poor in developing countries'. Working Paper for Commission on Macroeconomics and Health.

Dugger, C.W. 2005. 'African food for Africa's starving is roadblocked in Congress', *New York Times*, 12 October.

FAO. 2003. *The State of Food Insecurity in the World: Monitoring Progress towards the World Food Summit and Millennium Development Goals*. Rome: FAO.

FAO. 2004. *Annual Hunger Report: The State of Food Insecurity in the World*. Rome: FAO.

FAO/WHO. 1992. International Conference on Nutrition. Final report of the conference. Rome.

Global Forum for Research 2004. *The 10/90 Report on Health Research 2003–2004*. Geneva: Global Forum for Research.

Global Health Watch. 2005–6. *Global Heath Watch: An Alternative World Health Report*. Available at <http://www.ghwatch.org/> accessed September 2005.

Hagopian, A., Ofosu, A., Fatusi, A., Biritwum, R., Essel, A., Hart, L. and Watts, C. 2005. 'The flight of physicians from West Africa: Views of African physicians and implications for policy', *Social Science & Medicine*, 61 (8), 1750–60.

Hales, S., Howden-Chapman, P., Salmond, C., Woodward, A. and Mackenbach, J. 1999. 'National infant mortality rates in relation to gross national product and distribution of income', *Lancet*, 354 (9195), 2047.

Humphreys, M. 2005. *Economics and Violent Conflict*. Cambridge, MA. Available at <http://www.preventconflict.org/portal/economics/Essay.pdf> accessed September 2005.

International Rescue Committee. 2004. *Mortality in the Democratic Republic of Congo: Results from a Nationwide Survey*. New York. Available at <http://www.theirc.org/pdf/DRC_MortalitySurvey2004_RB_8Dec04.pdf>.

IOM (Institute of Medicine). 2003. *Microbial Threats to Health: Emergence, Detection, and Response*. Board on Global Health, US Institute of Medicine.

Kaferstein, F.K., Motarjemi, Y. and Bettcher, D.W. 1997. 'Foodborne disease control: A transnational challenge', *Emerging Infectious Diseases*, 3 (4), 503–10.

Lee, K. 2002. 'Introduction'. In K. Lee (ed.), *Health Impacts of Globalization: Towards Global Governance*. London: Palgrave Macmillan.

Lee, K. and Yach, D. 2007. 'Globalization and health'. In M. Merson, R. Black and A. Mills (eds), *International Public Health: Diseases, Programs, Systems and Policies*. Jones & Bartlett, in press.

Leeder, S., Raymond, S. and Greenberg, H. 2003. *A Race against Time: The Challenge of Cardiovascular Disease in Developing Economies*. New York: Columbia University.

Lynch, J. and Smith, G.D. 2005. 'A life course approach to chronic disease epidemiology', *Annual Review of Public Health*, 26, 1–35.

McBride, S. and Wiseman, J. 2000. 'Introduction'. In S. McBride and J. Wiseman (eds), *Globalization and Its Discontents*. Basingstoke: Macmillan.

McMurray, C. and Smith, R. 2001. *Diseases of Globalization: Socioeconomic Transition and Health*. London: Earthscan Publications.

Marshall, S.J. 2004. 'Developing countries face double burden of disease', *Bulletin of the World Health Organization*, 82 (7), 556.

Monteiro, C.A., Conde, W.L. and Popkin, B.M. 2000a. 'The burden of disease from undernutrition and overnutrition in countries undergoing rapid nutrition transition: A view from Brazil', *American Journal of Public Health*, 94 (3), 433–4.

Monteiro, C.A., D'A Benicio, M.H., Conde, W.L. and Popkin, B.M. 2000b. 'Shifting obesity trends in Brazil', *European Journal of Clinical Nutrition*, 54 (4), 342–6.

Montgomery, K. 2005. 'The demographic transition'. Department of Geography and Geology. University of Wisconsin. Available at <http://www.uwmc.uwc.edu/geography/Demotrans/demtran.htm> accessed September 2005.

Murphy, S. and McAfee, K. 2005. *U.S. Food Aid: Time to Get It Right*. The Institute for Agriculture and Trade Policy.

Murray, C.J. and Lopez, A.D. 1997a. 'Global mortality, disability, and the contribution of risk factors: Global Burden of Disease Study', *Lancet*, 349 (9063), 1436–42.

Murray, Q.L. and Lopez, A.D. 1997b. *The Global Burden of Disease*. Vol. 1. Cambridge, MA: Harvard School of Public Health.

OECD. 1996. *The Knowledge Based Economy*. Paris: OECD.

Omran, A.R. 1971. 'The epidemiologic transition: A theory of the epidemiology of population change', *Milbank Memorial Fund Quarterly*, 49, 509–38.

Pakenham-Walsh, N., Priestly, C. and Smith, R. 1997. 'Meeting the information needs of health workers in developing countries', *British Medical Journal*, 314 (7074), 90.

PHM (The People's Health Movement). 2005. Available at <http://www.phmovement.org/> accessed September 2005.

Popkin, B.M. and Doak, C.M. 1998. 'The obesity epidemic is a worldwide phenomenon', *Nutrition Reviews*, 56 (4 Pt 1), 106–14.

Rotimi, C., Okosun, I., Johnson, L. et al. 1999. 'The distribution and mortality impact of chronic energy deficiency among adult Nigerian men and women', *European Journal of Clinical Nutrition*, 53 (9), 734–9.

Ruger, J.P. and Yach, D. 2005. 'Global functions at the World Health Organization', *British Medical Journal*, 330 (7500), 1099–100.

Sacks, J. 2005. *End of Poverty: Economic Possibilities for Our Time*. London: A. Lane.

Save the Children. 2005. 'Whose charity, Africa's aid to NHS'. Briefing. Save the Children, in conjunction with the health charity Medact. Available at <http://www.medact.org/content/Skills%20drain/Whose%20charity%204%20page.pdf> accessed September 2005.

Schroeder, D.G., Martorell, R. and Flores, R. 1999. 'Infant and child growth and fatness and fat distribution in Guatemalan adults', *American Journal of Epidemiology*, 149 (2), 177–85.

Seidell, J.C. 2005. 'Epidemiology of obesity', *Seminars in Vascular Medicine*, 5 (1), 3–14.

Sen, A. 1999. 'Perspective of freedom'. In A. Sen (ed.), *Development as Freedom*. New York: Alfred A. Knopf.

Sivard, R.L. 1996. *World Military and Social Expenditures 1996*. Washington, DC: World Priorities Inc.

Stevens, J., Cai, J., Pamuk, E.R., Williamson, D.F., Thun, M.J. and Wood, J.L. 1998. 'The effect of age on the association between body-mass index and mortality', *New England Journal of Medicine*, 338 (1), 1–7.

Stilwell, B., Diallo, K., Zurn, P., Dal Poz, M.R., Adams, O. and Buchan, J. 2003. 'Developing evidence-based ethical policies on the migration of health workers: Conceptual and practical challenges', *Human Resources for Health*, 1 (1), 8.

Stockholm International Peace Research Institute. 2002. *Yearbook 2002: Armaments, Disarmament and International Security*. Oxford: Oxford University Press.

UN. 2005. *Millennium Development Goals Report*. New York: UN.

UNAIDS/WHO. 2004. *AIDS epidemic update: December 2004*. Geneva: WHO.

UNDP. 1999. *Human Development Report: Globalization with a Human Face*. UNDP.

UNDP. 2005.*Human Development Report: International Cooperation at a Crossroads – Aid, Trade and Security in an Unequal World*. UNDP.

UN Standing Committee on Nutrition. 2000. *Fourth Report on the World Nutrition Situation: Nutrition Throughout the Life Cycle*. Geneva: United Nations.

Wagner, C.S., Brahmakulam, I., Jackson, B., Wong, A. and Yoda, T. 2001. *Science and Technology Collaboration: Building Capacity in Developing Countries?* Santa Monica, CA: RAND. Available at <www.rand.org/publications/MR/MR1357.0/> accessed October 2005.

Wagstaff, A. 2002. 'Poverty and health sector inequalities', *Bulletin of the World Health Organization*, 80 (2), 97–105.

WHO. 2001. *WHO Global Strategy for Containment of Antimicrobial Resistance*. Geneva: WHO.

WHO. 2002. *World Health Report, 2002: Reducing Risks, Promoting Healthy Life*. Geneva: WHO.

WHO. 2003a. *World Health Report, 2003: Shaping the Future*. Geneva: WHO.

WHO. 2003b. *Emerging Issues in Water and Infectious Diseases*. Geneva: WHO.

WHO. 2003c. *WHO Framework Convention on Tobacco Control*. Geneva: WHO. Available at <http://www.who.int/tobacco/framework/en/> accessed September 2005.

WHO. 2005a. *Preventing Chronic Diseases: A Vital Investment*. Geneva: WHO.

WHO. 2005b. 'Cumulative number of confirmed human cases of Avian Influenza reported to WHO', 29 September. Available at <http://www.who.int/csr/disease/avian_influenza/country/cases_table_2005_09_29/en/index.html> accessed October 2005.

WHO. 2005c. 'Avian Influenza fact sheet'. Available at <http://www.who.int/csr/don/2004_01_15/en/> accessed October 2005.

Woodward, D., Drager, N., Beaglehole, R. and Lipson, D. 2001. 'Globalization and health: A framework for analysis and action', *Bulletin of the World Health Organization*, 79 (9), 875–81.

World Bank. 2002. *Constructing Knowledge Societies: New Challenges for Tertiary Education*. Washington, DC: World Bank.

Yach, D. and Beaglehole, R. 2004. 'Globalization of risks for chronic diseases demands global solutions', *Perspectives on Global Development and Technology*, 3 (1–2).

Yach, D. and Hawkes, C. 2004. *Towards a WHO Longterm Strategy for Prevention and Control of Leading Chronic Diseases*. Geneva: WHO.

Part III

Major Issues and Conclusions

Introduction to Part III

George Ritzer

This part opens with several chapters devoted to problematic aspects of globalization (although Part II dealt with its share of problems – ill health in a global context, for example) – inequality, corruption, sexuality, war and terrorism. The penultimate chapter examines, given the many problems associated with globalization, forms of resistance to it and the final chapter involves a sweeping look into the future(s) of globalization.

Given the importance of the relationship between globalization and inequality, we devote two chapters to it. There is another reason for devoting two chapters to this issue – the authors of each are the major protagonists in a crucial debate in this area over whether globalization is related to the continuing salience of (Korzeniewicz and Moran), or a meaningful decline in (Firebaugh and Goesling), global inequality. It may well be that this is *the* issue in the entire field of globalization and it is interesting to note that, as McGrew anticipated in the first chapter in this volume, it is a highly contested one. It is also, as discussed by Babones (Chapter 7), a methodological issue. Perhaps above all, it is, as contended by Korzeniewicz and Moran, a theoretical issue (see Robinson, Chapter 6) which, in their view, pits (world) system theory against modernization theory.

Firebaugh and Goesling address three forms of global inequality – income, health and education – although their focus is clearly on income. They examine several competing explanations of increasing and declining income inequality. Their preferred position is that the spread of industrialization leads to the industrialization (modernization?) of poorer regions of the world and the resulting economic gains there lead, in turn, to an overall reduction in global income inequality. This is based on several methodological positions, including measuring income on the basis of 'purchasing power parity' (PPP) as opposed to the measure based on 'official exchange rates' (FX) preferred by Korzeniewicz and Moran. They argue that the consensus favours their position, although Babones offers a view that supports the approach of Korzeniewicz and Moran.

Firebaugh and Goesling also see a decline in recent years in between-nation inequality in health, although the continuation of that pattern is threatened by the HIV/AIDS epidemic. However, even with the decline, great disparities remain between (and within) nations in terms of health. There is also a decline in the last 50 years or so in between-nation inequality in educational attainment.

In terms of the future, in the short run they foresee a further decline in global income inequality in the early twenty-first century because poor countries will see a bulge in working age population while rich countries will witness a bulge in the elderly population. A second factor is the continued economic renaissance in Asia. But the latter, in the longer run, will lead to an exacerbation in income inequality as the average income in Asia comes to exceed the world average. The scenarios for the future of health and educational inequality are more ambiguous.

Korzeniewicz and Moran focus their attention on economic inequality and report the differences between their conclusions on this issue (using FX-based data) versus those of Firebaugh and Goesling (using PPP-based data). While there are technical issues involved here, they choose to focus on theoretical differences, differences in the two ways of thinking. They argue that Firebaugh and Goesling are interested in 'differences between populations in their relative access to welfare', whereas they focus on 'relations between populations'. Firebaugh and Goesling are seen, given the centrality they accord to industrialization, as employing modernization theory which leads to a focus on individual nations and the degree to which they have, or have not, modernized or industrialized. In contrast, Korzeniewicz and Moran adopt a more systemic – especially world-system – approach that leads to a focus on overall patterns of global interaction (e.g. the integration of labour markets on a global scale).

Korzeniewicz and Moran compare the economics of Simon Kuznets (1955) which is consistent with a modernization approach, to that of Joseph Schumpeter which is more consistent with their (world) system approach. Specifically, Schumpeter's (1950) thinking on 'creative destruction' leads to a view of constant change rather than one of modern equilibrium. In fact, they argue that combining the insights of Kuznets and Schumpeter leads to a view of the world as involved in a 'constant drive towards rising inequality', but how that plays out in specific nations depends on the actions of various institutions. Their key point, however, is that as relational systems, institutions have often served to reduce inequality within high income nations while increasing between-nation inequality through the exclusion of poorer nations. Such a systemic, institutional approach seems to imply that the best we can hope for in the future is a different global configuration of inequality; a significant decline, let alone disappearance, of such inequality would be indicative of a substantial transformation of the institutional processes that have characterized the development of the world-economy over the last 200 years.

Warner begins with the widespread assumption that globalization leads to a decline in corruption (defined rather narrowly as 'misuse of public office for private gain'). The view is that globalization is more likely to uncover corruption because firms and the nation-state are subjected to free market pressures and the openness of such a market. Furthermore, it is assumed that states will try to clean things up in order to attract more international business and investment, the firm will not be able to afford the added costs of corruption because of greater global competition, politicians will find it more difficult to be corrupt if bids for public procurement are open to foreign firms, because of moral pressure from various NGOs that crusade against corruption (e.g. Transparency International, World Bank) on the basis of the belief that it is bad for democratic values, economic development and business in general, and finally because states are more involved in international organizations and networks where there are strong anti-corruption norms (largely derived from Western nations, especially the United States). Warner accords the United States a central role in the global efforts to curb corruption. The United States has an anti-corruption law – Foreign Corrupt Practices Law – and Warner sees the US as trying to internationalize such prohibitions against corruption. She argues that there is a comparative lack of corruption in the United States and this is also aided by the fact that there are stringent requirements for firms to be listed on the US Stock Exchange, US efforts to curb global corruption are no longer impeded by privileging anti-communist regimes and looking the other way when it is clear that corruption exists in them, and more recently anti-terrorist banking laws have exposed still other transactions to inspection. While there are moral issues involved in this, from a pragmatic point of view, if the United States operates under such restraints on corruption, it needs other nations to do so or it will be at a competitive disadvantage. The efforts of the United States have met with some success. In 1997 the OECD Anti-bribery Convention was enacted and by 2004 there were 35 nations on board.

However, globalization (as well as US efforts) does not seem to lead to a decline in corruption, but in fact it creates both new means and incentives for corruption. First, increased global competition over exports leads to the increased need to use bribery as a business tool in order to beat out rivals. Second, politicians can gain much more from corruption because of the increased involvement of foreign firms and their eagerness to gain new business. Third, international organizations lack enforcement powers (in fact, OECD not only tolerates, but uses, corruption to expedite such transactions as weapons sales) and some (WTO) have no rules whatsoever on corruption. Finally, anti-corruption norms are often circumscribed by states' economic and geo-political interests and by the fact that many of the world's growing economic powers (especially China which Warner labels a 'corrupt country') do not share those norms. Furthermore, efforts to reduce global corruption are hurt when we learn that the UN, which is supposed to be part of the solution, is itself in fact engaged in corruption (e.g. the 'Oil for Food' scandal in Iraq that involved, among others, the son of the former UN Secretary-General).

However, Warner wonders whether we are now at a global 'tipping point' with corruption beginning to decline. There are various global movements against corruption. Transparency International (TI) makes public the varying degrees of corruption in almost all countries. It also publishes the TI Corruption Index. Others involved in such efforts include Global Witness and the Center for Public Integrity. Pressure from TI, as well as new leadership, is changing the WTO and leading it to adopt a stronger anti-corruption position. The United States has been key here in coordinating efforts that led to the OECD's 1997 Anti-bribery Convention, as well as in the Millennium Challenge Corporation which only gives money to those nations that practise 'good governance'. That is, they must govern justly, invest in their citizens, encourage economic freedom and control corruption. (The problem with much of this is that it is US definitions of what constitutes good governance that prevail and it ignores the fact that corruption is far from being unknown in the United States and in its global dealings.)

Also pointing to the idea that we may be approaching a tipping point on corruption are the increasing number of international organizations with anti-bribery and anti-corruption policies, successful prosecutions of corruption which would never have occurred in the past (Montesinos in Peru and involving former Peruvian President Fujimori; Elf Aquitaine in France), new banking and accounting laws (e.g. Sarbanes–Oxley in the United States, 2002) making it easier for officials to find and deal with corruption, initiatives by private industry to limit corruption (e.g. Extractive Industries Transparency Initiative), and regional and international integration leading to a decline in corruption (although organizations like the EU have conventions that lack force and, in any case, tolerate corruption).

However, all of these movements and efforts against corruption are counterbalanced by the fact that globalization encourages corruption in various ways. In fact, corruption can be seen as not being in opposition to global export markets, but an integral part of them. As mentioned above, globalization in fact greatly increases the magnitude of the rewards to be derived from successful bribes. And there are many incentives to state officials not to upset the status quo which, among many other things, includes bribery. Perversely, globalization leads to an increase in bribery because it makes more widespread knowledge of the existence of these bribes and their utility.

Overall, Warner concludes that while there have been gains, much more needs to be done in order to really turn the tide against global corruption. The fact is that corruption continues to advantage firms (they get things like exclusive contracts and market access) and politicians (who get resources that help them obtain or maintain power).

Farr examines the relationship between sexuality (and gender) and globalization. She makes the interesting point that globalization privileges the heteronormative and the masculine. The powerful players – nation-states and TNCs – are emphasized in globalization and thought of as masculine, while those that are dependent or local are de-emphasized and associated with feminine, as well as queer, worlds. More generally women and other sexual minorities are under-analysed in the globalization literature. All of this is aided by the propensity to conceptualize both globalization and sexuality in terms of modern binaries. Thus, she argues, like most other students of globalization, we need to think in terms of heterogenization, glocalization or complex connectivity (Tomlinson). However, Farr's argument is weakened here by the fact that, as we have seen throughout this volume, she like most others is adopting the overwhelmingly predominant, but narrow and simplistic, way in which globalization is viewed today.

Farr looks at various aspects of the relationship between sexuality and globalization. First, there are the increasing global flows of gays; the gay ethnoscape (Appadurai 1996). This includes increases in both gay and lesbian tourism. While tourism is increasingly global, it continues to represent distinctive problems for women and homosexuals. For example, it continues to be difficult for women to travel alone. And homophobia continues to plague gay and lesbian tourists. Then there is the seemingly increasing popularity of sex tourism where both straights and gays travel the world to have sex with exotic, often racialized others. Natives are commodified and relations of dominance are reinforced, often through the degradation of these people.

Migration involves sexuality in various ways. For example, the massive migration of women from South to North often involves either domestic or sex work. In the South, a similar process is involved in migration from rural to urban centres. To survive the hazards involved in this movement, women rely heavily on various survival circuits. Of special interest and importance is sex trafficking with over one million largely women and children transported transnationally (and many more intra-nationally) for the purposes of prostitution. This is a multi-billion dollar industry that is animated by, and reinforces, social inequality since the major sources of sex workers tend to be poor, developing countries and their destinations are likely to be well-to-do developed countries. The sex industry functions well as a loosely organized, flexible network that operates both within nations and transnationally. As with many other things, it is relatively easy to arrange for sex workers to cross freely national borders.

Farr sees a global war on sexual minorities and female migrants. A key factor in this is the rise of an interrelated set of strongly homophobic and sexist 'isms': nationalism, nativism, fundamentalism and patriarchalism. Women are also very likely to be the victims in wars started and conducted by men. Globalization brings with it increasing border crossings and borders are often sites of conflict and contention that is often gendered and sexualized in nature. In other words, borders are sites, in Appadurai's terms, of disjunctures in the flows of people.

There are a few hopeful signs in this realm. Collective resistance is aided by INGOs devoted to gender and sexuality issues. There are global networks that help women and gays gain a sense of identity and community, as well as helping them to deal with more concrete issues such as AIDS. Poor women use a variety of survival strategies to capitalize on the very global linkages that exploit them. In fact, some use sex (and other forms of work) as an advancement strategy. Thus, there are new opportunities and hopes in globalization, but new problems and inequities have arisen that are simply added to those that pre-date globalization and continue to plague women and sexual minorities.

While we touched on war in Part II, especially information war, it is the focal concern in Schneider's chapter. As with most analyses of globalization, Schneider focuses on economics, in this case the economic preconditions of war. He argues that there are two contrasting positions on this. The first is *commercial liberalism* where the view is that globalization has a pacifying effect on states and inter-state relationships. The view here is 'peace-through-trade' and a well-known example is Thomas Friedman's argument (shown by later events in the old Yugoslavia to be false) that no two nations that have McDonald's have ever gone to war with one another. The second is the *sceptical* view that in various ways globalization increases the likelihood of war. Included here would be Marx's argument that capitalism is inevitably global and that the contradictions within it point in the direction of global war; Lenin's contention that imperialism brings with it the likelihood of war between oppressor and oppressed; dependency theory's view that economic imbalances lead to civil strife; that increased trade, especially the arms trade, associated with globalization leads, sometimes unwittingly, to the arming of potential opponents; and finally that globalization destabilizes developing countries making all sorts of strife more likely.

Schneider offers an alternative, revised liberal theory of peace, to these positions that he calls a *distributional theory of liberal peace*. Its premises are that at the international level, globalization can lead to an increase in the likelihood of war in those countries with a strong praetorian sector. The military engages in external warfare to increase tax revenues devoted to it and to enhance its influence at home. Domestically, globalization creates a short-term risk of war as long as the costs of foreign economic liberalization are larger than the long-run benefits of globalization for the population. Overall he argues that the increase in global trade is a necessary, but not a sufficient, condition (contra commercial liberalism) for domestic and international peace.

Among the implications of this view are that we cannot simply assume that war declines with globalization because it will prove too costly. We need to look at why leaders are simultaneously interested both in commercial bonds *and* in waging war. Another way to put this is the need to look at the interaction between the pacifying and war-engendering effects of globalization. For example, while loss of business and income may be a deterrent to war, the cheapening of armaments as a result of expanded global trade makes war more likely as does the time-space compression associated with globalization. Modern technology brings enemies closer and greatly reduces the time available to make decisions about whether or not to go to war. Globalization is an ambiguous force. For example, it can reduce internal strife by increasing homogeneity at home, but it can increase it globally when attempts are made to foist that homogeneity on other nations. Globalization is no panacea for peace.

Closely related to war, especially post-9/11, is the terrorism and war on it analysed by Martin. He argues that 9/11 ushered in a new, or at least a more advanced, form of terrorism. Previous terrorists of the modern era tended to be nationalists fighting self-described wars of national liberation, adherents of some variant of Marxian ideology or amalgams of these two characteristics. Today's terrorists tend not to be tied to any particular nation and most are certainly not associated with Marxian ideology. New political arrangements (e.g. the EU) make it easier for terrorists to cross borders. They are heavily influenced by new technologies and linkages between cultures that make it much easier to disseminate people, information and influence over much larger global audiences. Unlike earlier terrorists (except for Jewish terrorists in the era of the British mandate), the new terrorists are much more motivated by religion (especially Islam) and religious differences. They are also animated by global, especially North–South, disparities in wealth and poverty. Martin seems to accept Huntington's (1996) controversial ideas on civilizational fault lines, especially between Islam and the West, as a cause of terrorism. Another factor is the existence of nations (like Afghanistan and Pakistan) with areas that are largely free of governmental control and therefore constitute excellent areas for headquarters for terrorist groups. Targets of terrorists are increasingly outside their base of operations and they are often chosen because of their importance as international symbols (the World Trade Center and the Pentagon) and in many cases in order to maximize casualties. Large numbers of casualties in attacks on global symbols are likely to bring the global media attention (and spectacle; see Kellner and Pierce, in Part II) that is of such great importance to today's terrorists.

Of course Al-Qaeda is the paradigm of the new terrorism. It is stateless, lacks even a quasi-military hierarchy, is motivated by religious fundamentalism, champions only fellow-believers, is globalized and is in the process of being transformed into an ideology – 'Qaedaism' – that promises to be more versatile and threatening than a tangible network of believers. The fear is that Al-Qaeda is being 'cloned' and just as the war in Afghanistan gave birth to Al-Qaeda, clones are emerging from the war in Iraq.

The war on terrorism has led to a variety of new strategies, many of them morally and legally highly questionable. These include using unconventional groups and methods to wage war against terrorists, as well as new customs protocols and surveillance over many people, including large numbers of innocent citizens. The US Patriot Act has been particularly controversial because it has made it easier, among other things, to access private records, e-mails and related address books, made it possible to wiretap any phone a suspect may use and created nationwide search warrants where it is possible to search multiple premises.

Terrorist attacks in recent years are not more numerous or frequent than in previous epochs, but they are more spectacular, more deadly, involve greater patience and planning, involve pre-positioned sleepers and the use of advanced technologies that permit broad dissemination of messages and (coded) instructions. Globalized terrorism is a central attribute of the contemporary era and globalization creates an environment that encourages the new terrorism to operate globally.

All of the problems discussed not only in this part of the book, but earlier, lead to the issue discussed by Kahn and Kellner of resistance to globalization. Resistance, like globalization itself, is seen as highly complex, contradictory and ambiguous, ranging from the radically progressive to the reactionary and conservative (including frontier-style self-determination, isolationism, fundamentalism, neo-fascism and ultra-nationalism). In addition to immediate gains, the anti-globalization movement may constitute the beginning of a global civil society, of a new public sphere, that might uphold such values as autonomy, democracy, peace, ecological sustainability and social justice. While the anti-globalization forces have tended to portray globalization in a negative light (as top-down, neoliberal capitalism, imperialism and terror war; involving the McDonaldization of the planet, and creating disequilibrating social changes), they are themselves products of globalization that survive by using such globe-straddling technologies as the Internet.

The anti-globalization movement can be said to have begun in 1993. It has been highly mobile, continually changing its style, messages and constituencies. Many individuals, groups, social movements and issues are loosely combined in the anti-globalization movement. However, Kahn and Kellner prefer to move away from using the concept of the anti-globalization movement to globalization from below (as well as above). For one thing, the movement is not, as we have seen, opposed to all aspects of globalization. It is opposed to some varieties (e.g. neoliberal) and is itself a form of globalization, a form emanating from below rather than above. Another new label is 'movement of movements', especially tied to the World Social Forum.

Kahn and Kellner devote much attention to the technopolitics of resistance, especially those involving the Internet. These are new terrains for political struggle and places where new voices can be heard. The technology is highly democratic and generally decommodified. It is a place where campaigns can be waged against global corporations by, for example, hacking into their websites. Other wholly or primarily web-based forms of resistance include McSpotlight, the Clean Clothes Campaign, the campaign waged in 2004 that led to the ousting of a pro-Iraq War regime in Spain, the paradigmatic anti-globalization activities in Seattle in 1999, which led to the formation of the Independent Media Center and later Indymedia.com. The latter has become a/the major alternative media form with 160 centres in 60 countries. It is devoted to presenting media images and ideas not represented in the mainstream media. Then there are the Hacktivists who can create havoc on the Internet and perhaps one day will cause a 'digital Pearl Harbor'.

Kahn and Kellner close with a review of several theories involving resistance (Polanyi's ideas on countermovements; Gramsci on hegemony/counter-hegemony; Hardt and Negri on empire/multitude; Barber on McWorld and Jihad), but they find them all wanting for one reason or another and too limited. They end by calling for more complex, dialectical and critical theories of global resistance that avoid the extremes of either globophobia or globophilia.

The volume concludes with Bryan Turner's wide-ranging thoughts on the future of globalization(s). Turner argues that globalization studies have in the past been overly optimistic, although there were various critiques (of McDonaldization, Americanization, 'nothing', risk, empire and so on). However, pre-9/11 optimism about globalization has declined and the negatives associated with it – urban violence (Paris in 2005), slavery, terrorism, international crime, tourist sex and global epidemics – have been increasingly likely to take centre stage.

He adopts a neo-Malthusian approach that looks at the 'complex interaction between the clash of civilizations, terrorism, changing population structure, agency and migration, pollution and environmental crisis'. He also draws on Foucault, especially on the body and population, but adds a political economy of agency and resources to his theory.

On these bases Turner makes a variety of predictions about the future of globalization both negative (e.g. new wars) and positive (increase in human rights legislation). In the realm of bio-economic globalization, he worries about the increasing globalization of infectious diseases, the growing role of the medical-industrial complex which is involved in various inequalities including those involved in the global market for body parts, the focus on the commercial aspects of genetic research and ultimately corporate control over genetic codes and their use (and abuse).

He also discusses the coming gerontological revolution with the promise of the slowing down or even halting of the ageing of the population. This would obviously create huge problems for an already over-populated and ageing globe. Indefinite life spans would lead to an acute Malthusian crisis with such disasters as increasing resource depletion, increasing pollution of various types and the greater likelihood of war caused by population pressures and the resulting ills. Ironically, the global threats posed by increasing population might be mitigated by another global threat – pandemics – that could dramatically reduce populations, especially among the elderly. In either, or any, case, globalization will make catastrophes more general, immediate and profound. There is the possibility of a 'Mad Max' world and it is already with us today in Kabul and Baghdad. Other ingredients of a neo-Malthusian crisis are already here including alienated people, drug dependency, civil disruption, environmental decay, control by war lords, new wars and religio-political extremism. Such a crisis will adversely affect democratic societies, draining them of their democratic principles and civil liberties. While there will be juridical efforts to deal with these problems, it is unlikely that they can contain the impending global anarchy.

Thus, the book ends with a highly critical, dystopian view of the future of globalization. Overall, this volume has presented much information and many perspectives on globalization, as well as many of its pros and cons. It is up to the readers of this volume to review that vast body of material and to come to their own conclusions about the likely futures of globalization and about Turner's dystopian conclusions about that future. One thing seems abundantly clear: given the great complexity of globalization, and the likelihood that it will increase, it is unlikely that any single scenario will do more than capture a small portion of that future. Complex scenarios, probably lots of them, are needed in order to get a better sense of the complex future of such a complicated and multifaceted process as globalization.

References

Appadurai, A. 1996. *Modernity at Large: Cultural Dimension of Globalization*. Minneapolis: University of Minnesota Press.

Friedman, T. 2005. *The World Is Flat*. New York: Farrar, Strauss and Giroux.

Huntington, S. 1996. *The Clash of Civilizations and the Remaking of the World Order*. New York: Simon and Schuster.

Kuznets, S. 1955. 'Economic growth and income inequality', *American Economic Review*, 45, 1–28.

Schumpeter, J. 1950. *Capitalism, Socialism and Democracy*, 3rd edn. New York: Harper and Brothers.

Chapter 28

Globalization and Global Inequalities: Recent Trends

GLENN FIREBAUGH AND BRIAN GOESLING

GLOBAL INEQUALITY

One of the most contentious aspects of the globalization debate focuses on globalization's effect on global inequality, especially its effect on global income inequality. Globalization critics and defenders alike point to global inequality as key to their argument: critics aver that globalization has worsened inequality, while defenders aver the opposite. All sides agree that the 'problem of global inequality has become one of the most pressing and contentious issues on the global agenda' (Held and McGrew 2000: 27). So it is important to know the inequality trends – the point of this chapter.

The question of whether global inequality is rising or declining has been hotly debated among academics, international organizations, political activists and others. Among academics, views have changed dramatically in the last few years. As recently as 2001, Robert Wade probably represented the majority view when he wrote in *The Economist* that 'New evidence suggests global inequality is worsening rapidly' (Wade 2001: 72). That claim was soon called into question by a number of empirical studies which, using improved methods and newly available data, concluded that the level of income inequality in the world has been declining at least since 1980. Other studies went even further, arguing that if global inequality is expanded beyond income to include measures such as life expectancy, the reduction in global inequality began well before 1980.

Although it is not our purpose in this chapter to resolve the debate over the consequences of globalization for global inequality – the issue is a vexed one, and we could not do it justice in the space allotted – we can bring evidence to bear on the issue by reviewing the latest evidence regarding trends in global inequality. The chapter is laid out as follows. We begin by defining key terms. We turn next to broad arguments about the consequences of globalization for global inequality.

Does globalization tend to be a levelling process, or does it tend to worsen global inequality? In this section we try to show that globalization can be either a compressing or dilating force, to be determined empirically.

The bulk of the chapter then is devoted to describing the empirical evidence on global inequality trends over the globalizing decades of the late twentieth century. From this description alone we cannot of course prove that the global inequality trends in the late twentieth century were caused by globalization, but we can at least narrow the range of claims that are plausible regarding globalization's consequences in the recent era. We examine trends in global inequality in three basic domains: income, health and education. We also examine the trend in global inequality using the United Nation's Human Development Index or HDI – a composite index of human well-being measured on the basis of income, education and life expectancy. We conclude with brief speculation about the future direction of global inequality in the new century.

INEQUALITY

Inequality refers to the disproportionate distribution of some quantity X across units. Most often the units are individuals or households, but the unit could be men and women (gender inequality), regions (regional inequality), countries (between-nation inequality) and so on. The quantity X is something to which we attach value or disvalue – otherwise its unequal distribution would be no cause for notice. Thus social scientists have paid particular attention to worldwide inequality in the distribution of income, in the distribution of health (life expectancy, mortality and morbidity) and in the distribution of education (for example, school enrolment rates, literacy). Those are the domains of inequality that we focus on in this chapter.

Global inequality refers to the disproportionate distribution of X across all the world's citizens. Global income inequality, for example, refers to the disproportionate distribution of income across all the world's individuals or households. It is important to be clear on this point, since loose definitions of global inequality have led to much confusion. Suppose we have income data for every individual or household in the world. Then we could compute the variance of that income and, if we can compute variance, we can also measure inequality (by dividing the standard deviation by the mean, for example – that is one way to measure inequality).

Confusion has come about when writers have failed to conceptualize global inequality in a precise way, as applying to inequality in a *global distribution of X across individuals*. For example, in recent decades income inequality has been rising in the United States and in a number of other Western nations, in Russia and most of the former Soviet Republics, in China, in India and so on. This phenomenon is sometimes referred to as 'rising global income inequality', as a sort of shorthand for the notion that income inequality is rising in nations all over the globe. That loose usage of the term global inequality muddies the water, however, since global income inequality defined more accurately – again, as inequality in the distribution of income across all the world's citizens – is not rising. It is not rising because (as we see subsequently) the effects of rising within-nation inequality have been more than offset by the compression of between-nation income inequality due to the rapid growth of income in Asian countries such as China and India where, historically, the majority of the world's poor live.

IS GLOBALIZATION A LEVELLING PROCESS?

There are apparently about as many views on how globalization affects global inequality as there are people writing about globalization and inequality. It is possible, however, to classify the arguments into several very broad categories. First we separate the inequality-boosting arguments (that globalization tends to worsen global inequality) from the inequality-compressing arguments. Within both schools of thought there are different views on the central mechanisms by which globalization boosts or compresses global inequality. On the basis of those theorized mechanisms we can further divide the inequality-boosting and inequality-compressing perspectives to identify in very general terms the essential approaches that can be taken to the question of whether globalization has tended to exacerbate or diminish global inequalities. For convenience, we illustrate the arguments using the example of inequality in the distribution of global income. The arguments may be different for global inequality in health or education, as we describe below.

Globalization boosts global inequality

By globalization we are referring primarily to economic globalization, or the increased economic interconnectedness of localities, especially the deepening of economic ties across countries through cross-country trade and capital movement. Other forms of globalization – such as political and cultural globalization – might be closely linked to economic globalization, but our focus here is on the inequality consequences of deepening *economic* links.

One possibility is that economic globalization boosts global inequality by boosting world productivity, thus enlarging the surplus that elites can appropriate. Schematically, the argument is:

Scheme I.   Globalization → Rising world productivity → Greater world surplus → Greater global income inequality

The last part of the argument – that rising surplus leads to greater income inequality – could be called the Lenski principle. In his classic book *Power and Privilege*, Gerhard Lenski noted that very poor subsistence societies have relatively low levels of inequality because there is little surplus for the elites to appropriate. As societies become richer, however, there is more surplus for the elites to appropriate so that – up to a point (see Lenski 1966) – income inequality rises with economic growth.

The globalization → rising productivity → rising global inequality argument, then, is the Lenski principle writ large – applied to the whole world. The Lenski principle applied globally means that we expect to see growth in global income inequality because the rich are becoming richer, or a higher percentage of people are becoming rich, as opposed to an increase in the poverty rate, or a decline in the incomes of the poor.

However, the Lenski argument is rarely put forth by those who argue that globalization boosts global inequality. The more popular argument is that globalization boosts global inequality, not by raising those at the top, but by simultaneously raising those at the top and lowering those at the bottom. In this view economic globalization boosts inequality, not by boosting world production, but by increasing the reach or leverage of elites:

Scheme II.   Globalization → Greater reach of the elites → Greater rate of appropriation of surplus by elites → Greater global income inequality

There are various views on how globalization operates to increase the rate of appropriation by elites, ranging from the old notion of unequal benefits from exchange of goods (e.g. Emmanuel 1972) to newer ideas about an emerging knowledge-based global economy that is stacked in favour of the rich (e.g. Castells 1998).

It is important to note that the two very broad lines of argument in Schemes I and II are not mutually exclusive. It is possible for globalization to raise global income inequality both by increasing the world surplus *and* by increasing the rate of appropriation of that surplus by the rich. The most popular arguments for globalization as inequality-boosting, however, tend to be along the lines of Scheme II. This is somewhat puzzling, since it is harder to square Scheme II *by itself* with the empirical evidence over recent decades. Specifically, if global income inequality were increasing because the poor are obtaining a smaller slice of a *fixed* per capita income pie for the world, then world poverty should be rising. Yet that is not the case: Although there is some debate over the *rate* at which poverty is falling, it is clear that the world poverty rate has fallen over recent decades (Bourguignon and Morrisson 2002; Ravallion 2004). This is not to suggest that poverty is falling in all regions of the world. Poverty is on the rise in some regions of sub-Saharan Africa, for example. Even in this case, however, it is not clear that globalization is the culprit, since regions of decline are not necessarily globalizing.

The most promising arguments for globalization → greater global income inequality, then, are those along the lines of Scheme I, or some combination of Scheme I and Scheme II. If globalization is boosting global income inequality, it is because globalization is increasing the incomes of the rich or the non-poor, not because globalization is reducing the incomes of the poor, as is sometimes claimed.

Globalization compresses global inequality

Arguments that globalization compresses global income inequality focus on the global diffusion of productive assets implied by globalization. In its general form, the model is:

Scheme IIIa: Globalization → Faster diffusion of production technologies to poorer regions → Uneven economic growth rates favouring poorer regions → Reduced global income inequality

By hastening the diffusion of production technologies across regions and countries, globalization should reduce global income inequality by tending to level out regional differences in productivity around the world. As DeLong (1988: 1138) puts it in the *American Economic Review*:

> Economists have always expected the 'convergence' of national productivity levels. The theoretical logic behind this belief is powerful. The per capita income edge of the West is based on its application of the storehouse of industrial and administrative technology of the Industrial Revolution. . . . The benefits of tapping this storehouse are great, so nations will strain every nerve to assimilate modern technology and their incomes will converge to those of industrial nations.

It is important to note that the diffusion argument is historically dependent. At the early stages of a technological revolution, the dominant diffusion pattern is likely to be from rich regions to other rich regions. If so, then uneven regional growth rates favour the rich, resulting in greater global income inequality:

Scheme IIIb: Globalization → Faster diffusion of production technologies to richer regions → Uneven economic growth rates favouring richer regions → Greater global income inequality

Indeed, as we see subsequently, the extreme global income inequality we see today is the result of highly uneven regional growth rates during the nineteenth and earlier twentieth centuries, as the West spurted ahead and Asia and Africa lagged badly behind. During this period, then, the latter part of Scheme IIIb prevailed (see Firebaugh 2003: Figure 2.2):

Spread of industrialization → Industrialization of richer regions → Greater income inequality

The issue today is whether diffusion is predominantly along the lines of Scheme IIIa or IIIb. Firebaugh (2003: Figure 2.2; see also Amsden 2001) argues that it is along the lines of IIIa:

Spread of industrialization → Industrialization of poorer regions → Reduced income inequality

Castells (1998) and others disagree, arguing that the economic impact of the spread of industrialization to poor countries in today's world is overshadowed by the impact of an emerging information-based global economy where 'the fundamental source of wealth generation lies in an ability to create new knowledge and apply it to every realm of human activity by means of enhanced technological and organizational procedures of information processing' (Castells 1993: 20). Because richer regions have a decided advantage in this information race, technological diffusion in today's world will continue to exacerbate global income inequality, just as it did in the nineteenth and early twentieth centuries. As Castells puts it (1998: 344, emphasis added), 'inequality and polarization are *prescripted* in the dynamics of informational capitalism'.

If Castells is right, then we expect to find evidence of rising global income inequality due to rising income inequality across regions and nations. We turn now to the relevant empirical evidence.

GLOBAL INCOME INEQUALITY

Evolution of global income inequality

The massive global income inequality that we see today – in which average incomes in the world's very richest countries are 20–30 times greater than average incomes in the world's very poorest countries – is the legacy of uneven regional growth patterns that began with the first Industrial Revolution in England in the late eighteenth century. Although income data for this period are admittedly sketchy, it is generally agreed that in the early nineteenth century average income in the world's richest regions was no more than about three times greater than average income in the poorest regions. Even if these estimates are off by a factor of two, we can be confident that global inequality today greatly exceeds the level of two centuries ago, since the current level of inequality would not have been possible given the income levels of the early nineteenth century. It follows that the period since the early nineteenth century has been characterized by 'divergence, big-time' (Pritchett 1997).

Maddison's (1995) painstaking work is the standard source for world and regional income estimates for the nineteenth (since 1820) century and first half of the twentieth century. Bourguignon and Morrisson (2002) use Maddison's data to trace the over-time trends in within-nation, between-nation and global income inequality from 1820 to 1992. They find that in the early nineteenth century the vast majority of global income inequality was within-nation inequality, not between-nation inequality. Over the nineteenth and early twentieth centuries, however, between-nation income inequality surged (Bourguignon and Morrisson 2002: Table 2) as the world split into three income camps (Firebaugh 2003: Table 1.1): a fast-growing West, a middle group consisting of Latin America and Eastern Europe where incomes grew roughly at the world average, and a lagging Asia and Africa. Because it was the richer regions that were growing faster, this unevenness in growth rates resulted in rising global income inequality.

The rise of the West and the lagging behind of Asia and Africa resulted in the global income inequality that we see today, which differs in three important respects from the global inequality of two centuries ago. First, today's global income inequality is much greater – reflecting the big-time historical divergence noted by Pritchett. Second, global income inequality today is formed around a much higher income average – reflecting the dramatic growth of the world's productivity over the past two centuries. Third, in contrast to the early nineteenth century, global income inequality today lies largely between, not within, countries. Indeed, decompositions of global income inequality indicate that eliminating all within-nation income inequality would reduce global income inequality by no more than one-third (Firebaugh 2003: Table 5.1; Goesling 2001). In other words, at least two-thirds of global income inequality lies between nations.

Because the disproportionate distribution of income across the world's citizens is due primarily to the disproportionate distribution of average income across nations (that is, to between-nation income inequality), the trend in global income inequality is primarily determined by the trend in between-nation income inequality. That is the reason it is inappropriate to infer that global income inequality must be rising because it is rising within so many nations. The evidence points instead towards steady or – more likely – declining global income inequality over the globalizing period of the late twentieth century, as we now see.

Global income inequality over recent decades

Economic and sociological studies of income inequality traditionally have focused on inequality within nations – on why inequality is higher in some nations, on the consequences of high (and low) inequality and on why inequality changes. Some studies examine trends in a single country over time, while others are cross-national in design, studying multiple countries at one point in time or over time. There is growing interest now in between-nation income inequality, that is, *inequality in average income across nations*. This interest in between-nation inequality reflects a growing recognition that, because between-nation inequality is the larger component of global income inequality, the between-nation trend holds the key to the global trend.

There are two types of between-nation income inequality (Firebaugh 1999). One type – call it nation-weighted inequality – weights each nation the same, so an individual in Luxembourg counts as much as about 3,000 Chinese. The second type – call it population-weighted inequality – weights countries by their population size, so each individual counts the same. Studies consistently find that population-weighted between-nation income inequality has been falling in recent decades (Bhalla 2002; Boltho and Toniolo 1999; Dev Bhatta 2002: Table 2; Firebaugh 2003; Firebaugh and Goesling 2004; Goesling 2001; Melchior et al. 2000: Diagram 2.2; Sala-i-Martin 2002; Summers and Heston 1999: Figure 16.3). Nation-weighted between-nation income inequality, by contrast, has been increasing (e.g. Firebaugh 2003: Chapter 7), indicating that per capita income growth in the average poor country has been slower than the overall average for all countries. This finding is not surprising, since there are many small poor countries in sub-Saharan Africa with slow or negative growth rates over this period.

Importantly, though, *many more people* live in poor countries with faster-than-world average income growth (for example, China and India: see Firebaugh and Goesling 2004), so *population-weighted* income inequality is declining across nations. Again, global inequality refers to inequality across the world's citizens, where each citizen is weighted equally. To reach defensible conclusions about global income inequality, then, we must use population-weighted, *not* nation-weighted, between-nation income inequality (see Firebaugh 2003: Chapters 7 and 9 for appropriate formulas). Estimates of global inequality on the basis of nation-weighted inequality are likely to be severely biased due to vast national differences in population size. This is one source of confusion leading to the claim that global income inequality is still rising (e.g. Wade 2001: 73).

The changing nature of global income inequality

An emerging theme in the literature is that the spatial nature of global income inequality is changing. After two centuries of growth, global inequality appears to have levelled off and then declined in recent decades. As noted above, this reversal in the global trend has been caused by declining income inequality across nations, as large poor nations in Asia have experienced faster-than-world-average income growth. At the same time, income inequality within nations – which had generally declined over the first part of the twentieth century (Bourguignon and Morrisson 2002) – is now rising in many nations.

This pattern of declining income inequality across nations and rising income inequality within nations (Goesling 2001) implies that nations are receding in importance as economic units, just as one might expect in a globalizing economy. Because the highly uneven income growth of the nineteenth and early twentieth centuries was largely country-based – richer countries grew faster than poorer ones – global income inequality increasingly became between-nation income inequality. The result is the passport principle – that what matters most for your income is the nationality on your passport.

However, the waning decades of the twentieth century witnessed the emergence of a new geography of global income inequality (Firebaugh 2003) where income inequality is rising within nations and shrinking across them. If this pattern continues then the passport principle will become less important in the determination of individuals' incomes in the twenty-first century.

As a final point on global income inequality, we note that the major challenge for future research on this issue is data reliability. Measurement issues are pretty well settled in terms of theory, if not in practice. There is general consensus on how to measure and decompose income inequality. There is also consensus that income should be measured cross-nationally in terms of purchasing power parity and not official exchange rates. As Nuxoll (1994: 1424) and many others have warned, 'exchange rates cannot be used to compare income levels of different nations' because exchange rates do not calibrate currencies very well (see Firebaugh 2003: Chapter 3, for an extended discussion; see Korzeniewicz and Moran 2000 for an alternative view). Although these issues have been settled in theory, practical problems remain in the collection of income data. Almost all studies rely on national account (production) data, although there is some debate over whether such production data are superior to data from household consumption surveys. Production data tend to overstate poverty reduction in the world whereas consumption surveys tend to understate poverty reduction (Deaton 2005), so production data tend to indicate sharper declines in inequality than do consumption data. In the final analysis, our measurements and decompositions are only as reliable as the data we input, and that is where much of the effort should be expended in future research on global income inequality.

OTHER GLOBAL INEQUALITIES

Global inequality does not begin and end with income inequality. In his review article on world inequality and globalization, Sutcliffe (2004: 33) concludes that 'it is futile to summarize anything as complicated as world inequality in a single figure. The world is made up of innumerable specific inequalities; whenever anything changes, then some of these get worse and some get better.' In the same way, critics often charge studies of global income inequality of glossing over other costs of globalization such as environmental degradation, increasing social isolation and alienation, and worsening population health. It is possible that other types of global inequality have recently increased even though global income inequality has apparently declined.

To address these concerns, a growing number of studies look at inequalities in health, education and other important social domains in addition to inequality in income. For example, Kenny (2004) analyses trends in between-nation inequality for more than a dozen quality of life indicators, including several measures of health and education.

These analyses also reflect current views of inequality as consisting of more than just disparities in income and material well-being – views heavily influenced by the work of Nobel Prize-winning economist Amartya Sen (1999) and others. Sen has long argued that the most important aspect of inequality is inequality in personal freedoms. Income inequality may contribute to inequality in personal freedoms, since low income tends to constrain the types of freedoms people enjoy, but other factors such as health, education, political participation and so on are also critically important. In this section we focus on two of these factors, health and education.

Global health inequality

There are large disparities in health among the world's population in addition to disparities in income. Life expectancy ranges from the high 70s or low 80s in nations in the West and East Asia to less than 50 in parts of sub-Saharan Africa. There are also large disparities in health among individuals within nations, especially between people with different racial/ethnic and socioeconomic backgrounds.

However, global health inequality also differs from global income inequality in several important ways. For one, although disparities in health between nations are large, they are generally *smaller* than disparities in income and wealth. Whereas average incomes in the world's richest nations are at least 20–30 times greater than average incomes in the poorest nations, average health (as measured by common indicators such as life expectancy or the infant mortality rate) is not 20–30 times better in the healthiest nations than in nations where health is relatively poor. Rather, life expectancy in the world's richest and poorest nations differs at most by a factor of two. Put another way, there is relatively less 'surplus' health in the world than surplus economic production, so levels of inequality in health tend to be relatively lower. This is not to diminish the significance of inequalities in health, but rather to highlight the severity of modern-day inequalities in income and wealth.

Trends in health inequality are also relatively less governed by zero-sum mechanisms, in that health improvements in one nation typically do not come at the expense of declining health in another nation (see Scheme II above). Rather, as we will see, health has improved over the long run in nations worldwide, though sporadic epidemics such as the current HIV/AIDS crisis in Africa have occasionally halted or reversed this progress in selected nations and regions. The extent and timing of population health improvements has also varied markedly between nations and regions.

It is also important to note that nations with the highest income levels do not necessarily have the best population health. Health is better on average in rich nations than in poor nations, but the correlation between health and wealth is not one-to-one. To illustrate, consider that the United States ranks near the top of the world in gross domestic product (GDP) per capita but only 27th in life expectancy (UNDP 2004). On the other hand, nations such as Costa Rica, Slovenia and Cuba have achieved levels of life expectancy comparable to those in rich Western nations despite substantially lower income levels.

A final difference between global health inequality and global income inequality is that the pathways or mechanisms linking globalization and health are likely different from those linking globalization and wealth. The diffusion of production technologies may influence global health inequality indirectly through its effects of global income inequality (see Schemes IIIa and IIIb above), but equally if not more important is the diffusion of medical knowledge and technology, health-promoting behaviours and public health improvements (Deaton 2004). Indeed, it is likely that political and cultural globalization have had a greater impact on global health inequality than has the deepening of global economic links.

Recent studies of global health inequality have focused mostly on the trend in between-nation inequality, leaving out trends in health inequality within nations. The trend in between-nation health inequality over the nineteenth and early twentieth centuries paralleled the trend in income inequality, increasing very sharply. In the early nineteenth century, differences in health between nations were smaller than they were later in the century, with life expectancy ranging from the low 20s in the least-healthy nations to the low 40s in the healthiest nations. But then a 'mortality revolution' (Easterlin 1996) swept through the West, due to rising living standards, public health improvements, and advancing medical knowledge and technology. Mortality rates plunged and life expectancy shot up. Since the early nineteenth century, life expectancy for the world as a whole has more than doubled, from roughly 30 years to nearly 70 years (Riley 2001). But because the initial gains in life expectancy were concentrated primarily in the West, the level of inequality in health between nations ballooned (Bourguignon and Morrisson 2002: Figure 3).

In the twentieth century the 'mortality revolution' spread out from the West to other world regions, due in large measure to the diffusion of health-promoting ideas, technologies and practices. The largest gains in life expectancy in the second half of the twentieth century were achieved by nations in Asia, Latin America and the Caribbean, and Africa, which had previously lagged behind. As a result, the trend of increasing inequality in health between nations stalled in the middle of the twentieth century, and then reversed course. In his recent analysis of trends in the international distribution of life expectancy, Wilson (2001) reports that between-nation health inequality fell sharply from 1950 to 2000. The long-term trend in health inequality between nations has thus followed an inverted-U shaped pattern, increasing through the nineteenth and early twentieth centuries, and then declining steadily thereafter.

The most distressing feature of the recent trend in between-nation health inequality has been the negative impact on life expectancy and population health of the HIV/AIDS crisis in sub-Saharan Africa. In the 1990s, life expectancy for sub-Saharan Africa as a whole *declined* by nearly 5 years, reversing much of the progress achieved in the 1970s and 1980s. The difference in life expectancy between sub-Saharan Africa and other world regions has also begun to widen, to the point that the overall level of inequality between nations may again be increasing (Goesling and Firebaugh 2004; Neumayer 2004). The trend of declining between-nation health inequality that started in the mid-twentieth century will be arrested or reversed if the HIV/AIDS epidemic is not halted.

Determining the direction of the trend in *global* health inequality will require augmenting these studies of between-nation inequality with similar analyses of health inequality within nations (e.g. Pradhan et al. 2003). It is likely that within-nation health inequality has declined over the long run, as long-term gains in life expectancy have typically been associated with a declining variance in health outcomes among individuals within nations (Wilmoth and Horuichi 1999). However, recent trends in within-nation health inequality appear to be stable or even increasing, at least in the few (mostly Western) nations for which data are available. Future studies of global health inequality must determine the trend in within-nation inequality more precisely using data for a broader range of nations. A best guess on the basis of the limited evidence currently available is that global health inequality has been declining since at least the mid-twentieth century, with the pace of decline slowing markedly over the past 10–15 years. Regardless of the direction of the overall trend, it is clear that large disparities in health persist both within and between nations.

Global educational inequality

Global educational inequality has many of the same features as global health inequality. Disparities in educational attainment and achievement between nations are generally smaller than disparities in income and wealth, and improvements in education in one nation typically do not come at the expense of declining education in another nation. Education and health are also similar in that nations with the highest incomes levels do not necessarily have the best-educated populations or the highest-achieving students. For example, the United States typically falls below several other European and Asian nations in international student achievement tests, just as it falls below 20–30 other nations in international rankings by population health indicators (see above).

Like global health inequality, global educational inequality is equally if not more sensitive to trends in political and cultural globalization than to the deepening of global economic links. Indeed, some scholars see cultural globalization as the mainspring behind recent trends in global educational inequality (e.g. Meyer 2004), and the global diffusion of various educational institutions, teaching practices, curricula and technologies has emerged as a main recent theme in the education literature (Baker and LeTendre 2005).

Perhaps the main education story of the past two centuries is the great expansion of mass education in nations worldwide. Two centuries ago, formal education was common only among the world's elites. Today, more than 90 per cent of the world's children receive at least some amount of formal education, and more than 80 per cent stay in school through the early secondary grades (UNESCO 2005). In many nations, it is common for people to spend up to 16 years or more (or roughly 20–25 per cent of their lifetimes) attending school.

Despite this overall global expansion, trends in education have varied greatly between regions and nations, and inequality in educational attainment between nations has over the long run waxed and waned. What are the long-term trends? The best available historical evidence suggests that the nineteenth century and first half of the twentieth century were periods of increasing inequality between nations, whereas in the second half of the twentieth century inequality declined. Inequality increased in the earlier period because the expansion of mass education began in the West – first in north-western Europe, and then spreading east and south. The United States was also an early leader. By the end of the nineteenth century, large national education systems had been established in nations throughout the West, and primary school enrolment rates were in many areas greater than 50–60 per cent (Benavot and Riddle 1988).

Education levels continued to push upward in Western nations through the twentieth century, with the expansion of both high school and college education. But the main story of the twentieth century is not what happened in the West, but rather the expansion of mass education in other world regions, particularly in the post-World War II period. In the second half of the twentieth century, school enrolments surged in nations worldwide, with the largest gains occurring in regions which had previously lagged behind, such as south Asia and sub-Saharan Africa. As a result of this global expansion, the level of inequality in educational attainment between nations declined rapidly.

It is important to note that figures on educational attainment do not account for differences between nations in the content or quality of schooling, so it is possible that trends in school quality or student achievement have changed in different ways. In addition, although the past half-century has witnessed a sharp convergence in average attainment levels between nations, large cross-country disparities remain. For example, whereas many children in the United States can now expect to attend school for 15 years or more, children in poor nations such as Mali in Africa can expect perhaps 5 years of formal schooling (UNESCO 2005: Table 11).

Given the sharp declines in both educational inequality and health inequality between nations in the second half of the twentieth century, it is not surprising that composite indexes of development such as the popular United Nations Human Development Index (HDI) – a weighted average of life expectancy, average national income, adult literacy and school enrolment rates – also register a trend of declining inequality between nations. Evidence on long-term trends in the HDI show that the global average HDI went up over the course of the twentieth century but that inequality in the HDI between nations went down (Firebaugh 2003: Figure 6.8). Much of the decline in HDI inequality must be due to declining inequality in education or health, since the level of income inequality between nations has declined only recently.

So far we have focused only on the trend in between-nation inequality. What is the trend in total *global* inequality? A confident assessment of this question still awaits future research, but the bulk of current evidence suggests that global educational inequality declined over the second half of the twentieth century, at least in terms of inequality in educational attainment. Studies of within-nation inequality suggest that the variance in educational attainment among individuals within nations *declines* as national education systems expand, such that higher average attainment levels are associated with *lower* within-nation inequality. Because the second half of the twentieth century was generally a period of increasing educational attainment in nations worldwide, this suggests that within-nation educational inequality has also recently declined. Global educational inequality is the sum of inequality between nations plus the average level of within-nation inequality, so declining between-nation and within-nation inequality imply declining inequality globally. Whether a similar trend holds for other dimensions of education such as educational resources, school quality or student achievement is unknown.

THE FUTURE OF GLOBAL INEQUALITY

Assuming no cataclysmic economic collapse or global war, the most likely scenario is that global income inequality will continue to decline in the early decades of the twenty-first century. There are two principal reasons for this optimism. First, change in the age structures of poor and rich countries will tend to compress between-nation income inequality over the next few decades. As Williamson (1998) notes, during the demographic transition the age structure of a population moves through three stages: a bulge in dependent children, then a bulge in the working-age population and finally a bulge in the elderly. In the early parts of the twenty-first century most poor countries will find themselves in the second stage (due to the current decline in their birth rates) and most rich countries will find themselves in the third stage. So we expect growth in the working-age population to exceed growth in the total population in poor countries, and the opposite to occur in rich countries, resulting in an advantaged position for poor countries with regard to the translation of rising worker productivity into rising per capita income (see Firebaugh 2003: Chapter 11 for further discussion of this 'demographic windfall' hypothesis).

The second reason for optimism is that we expect the economic renaissance of Asia to continue. Although it is unlikely that income growth in China will maintain the torrid pace of recent decades, we can expect incomes in China and other poor Asian countries to continue to grow at a faster-than-world-average rate as the region continues to industrialize. This bodes well in the short run for the compression of global income inequality, since most of the world's people live in Asia, and incomes in Asia tend to be below the world average.

In the longer run, however, continued faster-than-world-average income growth in China and the rest of Asia will exacerbate income inequality, since average income in Asia eventually will exceed average income for the world as a whole. According to Sala-i-Martin's (2002) calculations, if the income growth patterns of the last two decades were to continue – that is, dramatic growth in Asia combined with slow growth in Latin America and stagnation in sub-Saharan Africa – then global income inequality would resume its long-term upward trend once again within the next two decades.

The lesson to be drawn from these considerations is that we can anticipate continued decline in global income inequality over the next few decades, but in the long run the lagging economies of Africa and (to a lesser extent) Latin America hold the key to continued compression of global income distribution. In the middle of the twentieth century, Asia and sub-Saharan Africa were roughly comparable in terms of average income. Since then Asia has surged economically while sub-Saharan Africa has foundered. Because sub-Saharan Africa has become an economic outlier, the direction of global income inequality in the twenty-first century will depend heavily on what happens in sub-Saharan Africa. Once incomes in Asia approach the world average, continued compression of global income inequality will be very difficult to achieve in the absence of economic progress in Africa.

Global health inequality will also rise or fall with sub-Saharan Africa, and in particular with trends in HIV/AIDS. The United Nations estimates that HIV/AIDS rates will peak in Africa within the next 10–15 years (UNPD 2003). If so, then we expect global health inequality to increase through the first few decades of the twenty-first century (owing to declining population health in sub-Saharan Africa) and then decline thereafter. But if the HIV/AIDS estimates are off mark, or if the epidemic gains force in other world regions, then a trend of rising global health inequality will likely persist through the middle of the twenty-first century (Neumayer 2004: Figure 1). In addition, as levels of population health between other world regions continue to converge, we expect *within*-nation health inequality to play an increasingly important role in determining the direction of the global trend. The best studies of global within-nation inequality await future research, but it may be that within-nation inequality is either stable or increasing. If so, future global health inequality may be defined more by disparities within nations than between nations.

Finally, the main question regarding future global educational inequality is whether sharply declining inequality in educational attainment levels will be matched by declining inequality in other dimensions of education such as educational resources, school quality, student achievement and so on. Inequality in attainment levels will decline as mass education systems continue to expand in nations world-wide. Less certain is whether this expansion will also entail improvements in school quality and educational resources, especially in low-income countries. Parity in the features and organization of national education systems does not guarantee parity in educational outcomes, and it is possible that future global educational inequality will consist of relatively small disparities in attainment levels between countries but much larger disparities in school quality and student achievement. This in some sense would represent declining global educational inequality, but the achievement would ring very hollow.

Acknowledgments

This chapter was written when Firebaugh was a visiting scholar at Harvard University (on leave from the Pennsylvania State University) and Goesling was a post-doctoral research fellow at the University of Michigan.

References

Amsden, A.H. 2001. *The Rise of 'the Rest': Challenges to the West from Late-Industrializing Economies*. Oxford: Oxford University Press.

Baker, D.P. and LeTendre, G.K. 2005. *National Differences, Global Similarities: World Culture and the Future of Schooling*. Stanford, CA: Stanford University Press.

Benavot, A. and Riddle, P. 1988. 'The expansion of primary education, 1870–1940: Trends and Issues', *Sociology of Education*, 61, 191–210.

Bhalla, S.S. 2002. *Imagine There's No Country: Poverty, Inequality, and Growth in the Era of Globalization*. Washington, DC: Institute for International Economics.

Boltho, A. and Toniolo, G. 1999. 'The assessment: The twentieth century – achievements, failures, lessons', *Oxford Review of Economic Policy*, 15, 1–17.

Bourguignon, F. and Morrisson, C. 2002. 'Inequality among world citizens: 1820–1992', *American Economic Review*, 92, 727–44.

Castells, M. 1993. 'The informational economy and the new international division of labor'. In M. Carnoy, M. Castells, S.S. Cohen and F.H. Cardoso (eds), *The New Global Economy in the Information Age*, Chapter 2. University Park: Pennsylvania State University Press.

Castells, M. 1998. *End of Millennium*. Malden, MA: Blackwell.

Deaton, A. 2004. 'Health in an age of globalization'. In S.M. Collins and C. Graham (eds), *Brookings Trade Forum 2004: Globalization, Poverty, and Inequality*, 83–110. Washington, DC: Brookings Institution Press.

Deaton, A. 2005. 'Measuring poverty in a growing world (or measuring growth in a poor world)', *The Review of Economics and Statistics*, 87, 1–19.

De Long, J.B. 1988. 'Productivity growth, convergence, and welfare: Comment', *American Economic Review*, 78, 1138–54.

Dev Bhatta, S. 2002. 'Has the increase in world-wide openness to trade worsened global income inequality?' *Papers in Regional Science*, 81, 177–96.

Easterlin, R.A. 1996. *Growth Triumphant*. Ann Arbor: University of Michigan Press.

Emmanuel, A. 1972. *Unequal Exchange: A Study of the Imperialism of Trade*. New York: Monthly Review Press.

Firebaugh, G. 1999. 'Empirics of world income inequality', *American Journal of Sociology*, 104, 1597–630.

Firebaugh, G. 2003. *The New Geography of Global Income Inequality*. Cambridge, MA: Harvard University Press.

Firebaugh, G. and Goesling, B. 2004. 'Accounting for the recent decline in global income inequality', *American Journal of Sociology*, 110, 283–312.

Goesling, B. 2001. 'Changing income inequalities within and between nations: New evidence', *American Sociological Review*, 66, 745–61.

Goesling, B. and Firebaugh, G. 2004. 'The trend in international health inequality', *Population and Development Review*, 30, 131–46.

Held, D. and McGrew, A. (eds) 2000. *The Global Transformations Reader*. Cambridge: Polity Press.

Kenny, C. 2004. 'Why are we worried about income? Nearly everything that matters is converging', *World Development*, 33, 1–19.

Korzeniewicz, R.P. and Moran, T.P. 2000. 'Measuring world income inequalities', *American Journal of Sociology*, 106, 209–14.

Lenski, G. 1966. *Power and Privilege: A Theory of Stratification*. New York: McGraw-Hill.

Maddison, A. 1995. *Monitoring the World Economy 1820–1992*. Paris: OECD.

Melchior, A., Telle, K. and Wiig, H. 2000. *Globalization and Inequality: World Income Distribution and Living Standards, 1960–1998*. Oslo, Norway: Royal Norwegian Ministry of Foreign Affairs, Studies of Foreign Policy Issues.

Meyer, J.W. 2004. 'The nation as Babbitt: How countries conform', *Contexts*, 3, 42–7.

Mullis, I.V.S., Martin, M.O., Gonzalez, E.J. and Chrostowski, S.J. 2004. *TIMSS 2003 International Mathematics Report*. Chestnut Hill, MA: TIMSS & PIRLS International Study Center, Boston College.

Neumayer, E. 2004. 'HIV/AIDS and cross-national convergence in life expectancy', *Population and Development Review*, 30, 727–42.

Nuxoll, D. 1994. 'Differences in relative prices and international differences in growth rates', *American Economic Review*, 84, 1423–36.

Pradhan, M., Sahn, D.E. and Younger, S.D. 2003. 'Decomposing world health inequality', *Journal of Health Economics*, 22, 271–93.

Pritchett, L. 1997. 'Divergence, big time', *Journal of Economic Perspectives*, 11, 3–17.

Ravallion, M. 2004. 'Competing concepts of inequality in the globalization debate'. In S.M. Collins and C. Graham (eds), *Brookings Trade Forum 2004: Globalization, Poverty, and Inequality*, 1–38. Washington, DC: Brookings Institution Press.

Riley, J.C. 2001. *Rising Life Expectancy*. Cambridge: Cambridge University Press.

Sala-i-Martin, X. 2002. 'The disturbing "rise" of global income inequality', National Bureau of Economic Research (NBER) Working Paper No. 8904.

Sen, A. 1999. *Development as Freedom*. New York: Anchor Books.

Summers, R. and Heston, A. 1999. 'The world distribution of well-being dissected'. In Alan Heston and Robert E. Lipsey (eds.), *International and Interarea Comparisons of Income, Output, and Prices*, 479–503. Chicago: University of Chicago Press.

Sutcliffe, B. 2004. 'World inequality and globalization', *Oxford Review of Economic Policy*, 20, 15–37.

UNDP (United Nations Development Program). 2004. *Human Development Report 2004*. New York: United Nations Development Program.

UNESCO (United Nations Educational, Cultural, and Scientific Organization). 2005. *Global Education Digest 2005*. Montreal: UNESCO Institute for Statistics.

UNPD (United Nations Population Division). 2003. *World Population Prospects: The 2002 Revision. Highlights*. New York: United Nations.

Wade, R.H. 2001. 'Global inequality: Winners and losers', *The Economist*, 28 April, 72–4.

Williamson, J.G. 1998. 'Growth, distribution, and demography: Some lessons from history', *Explorations in Economic History*, 35, 241–71.

Wilmoth, J.R. and Horiuchi, S. 1999. 'Rectangularization revisited: Variability of age at death within human populations', *Demography*, 36, 475–96.

Wilson, C. 2001. 'On the scale of global demographic convergence, 1950–2000', *Population and Development Review*, 27, 155–71.

Further reading

Allison, P. 1978. 'Measures of inequality', *American Sociological Review*, 43, 865–80.

Dollar, D. and Kraay, A. 2002. 'Spreading the wealth', *Foreign Affairs*, 81, 120–33.

Galbraith, J.K. 2002. 'A perfect crime: Inequality in the age of globalization', *Daedalus*, 131, 11–25.

Melchior, A. and Telle, K. 2001. 'Global income distribution 1965–98: Convergence and marginalisation', *Forum for Development Studies*, 1, 75–98.

Milanovic, B. 2002. 'True world income distribution, 1988 and 1993: First calculation based on household survey alone', *Economic Journal*, 112, 51–92.

Milanovic, B. 2005. *Worlds Apart: Measuring International and Global Inequality*. Princeton, NJ: Princeton University Press.

Schultz, T.P. 1998. 'Inequality in the distribution of personal income in the world: How it is changing and why', *Journal of Population Economics*, 11, 307–44.

Wade, R.H. 2004. 'Is globalization reducing poverty and inequality?' *World Development*, 32, 567–89.

Chapter 29

World Inequality in the Twenty-first Century: Patterns and Tendencies

Roberto Patricio Korzeniewicz and Timothy Patrick Moran

General interest in patterns of economic inequality has grown significantly over the last two decades, due in large part to public concerns and debates about the distribution of winners and losers over the course of globalization – the tension involved with negotiating perceived benefits in the face of profound social and economic inequalities. In Atkinson's (1995) often-cited line, inequality has 'come in from the cold', resurfacing as a fundamental concern across the social sciences. In this contribution, we summarize and critically examine some of the complex debates within the social sciences over the impact of globalization on inequality between and within nations.

While most studies have come to acknowledge the long-term rise of between-country inequality over the nineteenth and twentieth centuries, and that this inequality constitutes today the single most important dimension of global stratification (for example, as shown by calculating the relevant weight of between-country inequalities to overall world inequality), there is an intense debate over trends in between-country inequality over the last two decades. For some, globalization has led to rising between-country inequality while for others globalization of production has led to considerable convergence. Debates on within-country inequalities also have been intense, particularly over whether and to what an extent 'globalization' and greater market integration over the past decades has led to an upsurge in inequality.

In the first two sections that follow, we shed light on these debates by focusing on the empirical and methodological underpinnings of these controversies. In the third section we argue that there is remarkably little substantive theorizing about the processes underlying either polarization or convergence in the world economy. Similarly, theoretical frameworks are lacking from which to integrate the various national trajectories described in the within-country studies. While various studies have enhanced our understanding of specific dimensions of inequality, then,

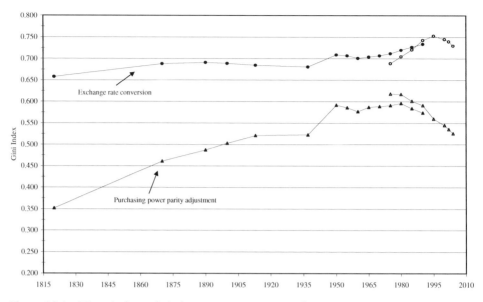

Figure 29.1   Historical trends in between-country inequality: 1820–2004
Sources: Authors' calculations based on: 1820–1990 series, Maddison (1995), $n = 24$; 1975–2005 series, World Bank (2006), $n = 107$.

relatively less efforts have gone into theorizing inequality as a complex set of interactions that have unfolded over space and time as a truly *world historical* phenomenon. The underlying assumption of many studies, but also the constraining institutional reality of even how relevant data are collected, is that the nation-state constitutes the crucial and only possible unit of analysis. We conclude our contribution by advancing the proposition that shifting the unit of analysis from the nation-state to the world as a whole allows us to raise more productive hypotheses about the past and future of inequality not only at the global, but also at the national or local scale.

BETWEEN-COUNTRY INEQUALITY: DIVERGENCE OR CONVERGENCE?

The available empirical data on inequality between countries unequivocally shows that the global expansion of markets and/or capitalism over the past two centuries has been accompanied by a significant rise of such inequality (see Figure 29.1). Precise estimates of the timing and extent of this rise in inequality differ: some studies (e.g. Pritchett 1997; Davis 2001; Milanovic 2005) consider the rise to have originated in the nineteenth century, while others (e.g. Wallerstein 1974) trace the development of inequality to the very origins of the modern world-system.[1] Most studies agree that by the late twentieth-century inequality between countries had become comparatively higher than most observed distributions (e.g. inequality within countries), and there is a consensus that inequality between nations accounts for the largest share of overall inequality.[2]

On the other hand, there is contention over whether these inequalities continued to grow or declined in the latter part of the twentieth century. In an earlier study, Korzeniewicz and Moran (1997) emphasized the continuing increase in between-country inequality in the late 1980s and early 1990s.[3] In a more recent contribution, Milanovic (2005) concludes that while *global* inequality (combining data on between- and within-country inequality) has remained rather stable, inequality *between* countries declined slightly over the last two decades of the twentieth century – but that this decline is smaller if we take into consideration growing regional disparities within China, and disappears altogether if China is excluded from the sample. Similarly, Wade (2004: 581) argues that by several measures, world inequality has been increasing over the last two decades; by one measure, average incomes per capita adjusted by purchasing power parities (PPP), between-country inequality has declined, '[b]ut take out China and even this measure shows widening inequality'. Firebaugh (2003; see also Firebaugh and Goesling 2004) dismisses these more qualified results with a more assertive emphasis on the declining magnitude of between-country inequalities.

Interpretations of recent trends in inequality are highly sensitive to the indicators and sampling procedures used by observers. Most studies showing a pronounced late twentieth-century decline in income inequalities between nations (e.g. Firebaugh 2003) tend to use national income data adjusted by PPP, while studies relying on exchange rate (FX)-based data (e.g. Korzeniewicz and Moran 1997) show income inequality rising until the mid-1990s.[4] Figure 29.1 represents these trends: PPP-based data show inequality between nations reaching a peak in the 1950s–1960s, and declining thereafter (although not yet below the levels reached around World War II). FX-based data, on the other hand, show inequality rising until the mid-1990s, to then decline slightly after 1995 (although not yet below the levels reached around 1980). PPP-based data increase the national income of poorer nations (particularly China),[5] thereby magnifying the rise of inequality of the nineteenth and early twentieth centuries and showing a decline in the late twentieth century, while FX-based data show a smaller increase in inequality in the earlier period, starting from a higher rate, and a less dramatic decline in the late twentieth century (see Figure 29.1).[6]

Beyond the technical issues surrounding the production of PPP and FX-based data, debates over which of these indicators is most relevant to the study of inequality reflect different ways of thinking about the meaning of income as an indicator. For authors such as Firebaugh (2003), data on income distribution are explored primarily to assess differences between populations in their relative access to welfare. For others, data on income distribution provide a lens through which to examine relations between populations: hence, Arrighi and Bonini (2005: 15) indicate that 'persistent differences in income . . . measure differences in wealth, that is, in the purchasing power or command wielded by a particular individual, group, or community over natural resources and the products and labor of other individuals, groups and communities'.[7] The choice of PPP- and FX-based indicators, then, should be informed by the theoretical questions informing the exploration of income data.

But let's leave aside for the moment the issue of trends in between-country inequality over the last two decades, and return to this topic after identifying some key, broader features of how the relationship between between-country inequality and globalization is theorized (or not) in the literature.

We should begin by noting that changes in levels of inequality between countries, characterized by a rather sustained rise in inequality, have been very gradual. This is striking in and of itself, as the period and countries considered in Figure 29.1 have been characterized by major shifts in the organization of production and consumption, widely different approaches to state regulation of markets, two World Wars and revolutionary change (in different directions over time) among large swaths of the world's population (e.g. Russia and China). Despite the turbulence implied in these transformations, and, observers might expect, their significant impact on global interaction, overall inequality between countries, as an output of global interaction, retained a remarkable stability. We would contend that inequality between countries in this sense is indicative of a system that for much of the last two centuries reached equilibrium, manifested in the long-term, gradual increase of world inequality.

To say that interactions between countries have constituted a system that reached equilibrium through most of the nineteenth and twentieth centuries is not to say that within this system there was rigidity and stability in the trajectories of individual countries during the same period. To the contrary, trends in inequality over the last two centuries indicate a considerable amount of mobility for individual nations. In the nineteenth century, for example, what are often ethnocentrically labelled as 'countries of recent settlement' (e.g. Argentina, Australia, Canada, New Zealand and the United States), were characterized by very high rates of economic growth. In the late nineteenth and early twentieth centuries, much of Scandinavia likewise experienced growth in national income and standards of living. Japan stood out in terms of its rapid economic ascendancy after World War II, and was joined (particularly after the 1970s) by the so-called 'East Asian Tigers'.

In short, since the early nineteenth century, we see both (1) a long-term stability of inequality (as indicated by groups of countries that have remained 'poor' and 'wealthy' over two centuries), and (2) persistently, individual cases of 'successful' upward mobility between these groups of countries. In this sense, individual mobility was consistent with the secular (and systemic) rise of inequality between nations. One aim, then, should be to theorize/understand the processes by which the distribution of world wealth can remain stable (i.e. be systemic) and simultaneously change from one moment to the next (i.e. be historical) – how states can move up and down as the system stays the same.

There have been two prevailing approaches to theorizing these processes. In one approach, deeply rooted in the social sciences, inequality is viewed as a consequence of time lags in the process of modernization. In the various versions of this approach, wealth is a consequence of modernization, and the achievement of wealth by nations is indicative of relative success in embracing key elements of modernization. Usually depending on the disciplinary background of the observer, favoured elements might include industrialization, free enterprise, rationality, efficient state institutions, democracy, social capital and so forth. In this approach, inequality appears as a transitional phenomena, marking the distance between the nations that have already embraced modernization successfully (attaining wealth) and those that are yet to do so (remaining in poverty). Over time, as all nations converge towards universal practices and modes of thought, inequality is bound to disappear.

A recent example of this approach is provided by the work of Glenn Firebaugh. According to Firebaugh (2003: 174), the rise (through most of the nineteenth century and the first half of the twentieth century) and decline (in the second half of the twentieth century) of inequalities between nations are explained primarily by the uneven spread of industrialization: 'the most important cause of the inequality transition is the spread of industrialization to poor nations . . . because industrialization took root first in richer nations, the spread of industrialization has boosted inequality across nations . . . Now, however, the diffusion of industrialization works to compress inequality across nations.' In this interpretation, nations tend to be perceived as independent and autonomous entities that embark, albeit with differences in timing, in a universal process of transformation from tradition into modernity. Appropriate institutions are the main force allowing for effective industrialization, and the adoption of such institutions is facilitated by globalization.[8]

An alternative approach has focused on the relational aspects that have characterized the systemic rise of inequality. In such approaches, inequality is viewed as a consequence of the comparative advantages that some nations have gained over others in their interaction. The relevant unit of analysis shifts from individual nations to overall patterns of interaction, and inequality becomes an expression of the inextricable links between success in some cases and failure in others.

An example of this alternative approach is provided by the work of Mike Davis. Davis (2001) focuses on the role of famines in the 'making of the Third World' over the late nineteenth century. As indicated by Davis (2001: 9):

> we are not dealing . . . with 'lands of famine' becalmed in stagnant backwaters of world history, but with the fate of tropical humanity at the precise moment (1870–1914) when its labor and products were being dynamically conscripted into a London-centered world economy. Millions died, not outside the 'modern world system', but in the very process of being forcibly incorporated into its economic and political structures.

For Davis (2001: 289–90), 'the forcible incorporation of smallholder production into commodity and financial circuits controlled from overseas tended to undermine traditional food security', while 'the integration of millions of tropical cultivators into the world market during the late nineteenth century was accompanied by a dramatic deterioration in their terms of trade', and 'formal and informal Victorian imperialism, backed up by the supernational automatism of the Gold Standard, confiscated local fiscal autonomy and impeded state-level developmental responses – especially investments in water conservancy and irrigation – that might have reduced vulnerability to climate shocks'. As opposed to the modernization approach, then, the emphasis here is on how the expansion of wealth-generating activities went hand-in-hand with the destruction of existing patterns of production and institutional arrangements.

Of course, these two approaches do not exhaust the range of approaches that characterize the study of the relationship between globalization and inequality. A crucial contribution has been the work of Jeffrey Williamson. While O'Rourke and Williamson (1999) appear to agree that the world as a whole was characterized by high levels of inequality during the nineteenth century wave of globalization, they focus on convergence among wealthier nations (what the authors label 'the Atlantic economy').

> Convergence was ubiquitous in the late-nineteenth-century Atlantic economy, but it was mostly a story about labor-abundant Europe with lower workers' living standards catching up with the labor-scarce New World with higher workers' living standards, and of Argentina and Canada catching up with Australia and the United States. It was less a story about European industrial latecomers catching up with European Industrial leaders. (O'Rourke and Williamson 1999: 15–16)

For O'Rourke and Williamson, convergence within the Atlantic economy ended in the interwar period when globalization gave way to more autarchic policies that greatly constrained global flows of commodities and labour. Furthermore, they are careful to note that not all countries experienced the consequences of greater world market integration in the same manner, for the impact of this integration depended on the particular constellation of factors of production and institutional response that characterized different countries (as we will see in the next section, a parallel argument can be made with trends in within-country inequality today).

Although limited to the 'Atlantic' economy (and perhaps even the authors in question should be more careful about not extrapolating their conclusions to the nineteenth century world economy as a whole), O'Rourke and Williamson make a crucial observation. Divergence and convergence in the global distribution of income most centrally involves the extent to which labour markets are integrated on a global scale. Late nineteenth century globalization generated convergence in incomes among the wealthier nations in the world economy because it involved world migration flows that produced greater integration (at least among this limited group of nations). The restriction of such flows in the twentieth century reduced global labour market integration and strengthened – or, more accurately, reconstituted – labour market segmentation along national boundaries.

Clearly, debates over the current impact of globalization on between-country inequality should take into account this particular relational dimension of recent developments. Regardless of whether using a PPP- or FX-based indicator to measure contemporary trends in income distribution, continued high rates of growth in India and China would result in further declines in between-country inequality. As we argue in greater detail in the third section below, such an outcome should be read, by those interested in shifting patterns of global interaction, not merely as indicative of growing industrialization in peripheral areas, but as a shift in the basic characteristics of operation of the world economy. Before moving to this discussion, however, we shall briefly consider recent trends in within-country inequality.

WITHIN-COUNTRY INEQUALITY: SHIFTING PATTERNS OF INEQUALITY AND GROWTH?

While the majority of the world's inequality is generated by between-nation disparities, social science research since the 1950s (greatly influenced by the work of Simon Kuznets: see Moran 2005) has paid considerable attention to trends in income inequality within countries. Built upon, and further constructing, the assumption that national units constitute the relevant unit of analysis for the study of inequality, this research is itself part and parcel of the trends discussed in the first part of this chapter.

For example, much of the research in question focused on nationally integrated markets (generally in wealthier countries) in order to model the relative importance of key variables (e.g. human or social capital) in explaining relative access to income, while paying considerably less attention to the continued relevance of ascriptive characteristics (e.g. nation of birth) in shaping integration and exclusion. At a more empirical level, the assumptions of this research both built upon, and further encouraged, the construction of national data on labour markets and income distribution – these data themselves constrained more and less practical ways of constructing units of observation when raising questions about patterns of income distribution.

In within-country inequality studies, regression analysis often is used to estimate the effects of various national characteristics (e.g. income level, type of political system) on a nation's level of inequality. And like the between-country studies just outlined, those seeking to find overall patterns of within-country inequality find mixed results – some argue that, on average, national inequality changes very little over time (Li et al. 1998), while others suggest that such inequalities are markedly increasing (UNDP 2005). The majority of cross-national studies analysing the latest data, however, find no simple, systematic relationship between average income levels and/or subsequent growth and changes in income inequality for nations on average (Anand and Kanbur 1993; Bruno et al. 1998; Deininger and Squire 1996, 1998; Kim 1997; Li et al. 1998; Lipton 1997; Ram 1997; Ravallion 1995). One of the most important indirect conclusions of these studies is that levels of within-country inequality vary significantly by region. In broad terms, Latin America and to some extent sub-Saharan Africa (although data is more sketchy here) register the highest levels of inequality in the world, while Asia and some of the high-income countries of the global North register the lowest.

Yet even within these broad regional tendencies, we see considerable variation in how different degrees of market integration have interacted among nations with particular constellations of factor endowments and specific institutional arrangements to result in different patterns of distributional change within nations. This means that rather than a single pattern among nations according to their level of income or of world market integration, we should expect variations in the trajectories of within-country inequality over the last 20 years.

Inequality in the global North

In the early 1980s researchers in the United States and the United Kingdom began to notice that, after a long period of relative stability, the distribution of income was becoming noticeably more unequal. This phenomenon, coined the 'great U-turn' by Harrison and Bluestone (1988), has spurred a vigorous and wide-ranging search for the socioeconomic version of the 'smoking gun' (Gustafsson and Johansson 1999). The overarching characteristic of the literature since the 1980s is its emphasis on answering two interrelated questions: (1) To what extent are various forms of economic restructuring driving inequalities in the global North? (2) To what extent are political contexts and institutional configurations impacting the distribution process?

Most arguments concerning inequality in the global North tend to implicate various forms of economic restructuring – shifting patterns of trade, increased capital and labour mobility, increased economic competition (deindustrialization), the rise of the skill-based economy – that fall under the 'globalization' rubric (Alderson and Nielsen 2002). The conventional argument is that the combined impact of these changes has drastically altered the relative demand for and supply of skilled and unskilled workers, generating downward pressures on the wages of the unskilled, while dramatically increasing returns to the skilled (Berman et al. 1994; Bound and Johnson 1992; Katz and Autor 2000; Murphy and Welch 1993). This in turn creates a bifurcated earnings distribution: falling (or at least stagnating) wages at the bottom combine with rapidly rising wages at the very top to produce a distribution where the middle is increasingly 'hollowed out'. This bifurcation in earnings then acts as the driving force behind rising income inequality between households (Bluestone and Harrison 1982; Harrison and Bluestone 1988).

Since economic restructuring like the sort described above characterizes the global North more broadly, both academic and popular interpretations tend to discuss rising inequality as a nearly universal outcome of these processes in the 1980s and 1990s (Friedman 2000; Smeeding 2002). As summarized by Ram (1997: 577), '[t]he somewhat cheerless distributional position recently noted for the U.S. seems to characterize most of the postwar developed world'. Yet scholars have begun to question the extent to which trends in the United States and United Kingdom were replicated throughout the global North, arguing that technological change has been less skill-based in parts of Europe than in the United States and United Kingdom, and that returns to education and skill increased less sharply in these areas (because the supply of skilled workers increased faster), leading to 'less of an increase, or even no change' in wage inequality in these countries (Acemoglu 2002: 1).

Another line of interpretation has emerged around the general idea that political contexts and institutional frameworks have important distributional consequences. Some argue, for example, that European labour policies and wage-setting institutions mitigate the tendency towards increasing earnings inequality (Acemoglu 2002; Blau and Kahn 1996; Freeman and Katz 1995; Nickell and Bell 1996). In particular, many studies find that labour union density significantly reduces inequality (Alderson and Nielsen 2002; Freeman 1993; Gustafsson and Johansson 1999), and that strong leftist government (Bradley et al. 2003; Brady 2003; Kelly 2004), high levels of democratic participation (Mueller and Stratman 2003) and low public tolerance for inequality (Lambert et al. 2003) are all associated with more equal income distributions.

Applying new statistical techniques to the income surveys of the Luxembourg Income Study (LIS), for example, Moran (2006) finds that, while inequality did surge in the United States and United Kingdom, the prevailing pattern in the global North is the one found in Continental Europe (and Canada) where relatively moderate levels of inequality have held constant over the last 20 years (with a few countries experiencing declining levels of inequality). Figure 29.2 plots the inequality trends for five selected high-income countries, illustrating these contrasting patterns. As seen in the figure, there are large differences in inequality trajectories for rich nations, suggesting that 'globalization' has not usurped the importance of national policy or led to the insignificance of the state; as in the late nineteenth century in

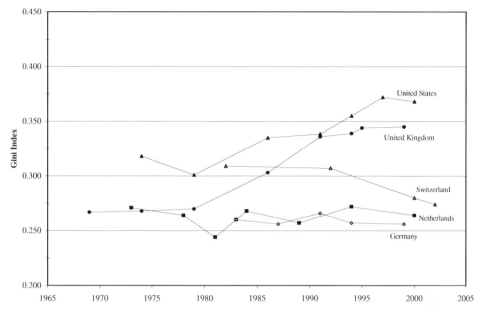

Figure 29.2 Inequality trends for selected high-income countries
Notes: Gini indices based on households' net disposable income.
Source: Luxembourg Income Study, Moran (2006).

our earlier discussion, these patterns suggest that even with similar degrees of integration into world markets, not all high-income countries follow a single, common trajectory.

China and India

China and India are widely described as the success stories of globalization, and indeed their sustained growth over the last two decades is well documented. Yet it is worthwhile noting that here, too, the particular path followed by each country has not been the same. Overall, the available data (limited as they are) suggest that growth in China has been accompanied by a considerable increase in within-country inequalities during transition (see, e.g., Hauser and Xie 2005; Khan and Riskin 2005; Meng 2004; Meng et al. 2005). While in India, a long time series of household consumption data collected by the National Sample Survey Organization (NSSO) shows much greater stability in overall within-country inequality (see Figure 29.3).[9] In China, increases in inequality are most pronounced among urban households, while in India distributional stability – if not declining levels of inequality – exists in both the rural and urban populations.

High rates of per capita income growth suggest large, sweeping gains across these highly populated nations, but a closer look reveals these gains to be unequally distributed within both China and India, between urban and rural areas, and between more and less affluent regions of the countries. Table 29.1 provides some indications of the complex forces shaping inequality in China. The table presents income and expenditure data across selected provinces for 2003. The provinces are divided

National Estimates

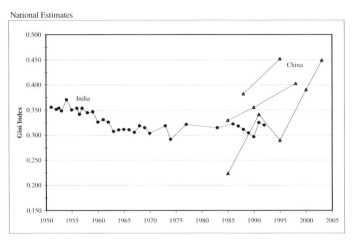

Rural Households

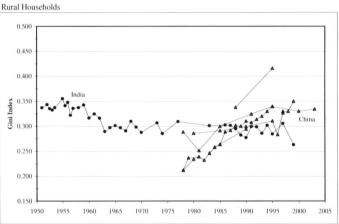

Urban Households

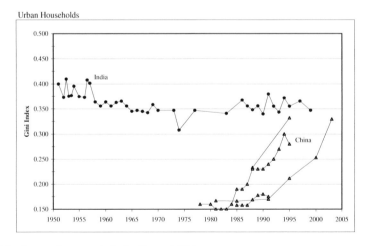

Figure 29.3 Inequality trends in India and China
Notes: One series, one survey for India, Gini indices based on households' consumption.
Multiple series, two surveys for China, Gini indices based on households' disposable
income.
Source: WIID (2005).

geographically between the south-eastern coast – where economic reforms were intentionally designed to 'develop' these now more affluent areas first – and the much poorer western interior. Vast rural–urban inequalities are well documented in China (see Skinner 1994) and the figures in Table 29.1 evidence this trend. In Shanghai province, for example, the average urban household has approximately 45 per cent more disposable income than the average rural household; in Jiangsu the average urban household has 46 per cent more. The rural/urban ratios are much larger in the wealthier provinces than they are in the poorer interior.

The figures in Table 29.1 are further divided by rural and urban households *within* each province (thus controlling somewhat for the differential size of these populations across regions), revealing that the degree to which labour markets are integrated into the global scale has important sub-national dynamics. Living expenditures and disposable incomes are much higher for both rural and urban households – sometimes twice as high or more – in the four coastal provinces than in the interior ones. While there is wide differentiation of incomes across regions, the sources of income are also much different. In the wealthier coastal areas, much higher percentages of rural household income are derived from wages and salary, but for urban households, these figures are comparable.

Similarly, in India high national growth rates belie considerable regional variation in living standards, where inequalities between states interact with income- and gender-based inequalities. Table 29.2 compares several education and health measures across selected Indian states in the 1998–9 period. Literacy rates in Kerala, for example, are in line with those seen in Mexico (although the gender gap is larger in Kerala), while rates in Bihar (including the gender gap) are lower than those in the Sudan. That 94 per cent of births in Kerala are attended by a health professional (the same as Venezuela) stands in stark contrast to the 23 per cent in Bihar, which is a lower percentage than Rwanda and Haiti. Similarly, the under-five mortality rate for India as a whole is about the same as Ghana, but in Kerala it is less than Argentina and Russia, and in Madhya Pradesh it is greater than Kenya and Senegal.[10] In India, as in many parts of the world, it is not just where you live, but where you live and if you are a girl or a boy. In Bihar, Rajasthan and Madhya Pradesh, less than half of females over 6 years old are literate, and the majority of women never went to school.

The large variance around the national averages in both China and India shows how national-level measures, and broader discussions of these country's 'globalization' processes, miss key distributional dynamics. Important rural/urban and inter-regional segmentations underlie overall national patterns, illustrating how various sub-national production processes and institutional responses create multiple distributional outcomes, and reflecting how different Chinese and Indian labour markets are differentially integrating into the world economy.

East Asia and Latin America

It is now widely argued under the rubric of an 'East Asian Miracle' that the countries in this region were able to experience rapid economic growth without significant increases in inequality in the last half of the twentieth century (Birdsall et al. 1997; Fei et al. 1979; Findley and Wellisz 1993; World Bank 1993). This 'growth with equity'

Table 29.1 Economic measures in China by selected regions, 2003

	Rural households				Urban households				Rural/Urban ratio	
	Living expenditures	Disposable income	Income from wages and salary	% Income from wages and salary	Living expenditures	Disposable income	Income from wages and salary	% Income from wages and salary	Expend.	Income
(Figures are yuan, per capita)										
National average	1,943	2,622	918	0.35	6,511	8,472	6,410	0.76	0.30	0.31
South-eastern, coastal regions										
Shanghai	5,670	6,654	5,252	0.79	11,040	14,867	11,526	0.78	0.51	0.45
Guangdong	2,927	4,055	1,966	0.48	9,636	12,380	10,413	0.84	0.30	0.33
Zhejiang	4,258	5,389	2,575	0.48	9,713	13,180	9,693	0.74	0.44	0.41
Jiangsu	2,704	4,239	2,189	0.52	6,709	9,262	6,091	0.66	0.40	0.46
Western, interior regions										
Guizhou	1,185	1,565	459	0.29	4,949	6,569	4,669	0.71	0.24	0.24
Yunnan	1,406	1,697	318	0.19	6,024	7,644	5,854	0.77	0.23	0.22
Gansu	1,337	1,673	489	0.29	5,299	6,657	5,269	0.79	0.25	0.25
Xinjiang	1,465	2,106	140	0.07	5,541	7,174	6,220	0.87	0.26	0.29

Source: Author's calculations, National Bureau of Statistics of China (2004).

Table 29.2 Education and health measures in India by selected states, 1998–1999

Measure	India	Kerala (South)	Goa (West)	Bihar (East)	Rajasthan (North)	Madhya Pradesh (Central)
Literate population, over 6 years old (%)						
Female	51	85	75	35	37	45
Male	75	93	89	63	72	72
Years of schooling (median)						
Female	2	7	7	0	0	0
Male	6	8	8	4	5	5
Births attended by health professional (%)	42	94	91	23	36	30
Children receiving all vaccinations (%)	42	80	83	17	14	25
Under-5 mortality (per 1,000 live births)	95	19	47	105	115	138

Source: IIPS and ORC Macro (2000).

pattern is usually juxtaposed with its socio-economic opposite in Latin America where recurrent economic recessions since the 1960s coincide with persistently high levels of inequality (Hoffman and Centeno 2003; Korzeniewicz and Smith 2000; Morley 1995). As indicated by Williamson (1991: 10), 'the initial Latin inequality may create a path-dependent inegalitarian regime throughout the Latin industrial revolution, just as the initial East Asian equality may create a path-dependent egalitarian regime throughout the East Asian industrial revolution'. In Figure 29.4, we plot inequality trends in select countries illustrating the contrasting regional trends.

Lower initial inequality in East Asia is generally attributed to major reforms following World War II that confiscated and redistributed land and other assets, and imposed progressive taxation on wealth. For some countries, such government policies reflected a concerted 'shared growth' approach to development that struck a more equal balance between rural and urban public investment – wide adoption of Green Revolution technology, high investments in rural infrastructure, limited taxation of agriculture – allowing rural incomes and productivity to rise more rapidly in East Asia than in other regions, and thereby lessening the distributional impact of rural–urban disparities. For example, the government in Indonesia used rice and fertilizer price policies to raise rural incomes, and in Malaysia introduced explicit wealth-sharing programmes to improve the lot of ethnic Malays relative to the better-off ethnic Chinese (World Bank 1993).

In the subsequent decades, inequality remained low not only because of continued investment in rural non-agricultural activities, but also because of the East Asian commitment to equitable access to education, which led to a rapid deepening of skills among the working population and widespread increases in human capital.

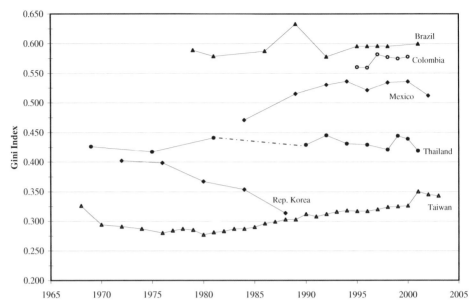

Figure 29.4 Inequality trends for selected East Asian and Latin American countries
Notes: Gini indices based on households' disposable income (Mexico, Taiwan); households' gross income (Brazil, Colombia, Thailand); individuals' gross earning (Korea). Data for Thailand are from the same survey but missing from 1982–9.
Source: WIID (2005).

The East Asian pattern sits in stark contrast to the persistent inequality characterizing Latin America. Here, income polarization is historically grounded in a highly unequal distribution of land and access to educational opportunities. Lack of significant land reform, combined with industrialization and urbanization transitions which excluded the poorest sectors of the population from educational opportunities and steady employment, has led to a concentration of the gains derived from economic expansion among skilled and/or organized workers (Edwards 1995; Korzeniewicz and Smith 2000; Lustig 1995; Morley 1995). Furthermore, as opposed to expanding legislative protection, recurrent economic recessions since the 1960s have been accompanied by sharp cuts in social spending that eroded the non-wage income of the poor (Edwards 1995; Rosenthal 1996). Finally, recent analyses indicate that the employment opportunities generated by market reforms and trade liberalization are widening income gaps between skilled/educated workers and unskilled/informal workers. In Latin America, these different elements have combined to produce highly unbalanced economic growth, and persistent and often deepening inequality.

PARTS AND THE WHOLE: THEORIZING WORLD HISTORICAL INEQUALITY

As summarized above, the recent literature has produced valuable insights on such diverse issues as the social effects of rising inequality (particularly in the United

States but elsewhere as well), the relationship between rising inequality in some wealthy countries and new patterns of production (e.g. the decline of manufacturing and the growth of the service sector), and regional patterns of inequality (such as the 'growth with equity' phenomena in East Asia and the 'persistent inequality' pattern of Latin America). These insights have enhanced our understanding of these specific dimensions of inequality.

Yet as in 'The Blind Men and the Elephant' metaphor, existing studies of both between- and within-country inequalities can be 'partly in the right' in describing what they perceive. But they are 'in the right' only within the particular boundaries of the sphere they choose to describe, and with the specific scopes (e.g. data, techniques, assumptions) through which observations are made. Hence, various 'parts' are adequately described, but what is required is an alternative way of theorizing this whole, that is, to account for inequality as a complex set of interactions (e.g. occurring simultaneously within- and between-countries) that have unfolded over space and time as a truly *world historical* phenomenon.

To begin constructing such an explanation, we draw some elements of the arguments advanced by Simon Kuznets (1955), who argued that inequality within nations rises in the early stages of economic growth, becomes more pronounced at intermediate levels of development and decreases thereafter as countries become wealthy. Kuznets attributed this pattern to (1) the compositional effects of population shifts from rural to urban sectors; and (2) institutional development shifting power among different factors of production.

Theories bear the imprint of the times in which they are constructed. Formulated when capitalist development was assumed to be concomitant with industrialization, and industrialization was conceived as the highest stage of such development, Kuznets' hypothesis on the relationship between capitalist development and inequality assumed that this relationship took place within a single transition of individual nations (from the production of raw materials to the production of manufactures, or from rural to urban societies, or from traditional to modern arrangements). Both the demographic transition and the institutional transformations that were predicted to follow were assumed by Kuznets to be embedded within this universal process of national transitions to modernity. Modernization, then, entailed a nationally based transformation (i.e. nations constituted the appropriate unit of analysis), and a singular, universal transition between two distinct distributional arrays (rural and urban) (some recent authors, such as Firebaugh 2003, continue to share this 'modernization' paradigm).

But there are important alternative ways of understanding capitalism. In a key and influential contribution, Joseph Schumpeter suggests that instead of a single transition from one state of equilibrium to another, we should conceive of capitalism as entailing continuous transformation.[11] For Schumpeter (1942: 82–3),

> [c]apitalism . . . is by nature a form or method of economic change and not only never is but never can be stationary . . . The opening up of new markets, foreign or domestic, and the organizational development from the craft shop and factory to such concerns as U.S. Steel illustrate the same process of industrial mutation – if I may use that biological term – that incessantly revolutionizes the economic structure from within, incessantly destroying the old one, incessantly creating a new one. This process of

> Creative Destruction is the essential fact about capitalism. It is what capitalism consists in and what every capitalist concern has got to live in.[12]

In the Schumpeterian model, the introduction and clustering of innovations disturb existing economic and social arrangements. Over time, this is the fundamental process driving cycles of prosperity (characterized by intense investment in new productive opportunities) and depression (characterized by the broader absorption of innovative practices and the elimination of older activities).

In recent decades, Schumpeter's insights have been influential within a number of economic growth perspectives.[13] Endogenous growth theory, for example, brought renewed attention to the 'virtuous cycles' (e.g. involving investments either in human capital and/or research and development) that enhance the ability of wealthy nations to continue to grow through technological innovations (for various formulations of such arguments, see Aghion and Howitt 1992, 1997; Barro and Sala-i-Martin 1995; Romer 1990). Deploying these insights within a world-systems approach, Arrighi and Drangel (1986: 20) suggest that Schumpeter's arguments can be read 'as a description of core–periphery relations in space, instead of a description of A–B phases in time'.

Here, we want to indicate that Schumpeter's interpretation of the (a) revolutionary and (b) destructive character of capitalist development has profound implications for understanding world historical patterns of inequality. After replacing the 'modernization' assumptions of the original inverted U-curve hypothesis with a Schumpeterian emphasis on capitalist economic growth as entailing constant 'creative destruction', any long-term stability (such as assumed by Kuznets) following the overall transition from the distributional array 'traditional' to the distributional array 'modern' can only be expected to be brief. Indeed, any apparent 'span of comparative quiet' constitutes an extraordinary respite from the 'discrete rushes' of transformation that characterize capitalism over time.

In other words, if, indeed, capitalism and economic growth involve 'incessantly revolutioniz[ing] the economic structure from within, incessantly destroying the old one, incessantly creating a new one', we should substantially revise our depiction of the pattern of demographic transitions between distributional arrays that is most likely to prevail. Rather than a single and fundamental transition between two distinct distributional arrays (culminating in universal 'modernization'), we should expect capitalism and economic growth to result in multiple and overlapping demographic transitions between many distributional arrays that never cease to emerge anew, prevail for a time and eventually be left behind – a process we might characterize as generating a 'constant drive towards inequality'.[14]

To the extent that Schumpeter's version of 'creative destruction' accurately captures key features of capitalism, capitalist economic growth entails the continuing prevalence of the compositional effects that result from constantly shifting populations across distributional arrays. In this sense, to the extent that an 'emerging' array is characterized by higher income levels of its participants (relative to previous arrays), processes of demographic transition between such arrays produce a 'constant drive towards inequality', even if (as emphasized by Kuznets) the distribution within 'emerging' arrays is more egalitarian than that of preceding arrays. Capturing such outcomes, however, requires observers to focus not on states of equilibrium, but on processes of change.[15]

Indeed, such a 'constant drive towards inequality' would help explain the long-term stability of high levels of inequality between countries and the constraints on upward mobility faced by nations in the world economy. Historically, policy-makers and business entrepreneurs in some nations have been able to design innovative strategies of growth that exploit the rigidities of prevailing economic and institutional arrangements (along similar lines, see Arrighi and Drangel 1986). On occasion, such innovative strategies have generated sufficient momentum to allow for significant upward mobility in the world economy of individual nations (such as Canada or Australia in the nineteenth century, Sweden and other Scandinavian countries in the late nineteenth century, Japan in the 1950s, South Korea in the 1980s and 1990s). But in the wake of all such successful transitions policy-makers in international agencies and in poorer countries have strived to follow on the track of innovators and catch up with wealthy nations by adopting whatever panacea seeks to distil the key ingredients of the success story of the moment. These efforts at diffusion have invariably been less successful, as efforts to generalize such strategies end up diluting, precisely, the innovative character of the original strategies. Furthermore, the very process of innovation, as Schumpeter tells us, serves to 'incessantly destroy' established arrangements, contributing to the constant relative impoverishment of those areas of the world economy in which such arrangements are more prevalent. Rather than simple industrialization, or a universal transition from tradition to modernity, successful economic growth historically has involved meeting a moving target of innovative practices.

Formulating the relationship between economic growth and inequality in this manner also helps our understanding of the recent increase in inequality across several wealthy countries. While rising inequality in wealthy countries was indeed difficult to explain within a modernization paradigm that saw urbanization and industrialization as a final endpoint, this rising inequality can be more elegantly explained within the type of framework we are proposing here. Indeed, processes of Schumpeterian innovation have led to technological changes that have pushed large sectors of the labour force in wealthy nations out of the type of jobs and social arrangements that Kuznets envisioned as key to the growing empowerment of labour that would accompany urbanization. Deindustrialization and the rise of the service sector, as emphasized by much of the literature, will be accompanied by new patterns of stratification in the labour force.

Institutional practices are key in altering the distribution of competitive pressures across the world economy. Collective actors and states can have a significant impact in accentuating or diminishing the constant drive towards inequality by (a) modifying the extent to which different sectors within a distributional array are included/excluded from processes of growth; and (b) shaping the distribution of the gains and losses that result from such growth. Hence, the precise manner in which institutional and political processes intervene most effectively itself varies through time and across place – from tax and/or wage-setting policies, to strategies that promote or hinder the acquisition of skills among different sectors of the population, to regulating entry into markets. In this sense, while creative destruction leads to the constant drive towards inequality identified above, economic growth takes place within institutional arrangements that have a direct impact on the distribution of resources among different groups of people.

From the point of view of the argument advanced in this essay, for example, the decline in inequality experienced in several wealthy countries earlier in the twentieth century can be interpreted to a large extent as the consequence of the introduction of wage-setting institutions among the countries in question. True, much of the literature emphasizes the importance of macroeconomic trends that enhanced the demand for unskilled labour (thereby reducing wage differentials), unionization or favourable state policies (see, for example, Galbraith and Berner 2001). But also of crucial importance was the introduction of restrictive international migration policies that reduced competitive pressures in national labour markets (e.g. see Williamson 1991), and provided opportunities for (some but not other) rural populations to rapidly enhance their incomes by moving to urban areas, thereby contributing further to declines in within-country inequality in wealthier nations.[16]

The trend towards declining inequality that characterized wealthy countries in the mid-twentieth century, the more recent East Asian trajectory and the current continental European pattern, all provide evidence as to the impact of institutions in altering the relationship between growth and inequality.[17] The three trajectories all suggest that institutional arrangements indeed can modify the extent to which different sectors within a distribution are included/excluded from processes of growth, thereby ameliorating the 'constant drive towards rising inequality' that might characterize economic growth.

The manner in which institutions intervene most effectively varies from case to case. In the mid-twentieth century trajectory, restrictive migration policies had a significant impact in reducing competitive pressures among the unskilled. In East Asia, as we indicated earlier in the chapter, intervention aimed at promoting the incorporation of new technologies into agriculture or facilitating access to new skills by the rural population or recent rural migrants. In continental Europe, the expansion of access to skills and to education was accompanied by trade union and government efforts to restrain wage gaps between the skilled and unskilled. What all these instances share in common, is that institutional efforts played a significant role in facilitating the inclusion of sectors of the population that were left behind as an outcome of processes of capitalist innovation and growth.[18]

But institutions should be understood as *relational* mechanisms of regulation, operating *within* countries while simultaneously shaping interactions and flows *between* nations. In this sense, the same institutional mechanisms through which inequality historically has been reduced within nations often have accentuated the exclusion from wealthy markets of populations from poorer countries.[19]

In other words, institutions often displace competitive pressures from one population into others. For example, even Olson (1982: 163) acknowledges, in the particular case of South Africa, that '[t]he denial of various skilled and semi-skilled jobs to Africans not only raised the wages of the European (and sometimes Coloureds and Asian) workers, but it also crowded more labor into the areas that remained open to Africans, making the wages there lower than they would otherwise be'. The same observation can be extended to other situations. Boserup (1970), for example, contends that over the initial process of economic growth, males were often able to use property rights and institutional arrangements as a means for obtaining significant competitive advantages over women. Davis (2001) argues that colonialist expansion in the nineteenth century entailed a strengthening of state capacity in wealthy countries and a dismantling of such a capacity in what became (to a significant extent, *through* such an uneven process) the Third World.[20] The situations differ in character, but they converge in underscoring the crucial role of institutions in shaping competitive pressures and the markets thereby constituted.

To use a broader and most significant example, greater national regulation of international migration after the early twentieth century certainly reduced competitive pressures among workers within wealthy nations (and thereby contributed to the declining phase of within-country income inequality observed by Kuznets in his original study). But at the same time the constraints imposed on international migration accentuated competitive pressures in labour markets elsewhere in the world, and in the process eliminated for much of the twentieth century one crucial set of mechanisms for reducing the income gap between countries (i.e. the transfer of populations from poor to wealthy nations and the transfer of income – e.g. through remittances – from wealthy to poor areas).[21]

This segmentation of the world labour market goes far in explaining the divide between wealthy and poor countries in the last two centuries. As we have indicated earlier, its development went hand-in-hand with the formulation of twentieth-century social science approaches that naturalized this segmentation by uncritically assuming the national boundaries that constituted segmentation to provide the only reasonable boundaries for constituting social inquiry. From the point of view of world income inequalities, what today we call globalization has served to challenge this segmentation and its accompanying assumptions.

This challenge has not emerged subtly and gradually; like an elephant in a china shop, it has altered dramatically existing expectations about the stability of prevailing arrangements. Over the long twentieth century, institutional arrangements and market mechanisms generally combined in ways that reduced inequality within high income nations, by simultaneously generating or strengthening constraints that accentuated inequalities between nations. From the point of view of world labour market segmentation, growing income disparities between nations generated strong incentives and opportunities (e.g. drastically lower wages in poor countries or more limited market regulation) for 'outsourcing' skilled and unskilled jobs to peripheral countries in a 'market bypass' that in effect has been overcoming twentieth century constraints on labour flows. In this sense, the high rates of economic growth that have characterized China and India in recent years are indicative of a breakdown of existing forms of segmentation, a breakdown that can potentially give way to significant convergence between poor and wealthy populations in the world economy.

But convergence is likely to entail a trade-off between within- and between-country inequality, and such a trade-off is at the heart of current tensions and debates over the future of 'globalization'. Late nineteenth-century globalization entailed both the expansion of markets and their simultaneous regulation (Karl Polanyi's 'double movement'), and eventually led to what some (e.g. O'Rourke and Williamson 1999) have characterized as a period of greater national autarchy.[22] The current competitive pressures unleashed by the growth of China and India could generate a backlash of protectionism, in an effort to reconstitute greater segmentation.

But growth in China and India could continue at high rates, in which case not only would inequality between nations undergo a significant decline: in fact, such a decline would be indicative of an end to the equilibrium that characterized the development of the world economy as a system. For as opposed to earlier individual transitions and trajectories of national mobility that characterized the history of this world economy, the continued rise of China and India at current rates would challenge the segmentation of the world labour market through national boundaries – a segmentation that was at the very heart of the trends we have observed in relation to world inequality over the development of the modern world-economy.[23]

CONCLUSIONS

This contribution has argued that economic growth, unfolding through institutions embedded in time and space, produces a constant drive towards inequality that results in a multiple and overlapping matrix of distributional arrays, an overall income distribution (e.g. within- and between-countries) that is both systemic and historical. Conceiving of world inequality in such a way allows us to understand why studies focusing on partial aspects of this phenomenon (or drawing on data constructed within the boundaries of the nation-state as the most relevant and sole unit of analysis) can generate contending interpretations on trends in the impact of globalization on between- and within-country inequality.

If indeed we are experiencing the transformation of the modern world economy (and this transformation is not yet certain), it is difficult to foresee what patterns in inequality would follow such a systemic change. Will new equilibria be attained? Will regional and other forms of within-country inequality increase in relative and/ or absolute terms? How will world markets interact with regulation from national governments and supranational agencies to produce new institutional configurations? Will these arrangements provide people around the world with greater freedom? These questions underline that in thinking about patterns and tendencies in world inequality as we move further into the new millennium we might deal, indeed, with a different elephant altogether.

Facing such systemic change, it is perhaps futile to anticipate future developments by drawing primarily on the experiences of past trajectories. Such experiences will continue to be relevant only to the extent that current trends are reversed and boundaries (perhaps no longer solely national) between poor and wealthy populations are once again reinforced. If not, contemporary observers 50 years hence are likely to revisit contemporary debates on globalization and inequality, if at all, only to recall with their bemused audiences the short-sighted perspectives of their naive predecessors.

Notes

1   Illustrating this divergent interpretation, contrast Adam Smith's (1976: 16) assertion in the 1770s that 'the accommodation of an European prince does not always so much exceed that of an industrious and frugal peasant, as the accommodation of the latter

exceeds that of many an African king', to Mike Davis's (2001: 16) recent indication that until the latter half of the nineteenth century '[t]he differences in living standards, say, between a French sans-culotte and Deccan farmer were relatively insignificant compared to the gulf that separated both from their ruling classes'.

2 Milanovic (n.d.: 27), for example, notes that 'the current dollar inequality . . . reaches a Gini of 80 [*sic*] in 1993 . . . the highest income or expenditure Gini coefficient ever reported'. In a detailed combination of within- and between-country data, Milanovic (n.d.: 34) calculates inequality between countries to account for roughly two-thirds of overall world inequality in 1993.

3 Lindert and Williamson (2001) observe rising inequality between nations, but argue that the forces usually identified as 'globalization' have tended to reduce rather than enhance such inequality.

4 The PPP adjustment of national income data aims at recalculating the estimated volume and value of the production of goods and services. The basic principle of such an adjustment is that goods and services are undervalued in poorer countries. The actual process of conducting such estimates is extremely complicated and expensive, and the collection of the relevant data has been irregular and fairly infrequent. We examine these issues in great detail in Korzeniewicz et al. (2004).

5 Firebaugh (2003: 148) himself notes that '[w]hen China is removed . . . the annual rate of income growth for LDCs falls to 2.3 percent, which is lower than the growth rate for industrial market nations – again pointing to the importance of China in determining the direction of the trend in between-nation income inequality.'

6 Additionally, the current mode of adjusting national income data by PPP is certainly unwarranted to study historical trends in inequality, as a single benchmark adjustment is made for contemporary data, and the same adjustment is projected back for 200 years. By this procedure, the relative weight of the PPP adjustment increases significantly over time (explaining why the rise in world income inequalities is made more dramatic by the use of PPP data).

7 For a similar point, as indicated in the late eighteenth century by Adam Smith (1976), '[h]alf an ounce of silver at Canton in China may command a greater quantity both of labour and of the necessaries and conveniences of life, than an ounce at London. A commodity, therefore, which sells for half an ounce of silver at Canton may there be really dearer, of more importance to the man who possess it there, than a commodity which sells for an ounce at London is to the man who possess it at London. If a London merchant, however, can buy at Canton for half an ounce of silver, a commodity which he can afterwards sell at London for an ounce, he gains a hundred per cent by the bargain, just as much as if an ounce of silver was at London exactly of the same value as at Canton. It is of no importance to him that half an ounce of silver at Canton would have given him the command of more labour and of a greater quantity of the necessaries and conveniences of life than an ounce can do at London. An ounce at London will always give him the command of double the quantity of all these, which half an ounce could have done there, and this is precisely what he wants.'

8 Firebaugh contends that his theorization represents a significant challenge to what he calls 'the Trade Protest Model'. Firebaugh (2003: 16) indicates that the arguments of this model can be characterized as:

Globalization → global inequality

By contrast, Firebaugh (2003: 194) characterizes his own theoretical approach as:

Globalization → Narrowing of institutional differences across nations → Reduction in between-nation inequality → Reduction in global inequality

As we discuss in this chapter, this 'approach' tends to ignore key contributions and debates on the relationship between globalization and inequality.

9 The quality and comparability of these data is questionable at the very best, and Figure 29.3 should be read with exceptional care, especially for China. For example, in the Rural Household Survey, selected households are asked to keep a written record of their incomes and expenditures, automatically excluding the significantly large (and poor) illiterate population. In the Urban Household Survey, only residents with urban status are surveyed, thus excluding the significantly large (and poor) rural to urban migrant population. In all cases, non-trivial changes in measurement and methodology over the years would cause the Gini index to shift irrespective of shifts in the underlying income distributions. In both China and India, overall distribution estimates are derived via procedures that pool rural and urban distributions using population shares as weights.

10 Data for these country comparisons are taken from the 2005 *Human Development Report*.

11 A similar interpretation, albeit with a different account of the intervening mechanisms at hand, is advanced more recently by Baumol (2002: viii), who argues that 'what differentiates the prototype capitalist economy most sharply from all other economic systems is free-market pressures that force firms into a continuing process of innovation, because it becomes a matter of life and death for many of them. The static efficiency properties that are stressed by standard welfare economics are emphatically not the most important qualities of capitalist economies.' For a related perspective, see also North (1981): '[t]he major source of changes in an economy over time is structural change in the parameters held constant by the economist – technology, population, property rights, and government control over resources'.

12 Kuznets (1940) was critical in his own review of Schumpeter's work on business cycles, indicating doubts about the empirical accuracy of Schumpeter's account in regard to the clustering of innovations in cycles. There is a vast literature and extensive debates on the existence of periodic cycles of innovation, their causes and implications (see, for example, Aghion and Howitt 1992, 1997; Dinopoulos and Segerstrom 1999; Forbes 2000; Francois and Lloyd-Ellis 2003; Goldstein 1988; Maddison 1982; Mansfield 1983; Rostow 1978; Thompson 1990). While these debates are important, whether the type of innovations emphasized in this chapter can be observed in cycles is not central to our arguments regarding the impact of change on inequality.

13 In fact, Schumpeter has had a tremendous impact across the social sciences. Recently, his ideas have been incorporated in research ranging from the workings of democracy to outsourcing and other 'globalization' issues. For our purposes here, we are focusing on his more detailed arguments concerning processes of creative destruction.

14 Among such multiple and overlapping transitions, those characterized by most unbalanced growth are of course most likely to result in rapidly rising inequality (Williamson 1991).

15 We should note that such a perspective on the character of economic growth is already fairly common among several approaches in the social sciences. For example, even in his earlier formulations of a world-systems approach, Wallerstein (1989: 71) emphasized that the unequal exchange that characterized core and peripheral countries was not necessarily centred on an agricultural/industrial divide: '[w]hat products are exchanged in . . . "unequal exchange" are a function of world technology. If in the sixteenth century, peripheral Poland traded its wheat for core Holland's textiles, in the mid-twentieth-century world, peripheral countries are often textile producers whereas core countries export wheat as well as electronic equipment. The point is that we should not identify any particular product with a structural sector of the world-economy but rather observe the wage patterns and margins of profit of particular products at particular moments

of time to understand who does what in the system.' Arrighi and Drangel (1986: 56) explicitly sought to bring a Schumpeterian emphasis on processes of creative destruction to reconceptualize world economic zones (periphery, semi-periphery and core) and the characteristics of productive characteristics in each, concluding in fact that 'the industrialization of the semiperiphery and periphery has ultimately been a channel, not of subversion, but of reproduction of the hierarchy of the world-economy'. Partly reflecting Arrighi's influence in reformulating this particular aspect of a world-systems approach, Wallerstein (1996) himself would later emphasize to a greater extent the impact of processes of 'creative destruction' on product cycles and the spatial organization of production and consumption in the world economy.

16 Williamson (1991: 17), for example, argues that declining inequality in industrialized countries after the 1930s was chiefly the outcome of pre-fisc forces altering returns to skilled and unskilled sectors of the labour force in favour of the latter, and indicates that key to these forces was 'an erosion in the premium on . . . skills, and [a] relative increase in unskilled labor scarcity'.

17 Thus, 'the institutional and economic arrangements which make the human capital accumulation response rapid in some countries (like East Asia) and slower in others (like Latin America) clearly will play a role in determining whether a Kuznets curve will be more pronounced in some countries compared with others' (Williamson 1991: 27).

18 Observers often note that efforts to provide protection to lagging sectors of the population through market regulation eventually are bound to fail. But Polanyi (1957: 36) reminds us that 'such a view seems to miss the point altogether. Why should the ultimate victory of a trend be taken as a proof of the ineffectiveness of the efforts to slow down its progress? And why should the purpose of these measures not be seen precisely in that which they achieved, i.e., in the slowing down of the rate of change? . . . The rate of change is often of no less importance than the direction of the change itself; but while the latter frequently does not depend upon our volition, it is the rate at which we allow change to take place which well may depend upon us.'

19 Such an outcome would not have been surprising to Adam Smith, who in a different context understood combinations restricting entry to markets as efforts by producers and traders in wealthy areas to limit competition (so as to maintain relatively higher wages and profits). Tilly (1998: 91) refers to such arrangements as opportunity hoarding: '[w]hen members of a categorically bounded network acquire access to a resource that is valuable, renewable, subject to monopoly, supportive of network activities, and enhanced by the network's modus operandi, network members regularly hoard their access to the resource, creating beliefs and practices that sustain their control. As in exploitation, a boundary separates beneficiaries from others, while unequal relations across the boundary connect them.'

20 We should note that although O'Rourke and Williamson (1999) emphasize the relational aspect of development in the 'Atlantic' economy, they pay less attention to the story of how differences in the development of state capacity in wealthier and poorer countries was a crucial aspect of nineteenth-century globalization.

21 Thus, a recent study indicates that 'even a small liberalization of international migration restrictions' would have a significant impact in alleviating poverty, enhancing efficiency and reducing the income gap between poor and wealthy nations (Moses and Letnes 2004: 1609; along similar lines, see also Adams and Page 2005). In this sense, it is important to recognize (as Adam Smith certainly did) that for some disadvantaged populations, greater access to markets becomes an effective strategy for challenging existing inequalities.

22 Although, we should emphasize, what many view as a retreat from globalization through most of the twentieth century, actually involved the continued advance of common

patterns of thought and behaviour. To take but one example, national state building through the twentieth century involved the construction of rational institutions and procedures (in the operation of both markets and governments) that were key to facilitating commodity, financial and policy-making flows in the latter part of the century.

23 This is probably what Wallerstein (1974: 127) aimed at in indicating that '[f]ree labor is the form of labor control used for skilled work in core countries whereas coerced labor is used for less skilled work in peripheral areas. The combination thereof is the essence of capitalism. When labor is everywhere free, we shall have socialism.'

References

Acemoglu, D. 2002. 'Cross-country inequality trends', Luxembourg Income Study Working Paper No. 296.

Adams, R.H. Jr and Page, J. 2005. 'Do international migration and remittances reduce poverty in developing countries?' *World Development*, 33, 1645–69.

Aghion, P. and Howitt, P. 1992. 'A model of growth through creative destruction', *Econometrica*, 60, 323–51.

Aghion, P. and Howitt, P. 1997. *Endogenous Growth Theory*. Cambridge, MA: MIT Press.

Alderson, A.A. and Nielsen, F. 2002. 'Globalization and the great U-turn: Income inequality trends in 16 OECD countries', *American Journal of Sociology*, 107, 1244–99.

Anand, S. and Kanbur, S.M.R. 1993. 'Inequality and development: A critique', *Journal of Development Economics*, 41, 19–43.

Arrighi, G. and Bonini, A.N. 2005. 'The political sociology of world income inequality', Paper presented at the annual meeting of the American Sociological Association, Philadelphia (August).

Arrighi, G. and Drangel, J. 1986. 'The stratification of the world-economy: An exploration of the semiperipheral zone', *Review*, X (1) (Summer), 9–74.

Atkinson, A. 1995. *Incomes and the Welfare State: Essays on Britain and Europe*. Cambridge: Cambridge University Press.

Barro, R.J. and Sala-i-Martin, X. 1995. *Economic Growth*. Cambridge, MA: MIT Press.

Baumol, W.J. 2002. *The Free-Market Innovation Machine: Analyzing the Growth Miracle of Capitalism*. Princeton, NJ: Princeton University Press.

Berman, E., Bound, J. and Griliches, Z. 1994. 'Changes in the demand for skilled labor within U.S. manufacturing: Evidence from the Annual Survey of Manufacturers', *Quarterly Journal of Economics*, 109, 367–97.

Birdsall, N., Ross, D. and Sabot, R. 1997. 'Education, growth and inequality'. In N. Birdsall and F. Jaspersen (eds), *Pathways to Growth: Comparing East Asia and Latin America*, 93–130. Washington, DC: Inter-American Development Bank.

Blau, F.D. and Kahn, L.M. 1996. 'International differences in male wage inequality: Institutions versus market forces', *Journal of Political Economy*, 104, 791–837.

Bluestone, B. and Harrison, B. 1982. *The Deindustrialization of America*. New York: Basic Books.

Boserup, E. 1970. *Women's Role in Economic Development*. London: Allen and Unwin.

Bound, J. and Johnson, G. 1992. 'Changes in the structure of wages in the 1980s: An evaluation of alternative explanations', *American Economic Review*, 82, 371–92.

Bourguignon, F. and Morrison, C. 2002. 'Inequality among world citizens, 1820–1992', *American Economic Review*, 92, 727–44.

Bradley, D., Huber, E., Moller, S., Nielsen, F. and Stephens, J.D. 2003. 'Distribution and redistribution in postindustrial democracies', *World Politics*, 55, 193–230.

Brady, D. 2003. 'The politics of poverty: Left political institutions, the welfare state, and poverty', *Social Forces*, 82, 557–88.

Bruno, M., Ravallion, M. and Squire, L. 1998. 'Equity and growth in developing countries: Old and new perspectives on the policy issues'. In V. Tanzi and Ke-Young Chu (eds), *Income Distribution and High Quality Growth*, 117–46. Cambridge, MA: MIT Press.

Davis, M. 2001. Late *Victorian Holocausts: El Niño Famines and the Making of the Third World*. London: Verso.

Deininger, K. and Squire, L. 1996. 'A new data set measuring income inequality', *The World Bank Economic Review*, 10, 565–91.

Deininger, K. and Squire, L. 1998. 'New ways of looking at old issues: Inequality and growth', *Journal of Development Economics*, 57, 259–87.

Dinopoulos, E. and Segerstrom, P. 1999. 'A Schumpeterian model of protection and relative wages', *American Economic Review*, 89, 450–72.

Edwards, S. 1995. *Crisis and Reform in Latin America: From Despair to Hope*. New York: Oxford University Press.

Fei, J.C.H., Ranis, G. and Kuo, S.W.Y. 1979. *Growth with Equity: The Taiwan Case*. New York: Oxford University Press.

Findley, R. and Wellisz, S. 1993. *Five Small Open Economies*. Oxford: Oxford University Press.

Firebaugh, G. 1992. 'Growth effects of foreign and domestic investment', *American Journal of Sociology*, 98, 105–30.

Firebaugh, G. 2003. *The New Geography of Global Income Inequality*. Cambridge, MA: Harvard University Press.

Firebaugh, G. and Goesling, B. 2004. 'Accounting for the recent decline in global income inequality', *American Journal of Sociology*, 110, 283–312.

Forbes, K.J. 2000. 'A reassessment of the relationship between inequality and growth', *American Economic Review*, 90, 869–87.

Francois, P. and Lloyd-Ellis, H. 2003. 'Animal spirits through creative destruction', *American Economic Review*, 93, 530–50.

Freeman, R.B. 1993. 'How much has de-unionization contributed to the rise in male earnings inequality?' In S.H. Danziger and P. Gottschalk (eds), *Uneven Tides: Rising Inequality in America*, 133–63. New York: Russell Sage Foundation.

Freeman, R.B. and Katz, L.F. (eds) 1995. *Differences and Changes in Wage Structures*. Chicago, IL: University of Chicago Press.

Friedman, T.L. 2000. *The Lexus and the Olive Tree*. New York: Farrar, Straus, and Giroux.

Galbraith, J.K. 2001. 'The macroeconomics of income distribution'. In J.K. Galbraith and M. Berner (eds), *Inequality and Industrial Change: A Global View*, 3–15. New York: Cambridge University Press.

Galbraith, J.K. and Berner, M. (eds) 2001. *Inequality and Industrial Change: A Global View*. New York: Cambridge University Press.

Goldstein, J. 1988. *Long Cycles: Prosperity and War in the Modern Age*. New Haven: Yale University Press.

Gustafsson, B. and Johansson, M. 1999. 'In search of smoking guns: What makes income inequality vary over time in different countries?' *American Sociological Review*, 64, 585–605.

Harrison, B. and Bluestone, B. 1988. *The Great U-Turn*. New York: Basic Books.

Hauser, S.M. and Xie, Y. 2005. 'Temporal and regional variation in earnings inequality: Urban China in transition between 1988 and 1995', *Social Science Research*, 34, 44–79.

Hoffman, K. and Centeno, M.A. 2003. 'The lopsided continent: Inequality in Latin America', *Annual Review of Sociology*, 29, 363–90.

IIPS (International Institute for Population Sciences) and ORC Macro. 2000. *National Family Health Survey (NFHS-2), 1998-99: India*. Mumbai: IIPS.

Katz, L.F. and Autor, D. 2000. 'Changes in the wage structure and earnings inequality'. In O. Ashenfelter and D. Card (eds), *The Handbook of Labor Economics*, Volume 3, Chapter 26. Amsterdam: Elsevier.

Kelly, N.J. 2004. 'Does politics matter? Policy and government's equalizing influence in the United States', *American Politics Research*, 32, 264–84.

Khan, A.R. and Riskin, C. 2005. 'China's household income and its distribution, 1995 and 2002', *China Quarterly*, 182, 356–84.

Kim, K.S. 1997. 'Income distribution and poverty: An interregional comparison', *World Development*, 25, 1909–24.

Korzeniewicz, R.P. and Moran, T.P. 1997. 'World-economic trends in the distribution of income, 1965–1992', *American Journal of Sociology*, 102, 1000–39.

Korzeniewicz, R.P. and Moran, T.P. 2005. 'Theorizing the relationship between inequality and economic growth', *Theory and Society*, 34, 277–316.

Korzeniewicz, R.P. and Smith, W.C. 2000. 'Growth, poverty, and inequality in Latin America: Searching for the high road', *Latin American Research Review*, 35, 7–54.

Korzeniewicz, R.P., Stach, A., Patil, V. and Moran, T.P. 2004. 'Measuring national income: A critical assessment', *Comparative Studies in Society and History*, 46 (3), 535–86.

Kuznets, S. 1940. 'Schumpeter's business cycles', *American Economic Review*, 30, 257–71.

Kuznets, S. 1955. 'Economic growth and income inequality', *American Economic Review*, 45, 1–28.

Kuznets, S. 1963. 'Quantitative aspects of economic growth of nations: III, Distribution of income by size', *Economic Development and Cultural Change*, 11, 1–80.

Lambert, P.J., Millimet, D.L. and Slottje, D. 2003. 'Inequality aversion and the natural rate of subjective inequality', *Journal of Public Economics*, 87, 1061–90.

Li, H., Squire, L. and Zou, H.-F. 1998. 'Explaining international and intertemporal variations in income inequality', *Economic Journal*, 108, 26–43.

Lindert, P.H. and Williamson, J.G. 2001. 'Does globalization make the world more unequal?' Paper presented at the NBER Globalization in Historical Perspective conference (Santa Barbara, March).

Lipton, M. 1997. 'Editorial: Poverty – Are there holes in the consensus?' *World Development*, 25, 1003–7.

Lustig, N. 1995. 'Introduction'. In N. Lustig (ed.), *Coping with Austerity: Poverty and Inequality in Latin America*, 1–41. Washington, DC: Brookings Institute.

Maddison, A. 1982. *Phases of Capitalist Development*. New York: Oxford University Press.

Maddison, A. 1995. *Monitoring the World Economy, 1820–1992*. Paris: OECD.

Mansfield, E. 1983. 'Long waves and technological innovation', *American Economic Review*, 73: 141–5.

Meng, X. 2004. 'Economic restructuring and income inequality in urban China', *Review of Income and Wealth*, 50, 357–79.

Meng, X., Gregory, R. and Wang, Y. 2005. 'Poverty, inequality, and growth in urban China, 1986–2000', *Journal of Comparative Economics*, 33, 710–29.

Milanovic, B. 2003. 'The two faces of globalization: Against globalization as we know it', *World Development*, 31, 667–83.

Milanovic, B. 2005. *Worlds Apart: Measuring International and Global Inequality*. Princeton, NJ: Princeton University Press.

Milanovic, B. n.d. 'True world income distribution, 1988 and 1993: First calculation based on household surveys alone'. World Bank, Development Research Group.

Milner, M. Jr. 1987. 'Theories of inequality: An overview and a strategy for synthesis', *Social Forces*, 65, 1053–89.

Moran, T.P. 2005. 'Kuznets's inverted u-curve hypothesis: The rise, demise, and continued relevance of a socioeconomic law', *Sociological Forum*, 20, 209–43.

Moran, T.P. 2006. 'Statistical inference and patterns of inequality in the global North', *Social Forces*, 84, 1799–1818.

Morley, S.A. 1995. *Poverty and Inequality in Latin America: The Impact of Adjustment and Recovery in the 1980s*. Baltimore, MD: The Johns Hopkins University Press.

Moses, J.W. and Letnes, B. 2004. 'The economic costs to international labor restrictions: Revisiting the empirical discussion', *World Development*, 32, 1609–26.

Mueller, D.C. and Stratmann, T. 2003. 'The economic effects of democratic participation', *Journal of Public Economics*, 87, 2129–55.

Murphy, K.M. and Welch, F. 1993. 'Industrial change and the rising importance of skill'. In S.H. Danziger and P. Gottschalk (eds), *Uneven Tides: Rising Inequality in America*, 101–32. New York: Russell Sage Foundation.

National Bureau of Statistics of China. 2004. *China Statistical Yearbook*. Beijing: China Statistics Press.

Nickell, S. and Bell, B. 1996. 'The collapse in demand for the unskilled and unemployed across the OECD', *Oxford Review of Economic Policy*, 11, 40–62.

North, D.C. 1981. *Structure and Change in Economic History*. New York: W.W. Norton.

Olson, M. 1982. *The Rise and Decline of Nations*. New Haven, CT: Yale University Press.

O'Rourke, K.H. and Williamson, J.G. 1999. *Globalization and History: The Evolution of a Nineteenth-Century Atlantic Economy*. Cambridge, MA: MIT Press.

Polanyi, K. 1957 [1944]. *The Great Transformation: The Political and Economic Origins of our Time*. Boston: Beacon Press.

Pritchett, L. 1997. 'Divergence, big time', *Journal of Economic Perspectives*, 11, 3–17.

Ram, R. 1989. 'Level of development and income inequality: An extension of Kuznets hypothesis to the world-economy', *Kyklos*, 42, 73–88.

Ram, R. 1997. 'Level of economic development and income inequality: Evidence from the postwar developed world', *Southern Economic Journal*, 64, 576–83.

Ravallion, M. 1995. 'Growth and poverty: Evidence for developing countries in the 1980s', *Economics Letters*, 48, 411–17.

Romer, P. 1990. 'Endogenous technological growth', *Journal of Political Economy*, 98, 71–102.

Rosenthal, G. 1996. 'On poverty and inequality in Latin America', *Journal of Interamerican Studies and World Affairs*, 38, 15–38.

Rostow, W.W. 1978. *The World Economy: History and Prospect*. Austin: University of Texas Press.

Schumpeter, J.A. 1942. *Capitalism, Socialism and Democracy*. New York: Harper and Row.

Skinner, W.G. 1994. 'Differential development in Lingnan'. In T.P. Lyons and V. Nee (eds), *The Economic Transformation of South China: Reform and Development in the Post-Mao Era*. Ithaca, NY: Cornell University Press.

Smeeding, T. 2002. 'Globalization, inequality, and the rich countries of the G-20: Evidence from the Luxembourg Income Study', Luxembourg Income Study Working Paper No. 320.

Smith, A. 1976 [1776]. *An Inquiry into the Nature and Causes of the Wealth of Nations*. Chicago: University of Chicago Press.

Thompson, W.R. 1990. 'Long waves, technological innovation, and relative decline', *International Organization*, 44, 201–33.

Tilly, C. 1998. *Durable Inequality*. Berkeley: University of California Press.

Topel, R. 1994. 'Regional labor markets and the determinants of wage inequality', *American Economic Review*, 84, 17–22.

UNDP (United Nations Development Programme). 2005. *Human Development Report 2005: International Cooperation at a Crossroads*. New York: Oxford University Press.

Wade, R.H. 2004. 'Is globalization reducing poverty and inequality?' *World Development*, 32, 567–89.

Wallerstein, I. 1974. *The Modern World System*. New York: Academic Press.

Wallerstein, I. 1989 [1975]. 'Dependence in an interdependent world: The limited possibilities of transformation within the capitalist world-economy'. In I. Wallerstein (ed.), *The Capitalist World-Economy*, 66–94. Cambridge: Cambridge University Press.

Wallerstein, I. 1996 [1983]. *Historical Capitalism with Capitalist Civilization*. London: Verso.

WIID (World Income Inequality Database). 2005. UNU-WIDER, Version 2.0a.

Williamson, J.G. 1991. *Inequality, Poverty, and History: The Kuznets Memorial Lectures of the Economic Growth Center, Yale University*. New York: Basil Blackwell.

World Bank. 1993. *The East Asian Miracle*. New York: Oxford University Press.

World Bank. 1998. *World Development Indicators on CD-ROM*. Washington, DC: World Bank.

World Bank. 2006. *World Development Indicators on CD-ROM*. Washington, DC: World Bank.

Chapter 30

Globalization and Corruption

Carolyn Warner

Globalization has helped to expose the extent to which corruption is embedded in international economic exchanges. This has led some to think that globalization inevitably reduces corruption by first revealing it and then subjecting firms and states to bribery-discouraging pressures from the free market. However, for as much as globalization helps to reduce corruption, its effects on corruption are not inherently in the presumed positive direction. Globalization creates incentives and new means for corruption, the standard definition of which is the misuse of public office for private gain (Philp 1997; Gerring and Thacker 2005; Scott 1972).

The standard expectation is that more international trade decreases corruption because states, now competing globally, have to present clean business environments to attract business. In addition, firms in any particular country, now subject to competitive pressure from foreign firms, cannot sustain the costs which corruption adds to their operating expenses. Thus, the free trade which is part and parcel of globalization is supposed to dampen corruption. It raises competitive pressures on firms, which lowers their ability to tolerate the costs of corruption that they may have been paying. If free trade also includes an agreement to open up states' public procurement practices to bids from foreign firms, then politicians and bureaucrats should also find it harder to continue corrupt practices. In this virtuous path, even under domestic policing and judicial systems which haven't changed, everyone should have less incentive to engage in corruption: there is less profit in it (Ades and Di Tella 1999: 988; Krueger 1974).

Furthermore, globalization has seen the proliferation of non-governmental organizations (NGOs), several of which have been prominent in crusading against corruption by exposing it and by pressuring firms and states to take corrective measures. NGOs such as Transparency International and even some international organizations, such as the World Bank, have pointed out that corruption is not just bad for democratic values, it is also bad for economic development and business. They have lobbied governments and firms to adopt anti-corruption measures, and have had some success in getting corruption onto the international agenda.

Globalization also exposes more states to anti-corruption norms, because an inherent feature of globalization is increased state membership in international organizations and networks. The assumption is that these international networks, being dominated by the wealthy Western states, which have anti-corruption norms of their own, contain and transmit anti-corruption norms (Sandholtz and Gray 2003). Indeed, corruption should be receding in international economic transactions because the dominant power in the international system, the United States, has been striving to internationalize its own anti-bribery law, the Foreign Corrupt Practices Act (FCPA). Originating in reaction to discoveries, via the uncovering of Watergate slush funds, of widespread bribery by US firms in their foreign dealings, it has been amended and tightened. Given that no elected official in the United States wants to be seen as condoning corruption, the FCPA has proven impossible to repeal. Because of that, US firms as well as agencies of the US government were compelled to turn their energies towards having other states adopt a similar law. The US view was that everyone ought to be equally constrained from using bribery in foreign business transactions, so that US firms, vulnerable to prosecution at home for using bribery abroad, were not at a disadvantage. Success of a sort came in 1997, with the adoption of the OECD Anti-bribery Convention, and ratification of it by all 35 signatories by 2004. There have been reviews of all countries' implementation and enforcement and follow-up reviews have taken place or been scheduled. Results are transparent, in that they are posted on the OECD's website (www.oecd.org). In addition, the United States has relatively stringent requirements for firms to be listed on US stock exchanges. Over the years, those exchanges have become a locus of international trade, as numerous foreign firms list on them. Thus, globalization is exposing firms around the world to the laws of the United States. This should have a damping effect on the extent of bribery and corruption in international economic transactions.

Just as globalization got a large boost with the collapse of the Soviet Union and increased economic openness of China, so too did anti-corruption efforts: they were no longer impeded by the privileging of anti-Communist policies, and, since 2001, have been aided by anti-terrorist banking laws exposing other transactions to inspection (Naylor 2002; Palan 2003).

However, the standard view that globalization decreases corruption has been confounded by the perverse effect of increased competition in the international export markets increasing the utility of bribery as a business tool and increasing the utility of corruption as a means for politicians to extract resources from foreign firms; and by the fact that international trade and political activity takes place increasingly under rules governed by international organizations which lack real enforcement powers. It is because of that that OECD states can (and do) use or tolerate corruption when it facilitates geo-political or economic interests, such as national security or weapons sales. Furthermore, the reputed engine of globalization, the World Trade Organization (WTO), has no rules concerning corruption in international trade and government contracting. OECD states have even institutionalized the underwriting of corrupt transactions. It is inaccurate to speak of international anti-corruption norms – they are circumscribed by the concrete economic and geo-political interests of the very states which are said to promulgate them, and are not shared by many of the world's rising economic and political powers.

Specifically, corruption continues despite globalization because competition has become fierce, especially in energy, infrastructure and weapons; by there being increased economic competition in already corrupt countries (e.g. the opening of the East bloc and Russia); by loopholes in the OECD anti-bribery convention (including tax deductions for 'grease' payments and excluding payments to political parties); by legal jurisdictions largely still being national and by international organizations and conventions having limited or no enforcement powers (enforcement is left to states which may have little interest in enforcement or no capacity to do so); by arms and economic embargoes which create incentives for black markets and corruption; sometimes merely by the political sensitivity of the transaction and individuals involved; by the emergence of a corrupt country, China, as a world economic power; and by the resistance of most states to anti-corruption efforts (Manion 2004; Sun 2004; Abbott 2001; Transparency International 2004).

It is clear that part of globalization has been the apparent increase in international organizations taking on governing and trade tasks which used to be the purview of sovereign states. The UN's 'oil for food' programme for Iraq is one example; the WTO's regulation of trade between most countries of the world is another. The UN also has been the locus of arms embargo enforcement. Yet these organizations often become part of the problem, as the UN oil for food programme has shown, as the scandal of UN head Kofi Anan's son obtaining UN contracts, the EU Commission being plagued by mismanagement and nepotism, and the Coalition Provisional Authority turning a blind eye on corruption in contracting in Iraq. In addition, international organizations sometimes become the repositories for leaders with dubious domestic records. The European Union's Commission, the Organization of American States (OAS), the World Economic Forum, the North Atlantic Treaty Organization, all have had leaders and officials whose corrupt or dubious activities in their country of origin surfaced during their tenure in the international organization.

This chapter first discusses the expectations and indications that globalization has introduced dynamics which help to reduce corruption, then analyses the contrary. It moves to an analysis of whether a tipping game might be in the offing, with dynamics shifting from those in which corruption is the norm to those in which it is not, and concludes with some reflections on the tensions between globalization, and the economic and political interests of industry and politicians.

GLOBALIZATION AGAINST CORRUPTION

Globalization seems to have brought with it some efforts to globalize anti-corruption policies and practices. Symptomatic of this is Transparency International (TI), founded in 1993 by a German businessman, Peter Eigen, who decided to rally against corrupt practices in international business. His first tactic, and the one for which TI is most widely known, was to make public the varying degrees of corruptness of almost all countries in the world. While the TI Corruption Perception Index makes no claim to being a scientific measure of corruption, it does make transparent what had previously been a taboo subject: corruption, and it does challenge the international stature of some countries which find themselves further down the rankings than their moral posturing and level of economic development would lead one to expect. Perhaps more importantly, TI has been a persistent lobbyist to inter-national organizations when trade and other agreements are being established. As Abbott and Snidal (2002) note, TI's efforts were critical to the adoption of the OECD Anti-bribery Convention, and they continue to be important in pressuring states to implement and enforce the convention. TI has likewise been an important player in OAS, World Bank, International Monetary Fund (IMF) and WTO meet-ings on anti-bribery and corruption policies. It is not the only international NGO which has emerged: others, such as Global Witness and the Center for Public Integ-rity, have been active.

The United States has been a major player in efforts to internationalize the US FCPA, and its efforts to do so seem to coincide with a rapidly globalizing interna-tional economy. The fall of the Soviet Union brought new business opportunities in corrupt countries, and US firms wanted everyone else to be shackled with the same competitive restraint they were: anti-bribery laws. The US government coor-dinated efforts which led to the 1997 OECD Anti-bribery Convention. The United States has also attempted to reduce corruption through the creation and practices of the Millennium Challenge Corporation, a para-public foreign aid agency which is only to give aid to those countries which demonstrate good governance, as defined by the United States: those countries which are seen to be 'governing justly, invest-ing in their citizens, and encouraging economic freedom' qualify for aid. As part of that assessment, countries are evaluated on their control of corruption (Millennium Challenge Corporation 2005).

Another important international institution has been the World Bank, an inter-national organization which is seen to be an integral part of globalization. The Bank had, for decades, tolerated corruption in developing countries because it assumed that corruption, by enabling firms to get around red tape, facilitated economic development. The Bank also justified its stance by noting it was respecting local traditions. Coincident with the fall of the Berlin Wall in 1989 came 'a turning point' at the Bank: its African 'development experts called for a rethinking of policy' (Abbott and Snidal 2002: 10). Yet it took several other key events in order to have this epitome of globalization reconsider its stance on corruption. First, it took the founding and then persistent lobbying of TI to goad the Bank into adopting anti-corruption policies. TI founder Peter Eigen used to work for the World Bank but, dissatisfied with the Bank's tolerance of corruption, left it and then established TI. Second, it took a change in leadership. With his arrival in 1996, James Wolfensohn used his presidency of the Bank to start to change the Bank's stance. It remains to be seen whether Paul Wolfowitz (President, June 2005–) will give the Bank's anti-corruption measures the same attention.

Those who think globalization promotes anti-corruption measures can point to the fact that by the late 1990s, many major international organizations had anti-bribery and/or anti-corruption policies of some sort: the UN, the development banks, the IMF, the OAS, the Council of Europe, the European Union, as well as the OECD. Anti-corruption measures are being written into the North–South American free trade agreement. They can also point to successful prosecutions of corruption which in previous decades would never have seen the light of day, such as the Montesinos case in Peru (exposing a thick network of corrupt transactions and reaching all the way to then President Alberto Fujimori) and the Elf Aquitaine case in France (the then state-owned oil company was at the centre of major international bribery cases ranging from Germany to Taiwan and parts of Africa and including some of the highest ranking officials and politicians in France). They can point to banking and accounting laws, such as the 2002 Sarbannes–Oxley Act of the United States, which make it easier for magistrates to find and sequester laundered money (Naylor 2002) or discover fraudulent transactions. Private enterprise has also initiated anti-corruption efforts, most notably the Extractive Industries Transparency Initiative (see below).

Regional or international economic integration has been a significant element in globalization. It has been said to reduce corruption, by improving norms of business and government practice and, through economic competition, making corruption's drag on the economy more noticeable. These macro level trends may exist in theory, but at the micro level, they often fail to obtain. International economic integration tends to remove barriers to trade and increase economic competition but fails to install effective regulatory and enforcement agencies. Some have pointed to the EU's Convention against Corruption as evidence that the EU promotes norms of clean government (Sandholtz and Gray 2003, 772; Gerring and Thacker 2005). But the Convention does not have the force of law, and it merely masks a more significant but informal convention, the one which agrees to tolerate corruption because to expose it would be to undermine further the tenuous popularity of EU institutions. If anything, the EU (to say nothing of the UN) should lead us to question whether international organizations promote norms of clean government.

The EU can serve as a microcosm of globalization: there is a fairly free flow of capital, labour and goods, with supranational oversight institutions, and a number of states which not only seem to have norms against corruption, but also score very high in international anti-corruption indices. Risks to corrupt activities would seem to be high. But, as the European Union's experience shows, these risks may exist in theory, but not, at least for many years, in practice. The risks, so far, have been minimal: additional oversight is trivial, penalties negligible, and competitors seldom wind up having an incentive to protest malfeasance. Opportunities have the same source: an inadequate international legal system, enforcement largely left to the very governments which may be directly involved in corruption and low risk of discovery and penalty, partly because the states seldom if ever intervene in each other's affairs. In addition, firms, including newcomers to a market, sometimes find it cheaper to pay a bribe as part of a collusive arrangement than to confront the costs of a competitive market. Indeed, contractors looking for more business may be willing to pay 'commissions', bribes or kickbacks in order to establish themselves in a new market. Also, due to their characteristics, some sectors do not have a plethora of available competitors, so those firms which enter the market can easily be incorporated into the corrupt distribution network.

Even if globalization is encouraging and facilitating some reduction in corruption, it is also doing the opposite, and it is worth understanding how that happens.

WHY GLOBALIZATION ENCOURAGES CORRUPTION

Competition and corruption

Globalization has brought more firms and governments from more parts of the world into more frequent contact for economic exchange. Corruption has followed.

Firms do what is expedient for business, and if bribery lands contracts, gains market access and moves goods, whereas honesty doesn't, the incentives to use bribery are strong. Western politicians and firms claim that bribery is a 'must' in many parts of the world; non-Western politicians and firms claim that their Western counterparts are only too ready to bribe. Either way, given the spread of capitalism and the growth of so-called emerging markets, there are more and not less instances in which '[p]owerful actors are motivated to penetrate government wherever possible, if not to gain privileged access to government contracts, then – and more commonly in the developed democracies – to affect the rules of competition in ways favorable to them' (Warren 2004: 340).

Fierce competition by firms and their home states for export markets has given rise to markets which economists might say are characterized by 'market failure', particularly in the realm of infrastructure projects, arms and oil. I suggest that corruption is not in opposition to the export market, it is a feature, a tool, of it. The more profitable the market, the more demand there will be to participate in it, to gain a large share of it. As demand goes up (when, for instance, there are more competitors in the international construction industry and when traditional markets saturate), the price of getting into the market goes up. This includes legally permitted 'offsets', and also illegal bribes. In some sectors, such as the manufacture of commercial planes, arms, oil and utility infrastructure, the stakes (profits, rents) are very high; and firms and states have the perception that winning any particular contract is critical for gaining substantial market share and for maintaining and increasing domestic employment and economic growth. Because of that, as economic competition *increases*, firms are willing to pay bribes up to the point where the cost (including nearly negligible risks of prosecution) matches the profits. Their domestic governments are willing to overlook or indirectly subsidize the bribes (through export credits) in order to help their firms land contracts.

Competition carries with it countervailing pressures. More competition means that expenses, including taxes, matter more. This means, in turn, that firms have an increased incentive to bribe their way out of taxes; more competition also means that cartels have a higher value to all the firms which are included in them, even if, under the new trade regime, cartels run a greater risk of discovery and disruption (because more firms can try to enter the market; cf. European Commission 1997: 38–41).

Free trade and ensuing competition may not reach into all areas vulnerable to corruption. Even under competitive rules, states retain discretion over actions with large financial repercussions for firms, among them, tax decisions, zoning regulations, authorizations of the sale or purchase of arms etc. More free trade may spur demand for the development of agricultural land, which may require a change in zoning laws. Politicians on the relevant councils and committees may extract fees for their 'services'.

Petty corruption, such as bribing customs officials, also thrives with globalization. Clearly, as competition gets keener, access to markets becomes more significant, so customs officials can charge more for access to that market. Recognizing and, in a way, legitimizing this practice, the OECD Anti-bribery Convention, as well as most national anti-corruption legislation, exempts from prosecution 'facilitation payments' to speed market access.

The apparent opposite of competition, economic and weapons embargoes, also facilitate the creation of new circuits of corruption.

Embargoes

Arms and other embargoes to lucrative (often oil) markets do nothing but force the (already prone-to-corruption) transactions market underground, making corruption inevitable. The corruption of the UN-run Oil for Food programme, for Iraq, is a stellar case in point. In addition, virtually all major arms exporting countries violated the UN arms embargo against Iraq; Iran benefited from an extraordinarily complicated evasion of weapons sale bans (courtesy not just of the United States and the United Kingdom, but France, Germany, Saudi Arabia and Israel). Bribes are paid not just to facilitate the sale between states but also to buy or reward the complicity of home country politicians. Firms take advantage of regional economic integration to use subsidiaries to move weapons which, when they leave one country, are usually declared to be going to a false destination (Marion 1990: 117–18).

Using corruption to promote national champions and institutionalizing the means to do so

Despite the fact that the largest firms based in any OECD country are usually multinationals and have their tax liabilities spread across numerous jurisdictions, domestic governments still regard them as their national champions. There has been a trend for states, in the name of the free market, prosperity and national defence, to promote their industries' exports. This has two effects related to corruption: first, supply starts to push demand. Markets are created artificially, and states are tempted to bribe or condone bribes for the sake of their firms' international market share. The corrupt practices of Elf, the French oil firm, the alleged corruption in, and the UK government's quashing, of all efforts to investigate and make public findings about, major UK arms sales to Saudi Arabia, the huge infrastructure projects in less developing countries promoted by Western states and their construction industries, all illustrate this phenomenon of supply pushing demand, and an accompanying willingness to overlook corruption for the sake of market share. Second, the states establish institutions which facilitate networks between potential buyers and sellers, in order to support their export industries (Warner 2007).

Export credit guarantees to home firms and development aid to foreign governments are typical means by which the OECD countries have supported corruption in international economic transactions. While EU states have regulated themselves to limit state subsidies to their own industries, they have left the international market virtually regulation free.[1] Another government strategy for increasing domestic economic and political revenue, which is not technically corrupt but which can foster corruption, is increasing the level of aid given to a country in order that it can purchase weapons or infrastructure projects from the donor country. The United Kingdom provides an example of how it works. In 1988–9, the United Kingdom's aid to Nigeria was £6.3 million. In 1989–90, UK aid increased tenfold, to £67.7 million. Also in 1990, the United Kingdom negotiated the sale of eighty 'made in the UK' Vickers tanks to Nigeria for at least £50 million. 'A Whitehall spokeswoman said £59.4 million of this aid was to finance essential imports. She insisted there was no link between the aid increase and the arms deal' (Elliott et al. 1994). Rather than force Nigeria's corrupt president, the now late Sani Abacha, to pay for the tanks, or for the 'essential foreign aid' which the oil-rich country should not have needed, with funds he had sequestered in Swiss banks, by way of UK banks, the UK government coddled the Nigerian ruler, used public money to facilitate sales for the UK's privatized defence industry and foisted the costs onto UK taxpayers. In essence, the scheme is not unlike that of politicians inflating a contract by an amount more than sufficient for the contractor(s) to pay the required kickback and make a hefty profit at the same time. Significantly, research by the NGO World Development Movement found that between the 1980s and 1990s, foreign aid to 'eight of the largest buyers of British arms, including Oman and Indonesia, has risen while aid overall has fallen by 20 per cent. Last year alone, as aid to Africa was cut, ECGD [Export Credits Guarantee Department] increased by five times its financial backing for arms sales to "risky markets".' In 1984, India used its UK foreign aid to purchase 21 UK military helicopters. In 1993, two months after Foreign secretary Douglas Hurd promised Indonesia £500 million in aid, Indonesia agreed to a £65 million 'soft loan' for a power station (Bellamy 1994; Davis 2002: 125). This process appears to have accelerated as weapons sales became ever more competitive, and from the perspective of politicians, had the benefit of ostensibly providing business for their infrastructure contractors too. The system sets up an absurd cycle: for rulers of developing countries, the more subsidies there are for contractors, the more they will have bidders for their contracts, the more the bidders will be compelled, due to intense competition, to offer bribes. In addition, the cost effectiveness of such programmes is dubious at best, and the ease with which buyers can obtain weapons enables them to engage in behaviour which the export-credits are there to off-set: the risk for the sellers of civil wars, currency crises etc. (Cooper 1997: 143; World Development Movement 1995: 22). In 2005, the United States gave Pakistan $3 billion in military and economic aid to enable it to buy up to 24 F-16 jets, so Lockheed-Martin would have additional orders for a plant in Texas which Lockheed-Martin was threatening to close down (*Financial Times* 2005). For Lockheed-Martin, this has the added benefit of impelling Pakistan's rival India to place a large order for F-16s.

Bad press and some effort to implement the OECD Anti-bribery Convention have prompted a number of states to make slight changes to their export credit guarantee practices. As an example, the UK's ECGA now requires firms receiving funds to sign a document saying that they did not knowingly use bribes to obtain the contract to be subsidized by the ECGA. However, OECD states have done nothing to change their efforts to promote weapons sales, save disengage from some of the direct marketing, nor have they made changes in how they help their oil industries land contracts, or promote sales of other exports.

The banks of the OECD countries have long profited from their role as repositories for illicitly gained funds; globalization has only meant that they can now do so via offshore transactions (Naylor 2002; Palan 2004).

Incentives to government officials reward the status quo. First, it takes an enormous amount of time and money to investigate and prosecute corruption. Second, doing so renders public actions and expenditures that those involved might have preferred had been kept confidential. Firms and governments prefer that things such as amounts of bribes, names of intermediaries, remain secret. Third, prosecution of major multinationals is akin to biting the hand that feeds the politicians. Fourth, the OECD Convention's mandate to prosecute despite possible economic repercussions loses out to the economic argument that if 'their' companies aren't bribing, then rival states' companies will anyway, and will therefore win the contracts. The 'what's good for the multinational is good for the domestic economy' argument is irresistible to politicians, particularly when the corruption occurs offshore, out of sight of constituents and practically off limits to domestic investigative agencies. The same logic holds for the bureaucrats who supposedly regulate the industries in question. Fifth, even though globalization deterritorializes capital and sometimes culture, elections are still nation-state based. That goes for the European Parliament as well. Elections to it are still held by and within each member state; politicians do not run in transnational political parties, and the elections have become referenda on domestic politics, with jobs and the economy being key issues. Hence, the promoting of national industries is critical to the electoral success of politicians.

Exacerbating those pressures is the fact that globalization has not done away with one of the key factors fuelling corruption: the demand by politicians and parties for campaign and party financing. Many of the corruption cases in Western Europe have involved efforts by politicians and their parties to obtain more financing. When they are blocked from getting the funds legally, say, through caps on donations and limited state funding, they get it through requiring kickbacks on government contracts or retro-commissions from bribes paid for overseas contracts. While the percentages may or may not be large, ranging from 2 to 50 per cent, the more globalized economy has merely provided another realm from which funds can be purloined. Combine that with more sophisticated offshore financial sectors, and restricted jurisdictions of national judiciaries, and the result is anything but less corruption.

Corruption needs secrecy, and in many major international economic sectors, such as infrastructure projects, oil and arms trade, it has it, courtesy of 'national interest' and 'defence secrecy'. With the exception of Sweden (after a 1986 arms export corruption scandal), OECD countries seldom fully disclose the terms of weapons sales. Information is provided 'on an unofficial and selective basis', oversight by elected parliaments is rare and media coverage is regarded as a nuisance, at best (Gibbs 1995; Davis 2002). Despite claims of being democratic, OECD governments keep to themselves information such as 'to which countries and in what quantities goods such as artillery shells, land mines and cluster bombs have been licensed for export' (British House of Commons 1996: pr. K8.13). Oil companies have protested efforts to have them 'publish what they pay' in bribes (always called commissions, see below) or reveal their financial circuits. A TotalFinaElf spokesman said that 'Whether it's the oil industry or any other industry, obviously you wouldn't want your competitors to know what you pay. It's not that we're against it, or that there's something to hide; it's just the standard' (International Consortium of Investigative Journalists 2002: 10). Infrastructure projects are seldom decided by transparent processes; with neither the governments nor the firms involved having an incentive to share their pricing and payment information with the public or each other. The legitimate procedures in place to maintain corporate secrecy provide a cover for corruption.

Even in a country with a stronger tradition than most of public oversight by way of parliamentary committees, the unwillingness to investigate possible corruption in overseas exports is strong. The economic and political costs are deemed too great. The United Kingdom has refused to make results public of one investigation into a shady arms deal with Saudi Arabia, on the grounds that the publication would have annoyed the Saudis, and terminated another on the grounds that it jeopardized jobs and national security. This is the same state that, in other contexts, lectures or 'advises' new democracies on the importance of transparency, openness and other anti-corruption policies in government and in economic transactions. As an OECD review noted (2005), the United Kingdom, for all its extensive overseas trade activities, had not yet investigated or prosecuted anyone for bribery of foreign officials.

Globalization and the market for bribes

In some ways, globalization has merely spread the knowledge that bribes are necessary to facilitate transactions. Often, these are euphemistically known as 'commissions'. As one managing director of a UK weapons manufacturer said, 'Commissions make the world go round. There's nothing illegal about them. I don't know of a [Saudi] Royal who'll get out of bed for less than 5%' (John Hoakes, of Thorn EMI, quoted in the *Guardian*, 14 November 1994). Some argue that commissions should not be called bribes, they are instead like brokerage or realtor fees – a payment to someone who makes a deal happen, who finds terms on which buyer and seller can agree. Yet commissions support corruption. When the commission is 25 per cent of the contract, and when it is not transparent where all the money from that commission goes, is it really just a commission? Commissions are used to purchase the award of contracts, even and often especially in competitive markets (where there is competition between suppliers). A French official in the finance ministry said that 'They go up in certain Asian countries for some types of transactions, because there is very strong competition' (Plouvier 1992). An industrialist noted that sometimes the commissions, which are often turned to private ends by the recipient, reach 45 per cent of the contract in highly competitive markets because it is necessary 'to coax' the client (Isnard 1998).

Globalization has not done away with the middlemen necessary to conduct corrupt international economic transactions. They advertise themselves as being connected to the right people in the right places and they stress that without their intervention, Western firms will get nowhere. They rely on the personalistic nature of much of politics and business, and given lack of familiarity and contacts in the countries in which they wish to land contracts, firms and states believe them. When an intermediary is paid a commission, he/she routinely gives part of it to key officials and leaders in the country awarding the contract. Often, part of the commission makes its way back to the home country by way of the foreign bank accounts of key politicians and industry leaders. For example, one of the French state's oil company intermediaries, André Guelfi, estimated that of the $100 million Elf paid him in commissions for the various contracts he brokered, he spent $70 million paying third parties, including political leaders (Van Ruymbeke 2002: 372–87). Intermediaries also 'isolate businessmen [and states] from unpleasant truths' (Rose-Ackerman 1978: 193). Using an intermediary keeps the corruption at arms length.

As a French exporter said, 'One is not too curious neither about the real power that is behind [the deals], nor about the real recipient of the funds' (Plouvier 1992). Commissions may reach extraordinary heights in order to buy the compliance of the intermediary. When the intermediaries become the targets of judicial investigations, they often find comfortable exile in an OECD country.

IS THE TIDE TURNING?

Corruption in international economic exchange thrives on a collective action problem: firms and governments might prefer not to pay bribes, so as to reap higher profits, but can't trust others not to bribe. The OECD Convention is a case in point: 35 countries had signed and ratified it by 2004, a number too large for easy monitoring. Furthermore, within each state there are thousands of exporting firms, too many for effective monitoring by the group of each group member's adherence to the agreement. As Transparency International (2002: 7) notes, 'there are more than 60,000 multinational corporations operating around the world with more than 600,000 foreign affiliates'. The Convention's failure is evident in statistics on bribe paying. Italy has ratified the Convention, but on a scale of 10–0, in which 10 is *least likely to bribe*, Italy's firms are ranked 4.1; France's 5.5; firms from the United States, notwithstanding its Foreign Corrupt Practices Act, 5.3; and Germany's firms, 6.3 (Transparency International 2002). Construction and public works contracts are the sectors in which bribery was most likely to take place, followed closely by the arms and oil and gas sectors (these same sectors were judged, in that same order, to be those where the biggest bribes were made). Even though most of the EU countries have ratified the OECD Convention and agreed to an EU statement (with no force of law) about being opposed to corruption, international organizations are inherently bad at policing their members; enforcement is largely left to the individual, highly self-interested states' authorities, who often find bribery for export market access an acceptable evil. And in this exemplar of international coordination to reduce bribery and corruption, even with external 'peer' review, some signatory states are uncooperative. The United Kingdom and Japan have recently been singled out as having poor enforcement records. Of the 35 signatories, only four have investigated or prosecuted more than one case.

It is tempting to think that corruption in the international political economy is at a tipping point: despite the many factors encouraging corruption, 30 OECD states and five others have signed on to the OECD anti-bribery convention, OECD firms are becoming aware of possible penalties, a few OECD states' judiciaries are investigating and prosecuting egregious cases of bribery, some major firms, spearheaded by BP, have signed on to the Extractive Industries Transparency Initiative, the World Bank and the IMF have made corruption reduction a recognized policy area, and NGOs such as Transparency International and Global Witness have made corruption an international issue. Could it be that the tide is turning, and corruption will recede?

For that to occur, not only do states and firms have to recognize that bribery and corruption is not in their interest, but a major coordination problem has to be solved. International trade is interdependent on norms, not merely on economic and political conditions. The necessary coordination relies on a particular kind of inter-dependence: that of the expectations of each about the expectations and thus behaviour of the others involved in a transaction. In a tipping game, no one is willing to be first to abandon these practices: it would be irrational for any one firm to move unilaterally away from the status quo (Mackie 1996; Laitin 1994: 626). For firms and the Western states which back them up, the key assumptions that sustain the corrupt exchanges are: (1) firms believe they have to bribe in order to land contracts; (2) they want the contracts and know that other firms do also; (3) they think that if they do not bribe, they will lose to their competitors; (4) they believe there is a low risk of discovery and penalty and a high benefit of bribery and profit. For government officials who ask for bribes, the key assumptions which sustain the corrupt exchanges are: (1) if they ask for a bribe, firms will pay; (2) no risk or enforcement costs and penalties; (3) if they don't, others will, thus putting them at a competitive disadvantage; (4) if one firm refuses to pay, another can easily be found that will. Some significant number of states including the significant world powers, and some significant number of firms, including the significant multination-als, would need to expect that others expect that the norm is uncorrupt interaction. They each and all would need to believe that the likelihood of others cheating (resorting to bribery and corruption) is extremely low, and very costly. There needs to be a convention shift. I suggest that this is not likely to obtain. The corruption abolition campaign has been limited in scope, ignoring as it does the WTO and the less developed countries, several key major powers have no scruples about using corruption to land contracts (e.g. India, China; Transparency International 2004), loopholes to the US FCPA and the implementing legislation of the OECD conven-tion are plentiful, and enforcement has been erratic. Furthermore, to the extent that Western firms sign on to anti-bribery practices, that raises the profitability of bribery for those that do not, giving the latter a competitive edge, and thus impels the Western firms to find some way around the OECD Anti-bribery Convention. In contrast to other tipping games, it is not the case that the greater the proportion of firms and states which eschew bribery and corruption, the less are those activities advantageous in securing foreign contracts. While this may be contrary to economic wisdom, which holds that corruption is like an extra tax (in the long run everyone pays), it is in keeping with micro-economic and political logic. In the short run, powerful interests benefit, in part because they can shift the burden of the corrup-tion tax onto others.

The much-touted US FCPA and the OECD Anti-bribery Convention have only as much bite as states wish to give them. Just as the United Kingdom has yet to prosecute anyone under its OECD legislation, the United States has only, since 1977, prosecuted 100 cases and many of those involve the same firms. That would indicate that penalties are quite low relative to the benefits of corruption, and that firms estimate they have a very good chance of being undetected. In addition, states themselves openly allow circumventions of the law: US firms can apply to the Justice Department and the Securities and Exchange Commission for permission to make dubious payments to foreign officials in order to land contracts. One such example is that of Goldman Sachs in 2004 getting permission to pay a $67 million 'donation' to Chinese officials in order to land a joint-venture banking operation there. The 'donation' was to help cover investor losses of firm which had gone bankrupt after embezzling most of its investors' money. The donation, as it were, most likely went into a legal (for China) account before being dispersed to final recipients. In essence, Goldman Sachs could say they were not bribing foreign officials. However, the bankrupt firm, Hainan Securities, was completely unrelated to the securities firm Goldman Sachs was trying to set up, and yet had been linked to an official, Fang Feng Lei, to whom Goldman Sachs additionally made a $100 million loan and who was to be chairman of the new joint venture investment banking firm, Goldman Sachs Gaohua Securities (Barboza 2005). The US FCPA and the OECD Anti-bribery Convention may merely cause the corruption to go down one level, to where it is camouflaged by a variety of first order legal, albeit odd, transactions. States themselves establish complicated rules which legalize offshore banking and other financial transactions (Palan 2003).

Furthermore, the United States is undermining its efforts to compel other countries to abide by the OECD rules when it refuses to investigate corruption within the contracting practices of the Coalition Provisional Authority (CPA) in Iraq, when it ignores bribery and corruption allegations against Halliburton and its subsidiaries, when it condones or sponsors illegal drugs and weapons sales, and when it tries to block new governments in developing countries from re-visiting major contracts which may have been won by US firms through corruption. The United States has cleverly claimed that the CPA was not an arm of the US government because it was a multinational governing coalition (Hirsch 2005), so it has blocked the prosecution of firms which may have defrauded the US government of hundreds of millions of dollars. The senior army procurement officer who questioned the dubious practices of Halliburton and the contract award process has faced retribution, while the Republican Congressional majority has stymied efforts to investigate. By 2005, Halliburton had been awarded over $10 billion in US government contracts for reconstruction in Iraq, with at least 10 per cent of that being of questionable use or entirely unaccounted for (Bodzin, 2005; Griffiths, 2005; Waxman and Dorgan 2005).

In 1998, when Pakistan, under the new and short-lived government of Nawaz Sharif, challenged the Western-dominated electricity consortium Hubco for having allegedly bribed Pakistan's previous prime minister, Benazir Bhutto, and for recovering those costs by overcharging on electricity rates, the World Bank, ten US Senators and the UK government, to name a few, intervened to block Pakistan's efforts. Under the previous agreement, Hubco built, owned and operated a 1,200 MW power plant on the Hab river. Pakistan's new audit agency, the Accountability Bureau, alleged that that Hubco's project costs were inflated by over $400 million; there were other plausible allegations of kickbacks to Bhutto and her cohorts. (The Accountability Bureau had been established by Sharif to investigate corruption under Bhutto.) Spurred on by a US energy firm with interests in the project, and motivated by a similar situation in India involving now bankrupt Enron, the US Senators wrote to the World Bank, which had provided a controversial and scarcely used underwriting provision to cover approximately one-third of the $1.5 billion project (for reasons of 'political risk'). In their letter, the Senators complained that Pakistan's actions were part of 'an alarming trend in several developing countries where federal and state governments use unproven allegations of corruption, collusion and even nepotism to rewrite existing commercial contracts'. The World Bank concurred (Fidler 2000; Hawley 2003). Once Sharif was deposed by military dictator and US ally

Pervez Musharraf, Pakistan settled its dispute over the electricity rates and withdrew its case against the Hubco consortium and officials. The post-Suharto government of Indonesia faced a similar situation when it tried to renegotiate contracts that had all the hallmarks of Suharto's corruption.

These examples show that the United States is undercutting the momentum towards an equilibrium shift to a much less corrupt international business environment. Corruption continues because firms and politicians correctly perceive that the level of coordination and cooperation needed to end bribery will not materialize. As a former Costa Rican prosecutor said of several major corruption cases that occurred in Costa Rica in the early 2000s, 'Corruption continues to be to world business what doping is to high-level athletics and sports. Many enterprises are aware of the risks of corruption, and have probably the will to renounce to it, but only if all other competitors also give up kickbacks to get contracts' (Godoy 2004).

Yet what are the possibilities for such a shift taking place in particular economic sectors? Take, for example, what might be a tipping game in the energy and mining sectors. The corrupt way of doing business is being challenged by several NGOs and a core of extractive industry firms, such as BP. Through the Extractive Industries Transparency Initiative, allegedly launched by the Blair government but apparently more the work of BP, some of the extractive industry firms have succeeded in getting several countries to agree to publish what they receive for mining and oil concessions, and several firms to agree to publish what they pay for those. Participation is far from universal or inclusive, and has no enforcement or penalty mechanisms. It is unlikely to alter the current 'rules' in the extractive industries game, which stipulate that the firm which does not bribe does not do business. Combined with secrecy incentives in the West, firms doing business in less developed countries may have little incentive to 'publish what you pay' for access to a market, for landing a contract: when BP did so, it was almost thrown out of the Congo; its competitors, unwilling to do so, were not. The Congo has not signed on to the EITI; at the time of writing, only five have (Azerbaijan, Ghana, Kyrgyz Republic, Nigeria, and Trinidad and Tobago), and only two other countries (Peru, and São Tomé and Príncipe), as well as the Congo, have engaged in tentative negotiations. Conspicuously absent from the companies which have signed onto the agreement are ENEL/ENI, the Italian energy conglomerate, China's national oil company (China National Petroleum or Sinopec) and Japan's (Japan National Oil Corporation).

Despite this somewhat discouraging start (though some would say that it started at all is encouraging), a tipping game may be possible, with a shift from opaque to transparent practices within particular countries. Why? Because in any one country, the signatory government and a prominent set of companies have declared a change in practices. This is one of the key components of creating the coordination of expectations necessary to tip the balance. The signatory countries have agreed to independent audits adhering to internationally recognized standards, in order to reconcile payments and revenues. Granted, this is an unstable condition, and any number of factors could defeat the coordination of expectations. There are no enforcement mechanisms, and a secret bribe from one of the non-signatory companies could sway the leadership, or one of the signatory companies may decide the EITI is not credible, and so will return to secrecy. Furthermore, if politicians and officials in other countries are 'benefiting' from corruption, why should the elites of any one country forgo it?

It may be that anti-corruption efforts will have to proceed sector by sector. There is less chance it will happen in the large infrastructure sector, since that would be covered by WTO rules, and the WTO has, for various reasons, studiously avoided anti-bribery and corruption campaigns and rules (Abbott 2001).

CONCLUSION

As globalization has shown, corruption is not something that is automatically swept away by it. Reducing corruption requires a concerted effort by activists, judiciaries, industries and politicians. Yet the efforts of the former two are often stymied by the interests of the latter two. Industries will refuse to use bribery only when the risks of being caught, and the penalties applied, are quite high relative to the potential profit of bribery. In light of the enormous number of transnational transactions which occur on a daily basis, versus the number of investigations and prosecutions of bribery, the risks are still quite low. Penalties applied are, in most cases, trivial, and are likely to remain so. Politicians will only crack down on bribery when doing so does not affect their ability to raise campaign funds, does not hamper their national champions in the global market and has some value at the polls. Globalization has not enabled politicians to raise more campaign and party financing legally, it has only increased the extent to which politicians must cater to their nationals (multinationals) in order to retain some jobs and tax revenue in their districts, and has not altered the fact that corruption is seldom the key concern of voters when they go to the polls. And for those countries which are not electoral democracies, globalization has yet to penalize the kleptocratic behaviour of their leaders. Finally, it has not altered a fundamental aspect of economic and political activity: firms competing for business and politicians competing for power can, through corruption, give each other what they want. The firms get exclusive contracts and market access, the politicians get resources which facilitate their bid for power.

Note

1   There has been pressure in recent years to reach agreements limiting export subsidies, but, as usual in international accords, the rules and enforcement provisions are weak. Aid which is given with strings attached (for example, funds for a project are donated with the restriction that the receiving country award contracts for the project exclusively to firms from the donor country) has been exempt from the rules (Moravcsik 1989: 181).

References

Abbott, K.W. 2001. 'Rule-making in the WTO: Lessons from the case of bribery and corruption', *Journal of International Economic Law*, 275–96.

Abbott, K.W. and Snidal, D. 2002. 'Values and interests: International legalization in the fight against corruption', *Journal of Legal Studies*, 31 (141), 1–30.

Ades, A. and Di Tella, R. 1999. 'Rents, competition and corruption', *American Economic Review*, 89 (4), 982–93.

Barboza, D. 2005. '"Donation" and insider open China for Goldman', *International Herald Tribune*, 5 March.

Bellamy, C. 1994. 'Campaign condemns arms sales subsidies', *The Independent*, 15 November.

Bodzin, S. 2005. 'Pentagon aided Halliburton, official charges', *Los Angeles Times*, 28 June, A12.

Cooper, N. 1997. *The Business of Death*. London: Tauris Academic.

Davis, I. 2002. *The Regulation of Arms and Dual-Use Exports: Germany, Sweden and the UK*. New York: Oxford University Press.

Elliott, C., Fairhall, D. and White, M. 1994. 'Fresh pressure on arms deals', *The Manchester Guardian Weekly*, 20 November.

European Commission. 1997. *Impact on Competition and Scale Effects: Competition Issues*. The Single Market Review Subseries V: Vol. 3. Luxembourg: Office for Official Publications of the European Communities.

Fidler, S. 2000. 'US steps up pressure over power project', *Financial Times*, 8 March.

Financial Times. 2005. 'Economic reasons for F-16 sale?', 27 March.

Gerring, J. and Thacker, S. 2005. 'Do Neoliberal policies deter corruption?' *International Organization*, Winter, 59, 233–54.

Gibbs, D. 1995. 'Secrecy and international relations', *Journal of Peace Research*, 32 (2), 213–28.

Godoy, J. 2004. 'Corruption in France, the more things change . . .', *Inter-Press Service*, 14 December.

Griffiths, K. 2005. 'Oh what a lovely war on terror it's been for Halliburton', *The Independent*, 27 March.

Hawley, S. 2003. 'Turning a blind eye: Corruption and the UK Export Credits Guarantee Department', Dorset: The Corner House. Available at <http://www.thecornerhouse.org.uk/document/correcgd.html>.

Hirsch, M. with Dehghanpisheh, B. 2005. 'Follow the money', *Newsweek*, 4 April, 34–5.

House of Commons, The Right Honourable Sir Richard Scott (1996). *Report of the Inquiry into the Export of Defence Equipment and Dual-Use Goods to Iraq and Related Prosecutions: Return to an Address of the Honourable of the House of Commons Dated 15 February*, HC 1995/96. London: HMSO.

International Consortium of Investigative Journalists. 2002. *Greasing the Skids of Corruption*. Washington, DC: Center for Public Integrity.

Isnard, J. 1998. 'Fournisseur et client sont complices', *Le Monde*, 14 March.

Krueger, A.O. 1974. 'The political economy of the rent-seeking society', *American Economic Review*, 64 (3), 291–303.

Laitin, D. 1994. 'The Tower of Babel as a coordination game', *American Political Science Review*, 88 (3), 622–34.

Mackie, G. 1996. 'Ending footbinding and infibulation: A convention account', *American Sociological Review*, 61 (6), 999–1017.

Marion, P. 1990. *Le Pouvoir sans Visage. Le complexe militaro-industriel*. Paris: Calmann-Lévy.

Manion, M. 2004. *Corruption by Design*. Cambridge, MA: Harvard University Press.

Millennium Challenge Corporation. 2005. Report on the Criteria and Methodology for Determining the Eligibility of Candidate Countries for Millennium Challenge Account Assistance in FY 2005. Millennium Challenge Account. Available at <http://www.mca.

gov/about_us/congressional_reports/Report%20to%20Congress%20on%20Criteria%20 and%20Methodology%20FY051.pdf>.

Moravcsik, A.M. 1989. 'Disciplining Trade Finance: The OECD Export Credit Arrangement', *International Organization*, 43 (1) (Winter), 173–205.

Naylor, R.T. 2002. *Wages of Crime*. Ithaca, NY: Cornell University Press.

OECD, Directorate for Financial and Enterprise Affairs. 2005. *United Kingdom: Phase 2. Report on the Application of the Convention on Combating Bribery of Foreign Public Officials in International Business Transactions and the 1997 Recommendations on Combating Bribery in International Business Transactions.* Paris: OECD.

Palan, R. 2003. *The Offshore World*. Ithaca, NY: Cornell University Press.

Philp, M. 1997. 'Defining political corruption'. In P. Heywood (ed.), *Political Corruption*. Oxford: Blackwell.

Plouvier, E. 1992. 'Corruption à la française III', *Le Monde*, 15 October.

Rose-Ackerman, S. 1978. *Corruption: A Study in Political Economy*. New York: Academic Press.

Sandholtz, W. and Gray, M.M. 2003. 'International Integration and National Corruption', *International Organization*, 57 (4), 761–800.

Scott, J.C. 1972. *Comparative Political Corruption*. Englewood Cliffs, NJ: Prentice-Hall.

Sun, Y. 2004. *Corruption and Market in Contemporory China*. Ithaca, NY: Cornell University Press.

Transparency International. 2002. 'Transparency International Bribe Payers Index 2002'; Berlin. Available at <http://www.transparency.org/cpi/2002/bpi2002.en.html>.

Transparency International. 2004. 'Corruption Perceptions Index'. Available at <http://www.transparency.org/cpi/2004/cpi2004.en.html#cpi2004>.

Van Ruymbeke, R. 2002. *Ordonnance de Renvoi devant le Tribunal Correctionnel de Non-Lieu Partiel et de Requalification.* No. du Parquet 9418769211, No. Instruction 2039/94/29 Procédure Correctionnelle. Cour d'Appel de Paris. Tribunal de Grand Instance de Paris. 13 December.

Warner, C.M. 2007. *The Best System Money Can Buy: Corruption in the European Union*. Ithaca, NY: Cornell University Press.

Warren, M.E. 2004. 'What does corruption mean in a democracy', *American Journal of Political Science*, 48 (2), 328–43.

Waxman, H.A. and Dorgan, B.L. 2005. *Halliburton's Questioned and Unsupported Costs in Iraq exceed $1.4 Billion*. Joint Report of the United States House of Representatives Committee on Government Reform Minority Staff Special Investigations Division and United States Senate Democratic Policy Committee. Washington, DC. Available at <http://www.democrats.reform.house.gov/Documents/20050627140010-82879.pdf>.

World Development Movement. 1995. *Gunrunners Gold: How the Public's Money Finances Arms Sales*. London: WDM.

Further reading

Della Porta, D. and Rose-Ackerman, S. (eds) 2002. *Corrupt Exchanges: Empirical Themes in the Politics and Political Economy of Corruption*. Baden-Baden: Nomos Verlagsgesellschaft.

Elliott, K.A. (ed.) 1997. *Corruption and the Global Economy*. Washington, DC: Institute for International Economics.

Warner, C.M. 2007. *The Best System Money Can Buy: Corruption in the European Union*. Ithaca, NY: Cornell University Press.

Chapter 31

Globalization and Sexuality

KATHRYN FARR

INTRODUCTION

This chapter provides an overview of the major issues and perspectives in the literature on globalization and sexuality. Like other difference, sexuality is an important but complicated mediator of globalization processes and effects. To begin with, the meaning of sexuality in the globalization literature is not fixed. In most of this literature, sexuality refers to homosexuality and other forms of sexual dissidence, but heterosexual and gender-related issues are the focus of some work. And, throughout, definitions of and distinctions between 'sexuality', 'gender' and 'sex' are fuzzy or absent. Adding to these complexities is that the most visible literature on globalization foregrounds heteronormative and masculinist narratives, leaving the sexually dissident and 'the feminized' in the shadows. This chapter, then, actually *re*focuses the analytical gaze, first, by briefly addressing perspectives through which the study of sexuality and globalization is obscured as well as advanced; and second, by examining in greater depth, major issues addressed in the globalization and sexuality literature. These are as follows: culture, identity and cosmopolitan 'gayness'; travel and tourism; migration, production and commodification; nationalism, citizenship and nation-state conflict; communication connections – the virtual and the actual; and collective resistance and situated strategies.

CENTRING SEXUALITIES IN GLOBALIZATION STUDIES: PROBLEMS AND PERSPECTIVES

'Outing' dominant globalization narratives

Queer and feminist globalization scholars often contend that the most visible literature on globalization foregrounds heteronormative and masculinist narratives. In part, such narratives result from the tendency of 'experts' to see globalization as an economic and market-oriented phenomenon, and the 'rugged individual' who moves the market forward as male and masculine. The dominant paradigm also suggests that globalization travels one way, from the most powerful and affluent (and thus masculinized) nation-states and multinationals to the 'lesser', dependent (and thus feminized) nation-states. Localities – so much a part of the feminine world and important as well in understanding queer culture – are also deemed of lesser significance in the globalized world.

Noting the emphasis on the global over the local and the corporate elite over labour, Saskia Sassen contends that dominant globalization narratives privilege 'hypermobility, international communication and the neutralization of distance and place . . . information over the workers who produce it . . . and the new transnational corporate culture over the other jobs upon which it rests' (2002: 254). As such, the labour and situated cultural production of women and sexual minorities is under-analysed. And, when discussed, domestic work is commonly imagined within the heterosexual family; family roles are broken down as feminine and masculine, or as those held by heterosexual women and men. Here and elsewhere, implied assumptions and confusion about links between sexuality and gender abound.

Problematizing sexuality and gender

It is almost impossible to discuss sexuality without discussing 'characterological' gender, as the two are so often intertwined. In the globalization literature, however, 'gender' is typically used as a proxy for 'women' or 'female/male', and its characterological meaning – essentialist characteristics that are believed to be representative or typical of femaleness/maleness – is overlooked. Whether or not a particular culture formally recognizes gender (as in feminine and masculine), in most cultures essentialist distinctions between women and men are made. And typically, there is an assumed match between characterological gender and sexual identity. That is, the heteronormative belief is that masculine men are heterosexual, whereas homosexual men are feminine, and heterosexual women are feminine, whereas homosexual women are masculine. Note here that in this juxtapositioning, gender defines sexuality for straight men, whereas for the remaining three types, sexuality defines gender. For the latter three, it would appear, then, that control of gender requires control of sexuality. Certainly, efforts to control both sexuality and women, and more pointedly women's sexuality, are pervasive, and figure as well into current globalization-related activity. More important for men, however, is the control of gender, that is, the insistence on masculinity (a putative signifier of heterosexuality), but with little other control of male heterosexual behaviour.

Additionally, gender *deviance* (personified in the masculine woman or feminine man) is often treated as a marker of homosexuality or other sexual dissidence, for example, the assumption that a masculine woman must be a lesbian. To add further complexity, gendered metaphors are often reflected in descriptions of nation-states themselves as either 'masculine' (competitive, powerful, modern, conquering) or 'feminine' (passive, powerless, traditional, conquered). Both sexual and gender dissidence are threatening to dominant imaginaries of globalization and of the 'successful' nation-state, as well as to the patriarchal family that reproduces the population to carry out and support global and state projects.

Finally, for both 'gender' and 'sexuality' there is a heavy reliance in Western (but not all other) cultures on binaries. That is, in typical Western terms, gender is portrayed as feminine *or* masculine, and sexuality as homosexual *or* heterosexual; in each case, greater value is placed on the latter side of the binary. And the binaries are seen as the difference, thus overshadowing intra-difference.

FRAMING SEXUALITIES AND GLOBALIZATION

Continua and multiples

Sexuality-focused globalization perspectives typically eschew universalisms, essentialisms and binaries. Universal declarations, the argument goes, belie historical, material and cultural differences, and essentialist descriptions conceal the reality of varying social constructions of sexuality. Binaries also simplify and camouflage difference, positing opposites, such as Western versus non-Western or developing versus developed nations, and global versus local. The call is for greater recognition of continua and multiples, in regard to sexuality as well as globalization. The use of the plural term 'sexualities', for example, expands and complicates understandings of sexual identity or orientation. And, according to one author, the replacement of 'gay and lesbian' with 'queer' problematizes not only sexual relations, but also what it *means* to be homosexual, for example, a way of being, an identity, a behaviour, certain attitudes or values (Altman 1996a: 6).

In one illustration, Katie King describes the unsuccessful attempt at the UN's 1995 Beijing World Conference on Women to construct lesbianism as an inclusive global category, and questions whether or not the term 'lesbian' or any such wording would work 'as a meta-term under which local sexualities can be displayed'. 'Is this possible,' she asks rhetorically, 'in an anti-essentialist feminist politics?' (2002: 33). Moreover, as King points out, the terms 'lesbian' and 'feminist' have varied meanings across cultures. But, the politics here, she continues, are complex: both using and *not* using these terms constitute political acts. And, in some cases, King suggests, usage is economically rather than politically motivated; the term 'bisexual', for example, has 'currency in a globalized economy of niche markets', that is, where the effort is to broaden the niche as much as possible (2002: 42).

The local, global and transnational

For some feminist and queer scholars, sexuality and globalization are best understood by focusing on the global–local mix – variously conceptualized as hybridity, homogenization or 'glocalization'.[1] In their anthology, Berry, Martin and Yue offer a collection of articles on cultures in queer Asia that give credence to the reality of glocalization, or, as one reviewer put it, the 'localization and indigenization of globally mobile understandings of sexuality' (Hughes 2005).

A number of feminist, queer and other *cultural* scholars, however, have suggested that these 'mix' conceptualizations simplify the relational character of the global and local *and* fail to account for the unique cultural forms that develop in different sites. Cultural studies scholar John Tomlinson (1999), for example, faults what he calls the 'homogenization' hypothesis, preferring instead to emphasize more nuanced understandings of links between the global and local in his conceptualization of 'complex connectivity'. Relatedly, globalization theorist Arjun Appadurai notes that the global and local 'feed and reinforce each other' in the construction of 'situated cultures'. Appadurai's vision of globalization components as 'scapes' highlights movement and flows – in ethnoscapes, consisting of the 'landscapes of persons who constitute the shifting world in which we live', both identity and the cultural are embedded, and around ideoscapes, or 'ideologies of states and counter-ideologies of movements', around which political cultures and counter-cultures are organized. Appadurai's model also emphasizes disjunctures and ruptures in scapes and flows, and thus fits well with examinations of how (sexual) difference and dissidence is expressed and received, organized and re-organized.[2]

Complementing a 'shifting worlds' theme at the structural level is Grewal and Kaplan's concept of 'scattered hegemonies'. Here, the authors point out that in the past, feminist thinking has often relied on meta-terms (such as capitalism and patriarchy) and singular realities. The need, according to these authors, is to 'articulate the relationship of gender to scattered hegemonies such as global economic structures, patriarchal nationalism, "authentic" forms of tradition, local structures of domination, and legal-juridical oppression on multiple levels' (1994: 17).

Some feminist and queer scholars have embedded their theoretical emphasis in language, identifying as 'transnational' rather than 'global' theorists. As transnational feminist scholars Grewal and Kaplan suggest, the 'transnational' attends to linkages across cultural contexts and highlights the importance of social structure and the state, as well as its alliances with global capital. And, says sexualities scholar Evelyn Blackwood, 'transnational sexualities' goes beyond the local–global divide, which typically posits a binary between 'traditional or oppressed sexualities' versus a 'Western-defined liberated gayness' (2005: 221). Sexualities scholars also note that transnational analyses attend to connections and flows that traverse a variety of locations, including not only those of class, gender and ethnicity, but also of urban, rural and other geographics (see, for example, Collins 2005). Finally, transnational scholars tend to avoid over-reliance on 'victim' narratives, and stress the importance of giving voice to agency and visibility to acts of resistance on the part of exploited people around the world.

CULTURE, IDENTITY AND COSMOPOLITAN 'GAYNESS'

According to Manuel Castells (1997), the pursuit of identity is the primary source of social meaning in a globalized world focused on flows of wealth, power and (external) images. Queer scholars have built on Castells' general argument by pointing out that in synchrony with the post-industrial arrival of globalized 'commodity capitalism', gay identity has moved from a minority status to a cultural or lifestyle signification (Pellegrini 2002; Lowe 1995; Tomlinson 1999). In support of this argument are the territorial gay (or queer) communities that have coalesced and become visible in a variety of localities, providing for their gay inhabitants a sense of community and lifestyle-aligned identity. Gay urban communities and the lifestyles within them are imagined as cosmopolitan – that is, as privileged, sophisticated, knowledgeable about diverse cultural experiences and comfortable with diverse cultural groups (Hannerz 1996). Modern gay communities are also largely urban, white, middle class and male, but beyond that, portrayals vary.

Some believe that globalization has led to the 'homogenization' and, more specifically, the 'Americanization' of gay culture throughout the world. Researcher Dennis Altman, for instance, argues that, while there are indigenous components of gay cultures in particular locales, modern 'queerness' reflects 'American fashion and intellectual style: young, upwardly mobile, sexually adventurous, with an in-your-face attitude toward traditional restrictions . . .' (1996b: 77). But others disagree, noting that globalization flows are uneven, as are their impacts on particular places, and that numerous variations in sexual cultures have been documented (Binnie 2004). Also, like other ethnoscapes, gay culture moves across borders, frequently changing course as it comes into contact with new populations, situations and places. And, in gay diasporas, residents construct cultures that reflect both their national culture of origin and that of their adopted home. Various ethnographic studies highlight the agency that indigenous, as well as diasporic, gays display in shaping sexual cultures (see, for example, articles in Cruz-Malave and Manalansan 2002b).

Others question the narration of gay culture as strictly cosmopolitan, pointing out that while urban gays may embrace an imaginary of acceptance of other, in reality their communities are often inaccessible to or marginalize many 'others', including working class and rural gay men and all lesbians. As Gabriel Giorgi notes, for example, the motto that 'everything is gay in this neighborhood now' applies only to male gayness, and on the occasions in which it 'traverses the scenario', the lesbian body stands out for its representational rarity (2002: 67).

Transformed from a 'seedy,' hetero-*sex* tourist site to a 'cosmopolitized' gay tourist district in Manila, Malate is illustrative of several of the above points. Gay entrepreneurs in Malate fit with the cosmopolitan imaginary, as they welcome foreign, typically privileged gay consumers. Yet the working-class Filipino gay men (referred to as hosts) who travel there to provide guide and companion services to tourists cannot afford to live in Malate. In an interesting turn, the hosts exhibit their own ethno-biases, most consistently expressed as a sexual preference for foreigners (or 'foreignness') over privileged gay Filipinos, whom they see as elitist and sexually reserved.

The services provided by this imported labour pool may include sex, but, as Dana Collins found in her interviews with them, the hosts identified not as sex workers, but rather as ' "legitimate" gay men, who genuinely desire other men and who want to participate in cosmopolitan urban gay life; that is, they have both class aspirations and gay desire' (2005: 188). Sex work, the hosts told Collins, involves women selling sex to men out of need rather than desire. But in spite of their own distancing from sex work and their upward aspirations, hosts were often excluded and marginalized by gay residents and entrepreneurs in Malate. They were not, for example, allowed into some establishments unless accompanied by a consumer-tourist. Nevertheless, the hosts saw Malate as public-visibility space where they could 'become the type of gay men that they want[ed] to be' (2005: 191). That is, through place, they constructed social identity by performing it. But this identity, and the culture to which it is tied, was not necessarily place-bound; it also travelled and transformed via the hosts to other parts of Manila, and at times outside of the Philippines.

Of concern to some queer scholars is that queers are buying into a commodified gayness as consumers and entrepreneurs, both of whose interests are 'allied with corporate multinational interests' (Puar 2002: 133). Altman (2001) fears that gays have become 'cultural dupes', willingly buying into a global gay culture constructed for the market, and perhaps seduced by an imaginary of social acceptance. Consumer capitalism has become more tolerant of diversity, but, as Miranda Joseph (2002) points out, promoters of global, free-market capitalism are just that, and are typically *not* concerned with the liberation of oppressed minorities. Jasbir Kaur Puar (2002: 133) provides an example of an inclusiveness contradiction in the November 1998 kick-off of a Levi Strauss campaign targeting gay and lesbian consumers – a campaign supported and applauded by many gays and lesbians, *but* which took place at the same time as the call for a boycott of Levi Strauss in protest of its unfair labour practices.

For gays, the construction of cosmopolitan identity involves the negotiation of other contradictions. Puar goes on to note that the 'binaried discussion on queer consumption' problematizes 'queer visibility – either visibility achieved through the marketplace is politically suspect [cultural dupes] or visibility in the marketplace is a sign of progress in the realm of acceptability [assimilation and perhaps the repudiation of difference]' (2002: 111). Does, some ask, an assimilationist model de-politicize gay culture, taking the focus away from the systemic discrimination that gays still face and the homophobia that, some argue, has also been globalized? Ann Pelligrini (2002) presents a more positive point of view, arguing that the 'commodification of gayness' does not negate gay politics, but rather is among its political 'operating conditions and constraints'.

While some argue that the 'cultural dupes' hypothesis lacks empirical validation, or, at the least, overstates the problem, there seems to be no question about cities' use of diversity, including gayness, as cultural capital. The commodification of space, in one view, is reflected in the efforts of nation-states and cities to compete for capital in high-tech and other industries. According to Dereka Rushbrook, nowhere is this more evident than in smaller, 'secondary' cities (as opposed to world or global cities, such as New York, London, Tokyo) which promote themselves as centres of modernity and cosmopolitan culture, including ethnic diversity; increasingly, Rushbrook (2002) argues, 'queer space' operates as one form of ethnic diversity. And gay culture, especially when it is concentrated in a particular neighbourhood or district, is regularly marketed to straight visitors as voyeur- or participant-consumers. The greater public visibility of gay culture today opens it up to the straight gaze, providing another standpoint from which a gay imaginary can be constructed.

Sassen provides a slightly different view, noting that large Western cities are clearly 'inscribed with the dominant corporate culture, but also with a multiplicity of other cultures and identities', and 'the dominant culture can encompass only part of the city' (1998: xxxi). Although diverse ethnic cultures can be infused with (dominant) corporate culture, it is useful to keep in mind that the economic is only one part, and not necessarily the most relevant part, of culture and identity.

Travel and Tourism

Although 'globalization champions the free movement of capital and goods', as author Jon Binnie notes, 'the free movement of persons is more problematic' (2004: 10). A distinction is made, for example, between travellers or tourists (affluent, cosmopolitan visitors) and migrants (poor, homeless foreigners). And, while touring or travelling across borders is often considered a citizen's right, migration across borders is not. Yet the traveller-tourist's welcoming is far from guaranteed – it also is mediated by difference, not the least of which are gender and sexuality.

Gay men and women of all sexualities may travel to escape their culture's discriminatory or confining social controls – which may be re-enacted in more widespread restrictions on or biases against their travelling. While globalization has opened up some business travel opportunities for professional women, women (both heterosexual and lesbian) travelling independently and recreationally are still subject to normative gender proscriptions, which often imply that among other things, they are 'fair sexual game'. And gay men (particularly with the globalization of HIV/ AIDS) are often discouraged and sometimes prevented from travelling across national borders. It was only in 1990, for instance, that the United States passed legislation eliminating the open-ended category of 'sexual deviancy' as a reason to deny entry into the country (Puar 2002: 126). As Giorgi puts it, at the same time that borders have opened up to travellers, 'homophobia appears as a limit or border' (2002: 72).

Neither sexism nor homophobia, however, necessarily trumps economic opportunism, and women and gay men are increasingly targeted by the travel-tourism industry as it broadens its search for lucrative niche markets.

Tourism as a development strategy

For many developing and some transitional countries, tourism is increasingly touted as a pathway out of poverty and debt. Global funding institutions such as the World Bank (WB) and the International Monetary Fund (IMF) have been adamant about the need for heavily indebted countries to build up their tourism sectors in order to secure debt-repayment revenues. Critics have expressed concerns about tourism's negative effects on poor countries, including environmental damage and disruption of local culture and traditions. Additionally, cultural images of tourist destinations in developing countries (and the often sexualized and racialized native 'others' who inhabit them) are commonly culled by foreign marketers, without any local input or control.

The globalized tourism boom (in 2004, there was an all-time high of 760 million tourist arrivals worldwide, and an expectation of 1.56 billion by 2020)[3] has had important gender and sexuality effects – for both tourists and those commodified for tourists.

Gay tourism

Recent data indicate that gay and lesbian travel accounts for about 10 per cent of the US travel industry and is valued at about $54 billion annually (Puar 2002: 110).

In order to reach these potential customers, some 1,200 gay and gay-friendly travel agencies have linked up with the International Lesbian and Gay Association (ILGA). And the gay travel magazine *Out and About*, another venue for reaching tourists, now has 10,000 subscribers (Puar 2002: 105).

Whether independently, or through a tour or cruise, gay and lesbian tourism is on the upswing. In the early 1990s, when the general cruise market was slipping, gay and lesbian cruises continued to do well, and by the end of the 1990s, more than 300 travel agencies were organizing gay and lesbian cruises. Olivia Cruises and Resorts, which organizes cruises for lesbians, saw its revenues go from $1.5 million in 1990 to just under $6 million in 1996 (Puar 2002: 105). But gay and lesbian cruise tourism has not been trouble-free. In 1998, the Cayman Islands refused to allow a gay cruise ship carrying over 90 men to dock for a one-day visit, stating in a letter to the cruise organizer that based upon research and experience, they could not count on this group to 'uphold appropriate standards of behavior' (BBC 1998: 1). And in 2000, when a gay male cruise ship stopped for a day of shopping and sight-seeing in the Turkish port of Kuşadası, local police ordered passengers already in town back to their ship, and forbid those on the ship from disembarking (PlanetOut 2000). Homophobic reactions to gay tourism have targeted lesbians as well. In 1998, a lesbian cruise ship carrying about 800 passengers was boycotted by angry protestors as it docked at Nassau in the Bahamas; few of the passengers got off the ship to go into town (CNN 1998).

Less has been written about lesbian than gay male tourism. There are, however, specific organized travel venues and tourist sites which cater to lesbians. Perhaps most notable among the latter is the Greek island of Lesvos and its town of Eresos, the birthplace of the archetype lesbian Sappho. Each summer, over 1,000 lesbians travel there and participate in a celebratory women's community, described by one tourist-journalist as 'a row of lesbians stretching 200 meters along the shore', writing, painting, weaving, swimming and slumbering, and having 'travelled from all over the world' in order to 'pay homage to one of the few remaining bastions saluting the fact, legends and symbols of lesbian history' (Dewhurst 1990: 11, 12).

There is also a market for lesbians and gay men who want to travel to gay-friendly sites and learn about gay-friendly resources, but are not looking for a gay group with which to travel. One tour organizer, Family Abroad, attempts to capture both gay tourists who do and do not wish to travel as gay with this advertising message: 'Don't think that all gay trips are centered around your sexual orientation. Our vacations allow you to celebrate your sexual orientation, but they also allow you the freedom to forget about it entirely' (Puar 2002: 109).

Sex tourism

In spite of the fact that most gay tourists engage in 'regular' tourism (although, as some have noted, regular tourism is often sexualized in travel ads), most of the media attention is focused on gay men's *sex* tourism, written, as Binnie puts it, through 'discourses . . . that pathologize western gay men as predatory paeodphiles' (2004: 1). Even though purchased sex with children is far more common among heterosexual than gay men, the predator and paedophile identities are much less frequently applied to men who buy sex with girl children. Relatedly, the spread of HIV/AIDS is commonly linked in the media to gay male sex tourists, or to the female prostitutes who serve straight men, even though there is evidence that around the world, sexually-transmitted HIV/AIDS usually goes *from* heterosexual men to sex workers, as well as to their wives and girlfriends. Also, heterosexual male sex customers' fear of HIV/AIDS (along with myths about the 'restorative power' of sex with a virgin) has led to their greater demand for younger and younger girls, causing the rate of HIV/AIDS to spiral among these prostituted children.

In the late 1960s, (hetero)sex tourism gained popularity with Japanese men, and marketers scrambled to take advantage of what was largely thought of as a normative or conventional demand. Within a few years, Japanese travel groups were offering sex tours to Thailand, Taiwan, Korea and the Philippines. A number of private businesses in Japan also began offering their male employees 'weekend sex holidays' as part of their annual bonus (Human Rights Watch 2000; Barry 1995). With the growth of international business travel, both the sex customer base and the number of tour sites have increased. In fact, globalization has fostered a sizeable migratory male labour population in general, providing an even more expansive, class-diverse and largely heterosexual customer base for the sex market.

Gay or straight, male sex tourists often seek sex with 'exotic', racialized 'others'. In their particular sexualized portrayals of ethnic and racial others, sex industries today reinforce historical relations of dominance, often through degradation of the other. Historically, Kempadoo argues, it was 'enslaved, indentured and colonized womanhood . . . [who] came to represent uninhibited and unrestricted sexual intercourse' (1998: 10). But, privilege (or 'the cosmopolitan') is also found among gay male customers, and their racism is played out on the commodified male native, maintaining as one author puts it, a 'queer modern-versus-primitive native binary' (Puar 2002: 113).

Discussions of globalization, tourism and the appropriation of culture, or of changes in culture as it moves across borders, commonly focus on consumption rather than production. When global production is addressed, the role of technology and technological elites is often given more attention than that of working- or poverty-class labour. Conversely, some argue, globalization itself 'needs to be understood first and foremost as a phenomenon driven by migrant labor, not simply as a question of cultural flows' (Puar 2002: 127, referring to Spivak 1996).

MIGRATION, PRODUCTION AND COMMODIFICATION

A key component of globalization is the work-related mass migration of people, both across and within nation-states. The largest share of this mass is female migratory labour, most notably women migrating from the 'South' to the 'North' for domestic or sex work; and in the 'South', from rural to urban sites for sex work, and service or factory jobs (often in multinational or Western-owned companies).

This migratory female labour, Sassen observes, is involved in two trajectories: the global city and survival circuits. In the *global city*, management professions require and a management class demands more and more low-end service and domestic work. Most of the migratory women are also utilizing *survival circuits* that 'have emerged in response to the "deepening misery of the global south"', particularly in countries 'struggling on the periphery of the global system with debt and poverty', and that consist largely of 'trafficked low-wage workers, and prostitutes or migrants who send remittances home' (Sassen 2002: 255). Prior to the 1990s, domestic and sex workers came largely from developing countries, but since the fall of the Soviet Union, women from the former Soviet republics and other Eastern Europe countries have begun to make up a larger share of this labour pool.

Migratory female labour carries gender disjuncture on its back. Across many cultures, gender norms insist that woman's place is in or near the home where she can care for her family. As Cynthia Enloe notes, 'in many societies, being feminine has meant sticking close to home' (2000: 21). Instead, the migratory woman – as nanny, maid or caretaker of the elderly – performs domestic duties for other families and serves as the breadwinner for her own. In fact, indebted nation-states, desperate for revenues, often prefer to outsource female labour because, they reason, women will be more likely than men to send earnings back home. And they are right (see Ehrenreich and Hochschild 2002). Gender caretaking prescriptions for women do work to the advantage of the nation-state, and gender disjuncture in this instance can be rationalized. That is, because she is doing women's work and it is theoretically temporary, the migratory female domestic can retain normative categorical (feminine) gender status. And the migratory sex worker? Although she too sends earnings home when possible and contributes to the build-up of the tourism industry in the country in which she works, her gender transgression is substantial.

Sex trafficking

An estimated one million women and children are annually trafficked transnationally into prostitution; many more are trafficked internally, most typically from rural to urban settings. Sex trafficking is a multi-billion dollar industry, with illegal profits behind only those from the drugs and weapons trades. The industry's (human) commodity, often obtained initially for free, can be sold, used and resold without her permission or even her knowledge. Typically, new recruits are led to believe that there is a legitimate job (e.g. nanny, maid, waitress, dancer) awaiting them in another country or city; those who do know that the job is sex work are rarely aware of the enslaved and deplorable work and living conditions to which they will be subjected. Others, sometimes children as young as eight and nine, are sold by poor families (also often duped by traffickers), abducted from their school or neighbourhood, or even drugged and transported to a foreign destination (see Farr 2005).

Upon arrival, traffickers tell the woman or child that she is indebted to them for her travel and employment arrangements, and must work this debt off through prostitution – a system known as debt bondage. For women trafficked overseas to affluent countries such as the United States, Canada and Japan, debts are notoriously high, averaging around $25,000–$30,000; monthly charges for room and board, along with other fees and fines, are also taken out of their earnings. The women typically work long hours, serve many customers a day and are subject to violence and abuse from their employer. Some women escape their traffickers, and some eventually do pay off their debt and are freed, but others remain in brothels for years. Many never recover – ashamed or forbidden to return home because of the stigma and dishonour associated with prostitution, or sick with HIV/AIDS or another illness.

Sex trafficking operates at some level in every region and virtually every country. Canada, the United States, most Western European countries, Australia, Japan and some Persian gulf states are major destination sites. Source sites tend to be either poor, developing countries, or, like the former Soviet republics, countries in transition from socialist to market economies. Many source countries are indebted to the IMF or the WB, and are pressured to go along with structural adjustment and austerity plans as development strategies.

The sex trafficking industry relies on a number of players, including recruiters, brokers, employment and travel agents, document thieves and forgers, transporters or escorts, brothel owners or managers, guards and extorters. These roles can be played by myriad actors, for example, temporary or one-time-for-hire workers, individual or partner entrepreneurs (both criminal and non-criminal), specialized gangs, organized crimes groups, such as the Russian mafia and the Japanese Yakuza, and 'corrupt guardians', such as the police, border guards or immigration employees. The industry itself consists of loosely organized, flexible internal and transnational networks of many sizes and with a variety of linkages. It features open global trade, and it easily crosses borders, moving money and people around the world with the use of efficient, advanced technologies. That is, it operates like any other big business in the globalized market economy (Farr 2005).

Coercion, deception and abuse, however, are found in all forms of human trafficking. In fact, some argue that an over-focus on sex work migration obscures the plight of many women and children who are trafficked across borders into other kinds of enslaved labour (Nathan 2005).

NATIONALISM, CITIZENSHIP AND NATION-STATE CONFLICT

Liberal nation-state democracy is arguably the central imaginary of globalization politics today (Kempny 1999–2000), and it often serves as a litmus test in a determination by Western and multinational powers as to whether or not a country is deserving of aid. At the same time, many argue, globalization has led to a decline in nation-state sovereignty, making it difficult for some states to live up to their responsibilities to care for and protect the rights of their citizens. In turn, according to Castells (Kreisler 2001), nation-state crisis threatens the very essence of liberal political democracy, as citizens lose confidence in their governments and increasingly rely on collective, but often fragmented, identity groups for stability.

As a reaction to the growing invasions of globalization, with a seeming loss of sovereignty and territoriality, *and* with collective identity (or Appadurai's ethnoscapes) as a new marker, invigorated nationalisms and nativisms have appeared around the world. These developments are particularly problematic for women and gays. Historically, as part of the social contract between a nation and its citizens, women and gays, like other marginalized groups, have relied on their country to protect their rights and welfare; nationalisms undermine these guarantees. Under nationalisms, national-cultural identity is the primary, if not the only, identity that matters, and it becomes dangerous to question the state should it discriminate against or fail to address an issue important to women or gays.

Additionally, control of non-reproductive sex and sexual desire (along with homosexuality in general) has been a basic component of nationalisms; the absence of such control is seen as a threat to the 'reproduction of the heterosexual familial narrative of the Nation/State' (Conrad 2001: 16). Yet, as Binnie notes, the sexual morals of the transnational class are a non-issue. In a related, gendered disjuncture, the non-reproductive sexual desires and behaviours of heterosexual soldiers and revolutionary forces continue to be seen as normative, while the prostitute who services them is morally condemned.

Nationalisms have historically been based on fundamentalist and patriarchal ideologies that underlie repressive actions towards women and sexual minorities. When a nation is also under duress, recovering from colonial rule or internal warfare, nationalisms can be *intensely* fundamentalist and patriarchal. In postwar Croatia, for example, rebuilding has included not only a move to a market economy, but also the development of a national identity that showcases the patriarchal family. Women are the reproducers of the nation, men rule and the state itself is the supra-family. 'Sexism and homophobia', states researcher Tatjana Pavlovic, 'are correlates of this national chauvinism'. As he relates to the family, Pavlovic continues, the 'homosexual is a dark counterpart of the hypermasculine father/defender/ warrior' (1999: 134).

Reflecting on narratives connecting nationalism and masculinity, Enloe suggests that as 'protectors of the nation', men are expected to place excessive controls on women's behaviour. Deviance from patriarchal norms may be taken as a sign of women's disloyalty to the nation. Enloe suggests, for example, that criticisms of the veil are often tagged as a national betrayal, or as pro-Western, but *not* as a threat to male dominance or patriarchal control. She says:

> What is striking about . . . arguments over whether a veiled woman is strengthening her nation or betraying it is that they are so important *to men* in their communities. One is hard-pressed to think of an equally heated debate in any national community about men's attire – or diet or linguistic style – in which women have had so predominant a role to play. (Enloe 2000: 53)

Parts of women's and minorities' historical political struggles, of course, have been assimilationist, and integration may be predicated on acceptance of a nationalist discourse. Researcher Lisa Duggan argues that while some gay politics have been assimilationist, others are themselves nationalist. Commenting on gay politics that insist on queers' public taking of an essentialist queer identity, Duggan argues that 'Outers generally not only believe in the existence of a gay nation, but are confident of their ability to identify its members and of their authority to do so' (2002: 221). To many, this fixed stand ignores sexuality diversity and poses dilemmas for gays and lesbians with multiple identities and allegiances.

Global assault on minorities and immigrants

Of the many 'contexts for violence', in Appadurai's view, 'the most difficult one is the worldwide assault against minorities of all kinds . . . ' (2001: 4). Various nativisms complement nationalisms, springing up in reaction to uncertainties about identity and economic well-being fostered by globalization. In many countries,

Appadurai states further, minorities 'are metaphors of the betrayal of the classical national project', and are also scapegoats for 'rising expectations, cruel markets, corrupt state agencies . . . and arrogant interventions from the outside' (2001: 6–7). Sexual minorities are among the victims of repression and hate. And women become pawns in intra-state conflict in specific, gendered ways.

Women as victims of men's wars

Rape, enslaved prostitution and other kinds of sexual violence against women have always been a regular part of warfare – intra-state, inter-state or world. Today, with their post-colonial ethnic divisions, intense concern about cultural identity and uncertainty about their place in the global economy, some developing and transition states have become embroiled in very violent intra-state warfare. In these conflicts, women are raped and assaulted by government soldiers, militias and insurgents, and eventually peace-keeping troops from all over the world. For combatants, the raping of the (male) enemy's woman-possession is often intended to humiliate and intimidate him, and in some cases, to impurify the enemy's ethnic, racial or religious identity (one of several strategies for ethnic cleansing or symbolic genocide). In many such cases (e.g. Kosovo, Rwanda, Sudan), Western nations and global bodies have not responded to genocidal rape and assault, or have responded too late with too little.

Analyses of some intra-state conflicts have shown the interplay of culturally drawn manipulations of gender and sexuality. Using Sri Lanka's armed conflict as an example, Yasmin Tambiah describes how militarization 'entrenches gender performances and heteronormative schemes while enabling women to transgress these' (2005: 243). The women's wing of the insurgent Liberation Tigers of Tamil Eelam (fighting against the Sri Lankan government in the early 2000s) issued a 'feminine' dress code for civilian women, following several reports of the sexual abuse of women at military checkpoints. The dress code was narrated as a technique for blaming 'non-wifely-dressed' women for their own abuse, *and* for preserving Tamil 'cultural' ways. A further advisory directed women soldiers themselves to comply with the dress code when not wearing their military uniforms, *and* to be tolerant of 'unwelcome sexual attention from male peers and superiors'. To fail to do one or the other would be seen, Tambiah learned, as a sign that the female soldier was a lesbian (and already de-feminized by way of being a soldier) and thus at risk of dismissal from military service (Tambiah 2005: 245).

Borders as sites of contention and violence

While 'borderless' is often used as a metaphor for globalization, borders are both real and symbolic sites of uncertainty and danger for those migrating (voluntarily or involuntarily) to and across them. Under globalization, migrants may be expected and needed, but not necessarily welcomed, by the receiving country. And, as Appadurai contends, 'the crossing by migrants can produce new and aggressive forms of minority-driven terror' (Baldauf and Hoeller 1998: 3). Migration disrupts the policing of borders and thus challenges not only containment, but sovereignty itself; moreover confusion about the illegality and legality of some border crossings causes further tension.

Border are sites of potential gendered and sexualized violence in several ways. Women are at particular risk of rape and assault during their border crossings. Kevin Bales describes, for example, the border between Thailand and Myanmar, where women are bought and sold for the sex industry, as 'especially chaotic and dangerous'. Some parts of this border are controlled by the Burmese military, and other parts by tribal militias and warlords. Sexually enslaved women who have escaped or have been discarded by brothel owners are often re-victimized at the border. As Bales explains, these 'deportees' are usually held in cells at the border for several days, where they are often sexually and physically abused by immigration police. Then police notify traffickers of the exact time and place of deportation. 'On the day of deportation the prisoners are driven . . . along the border into the countryside . . . and then pushed out of the cattle trucks in which they are transported' and, as 'the immigration police drive away, the deportees are approached by agents and brokers' who offer them prostitution work and transportation back to it (Bales 1999: 67–8).

Additionally, some of the most insecure and dangerous refugee camps are located near borders. Teeming with large, displaced populations – the great majority of whom are women and children – who have typically fled extreme violence in their own country, these camps put women at risk of rape and assault by soldiers, roving bandits, camp guards and even fellow refugees. Gender roles may also increase women's risk of sexual assault. Such has been the case for women refugees in Kenya, whose firewood-gathering role requires them to go outside the camps. Recent firewood-delivery projects which provide alternatives to women's foraging for firewood outside camps have shown some success in reducing the number of rapes (PeaceWomen 2002).

Among those making legal border crossings, gay men and lesbians face homophobic risks of discrimination and violence. Border crossing without hassle or worse may best be achieved by passing as straight and gender-appropriate (a masculine man or feminine woman). Also, other statuses – for example, middle class, white, tourist – may cushion border crossings for gay men and lesbians. As Puar notes, the policing hand falls more heavily on gay travellers who don't fit with the 'good homosexual' image (2002: 126).

Thus, both sexuality and gender (sometimes intertwined) are important to an analysis of borders as rupture sites, and to border crossings as disjunctive flows. Whereas physical territorialized space is clearly not borderless, cyberspace may come closer to this globalization imaginary. Yet, even here, borders, or at least boundaries, are constructed and re-constructed.

COMMUNICATION CONNECTIONS: THE VIRTUAL AND THE ACTUAL

Cyberspace and virtual communities

Queers have arguably taken the lead in using cyberspace to construct identities through queer virtual communities (Gauntlett 1999). Through the Internet, queers can choose from and connect with an array of virtual sites, allowing them to become 'citizens' of the global queer world, or providing them with a more local and familiar virtual experience. The latter may appeal to diasporic queers hoping to connect with queers and queer culture from their native country. And, like territorially located communities, virtual communities may be glocalized, with the mix in a constant state of flux as the virtual moves rapidly through the universe (see Berry et al. 2003).

The Internet also provides a safe and anonymous connection among sexual minorities – feelings can be expressed, identities can be revealed and relationships can be imagined in cyberspace, but not necessarily voiced or acted out in everyday life. In fact, as Puar notes, in imaginaries of the global gay traveller, the 'cosmopolitan queer subject is . . . interestingly, a closeted one' (2002: 109). However, communications on the web can lead to real-life encounters. In fact, some use the Internet as a way to meet people; as Daniel Tsang has pointed out, for some gay males, 'electronic cruising has replaced bar hopping' (1996: 155). And, as Binnie further suggests, 'Cyberspace collapses spatial scales – it is where the global is [potentially] most approximate, most intimate' (2004: 42).

There are, however, cyberspace limitations. Access to the Internet is heavily class-based, requiring both financial resources and technical knowledge. And in cultures where their education, income and independence are restricted, women are less likely than men to have cyberspace access. Also, numerous websites give voice to homophobic and sexist messages of hate and violence towards gay men and lesbians, and women in general.

Advertising places, events and services

Increasingly, through the Internet and other media venues, places are advertised not only as gay-friendly, but as 'gay'. Such is the case for the new gay quarter, Chueca, in Madrid. As Giorgi points out, Chueca, 'like other metropolitan gay territories – fragments of the discourse of global mobility – projects a sense of cosmopolitanism and erasure of difference', which, he points out, is 'soon revealed as highly problematic' (2002: 67). Chueca is advertised most vividly in guidebooks for gays, but it is also promoted as an object of observational tourism for non-gays. However, there may be conflict between promoting a particular public gay space and imaging a nation-state as gay-friendly. As Giorgi notes, in 1996, the Spanish Tourism Institute published a gay guidebook entitled *Gay Spain: Feel the Passion*, which was quickly withdrawn by the incoming Spanish government.

Gay global events also benefit from communication advances and mass advertising that sells not only material goods and services, but also gay culture and identity. Tensions often arise from efforts to combine these various and in some ways disparate offerings. Controversy over the highly publicized Gay and Lesbian Mardi Gras held annually in Sydney, Australia provides one example. While the Mardi Gras does much to affirm gay identity and cultures, it is also a commercial event, dependent on its ability to sell itself to a broad set of consumers. The author of one international gay guidebook opines that 'A visit to Mardi Gras is an absolute once-in-a-lifetime must for every gay travelling man' and that, moreover, 'Sydney is the gay capital of the South Pacific' (Markwell 2002). Although the 1998 Mardi Gras brought in an estimated $55 million, it lost money in 2002. The number of attendees was lower than had been expected, and the event was criticized by some gays and lesbians as elitist, catering primarily to Western, white gay men, and beholden to its corporate sponsors.

Global advertising through the Internet and other media venues also offers consumers opportunities to purchase sexualized bodies, for the most part, those of women and girls. A plethora of Internet sites, for example, sell prostitutes, brides and other sex-servicing women from and to all parts of the world. With the expansion of global travel and providers of it, women can be efficiently delivered to consumers, or consumers can travel to their situated purchase. Travel though is not always necessary as sex services can also be advertised, purchased *and* experienced through the Internet or telephone.

As Appadurai (2005) points out, however, media consumption can also bring forth agency and resistance. Consumers may make more informed and responsible choices as a result of their Internet exposure. Moreover, the Internet is now routinely used by feminist and gay and lesbian activists to put out and share information and to network with others working towards progressive social change.

COLLECTIVE RESISTANCES AND SITUATED STRATEGIES

Although global capitalism may provoke some people's interest in radical social change, institutionalized systems are inherently change-resistant. And, as author and gay and lesbian activist Urvashi Vaid[4] points out, the 'pursuit of civil rights [for sexual minorities] does not challenge fundamental inequalities' in a world 'built upon an exploitative, inherently racist economic system, in which the family is by definition heterosexist and patriarchal' (Mathur and Das 1997: 2–3).

However, a number of global social movements – feminist, environmental, labour, human rights and civil rights – have challenged hegemonic global capitalism. Such movements have been facilitated by grassroots work, and by myriad local and global NGOs that have sprung up around the world to work on specific gender and sexuality issues. Particularly notable is the growth of cross-issue coalitions that have found enough common ground to provide one another with support. According to Cruz-Malave and Manalansan, for example, the 'increased global visibility of queer sexualities and cultures has also generated multiple opportunities for queer political intervention through an equally globalized coalition politics', and it has 'compelled queer activists, feminists and legal scholars, to come together cross-nationally in order to confront violations of human rights of queers around the globe in organizations such as ILGA (International Lesbian and Gay Association) and the IGLHRC (International Gay and Lesbian Human Rights Commission)' (2002a: 2, 3). Although varying by culture, the framing of issue discourses also hints at coalition forces. Cindy Patton (2002), for instance, shows how Taiwanese gays' and lesbians' human rights discourse was generated from a feminist and women's rights discourse, unlike in the United States where gay rights were more closely linked to race and civil rights movements, and as such, gays and lesbians were constructed as (or more like) a minority.

Global networks often serve both personal and public ends – strengthening a sense of identity and community *and* working towards social change. In fact, at gay and lesbian events around the world, political activism shares the stage not only with gay cultural transmission and identity building, but also with tourism, as attendees have the opportunity to experience new recreational spaces. In other situations, rights activism or identity building springs from an issue of relevance to a particular group. The globalization of HIV/AIDS, for example, has mobilized many gay men to join transnational networks and work for AIDS prevention and treatment. And, as Altman notes, global connections formed through AIDS activism have also enhanced gay identity, leaving individual gay men with a view of themselves as part of a transnational 'gay world' (1996a: 4).

Particular collective or individual work strategies constitute another form of resistance. In her research on sex tourism, for example, Denise Brennan found that many poor women in the Dominican Republic migrated to Sosua, a popular Dominican resort town, to work there in the sex trade (a survival strategy). Their 'performance' often included pretending to be in love with carefully selected (usually European) clients – sometimes several at the same time – with the hope of migrating to a better life through marriage. Brennan argues that 'these women are engaged in an economic strategy that is both familiar and altogether new: they are attempting to capitalize on the very global linkages that exploit them'. These poor women, Brennan continues, 'are not simply using sex work . . . as a survival strategy; they are using it as an *advancement* strategy' (2002: 154–5).

Globalization provides (gendered) women and sexual dissidents around the world with opportunities to build across-border communities, transmit cultural material, strengthen identities and experience new places. Yet it also provokes old and new hostilities and inequities. Through organized and informal acts of resistance and political work, women and gays and lesbians are using globalized opportunities to survive and advance, as well as to work for social justice and equity.

Notes

1 The term 'glocalization', first popularized in English by British sociologist Roland Robertson in the 1990s, is now used regularly in the globalization literature.
2 Quotes available at <http://www.indiana.edu/~wanthro/appadurai.htm>, retrieved 17 June 2005. See, for examples of these and other of Appadurai's conceptualizations, Baldauf and Hoeller (1998). Interview with Arjun Appadurai, available at <http://www.appadurai.com/interviews_baladauf.htm>; Appadurai (1990, 1995).
3 Tourism data are available through <http://www.world-tourism.org>.
4 Urvashi Vaid is a former head of the National Gay and Lesbian Task Force and the author of *Virtual Equality: The Mainstreaming of Gay and Lesbian Liberation* (Garden City, NY: Anchor, 1996).

References

Altman, D. 2001. *Global Sex*. Chicago: University of Chicago Press.
Altman, D. 1996a. 'On global queering', *Australian Humanities Review* (July), available at <http://www.lib.latrobe.edu.au/AHR/archive/Issue-July-1996/altman.html>.

Altman, D. 1996b. 'Rupture or continuity: the internationalization of gay identities', *Social Text*, 14 (3), 77–94 (quoted in Binnie 2004).

Appadurai, A. 1990. 'Disjuncture and difference in the global cultural economy'. In M. Featherstone (ed.), *Global Culture: Nationalism, Globalisation and Modernity*, 295–310. London: Sage.

Appadurai, A. 1995. 'The production of locality'. In R. Fardon (ed.), *Counterworks: Managing the Diversity of Knowledge*, 204–25. London: Routledge.

Appadurai, A. 2001. 'New logics of violence', available at <http://www.india-seminar.com/2001/ 503/503%20arjun%20apadurai.htm>.

Appadurai, A. 2005. 'Basic concepts and accomplishments', available at <http://www.indiana.edu/~wanthro/appadurai.htm>, retrieved 17 June 2005.

Baldauf, A. and Hoeller, C. (interviewers) 1998. Interview with Arjun Appadurai, available at <http://www.appadurai.com/interviews_baladauf.htm>.

Bales, K. 1999. *Disposable People: New Slavery in the Global Economy*. Berkeley: University of California Press.

Barry, K. 1995. *The Prostitution of Sexuality*. New York: New York University Press.

BBC 1998. 'Gay cruise banned from Caribbean island', *BBC News Online*, 8 January, available at <http://news/bbc/co.uk/1/low/despatches/45246.stm>.

Berry, C., Martin, F. and Yue, A. (eds). 2003. *Mobile Cultures: New Media in Queer Asia*. London: Duke University Press.

Binnie, J. 2004. *The Globalization of Sexuality*. London: Sage.

Blackwood, E. 2005. 'Transnational sexualities in one place: Indonesian readings', *Gender and Society*, 19 (2), 221–42.

Brennan, D. 2002. 'Selling sex for visas: Sex tourism as a stepping-stone to international migration'. In B. Ehrenreich and A.R. Hochschild (eds), *Global Woman: Nannies, Maids, and Sex Workers in the New Economy*, 154–68. New York: Henry Holt.

Castells, M. 1997: *The Power of Identity*, Vol. 2 of *The Information Age: Economy, Society and Culture*. Oxford: Blackwell.

CNN 1998. 'Bahamians protest arrival of lesbian cruise ship in continuing debate over gay tourism in Caribbean', CNN, 14 April, available at <http://www.cnn.com/TRAVEL/NEWS/9804/14/bahamas.gay/>.

Collins, D. 2005. 'Identity, mobility, and urban place-making: Exploring gay life in Manila', *Gender & Society*, 19 (2), 180–98.

Conrad, K. 2001. 'Queer treasons: Homosexuality and Irish national identity', *Cultural Studies*, 15 (1), 124–37 (quoted in Binnie 2002: 16).

Cruz-Malave, A. and Manalansan IV, M.F. 2002a. 'Introduction: Dissident sexualities/alternative globalisms'. In A. Cruz-Malave and M.F. Manalanson IV (eds), *Queer Globalizations: Citizenship and the Afterlife of Colonialism*, 1–10. New York: New York University Press.

Cruz-Malave, A. and Manalanson IV, M.F. (eds) 2002b. *Queer Globalizations: Citizenship and the Afterlife of Colonialism*. New York: New York University Press.

Dewhurst, T. 1990. 'Getting back to our roots on a lesbian oasis', *Pink Paper*, 11, 12 (quoted in Kantsa 2002).

Duggan, L. 2002. 'Making it perfectly queer'. In I. Grewal and C. Kaplan (eds), *An Introduction to Women's Studies: Gender in a Transnational World*, 219–23. New York: McGraw-Hill (first appeared in *Socialist Review*, 1992, 22 (1), 11, 13–22, 26–31).

Ehrenreich, B. and Hochschild, A.R. 2002. 'Introduction'. In B. Ehrenreich and A.R. Hochschild (eds), *Global Woman: Nannies, Maids, and Sex Workers in the New Economy*, 1–13. New York: Henry Holt.

Enloe, C. 2000 [1990]. *Bananas, Beaches and Bases: Making Feminist Sense of International Politics*. Berkeley: University of California Press.

Farr, K. 2005. *Sex Trafficking: The Global Market in Women and Children*. (Contemporary Social Issues, series ed. George Ritzer). New York: Worth.

Gauntlett, D. 1999. 'Digital sexualities: A guide to internet resources', *Sexualities*, 2 (3), 327–32.

Giorgi, G. 2002. 'Madrid en transito: Travelers, visibility, and gay identity'. In J.K. Puar (ed.), *Gay and Lesbian Quarterly*, 8 (1–2): *Queer Tourism: Geographies of Globalization*, 57–79.

Grewal, I. and Kaplan, C. 1994. 'Introduction: Transnational feminist practices and questions of postmodernity'. In I. Grewal and C. Kaplan (eds), *Scattered Hegemonies: Postmodernity and Transnational Feminist Practices*, 1–33. Minneapolis: University of Minnesota Press.

Hannerz, U. 1996. *Transnational Connections: Culture, People, Places*. London: Routledge.

Hughes, G. 2005. 'Review of Berry, C., F. Martin, and A. Yue (eds). 2003: *Mobile Cultures: New Media in Queer Asia*'. London: Duke University Press, available at <http://reviews.media-culture.org>.

Human Rights Watch 2000. 'Owed justice: Thai women trafficked into debt bondage in Japan', September, available at <http://www.hrw.org/reports/2000/japan>.

Joseph, M. 2002. 'Family affairs: The discourse of global/localization'. In A. Cruz-Malave and M.F. Manalanson IV (eds), *Queer Globalizations: Citizenship and the Afterlife of Colonialism*, 71–99. New York: New York University Press.

Kantsa, V. 2002. ' "Certain places have different energy": Spatial transformations in Eresos, Lesvos'. In J.K. Puar (ed.), *Gay and Lesbian Quarterly*, 8 (1–2): *Queer Tourism: Geographies of Globalization*, 47–8.

Kempadoo, K. 1998. 'Introduction'. In K. Kempadoo and J. Doezema (eds), *Global Sex Workers: Rights, Resistance, and Redefinition*, 1–28. New York: Routledge.

Kempny, M. 1999–2000. 'Globalization of democracy and conditions for democratic community in the glocalized world, 4. Cultures of Democracy and Democratization: Israel, Eastern Europe and Beyond', seminar. Center for Russian, Central and East European Studies and the Allen and Joan Bildner Center for the Study of Jewish Life. Rutgers University, available at <http://www.rci.rutgers.edu/~culdemsm/Kempny.htm>.

King, K. 2002. ' "There are no lesbians here": Lesbianisms, feminisms, and global gay formations'. In A. Cruz-Malave and M.F. Manalanson IV (eds), *Queer Globalizations: Citizenship and the Afterlife of Colonialism*, 33–45. New York: New York University Press.

Kreisler, H. 2001. 'Identity and change in the network society: Conversation with Manuel Castells', available at <http://globetrotter.berkeley.edu/people/Castells/castells-con5.html>.

Lowe, D.M. 1995. *The Body in Late-Capitalist USA*. Durham, NC: Duke University Press.

Markwell, K. 2002. 'Mardi Gras tourism and the construction of Sydney as an international gay and lesbian city'. In J.K. Puar (ed.), *Gay and Lesbian Quarterly*, 8 (1–2): *Queer Tourism: Geographies of Globalization*, 81–99.

Mathur, C. and Das, A. 1997. 'Equality, identity and factoring the left back into the political equation: An interview with Urvashi Vaid', *Samar* 7 (Winter), 2–3, available at <http://www.samarmagazine.org/archive/article.php?id=85>.

Nathan, D. 2005. 'Oversexed: Forced labor isn't just about brothels', *The Nation*, 281 (6), 29 August 29–5 September, 27–30.

Patton, A. 2002. 'Stealth bombers of desire: The globalization of "alterity" in emerging democracies'. In A. Cruz-Malave and M.F. Manalanson IV (eds), *Queer Globalizations: Citizenship and the Afterlife of Colonialism*, 195–218. New York: New York University Press.

Pavlovic, T. 1999. 'Women in Croatia: Feminists, nationalists, and homosexualities'. In S.P. Ramet (ed.), *Gender Politics in the Western Balkans: Women and Society in*

Yugoslavia and the Yugoslav Successor States, 131–52. University Park: The Pennsylvania State University Press.

PeaceWomen 2002. 'Firewood project reduces rape incidents in Kenya', *Agence France-Presse*, 20 June, available at <http://www.peacewomen.org/news/June/kenya.html>.

Pellegrini, A. 2002. 'Consuming lifestyle: Commodity capitalism and transformations in gay identity. In A. Cruz-Malave and M.F. Manalanson IV (eds), *Queer Globalizations: Citizenship and the Afterlife of Colonialism*, 134–45. New York: New York University Press.

PlanetOut 2000. 'Gay cruise fiasco in Turkey', *PlanetOut*, 7 September, available at <http://www.PlanetOut.com>.

Puar, J.K. 2002. 'Circuits of queer mobility: Tourism, travel and globalization. In J.K. Puar (ed.), *Gay and Lesbian Quarterly*, 8 (1–2): *Queer Tourism: Geographies of Globalization*, 101–37.

Rushbrook, D. 2002. 'Cities, queer space, and the cosmopolitan tourist'. In J.K. Puar (ed.), *Gay and Lesbian Quarterly*, 8 (1–2): *Queer Tourism: Geographies of Globalization*, 183–206.

Sassen, S. 1998. *Globalization and Its Discontents*. New York: New Press.

Sassen, S. 2002. 'Global cities and survival circuits'. In B. Ehrenreich and A.R. Hochschild (eds), *Global Woman: Nannies, Maids, and Sex Workers in the New Economy*, 254–74. New York: Henry Holt.

Spivak, G.C. 1996. 'Diasporas old and new: Women in the transnational world', *Textual Practice*, 10, 245–69.

Tambiah, Y. 2005. 'Turncoat bodies: Sexuality and sex work under militarization in Sri Lanka', *Gender & Society*, 19 (2), 243–61.

Tomlinson, J. 1999. *Globalization and Culture*. Chicago: University of Chicago Press.

Tsang, D. 1996. 'Notes on queer 'n' Asian virtual sex'. In R. Leong (ed.), *Asian American Sexualities: Dimensions of the Gay and Lesbian Experience*, 153–62. London: Routledge (quoted in Binnie 2002: 46).

Chapter 32

War in the Era of Economic Globalization

Gerald Schneider

Introduction

The debate on the pros and cons of globalization has revived the debate on whether or not increased economic, political and social linkages between nation-states influence the risk of war both *within* and *between* states. As this chapter shows, the globalization debate has mainly focused on the economic preconditions of war and peace. Within this discussion, two positions are at loggerheads with each other; each of them has a distinguished track record in the history of political thinking. Commercial liberalism, the globalization friendly perspective, mainly relates to the pacifying effect that the exchange of goods and services across states allegedly has. A statement, which Vernon Smith (2004: 638) attributes to the French journalist Fredric Bastiat, succinctly summarizes the peace-through-trade hypothesis of commercial liberalism: 'If goods don't cross borders, soldiers will'. In a masterful treatise on the liberal sources of peace, Russett and Oneal (2001) trace this belief back to Kant and expect in line with the Königsberg philosopher that a tripod of forces – democracy, economic interdependence and membership in international organizations – are key causes of peace. As I have outlined elsewhere (Schneider et al. 2003), the author of *Perpetual Peace* had a predecessor in other enlightenment philosophers like Montesquieu as well as medieval and ancient writers.

A current popular version of commercial liberalism is traceable to *New York Times* columnist Thomas Friedman (1996, 1999). In a notorious commentary he paraphrased the main tenet of the literature on the Kantian democratic peace hypothesis. According to this important theoretical and empirical perspective, democracies do not engage in massive armed violence against each other. In Friedman's revised view, no two countries that possess a McDonald's ever fought a war against each other. As Wheen (2004: 241) points out in an entertaining polemic, Friedman's prophecy already experienced its death blow during the Kosovo war when US-led forces bombarded Belgrade, a capital 'with no fewer than seven branches of McDonald's'. Interestingly, Friedman tried to save face through the argument that what he considered to be weak Serbian resistance proved his 'Golden Arches Theory of Conflict Prevention' to be correct after all: 'It turns out in the end the Serbs wanted to wait in line for burgers, not for Kosovo' (cited in Wheen 2004: 241). There is no sign that this intellectual *volte-face* diminished the political influence of the *NYT* columnist.

It seems like an odd coincidence that another bold prediction by a proponent of commercial liberalism endured a similar fate. Angell (1910), winner of the 1933 Nobel Peace Prize, forecast just 4 years before the outbreak of World War I that engaging in armed conflict amounts to an illusion that would only seem attractive to a foolish and irrational government. Retrospectively, Keynes (1919) described the period during which 'The Great Illusion' was written as an 'extraordinary episode' of economic globalization.

The sceptical viewpoint has some of its intellectual roots in anti-capitalist religious writing and especially the various traditions of Marxist thinking. Marx and Engels had advanced the perspective that the contradictions of capitalism and thus also of one of its key components, free trade, would result in class warfare. Marx (1848) welcomed free trade because of its alleged destructive nature that pushes the antagonism between capitalists and workers to the extreme. The Leninist theory of imperialism developed this argument further and argued that the search for new markets would result in global tensions that ultimately culminate in an armed struggle between the oppressors and the oppressed around the world. Economic globalization would thus result in global war (Lenin 1921 [1917]).

Dependency theories qualified this view, pointing out that class interests are not uniform in the north and the south of the world economy (e.g. Amin 1976; Cardoso and Falleto 1969). Galtung's (1971) theory of 'structural' imperialism, for instance, perceived a global revolution as unlikely because of conflicting interests between the workers in the industrialized world and their counterparts in the developing world. In the 1970s and early 1980s the debate on the role of global economic integration took an empirical turn, when political sociologists started to examine the effects of trade and investment on developing countries (e.g. Bornschier et al. 1978). One of their main fears was that increased foreign direct investment mainly profits the owners of those firms that do not produce for the internal market. This 'penetration' of fragile markets by multinational corporations aggravates, in the *dependencia* view, economic imbalances and social inequality as the northern profiteers of globalization do not reinvest their earnings in the developing world. The resulting misery makes civil strife almost inevitable.

Interestingly, politically conservative authors like Waltz (1979) and Gowa (1994) offered similarly gloomy predictions about the impact of economic integration on the likelihood of interstate war. In the view of these so-called neo-realists, growing economic exchanges make an economy more efficient. This has the perverse effect that, by engaging in increased trade, one unwillingly arms a potential opponent.

Sceptical arguments popped up again in the 1990s, a period during which, according to Rodrik (1994), an extraordinary 'rush to free trade' shattered the developing world. The capitalist trend invited the accusation that global economic integration destabilizes the open countries (e.g. Chua 2002). Brennan (2003: 50) wrote in this vein that 'globalization . . . visits terrors on the South and on the future, directly through war, starvation and exploitation, and indirectly through the destruction of the atmosphere'. A more nuanced perspective is offered by Stiglitz 2002: 67). He believes that the uniform application of globalization precepts by the International Monetary Fund has undermined fragile societies in the developing world. In his view, 'liberalization – especially when undertaken prematurely, before strong financial institutions are in place – increased instability . . . one fact remains clear: instability is not only bad for economic growth, but the costs of the instability are disproportionately borne by the poor'.

This chapter will first provide a theoretical rationale for the two competing perspectives and argue that they are reconcilable with what the author calls the distributional theory of liberal peace. This approach maintains that for the international level globalization can increase the risk of war in societies in which a praetorian sector is sufficiently strong. In order to maintain its influence at home and to channel tax money into its own pocket, the military is interested in increased hostilities with the outside world (Schneider and Schultze 2003, 2005).

Domestically, the distributional version of commercial liberalism expects that the integration of a society into the world market reduces the income of the less competitive parts of the economy. This effect of globalization creates a short-run risk of war as long as the costs of foreign economic liberalization are larger than the growing benefits that globalization has for the whole population in the long run (Bussmann et al. 2003, 2005; Bussmann and Schneider 2007).

These qualifications do not amount to a rejection of commercial liberalism. On the contrary, the most recent research on the impact of globalization on the risk of both international and domestic conflict stresses that the increased costs of conflict in times of growing economic bonds are a necessary, but not a sufficient, condition for both domestic and international peace. This chapter will first outline the causal mechanism through which globalization acts as a source of cooperation and conflict. I will start out the discussion with a summary of the main explanations and move then to the empirical research on this topic. The chapter concludes with a critical survey of the challenges that the revised liberal theory of peace faces. I will also discuss how other, but unfortunately less researched, facets of globalization – a growing number of states, the proliferation of weapons of mass destruction, expanding social ties between states and increasing cultural homogeneity – influence the risk of war.

THE CLASSICAL ARGUMENTS AND THEIR QUALIFICATION

The theoretical basis of commercial liberalism is a simple opportunity cost argument. In Polachek's (1980) classic statement, globalization lowers the likelihood of armed violence between states because growing interdependence renders warfare more costly. His formal conclusion on the pacifying effect of global economic integration has its theoretical basis in Ricardo's theorem on comparative advantage. As this standard argument of globalization advocates goes, states should have a unilateral incentive to open up their economies to free trade. Specialization in the production of those goods in which a nation possesses a comparative advantage increases imports and exports; the income of the average citizen should in return grow (Fisher 2003). Yet, as the political economy literature maintains, the economic well-being of their population is not necessarily the top priority of political leaders (e.g. Hillman 1989). If globalization induces political changes such as democratization or a strengthening of the political opposition, both elected and non-elected leaders might opt against it. The remainder of this section shows how such political considerations qualify the unconditional peace-through-globalization hypothesis that can be derived from classical economics.

Interstate war

Most studies on the impact of globalization on the likelihood of violent conflict address interstate war as the outcome variable. Only a few studies have, however, devoted some energy to the question of how the opportunism of politicians disrupts the optimism of commercial liberalism. Recent theoretical developments advance a more strategic version of Polachek's expectation that serves as a deterrent against the usage of armed force (Gartzke et al. 2001). Yet the argument boils down to the conviction that governments of states that are highly integrated are better able to 'signal' their true intentions than leaders of closed economies. This advantage arises because the foreign policy a government pursues gains in credibility with the size of the opportunity costs that political violence would create. The model of Gartzke et al. is similar to an argument that Morrow (1999) sketches. In his view, trade is a variable that potential belligerents can easily observe. Although leaders might use trade flows as an instrument to signal their resolve in a dispute, economic interactions always also reflect the level of hostility between states. If economic leaders of one state anticipate conflict with another state, they will thus automatically reduce their exchanges with their economic partner. Although trade might thus be negatively correlated with conflict, the 'true' explanation of peace or conflict lies in some other attribute that characterizes the relations between two states. In other words, globalization might just be a manifestation, but not necessarily a cause, of peace. Gowa (1994) and other neo-realists have accordingly maintained the traditional 'trade follows the flag' argument. She argued in a further development of the structural realist view of Waltz (1979) that alliance configurations and especially multipolar world systems are more prone to conflict than bipolar ones and that these patterns determine who trades with whom. Globalization would thus be nothing else than the outflow of security considerations. Morrow (1997) has shown, against this realist determinism, that bilateral economic exchanges are also possible between adversaries.

A convincing version of the liberalist cause should motivate both war and economic openness as policy instruments that governments can simultaneously manipulate. One possibility is to move away from 'states' as the ultimate arbiter in trade policy-making and to also consider those actors whose interaction affects government trade orientations: employers and employees. Ironically, proponents of the peace-through-trade nexus often advocate in other contexts the wish that theoretical analyses should look at the real motivation for politicians to engage in peaceful or conflictual relations with other states. Most studies on this relationship, however, are implicitly mercantilist and assume that governments are simply aggregating the welfare of their citizens. To overcome this outmoded hypothesis, Schneider and Schultze (2003, 2005) have disaggregated the state and analysed the trade–conflict nexus in a more complex trade policy model. Their refinement of commercial liberalism stresses the redistributive aspects of foreign economic liberalization and distinguishes between the export, the import-competing and the military sector as the crucial actors within a society. Hence, this political economy re-statement of the classical argument assumes that the 'military–industrial complex' is just living on the taxes that the two productive sectors within the economy provide. Because globalization increases the tax base of a state, the military is in favour of both foreign economic liberalization and increased violence since only military tensions can justify increases in the defence budget. If the government wants to keep the military happy, it will thus become more hostile in its interactions with other states even in times of growing economic interdependence. Yet there are limitations to belligerence in an era of globalization. The costs of heavy fighting might outweigh the benefits of growing economic ties, turning the export sector away from its tacit alliance with the military. In the event that war becomes, in return, too costly for the governments because both the export and the import-competing sector suffer under it, leaders will move towards a more peaceful course of interaction. We can thus expect that opportunistic governments that take the wishes of the military into account will rather fight short conflicts that do not hurt the economy too much and that are not directed against main trading partners. Furthermore, if the military is politically weak, the opportunity cost model of Polachek is confirmed: states are more peaceful in times of expanding economic ties.

Civil war

According to neoclassical economics, the precepts of commercial liberalism should also hold domestically. Nations that embark on a course of foreign economic liberalization should, on average, be more peaceful because economic openness creates growth and jobs, rendering distributive conflicts less severe. Yet the way to economic openness is not a smooth one; it redistributes income from the losers to the winners of globalization. In the industrialized world, the winners are largely well-educated and capital owners. This is at least what we can expect from the Heckscher–Ohlin and the related Stolper–Samuelson models of trade policy-making (e.g. Deardorff 1994). This standard analytical framework distinguishes between the different factors of production and argues that the abundant factor within an economy will profit from increasing trade. The abundant factor in the 'North' of the world is capital; labour, especially unskilled workers, will, conversely, lose jobs because capital can easily be transferred to another country with lower wage costs. However, as labour rather than capital is abundant in the developing world, globalization has opened up another cleavage according to this theory. Unskilled workers are thus the potential winners of globalization, and it is no surprise in this light that especially governments from the Southern hemisphere have called for another world trade round and thus an intensification of globalization. Some studies that assessed the *dependencia* arguments point out that the developing world is the main profiteer of globalization (e.g. Firebaugh 1992; de Soysa and Oneal 1999).

A further conflict arises at least in the short run between the export and the import-competing sectors of the economy. The Ricardo–Viner model, also dubbed the sector-specific model, maintains that factors are not completely mobile between industries. While both workers and employers will call for a further liberalization of the economy, their counterparts in the less competitive import-competing sectors will oppose such a move towards more globalization. As the short-run costs of liberalization clearly outweigh the benefits, the potential losers in the import-competing industries will counter the demands of the beneficiaries of increasing economic bonds with other states. The risk that the dispute over globalization escalates into violence will be especially severe for countries in which the government does not compensate the victims of globalization (Bussmann et al. 2005).

A related hypothesis attributes the source of instability to the uniform application of the 'Washington consensus' and thus the precepts that the International Monetary Fund and other international actors have sold throughout the past decades to the governments of developing countries in exchange for foreign economic assistance. In the meantime, the Bretton Woods institutions and, among them, especially the World Bank have distanced themselves from the precepts of the 'Washington consensus' to some extent. During the 1980s and 1990s globalization à la IMF entailed a retrenchment of state activities and a turn away from protectionist policies. As a radical austerity programme or foreign economic liberalization undoubtedly meet public resistance, public protests and eruptions of political violence should have accompanied the implementation of the IMF programmes. Yet, up to now, no clear evidence links IMF programmes to political instability and civil unrest (Bussmann et al. 2005). This might, however, also be a consequence of a lack of a sound database on the structural adjustment programmes and the negotiations that the IMF and other institutions have held with debtor countries. Bussmann et al. (2005) report a contemporaneous relationship between IMF programmes and domestic instability but caution about the causality behind this correlation. Be that as it may, it seems quite indicative that policy-makers, civil servants and the public know so little about how globalization was implemented throughout the past decades around the world and what kind of social impact these programmes had.

THE EMPIRICAL RECORD

The companion argument to commercial liberalism, the democratic peace hypothesis, according to which democracy reduces the likelihood of conflict in jointly democratic pairs of states, has survived many challenges by outstanding theorists and methodologists. The track record of the related 'peace through globalization' literature is more ambiguous. One of the problems with the empirical studies is simply measurement. Conflict researchers have not yet come up with a definition of globalization that is completely satisfactory. The typical indicator for economic openness, the trade-through-GDP ratio, suffers from two limitations. First, it covers only one dimension of globalization and, by some accounts, not the most problematic one (Stiglitz 2004). Second, trade is an outcome variable and only indirectly reflects the political decision of whether or not a country should open itself to global competition; indicators that take the policies into account should be a more precise manifestation of the degree to which a country has embarked on a course of foreign economic liberalization (Martin 2005). Similar measurement problems exist for the dependent variable. Although earlier studies also looked at the impact of war on a continuous scale of cooperative and conflictive events (Gasiorowski and Polachek 1982; Gasiorowski 1986; Pevehouse 2004), most of the recent studies conceive of war as an event that can be separated clearly from peace. The resulting dummy variable is, however, not innocuous, as the number of wars a country experiences really depends on the fatality threshold that one uses to qualify interstate or intra-state relations. Large-scale wars are also – fortunately – rare events, rendering the application of standard statistical techniques highly problematic (King and Zeng 2001).

This section will survey the empirical findings that have been put forward during the past few years, often simply by using the trade-through-GDP ratio. Most of these studies are quantitative by nature; Ripsman and Blanchard (2003) summarize the state of art in qualitative studies.

International war

The publication in 1996 of two articles in *Journal of Peace Research* relaunched the debate on whether increasing economic exchanges between states decrease the likelihood of conflict between states. Oneal et al. (1996: 23) presented results that strongly supported the position of commercial liberalism. These liberalist authors examined a selection of all pairs of states from 1950 to 1985 and concluded based on their statistical analysis that 'the pacific benefits of interdependence have not been sufficiently appreciated'. Barbieri (1996), by contrast, claimed in a similarly designed empirical study that the impact of growing trade bonds on conflict is positive. Globalization should thus render states more belligerent rather than more peaceful, as liberalists claim.

Barbieri's monograph *The Liberal Illusion* qualified this argument somewhat, but still maintained: 'the evidence indicates that interdependent dyads are more likely to experience the most extreme form of conflict' (Barbieri 2002: 121). Oneal and Russett (1999) have responded to this challenge with a thorough reanalysis of their own and Barbieri's data. They show that the latter's usage of several highly inter-correlated explanatory variables might have rendered her analysis unreliable. The author does not know of any published study that was able to replicate the negative association between economic interdependence and peace that Barbieri found. Most other studies support the liberalist cause. Dorussen (2004) particularly demonstrates that the strategic nature of the traded goods matters considerably in the trade–conflict nexus. Exchanges in goods for which production needs particular expertise have particularly peaceful effects, while the impact of trade in goods like primary commodities that could also be appropriated by force is less strong. Keshk et al. (2004) furthermore show with the help of a simultaneous equation model that the influence of trade on war is not significant, but that conflict in return inhibits trade. This latter result probably also solves the dispute on the effects of war on global economic interactions. Barbieri and Levy (1999) first claimed, in an examination of a limited number of dyads, that the effect of war is negligible. Based on a larger sample of pairs of states, Anderton and Carter (2001a, b) came, however, to the opposite conclusion.

Another problem in the empirical study of the trade–conflict interrelationship is the choice of the appropriate unit of analysis. Domke (1988) examines the conflict-propensity of states and not dyads and finds considerable support for the thesis of Rosecrance (1986) that trading states are more peaceful than more autarkic nations. Barbieri (2002), relying on a more convincing methodology, corroborates these findings. This makes it mandatory to figure out why she comes to the opposite result in the analysis of pairs of states. One possibility might be that dyadic analyses allow a researcher to account for 'asymmetric interdependence' between countries much better than examinations that focus on the state as the unit of analysis. In the perspective of *dependencia* theorists, pairs of states that face such 'unequal' trade relationships should face a particularly high risk of conflict. The results of Oneal and Russett (1999), however, cast doubt on the finding of Barbieri (1996) that unbalanced exchanges are particularly risky. It might be more worthwhile, therefore, to look at the overall inclusion of a state into the multilateral trading system as a possible source of conflict in the future.

These controversies show that the debate on commercial liberalism is far from being over. Although most results seem to support or at least not contradict the tenets of commercial liberalism, there is still a need for studies that use other indicators than trade to gauge the impact of globalization on interstate relations. Only a few studies have started to look at the pacific effect of foreign direct investment, confirming (up to now) the optimism of the liberal viewpoint (Bussmann and Wild 2004).

One problem of these statistical studies is reversed causality and thus the possibility that war is the real explanatory variable and the facets of globalization are what should be explained. This is especially the case with studies on the impact of investment on armed conflict because one could easily theorize that a rational investor will move money only to countries for which no armed conflict is foreseeable. Some studies such as the paper by Keshk et al. (2004) deal with the issue, but applications of this or similar methodologies to the role of financial flows on war are lacking.

Civil war

Empirical studies on the impact of globalization on the likelihood of conflict within states are rare. Some studies on this topic were published in the 1970s and 1980s when the *dependencia* arguments enjoyed widespread support in academia and government circles. According to the conventional wisdom of this period, foreign direct investment and other manifestations of global economic interdependence destabilize emerging economies. The reasons for this hypothesis largely rest on the implicit assumption that the benefits of global economic exchanges are unequal and reach mainly those who are already in a privileged position within society. Yet the empirical evidence for these hypotheses is rather limited, as Hegre et al. (2003) show that globalization indeed pacifies intrastate relations. Harff (2003) reports that governments of open economies are less likely to initiate genocides. These results are in accordance with the findings of Bussmann et al. (2005) as well as Bussmann and Schneider (2007).

The suspicion of some globalization sceptics that capital account rather than trade openness increases the likelihood of domestic conflict seems a more promising research hypothesis. As Stiglitz (2004: 60) writes, 'Most of the critics of capital-market liberalization are not as concerned about foreign direct investment (FDI) as they are about short-term financial flows. It is the latter which many fear as particularly destabilizing.' In this view, capital-account liberalization unnecessarily exposes countries to the risk of economic shocks which in return renders violent forms of protest more likely. Bussmann and Schneider (2007) cannot find support for this thesis, noting, however, the limitations of the currently available data.

Yet the lack of statistical significance does not imply that domestic effects of globalization are always positive. Bussmann et al. (2005) offer considerable support for the thesis that foreign economic liberalization increases the short-run risk of conflict while its long-term impact might be positive. This double-edged tendency is particularly pronounced in sub-Saharan Africa which endured in the 1980s and 1990s both increased globalization and a high incidence of civil war. Obviously, revolts against foreign economic liberalization aggravate the development problems of these states, as the World Bank report on civil war sadly shows (Collier et al. 2003). Bayer and Rupert (2004) estimate that civil wars destroyed around one-third of all bilateral trade between states in the post-World War II era. This all supports the contention of Stiglitz and other sceptics that foreign economic liberalization has to be carefully implemented in order to avoid the negative side-effects of globalization.

THE WAY AHEAD IN THE LIBERAL THEORY OF PEACE

The main challenge for commercial liberalism is still theoretical. We do not know how exactly politicians react to the demands by exporters, importers and other social forces. A politician who faces a re-election challenge will probably heed such voices and carefully balance the interests of the competing sectors against each other. As we have long known, globalization can act as a deterrent against the use of force because it increases the opportunity costs of war. One of the main problems of this important proposition is that it lacks a motivation for both trade and war. This deficiency renders the hypothesis almost tautological. As liberalists associate with globalization a diminishing attractiveness of waging war, raising the level of hostility is purely irrational or, to use Angell's word, a 'Great Illusion'.

Convincing theories of how globalization affects armed conflict need to refrain from defining the cause for war away by simply assuming that it becomes increasingly costly. They rather need to motivate the conditions under which leaders are simultaneously interested in commercial bonds and in waging war. As I have argued in this chapter, an analysis of the redistributive effects of global economic integration can serve as an analytical basis for non-tautological theories of globalization and peace. Another possibility is to look at the efficiency gains that increasing commercial ties have for a society and its military sector. No clear model has yet been developed for the assessment of these countervailing influences of growing cost of war and the efficiency gains in the usage of armed force. Future restatements of commercial liberalism have to take into account how the pacifying effect of globalization interacts with the war-mongering effects of the very same process. This work will be particularly relevant for the analysis of those states in which the military plays an important role.

Globalization similarly makes armament cheaper and, due to technological progress, increases the threat that emanates from isolated states or marginalized terrorist groups. In other words, the costs of fighting a war decrease in times of globalization although the very same process makes governments more vulnerable by increasing the opportunity costs of warfare. We do not know how rebel leaders, politicians and governments evaluate the incentives and disincentives to wage war against each other. It is, however, easily conceivable that globalization increases for some the attractiveness of using armed force. In a time of shrinking distances, disgruntled actors that only posed local or regional risks in the pre-globalization period increasingly enter the centre stage in world politics and create truly global security problems. The most striking example is obviously the Al-Qaeda terrorist network which attacked some of the symbols of global capitalism like the World Trade Center to declare its war on the United States and the Western world on 11 September 2001. In the view of one observer, 'this episode defies globalization kitsch and the comfortable illusion that all is well in the world of Ronald McDonald' (Pieterse 2002: 24). Although anarchists and other revolutionaries engaged in what is nowadays called 'transnational terrorism' at the end of the nineteenth century, their killing spree was, by and large, restricted to monarchs and highly ranked politicians. One hundred years later, the killing has become so random that Beck's (1999) phrase of a 'world risk society' seems certainly justified for the domain of human security.

Globalization is thus no panacea for peace, as some liberalists might claim. It rather is an ambiguous force of change that 'simultaneously creates friends and enemies, wealth and poverty, and growing divisions between "haves" and "have-nots"' (Kellner 2002: 291). Admittedly, most published studies show that the direct impact of globalization on the likelihood of war is negative. Increasing interactions between states render political leaders, on average, apparently more cautious about using force. Political violence endangers what they cherish the most – their tenure. Yet globalization has some side effects which may increase the likelihood of conflict in some instances.

The growing social bonds between people created by globalization can have a further double-sided effect. Karl Deutsch and his co-authors (1957) proposed in an influential monograph the thesis that economic linkages and social interactions between different populations foster the development of a 'sense of community' according to which the resolution of conflict through the usage of political violence becomes unthinkable. Ample evidence against this liberalist vision indicates that growing social integration is not a necessary cause for peace. The emergence of anti-immigration parties, racial abuse and other forms of nearly violent reactions to multiculturalism indicate that the relationship between social integration and peace is not linearly positive. On the contrary, the growing heterogeneity of the population that immigration brings about decreases the effectiveness of the state in providing public goods. Some even show that the likelihood of conflict is higher in ethnically or religiously diverse countries (Reynal-Querol 2002). Others demonstrate that globalization may ease these tensions somehow. As Alesina and Spolaore (2003) argue, economic globalization causes political disintegration, leading to a larger number of nation-states. As the average size of the state decreases, public goods are provided more efficiently. Because citizens no longer have to fear that they subsidize people with another background through their taxes, the functioning of welfare states and the redistribution of income are, in this view, also easier in these small, ethnically homogeneous countries.

If this growing uniformity at the national level decreases social envy and racism, we could expect that global integration makes the world more peaceful by way of political disintegration and increasing cultural uniformity *within* ethnically or religiously defined states. Yet this regionalization coincides with the trend towards cultural homogeneity at the global level. Various developments like the end of the Cold War and the internationalization of mass media as well as the globalization of the entertainment industry have reinforced this parallel process. At least since the breakdown of the Berlin Wall, the United States is the only nation-state that militarily and culturally has a global reach. This precarious position has predictably met considerable resistance. Huntington (1993, 2000) has especially warned that the trend towards cultural homogeneity within nation-states and civilizations increases the risk of conflict as other cultures question the legitimacy of the United States as the sole superpower: '. . . the leaders of countries with at least two-thirds or more of the world's people – Chinese, Russians, Indians, Arabs, Muslims, Africans – see the United States as the single greatest external threat to their societies' (Huntington 2000: 7). It is pure speculation to forecast which one of the two trends will be more influential in the future – the peace-fostering homogenization at the state or the conflict-inducing homogenization of culture at the global level of interaction. Yet these countervailing trends indicate that globalization is an ambiguous phenomenon. If we want to understand the effect of economic and other forms of integration around the globe, we need to move beyond naive optimism as well as cynical pessimism that have shaped the debate on globalization for too long.

Acknowledgments

I would like to thank my co-authors over the past few years on this topic, especially Katherine Barbieri, Margit Bussmann, Nils Petter Gleditsch and Günther Schulze. This chapter summarizes our joint work and other contemporary thinking on globalization and war. I have also profited from comments by John Oneal on an early draft of this chapter. It is part of the Polarization and Conflict Project CIT-2-CT-2004-506084 funded by the European Commission-DG Research Sixth Framework Programme. This chapter reflects only the author's views and the Community is not liable for any use that may be made of the information contained therein.

References

Alesina, A. and Spolaore, E. 2003. *The Size of Nations*. Cambridge, MA: MIT Press.
Amin, S. 1976. *Unequal Development*. New York: Monthly Review.
Anderton, C. and Carter, J.R. 2001a. 'The impact of war on trade: An interrupted times-series study', *Journal of Peace Research*, 38 (4), 445–57.
Anderton, C. and Carter, J.R. 2001b. 'On disruption of trade by war: A reply to Barbieri & Levy', *Journal of Peace Research*, 38 (5), 625–8.

Angell, N. 1910. *The Great Illusion: A Study of the Relation of Military Power in Nations to their Economic and Social Advantages*. London: Heinemann.

Barbieri, K. 1996. 'Economic interdependence: A path to peace or source of interstate conflict? *Journal of Peace Research*, 33 (1), 29–49.

Barbieri, K. 2002. *The Liberal Illusion*. Ann Arbor: University of Michigan Press.

Barbieri, K. and Levy, J.S. 1999. 'Sleeping with the enemy: The impact of war on trade', *Journal of Peace Research*, 36 (4), 463–79.

Bayer, R. and Rupert, M.C. 2004. 'Effects of civil wars on international trade, 1950–92', *Journal of Peace Research*, 41 (6), 699–713.

Beck, U. 1999. *World Risk Society*. Cambridge: Polity Press.

Bornschier, V., Chase-Dunn, C. and Rubinson, R. 1978. 'Crossnational evidence of the effects of foreign investment and aid on economic growth and inequality: A survey of findings and a reanalysis', *American Journal of Sociology*, 84 (3), 651–83.

Brennan, T. 2003. *Globalization and its Terrors*. London: Routledge.

Bussmann, M. and Schneider, G. 2005. 'Foreign Economic Liberalization and Civil War'. Unpublished manuscript, University of Konstanz.

Bussmann, M., Schneider, G. and Scheuthle, H. 2003. 'Die "Friedensdividende" der Globalisierung: Außenwirtschaftliche Öffnung und innenpolitische Instabilität', *Politische Vierteljahresschrift*, 44 (3), 302–24.

Bussmann, M., Schneider, G. and Wiesehomeier, N. 2005. 'Foreign economic liberalization and peace: The case of sub-Saharan Africa', *European Journal of International Relations*, 11 (4), 551–79.

Bussmann, M. and Schneider, G. 2007. 'When Globalization Discontent Turns Violent: Foreign Economic Liberalization and Civil War', *International Studies Quarterly*, 51 (1), 79–97.

Bussmann, M. and Wild, H. 2004. 'Foreign Direct Investment and Militarized Conflict'. Unpublished manuscript, University of Konstanz.

Cardoso, F.H. and Falleto, E. 1979 [1969]. *Dependency and Development in Latin America* (translated by University of California Press). Berkeley: University of California Press.

Chua, A. 2002. *World on Fire: How Exporting Free Market Democracy Breeds Ethnical Hatred and Global Instability*. New York: Doubleday.

Collier, P., Elliot, V.L., Hegre, H., Hoeffler, A., Reynal-Querol, M. and Sambanis, N. 2003. *Breaking the Conflict Trap: Civil War and Development Policy*. Washington, DC: World Bank; Oxford: Oxford University Press.

Deardorff, A.V. 1994. *The Stolper-Samuelson Theorem: A Golden Jubilee*. Ann Arbor: University of Michigan Press.

De Soysa, I. and Oneal, J.R. 1999. 'Boon or bane? Reassessing the effects of foreign capital on economic growth', *American Sociological Review*, 64 (5), 766–82.

Deutsch, K.W., Burrel, S., Kann, R., Lee, M., Lichterman, M., Lindgren, R., Loewenheim, F. and van Wagenen, R. 1957. *Political Community and the North Atlantic Area*. Princeton, NJ: Princeton University Press.

Domke, W.K. 1988. *War and the Changing Global System*. New Haven, CT: Yale University Press.

Dorussen, H. 2004. 'Heterogeneous trade interests and conflict: It matters what you trade with whom'. Unpublished manuscript, University of Essex.

Firebaugh, G. 1992. 'Growth effects of foreign and domestic investment', *American Journal of Sociology*, 98 (July), 105–30.

Fisher, S. 2003. 'Globalization and its challenges', *American Economic Review*, 93 (2), 1–30.

Friedman, T.L. 1996. 'Big Mac I'. *New York Times*, 8 December.

Friedman, T.L. 1999. *The Lexus and the Olive Tree*. New York: Farrar, Straus and Giroux.

Galtung, J. 1971. 'A structural theory of imperialism', *Journal of Peace Research*, 8, 81–117.

Gartzke, E., Li, Q. and Boehmer, C. 2001. 'Investing in the peace: Economic interdependence and international conflict', *International Organization*, 55, 391–438.

Gasiorowski, M. 1986. 'Economic interdependence and international conflict: Some cross-national evidence', *International Studies Quarterly*, 30 (1), 23–8.

Gasiorowski, M. and Polachek, S.W. 1982. 'Conflict and interdependence: East-West trade and linkages in the era of détente', *Journal of Conflict Resolution*, 26 (4), 709–29.

Gowa, J. 1994. *Allies, Adversaries, and International Trade*. Princeton, NJ: Princeton University Press.

Harff, B. 2003. 'No lessons learned from the Holocaust? Assessing risks of genocide and political mass murder since 1955', *American Political Science Review*, 97 (1), 57–73.

Hegre, H., Gissinger, R. and Gleditsch, N.P. 2003. 'Globalization and internal conflict'. In G. Schneider, K. Barbieri and N.P. Gleditsch (eds), *Globalisation and Armed Conflict*, 251–75. Lanham, MD: Rowman and Littlefield.

Hillman, A.L. 1989. *The Political Economy of Protection*. Chur: Harwood.

Huntington, S.P. 1993. 'The clash of civilization', *Foreign Affairs*, 72 (Summer), 22–49.

Huntington, S.P. 2000. 'Culture, power, and democracy'. In M.F. Plattner and A. Smolar (eds), *Globalization, Power, and Democracy*, 3–13. Baltimore, MD: The Johns Hopkins University Press.

Kellner, D. 2002. 'Theorizing globalization', *Sociological Theory*, 20 (3), 285–305.

Keshk, O.M., Pollins, B.M. and Reuveny, R. 2004. 'Trade still follows the flag: The primacy of politics in a simultaneous model of interdependence and armed conflict', *Journal of Politics*, 66, 1155–79.

Keynes, J.M. 1919. *The Economic Consequences of the Peace*. London: Macmillan.

King, G. and Zeng, L. 2001. 'Explaining rare events in international relations', *International Organization*, 55 (3), 693–715.

Lenin, V.I. 1921. *Der Imperialismus als jüngste Etappe des Kapitalismus*. Hamburg: Cahnbley (Original work published 1917 as *Imperializm kak novejsij etap kapitalizma*, Petrograd: Shisn i Snanije).

Martin, C.W. 2005. *Die doppelte Transformation. Demokratie und Außenwirtschaftsliberalisierung in Entwicklungsländern*. Wiesbaden: Sozialwissenschaftlicher Verlag.

Marx, K. 1848. 'Discours sur la question du libre-échange'. Speech held during the reunion of the *Association démocratique de Bruxelles*. 7 January 1848; available at <http://www.marxists.org/francais/> accessed February 2005.

Morrow, J.D. 1997. 'When do "relative gains" impede trade?' *Journal of Conflict Resolution*, 41 (1), 12–37.

Morrow, J.D. 1999. 'How could trade affect conflict?' *Journal of Peace Research*, 36 (4), 481–9.

Oneal, J.R., Oneal, F., Maoz, Z. and Russett, B. 1996. 'The liberal peace: Interdependence, democracy and international conflict, 1950–1986', *Journal of Peace Research*, 33 (1), 11–28.

Oneal, J.R. and Russett, B.M. 1999. 'Assessing the liberal peace with alternative specifications: Trade still reduces conflict', *Journal of Peace Research*, 36 (4), 423–42.

Pevehouse, J.C. 2004. 'Interdependence theory and the measurement of international conflict', *Journal of Politics*, 66 (2), 247–66.

Pieterse, J.N. 2002. 'Globalization, kitsch and conflict: Technologies of work, war and politics', *Review of International Political Economy*, 9 (2), 1–36.

Polachek, S.W. 1980. 'Conflict and trade', *Journal of Conflict Resolution*, 24 (1), 57–78.

Reynal-Querol, M. 2002. 'Ethnicity, political systems, and civil wars', *Journal of Conflict Resolution*, 46 (1), 29–54.

Ripsman, N.M. and Blanchard, J.-M.F. 2003. 'Qualitative research on economic interdependence and conflict: Overcoming methodological hurdles'. In E.D. Mansfield and B.M. Pollins (eds), *Economic Interdependence and International Conflict*, 310–23. Ann Arbor: University of Michigan Press.

Rodrik, D. 1994. 'The rush to free trade in the developing world: Why so late? Why now? Will it last? In S. Haggard and S.B. Webb (eds), *Voting for Reform: Democracy, Political Liberalization, and Economic Adjustment*. New York: Oxford University Press.

Rosecrance, R. 1986. *The Rise of the Trading State: Commerce and Conquest in the Modern World*. New York: Basic Books.

Russett, B. and Oneal, J.R. 2001. *Triangulating Peace: Democracy, Interdependence, and International Organizations*. New York: Norton.

Schneider, G. and Schulze, G. 2003. 'The domestic roots of commercial liberalism: A sector-specific approach'. In G. Schneider, K. Barbieri and N.P. Gleditsch (eds), *Globalisation and Armed Conflict*, 103–22. Lanham, MD: Rowman and Littlefield.

Schneider, G. and Schulze, G. 2005. 'Trade and conflict: A restatement'. Unpublished manuscript, University of Konstanz.

Schneider, G., Barbieri, K. and Gleditsch, N.P. 2003. 'Does globalization contribute to peace? A critical survey of the theoretical and formal literature'. In G. Schneider, K. Barbieri and N.P. Gleditsch (eds), *Globalisation and Armed Conflict*, 3–29. Lanham, MD: Rowman and Littlefield.

Smith, V.L. 2004. 'Expert panel ranking'. In B. Lomborg (ed.), *Global Crises, Global Solutions*, 630–8. Cambridge: Cambridge University Press.

Stiglitz, J.E. 2002. *Globalization and its Discontents*. London: Allen Lane.

Stiglitz, J.E. 2004. 'Capital-market liberalization, globalization, and the IMF', *Oxford Review of Economic Policy*, 20, 57–71.

Waltz, K. 1979. *Theory of International Politics*. Reading, MA: Addison-Wesley.

Wheen, F. 2004. *How Mumbo-Jumbo Conquered the World*. London: Harper Perennial.

Further reading

Mansfield, E.D. and Pollins, B.M. (eds) 2003. *Economic Interdependence and International Conflict*. Ann Arbor: University of Michigan Press.

Schneider, G., Barbieri, K. and Gleditsch, N.P. (eds) 2003. *Globalization and Armed Conflict*. Lanham, MD: Rowman and Littlefield.

Chapter 33

Globalization and International Terrorism

Gus Martin

The Security Council, reaffirming the principles and purposes of the Charter of the United Nations, determined to combat by all means threats to international peace and security caused by terrorist acts, recognizing the inherent right of individual or collective self-defence in accordance with the Charter, unequivocally condemns in the strongest terms the horrifying terrorist attacks which took place on 11 September 2001; calls on all States to work together urgently to bring to justice the perpetrators, organizers and sponsors of these terrorist attacks and stresses that those responsible for aiding, supporting or harbouring the perpetrators, organizers and sponsors of these acts will be held accountable; . . . expresses its readiness to take all necessary steps to respond to the terrorist attacks of 11 September 2001, and to combat all forms of terrorism, in accordance with its responsibilities under the Charter of the United Nations. (United Nations Security Council, Resolution 1368 (2001), 12 September 2001)

United Nations Resolution 1368 symbolizes a moment of global solidarity against the perpetrators of mass casualty terrorism. At that moment, it seemed that the family of nations was prepared to form a united front against terrorism that would work cooperatively to defeat terrorist networks, and support 'the inherent right of individual or collective self-defence'. Unfortunately, such solidarity was fleeting, and cracks appeared in the alliance in the aftermath of the invasions of Afghanistan and Iraq.

The terrorist attacks of 11 September 2001 heralded the advent of a new era of globalized terrorism. A fresh breed of extremists who are quite willing to sacrifice themselves and others on the world's stage characterizes this new era. This new generation became very adept at broadcasting their motives and actions to global audiences via graphic images posted on the Internet, and audio-visual communiqués delivered to cable news networks. Modern extremists also demonstrated an eagerness to acquire highly destructive weapons technologies, and to use these technologies to inflict maximum casualties on civilian populations and passive security targets. Although religious zealotry is the primary motivation (and justification) behind much of the New Terrorism, there are indications that nationalists and other secular extremists are similarly willing to engage in mass casualty terrorism and broadcasted violence. For example, many mass casualty and broadcasted incidents in Iraq, and lethal 'martyrdom' operations in Israel, were the work of secular nationalists – a fact which suggests that the relative notoriety and success achieved from the tactics of their religious counterparts have encouraged secular terrorists to copy them.

Although international terrorism is certainly not a new phenomenon, its organizational, operational and motivational profiles have changed significantly in the newly globalized world. One of the central attributes of the New Terrorism is its influence on the affairs of the global community. In this new era, advanced communications technologies such as the Internet and cable news outlets confer an unprecedented ability for terrorists to influence the international community quickly, cheaply, and with little risk to the extremists themselves. Media-savvy terrorists calculate how to use modern information technologies to their benefit. Because '[n]ewsprint and air-time are . . . the coin of the realm in the terrorists' mindset . . . little distinction or discrimination is made between good or bad publicity' (Hoffman 1998: 176). Thus, the modern era is one of immense potential for dedicated extremists who possess sophisticated technical, operational and public relations skills. In addition, self-supported terrorist networks have emerged within the context of modern integrated economies and regional trade areas. These new attributes define *globalized terrorism*.

This chapter examines the threat from terrorism in the age of globalization, and argues that modern globalized terrorism is a more advanced manifestation – in essence, an upgrading – of recent cycles of international violence. The focal point is an analysis of globalized terrorism and the considerable challenges posed by this phenomenon. The discussion begins with an analysis of political violence in the era of globalization, including a contextual assessment of the relationship between 'civilizational' tensions in the global environment and the New Terrorism. An examination of the operational environment for globalized terrorism is presented to complement the preceding civilizational analysis. An investigation of the new war against terrorism includes an analysis of asymmetrical methods, the use of high-yield weapons, and the role of broadly drawn ideological precepts. To further our understanding of the near future of global political violence, the implications of the Qaeda archetype are identified and evaluated. Finally, an assessment is made of emergent challenges emanating from lessons learned from the '9/11' and '3/11' attacks in the United States and Spain.

UNDERSTANDING GLOBALIZED TERRORISM

In many respects, the contemporary international environment is perfectly configured to facilitate transnational political violence. New political and economic alignments such as the European Union and the expansion of NATO provide revolutionaries with the ability to cross national borders under minimal restrictions to attack highly symbolic targets. Current political and economic alignments also afford violent extremists with an opportunity to influence a much broader audience than could their predecessors. Advanced communications technologies augment the ability of the media to consistently broadcast, and seamlessly disseminate, images and information on terrorist incidents and objectives. Such reporting becomes particularly pervasive when political violence is deemed sufficiently spectacular to garner the attention of the global community. In effect,

> with the assistance of media, terrorism reaches a much broader, sometimes global audience – and in an era in which most people (at least in the United States) get their political information from television, mass-mediated depictions of terrorism can have a profound effect upon the way we think about and engage in discourse about terrorism. (Tuman 2003: 115)

By definition, international terrorism is a specific typology characterized by explicit international implications. Strategically, these international 'spillovers' have long been a feature of modern terrorism, with dedicated revolutionaries regularly selecting internationally symbolic targets to carry out high-profile strikes. The calculation for stirring international ramifications centres on two alternative courses of action: either launching operations outside of the perpetrator's home country, or conducting local operations against targets with internationally symbolic personas. By executing violent international spillovers on behalf of their struggle, extremists effectively garner the attention of a much broader and more influential global audience. Operatives who attack adversaries in regions far from the origin of their grievances and the centre of their conflict do so as a deliberate strategy because:

> Those who engage in political violence on an international scale do so with the expectation that it will have a positive effect on their cause at home – thus reasoning that international exposure will bring about compensation for perceived injustices. (Martin 2003: 220).

In the modern era, the first international terrorists were nationalists fighting self-described wars of national liberation, or the adherents of some variant of Marxist ideology, or an amalgam of both tendencies. Many recent examples exist of nationalists crossing international borders to assault symbolic representations of their perceived oppressor. There are also many examples of violence committed by ideological extremists, usually nihilistic West European Marxists, acting in solidarity with their championed oppressed group in the Third World. The Red Army Faction, Ilich Sanchez (aka Carlos), Leila Khaled and Abu Nidal are good case studies of violent extremists who operated across state borders to wage their wars in the international domain.

Contemporary globalized terrorism is conceptually akin to international terrorism, but it integrates additional definitional elements that are influenced by new technologies and unprecedented cultural interlinkages peculiar to the modern era. Globalized terrorism incorporates many technology-driven potentialities such as immediate information dissemination, vastly enhanced influence over much larger audiences and all of the attributes of the New Terrorism (discussed further below). These potentialities, if skilfully coordinated, provide unprecedented opportunities for small groups of violent extremists to broadly influence targeted audiences.

CONTEXTUAL ENVIRONMENT: CIVILIZATIONAL FAULT LINES

Conceptually, modern globalization is the culmination of an environment that arose during the 1990s because of the confluence of global political and economic events. Politically, the failure of Communism and the disintegrations of the Soviet Union and Eastern bloc heralded the beginning of a realigned international order. Afterward, the process began of integrating newly independent European and Asian nations into regional systems and the global community. The failure of revolutionary Marxism occurred during the advent of global economic integration, and it is patently plausible that the emerging global economy would have hastened Communism's demise had the Soviet-led system not imploded politically. Perhaps the most significant feature of the new global economy is that it became *truly* global, and affected national and regional trade policies – as well as cultures – everywhere. Experts have long argued that cultural and political readjustments must occur in the wake of strong economic performance and integration (Lewis and Harris 1992). Consequently, nations must necessarily align themselves within the framework of the global economy, or face isolation. As Rosenau (1997) explains rather clearly, cultural and economic processes that are unimpeded by national territory or official jurisdictional constraints distinguish globalization.

In his influential article 'The Clash of Civilizations?' Samuel P. Huntington (1993) prognosticated that the principal attributes of the global system would be the decline of ideologies and the concomitant centrality of ethnic and religious identities. Because these cultural identities represent transnational 'fault lines', he projected that future conflicts would be civilizational rather than ideological. According to Huntington's thesis, the global processes of economic and social modernization and change have expanded people's cultural identities beyond local and national boundaries. As cultural and ethno-national identity become transnational norms, friction along civilizational fault lines will inevitably lead to competition and conflict. Hence, when commercial and cultural products from one civilization penetrate the market of another civilization, some degree of backlash will follow.

Huntington's thesis, while open to criticism, successfully stimulated a vigorous debate and produced a rich body of commentary in academic, practitioner and popular literature. The principal subject of discussion has been whether the new millennium will be an era of globalized politics, wherein contending political and cultural blocs clash on issues that were previously resolved domestically or diplomatically between small groups of nations. As noted by some writers, Huntington's thesis was only partially correct, because some civilizational fault lines actually rupture *within* civilizations. Thus, wars in Yugoslavia and elsewhere will continue to be waged among religious and ethnic groups who share some degree of civilizational commonality (such as ethnicity), but whose commonality breaks down along other fault lines (such as religion) (Hoffman 2002). A significant focus in this literature investigates whether the fault line between the West and Islamic countries has already fractured, and whether the 9/11-induced war on terrorism portends an era of civilizational conflict between Western and Islamic cultures. For example, Benjamin Barber (2001) in *Jihad vs. McWorld* queries whether the 'parochial hatreds' evidenced in religious and ethnic tribalist worldviews, and the 'universalist' tendencies of Western commercialism, will inevitably weaken democracy and the pre-eminence of nations. In light of the attacks of 11 September 2001,

> The collision between the forces of disintegral tribalism and reactionary fundamen-talism . . . and the forces of integrative modernization and aggressive economic and cultural globalization . . . has been brutally exacerbated by the dialectical interdepend-ence of these two seemingly oppositional sets of forces. (Barber 2001: xii)

Although Barber and many other experts agree that the most serious and endur-ing global fractures emanate from the threat posed by adherents of the New Terrorism, one additional contextual consideration must be addressed. Arguably, the much-discussed Western/Islamic fault line is but one indicator of tension within a broader and deeper stratum. In recent decades, the ideological East–West conflict has been supplanted by political, cultural and economic tensions between the devel-oped North (the West of the Soviet era) and the developing South (the former Third World). As national economies become increasingly interdependent, the existing relationship between the developed and developing worlds suggests that the benefits of globalization are weighted in favour of the wealthy economies of the West. Developing nations often cannot attract the interest of investors for the simple reason that they frequently possess ineffectual institutions and few profitable products (Scott 2001).

The West's insistence on market development is arguably a cultural and ideologi-cal presumption which produces cultural tensions when open markets result in an influx of Western culture and goods. Stephen Marglin (2003) supports this thesis in his critique of international development, stating that entire indigenous cultures and communities have been placed at risk by the global market system. He observes, in part, that Western culture and self-interest have created tensions in the developing world among people and cultures who do not share the West's imposition of its universalist worldview. Thus, some problems in developing nations are exacerbated by globalized economic, cultural and political trends that have a significant impact on non-Western regions.

Symbolic of the possible future of developed–developing world tensions is the abortive September 2003 meeting of the World Trade Organization in Cancun, Mexico, which broke down largely because of what Rorden Wilkinson (2004) has termed an agricultural fault line. Where might friction along this and other fault lines lead? With the American economy strained by the war on terrorism and increased government spending, further strains could come from protectionist policies by the United States or its developed allies (Summers 2004).

OPERATIONAL ENVIRONMENT: GLOBALIZATION AND TERRORISM

The foregoing civilizational analysis highlights some of the preconditions for ter-rorism and conflict that are endemic to the era of globalization. According to a number of experts, many of these tensions are exacerbated by chronic poverty and instability. For example, Paul Collier (2003) writes that the root causes of civil war are found in economic deprivation and struggles for control over natural resources. Experts are not unanimous in this assessment (Pipes 2002), but the fact is that many indigenous populations in the developing world live under authoritarian regimes that cannot adequately absorb growing numbers of young workers into their economies. Large numbers of people are either unemployed or under-employed, and young educated skilled workers often emigrate to vigorous economies for employment, thus creating a brain drain that cannot be restored. This process can produce domestic destabilization. In this regard, internal conflicts can be affected by the continuing intensification of the forces of globalization.

When such conflicts constrain or neutralize the ability of governments to control broad swaths of their own territory, terrorists are presented with an excellent opportunity to establish zones of refuge within these territories. For example, extremists have operated relatively openly in the Northwest Frontier Province of Pakistan, Kashmir, Taliban Afghanistan, post-Baathist Iraq, Chechnya and the historic terrorist refuge in Lebanon's Beka'a Valley. The new global environment therefore rather naturally incorporates potential security threats from enterprising terrorists who can identify and operate within uncontrolled regions that have only a modicum of state authority. Whether developed countries can engage poor or failing states depends on the degree to which the European Union, the United States and other developed nations can coordinate a global response to alleviating conditions that incubate violent extremism (Crocker 2003).

INFORMATIONAL ENVIRONMENT: THE ROLE OF THE MEDIA

The information revolution is a quintessential example of globalization. Conceptually, 'the media' no longer refers to traditionally local and national press agencies, but now consists of cable news agencies and Internet 'bloggers' who offer globalized and minimally regulated forums for news, political opinion and speculation. In particular, global cable news agencies such as Al-Jazeera in Qatar, CNN in the United States and Sky News in the United Kingdom broadcast televised and online news instantaneously to many millions of viewers. Images of political violence are observed across the globe by large populations, thus bringing them into the scope of interest (and influence) of revolutionaries.

Experts have long evaluated the impact of broadcast violence on populations and nations, as well as the calculated manipulation of broadcasts by extremist movements (Paletz and Schmid 1992). With the advent of the globalized media, these movements have become adept at disseminating their message via a combination of violence against symbolic targets, and carefully planted communiqués. For example, Al-Jazeera received numerous audio and video communiqués from Osama bin Laden and other Islamist revolutionaries. In addition, members of the Iraqi resistance regularly delivered photographs and videotapes of their hostages and attacks against US and allied forces. These images and messages illustrate the enormous potential for globalizing 'propaganda by the deed' by dedicated revolutionaries.

THE NEW WAR

During the previous era of the 'old' terrorism, violent extremists were motivated by ethno-nationalist aspirations and the predominating Cold War ideologies. Marxist-inspired terrorists waged bloody campaigns in Europe, Latin America and elsewhere. Excellent case studies of aggressive postwar revolutionary movements are found in Germany's Red Army Faction, Italy's Red Brigades, Argentina's Montoneros and Uruguay's Tupamaros – all of whom participated in Marxist-inspired urban terrorism. Many ethno-nationalist movements also adopted Marxism as a binding ideology, although most nationalists clearly used revolutionary ideologies to focus their cadres on their political cause. The Irish Republican Army (IRA) and several factions of the Palestine Liberation Organization (PLO) are important examples of this blending of Marxism and nationalism during the previous era of terrorism. Interestingly, there were few examples of the incorporation of religious precepts as a primary motivation during the previous terrorist environment. One historical example of the amalgamation of religion and nationalism occurred during the Jewish terrorist campaign against the British Mandate in Palestine.

Contemporary globalized terrorism, as evidenced by stateless networks such as Al-Qaeda, is no longer constrained by narrowly drawn ideological imperatives or the quality of support from sympathetic state sponsors. Revolutionary movements now have the ability to wage their wars independently on a global battlefield under broadly drawn precepts such as pan-religious revolution. Very real scenarios involving the use of high-yield armaments and weapons of mass destruction have arisen because of the unique attributes of globalization. Threats posed in the post-9/11 world include the potential proliferation of Russian weapons, nuclear-armed developing nations, components for radiological 'dirty' bombs, and ingredients for biological and chemical weapons (Newhouse 2002). In his article, 'The Five Wars of Globalization', Moises Naím (2003: 28) observes that Al-Qaeda is an excellent example of how difficult it is for states to combat 'stateless, decentralized networks that move freely, quickly, and stealthily across national borders to engage in terror'. Naím points out that the Al-Qaeda phenomenon is but one war that is occurring in concert with other wars, involving networks that trade in drugs, arms, intellectual property, people and money. From the perspective of violent extremists, such an environment is conducive to their overall strategy to wage global war against their adversaries.

It is instructive to review the historical context of globalized terrorism, and identify the interrelated attributes of the New Terrorism in a globalized environment. Immediately prior to the Al-Qaeda attacks against the United States on 11 September 2001, experts hypothesized that a New Terrorism would soon emerge as the principal exemplar for international terrorism. During the 1990s, many commentators argued that this emergent model – a new archetype – would presage the onset of a reconfigured terrorist environment, heralding a paradigm shift for future threat scenarios. A paradigm shift was also predicted for future policies on how to thwart a fresh generation of violent extremists. As explained by Jessica Stern (1999), the new terrorists are quite willing to wage asymmetrical warfare using nuclear, biological and chemical weapons against mass populations. In addition, new technologies allow violent extremists access to information and vastly enhanced communications capabilities. The most vigorous aspect of this debate centred on an expected confluence of new threat scenarios, such as religious fundamentalism, asymmetrical warfare, the use of weapons of mass destruction and cell-based organizational models (Hoffman 1997).

Several incidents prior to 9/11 supported the hypothesized emergence of the New Terrorism:

- February 1993. A car bomb exploded in the garage of the New York World Trade Center, killing six people and wounding more than 1,000 others.
- June 1996. In Dhahran, Saudi Arabia, a truck bomb destroyed a US military barracks.
- August 1998. Synchronized vehicular bombs severely damaged the US embassies in Nairobi, Kenya and Dar es Salaam, Tanzania. The Kenyan bomb killed 213 people and injured about 4,000. The Tanzanian bomb killed 12 people and injured 85.
- October 2000. A suicide boat bomb severely damaged the US Navy destroyer *Cole* in Aden, Yemen. Dozens of sailors were killed or injured.

These attacks epitomized the central elements of the new globalized environment – stateless networking, religious motivation, unanticipated targets and maximized casualties. They also evidenced the globalized operational doctrine of modern terrorists, particularly their willingness to strike symbolic and highly populated targets in far-flung corners of the globe. Such attacks were an initial confirmation that terrorist movements are adept at pre-positioning their adherents in cells located in Western and developing world countries, thereby creating a fluid global network of loosely connected operatives.

The theory of the New Terrorism became fully operationalized by the attacks on 11 September 2001 and thereafter:

- September 2001. Four aircraft were hijacked in the United States. One airliner crashed into rural Pennsylvania, two crashed into the World Trade Center in New York City and one crashed into the Pentagon. Thousands died in the attacks.
- October 2002. Terrorists struck a tourist area on the Indonesian island of Bali, killing or injuring hundreds of people, mostly Australian tourists.
- November 2002. Terrorists destroyed an Israeli-owned resort hotel in Mombasa, Kenya.
- March 2004. Bombs placed aboard commuter trains in Spain killed 191 civilians and wounded more than 1,800.

As hypothesized during the theoretical debate of the 1990s, and substantiated by the foregoing incidents, the New Terrorism operationally exhibits asymmetrical methods, the use of high-yield weapons and broadly drawn ideological precepts (in these cases, religious precepts). It is instructive to review these characteristics.

Asymmetrical methods

In recent decades, international terrorism was an insurgent methodology undertaken by small bands of extremists who wished primarily to garner the attention of the world – in effect, by engaging in transnational 'armed propaganda'. Although organizations such as the IRA and the PLO regularly struck their enemies on territories outside of their homelands (often spectacularly), they largely did so to engender international and domestic pressure against their adversaries. In the modern era, the strategic rationale for transnational terrorism, and indeed the perceived efficacy of such attacks, is no longer solely a matter of armed propaganda. It is now evident that the predictions of a metamorphosis of terrorist violence from pinprick assaults into an asymmetrical mode of warfare have become reality.

The doctrine of asymmetrical warfare, as developed since the 1990s, holds that terrorists are attempting to acquire, and indeed use, weapons of mass destruction and other high-yield weapons technologies. Strategically, they identify and plan attacks on unexpected targets using creative methods and tactics, including new technology-driven strikes. For example, one threat scenario envisions terrorists engaging in piracy, and taking to the high seas to attack freighters or other maritime targets (Luft and Korin 2004). Alternatively, enterprising extremists can utilize the Internet to launch cyber attacks that will disrupt financial, security and communications centres. Thus, the New Terrorism incorporates asymmetric threats that were hitherto unimaginable (Freedman 2003).

The use of high-yield weapons

Since the time of Narodnaya Volya in Russia during the nineteenth century and the anarchists in Europe and North America during the same period, the bomb and the gun have been ubiquitous staples in the terrorist arsenal. These weapons continue to be ubiquitous in the era of the New Terrorism, with one significant distinction: the technologies of killing have been improved by orders of magnitude. High-powered rifles such as the AK-47, and high-yield explosives such as Semtex *plastique*, provide much more destructive potential than in prior generations. Yet these are relatively commonplace weapons. Other weapons technologies, and available technologies that can be converted into weapons, are much more destructive. Radiological, chemical, biological and nuclear weapons pose very real scenarios of catastrophic destruction (Laqueur 1999: 254). For example, the conversion of airliners into ballistic missiles is a proven threat. The suicidal use of airliners as missiles was unsuccessfully attempted in December 1994 when Algerian terrorists hijacked Air France Flight 8969, and successfully implemented on 11 September 2001. Another scenario is the detonation of vehicular bombs laden with radiological, chemical or biological agents.

Who would use such weapons? Why would they do so? Are they not killing innocents rather than true enemies? During the 1990s, it became clear that moral imperatives – which had previously constrained terrorists to committing surgical strikes against symbolic targets – were no longer restrictive considerations. One reason for this transition is the religious justification that one's actions will please God, no matter how violent those actions are. Recently, many young violent Islamists have adopted this rationale. Another reason is the persistent perception among extremists that only by creating an intolerable environment will their grievances be addressed. Entire populations are now legitimate targets, and the infliction of catastrophic casualties upon them is both acceptable and desirable. If one accepts the premise that terrorists consider terrorism to be a legitimate mode for asymmetrical war fighting, it becomes apparent that such weapons, if applied decisively and homicidally, could influence the behaviour of entire nations. In this context, revolutionaries would become quite willing to build arsenals of weapons of mass destruction for the simple reason that they have proven to be quite effective.

Broadly drawn ideological precepts

In the post-9/11 world, extremists who possess a global revolutionary design are typically motivated by religious fervour; it has become the predominant motivation for international violence. With the collapse of the Eastern bloc, the classical ideologies of the fringe left and fringe right – while still popular among some secular activists and revolutionaries – are no longer ascendant. Very few conflicts remain that are inspired by admixtures of transnational secular ideologies and ethno-nationalist extremism.

Al-Qaeda and its comrades-in-arms are obvious examples of movements that adopt fundamentalist religion as the binding motivation for their global revolution. Among violent Islamists, a global sense of common cause has resulted in terrorist attacks in Africa, Asia, Europe, the Middle East and North America. Cells of religious revolutionaries have been identified in each of these regions. Significantly, a number of domestic ethno-nationalist revolutionary movements have linked their nationalistic identities to religion, much as the previous generation linked their identities to Marxism. Of course, many nationalists remain primarily secular in their worldview, but examples of nationalists who have incorporated religious precepts into their movements include violent extremists in Indonesia, Israel, Chechnya and Kashmir. Experts and scholars predicted all of these tendencies during the debates on the New Terrorism in the 1990s, when they foresaw a significant increase in the incidence of religious terrorism as the ideological foundation for globalized violence (Laqueur 1996).

THE CASE OF AL-QAEDA: AN ARCHETYPE FOR GLOBALIZED TERROR?

Among Western nations, Al-Qaeda ('the Base') is the modern era's archetypal globalized terrorist network. However, many residents of the Muslim world possess another perception of Al-Qaeda, particularly the social and religious undercurrents represented by the movement. What is Al-Qaeda? Is it a quintessentially terrorist archetype, as presumed in the developed world? Alternatively, does the movement represent a civilizational conflict which is the embodiment of pan-Islamic revolution? As explained by Mustafa Al Sayyid (2002), the concept of *terrorism* is frequently defined differently among many people in the Muslim world vis-à-vis the West. The result is that there have arisen fundamental divergences in analysis and communication between Westerners and Muslims.

Al-Qaeda certainly is a stateless revolutionary movement that receives little or no state sponsorship, has no quasi-military hierarchy, is motivated by religious fundamentalism, champions only fellow-believers and claims no homeland or national territory. It is also a globalized phenomenon, and is no longer solely a network inspired by Osama bin Laden – in essence, it has become an ideology. As an ideology, 'Qaedaism' is an intangible idea, and is therefore more versatile than the tangible network of Al-Qaeda (Burke 2004). Because of these factors, it does represent an archetypal revolutionary model for the modern global political environment.

Birth of the phenomenon

Because the Qaeda phenomenon is an archetype, it is critically important to understand the nature and consequences of its origin. This is an especially significant investigation because of the character of the insurgency that occurred later in occupied Iraq, and the consequences which will arise therefrom.

Al-Qaeda was born from the war against the Soviet invasion of Afghanistan during the 1980s. Muslim fighters from throughout the world joined their Afghan comrades in a holy *jihad* against the Soviet army. These foreign fighters are known as 'Afghan Arabs', and became legendary in the Muslim world. During the war, the United States and United Kingdom actively supported indigenous Afghan *mujahideen* (holy warriors) and foreign Afghan Arabs, including Osama bin Laden and other leaders who were proficient at building resistance networks (Reeve 1999). Bin Laden was a particularly skilful coordinator of money and arms deals, which made him a very useful asset in the US effort to inflict as much damage as possible on the Soviets.

Of central significance was the forming of Al-Qaeda by Osama bin Laden during the war and its expansion around the globe thereafter. When the Soviets withdrew from Afghanistan after losing 15,000 soldiers, many Afghan Arabs continued their *jihad*, this time against secular governments and Western influences. Some became internationalists, and one example of this ongoing struggle was the presence of *mujahideen* fighters during the war in Bosnia. Many other Afghan Arabs and members of Al-Qaeda returned to their homelands to organize fundamentalist movements in central Asia, South-east Asia, North Africa, the Middle East and Europe. Muslim groups in these regions received financial and organizational support, and new networks of fundamentalists were indoctrinated and formed. There are many examples of financial and operational support from Al-Qaeda and the Afghan Arabs in the planning and implementation of terrorist attacks and other violent incidents.

Religious nihilism

During the previous era of terrorism, many movements exhibited solidarity over broad ideological concepts, but did not present a cohesive vision for the post-revolutionary order. Nationalistic movements such as the Basque ETA and the IRA tended to be rather coherent in their stated goals, usually advocating independence or some degree of self-determination. On the other hand, purely ideological movements such as the Red Brigades and Red Army Faction were much more nihilistic in their goals. They were clear about their desire to overthrow Western capitalism (in solidarity with nationalists in the developing world), but they offered no reasoned articulation of the attributes of the new order.

The stated goals of Al-Qaeda and other Islamists are also nihilistic in two senses: first, their followers intend to defeat what they define as apostate or infidel influences on the pan-Islamic nation. Second, they offer little clarity about what kind of new society will be built upon the rubble of the old. Adherents vaguely refer to creating a post-revolutionary religious society governed under the precepts of the Holy Quran, with secular governments giving way to sectarian fundamentalist leadership. However, such vision is of secondary importance to the immediate concern of waging a globalized holy war.

The fundamentalist strain of nihilism creates an environment wherein the only concrete agenda is to send forth cadres to fight and die for a global Islamist revolution, thereby eliminating the influences of non-fundamentalist apostasies on the faithful. Little regard is given to promoting a specific vision for the new order, which is not an atypical stratagem among internationalist revolutionaries. It is comparable to the priorities established by secular anarchists and nihilists of previous generations, many of whom waged 'revolution for revolution's sake'. In essence, destruction of the existing order is paramount because the system is fundamentally corrupt and oppressive toward the championed group, and for their sake, it cannot be permitted to exist.

Many of these themes resonate among young religious activists. For some, the Islamist analysis provides answers to their questions and discontent about political repression, poverty, exploitation and the role of religious faith in remedying these conditions. Thus, whereas non-Islamists decry the violence of radical movements such as Al-Qaeda, Islamist intellectuals and activists feel championed by these movements.

Theory into practice: The cloning of Al-Qaeda

Al-Qaeda is the organizational and operational model for the new millennium. Since its origin in the Islamist crucible of Afghanistan, Al-Qaeda has proven itself more than simply a globalized network of stateless revolutionaries. It became truly a *phenomenon* of the modern era, both concretely (as a network) and abstractly (as an idea). In one sense, Al-Qaeda has demonstrated its ability to strike its enemies very hard by mastering the art of asymmetrical warfare. In another sense – one which was not readily apparent to Westerners until the war in Iraq – the Qaeda phenomenon became transformed into a concept and an ideology that will be replicated by other dedicated Islamist activists. Many have been inspired by its example and by the success of its methods. For example, large numbers of young non-Iraqis who volunteered to resist the US-led occupation did so under a broad Islamist banner, and one may conclude that these new fighters represent the progeny of the Qaedaist model.

Although Al-Qaeda-like cells have been dismantled around the globe, many more remain active and new cells continue to be positioned. Even if the first-generation network is destroyed, it is highly improbable that the ideology and phenomenon will also be destroyed. As an archetypical model, Al-Qaeda's strength lies in the fact that it is a symbolic *beginning* rather than an end in itself.

For these reasons, Al-Qaeda 'clones' arose to wage globalized warfare, and continue to recruit and indoctrinate new cadres and cells. Yet why would a new generation of fighters join this struggle? Where lays the inspiration to wage war against secular governments and the West? Is there a seminal event, or identifiable enemy, which serves to reinflame and reinvigorate the Islamists' *jihad*? From the perspective of prospective *mujahideen*, the answers to these questions are found in the war against terrorism, a war in which the occupation of Iraq, and the presence of Western soldiers in other Muslim countries, mobilized Islamist activists in much the same manner as the Soviet war in Afghanistan. In effect, a new generation of Afghan Arabs was born from the insurgency in Iraq (Bergen 2004).

The cloning of Al-Qaeda has accelerated, as evidenced by important parallels drawn between the US-led wars in Iraq and Afghanistan, and the Soviet war in Afghanistan. Although it is erroneous to conclude that the US-led and Soviet conflicts are *identical* cases, in both circumstances the following patterns occurred:

- Conventional armies overran weaker opponents, thus occupying the country in short order.
- The indigenous central authority collapsed, necessitating foreign occupation forces to provide security. During critical periods of the occupations, the sole burden of security fell upon the occupiers.
- Indigenous security forces were organized, but proved marginally effective and often unreliable for long periods in broad swaths of the countryside.
- Unconventional insurgencies commenced, growing in scope, strength and popularity despite the best efforts of occupying forces to neutralize the guerrillas.
- Mistakes were made during the suppression campaigns, and innocent civilians were killed. In the case of the Soviet war, civilians were deliberately targeted. For both the Soviets and the Americans in Iraq, rumours and images of torture, illegal killings, desecrations and casualties were broadcast to the world.
- Foreign fighters swarmed to the fray, fighting in solidarity with the indigenous insurgents.
- Among the insurgents, religious fundamentalists became feared and effective fighters, often engaging in acts of terrorism and suicidal attacks. Many foreign fighters adopted the mantle of *mujahideen*, thereby defining their wars as holy *jihads* against invading unbelievers.
- In both cases, the international community strongly criticized the invasions, occupations and the ongoing unconventional wars.

These similarities created two generations of global revolutionaries. First, an older generation of Islamists who found a way to fight, hurt and defeat (in the case of the anti-Soviet *jihad*) strong adversaries. Second, a younger generation who were incensed by the manner in which the US-led war on terrorism was waged, particularly the invasion of Iraq. Within this context, an important observation must be considered: the old Nasser-inspired generation's experiments with pan-Arab nationalism and socialism proved to be marginally effective against Israeli and Western adversaries. They also resulted in little prosperity and political liberty for young Muslims. Therefore, many young Muslim activists are attracted to Islamist tendencies, with the result that they exhibit great respect for the first generation of Afghan Arabs. In comparison, the secular nationalists and socialists no longer inspire the young towards action. In the era of globalized terrorism, it is likely that young volunteers will continue to join the Islamist movement and emulate the Qaeda model.

NEW CHALLENGES IN A NEW ERA

On 28 February 2005, the United States released a communiqué sent by Osama bin Laden to Musab al-Zarqawi, in which bin Laden encouraged the Iraq-based Jordanian to attack targets outside of Iraq. Al-Zarqawi's group was induced to undertake attacks in Europe and the United States. This communiqué illustrates how uncomplicated the process is for establishing fraternal associations and cooperation among internationalist revolutionaries in the new era – all accomplished without the need to establish complex command or logistical protocols. Other documents have been captured that are essentially 'how to' manuals on waging asymmetrical campaigns (Alcott and Babajanov 2003).

Identifiably hierarchical lines of authority, modelled after quasi-military configurations, no longer characterize revolutionary networks. In contrast, networks such as Al-Qaeda have adopted cell-based organizational models as an operational strategy. Cell-based networks are 'stateless revolutions' in the sense that they have no homeland which serves as an operational base, little or no state sponsorship, and they support themselves through logistical and financial pipelines. Decentralized support networks funnel information and logistical support to these cells. The obvious advantage of having a flat organizational structure is that there is no central leadership or operational node that can be targeted by adversaries. Hence, when one cell or leadership group is eliminated, others are likely to be minimally affected and remain intact.

Because of the cell-based and transnational aspects of the New Terrorism, leaders such as bin Laden and al-Zarqawi symbolize a new model of mentorship for potential fighters, regardless of whether they in fact exercise operational management over dispersed cadres and cells. Many Islamic activists are inspired as much from leadership by example as they are by receiving direct orders, as shown in the statements of terrorists during interviews and other communications (Post et al. 2003). Consequently, the terrorist environment of the new millennium is inherently globalized, exhibits decentralized command and control, successfully propagandizes Western intervention in the 'Muslim Nation' and possesses a symbolic leadership which inspires the faithful by example.

This type of environment poses an unprecedented challenge to the global community, for the war on globalized terrorism is unlike any previous war. Domestic security forces have identified and disrupted cells and networks that are linked to operatives and ideological comrades in other countries. This fact has necessitated counterterrorist cooperation and coordination among nations. However, there has been significant disagreement on many measures used in the war. For example, in order to combat the global nature of terrorism, the United States and a few allies conducted overt military operations using conventional forces in Afghanistan and

Iraq, as well as covert incursions, but in the end generated strong protests from many nations for doing so.

Fighting shadow wars on a globalized battlefield

When political conflict spills over into the international domain, the revolutionaries cross borders to engage in operations in a third country, or they select domestic targets that are internationally symbolic. In either scenario, operatives disseminate their message to a global audience by selecting high-value targets. Such targets are chosen as a calculation that certain methods produce maximized international propaganda dissemination. Logically, spectacular attacks in third countries will result in enhanced media exposure, and will optimally create political crises in the afflicted countries or regions. Terrorists calculate that significant attacks against prime targets will foment serious implications, especially if carried out in foreign countries. This outcome occurred in the aftermath of the 11 March 2004 bombings of Spanish trains by Islamist terrorists – the outcomes were that a new Spanish government was elected, Spain quickly withdrew its soldiers from Iraq and European public opinion became increasingly critical of the occupation. How should nations respond to this strategy? Which tactics are optimal?

Whether conventional invasions and occupations have a lasting effect on motivated fighters is questionable, because violent extremists in the era of the New Terrorism do not field conventional armies. In many ways, the principal front in the war centres on safe houses, urban expatriate communities, financial institutions and bases in remote regions. Waging war against amorphous terrorist networks involves the deployment of a variety of national security agencies, including military, paramilitary, law enforcement and intelligence assets. In this shadow war, unconventional covert operations conducted domestically and internationally are a norm rather than an exception, and many practices – such as kidnappings, renditions and interrogations – have resulted in widespread political criticism among erstwhile supporters. Regardless of the extent of these political and policy challenges, governments have no choice but to design innovative responses to counter this deadly globalized environment.

Experts and the extremists themselves now understand that dedicated adherents of championed causes can critically disrupt domestic environments, national policies and international relations in an unprecedented manner. For example, the attacks in Spain on 11 March 2004 significantly affected Spain's domestic and international political milieu. The fact is that terrorists no longer simply seek to force symbolic 'big splashes' onto the international agenda – they are now willing to confront directly Western interests as a practical warfighting strategy (Lesser 1999: 94). This is the only manner in which they can realistically engage the enormous power wielded by Western nations. The fundamental fact is that many terrorists consider themselves to be at war, that the most logical methodology is asymmetrical disruption and that they stand a good chance of inciting an environment which will influence their adversaries' behaviour.

Given these considerations, unconventional and imaginative strategies are critical for the successful neutralization of globalized revolutionary violence. For example, the new stateless revolutionaries utilize financial and logistical networks that are difficult to identify, penetrate and disrupt. Since these networks operate across state borders, and are independent of governmental benefactors, intergovernmental cooperation is required to dismantle them. The globalized battlefield also mandates the implementation of anti-terrorist procedures such as enhanced security technologies at national *entrepôts*, new customs protocols and hardening of symbolic facilities. Sensitive, and somewhat controversial, surveillance technologies have been deployed to monitor cell phones, Internet communications and other modes of communication among extremists. Old lessons must also be scrutinized and revised. In particular, experts believe that soldiers and policy makers must relearn counter-insurgency warfare (Tomes 2004).

POSTSCRIPT: LESSONS FROM 9/11 AND 3/11

The 11 September 2001 and 11 March 2004 attacks in the United States and Spain were, by any measure, extremely powerful attacks. They had an immediate impact on the behaviour of nations, and shaped the security environment of the new millennium. Both attacks demonstrated patience, meticulous planning and ruthless execution by true believers.

Lessons from the attacks of 9/11 and 3/11 clearly suggest that international cooperation is essential, and that domestic security policies should be carefully designed. Internationally, the shadow war against terrorist cells is but one of several policy options. Former American Secretary of State Colin Powell (2004) has consistently argued that broad cooperative strategies must be designed to create multilateral partnerships. According to Powell and others, such partnerships go beyond the war on terrorism. In addition, new arms control and non-proliferation regimes are essential for securing WMD arsenals (Carter 2004). Domestically, laws such as the USA Patriot Act in the United States were designed to enhance and expand the scope of legal authority for domestic security. Security legislation in democracies is deemed by proponents to be necessary to disrupt terrorist conspiracies and networks. However, critics have raised strong concerns about whether the promised good of domestic security has been pursued at the expense of civil liberties. Critics of the USA Patriot Act argue that the following provisions are potentially incompatible with civil liberties protections:

- Modified standards for government surveillance, making it easier for federal agencies to access private records.
- Revised standards for electronic surveillance, making it easier to access e-mail and electronic address books.
- Adoption of 'roving wiretaps', which permit law enforcement agencies to tap a suspect's telephone conversations on any telephone which they may use.
- Adoption of nationwide search warrants, which grant broad authority for law enforcement agencies to search a suspect's premises or person at multiple locations.

The post-9/11 and post-3/11 environment is one wherein asymmetrical attacks in the international domain are generally neither greater in number, nor more frequent, than during the heyday of the old terrorism in the latter quarter of the twentieth century. However, incidents in the new millennium are more spectacular and more deadly than most examples from the previous era. New terrorist networks are quite patient in their planning and execution of attacks. Months or years pass between mass-casualty attacks, but when they occur, they have been quite devastating. Arrests in Europe and elsewhere indicate that 'sleepers' have been pre-positioned around the world, and have been successful at blending in as residents until the time when they are activated. Furthermore, the skilful use of information technologies permits broad dissemination of the revolutionaries' message, replete with video and audio feeds and tapes.

These trends indicate that globalized terrorism has become a central attribute of the modern era. The Qaedaist model has exhibited versatility, resilience and patience in the prosecution of their war against secular governments and foreign influences. Symbolic leaders inspire fellow believers, and indignation arising from the war on terrorism attracts new recruits to the cause. Absent a dramatic transformation within the Islamist movement, or a civilizational reconciliation between Western and Muslim perceptions, there is certain to be a prolongation of the New Terrorism and the war on terrorism. Moreover, and ominously, the environment which nurtures such conflict has become globalized.

References

Al Sayyid, M. 2002. 'Mixed message: Arab and Muslim response to "terrorism"', *The Washington Quarterly*, 25 (2), 177–90.

Alcott, M.B. and Babajanov, B. 2003. 'The terrorist notebooks', *Foreign Policy* (March/April), 31–40.

Barber, B.R. 2001. *Jihad vs. McWorld*. New York: Ballantine Books.

Bergen, P. 2004. 'Backdraft: how the war in Iraq has fueled Al Qaeda and ignited its dream of global jihad', *Mother Jones* (July/August), 41–5.

Burke, J. 2004. 'Al Qaeda', *Foreign Policy* (May/June), 18–26.

Carter, A.B. 2004. 'How to counter WMD', *Foreign Affairs*, 83 (5) (September/October), 72–85.

Collier, P. 2003. 'The market for civil war', *Foreign Policy* (May/June), 136, 32–44.

Crocker, C.A. 2003. 'Engaging failing states', *Foreign Affairs*, 82 (5) (September/October), 32–44.

Freedman, L. 2003. 'Think again: War', *Foreign Policy* (July/August), 137, 16–24.

Hoffman, B. 1997. 'The confluence of international and domestic trends in terrorism', *Terrorism and Political Violence*, 9 (1) (Summer), 1–15.

Hoffman, B. 1998. *Inside Terrorism*. New York: Columbia University Press.

Hoffman, S. 2002. 'Clash of globalizations', *Foreign Affairs*, 81 (3) (July-August), 104–15.

Huntington, S.P. 1993. 'The clash of civilizations?' *Foreign Affairs*, 72 (3) (Summer 1993), 24–49.

Laqueur, W. 1996. 'Postmodern terrorism: New rules for an old game', *Foreign Affairs*, 75 (5) (September/October), 24–36.

Laqueur, W. 1999. *The New Terrorism: Fanaticism and the Arms of Mass Destruction*. New York: Oxford University Press.

Lesser, I.O. 1999. 'Countering the new terrorism: Implications for strategy.' In I.O. Lesser et al. (eds), *Countering the New Terrorism*, 94. Santa Monica, CA: RAND.

Lewis, W.W. and Harris, M. 1992. 'Why globalization must prevail', *The McKinsey Quarterly* No. 2, 115ff.

Luft, G. and Korin, A. 2004. 'Terrorism goes to sea', *Foreign Affairs*, 83 (6) (November/December), 61–71.

Marglin, S.A. 2003. 'Development as poison: Rethinking the Western model of modernity', *Harvard International Review*, 25 (1) (Spring), 70–5.

Martin, G. 2003. *Understanding Terrorism: Challenges, Perspectives, and Issues*. Thousand Oaks, CA: Sage Publications.

Naím, M. 2003. 'The five wars of globalization', *Foreign Policy* (January/February), 28–37.

Newhouse, J. 2002. 'The threats America faces', *World Policy Journal* (Summer), 37–50.

Paletz, D. and Schmid, A. 1992. *Terrorism and the Media*. Newbury Park, CA: Sage Publications.

Pipes, D. 2002. 'God and mammon: Does poverty cause militant Islam?' *The National Interest* (Winter 2001/2), 14–21.

Post, J.M., Sprinzak, E. and Denny, L. 2003. 'The terrorists in their own words: Interviews with 35 incarcerated Middle Eastern terrorists', *Terrorism and Political Violence* (Spring), 171–84.

Powell, C.L. 2004. 'A strategy of partnerships', *Foreign Affairs*, 83 (1) (January/February), 22–34.

Reeve, S. 1999. *The New Jackals: Ramzi Yousef, Osama bin Laden and the Future of Terrorism*. Boston: Northeastern University Press.

Rosenau, J.N. 1997. 'The complexities and contradictions of globalization', *Current History* (November 1997), 360–4.

Scott, B.R. 2001. 'The great divide in the global village', *Foreign Affairs*, 80 (1) (January/February), 160–77.

Stern, J. 1999. *The Ultimate Terrorists*. Cambridge, MA: Harvard University Press.

Summers, L. 2004. 'America Overdrawn.' *Foreign Policy*. (July/August), 47-49.

Tomes, R.R. 2004. 'Relearning counterinsurgency warfare', *Parameters* (Spring), 16–28.

Tuman, J.S. 2003. *Communicating Terror: The Rhetorical Dimensions of Terrorism*. Thousand Oaks, CA: Sage Publications.

Wilkinson, R. 2004. 'Crisis in Cancún', *Global Governance: A Review of Multilateralism and International Organizations*, 10 (2) (April–June), 149–55.

Chapter 34

Resisting Globalization

RICHARD KAHN AND DOUGLAS KELLNER

The current forms and scope of worldwide resistance to globalization policies and processes is one of the most important political developments of the last decade. However, to speak singularly of 'resistance' is itself something of a misnomer. For just as globalization must ultimately be recognized as comprising a multiplicity of forces and trajectories, including both negative and positive dimensions, so too must the resistance to globalization be understood as pertaining to highly complex, contradictory and sometimes ambiguous varieties of struggles that range from the radically progressive to the reactionary and conservative.

'Globalization' itself is one of the most highly contested terms of the present era with passionate advocates and militant critics (Kellner 2002). By the nineteenth century debates raged over whether the global reach of the capitalist market system and the disruptions it brought were producing a beneficial 'wealth of nations' (i.e. Adam Smith) or producing an era of exploitation and imperialism (i.e. Karl Marx). For the Marxist tradition, globalization has since signified an oppressive hegemony of capital, and after the Great Depression and World War II many critics have discussed the manner in which a discourse of 'modernization' emerged to celebrate the growth of a globalized capitalist market system against its ideological and geopolitical competitor, state communism. Counterhegemonic national liberation movements and attempts to develop a 'Third Way' against capitalism and communism marked the post-World War II epoch up until the 1990s and the collapse of communism.

Perhaps the most noted form of resistance to globalization at the end of the twentieth century was first popularly termed the 'anti-globalization movement', which can be seen as attempting to constitute the beginnings of a global civil society that might produce new public spheres of political debate and cosmopolitan culture, as it upholds values of autonomy, democracy, peace, ecological sustainability, equality and social justice. Around the turn of the new millennium activists began to more specifically describe their opposition to certain aspects and forms of globalization, thereby identifying the possibility of positive forms of globalization. As we shall see below, this resulted in terms like the 'anti-corporate globalization movement' and the 'social justice movement' gaining currency. Still, many activists have tended to portray globalization in a largely negative fashion. For them, globalization is often considered as being more or less equivalent with programmes of top-down neoliberal capitalism, imperialism and terror war, McDonaldization (Ritzer 2004) of the planet by transnational corporations who exist only for profit and the states that cater to them, as well as dis-equilibrating cultural change resulting from the global proliferation and migration of Western/Northern science and technology. On the other hand, perhaps due to the significant political involvement of youth throughout the movement, the use of new media associated with the Internet has been key in helping anti-corporate globalizers to coordinate protests, proliferate counter-messages and manifest oppositional technopolitics and subcultures (see Kahn and Kellner 2003). Thus, the anti-globalization movement's relationship to contemporary technology must itself be considered contested and complex, if not contradictory in some aspects.

The anti-corporate globalization movement initially began to receive widespread recognition in 1999, when the first in an ongoing series of large international protests was staged. These protests, which have often taken the name of the date on which they occurred (e.g. J16 for 'June 16th') or the central city which they have occupied (e.g. 'Battle for Seattle'), have continued to erupt outside almost every major international political and economic meeting. Protesters see economic policy-making institutions such as the World Trade Organization (WTO), the World Bank, the International Monetary Fund (IMF), as well as conferences such as the Davos World Economic Forum and the G8 Summits, as central to the growth and future planning of unjust globalization and have accordingly made protest of their major meetings a priority. Additionally, since 9/11, the anti-globalization movement has increasingly become associated with targeting the militarist policies of the Bush and Blair administrations as part of a growing anti-war grassroots movement. Indeed, on 15 February 2003, an anti-war/globalization protest was convened that brought together an estimated 15 million people in some 60 countries worldwide, which resulted in media outlets such as the *New York Times* referring to the unprecedented resistance as the 'other superpower'.

The manner in which the anti-globalization movement has remained mobile, changing its styles, messages and constituencies depending on the situation, is one of its more important features. Scholars have often noted how the anti-corporate globalization movement is marked by the convergence and collection of political and cultural organizations involving more traditional political structures such as unions and parties, as well as non-governmental organizations (NGOs), along with a wide-range of citizen's groups and individual persons representing what have been termed the 'new social movements' (see the studies in Aronowitz and Gautney 2003). Hence, the anti-capitalist globalization movement has been portrayed as an evolution of modern political rights struggles in which all manner of identity and single-issue politics have become loosely linked, and to some degree hybridized, in joint contest against the rapacity of transnational neoliberalism as they fight for further extensions of universal human rights and a sustainable planetary ecology.

In as much as neoliberal globalization represents a continuation of the sort of modernization agenda that Western and Northern states began to propound in less developed countries following World War II, and especially since the reformation of the Organization for Economic Co-operation and Development (OECD) in the early 1960s, there are reasons to link the resistance of today's new social movements to a number of historical precedents. These include earlier examples of resistance to burgeoning globalization such as Latin American popular education programmes and the rise of African nationalism in the 1950s and 1960s, South-east Asia's Chipko movement, Chico Mendes's unionization against Amazonian rain forest destruction and China's Tiananmen Square democracy movement in the 1980s, the 56 'IMF riots' that occurred in Latin America, the Caribbean, Africa, Europe and the Middle East from 1985 to 1992, and manifestations of resistance such as the formation of the Movement for the Survival of Ogoni People in 1991 to fight Shell Oil in Nigeria, as well as the election of a self-determining Government of National Unity in South Africa and the emergence of the Zapatista Army of National Liberation in Chiapas, Mexico in 1994. Whereas some of these resistance movements were regionalized and based their approach in local traditions, which they utilized to contest the negative and colonizing influences of unrestrained capitalist development, others such as the Zapatistas have demonstrated a closer resemblance to recent mass-mobilizations against capitalist globalization through their mix of violent and non-violent protest, attempts to form solidarity with a myriad of oppressed peoples and groups around the world, and their subversion of new media (e.g. the Internet) which they incorporate as weapons in the furtherance of resistant goals.

Undeniably, much of the resistance to globalization today cannot be understood apart from its use of the new technologies associated with the Internet. It is for this reason, as well as for more ideological reasons such as the fact that many involved in the so-called 'anti-globalization movement' actually desire something like the globalization of positive values and culture, that many scholars and activists have begun to reject the moniker of 'anti-globalization' altogether. Instead, people often speak of 'globalization from below' as opposed to 'globalization from above', of anti-capitalist or anti-corporate globalization, of the 'alter-globalization movement' and of 'alternative globalizations', of the 'global justice movement' or the 'movement of movements'. The latter is particularly used to express the political idea of a global solidarity based in the tremendous diversity of resistance to be found to today's mainstream ruling practices, neoliberal capitalist economics, repressive cultural norms and other aspects of global society that appear to augment the divides between rich and poor and oppressor and oppressed. Notably, since 2001, the World Social Forum has been held as a sort of annual counter-summit to the World Economic Forum. With its motto of 'Another World is Possible', attendance in the many tens of thousands hailing from over 100 countries and highly inclusive nature that involves diverse representatives from all manner of progressive groups and causes, many have come to highlight the World Social Forum as a prominent example of the movement of movements that can characterize an alternative to capitalist globalization (see Hardt 2002).

The new movements against capitalist globalization, then, have placed issues like global justice and environmental destruction squarely in the centre of the important political concerns of our time. Whereas the mainstream media failed to vigorously debate or even report on globalization until the eruption of a vigorous anti-corporate globalization movement and rarely, if ever, critically discussed the activities of the WTO, the World Bank and the IMF, there is now a widely circulating critical discourse and controversy over these institutions. Stung by criticisms, representatives of the World Bank in particular are pledging reform, and pressures are mounting concerning proper and improper roles for the major global institutions, highlighting their limitations and deficiencies and the need for reforms such as debt relief for overburdened developing countries to solve some of their fiscal and social problems. In fact, this highlights that another aspect of the current resistance to globalization is that it works both to counter and reform it at once, with some social movements working for direct and participatory democracy and autonomous communities (sometimes utilizing alternative economic structures such as 'local exchange trading systems'), on the one hand, while others seek truly representative and democratically accountable national and global political structures, on the other.

Resistance to globalization is also occurring in the form of extreme right political movements that seek to defend ideas such as frontier-style self-determination, national isolationism and fundamentalist culture against what they perceive as the growing imposition of total global governance, in some cases, or modern liberal and secular culture, in others. Since the 1990s, there has been a dramatic rise in fascist groups and ultra-nationalist and xenophobic politics in European countries, with nations such as France, Italy, Austria, Belgium and Norway having seen over 15 per cent of the popular vote captured by politicians representing these ideological aims. Indeed, xenophobia is also growing in the United States with the rise of groups such as the Minutemen, who as armed vigilantes patrol the border zone with Mexico in order to prevent illegal entry and who additionally monitor corporations and the government for violations of tax, immigration and employment laws. Further, the United States possesses a significant far right population that fights for individualist liberties such as the right to bear arms, live free from governmental intrusions into private affairs and possess inalienable private property, which it sees as under threat from a global conspiracy of political institutions that seek one form or another of the globalization of a New World Order. Finally, against the globalization of Western culture and political norms, the last few decades have seen the rise of highly conservative and reactionary forms of religious fundamentalism. In particular, Islamic fundamentalism has been portrayed as a major opponent of globalization, with groups such as the Taliban in Afghanistan signifying an extreme form of resistance to the globalization of modern secular culture and democratic politics. Yet, as the Taliban is also associated with Osama bin Laden and his Al-Qaeda network, who actively use new media technologies to promote their cause and who seek in their own image a 'global jihad movement', it is clear that even here resistance must be revealed as embodying a myriad of complexities and contradictions.

It would thus be incorrect to perceive a simple dichotomy between globalization processes and its resisters. Just as there are positive and negative dimensions to globalization, the same can be said of the various forces which seek to resist it. Thus, in understanding the resistance to globalization, one needs to be context specific and look for the variety of forms of struggle – including individuals practising lifestyle politics, civic groups and grassroots activist networks, nongovernmental and transnational social movement organizations, as well as more national groups and parties – that are often combined in producing resistance events and which comprise a broad spectrum of resistance to globalization.

TECHNOPOLITICS OF RESISTANCE

Significant contemporary political struggles against globalization are mediated by technopolitics, in which new technologies such as computers and the Internet are used to advance political goals (Kellner 2003a; Kahn and Kellner 2005). To some extent, politics in the modern era have always been mediated by technology, with the printing press, photography, film, and radio and television playing crucial roles in politics and all realms of social life, as Marshall McLuhan, Harold Innis, Lewis Mumford and others have long argued and documented. Today, participation in representative democracies is mediated by technology, and as the disastrous failure of computerized e-voting machines in the US 2000 and 2004 presidential elections and the grassroots online response has dramatized, computers themselves are now crucial political tools for competing groups as they attempt to access state power. Further, international organizations like Third World Network, Mexican Action Network on Free Trade and Globalise Resistance are able to influence global policy making in large part because of the coalition-building and informative power their websites and list-serves have brought to them.

What is especially novel about computer and information technology mediated politics is that information can be instantly communicated to large numbers of individuals throughout the world who become connected to one another via computer networks. The Internet is also potentially interactive, facilitating discussion, debate, and online and archived discussion. It is also increasingly multimedia in scope, allowing the dissemination of images, sounds, video and other cultural forms and it has likewise begun to produce its own styles. Moreover, the use of computer technology and networks is becoming a normalized aspect of politics, just as the broadcasting media were some decades ago. The use of computer-mediated technology for technopolitics, however, opens new terrains of political struggle for voices and groups excluded from the mainstream media and thus increases potential for intervention by oppositional groups, potentially expanding the scope of democratization and challenging the naturalization of free trade agreements and neoliberal capitalism.

Given the extent to which capital and its logic of commodification have colonized ever more areas of everyday life in recent years, it is somewhat astonishing that cyberspace is by and large decommodified for large numbers of people – at least in the overdeveloped countries like the United States. On the other hand, using computers, transforming information into data-packets that can be sent through networks and hooking oneself up to computer networks, involves a form of commodified activity, inserting the user in networks and technology that are at the forefront of the information revolution and global restructuring of capital. Thus the Internet is highly ambiguous from the perspective of global commodification, as from other perspectives, even as it is notable for being a major tool in the production of resistance to globalization.

There have been many campaigns against the excesses of global capitalist corporations such as Nike and McDonald's. Hackers attacked Nike's site in June 2000 and substituted a 'global justice' message for Nike's corporate hype. Many anti-Nike websites and list-serves have emerged, helping groups struggling against Nike's labour practices circulate information and organize movements against Nike, which have forced them to modify their labour practices.

A British group, London Greenpeace, that created an anti-McDonald's website against the food corporation and then distributed the information through digital and print media, has received significant attention. This site was developed by supporters of two British activists, Helen Steel and Dave Morris, who were sued by McDonald's for distributing leaflets denouncing the corporation's low wages, advertising practices, involvement in deforestation, cruel treatment of animals and patronage of an unhealthy diet. The activists counterattacked and with help from supporters, organized a McLibel campaign, assembled a McSpotlight website with a tremendous amount of information criticizing the corporation and mobilized experts to testify and confirm their criticisms (see www.mcspotlight.org). The three-year civil trial, the UK's longest ever, ended ambiguously on 19 June 1997, with the judge defending some of McDonald's claims against the activists, while substantiating some of the activists' criticisms.

The case created unprecedented bad publicity for McDonald's which was disseminated throughout the world via Internet websites, mailing lists and discussion groups. The McLibel/McSpotlight group claims that their website was accessed over 15 million times and was visited over 2 million times in the month of the verdict alone. Additionally, the newspaper *The Guardian* reported that the site 'claimed to be the most comprehensive source of information on a multinational corporation ever assembled' and was part of one of the more successful anti-corporate campaigns to have been undertaken.

On the whole, websites critical of global capitalist corporations have disseminated a tremendous amount of information. Many labour organizations are also beginning to make use of the new technologies. The Clean Clothes Campaign, a movement started by Dutch women in 1990 in support of Filipino garment workers, has supported strikes throughout the world, exposing exploitative working conditions. In 1997, activists involved in Korean workers' strikes and the Merseyside dock strike in England used websites to promote international solidarity. In like manner, representatives of major US labour organizations have indicated how useful e-mail, faxes, websites and the Internet have been to their struggles and, in particular, indicated how such technopolitics helped organize demonstrations or strikes in favour of striking English or Australian dockworkers, as when US longshoremen organized strikes to boycott ships carrying material loaded by scab workers. Technopolitics thus helps labour create global alliances in order to combat increasingly transnational corporations.

Indeed, one can argue that against the capitalist organization of neoliberal globalization, a Fifth International, to use Waterman's phrase (1992), of computer-mediated activism is emerging that is qualitatively different from the party-based socialist and communist Internationals of the past. Advances in personal, mobile informational technology are rapidly providing the structural elements for the existence of fresh kinds of highly informed, autonomous communities that coalesce around local lifestyle choices, global political demands and everything in between. As the virtual-community theorist Howard Rheingold (2002) describes, these multiple networks of connected citizens and activists transform the 'dumb mobs' of totalitarian states into 'smart mobs' of socially active personages linked by notebook computers, PDA devices, Internet cell phones, pagers and global positioning systems (GPS). Increasingly, this is being done with great political effect. For instance, these technologies were put to use in a March 2004 mobilization in Spain that spontaneously organized the population to vote out the existing conservative government and replace it with an anti-war, socialist party. Thus, while emergent mobile technology provides yet another impetus towards experimental identity construction and identity politics, such networking also links individuals up with diverse communities such as labour, feminist, ecological, black bloc anarchist, and anti-racism and war organizations, along with peasant movements like Via Campesina, and various anti-capitalist groups, thereby providing the evolving basis for a democratic politics of alliance and solidarity to overcome the limitations of postmodern identity politics.

Of course, one of the most instructive examples of the use of the Internet to foster collective networks of struggle against the excesses of corporate capitalism occurred in the protests in Seattle and throughout the world against the WTO meeting in December 1999, which has resulted in the subsequent emergence of worldwide anti-globalization and alter-globalization movements. Behind the Seattle actions was a burgeoning global protest movement that was experimenting with the Internet to organize resistance to the institutions of capitalist globalization and champion democratization. In the build-up to the 1999 Seattle demonstrations, many websites generated anti-WTO material and numerous mailing lists used the Internet to distribute critical material and to organize the protest. The result was the mobilization of caravans from throughout the United States to take protestors to Seattle, as well as contingents of activists throughout the world. Many of the protestors had never met and were recruited through the Internet. For the first time ever, labour, environmentalist, feminist, anti-capitalist, animal rights, anarchist and other groups organized to protest against aspects of globalization and to form new alliances and solidarities for future struggles. In addition, demonstrations took place throughout the world, and a proliferation of anti-WTO material against the extremely secret group spread throughout the Internet.

Furthermore, the Internet provided critical coverage of the event, documentation of the various groups' protests and debate over the WTO and globalization. Indeed, it was at this event that a collective of alternative and independent media organizations and activists formed the first Independent Media Center, resulting in the website Indymedia.org which has since grown to be perhaps the most major form of alternative media, as Indymedia includes over 160 such centres in some 60 countries worldwide. In Seattle, whereas the mainstream media presented the IMF protests as 'anti-trade', featured the incidents of anarchist violence against property and minimized police brutality against demonstrators, Indymedia provided the Internet with pictures, audio, video, eyewitness accounts and reports of police viciousness and the generally peaceful and non-violent nature of the protests. While the mainstream media framed the Seattle anti-WTO activities negatively and privileged suspect spokespeople like Patrick Buchanan as critics of globalization, Internet-based media provided multiple representations of the demonstrations, advanced reflective discussion of the WTO and globalization, and presented a diversity of critical perspectives.

On the other hand, it must be pointed out that extreme right-wing and reactionary forces can and have used the Internet to promote their political agendas as well. One can easily access an exotic witch's brew of websites maintained by the Ku Klux Klan and myriad neo-Nazi assemblages, including the Aryan Nation and various militia groups. Internet discussion lists also disperse these views and right-wing extremists are aggressively active on many computer forums. These types of organizations are hardly harmless, having carried out terrorism of various sorts extending from church burnings to the bombings of public buildings. Adopting quasi-Leninist discourse and tactics for ultra-right causes, such groups have been successful in recruiting working-class members devastated by the developments of global capitalism, which has resulted in widespread unemployment for traditional forms of industrial, agricultural and unskilled labour. Moreover, extremist websites have influenced alienated middle-class youth as well (a 1999 HBO documentary 'Hate on the Internet' provides a disturbing number of examples of how extremist websites influenced disaffected youth to commit hate crimes). An additional twist in the saga of technopolitics seems to be that allegedly 'terrorist' groups are now also increasingly using the Internet and websites to organize and promote their causes, as has been alleged of Al-Qaeda in particular, which encrypted and posted instructions to operatives on websites like Alneda.com and Qal3ah.net prior to their discovery by the US government.

While former Bush administration cybersecurity czar, Richard Clarke, has warned of a 'digital Pearl Harbor' that would result from terrorists using the Internet to attack key corporate and government computer systems with machine disabling codes known as network 'worms', such has yet to arise. Al-Qaeda computers have been seized, however, that demonstrate their intention to train 'hackers' – a term which initially meant someone who made creative innovations in computer systems but which has increasingly come to denote someone engaged in malicious online activities – that would write and propagate computer worms and viruses in this manner. Additionally, hackers such as Melhacker, who has publicly supported Al-Qaeda and promised to release a 'super worm' upon the invasion of Iraq, are actively involved in extreme right cyber-resistance.

On the other hand, progressive hackers called 'hacktivists' have grouped together as a global movement under the banner of HOPE, which stands for 'Hackers On Planet Earth'. Hactivists have involved themselves in creating open source software programs that can be used freely to circumvent attempts by government and corporations to control the Internet experience, and have been key in cracking commercial software authentication codes towards making programs available freely online. Wireless network hackers often deploy their skills towards developing a database of 'freenets' that, if not always free of costs, represent real opportunities for local communities to share online connections and corporate fees. Such freenets represent inclusive resources that are developed by communities for their own needs and involve values like conviviality and culture, education, economic equity and sustainability that have been found to be progressive hallmarks of online communities generally.

Hactivists are also directly involved in the immediate political battles played out around the dynamically globalized world. Hactivists such as The Mixter, from Germany, who authored the program Tribe Floodnet that shut down the website for the World Economic Forum in January 2002 and which has been utilized by militant activists like Stop Huntingdon Animal Cruelty (SHAC) against corporations related to vivisection company Huntingdon Life Sciences, routinely use their hacking skills to cause disruption of governmental and corporate presences online. On 12 July 2002, the homepage for the *USA Today* website was hacked and altered content was presented to the public, leaving *USA Today* to join such other media magnets as the *New York Times* and Yahoo as the corporate victims of a media hack. In February 2003, immediately following the destruction of the Space Shuttle Columbia, a group calling themselves Trippin Smurfs hacked NASA's servers for the third time in three months. In each case, security was compromised and the web servers were defaced with anti-war political messages. Another repeated victim of hacks is the Recording Industry Association of America (RIAA), which because of its attempt to legislate P2P (peer-to-peer) music trading has become anathema to Internet hactivists. A sixth attack upon the RIAA website in January 2003 posted bogus press releases and even provided music files for free downloading.

THEORIZING GLOBAL RESISTANCE

While scholars and others have shown a tremendous interest in theorizing globalization throughout the 1990s and up to the present, and while there is a healthy body of literature describing new social movements since the 1980s, it is only recently that the resistance to globalization proper has begun to warrant equal interest and debate (Appadurai 2000; Aronowitz and Gautney 2003). Still, there are a number of concepts and frameworks that have begun to be used in order to characterize global resistance that are worthy of summary here.

Some scholars have returned to the work of Karl Polanyi (1944), finding in his idea of countermovements a workable framework for understanding contemporary resistance movements. In this way, movements towards greater neoliberalization and corporatization of the economy as part of a general trend towards the globalization of politics are perceived as generating countermovements that are arising to protect people and society against market dominance. These countermovements are based in mutual solidarity and are conflictual and defensive of the non-market oriented social relations and institutions in which countermovement actors exist. Yet it has been argued by scholars such as James Mittelman (2000) that the transposition of Polyani's theory onto the movements which have arisen to resist globalization is problematic in at least two ways. First, it assumes a united front where there is not one to be found, as it collects the diversity of new social movements and identity positions into a homogenizing political space. This is not to say that solidarities do not exist, or that there are not at times common foes, but as pro-global justice movement theorist George Monbiot has written in a 2003 article for the *Guardian* newspaper, a major division exists in the movement between 'diversalists' who desire a plurality of struggles and the 'universalists' who seek to organize under a singular leadership.

A second problem with applying Polyani's theory to today's resistance is its reliance upon notions of organizational structure. As critics point out, certainly many NGOs and political groups do resist in an organized way. But it is not clear that the movement on the whole does, or even can do so, despite the formative attempts of new global institutional summits such as the World Social Forum – which despite its often positive valorization has come up for critique from notable *No Logo* theorist/activist Naomi Klein (2002), who challenged the forum's billing as an opportunity 'to whip the chaos on the streets into a structured shape' as contrary to the movement's mobility and diversity, which she felt should instead be loosely 'hotlinked' like websites on a network. Further, over-emphasizing the organized quality of today's resistance to globalization overlooks the many resistances people are making in their everyday lives and culture, whether by altering their behaviour as consumers or engaging in acts of cultural dissent such as culture jamming or subcultural participation.

Another theorist often employed to illustrate current resistances is Antonio Gramsci, who developed a theory of hegemony and counterhegemony that has proven especially fruitful for understanding the relationship between transnational state actors and grassroots and other popular forms of contestation and social transformation. Put simply, Gramsci felt social stability was achieved through the mixture of dominant force and the formation of and consent to the ideology of ruling groups who form hegemonic blocs across a wide range of institutions. Against this, he felt that counterhegemonic forces, groups and ideas form their own blocs and so serve to challenge hegemonies in the quest for power. In recent theories such as those that pit globalization from above against globalization from below (Falk 1999, 2000; Brecher et al. 2000; Brecher 2003), one can see the neo-Gramscian influence in understanding new social movement resistance to hegemonic orders of neoliberalism and market capitalism, as well as of patriarchy, racism, industrialism and other ruling ideologies. However, for all of its efficacy this model can also occlude the complexities of actual resistance. As Raymond Williams has echoed in a different context, applications of Gramscian hegemony theory to global resistances often devolve into one form or another of reductive base-superstructure analyses in which there is theorized only an hegemony and a counterhegemonic movement in opposition to it. Rather, as we have seen, each is multiple and multifaceted, containing a variety of contradictions and potentials.

In this respect, a promising theory of globalization and resistance is offered by Michael Hardt and Antonio Negri's *Empire* (2000) and *Multitude* (2004). For Hardt and Negri, globalization is characterized by a new imperialistic logic that conducts virtuous wars and makes decisions over who is to live and who is to die. They see it as a complex process that involves a multidimensional mixture of expansions of the global economy and capitalist market system, new technologies and media, expanded judicial and legal modes of governance, and emergent modes of power, sovereignty and resistance. Yet, as a global order of power in an age of nation-states, it transcends and is not traceable to any particular centre of power or state capital. Rather, they believe it is maintained hegemonically by the consent of the 'multitudes', some of whom they optimistically note are producing alternatives by deserting from mainstream order, migrating to points of struggle and attempting to achieve a counter-Empire based on global citizenship, living wages for all and other progressive political agendas.

Hardt and Negri have engendered their share of criticism, partly for being unprogrammatic and partly for having failed to account for the role of American exceptionalism and militarism in global empire, but their theory rises above many other competing accounts that tend to be too uncritically binary in their opposition of globalization and its discontents. Thus, Benjamin Barber (1998) describes the strife between McWorld and Jihad, contrasting the homogeneous, commercial and Americanized tendencies of the global economy and culture to traditional cultures which are often resistant to globalization. Likewise, Thomas Friedman (1999) makes a more benign distinction between what he calls the 'Lexus' and the 'Olive Tree'. The former is a symbol of modernization, of affluence and luxury, and of Westernized consumption, contrasted with the olive tree that is a symbol of roots, tradition, place and stable community.

Barber, however, is too negative towards McWorld and Jihad, and does not adequately describe the democratic and progressive forces within both. Although Barber recognizes a dialectic of McWorld and Jihad, he opposes both to democracy, failing to perceive how they each generate their own democratic forces and tendencies, as well as oppose and undermine democratization in their own right. Within the Western democracies, for instance, there is not just top-down homogenization and corporate domination, but also globalization from below and a multitude of social movements that desire alternatives to capitalist globalization. Thus, it is not only traditionalist, non-Western forces of Jihad that oppose McWorld. Likewise, Jihad contains progressive forces along with the reactionary Islamic fundamentalists, who are now the most demonized elements of the contemporary era. Like McWorld, Jihad has its contradictions and its potential for democratization, as well as elements of domination and destruction.

Friedman, by contrast, is too uncritical of globalization and fails to perceive the depth of the oppressive features of globalization and breadth and extent of resistance and opposition to it. In particular, he fails to articulate contradictions between capitalism and democracy, and the ways that globalization and its economic logic undermines democracy as well as circulates it. Likewise, he does not grasp the virulence of the pre-modern and Jihadist tendencies that he blithely identifies with the olive tree, and the reasons why globalization and the West are so strongly resisted in many parts of the world.

Ultimately, what is required is a critical theory of globalization and its resistance that articulates the complexity of globalization and of the movements resisting it. Such a dialectical theory would avoid globophobia and globophilia, or dualistic optics that oppose a 'good' globalization from below to a 'bad' globalization from above. Additionally, it would avoid determinism and pessimism, while acknowledging the power of state corporate globalization and its destructive tendencies, as well as the idealized celebration of anti-global forces. Finally, a critical theory of globalization would articulate the dialectic of the global and the local, recognizing resistance and domination as complex and multilayered forces and events. Unquestionably, the struggle over globalization is one of the defining issues of our time whose dynamics will surely influence the course of the next century. Movements of resistance are continually arising and changing, even as technological inventions proliferate throughout the world and produce a global media culture, while economic crises, natural disasters, militarism and war threaten to undermine the global order. Therefore, theories of globalization and resistance must ultimately remain sensitive to ongoing change, be rigorously critical and so overcome the tendency towards being either dogmatic or overly explanative.

References

Appadurai, A. 2000. 'Grassroots globalization and the research imagination', *Public Culture*, 12 (1), 1–19.

Aronowitz, S. and Gautney, H. (eds) 2003. *Implicating Empire: Globalization and Resistance in the 21st Century World Order*. New York: Basic Books.

Barber, B.R. 1998. *A Place for Us: How to Make Society Civil and Democracy Strong*. New York: Hill and Wang.

Brecher, J.T. 2003. 'Globalization today'. In S. Aronowitz and H. Gautney (eds), *Implicating Empire: Globalization and Resistance in the 21st Century World Order*, 199–210. New York: Basic Books.

Brecher, J., Costello, T. and Smith, B. 2000. *Globalization from Below*. Boston, MA: South End.

Cvetkovich, A. and Kellner, D. 1997. *Articulating the Global and the Local: Globalization and Cultural Studies*. Boulder, CO: Westview Press.

Falk, R. 1999. *Predatory Globalization*. Oxford: Blackwell.

Falk, R. 2000. 'Resisting "globalization from above" through "globalization from below"'. In B. Gills (ed.), *Globalization and the Politics of Resistance*. London: Macmillan.

Friedman, T. 1999. *The Lexus and the Olive Tree*. New York: Farrar, Strauss and Giroux.

Hardt, M. 2002. 'Porto Allegre: Today's Bandung?' *New Left Review*, 14 (March-April).

Hardt, M. and Negri, A. 2000. *Empire*. Cambridge, MA: Harvard University Press.

Hardt, M. and Negri, A. 2004. *Multitude: War and Democracy in the Age of Empire*. New York: Penguin Press.

Kahn, R. and Kellner, D. 2003. 'New media, Internet activism, and blogging'. In D. Muggleton (ed.), *The Post-Subcultures Reader*, 299–314. London: Berg.

Kahn, R. and Kellner, D. 2005. 'Oppositional politics and the Internet: A critical/ reconstructive approach', *Cultural Politics*, 1 (1), 75–100.

Kellner, D. 2002. 'Theorizing globalization', *Sociological Theory*, 20 (3) (November), 285–305.

Kellner, D. 2003a. 'Globalization, technopolitics, and revolution'. In J. Foran (ed.), *The Future of Revolutions: Rethinking Radical Change in the Age of Globalization*, 180–94. London: Zed Books.

Kellner, D. 2003b. *From 9/11 to Terror War: The Dangers of the Bush Legacy*, New York: Rowman and Littlefield.

Klein, N. 2002. 'Farewell to the end of history: Organization and vision in anti-corporate movements', *Socialist Register 2002*, 1–13.

Mittelman, J. 2000. *The Globalization Syndrome: Transformation and Resistance*. Princeton, NJ: Princeton University Press.

Polanyi, K. 1944. *The Great Transformation*. New York: Toronto, Farrar, and Rinehart.

Rheingold, H. 2002. *Smart Mobs: The Next Social Revolution*. Cambridge, MA: Perseus.

Ritzer, G. 2004. *The McDonaldization of Society*. Revised New Century edn. Thousand Oaks, CA: Sage Publications.

Waterman, P. 1992. 'International labour communication by computer: The fifth international?' Working Paper Series 129. The Hague: Institute of Social Studies.

Further reading

Amoore, L. (ed.) 2005. *The Global Resistance Reader*. New York: Routledge.

Barlow, M. and Clarke, T. 2001. *Global Showdown: How the New Activists are Fighting Global Corporate Rule*. Toronto: Stoddart Publishing Co.

Broad, R. 2002. *Global Backlash: Citizen Initiatives for a Just World Economy*. Lanham, MD: Rowman and Littlefield.

Hayden, P. and el-Ojeili, C. (eds) 2005. *Confronting Globalization: Humanity, Justice and the Renewal of Politics*. New York: Palgrave Macmillan.

Smith, J. and Johnston, H. (eds) 2002. *Globalization and Resistance: Transnational Dimensions of Social Movements*. Lanham, MD: Rowman and Littlefield.

Stiglitz, J.E. 2002. *Globalization and Its Discontents*. New York: W.W. Norton.

Chapter 35

The Futures of Globalization

Bryan S. Turner

Introduction: Defining the Field

Theories of globalization have been the dominant paradigm in sociology for at least two decades, but certain features of the globalization debate have been part of sociological discourse for much longer. In mainstream academic sociology, one of the earliest publications on the topic was by W.E. Moore (1966) in his 'Global sociology: The world as a singular system'. He argued that sociology was becoming a global science and that 'the life of the individual anywhere is affected by events and processes everywhere' (Moore 1966: 482). 'Globalization' refers then to the process by which the world becomes a single place, and hence the volume and depth of social interconnectedness are greatly increased. Globalization is the compression of social space (Giddens 1990). The analysis of the future of globalization will have to address the consequences, both intended and more commonly unintended, of these processes of temporal and spatial compression.

In the 1960s Marshall McLuhan (1967) had introduced an influential vocabulary to describe the role of 'the global village' in the analysis of culture and mass media in order to understand how the world was shrinking as a result of new technologies of communication. The globalization literature grew apace in the 1970s and 1980s, mainly within the sociology of religion where religious revivalism was increasingly seen as a global process (Beckford and Luckmann 1989; Robertson 1987). By the 1990s globalization had been identified as 'the central concept' of sociology (Robertson 1990).

Although there is now a large and expanding body of literature on globalization, theories of these global processes are characterized by certain persistent deficiencies, especially in terms of explanatory power and precision. This discussion is concerned with the future of globalization processes rather than with the future of globalization theory, but of course the two issues are inevitably interconnected. If we are to think effectively about globalization's futures, it is helpful intellectually to consider briefly some of the difficulties and shortcomings of existing theories in the sociological literature. In this commentary, the range of the debate about the nature of globalization is extended through a sociological interpretation of its likely futures. Because futurology is generally speaking merely an extrapolation from present trends, many of these social transformations are of course already upon us.

Religious dimensions of globalization have been neglected, and most explanations focus broadly on technological and economic causes (Beyer 1994; Turner 1994). For example, while Ulrich Beck (2000: 53) clearly recognizes the importance of cultural globalization and 'ideoscapes', *What Is Globalization?* contains no discussion of fundamentalism, Islamic radicalism or religion in general. Sociologists have in addition had little to say about military globalization or about warfare. The impact of war and militarism on the origins and development of globalization has thus been neglected (Black 1998), and yet they have played a crucial part, especially with the rise of world wars, in transforming the international order into a global system. In the globalization literature, there has developed an unfortunate gap between sociological and international relations theory. Religion and military violence are therefore important causal aspects of globalization processes.

In mainstream sociology, the most influential writer on the importance of religion in globalization has been Roland Robertson (1992), who complained with some justification that analysts had overstated the economic nature of globalization (free trade, neoliberalism, financial deregulation, and integrated production and management systems) to the neglect of its social and cultural characteristics, especially its religious dimensions. Theories that emphasize the technological and economic causes of globalization (such as computerization of information and communication or economic and fiscal deregulation in the neoliberal revolution of the 1970s) show little appreciation of long-term cultural, religious and social conditions. These theories tend to be somewhat simple versions of technological determinism. Whereas Ulrich Beck (1992) and Anthony Giddens (1990) have approached globalization as an aspect of late modernity (and therefore as related to risk society and reflexive modernization), Robertson has been concerned with long-term cultural developments. These include the unification of global time, the spread of the Gregorian calendar, the rise of world religions, the growth of human rights values and institutions and the globalization of sport. In short, we also need to attend to the various dimensions of globalization and their causal priority: such dimensions as the economic and technological (including global markets of goods, services and labour); the informational and cultural (such as global knowledge, religious revival movements and radical fundamentalism); the legal and political (human rights, legal pluralism and legal regulation of trade); and the medical and health aspects (such as epidemics). We can simplify this discussion by suggesting that globalization has four major dimensions: economic, cultural, technological and political. Any comprehensive analysis of the futures of globalization would have to consider all four dimensions and their interaction, but this overview has of necessity to be more selective in its treatment of issues. Furthermore, this analysis will be primarily concerned with the negative and unintended consequences of these four broad aspects of global society.

Perhaps one consistent weakness of sociological views of globalization has been their persistently optimistic, and frequently naive assumptions about the causes and consequences of globalization. There are of course existing criticisms of globalization that have identified its negative features. For example, it has been claimed that globalization is basically the spread of rational models of organization that produce cultural standardization. McDonaldization is the classic example (Ritzer 1993). Globalization produces a standardized world, not simply of commodities, but also of traditions and cultures. Globalization empties out social content, evaporates cultural differences and eliminates authenticity. The result is cultural nothingness (Ritzer 2004). Anti-globalization theorists and activists who obviously share this view oppose globalization as the imposition of Western economic hegemony. Beck has associated globalization with risk society, thereby exploring its negative impact on social structures and everyday life. These existing criticisms of globalization theory have been brought into sharper focus by the recent interest in 'empire' (Hardt and Negri 2000) and the question of global military conflict is therefore closely allied to arguments about the rise of an American empire. Niall Ferguson (2004) in *Colossus* claims that American imperialism has a long history, but there is a persistent sense that imperialism and democracy do not go together, and hence America is an empire in denial. Recent studies of emerging imperial power suggest that global governance requires an imperial policeman to regulate local conflicts and regional wars. If Ferguson is correct, globalization will require new systems of regulation and domination which cannot be provided by nation-states.

While there are important criticisms of globalization (as process rather than merely as theory) in the evolving literature on globalization, the attack on the World Trade Center, the subsequent 'war on terrorism' and more recently the bombings in Madrid and London have transformed the study of globalization. International terrorism has, at least for the foreseeable future, eclipsed erstwhile naively optimistic views of globalization as merely a positive extension of modernization. There is currently therefore a greater interest in the negative aspects of globalization, namely of urban violence, slavery, terrorism, international crime, tourist sex and global epidemics. In response to this negative but more realistic assessment of globalization, I develop what can be regarded as a neo-Malthusian theory that examines the complex interaction between the clash of civilizations, terrorism, changing population structure, ageing and migration, pollution and environmental crisis.

The futures of globalization will require the colonial and imperial exploitation of outer space, because the earth's resources will be too depleted to support future population growth. If the earth's resources are finite, then space exploration must have a significant economic and military role in the development of global society. This dystopic vision was perhaps first articulated by H.G. Wells in his *The Time Machine* which was a major contribution to futurology. Wells also played a significant role in the development of human rights when in a series of letters to *The Times* in October 1939 he helped to create a bill of rights against totalitarian regimes (Robertson 2002). The future of globalization will involve a significant increase in the disruption of civil society through 'new wars', and a variety of attempts to secure the rule of law, including the globalization of rights. These civil conflicts will have diverse manifestations, but a common set of causes.

This analysis of the futures of globalization has the following general features. First, it draws on the work of Michel Foucault to place the body and populations at the centre of any picture of the future, and hence this discussion will deal extensively with medical technology, population changes, ageing demographic structures, disease and drugs (Turner 2004). One problem with Foucault's theory was the lack of a genuine political economy, namely a concern for governmentality in terms of pension funds, investment in regenerative medicine, research budgets for stem cell development and so forth. By combining Foucault and the political economy of ageing and resources, it is possible to develop a general framework for a neo-Malthusian sociology of globalization that attempts to grasp the interconnections between the following conditions: waste, environmental damage and the depletion of natural resources; the growth of radical politics, new wars and the alienation of youth; the growing importance of human rights responses to failed states and civil war; and the centrality of religious imagination and religious violence to global change. The aim is to understand how the changing structure of populations has interacted with capitalist markets to produce a new age of violence, and hence a key component of the future of globalization must be to consider the emergence of dystopic cosmologies, that will resemble the depraved consciousness of plague-ridden medieval society or the extraordinary baroque mentality of the Post-Reformation world.

CULTURAL GLOBALIZATION: RELIGION AND THE CLASH OF CIVILIZATIONS

The modern economy requires considerable labour mobility, and hence it requires open, porous state boundaries. The globalization of the labour market creates cultural diversity, and cultural diversity has become essentially religious diversity. Against this rising hybridity, the nation-state has sought to protect its sovereignty and to retain a largely homogeneous civil society. There is therefore a tension between the global economy and the territoriality of the nation-state. One traditional solution has been to develop multicultural policies, but for various reasons multiculturalism is under attack (Glazer 1997). It is, for example, largely incompatible with religious fundamentalism, because fundamentalist theologians recognize that such hybridity erodes the purity (that is the fundamentals) of religious orthodoxy.

One perspective on global hybridity emphasizes the growing clash of civilizations in which the conflict between religions defines the boundaries of the political. Samuel Huntington's article on 'the clash of civilizations' in *Foreign Affairs* (1993) has shaped much of the academic debate about inter-cultural understanding for almost a decade. In the post-9/11 world, Huntington's bleak analysis of the development of micro fault-line conflicts and macro core state conflicts has captured the mood of foreign policy in the West in the era of the 'war on terror'. Huntington of course believes that the major division is between the Christian West and the Muslim world. More recently, he has even more openly spoken about 'the age of Muslim Wars' and widespread Muslim grievance and hostility towards the United States (Huntington 1996). Any attempt to engage with Islamic civilization is now seen as a 'war for Muslim minds'. Globalization will continue to have contradictory consequences for religion: increasing pluralism and hybridity, growing fundamentalism and evolving importance of religious idioms as political ideologies. Globalization has had the further paradoxical effect of making religions (via their religious leaders and elites) more self-conscious of themselves as 'world religions', that is 'modern conditions have made religions more self-consciously global in character' (Smart 1989: 556). We can trace this development of a global consciousness of a system of religions back, for example, to the World's Parliament of Religions in 1893.

The development of religious pluralism or the emergence of a religious super-market represents a consumer secularism in which religious forms are hybrid. Globalization produces cultural hybridization, because the interaction of different cultures through migration and the growth of diasporic communities creates, pri-marily in global cities, a shared cultural complexity (Appadurai 2003). These hybrid forms of religion are often constructed self-consciously and they are closely related to youth movements and to generational politics. Global, hybrid religiosity is a form of religious popular culture. In the United States, sociologists have identified the emergence of a 'quest culture' that attempts to find meaning in various and diverse traditions. The result is religious hybridity. The mechanism by which these hybrid religious styles emerge is through a 'spiritual market place' (Roof 1993, 1999). These quest cultures have been critically evaluated as forms of expressive indivi-dualism, because they are related to what Talcott Parsons called the 'expressive revolution' (Parsons 1974). New age communities have become a popular topic of sociological research (Heelas 1996), but we need to understand more precisely how these spiritual marketplaces function globally and how they are connected electroni-cally through the Net (Dawson and Hennebry 2003).

Sociologists have in the debate about religious globalization narrowly focused on fundamentalism. Indeed, the growth of religious fundamentalism is often regarded as the principal consequence of globalization (as the most recent aspect of moderni-zation). Fundamentalism has been a common development in the three Abrahamic religions, but it is also present in various reform movements in Buddhism (Marty and Appleby 1995). Religious fundamentalism is often defined as traditionalism because it is seen to be anti-modern. This view pervades Frank Lechner and John Boli's *The Globalization Reader* (2004: 326–60). There is obviously evidence to show how fundamentalism has attempted to contain the growth of cultural hybridi-zation, to preserve what is seen to be the pristine, authentic faith, to sustain religious authority and orthodoxy, and in particular to curb the growth of women's social and political autonomy. This view is questionable for two main reasons. First, fun-damentalist movements employ the full range of modern means of communication and organization and secondly they are specifically anti-traditionalist in rejecting the taken-for-granted assumptions of traditional practice (Turner 2003). In Islam, since the formation of the Muslim Brothers in the 1920s, fundamentalists have consistently rejected traditional religion, specifically Sufism. If we consider funda-mentalism as a verb, 'to fundamentalize', then religious traditions can be seen as strategies of alternative modernity, not a return to tradition (Turner 2002).

The growth of higher education and student movements has been important in the evolution of 'political religions'. The case of Islamic fundamentalism and politi-cal Islam is the classic illustration. With the decline of communism, radical religion has replaced secular politics as the rallying point of those who have experienced social alienation. It is of course important to distinguish between the training of different social strata with respect to universities, technical colleges and religious institutions. This argument – religion as an expression of the social disappoint-ment and dislocation of economic change – is now inevitably associated with the

Huntington thesis and with the 'Jihad vs. McWorld' dichotomy (Barber 2001). The process of 'securitization' in Europe and North America and the development of the friend/foe approach to foreign policy has produced significant forms of political 'blowback'. Although the clash of civilizations thesis has been the subject of bitter criticism, it is evident that fundamentalist religions are incompatible with cultural diversity, legal pluralism and multiculturalism. Fundamentalism is generally hostile to inter-cultural marriage, secular education, tolerance for 'deviant' sexuality and women's involvement in the public sphere, that is, it is hostile to the conditions that make multicultural global cities feasible as spaces to inhabit. High rates of intermarriage between separate communities are a condition of successful social integration in multicultural societies, but fundamentalism undermines such conditions. In July 2005 the Muslim Council of Indonesia issued legal pronouncements (*fatwa*) banning mixed marriages, interfaith prayers and religious pluralism. The hybridization of cultures that is one consequence of globalization is not compatible with the defence of religious exclusivity.

TECHNO-MILITARY GLOBALIZATION: TERRORISM AND NEW WARS

The impact of military technology, militarism and war on the shape and direction of globalization has been neglected in the primary literature on globalization. The principal exceptions are *War and Modernity* (Joas 2003) and *War and Power in the 21st Century* (Hirst 2001). War and military technology are major causes of globalization because they determined the conditions of social development in the twentieth century. The spread of nuclear weapons shaped the conditions of warfare and produced the Cold War. Constant innovation in military technology shaped the economic growth of the Western world. However, it is said that there has been a revolution in military affairs (Cohen 1966), because the military platforms of existing forces – tanks, planes and ships – are obsolete. In the recent sociology of the military, there has been an important debate about the distinction between old and new wars, that provides a valuable insight into ethnic-cleansing and genocide. In particular, the concept of new wars is helpful in thinking about the increased vulnerability of women in civil conflicts. Military conflict has the effect of disrupting and eroding political boundaries, and 'new wars' will be an increasing feature of violence under global conditions (Münkler 2005).

Old wars or 'bourgeois wars' are said to be characteristic of the international system that was created by the Treaty of Westphalia of 1648, involving military conflict between armies that were recruited and trained by nation-states. In conventional inter-states wars involving large set battles and military manoeuvres, sexual violence against women on enemy territory was dysfunctional in terms of strategic, rational, military objectives. Attacks on civilian populations interfered with the primary objective of war, which was the decisive defeat of an opposing army by direct military engagement. Harassing civilian populations only constrained military mobility on the battle field and delayed direct engagement with an opposing army. Within these conventional inter-state wars, the development of international law to protect civilians was perfectly compatible with conventional military objectives. In new wars, this military logic – its strategic rationality – evaporates, and systematic rape of women (so-called 'camp rape'), and systematic violence towards civilians generally, become functional activities in the erosion of civil authorities and destruction of civil society. In bourgeois wars, rape was common but unplanned; in bourgeois wars, rape is systematic and constitutive of military violence. Therefore, in bourgeois wars, the majority of casualties were military personnel; in new wars, the casualties are almost entirely civilian. New wars involve the sexualization of violence, because civil society can be destroyed through a systematic attack on the reproduction of its population. Mass sexual violence has a symbolic political meaning, namely that men can no longer protect their women. Another characteristic of such wars is the growing use of children as cheap and biddable combat troops. These wars are in large measure the product of failed states and the reduced cost of military equipment, such as the widespread use of the Kalashnikov rifle. One consequence of new wars in Africa, especially in the Congo, has been growing distrust of and hostility towards children. Child soldiers have played a major role in civil conflicts throughout Africa and are no longer regarded as innocent victims of war. The extended family has largely broken down in central Africa leaving many children without care and support. In cities such as Kinshasa, there has been a sudden increase in witchcraft accusations against marginalized children. Indigenous evangelical churches play an important role in exorcising possessed children, and hence there is a causal connection between state failure, new wars and generational disruption. In Africa and Latin America, globalization is closely associated with religious revivalism such as Pentecostalism (Lehmann 1996; Martin 2002).

New wars have occurred and are occurring in Afghanistan, Bosnia, Chechnya, Myanmar, East Timor and the Sudan. In these wars, the military institutions and technologies of nation-states, especially of America, are largely irrelevant to the conduct of new wars, a situation which is illustrated by the inability of coalition forces to contain violence in Baghdad. Tanks are relatively useless against suicide bombers mingling with urban crowds on urban subways. New wars, not bourgeois wars, will characterize the future of globalization, because nuclear wars between nation-states cannot be successfully pursued without mutual destruction.

POLITICAL GLOBALIZATION: THE JURIDICAL REVOLUTION

Human rights legislation and institutions such as the international court of justice have been responses to the humanitarian crises of world wars. The 'juridical revolution' of the twentieth century, involving the international recognition of human rights as formulated in the United Nations Declaration, is a major example of the general process of legal globalization (Ignatieff 2002; Woodiwiss 2003).

There have been several stages in the development of human rights. In the final quarter of the eighteenth century, American independence from Britain and the French Revolution in overthrowing despotic monarchy established the liberty of the individual as a constraint on the powers of the state. Immanuel Kant defined 'enlightenment' as freedom from tutelage to think and act as an autonomous individual. Enlightenment ideas had a significant impact on the French Revolution, which proclaimed the famous ideas of liberty, equality and fraternity. The essential principle behind the English, American and French revolutions was that human beings should not be subject to arbitrary and tyrannical powers.

The second stage was marked by the Nuremberg trials in which the Nazi crimes against the Jews came to be defined as 'crimes against humanity' and Article 6 (c) of the Nuremberg Charter established the legal grounds by which those responsible for torture and genocide would be prosecuted in an international court of justice. These human rights laws recognized individuals as victims of state crimes, and made special provisions for political refugees. Throughout the Cold War, human rights became part of the rhetorical struggle with the Soviet Union. International protection of refugees was an aspect of Cold War international relations, where acceptance of refugees was an aspect of this ideological struggle. With the fall of the Soviet Union in 1992, Western nations, supported by neoliberal economic strategies, came to regard refugees as a threat to national culture and economic growth. With the end of the Cold War, there is greater emphasis on asylum abuse, people trafficking, repatriation, burden sharing and short-term protection. The decline of universal norms regulating the flow of people on the part of states has seen a growth in voluntary-sector responses from international non-governmental organizations (INGOs) and non-governmental organizations (NGOs), especially in the care of women and children who constitute the overwhelming majority of refugees. Human rights abuse by states appears to be the main cause of displacement and forced migration.

In the late twentieth century, there has been an age of enforcement including truth commissions in post-Apartheid South Africa, the extradition of Pinochet, the occupation of East Timor by UN troops, the Lockerbie verdict, the Japanese apology for war-time treatment of 'comfort women' and the trial of Slobadan Milosevic. These legal and political efforts to enforce human rights conventions are seen to counteract the criticism that human rights are not justiciable without world government. However, the international failure to act effectively over the Darfur crisis in western Sudan in 2003–4 illustrates the argument that the UN is reluctant to intervene in situations where the interests of the major powers are not at stake, and that the UN is ineffectual without the direct involvement of US military force.

Despite the political difficulties that have surrounded UN involvement in Rwanda (1994), Kosovo (1999) and Darfur (2004), there is increasing willingness to intervene against despotic governments and to support humanitarian intervention to protect civilians. These are examples of human rights wars. What has changed historically to make human rights a prominent feature of global attempts to regulate violence? First, the globalization of communications has created opportunities for criticism of government actions, and these channels cannot be easily regulated or scrutinized by governments. The development of photography has facilitated the rapid communication of war crimes and military violence. Media coverage of the Vietnam War (1965–73) was an important turning point in the creation of global audiences of war. Newspapers such as *Al-Jazeera* and countless websites provided an alternative view of the war in Iraq (Mann 2003). Secondly, technological changes in warfare have made civilians increasingly the target of military conflict. The bombing of civilians in the Basque town of Guernica in 1937 during the Spanish Civil War (1936–9) has become the symbol of such atrocities. The carnage of the Second World War and the genocide of Jews, gypsies, homosexuals, the disabled,

Armenians, the mentally ill and so forth were important and direct causes of twentieth-century human rights legislation.

The recognition of civilian individuals rather than states as victims of war has been a major achievement of human rights legislation. The human rights movement has flourished alongside the erosion of the strong Westphalian doctrine of state sovereignty and the ascendancy of the status of the individual as a victim of war between and within states. In the aftermath of the First World War, the Allies upheld the traditional legal view that only states were the legitimate subjects of international law. The recognition of the responsibility of states towards individuals has underpinned the development of theories of reparations, that is of making good again (*Wiedergutmachung*). For example, rape has been historically regarded as simply an inevitable outcome of war, but in 2001 the International Tribunal for the former Yugoslavia found three Serbian soldiers guilty of rape as a crime against humanity. The development of the sovereignty of individuals and the responsibility of states to maintain the well-being of citizens are two important consequences of globalization. While states may regard rape in war as a crime, the sexual abuse of women and children is a common pattern of new wars.

BIO-ECONOMIC GLOBALIZATION: INFECTIOUS DISEASE AND ORGAN TRANSPLANTS

By the 1970s it was assumed that the conquest of disease in Western societies would require the development of drugs which would delay or manage old age. As medical attention moved from acute to chronic disease, preventative medicine and health education came to focus on the containment of such conditions as diabetes, stroke and heart disease, which were seen to be related more to lifestyle rather than to genetic legacy. These assumptions were severely challenged in the 1980s by the emergence of the HIV/AIDS epidemic. First reported in 1979, HIV spread rapidly among the gay and homosexual communities of North America, Europe and Australia, and subsequently to heterosexual couples and finally to drug users who shared needles. AIDS is simply one illustration of a dramatic globalization of disease.

In previous centuries, while plagues were spread by migration and trade, diseases remained relatively specific to geographical niches. With the growth of world tourism and trade, the global risk of infectious disease has increased rapidly. Global influenza epidemics now spread almost instantaneously. There is widespread anxiety about the development of a variety of new conditions that are difficult to diagnose and classify, complex in their functions and diffusion, and resistant to conventional medical treatment. The list of such conditions now includes the eruption of newly discovered diseases such as hantavirus, the migration of diseases to new areas such as cholera in Latin America, diseases produced by new technologies such as toxic shock syndrome and Legionnaires' Disease, and diseases which spring from animals to humans such as AIDS and SARS. A unique form of pneumonia, SARS is caused by an influenza-type virus rather than by bacteria. The World Health Organization warned that SARS was moving across the world with 'the speed of a jet'. By early April 2003, there were 1,268 reported cases and 61 deaths in Hong Kong. Having infected hundreds of people in China and Vietnam, the condition spread quickly to North America and Europe, being carried mainly by airline passengers who were leaving Asia through Singapore and Hong Kong. SARS had subsequently a major impact on the Asian economy and led many air carriers in the region to cancel flights as governments warned their citizens not to travel. Similarly in 1999 the West Nile Virus (WNV) arrived in New York and the epidemic has been growing as it moves westwards. In 2002 the virus caused 4,156 confirmed cases and 284 deaths. WNV was expected to arrive in the densely populated areas of California by 2004, where mosquitoes are efficient carriers of the infection.

These problems have, along with Ebola, Marburg virus, Lassa fever and swine flu, generated a concern for 'the coming plagues' as a consequence of globalization (Garrett 1995). Many health agencies are now predicting that a world pandemic is highly likely in the event of avian flu spreading through the human population within the next decade and that such an outbreak would kill between 180 and 300 million people (Garrett 2005). If the current H5N1 strain produced a pandemic on the same scale as the 1918–19 flu outbreak, then approximately 1.7 million Americans would die. There is currently little protection against such an outbreak because there is a scarcity of relevant vaccines and the world's public health systems have long been in decline, because neoliberal policies have encouraged private insurance not public health. The economic consequences and social disruption of a pandemic would be enormous. The crisis resulting from a pandemic would require determined and concerted international cooperation, but there is currently little preparedness for the social damage that a pandemic would create. The globalization of infectious disease is produced by the rapid transportation of people and goods, population density and growing dependency on intensive livestock production. In particular, the transportation of animals and animal products has created ideal conditions for the transport of fungi, viruses and bacteria that produce devastating sickness in both human and animal populations (Karesh and Cook 2005).

Modern society is often described as a medical–industrial complex, because the human body can be broken down into parts that in turn become commodities. These social changes have their specific roots in commercial applications of genetic research, but perhaps a more dramatic and emotive illustration of commercialization is the emergence of a world market in kidney sales from poor to rich countries. It is controversial because its supporters argue that this organ exchange provides immediate cash benefits for the donating family while the sick receive a much-needed organ donation. Critics argue that organs typically come from women of poor countries who donate them to men in rich societies. These women do not receive adequate medical support after donation and often suffer from infections and exhaustion, and the costs of drugs to suppress the immune system of recipients represents a significant economic burden on recipient families.

Organ donation is in formal terms voluntary, but in practice kidney donation is a response to extreme poverty. Impoverished Indian women are often forced to sell a kidney in order to feed their families, but donations have not always been voluntary or with the patient's consent. Before the end of South African Apartheid, human tissues and organs were harvested from people in intensive care units without the knowledge of their families (Scheper-Hughes 2001a, 2001b). These practices raise difficult moral and political questions, because families that donate organs clearly need the injection of cash that such transactions produce, but the exchanges are typically unequal. In the future, kidney disease will more likely be treated by therapeutic cloning.

Global markets in organ sales have been of considerable interest to medical sociologists, who have generally been critical of organ sales and bio-harvesting from remote and isolated aboriginal communities. Given the social inequalities of the existing market, therapeutic cloning would be a significant medical advance and would probably undermine the market for human organs. In practice, such medical improvements in the developed world are unlikely to help Third World societies until more fundamental social and economic improvements take place.

The tensions between legal and economic regulation are particularly problematic in the control of the sale of human organs. The potential marketization of women's bodies by reproductive technologies was early recognized by feminist critics, but Internet marketing of surrogate mothers and human gametes is now a global phenomenon. The technology of the Internet promotes the globalization of the marketing of the human body, which in turn was made possible through new reproductive technologies, and presents the greatest challenge to any attempt to regulate the market through the imposition of ethical standards upheld by law. The global market in human organs is consequently anomic. The next regulatory problem arising in this medical field is the corporate control of genetic codes via patenting. Such patents are important because they make the global sale of genetic information commercially viable, but they also insure that the economic inequalities between the developed and developing world will continue. The contemporary global conflict over stem-cell research illustrates the tensions between national politics, international regulation and corporate profits. In Singapore and South Korea, where legal regulation of stem cell and related biological research fields is permissive, there is an increasing possibility that such global scientific competition will result in the cloning of human beings. This outcome will have major moral and legal implications for what is human and posthuman (Fukuyama 2002).

BIO-ECONOMIC GLOBALIZATION: THE GERONTOLOGICAL REVOLUTION

The demographic revolution and the greying of populations are worldwide phenomena with significant consequences for the global economy, welfare policies and defence strategies. Ageing populations mean that there are significant shortages in the labour markets of the advanced societies and the future implications of ageing for investment, pensions and economic stagnation are significant. The advanced economies (in North America, Europe and Japan) have become dependent on labour migration, both legal and illegal, to solve labour shortages. However, advances in biological sciences have created an expectation that ageing could be delayed, if not cancelled. In conventional gerontology, the question about 'living forever' might in practical terms mean living a full life and achieving the average expectation of life. More recently, there has been considerable speculation as to whether medical science through stem-cell research could in fact reverse the ageing process. Between the 1960s and 1980s the view put forward by biologists was that normal cells had a 'replicative senescence', that is, normal tissues can only divide a finite number of times before entering a stage of advanced quiescence. Cells were observed *in vitro* in a process of natural senescence, and eventually experiments *in vivo* produced a distinction between normal and pathological cells in terms of division. It is paradoxical that pathological cells appear to have no necessary limitation on replication, and 'immortalization' is the distinctive feature of a pathological cell line. By extrapolation, biologists concluded that finite cell division meant that the ageing of the whole organism was inevitable. These research findings confirmed the traditional view that human life had an intrinsic and predetermined limit. Only pathology described how certain cells might out survive the otherwise inescapable senescence of normal cellular life.

This biological framework of ageing was eventually disrupted by the discovery that some isolated human embryonic cells were capable of continuous division in culture, and showed no evidence of a replicative crisis. Certain non-pathological cells (or stem cells) were capable of indefinite division, and hence were 'immortalized'. The cultivation of these cells as an experimental form of life has challenged existing assumptions about the boundaries between the normal and the pathological, and between life and death. Stem cell research begins to define the arena within the body that has reserves of renewable tissue, indicating that the limits of biological growth are not fixed or inflexible. The body has a surplus of stem cells capable of survival beyond the death of the organism. With these developments in bio-gerontology, the capacity of regenerative medicine to expand the 'natural' limits of life becomes a plausible aspect of contemporary medicine. This new interpretation of replication locates ageing as a shifting threshold between surplus and waste, between obsolescence and renewal, between death and immortality.

The ageing of the developed world is regarded by economists in the World Bank as a threat to economic growth, and hence there is much political excitement about the possibilities of stem cell research as an aspect of regenerative medicine. Companies operating in tourist destinations as far afield as the Caribbean and Malaysia are already offering regenerative medicine as components of holiday packages, designed to alleviate the negative consequences of degenerative diseases such as multiple sclerosis or diabetes. Holiday packages will come to include cosmetic and regenerative medicine as part of the world cruise for the super-rich. The idea of gerontological tourism offering rest, cure and rejuvenation might also become an addendum to sexual tourism in the world of advanced bio-capitalism. One sign of the times was an academic event hosted by Cambridge University Life Extension and Rejuvenation Society in October 2004 in which Dr Aubrey de Grey announced that human beings could 'live forever', by which he meant that within 25 years medical science will possess the capacity to repair all known effects of ageing. The average age at death of people born thereafter would exceed 5,000 years.

Such expectations are literally fantastic. In fact the scientific expectations of significant breakthroughs in the treatment of disease and significant profits by the large pharmaceutical companies after the decoding of the human genome in 2001 were not fulfilled. The pharmaceutical industry has been reluctant to invest in new products that were designed for conditions that affect small numbers of people. The fears associated with 'personalized medicine' have begun to disappear, because it is obvious that there are generic processes from which the genomics companies can profit. However, genetics-based medicine is poised to find better diagnostic tests for disease and generic solutions to such conditions as diabetes, Alzheimer's disease, heart problems and breast cancer. These advances will undoubtedly enhance life expectancy and have significant implications for the shape of the world's population in terms of age structure.

The human consequences of these medical innovations and demographic changes will be rapid and radical, but little systematic thought has been given to the social and political consequences of enhanced longevity. Although it is mere speculation, it is reasonable to assume that the social outcomes of new patterns of ageing will be revolutionary. Increasing world inequality between the rejuvenated North and the naturally ageing South would further inflame frustration and resentment of deprived social groups against wealthy aged populations. Under existing economic conditions, labour markets will be unable to cope with the increasing number of ageing survivors and there would be major crises in housing markets. The food supply would be unable to keep up with population expansion and there will be increasing dependence on the use of genetically modified food. As environmental pollution increases, nation-states will have to struggle to maintain natural resources to support their own populations. In addition to national conflicts, there would be intergenerational conflicts over resources, in which existing economic crises around pensions and housing would increase. The elderly would be increasingly uninsurable and would need to work indefinitely to support themselves and their families in old age. If we assume that while the application of genetic sciences could reduce mortality, it would, at least in the short term, increase morbidity as chronic illness and geriatric diseases increased. The burden of dependency would have negative consequences for healthcare systems and economic growth. Since longevity does not in itself result in greater happiness, elderly populations would be drug-dependent. The main driving force in the economy would be from genetic research and its applications in pharmaceutical industries. A pharmaceutical product can be profitable when applied to a chronic condition which it does not cure, but where it helps the patient to survive in a relationship of complete dependency on the new drug. The aim of commercial pharmacy is not to cure but to assist survival. There are strong economic reasons to promote longevity, provided it is longevity with increasing morbidity.

The prospect of indefinite life would thus raise an acute Malthusian crisis. These changes imply an important change from early to late modernity. In the early stages of capitalism, the role of medical science was to improve healthcare to make the working class healthy in order to have an efficient labour force. Late capitalism does not need a large permanent labour force at full employment and working full time, because technology has made labour more efficient. In the new biotechnological environment, disease is no longer a negative force in the economy but on the contrary an aspect of the factors of production. The economy will increasingly depend on the demand for products to manage the chronic illness of a population condemned to 'live forever'. These assumptions about the dominance of chronic illness will be periodically undermined by pandemics that will assist in reducing the world's population pressures. The relationship between pandemics and ageing will produce uncertain and contradictory outcomes for the global economy.

This Malthusian crisis has been brilliantly conceptualized by Nicholas Georgescu-Roegen (1971) in his *The Entropy Law and the Economic Process* where he argues that the exhaustion of the earth's resources cannot be finally overcome by economic growth, because waste is an unavoidable law of nature, and the economic process merely accelerates the realization of this law. The economic process involves an inevitable degradation and depletion of resources. Economics has strangely neglected the problem of the scarcity of natural resources and Georgescu-Roegen attempted to develop an economic science based on assumptions about biological evolution and the economic process of production and consumption as parallel and interconnected processes. Following the biologist Alfred Lotka, he noted that humans like other animals use their organs to enhance their enjoyment of life. All animals are born with these organs that Lotka called endosomatic instruments, but man is the only creature who uses organs that are not part of his biological constitution. These are his exosomatic instruments. In economic terms, these exosomatic instruments are in fact simply capital equipment. This bio-economic understanding of human beings can be combined with the philosophical anthropology of Arnold Gehlen to argue that human beings are poorly equipped with endosomatic instruments and hence have to build institutions to protect themselves and to create their social world. These exosomatic instruments are inherently precarious and the somatic condition of human beings is vulnerable. Therefore the logical situation of human beings has one major problem, namely scarcity and the resulting social conflict over resources (Turner and Rojek 2001).

Georgescu-Roegen conceptualizes this state of scarcity in terms of the production of waste in the economic process, namely the inevitable depletion of resources and the pollution of our environment that are associated with population growth. In his entropic economics, Georgescu-Roegen rejected Karl Marx's solution that the socialization of the means of production by communism could overcome the social class conflict resulting from the struggle over scarce resources, and rejected the idea that endless technological innovation can enhance our resources and reduce the expenditure of labour in relation to leisure time and consumption. In this economic interpretation of waste, the depletion of resources is inevitable, and hence social conflict results from scarcity and overpopulation. Environmental depletion has been rapid and profound. For example, in a period of some 40 years, the forest cover in Thailand was reduced from 65 per cent to 15 per cent resulting in catastrophic flooding, pollution of rivers and decline in soil quality. The proposal that we could 'live forever', even if that means an extra decade for rich nations, can only increase the rate at which resources are depleted and pollution increased, and it would inevitably lead to war.

CONCLUSION: WASTE, WAR AND WARRIORS

We can now summarize this neo-Malthusian argument by claiming that globalization by creating global interconnectedness increases the social impact of technological change. Global social change will be increasingly negative, because it will magnify entropic waste. Globalization of tourism, transport and exchange, together with increasing population density, produces environmental degradation and major epidemics that cannot be easily contained. If a pandemic is inevitable under these circumstances, there will be major economic crises and the resulting social disruption will further enhance the possibilities of civil and military conflict. The surplus of unemployed and underemployed young men is a major causal factor in the global development of new wars, that will bring with them social breakdown. Sociologists have begun to talk about the destructive social role of the 'overpopulation warrior' (Diessenbacher 1998) whose presence has caused havoc in the Congo, Myanmar, southern Thailand, Cambodia and central Asia. Social disruption in the advanced societies is also closely related to the absence of adequate social roles for young men in economies that are outsourced and that no longer need permanent, mass labour supplies. Casualization of employment, underemployment and low status leads to lack of respect, low social capital and marginalization from citizenship institutions. The London bombers were not impoverished, but their social alienation was expressed through their sense of not being UK subjects, and hence the Islamic *ummah* offered some subjective notion of inclusion and purpose.

Environmental crisis will become an increasingly significant determinant of the economic viability of nation-states, but it is doubtful whether there are such things as 'natural disasters'. The loss of life in the tsunami of 2004 was in part a consequence of the absence of an early warning system. The flooding of New Orleans in 2005 was a consequence of failed levees and inadequate planning, but it was also a consequence of global warming, and the resulting social chaos and collapse of civil order can be taken as one illustration of the social and political disruptions that will flow from further globalization. Deforestation is clearly a man-made disaster that will cause sea levels to rise as the ice cap defrosts and sea temperatures rise. It is likely, not only that many small Pacific islands will simply disappear, but low-lying areas of Europe, such as the English fens, will be under water. These environmental changes will increase scarcity and make conflict over water and land more prominent in civil conflict. War and waste will be significant driving features of the futures of globalization.

In the past, catastrophes such as the Black Death, the fire of London and the Lisbon earthquake produced major religious responses. The very concept of theodicy in the philosophy of Leibniz attempted to explain such disasters, and was adopted by Max Weber in his analysis of religious ideologies. For example, the Asian tsunami resulted in a powerful religious response in fundamentalist circles in Indonesia, where video-tapes were soon available showing that the natural disaster was a punishment from God for human wickedness in Thailand and elsewhere. Human failure to adhere strictly to religious law (the Shari'a) was allegedly the real cause of natural catastrophe. In medieval Europe, the Black Death of the fourteenth century, which was carried by the intercontinental trade and warfare, resulted in the deaths of one-third of the population of Europe. The plague broke out in 1346 among the armies of a Mongol prince who was attacking the Crimea. Despite the limitations of trade routes, even Greenland suffered from the epidemic. The plague which became a persistent but unpredictable feature of society, brought about a new consciousness, namely a macabre sense of the persistent presence of a malevolent force bringing certain destruction, evil and death. The baroque imagination of the post-Reformation Europe sought to explain the catastrophe of Lutheranism. Comparisons with modern epidemics and their complex social and political history such as malaria are useful from an historical and sociological perspective. The impact of tuberculosis would be another example of a disease that created a new consciousness and culture, especially among the intellectual elite (Dormandy 1999). The globalization of disease was powerfully illustrated in 1918 with the outbreak of the Spanish influenza pandemic that killed 25 million people in 6 months – about three times the number of deaths of World War I. In 1920, an epidemic of encephalitis lethargica and a further outbreak of influenza followed. These epidemics were rapid and global, because the war had brought about worldwide movements of peoples. As a consequence influenza spread rapidly among US troops based in Europe, and between September and October 1918, 20 per cent of the US army was sick and 24,000 soldiers died of flu compared to 34,000 killed in battle. In the 1920s in response to the mass slaughter of young men in the trenches, there was a significant expansion of interest in spiritualism Europe in which figures like Conan Doyle became involved in the collective attempt to reach the departed. Wartime horror produced a widespread need to communicate with the dead, especially where grieving relatives could not locate the bodies of their loved ones.

From these examples, it is evident that there is no clear point that divides global history between simple and reflexive modernity, between stable and mobile societies. Popular images or metaphors of AIDS are not far removed from the baroque vision of death (Ziegler 1998). While there are forms of social continuity, globalization will make catastrophes more general, immediate and profound. The pandemics of the future, precisely because the world is interconnected but lacks any effective global governance, will destroy millions of people, undermine whole societies and threaten civilized life. If the current weakness of the United Nations continues, it is unlikely that any single society, such as the United States, could act as a global policeman, or a global doctor. In the context of uncontrollable pandemics and famines, we can expect millenarian movements and fantastic cults to flourish once more in the era of global catastrophes. In this respect, the future of globalization will resemble not the *Brave New World* of Huxley or that of Orwell in *Nineteen Eighty-Four*, but the world of Mad Max with roaming armies of displaced men in search of gasoline, armaments and drugs, where small fortified hamlets of the rich and powerful would seek shelter, and secure religious meaning from their cults and prophets. This future world is already coming into existence in Kinshasa, Kabul, Baghdad, Manipur, the Fergana valley and Groznyy, where the ingredients of the global neo-Malthusian crisis – infectious disease, alienated men, drug dependency, civil disruption, environmental decay, control by war lords and new wars, and religio-political extremism – are being unwittingly assembled. These new-war conflict zones are the outposts of empire that will drain away the resources of democratic societies and erode the civil liberties of their citizens. It is unlikely that the juridical revolution can contain such pressing global anarchy.

References

Appadurai, A. (ed.) 2003. *Globalization*. Durham: Duke University Press.
Barber, B. 2001. *Jihad vs McWorld*. New York: Random House.
Beck, U. 1992. *Risk Society: Towards a New Modernity*. London: Sage.
Beck, U. 2000. *What Is Globalization?* Cambridge: Polity Press.
Beckford, J. and Luckmann, T. (eds) 1989. *The Changing Face of Religion*. London: Sage.

Beyer, P. 1994. *Religion and Globalization*. London: Sage.

Black, J. 1998. *War and the World: Military Power and the Fate of Continents 1450–2000*. New Haven, CT: Yale University Press.

Cohen , E.A. 1996. 'A revolution in warfare', *Foreign Affairs*, March–April, 37–54.

Dawson, L.L. and Hennebry, J. 2003. 'New religions and the Internet: Recruiting in a new public space'. In L.L. Dawson (ed.), *Cults and New Religious Movements*, 271–91. Oxford: Blackwell.

Diessenbacher, H. 1998. *Kriege der Zukunft: Die Bevolkerungsexploosion gefahrdet den Frieden*. Munich: Hanser.

Dormandy, T. 1999. *The White Death: The History of Tuberculosis*. London: Hambledon Press.

Ferguson, N. 2004. *Colossus: The Rise and Fall of the American Empire*. London: Allen Lane.

Foucault, M. 1977. *Discipline and Punish: The Birth of the Clinic*. London: Tavistock.

Fukuyama, F. 2002. *Our Posthuman Future: Consequences of the Biotechnology Revolution*. New York: Farrar, Straus and Giroux.

Garrett, I. 1995. *The Coming Plague: Newly Emerging Diseases in a World Out of Balance*, London: Virago.

Garrett, L. 2005. 'The next pandemic?' *Foreign Affairs*, July–August, 3–23.

Georgescu-Roegen, N. 1971. *The Entropy Law and the Economic Process*. Cambridge, MA: Harvard University Press.

Giddens, A. 1990. *The Consequences of Modernity*. Cambridge: Polity Press.

Glazer, N. 1997. *We Are All Multiculturalists Now*. Cambridge, MA: Harvard University Press.

Hardt, M. and Negri, A. 2000. *Empire*. Cambridge, MA: Harvard University Press.

Heelas, P. 1996. *The New Age Movement*. Oxford: Blackwell.

Hirst, P. 2001. *War and Power in the 21st Century*. Cambridge: Polity Press.

Huntington, S. 1993. 'The clash of civilizations', *Foreign Affairs*, 72 (3), 22–48.

Huntington, S. 1996. *The Clash of Civilizations: Remaking of World Order*. New York: Touchstone.

Ignatieff, M. 2002. *Human Rights as Politics and Idolatry*. Princeton, NJ: Princeton University Press.

Joas, H. 2003. *War and Modernity*. Cambridge: Polity Press.

Karesh, W.B. and Cook, R.A. 2005. 'The human-animal link', *Foreign Affairs*, July–August, 38–50.

Lechner, F.J. and Boli, J. (eds) 2004. *The Globalization Reader*. Oxford: Blackwell.

Lehmann, D. 1996. *The Struggle for the Spirit: Religious Transformation and Popular Culture in Brazil and Latin America*. Cambridge: Polity Press.

McLuhan, M. 1967. *The Medium Is the Massage*. San Francisco: Hardwired.

Malthus, T. 1970. *Essay on the Principle of Population as it Affects the Future Improvement of Society*. Harmondsworth: Penguin.

Mandaville, P. 2001. *Transnational Muslim Politics*. London: Routledge.

Mann, M. 2003. *Incoherent Empire*. London: Verso.

Martin, D. 2002. *Pentecostalism: The World their Parish*. Oxford: Blackwell.

Marty, E. and Appleby, R.S. (eds) 1995. *Fundamentalism and Society*. Chicago: University of Chicago Press.

Moore, W.E. 1966. 'Global sociology: The world as a singular system', *American Journal of Sociology*, 71 (March), 475–82.

Münkler, H. 2005. *The New Wars*. Cambridge: Polity Press.

Parsons, T. 1974. 'Religion in postindustrial America: The problem of secularization', *Social Research*, 51 (1–2), 193–225.

Ritzer, G. 1993. *The McDonaldization of Society*. London: Sage.

Ritzer, G. 2004. *The Globalization of Nothing*, London: Sage.

Robertson, G. 2002. *Crimes against Humanity: The Struggle for Global Justice*. New York: New Press.

Robertson, R. 1987. 'From secularisation to globalisation', *Journal of Oriental Studies*, 26, 28–32.

Robertson, R. 1990. 'Mapping the global condition: Globalization as the central concept', *Theory Culture and Society*, 72 (2–3), 15–30.

Robertson, R. 1992. *Globalization: Social Theory and Global Culture*. London: Sage.

Roof, W.C. 1993. *A Generation of Seekers: The Spiritual Journeys of the Baby Boom Generation*. San Francisco: Harper.

Roof, W.C. 1999. *Spiritual Marketplace: Baby Boomers and the Remaking of American Religion*. Princeton, NJ: Princeton University Press.

Scheper-Hughes, N. 2001a. 'Neo-cannibalism: The global trade in human organs', *The Hedgehog Review*, 3 (2), 7–52.

Scheper-Hughes, N. 2001b. 'Commodity fetishism in organs trafficking', *Body and Society*, 7 (2–3), 31–62.

Smart, N. 1989. *The World's Religions*. Cambridge: Cambridge University Press.

Turner, B.S. 1994. *Orientalism, Postmodernism and Globalism*. London: Routledge.

Turner, B.S. 2002. 'Sovereignty and emergency: Political theology, Islam and American conservatism', *Theory Culture and Society*, 19 (4), 103–19.

Turner, B.S. 2003. 'Class, generation and Islamism: Towards a global sociology of political Islam', *British Journal of Sociology*, 54 (1), 139–47.

Turner, B.S. 2004. *The New Medical Sociology*. New York: W.W. Norton.

Turner, B. and Rojek, C. 2001. *Society and Culture*. London: Sage.

Woodiwiss, A. 2003. *Making Human Rights Work Globally*. London: Glasshouse Press.

Ziegler, P. 1998. *The Black Death*. London: Penguin.

Subject Index

Author Index

Printed in the USA/Agawam, MA
January 9, 2013

571798.035